Search and Seizure Checklists

2017 Edition
Issued in December 2017

Prepared by the Publisher's Editorial Staff

LC 87-33845
ISSN 1045-8719
ISBN 978-0-314-84523-8

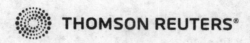 THOMSON REUTERS®

For Customer Assistance Call 1-800-328-4880

Mat #41883553

LC 87-33845
ISSN 1045-8719
ISBN 978-0-314-84523-8

Introduction to the December 2017 Edition

This quick-reference guide provides you with instant access to the latest and most important developments in the highly volatile field of search and seizure law, including:
- Arrest
- Standing
- Forfeiture
- Derivative evidence
- Exclusionary rule
- Justification to seize
- Warrantless searches
- Stop and frisk
- Vehicle searches
- Border and immigration searches
- Searches under exigent circumstances
- Observations made by officers inside and outside the curtilage of a house
- Airport searches

Highlights to the December 2017 edition include coverage of the U.S. Supreme Court decision in the following case:
- *City of Los Angeles v. Mendez*, 137 S. Ct. 1539, 198 L. Ed. 2d 52 (2017)

Introduction to the December 2017 Edition

This quick-reference guide provides you with instant access to the latest and most important developments in the highly volatile field of search and seizure law, including:

- Arrest
- Standing
- Forfeiture
- Derivative evidence
- Exclusionary rule
- Justification to seize
- Warrantless searches
- Stop and frisk
- Vehicle searches
- Border and immigration searches
- Searches under exigent circumstances
- Observations made by officers inside and outside the curtilage of a house
- Airport searches

Highlights to the December 2017 edition include coverage of the U.S. Supreme Court decision in the following case:

- City of Los Angeles v. Mendez, 137 S.Ct. 1539, 198 L. Ed. 2d 52 (2017)

THOMSON REUTERS PROVIEW™

This title is one of many now available on your tablet as an eBook.

Take your research mobile. Powered by the Thomson Reuters ProView™ app, our eBooks deliver the same trusted content as your print resources, but in a compact, on-the-go format.

ProView eBooks are designed for the way you work. You can add your own notes and highlights to the text, and all of your annotations will transfer electronically to every new edition of your eBook.

You can also instantly verify primary authority with built-in links to WestlawNext® and KeyCite®, so you can be confident that you're accessing the most current and accurate information.

To find out more about ProView eBooks and available discounts, call 1-800-344-5009.

RELATED PRODUCTS

For each publication, its corresponding Westlaw database identifier is listed in parentheses

CRIMINAL LITIGATION & PROCEDURE

Everytrial Criminal Defense Resource Book (CRDEFRB)
Barbara Bergman and Nancy Hollander

Federal Rules of Criminal Procedure 2d (US-RULES)
Publisher's Editorial Staff

Federal Jury Practice and Instructions, 5th and 6th, volumes 1 through 2B (FED-JI)
Kevin F. O'Malley, Jay E. Grenig, and William C. Lee

Federal Jury Practice and Instructions: Jury Instructions Companion Handbook
Kevin F. O'Malley, Jay E. Grenig, and William C. Lee

Federal Sentencing Guidelines Handbook
Roger Haines, Frank Bowman III, and Jennifer Woll

Grand Jury Law & Practice 2d (GRJURLAW)
Sara Sun Beale, James Felman, and Michael Elston

Guidebook to Freedom of Information and Privacy Act
Cornish Hitchcock

Jurywork Systematic Techniques 2d (JURYWORK)
National Jury Project

LaFave Search and Seizure 4th (SEARCHSZR)
Wayne R. LaFave

Law of Confessions 2d (LAWCONFESS)
David Nissman; Ed Hagen

Professional Responsibility in Criminal Defense Practice 3d Edition (PRCRIMDEF)
John Wesley Hall, Jr.

Representation of Witnesses Before Federal Grand Juries
National Lawyers Guild and Rikki J. Klieman and John W. Thomas

Rights of Juveniles 2d: The Juvenile Justice System (RTSJUVEN)
Samuel Davis

Uncharged Misconduct Evidence (UNMEV)
Edward J. Imwinkelried

Wharton's Criminal Procedure 13th
Charles Torcia

Wharton's Criminal Procedure 14th
Barbara Bergman, Teri Duncan and Melissa Stephenson

White Collar Crime 2d (WCCR)
Joel Androphy

EXPERT WITNESS & EVIDENCE

Cross Examining Experts in the Behavioral Sciences (BEHSCI)
Terence W. Campbell and Demosthenes Lorandos

e-Discovery and Digital Evidence (EDISCOVERY)
Jay E. Grenig, William C. Gleisner, Troy Larson and John L. Carroll

Expert Witnesses: Business and Economy
Publisher's Editorial Staff

Eyewitness Identification Legal and Practical Problems (EYEWITN)
Larry Vogelman and David Ruoff

Firearms Law Deskbook (FALDB)
Stephen P. Halbrook

Intoxication Test Evidence 2d (INTOX)
Edward Fitzgerald

The Law of Electronic Surveillance (ELECTRSURV)
James G. Carr and Patricia Bellia

Modern Scientific Evidence: Forensics (MODSCIEVID)
David L. Faigman, Edward K. Cheng, Michael J. Saks, and Joseph Sanders

Psychological and Scientific Evidence in Criminal Trials
Publisher's Editorial Staff

Uncharged Misconduct Evidence (UNMEV)
Edward J. Imwinkelried

Wharton's Criminal Evidence 15th (CRIMEVID)
Barbara Bergman and Teri Duncan

CRIMINAL INVESTIGATIONS

Checklists for Searches and Seizures in Public Schools (SRCHSCHLS)
John VanDyke and Melvin Sakurai

Guidebook to Freedom of Information and Privacy Act
Cornish Hitchcock

LaFave Search and Seizure 4th (SEARCHSZR)
Wayne R. LaFave

National Security Investigation and Prosecution (NSIAP)
David Kris and J. Douglas Wilson

Search Warrant Law Deskbook (SRCHWARLAW)
John Burkoff

Searches & Seizures Arrests and Confessions 2d (SSAC)

William E. Ringel and Publisher's Editorial Staff

Search and Seizure Checklists (SSLIST)
Publisher's Editorial Staff

Search and Seizure Law Report
John M. Burkoff

The Law of Electronic Surveillance (ELECTRSURV)
James Carr and Patricia Bellia

Vehicle Search Law Deskbook (VEHSRCH)
Christian Fisanick

Warrantless Search Law Deskbook (WARLESSRC)
Publisher's Editorial Staff

Wiretapping and Eavesdropping 3d
Clifford S. Fishman and Anne T. McKenna

SUBSTANTIVE CRIMINAL LAW

Banking Crimes (BANKCRIMES)
John K. Villa

Crimes of Violence: Homicide and Assault
F. Lee Bailey and Kenneth J. Fishman

Crimes of Violence: Rape and Other Sex Crimes
F. Lee Bailey and Kenneth J. Fishman

Criminal Defense Ethics 2d (DEFETHICS)
John Burkoff

Criminal Law Defenses (CRLDEF)
Paul H. Robinson

Criminal Law Digest 3d
Publisher's Editorial Staff

Criminal Practice Manual (CRPMAN)
Publisher's Editorial Staff

Criminal Practice Guide (CRPGUIDE)
Publisher's Editorial Staff

Drinking/Driving Litigation Criminal and Civil 2d (DRNKDRIVING)
Flem Whited

Drinking/Driving Litigation Criminal and Civil Trial Notebook (DDTRIALNB)
Flem Whited

Drug Abuse and the Law Sourcebook (DRUGAB)
Gerald Uelman

Handling Drunk Driving Cases 2d (HDRUNKDR)
Edward Fiandach

Handling Misdemeanor Cases 2d (HANDLMISD)
F. Lee Bailey and Kenneth J. Fishman

Handling Narcotic and Drug Cases (NARC-DRUG)
F. Lee Bailey and Kenneth J. Fishman

Hate Crimes Law (HATECRIMES)
Zachary Wolfe, Editor

LaFave Substantive Criminal Law, 2d (SUBCRL)
Wayne R. LaFave

Prisoners and the Law
Ira Robbins

Prosecutorial Misconduct 2d (PROSMIS)
Bennett Gershman

Rights of Prisoners 3d (RGTSPRISON)
Michael B. Mushlin

Wharton's Criminal Law 15th (CRIMLAW)
Charles Torcia

WHITE COLLAR CRIME

Banking Crimes (BANKCRIMES)
John K. Villa

Bromberg and Lowenfels on Securities Fraud and Commodities Fraud 2d (SECBROMLOW)
Alan R. Bromberg and Lewis D. Lowenfels

Civil and Criminal Forfeiture
Steven L. Kessler

Cybercrime Law Report (CYBERCRLR)
Anne T. McKenna

e-Discovery and Digital Evidence (EDISCOVERY)
Jay E. Grenig, William C. Gleisner, Troy Larson and John L. Carroll

Expert Witnesses: Business and Economy
Publisher's Editorial Staff

Property Investigation Checklists: Uncovering Insurance Fraud 9th (PROPICHK)
Michael H. Boyer

Securities Law Series Vols. 18 & 18A: Insider Trading Regulation, Enforcement and Prevention (INSIDETRAD)

Donald C. Langevoort

Securities Law Series Vol. 21: Securities Crimes (SECCRIM)
Marvin Pickholz

Securities Law Series Vols. 27 & 27A: Securities Litigation: Forms & Analysis (SECLITFRMS)
Alston & Bird, LLP

Securities Litigation Report (GLSLR)
Publisher's Editorial Staff

White Collar Crime 2d (WCCR)
Joel Androphy

White Collar Crime Reporter [Andrews Litigation Reporter] (ANWCCR)
Robert W. McSherry

DUI PRACTICE

California Drunk Driving Defense
Lawrence E. Taylor

Drinking/Driving Litigation Criminal and Civil 2d (DRNKDRIVING)
Flem Whited

Drinking/Driving Litigation Criminal and Civil Trial Notebook (DDTRIALNB)
Flem Whited

Drinking/Driving Law Newsletter (DDLAWLET)
Flem Whited

Drug Testing Legal Manual and Practice Aids (DRUGTSTMAN)
Kevin Zeese

Drug Abuse and the Law Sourcebook (DRUGAB)
Gerald Uelman

Handling Misdemeanor Cases 2d (HANDLMISD)
F. Lee Bailey and Kenneth J. Fishman

Handling Narcotic and Drug Cases (NARC-DRUG)
F. Lee Bailey and Kenneth J. Fishman

Handling Drunk Driving Cases 2d (HDRUNKDR)
Edward Fiandach

Handling the DWI Case in New York (HDWINY)
Peter Gerstenzang and Eric Sills

Intoxication Test Evidence 2d (INTOX)
Edward Fitzgerald

New York Driving While Intoxicated 2d (NYDWI)

Edward Fiandach

New York DWI Defense Forms (NYDWIFM)

James F. Orr and Michael S. Taheri

New York Vehicle and Traffic Law 2d (NYVEH)

James Rose

POSTCONVICTION & APPELLATE PRACTICE

Federal Criminal Appeals

by Publisher's Editorial Staff

Federal Postconviction Remedies and Relief Handbook with Forms (FEDPCREM)

Donald Wilkes

Habeas Corpus Checklists

by Ira P. Robbins

Handling Criminal Appeals

by Jonathan M. Purver and Lawrence E. Taylor

Ineffective Assistance of Counsel (INASCNSL)

by John M. Burkoff and Nancy M. Burkoff

Law of Sentencing 2d (LAWSENT)

by Arthur Campbell

Postconviction Remedies (PCREM)

by Brian R. Means

Proscecutorial Misconduct 2d (PROSMIS)

by Bennett L. Gershman

State Postconviction Remedies and Relief with Forms

by Donald Wilkes

The Law of Probation and Parole

Publisher's Editorial Staff

JOURNALS & NEWSLETTERS

Arrest Law Bulletin (QNLNALB)

Publisher's Editorial Staff

Americans With Disabilities: Practice and Compliance Manual Newsletter

Publisher's Editorial Staff

Computer Crime and Technology in Law Enforcement (QNLNCCT)

Publisher's Editorial Staff

Criminal Law Bulletin (CRIMLAWBUL)

James Robertson

Criminal Law News (CRIMLWNEWS)
Publisher's Editorial Staff

Criminal Practice Guide (CRPGUIDE)
Publisher's Editorial Staff

Criminal Practice Report (CRPREPORT)
Publisher's Editorial Staff

Cybercrime Law Report (CYBERCRLR)
Anne T. McKenna

Drinking/Driving Law Newsletter (DDLAWLET)
Flem Whited

Investigative Stops Law Bulletin (QNLNISL)
Publisher's Editorial Staff

Narcotics Law Bulletin (QNLNNL)
Publisher's Editorial Staff

Police Misconduct and Civil Rights Law Report
National Lawyers Guild
G. Flint Taylor, Clifford Zimmerman and Ben Elson, Editors

School Law Bulletin (QNLNSL)
Publisher's Editorial Staff

School Law Bulletin (QNLNSL)
Publisher's Editorial Staff

Search and Seizure Bulletin (QNLNSSL)
Publisher's Editorial Staff

Search and Seizure Law Report
John M. Burkoff

Securities Litigation Report (GLSLR)
Publisher's Editorial Staff

White Collar Crime Reporter [Andrews Litigation Reporter] (ANWCCR)
Robert W. McSherry

FORMS

Complete Manual of Criminal Forms 3d (CMCRF)
F. Lee Bailey and Kenneth J. Fishman

New York DWI Defense Forms (NYDWIFM)
James F. Orr and Michael S. Taheri

Securities Law Series Vols. 27 & 27A: Securities Litigation: Forms & Analysis (SECLITFRMS)
Alston & Bird, LLP

White Collar Crime 2d (WCCR)
Joel Androphy

CIVIL RIGHTS LAW & PRACTICE

**Americans With Disabilities: Practice and Compliance Manual
(AMDISPCM)**
Publisher's Editorial Staff

Blue's Guide to Jury Selection (BLUEJURYGD)
Lisa Blue and Robert Hirschhorn

Civil Rights and Civil Liberties Litigation: The Law of Section 1983
Sheldon Nahmod

Civil Rights Litigation and Attorney Fees Annual Handbook
National Lawyers Guild
Steven Saltzman, Editor

Disabilities and the Law
Laura Rothstein and Julia Rothstein

Education Law: First Amendment Due Process and Discrimination Litigation (EDULAW)
Ronna Greff Schneider

Federal Civil Rights Acts (FCIVRTACTS)
Rodney Smolla

**Federal Jury Practice and Instructions: Jury Instructions Companion
Handbook**
Publisher's Editorial Staff

Government Discrimination (GOVDISCRIM)
James Kushner

Housing Discrimination Law and Litigation (HDISLL)
Robert Schwemm

Housing Discrimination Practice Manual (HDISPRMAN)
John Relman

Legal Aspects of AIDS
Donald Hermann and William Schurgin

Lesbian, Gay, Bisexual and Transgender Family Law (LGFAMLAW)
Courtney Joslin and Shannon Minter

Police Misconduct and Civil Rights Law Report
National Lawyers Guild
G. Flint Taylor, Clifford Zimmerman and Ben Elson, Editors

Police Misconduct Law and Litigation 3d (POLICEMISC)
Michael Avery, David Rudovsky and Karen Blum

EDUCATION LAW

STATE SPECIFIC

Michigan Criminal Law and Procedure with Forms, 2d (MICRIM)
Timothy Baughman

Michigan Criminal Law and Procedure with Forms Practice Deskbook (MICRIMPD)
Timothy Baughman

Michigan Criminal Law and Procedure with Forms Search and Seizure (MICRIMSS)
Timothy Baughman

New York Charges to the Jury and Requests to Charge in a Criminal Case (CTJNY)
Howard Leventhal and Publisher's Editorial Staff

New York Court of Appeals on Criminal Law 2d
William Donnino

New York Criminal Law 3d (NYPRAC-CRIM)
Richard A. Greenberg, Martin Marcus, Lynn W. Fahey, and Eve Cary

New York Driving While Intoxicated 2d (NYDWI)
Edward Fiandach

New York DWI Defense Forms (NYDWIFM)
James F. Orr and Michael S. Taheri

New York Vehicle and Traffic Law 2d (NYVEH)
James Rose

Village, Town and District Courts in New York
Robert Bogle, James Morris, Thomas Liotti and Maryrita Dobiel

West's State Practice Series

West has specialized criminal and civil practice and procedure volumes available for many states. Please visit www.west.thomson.com for full details on titles in the following states:
AL, AK, AZ, CO, CT, FL, IA, IL, IN, KY, LA, MA, MD, ME, MI, MN, MO, MS, NE, NJ, NY, NC, OH, OK, PA, TN, TX, UT, VA, WA, WI

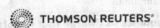

Table of Contents

CHAPTER 1. BASIC DEFINITIONS: SEARCH, SEIZURE, AND THE EXCLUSIONARY RULE

CHAPTER 2. SEARCH

CHAPTER 3. SEIZURE

CHAPTER 4. ARREST

CHAPTER 5. SEARCH WARRANT REQUIREMENTS

CHAPTER 6.   WARRANTLESS SEARCHES

CHAPTER 7.   SEARCHES INCIDENT TO ARREST

CHAPTER 8.   EXIGENT CIRCUMSTANCES

CHAPTER 9. STOP AND FRISK

CHAPTER 10. VEHICLE STOPS

CHAPTER 11. VEHICLE SEARCHES

CHAPTER 12. CONTAINER AND LUGGAGE SEARCHES

CHAPTER 13. INVENTORY SEARCHES

CHAPTER 17. CONSENT

CHAPTER 18. BORDER AND IMMIGRATION STOPS AND SEARCHES

CHAPTER 19. DEPARTMENT OF HOMELAND SECURITY SEARCHES AND SEIZURES

required in criminal cases but not in civil administrative proceedings

§ 19:3   Suppression: Illegally seized evidence may be admitted in deportation hearings

CHAPTER 20. BOAT STOPS AND SEARCHES

§ 20:1   Standard: The Fourth Amendment applies to stops and searches conducted by governmental agents within the jurisdiction of the United States, on the high seas, and in foreign waters

§ 20:2   Document stops in inland waters: Customs officials may stop a boat in inland waters without reasonable suspicion and board it to inspect its documentation

§ 20:3   Investigatory stops in inland waters: Customs officials having a reasonable suspicion that illegal activity is occurring on a vessel in inland waters may make an investigatory stop of the vessel

§ 20:4   Searches in inland waters: Warrantless searches in inland waters are permissible when probable cause and exigent circumstances exist

§ 20:5   Border searches: A search of a vessel that has crossed into the territory of the United States is subject to border search standards if the search takes place in an area contiguous to, or a functional equivalent of, the border

§ 20:6   American vessels on the high seas: United States registered vessels on the high seas are subject to routine safety or documentation inspections

§ 20:7   Foreign vessels on the high seas: The Coast Guard may stop and search a foreign vessel on the high seas if it has a reasonable suspicion that those aboard the vessel are involved in criminal activity

§ 20:8   American vessels in foreign waters: Unless the sovereign power involved objects, the Coast Guard has the authority to stop and search United States vessels in foreign waters on a showing of probable cause coupled with exigent circumstances

§ 20:9   Scope of searches: The Coast Guard may not search a private area of a ship unless it has a reasonable suspicion that the area contains seizable items

CHAPTER 33. BURDENS OF PROOF

CHAPTER 34. DERIVATIVE EVIDENCE: THE FRUIT OF THE POISONOUS TREE DOCTRINE

Chapter 1

Basic Definitions: Search, Seizure, and the Exclusionary Rule

Research References

West's Key Number Digest

§ 1:1 Constitutional law: The Fourth Amendment, as applied to the states through the Fourteenth Amendment, governs the law of searches and seizures

U.S. Constitution

- "The right of the people to be secure in their persons, houses, papers, and effects, against unreasonable searches and seizures, shall not be violated and no warrants shall issue, but upon probable cause, supported by oath or affirmation, and particularly describing the place to be searched, and the persons or things to be seized." U.S. Const. amend. IV.

Supreme Court

- "It is well settled that the Fourth Amendment's protection extends beyond the sphere of criminal investigations." *City of Ontario, Cal. v. Quon*, 560 U.S. 746, 130 S. Ct. 2619, 2627, 177 L. Ed. 2d 216, 30 I.E.R. Cas. (BNA) 1345, 93 Empl. Prac. Dec. (CCH) P 43907, 159 Lab. Cas. (CCH) P 61011 (2010).
- "We need not pick and choose among the dicta: Neither *Di Re* nor the cases following it held that violations of state arrest law are also violations of the Fourth Amendment, and our more recent decisions, discussed above, have indicated that when States go above the Fourth Amendment minimum, the Constitution's protections concerning search and seizure remain the same." *Virginia v. Moore*, 553 U.S. 164, 173, 128 S. Ct. 1598, 1605, 170 L. Ed. 2d 559 (2008).
- "In deciding whether a challenged governmental action violates the Amendment, we have taken care to inquire whether the action was regarded as an unlawful search and seizure when the Amendment was framed." *Florida v. White*, 526 U.S. 559, 563, 119 S. Ct. 1555, 143 L. Ed. 2d 748 (1999).
- "The Fourth Amendment guarantees: The right of the

people to be secure in their persons, houses, papers, and effects, against unreasonable searches and seizures, shall not be violated, and no Warrants shall issue, but upon probable cause, supported by Oath or affirmation, and particularly describing the place to be searched, and the persons or things to be seized. The Amendment protects persons against unreasonable searches of their persons and houses and thus indicates that the Fourth Amendment is a personal right that must be invoked by an individual." *Minnesota v. Carter*, 525 U.S. 83, 88, 119 S. Ct. 469, 142 L. Ed. 2d 373 (1998).

- "The Fourth Amendment requires government to respect the right of the people to be secure in their persons against unreasonable searches and seizures. This restraint on government conduct generally bars officials from undertaking a search or seizure absent individualized suspicion. Searches conducted without grounds for suspicion of particular individuals have been upheld, however, in certain limited circumstances. These circumstances include brief stops for questioning or observation at a fixed Border Patrol checkpoint or at a sobriety checkpoint and administrative inspections in closely regulated businesses." *Chandler v. Miller*, 520 U.S. 305, 308, 117 S. Ct. 1295, 137 L. Ed. 2d 513, 12 I.E.R. Cas. (BNA) 1233, 145 A.L.R. Fed. 657 (1997).

- "We have long held that the touchstone of the Fourth Amendment is reasonableness. Reasonableness, in turn, is measured in objective terms by examining the totality of the circumstances. In applying this test we have consistently eschewed bright-line rules, instead emphasizing the fact-specific nature of the reasonableness inquiry." *Ohio v. Robinette*, 519 U.S. 33, 39, 117 S. Ct. 417, 136 L. Ed. 2d 347, 148 A.L.R. Fed. 739 (1996).

- "The Fourth Amendment to the Constitution protects the right of the people to be secure in their persons, houses, papers, and effects, against unreasonable searches and seizures. In evaluating the scope of this right, we have looked to the traditional protections against unreasonable searches and seizures afforded by the common law at the time of the framing. Although the underlying command of the Fourth Amendment is always that searches and seizures be reasonable." *Wilson v. Arkansas*, 514 U.S. 927, 931, 115 S. Ct. 1914, 131 L. Ed. 2d 976 (1995).

- "[T]he text of the Fourth Amendment, its history, and our cases discussing the application of the constitution to aliens and extraterritorially [sic] require rejection of respondent's claim. At the time of the search, he was a citizen and resident of Mexico with no voluntary attachment to the United States, and the place searched was located in Mexico. Under these circumstances, the Fourth Amendment has no application." *U.S. v. Verdugo-Urquidez*, 494 U.S. 259, 275, 110 S. Ct. 1056, 108 L. Ed. 2d 222 (1990).
- "Since the Fourth Amendment's right of privacy has been declared enforceable against the States through the Due Process Clause of the Fourteenth Amendment, it is enforceable against them by the same sanction of exclusion as is used against the Federal Government." *Mapp v. Ohio*, 367 U.S. 643, 655, 81 S. Ct. 1684, 6 L. Ed. 2d 1081, 86 Ohio L. Abs. 513, 84 A.L.R.2d 933 (1961).

First Circuit

- "Although individualized suspicion is normally required for a car stop and 'probable cause' is required for an arrest, the Fourth Amendment rubric is 'reasonableness.' " *U.S. v. William*, 603 F.3d 66 (1st Cir. 2010).
- "Fourth Amendment rights are not mere second-class rights but belong in the catalog of indispensable freedoms. Among deprivations of rights, none is so effective in cowing a population, crushing the spirit of the individual and putting terror in every heart. Uncontrolled search and seizure is one of the first and most effective weapons in the arsenal of every arbitrary government. . . . But the right to be secure against searches and seizures is one of the most difficult to protect. Since the officers are themselves the chief invaders, there is no enforcement outside of court. . . . Courts can protect the innocent against such invasions only indirectly and through the medium of excluding evidence obtained against those who frequently are guilty." *U.S. v. Khounsavanh*, 113 F.3d 279, 285 (1st Cir. 1997).

Sixth Circuit

- "The touchstone of the Fourth Amendment is

reasonableness. . . . The reasonableness determination hinges upon objective factors, not the actual subjective motivation of the officer(s) involved." *U.S. v. Saucedo*, 226 F.3d 782, 789, 2000 FED App. 0315P (6th Cir. 2000).

- "The Fourth Amendment safeguards the privacy of individuals against arbitrary and unwarranted governmental intrusions by providing that the right of the people to be secure in their persons, houses, papers, and effects against unreasonable searches and seizures, shall not be violated. However, the Fourth Amendment does not proscribe all searches and seizures, but only those that are unreasonable." *Knox County Educ. Ass'n v. Knox County Bd. of Educ.*, 158 F.3d 361, 371, 130 Ed. Law Rep. 62, 14 I.E.R. Cas. (BNA) 609 (6th Cir. 1998).

Seventh Circuit

- "It is true that the Fourth Amendment protects police officers, not just ordinary citizens. This does not mean, however, that every order a police officer feels compelled to obey amounts to a seizure. *Gwynn v. City of Phila.*, 719 F.3d 295, 300 (3d Cir.2013). . . . The Fourth Amendment does not protect against the threat of job loss. So while an officer in Carter's position may have feared job-related consequences if he were to leave the residence without being patted down and searched, the potential for work-related discipline is not sufficient to succeed on a Fourth Amendment claim." *Carter v. City of Milwaukee*, 743 F.3d 540 (7th Cir. 2014).

- "The fourth amendment does not require police to follow their normal record-keeping procedures (or for that matter any state statute). . . ." *U.S. v. Billian*, 600 F.3d 791 (7th Cir. 2010).

- "With the exception of limited circumstances such as administrative searches, certain roadside checkpoints, and a narrow class of drug testing, a search or seizure is ordinarily considered unreasonable absent individualized suspicion of wrongdoing." *U.S. v. Taylor*, 596 F.3d 373 (7th Cir. 2010).

- "The Fourth Amendment provides that [t]he right of the people to be secure in their persons against unreasonable searches and seizures, shall not be violated, and no warrants shall issue, but upon probable cause. To determine whether a search is reasonable requires a

balancing of the need for the particular search against
the invasion of personal rights that the search entails.
Courts must consider the scope of the particular intrusion, the manner in which it is conducted, the justification for initiating it, and the place in which it is
conducted." *Kraushaar v. Flanigan*, 45 F.3d 1040, 1045
(7th Cir. 1995).

Ninth Circuit

- "[T]he Fourth Amendment does not directly govern the
  conduct of tribal governments. Nonetheless, the Indian
  Civil Rights Act ("ICRA") imposes an 'identical limitation' on tribal government conduct as the Fourth
  Amendment. Thus, we analyze the reasonableness of
  the stop under well developed Fourth Amendment precedent, which nets the same result as an analysis under
  ICRA." *U.S. v. Becerra-Garcia*, 397 F.3d 1167 (9th Cir.
  2005).

- "Individuals who have been arrested without a warrant
  and brought to a detention facility are subject to
  custodial detention involving isolation in a cell inter-
  spersed with the various administrative procedures of
  the booking process prior to arraignment or a probable
  cause hearing. We are persuaded by precedent which
  applies the Fourth Amendment standard to assess the
  constitutionality of the duration of or legal justification
  for a prolonged warrantless, post-arrest, pre-
  arraignment custody that the Fourth Amendment
  should also apply to evaluate the condition of such
  custody." *Pierce v. Multnomah County, Or.*, 76 F.3d
  1032, 1043 (9th Cir. 1996).

- "In *Verdugo-Urquidez*, the Court held that the Fourth
  Amendment does not apply to the search and seizure by
  United States agents of property owned by a Mexican
  citizen and located in his Mexican residence. The Court
  observed that the Fourth Amendment, by contrast with
  the Fifth and Sixth Amendments, extends its reach only
  to the people. The Court noted that the people seems to
  have been a term of art employed in select parts of the
  Constitution that refers to a class of persons who are
  part of a national community or who have otherwise
  developed sufficient connection with this country to be
  considered part of that community. Thus, the Court

reasoned, the purpose of the Fourth Amendment was to protect the people of the United States against arbitrary action by their own Government, and not to restrain the actions of the Federal Government against aliens outside of the United States territory." *Wang v. Reno*, 81 F.3d 808, 816–17 (9th Cir. 1996).

§ 1:2 Interests protected: The Fourth Amendment protects the reasonable privacy interests of individuals

Supreme Court

- "We have repeatedly told courts . . . not to define clearly established law at a high level of generality. The dispositive question is whether the violative nature of *particular* conduct is clearly established. This inquiry must be undertaken in light of the specific context of the case, not as a broad general proposition. Such specificity is especially important in the Fourth Amendment context, where the Court has recognized that it is sometimes difficult for an officer to determine how the relevant legal doctrine, here excessive force, will apply to the factual situation the officer confronts." *Mullenix v. Luna*, 136 S. Ct. 305, 308, 193 L. Ed. 2d 255 (2015) (inner quotations and citations omitted).
- "Here, the right in question is not the general right to be free from retaliation for one's speech, but the more specific right to be free from a retaliatory arrest that is otherwise supported by probable cause. This Court has never held that there is such a right." *Reichle v. Howards*, 566 U.S. 658, 132 S. Ct. 2088, 2094, 182 L. Ed. 2d 985 (2012).
- "Our Fourth Amendment analysis embraces two questions. First, we ask whether the individual, by his conduct, has exhibited an actual expectation of privacy; that is, whether he has shown that he sought to preserve something as private. . . . Second, we inquire whether the individual's expectation of privacy is one that society is prepared to recognize as reasonable." *Bond v. U.S.*, 529 U.S. 334, 338, 120 S. Ct. 1462, 146 L. Ed. 2d 365 (2000).
- "Property used for commercial purposes is treated differently for Fourth Amendment purposes than residen-

tial property. An expectation of privacy in commercial premises, however, is different from, and indeed less than, a similar expectation in an individual's home." *Minnesota v. Carter*, 525 U.S. 83, 90, 119 S. Ct. 469, 142 L. Ed. 2d 373 (1998).

- "[T]he seizure of an object in plain view does not involve an intrusion on privacy. If the interest in privacy has been invaded, the violation must have occurred before the object came into plain view and there is no need for an inadvertence limitation on seizures to condemn it. The prohibition against general searches and general warrants serves primarily as a protection against unjustified intrusions on privacy. But reliance on privacy concerns that support that prohibition is misplaced when the inquiry concerns the scope of an exception that merely authorizes an officer with a lawful right of access to an item to seize it without a warrant." *Horton v. California*, 496 U.S. 128, 141–42, 110 S. Ct. 2301, 110 L. Ed. 2d 112 (1990).

- "The warrantless search and seizure of the garbage bags left at the curb outside the [Defendant's] house would violate the Fourth Amendment only if respondents manifested a subjective expectation of privacy in their garbage that society accepts as objectively reasonable. It may be that respondents did not expect that the contents of their garbage bags would become known to the police or other members of the public. An expectation of privacy does not give rise to Fourth Amendment protection, however, unless society is prepared to accept that expectation as objectively reasonable. Accordingly, having deposited their garbage in an area particularly suited for public inspection and, in a manner of speaking, public consumption, for the express purpose of having strangers take it respondents could have had no reasonable expectation of privacy in the inculpatory items that they discarded." *California v. Greenwood*, 486 U.S. 35, 39, 108 S. Ct. 1625, 100 L. Ed. 2d 30 (1988).

- "In an age where private and commercial flight in the public airways is routine, it is unreasonable for respondent to expect that his marijuana plants were constitutionally protected from being observed with the naked eye from an altitude of 1,000 feet. The Fourth Amendment simply does not require the police traveling in the public airways at this altitude to obtain a warrant in order to observe what is visible to the naked eye." *California v. Ciraolo*, 476 U.S. 207, 212–13, 106 S. Ct. 1809, 90 L. Ed. 2d 210 (1986).

- "The Fourth Amendment protects legitimate expectations of privacy rather than simply places. If the inspection by police does not intrude upon a legitimate expectation of privacy, there is no search subject to the Warrant Clause." *Illinois v. Andreas*, 463 U.S. 765, 771, 103 S. Ct. 3319, 77 L. Ed. 2d 1003 (1983).

- "[C]apacity to claim the protection of the Fourth Amendment depends not upon a property right in the invaded place but upon whether the person who claims the protection of the Amendment has a legitimate expectation of privacy in the invaded place." *Rakas v. Illinois*, 439 U.S. 128, 143, 99 S. Ct. 421, 58 L. Ed. 2d 387 (1978).

- "[T]he Fourth Amendment protects people, not places. What a person knowingly exposes to the public, even in his own home or office, is not a subject of Fourth Amendment protection. . . . But what he seeks to preserve as private, even in an area accessible to the public, may be constitutionally protected." *Katz v. U.S.*, 389 U.S. 347, 351–52, 88 S. Ct. 507, 19 L. Ed. 2d 576 (1967).

First Circuit

- "We agree that, at least in theory, privacy interests in not being overheard may be greater than in not being seen, and vice versa, depending on the circumstances of the case. We have recognized that, as a general matter, whether an individual has a reasonable expectation of privacy may depend in part on the nature of the government intrusion. . . . [However] we conclude that, considering the totality of the circumstances, [defendant] had no reasonable expectation that he would be free from audio surveillance during his brief visit to another person's motel room." *U.S. v. Larios*, 593 F.3d 82 (1st Cir. 2010).

Fourth Circuit

- "Our nation's historic aversion to the warrantless searches of dwelling houses and residences reaches its zenith when such searches are conducted at night.

Nighttime searches have long been recognized as more intrusive than searches conducted during the day. In fact, the Supreme Court has deemed it 'difficult to imagine a more severe invasion of privacy than the nighttime intrusion into a private home.' That proposition is valid because, during the nighttime hours, searches of dwellings by government agents tend to involve 'rousing the residents out of their beds, and forcing them to stand by in indignity in their night clothes,' all of which 'smack[s] of a police state lacking in the respect for' individual privacy rights. Thus, warrantless nighttime searches of homes were characterized by the second Justice Harlan as creating 'a grave constitutional question.' . . . At bottom, Yanez's suppression motion implicates a simple rule: a daytime warrant does not authorize a nighttime search. The government implies that 5:00 a.m. essentially is 'close enough' to 6:00 a.m. in the eyes of the Fourth Amendment. Notably, however, as John Adams observed in successfully defending British soldiers charged in the Boston Massacre, '[f]acts are stubborn things.' And the stubbornest fact here is that 5:00 a.m. is not 6:00 a.m. At 6:00 a.m., the warrant sanctioned the ICE agents to enter into the Premises. At 5:00 a.m., the warrant did not permit such an entry. Because the nighttime execution of the daytime warrant violated Yanez's Fourth Amendment rights, as it was executed without consent or exigent circumstances, we must turn to the question of whether the agents egregiously violated Yanez's Fourth Amendment rights." *Yanez-Marquez v. Lynch*, 789 F.3d 434, 465–69 (4th Cir. 2015) (citations omitted).

- "The policy clearly stated that FBIS would audit, inspect, and/or monitor employees' use of the Internet, including all file transfers, all websites visited, and all e-mail messages, as deemed appropriate. . . . This policy placed employees on notice that they could not reasonably expect that their Internet activity would be private. Therefore, regardless of whether [Defendant] subjectively believed that the files he transferred from the Internet were private, such a belief was not objectively reasonable. . . ." *U.S. v. Simons*, 206 F.3d 392, 398 (4th Cir. 2000).

Fifth Circuit

- "[T]he following factors are considered in the determination whether an interest is protected by the fourth amendment: whether the defendant has a possessory interest in the thing seized or the place searched, whether he has the right to exclude others from that place, whether he has exhibited a subjective expectation of privacy that it would remain free from governmental intrusion, whether he took normal precautions to maintain privacy and whether he was legitimately on the premises." *U.S. v. Vega*, 221 F.3d 789, 795–96, 54 Fed. R. Evid. Serv. 1502 (5th Cir. 2000).

- "As with all explorations of Fourth Amendment jurisprudence addressing the validity of searches, whether a constitutional interest has been violated depends on whether the questioned governmental conduct infringed upon a reasonable expectation of privacy. The constitution does not guarantee that a citizen will never be subjected to any search, but rather that a citizen is entitled to be free from unreasonable searches." *U.S. v. Jenkins*, 46 F.3d 447, 454 (5th Cir. 1995).

Sixth Circuit

- "Since the Supreme Court's decision in *Katz v. United States*. . . .the touchstone of Fourth Amendment analysis has been the question whether a person has a constitutionally protected reasonable expectation of privacy. . . . . If a person cannot establish a reasonable expectation of privacy, then the government's search of his property simply does not implicate the Fourth Amendment." *U.S. v. Rapanos*, 115 F.3d 367, 374, 44 Env't. Rep. Cas. (BNA) 2097, 27 Envtl. L. Rep. 20961, 1997 FED App. 0165P (6th Cir. 1997).

Seventh Circuit

- "The Constitution forbids not all searches and seizures, but only 'unreasonable searches and seizures.' " *Penn, LLC v. Prosper Business Development Corp.*, 991 F. Supp. 2d 981 (S.D. Ohio 2014), aff'd in part, rev'd in part and remanded on other grounds, 600 Fed. Appx. 393 (6th Cir. 2015) (citations omitted).

- "[Defendant] did not have a reasonable expectation of privacy in the Mustang after he turned it over to the

shipper. The doors were left unlocked, the driver of the
car carrier was given the keys, and [defendant] knew
that the driver would enter the Mustang and drive it.
We conclude that no one could have a reasonable
expectation of privacy in the contents of a vehicle under
those circumstances. . . . That the drugs were hidden
in a secret compartment in the car clearly evinces
[defendant]'s subjective desire that the drugs not be
discovered. But [defendant] must also show that his
expectation of privacy was objectively reasonable—the
simple act of hiding something will not necessarily trigger Fourth Amendment protections." *U.S. v. Crowder*,
588 F.3d 929 (7th Cir. 2009).

Eighth Circuit

- "The question of whether a person has a constitutionally protected reasonable expectation of privacy in an
area requires us to ask (1) whether the individual
manifested a subjective expectation of privacy in the
area; and (2) whether society is willing to recognize the
expectation as reasonable." *U.S. v. Mathias*, 721 F.3d
952 (8th Cir. 2013).

- "Justifiable eviction terminates a hotel occupant's reasonable expectation of privacy in the room under the
Fourth Amendment; an individual cannot assert an
expectation of being free from police intrusion upon his
solitude and privacy in a place from which he has been
justifiably expelled." *U.S. v. Molsbarger*, 551 F.3d 809
(8th Cir. 2009).

- "The Fourth Amendment protects an individual's reasonable expectation of privacy from unauthorized
intrusion. . . . Where an individual possesses a reasonable expectation of privacy—such as in his home—the
government must generally obtain a warrant before
conducting a search." *U.S. v. Madrid*, 152 F.3d 1034,
1037 (8th Cir. 1998).

Ninth Circuit

- "It's well established that 'a seizure lawful at its inception can nevertheless violate the Fourth Amendment
because its manner of execution unreasonably infringes
possessory interests.' For example, in *United States v.
Dass*, officers validly seized packages that they sus-

pected contained marijuana. But we held that the length of the warrantless seizures—in that case, between seven to twenty-three days—violated the Fourth Amendment. The parties agree that the LAPD could impound—and, therefore, seize—Brewster's vehicle under section 14602.6(a)(1) pursuant to the community caretaking exception to the Fourth Amendment. The exigency that justified the seizure vanished once the vehicle arrived in impound and Brewster showed up with proof of ownership and a valid driver's license. The question we must consider is whether the Fourth Amendment required further authorization for the LAPD to hold the vehicle for 30 days. . .. Because a 30-day impound is a 'meaningful interference with an individual's possessory interests in [his] property,' the Fourth Amendment is implicated when a vehicle is impounded under section 14602.6(a). The district court found that such a seizure doesn't present a Fourth Amendment problem because 'the state has an important interest in . . . keeping unlicensed drivers from driving illegally.' But that is beside the point. The Fourth Amendment 'is implicated by a delay in returning the property, whether the property was seized for a criminal investigation, to protect the public, or to punish the individual.' The Fourth Amendment doesn't become irrelevant once an initial seizure has run its course. A seizure is justified under the Fourth Amendment only to the extent that the government's justification holds force. Thereafter, the government must cease the seizure or secure a new justification. Appellees have provided no justification here. . . . The 30-day impound of Brewster's vehicle constituted a seizure that required compliance with the Fourth Amendment. Appellees argue that this result frustrates the state legislature's intent to impose a penalty on unlicensed drivers. We have no occasion to decide whether this objective is lawful. The police could impound a vehicle under section 22651(p), which authorizes impoundment when the driver doesn't have a valid license. Section 22651(p) doesn't have a mandatory 30-day hold period, thus avoiding the Fourth Amendment problem presented by section 14602.6(a)." *Brewster v. Beck*, 859 F.3d 1194, 1196–98 (9th Cir. 2017) (citations omitted).

- "Individuals may have a reasonable expectation of privacy against intrusions by police into their offices, but, unlike the nearly absolute protection of a residence, the great variety of work environments requires analysis of reasonable expectations on a case-by-case basis. A reasonable expectation of privacy does not arise ex officio, but must be established with respect to the person in question." *U.S. v. SDI Future Health, Inc.*, 568 F.3d 684, 103 A.F.T.R.2d 2009-2436 (9th Cir. 2009).

Eleventh Circuit

- "The Supreme Court long has recognized that the Fourth Amendment's guarantee of freedom from warrantless searches and seizures is not premised on arcane concepts of property and possessory interests; instead, the Fourth Amendment protects an individual in those places where she can demonstrate a reasonable expectation of privacy against government intrusion." *U.S. v. Cooper*, 203 F.3d 1279, 1283–84 (11th Cir. 2000).

§ 1:3   Houses: An individual has a high expectation of privacy in a residence

Supreme Court

- "At the very core of the Fourth Amendment stands the right of a man to retreat into his own home and there be free from unreasonable governmental intrusion. . . .With few exceptions, the question whether a warrantless search of a home is reasonable and hence constitutional must be answered no." *Kyllo v. U.S.*, 533 U.S. 27, 121 S. Ct. 2038, 2041, 150 L. Ed. 2d 94 (2001).
- "We think that obtaining by sense-enhancing technology any information regarding the interior of the home that could not otherwise have been obtained without physical intrusion into a constitutionally protected area. . .constitutes a search—at least where (as here) the technology in question is not in general public use. . . .On the basis of this criterion, the information obtained by the thermal imager in this case was the product of a search." *Kyllo v. U.S.*, 533 U.S. 27, 121 S. Ct. 2038, 2043, 150 L. Ed. 2d 94 (2001).
- "[W]e have held that in some circumstances a person may have a legitimate expectation of privacy in the

house of someone else. In *Minnesota v. Olson*. . .for example, we decided that an overnight guest in a house had the sort of expectation of privacy that the Fourth Amendment protects. . . . Thus an overnight guest in a home may claim the protection of the Fourth Amendment, but one who is merely present with the consent of the householder may not." *Minnesota v. Carter*, 525 U.S. 83, 89–90, 119 S. Ct. 469, 142 L. Ed. 2d 373 (1998).

- "It is axiomatic that the physical entry of the home is the chief evil against which the wording of the Fourth Amendment is directed. And a principal protection against unnecessary intrusions into private dwellings is the warrant requirement imposed by the Fourth Amendment on agents of the government who seek to enter the home for purposes of search or arrest." *Welsh v. Wisconsin*, 466 U.S. 740, 748, 104 S. Ct. 2091, 80 L. Ed. 2d 732 (1984).

- "[T]he Fourth Amendment to the United States Constitution. . .prohibits the police from making a warrantless and nonconsensual entry into a suspect's home in order to make a routine felony arrest. [T]he Fourth Amendment has drawn a firm line at the entrance to the house. Absent exigent circumstances, that threshold may not reasonably be crossed without a warrant." *Payton v. New York*, 445 U.S. 573, 576, 100 S. Ct. 1371, 63 L. Ed. 2d 639 (1980).

First Circuit

- "The government cites no case in which a resident of a single-family structure was found to lack a reasonable expectation of privacy, relative to outsiders, in the common areas of his or her house. Instead, it points to inapposite cases involving duplexes or larger buildings in which tenants lived in separate, fully self-contained units. Similarly, the district court mistakenly adopted the frame of reference for multi-unit buildings in observing that Werra lacked a privacy interest in the foyer because others living in the house could pass through the entryway without his permission. The inability to exclude cohabitants from shared spaces within a traditional home does not on its own eliminate a resident's privacy interest in keeping outsiders from barging through the front door. Individuals routinely bring friends into their homes without the consent of every family member who resides there, and such unilateral decisions do not convert the hallway or entrance of a private home into a public space. There is no evidence that people who did not live at 63 Menlo Street routinely entered without the consent of a resident, which might have undermined the presumption of privacy that normally attends the interior of a residence." *U.S. v. Werra*, 638 F.3d 326 (1st Cir. 2011).

- "We agree that, at least in theory, privacy interests in not being overheard may be greater than in not being seen, and vice versa, depending on the circumstances of the case. We have recognized that, as a general matter, whether an individual has a reasonable expectation of privacy may depend in part on the nature of the government intrusion. . . . [However] we conclude that, considering the totality of the circumstances, [defendant] had no reasonable expectation that he would be free from audio surveillance during his brief visit to another person's motel room." *U.S. v. Larios*, 593 F.3d 82 (1st Cir. 2010).

- "The record shows that [defendant] had lived with [his girlfriend] in the apartment since April 2002, at least when they were not fighting, and that he kept his possessions there. As such, he had a reasonable expectation of privacy in the apartment and could object to the continuing search of his residence, even if it was also [the girlfriend's] primary residence. The apartment was his home at the time of the search, and he was entitled to Fourth Amendment protection of his home." *U.S. v. Paradis*, 351 F.3d 21 (1st Cir. 2003).

Second Circuit

- "The Fourth Amendment's warrant requirement protects one's privacy interest in home or property. Absent exigent circumstances or some other exception, the police must obtain a warrant before they enter the home to conduct a search or otherwise intrude on an individual's legitimate expectation of privacy." *U.S. v. Gori*, 230 F.3d 44, 50 (2d Cir. 2000).

Fourth Circuit

- "Our nation's historic aversion to the warrantless

searches of dwelling houses and residences reaches its
zenith when such searches are conducted at night.
Nighttime searches have long been recognized as more
intrusive than searches conducted during the day. In
fact, the Supreme Court has deemed it 'difficult to
imagine a more severe invasion of privacy than the
nighttime intrusion into a private home.' That proposition is valid because, during the nighttime hours,
searches of dwellings by government agents tend to
involve 'rousing the residents out of their beds, and
forcing them to stand by in indignity in their night
clothes,' all of which 'smack[s] of a police state lacking
in the respect for' individual privacy rights. Thus, warrantless nighttime searches of homes were characterized by the second Justice Harlan as creating 'a grave
constitutional question.' Rule 41 of the Federal Rules of
Criminal Procedure implements the Fourth Amendment's protections against warrantless searches. It
provides that a judicial officer must issue a search warrant if a federal law enforcement officer or an attorney
for the government presents an affidavit or other information showing probable cause to search a property.
Additionally, Rule 41 sets forth procedures controlling
the time at which a warrant may be executed, reflecting
that 'increasingly severe standards of probable cause
are necessary to justify increasingly intrusive searches.'
Once issued, a warrant can normally be executed solely
'in the daytime,' between 6:00 a.m. and 10:00 p.m., 'unless the judge for good cause expressly authorizes execution' during the night. Good cause for a nighttime
warrant might exist, for example, where necessary to
prevent the destruction of evidence. Because of the separate, heightened burden of proof required for issuance
of a nighttime warrant, the existence of a daytime warrant ordinarily does not justify a nighttime search. . . .
Following the persuasive decisions of the Third and
Tenth Circuits, as well as the Supreme Court's decision
in *Jones* where the Court accepted that the government's concession that a nighttime search conducted
pursuant to a daytime warrant violated the Fourth
Amendment, we hold that the nighttime execution of a
daytime warrant violates the Fourth Amendment,
absent consent or exigent circumstances. Applying the

foregoing principles to Yanez's Fourth Amendment timing claim reveals that the 5:00 a.m. search of the Premises violated the Fourth Amendment. . . . At bottom, Yanez's suppression motion implicates a simple rule: a daytime warrant does not authorize a nighttime search. The government implies that 5:00 a.m. essentially is 'close enough' to 6:00 a.m. in the eyes of the Fourth Amendment. Notably, however, as John Adams observed in successfully defending British soldiers charged in the Boston Massacre, '[f]acts are stubborn things.' And the stubbornest fact here is that 5:00 a.m. is not 6:00 a.m. At 6:00 a.m., the warrant sanctioned the ICE agents to enter into the Premises. At 5:00 a.m., the warrant did not permit such an entry. Because the nighttime execution of the daytime warrant violated Yanez's Fourth Amendment rights, as it was executed without consent or exigent circumstances, we must turn to the question of whether the agents egregiously violated Yanez's Fourth Amendment rights." *Yanez-Marquez v. Lynch*, 789 F.3d 434, 465–69 (4th Cir. 2015) (citations omitted).

Seventh Circuit

- "It is by now well-established that Fourth Amendment protections extend to temporary dwellings such as hotel rooms." *U.S. v. Brack*, 188 F.3d 748, 755 (7th Cir. 1999).
- "A person's expectation of privacy is legitimate only if it is one that society is willing to accept. . . . A person can have a legally sufficient interest in a place other than his own home so that the Fourth Amendment protects him from an unreasonable government intrusion into that place. . . . Accordingly, the Supreme Court has recognized that overnight guests have a legitimate expectation of privacy in their hosts' homes." *Terry v. Martin*, 120 F.3d 661, 663 (7th Cir. 1997).

Eighth Circuit

- "Under our precedent, once an individual is lawfully ejected from a hotel, the rental period terminates and 'control over the hotel room revert[s] to the management.' [. . . .] Thus, at the time the officers forcibly entered the hotel room at [the security guard's] request, [the co-defendant] had no reasonable expectation of privacy in the hotel room, and the subsequent search of the room did not violate his Fourth Amendment rights." *U.S. v. Bohmont*, 413 Fed. Appx. 946 (8th Cir. 2011).

- "[The defendant's] expectation of privacy in [the co-defendant's] hotel room is even more attenuated. [The defendant] did not rent the room, and the district court determined that he was not [the co-defendant's] overnight guest but rather was nothing more than [a] 'mere visitor[ ] in the room.' This distinction deprives [the defendant] of a protected privacy interest in the hotel room; although 'an overnight guest in a home may claim the protection of the Fourth Amendment, . . . one who is merely present with the consent of the householder may not.' . . . Having carefully reviewed the record, we conclude that the district court's determination that [the defendant] was a 'mere visitor' is not clearly erroneous. The finding is further supported by [a witness's] testimony that he went to the hotel room to purchase automobile rims from [the defendant], indicating that [the defendant] was present in the room for purposes of carrying out a commercial transaction. As noted by the Supreme Court, individuals have less of an expectation of privacy in commercial property than in residential property. . . . The *Sturgis* court relied on the facts that the defendant did not rent the room, was not an overnight guest, and was present only to deal drugs—a commercial activity—to hold that the defendant had no interest in the room protected by the Fourth Amendment. . . . [The defendant in this case] is in the same position as the defendant in *Sturgis,* and we are bound by its holdings. [The defendant] had no reasonable expectation of privacy in [the co-defendant's] room, and therefore his Fourth Amendment rights were not violated by the officers' search." *U.S. v. Bohmont*, 413 Fed. Appx. 946 (8th Cir. 2011) (citations omitted).
- "The Fourth Amendment has drawn a firm line at the entrance to the house. . . and it is designed to prevent, not simply to redress, unlawful police action." *U.S. v. Madrid*, 152 F.3d 1034, 1037 (8th Cir. 1998).
- "In *Payton*, the Supreme Court explained that no zone of privacy is more clearly defined than a person's home: The Fourth Amendment has drawn a firm line at the

entrance to the house. Absent exigent circumstances, that threshold may not reasonably be crossed without a warrant. . . . The same protection against unreasonable searches and seizures extends to a person's privacy in temporary dwelling places such as hotel or motel rooms." *U.S. v. Conner*, 127 F.3d 663, 666 (8th Cir. 1997).

Ninth Circuit

- "That same rationale applies when the police violate *Payton* by ordering a suspect to exit his home at gunpoint. The home receives special constitutional protection in part because 'at the very core of the Fourth Amendment stands the right of a man to retreat into his own home and there be free from unreasonable governmental intrusion.' When the police unreasonably intrude upon that interest by ordering a suspect to exit his home at gunpoint, the suspect's opportunity to collect himself before venturing out in public is certainly diminished, if not eliminated altogether. In this context, too, *Payton*'s protection of the privacy and sanctity of the home would be incomplete if it didn't extend to the person of a suspect forced to abandon the refuge of his home involuntarily." *U.S. v. Nora*, 765 F.3d 1049 (9th Cir. 2014) (citations omitted).

  "[Defendant]'s decision to open the property to public view by listing it for sale with the realty company manifested little, if any, subjective expectation of privacy, and whatever expectation of privacy they may have held subjectively was not objectively reasonable." *U.S. v. Schlotzhauer*, 356 Fed. Appx. 56 (9th Cir. 2009).

- "[Defendant's] rental period had yet to expire when the police searched his room. According to our precedent, unless his occupancy had been lawfully terminated when the police conducted their search, [defendant] retained a reasonable expectation of privacy in the room. The critical determination is whether or not management had justifiably terminated [defendant's] control of the room through private acts of dominion. It is undisputed in this case that the motel's manager took no affirmative steps to repossess the room once she learned that it had been reserved with a stolen credit card. To the contrary, she simply asked the police to investigate the matter, and would have evicted [defendant] only if he later failed to provide either a satisfactory explanation or another form of payment. . . . [T]he manager did not ask the police to evict [defendant]. Rather, the motel continued to recognize [defendant's] privacy rights, and planned to do so until [defendant] had the opportunity to speak with management. The government's argument that [defendant's] eviction was 'inevitable' misses the point. [Defendant] was still in possession of the room when the police entered and searched the premises, and that is the point in time when we determine the existence of any Fourth Amendment violation." *U.S. v. Bautista*, 362 F.3d 584 (9th Cir. 2004).

- "The Fourth Amendment's prohibition on warrantless entry into an individual's home does not apply to arrests made at the doorway, because the doorway is considered a public place." *LaLonde v. County of Riverside*, 204 F.3d 947, 955 (9th Cir. 2000).

- "Nowhere is the protective force of the Fourth Amendment more powerful than it is when the sanctity of the home is involved. The sanctity of a person's home, perhaps our last real retreat in this technological age, lies at the very core of the rights which animate the Amendment. Therefore, we have been adamant in our demand that absent exigent circumstances a warrant will be required before a person's home is invaded by the authorities." *U.S. v. Albrektsen*, 151 F.3d 951, 953 (9th Cir. 1998).

Tenth Circuit

- "An individual does not have to be settled at a location to have a reasonable expectation of privacy; a simple overnight guest has Fourth Amendment standing. Yet, not every individual legitimately on the premises has such a reasonable expectation. A social guest who does not stay overnight has a reasonable expectation of privacy; a social guest has a degree of acceptance into the household." *U.S. v. Poe*, 556 F.3d 1113 (10th Cir. 2009).

- "Until [homeowner] departed for work, she and [defendant] were in the home together for the entire time of the bounty hunters' surveillance. When she left, after

10:00 p.m., she permitted [defendant] to remain. Until a month earlier, [defendant] had lived at the residence with [homeowner]. He had lived there for a year and a half and, with her knowledge, had a key. She knew that [defendant] was expecting a drug customer at the house. [Homeowner] shared all of this information with the bounty hunters and never indicated that she did not want [defendant] in the house or that he was there without her permission. Further, [defendant] was a regular visitor since he had moved out, and the bounty hunters witnessed [defendant] invite another visitor into the house. Each of these factors weighs in favor of concluding that [defendant] had an ongoing and meaningful connection to [homeowner's] home as a social guest." *U.S. v. Poe*, 556 F.3d 1113 (10th Cir. 2009).

- "It is well settled that an individual's Fourth Amendment interest in freedom from governmental intrusion into the home is particularly strong, as this interest is rooted in the very language of the Fourth Amendment." *U.S. v. King*, 222 F.3d 1280, 1284 (10th Cir. 2000).

§ 1:4   Automobiles: An automobile affords a lesser expectation of privacy than a house for Fourth Amendment purposes

<u>Supreme Court</u>

- "Although we have recognized that a motorist's privacy interest in his vehicle is less substantial than in his home, the former interest is nevertheless important and deserving of constitutional protection." *Arizona v. Gant*, 556 U.S. 332, 129 S. Ct. 1710, 173 L. Ed. 2d 485, 47 A.L.R. Fed. 2d 657 (2009).

- "Our first cases establishing the automobile exception to the Fourth Amendment's warrant requirement were based on the automobile's ready mobility, an exigency sufficient to excuse failure to obtain a search warrant once probable cause to conduct the search is clear. More recent cases provide a further justification: the individual's reduced expectation of privacy in an automobile, owing to its pervasive regulation. If a car is readily mobile and probable cause exists to believe it contains contraband, the Fourth Amendment thus permits police to search the vehicle without more." *Pennsylvania v.*

Labron, 518 U.S. 938, 940, 116 S. Ct. 2485, 135 L. Ed. 2d 1031 (1996).

- "When a vehicle is being used on the highways, or if it is readily capable of such use and is found stationary in a place not regularly used for residential purposes— temporary or otherwise—the two justifications for the vehicle exception come into play. First, the vehicle is obviously readily mobile by the turn of an ignition key, if not actually moving. Second, there is a reduced expectation of privacy stemming from its use as a licensed motor vehicle subject to a range of police regulation inapplicable to a fixed dwelling. While it is true that respondent's vehicle possessed some, if not many of the attributes of a home, it is equally clear that the vehicle falls clearly within the scope of the exception laid down in *Carroll*. Like the automobile in *Carroll*, respondent's motor home was readily mobile. Furthermore, the vehicle was licensed to operate on public streets; [was] serviced in public places; and [was] subject to extensive regulation and inspection. And the vehicle was so situated that an objective observer would conclude that it was being used not as a residence, but as a vehicle." *California v. Carney*, 471 U.S. 386, 392–93, 105 S. Ct. 2066, 85 L. Ed. 2d 406 (1985).

- "It is unnecessary for us to decide here whether the same expectations of privacy are warranted in a car as would be justified in a dwelling place in analogous circumstances. We have on numerous occasions pointed out that cars are not to be treated identically with houses or apartments for Fourth Amendment purposes." *Rakas v. Illinois*, 439 U.S. 128, 148, 99 S. Ct. 421, 58 L. Ed. 2d 387 (1978).

- "This Court has traditionally drawn a distinction between automobiles and homes or offices in relation to the Fourth Amendment. [T]he inherent mobility of automobiles creates circumstances of such exigency that, as a practical necessity, rigorous enforcement of the warrant requirement is impossible. Besides the element of mobility, less rigorous warrant requirements govern because the expectation of privacy with respect to one's automobile is significantly less than that relating to one's home or office. Automobiles, unlike homes, are subjected to pervasive and continuing governmental regulation and controls, including periodic inspection and licensing requirements. The expectation of privacy as to automobiles is further diminished by the obviously public nature of automobile travel." *South Dakota v. Opperman*, 428 U.S. 364, 367–68, 96 S. Ct. 3092, 49 L. Ed. 2d 1000 (1976).

First Circuit

- "The search of one's person is more intrusive on the rights protected by the Fourth Amendment than the search of an automobile. Hence, circumstances which could justify a warrantless search of an automobile will not necessarily justify a warrantless search of a person." *U.S. v. Schiavo*, 29 F.3d 6, 9–10 (1st Cir. 1994).

Second Circuit

- "[C]itizens' reasonable expectations of privacy in their vehicles are reduced by the far-reaching web of state and federal regulations that covers not only vehicles but also our nation's roadways. As a result, warrantless searches of readily mobile vehicles, when based on probable cause, are reasonable under the Fourth Amendment." *U.S. v. Navas*, 597 F.3d 492 (2d Cir. 2010).

Fourth Circuit

- "It is axiomatic, of course, that one has a lesser expectation of privacy in a motor vehicle, in part because its function is transportation and it seldom serves as one's residence or as the repository of personal effects. Because of this, and the fact that vehicular travel is, of necessity, highly regulated, individuals traveling in vehicles must expect that the State, in enforcing its regulations, will intrude to some extent on their privacy." *U.S. v. Stanfield*, 109 F.3d 976, 982 (4th Cir. 1997).
- "The Fourth Amendment's protection of an individual's effects is preserved by the requirement that searches and seizures be conducted pursuant to a warrant issued by an independent judicial officer. One of the earliest exceptions to the warrant requirement was the automobile exception at issue in this case. the Court recognized that privacy interests in an automobile are constitution-

ally protected; however, that the automobile's ready mobility justifies a lesser degree of protection of those interests than would be afforded by a stationary structure. That a motor vehicle is readily mobile does not, however, mean that it may be seized and searched upon a mere pretext. As the Court made clear in *Carroll*, the measure of legality of such a seizure is, therefore, that the seizing officer shall have reasonable or probable cause for believing that the automobile which he stops and seizes has contraband therein which is being illegally transported." *U.S. v. Jones*, 31 F.3d 1304, 1312 (4th Cir. 1994).

Fifth Circuit

- "[T]he critical issue in this case is not whether there was probable cause for the search, but whether the trailer was more like a house or automobile for purposes of the Fourth Amendment. The Supreme Court has held that the warrantless search of a mobile home was within the automobile exception to the warrant requirement." *U.S. v. Ervin*, 907 F.2d 1534, 1538 (5th Cir. 1990).

Seventh Circuit

- "[T]here is no legitimate expectation of privacy shielding that portion of the interior of an automobile which may be viewed from outside the vehicle by either inquisitive passersby or diligent police officers." *U.S. v. Brown*, 79 F.3d 1499, 1508 (7th Cir. 1996).
- "[I]t is generally recognized that the privacy interest of people who are in transit on public thoroughfares are substantially less than those that attach to fixed dwellings." *U.S. v. Rem*, 984 F.2d 806, 812 (7th Cir. 1993).
- "Although it is well-established that citizens have a reasonable, albeit diminished, expectation of privacy in their automobiles, one may argue that any expectation of privacy is not reasonable once a person has subjected the automobile to search. The protections associated with the Fourth Amendment, however, are tied to objective reasonableness and merely lowering one's subjective expectations does not cause the constitutional protections to disappear." *McGann v. Northeast Illinois*

Regional Commuter R.R. Corp., 8 F.3d 1174, 1182, 8 I.E.R. Cas. (BNA) 1697, 9 I.E.R. Cas. (BNA) 827 (7th Cir. 1993).

<u>Ninth Circuit</u>

- "Expectation of privacy in an automobile is significantly different from the expectation of privacy within a home." *U.S. v. Ordaz*, 145 F.3d 1111, 1112 (9th Cir. 1998).

<u>Tenth Circuit</u>

- "[I]f society is willing to recognize as reasonable an expectation of privacy in an automobile in general, it cannot deny such recognition to particular compartments within that vehicle. The fact that secret compartments are most often used to conceal narcotics, weapons, or large amounts of cash does not alter the analysis; such *post hoc* rationalization subverts the purpose of the Fourth Amendment protection against unreasonable searches. Although an automobile is not accorded the same level of privacy protection as a permanent dwelling, if it is to be protected at all, there appears no reason to treat searches of secret compartments within the vehicle on any different basis than searches of the glove compartment or trunk." *U.S. v. Soto*, 988 F.2d 1548, 1554 (10th Cir. 1993).

- "Although the appellants point out that they took turns sleeping in the car during the return leg of their trip, we do not believe that the Supreme Court intended that any time an accused takes a long distance road trip in a car, the car is to be treated like a home for Fourth Amendment purposes. The point remains that regardless of whether it is driven across town or across the country, a car does not envelope its occupants in a house-like cloak of Fourth Amendment protection." *U.S. v. Jefferson*, 925 F.2d 1242, 1251, 32 Fed. R. Evid. Serv. 916 (10th Cir. 1991).

§ 1:5　Seizable items: The Fourth Amendment governs searches for contraband, fruits of criminal activity, instrumentalities, and evidence of crime

<u>Supreme Court</u>

- "[A]n officer who happens to come across an individual's property in a public area could seize it only if Fourth Amendment standards are satisfied—for example, if the items are evidence of a crime or contraband." *Soldal v. Cook County, Ill.*, 506 U.S. 56, 68, 113 S. Ct. 538, 121 L. Ed. 2d 450 (1992).

- "Under existing law, valid warrants may be issued to search *any* property, whether or not occupied by a third party, at which there is probable cause to believe that fruits, instrumentalities, or evidence of a crime will be found." *Zurcher v. Stanford Daily*, 436 U.S. 547, 554, 98 S. Ct. 1970, 56 L. Ed. 2d 525, 3 Media L. Rep. (BNA) 2377 (1978).

- "The requirements of the Fourth Amendment can secure the same protection of privacy whether the search is for mere evidence or for fruits, instrumentalities or contraband. There must, of course, be a nexus between the item to be seized and criminal behavior. Thus in the case of mere evidence, probable cause must be examined in terms of cause to believe that the evidence sought will aid in a particular apprehension or conviction." *Warden, Md. Penitentiary v. Hayden*, 387 U.S. 294, 306–07, 87 S. Ct. 1642, 18 L. Ed. 2d 782 (1967).

First Circuit

- "The incriminating nature of the evidence is immediately apparent, if the officer, upon observing the evidence, has probable cause to believe the item is contraband or evidence of a crime. A practical nontechnical probability that incriminating evidence is involved is all that is required." *U.S. v. McCarthy*, 77 F.3d 522, 534 (1st Cir. 1996).

Fourth Circuit

- "Other jurisdictions have held that a vehicle which has been used in a robbery may be seized without a warrant as evidence or as an instrumentality of a crime, particularly when it is parked on a public street." *U.S. v. Patterson*, 150 F.3d 382, 386, 49 Fed. R. Evid. Serv. 1271 (4th Cir. 1998).

Fifth Circuit

- "The general rule under the Fourth Amendment is that

27

any and all contraband, instrumentalities, and evidence of crimes may be seized based on probable cause." *Wallace v. Wellborn*, 204 F.3d 165, 167 (5th Cir. 2000).

Sixth Circuit

- "[P]robable cause means a reasonable ground for belief that the item seized is contraband or evidence of a crime." *U.S. v. Baro*, 15 F.3d 563, 567, 1994 FED App. 0029P (6th Cir. 1994).

Seventh Circuit

- "Although a person may possess a privacy interest in the contents of personal luggage, he may forfeit that interest by abandoning the luggage. Fourth Amendment protection does not extend to abandoned property." *Bond v. U.S.*, 77 F.3d 1009, 1013 (7th Cir. 1996).
- "Thinking a metal object might be a weapon does not meet the standard for plain view. The only item immediately apparent was a shiny chrome metal object of some kind. In order to determine what it was—in order to determine that it was a gun and not, say, a flashlight—[the] Officer had to further open the bag. The weapon (plus another gun and other incriminating items) then found was the product of a search, not something merely seized because it was in plain view. This is a close question. It was probably reasonable to suppose the shiny object was a gun. But because that fact was not immediately apparent [the] Officer['s] search of the bag without a warrant (assuming no other valid exception) violated [Defendant]'s constitutionally protected privacy interests under the Fourth Amendment." *U.S. v. Brown*, 79 F.3d 1499, 1509 (7th Cir. 1996).
- "The plain view doctrine is often considered an exception to the general rule that warrantless searches are presumptively unreasonable, but this characterization overlooks the important difference between searches and seizures. If an article is already in plain view, neither its observation nor its seizure would involve any invasion of privacy. A seizure of the article, however, would obviously invade the owner's possessory interest." *U.S. v. Brown*, 79 F.3d 1499, 1508 (7th Cir. 1996).

Tenth Circuit

- "The Fourth Amendment's requirement that a warrant particularly describe the things to be seized prevents a general, exploratory rummaging in a person's belongings and makes general searches impossible and prevents the seizure of one thing under a warrant describing another. As to what is to be taken, nothing is left to the discretion of the officer executing the warrant. The particularity requirement also ensures that a search is confined in scope to particularly described evidence relating to a specific crime for which there is demonstrated probable cause." *U.S. v. Janus Industries*, 48 F.3d 1548, 1553–54 (10th Cir. 1995).
- "[A] warrantless search and seizure of abandoned property is not unreasonable under the Fourth Amendment. It is not unreasonable because when individuals voluntarily abandon property, they forfeit any expectation of privacy in it that they might have had." *U.S. v. Austin*, 66 F.3d 1115, 1118 (10th Cir. 1995).

D.C. Circuit

- "We begin with the demise of Wrinkles. 'Every circuit that has considered the issue has held that the killing of a companion dog constitutes a "seizure" within the meaning of the Fourth Amendment.' Those circuits have invariably concluded that 'the use of deadly force against a household pet is reasonable only if the pet poses an immediate danger and the use of force is unavoidable.' As in any Fourth Amendment case, '[w]e analyze [the] question [of whether a pet constitutes an imminent threat] from the perspective "of a reasonable officer on the scene, rather than with the 20/20 vision of hindsight."' This analysis 'allow[s] for the fact that police officers are often forced to make split-second judgments—in circumstances that are tense, uncertain, and rapidly evolving—about the amount of force that is necessary in a particular situation.' " *Robinson v. Pezzat*, 818 F.3d 1, 7–8 (D.C. Cir. 2016) (citations omitted).

§ 1:6 Scope of seizure: Seizure includes both the collection of evidence and the detention of individuals

Supreme Court

- "Where, as here, the excessive force claim arises in the context of an arrest or investigatory stop of a free citizen, it is most properly characterized as one invoking the protections of the Fourth Amendment, which guarantees citizens the right to be secure in their persons against unreasonable seizures of the person." *Graham v. Connor*, 490 U.S. 386, 394, 109 S. Ct. 1865, 104 L. Ed. 2d 443 (1989).

- "A seizure affects only the person's possessory interests; a search affects a person's privacy interests." *Segura v. U.S.*, 468 U.S. 796, 806, 104 S. Ct. 3380, 82 L. Ed. 2d 599 (1984).

- "Although in the context of personal property, and particularly containers, the Fourth Amendment challenge is typically to the subsequent search of the container rather than to its initial seizure by the authorities, our cases reveal some general principles regarding seizures. In the ordinary case, the Court has viewed a seizure of personal property as *per se* unreasonable within the meaning of the Fourth Amendment unless it is accomplished pursuant to a judicial warrant issued upon probable cause and particularly describing the items to be seized. Where law enforcement authorities have probable cause to believe that a container holds contraband or evidence of a crime, but have not secured a warrant, the Court has interpreted the Amendment to permit seizure of the property, pending issuance of a warrant to examine its contents, if the exigencies of the circumstances demand it or some other recognized exception to the warrant requirement is present. [W]hen an officer's observations lead him reasonably to believe that a traveler is carrying luggage that contains narcotics, the principles of *Terry* and its progeny would permit the officer to detain the luggage briefly to investigate the circumstances that aroused his suspicion, provided that the investigative detention is properly limited in scope." *U.S. v. Place*, 462 U.S. 696, 701, 706, 103 S. Ct. 2637, 77 L. Ed. 2d 110 (1983).

- "[T]he detention of the respondent against his will constituted a seizure of his person, and the Fourth Amendment guarantee of freedom from unreasonable searches and seizures is clearly implicated. Nothing is more clear than that the Fourth Amendment was meant to prevent wholesale intrusions upon the personal security of our citizenry, whether these intrusions be termed arrests or investigatory detentions." *Cupp v. Murphy*, 412 U.S. 291, 294, 93 S. Ct. 2000, 36 L. Ed. 2d 900 (1973).

- "It is quite plain that the Fourth Amendment governs seizures of the person which do not eventuate in a trip to the station house and prosecution for crime—arrests in traditional terminology. It must be recognized that whenever a police officer accosts an individual and restrains his freedom to walk away, he has seized that person." *Terry v. Ohio*, 392 U.S. 1, 16, 88 S. Ct. 1868, 20 L. Ed. 2d 889 (1968).

Third Circuit

- "A person is seized for Fourth Amendment purposes only if he is detained by means intentionally applied to terminate his freedom of movement. A seizure occurs even when an unintended person is the object of detention, so long as the means of detention are intentionally applied to that person." *Berg v. County of Allegheny*, 219 F.3d 261, 269 (3d Cir. 2000).

- "Although the Supreme Court has repeatedly defined when a Fourth Amendment seizure occurs or begins, it has not determined when that seizure ends and Fourth Amendment protections no longer apply. We also have left open that question. It is beyond dispute that the Fourth Amendment has been construed to include events both before and after a formal arrest. . . . This case, however, concerns the other end of the Fourth Amendment continuum—post-conviction incarceration. Although Fourth Amendment seizure principles may in some circumstances have implications in the period between arrest and trial, we conclude that. . .post-trial incarceration does not qualify as a Fourth Amendment seizure." *Torres v. McLaughlin*, 163 F.3d 169, 174 (3d Cir. 1998).

Fourth Circuit

- "A Fourth Amendment seizure occurs whenever there is a governmental termination of freedom of movement through means intentionally applied. . . . The Court held in *Brower* that if the police purposely detain a person under the mistaken impression that he is some-

one else, they have seized him under the Fourth
Amendment. A seizure occurs even when an unintended
person or thing is the object of the detention or taking."
Vathekan v. Prince George's County, 154 F.3d 173, 178
(4th Cir. 1998).

Sixth Circuit

- "A seizure of property occurs when there is some
  meaningful interference with an individual's possessory
  interests in that property." *Bonds v. Cox*, 20 F.3d 697,
  701, 1994 FED App. 0106P (6th Cir. 1994).

Eighth Circuit

- "Police seize a person by engaging in conduct that would
  make a reasonable person feel he was not free to leave.
  . . . Other courts have recognized dispatching a police
  dog to find, bite, and detain a suspect may constitute a
  seizure . . .— order for police actions to constitute a
  seizure, the police must make physical contact with the
  suspect, or the suspect must acquiesce to an assertion
  of police authority." *Mettler v. Whitledge*, 165 F.3d 1197,
  1203–04 (8th Cir. 1999).

Ninth Circuit

- "Today, we reemphasize that the Fourth Amendment
  protects property as well as privacy and that the key to
  discerning a constitutional violation under that amendment is the intrusion on the people's security from
  governmental interference. We hold that [Defendant]'s
  statutory and Fourth Amendment rights were violated
  by the intrusion of government agents into his home
  during the early morning hours, without compliance
  with knock and announce requirements." *U.S. v. Becker*,
  23 F.3d 1537, 1541 (9th Cir. 1994).

Tenth Circuit

- "Violation of the Fourth Amendment requires an
  intentional acquisition of physical control. A seizure occurs even when an unintended person or thing is the
  object of the detention or taking, but the detention or
  taking itself must be willful." *Childress v. City of
  Arapaho*, 210 F.3d 1154, 1156 (10th Cir. 2000).
- "[T]he Fourth Amendment governs the period of confine-

ment between arrest without a warrant and the preliminary hearing at which a determination of probable cause is made, while due process regulates the period of confinement after the initial determination of probable cause." *Gaylor v. Does*, 105 F.3d 572, 574–75 (10th Cir. 1997).

- "A seizure of property occurs when there is some meaningful interference with an individual's possessory interests in that property. [S]eizures of property are subject to Fourth Amendment scrutiny even though no search within the meaning of the Amendment has taken place. Fourth Amendment safeguards apply to commercial premises as well as homes. Further, an individual and his private property are fully protected by the Fourth Amendment even when the individual is not suspected of criminal activity." *Winters v. Board of County Com'rs*, 4 F.3d 848, 853 (10th Cir. 1993).

§ 1:7 Probable cause defined: Probable cause means evidence which would lead a reasonable person to believe that an offense has been or is being committed or that seizable objects are in the place to be searched

Supreme Court

- "Perhaps the best that can be said generally about the required knowledge component of probable cause for a law enforcement officer's evidence search is that it raise a 'fair probability' or a 'substantial chance' of discovering evidence of criminal activity. (citations omitted) The lesser standard for school searches could as readily be described as a moderate chance of finding evidence of wrongdoing." *Safford Unified School Dist. No. 1 v. Redding*, 557 U.S. 364, 129 S. Ct. 2633, 174 L. Ed. 2d 354, 245 Ed. Law Rep. 626 (2009).
- "Articulating precisely what reasonable suspicion and probable cause mean is not possible. They are commonsense, nontechnical conceptions that deal with the factual and practical considerations of everyday life on which reasonable and prudent men, not legal technicians, act. As such, the standards are not readily, or even usefully, reduced to a neat set of legal rules." *Ornelas v. U.S.*, 517 U.S. 690, 695–96, 116 S. Ct. 1657, 134 L. Ed. 2d 911 (1996).

33

- "We think independent appellate review of these ultimate determinations of reasonable suspicion and probable cause is consistent with the position we have taken in past cases. We have never, when reviewing a probable-cause or reasonable-suspicion determination ourselves, expressly deferred to the trial court's determination. A policy of sweeping deference would permit, in the absence of any significant difference in the facts, the Fourth Amendment's incidence to turn on whether different trial judges draw general conclusions that the facts are sufficient or insufficient to constitute probable cause. Such varied results would be inconsistent with the idea of a unitary system of law. This, if a matter-of-course, would be unacceptable. In addition, the legal rules for probable cause and reasonable suspicion acquire content only through application. Independent review is therefore necessary if appellate courts are to maintain control of, and to clarify the legal principles. Finally, de novo review tends to unify precedent and will come closer to providing law enforcement officers with a defined set of rules which, in most instances, makes it possible to reach a correct determination beforehand as to whether an invasion of privacy is justified in the interest of law enforcement." *Ornelas v. U.S.*, 517 U.S. 690, 697–98, 116 S. Ct. 1657, 134 L. Ed. 2d 911 (1996).

- "[P]robable cause is a fluid concept—turning on the assessment of probabilities in particular factual contexts—not readily, or even usefully, reduced to a neat set of legal rules. While an effort to fix some general, numerically precise degree of certainty corresponding to probable cause may not be helpful, it is clear that only the probability, and not a prima facie showing, of criminal activity is the standard of probable cause." *Illinois v. Gates*, 462 U.S. 213, 232, 235, 103 S. Ct. 2317, 76 L. Ed. 2d 527 (1983).

- "[P]robable cause is a flexible, common-sense standard. It merely requires that the facts available to the officer would warrant a man of reasonable caution in the belief that certain items may be contraband or stolen property or useful as evidence of a crime; it does not demand any showing that such belief be correct or more likely true than false. A practical, nontechnical probability that incriminating evidence is involved is all that is required." *Texas v. Brown*, 460 U.S. 730, 742, 103 S. Ct. 1535, 75 L. Ed. 2d 502 (1983).

- "[Probable cause] mean[s] more than bare suspicion: Probable cause exists where the facts and circumstances within their [the Officers'] knowledge and of which they had reasonably trustworthy information [are] sufficient in themselves to warrant a man of reasonable caution in the belief that an offense has been or is being committed." *Brinegar v. U.S.*, 338 U.S. 160, 175, 69 S. Ct. 1302, 93 L. Ed. 1879 (1949).

Fourth Circuit

- "Accepting the allegations of the complaint as true, Goines, though having speech and other physical difficulties, exhibited no signs of mental illness and made no threats to harm himself or others, but instead sought the help of the police to avoid a confrontation and potential fight with a neighbor who had spliced into Goines' cable line. Under these facts, the Officers lacked probable cause for an emergency mental-health detention[.] . . . Probable cause, of course, is a 'fluid concept that cannot be reduced to a neat set of legal rules,' and our cases applying the concept in the mental-health context are perhaps not easily reduced to bright-line rules. Nonetheless, the facts as alleged by Goines— the involuntary detention of a man with physical disabilities who exhibited no signs of mental illness and made no threats of harm—are sufficiently beyond the realm of probable cause that no reasonable police officer would find them adequate." *Goines v. Valley Community Services Bd.*, 822 F.3d 159, 170 (4th Cir. 2016) (citation omitted).
- "Probable cause is simply not so exacting a standard that it requires a dog to be able to pinpoint the location of drugs within a foot or two. Instead, it is a 'commonsense' conception that deals with 'the factual and practical considerations of everyday life.'" *U.S. v. Kelly*, 592 F.3d 586 (4th Cir. 2010).

Fifth Circuit

- "A person's mere propinquity to others independently suspected of criminal activity does not, without more, give rise to probable cause to search that person. Where the standard is probable cause, a search or seizure of a person must be supported by probable cause particularized with respect to that person. However, proximity is not irrelevant; reasonable inferences may be drawn from a person's connection to the criminal activity." *U.S. v. Hearn*, 563 F.3d 95 (5th Cir. 2009).

- "It is almost a tautology to say that determining whether probable cause existed involves a matter of probabilities, but it nevertheless fairly describes the analysis we undertake. . . . The probable cause issue must be analyzed under the totality of the circumstances as to whether there is a fair probability that a crime occurred. . . . Although the fair probability must certainly be more than a bare suspicion. . . .our court has rejected the notion that the government must show that a reasonable person would have thought, by a preponderance of the evidence, that a defendant committed a crime. . . . In short, the requisite fair probability is something more than a bare suspicion, but need not reach the fifty percent mark." *U.S. v. Garcia*, 179 F.3d 265, 268–69 (5th Cir. 1999).

Sixth Circuit

- "Probable cause does not require police officers to establish a prima facie case that a crime has occurred or is occurring." *Young v. Owens*, 577 Fed. Appx. 410 (6th Cir. 2014).

"The real question, then, is this: at what point does a body of evidence amassed by a police officer against a particular suspect cross the line from merely raising a suspicion to establishing probable cause? In many respects, this raises a difficult epistemological problem. As Descartes famously observed, to the skeptic, any proposition—no matter how seemingly certain—carries with it a degree of doubt. But judges are not philosophers. To find probable cause, the law does not require that we rule out every conceivable explanation other than a suspect's illegal conduct. Instead, we need only consider whether there are facts that, given the factual and practical considerations of everyday life, could lead a reasonable person to believe that an illegal act has occurred or is about to occur." *U.S. v. Strick-*

land, 144 F.3d 412, 416, 1998 FED App. 0150P (6th Cir. 1998).

Seventh Circuit

- "Probable cause is an absolute defense to any claim under § 1983 for wrongful arrest or false imprisonment." *Bailey v. City of Chicago*, 779 F.3d 689 (7th Cir. 2015), cert. denied, 136 S. Ct. 200, 193 L. Ed. 2d 129 (2015). "While being present in a high-crime area cannot, in and of itself, support a particularized suspicion that a subject is committing a crime, an officer is permitted to consider a location's characteristics when assessing a situation." *U.S. v. Oglesby*, 597 F.3d 891 (7th Cir. 2010).
- "The rule of probable cause is a practical, nontechnical conception that affords the best compromise between the interests of individual liberty and effective law enforcement. . . .Contrary to what its name might seem to suggest, probable cause demands even less than probability. . . ." *Woods v. City of Chicago*, 234 F.3d 979, 996, 55 Fed. R. Evid. Serv. 912 (7th Cir. 2000).
- "The Supreme Court has refused to define probable cause, saying that whether it has been established varies with the facts of each case." *U.S. v. Roth*, 201 F.3d 888, 892 (7th Cir. 2000).

Eighth Circuit

- "Arresting officers are not required to witness actual criminal activity or have collected enough evidence so as to justify a conviction for there to be a legitimate finding of probable cause to justify a warrantless arrest. Instead, the mere 'probability or substantial chance of criminal activity, rather than an actual showing of criminal activity,' is all that is required. In making a probable cause determination, '[l]aw enforcement officers have substantial latitude in interpreting and drawing inferences from factual circumstances.'" *U.S. v. Winarske*, 715 F.3d 1063, 1067 (8th Cir. 2013) (citations omitted).
- "Probable cause may be based on the collective knowledge of all law enforcement officers involved in an investigation and need not be based solely upon the information within the knowledge of the officer on the scene if there is some degree of communication." *U.S. v. Wells*, 347 F.3d 280 (8th Cir. 2003).

- "In determining whether probable cause exists, we do not evaluate each piece of information independently; rather, we consider all of the facts for their cumulative meaning." *U.S. v. Nation*, 243 F.3d 467, 470, 56 Fed. R. Evid. Serv. 863 (8th Cir. 2001).
- "Probable cause to search exists where the known facts and circumstances are sufficient to warrant a man of reasonable prudence in the belief that contraband or evidence of a crime will be found. . . . We must consider the events leading up to the search and then decide whether these historical facts, viewed from the standpoint of an objectively reasonable police officer, amount to reasonable suspicion or probable cause." *U.S. v. Payne*, 119 F.3d 637, 642 (8th Cir. 1997).

Tenth Circuit

- "Probable cause doesn't require proof that something is more likely true than false. It requires only a 'fair probability,' a standard understood to mean something more than a 'bare suspicion' but less than a preponderance of the evidence at hand." *U.S. v. Denson*, 775 F.3d 1214, 1217 (10th Cir. 2014), cert. denied, 135 S. Ct. 2064, 191 L. Ed. 2d 967 (2015).
- "Probable cause to arrest exists when an officer, considering the totality of the circumstances before him, is led to a reasonable belief that an offense has been or is being committed by the suspect." *U.S. v. Allen*, 235 F.3d 482, 488 (10th Cir. 2000).

Eleventh Circuit

- "Probable cause requires more than mere suspicion, but does not require convincing proof. . . . The facts necessary to establish probable cause need not reach the standard of conclusiveness and probability as the facts necessary to support a conviction. In determining whether probable cause exists, we deal with probabilities. . .which are the factual and practical considerations of everyday life on which reasonable and prudent men, not legal technicians, act." *Rankin v. Evans*, 133 F.3d 1425, 1435, 39 Fed. R. Serv. 3d 1139 (11th Cir. 1998).

§ 1:8 Remedy: The principal remedy for unconstitutional police action is to exclude the illegally obtained evidence from admission in a criminal prosecution

Supreme Court

- "The Fourth Amendment protects the right to be free from 'unreasonable searches and seizures,' but it is silent about how this right is to be enforced. To supplement the bare text, this Court created the exclusionary rule, a deterrent sanction that bars the prosecution from introducing evidence obtained by way of a Fourth Amendment violation. The question here is whether to apply this sanction when the police conduct a search in compliance with binding precedent that is later overruled. Because suppression would do nothing to deter police misconduct in these circumstances, and because it would come at a high cost to both the truth and the public safety, we hold that searches conducted in objectively reasonable reliance on binding appellate precedent are not subject to the exclusionary rule." *Davis v. U.S.*, 564 U.S. 229, 131 S. Ct. 2419, 2423–24, 180 L. Ed. 2d 285, 68 A.L.R. Fed. 2d 665 (2011).
- "Real deterrent value is a 'necessary condition for exclusion,' but it is not 'a sufficient' one. The analysis must also account for the 'substantial social costs' generated by the rule. Exclusion exacts a heavy toll on both the judicial system and society at large. It almost always requires courts to ignore reliable, trustworthy evidence bearing on guilt or innocence. And its bottom-line effect, in many cases, is to suppress the truth and set the criminal loose in the community without punishment. Our cases hold that society must swallow this bitter pill when necessary, but only as a 'last resort.' For exclusion to be appropriate, the deterrence benefits of suppression must outweigh its heavy costs." *Davis v. U.S.*, 564 U.S. 229, 131 S. Ct. 2419, 2427, 180 L. Ed. 2d 285, 68 A.L.R. Fed. 2d 665 (2011) (citations omitted).
- "[T]he exclusionary rule is 'not a personal constitutional right.' It is a 'judicially created' sanction, specifically designed as a 'windfall' remedy to deter future Fourth Amendment violations." *Davis v. U.S.*, 564 U.S. 229, 131 S. Ct. 2419, 2433–34, 180 L. Ed. 2d 285, 68 A.L.R. Fed. 2d 665 (2011) (citations omitted).

- "Police practices trigger the harsh sanction of exclusion only when they are deliberate enough to yield '[meaningful]' deterrence, and culpable enough to be 'worth the price paid by the justice system.' The conduct of the officers here was neither of these things. The officers who conducted the search did not violate [the defendant's] Fourth Amendment rights deliberately, recklessly, or with gross negligence. Nor does this case involve any 'recurring or systemic negligence' on the part of law enforcement. The police acted in strict compliance with binding precedent, and their behavior was not wrongful. Unless the exclusionary rule is to become a strict-liability regime, it can have no application in this case. About all that exclusion would deter in this case is conscientious police work. . . . An officer who conducts a search in reliance on binding appellate precedent does no more than '"ac[t] as a reasonable officer would and should act"' under the circumstances. The deterrent effect of exclusion in such a case can only be to discourage the officer from '"do[ing] his duty."'" *Davis v. U.S.*, 564 U.S. 229, 131 S. Ct. 2419, 2428–29, 180 L. Ed. 2d 285, 68 A.L.R. Fed. 2d 665 (2011).

- "It is one thing for the criminal 'to go free because the constable has blundered.' It is quite another to set the criminal free because the constable has scrupulously adhered to governing law." *Davis v. U.S.*, 564 U.S. 229, 131 S. Ct. 2419, 2434, 180 L. Ed. 2d 285, 68 A.L.R. Fed. 2d 665 (2011) (citation omitted).

- "The Fifth Amendment guarantees that no person shall be compelled to give evidence against himself, and so is violated whenever a truly coerced confession is introduced at trial, whether by way of impeachment or otherwise. The Fourth Amendment, on the other hand, guarantees that no person shall be subjected to unreasonable searches or seizures, and says nothing about excluding their fruits from evidence; exclusion comes by way of deterrent sanction rather than to avoid violation of the substantive guarantee. Inadmissibility has not been automatic, therefore, but we have instead applied an exclusionary-rule balancing test." *Kansas v. Ventris*, 556 U.S. 586, 129 S. Ct. 1841, 1845, 173 L. Ed. 2d 801 (2009) (citation omitted).

- "In analyzing the applicability of the exclusionary rule,

the actions of all the police officers involved must be considered. It is necessary to consider the objective reasonableness, not only of the officers who eventually executed a warrant, but also of the officers who originally obtained it or who provided information material to the probable-cause determination. The fact that a Fourth Amendment violation occurred—*i.e.,* that a search or arrest was unreasonable—does not necessarily mean that the exclusionary rule applies. Indeed, exclusion has always been our last resort, not our first impulse. The rule is not an individual right and applies only where its deterrent effect outweighs the substantial cost of letting guilty and possibly dangerous defendants go free. For example, it does not apply if police acted in objectively reasonable reliance on an invalid warrant. The extent to which the exclusionary rule is justified by its deterrent effect varies with the degree of law enforcement culpability. To trigger the exclusionary rule, police conduct must be sufficiently deliberate that exclusion can meaningfully deter it, and sufficiently culpable that such deterrence is worth the price paid by the justice system. The pertinent analysis is objective, not an inquiry into the arresting officers' subjective awareness. When police mistakes leading to an unlawful search are the result of isolated negligence attenuated from the search, rather than systemic error or reckless disregard of constitutional requirements, the exclusionary rule does not apply." *Herring v. U.S.,* 555 U.S. 135, 129 S. Ct. 695, 172 L. Ed. 2d 496 (2009).

- "The question whether the exclusionary rule's remedy is appropriate in a particular context has long been regarded as an issue separate from the question whether the Fourth Amendment rights of the party seeking to invoke the rule were violated by police conduct." *Arizona v. Evans,* 514 U.S. 1, 10, 115 S. Ct. 1185, 131 L. Ed. 2d 34 (1995).
- "The exclusionary rule prohibits introduction into evidence of tangible materials seized during an unlawful search and of testimony concerning knowledge acquired during an unlawful search." *Murray v. U.S.,* 487 U.S. 533, 536, 108 S. Ct. 2529, 101 L. Ed. 2d 472 (1988).
- "In the absence of an allegation that the magistrate abandoned his detached and neutral role, suppression

is appropriate only if the officers were dishonest or reckless in preparing their affidavit or could not have harbored an objectively reasonable belief in the existence of probable cause." *U.S. v. Leon*, 468 U.S. 897, 926, 104 S. Ct. 3405, 82 L. Ed. 2d 677 (1984).

- "[S]uppression of evidence obtained pursuant to a warrant should be ordered only on a case-by-case basis and only in those unusual cases in which exclusion will further the purposes of the exclusionary rule." *U.S. v. Leon*, 468 U.S. 897, 918, 104 S. Ct. 3405, 82 L. Ed. 2d 677 (1984).

- "[T]he exclusionary rule should not be applied when the officer conducting the search acted in objectively reasonable reliance on a warrant issued by a detached and neutral magistrate that subsequently is determined to be invalid." *Massachusetts v. Sheppard*, 468 U.S. 981, 987–88, 104 S. Ct. 3424, 82 L. Ed. 2d 737 (1984).

- "The deterrent purpose of the exclusionary rule necessarily assumes that the police have engaged in willful, or at the very least negligent, conduct which has deprived the defendant of some right. By refusing to admit evidence gained as a result of such conduct, the courts hope to instill in those particular investigating officers, or in their future counterparts, a greater degree of care toward the rights of an accused." *Michigan v. Tucker*, 417 U.S. 433, 447, 94 S. Ct. 2357, 41 L. Ed. 2d 182 (1974).

- "The Government cannot violate the Fourth Amendment—in the only way in which the Government can do anything, namely through its agents—and use the fruits of such unlawful conduct to secure a conviction. Nor can the Government make indirect use of such evidence for its case, or support a conviction on evidence obtained through leads from the unlawfully obtained evidence. . . . All these methods are outlawed, and convictions obtained by means of them are invalidated, because they encourage the kind of society that is obnoxious to free men." *Walder v. U.S.*, 347 U.S. 62, 64–65, 74 S. Ct. 354, 98 L. Ed. 503 (1954).

First Circuit

- "The key precedent is *Hudson*. There, the Supreme Court squarely addressed whether a violation of the knock-and-announce rule might justify the exclusion of evidence seized. Noting that exclusion of evidence 'has always been [a] last resort, not [a] first impulse,' the Court held the exclusionary rule inapplicable to knock-and-announce violations. In taking this position, the Court noted two independent requirements for applying the exclusionary rule and explained why a knock-and-announce violation could never meet those requirements. To begin, the Court deemed but-for causation 'a necessary. . .condition for suppression.' In other words, there must be a causal link between the constitutional violation alleged and the discovery of the evidence seized. In the Court's view, a violation of the knock-and-announce rule could never achieve this benchmark; whether the officers knocked or not, the evidence would inevitably be discovered during the subsequent (valid) search. The *Hudson* Court set out a second condition for applying the exclusionary rule: that the beneficial effects of exclusion outweigh its social costs. In explaining why application of the exclusionary rule to knock-and-announce violations would be costly, the Court worried about a possible flurry of knock-and-announce litigation from prisoners seeking a 'get-out-of-jail-free card,' the potential for increased violence against officers hesitant to enter unannounced for fear that gathered evidence would be suppressed, and the potential for the destruction of evidence by those inside the dwelling. As against these substantial costs, the only benefit from exclusion would be the deterrence of police misconduct. Because the costs of using the exclusionary rule to remedy knock-and-announce violations would so clearly outweigh any corresponding benefits, the Court found this second requirement unmet." *U.S. v. Garcia-Hernandez*, 659 F.3d 108, 112 (1st Cir. 2011) (citations omitted).

Second Circuit

- "Although 18 U.S.C. § 2515 states that illegally obtained wire or oral communications may not be 'received in evidence in any trial,' the Government contends that we should nonetheless approve use of such communications for impeachment purposes, following the Supreme Court's use for impeachment purposes of evidence obtained in violation of the Fourth Amendment. As noted by the District Court in its written decision, the Senate Judiciary Committee report on the bill that became Title III states that Congress did not intend to 'press the scope of the suppression [rule] beyond present search and seizure law.' The report explicitly cites *Walder*. All of the circuits that have considered the issue have held that unlawfully obtained wiretap evidence may be used by the prosecution for impeachment in a criminal case. The Tenth Circuit has prohibited discovery of illegally obtained wiretap evidence in a civil case, distinguishing the cases permitting prosecution use for impeachment purposes in a criminal case on the ground that the exclusionary rule, which *Walder* declined to apply to Fourth Amendment violations, did not apply to private individuals. We agree with the courts applying the *Walder* rationale to evidence obtained in violation of Title III. As the First Circuit has pointed out, section 2515 cannot always be applied literally because doing so would preclude the use of illegally obtained wiretap evidence in a prosecution for violating Title III itself. And, as the Eighth Circuit has stated, 'It makes no sense for evidence obtained in violation of a mere statute to be more severely restricted than evidence obtained in violation of the Constitution. At the time the statute was enacted, evidence obtained in violation of the Fourth Amendment could be used for impeachment purposes. It is reasonable to assume that Congress had this background in mind when the statute was passed, and that, in the absence of an express statement, it did not intend to draw the line of exclusion in a different place.' " *U.S. v. Simels*, 654 F.3d 161, 169–70 (2d Cir. 2011) (citations omitted).

Third Circuit

- "The exclusionary rule serves to deter constitutional violations by denying the government the benefit of those violations, and accordingly, the application of the rule has been restricted to those areas where its remedial objectives are thought most efficaciously served." *U.S. v. Pelullo*, 173 F.3d 131, 136 (3d Cir. 1999).

Fourth Circuit

- "In our case, the IJ, the BIA, and the Attorney General all agree that the exclusionary rule applies in removal proceedings to egregious violations of the Fourth Amendment. Although we have not had occasion to consider the application of the exclusionary rule in removal proceedings in a published opinion, we are in agreement with those courts that have concluded that the rule applies to egregious violations of the Fourth Amendment. To hold otherwise would give no effect to the language used by the Supreme Court in *Lopez–Mendoza* expressing concern over fundamentally unfair methods of obtaining evidence and would ignore the fact that eight justices in *Lopez–Mendoza* seem to have agreed that the exclusionary rule applies in removal proceedings in some form. Moreover, even assuming the Court's limitation in *Lopez–Mendoza* could be construed as dicta, we simply cannot ignore the import of the language used by the Supreme Court in that case. Accordingly, we hold that the exclusionary rule applies in removal proceedings where the challenged evidence has been obtained by 'egregious violations of [the] Fourth Amendment . . . that might transgress notions of fundamental fairness and undermine the probative value of the evidence obtained.' Under this holding, an alien seeking the application of the exclusionary rule to a Fourth Amendment claim in a removal hearing faces two hurdles at the *prima facie* case stage. First, she must allege facts that state a violation of her rights under the Fourth Amendment. Second, the alien must show that the alleged violation of the Fourth Amendment was egregious. To get an evidentiary hearing, the alien must satisfy both prongs. If an evidentiary hearing is warranted, the alien will have the opportunity to present testimony and evidence in support of her Fourth Amendment claim. Upon the establishment of a *prima facie* case, the burden of proof shifts to the government to demonstrate why the IJ should admit the challenged evidence. A court reviewing the alien's claim may, but is not required to, address both the constitutional and egregiousness prongs. Like a § 1983 qualified immunity inquiry, the court can choose to decline to address whether a Fourth Amendment violation has occurred and first address whether the egregiousness prong has been satisfied. Thus, if the alien fails to allege facts sufficient to show that an immigration official has violated the Fourth Amendment, relief can be denied alone on that basis. Alternatively, relief can be denied where the alien fails to allege facts that an immigration official egregiously violated the Fourth Amendment. If there is an evidentiary hearing on the alien's claim, relief can be denied if the alien fails to meet her evidentiary burden on either prong." *Yanez-Marquez v. Lynch*, 789 F.3d 434, 450–51 (4th Cir. 2015) (citations omitted).

- "In our case, the IJ, the BIA, and the Attorney General all agree that the exclusionary rule applies in removal proceedings to egregious violations of the Fourth Amendment. . . . To hold otherwise would give no effect to the language used by the Supreme Court in *Lopez–Mendoza* expressing concern over fundamentally unfair methods of obtaining evidence and would ignore the fact that eight justices in *Lopez–Mendoza* seem to have agreed that the exclusionary rule applies in removal proceedings in some form. Moreover, even assuming the Court's limitation in *Lopez–Mendoza* could be construed as dicta, we simply cannot ignore the import of the language used by the Supreme Court in that case. Accordingly, we hold that the exclusionary rule applies in removal proceedings where the challenged evidence has been obtained by 'egregious violations of [the] Fourth Amendment . . . that might transgress notions of fundamental fairness and undermine the probative value of the evidence obtained.' Under this holding, an alien seeking the application of the exclusionary rule to a Fourth Amendment claim in a removal hearing faces two hurdles at the *prima facie* case stage. First, she must allege facts that state a violation of her rights under the Fourth Amendment. Second, the alien must show that the alleged violation of the Fourth Amendment was egregious. To get an evidentiary hearing, the alien must satisfy both prongs. If an evidentiary hearing is warranted, the alien will have the opportunity to present testimony and evidence in support of her Fourth Amendment claim. Upon the establishment of a *prima facie* case, the burden of proof shifts to the government to demonstrate why the IJ should admit the challenged evidence." *Yanez-Marquez v. Lynch*, 789 F.3d 434, 450–51 (4th Cir. 2015) (citations omitted).

- "As noted above, the question of egregiousness turns on an evaluation of the totality of the circumstances. There are two circumstances that support Yanez's egregiousness claim. The first is that the Fourth Amendment violation occurred in her home, where her privacy interests are strong. The second is that the entry occurred during the night, a time of day jealously protected by the Supreme Court. On the other side of the ledger, several factors weigh in the government's favor. There is no evidence that the ICE agents threatened, coerced, or physically abused Yanez, or promised her anything for her cooperation. Unlike Umana and Mendoza, she was never handcuffed and was allowed to remain at the Premises following the search. There is no evidence of diminished capacity on the part of Yanez, or that the questioning of her was particularly lengthy. Also, there is nothing in the record to suggest that the agents were motivated by racial considerations, and there is no evidence of improper intent on the part of the agents. While the totality scales at this point tilt in the government's favor, two additional facts seal Yanez's fate: (1) the ICE agents prepared a valid search warrant; and (2) the magistrate judge found the existence of probable cause to search the Premises in the daytime. As to the validity of the warrant, Agent Coker prepared a detailed and thorough affidavit laying out the facts in support of probable cause to believe that illegal aliens (and evidence of the harboring of illegal aliens) would be found in the Premises during a search. Yanez makes no challenge to the accuracy of the facts set forth in Agent Coker's affidavit, other than the description of the Premises as a single-story, single-family home. Under such circumstances, there simply is no doubt that the warrant was facially valid. . . . Put another way, if law enforcement officers do not attempt to secure a valid warrant supported by a magistrate judge's probable cause finding (as in *Cotzojay*), their conduct is more egregious than law enforcement officers who take the time to prepare a valid warrant and present it to a magistrate judge for a probable cause finding. In the latter case, the law enforcement officers' conduct is less offensive—they have sought and received authorization for a privacy interest invasion—while in the former case, the law enforcement officers' conduct borders on abhorrent, which renders the intrusion more severe and, hence, egregious." *Yanez-Marquez v. Lynch*, 789 F.3d 434, 469–71 (4th Cir. 2015) (citations omitted).

- "Blanket suppression is. . . appropriate where the warrant application merely serves as a subterfuge masking the officers' lack of probable cause for a general search, or where the officers flagrantly disregard the terms of the warrant. Indeed, blanket suppression is warranted where the officers engage in a fishing expedition for the discovery of incriminating evidence. Nevertheless, blanket suppression is an extraordinary remedy that should be used only when the violations of the warrant's requirements are so extreme that the search is essentially transformed into an impermissible general search. Even where officers exceed the bounds of their authority pursuant to the warrant, a search is not invalidated in its entirety merely because some seized items were not identified in the warrant. Nor is blanket suppression appropriate where the agents exceed the limits of their authority under the warrant based on practicality considerations or mistake." *U.S. v. Uzenski*, 434 F.3d 690, 69 Fed. R. Evid. Serv. 274 (4th Cir. 2006).

Fifth Circuit

- "The exclusionary rule requires that evidence obtained in violation of the Fourth Amendment cannot be used in a criminal proceeding against the victim of an illegal search." *U.S. v. Paige*, 136 F.3d 1012, 1017 (5th Cir. 1998).

Sixth Circuit

- "Defendant was a passenger in a vehicle that was pulled over for driving with a broken taillight. When asked for identification, the driver immediately admitted that he did not have a valid license—a misdemeanor criminal offense. The driver was arrested and locked in the back of the patrol car. At that point, officers returned to the vehicle to 'make contact' with Defendant, who was still seated in the passenger seat. The officers did not have any reason to suspect that Defendant was engaged in any criminal activity or that Defendant was armed and dangerous. Nevertheless, the officers ordered Defendant out of the vehicle and told him to put his hands on his head with his fingers interlaced. Officers then began to escort Defendant to the patrol car to search him for weapons and/or drugs. While Defendant was being escorted to the patrol car for a 'pat down' search, he broke free and ran away. The officers pursued Defendant, but did not make any audible commands for him to stop. After Defendant was chased and apprehended by officers, he was searched and found to be carrying a pistol and two bags of hashish, a derivative of marijuana. . . . We agree with the district court that the firearm and the hashish recovered during the search are inadmissible because they were recovered in violation of Defendant's Fourth Amendment rights. The district court correctly determined that the purpose of the traffic stop had been accomplished after the driver was arrested, and Defendant was unlawfully detained after the traffic stop was completed. We further agree with the district court's finding that the officers lacked reasonable suspicion to justify prolonging the traffic stop. Under the circumstances, the officers should have advised Defendant that the vehicle was being impounded and informed Defendant that he was free to go." *U.S. v. Cheatham*, 577 Fed. Appx. 500 (6th Cir. 2014) (citations omitted).

"In order to effect a traffic stop, an officer must possess either probable cause of a civil infraction or reasonable suspicion of criminal activity. . . . We primarily enforce these standards through the exclusionary rule, which requires the suppression of any evidence seized during a vehicle search premised on an illegal traffic stop." *U.S. v. Lyons*, 687 F.3d 754, 763 (6th Cir. 2012).

- "The exclusionary rule is designed to deter police misconduct rather than to punish the errors of judges and magistrates. . . . We do not exclude evidence, absent constitutional violations, unless the exclusion furthers the purpose of the exclusionary rule. . . ." *U.S. v. Chaar*, 137 F.3d 359, 361, 1998 FED App. 0052P (6th Cir. 1998).

Seventh Circuit

- "The exclusionary rule is used in only a subset of all constitutional violations—and excessive force in making an arrest or seizure is not a basis for the exclusion of evidence." *Evans v. Poskon*, 603 F.3d 362 (7th Cir. 2010).
- "The exclusionary rule is a judicially created remedy designed to safeguard Fourth Amendment rights generally through its deterrent effect, rather than a personal constitutional right of the party aggrieved. . . .Because the exclusionary rule is designed to deter official misconduct, and not to remedy individual constitutional violations, its application is restricted to those areas where its remedial objectives are thought most efficaciously served. . . . In order to determine whether the exclusionary rule should bar the introduction of evidence seized in violation of the Fourth Amendment at a sentencing hearing, we must weigh the additional deterrent benefit to be gained by applying the rule at sentencing against the costs such an application would impose on sentencing proceedings and on the goal of achieving fair, accurate, and individualized sentences." *U.S. v. Brimah*, 214 F.3d 854, 857 (7th Cir. 2000).
- "The exclusionary rule is a judicially created remedy, aimed at curbing overly zealous police action. It tells police that if they obtain evidenqe illegally, they will not ordinarily be allowed to use it against the suspect they are after." *U.S. v. Swift*, 220 F.3d 502, 506–07 (7th Cir. 2000).
- "Any application of the exclusionary rule necessarily requires consideration of society's competing interests in deterring illegal police conduct and providing juries with all of the evidence relevant to a defendant's guilt. The Supreme Court has determined that the interest of society in deterring unlawful police conduct and the public interest in having juries receive all probative evidence of a crime are properly balanced by putting the police in the same, not a worse, position that they would have been in if no police error or misconduct had occurred." *U.S. v. Liss*, 103 F.3d 617, 621 (7th Cir. 1997).

Ninth Circuit
- "Suppression of evidence obtained through a search that violates Federal Rule of Criminal Procedure 41 [requiring that officers leave a copy of the search warrant at

the presmises searched or with the person in possession of those premises] is required only if: 1) the violation rises to a 'constitutional magnitude;' 2) the defendant was prejudiced, in the sense that the search would not have occurred or would not have been so abrasive if law enforcement had followed the Rule; or 3) officers acted in 'intentional and deliberate disregard' of a provision in the Rule." *U.S. v. Martinez-Garcia*, 397 F.3d 1205 (9th Cir. 2005).

Tenth Circuit

- "[T]he affidavit in support of the no-knock search warrant presented facts that established past possession of firearms and small amounts of marijuana, and present evidence of the same. Officers failed to present any evidence of past violent behavior that would indicate a potential for present violence or futility, or any other evidence that would provide a reason to believe [defendants] would be violent. In light of our clear precedent providing that mere allegations of the presence of a firearm are insufficient to support a no-knock entry, we cannot say that law enforcement officers' reliance on the state judge's authorization was objectively reasonable. Therefore we conclude that law enforcement officers are not entitled to a good-faith exception to suppression of evidence in this case." *U.S. v. Nielson*, 415 F.3d 1195 (10th Cir. 2005).

D.C. Circuit

- "[A] criminal defendant is assured by the trial right of the exclusionary rule, where it applies. . .that no evidence seized in violation of the Fourth Amendment will be introduced at his trial unless he consents." *U.S. v. Gale*, 136 F.3d 192, 195 (D.C. Cir. 1998).

§ 1:9 Exceptions: Several exceptions to the exclusionary rule have been developed

Supreme Court

- "When the police exhibit 'deliberate,' 'reckless,' or 'grossly negligent' disregard for Fourth Amendment rights, the deterrent value of exclusion is strong and tends to outweigh the resulting costs. But when the po-

lice act with an objectively 'reasonable good-faith belief'
that their conduct is lawful, or when their conduct
involves only simple, 'isolated' negligence, the 'deterrence rationale loses much of its force,' and exclusion
cannot 'pay its way.' " *Davis v. U.S.*, 564 U.S. 229, 131
S. Ct. 2419, 2427–28, 180 L. Ed. 2d 285, 68 A.L.R. Fed.
2d 665 (2011) (citations omitted).

- "This case presents the question whether the exclusionary rule, which generally prohibits the introduction at
  criminal trial of evidence obtained in violation of a
  defendant's Fourth Amendment rights, applies in parole revocation hearings. We hold that it does not."
  Pennsylvania Bd. of Probation and Parole v. Scott, 524
  U.S. 357, 359, 118 S. Ct. 2014, 141 L. Ed. 2d 344 (1998).

- "[T]he practice of denying criminal defendants an
  exclusionary remedy from Fourth Amendment violations when those errors occur despite the good faith of
  the Government actors does not require the affirmance
  of petitioner's conviction in this case. Finding the deterrent remedy of suppression not compelled by the Fourth
  Amendment that case specifically relied on the objectionable collateral consequence of the interference with
  the criminal justice system's truth-finding function in
  requiring a blanket exclusionary remedy for all violations and the relative ineffectiveness of such remedy to
  deter future Fourth Amendment violations in particular
  cases." *Ryder v. U.S.*, 515 U.S. 177, 185–86, 115 S. Ct.
  2031, 132 L. Ed. 2d 136 (1995).

- "The question whether the exclusionary rule's remedy
  is appropriate in a particular context has long been
  regarded as an issue separate from the question
  whether the Fourth Amendment rights of the party
  seeking to invoke the rule were violated by police
  conduct. The exclusionary rule operates as a judicially
  created remedy designed to safeguard against future
  violations of Fourth Amendment rights through the
  rule's general deterrent effect. As with any remedial device, the rule's application has been restricted to those
  instances where its remedial objectives are thought
  most efficaciously served. Where the exclusionary rule
  does not result in appreciable deterrence, then, clearly,
  its use is unwarranted." *Arizona v. Evans*, 514 U.S. 1,
  10–11, 115 S. Ct. 1185, 131 L. Ed. 2d 34 (1995).

- "[T]he Fourth Amendment exclusionary rule does not apply to grand jury proceedings. Permitting witnesses to invoke the exclusionary rule would delay and disrupt grand jury proceedings by requiring adversarial hearings on peripheral matters and would effectively transform such proceedings into preliminary trials on the merits." *U.S. v. R. Enterprises, Inc.*, 498 U.S. 292, 298, 111 S. Ct. 722, 112 L. Ed. 2d 795 (1991).

- "Important as it is to protect the Fourth Amendment rights of all persons, there is no convincing indication that application of the exclusionary rule in civil deportation proceedings will contribute materially to that end." *I.N.S. v. Lopez-Mendoza*, 468 U.S. 1032, 1046, 104 S. Ct. 3479, 82 L. Ed. 2d 778 (1984).

- "When the challenged evidence has an independent source, exclusion of such evidence would put the police in a worse position than they would have been in absent any error or violation. There is a functional similarity between these two doctrines in that exclusion of evidence that would inevitably have been discovered would also put the government in a worse position, because the police would have obtained that evidence if no misconduct had taken place. Thus, while the independent source exception would not justify admission of evidence in this case, its rationale is wholly consistent with and justifies our adoption of the ultimate or inevitable discovery exception to the Exclusionary Rule." *Nix v. Williams*, 467 U.S. 431, 443–44, 104 S. Ct. 2501, 81 L. Ed. 2d 377 (1984).

- "[T]he Fourth Amendment exclusionary rule should be modified so as not to bar the use in the prosecution's case-in-chief of evidence obtained by officers acting in reasonable reliance on a search warrant issued by a detached and neutral magistrate but ultimately found to be unsupported by probable cause." *U.S. v. Leon*, 468 U.S. 897, 900, 104 S. Ct. 3405, 82 L. Ed. 2d 677 (1984).

- "[W]here the State has provided an opportunity for full and fair litigation of a Fourth Amendment claim, a state prisoner may not be granted federal habeas corpus relief on the ground that evidence obtained in an unconstitutional search or seizure was introduced at his trial. In this context the contribution of the exclusionary rule, if any, to the effectuation of the Fourth Amendment is

minimal and the substantial societal costs of application of the rule persist with special force." *Stone v. Powell*,
428 U.S. 465, 494–95, 96 S. Ct. 3037, 49 L. Ed. 2d 1067
(1976).

First Circuit

- "[T]he exclusionary rule based in the Fourth Amendment normally does not apply in deportation
  proceedings. Nevertheless, INS regulations do contemplate the suppression of illegally seized evidence in
  cases involving 'egregious violations of the Fourth
  Amendment or other liberties that might transgress notions of fundamental fairness and undermine the probative value of the evidence obtained.' " *Ruckbi v. I.N.S.*,
  285 F.3d 120 (1st Cir. 2002).

Second Circuit

- "Although 18 U.S.C. § 2515 states that illegally obtained
  wire or oral communications may not be 'received in evidence in any trial,' the Government contends that we
  should nonetheless approve use of such communications for impeachment purposes, following the Supreme
  Court's use for impeachment purposes of evidence
  obtained in violation of the Fourth Amendment. As
  noted by the District Court in its written decision, the
  Senate Judiciary Committee report on the bill that
  became Title III states that Congress did not intend to
  'press the scope of the suppression [rule] beyond present search and seizure law.' The report explicitly cites
  Walder. All of the circuits that have considered the issue have held that unlawfully obtained wiretap evidence may be used by the prosecution for impeachment
  in a criminal case. The Tenth Circuit has prohibited
  discovery of illegally obtained wiretap evidence in a
  civil case, distinguishing the cases permitting prosecution use for impeachment purposes in a criminal case
  on the ground that the exclusionary rule, which *Walder*
  declined to apply to Fourth Amendment violations, did
  not apply to private individuals. We agree with the
  courts applying the *Walder* rationale to evidence
  obtained in violation of Title III. As the First Circuit
  has pointed out, section 2515 cannot always be applied
  literally because doing so would preclude the use of il-

legally obtained wiretap evidence in a prosecution for violating Title III itself. And, as the Eighth Circuit has stated, 'It makes no sense for evidence obtained in violation of a mere statute to be more severely restricted than evidence obtained in violation of the Constitution. At the time the statute was enacted, evidence obtained in violation of the Fourth Amendment could be used for impeachment purposes. It is reasonable to assume that Congress had this background in mind when the statute was passed, and that, in the absence of an express statement, it did not intend to draw the line of exclusion in a different place.' " *U.S. v. Simels*, 654 F.3d 161, 169–70 (2d Cir. 2011) (citations omitted).

- "If. . . .the exclusionary rule does not result in appreciable deterrence, then, clearly, its use. . .is unwarranted. . . . The Supreme Court has refused for that reason to extend the exclusionary rule to non-criminal contexts, including civil tax proceedings. . .habeas proceedings. . .grand jury proceedings. . .INS deportation proceedings. . .and parole revocation proceedings. . . ." *Townes v. City of New York*, 176 F.3d 138, 145–46 (2d Cir. 1999).

Third Circuit

- "Courts have developed a number of exceptions to the exclusionary rule, including the independent source, inevitable discovery, and attenuation doctrines, and a good faith exception. . . . The independent source, inevitable discovery, and attenuation doctrines recognize that where the causal link between the constitutional violation and later-revealed evidence is tenuous or, indeed, non-existent, the later-revealed evidence can be said to be untarnished by the constitutional violation and therefore may be admissible." *U.S. v. Pelullo*, 173 F.3d 131, 136 (3d Cir. 1999).

Fourth Circuit

- "In sum, because the reasoning of Scott applies equally to supervised release revocation proceedings as to parole revocation proceedings, and to federal proceedings as to state proceedings, we agree with the district court that Scott requires that the exclusionary rule not be extended to federal supervised release revocation proceedings." *U.S. v. Armstrong*, 187 F.3d 392, 394 (4th Cir. 1999).

Fifth Circuit

- "(T)he district court denied (the) motion to suppress, ruling that even if a statutory violation had occurred, suppression was unavailable because the Fourth Amendment is not implicated by a pen register . . . We agree. (Defendant) has identified no statutory provision empowering this court to suppress evidence collected in violation of the pen-trap statute. Yet the pen-trap statute provides for fines and imprisonment for knowing violations . . . In contrast, the wire-tap statute specifically provides for an exclusionary remedy when the statutory requirements are not met . . . In our case, Congress has determined that the benefits of an exclusionary rule do not outweigh its substantial social costs . . . Compare this with the wiretap statute, which does provide for an exclusionary remedy . . . The Eleventh Circuit agrees. In *Thompson*, relying in part on our *Kington* decision, it refused to extend the exclusionary rule to statutory violations of the pen-trap statute. We join our sister circuit in concluding that the district court properly denied (the) motion to suppress as a matter of law." *U.S. v. German*, 486 F.3d 849 (5th Cir. 2007).

- "The Supreme Court has never applied the exclusionary rule to civil cases, state or federal. . . . It is true that the exclusionary rule applies in forfeiture proceedings. . . . This is because forfeiture is considered to be a criminal or quasi-criminal sanction. . . . This circuit has stated that because forfeiture is clearly a penalty for transgressing criminal laws, exclusion of illegally seized evidence is thought to obtain the same deterrent effect as exclusion in a criminal proceeding." *Wren v. Towe*, 130 F.3d 1154, 1158 (5th Cir. 1997).

Sixth Circuit

- "The deterrence rationale for the exclusionary rule limits and guides its reach. Evidence will not be excluded. . .unless the illegality is at least the but for cause of the discovery of the evidence, unless that is the challenged evidence is in some sense the product of illegal governmental activity. For there is little to deter if the officers' conduct is not the unattenuated causation of the evidentiary discovery. And even if recovered evidence *is* the product of illegality, it will be suppressed only where doing so yields deterrence benefits that sufficiently outweigh the substantial social costs associated with exclusion." *U.S. v. Figueredo-Diaz*, 718 F.3d 568, 574 (6th Cir. 2013) (inner quotations and citations omitted).

Eighth Circuit

- "The exclusionary rule does not apply when police make a seizure in objectively reasonable reliance on binding judicial precedent. Before the *Rodriguez* decision in 2015, binding precedent from this circuit held that 'even without reasonable suspicion following the completion of a traffic stop, seizures of less than ten minutes [were permissible] as de minimis intrusions [and did] not amount to an unreasonable seizure.' Meisel's actions fell squarely within the conduct permitted by this binding precedent. Ahumada argues that there was no reasonable reliance on precedent, because the North Dakota Supreme Court stated flatly in *State v. Fields*, that '[o]nce the purposes of the initial traffic stop are completed, a continued seizure of a traffic violator violates the Fourth Amendment unless the officer has a reasonable suspicion for believing that criminal activity is afoot.' The North Dakota court, however, cited a decision of this court, *United States v. Jones*, in support of its statement, and *Fields* involved a detention of thirty minutes after the completion of a traffic stop. A reasonable officer, therefore, need not have read *Fields* to reject this court's view on de minimis intrusions. In any event, a reasonable officer investigating a possible federal drug trafficking offense presumably is entitled to rely on binding federal precedent from the relevant judicial circuit. Accordingly, suppression of evidence is not justified, even assuming that the trooper lacked reasonable suspicion to extend the stop under the rule announced in *Rodriguez*." *United States v. Ahumada*, 858 F.3d 1138, 1140 (8th Cir. 2017) (citations omitted).
- "The government concedes on appeal that the search warrant. . .was not supported by probable cause.

Under *Leon*, however, evidence obtained pursuant to a search warrant that is later found to be invalid is not suppressed if the executing officers reasonably relied in good faith on the issuing court's determination of probable cause and technical sufficiency." *U.S. v. Herron*, 215 F.3d 812, 814 (8th Cir. 2000).

Tenth Circuit

- "An executing officer is generally presumed to be acting in good-faith reliance upon a warrant. However, this presumption is not absolute. There are four situations in which the presumption of good faith and, consequently, the good-faith exception to the exclusionary rule do not apply: (1) when the issuing magistrate was misled by an affidavit containing false information or information that the affiant would have known was false if not for his reckless disregard of the truth; (2) when the issuing magistrate wholly abandon[s her] judicial role; (3) when the affidavit in support of the warrant is so lacking in indicia of probable cause as to render official belief in its existence entirely unreasonable; and (4) when a warrant is so facially deficient that the executing officer could not reasonably believe it was valid." *U.S. v. Augustine*, 742 F.3d 1258 (10th Cir. 2014) (inner quotations and citations omitted).

- "[T]he good-faith exception to the exclusionary rule applies when an officer acts in reasonable reliance upon our settled case law that is later made unconstitutional by the Supreme Court." *U.S. v. Davis*, 590 F.3d 847 (10th Cir. 2009).

- "[W]hen evidence of an individual's identity is discovered through routine booking procedures incident to an unlawful arrest, that evidence is not suppressed unless the arrest was purposefully exploited to learn the identity." *U.S. v. Pena-Montes*, 589 F.3d 1048 (10th Cir. 2009).

- "Under Stone, habeas relief shall not be granted on the ground that the trial court admitted evidence obtained in violation of the Fourth Amendment despite the judicially-created exclusionary rule, provided that the defendant had an opportunity for full and fair litigation of the Fourth Amendment claim." *Smallwood v. Gibson*, 191 F.3d 1257, 1265 (10th Cir. 1999).

Chapter 2

Search

Research References

West's Key Number Digest

Searches and Seizures ☞13, 23, 26

KeyCite®: Cases and other legal materials listed in KeyCite Scope can be
researched through the KeyCite service on Westlaw®. Use KeyCite to
check citations for form, parallel references, prior and later history, and
comprehensive citator information, including citations to other decisions
and secondary materials.

---

§ 2:1   Scope of protection: The Fourth Amendment prohibition against unreasonable searches protects an individual's legitimate and reasonable expectation of privacy

Supreme Court

- "It would be foolish to contend that the degree of privacy
  secured to citizens by the Fourth Amendment has been
  entirely unaffected by the advance of technology. For
  example. . .the technology enabling human flight has
  exposed to public view (and hence, we have said, to official observation) uncovered portions of the house and

its curtilage that once were private." *Kyllo v. U.S.*, 533 U.S. 27, 121 S. Ct. 2038, 2043, 150 L. Ed. 2d 94 (2001).

- "The Fourth Amendment requires that searches and seizures be reasonable. A search or seizure is ordinarily unreasonable in the absence of individualized suspicion of wrongdoing. . . .While such suspicion is not an irreducible component of reasonableness. . .we have recognized only limited circumstances in which the usual rule does not apply. For example, we have upheld certain regimes of suspicionless searches where the program was designed to serve special needs, beyond the normal need for law enforcement." *City of Indianapolis v. Edmond*, 531 U.S. 32, 37, 121 S. Ct. 447, 148 L. Ed. 2d 333 (2000).

- "Because it is clear that the collection and testing of urine intrudes upon expectations of privacy that society has long recognized as reasonable, the Federal Courts of Appeals have concluded unanimously, and we agree, that these intrusions must be deemed searches under the Fourth Amendment." *Skinner v. Railway Labor Executives' Ass'n*, 489 U.S. 602, 617, 109 S. Ct. 1402, 103 L. Ed. 2d 639, 4 I.E.R. Cas. (BNA) 224, 130 L.R.R.M. (BNA) 2857, 13 O.S.H. Cas. (BNA) 2065, 49 Empl. Prac. Dec. (CCH) P 38791, 111 Lab. Cas. (CCH) P 11001, 1989 O.S.H. Dec. (CCH) P 28476 (1989).

- "A search occurs when an expectation of privacy that society is prepared to consider reasonable is infringed." *U.S. v. Jacobsen*, 466 U.S. 109, 113, 104 S. Ct. 1652, 80 L. Ed. 2d 85 (1984).

- "In assessing the degree to which a search infringes upon individual privacy, the Court has given weight to such factors as the intention of the Framers of the Fourth Amendment, the uses to which the individual has put a location, and our societal understanding that certain areas deserve the most scrupulous protection from government invasion." *Oliver v. U.S.*, 466 U.S. 170, 178, 104 S. Ct. 1735, 80 L. Ed. 2d 214 (1984).

- "The Fourth Amendment protects legitimate expectations of privacy rather than simply places. If the inspection by police does not intrude upon a legitimate expectation of privacy, there is no search subject to the Warrant Clause." *Illinois v. Andreas*, 463 U.S. 765, 771, 103 S. Ct. 3319, 77 L. Ed. 2d 1003 (1983).

- "The person in legal possession of a good seized during an illegal search has not necessarily been subject to a Fourth Amendment deprivation. [L]egal possession of a seized good is not a proxy for determining whether the owner had a Fourth Amendment interest, for it does not invariably represent the protected Fourth Amendment interest. This Court has repeatedly repudiated the notion that arcane distinctions developed in property tort law ought to control our Fourth Amendment inquiry." *U. S. v. Salvucci*, 448 U.S. 83, 91, 100 S. Ct. 2547, 65 L. Ed. 2d 619 (1980).

- "[C]apacity to claim the protection of the Fourth Amendment depends not upon a property right in the invaded place but upon whether the person who claims the protection of the Amendment has a legitimate expectation of privacy in the invaded place." *Rakas v. Illinois*, 439 U.S. 128, 143, 99 S. Ct. 421, 58 L. Ed. 2d 387 (1978).

- "[T]he Fourth Amendment protects people, not places. What a person knowingly exposes to the public, even in his own home or office, is not a subject of Fourth Amendment protection. But what he seeks to preserve as private, even in an area accessible to the public, may be constitutionally protected." *Katz v. U.S.*, 389 U.S. 347, 351–52, 88 S. Ct. 507, 19 L. Ed. 2d 576 (1967).

Second Circuit

- "The underlying command of the Fourth Amendment is always that searches and seizures be reasonable, and what is reasonable depends on the context within which a search takes place." *Gudema v. Nassau County*, 163 F.3d 717, 722 (2d Cir. 1998).

Fifth Circuit

- "Generally, the Fourth Amendment's guarantees apply in both criminal and civil contexts. In addition, our sister circuits have held that the Fourth Amendment applies when government officials execute a mental health warrant. Thus, we apply Fourth Amendment standards to this case, while observing that, although it has not been timely argued here, the balance struck in the criminal context between an individual's rights and the government's law enforcement imperatives may require modification in the field of mental health activity." *Linbrugger v. Abercia*, 363 F.3d 537 (5th Cir. 2004).

Seventh Circuit

- "The Constitution forbids not all searches and seizures, but only 'unreasonable searches and seizures.'" *Carter v. City of Milwaukee*, 743 F.3d 540 (7th Cir. 2014) (citations omitted).

- "Because the basic purpose of the Fourth Amendment is to safeguard the privacy and security of individuals against arbitrary invasions by governmental officials, the amendment's prohibition against unreasonable searches and seizures protects against warrantless intrusions during civil as well as criminal investigations by the government. Thus, the strictures of the Fourth Amendment apply to child welfare workers, as well as all other governmental employees. The threshold consideration in a Fourth Amendment inquiry is whether the governmental conduct in question constitutes a search or seizure within the meaning of the amendment's text. In this case, defendants... , with the assistance of the police, investigated allegations of child abuse on the premises of [a private school]. As part of that investigation, they took John Doe Jr. into custody to interview him. We think it is clear that the foregoing actions constitute both a search and a seizure under the Fourth Amendment." *Doe v. Heck*, 327 F.3d 492 (7th Cir. 2003), as amended on denial of reh'g, (May 15, 2003).

- "... [A] person has no expectation of privacy in a photograph of his face." *U.S. v. Emmett*, 321 F.3d 669 (7th Cir. 2003).

Eighth Circuit

- "[S]tate law 'can be relevant in determining what is reasonable under the Fourth Amendment' ... Statutes, which are 'prima facie evidence of what society as a whole regards as reasonable,' are among the sources courts should look to in assessing the reasonableness of governmental action." *U.S. v. Belcher*, 288 F.3d 1068 (8th Cir. 2002).

Ninth Circuit

- "The compulsory extraction of blood for DNA profiling unquestionably implicates the right to personal security embodied in the Fourth Amendment, and thus constitutes a search within the meaning of the Constitution. Of course, the fact that such extraction constitutes a search is hardly dispositive, as the Fourth Amendment does not proscribe all searches and seizures. It would be foolish to contend that the degree of privacy secured to citizens by the Fourth Amendment has been entirely unaffected by the advance of technology." *Ellison v. Nevada*, 299 Fed. Appx. 730 (9th Cir. 2008).

- "Appellants contend that the home visits are searches because they are highly intrusive and their purpose is to discover evidence of welfare fraud . . . Here. . .all prospective welfare beneficiaries are subject to mandatory home visits for the purpose of verifying eligibility, and not as part of a criminal investigation. The investigators conduct an in-home interview and "walk through," looking for inconsistencies between the prospective beneficiary's application and her actual living conditions . . . . (T)he home visits are conducted with the applicant's consent, and if consent is denied, the visit will not occur . . . (T)here is no penalty for refusing to consent to the home visit, other than denial of benefits . . . . The fact that the D.A. investigators who make the Project 100% home visits are sworn peace officers does not cause the home visits to rise to the level of a "search in the traditional criminal law context" because the visits' underlying purpose remains the determination of welfare eligibility . . . . Therefore. . .we conclude that the. . .home visits do not qualify as searches within the meaning of the Fourth Amendment." *Sanchez v. County of San Diego*, 464 F.3d 916 (9th Cir. 2006).

- "As early as the mid-60's the Supreme Court considered it settled law that the Fourth Amendment protects a person's property when he places it in his office, and that when he puts something in his filing cabinet or in his desk drawer. . .he has the right to know it will be secure from an unreasonable search or an unreasonable seizure." *Ortega v. O'Connor*, 146 F.3d 1149, 1157, 14 I.E.R. Cas. (BNA) 97 (9th Cir. 1998).

Tenth Circuit

- "The Fourth Amendment protects against unreasonable searches and seizures. Generally, a seizure made without individualized suspicion of wrongdoing is unreasonable. . . . But the 'touchstone of the Fourth Amendment is reasonableness, not individualized suspicion.' Accordingly, the Supreme Court has carved out exceptions to the general rule where the primary purpose of a group seizure went beyond ordinary crime control. . . . In those situations, the Court has not required individualized reasonable suspicion, instead favoring a group-level balance of interests, weighing the public interest against intrusions on individuals' liberty." *U.S. v. Paetsch*, 782 F.3d 1162, 1168–69 (10th Cir. 2015), cert. denied, 136 S. Ct. 195, 193 L. Ed. 2d 153 (2015) (citations omitted).
- "The Supreme Court has recognized that what a person knowingly exposes to the public, even in his own home or office, is not a subject of Fourth Amendment protection. . . . If a person knowingly exposes statements to the plain view of outsiders, such statements are not protected under the Fourth Amendment because the speaker has not exhibited an intention to keep them to himself. . . . As the Court noted, the risk of being overheard . . . is . . . inherent in the conditions of human society. It is the kind of risk we necessarily assume whenever we speak. . . . This principle applies with equal force to statements knowingly exposed to government informants." *U.S. v. Longoria*, 177 F.3d 1179, 1182 (10th Cir. 1999).

Eleventh Circuit

- "The evidence, interpreted in the light most favorable to [plaintiff medical office manager], is sufficient for a jury to conclude that her Fourth Amendment rights were violated [by probation officer's unwarranted entry into medical office in search of probationer for whom arrest warrant had been issued]. Though physical entry of the home is the chief evil against which the wording of the Fourth Amendment is directed, its protection extends to any area in which an individual has a reasonable expectation of privacy. Offices and other workplaces are among the areas in which individuals may enjoy such a reasonable expectation of privacy.

Absent exigent circumstances, police must have a search warrant to enter any area in a place of business that is off-limits to the general public. . . . [Probation officer's] mere entry into the office was enough to violate the Fourth Amendment. [Officer] did not have a search warrant, and can point to no exigency justifying his search. Consequently, even if a factually similar case did not exist, his actions would still have violated rights that are clearly established under these general statements of principle." *O'Rourke v. Hayes*, 378 F.3d 1201 (11th Cir. 2004).

- "The Supreme Court long has recognized that the Fourth Amendment's guarantee of freedom from warrantless searches and seizures is not premised on arcane concepts of property and possessory interests; instead, the Fourth Amendment protects an individual in those places where she can demonstrate a reasonable expectation of privacy against government intrusion." *U.S. v. Cooper*, 203 F.3d 1279, 1283–84 (11th Cir. 2000).

- "The general rule is that warrantless searches are presumptively unreasonable. . . . The courts have, however, fashioned exceptions to the general rule, recognizing that in certain limited situations the government's interest in conducting a search without a warrant may outweigh the individual's privacy interest." *U.S. v. Gordon*, 231 F.3d 750, 754 (11th Cir. 2000).

§ 2:2 Test: The individual must exhibit a reasonable expectation of privacy

Supreme Court

- "Furthermore, and again on the assumption that Quon had a reasonable expectation of privacy in the contents of his messages, the extent of an expectation is relevant to assessing whether the search was too intrusive. Even if he could assume some level of privacy would inhere in his messages, it would not have been reasonable for Quon to conclude that his messages were in all circumstances immune from scrutiny. . . . This Court has 'repeatedly refused to declare that only the least intrusive search practicable can be reasonable under the Fourth Amendment.' That rationale 'could raise insuperable barriers to the exercise of virtually all search-and-seizure powers,' because 'judges engaged in *post hoc* evaluations of government conduct can almost always imagine some alternative means by which the objectives of the government might have been accomplished[.]' The analytic errors of the Court of Appeals in this case illustrate the necessity of this principle. Even assuming there were ways that OPD could have performed the search that would have been less intrusive, it does not follow that the search as conducted was unreasonable." *City of Ontario, Cal. v. Quon*, 560 U.S. 746, 130 S. Ct. 2619, 2632, 177 L. Ed. 2d 216, 30 I.E.R. Cas. (BNA) 1345, 93 Empl. Prac. Dec. (CCH) P 43907, 159 Lab. Cas. (CCH) P 61011 (2010) (citations and internal quotations omitted).

- "[Plaintiff]'s subjective expectation of privacy against such a [strip] search is inherent in her account of it as embarrassing, frightening, and humiliating. The reasonableness of her expectation (required by the Fourth Amendment standard) is indicated by the consistent experiences of other young people similarly searched, whose adolescent vulnerability intensifies the patent intrusiveness of the exposure." *Safford Unified School Dist. No. 1 v. Redding*, 557 U.S. 364, 129 S. Ct. 2633, 174 L. Ed. 2d 354, 245 Ed. Law Rep. 626 (2009).
- "Our Fourth Amendment analysis embraces two questions. First, we ask whether the individual, by his conduct, has exhibited an actual expectation of privacy; that is, whether he has shown that he sought to preserve something as private. . . . Second, we inquire whether the individual's expectation of privacy is one that society is prepared to recognize as reasonable." *Bond v. U.S.*, 529 U.S. 334, 338, 120 S. Ct. 1462, 146 L. Ed. 2d 365 (2000).
- "It has long been the rule that a defendant can urge the suppression of evidence obtained in violation of the Fourth Amendment only if that defendant demonstrates that *his* Fourth Amendment rights were violated by the challenged search or seizure. Expectations of privacy and property interests govern the analysis of Fourth Amendment search and seizure claims. Participants in a criminal conspiracy may have such expectations or interests, but the conspiracy itself neither adds nor

detracts from them." *U.S. v. Padilla*, 508 U.S. 77, 81, 113 S. Ct. 1936, 123 L. Ed. 2d 635 (1993).

- "We have never intimated, however, that whether or not a search is reasonable within the meaning of the Fourth Amendment depends on the law of the particular State in which the search occurs. We have emphasized instead that the Fourth Amendment analysis must turn on such factors as our societal understanding that certain areas deserve the most scrupulous protection from government invasion." *California v. Greenwood*, 486 U.S. 35, 43, 108 S. Ct. 1625, 100 L. Ed. 2d 30 (1988).

- "We simply decline to use possession of a seized good as a substitute for a factual finding that the owner of the good had a legitimate expectation of privacy in the area searched." *U. S. v. Salvucci*, 448 U.S. 83, 92, 100 S. Ct. 2547, 65 L. Ed. 2d 619 (1980).

- "[T]his Court uniformly has held that the application of the Fourth Amendment depends on whether the person invoking its protection can claim a justifiable, a reasonable, or a legitimate expectation of privacy that has been invaded by government action. This inquiry normally embraces two discrete questions. The first is whether the individual, by his conduct, has exhibited an actual (subjective) expectation of privacy. The second question is whether the individual's subjective expectation of privacy is one that society is prepared to recognize as reasonable, whether the individual's expectation, viewed objectively, is justifiable under the circumstances." *Smith v. Maryland*, 442 U.S. 735, 740, 99 S. Ct. 2577, 61 L. Ed. 2d 220 (1979).

- "[T]here is a twofold requirement, first that a person have exhibited an actual (subjective) expectation of privacy and, second, that the expectation be one that society is prepared to recognize as reasonable. Thus, a man's home is, for most purposes, a place where he expects privacy, but objects, activities, or statements that he exposes to the plain view of outsiders are not protected because no intention to keep them to himself has been exhibited. On the other hand, conversations in the open would not be protected against being overheard, for the expectation of privacy under the circumstances would be unreasonable." *Katz v. U.S.*, 389 U.S.

347, 361, 88 S. Ct. 507, 19 L. Ed. 2d 576 (1967) (Harlan, J., *concurring*).

Second Circuit

- "Although both defendants had a sufficient relationship to the premises and each other to permit them to establish a legitimate expectation of privacy in the Edgewood Avenue apartment, that does not end the inquiry. Defendants must also establish that they took advantage of that opportunity for privacy at the time of the window search by the police. Although society generally respects a person's expectations of privacy in a dwelling, what a person chooses voluntarily to expose to public view thereby loses its Fourth Amendment protection. . . . Generally, the police are free to observe whatever may be seen from a place where they are entitled to be." *U.S. v. Fields*, 113 F.3d 313, 321 (2d Cir. 1997).

Third Circuit

- "[A]n alien charged with illegal reentry has no possessory or proprietary interest in his/her immigration file or the documentary evidence contained in that file. Similarly, an alien has no reasonable expectation of privacy in a file that is maintained solely by a government agency for official purposes and kept in the custody of that agency." *U.S. v. Bowley*, 435 F.3d 426 (3d Cir. 2006), as amended, (Feb. 17, 2006).

Fourth Circuit

- "It is well-established that a criminal defendant does not have standing to contest the search of a third party unless he can show he had a reasonable expectation of privacy in the area searched or the property seized. [Defendant] contends that he had just such a legitimate expectation of privacy in the Oldsmobile because he was a supervisor and thus maintained considerable control over the vehicle. This coconspirator exception to the rule of standing was squarely rejected in *United States v. Padilla*. No expectation of privacy is created simply because one has a supervisory role in the conspiracy or joint control over the place or property involved in the search or seizure." *U.S. v. Al-Talib*, 55 F.3d 923, 930–31, 141 A.L.R. Fed. 679 (4th Cir. 1995).

Fifth Circuit

- "The Fourth Amendment does not provide blanket protection against searches. . .on private property. Rather, the Fourth Amendment protects only those areas in which. . .citizens have a reasonable expectation of privacy. . . . Although it no doubt can be said that our constitutional precedent on the concept of reasonable expectation of privacy comprises an amorphous realm, this concept nonetheless plays the crucial gatekeeping role in our inquiry, allowing us to separate that which falls within the ambit of the Fourth Amendment from that which does not. Only if governmental activity intrudes upon a reasonable expectation of privacy in a significant way does the activity constitute a search for Fourth Amendment purposes." *U.S. v. Paige*, 136 F.3d 1012, 1018 (5th Cir. 1998).

Sixth Circuit

- "There is no question that [defendant], as a tenant, had a possessory interest in the common hallway and stairway of his duplex and the right generally to exclude anyone who was not a tenant. But because [defendant] made no effort to maintain his privacy in the common hallway and stairway, he did not have an objectively reasonable expectation of privacy in those areas. Both doors on the first floor were not only unlocked but also ajar. By not locking the duplex's doors, [defendant] did nothing to indicate to the officers that they were not welcome in the common areas. Moreover, without being able to pass through the hallway and stairway, there was no visible way for the police or anyone else to alert the duplex tenants of their presence. There was no intercom system, and [tenant] testified that she was not sure if there was a doorbell. Perhaps the officers could have used the side door, but we are not prepared to impose a burden on police officers to walk around apartment buildings in search of a different entrance when the front entrance is unlocked. How would officers ever know which entrance is the 'right' entrance for Fourth Amendment purposes? Nothing in these circumstances indicates that [defendant] had a reasonable expectation of privacy in the hallway and stairway." *U.S. v. Dillard*, 438 F.3d 675, 2006 FED App. 0073P (6th Cir. 2006).

Seventh Circuit

- "[Defendant] did not have a reasonable expectation of privacy in the Mustang after he turned it over to the shipper. The doors were left unlocked, the driver of the car carrier was given the keys, and [defendant] knew that the driver would enter the Mustang and drive it. We conclude that no one could have a reasonable expectation of privacy in the contents of a vehicle under those circumstances. . . . . That the drugs were hidden in a secret compartment in the car clearly evinces [defendant]'s subjective desire that the drugs not be discovered. But [defendant] must also show that his expectation of privacy was objectively reasonable—the simple act of hiding something will not necessarily trigger Fourth Amendment protections." *U.S. v. Crowder*, 588 F.3d 929 (7th Cir. 2009).

- "After [defendants] were arrested, a Spanish speaking interpreter. . . interviewed the defendants in Spanish and asked them the questions necessary to complete booking forms. Based upon these interviews, [the interpreter] compared the voices of [defendants] with voices that she had heard during the wire surveillance. . . . The subsequent evaluation of the defendants' voices did not violate the Fourth Amendment. The United States Supreme Court has held that people do not have a reasonable expectation of privacy in their voices. Moreover, federal courts have consistently recognized that law enforcement officers may question an arrested person to collect booking information incident to processing him or her for arrest and custody. In addition, the comparison of the defendants' voices with those on the tapes falls within the 'plain hearing' exception to the search warrant requirement." *U.S. v. Ceballos*, 385 F.3d 1120, 65 Fed. R. Evid. Serv. 629 (7th Cir. 2004).

Eighth Circuit

- "A defendant, justifiably evicted from his hotel room, has no reasonable expectation of privacy in the room under the Fourth Amendment and police may justifiably enter the room to assist the hotel manager in expelling the individuals in an orderly fashion." *U.S. v. Molsbarger*, 551 F.3d 809 (8th Cir. 2009).

- "Not every investigatory encounter. . .rises to the level

of a Fourth Amendment search or seizure. A search within the meaning of the Amendment occurs when an expectation of privacy that society is prepared to consider reasonable is infringed. . . ." *U.S. v. Roby*, 122 F.3d 1120, 1123 (8th Cir. 1997).

Ninth Circuit

- "The Fourth Amendment does not protect a defendant from a warrantless search of property that he stole, because regardless of whether he expects to maintain privacy in the contents of the stolen property, such an expectation is not one that 'society is prepared to accept as reasonable.' A legitimate expectation of privacy means more than a subjective expectation of not being discovered. . . Whatever possessory interest a thief may have, that interest is subordinate to the rights of the owner, and in this case, the business supply store, from which [defendant] fraudulently obtained the computer, not only consented to the police examination of the laptop's hard drive, but also specifically requested that the police examine it before returning it, to protect the store from accidentally coming into possession of material the store did not want—like child pornography." *U.S. v. Caymen*, 404 F.3d 1196 (9th Cir. 2005).
- "[Defendant] procured this room through deliberate and calculated fraud. . . . Nevertheless, in the Ninth Circuit, the rule is that even if the occupant of a hotel room has procured that room by fraud, the occupant's protected Fourth Amendment expectation of privacy is not finally extinguished until the hotel justifiably takes 'affirmative steps to repossess the room.'" *U.S. v. Cunag*, 386 F.3d 888 (9th Cir. 2004).
- "The Fourth Amendment protects against intrusions into an individual's zone of privacy. In general, an American depositor has no reasonable expectation of privacy in copies of his or her bank records, such as checks, deposit slips, and financial statements maintained by the bank. A depositor takes the risk, in revealing his affairs to another, that the information will be conveyed by that person to the Government. Where an individual's Fourth Amendment rights are not implicated, obtaining the documents does not violate his or her rights, even if the documents lead to indictment."

In re Grand Jury Proceedings, 40 F.3d 959, 962–63 (9th Cir. 1994).

Tenth Circuit

- "The Fourth Amendment right of privacy is a personal right. . . .It cannot be vicariously asserted. . . .Thus, the proper inquiry is whether the challenged action violated the Fourth Amendment rights of the criminal defendant making the challenge." *U.S. v. Allen*, 235 F.3d 482, 489 (10th Cir. 2000).
- "A warrantless search is unreasonable, and therefore unconstitutional, if the defendant has a legitimate expectation of privacy in the area searched. . . . The ultimate question is whether one's claim to privacy from the government intrusion is reasonable in light of all the surrounding circumstances." *U.S. v. Anderson*, 154 F.3d 1225, 1229 (10th Cir. 1998).

Eleventh Circuit

- ". . . The Fourth Amendment's prohibition against unreasonable searches and seizures 'protects an individual in those places where [he] can demonstrate a reasonable expectation of privacy against government intrusion,' and 'only individuals who actually enjoy the reasonable expectation of privacy have standing to challenge the validity of a government search.' [citation omitted] . . . Accordingly, the threshold issue in this case is whether [defendant] had a legitimate expectation of privacy in the contents of his personal laptop computer when it was connected to the [military] base network from his dorm room. [citation omitted] . . . [Defendant] has not shown a legitimate expectation of privacy in his computer files. . . . [His] files were 'shared' over the entire base network, and. . .everyone on the network had access to all of his files and could observe them in exactly the same manner as [military officials] did. [R]ather than analyzing the military official's actions as a search of [defendant's] personal computer in his private dorm room, it is more accurate to say that the authorities conducted a search of the military network, and [defendant's] computer files were a part of that network. [Defendant's] files were exposed to thousands of individuals with network access, and the military authorities encountered the files without employing any special means or intruding into any area [that defendant] could reasonably expect would remain private. The contents of his computer's hard drive were akin to items stored in the unsecured common areas of a multi-unit apartment building or put in a dumpster accessible to the public. Because his expectation of privacy was unreasonable[, defendant] suffered no violation of his Fourth Amendment rights when his computer files were searched through the computer's connection to the base network. . . ." *U.S. v. King*, 509 F.3d 1338, 1341–1343 (11th Cir. 2007).

§ 2:3 Balancing test: In determining the applicability of the Fourth Amendment, the court may balance the public interest against the degree of the intrusion

<u>Supreme Court</u>

- "A breath test does not 'implicat[e] significant privacy concerns.' Blood tests are a different matter. . . . Blood tests are significantly more intrusive, and their reasonableness must be judged in light of the availability of the less invasive alternative of a breath test. . . . Breath tests have been in common use for many years. Their results are admissible in court and are widely credited by juries, and respondents do not dispute their accuracy or utility. What, then, is the justification for warrantless blood tests? One advantage of blood tests is their ability to detect not just alcohol but also other substances that can impair a driver's ability to operate a car safely. A breath test cannot do this, but police have other measures at their disposal when they have reason to believe that a motorist may be under the influence of some other substance (for example, if a breath test indicates that a clearly impaired motorist has little if any alcohol in his blood). Nothing prevents the police from seeking a warrant for a blood test when there is sufficient time to do so in the particular circumstances or from relying on the exigent circumstances exception to the warrant requirement when there is not. . . . Because breath tests are significantly less intrusive than blood tests and in most cases amply serve law enforcement interests, we conclude that a breath test, but not a blood test, may be administered as a search incident to a lawful arrest for drunk driving. As in all cases involving reasonable searches incident to arrest, a warrant is not needed in this situation." *Birchfield v. North Dakota*, 136 S. Ct. 2160, 2178, 2184, 2185, 195 L. Ed. 2d 560 (2016) (citation omitted).

- "It can be agreed that using a buccal swab on the inner tissues of a person's cheek in order to obtain DNA samples is a search. Virtually any intrusio[n] into the human body will work an invasion of cherished personal security that is subject to constitutional scrutiny. The Court has applied the Fourth Amendment to police efforts to draw blood, scraping an arrestee's fingernails to obtain trace evidence, and even to a breathalyzer test, which generally requires the production of alveolar or deep lung breath for chemical analysis. A buccal swab is a far more gentle process than a venipuncture to draw blood. It involves but a light touch on the inside of the cheek; and although it can be deemed a search within the body of the arrestee, it requires no surgical intrusions beneath the skin. The fact than an intrusion is negligible is of central relevance to determining reasonableness, although it is still a search as the law defines that term. . . . The legitimate government interest served by the Maryland DNA Collection Act is one that is well established: the need for law enforcement officers in a safe and accurate way to process and identify the persons and possessions they must take into custody. It is beyond dispute that probable cause provides legal justification for arresting a person suspected of crime, and for a brief period of detention to take the administrative steps incident to arrest. . . . [i]n every criminal case, it is known and must be known who has been arrested and who is being tried. An individual's identity is more than just his name or Social Security number, and the government's interest in identification goes beyond ensuring that the proper name is typed on the indictment. Identity has never been considered limited to the name on the arrestee's birth certificate. In fact, a name is of little value compared to the real interest in identification at stake when an individual is brought into custody. It is a well

recognized aspect of criminal conduct that the perpetrator will take unusual steps to conceal not only his
conduct, but also his identity. Disguises used while committing a crime may be supplemented or replaced by
changed names, and even changed physical features.
An arrestee may be carrying a false ID or lie about his
identity and criminal history records. . . .can be inaccurate or incomplete. . . . Like a fingerprint, the 13
CODIS loci are not themselves evidence of any particular crime, in the way that a drug test can by itself be
evidence of illegal narcotics use. . . . Perhaps the most
direct historical analogue to the DNA technology used
to identify respondent is the familiar practice of
fingerprinting arrestees. From the advent of this
technique, courts had no trouble determining that
fingerprinting was a natural part of the administrative
steps incident to arrest. In the seminal case of *United
States v. Kelly,* Judge Augustus Hand wrote that routine fingerprinting did not violate the Fourth Amendment precisely because it fit within the accepted means
of processing an arrestee into custody . . . . We find no
ground in reason or authority for interfering with a
method of identifying persons charged with crime which
has now become widely known and frequently practiced.
By the middle of the 20th century, it was considered
elementary that a person in lawful custody may be
required to submit to photographing and fingerprinting
as part of routine identification processes. DNA identification is an advanced technique superior to fingerprinting in many ways, so much so that to insist on fingerprints as the norm would make little sense to either the
forensic expert or a layperson. The additional intrusion
upon the arrestee's privacy beyond that associated with
fingerprinting is not significant, and DNA is a markedly more accurate form of identifying arrestees."
Maryland v. King, 133 S. Ct. 1958, 1968–72, 1976, 186
L. Ed. 2d 1 (2013) (inner quotations and citations
omitted).

• "Fourth Amendment reasonableness 'is predominantly
an objective inquiry.' We ask whether 'the circumstances, viewed objectively, justify [the challenged]
action.' If so, that action was reasonable '*whatever* the
subjective intent' motivating the relevant officials. This

approach recognizes that the Fourth Amendment regulates conduct rather than thoughts, and it promotes evenhanded, uniform enforcement of the law. Two 'limited exception[s]' to this rule are our special-needs and administrative-search cases, where 'actual motivations' do matter." *Ashcroft v. al-Kidd*, 563 U.S. 731, 131 S. Ct. 2074, 2080–81, 179 L. Ed. 2d 1149 (2011) (citations omitted).

- "In determining whether a search or seizure is unreasonable, the Supreme Court begins with history and looks to statutes and common law of the founding era to determine the norms that the Fourth Amendment was meant to preserve. When history does not provide a conclusive answer to the reasonableness of search or seizure under the Fourth Amendment, the Supreme Court analyzes search or seizure in light of traditional standards of reasonableness by assessing, on the one hand, degree to which it intrudes on individual's privacy and, on the other, degree to which it is needed for promotion of legitimate governmental interests. The Fourth Amendment's meaning does not change with local law enforcement practices, even practices set by rule; while those practices vary from place to place and from time to time, the Fourth Amendment protections are not so variable and cannot be made to turn upon such trivialities. A State is free to prefer one search-and-seizure policy among range of constitutionally permissible options, but its choice of a more restrictive option does not render the less restrictive ones unreasonable, and hence violative of the Fourth Amendment. In determining what is reasonable under the Fourth Amendment, the Supreme Court gives great weight to the essential interest in readily administrable rules." *Virginia v. Moore*, 553 U.S. 164, 128 S. Ct. 1598, 170 L. Ed. 2d 559 (2008).

- "[R]ather than employing a per se rule of unreasonableness, we balance the privacy-related and law enforcement-related concerns to determine if the intrusion was reasonable." *Illinois v. McArthur*, 531 U.S. 326, 121 S. Ct. 946, 947, 148 L. Ed. 2d 838 (2001).

- "The Fourth Amendment protects the right of the people to be secure in their persons, houses, papers, and effects, against unreasonable searches and seizures. In determining whether a particular governmental action violates this provision, we inquire first whether the action was regarded as an unlawful search or seizure under the common law when the Amendment was framed. . . . Where that inquiry yields no answer, we must evaluate the search or seizure under traditional standards of reasonableness by assessing, on the one hand, the degree to which it intrudes upon an individual's privacy and, on the other, the degree to which it is needed for the promotion of legitimate governmental interests." *Wyoming v. Houghton*, 526 U.S. 295, 299–300, 119 S. Ct. 1297, 143 L. Ed. 2d 408 (1999).

- "Although the underlying command of the Fourth Amendment is always that searches and seizures be reasonable, what is reasonable depends on the context within which a search takes place. The determination of the standard of reasonableness governing any specific class of searches requires balancing the need to search against the invasion which the search entails. On one side of the balance are arrayed the individual's legitimate expectations of privacy and personal security; on the other, the government's need for effective methods to deal with breaches of public order." *New Jersey v. T.L.O.*, 469 U.S. 325, 337, 105 S. Ct. 733, 83 L. Ed. 2d 720, 21 Ed. Law Rep. 1122 (1985).

- "[T]he permissibility of a particular law enforcement practice is judged by balancing its intrusion on the individual's Fourth Amendment interests against its promotion of legitimate governmental interests. Implemented in this manner, the reasonableness standard usually requires, at a minimum, that the facts upon which an intrusion is based be capable of measurement against an objective standard, whether this be probable cause or a less stringent test. In those situations in which the balance of interests precludes insistence upon some quantum of individualized suspicion, other safeguards are generally relied upon to assure that the individual's reasonable expectation of privacy is not subject to the discretion of the official in the field." *Delaware v. Prouse*, 440 U.S. 648, 654–55, 99 S. Ct. 1391, 59 L. Ed. 2d 660 (1979).

- "In delineating the constitutional safeguards applicable in particular contexts, the Court has weighed the public interest against the Fourth Amendment interest of the individual." *U.S. v. Martinez-Fuerte*, 428 U.S. 543, 555, 96 S. Ct. 3074, 49 L. Ed. 2d 1116 (1976).

- "[T]here can be no ready test for determining reasonableness other than by balancing the need to search against the invasion which the search entails." *Camara v. Municipal Court of City and County of San Francisco*, 387 U.S. 523, 536–37, 87 S. Ct. 1727, 18 L. Ed. 2d 930 (1967).

First Circuit

- "Analyzing the propriety of a frisk involves a two-part inquiry, in which no single factor is controlling: first. . .one must determine whether the officer's action was justified at its inception, and second, whether the action taken was reasonably related in scope to the circumstances which justified the interference in the first place. . . . The court must consider the circumstances as a whole, and must balance the nature of the intrusion with the governmental interests that are served." *U.S. v. Cruz*, 156 F.3d 22, 26, 50 Fed. R. Evid. Serv. 212 (1st Cir. 1998).

Second Circuit

- "An inquiry into the reasonableness of a search focuses on whether the governmental interests advanced to justify the search outweigh the privacy interest impaired by the search." *In re Terrorist Bombings of U.S. Embassies in East Africa*, 553 F.3d 150 (2d Cir. 2009).

Third Circuit

- "The usual way in which judges interpreting the Fourth Amendment take account of the fact that searches vary in the degree to which they invade personal privacy is by requiring a higher degree of probable cause (to believe that the search will yield incriminating evidence), and by being more insistent that a warrant be obtained if at all feasible, the more intrusive the search is. But maybe in dealing with so intrusive a technique as television surveillance, other methods of control as well, such as banning the technique outright from use in the home in connection with minor crimes, will be required, in order to strike a proper balance between public safety and personal privacy. . . . But it does not follow that a judicial officer, in weighing the public interest, may properly take into account his or her personal opinion regarding the need for or the importance of the criminal provisions that appear to have been violated." *U.S. v. Williams*, 124 F.3d 411, 416–17 (3d Cir. 1997).

Fourth Circuit

- "Reasonableness is determined by weighing the public interest against the individual's right to personal security free from arbitrary interference by law officers. . . . The public interest. . .includes the substantial public concern for the safety of police officers lawfully carrying out the law enforcement effort." *U.S. v. Sakyi*, 160 F.3d 164, 167 (4th Cir. 1998).

- "Determining the reasonableness of a protective search involves balancing the officer's interest in self-protection against the intrusion on individual rights necessitated by the search. A police officer's interest in self-protection arises when he reasonably believes that a suspect is armed and dangerous; at that point, he has an interest in taking steps to assure himself that the person with whom he is dealing is not armed with a weapon that could unexpectedly and fatally be used against him. The steps taken by the officer for self-protection, however, necessarily intrude upon the individual's interest in personal security, which is protected from unreasonable governmental intrusion by the Fourth Amendment. To determine whether the intrusion was reasonable under the Fourth Amendment, a court must analyze the competing interests of the officer and the individual." *U.S. v. Baker*, 78 F.3d 135, 137–38 (4th Cir. 1996).

Fifth Circuit

- "The central inquiry under the Fourth Amendment is whether a search or seizure is reasonable under all the circumstances of a particular governmental invasion of a person's personal security. . . .To assess the reasonableness of a search or seizure, courts balance the governmental interest against the invasion which the search or seizure entails. . . .Balancing renders es-

sential a consideration of the context in which a Fourth
Amendment right is asserted." *Milligan v. City of Slidell*,
226 F.3d 652, 654, 147 Ed. Law Rep. 429 (5th Cir. 2000).

- "We deviate from this principle—that an arrest based
  on probable cause is reasonable under the Fourth
  Amendment—only when an arrest is conducted in an
  extraordinary manner, unusually harmful to an individual's privacy or even physical interests. . . . For
  example, it is necessary actually to perform a balancing
  analysis notwithstanding the existence of probable
  cause when a search or seizure involves deadly force,
  an unannounced entry into a home, entry into a home
  without a warrant, or physical penetration of the body."
  Atwater v. City of Lago Vista, 195 F.3d 242, 244–45 (5th
  Cir. 1999), aff'd, 532 U.S. 318, 121 S. Ct. 1536, 149 L.
  Ed. 2d 549 (2001).

Seventh Circuit

- "As a practical matter, it may be that when a suspicion-
  based search is workable, the needs of the government
  will never be strong enough to outweigh the privacy
  interests of the individual. Or, stated slightly differently, perhaps if a suspicion-based search is feasible,
  the government will have failed to show a special need
  that is important enough to override the individual's
  acknowledged privacy interest, sufficiently vital to suppress the Fourth Amendment's normal requirement of
  individualized suspicion." *Willis by Willis v. Anderson
  Community School Corp.*, 158 F.3d 415, 421, 130 Ed.
  Law Rep. 89 (7th Cir. 1998), as amended on denial of
  reh'g and reh'g en banc, (Oct. 28, 1998).

§ 2:4 Exceptions: There are a number of intrusions which do not constitute searches protected by the Fourth Amendment

Supreme Court

- "It is well established that a vehicle stop at a highway
  checkpoint effectuates a seizure within the meaning of
  the Fourth Amendment. . . . The fact that officers walk
  a narcotics-detection dog around the exterior of each
  car at the Indianapolis checkpoints does not transform
  the seizure into a search. . . . Just as in *Place*, an

exterior sniff of an automobile does not require entry
into the car and is not designed to disclose any information other than the presence or absence of narcotics.
. . .Like the dog sniff in *Place*, a sniff by a dog that
simply walks around a car is much less intrusive than a
typical search." *City of Indianapolis v. Edmond*, 531
U.S. 32, 40, 121 S. Ct. 447, 148 L. Ed. 2d 333 (2000).

- "A chemical test that merely discloses whether or not a
particular substance is cocaine does not compromise
any legitimate interest in privacy. This conclusion is
not dependent on the result of any particular test. It is
probably safe to assume that virtually all of the tests
conducted under circumstances comparable to those
disclosed by this record would result in a positive finding; in such cases, no legitimate interest has been
compromised. But even if the results are negative—
merely disclosing that the substance is something other
than cocaine—such a result reveals nothing of special
interest. Congress has decided—and there is no question about its power to do so—to treat the interest in
privately possessing cocaine as illegitimate; thus
governmental conduct that can reveal whether a
substance is cocaine, and no other arguably private fact,
compromises no legitimate privacy interest." *U.S. v.
Jacobsen*, 466 U.S. 109, 123, 104 S. Ct. 1652, 80 L. Ed.
2d 85 (1984).

- "It is beyond dispute that [the Officer's] action in shin-
ing his flashlight to illuminate the interior of [Defen-
dant's] car trenched [sic] upon no right secured to the
latter by the Fourth Amendment. Numerous other
courts have agreed that the use of artificial means to illuminate a darkened area simply does not constitute a
search, and thus triggers no Fourth Amendment
protection." *Texas v. Brown*, 460 U.S. 730, 739–40, 103
S. Ct. 1535, 75 L. Ed. 2d 502 (1983).

- "[T]he particular course of investigation that the agents
intended to pursue here—exposure of respondent's luggage, which was located in a public place, to a trained
canine—did not constitute a search within the meaning
of the Fourth Amendment." *U.S. v. Place*, 462 U.S. 696,
707, 103 S. Ct. 2637, 77 L. Ed. 2d 110 (1983).

- "[D]id monitoring the beeper signals complained of by
respondent invade any legitimate expectation of privacy

on his part? . . . . [W]e hold they did not. Since they did not, there was neither a search nor a seizure within the contemplation of the Fourth Amendment." *U.S. v. Knotts*, 460 U.S. 276, 285, 103 S. Ct. 1081, 75 L. Ed. 2d 55 (1983).

- "[P]etitioner in all probability entertained no actual expectation of privacy in the phone numbers he dialed, and even if he did, his expectation was not legitimate. The installation and use of a pen register, consequently, was not a search, and no warrant was required." *Smith v. Maryland*, 442 U.S. 735, 745–46, 99 S. Ct. 2577, 61 L. Ed. 2d 220 (1979).

- "Respondent urges that he has a Fourth Amendment interest in the records kept by the banks. Even if we direct our attention to the original checks and deposit slips, rather than to the microfilm copies actually viewed and obtained by means of the subpoena, we perceive no legitimate expectation of privacy in their contents." *U. S. v. Miller*, 1976-1 C.B. 535, 425 U.S. 435, 442, 96 S. Ct. 1619, 48 L. Ed. 2d 71, 76-1 U.S. Tax Cas. (CCH) P 9380, 37 A.F.T.R.2d 76-1261 (1976).

First Circuit

- "All that remains for us to consider with respect to Hillaire's challenge to the denial of his suppression motion is Hillaire's contention that the District Court erred in concluding that the warrantless swiping of the credit cards through the card reader was constitutional. We find no merit in this challenge, either. Hillaire contends that the District Court erred because credit cards are 'analogous to cell phones'—which generally cannot be searched without a warrant—due to the capacity of the magnetic strips on credit cards to store 'personal digital data.' In support of the argument, Hillaire asserts that the magnetic strips on credit cards store 'confidential financial information' and 'data concerning merchandise purchased,' including 'locations where the credit card was used' and 'types of merchandise purchased.' The only evidence presented on the matter in the District Court, however, showed that, except when magnetic strips are altered for criminal purposes, the magnetic strips 'contain[ ] only the card number and the expiration date, which [are] routinely given to retailers and

[are] visible on the front of the card.'" *United States v. Hillaire*, 857 F.3d 128, 129-30 (1st Cir. 2017) (citations omitted).

- "In Place, the Supreme Court held that a dog sniff of luggage in an airport was not a search. . . . [T]he important factor in applying Place is not whether the sniff occurs in a public place like an airport, but whether—as in an officer's plain view observation of contraband—the observing person or the sniffing canine are legally present at their vantage when their respective senses are aroused by obviously incriminating evidence." *U.S. v. Esquilin*, 208 F.3d 315, 318 (1st Cir. 2000) (abrogated on other grounds by, Missouri v. Seibert, 542 U.S. 600, 124 S. Ct. 2601, 159 L. Ed. 2d 643 (2004)).

Second Circuit

- "Canine sniffs are recognized as being less intrusive than a typical search used to determine the presence of contraband, and the practice of using trained dogs to sniff baggage at airports has been held not to constitute a search. . . . [I]nsofar as the presence of narcotics is revealed by a canine sniff, the Supreme Court has held that any interest in possessing contraband cannot be deemed legitimate, and thus, governmental conduct that only reveals the possession of contraband compromises no legitimate privacy interest. . . . This is because the expectation that certain facts will not come to the attention of the authorities is not the same as an interest in privacy that society is prepared to consider reasonable. However, while a canine sniff in an airport is not a search, it is quite another thing to say that a sniff can never be a search. The question always to be asked is whether the use of a trained dog intrudes on a legitimate expectation of privacy. While one generally has an expectation of privacy in the contents of personal luggage, this expectation is much diminished when the luggage is in the custody of an air carrier at a public airport." *U.S. v. Hayes*, 551 F.3d 138 (2d Cir. 2008).

Fourth Circuit

- "Rule 41 of the Federal Rules of Criminal Procedure implements the Fourth Amendment's protections

against warrantless searches. It provides that a judicial
officer must issue a search warrant if a federal law
enforcement officer or an attorney for the government
presents an affidavit or other information showing probable cause to search a property. Additionally, Rule 41
sets forth procedures controlling the time at which a
warrant may be executed, reflecting that 'increasingly
severe standards of probable cause are necessary to
justify increasingly intrusive searches.' Once issued, a
warrant can normally be executed solely 'in the daytime,' between 6:00 a.m. and 10:00 p.m., 'unless the
judge for good cause expressly authorizes execution'
during the night. Good cause for a nighttime warrant
might exist, for example, where necessary to prevent
the destruction of evidence. Because of the separate,
heightened burden of proof required for issuance of a
nighttime warrant, the existence of a daytime warrant
ordinarily does not justify a nighttime search. . . . In
so holding, we note that our court, in an unpublished
opinion, has treated a nighttime search conducted under
the aegis of a daytime warrant as a mere Rule 41 violation, rather than as an unconstitutional search. In
concluding that the defendant's suppression motion was
properly denied, the *Davis* court relied on precedent not
involving an unauthorized nighttime search, but rather
on precedent that states that a Rule 41 violation will
result in suppression only if the party seeking suppression suffered prejudice or the government intentionally
violated the rule. Some of our sister circuits have
employed that same standard in refusing to suppress
evidence obtained during unauthorized nighttime
searches. Those courts have considered factors such as:
whether good cause could have been shown for a nighttime warrant had one been requested; whether the executing officers believed in good faith they had authority
to conduct a nighttime search; whether the search was
executed a short time before or after nighttime; and
whether the search was in fact more abrasive because
it was conducted in the nighttime." *Yanez-Marquez v.
Lynch*, 789 F.3d 434, 465–66, 67-68 (4th Cir. 2015) (citations omitted).

- "[T]he Court has recognized a narrow exception to the
warrant requirement that permits a search even if the

police lack probable cause to suspect criminal activity. Indeed, the exception only applies when the police are *not* engaged in a criminal investigation, that is, it only applies when they are 'engaged in. . . community caretaking functions, totally divorced from the detection, investigation, or acquisition of evidence relating to the violation of a criminal statute.' The police do not need probable cause when engaged solely in community caretaking since 'the standard of probable cause is peculiarly related to criminal investigations, not routine, noncriminal procedures.' The Court has recognized the need for this community-caretaking exception because police often come into 'contact with vehicles for reasons related to the operation of vehicles themselves' and this 'often noncriminal contact with automobiles will bring local officials in plain view of evidence, fruits, or instrumentalities of a crime, or contraband.' . . .[An officer investigating an automobile accident involving an unconscious driver] testified, without contradiction, that he opened the glove compartment in hopes that he would find identifying information he could use to communicate more effectively with [the driver] so that he could assess [the driver's] medical condition and get his car out of the traffic lane. These efforts fall squarely within the parameters of the community-caretaking exception." *U.S. v. Johnson*, 410 F.3d 137 (4th Cir. 2005).

- "Only recently, we held that a police officer who was authorized to be at the front door of a house did not implicate or violate the Fourth Amendment when he walked three steps down the porch in order to look through a front window of the defendant's house and observed incriminating evidence. . . . Similarly, the Supreme Court has recognized, in somewhat analogous circumstances, that an officer's enhancing his position or ability to see objects otherwise in plain view is irrelevant to any Fourth Amendment analysis. . . . [I]n this case we hold that. . .[the] shift in position by a few steps for a few seconds to observe better what was in plain view did not meaningfully intrude on any privacy interest. . . ." *U.S. v. Jackson*, 131 F.3d 1105, 1110 (4th Cir. 1997).

- "No fence surrounded the [Defendant]'s home, nor was

the property posted to prohibit trespassing. [The Officer] arrived at the [Defendant]'s home on a ministerial mission to return a handgun to [Defendant], they approached the house from the driveway and proceeded directly to the front door. As they did so, the interior of the [Defendant]'s dining room was well lit and plainly visible through the picture window located directly adjacent to the front door. And, having exposed their dining room and its contents to anyone positioned at the front entranceway of their home, the [Defendant] possessed no reasonable expectation of privacy in the dining room or its openly visible contents. Accordingly, the observations [the Officers] made through the [Defendant]'s dining room window did not constitute a search within the meaning of the Fourth Amendment." *U.S. v. Taylor*, 90 F.3d 903, 909 (4th Cir. 1996).

Fifth Circuit

- "Wallace argues that the district court should have granted his motion to suppress because the government violated his Fourth Amendment rights when it accessed his phone's E911 location information—or prospective cell site data—pursuant to a court order supported by 'specific and articulable facts' rather than a warrant supported by probable cause. Ordinarily, 'evidence obtained in violation of the Fourth Amendment cannot be used in a criminal proceeding against the victim of the illegal search or seizure. This prohibition applies as well to the fruits of the illegally seized evidence.' '[A] Fourth Amendment search occurs when the government violates a subjective expectation of privacy that society recognizes as reasonable.' Whether obtaining prospective cell site data constitutes a search within the meaning of the Fourth Amendment is still an open question in this Circuit. . . .. There is little distinction between historical and prospective cell site data. As in *Historical Cell Site Data*, here the government sought 'the disclosure of the locations of cell site towers being accessed by [Wallace's] cell phone' as recorded in future records 'captured, stored, recorded and maintained by the phone companies in the ordinary course of business.' 'While this information is "prospective" in the sense that the records had not yet been created at the time the order was authorized, it is no different in substance from the historical cell site information . . . at the time it is transmitted to the government.' The information the government requested was, 'in fact, a stored, historical record because it [was] received by the cell phone service provider and stored, if only momentarily, before being forwarded to law enforcement officials.' We therefore conclude that like historical cell site information, prospective cell site data falls outside the purview of the Fourth Amendment. As such, 'the [Stored Communications Act's] authorization of § 2703(d) orders for [prospective] cell site information if an application meets the lesser "specific and articulable facts" standard, rather than the Fourth Amendment probable cause standard, is not per se unconstitutional.'" *United States v. Wallace*, 857 F.3d 685, 690-91 (5th Cir. 2017), opinion withdrawn and superseded, 866 F.3d 605 (5th Cir. 2017) (citations omitted).

- "The defendant, an employee of the City Fire Department, did not have an objectively reasonable expectation of privacy in his City-owned workplace computer, and thus, the examination of defendant's workplace computer by City officials did not constitute a search, for Fourth Amendment purposes." *U.S. v. Zimmerman*, 303 Fed. Appx. 207 (5th Cir. 2008).

Sixth Circuit

- "[U]sing seven hours of GPS location data to determine an individual's location (or a cell phone's location), so long as the tracking does not reveal movements within the home (or hotel room), does not cross the sacred threshold of the home, and thus cannot amount to a Fourth Amendment search." *United States v. Riley*, 858 F.3d 1012, 1018 (6th Cir. 2017).

- "This court has not previously addressed in a published opinion the question of whether an individual has a reasonable expectation of privacy in his license plate . . . No argument can be made that a motorist seeks to keep the information on his license plate private. The very purpose of a license plate number, like that of a Vehicle Identification Number, is to provide identifying information to law enforcement officials and others . . . Thus, so long as the officer had a right to be in a position to observe the defendant's license plate, any such observation and corresponding use of the information on the plate does not violate the Fourth Amendment." *U.S. v. Ellison*, 462 F.3d 557, 2006 FED App. 0339P (6th Cir. 2006).

- "[W]e do not regard the examination of appellant's hands under the ultraviolet light as a search within the meaning of the Fourth Amendment." *U.S. v. Ukomadu*, 236 F.3d 333, 338, 2001 FED App. 0006P (6th Cir. 2001).

Seventh Circuit

- "The court in *Villarreal* consistently referenced a reasonable expectation of privacy in 'closed containers.' . . . The Mustang at issue in this case can hardly be considered a 'closed container' analogous to the sealed drums in *Villarreal*. The doors to the Mustang were unlocked, the driver had the keys, and [defendant] knew that the driver would be opening the doors and driving the car." *U.S. v. Crowder*, 588 F.3d 929 (7th Cir. 2009).

- "The only issue is whether evidence obtained as a result of a tracking device attached to his car should have been suppressed as the fruit of an unconstitutional search . . . The Supreme Court has held that the mere tracking of a vehicle on public streets by means of a similar though less sophisticated device (a beeper) is not a search . . . But the Court left open the question whether installing the device in the vehicle converted the subsequent tracking into a search . . . GPS tracking is on the same side of the divide with the surveillance cameras and the satellite imaging, and if what they do is not searching in Fourth Amendment terms, neither is GPS tracking . . ." *U.S. v. Garcia*, 474 F.3d 994 (7th Cir. 2007).

Ninth Circuit

- "Under the 'community caretaking' doctrine, police may, without a warrant, impound and search a motor vehicle so long as they do so in conformance with the standardized procedures of the local police department and in furtherance of a community caretaking purpose, such as promoting public safety or the efficient flow of traffic. This requirement ensures that impoundments are conducted 'on the basis of something other than suspicion of evidence of criminal activity.' The government bears the burden of establishing that a vehicle's impoundment and search are justified under an exception to the warrant requirement. . . . This case thus turns on whether it was reasonable for Officer Donaldson to unlatch the air filter box in the engine compartment as part of the inventory search. We hold that it was. . . . 'Knowledge of the precise nature of the property helped guard against claims of theft, vandalism, or negligence. Such knowledge also helped to avert any danger to police or others that may have been posed by the property.' . . . Officer Donaldson's search of the engine cabin was motivated, at least in part, by concerns for the safety of the police or others. The air filter compartment was obviously large enough to hold a firearm, and could be opened by lifting the hood and releasing the latches on the box. Officer Donaldson testified that he commonly checks the air filter compartment because, based on his training and experience, 'criminals' hide contraband there such as narcotics and weapons. In light of this uncontradicted evidence that firearms and other weapons have been located in air filter compartments in the past, it is reasonable for the LVMPD to maintain an inventory search protocol that encompasses areas where weapons may be stored in a manner reasonably accessible to the owners of vehicles in the process of being impounded, or others who may have access to the vehicle after it is impounded. Officer Donaldson's search of the air filter compartment in this case was justified by the need to 'protect the public from the possibility that a revolver would fall into untrained or perhaps malicious hands.' In sum, the LVMPD inventory search policy appears to have been reasonably 'designed to produce an inventory,' and ensures sufficient uniformity to protect the owners and occupants of impounded vehicles from the risk that officers will exercise discretion in performing an inventory search only when they suspect they will uncover the fruits of criminal activity. Accordingly, the purposes underlying the requirement of a process to discourage inventory searches from becoming a 'ruse for a general rummaging' are satisfied with respect to the LVMPD policy at issue. In fulfilling his duty to search 'all containers,' Officer Donaldson acted within the parameters of LVMPD policy when he unlatched the air filter compartment. For this reason, the inventory search did not violate the Fourth Amendment[.]" *United States v. Torres*, 828 F.3d 1113, 1118, 1120-21 (9th Cir. 2016) (citations omitted).

- "Undercover operations, in which the agent is a so-called "invited informer," are not "searches" under the Fourth Amendment . . . Even though a conversation between an agent and a target may occur in an otherwise private environment, 'a person has no legitimate expectation of privacy in information he voluntarily turns over to third parties' . . . Here, NAMBLA (North American Man/Boy Love Association) invited (the agent) to join its group, participate in its holiday card program, attend its conferences, and participate in the privacy committee. He received access to other people, not access to files or information. In essence, NAMBLA invited (the agent) to join its social network; his conversations with other members were well within the scope of that invitation, and NAMBLA had no legitimate expectation of privacy in them." *U.S. v. Mayer*, 490 F.3d 1129 (9th Cir. 2007), opinion amended and superseded on denial of reh'g, 503 F.3d 740 (9th Cir. 2007).

- "We are presented with a question this court has not yet resolved: Does a license plate check by a law enforcement officer that reveals information about a person's car ownership, driver status and criminal record constitute a search under the Fourth Amendment? We agree with all the other courts that have considered the issue that it does not. We therefore hold that (defendant's) Fourth Amendment rights were not violated when (the officer) stopped the truck in which (defendant) was a passenger, asked him for identification and checked his driver's license or Oregon identification card with radio dispatch." *U.S. v. Diaz-Castaneda*, 494 F.3d 1146 (9th Cir. 2007).

- "Here, rather than making a visual inspection of the undercarriage of the Toyota 4Runner, the officers placed the magnetized electronic devices on the vehicle's undercarriage. . . . [N]o seizure occurred because the officers did not meaningfully interfere with [Defendant]'s possessory interest in the Toyota 4Runner." *U.S. v. McIver*, 186 F.3d 1119, 1127 (9th Cir. 1999).

- "We are also persuaded that the use of photographic equipment to gather evidence that could be lawfully observed by a law enforcement officer does not violate the Fourth Amendment. The use of a motion activated camera under these circumstances appears to us to be a prudent and efficient use of modern technology." *U.S. v. McIver*, 186 F.3d 1119, 1125 (9th Cir. 1999).

Tenth Circuit

- "(W)e see no violation of (defendant's) reasonable expectation of privacy in (the officer's) knock on his inner door. (The officer) first knocked several times on the storm door. When that elicited no response, he tried to be heard by knocking on the inner door, an act that required opening the storm door. We suspect that most visitors would have done the same. In our view, opening the storm door to knock on the inner door, even though the inner door was partially open, was not a Fourth Amendment intrusion because such action does not violate an occupant's reasonable expectation of privacy." *U.S. v. Walker*, 474 F.3d 1249 (10th Cir. 2007).

- "(W)e conclude (the officer's) insertion of his rifle into the interior of the (plaintiffs') home and following (a plaintiff's) movement with it was not a search because the rifle was incapable of obtaining information and did not obtain any information beyond that which was observed by (the officer) standing in the common area. Nor did the insertion of the rifle through the window enable (the officer) to see that which would not otherwise be visible." *Reeves v. Churchich*, 484 F.3d 1244 (10th Cir. 2007).

- "Even if (defendant) did possess a subjective expectation of privacy, his failure to take affirmative measures to limit other employees' access makes that expectation unreasonable . . . Those who bring personal material into public spaces, making no effort to shield that material from public view, cannot reasonably expect their personal materials to remain private . . . (Defendant) voluntarily moved his personal computer into a public space and took no measures to protect its contents from public inspection. Consequently, he did not enjoy a reasonable expectation of privacy and (the officer's) search worked no Fourth Amendment violation." *U.S. v.*

Barrows, 481 F.3d 1246, 154 Lab. Cas. (CCH) P 60394 (10th Cir. 2007).

- "Every search necessarily involves the use of sensory perception, i.e., touch, taste, smell, sight, or sound, but as case law teaches us, the use of sensory perception does not necessarily constitute a search. Logically then, as with sight and smell, not every manner of touch constitutes a search under the Fourth Amendment." *U.S. v. Nicholson*, 144 F.3d 632, 636 (10th Cir. 1998).

Chapter 3

Seizure

§ 3:15   Seizure under the Patriot Act: Warrant can be
          issued by court with subject matter jurisdiction,
          not just court with geographical jurisdiction
§ 3:16   Seizure under the Patriot Act: Duration of
          detention

Research References

West's Key Number Digest

Arrest ⊙63, 68; Automobiles ⊙349; Constitutional Law ⊙83; Criminal Law ⊙394.6, 1224; Customs Duties ⊙126; Searches and Seizures ⊙23, 25, 40, 44, 47, 52, 57, 101, 198

KeyCite®: Cases and other legal materials listed in KeyCite Scope can be researched through the KeyCite service on Westlaw®. Use KeyCite to check citations for form, parallel references, prior and later history, and comprehensive citator information, including citations to other decisions and secondary materials.

---

§ 3:1   Significance: When a person is seized, Fourth Amendment protections are invoked

Supreme Court

- "[The] petitioner Elijah Manuel was held in jail for some seven weeks after a judge relied on allegedly fabricated evidence to find probable cause that he had committed a crime. The primary question in this case is whether Manuel may bring a claim based on the Fourth Amendment to contest the legality of his pretrial confinement. Our answer follows from settled precedent. The Fourth Amendment, this Court has recognized, establishes 'the standards and procedures' governing pretrial detention. And those constitutional protections apply even after the start of 'legal process' in a criminal case—here, that is, after the judge's determination of probable cause. Accordingly, we hold today that Manuel may challenge his pretrial detention on the ground that it violated the Fourth Amendment. . . . [P]retrial detention can violate the Fourth Amendment not only when it precedes, but also when it follows, the start of legal process in a criminal case. The Fourth Amendment prohibits government officials from detaining a person in the absence of probable cause. That can happen when the police hold someone without any reason before the formal onset of a criminal proceeding. But it also can occur when legal process itself goes wrong—when, for example, a judge's probable-cause determination is predicated solely on a police officer's false statements. Then, too, a person is confined without constitutionally adequate justification. Legal process has gone forward, but it has done nothing to satisfy the Fourth Amendment's probable-cause requirement. . . . . Police officers initially arrested Manuel without probable cause, based solely on his possession of pills that had field tested negative for an illegal substance. So (putting timeliness issues aside) Manuel could bring a claim for wrongful arrest under the Fourth Amendment. And the same is true (again, disregarding timeliness) as to a claim for wrongful detention—because Manuel's subsequent weeks in custody were *also* unsupported by probable cause, and so *also* constitutionally unreasonable. . . . And that means Manuel's ensuing pretrial detention, no less than his original arrest, violated his Fourth Amendment rights. Or put just a bit differently: Legal process did not expunge Manuel's Fourth Amendment claim because the process he received failed to establish what that Amendment makes essential for pretrial detention—probable cause to believe he committed a crime." *Manuel v. City of Joliet, Ill.*, 137 S. Ct. 911, 914, 918–20 (2017) (citations omitted).

- "We have long understood that the Fourth Amendment's protection against unreasonable seizures includes seizure of the person. From the time of the founding to the present, the word seizure has meant a taking possession." *California v. Hodari D.*, 499 U.S. 621, 624, 111 S. Ct. 1547, 113 L. Ed. 2d 690 (1991).

- "Our cases make it clear that a seizure does not occur simply because a police officer approaches an individual and asks a few questions. So long as a reasonable person would feel free to disregard the police and go about his business, the encounter is consensual and no reasonable suspicion is required. The encounter will not trigger Fourth Amendment scrutiny unless it loses its consensual nature." *Florida v. Bostick*, 501 U.S. 429, 434, 111 S. Ct. 2382, 115 L. Ed. 2d 389 (1991).

- "While the very presence of a police car driving parallel to a running pedestrian could be somewhat intimidating, this kind of police presence does not, standing alone, constitute a seizure. Without more, the police conduct here—a brief acceleration to catch up with respondent, followed by a short drive alongside him—was not so intimidating that respondent could reasonably have believed that he was not free to disregard the police presence and go about his business." *Michigan v. Chesternut*, 486 U.S. 567, 575, 108 S. Ct. 1975, 100 L. Ed. 2d 565 (1988).

- "The simple language of the [Fourth] Amendment applies equally to seizures of persons and to seizures of property." *Payton v. New York*, 445 U.S. 573, 585, 100 S. Ct. 1371, 63 L. Ed. 2d 639 (1980).

- "It is quite plain that the Fourth Amendment governs 'seizures' of the person." *Terry v. Ohio*, 392 U.S. 1, 16, 88 S. Ct. 1868, 20 L. Ed. 2d 889 (1968).

First Circuit

- "*Brower* enunciates a rule that renders its egregious facts largely immaterial to the required Fourth Amendment inquiry into whether a roadblock seizure has occurred. Writing for the Court, Justice Scalia explained that a Fourth Amendment seizure occurs only when there is a governmental termination of freedom of movement through means intentionally applied explaining that it is enough for a seizure that a person be stopped by the very instrumentality set in motion or put in place to achieve that result." *Seekamp v. Michaud*, 109 F.3d 802, 805 (1st Cir. 1997).

- "Interaction between law enforcement officials and citizens generally falls within three tiers of Fourth Amendment analysis, depending on the level of police intrusion into a person's privacy. The first or lowest tier encompasses interaction of such minimally intrusive nature that it does not trigger the protections of the Fourth Amendment. The Supreme Court has repeatedly emphasized that not all personal intercourse between the police and citizens rises to the level of a stop or seizure. Police may approach citizens in public spaces and ask them questions without triggering the protections of the Fourth Amendment. Such police engagements need not find a basis in any articulable suspicion. Police conduct falls short of triggering Fourth Amendment protections when, from the totality of the circumstances, we determine that the subject of any police interaction would have felt free to terminate the conversation and proceed along his way." *U.S. v. Young*, 105 F.3d 1, 5–6, 46 Fed. R. Evid. Serv. 307 (1st Cir. 1997).

Third Circuit

- "Less than one month after being interrogated by police and accused of committing arson, Black flew from her home in California to Pennsylvania for her arraignment because an arrest warrant had been issued and she had been directed to return. She spent more than an hour being fingerprinted and photographed at a police station—and she was clearly not free to leave. Black was required to post unsecured bail of $50,000. She was told that the bond would be forfeited if she did not attend all court proceedings—compelling her to travel across the United States to attend pre-trial hearings. Even though Black was never incarcerated, that 'should not lead to the conclusion that a defendant released pre-trial is not still "seized" in the constitutionally relevant sense.' Further, the cloud of very serious charges demonstrates that Black was 'hardly freed from the state's control upon [her] release from a police officer's physical grip.' " *Black v. Montgomery County*, 835 F.3d 358, 367–68 (3d Cir. 2016), as amended, (Sept. 16, 2016) and cert. denied, 2017 WL 1540522 (U.S. 2017) (citations omitted).
- "A person is seized for Fourth Amendment purposes only if he is detained by means intentionally applied to terminate his freedom of movement. A seizure occurs even when an unintended person is the object of detention, so long as the means of detention are intentionally applied to that person." *Berg v. County of Allegheny*, 219 F.3d 261, 269 (3d Cir. 2000).
- "[T]he Supreme Court has clarified that seizures can be of different intensities. Thus, whereas an arrest that results in detention may be the most common type of seizure, an investigative stop that detains a citizen only momentarily also is a seizure." *Gallo v. City of Philadelphia*, 161 F.3d 217, 223 (3d Cir. 1998), as amended, (Dec. 7, 1998).

Sixth Circuit

- "The Fourth Amendment conditions warrants on probable cause and prohibits unreasonable seizures. A police officer violates those restrictions only when his deliberate or reckless falsehoods result in arrest and prosecution without probable cause. The resulting claim, what might be called an 'unreasonable prosecutorial seizure' claim, is traditionally known as a 'malicious prosecution' claim." *Newman v. Township of Hamburg*, 773 F.3d 769, 771–72 (6th Cir. 2014) (citations omitted).

- "We have held that '[t]he Fourth Amendment requires an official seizing and detaining a person for a psychiatric evaluation to have probable cause to believe that the person is dangerous to himself or others.'" *Hoover v. Walsh*, 682 F.3d 481, 500 (6th Cir. 2012) (citations omitted).

- "This Court has explained that there are three types of permissible encounters between the police and citizens: (1) the consensual encounter, which may be initiated without any objective level of suspicion; (2) the investigative detention, which, if non-consensual, must be supported by a reasonable, articulable suspicion of criminal activity; and (3) the arrest, valid only if supported by probable cause." *U.S. v. Waldon*, 206 F.3d 597, 602, 2000 FED App. 0059P (6th Cir. 2000).

- "The seizure of an individual takes place when by means of physical force or a show of authority, his freedom of movement is restrained." *Ingram v. City of Columbus*, 185 F.3d 579, 591, 1999 FED App. 0258P (6th Cir. 1999).

Seventh Circuit

- "Probable cause is an absolute defense to any claim under § 1983 for wrongful arrest or false imprisonment." *Bailey v. City of Chicago*, 779 F.3d 689, 694 (7th Cir. 2015), cert. denied, 136 S. Ct. 200, 193 L. Ed. 2d 129 (2015).

- "It is well-established that the Fourth Amendment does not prohibit all searches and seizures, but only those that are unreasonable. In *California v. Hodari D.* the Supreme Court applied a two-part test to decide whether a person had been seized such that Fourth Amendment protections are triggered (whether that seizure be an arrest, a *Terry* stop, or otherwise): first, determine whether any physical force simultaneously accompanied the officer's show of authority, and second, determine whether the defendant failed to comply with that show of authority. If no physical force accompanied the show of authority and a person chose to ignore or reject that show of authority, the defendant is not seized until the officer applied physical force and the person submitted to the officer's show of authority." *U.S. v. $32,400.00, in U.S. Currency*, 82 F.3d 135, 138 (7th Cir. 1996).

Ninth Circuit

- "For purposes of the Fourth Amendment, a seizure occurs when a law enforcement officer, by means of physical force or show of authority, in some way restrains the liberty of a citizen. . . . A police officer has restrained the liberty of the citizen if, taking into account all of the circumstances surrounding the encounter, the police conduct would have communicated to a reasonable person that he was not at liberty to ignore the police presence and go about his business." *U.S. v. Chan-Jimenez*, 125 F.3d 1324, 1326 (9th Cir. 1997) (rejected on other grounds by, U.S. v. Al Nasser, 555 F.3d 722 (9th Cir. 2009)).

- "The Fourth Amendment guards against unreasonable seizures of a person, including brief investigatory stops." *U.S. v. Garcia-Acuna*, 175 F.3d 1143, 1146 (9th Cir. 1999), as amended on denial of reh'g, (July 19, 1999).

Tenth Circuit

- ". . . . [N]either usage nor common-law tradition makes an *attempted* seizure a seizure." *Brooks v. Gaenzle*, 614 F.3d 1213, 1221 (10th Cir. 2010).

§ 3:2 Test: A person has been seized if, under the totality of the circumstances, a reasonable person would believe himself not free to go

Supreme Court

- "We think that under our recent decision in *Whren v. United States* the subjective intentions of the officer did not make the continued detention of respondent illegal under the Fourth Amendment. As we made clear in *Whren*, the fact that an officer does not have the state of mind which is hypothecated by the reasons which provide the legal justification for the officer's action does not invalidate the action taken as long as the circumstances, viewed objectively, justify that action. Subjective intentions play no role in ordinary, probable-cause Fourth Amendment analysis." *Ohio v. Robinette*, 519 U.S. 33, 38, 117 S. Ct. 417, 136 L. Ed. 2d 347, 148 A.L.R. Fed. 739 (1996).

- "When police attempt to question a person who is walking down the street or through an airport lobby, it makes sense to inquire whether a reasonable person would feel free to continue walking. But when the person is seated on a bus and has no desire to leave, the degree to which a reasonable person would feel that he or she could leave is not an accurate measure of the coercive effect of the encounter. Here, for example, the mere fact that [Defendant] did not feel free to leave the bus does not mean that the police seized him. [Defendant] was a passenger on a bus that was scheduled to depart. He would not have felt free to leave the bus even if the police had not been present. [Defendant's] movements were confined in a sense, but this was the natural result of his decision to take the bus; it says nothing about whether or not the police conduct at issue was coercive. In such a situation, the appropriate inquiry is whether a reasonable person would feel free to decline the officers' requests or otherwise terminate the encounter. [T]he crucial test is whether, taking into account all of the circumstances surrounding the encounter, the police conduct would have communicated to a reasonable person that he was not at liberty to ignore the police presence and go about his business." *Florida v. Bostick*, 501 U.S. 429, 435–37, 111 S. Ct. 2382, 115 L. Ed. 2d 389 (1991).

- "What is apparent from *Royer* and *Brown* is that police questioning, by itself, is unlikely to result in a Fourth Amendment violation. While most citizens will respond to a police request, the fact that people do so, and do so without being told they are free not to respond, hardly eliminates the consensual nature of the response. Unless the circumstances of the encounter are so intimidat-

ing as to demonstrate that a reasonable person would
have believed he was not free to leave if he had not
responded, one cannot say that the questioning resulted
in a detention under the Fourth Amendment. But if the
person refuses to answer and the police take additional
steps then the Fourth Amendment imposes some
minimal level of objective justification to validate the
detention or seizure." *I.N.S. v. Delgado*, 466 U.S. 210,
216–17, 104 S. Ct. 1758, 80 L. Ed. 2d 247 (1984).

- "[I]t is submitted that the entire encounter was consensual and hence [Defendant] was not being held against
his will at all. We find this submission untenable. Asking for and examining [Defendant's] ticket and his driver's license were no doubt permissible in themselves,
but when the officers identified themselves as narcotics
agents, told [him] that he was suspected of transporting
narcotics, and asked him to accompany them to the police room, while retaining his ticket and driver's license
and without indicating in any way that he was free to
depart, [Defendant] was effectively seized for the
purposes of the Fourth Amendment. These circumstances surely amount to a show of official authority
such that a reasonable person would have believed he
was not free to leave." *Florida v. Royer*, 460 U.S. 491,
501–02, 103 S. Ct. 1319, 75 L. Ed. 2d 229 (1983).

- "We conclude that a person has been seized within the
meaning of the Fourth Amendment only if, in view of
all of the circumstances surrounding the incident, a
reasonable person would have believed that he was not
free to leave. Examples of circumstances that might
indicate a seizure, even where the person did not attempt to leave, would be the threatening presence of
several officers, the display of a weapon by an officer,
some physical touching of the person of the citizen, or
the use of language or tone of voice indicating that
compliance with the officer's request might be
compelled. In the absence of some such evidence,
otherwise inoffensive contact between a member of the
public and the police cannot, as a matter of law, amount
to a seizure of that person." *U.S. v. Mendenhall*, 446
U.S. 544, 554–55, 100 S. Ct. 1870, 64 L. Ed. 2d 497
(1980).

- "It is quite plain that the Fourth Amendment governs

seizures of the person which do not eventuate in a trip to the station house and prosecution for crime—arrests in the traditional terminology. Only when the officer, by means of physical force or show of authority, has in some way restrained the liberty of a citizen may we conclude that a seizure has occurred." *Terry v. Ohio*, 392 U.S. 1, 16, 19 n.16, 88 S. Ct. 1868, 20 L. Ed. 2d 889 (1968).

Fourth Circuit

- "The government concedes that [Defendant] was 'seized' at the time of his initial detention. We agree that a seizure occurred here, because a reasonable person in [Defendant's] position would not have felt 'free to leave' the area of the building in which he was held, or otherwise to terminate the encounter with the officers. When the officers entered the building, they instructed [Defendant] to 'sit down,' informed him of his *Miranda* rights, and kept him confined to a limited area during the entire three-hour detention. Accordingly, the officers' actions effected a seizure of [Defendant], within the meaning of the Fourth Amendment." *U.S. v. Watson*, 703 F.3d 684 (4th Cir. 2013).

- "The Supreme Court has explained that a Fourth Amendment seizure requires 'an intentional acquisition of physical control' which occurs 'only when there is a governmental termination of freedom of movement *through means intentionally applied.*' . . . [The] government actor need not, however, seize an individual in the precise manner intended. . . . In other words, so long as the *instrumentality* is intended, a seizure occurs even if the *degree* of the instrumentality's effectiveness was unanticipated." *Melgar ex rel. Melgar v. Greene*, 593 F.3d 348 (4th Cir. 2010) (emphasis in original).

Fifth Circuit

- "Aldridge's argument is directed at the first *Terry* prong, namely, whether the officer's decision to stop the vehicle was justified at its inception. According to Aldridge, the tip regarding the purchase of iodine, a legal product, is insufficient, at least in this case, to establish reasonable suspicion without some additional investigatory work. Because the officers admittedly had no basis for the stop other than the tip from the veterinary clinic, he concludes that the stop was illegal. . . . . Aldridge's argument might have more force if the tip had come from a merchant reporting a single purchase of ordinary strength iodine. Here, however, the tippee reported the purchase of three bottles of highly concentrated iodine, following the purchase of numerous such bottles in the prior months. Based on previous discussions between Dr. Hada and the police concerning the typical sale of iodine in the clinic, it was reasonable for the officers to infer that the purchase of such a large quantity in a relatively short period of time indicated that the purchaser intended to use the iodine illegally, that is, for the production of methamphetamine. Indeed, as the district court noted, previous tips from the clinic had already resulted in the police shutting down a different methamphetamine manufacturing operation. Moreover, this same woman had purchased eleven pint sized bottles of concentrated iodine over the prior nine months. We therefore hold that the purchase of the three additional bottles of iodine, when viewed within the 'totality of the circumstances,' including the ongoing and previously reliable communication between the veterinary clinic and the police, provided reasonable suspicion sufficient to justify the stop." *U.S. v. Rains*, 615 F.3d 589, 595-96 (5th Cir. 2010) (citations omitted).

• "The Supreme Court requires lower courts to look at 'the totality of the circumstances' in evaluating whether or not the police had reasonable suspicion of criminal activity. The Court has interpreted this requirement as prohibiting the method of 'divide-and-conquer analysis,' under which a court examines and rejects individually each of a number of factors that the police cite as having created reasonable suspicion, instead of examining the factors jointly. Thus, it is improper for a court to refuse to find that reasonable suspicion existed because each of a set of circumstances has an innocent explanation. The proper question is whether or not the entire set of circumstances, taken together, created reasonable suspicion of criminal activity." *U.S. v. Pack*, 612 F.3d 341, 358 (5th Cir. 2010), opinion modified on denial of reh'g, U.S. v. Pack, 622 F.3d 383 (5th Cir. 2010) (citations omitted).

- "The court applied our totality-of-the-circumstances test, containing six factors: (1) the voluntariness of the defendant's custodial status; (2) the presence of coercive police procedures; (3) the extent and level of the defendant's cooperation with police; (4) his awareness of the right to refuse to consent; (5) his education and intelligence; and (6) his belief that no incriminating evidence will be found." *U.S. v. Hernandez*, 392 Fed. Appx. 350, 352 (5th Cir. 2010) (citations omitted).

Seventh Circuit

- "This is not the first time we have considered an officer's claim that he was seized while on the job; we considered several claims of unlawful seizure by officers in our *Driebel* decision. . . . [H]ere, no seizure occurred. Although [plaintiff] contends he was under criminal investigation, the record does not support him. . . . While [plaintiff] is not maintaining that he feared only job consequences, the bottom line is that a reasonable person in [plaintiff's] position would not have feared arrest or detention if he had declined to be patted down or searched. As we discussed, [plaintiff's supervisor] did not tell [plaintiff] he was the subject of a criminal investigation, nor is there any indication that he was. He did not read [plaintiff] his rights. He did not threaten arrest if [plaintiff] refused to be searched. He did not touch [plaintiff] to stop him from leaving. (He only came into contact with [plaintiff] during the pat-down.) There is also no evidence to support a finding that had [plaintiff] asked him to stop, the lieutenant would not have done so. . . . Although [plaintiff] may have felt it necessary to agree to the search because he needed to use the restroom badly, that does not mean he was seized by [his supervisor]. A reasonable officer in [plaintiff's] position would not have feared arrest or detention had he not complied. Therefore, we agree with the district court that [plaintiff] was not seized." *Carter v. City of Milwaukee*, 743 F.3d 540 (7th Cir. 2014).
- "The Fourth Amendment ensures that the right of the people to be secure in their persons, houses, papers, and effects, against unreasonable searches and seizures, shall not be violated. A Fourth Amendment seizure occurs when there is a governmental termination of

freedom of movement through means intentionally applied. . .such that a reasonable person would have believed that he was not free to leave. . . ." *Tesch v. County of Green Lake*, 157 F.3d 465, 472 (7th Cir. 1998).

- "The second approach articulated by the Supreme Court applies when the police approach an individual in a confined space such as a bus. In such a situation, it no longer makes sense to inquire whether a reasonable person would feel free to continue walking. Because a person on a bus or in an otherwise confining space has no desire to leave and would wish to remain even if police were not present, the degree to which a reasonable person would feel that he or she could leave is not an accurate measure of the coercive effect of the encounter. When a person's freedom of movement is restricted by a factor independent of police conduct—i.e., by his being a passenger on a bus the appropriate inquiry is whether a reasonable person would feel free to decline the officers' request or otherwise terminate the encounter." *U.S. v. Jerez*, 108 F.3d 684, 689 (7th Cir. 1997).

Eighth Circuit

- "[A]n officer does not seize a person by asking for license and registration if he does not 'convey a message that compliance with [his] request is required.' " *U.S. v. Lopez-Mendoza*, 601 F.3d 861 (8th Cir. 2010).
- "The government argues that [defendant] was never subjected to a Fourth Amendment seizure because he was given all his papers back and told that [officer] was 'all done with him.' The government further asserts that [defendant] was not subjected to the threatening presence of several officers, the display of any weapons, any physical touching, or the use of language or tone of voice indicating that compliance with [officer's] request was compelled. Instead, the tone of the exchange was cooperative and, at the time [officer] asked to search the SUV, [defendant] had everything he needed to continue on his journey. For Fourth Amendment purposes, a seizure occurs when a reasonable person would not feel free to leave. The district court concluded that [defendant's] inability to understand English, [officer's] statement 'before you take off,' and the fact that [officer] continued to talk to him and ask questions

while [defendant] was sitting in the back seat of the patrol car would reasonably lead a person in similar circumstances to believe that they were not yet free to leave. We agree. Most English-speaking people, and certainly [defendant], who was having trouble understanding [officer], would not have understood that the stop ended and a voluntary interaction with [officer] began." *U.S. v. Guerrero*, 374 F.3d 584 (8th Cir. 2004).

- "Circumstances indicative of a seizure may include a threatening presence of several officers, the display of a weapon by an officer, some physical touching of the person. . . .or the use of language or tone of voice indicating that compliance with the officer's request might be compelled. . . . In addition, when an officer, by means of physical force or show of authority, has in some way restrained the liberty of a citizen the court may conclude that a seizure has occurred." *U.S. v. Tovar-Valdivia*, 193 F.3d 1025, 1027 (8th Cir. 1999).

- "We begin by evaluating the issue of seizure. A seizure occurs when, in the totality of the circumstances surrounding the encounter, a reasonable person would believe that she is not free to leave. . . . Seizing luggage without asking consent, or in spite of a suspect's refusal to consent, or compelling a suspect to go to an interdiction room constitutes a show of authority and creates a reasonable belief that the suspect is not free to leave." *U.S. v. Pena-Saiz*, 161 F.3d 1175, 1177 (8th Cir. 1998).

Ninth Circuit

- "Determining whether to apply a subjective or objective test to police conduct is a practical exercise, not a metaphysical one. The purpose of either test is to avoid the kind of arbitrary and oppressive interference by law enforcement officials with the privacy and personal security of individuals' that the Fourth Amendment was intended to limit. That an encounter is *not* a seizure when a reasonable person would feel free to leave does not mean that an encounter *is* a seizure just because a reasonable person would not feel free to leave. In fact, the Court has expressly rejected such an inference. A Fourth Amendment seizure does not occur whenever there is a governmentally caused termination of an individual's freedom of movement (the innocent passerby), nor even whenever there is a governmentally caused and governmentally desired termination of an individual's freedom of movement (the fleeing felon), but only when there is a governmental termination of freedom of movement through means intentionally applied. The objective inquiry of whether a reasonable person would have believed that he was not free to leave, has been supplemented with a requirement that the detention be willful. This latter requirement arises because the Fourth Amendment addresses misuse of power, not the accidental effects of otherwise lawful government conduct." *U.S. v. Al Nasser*, 555 F.3d 722 (9th Cir. 2009).

- "A person is seized when he is meant to be stopped by [a particular law enforcement action] . . . and [is] so stopped. That is, a seizure occurs where a person is stopped by the very instrumentality set in motion or put in place in order to achieve that result." *U.S. v. Al Nasser*, 555 F.3d 722 (9th Cir. 2009).

- "We first address whether [Officer] Shaw's initial encounter with [defendant] constituted a seizure under the Fourth Amendment. . . . We conclude that although [Officer] Shaw conceded he suspected [defendant] of no criminal activity, [Officer] Shaw's initial encounter with [defendant] was not a seizure and did not implicate the Fourth Amendment. In approaching the scene, [Officer] Shaw parked his squad car a full car length behind [defendant]'s car so he did not block it. [Officer] Shaw did not activate his sirens or lights. [Officer] Shaw approached [defendant]'s car on foot, and did not brandish his flashlight as a weapon, but rather used it to illuminate the interior of [defendant]'s car. Although [Officer] Shaw was uniformed, with his baton and firearm visible, [Officer] Shaw did not touch either weapon during his encounter with [defendant]. [Officer] Shaw's initial questioning of [defendant] was brief and consensual, and the district court found that [Officer] Shaw was cordial and courteous. Under these circumstances, the district court correctly concluded that a reasonable person would have felt free to terminate the encounter and leave. . . . We next address whether [defendant] was seized during the search of his person . . . [.] . . . Even though [Officer] Shaw did not inform [defendant]

that he could refuse to consent to a search of his person,
[defendant] does not dispute the district court's finding
that he voluntarily consented to the search of his
person. And although [defendant] was seated in his car
with his car door closed when he gave this consent, a
reasonable person in [defendant]'s situation would have
understood that the police officer might ask him to exit
the vehicle in order to conduct the search because of
valid concerns for officer safety. [citation omitted]
Otherwise, the police officer would have been forced to
search the person through the car door window while
the driver remained seated in the car within easy reach
of any hidden weapons. [footnote omitted] [Defendant]'s
voluntary consent to the search of his person, however,
does not preclude the possibility that officer [Officer]
Shaw improperly seized [defendant] as events unfolded.
[citations omitted] If [Officer] Shaw and [Officer]
Pahlke's actions exceeded the scope of [defendant]'s
consent to the search of his person, such that a reasonable person in [defendant]'s situation would not have
felt free to depart if he so chose, then [Officer] Shaw
and [Officer] Pahlke seized [defendant]. [citations omit-
ted] . . . We have identified several non-exhaustive
situations where an officer's actions escalate a consensual encounter into a seizure: [a] '. . . a law enforcement officer, through coercion, physical force, or a show
of authority, . . . restricts the liberty of a person [cita-
tion and internal quotation marks omitted][;] [b] . . . a
threatening presence of several officers [;] [c] . . . a
display of a weapon by an officer[;] [d] . . . some physical touching of the person of the citizen[;] or [e] the use
of language or tone of voice indicating that compliance
with the officer's request might be compelled.' [citation
and internal quotation marks omitted] In Orhorhaghe
[v. I.N.S.], we identified several factors to consider in
determining if a person was seized, any one of which, if
present, could constitute a seizure: (1) the number of officers; (2) whether weapons were displayed; (3) whether
the encounter occurred in a public or non-public setting;
(4) whether the officer's tone or manner was authoritative, so as to imply that compliance would be compelled;
and (5) whether the officers informed the person of his
right to terminate the encounter. [citation omitted] . . .

Applying these factors, we conclude that under the total circumstances present in [defendant]'s case, [Officer] Shaw and [Officer] Pahlke's encounter with [defendant] escalated into a seizure. It is undisputed that neither [Officer] Shaw nor [Officer] Pahlke used physical force or a threat of physical force in their interaction with [defendant]. And the district court found that [Officer] Shaw was courteous and cordial when questioning [defendant]. Despite these findings, several facts support our conclusion that in the total circumstances a reasonable person in [defendant]'s shoes would not have felt at liberty to terminate the encounter with the police and leave. . . . First, although the encounter took place on a public street, it happened around 11:30 p.m. in lighting that required [Officer] Shaw to use a flashlight. Second, when [defendant] exited his car, he was confronted with two uniformed police officers. [citation omitted] And third, it is undisputed that neither [Officer] Pahlke, nor [Officer] Shaw, informed [defendant] of his right to terminate the encounter. [citation omitted] . . . Perhaps most important, the manner in which [Officer] Shaw searched [defendant]'s person was authoritative and implied that [defendant] 'was not free to decline his requests.' [citation omitted] [Officer] Pahlke testified that when [defendant] exited his car, [defendant]'s hands were raised. [citation omitted] And instead of searching [defendant] in front of, or nearby his car, [Officer] Shaw directed [defendant] to move away from his car, and continued directing [defendant] where to walk until the two reached [Officer] Shaw's squad car, a full car length away from the Taurus. Indeed, at one point, [defendant] testified that [Officer] Shaw 'corrected [[defendant]] to walk towards the back of [[Officer] Shaw's] car.' [citation omitted] . . . Additionally, [defendant] testified that when [Officer] Shaw searched him, his hands were on the top of [Officer] Shaw's squad car, with his back to [Officer] Shaw. [Defendant] indicated that [Officer] Shaw 'patted [him] all the way down' his body, and when [defendant] attempted to turn his head sideways, [Officer] Shaw instructed him to 'keep his head forward.' [Officer] Shaw's search appears to have exceeded a normal *Terry* frisk for weapons. [citation omitted] Instead, [Officer]

Shaw's search, and the manner in which it was conducted, put [defendant] in a position where a reasonable person would not have felt free to decline the requests and depart. Hence, the consensual search by [Officer] Shaw had escalated to a seizure of [defendant], whereby [defendant] could do nothing more than comply with [Officer] Shaw's orders. . . . Finally, [Officer] Pahlke's position during [Officer] Shaw's search of [defendant]'s person weighs in favor of finding a seizure. After [defendant] exited his car and began following [Officer] Shaw's directions to move away from it and towards [Officer] Shaw's squad car, [Officer] Pahlke positioned himself between [defendant] and his car. If [defendant] wanted to end his encounter with [Officer] Shaw and [Officer] Pahlke and leave, he would have had to either: (a) leave on foot, abandoning his unlocked car, with the driver's door partially open; or (b) navigate through or around [Officer] Pahlke to get back into his car. Neither option was realistic, especially considering [Officer] Pahlke and [Officer] Shaw outnumbered and outsized [defendant]. [citation and footnote omitted] . . . In sum, under the totality of the circumstances— [Officer] Shaw's authoritative manner and direction of [defendant] away from [defendant]'s car to another location, the publicized shootings by white Portland police officers of African-Americans, the widely distributed pamphlet with which [defendant] was familiar, instructing the public to comply with an officer's instructions, that [Officer] Shaw and [Officer] Pahlke outnumbered [defendant] two to one, the time of night and lighting in the area, that [Officer] Pahlke was blocking [defendant]'s entrance back into his car, and that neither [Officer] Pahlke, nor [Officer] Shaw, informed [defendant] he could terminate the encounter and leave—we conclude that a reasonable person would not have felt free to disregard [Officer] Shaw's directions, end the encounter with [Officer] Shaw and [Officer] Pahlke, and leave the scene. [citations omitted] We hold that [Officer] Shaw and [Officer] Pahlke exceeded the scope of [defendant]'s consent to search his person and seized him. . . . Having concluded that [Officer] Shaw and [Officer] Pahlke seized [defendant], we must determine if that seizure violated the Fourth Amendment. A seizure of a person is justified under the Fourth Amendment if law enforcement officers have reasonable suspicion that a person committed, or is about to commit, a crime. [citation omitted] Without reasonable suspicion, a person 'may not be detained even momentarily.' [citation omitted] . . . The government concedes that at the time [Officer] Shaw searched [defendant]'s person, neither [Officer] Shaw nor [Officer] Pahlke possessed reasonable suspicion or probable cause that [defendant] was engaged in criminal activity. Accordingly, [Officer] Shaw and [Officer] Pahlke's seizure of [defendant] violated the Fourth Amendment. [citation omitted]" *U.S. v. Washington*, 490 F.3d 765, 770–774 (9th Cir. 2007).

- "A reasonable person handcuffed for four hours in a locked security office after a narcotics search would have believed that she was not free to leave." *U.S. v. Juvenile (RRA-A)*, 229 F.3d 737, 743 (9th Cir. 2000).

Tenth Circuit

- " '[A]n individual is "seized" when he has an objective reason to believe that he is not free to terminate his conversation with the officer and proceed on his way.' 'The question of whether an encounter was consensual "calls for the refined judgment of the trial court."' Considering the totality of the circumstances here, that there were two uniformed police officers driving closely alongside Mr. Hernandez in the dark with no one else around, and that Mr. Hernandez did not stop walking until one officer asked him to stop even though he was answering the officers' questions, the district court did not err in concluding there was a show of authority by Officers Morghem and Walton sufficient to constitute a seizure under the Fourth Amendment." *United States v. Hernandez*, 847 F.3d 1257, 1266 (10th Cir. 2017) (citations omitted).

- "In *United States v. Mendenhall*, the Supreme Court further explained 'a person is seized only when, by means of physical force or a show of authority, *his freedom of movement is restrained.*' . . . . (emphasis added). In *Garner,* the Court applied this principle to a suspect flight situation where a police officer's fatal shooting of a fleeing suspect was deemed to constitute a

111

Fourth Amendment seizure on grounds that '[w]henever an officer restrains the freedom of a person to walk away, he has seized that person.' . . . The *Garner* Court also stated 'there can be no question that *apprehension by the use of deadly force* is a seizure subject to the reasonableness requirement of the Fourth Amendment.' . . . (emphasis added). Thus, from *Terry, Mendenhall*, and *Garner,* one can reasonably conclude a 'seizure' requires restraint of one's freedom of movement and includes apprehension or capture by deadly force. However, they do not stand for the proposition, as [the plaintiff] contends, that use of deadly force alone constitutes a seizure. Instead, it is clear restraint of freedom of movement must occur." *Brooks v. Gaenzle*, 614 F.3d 1213, 1219 (10th Cir. 2010).

- "In order to determine whether a particular encounter constitutes a seizure, a court must consider all the circumstances surrounding the encounter to determine whether the police conduct would have communicated to a reasonable person that the person was not free to decline the officers' requests or otherwise terminate the encounter." *U.S. v. Broomfield*, 201 F.3d 1270, 1274 (10th Cir. 2000).

Eleventh Circuit

- "[The defendant] manifested his subjective expectation of privacy by placing personal items inside the pillowcase and holding it shut in one hand. The fact that the pillowcase could not be fastened is not dispositive. The Supreme Court has recognized that 'a traveler who carries a toothbrush and a few articles of clothing in a paper bag or knotted scarf [may] claim an equal right to conceal his possessions from official inspection as the sophisticated executive with the locked attaché case.' . . . Where Mr. Epps's argument founders is on the objective component, because society is not willing to accept that his subjective privacy expectation was objectively reasonable. The Supreme Court has suggested in dictum that 'some containers (for example a kit of burglar tools or a gun case) by their very nature cannot support any reasonable expectation of privacy because their contents can be inferred from their outward appearance.' . . . In this case, considering the totality of the circumstances, the fact that the pillowcase contained dye packs and possibly other items associated with the bank robbery could 'be inferred from [its] outward appearance.' Deputy Kent saw Mr. Epps with a white bag in his hand, running away from a blue Cavalier parked at an angle with its driver's door open. The deputy knew that a blue Cavalier had been carjacked, and he believed that the carjacking was related to a bank robbery that had taken place in the same area just minutes before. After being directed to stop, the fleeing individual pointed a gun at the deputy. Upon closer inspection, the white bag was found to be a pillowcase with pink stains on it. Tellers frequently give bank robbers dye packs, which are designed to explode after the robbery and permanently mark the bills with ink . . . . Because the pillowcase's contents could be inferred from its outwardly visible stains and the circumstances under which the police obtained it, the pillowcase was one of those containers that 'by [its] very nature cannot support any reasonable expectation of privacy.' The pillowcase therefore fell outside the protective ambit of the Fourth Amendment, and the police did not violate Mr. Epps's constitutional rights when they opened the pillowcase without first obtaining a warrant." *U.S. v. Epps*, 613 F.3d 1093, 1098-99 (11th Cir. 2010).

§ 3:3 Test: Suspect must submit to show of authority for seizure to occur

Supreme Court

- "The word seizure readily bears the meaning of a laying on of hands or application of physical force to restrain movement, even when it is ultimately unsuccessful. (She seized the purse-snatcher, but he broke out of her grasp.) It does not remotely apply, however, to the prospect or a policeman yelling Stop, in the name of the law! at a fleeing form that continues to flee. That is no seizure. Nor can, the result respondent wishes to achieve be produced—indirectly, as it were—by suggesting that [the Officer's] uncomplied-with show of authority was a common-law arrest, and then appealing to the principle that all common-law arrests are

seizures. An arrest requires either physical force (as
described above) or, where that is absent, submission to
the assertion of authority." *California v. Hodari D.*, 499
U.S. 621, 626, 111 S. Ct. 1547, 113 L. Ed. 2d 690 (1991).

Second Circuit

- " 'A seizure . . . requires "either physical force . . . or,
where that is absent, submission to the assertion of [po-
lice] authority.'" It is undisputed that Officer Lattanzio
used no physical force. Therefore, Huertas was seized
only if he (1) 'submitted' (2) to an 'assertion of authority.'
We conclude that Huertas never 'submitted' to Officer
Lattanzio and was therefore never 'seized' within the
meaning of the Fourth Amendment. In light of this disposition, we need not consider whether the spotlighting
of Huertas by a police car going the wrong way down a
dark street constituted an 'assertion of authority.'
'Whether conduct constitutes submission to police
authority will depend . . . on "the totality of the circumstances—the whole picture."' Of particular relevance here, conduct that 'amount[s] to evasion of police authority' is 'not submission.'. . . . Huertas argues
that he 'submitted' to police authority by standing still
as Officer Lattanzio's police cruiser approached and by
answering Officer Lattanzio's questions. However, we
conclude that Huertas's behavior was akin to the
evasive actions in *Baldwin*, which did not constitute
submission. The defendant in *Baldwin* pulled his car to
the side of the road in response to a police cruiser's siren and flashing lights. 496 F.3d at 217. Both police officers walked toward Baldwin's car and ordered Baldwin
to show his hands. When he refused and just stared at
them, the officers drew their weapons and continued to
approach. As they neared, Baldwin sped off. When
Baldwin was apprehended, weapons and drug paraphernalia were found in his car. The trial court denied
Baldwin's motion to suppress the physical evidence on
the ground that it was discovered after an illegal
seizure. We affirmed on the ground that the temporary
stop did not constitute submission to police authority.
Rather, 'Baldwin's conduct, all circumstances considered, amounted to evasion of police authority, not
submission.' All circumstances considered, Huertas's

actions were likewise evasive, and maximized his chance of avoiding arrest. If Huertas had run as soon as he was illuminated by Officer Lattanzio's spotlight, he could expect Officer Lattanzio to give chase. By remaining still and answering questions, Huertas had a chance to quiet suspicion and hope that Officer Lattanzio would drive away after being satisfied with answers to his questions. But as soon as Huertas saw Officer Lattanzio getting out of his car, Huertas ran. Among the significant circumstances are the brevity of the interaction and the fact that Officer Lattanzio was never within reach of Huertas and able to physically restrain him. As in Baldwin, the totality of the circumstances indicate that the defendant was evading police authority, not submitting to it. Huertas was never seized, and the evidence was admissible." *United States v. Huertas*, 864 F.3d 214, 216-17 (2d Cir. 2017) (citations omitted).

Fourth Circuit

- "A defendant who flees the police in response to an assertion of authority has not been seized, and thus his Fourth Amendment rights are not implicated." *U.S. v. Brown*, 401 F.3d 588 (4th Cir. 2005).

Sixth Circuit

- "It would be an unnatural reading of the case law to hold that a defendant who is ordered to stop is not seized until he stops *and* complies with a subsequent order to raise his hands. If a subject is seized only if (1) 'a reasonable person would have believed that he was not free to leave,' and (2) the subject actually 'yield[s]' to the message that he is not free to leave, then for a person who is moving, to 'yield' most sensibly means to stop. To 'yield' cannot mean to comply with each subsequent order made by an officer after the subject's initial compliance. Indeed, if a person stopped and raised his hands at an officer's command but failed to obey a further command to spread his legs or to lie on the ground, we would not say that he had not been seized initially. It is enough to submit to an officer's initial command to stop and to remain stopped." *U.S. v. Johnson*, 620 F.3d 685, 691 (6th Cir. 2010) (citations omitted).

- "However, absent the intentional application of physical force, even if there is a show of authority and a reasonable person would not feel free to leave, in order for a seizure to occur there must also be submission to the show of authority." *U.S. v. Smith*, 594 F.3d 530 (6th Cir. 2010).

Seventh Circuit

- "A seizure triggering the Fourth Amendment's protections occurs only when government actors have, by means of physical force or show of authority. . .in some way restrained the liberty of a citizen. . . . It is, however, difficult to ascertain the precise moment a seizure occurs when law enforcement officers are pursuing an individual who is evading capture by driving or running away from police after a display of authority." *U.S. v. Bradley*, 196 F.3d 762, 767 (7th Cir. 1999).

Tenth Circuit

- "Fourth Amendment law recognizes three types of police-citizen encounters: (1) consensual encounters; (2) investigative detentions; and (3) arrests. Both detentions and arrests are seizures. Police must have reasonable suspicion of criminal activity for a detention and probable cause that a crime has been committed for an arrest. A police officer may seize someone either by physical force or a show of authority. As in this case, '[w]hen an officer does not apply physical force to restrain a subject, a Fourth Amendment seizure occurs only if (a) the officer shows his authority; and (b) the citizen "submits to the assertion of authority."' Because the ensuing analysis relies on whether Mr. Roberson submitted to an assertion of authority, additional legal background on that element follows. . . .. A show of authority alone is not a seizure 'without actual submission.' Actual submission depends on 'the view of a reasonable law enforcement officer' under 'the totality of the circumstances.' Submission 'requires, at minimum, that a suspect manifest compliance with police orders.'" *United States v. Roberson*, 864 F.3d 1118, 1121–22 (10th Cir. 2017) (citations omitted).
- "[T]he officers clearly showed their authority by raising their weapons and shouting 'hands up,' but Defendant—

although he may have frozen momentarily out of confusion—did not immediately manifest compliance with their orders. True, a reasonable officer shouting 'hands up' likely would have viewed Defendant as "seized" had Defendant simply sat still in the car without making furtive motions. Furthermore, had Defendant simply sat still in response to the officer's commands and allowed himself to be seized from the outset, the seizure may not have been valid. But here, . . . Defendant did not simply remain seated; rather, he began making furtive motions consistent with hiding—or worse, retrieving—a gun. Defendant did not manifest submission; quite the opposite, Defendant went from sitting still before being confronted by the officers, to moving furtively, directly contrary to the officers' commands. We hold Defendant did not submit to the officers' show of authority, and therefore was not 'seized' within the meaning of the Fourth Amendment, until he manifested compliance with the officers' orders—when he put his hands up." *U.S. v. Mosley*, 743 F.3d 1317 (10th Cir. 2014).

D.C. Circuit

- "For purposes of the Fourth Amendment a seizure occurs when physical force is used to restrain movement or when a person submits to an officer's 'show of authority.' The government concedes that the police made a show of authority when they ordered Brodie to put his hands on the car. But they claim that he didn't submit, arguing that the compliance was too 'momentary' to constitute submission. . . . We can see no basis for classifying Brodie's action—putting his hands on the car when told to do so by the police—as anything other than full compliance with the officer's request. Nothing suggests, for example, that the compliance was feigned. In fact, the district court found that 'Mr. Brodie put his hands on the car *and then* decided that he was going to run.' Nor does anything in the record suggest that Brodie had some ulterior purpose in putting his hands on the car, such as a belief that doing so would facilitate escape. Contrary to the government's position, the short duration of Brodie's submission means only that the seizure was brief, not that no seizure occurred.

Later acts of noncompliance do not negate a defendant's initial submission, so long as it was authentic." *U.S. v. Brodie*, 742 F.3d 1058 (D.C. Cir. 2014).

§ 3:4 Justification to seize—Arrest: An arrest or its functional equivalent must be based upon probable cause

Supreme Court

- "The probable-cause standard is incapable of precise definition or quantification into percentages because it deals with probabilities and depends on the totality of the circumstances. We have stated, however, that the substance of all the definitions of probable cause is a reasonable ground for belief of guilt, and that the belief of guilt must be particularized with respect to the person to be searched or seized. . . . To determine whether an officer had probable cause to arrest an individual, we examine the events leading up to the arrest, and then decide whether these historical facts, viewed from the standpoint of an objectively reasonable police officer, amount to probable cause." *Maryland v. Pringle*, 540 U.S. 366, 124 S. Ct. 795, 157 L. Ed. 2d 769 (2003).

- "The principal components of a determination of reasonable suspicion or probable cause will be the events which occurred leading up to the stop or search, and then the decision whether these historical facts, viewed from the standpoint of an objectively reasonable police officer, amount to reasonable suspicion or to probable cause. The first part of the analysis involves only a determination of historical facts, but the second is a mixed question of law and fact." *Ornelas v. U.S.*, 517 U.S. 690, 696, 116 S. Ct. 1657, 134 L. Ed. 2d 911 (1996).

- "[T]he general rule [is] that seizures of the person require probable cause to arrest." *Florida v. Royer*, 460 U.S. 491, 499, 103 S. Ct. 1319, 75 L. Ed. 2d 229 (1983).

- "[P]robable cause to arrest [Defendant] did not exist at the time he consented to the search of his luggage. The facts are that a nervous young man with two American Tourister bags paid cash for an airline ticket to a target city. These facts led to inquiry, which in turn revealed that the ticket had been bought under an assumed name. The proffered explanation did not satisfy the

officers. We cannot agree with the State, if this is its
position, that every nervous young man paying cash for
a ticket to New York City under an assumed name and
carrying two heavy American Tourister bags may be arrested and held to answer for a serious felony charge."
Florida v. Royer, 460 U.S. 491, 507, 103 S. Ct. 1319, 75
L. Ed. 2d 229 (1983).

- "[T]he general rule [is] that every arrest, and every
  seizure having the essential attributes of a formal arrest, is unreasonable unless it is supported by probable
  cause." *Michigan v. Summers*, 452 U.S. 692, 700, 101 S.
  Ct. 2587, 69 L. Ed. 2d 340 (1981).

- "[T]he entry into a home to conduct a search or make
  an arrest is unreasonable under the Fourth Amendment unless done pursuant to a warrant." *Steagald v.
  U.S.*, 451 U.S. 204, 211, 101 S. Ct. 1642, 68 L. Ed. 2d
  38 (1981).

- "[D]etention for custodial interrogation—regardless of
  its label—intrudes so severely on interests protected by
  the Fourth Amendment as necessarily to trigger the
  traditional safeguards against illegal arrest." *Dunaway
  v. New York*, 442 U.S. 200, 216, 99 S. Ct. 2248, 60 L.
  Ed. 2d 824 (1979).

- "Nothing is more clear than that the Fourth Amendment was meant to prevent wholesale intrusions upon
  the personal security of our citizenry, whether these
  intrusions be termed arrests or investigatory
  detentions." *Davis v. Mississippi*, 394 U.S. 721, 726–27,
  89 S. Ct. 1394, 22 L. Ed. 2d 676 (1969).

Fourth Circuit

- "Accepting the allegations of the complaint as true,
  Goines, though having speech and other physical difficulties, exhibited no signs of mental illness and made
  no threats to harm himself or others, but instead sought
  the help of the police to avoid a confrontation and
  potential fight with a neighbor who had spliced into
  Goines' cable line. Under these facts, the Officers lacked
  probable cause for an emergency mental-health
  detention[.] . . . Probable cause, of course, is a 'fluid
  concept that cannot be reduced to a neat set of legal
  rules,' and our cases applying the concept in the mental-
  health context are perhaps not easily reduced to bright-

line rules. Nonetheless, the facts as alleged by Goines—the involuntary detention of a man with physical disabilities who exhibited no signs of mental illness and made no threats of harm—are sufficiently beyond the realm of probable cause that no reasonable police officer would find them adequate." *Goines v. Valley Community Services Bd.*, 822 F.3d 159, 170 (4th Cir. 2016) (citation omitted).

Fifth Circuit

- "It is well established that under the Fourth Amendment a warrantless arrest must be based on probable cause." *U.S. v. Castro*, 166 F.3d 728, 733 (5th Cir. 1999).

Sixth Circuit

- "The Fourth Amendment conditions warrants on probable cause and prohibits unreasonable seizures. A police officer violates those restrictions only when his deliberate or reckless falsehoods result in arrest and prosecution without probable cause. The resulting claim, what might be called an 'unreasonable prosecutorial seizure' claim, is traditionally known as a 'malicious prosecution' claim." *Newman v. Township of Hamburg*, 773 F.3d 769, 771–72 (6th Cir. 2014) (citations omitted).
- "Defendant was a passenger in a vehicle that was pulled over for driving with a broken taillight. When asked for identification, the driver immediately admitted that he did not have a valid license—a misdemeanor criminal offense. The driver was arrested and locked in the back of the patrol car. At that point, officers returned to the vehicle to 'make contact' with Defendant, who was still seated in the passenger seat. The officers did not have any reason to suspect that Defendant was engaged in any criminal activity or that Defendant was armed and dangerous. Nevertheless, the officers ordered Defendant out of the vehicle and told him to put his hands on his head with his fingers interlaced. Officers then began to escort Defendant to the patrol car to search him for weapons and/or drugs. While Defendant was being escorted to the patrol car for a 'pat down' search, he broke free and ran away. The officers pursued Defendant, but did not make any audible commands for him

to stop. After Defendant was chased and apprehended by officers, he was searched and found to be carrying a pistol and two bags of hashish, a derivative of marijuana. . . . We agree with the district court that the firearm and the hashish recovered during the search are inadmissible because they were recovered in violation of Defendant's Fourth Amendment rights. The district court correctly determined that the purpose of the traffic stop had been accomplished after the driver was arrested, and Defendant was unlawfully detained after the traffic stop was completed. We further agree with the district court's finding that the officers lacked reasonable suspicion to justify prolonging the traffic stop. Under the circumstances, the officers should have advised Defendant that the vehicle was being impounded and informed Defendant that he was free to go." *U.S. v. Cheatham*, 577 Fed. Appx. 500, 501–02 (6th Cir. 2014) (citations omitted).

- "The threshold for probable cause is based upon factual and practical considerations of every day life that could lead a reasonable person to believe that there is a probability that an illegal act has occurred or is about to occur. . . .[A]n arresting officer must be able to articulate concrete facts from which the totality of the circumstances indicates that an arrest is warranted." *U.S. v. Reed*, 220 F.3d 476, 478, 2000 FED App. 0213A (6th Cir. 2000).

- "Applying. . . .Fourth Amendment jurisprudential principles to the case at hand, we hold that the district court erred in denying Defendant's motion to suppress the evidence where upon learning Defendant's identity and that she was not armed or carrying contraband (as determined by the patdown search), the Redford Police officers unreasonably seized Defendant by placing her in the police car and questioning her further; transporting her to the police station; detaining Defendant while at the police station; and questioning her further once there." *U.S. v. Butler*, 223 F.3d 368, 375, 2000 FED App. 0253P (6th Cir. 2000).

- "It is a well-settled principle of constitutional jurisprudence that an arrest without probable cause constitutes an unreasonable seizure in violation of the Fourth Amendment." *Ingram v. City of Columbus*, 185 F.3d 579, 592–93, 1999 FED App. 0258P (6th Cir. 1999).

- "An arrest without a warrant does not violate the Fourth Amendment if probable cause exists for the arresting officer's belief that a suspect has violated or is violating the law." *U.S. v. Strickland*, 144 F.3d 412, 415, 1998 FED App. 0150P (6th Cir. 1998).

Seventh Circuit

- "Probable cause is an absolute defense to any claim under § 1983 for wrongful arrest or false imprisonment." *Bailey v. City of Chicago*, 779 F.3d 689, 694 (7th Cir. 2015), cert. denied, 136 S. Ct. 200, 193 L. Ed. 2d 129 (2015).
- "Probable cause is itself a commonsense determination, measured under a reasonableness standard. . . . The existence of probable cause turns on the information known to the officers at the moment the arrest is made, not on subsequently-received information. . . . Consequently, as long as a reasonably credible witness or victim informs the police that someone has committed, or is committing, a crime, the officers have probable cause to place the alleged culprit under arrest. . . ." *Spiegel v. Cortese*, 196 F.3d 717, 723 (7th Cir. 1999), as amended, (Jan. 7, 2000).
- "We begin with a recognition that probable cause is a relatively fluid concept. It exists if at the moment the arrest was made . . . the facts and circumstances within the arresting officer's knowledge and of which he had reasonably trustworthy information were sufficient to warrant a prudent man in believing that the arrestee was committing, or had committed, a crime. . . . As an objective test, probable cause is less than a rule of more-likely-than-not, but how much less depends on the circumstances . . . including the factual and practical considerations of everyday life on which reasonable and prudent men, not legal technicians, act." *Tangwall v. Stuckey*, 135 F.3d 510, 518–19 (7th Cir. 1998).

§ 3:5   Justification to seize—Arrest: An arrest or its functional equivalent must be based upon probable cause—Arresting officer may rely upon fellow officer's probable cause determination

Fourth Circuit

- "Under the collective knowledge doctrine, the collective knowledge of the police can be used in two different situations to establish probable cause even when the arresting officer himself does not have sufficient personal knowledge to independently establish probable cause. The first situation arises when one officer with personal knowledge of facts sufficient to establish probable cause orders another officer, who does not have personal knowledge of those facts, to make an arrest. . . . In the second situation, an officer without independent knowledge of facts sufficient to establish probable cause makes an arrest, but the officer has been in communication with a group of officers that collectively has knowledge of facts sufficient to establish probable cause." *U.S. v. Joy*, 336 Fed. Appx. 337, 342 (4th Cir. 2009).

Fifth Circuit

- "Having determined there existed reasonable suspicion to stop Zuniga's vehicle, we now consider whether the collective knowledge doctrine provided the grounds for imputation of that information to Officer Pruit. Reasonable suspicion to stop a vehicle, or probable cause to conduct a search, may arise through the collective knowledge of the officers involved in the operation. Under the collective knowledge doctrine, an officer initiating the stop or conducting the search need not have personal knowledge of the evidence that gave rise to the reasonable suspicion or probable cause, so long as he is acting at the request of those who have the necessary information. In other words, the collective knowledge theory applies so long as there is 'some degree of communication' between the acting officer and the officer who has knowledge of the necessary facts. Here, Zuniga does not deny that officers could rely on the collective knowledge doctrine to transfer reasonable suspicion between each other. Instead, he falls back on his principal argument that the officers failed to establish any reasonable suspicion that could be transferred. As we discussed above, we do not agree. And although Officer Pruit's testimony shows that he only effected the stop at Sergeant Egger's instruction, his lack of personalized suspicion is 'immaterial . . . . because under the "collective knowledge" doctrine, [Officer Pruit] did not need to form [his] own suspicion.' The suspicion transferred by the law enforcement agents who observed Zuniga's traffic violation suffices." *United States v. Zuniga*, 860 F.3d 276, 282–83 (5th Cir. 2017) (citations omitted).

Sixth Circuit

- "[A]n officer may conduct a stop based on information obtained from fellow officers. This is known as the 'collective-knowledge doctrine.' When an officer executes a stop based in part on information obtained from another law-enforcement official, the doctrine imputes to the officer conducting the stop the knowledge of those with whom he communicated. '[I]f a flyer or bulletin has been issued on the basis of articulable facts supporting a reasonable suspicion that the wanted person has committed an offense, then reliance on that flyer or bulletin justifies a stop to check identification, to pose questions to the person, or to detain the person briefly while attempting to obtain further information.' However, 'if the flyer has been issued in the absence of a reasonable suspicion, then a stop in the objective reliance upon it violates the Fourth Amendment.' Furthermore, 'the stop that in fact occurred [must not be] significantly more intrusive than would have been permitted' based on the reasonable suspicion." *Brown v. Lewis*, 779 F.3d 401, 412–13 (6th Cir. 2015) (citations omitted).

- "Strict application of the collective-knowledge doctrine would result in a determination that the officers did not have reasonable suspicion to stop Brown. The 911 operator did overhear certain statements made by an intoxicated male which could potentially establish reasonable suspicion, namely his statements about hiding from the police and about wanting to 'kill that bitch.' But no one in the room took the statement seriously; all of the other voices on the call dispute, criticize or laugh at these statements. The statements could therefore support, at most, reasonable suspicion to stop the intoxicated male but no other individual in the house. The 911 operator, moreover, could hear the same intoxicated male voice, still within the house, after the officers saw Brown's car pull away from the house. Because the 911 operator knew that the intoxicated male—the sole individual for whom the police had reasonable suspicion—could not be in the car, the police did not have reasonable suspicion to stop the car." *Brown v. Lewis*, 779 F.3d 401, 413 (6th Cir. 2015)).

Eighth Circuit

- "The collective knowledge doctrine imputes the knowledge of all officers involved in an investigation upon the seizing officer in order to uphold 'an otherwise invalid search or seizure.' (citation omitted) . . . Applying the doctrine requires some degree of communication between the officer who possesses the incriminating knowledge and the officer who does not. . . . When officers function as a search team, it is appropriate to judge probable cause upon the basis of their combined knowledge, because 'we presume that the officers have shared relevant knowledge which informs the decision to seize evidence or to detain a particular person.' " *U.S. v. Banks*, 514 F.3d 769, 776 (8th Cir. 2008).

Ninth Circuit

- "Under the collective knowledge doctrine, Deputy Simpson permissibly relied on the fact that Agent Sanders had probable cause when he directed him to stop [defendant]. . . . [Defendant] argues that the collective knowledge doctrine does not apply because Agent Sanders and Deputy Simpson are not in the same department. . . . [However,] [t]he common knowledge doctrine applies irrespective of whether cooperating law enforcement officers are in different departments." *U.S. v. McCartney*, 357 Fed. Appx. 73 (9th Cir. 2009).
- "The collective knowledge doctrine is otherwise known as the 'fellow officer' rule." *U.S. v. Ramirez*, 473 F.3d 1026, 1032 (9th Cir. 2007).
- "We look to the collective knowledge of all the officers involved in the criminal investigation although all of the information known to the law enforcement officers involved in the investigation is not communicated to the officer who actually makes the stop. We agree with the Tenth Circuit that the collective knowledge rule applies where an officer makes an investigatory stop based

in part on information or directions from other law
enforcement officials." *U.S. v. Sutton*, 794 F.2d 1415,
1426 (9th Cir. 1986).

§ 3:6 Justification to seize—*Terry* stop: A stop must be based upon reasonable suspicion

Supreme Court

- "In *Terry*, we held that an officer may, consistent with
  the Fourth Amendment, conduct a brief, investigatory
  stop when the officer has a reasonable, articulable
  suspicion that criminal activity is afoot. . . . While reasonable suspicion is a less demanding standard than
  probable cause and requires a showing considerably
  less than preponderance of the evidence, the Fourth
  Amendment requires at least a minimal level of objective justification for making the stop. . . . The officer
  must be able to articulate more than an inchoate and
  unparticularized suspicion or hunch of criminal
  activity." *Illinois v. Wardlow*, 528 U.S. 119, 123–24, 120
  S. Ct. 673, 145 L. Ed. 2d 570 (2000).
- "We have described reasonable suspicion simply as a
  particularized and objective basis for suspecting the
  person stopped of criminal activity and probable cause
  to search as existing where the known facts and circumstances are sufficient to warrant a man of reasonable prudence in the belief that contraband or evidence
  of a crime will be found. We have cautioned that these
  two legal principles are not finely-tuned standards, comparable to the standards of proof beyond a reasonable
  doubt or of proof by a preponderance of the evidence.
  They are instead fluid concepts that take their substantive content from the particular contexts in which the
  standards are being assessed." *Ornelas v. U.S.*, 517 U.S.
  690, 696, 116 S. Ct. 1657, 134 L. Ed. 2d 911 (1996).
- "Reasonable suspicion is a less demanding standard
  than probable cause not only in the sense that reasonable suspicion can be established with information that
  is different in quantity or content than that required to
  establish probable cause, but also in the sense that reasonable suspicion can arise from information that is
  less reliable than that required to show probable cause.
  Both factors—quantity and quality—are considered in

the totality of the circumstances—the whole picture that must be taken into account when evaluating whether there is reasonable suspicion. Thus, if a tip has a relatively low degree of reliability, more information will be required to establish the requisite quantum of suspicion than would be required if the tip were more reliable." *Alabama v. White*, 496 U.S. 325, 330, 110 S. Ct. 2412, 110 L. Ed. 2d 301 (1990).

- "There is support in our cases for the view that the Fourth Amendment would permit seizures for the purpose of fingerprinting, if there is reasonable suspicion that the suspect has committed a criminal act, if there is a reasonable basis for believing that fingerprinting will establish or negate the suspect's connection with that crime, and if the procedure is carried out with dispatch. Of course, neither reasonable suspicion nor probable cause would suffice to permit the officers to make a warrantless entry into a person's house for the purpose of obtaining fingerprint identification." *Hayes v. Florida*, 470 U.S. 811, 817, 105 S. Ct. 1643, 84 L. Ed. 2d 705 (1985).

- "[N]ot all seizures of the person must be justified by probable cause to arrest for a crime. [C]ertain seizures are justifiable under the Fourth Amendment if there is articulable suspicion that a person has committed or is about to commit a crime. . . . Detentions may be investigative yet violative of the Fourth Amendment absent probable cause. In the name of investigating a person who is no more than suspected of criminal activity, the police may not carry out a full search of the person or of his automobile or other effects. Nor may the police seek to verify their suspicions by means that approach the conditions of arrest." *Florida v. Royer*, 460 U.S. 491, 498, 103 S. Ct. 1319, 75 L. Ed. 2d 229 (1983).

- "When the officers detained appellant for the purpose of requiring him to identify himself, they performed a seizure of his person subject to the requirements of the Fourth Amendment. In the absence of any basis for suspecting appellant of misconduct, the balance between the public interest and appellant's right to personal security and privacy tilts in favor of freedom from police interference." *Brown v. Texas*, 443 U.S. 47, 50, 99 S. Ct. 2637, 61 L. Ed. 2d 357 (1979).

127

- "[T]he Fourth Amendment allows a properly limited search or seizure on facts that do not constitute probable cause to arrest or to search for contraband or evidence of crime. . . . [W]hen an officer's observations lead him reasonably to suspect that a particular vehicle may contain aliens who are illegally in the country, he may stop the car briefly and investigate the circumstances that provoke suspicion." *U.S. v. Brignoni-Ponce*, 422 U.S. 873, 881, 95 S. Ct. 2574, 45 L. Ed. 2d 607 (1975).
- "[A] police officer may in appropriate circumstances and in an appropriate manner approach a person for purposes of investigating possible criminal behavior even though there is no probable cause to make an arrest." *Terry v. Ohio*, 392 U.S. 1, 22, 88 S. Ct. 1868, 20 L. Ed. 2d 889 (1968).

First Circuit

- "[A]lthough nothing in the record describes the precise length of time it took for Morales to exit the vehicle, approach its front, and open the hood, no reasonable reading of the facts could allow us to conclude that the duration of time in which these events occurred was anything but brief. Moreover, whatever its length, this sequence of events occurred immediately after the officers began to suspect that the car might be stolen, and it was a 'reasonable investigative approach' intended to dispel that suspicion." *U.S. v. Tiru-Plaza*, 766 F.3d 111, 117 (1st Cir. 2014) (citations omitted).
- "The reasonable suspicion standard is a protean one; it defies strict boundaries, requiring 'more than a visceral hunch about the presence of illegal activity, [but] less than probable cause.' 'In the last analysis, reasonable suspicion is more a concept than a constant: it deals with degrees of likelihood, not with certainties or near certainties.' " *U.S. v. Arthur*, 764 F.3d 92, 97 (1st Cir. 2014) (citations omitted).
- "We think it virtually unarguable that a reasonably prudent police officer, standing in Officer Golden's shoes and knowing what he knew, would have harbored such a suspicion. In light of the attendant circumstances, a failure to stop the men and question them briefly would have verged on a dereliction of duty. It follows that the

district court's decision upholding the lawfulness of the investigatory stop was free from error. To be sure, the stop occurred in a majority-minority neighborhood; and the physical description of a black man in dark, heavy clothing might fit a significant percentage of the local population on a late October day. We agree with the appellant that such a description, standing alone, would likely be insufficient to give rise to reasonable suspicion. But everything depends on context and, in this instance, the description did not stand alone. Officer Golden was entitled to rely on the description in combination with other clues: the precise number of robbers, the immediacy of the robbery, the suspects' close proximity to the crime scene, the direction in which the men were headed, and the dearth of others in the critical two-block area. The totality of the circumstances supported a logical inference that the appellant and his companion were the robbers." *U.S. v. Arthur*, 764 F.3d 92, 98 (1st Cir. 2014) (citations omitted).

- "Judicial review of investigatory stops, commonly known as *Terry* stops demands a two-tiered evaluation. First, the stop must be justified at its inception. Second, actions undertaken during the stop must be reasonably related in scope to the stop itself 'unless the police have a basis for expanding their investigation.' In the *Terry* milieu, reasonable suspicion is the touchstone for an initial stop. While reasonable suspicion is a fluid concept that lacks precise definition, it is common ground that 'reasonable suspicion requires more than a mere hunch but less than probable cause.' An inquiring court must examine the totality of the circumstances 'to see whether the detaining officer ha[d] a particularized and objective basis for suspecting legal wrongdoing.' At the second tier, the court must scrutinize 'whether the officer's subsequent actions were fairly responsive to the emerging tableau.' Although such actions ordinarily must bear some relation to the purpose of the initial stop, an officer 'may shift his focus and increase the scope of his investigation by degrees if his suspicions mount during the course of the detention.' " *U.S. v. Gates*, 709 F.3d 58 (1st Cir. 2013) (citations omitted).

Second Circuit

• "Because a stop must be justified 'at its inception,' we consider only the facts known to [Officer] McGinley that prompted him to give the cell phone orders. The facts McGinley offers to establish reasonable suspicion prior to the stop are: 1) Elting's presence in the company of an individual who (in some ways) met the description of a robbery suspect; 2) the proximity in time and space to the crime; and 3) Elting and Dancy looking over their shoulders at the police car following them. First, mere presence near someone who somewhat matches a vague description is not a reasonable basis for suspicion. . . . McGinley observed Elting in the company of Dancy, who "somewhat" matched the description broadcast over the radio. . . . While such a discrepancy does not necessarily defeat a finding of reasonable suspicion, the remaining description—thin, black, and male—is too vague in the circumstances here to justify a stop of anyone meeting it. Furthermore, the description did not mention a second assailant or accomplice, and Elting's mere presence in the company of a possible suspect is, standing alone, not enough for a stop. . . . Second, while they were found walking within several city blocks of the crime scene, such proximity was innocuous given the unremarkable nature of the area in question. . . . It would not have been unusual to find a thin, black male in downtown Poughkeepsie that Friday evening. The city itself is 33.5% African–American. Poughkeepsie's Main Street is aptly named, featuring a number of restaurants, businesses, and nightlife. Under the circumstances, the description fit too many people to constitute sufficient articulable facts on which to justify a forcible stop of Elting. Third, as the case law recognizes, in the circumstances here there is nothing suspicious about looking over one's shoulder at an approaching police car. . . . In the circumstances here, looking over one's shoulder at an officer in slow pursuit is not suspicious behavior. Indeed, it is natural for people to take an interest in police activity nearby 'out of a desire to avoid some minor misstep, such as a minor traffic violation, which would involve them unnecessarily with the police.' . . . Nor did Dancy or Elting exhibit nervous or evasive behavior of any kind. . . . Considering these facts together and under the 'totality of the circumstances,' we conclude that McGinley had no basis to suspect Elting of any legal wrongdoing. . . . On these facts, no reasonable police officer would have had reason to stop him, or prevent him from calling his mother, or throw him to the ground. Because subjective intentions are irrelevant to this analysis, we do not assess what was motivating this police officer when he decided to stop Elting. But we do know that, objectively speaking, he lacked reasonable suspicion, and so violated the Fourth Amendment by detaining Elting without an adequate basis. As a result of this suspicionless stop, an African–American teenager was arrested, jailed, and subjected to 'the humiliations of [an] unconstitutional search[ ].' Circumstances like these remind us that specificity in articulating the basis for a stop is necessary 'in part because according the police unfettered discretion to stop and frisk could lead to harassment of minority groups and "severely exacerbate police-community tensions."'" *Dancy v. McGinley*, 843 F.3d 93, 108–11 (2d Cir. 2016), 2016) (citations omitted).

- "Here, while the case is close, we find that the officers had reasonable suspicion for the stop of [defendant]. Responding to a dispatch that communicated the 911 caller's report of an assault in progress, possibly involving a weapon, the officers, despite not finding evidence of an assault in progress, confirmed that [defendant's] appearance matched the description of the suspect and that the [defendant] was present at the specified location. The officers' corroboration of information identifying the suspect is entitled to more weighty consideration in the context of an emergency 911 call. This follows from our holding that a 911 call reporting an ongoing emergency is accorded a higher degree of reliability and requires a lesser showing of corroboration." *U.S. v. Simmons*, 560 F.3d 98 (2d Cir. 2009).

Fourth Circuit

- "We have stated that when an investigative stop is based on unverified information provided by a known informant, a tip of this nature 'may alone justify a reasonable suspicion of criminal activity.' And when police obtain information corroborating such a tip, this circumstance adds significant support for a finding of reasonable suspicion. . . . The present case is governed by our decision in *Singh.* As in *Singh,* the officers here received a tip from a known informant that a certain convicted felon driving a white Lincoln Town Car could be found at a particular location with a gun in his possession. This tip alone may have supported a finding of reasonable suspicion. But the officers in the present case also had corroborated some of the information provided by the informant, namely, the presence of a white Lincoln Town Car at the described location and verification that Gardner was the owner of that vehicle. While the officers did not confirm that Gardner was a convicted felon before initiating the stop, every detail provided by a tipster need not be independently verified to support a finding of reasonable suspicion. Accordingly, we hold that the district court did not err in concluding that the traffic stop was supported by reasonable suspicion." *U.S. v. Gardner,* 823 F.3d 793, 799–800 (4th Cir. 2016) (citations omitted).

Fifth Circuit

- "An officer may, consistent with the Fourth Amendment, conduct a brief investigatory stop when the officer has a reasonable, articulable suspicion that criminal activity is afoot." *U.S. v. Jordan,* 232 F.3d 447, 448 (5th Cir. 2000).

Sixth Circuit

- "[In *Noble*], we were critical of nervousness as an indicator of dangerousness, noting that, because many law-abiding citizens are nervous during traffic stops, it is unreliable. . . . [W]hile we have cautioned against relying too heavily on nervousness as indicia of dangerousness, Pacheco's nervousness is another factor in the totality-of-the-circumstances analysis that supports a reasonable-suspicion finding. While '[n]ervous behavior, standing alone, is not enough to justify a *Terry* search,' nervousness is still relevant to the reasonable-suspicion calculus. And we have found reasonable suspicion in other cases based, in part, on the suspect's extraordinary nervousness that increased as the traffic stop progressed. In *Noble,* there was no testimony that the suspect became increasingly nervous. Here, in contrast, Trivette testified that Pacheco was 'extremely nervous,' and that as the stop progressed, Pacheco began glancing around the vehicle and rummaging through the glove box. Additionally, Noble did not avoid all eye contact with the officers, fidget with his pockets, or otherwise act as if he was concealing something. In contrast, Trivette testified that Pacheco 'wouldn't even make eye contact with [him]' and that 'he was fidgeting around' as he opened up the glove box and shuffled papers back and forth, removing nothing. Further, Trivette testified that Pacheco was looking down at the floorboard and over at the area between the console and his seat. Trivette claimed that, in his experience, this is an area where firearms are often concealed. He went on to say that Pacheco disregarded his presence and that 'it was like he was looking for like an avenue of escape almost.' The absence of these factors weighed against reasonable suspicion in *Noble*; their presence weighs in favor here." *United States v. Pacheco*, 841 F.3d 384, 391, 393 (6th Cir. 2016) (citations omitted).

- "The crux of the issue in this case is whether the phone call to the police stating 'that [Courtright] had come out of his room with a gun and threatened to shoot another resident's dog' was sufficient to establish probable cause for Courtright's arrest. . . . [B]ecause 'eyewitnesses' statements are based on firsthand observations, they are generally entitled to a presumption of reliability and veracity.' . . . [O]n the other hand, . . . the phone call was an individual's 'mere allegation' of criminal activity that 'may [have] create[d] reasonable suspicion justifying an investigative stop under [*Terry v. Ohio*], but [fell] short of creating probable cause absent some corroborating evidence of wrongdoing.' Although there is 'some tension' [in the case law], we recently clarified that 'those cases also contain an important limiting factor: Probable cause is created only by eyewitness allegations that are *reasonably trustworthy*, and thus probable cause does *not* exist where there is an apparent reason for the officer to believe that the eyewitness was lying, did not accurately describe what he had seen, or was in some fashion mistaken regarding his recollection.' . . . At best, Wolf had reasonable suspicion for an investigatory stop under *Terry v. Ohio*, at the time that he arrived at Courtright's room. Therefore, to legitimate an arrest of Courtright, Wolf would have needed to discover more information or evidence at the Traveler's Inn that would have established probable cause for an arrest." *Courtright v. City of Battle Creek*, 839 F.3d 513, 521–23 (6th Cir. 2016) (citations omitted).

- "It is well-settled that, standing alone, mere presence in a high crime area is insufficient 'to support a reasonable, particularized suspicion that the person is committing a crime.' However, 'the fact that the stop occurred in a "high crime area" [is] among the relevant contextual considerations in a *Terry* analysis.' The same is true with regard to the time of day: It is relevant without being independently dispositive. Similarly, 'nervous, evasive behavior is a pertinent factor in determining reasonable suspicion.' Although headlong flight is 'the consummate act of evasion,' it is clear that frantic flight from officers is not the only evasive act which will arouse an officer's reasonable suspicion. There are a number of ways in which an individual can attempt to evade the police. . . . In the same vein, once an individual is aware that police are behind him, his choice of a circular route or driving with no apparent destination may strike a trained officer as a similar attempt to avoid police attention. '[W]hen used by trained law enforcement officers, objective facts, meaningless to the untrained, can be combined with permissible deductions from such facts to form a legitimate basis for suspicion of a particular person and for action on that suspicion.' Of course, not every act taken to avoid contact with the police will support reasonable suspicion; for example, simply walking away from officers is clearly insufficient to support reasonable suspicion. As the Second Circuit has noted, 'circular driving in the dead of night in a high-crime area is suggestive' of criminal activity, but it may not be enough, without more, to support reasonable suspicion." *Hoover v. Walsh*, 682 F.3d 481, 495-96 (6th Cir. 2012) (citations omitted).

Seventh Circuit

- "Determining whether an officer had reasonable suspicion to support a *Terry* stop requires courts to examine

'the totality of the circumstances known to the officer at
the time of the stop, including the experience of the officer and the behavior and characteristics of the
suspect.' At the time Officer Newport conducted the
stop, he had information that a Marquis circled the auto
parts store parking lot multiple times near the close of
business. He believed that this conduct was consistent
with casing a business in order to commit a robbery. Officer Newport was also aware that the store had been
robbed within the last two months at closing time. The
Supreme Court has held that 'officers are not required
to ignore the relevant characteristics of a location in
determining whether the circumstances are sufficiently
suspicious to warrant further investigation.' While the
prior robbery does not make this area 'high crime' per
se, we believe it is a relevant contextual consideration.
. . . We recognize that there are factual disputes between Green and Officer Newport, and that the district
court refused to credit certain factual assertions by Officer Newport. But even construing the facts in Green's
favor, we cannot find that the police lacked 'minimal information' to warrant suspicion of criminal conduct."
Green v. Newport, 2017 WL 3599778, *3-4 (7th Cir. 2017)
(citations omitted).

- "The distinction between a consensual encounter, which
  does not implicate the Fourth Amendment, and an
  investigative stop, which does implicate the constitutional guarantee because it constitutes a seizure, is
  often difficult to discern. On one hand, the Supreme
  Court has recognized that 'mere police questioning does
  not constitute a seizure.' Accordingly, 'law enforcement
  officers do not violate the Fourth Amendment by merely
  approaching an individual on the street or in another
  public place, by asking him if he is willing to answer
  some questions, [or] by putting questions to him if the
  person is willing to listen.' A mere request for identification does not change a voluntary stop, which is outside
  the purview of the Fourth Amendment, into an investigatory stop. These principles do not change when an individual is seated in an automobile." *U.S. v. Shields*,
  789 F.3d 733, 743–44 (7th Cir. 2015), cert. denied, 136
  S. Ct. 420, 193 L. Ed. 2d 329 (2015) (citations omitted).

- "With respect to the duration of the stop, there is no

rigid time limit placed on *Terry* stops. And a defendant's actions can contribute to a permissible extension of the stop. . . . Likewise, assuming reasonable suspicion exists (as it did here), a reasonable delay attributable to arranging for a canine unit to conduct a sniff may permissibly extend the duration of a stop. At the outset of the stop, Ruiz gave answers which increased rather than allayed the officers' suspicions. Ruiz claimed to be parked in the driveway because he was interested in renting the house, but, as the district court noted, his "backing out of that driveway [after] the police car passed him . . . is inconsistent with looking at a house he might want to rent." Also suspicious was Ruiz's claim that he was at the mall to visit a furniture store, when he did not park within view of any furniture store and, unbeknownst to Ruiz, the officers had witnessed Ruiz meet with the subject of their narcotics investigation in the parking lot. The officers' suspicions were increased further by Ruiz's Texas driver's license, combined with his car being registered in Wisconsin and containing no personal items. In short, the first few minutes of the stop only served to increase the officers' reasonable suspicion that Ruiz was operating a trap car, and this justified further investigation by the officers. The remainder of the time in the driveway was devoted to Tapia's search of Ruiz's car and the officers' attempt to summon a canine unit for assistance. The district court found that Ruiz voluntarily consented to the search of his car. This finding is not challenged by Ruiz, and the finding was not clearly erroneous. In the words of the district court, Ruiz's voluntary consent to the search was 'consistent with the entire modus operandi . . . of the officers . . . mak[ing] this defendant feel as comfortable as possible while they were talking to him.' " *U.S. v. Ruiz*, 785 F.3d 1134, 1143–44 (7th Cir. 2015) (citations omitted).

- "While being present in a high-crime area cannot, in and of itself, support a particularized suspicion that a subject is committing a crime, an officer is permitted to consider a location's characteristics when assessing a situation." *U.S. v. Oglesby*, 597 F.3d 891 (7th Cir. 2010).
- "Police can sometimes consider otherwise innocent behavior in determining whether reasonable suspicion

exists to detain a person. Specifically, police observation of an individual, fitting a police dispatch description of a person involved in a disturbance, near in time and geographic location to the disturbance establishes a reasonable suspicion that the individual is the subject of the dispatch. Additionally, a person's flight upon seeing the police approach in a high crime area establishes reasonable suspicion to justify a *Terry* stop. A suspect's failure to halt upon police command to do so, as well as the suspect's apparent public intoxication further support a finding of reasonable suspicion." *U.S. v. Lenoir*, 318 F.3d 725 (7th Cir. 2003).

Eighth Circuit

- "Reasonable suspicion may be based in whole or in part on hearsay information. The Supreme Court long ago rejected the notion that reasonable suspicion 'can only be based on the officer's personal observation, rather than on information supplied by another person.' Police may rely on the tip of an informant, and the degree of corroboration required to establish reasonable suspicion depends on whether the informant's reliability has been established. The information here was provided by a security guard, an 'informant' who 'is not just any eyewitness.' Given the security guard's position and responsibility to his employer, the risk that he will pursue a private agenda or embarrass an honest patron is smaller than when a previously unknown citizen provides a tip. And especially in a situation like this one, where police officers work directly with private security guards to keep a location secure, the police have reasonable grounds to believe the guard." *U.S. v. Robinson*, 670 F.3d 874, 876-77 (8th Cir. 2012) (citations omitted).

- "Blocking a vehicle so its occupant is unable to leave during the course of an investigatory stop is reasonable to maintain the status quo while completing the purpose of the stop. . . . We conclude that blocking [Defendant]'s truck with the squad car resulted in a Fourth Amendment seizure. The seizure, however, was based on a reasonably articulable suspicion and satisfies the first prong of *Terry* that the initial stop be justified." *U.S. v. Tuley*, 161 F.3d 513, 515 (8th Cir. 1998).

<u>Ninth Circuit</u>

- "Thomas does not challenge Dillard's initial decision to stop and question him and Husky for a brief period. Campus police dispatch had informed Dillard that a man wearing the same color shirt as Thomas had pushed a woman in the very location Thomas and Husky were found, by the storage containers. This created a reasonable suspicion Thomas might have committed a simple assault or battery, possibly in the context of a domestic relationship. Dillard was entitled to detain Thomas briefly to investigate the report of potential criminal activity—a so-called *Terry* stop. In conducting the stop, Dillard also was permitted to ask Thomas for consent to search for weapons, known as a *Terry* frisk. As the word 'consent' implies, however, Thomas was free to decline Dillard's request. The nature of the interaction between Dillard and Thomas changed significantly, however, once Dillard unholstered his Taser, pointed it at Thomas and *ordered* Thomas to submit to a frisk for weapons. At that point, he exceeded the justification and authority for the *Terry* stop—to investigate a potential battery. Once Dillard demanded Thomas submit to a search for weapons, he needed a reasonable basis for believing Thomas might be armed and dangerous in order to continue detaining him for the search. . . . [W]hereas a *Terry* stop is justified by reasonable suspicion that criminal activity may be afoot, a frisk of a person for weapons requires reasonable suspicion that a suspect 'is armed and presently dangerous to the officer or to others.' 'A lawful frisk does not always flow from a justified stop.' " *Thomas v. Dillard*, 818 F.3d 864, 875–76 (9th Cir. 2016), as amended, (May 5, 2016) (citations omitted).
- "In assessing the totality of the circumstances, relevant considerations may include: observing a visible bulge in a person's clothing that could indicate the presence of a weapon; seeing a weapon in an area the suspect controls, such as a car; 'sudden movements' suggesting a potential assault or 'attempts to reach for an object that was not immediately visible'; 'evasive and deceptive responses' to an officer's questions about what an individual was up to; unnatural hand postures that suggest an effort to conceal a firearm; and whether the of-

ficer observes anything during an encounter with the suspect that would dispel the officer's suspicions regarding the suspect's potential involvement in a crime or likelihood of being armed. This last point is especially important. Even where certain facts might support reasonable suspicion a suspect is armed and dangerous when viewed initially or in isolation, a frisk is not justified when additional or subsequent facts dispel or negate the suspicion. Just as a suspicion must be reasonable and individualized, it must be based on the *totality* of the circumstances known to the officer. Officers may not cherry pick facts to justify the serious Fourth Amendment intrusion a frisk imposes." *Thomas v. Dillard*, 818 F.3d 864, 877 (9th Cir. 2016) (citations omitted).

- "[T]he *Terry* exception to the warrant requirement does not apply to in-home searches and seizures." *U.S. v. Struckman*, 603 F.3d 731, 738 (9th Cir. 2010).

- "The Fourth Amendment permits limited investigatory stops where there is some reasonable, articulable, and objective manifestation that the person seized is, or is about to be, engaged in criminal activities.. . . . In order to determine if reasonable suspicion existed to justify an investigatory stop, the court must consider the facts available to the officer at the moment of seizure." *U.S. v. Smith*, 217 F.3d 746, 749 (9th Cir. 2000).

- "[R]easonable suspicion must not be based on broad profiles which cast suspicion on entire categories of people. . . . The rationale upon which the reasonable suspicion doctrine is based, a doctrine that thwarts the notion of liberty and freedom from state intrusion in a mobile society, must be founded on an objective basis for suspecting that a particular person is engaged in criminal activity, lest we sweep many ordinary citizens into a generality of suspicious appearance merely on hunch.. . . Reasonable suspicion can not rest upon the hunch of an experienced officer, even if the hunch turns out right. The requirement of objective fact to support an inference of wrongdoing eliminates the need to deal with a police stop that rests on constitutional intuition." *U.S. v. Jimenez-Medina*, 173 F.3d 752, 756 (9th Cir. 1999).

Tenth Circuit

- "Police officers must have more than a 'hunch' to justify stopping an individual, but 'the likelihood of criminal activity need not rise to the level required for probable cause, and it falls considerably short of satisfying a preponderance of the evidence standard.' We have held that 'as long as [the detaining officer] has a particularized and objective basis for suspecting an individual may be involved in criminal activity, he may initiate an investigatory detention even if it is more likely than not that the individual is *not* involved in any illegality.' We apply an objective standard to determine whether the 'facts available to the officer at the moment of the seizure or the search [would] warrant a man of reasonable caution in the belief that the action taken was appropriate.' Due to their 'experience and specialized training,' we 'accord deference to an officer's ability to distinguish between innocent and suspicious actions.' 'Moreover, reasonable suspicion may be supported by an objectively reasonable good faith belief even if premised on factual error.' . . . Both this court and the Supreme Court have held that a suspect's unprovoked flight and other evasive behavior upon noticing police officers is a pertinent factor in determining reasonable suspicion." *U.S. v. Madrid*, 713 F.3d 1251, 1256-57 (10th Cir. 2013) (citations omitted).
- "In considering whether an investigative stop is reasonable, we conduct a two-step inquiry, asking first whether the detention was justified at its inception and, second, whether the agents' actions were reasonably related in scope to the circumstances initially justifying the detention." *U.S. v. De La Cruz*, 703 F.3d 1193 (10th Cir. 2013).
- "In *Florida v. Bostick*. . .the Supreme Court addressed a situation where the police boarded a bus and asked permission to search a passenger's luggage. The court remanded for further findings on the voluntariness of the defendant's alleged consent, but in doing so reiterated, We have consistently held that a refusal to cooperate, without more, does not furnish the minimal level of objective justification needed for a detention or seizure." *U.S. v. Garzon*, 119 F.3d 1446, 1451 (10th Cir. 1997).

Eleventh Circuit

- "[W]hile reasonable suspicion is a less demanding standard than probable cause and requires a showing considerably less than preponderance of the evidence, the Fourth Amendment requires at least a minimal level of objective justification for making the stop." *Jackson v. Sauls*, 206 F.3d 1156, 1165 (11th Cir. 2000).

§ 3:7   Justification to seize—Lesser intrusions: Some restrictions on a person's freedom of movement are permitted in the absence of probable cause or reasonable suspicion

Supreme Court

- "[T]he Fourth Amendment is [not] offended when Customs officials, acting pursuant to this statute and without any suspicion of wrongdoing, board for inspection of documents a vessel that is located in waters providing ready access to the open sea." *U.S. v. Villamonte-Marquez*, 462 U.S. 579, 580–81, 103 S. Ct. 2573, 77 L. Ed. 2d 22 (1983).

- "Against this important interest [officer safety] we are asked to weigh the intrusion into the driver's personal liberty occasioned not by the initial stop of the vehicle, which was admittedly justified, but by the order to get out of the car. We think this additional intrusion can only be described as *de minimis*. The driver is being asked to expose to view very little more of his person than is already exposed. The police have already lawfully decided that the driver shall be briefly detained; the only question is whether he shall spend that period sitting in the driver's seat of his car or standing alongside it. Not only is the insistence of the police on the latter choice not a serious intrusion upon the sanctity of the person, but it hardly rises to the level of a petty indignity. What is at most a mere inconvenience cannot prevail when balanced against legitimate concerns for the officer's safety." *Pennsylvania v. Mimms*, 434 U.S. 106, 111, 98 S. Ct. 330, 54 L. Ed. 2d 331 (1977).

- "[A] requirement that stops on major routes inland always be based on reasonable suspicion would be impractical because the flow of traffic tends to be too heavy to allow the particularized study of a given car that would enable it to be identified as a possible carrier of illegal aliens. While the need to make routine checkpoint stops is great, the consequent intrusion on Fourth Amendment interests is quite limited. Accordingly, we hold that the stops and questioning at issue may be made in the absence of any individualized suspicion at reasonably located checkpoints." *U.S. v. Martinez-Fuerte*, 428 U.S. 543, 557, 562, 96 S. Ct. 3074, 49 L. Ed. 2d 1116 (1976).

Second Circuit

- "The federal appellate courts that have considered this issue all appear to have concluded that the Constitution does not require either a reasonable basis or reasonable suspicion of wrongdoing by a suspect before the government can begin an undercover investigation of that person." *U.S. v. Harvey*, 991 F.2d 981, 990, 38 Fed. R. Evid. Serv. 1144 (2d Cir. 1993).

Fourth Circuit

- "The police conduct challenged in this case is [the officer's] decision to stop [Defendant] for the purpose of investigating whether he was trespassing. It is a stop at issue—not a frisk and not an arrest—either of which would have required more than [the officer] had here. 'Consideration of the extent of the intrusion abounds in modern Fourth Amendment doctrine.' *United States v. Chaidez*, 919 F.2d 1193, 1997 (7th Cir.1990). Indeed, it was only upon discovering an active warrant during the *Terry* stop, and searching [Defendant] incident to his undisputedly lawful arrest on that warrant, that [Defendant's] firearm was discovered." *U.S. v. Bumpers*, 705 F.3d 168 (4th Cir. 2013).

Sixth Circuit

- "A law enforcement officer is generally justified in stopping an individual and asking for identification when relying on information transmitted by a valid police bulletin." *U.S. v. Erwin*, 155 F.3d 818, 822, 1998 FED App. 0291P (6th Cir. 1998).

Seventh Circuit

- "The distinction between a consensual encounter, which does not implicate the Fourth Amendment, and an investigative stop, which does implicate the constitutional guarantee because it constitutes a seizure, is often difficult to discern. On one hand, the Supreme Court has recognized that 'mere police questioning does not constitute a seizure.' Accordingly, 'law enforcement officers do not violate the Fourth Amendment by merely approaching an individual on the street or in another public place, by asking him if he is willing to answer some questions, [or] by putting questions to him if the person is willing to listen.' A mere request for identification does not change a voluntary stop, which is outside the purview of the Fourth Amendment, into an investigatory stop. These principles do not change when an individual is seated in an automobile." *U.S. v. Shields*, 789 F.3d 733, 743–44 (7th Cir. 2015), cert. denied, 136 S. Ct. 420, 193 L. Ed. 2d 329 (2015) (citations omitted).

- "The use of a firearm and handcuffs undoubtedly puts Matz's encounter at the outer edge of a permissible *Terry* stop. As we have previously recognized, '[s]ubtle, and perhaps tenuous distinctions exist between a *Terry* stop, a *Terry* stop rapidly evolving into an arrest and a *de facto* arrest.' . . . Although the hallmarks of formal arrest such as applying handcuffs, drawing weapons, and placing suspects in police vehicles should not be the norm during an investigatory detention, all of those measures have been recognized as appropriate in certain circumstances. In evaluating whether the force used converted an encounter into a full arrest, we must consider whether the surrounding circumstances would support an officer's legitimate fear for personal safety. We must also take into account the suspect's own behavior in resisting an officer's efforts. . . . Not only were they outnumbered, they were approaching a moving vehicle containing individuals who had been with Salazar just moments beforehand. Given the possibility that Salazar was hidden inside the vehicle, their clear disadvantage attempting on foot to stop a moving vehicle, and the possibility, given the nature of Salazar's suspected crimes, that individuals in the car may have been armed, it was not unreasonable to draw weapons to safely effect the stop." *Matz v. Klotka*, 769 F.3d 517, 525–26 (7th Cir. 2014), petition for certiorari filed, 135 S. Ct. 1901, 191 L. Ed. 2d 765 (2015) (inner quotations and citations omitted).

143

Eighth Circuit

- "[Defendant] was not seized when the trooper approached the van, asked to see identification, and posed a few questions. There is no seizure when a police officer approaches an individual and asks questions or requests identification, as long as the officer does not convey that compliance is required." *U.S. v. Perez-Sosa*, 164 F.3d 1082, 1084, 50 Fed. R. Evid. Serv. 496 (8th Cir. 1998).

Ninth Circuit

- "Thomas does not challenge Dillard's initial decision to stop and question him and Husky for a brief period. Campus police dispatch had informed Dillard that a man wearing the same color shirt as Thomas had pushed a woman in the very location Thomas and Husky were found, by the storage containers. This created a reasonable suspicion Thomas might have committed a simple assault or battery, possibly in the context of a domestic relationship. Dillard was entitled to detain Thomas briefly to investigate the report of potential criminal activity—a so-called *Terry* stop. In conducting the stop, Dillard also was permitted to ask Thomas for consent to search for weapons, known as a *Terry* frisk. As the word 'consent' implies, however, Thomas was free to decline Dillard's request. The nature of the interaction between Dillard and Thomas changed significantly, however, once Dillard unholstered his Taser, pointed it at Thomas and *ordered* Thomas to submit to a frisk for weapons. At that point, he exceeded the justification and authority for the *Terry* stop—to investigate a potential battery. Once Dillard demanded Thomas submit to a search for weapons, he needed a reasonable basis for believing Thomas might be armed and dangerous in order to continue detaining him for the search. . . . [W]hereas a *Terry* stop is justified by reasonable suspicion that criminal activity may be afoot, a frisk of a person for weapons requires reasonable suspicion that a suspect 'is armed and presently dangerous to the officer or to others.' 'A lawful frisk does not always flow from a justified stop.' " *Thomas v. Dillard*, 818 F.3d 864, 875-76 (9th Cir. 2016), as amended, (May 5, 2016) (citations omitted).

§ 3:8 Justification to seize—Temporary detention of premises occupant allowed to ensure police officers' safety during the execution of a search warrant on the premises

Supreme Court

- "A spatial constraint defined by the immediate vicinity of the premises to be searched is therefore required for detentions incident to the execution of a search warrant. The police action permitted here—the search of a residence—has a spatial dimension, and so a spatial or geographical boundary can be used to determine the area within which both the search and detention incident to that search may occur. Limiting the rule in *Summers* to the area in which an occupant poses a real threat to the safe and efficient execution of a search warrant ensures that the scope of the detention incident to a search is confined to its underlying justification. Once an occupant is beyond the immediate vicinity of the premises to be searched, the search-related law enforcement interests are diminished and the intrusiveness of the detention is more severe. . . . Here, petitioner [who had driven one mile away from the premises] was detained at a point beyond any reasonable understanding of the immediate vicinity of the premises in question; and so this case presents neither the necessity nor the occasion to further define the meaning of immediate vicinity. In closer cases courts can consider a number of factors to determine whether an occupant was detained within the immediate vicinity of the premises to be searched, including the lawful limits of the premises, whether the occupant was within the line of sight of his dwelling, the ease of reentry from the occupant's location, and other relevant factors." *Bailey v. U.S.*, 568 U.S. 186, 133 S. Ct. 1031, 185 L. Ed. 2d 19 (2013).

- "[F]or Fourth Amendment purposes, we hold that a warrant to search for contraband founded on probable cause implicitly carries with it the limited authority to detain the occupants of the premises while a proper search is conducted. [I]t was lawful to require respondent to reenter and to remain in the house until evidence establishing probable cause to arrest him was found."

Michigan v. Summers, 452 U.S. 692, 705, 101 S. Ct. 2587, 69 L. Ed. 2d 340 (1981).

- "[It is possible that] the requirements of the Fourth Amendment could be met by narrowly circumscribed procedures for obtaining, during the course of a criminal investigation, the fingerprints of individuals for whom there is no probable cause to arrest." *Davis v. Mississippi*, 394 U.S. 721, 728, 89 S. Ct. 1394, 22 L. Ed. 2d 676 (1969).

Third Circuit

- "The Supreme Court has held that officers executing a search warrant lawfully may restrain persons present at the searched premises. . . . In *Summers*, the Supreme Court noted that a warrant to search for narcotics may give rise to sudden violence or frantic efforts to conceal or destroy evidence, and thus the risk of harm to officers and occupants alike is minimized if the officers routinely exercise unquestioned command of the situation. . . . The Supreme Court indicated that the officers might exceed their proper authority in an unusual case involving special circumstances, or possibly a prolonged detention, but the routine detention of residents while a search is conducted is constitutional." *Torres v. U.S.*, 200 F.3d 179, 185 (3d Cir. 1999).

Fourth Circuit

- "We need not belabor the point that [Defendant's] three-hour detention in a confined space and under constant police surveillance was a substantial intrusion on his Fourth Amendment rights. Against this substantial intrusion, we consider the law enforcement objectives underlying the officers' decision to detain [Defendant] while the search warrant was obtained, namely, the need to preserve evidence and the concern for officer safety. . . . We are not aware of any Supreme Court case or federal appellate decision permitting a three-hour detention of an occupant of a building who lacks any specific connection to suspected criminal activity, while police obtain a warrant to search that building. Moreover, the detention that occurred in the present case lasted significantly longer than any reasonable period the officers needed to alleviate potential threats to

their safety. At some point during [Defendant's] detention, likely close to its inception, any potential threat
that [Defendant] posed to the officers' safety had
dissipated. Thus, at that point, any reasonable justification for continuing to detain [Defendant] dissipated as
well. . . . . Thus, we conclude that Watson's three-hour
detention was unreasonable and constituted an unlawful custodial arrest in violation of his Fourth Amendment rights." *U.S. v. Watson*, 703 F.3d 684 (4th Cir.
2013).

Sixth Circuit

* "[T]he Supreme Court held that a warrant to search for
  contraband founded on probable cause implicitly carries
  with it the limited authority to detain the occupants of
  the premises while a proper search is conducted. In
  Summers, the Court reached its decision after concluding that exigent circumstances—such as the risk of
  flight and harm to the officers—outweighed the intrusion on the occupant's Fourth Amendment rights."
  Centanni v. Eight Unknown Officers, 15 F.3d 587,
  590–91, 1994 FED App. 0033P (6th Cir. 1994).

Seventh Circuit

* "A person who is not free to leave his home while officers are conducting a search is seized for Fourth
  Amendment purposes. . . .An official seizure is ordinarily unreasonable unless it is supported by probable
  cause, even where no formal arrest is made. . . .
  However, a warrant to search for contraband founded
  on probable cause implicitly carries with it the limited
  authority to detain the occupants of the premises while
  a proper search is conducted. . . . This is because there
  is a substantial law enforcement interest in preventing
  the flight of a suspect in the event that incriminating
  evidence is found, in protecting the safety of the officers, and in the orderly completion of the search which
  is facilitated by the presence of the suspects." *Jacobs v.
  City of Chicago*, 215 F.3d 758, 772, 46 Fed. R. Serv. 3d
  832 (7th Cir. 2000).

Eighth Circuit

* "While an investigative stop must be limited in scope

and manner, there is no litmus-paper test or sentence or paragraph rule to determine when, given the endless variations in facts and circumstances, police-citizen encounters exceed the bounds of mere investigative stops. It is well established, however, that police officers may handcuff a suspect and place him in a patrol car during an investigative stop in order to protect their personal safety and maintain the status quo." *U.S. v. Robinson*, 670 F.3d 874, 877 (8th Cir. 2012) (quotations and citations omitted).

Ninth Circuit

- "[W]hile detentions of occupants during the period of a search will under most circumstances prove to have been reasonable, a detention may be unreasonable in a particular instance either because the detention itself is improper or because it is carried out in an unreasonable manner." *Mena v. City of Simi Valley*, 226 F.3d 1031, 1039–40 (9th Cir. 2000).

- "In *Summers*, the Court held that a warrant to search for contraband founded on probable cause implicitly carries with it the limited authority to detain the occupants of the premises while a proper search is conducted. . . . It reached that conclusion relying on a line of cases upholding limited seizures of persons on less than probable cause. . . . In *Summers*, the Court suggested the existence of some limitations on its holding: special circumstances, or possibly a prolonged detention, might lead to a different conclusion in an unusual case. . . ." *Liston v. County of Riverside*, 120 F.3d 965, 977–78 (9th Cir. 1997), as amended, (Oct. 9, 1997).

Tenth Circuit

- "[U]nder *Summers,* an officer's authority to detain the occupant of a residence while searching for contraband pursuant to a warrant lasts only as long as the search is proper." *Harman v. Pollock*, 586 F.3d 1254 (10th Cir. 2009).

§ 3:9 Justification to seize—Pretrial detention

Supreme Court

- "[The] petitioner Elijah Manuel was held in jail for some seven weeks after a judge relied on allegedly fabricated evidence to find probable cause that he had committed a crime. The primary question in this case is whether Manuel may bring a claim based on the Fourth Amendment to contest the legality of his pretrial confinement. Our answer follows from settled precedent. The Fourth Amendment, this Court has recognized, establishes 'the standards and procedures' governing pretrial detention. And those constitutional protections apply even after the start of 'legal process' in a criminal case—here, that is, after the judge's determination of probable cause. Accordingly, we hold today that Manuel may challenge his pretrial detention on the ground that it violated the Fourth Amendment. . . . [P]retrial detention can violate the Fourth Amendment not only when it precedes, but also when it follows, the start of legal process in a criminal case. The Fourth Amendment prohibits government officials from detaining a person in the absence of probable cause. That can happen when the police hold someone without any reason before the formal onset of a criminal proceeding. But it also can occur when legal process itself goes wrong—when, for example, a judge's probable-cause determination is predicated solely on a police officer's false statements. Then, too, a person is confined without constitutionally adequate justification. Legal process has gone forward, but it has done nothing to satisfy the Fourth Amendment's probable-cause requirement. . . . Police officers initially arrested Manuel without probable cause, based solely on his possession of pills that had field tested negative for an illegal substance. So (putting timeliness issues aside) Manuel could bring a claim for wrongful arrest under the Fourth Amendment. And the same is true (again, disregarding timeliness) as to a claim for wrongful detention—because Manuel's subsequent weeks in custody were *also* unsupported by probable cause, and so *also* constitutionally unreasonable. . . . And that means Manuel's ensuing pretrial detention, no less than his original arrest, violated his Fourth Amendment rights. Or put just a bit differently: Legal process did not expunge Manuel's Fourth Amendment claim because the process he received failed to establish

what that Amendment makes essential for pretrial
detention—probable cause to believe he committed a
crime." *Manuel v. City of Joliet, Ill.*, 137 S. Ct. 911, 914,
918–20 (2017) (citations omitted).

§ 3:10 Seizure by force: A person is seized when the officer by means of physical force or show of authority terminates or restrains his freedom of movement through means intentionally applied

Supreme Court

- "A person is seized by the police and thus entitled to
challenge the government's action under the Fourth
Amendment when the officer, by means of physical force
or show of authority, terminates or restrains his
freedom of movement. Thus, an unintended person . . .
[may be] the object of the detention, so long as the
detention is willful and not merely the consequence of
an unknowing act. A police officer may make a seizure
by a show of authority and without the use of physical
force, but there is no seizure without actual submission;
otherwise, there is at most an attempted seizure, so far
as the Fourth Amendment is concerned. When the actions of the police do not show an unambiguous intent
to restrain or when an individual's submission to a show
of governmental authority takes the form of passive acquiescence, there needs to be some test for telling when
a seizure occurs in response to authority, and when it
does not. The test was devised by Justice Stewart in
United States v. Mendenhall, who wrote that a seizure
occurs if in view of all of the circumstances surrounding
the incident, a reasonable person would have believed
that he was not free to leave. Later on, the Court
adopted Justice Stewart's touchstone, see, *e.g., Hodari
D., Michigan v. Chesternut, INS v. Delgado,* but added
that when a person has no desire to leave for reasons
unrelated to the police presence, the coercive effect of
the encounter can be measured better by asking
whether a reasonable person would feel free to decline
the officers' requests or otherwise terminate the
encounter." *Brendlin v. California,* 551 U.S. 249,
254–55, 127 S. Ct. 2400, 2405–06, 168 L. Ed. 2d 132
(2007) (quotations and citations omitted).

Sixth Circuit

- "We have held that 'excessively forceful or unduly tight handcuffing is a constitutional violation under the Fourth Amendment' and that 'freedom from excessively forceful or unduly tight handcuffing is a clearly established right for purposes of qualified immunity.' To plead successfully a claim of excessively forceful handcuffing, the plaintiff must allege physical injury from the handcuffing. '[W]hen there is no allegation of physical injury, the handcuffing of an individual incident to a lawful arrest is insufficient as a matter of law to state a claim of excessive force under the Fourth Amendment.' " The extent of the physical injury suffered by the plaintiff need not be severe in order to sustain the excessive-force claim." *Courtright v. City of Battle Creek*, 839 F.3d 513, 518–19 (6th Cir. 2016) (citations omitted).

Ninth Circuit

- "In this case, the U.C. Davis police officers took aim and intentionally fired in the direction of a group of which Nelson was a member. Nelson was hit in the eye by a projectile filled with pepper spray and, after being struck, was rendered immobile until he was removed by an unknown individual. Nelson was both an object of intentional governmental force and his freedom of movement was limited as a result. Under these facts, Nelson was unquestionably seized under the Fourth Amendment. The officers argue that Nelson was not individually targeted by officers, and therefore his shooting was unintentional and incapable of causing a Fourth Amendment violation. This argument misapprehends the distinction between intentional and unintentional conduct that the Supreme Court has repeatedly held as determinative of the Fourth Amendment analysis. To constitute a seizure, the governmental conduct must be purposeful, and cannot be an unintentional act which merely has the effect of restraining the liberty of the plaintiff. The intentionality requirement is satisfied when the 'termination of freedom of movement [occurs] *through means intentionally applied.*' In the Court's opinion in *Brower,* such willful conduct is contrasted with the unknowing and unintentional act of accidentally pinning a fleeing felon to a wall with a police car when the brakes of an unoccupied police vehicle failed. For an act to be unintentional, the governmental conduct must lack the element of volition; an absence of concern regarding the ultimate recipient of the government's use of force does not negate volition. As *Brendlin* stated, "'an unintended person . . . [may be] the object of the detention," so long as the detention is "willful" and not merely the consequence of "an unknowing act.'" Regardless of whether Nelson was the specific object of governmental force, he and his fellow students were the undifferentiated objects of shots intentionally fired by the officers in the direction of that group. Although the officers may have intended that the projectiles explode over the students' heads or against a wall, the officers' conduct resulted in Nelson being hit by a projectile that they intentionally fired towards a group of which he was a member. Their conduct was intentional, it was aimed towards Nelson and his group, and it resulted in the application of physical force to Nelson's person as well as the termination of his movement. Nelson was therefore intentionally seized under the Fourth Amendment. The defendants contend that the intent of the officers was to hit the area around the students in order to douse them with pepper spray from the exploding pepperball projectiles in a tactic called 'area contamination.' Testimony from at least one officer, however, reveals that they were instructed by Wilson to 'shoot at the crowd,' and that at least one officer attempted to hit individual students within Nelson's group. Nonetheless, even were we to accept as true their contention on appeal that they intended to conduct area contamination, it is of no significance whether the expectation was to hit the group with the contents of the projectile or with the projectile itself. Whether the officers intended to subject the students to a shower of pepper spray via area contamination or intended to hit them with the pepperball projectiles themselves, the officers intentionally directed their use of force at the students. As the Supreme Court has recognized, a seizure occurs when an individual is 'stopped by the accidental discharge of a gun with which he was meant only to be bludgeoned, or by a bullet in the heart that was meant only for the leg.' Thus, the precise manner in which the officers' intentional use of force was ultimately experienced by Nelson does not affect the determination that a seizure has occurred. Although Nelson may have been struck in the eye with a pepperball that was intended to impact his body elsewhere, or was physically hit by the projectile when the officers sought only to spray him with its contents, the legal consequence of the officers' actions is that a seizure of Nelson occurred. The officers also argue that their actions could not constitute a seizure because their intent was to disperse the crowd. The Supreme Court has repeatedly held that the Fourth Amendment analysis is not a subjective one. 'The intent that counts under the Fourth Amendment is the intent [that] has been conveyed to the person confronted, and the criterion of willful restriction on freedom of movement is no invitation to look to subjective intent when determining who is seized.' Recently, the Court again emphasized that 'the Fourth Amendment regulates conduct rather than thoughts.' Whether the officers intended to encourage the partygoers to disperse is of no importance when determining whether a seizure occurred. The officers took aim and fired their weapons towards Nelson and his associates. Regardless of their motives, their application of force was a knowing and wilful act that terminated Nelson's freedom of movement. It unquestionably constituted a seizure under the Fourth Amendment." *Nelson v. City of Davis*, 685 F.3d 867, 875–78, 282 Ed. Law Rep. 80 (9th Cir. 2012) (citations omitted).

§ 3:11 Seizure by force: A seizure by force is reasonable if the totality of the circumstances justified the particular sort of force used

Supreme Court

- "Clearly established federal law does not prohibit a reasonable officer who arrives late to an ongoing police action in circumstances like this from assuming that proper procedures, such as officer identification, have already been followed. No settled Fourth Amendment principle requires that officer to second-guess the earlier

steps already taken by his or her fellow officers in instances like the one White confronted here." *White v.
Pauly*, 137 S. Ct. 548, 552, 196 L. Ed. 2d 463 (2017).

- "Determining whether the force used to effect a particular seizure is reasonable under the Fourth Amendment
  requires a careful balancing of the nature and quality
  of the intrusion on the individual's Fourth Amendment
  interests against the countervailing governmental
  interests at stake. Our Fourth Amendment jurisprudence has long recognized that the right to make an arrest or investigatory stop necessarily carries with it the
  right to use some degree of physical coercion or threat
  thereof to effect it. Because [t]he test of reasonableness
  under the Fourth Amendment is not capable of precise
  definition or mechanical application, however, its proper
  application requires careful attention to the facts and
  circumstances of each particular case, including the severity of the crime at issue, whether the suspect poses
  an immediate threat to the safety of the officers or others, and whether he is actively resisting arrest or attempting to evade arrest by flight.. . . . With respect to
  a claim of excessive force, the same standard of reasonableness at the moment applies: Not every push or
  shove, even if it may later seem unnecessary in the
  peace of a judge's chambers, violates the Fourth
  Amendment. The calculus of reasonableness must
  embody allowance for the fact that police officers are
  often forced to make split-second judgments—in circumstances that are tense, uncertain, and rapidly evolving—about the amount of force that is necessary in a
  particular situation. As in other Fourth Amendment
  contexts, however, the reasonableness inquiry in an
  excessive force case is an objective one: the question is
  whether the officers' actions are objectively reasonable
  in light of the facts and circumstances confronting them,
  without regard to their underlying intent or motivation.
  An officer's evil intentions will not make a Fourth
  Amendment violation out of an objectively reasonable
  use of force; nor will an officer's good intentions make
  an objectively unreasonable use of force constitutional."
  Graham v. Connor, 490 U.S. 386, 396–97, 109 S. Ct.
  1865, 1871–72, 104 L. Ed. 2d 443 (1989) (quotations
  and citations omitted).

● "It is insisted that the Fourth Amendment must be construed in light of the common-law rule, which allowed the use of whatever force was necessary to effect the arrest of a fleeing felon, though not a misdemeanant. . . . Most American jurisdictions also imposed a flat prohibition against the use of deadly force to stop a fleeing misdemeanant, coupled with a general privilege to use such force to stop a fleeing felon. The State and city argue that because this was the prevailing rule at the time of the adoption of the Fourth Amendment and for some time thereafter, and is still in force in some States, use of deadly force against a fleeing felon must be 'reasonable.' It is true that this Court has often looked to the common law in evaluating the reasonableness, for Fourth Amendment purposes, of police activity. On the other hand, it 'has not simply frozen into constitutional law those law enforcement practices that existed at the time of the Fourth Amendment's passage.' Because of sweeping change in the legal and technological context, reliance on the common-law rule in this case would be a mistaken literalism that ignores the purposes of a historical inquiry. It has been pointed out many times that the common-law rule is best understood in light of the fact that it arose at a time when virtually all felonies were punishable by death. 'Though effected without the protections and formalities of an orderly trial and conviction, the killing of a resisting or fleeing felon resulted in no greater consequences than those authorized for punishment of the felony of which the individual was charged or suspected.' Courts have also justified the common-law rule by emphasizing the relative dangerousness of felons. Neither of these justifications makes sense today. Almost all crimes formerly punishable by death no longer are or can be. And while in earlier times 'the gulf between the felonies and the minor offences was broad and deep,' today the distinction is minor and often arbitrary. Many crimes classified as misdemeanors, or nonexistent, at common law are now felonies. These changes have undermined the concept, which was questionable to begin with, that use of deadly force against a fleeing felon is merely a speedier execution of someone who has already forfeited his life. They have also made the assumption that a 'felon' is more dangerous than a misdemeanant untenable. Indeed, numerous misdemeanors involve conduct more dangerous than many felonies. . . . One other aspect of the common-law rule bears emphasis. It forbids the use of deadly force to apprehend a misdemeanant, condemning such action as disproportionately severe." *Tennessee v. Garner*, 471 U.S. 1, 12–19, 105 S. Ct. 1694, 1701–03, 85 L. Ed. 2d 1 (1985).

Second Circuit

- "Because a stop must be justified 'at its inception,' we consider only the facts known to [Officer] McGinley that prompted him to give the cell phone orders. The facts McGinley offers to establish reasonable suspicion prior to the stop are: 1) Elting's presence in the company of an individual who (in some ways) met the description of a robbery suspect; 2) the proximity in time and space to the crime; and 3) Elting and Dancy looking over their shoulders at the police car following them. First, mere presence near someone who somewhat matches a vague description is not a reasonable basis for suspicion. . . . McGinley observed Elting in the company of Dancy, who "somewhat" matched the description broadcast over the radio. . . . While such a discrepancy does not necessarily defeat a finding of reasonable suspicion, the remaining description—thin, black, and male—is too vague in the circumstances here to justify a stop of anyone meeting it. Furthermore, the description did not mention a second assailant or accomplice, and Elting's mere presence in the company of a possible suspect is, standing alone, not enough for a stop. . . . Second, while they were found walking within several city blocks of the crime scene, such proximity was innocuous given the unremarkable nature of the area in question. . . . It would not have been unusual to find a thin, black male in downtown Poughkeepsie that Friday evening. The city itself is 33.5% African–American. Poughkeepsie's Main Street is aptly named, featuring a number of restaurants, businesses, and nightlife. Under the circumstances, the description fit too many people to constitute sufficient articulable facts on which to justify a forcible stop of Elting. Third, as the case law recognizes, in the circumstances here there is nothing suspi-

cious about looking over one's shoulder at an approaching police car. . . . In the circumstances here, looking
over one's shoulder at an officer in slow pursuit is not
suspicious behavior. Indeed, it is natural for people to
take an interest in police activity nearby 'out of a desire
to avoid some minor misstep, such as a minor traffic
violation, which would involve them unnecessarily with
the police.' . . . Nor did Dancy or Elting exhibit nervous or evasive behavior of any kind. . . . Considering
these facts together and under the 'totality of the circumstances,' we conclude that McGinley had no basis to
suspect Elting of any legal wrongdoing. . . . On these
facts, no reasonable police officer would have had reason to stop him, or prevent him from calling his mother,
or throw him to the ground. Because subjective intentions are irrelevant to this analysis, we do not assess
what was motivating this police officer when he decided
to stop Elting. But we do know that, objectively speaking, he lacked reasonable suspicion, and so violated the
Fourth Amendment by detaining Elting without an adequate basis. As a result of this suspicionless stop, an
African–American teenager was arrested, jailed, and
subjected to 'the humiliations of [an] unconstitutional
search[ ].' Circumstances like these remind us that
specificity in articulating the basis for a stop is necessary 'in part because according the police unfettered
discretion to stop and frisk could lead to harassment of
minority groups and "severely exacerbate police-
community tensions." ' " *Dancy v. McGinley*, 843 F.3d
93, 108–11 (2d Cir. 2016) (citations omitted).

Ninth Circuit

- "A seizure results in a constitutional violation only if it
is unreasonable. Defendants contend that any seizure
here did not meet that standard. The determination of
unreasonableness requires us to decide 'whether the
totality of the circumstances justified a particular sort
of. . .seizure.' To resolve this question we must balance
'the nature and quality of the intrusion on the individual's Fourth Amendment interests against the countervailing governmental interests at stake.' When the
governmental interests at stake are substantial, a
greater intrusion upon the Fourth Amendment rights of

the person may be justified. Conversely, when the governmental interest is insubstantial, the application of even minimal force may be unreasonable. When balancing the degree of force used against the governmental interests, 'it is the *need* for force which is at the heart of the [analysis].' . . . The actual harm caused . . . 'is certainly relevant in evaluating the degree of the Fourth Amendment intrusion.' [In this case, we] conclude that both the risk of harm and the actual harm experienced by Nelson were significant and must be justified by substantial government interests. . . . To evaluate the need for the government's use of force against Nelson we consider a number of factors, including 'the severity of the crime at issue, whether . . . [Nelson] pose[d] an immediate threat to the safety of the officers or others, and whether he. . .actively resist[ed] arrest or attempt[ed] to evade arrest by flight.' " *Nelson v. City of Davis*, 685 F.3d 867, 878–79, 282 Ed. Law Rep. 80 (9th Cir. 2012) (citations omitted).

Eleventh Circuit

- "[E]ven if the complaint could be read to allege that Mr. Saunders disobeyed an order by lifting his head off the hot pavement, that minor transgression does not mean that the force allegedly used was a constitutionally permissible response, or that the agents are entitled to qualified immunity. The agents did not, by Mr. Saunders' account, merely exert some pressure to guide his head downward. Instead, they 'slammed' his head against the pavement with 'extreme force,' and, not surprisingly, this resulted in significant injuries to Mr. Saunders. The human skull is a relatively hearty vessel for the brain, but it will generally not fare well in a contest with hardened cement." *Saunders v. Duke*, 766 F.3d 1262, 1269 (11th Cir. 2014) (citations omitted).

D.C. Circuit

- "We begin with the demise of Wrinkles. 'Every circuit that has considered the issue has held that the killing of a companion dog constitutes a "seizure" within the meaning of the Fourth Amendment.' Those circuits have invariably concluded that 'the use of deadly force against a household pet is reasonable only if the pet poses an immediate danger and the use of force is unavoidable.' As in any Fourth Amendment case, '[w]e analyze [the] question [of whether a pet constitutes an imminent threat] from the perspective "of a reasonable officer on the scene, rather than with the 20/20 vision of hindsight."' This analysis 'allow[s] for the fact that police officers are often forced to make split-second judgments—in circumstances that are tense, uncertain, and rapidly evolving—about the amount of force that is necessary in a particular situation.'" *Robinson v. Pezzat*, 818 F.3d 1, 7–8 (D.C. Cir. 2016) (citations omitted).

§ 3:12 Nonseizures: Some encounters between citizens and police do not constitute seizures

Supreme Court

- "Even when law enforcement officers have no basis for suspecting a particular individual, they may pose questions, ask for identification, and request consent to search luggage—provided they do not induce cooperation by coercive means. [P]olice did not seize respondents when they boarded the bus and began questioning passengers. The officers gave the passengers no reason to believe that they were required to answer the officers' questions. When [the officer] approached respondents, he did not brandish a weapon or make any intimidating movements. He left the aisle free so that respondents could exit. He spoke to passengers one by one and in a polite, quiet voice. Nothing he said would suggest to a reasonable person that he or she was barred from leaving the bus or otherwise terminating the encounter." *U.S. v. Drayton*, 536 U.S. 194, 122 S. Ct. 2105, 153 L. Ed. 2d 242 (2002).

- "The narrow question before us is whether, with respect to a show of authority as with respect to application of physical force, a seizure occurs even though the subject does not yield. We hold that it does not." *California v. Hodari D.*, 499 U.S. 621, 626, 111 S. Ct. 1547, 113 L. Ed. 2d 690 (1991).

- "It is clear, in other words, that a Fourth Amendment seizure does not occur whenever there is a governmentally caused termination of an individual's freedom of movement (the innocent passerby), nor even whenever there is a governmentally caused and governmentally desired termination of an individual's freedom of movement (the fleeing felon), but only when there is a governmental termination of freedom of movement through means intentionally applied." *Brower v. County of Inyo*, 489 U.S. 593, 596, 109 S. Ct. 1378, 103 L. Ed. 2d 628 (1989).

- "[P]olice questioning, by itself, is unlikely to result in a Fourth Amendment violation. While most citizens will respond to a police request, the fact that people do so, and do so without being told they are free not to respond, hardly eliminates the consensual nature of the response." *I.N.S. v. Delgado*, 466 U.S. 210, 216, 104 S. Ct. 1758, 80 L. Ed. 2d 247 (1984).

- "[L]aw enforcement officers do not violate the Fourth Amendment by merely approaching an individual on the street or in another public place, by asking him if he is willing to answer some questions, by putting questions to him if the person is willing to listen, or by offering in evidence in a criminal prosecution his voluntary answers to such questions. Nor would the fact that the officer identifies himself as a police officer, without more, convert the encounter into a seizure requiring some level of objective justification. The person approached, however, need not answer any question put to him; indeed, he may decline to listen to the questions at all and may go on his way. He may not be detained even momentarily without reasonable, objective grounds for doing so; and his refusal to listen o r answer does not, without more, furnish those grounds." *Florida v. Royer*, 460 U.S. 491, 497, 498, 103 S. Ct. 1319, 75 L. Ed. 2d 229 (1983).

- "We conclude that a person has been seized within the meaning of the Fourth Amendment only if, in view of all of the circumstances surrounding the incident, a reasonable person would have believed that he was not free to leave. Examples of circumstances that might indicate a seizure, even where the person did not attempt to leave, would be the threatening presence of several officers, the display of a weapon by an officer, some physical touching of the person of the citizen, or the use of language or tone of voice indicating that compliance with the officer's request might be compelled. In the absence of some such evidence, otherwise inoffensive contact between a member of the public and the police cannot, as a matter of law, amount to a seizure of that person." *U.S. v. Mendenhall*, 446 U.S. 544, 554–55, 100 S. Ct. 1870, 64 L. Ed. 2d 497 (1980).

- "Obviously, not all personal intercourse between policemen and citizens involves seizures of persons. Only when the officer, by means of physical force or show of authority, has in some way restrained the liberty of a citizen may we conclude that a seizure has occurred." *Terry v. Ohio*, 392 U.S. 1, 19 n.16, 88 S. Ct. 1868, 20 L. Ed. 2d 889 (1968).

First Circuit

- "There are no colorable Fourth Amendment concerns where an officer simply asks a few questions to a civilian, who voluntarily allows the encounter to continue. Nor is an otherwise consensual encounter stripped of its consensual nature by the mere act of moving to a police office." *U.S. v. One Lot of U.S. Currency ($36,634)*, 103 F.3d 1048, 1053 (1st Cir. 1997).

Second Circuit

- "We hold that the issuance of a pre-arraignment, non-felony summons requiring a later court appearance, without further restrictions, does not constitute a Fourth Amendment seizure. This summons does no more than require [petitioner] to appear in court on a single occasion, and operates to effectuate due process." *Burg v. Gosselin*, 591 F.3d 95 (2d Cir. 2010).

Third Circuit

- "The District Court correctly concluded that [plaintiff]'s meeting with [police chief] did not constitute a seizure. [Plaintiff] reported to the police station voluntarily, and it does not appear that, after [plaintiff] arrived at the station, the meeting evolved into a seizure. . . . Granted, [plaintiff] does allege that [the police chief] gave him an ultimatum—resign or be named in a police report. Yet this ultimatum, though asking [plaintiff] to make a difficult decision, did not restrict his freedom of movement or otherwise prevent him from ending the

meeting. . . . In light of all of the circumstances surrounding this meeting, it seems that a reasonable
person in [plaintiff]'s position would have felt free to
end the encounter." *Fera v. Baldwin Borough*, 350 Fed.
Appx. 749 (3d Cir. 2009).

Fourth Circuit

- "[O]fficers remain free to seek cooperation from citizens
  on the street without being called upon to articulate
  any level of suspicion or justification for their
  encounters. The authority of police officers to initiate
  such police-citizen encounters is the same as, but no
  greater than, the authority of an ordinary citizen to approach another on the street and ask questions. By the
  same token, the citizen encountered in this manner has
  the right to ignore his interrogator and walk away."
  U.S. v. Burton, 228 F.3d 524, 527 (4th Cir. 2000).

Sixth Circuit

- ". . . Under *Fisher,* an officer's intentionally applied exertion of force directed at a vehicle to stop it effectuates
  a seizure of all occupants [including plaintiff/passenger]
  therein. Factually, the instant case is like *Fisher* in
  that it involved an officer's shooting at a moving vehicle
  in order to stop it, resulting in injury to the passenger.
  That *Fisher* does not mention whether the police were
  aware of the passenger's presence in the vehicle does
  not render *Fisher* inapplicable to the instant case. . . .
  [In *Troupe,* a]lthough a bullet struck the driver, it did
  not effect a seizure of the vehicle; it was the vehicle's
  later crash that stopped the vehicle and caused the
  death of the driver and a passenger, and injury to the
  other passenger. That is, the gunfire in *Troupe* did not
  cause the vehicle to stop, and there was thus no seizure.
  To be sure, the *Troupe* court did say, in the course of
  discussing whether there had been a seizure ['s]topping
  a vehicle's driver does not constitute a seizure of a
  passenger.' Here the intent to stop the vehicle was the
  same as in *Fisher,* and *Fisher* controls. By shooting at
  the driver of the moving car, he intended to stop the
  car, effectively seizing everyone inside, including the
  Plaintiff." *Rodriguez v. Passinault*, 637 F.3d 675 (6th
  Cir. 2011) (citations omitted).

- "We have held that law enforcement officers may approach an individual and ask general questions without having any reasonable suspicion of criminal activity, so long as the officers refrain from the type of intimidating behavior that would lead a reasonable person to believe that the person was not free to leave. . . . Whether an encounter between a police officer and a citizen is consensual depends on the officer's objective behavior, not on any subjective suspicion of criminal activity." *U.S. v. Waldon*, 206 F.3d 597, 603, 2000 FED App. 0059P (6th Cir. 2000).

Seventh Circuit

- " 'Even when law enforcement officers have no basis for suspecting a particular individual, they may pose questions, ask for identification, and request consent to search luggage—provided they do not induce cooperation by coercive means,' . . ., and a seizure hasn't taken place so long as 'a reasonable person would feel free to decline the officers' requests or otherwise terminate the encounter,' . . .. Radford, however, argues that she was intimidated by Mings, primarily because the [train] roomette was small, Mings weighed 170 pounds and was fully uniformed and equipped (he was wearing a holster with a gun in it), he was white and she was black, he was standing and she was sitting, he said he was investigating drug trafficking but didn't tell her she had a right to refuse to answer his questions or consent to a search of her handbags. . . . Her argument exaggerates the situation. Mings didn't enter the roomette before she consented to the search, his uniform with its accouterments established his identity as a police officer, he told her why he wanted to search her, there can't be a rule that a police officer is forbidden to speak to a person of another race, and since he didn't tell her that she had to answer his questions and didn't threaten her with arrest there was no need to tell her that she didn't have to answer his questions or consent to a search—that was implicit in his asking her questions without telling her that she was required to answer them. . . . It would have been better had Mings, like his counterpart in *Goodwin,* asked whether Radford was 'willing to answer some questions,' or like his counterpart in *Notorianni*, whether he 'could ask [her] some questions.' But there was nothing stopping her from asking Mings whether she was under arrest and had to answer his questions. In all likelihood she answered his questions because she knew the jig was up. She knew that she was carrying a substantial quantity of an illegal drug and that she had an arrest record for trafficking illegal immigrants and possessing marijuana. She probably guessed the police knew all this, and if so she probably also surmised that they knew the purpose of her train trip. She may well have realized that if she clammed up she would be greeted by police at the other stops on her trip, and at her final destination, by which time the police might have obtained a warrant to arrest and search her. Or she may have thought that answering questions and consenting to a search would allay suspicion, inducing the police to leave after a minimal search or even without searching at all." *United States v. Radford*, 856 F.3d 1147, 1149-50 (7th Cir. 2017) (citations omitted).

- "The distinction between a consensual encounter, which does not implicate the Fourth Amendment, and an investigative stop, which does implicate the constitutional guarantee because it constitutes a seizure, is often difficult to discern. On one hand, the Supreme Court has recognized that 'mere police questioning does not constitute a seizure.' Accordingly, 'law enforcement officers do not violate the Fourth Amendment by merely approaching an individual on the street or in another public place, by asking him if he is willing to answer some questions, [or] by putting questions to him if the person is willing to listen.' A mere request for identification does not change a voluntary stop, which is outside the purview of the Fourth Amendment, into an investigatory stop. These principles do not change when an individual is seated in an automobile." *U.S. v. Shields*, 789 F.3d 733, 743–44 (7th Cir. 2015), cert. denied, 136 S. Ct. 420, 193 L. Ed. 2d 329 (2015) (citations omitted).

- "The plaintiffs. . . .represent the interests of a young man who was killed and a young woman who was rendered disabled in a motorcycle accident that occurred during a police chase . . . . In the context of a police pursuit, a Fourth Amendment seizure does not occur unless an officer intentionally and forcibly halts the fleeing suspect . . . (W)e agree with the district court that no reasonable jury could find that (the officer) violated the appellants' Fourth Amendment rights . . . The appellants here have failed to bring forth any evidence that there was any contact between the motorcycle and Myers's police car . . . Even the most damning evidence of a nefarious motive (which this is not) does not overcome the fact that the plaintiffs have provided no evidence that any seizure within the meaning of the Fourth Amendment has occurred." *Steen v. Myers*, 486 F.3d 1017 (7th Cir. 2007).

Eighth Circuit

- "So long as a reasonable person would feel free to disregard the police and go about his business, the encounter is consensual and no reasonable suspicion is required. The encounter will not trigger Fourth Amendment scrutiny unless it loses its consensual nature. . . . Neither officer had his holster showing; both were in plain clothes; neither touched [Defendant] or blocked his way when telling him he could not enter the apartment; all three were in an open, public hallway; no one told [Defendant] he could not leave; and no one alleged that the officers spoke in harsh tones, raised their voices, or crowded [Defendant]. The facts indicate a lack of intimidation or threats." *U.S. v. Garcia*, 197 F.3d 1223, 1226 (8th Cir. 1999).

Tenth Circuit

- "Because a consensual encounter is voluntary, such an encounter does not constitute a seizure within the meaning of the Fourth Amendment. A consensual encounter is simply the voluntary cooperation of a private citizen in response to non-coercive questioning by a law enforcement official." *U.S. v. Patten*, 183 F.3d 1190, 1194 (10th Cir. 1999).
- "An encounter is consensual if the defendant is free to leave at any time during the encounter. . . . A person is seized only when that person has an objective reason to believe he or she is not free to end the conversation with the officer and proceed on his or her way. . . . The defendant's subjective belief that she was not free to

leave is not determinative. The correct test is whether a
reasonable person in the defendant's position would
believe she was not free to leave." *U.S. v. Torres-
Guevara*, 147 F.3d 1261, 1264 (10th Cir. 1998).

Eleventh Circuit

- "Law enforcement officers do not violate the Fourth
  Amendment simply by approaching an individual on
  the street or in some other public place and asking a
  question or asking for identification." *U.S. v. Caraballo*,
  595 F.3d 1214 (11th Cir. 2010).

- "A well-established principle of Fourth Amendment jurisprudence is that a seizure does not occur just because
  a police officer approaches a person and asks the person
  a few questions. . . . The Supreme Court, accordingly,
  has said that a bus check, where government agents
  board a bus and ask questions of the passengers, is not
  necessarily a seizure." *U.S. v. Smith*, 201 F.3d 1317,
  1321 (11th Cir. 2000).

§ 3:13   Seizure of personal property: Personal property may be subject to a limited warrantless seizure if there is reasonable suspicion that it contains seizable items

Supreme Court

- "[A]n officer who happens to come across an individual's
  property in a public area could seize it only if Fourth
  Amendment standards are satisfied—for example, if the
  items are evidence of a crime or contraband." *Soldal v.
  Cook County, Ill.*, 506 U.S. 56, 68, 113 S. Ct. 538, 121 L.
  Ed. 2d 450 (1992).

- "The plain view doctrine is often considered an exception to the general rule that warrantless searches are
  presumptively unreasonable, but this characterization
  overlooks the important difference between searches
  and seizures. If an article is already in plain view, neither its observation nor its seizure would involve any
  invasion of privacy. A seizure of the article, however,
  would obviously invade the owner's possessory interest.
  If plain view justifies an exception from an otherwise
  applicable warrant requirement, therefore, it must be
  an exception that is addressed to the concerns that are

implicated by seizures rather than by searches." *Horton v. California*, 496 U.S. 128, 133–34, 110 S. Ct. 2301, 110 L. Ed. 2d 112 (1990).

- "A seizure of property occurs when there is some meaningful interference with an individual's possessory interests in that property." *U.S. v. Jacobsen*, 466 U.S. 109, 113, 104 S. Ct. 1652, 80 L. Ed. 2d 85 (1984).

- "In the ordinary case, the Court has viewed a seizure of personal property as *per se* unreasonable within the meaning of the Fourth Amendment unless it is accomplished pursuant to a judicial warrant issued upon probable cause and particularly describing the items to be seized. . . . Where law enforcement authorities have probable cause to believe that a container holds contraband or evidence of a crime, but have not secured a warrant, the Court has interpreted the Amendment to permit seizure of the property, pending issuance of a warrant to examine its contents, if the exigencies of the circumstances demand it or some other recognized exception to the warrant requirement is present." *U.S. v. Place*, 462 U.S. 696, 701, 103 S. Ct. 2637, 77 L. Ed. 2d 110 (1983).

- "Given the fact that seizures of property can vary in intrusiveness, some brief detentions of personal effects may be so minimally intrusive of Fourth Amendment interests that strong countervailing governmental interests will justify a seizure based only on specific articulable facts that the property contains contraband or evidence of a crime." *U.S. v. Place*, 462 U.S. 696, 706, 103 S. Ct. 2637, 77 L. Ed. 2d 110 (1983).

- "[W]hen the police seize luggage from the suspect's custody, we think the limitations applicable to investigative detentions of the person should define the permissible scope of an investigative detention of the person's luggage on less than probable cause. Under this standard, it is clear that the police conduct here exceeded the permissible limits of a *Terry*-type investigative stop. The length of the detention of respondent's luggage alone precludes the conclusion that the seizure was reasonable in the absence of probable cause." *U.S. v. Place*, 462 U.S. 696, 708–09, 103 S. Ct. 2637, 77 L. Ed. 2d 110 (1983).

- "[I]t is well settled that objects such as weapons or

contraband found in a public place may be seized by the police without a warrant. The seizure of property in plain view involves no invasion of privacy and is presumptively reasonable, assuming that there is probable cause to associate the property with criminal activity." *Payton v. New York*, 445 U.S. 573, 586–87, 100 S. Ct. 1371, 63 L. Ed. 2d 639 (1980).

First Circuit

- "Defendant had no reasonable expectation of privacy with respect to the crack cocaine and the firearm he allegedly threw away while being pursued by police, as required to be able to challenge their seizure under the Fourth Amendment; defendant actively disowned any interest in the items." *U.S. v. Lipscomb*, 539 F.3d 32 (1st Cir. 2008).

- "If an initial entry is unlawful, then a defendant with an established Fourth Amendment interest in the premises searched need not also show an interest in the particular item seized. Here, though, the initial entry was lawful, so [defendant] has the burden of showing that he had a protectible Fourth Amendment interest in the gun. The district court correctly determined that [defendant] has established a Fourth Amendment interest in the gun. He purchased the gun, directed the purchase of ammunition for it, test fired the gun, and kept it in his home. The district court appropriately characterized the defendant's testimony regarding his ownership of the gun as 'less than uniform.' But the defendant did not disavow any ownership or control of the gun, and his testimony was certainly sufficient to allow him to assert a protectible interest in it. The mere fact that he claimed to have bought the gun as a gift for [his girlfriend] does not, by itself, work to extinguish his Fourth Amendment interest." *U.S. v. Paradis*, 351 F.3d 21 (1st Cir. 2003).

Second Circuit

- "[T]he making of the videotape [of plaintiff after his arrest] resulted in the seizure of [his] image. The Fourth Amendment seizure has long encompassed the seizure of intangibles as well as tangibles. . . . In this set of circumstances, the County's creation and dissemination of

the videotape implicate privacy interests that are
protected by the Fourth Amendment. . . . [Plaintiff's]
reasonable expectation of privacy on [Department of
Correction] grounds, however, was minimal. . . .Our inquiry does not end with the determination that [plain-
tiff's] privacy interests (although minimal) were implicated by the County's actions. . . . We therefore examine
the government purposes underlying the making and
release of the videotape. The County's purposes in making the videotape were the same as its purposes in
distributing the videotape to the media: the County created and distributed the videotape to inform the public
about its efforts to stop the abuse of disability benefits
by its employees. The fact that corrections officers—
public employees—were arrested on suspicion of grand
larceny is highly newsworthy and of great interest to
the public at large. Divulging the arrests also enhances
the transparency of the criminal justice system, and it
may deter others from attempting similar crimes.
Furthermore, allowing the public to view images of an
arrestee informs and enables members of the public
who may come forward with additional information relevant to the law enforcement investigation. . . . Although [plaintiff] possessed a privacy interest in not
having his 'perp walk' broadcast to the public, that
privacy interest was outweighed by the County's legitimate government purposes. Therefore, [plaintiff]
sustained no actionable Fourth Amendment injury."
Caldarola v. County of Westchester, 343 F.3d 570, 31
Media L. Rep. (BNA) 2291 (2d Cir. 2003).

Fourth Circuit

- "(Plaintiff) alleges that, without her consent, the
  Defendants conspired to publish a map that showed a
  public trail crossing her yard. Presley further alleges
  that, even after the Defendants realized their error,
  they did not correct it but rather criminally prosecuted
  her when she herself took measures to prevent tres-
  passes on her property . . . . Although she ultimately
  may not be able to prevail, (plaintiff) has. . .raised a
  Fourth Amendment seizure claim by alleging that
  private individuals, knowingly encouraged and aided by
  the Defendants, trespassed onto her property." *Presley
  v. City Of Charlottesville*, 464 F.3d 480 (4th Cir. 2006).

- "[D]ogs merit protection under the Fourth Amendment. The common law personal property rights that attached to dogs were at least as strong as those that have been held sufficient by the Court to qualify other objects as 'effects' entitled to Fourth Amendment protection. ... Accordingly, on the strength of the Constitution's text, of history, and of precedent, we hold that the plaintiffs' privately owned dogs were 'effects' subject to the protections of the Fourth Amendment." *Altman v. City of High Point, N.C.*, 330 F.3d 194 (4th Cir. 2003).

Fifth Circuit

- "The weapons were illegal because they were possessed by persons who had no lawful right to possess them. However, the officers who seized the weapons did not know at the time of the seizure the criminal histories of Roberts and Booth that would make their possession of the weapons illegal. Thus, the incriminating nature of the weapons was not apparent at the moment they were seized and removed from the apartment . . . . Nonetheless, we think the police were justified in temporarily seizing the weapons under these circumstances. The officers could see four individuals in the darkened room of the apartment. When Roberts walked back into the darkened room, Officer Clements saw a pistol magazine and loose ammunition rounds on the entertainment center where Roberts was headed. At that point, the officers asked Roberts to step away from the entertainment center, and they secured the other individuals against a wall, away from the ammunition. Roberts then told the officers that there was a gun under the couch. Though the officers moved all of the individuals against a wall, the danger posed to the officers by the firearms did not fully dissipate. The individuals were not handcuffed or otherwise incapacitated and in the event of a scuffle could have accessed the unsecured weapons. 'Common sense dictates that a firearm that could be accessed by someone at the scene and used against officers or others should be unloaded, and at least temporarily, kept in a safe place.' . . . The officers acted reasonably—the touchstone requirement of the Fourth Amendment—in seizing the weapons for the safety of themselves and the apartment's occupants. Accordingly, such a temporary seizure does not violate the Fourth Amendment." *U.S. v. Roberts*, 612 F.3d 306, 313-14 (5th Cir. 2010).

- "[A] governmental seizure of property—that is, some meaningful interference with an individual's possessory interest in that property. . . .is subject to Fourth Amendment scrutiny even if no search within the meaning of the Amendment takes place." *U.S. v. Paige*, 136 F.3d 1012, 1017 (5th Cir. 1998).

Sixth Circuit

- "The Supreme Court has established that one of the purposes of the prohibition on unreasonable seizures of property is the protection of the individual's property rights in the seized item. . . . However, the courts have yet to define the breadth of the Fourth Amendment's protection of property. . . . Whatever the breadth of Fourth Amendment protection of property interests, that protection is limited to the breadth of the meaning of the word seizure in the Fourth Amendment." *Fox v. Van Oosterum*, 176 F.3d 342, 350, 1999 FED App. 0164P (6th Cir. 1999).
- "The Supreme Court has only applied the meaningful interference with possessory interests definition of seizure to cases where there is no debate that the challenged act is one of taking property away from an individual and the issue is whether that act of taking property away constitutes a meaningful interference with possessory interests." *Fox v. Van Oosterum*, 176 F.3d 342, 351, 1999 FED App. 0164P (6th Cir. 1999).

Seventh Circuit

- "A seizure of property connotes some meaningful interference with an individual's possessory interests in that property. . . . We are talking now solely about the removal of the bag from the common luggage area of the bus. . . . [Defendant] had surrendered custody of the bag to Greyhound and no doubt realized that the bag would be transported to Indianapolis in the common luggage compartment of the bus. He could reasonably have foreseen that the bag would be handled, moved around, and even taken off the bus, whether at intermediate stops when the driver might need to remove the bag to sort and/or gain access to other luggage, or at a hub like St. Louis where the bag would have been transferred to another bus. He could have no reasonable expectation, in other words, that the bag would not be touched, handled, or even removed from the bus prior to the bag's arrival in Indianapolis." *U.S. v. Ward*, 144 F.3d 1024, 1032 (7th Cir. 1998).

Eighth Circuit

- "In *South Dakota v. Opperman,* the Supreme Court noted two common police practices. First, 'automobiles are frequently taken into police custody' in the interests of public safety and 'community caretaking functions.' Second, '[w]hen vehicles are impounded, local police departments generally follow a routine practice of securing and inventorying the automobiles' contents.' The Court concluded that, properly implemented, these practices do not run afoul of the Fourth Amendment's search warrant requirement. . . . In *Colorado v. Bertine,* a decision dealing primarily with an inventory search of a closed container, the Supreme Court also addressed the question whether the inventory search was unconstitutional because the police department regulations gave officers 'discretion to choose between impounding [defendant's] van and parking and locking it in a public parking space.' The Fourth Amendment permits exercise of such discretion, the Court concluded, 'so long as that discretion is exercised according to standard criteria and on the basis of something other than suspicion of evidence of criminal activity.' We interpreted and applied that ruling in *United States v. Petty*:

  Some degree of 'standardized criteria' or 'established routine' must regulate these police actions, which may be conducted without the safeguards of a warrant or probable cause, to ensure that impoundments and inventory searches are not merely a ruse for general rummaging in order to discover incriminating evidence.

  The requirement that discretion be fettered, however, has never meant that a decision to impound must be made in a 'totally mechanical' fashion. . . . It is not feasible for a police department to develop a policy that provides clear-cut guidance in every potential impoundment situation. . . . [T]estimony can be sufficient to establish police [impoundment] procedures. . . . So long as the officer's residual judgment is exercised based on legitimate concerns related to the purposes of an impoundment, his decision to impound a particular vehicle does not run afoul of the Constitution.

We agree with the district court that, although Officer King exercised some discretion in deciding that Arrocha's SUV must be towed, he acted within the degree of 'standardized criteria' or 'established routine' that our prior towing cases require. Arrocha further argues [he] 'was legally parked in a marked parking space' and 'did not interfere with the use of the real property by Quik-Trip.' We disagree. 'Police may take protective custody of a vehicle when they have arrested its occupants, even if it is lawfully parked and poses no public safety hazard.' Here, although Officer King did not consult QuikTrip employees before towing Arrocha's SUV, Officers King and Mason testified that the police had an informal agreement with QuikTrip that vehicles abandoned in its busy parking lot because of an arrest would be towed. This is the type of unwritten towing policy that suffices as standardized police procedure in the absence of evidence that an officer's exercise of this discretion in a particular case was 'merely a ruse for general rummaging in order to discover incriminating evidence.' . . . Finally, Arrocha complains that the 'officers did not allow Mr. Arrocha to contact anyone and therefore violated the Liberty tow policy.' But this is not a Fourth Amendment issue. 'Nothing in the Fourth Amendment requires a police department to allow an arrested person to arrange for another person to pick up his car to avoid impoundment and inventory.' 'The central question in evaluating the propriety of an inventory search is whether, in the totality of the circumstances, the search was reasonable.' Here, we agree with the district court that Officer King's decision to tow the SUV was a reasonable exercise of discretion that was sufficiently 'fettered' by standardized police procedures." *U.S. v. Arrocha*, 713 F.3d 1159, 1162–64 (8th Cir. 2013) (citations omitted).

- "Defendant relinquished his reasonable expectation of privacy over handgun by abandoning it under a tree." *U.S. v. Richardson*, 537 F.3d 951 (8th Cir. 2008).
- "[L]aw enforcement authorities must possess a reasonable suspicion based on articulable facts that a package

contains contraband before they may detain the package for investigation." *U.S. v. Vasquez*, 213 F.3d 425, 426, 55 Fed. R. Evid. Serv. 218 (8th Cir. 2000).

- "The warrantless search of an automobile, predicated on consent, may be expanded beyond the scope of the consent when it yields a basis for a reasonable articulable suspicion that additional contraband may be found in parts of the car not included in the consent." *U.S. v. Alverez*, 235 F.3d 1086, 1089 (8th Cir. 2000).

- "In the context of the Fourth Amendment, a seizure of property occurs whenever there is some meaningful interference with an individual's possessory interest in that property." *Johnson v. Outboard Marine Corp.*, 172 F.3d 531, 536 (8th Cir. 1999).

Ninth Circuit

- "Under the 'community caretaking' doctrine, police may, without a warrant, impound and search a motor vehicle so long as they do so in conformance with the standardized procedures of the local police department and in furtherance of a community caretaking purpose, such as promoting public safety or the efficient flow of traffic. This requirement ensures that impoundments are conducted 'on the basis of something other than suspicion of evidence of criminal activity.' The government bears the burden of establishing that a vehicle's impoundment and search are justified under an exception to the warrant requirement." *United States v. Torres*, 828 F.3d 1113, 1118 (9th Cir. 2016) (citations omitted).

- "The benchmark for the Fourth Amendment is reasonableness, which requires us to weigh the government's justification for its actions against the intrusion into the defendant's interests . . . . The government here certainly had important reasons for employing this unusual procedure in seizing the car . . . (T)he intrusion into (defendant's) Fourth Amendment interests was relatively mild . . . While the police may not use *excessive* force in conducting a search or seizure . . .the force here was minimal . . . . (T)he agent in the truck bumped the stationary car with "enough force. . .so that the *tap* was felt by Defendant to the extent that it caused him to get out of his car and examine his bumper" . . . . but the truck was moving at only 1 to 2 miles per hour and the tap caused no harm to the couple and left no scratch on the car. A tap is a use of force, to be sure, but it is hardly excessive. The staged collision involved just enough force to pull off the "drunk driver" ruse, without causing physical injury to the suspects . . . Nor was there anything unreasonable in the agents' choice of guile to seize the car, rather than taking it outright, as they were entitled to do . . . . 'We think it clearly improper for a government agent to gain access to [property] which *would otherwise be unavailable to him* by invoking the private individual's trust in his government . . . .' . . . This consideration is not implicated by the agents' actions here because they already had the authority to seize the car and arrest (defendant); their lies didn't have the effect of expanding their ostensible authority beyond the scope of their actual authority. The only consequence of their deceit was to treat (defendant) as a victim, rather than a criminal suspect-driving him to a hotel rather than immediately dragging him off to jail-and the only harm he suffered was being misled and subjected to the fright that comes from being the victim of a crime . . . . We find that the agents' actions in misleading (defendant) were reasonable in light of their vital interest in seizing the drugs and not exposing their investigation." *U.S. v. Alverez-Tejeda*, 491 F.3d 1013 (9th Cir. 2007).

Tenth Circuit

- "We hold that impoundment of a vehicle located on private property that is neither obstructing traffic nor creating an imminent threat to public safety is constitutional only if justified by both a standardized policy and a reasonable, non-pretextual community-caretaking rationale. Our holding, like that of a majority of circuits, recognizes that *Bertine* makes the existence of standardized criteria the touchstone of the inquiry into whether an impoundment is lawful. However, *Bertine* did not purport to overrule *Opperman,* and *Opperman* envisioned a situation in which an impoundment is immediately necessary, regardless of any other circumstances, in order to facilitate the flow of traffic or protect the public from an immediate harm. But to hold, as have the First, Third, and Fifth Circuits, that standard-

ized criteria are never relevant is to ignore the plain
language of *Bertine,* which holds that police discretion
to impound a vehicle is constitutional only '*so long as
that discretion is exercised according to standard
criteria.*' Our holding follows our prior circuit precedent
in *Taylor, Ibarra,* and *Maher* in recognizing the centrality of standardized criteria, yet allowing broader officer
discretion to protect public safety. Our requirement that
standardized criteria guide impoundments on private
property ensures that police discretion to impound
vehicles is cabined rather than uncontrolled. Imposing
heightened requirements on police who seize vehicles
from private property is consistent with our circuit precedent and caselaw from other circuits. Yet *Opperman*
establishes that if a vehicle is obstructing or impeding
traffic on public property, it can be impounded regardless of whether the impoundment is guided by standardized procedures. By recognizing that standardized
procedures need not justify impoundments of such
vehicles, our holding is also faithful to our circuit precedent holding that officers should be free to impound
vehicles that threaten public safety. For example, our
holding allows officers from a rural county lacking a
specific policy to impound a vehicle obstructing a
highway, if that impoundment is reasonable and not
pretextual, without fear of liability. Moreover, because
our holding requires all community-caretaking impoundments to be supported by a reasonable, non-
pretextual justification, it guards against arbitrary
impoundments. This rule ensures that even if the police
were to adopt a standardized policy of impounding all
vehicles whose owners receive traffic citations, such
impoundments could be invalidated as unreasonable
under our precedent. Protection against unreasonable
impoundments, even those conducted pursuant to a
standardized policy, is part and parcel of the Fourth
Amendment's guarantee against unreasonable searches
and seizures. Ascertaining whether an impoundment is
justified by a reasonable and legitimate, non-pretextual
community-caretaking rationale is not an easy task. We
note that courts have considered the following non-
exclusive list of factors: (1) whether the vehicle is on
public or private property; (2) if on private property,

whether the property owner has been consulted; (3) whether an alternative to impoundment exists (especially another person capable of driving the vehicle); (4) whether the vehicle is implicated in a crime; and (5) whether the vehicle's owner and/or driver have consented to the impoundment." *U.S. v. Sanders*, 796 F.3d 1241, 1248–50 (10th Cir. 2015) (citations omitted).

- "If the police detect a weapon or contraband during a *Terry* search, they are entitled to seize it. This is true whether the *Terry* search is a simple frisk or a limited search beyond the person of the suspect. . . . Thus, upon detection of a weapon or contraband the officer may reach into a pocket and seize the item." *U.S. v. Thomson*, 354 F.3d 1197 (10th Cir. 2003).

D.C. Circuit

- "We begin with the demise of Wrinkles. 'Every circuit that has considered the issue has held that the killing of a companion dog constitutes a "seizure" within the meaning of the Fourth Amendment.' Those circuits have invariably concluded that 'the use of deadly force against a household pet is reasonable only if the pet poses an immediate danger and the use of force is unavoidable.' As in any Fourth Amendment case, '[w]e analyze [the] question [of whether a pet constitutes an imminent threat] from the perspective "of a reasonable officer on the scene, rather than with the 20/20 vision of hindsight."' This analysis 'allow[s] for the fact that police officers are often forced to make split-second judgments—in circumstances that are tense, uncertain, and rapidly evolving—about the amount of force that is necessary in a particular situation.' " *Robinson v. Pezzat*, 818 F.3d 1, 7–8 (D.C. Cir. 2016) (citations omitted).

§ 3:14 Seizure of homes: A dwelling may be secured while a search warrant is obtained

Supreme Court

- "An officer's authority to detain incident to a search is categorical; it does not depend on the 'quantum of proof justifying detention or the extent of the intrusion to be imposed by the seizure.' " *Muehler v. Mena*, 544 U.S. 93, 125 S. Ct. 1465, 161 L. Ed. 2d 299 (2005).

- "[T]he police officers in this case had probable cause to believe that a home contained contraband, which was evidence of a crime. They reasonably believed that the home's resident, if left free of any restraint, would destroy that evidence. And they imposed a restraint that was both limited and tailored reasonably to secure law enforcement needs while protecting privacy interests. In our view, the restraint met the Fourth Amendment's demands." *Illinois v. McArthur*, 531 U.S. 326, 121 S. Ct. 946, 953, 148 L. Ed. 2d 838 (2001).
- "We have found no case in which this Court has held unlawful a temporary seizure that was supported by probable cause and was designed to prevent the loss of evidence while the police diligently obtained a warrant in a reasonable period of time." *Illinois v. McArthur*, 531 U.S. 326, 121 S. Ct. 946, 951, 148 L. Ed. 2d 838 (2001).
- "The Fourth Amendment, made applicable to the States by the Fourteenth provides in pertinent part that the right of the people to be secure in their persons, houses, papers, and effects, against unreasonable searches and seizures, shall not be violated. A seizure of property, we have explained, occurs when there is some meaningful interference with an individual's possessory interests in that property. In addition, we have emphasized that at the very core of the Fourth Amendment stands the right of a man to retreat into his own home." *Soldal v. Cook County, Ill.*, 506 U.S. 56, 61, 113 S. Ct. 538, 121 L. Ed. 2d 450 (1992).
- "As we have noted, however, a seizure affects only possessory interests, not privacy interests. Therefore, the heightened protection we accord privacy interests is simply not implicated where a *seizure* of premises, not a search, is at issue. We hold, therefore, that securing a dwelling, on the basis of probable cause, to prevent the destruction or removal of evidence while a search warrant is being sought is not itself an unreasonable seizure of either the dwelling or its contents." *Segura v. U.S.*, 468 U.S. 796, 810, 104 S. Ct. 3380, 82 L. Ed. 2d 599 (1984).
- "Securing of the premises from within, however, was no more an interference with the petitioners' possessory interests in the contents of the apartment than a

perimeter stakeout. In other words, the initial entry—
legal or not—does not affect the reasonableness of the
seizure. Under either method—entry and securing from
within or a perimeter stakeout—agents control the
apartment pending arrival of the warrant; both an
internal securing and a perimeter stakeout interefere to
the same extent with the possessory interests of the
owners." *Segura v. U.S.*, 468 U.S. 796, 811, 104 S. Ct.
3380, 82 L. Ed. 2d 599 (1984).

- "[W]here officers, having probable cause, enter premises,
  and with probable cause, arrest the occupants who have
  legitimate possessory interests in its contents and take
  them into custody and, for no more than the period here
  invoked, secure the premises from within to preserve
  the status quo while others, in good faith, are in the
  process of obtaining a warrant, they do not violate the
  Fourth Amendment's proscription against unreasonable
  seizures." *Segura v. U.S.*, 468 U.S. 796, 798, 104 S. Ct.
  3380, 82 L. Ed. 2d 599 (1984).

Fifth Circuit

- "*Summers*. . .holds that the police have limited authority to detain the occupant of a house without probable
  cause while the premises is searched, when the detention is neither prolonged nor unduly intrusive, and
  when police are executing a validly executed search
  warrant for contraband." *Heitschmidt v. City of Houston*,
  161 F.3d 834, 838 (5th Cir. 1998).

Sixth Circuit

- "[W]here an intrusion is justified, whether by warrant
  or by probable cause and exigent circumstances, police
  are temporarily placed in control of the premises and
  its occupants. It is as though the premises were given
  to the officers in trust for such time as may be required
  to execute their search in safety and then depart. Officers in unquestioned command of a dwelling may
  violate that trust and exceed the scope of the authority
  implicitly granted them by their warrant when they
  permit unauthorized invasions of privacy by third parties who have no connection to the search warrant or
  the officers' purposes for being on the premises. The
  warrant in this case implicitly authorized the police of-

ficers to control and secure the premises during their search for a generator. It did not implicitly authorize them to invite a private security officer to tour plaintiff's home for the purpose of finding General Motors property." *Bills v. Aseltine*, 958 F.2d 697, 704 (6th Cir. 1992).

Seventh Circuit

- "No decision of the Supreme Court, including those we discuss below and those discussed by the dissent, has ever held that police may conduct a *Terry* frisk of a house or an apartment—that is, approach it on nothing but a suspicion that something is amiss and conduct a brief warrantless search. The fact that the police had only the vaguest information about the apartment building and apartment 7 is critical to our analysis as a whole, because it reveals that the officers were in essence conducting a general search in the hopes that something would turn up—the very kind of search the Fourth Amendment was designed to regulate." *U.S. v. Johnson*, 170 F.3d 708, 714 (7th Cir. 1999).

- "Because our law and legal traditions long have recognized the special vulnerability of those awakened in the night by a police intrusion at their dwelling place, our Fourth Amendment jurisprudence counsels that, when a knock at the door comes in the dead of night, the nature and effect of the intrusion into the privacy of the dwelling place must be examined with the greatest of caution. Therefore, in recognizing the particular intrusiveness of nocturnal encounters with the police at one's dwelling, the courts of appeals have stressed the impact of such encounters on the individual dwelling there. For instance, our colleagues in the First Circuit have noted specifically that the reason for limiting nocturnal searches is to prevent abrupt intrusions on sleeping residents in the dark. Likewise, the Second Circuit has noted the peculiar abrasiveness of intrusions by law enforcement officials at night. And the Tenth Circuit, in *Harless v. Turner* invalidated an individual's consent to search because it was obtained after the individual was routed out of bed in the middle of the night." *U.S. v. Jerez*, 108 F.3d 684, 690–91 (7th Cir. 1997).

- "It is also beyond doubt that [Defendant] was seized during execution of the search warrant. A reasonable person in [Defendant]'s situation would not have felt free to leave. Moreover, [Defendant] was not detained pursuant to an arrest warrant. Nor does the government contend that the law enforcement officers had probable cause to detain her prior to discovering the cocaine. Thus, we are left to determine whether [Defendant]'s detention fits into one of the several exceptions to the probable cause requirement. In *Michigan v. Summers*, the Supreme Court held that for Fourth Amendment purposes, a warrant to search for contraband founded on probable cause implicitly carries with it the limited authority to detain the occupants of the premises while a proper search is conducted. In that case, police officers were about to execute a search warrant when they encountered the owner of the house coming down the front steps. Once the police had gained admittance to the house, they brought the owner into the house and detained him during execution of the search warrant. During the search, the police found narcotics in the basement and subsequently placed the owner under formal arrest." *U.S. v. Burns*, 37 F.3d 276, 279 (7th Cir. 1994).

Eighth Circuit

- "Here, [Defendant] was not on his front steps or even near his home. He was stopped three to five miles away, hand-cuffed, and taken back to his house. The intrusiveness of the detention was therefore much greater than in *Summers*. Further, none of the law enforcement interests set forth in *Summers* apply. [Defendant] was not aware that a search was about to be conducted and therefore did not pose a risk of flight. There was no risk of harm to the agents from [Defendant] in a car miles away from the premises. The agents could hardly claim an interest in orderly completing the search with [Defendant's] aid in view of the fact that they kept him handcuffed and outside the house during the entire search." *U.S. v. Hogan*, 25 F.3d 690, 693 (8th Cir. 1994).

§ 3:15 Seizure under the Patriot Act: Warrant can be issued by court with subject matter jurisdiction, not just court with geographical jurisdiction

Seventh Circuit

- "The Uniting and Strengthening America by Providing Appropriate Tools to Intercept and Obstruct Terrorism Act (USA Patriot Act) made two significant changes to the statute governing seizure of electronic communications, by broadening the government's ability to obtain warrants for such communications: (1) search warrants could be issued using the procedures described in criminal procedure rules, rather than under those rules, and (2) search warrants could be issued by a court with jurisdiction over the offense under investigation, rather than exclusively by the court with geographical jurisdiction of the electronic property sought by the warrant." *U.S. v. Berkos*, 543 F.3d 392 (7th Cir. 2008).

§ 3:16 Seizure under the Patriot Act: Duration of detention

D.C. Circuit

- "[W]e turn to the argument that [defendant] must now be released according to longstanding law of war principles because the conflict with the Taliban has allegedly ended. . . . Even so, we do not rest our resolution of this issue on international law or mere common sense. The determination of when hostilities have ceased is a political decision, and we defer to the Executive's opinion on the matter, at least in the absence of an authoritative congressional declaration purporting to terminate the war. (citations omitted) . . . A clear statement requirement is at odds with the wide deference the judiciary is obliged to give to the democratic branches with regard to questions concerning national security. In the absence of a determination by the political branches that hostilities in Afghanistan have ceased, [defendant]'s continued detention is justified." *Al-Bihani v. Obama*, 590 F.3d 866 (D.C. Cir. 2010).

KeyCite®: Cases and other legal materials listed in KeyCite Scope can be researched through the KeyCite service on Westlaw. Use KeyCite to check citations for formal parallel references, prior and later history, and comprehensive citator information, including citations to other decisions and secondary materials.

Chapter 4

Arrest

Research References

West's Key Number Digest

Arrest ⚷63, 68, 70; Constitutional Law ⚷262; Courts ⚷495; Criminal Law ⚷217; Searches and Seizures ⚷24 to 25, 42, 113, 192

§ 4:1 Definition: An individual has been arrested when he is not free to go, whether or not formal words of arrest are used

Supreme Court

- "The officers had [Defendant's] ticket, they had his identification, and they had seized his luggage. [He] was never informed that he was free to board his plane if he so chose, and he reasonably believed that he was being detained. At least as of that moment, any consensual aspects of the encounter had evaporated. . . . As a practical matter, [Defendant] was under arrest. Consistent with this conclusion, the State conceded that [Defendant] would not have been free to leave the interrogation room had he asked to do so." *Florida v. Royer*, 460 U.S. 491, 503, 103 S. Ct. 1319, 75 L. Ed. 2d 229 (1983).

- "[D]etention for custodial interrogation—regardless of its label—intrudes so severely on interests protected by the Fourth Amendment as necessarily to trigger the traditional safeguards against illegal arrest." *Dunaway v. New York*, 442 U.S. 200, 216, 99 S. Ct. 2248, 60 L. Ed. 2d 824 (1979).

- "Nothing is more clear than that the Fourth Amendment was meant to prevent wholesale intrusions upon the personal security of our citizenry, whether these intrusions be termed arrests or investigatory detentions." *Davis v. Mississippi*, 394 U.S. 721, 726–27, 89 S. Ct. 1394, 22 L. Ed. 2d 676 (1969).

First Circuit

- "We appreciate 'that few people . . . would ever feel free to walk away from any police question.' But that reality obviously does not mean that every police-citizen encounter results in a show of authority for Fourth Amendment purposes. The 'free to leave' test thus focuses on whether the conduct of law enforcement '*objectively* communicate[s] that [law enforcement] is exercising [its] official authority to restrain the individual's liberty of movement.' The Supreme Court has identified several characteristics of an encounter with law enforcement that might indicate that there was a show of authority. These characteristics include: '[1] the threatening presence of several officers, [2] the display of a weapon by an officer, [3] some physical touching of the person of the citizen, or [4] the use of language or tone of voice indicating that compliance with the officer's request might be compelled.' " *U.S. v. Fields*, 823 F.3d 20, 25 (1st Cir. 2016) (citations omitted).

- "An arrest occurs when an officer, acting on probable cause that an individual has committed a crime, detains that individual as a suspect." *U.S. v. Young*, 105 F.3d 1, 6, 46 Fed. R. Evid. Serv. 307 (1st Cir. 1997).

Second Circuit

- "A seizure occurs when (1) a person obeys a police officer's order to stop or (2) a person that does not submit to an officer's show of authority is physically restrained. A police officer's order to stop constitutes a seizure if a reasonable person would have believed that he was not free to leave, and the person complies with the officer's order to stop. The grounds for a stop must exist at the time of the seizure. The grounds for a stop may be based on events that occur after the order to stop is given. Reasonable suspicion must arise before a search or seizure is actually effected. Flight in response to an order to stop is relevant to the reasonableness of a stop because it precedes the seizure, which occurs when the fleeing suspect is physically apprehended. Conversely, a person's compliance with an officer's order to stop where a reasonable person would not feel free to leave is a seizure, and sets the point in time for evaluating the presence of reasonable suspicion for the stop." *U.S. v. Simmons*, 560 F.3d 98 (2d Cir. 2009).

Third Circuit

- "The point at which an arrest occurs has been the subject of considerable judicial line-drawing. . . . In the most recent decision on the issue, the Supreme Court in *California v. Hodari D.* . . .explained that an arrest

185

requires either physical force. . . .or, where that is absent, submission to the assertion of authority." *Sharrar v. Felsing*, 128 F.3d 810, 819 (3d Cir. 1997).

- "In holding that the Fourth Amendment governed that case, the *Graham* Court implicitly held that an arrest is a continuing event that does not end as soon as a suspect is first restrained. Moreover, because *Graham* was handcuffed at the time of his assault, *Graham* shows that handcuffing is not necessarily the point at which a seizure ends for purposes of the application of the Fourth Amendment." *U.S. v. Johnstone*, 107 F.3d 200, 205 (3d Cir. 1997).

- "While [Defendant] emphasizes the fact that he was not free to leave the scene, this does not mark the point where a *Terry* stop escalates into an arrest, since in neither a stop nor an arrest is a suspect free to leave. Clearly, a *Terry* stop is a seizure and one seized is by definition not free to leave. Of course, we distinguish the length of time a suspect may be detained before the detention becomes a full-scale arrest, which we consider as a factor in evaluating the reasonableness of the detention as a whole in light of the circumstances." *U.S. v. Edwards*, 53 F.3d 616, 619–20 (3d Cir. 1995).

Sixth Circuit

- "To determine whether an investigative detention has crossed the line and become an arrest, this court considers factors such as the transportation of the detainee to another location, significant restraints on the detainee's freedom of movement involving physical confinement or other coercion preventing the detainee from leaving police custody, and the use of weapons or bodily force. . . .But there is no bright line that distinguishes an investigative detention from an arrest. . . . In the present case, the district court did not clearly err in finding that before defendants gave their consent to search the motel room, they were (1) stopped by four DEA agents brandishing firearms, (2) handcuffed, (3) placed into the backseats of separate DEA vehicles, (4) transported from the scene of the stop, (5) read their *Miranda* rights, and (6) questioned. The government. . . argues that all these measures were reasonably necessary for the protection of the DEA agents. The seizure in the present case, however, was more like an arrest than the seizure this court considered in *Houston*. In addition to taking the same protective measures as did the police officers in *Houston*, the DEA agents in the present case transported defendants from the scene of the stop and read them their *Miranda* rights. Each of these additional measures made the seizure more like an arrest. Moreover, in this case, defendants were not suspected of anything so dangerous as shooting a police officer, as was the case in *Houston*. . . . We therefore agree with the district court that the DEA agents had arrested defendants by the time defendants consented to the search of the motel room. Because the DEA agents lacked probable cause, the arrest was unlawful." *U.S. v. Lopez-Arias*, 344 F.3d 623, 2003 FED App. 0336P (6th Cir. 2003).

- "There is no doubt that at some point in the investigative process, police procedures can qualitatively and quantitatively be so intrusive with respect to a suspect's freedom of movement and privacy interests as to trigger the full protection of the Fourth and Fourteenth Amendments. And our view continues to be that the line is crossed when the police, without probable cause or a warrant, forcibly remove a person from his home or other place in which he is entitled to be and transport him to the police station, where he is detained, although briefly, for investigative purposes. We adhere to the view that such seizures, at least where not under judicial supervision, are sufficiently like arrests to invoke the traditional rule that arrests may constitutionally be made only on probable cause." *U.S. v. Obasa*, 15 F.3d 603, 608, 1994 FED App. 0035P (6th Cir. 1994).

Seventh Circuit

- "On the 'custodial' side of the ledger, the officers failed to inform Ruiz that he was not under arrest and was free to leave. Also, the manner in which the officers' vehicles—unmarked though they may have been— flanked Ruiz's car in the driveway and during the drive to the station subtly undermined the message that Ruiz was free to leave. Ruiz was asked to move from the driveway to the police station, although any custodial aspect of this was mitigated by the fact that Ruiz consented to the relocation (whether this consent was voluntary will be discussed below), and was permitted to drive his own car. On the 'non-custodial' side of the ledger, the entire encounter took place in public view. The district court found that the officers spoke to Ruiz in a calm, courteous manner throughout the encounter, which was designed to make Ruiz feel at ease. The officers were in plainclothes, with no display of weapons or force. The officers' unmarked vehicles did not block the driveway, and the marked squad car was parked across the street, two houses away. The Gurnee police officer in the squad car did not approach the driveway at any time, and she drove away in a different direction when Ruiz and the officers left the area. As the district court noted, the fact that the officers let Ruiz drive his own car to the station and retain possession of his driver's license and phones is a strong indicator that Ruiz was not in custody. When he arrived at the police station, Ruiz parked in a public lot rather than a secure lot. The subsequent conversation between Bakewell and Ruiz occurred beside Ruiz's car in the public lot. On balance, we think that Ruiz was not in custody prior to being *Mirandized* at the station." *U.S. v. Ruiz*, 785 F.3d 1134, 1145 (7th Cir. 2015).

- "In *Kernats v. O'Sullivan* we recognized that under this test, a fleeing suspect—even one who is confronted with an obvious show of authority—is not seized until his freedom of movement is terminated by intentional application of physical force or by the suspect's submission to the asserted authority. We have also recognized that neither a police officer who chases a suspect unsuccessfully nor an officer who yells stop at a fleeing person has effected a seizure." *U.S. v. $32,400.00, in U.S. Currency*, 82 F.3d 135, 139 (7th Cir. 1996).

Ninth Circuit

- "The officers handcuffed Sialoi Sialoi Jr. and placed him in the back of the police car after he pleaded with the officers to stop pointing their weapons at the children. Sialoi Sialoi Jr. did 'raise his voice' and initially refused to raise his hands when directed to do so by the police, but he calmed down within a matter of minutes and complied with the officers' requests when they approached him for the purpose of handcuffing him. As with the three teenagers, the factors set forth in *Washington* compel the conclusion that a rational jury could find that the officers' conduct with respect to Sialoi Sialoi Jr. amounted to an arrest. Similarly to G.S., T.O.S., and B.F., the officers patted Sialoi Sialoi Jr. down, handcuffed him, and placed him in the back of a police car. By this time, over twenty officers had arrived at the scene, many of whom had their weapons drawn and trained on the plaintiffs. The defendants argue that the seizure of Sialoi Sialoi Jr. was a mere detention because he was initially uncooperative. We cannot say, however, as defendants argue, that Sialoi Sialoi Jr.'s temporary refusal to raise his hands and initial objection to the officers' tactics would as a matter of law prevent a rational jury from concluding that he was arrested. To the contrary—in cases in which we have relied on an individual's non-compliance with officers' commands to hold as a matter of law that an arrest did not occur, the individual demonstrated far greater, and far more dangerous, defiance. Accordingly, taking the facts in the light most favorable to Sialoi Sialoi Jr., the officers' conduct amounted to an arrest." *Sialoi v. City of San Diego*, 823 F.3d 1223, 1233–34 (9th Cir. 2016) (citations omitted).

- "There is no bright-line rule to determine when an investigatory stop becomes an arrest. Rather, in determining whether stops have turned into arrests, courts consider the totality of the circumstances. As might be expected, the ultimate decision in such cases is fact-specific. In looking at the totality of the circumstances, we consider both the intrusiveness of the stop, i.e., the aggressiveness of the police methods and how much the plaintiff's liberty was restricted and the justification for the use of such tactics, i.e., whether the officer had sufficient basis to fear for his safety to warrant the intrusiveness of the action taken. In short, we decide whether the police action constitutes a *Terry* stop or an arrest by evaluating not only how intrusive the stop was, but also whether the methods used were reasonable given the specific circumstances. As a result, we have held that while certain police actions constitute an arrest in certain circumstances, e.g., where the

suspects are cooperative, those same actions may not
constitute an arrest where the suspect is uncooperative
or the police have specific reasons to believe that a serious threat to the safety of the officers exists. The relevant inquiry is always one of reasonableness under the
circumstances." *Washington v. Lambert*, 98 F.3d 1181,
1185 (9th Cir. 1996).

Tenth Circuit

- "An arrest occurs when the police use a show of official
  authority such that a reasonable person would have
  believed he was not free to leave." *U.S. v. Edwards*, 632
  F.3d 633, 639 (10th Cir. 2001).

- "However, after approximately 5:00 a.m. there was no
  reasonable basis for keeping [Defendants] in handcuffs.
  Therefore, we must conclude that at that point their
  detention became an unlawful arrest. [Defendant] was
  unlawfully arrested after she was transported from the
  scene of the stop to the police station. Transportation of
  a defendant to the police station can not be justified
  absent probable cause to believe the defendant committed a crime." *U.S. v. Shareef*, 100 F.3d 1491, 1508 (10th
  Cir. 1996).

D.C. Circuit

- "For purposes of the Fourth Amendment, a stop that is
  unduly prolonged or intrusive transforms from an
  investigative stop into an arrest requiring probable
  cause. The point at which an investigative stop becomes
  an arrest is not marked with a bright line. Rather, the
  Court has 'emphasized the need to consider the law
  enforcement purposes to be served by the stop as well
  as the time reasonably needed to effectuate those
  purposes.' In other words, investigative detention must
  last 'no longer than is necessary to effectuate the
  purpose of the stop.' . . . . Relevant to that inquiry, and
  particularly germane on these alleged facts, is 'whether
  the police diligently pursued a means of investigation
  that was likely to confirm or dispel their suspicions
  quickly, during which time it was necessary to detain
  the defendant.' An investigatory stop 'to maintain the
  status quo momentarily while obtaining more information' would have been 'most reasonable in light of the

facts known to [Lee] at the time.' Hall's complaint alleges that Lee did not, however, undertake even the most basic means of investigation that could 'confirm or dispel [her] suspicions quickly.' Officer Lee did not attempt to verify Cities' contentions before handcuffing Hall, forcibly removing her from the bar, and putting her in the police cruiser. And Lee failed to ask simple questions that might have uncovered that Hall had already provided her credit card, Cities may have already charged $935.04 to that card, Hall never actually refused to pay or left under circumstances suggesting she did not intend to return to settle her bill, and Hall's friends were still present and might have had the authority and intention to pay or to contact Hall to confirm her intentions. Moreover, Lee detained Hall for forty-five minutes, which a jury could find to be far longer than reasonably necessary to effectuate the purposes of an investigative stop, particularly given that the police found Hall close to Cities and all the relevant witnesses. On the facts as alleged, Officer Lee's detention of Hall amounted to an arrest. . . . We are mindful that courts should not indulge in 'unrealistic second-guessing' of an officer's assessment in a 'swiftly developing situation.' But here, on the facts as pleaded, the matter was quickly resolved once the police asked Hall a few, basic questions. In other words, we need not indulge any counterfactuals. Another officer's actions at the scene show that, if Officer Lee had simply asked Hall about the bill Cities claimed that Hall refused to pay, Lee quickly would have discovered that Hall's arrest and detention were unnecessary and unjustified." *Hall v. District of Columbia*, 867 F.3d 138, 153 (D.C. Cir. 2017) (citations omitted).

§ 4:2 Standard: An arrest must be based upon probable cause

Supreme Court

- "*Atwater* addressed the perhaps more fundamental question of who may be deprived of liberty and taken to jail in the first place. The case involved a woman who was arrested after a police officer noticed neither she nor her children were wearing their seatbelts. The ar-

191

restee argued the Fourth Amendment prohibited her custodial arrest without a warrant when an offense could not result in jail time and there was no compelling need for immediate detention. The Court held that a Fourth Amendment restriction on this power would put officers in an 'almost impossible spot.' Their ability to arrest a suspect would depend in some cases on the precise weight of drugs in his pocket, whether he was a repeat offender, and the scope of what counted as a compelling need to detain someone. The Court rejected the proposition that the Fourth Amendment barred custodial arrests in a set of these cases as a matter of constitutional law. It ruled, based on established principles, that officers may make an arrest based upon probable cause to believe the person has committed a criminal offense in their presence. The Court stated that 'a responsible Fourth Amendment balance is not well served by standards requiring sensitive, case-by-case determinations of government need, lest every discretionary judgment in the field be converted into an occasion for constitutional review.'" *Florence v. Board of Chosen Freeholders of County of Burlington*, 566 U.S. 318, 132 S. Ct. 1510, 1517–18, 182 L. Ed. 2d 566 (2012) (citations omitted).

- "[A]n arresting officer's state of mind (except for the facts that he knows) is irrelevant to the existence of probable cause. That is to say, his subjective reason for making the arrest need not be the criminal offense as to which the known facts provide probable cause. As we have repeatedly explained, 'the fact that the officer does not have the state of mind which is hypothecated by the reasons which provide the legal justification for the officer's action does not invalidate the action taken as long as the circumstances, viewed objectively, justify that action.'. . . The rule that the offense establishing probable cause must be 'closely related' to, and based on the same conduct as, the offense identified by the arresting officer at the time of arrest is inconsistent with this precedent." *Devenpeck v. Alford*, 543 U.S. 146, 125 S. Ct. 588, 160 L. Ed. 2d 537 (2004).

- "The question is whether the Fourth Amendment forbids a warrantless arrest for a minor criminal offense, such as a misdemeanor seatbelt violation punishable only by a fine. We hold that it does not." *Atwater v. City of Lago Vista*, 532 U.S. 318, 121 S. Ct. 1536, 1541, 149 L. Ed. 2d 549 (2001).

- "Articulating precisely what reasonable suspicion and probable cause mean is not possible. They are commonsense, nontechnical conceptions that deal with the factual and practical considerations of everyday life on which reasonable and prudent men, not legal technicians, act. As such, the standards are not readily, or even usefully, reduced to a neat set of legal rules." *Ornelas v. U.S.*, 517 U.S. 690, 695–96, 116 S. Ct. 1657, 134 L. Ed. 2d 911 (1996).

- "[P]robable cause to arrest [Defendant] did not exist at the time he consented to the search of his luggage. The facts are that a nervous young man with two American Tourister bags paid cash for an airline ticket to a target city. These facts led to inquiry, which in turn revealed that the ticket had been bought under an assumed name. The proffered explanation did not satisfy the officers. We cannot agree with the State, if this is its position, that every nervous young man paying cash for a ticket to New York City under an assumed name and carrying two heavy American Tourister bags may be arrested and held to answer for a serious felony charge." *Florida v. Royer*, 460 U.S. 491, 507, 103 S. Ct. 1319, 75 L. Ed. 2d 229 (1983).

- "[T]he general rule [is] that every arrest, and every seizure having the essential attributes of a formal arrest, is unreasonable unless it is supported by probable cause." *Michigan v. Summers*, 452 U.S. 692, 700, 101 S. Ct. 2587, 69 L. Ed. 2d 340 (1981).

- "[P]robable cause to justify an arrest means facts and circumstances within the officer's knowledge that are sufficient to warrant a prudent person, or one of reasonable caution, in believing, in the circumstances shown, that the suspect has committed, is committing, or is about to commit an offense." *Michigan v. DeFillippo*, 443 U.S. 31, 37, 99 S. Ct. 2627, 61 L. Ed. 2d 343 (1979).

- "Where the standard is probable cause, a search or seizure of a person must be supported by probable cause particularized with respect to that person. This requirement cannot be undercut or avoided by simply pointing to the fact that coincidentally there exists probable cause to search or seize another or to search the premises where the person may happen to be." *Ybarra v. Illinois*, 444 U.S. 85, 91, 100 S. Ct. 338, 62 L. Ed. 2d 238 (1979).

- "[G]ood faith on the part of the arresting officers is not enough. Probable cause exists if the facts and circumstances known to the officer warrant a prudent man in believing that the offense has been committed." *Henry v. U.S.*, 361 U.S. 98, 102, 80 S. Ct. 168, 4 L. Ed. 2d 134 (1959).

First Circuit

- "Where warrantless arrests for criminal offenses are concerned, the Fourth Amendment is satisfied if the arresting officer had probable cause and the arrest was reasonable under the totality of the circumstances." *Diaz v. City of Fitchburg*, 176 F.3d 560, 563 (1st Cir. 1999).

Second Circuit

- "A police officer ordinarily has probable cause to arrest when he or she 'ha[s] knowledge of, or reasonably trustworthy information as to, facts and circumstances that are sufficient to warrant a person of reasonable caution in the belief that an offense has been or is being committed by the person to be arrested.' An officer's assessment in this regard need not 'be perfect' because 'the Fourth Amendment allows for some mistakes on the part of government officials,' including 'reasonable mistakes of law.'. . . .Officer Aybar's probable-cause determination was predicated on the New York open-container law, which provides that '[n]o person shall drink or consume an alcoholic beverage, or possess, with intent to drink or consume, an open container containing an alcoholic beverage in any public place,' where 'public place' is defined, in pertinent part, as '[a] place to which the public or a substantial group of persons has access, including, but not limited to, any highway, street, road, sidewalk, parking area, shopping area, place of amusement, playground, park or beach located within the city,' Diaz argues that the apartment-building stairwell where he was found with an open container of alcohol is not a 'public place' because, although it is a common area, it is located within a locked residential building. In his view, canons of construction such as *ejusdem generis* and *noscitur a sociis* support his construction of the open-container law. But as the district court correctly acknowledged, the question presented here is not whether a common area of an apartment such as a stairwell constitutes a public place within the meaning of the open-container law, but only whether Officer Aybar had an objectively reasonable belief that it so qualified. . . . .We think that Officer Aybar's belief that the apartment-building stairwell qualified as a 'public place' within the meaning of the open-container law was an objectively reasonable prediction of the scope of the law when it was made. [H]er assessment was premised on a reasonable interpretation of an ambiguous state law, the scope of which had not yet been clarified. Even now, the New York Court of Appeals has not addressed whether a common area inside an apartment building is a 'public place' within the meaning of the open-container law, and the other New York courts that have done so have reached conflicting conclusions. In light of these conflicting precedents, Officer Aybar's belief that an apartment-building stairwell is a public place within the meaning of the open-container law was a reasonable, even if mistaken, assessment of the scope of that law at the time it was made. Thus, contrary to Diaz's contention, Officer Aybar had probable cause to believe that Diaz had violated the open-container law." *United States v. Diaz*, 854 F.3d 197, 202–205 (2d Cir. 2017) (citations and footnotes omitted).

• "The existence of probable cause to arrest—even for a crime other than the one identified by the arresting officer—will defeat a claim of false arrest under the Fourth Amendment. 'Probable cause to arrest exists when the arresting officer has knowledge or reasonably trustworthy information of facts and circumstances that are sufficient to warrant a person of reasonable caution in the belief that the person to be arrested has committed or is committing a crime.' Probable cause is a 'fluid' standard that 'does not demand hard certainties or mechanistic inquiries'; nor does it 'demand that an officer's good-faith belief that a suspect has committed or is committing a crime be correct or more likely true than false.' Rather, it requires only facts establishing 'the kind of fair probability' on which a 'reasonable and prudent' person, as opposed to a 'legal technician[ ],' would rely." *Figueroa v. Mazza*, 825 F.3d 89, 99 (2d Cir. 2016) (citations omitted).

- "On the facts viewed in the light most favorable to Ms. Simpson, a passenger was stuck on the lift at the front of the bus. The bus driver directed the crowd, which included Officer Nelson and Ms. Simpson, to 'Go around, go around' to the back entrance of the bus, and he opened the back doors. Ms. Simpson and the other passengers then moved to the back entrance and boarded. Once on the bus, Ms. Simpson waited in line behind other passengers to swipe her MetroCard. Officer Nelson stopped Ms. Simpson, ordered her not to pay her bus fare, and demanded that she follow him off the bus. On these facts, no reasonable officer could have concluded that Ms. Simpson intended to commit theft of services any more than a reasonable officer could have concluded that a person at the grocery store directed to a checkout counter and waiting in line to pay for produce intended to commit petit larceny. Add to this scenario the reasonable inference that Officer Nelson (1) was upset by having been rebuffed and (2) was merely demonstrating his dominance, and any pretense of reasonableness flies out the window." *Simpson v. City of New York*, 793 F.3d 259, 269 (2d Cir. 2015).

- "In order to have a reasonable belief that probable cause exists, an officer need not anticipate or investigate every possible defense that a person suspected of violating the law may have, and an officer may have probable cause despite knowledge of facts that create an arguable defense. On the other hand, as *Cox* and *Papineau* clearly establish, an officer may not constitutionally arrest a demonstrator when he is personally aware that responsible officials have implicitly or explicitly authorized the very conduct for which he seeks to make the arrest. As the Seventh Circuit has held, '[o]nce a police officer discovers sufficient facts to establish probable cause, she has no constitutional obligation to conduct any further investigation in the hope of discovering exculpatory evidence,' but '[a] police officer may not ignore conclusively established evidence of the existence of an affirmative defense.' Taking plaintiffs' allegations as true, as we must, we believe that they have adequately alleged actionable conduct. Plaintiffs have alleged that the police directed the demonstrators' activity along the route of their march, at times specifically condoning, or even directing, behavior that on its face would violate traffic laws. . . . [T]he police then retreated back onto the Bridge in a way that would reasonably have been understood, and was understood, by the bulk of the demonstrators to be a continuation of the earlier practice of allowing the march to proceed in violation of normal traffic rules." *Garcia v. Does*, 764 F.3d 170, 181–82 (2d Cir. 2014) (citations omitted).

Third Circuit

- "Based on the standard set by the Supreme Court in *Beck*, the district court erred in concluding that there was probable cause to arrest and search [Defendant] prior to the discovery of the guns. The mere fact that [Defendant] is black and the perpetrators had been described as two black males is plainly insufficient. . . . Moreover, the match between the description of the perpetrators' car. . .and the vehicle in which [Defendant] was spotted. . .was far from precise. . . . Nor is probable cause established by either the location or time of the stop. . . . In other words, armed with information that two black males driving a black sports car were believed to have committed three robberies in the area some relatively short time earlier, [the] Officer. . .could not justifiably arrest any African-American man who happened to drive by in any type of black sports car." *U.S. v. Kithcart*, 134 F.3d 529, 531–32 (3d Cir. 1998).

Fifth Circuit

- "As a general matter, the detention of a witness that is indistinguishable from custodial interrogation requires no less probable cause than a traditional arrest." *Lincoln v. Barnes*, 855 F.3d 297, 304 (5th Cir. 2017) (citations omitted).

Sixth Circuit

- "The crux of the issue in this case is whether the phone call to the police stating 'that [Courtright] had come out of his room with a gun and threatened to shoot another resident's dog' was sufficient to establish probable cause for Courtright's arrest. . . . [B]ecause 'eyewitnesses' statements are based on firsthand observations, they are generally entitled to a presumption of reliability and veracity.' . . . [O]n the other hand, . . . the phone call was an individual's 'mere allegation' of criminal activity that 'may [have] create[d] reasonable suspicion justifying an investigative stop under [*Terry v. Ohio*], but [fell] short of creating probable cause absent some corroborating evidence of wrongdoing.' Although there is 'some tension' [in the case law], we recently clarified that 'those cases also contain an important limiting factor: Probable cause is created only by eyewitness allegations that are *reasonably trustworthy*, and thus probable cause does *not* exist where there is an apparent reason for the officer to believe that the eyewitness was lying, did not accurately describe what he had seen, or was in some fashion mistaken regarding his recollection.' . . . At best, Wolf had reasonable suspicion for an investigatory stop under *Terry v. Ohio*, at the time that he arrived at Courtright's room. Therefore, to legitimate an arrest of Courtright, Wolf would have needed to discover more information or evidence at the Traveler's Inn that would have established probable cause for an arrest." *Courtright v. City of Battle Creek*, 839 F.3d 513, 521–23 (6th Cir. 2016) (citations omitted).
- "Probable cause could not have been based on Smith's words. Ohio courts have not treated speech alone as an act for purposes of the statute. Hence, the only relevant affirmative act was Smith withdrawing her hand when Officer Murphy grabbed it. Drawing all reasonable inferences in Smith's favor, this withdrawal may have been simply an involuntary reaction to an unexpected touch. And, giving Smith the benefit of the doubt, she had no intention of obstructing the officers in their duties. Nor did she delay them for more than a few seconds. After pulling her hand away, she walked downstairs as directed and did not resist being handcuffed. In sum, on the facts as Smith relates them, her conduct did not provide probable cause to arrest her

for obstructing official business in violation of Ohio law. Hence, the officers arrested her in violation of the Fourth Amendment." *Smith v. City of Wyoming*, 821 F.3d 697, 716 (6th Cir. 2016) (citation omitted).

- "The Fourth Amendment conditions warrants on probable cause and prohibits unreasonable seizures. A police officer violates those restrictions only when his deliberate or reckless falsehoods result in arrest and prosecution without probable cause. The resulting claim, what might be called an 'unreasonable prosecutorial seizure' claim, is traditionally known as a 'malicious prosecution' claim." *Newman v. Township of Hamburg*, 773 F.3d 769, 771–72 (6th Cir. 2014) (citations omitted).

- "Defendant was a passenger in a vehicle that was pulled over for driving with a broken taillight. When asked for identification, the driver immediately admitted that he did not have a valid license—a misdemeanor criminal offense. The driver was arrested and locked in the back of the patrol car. At that point, officers returned to the vehicle to 'make contact' with Defendant, who was still seated in the passenger seat. The officers did not have any reason to suspect that Defendant was engaged in any criminal activity or that Defendant was armed and dangerous. Nevertheless, the officers ordered Defendant out of the vehicle and told him to put his hands on his head with his fingers interlaced. Officers then began to escort Defendant to the patrol car to search him for weapons and/or drugs. While Defendant was being escorted to the patrol car for a 'pat down' search, he broke free and ran away. The officers pursued Defendant, but did not make any audible commands for him to stop. After Defendant was chased and apprehended by officers, he was searched and found to be carrying a pistol and two bags of hashish, a derivative of marijuana. . . . We agree with the district court that the firearm and the hashish recovered during the search are inadmissible because they were recovered in violation of Defendant's Fourth Amendment rights. The district court correctly determined that the purpose of the traffic stop had been accomplished after the driver was arrested, and Defendant was unlawfully detained after the traffic stop was completed. We further agree with the district court's finding that the officers lacked reasonable suspicion to justify prolonging the traffic stop. Under the circumstances, the officers should have advised Defendant that the vehicle was being impounded and informed Defendant that he was free to go." *U.S. v. Cheatham*, 577 Fed. Appx. 500, 501–20 (6th Cir. 2014) (citations omitted).

Seventh Circuit

- "Probable cause is an absolute defense to any claim under § 1983 for wrongful arrest or false imprisonment." *Bailey v. City of Chicago*, 779 F.3d 689, 694 (7th Cir. 2015), cert. denied, 136 S. Ct. 200, 193 L. Ed. 2d 129 (2015).

- "While it is true that the testimony of a single, impartial eyewitness is sufficient to support probable cause, there is no corresponding rule to account for identifications obtained from persons who were not eyewitnesses to an event but viewed video footage afterwards." *Bailey v. City of Chicago*, 779 F.3d 689, 694 (7th Cir. 2015), cert. denied, 136 S. Ct. 200, 193 L. Ed. 2d 129 (2015) (citation omitted).

- "The government contends that this case is governed by the 'collective knowledge doctrine,' under which the police who actually make the arrest need not personally know all the facts that constitute probable cause if they reasonably are acting at the direction of another officer or police agency. In that case, the arrest is proper so long as the knowledge of the officer directing the arrest, or the collective knowledge of the agency he works for, is sufficient to constitute probable cause. . . . Courts have applied the collective knowledge doctrine in two situations: first, when information from one jurisdiction is actually relayed to officers or agencies in another jurisdiction to permit coordination of investigations and the speedy apprehension of fleeing suspects, . . . and second, when officers are in communication with each other while working together at a scene. In the latter group of cases, the knowledge of the officers may be imputed to one another even when there is no express testimony that the specific or detailed information creating the justification for a stop was conveyed (though of course the information actually possessed by the of-

ficers must be sufficient to justify the stop or arrest)."
U.S. v. Parra, 402 F.3d 752, 66 Fed. R. Evid. Serv. 1088
(7th Cir. 2005).

- "Arrest for a minor, non-jailable offense does not violate
  the Fourth Amendment. When officers have probable
  cause to believe that an individual has committed an offense in their presence, they may arrest the offender. . .
  . *Atwater* makes clear that even non-violent misdemeanor offenses, such as unauthorized ticket sales, can
  support an arrest under the Fourth Amendment, as
  long as the officer had probable cause to believe the offense had been committed." *Chortek v. City of Milwaukee*,
  356 F.3d 740 (7th Cir. 2004).

- "In order to have probable cause for an arrest, law
  enforcement agents must reasonably believe, in light of
  the facts and circumstances within their knowledge at
  the time of the arrest, that the suspect had committed
  or was committing an offense. . . .The probable cause
  standard is a flexible, practical common-sense one
  which is met if the facts are sufficient to warrant a
  person of reasonable caution to believe that an offense
  has been or is being committed." *U.S. v. Hayes*, 236
  F.3d 891, 894 (7th Cir. 2001).

- "A police officer has probable cause to arrest when, at
  the moment the decision is made, the facts and circumstances within her knowledge and of which she has reasonably trustworthy information would warrant a
  prudent person in believing that the suspect had committed or was committing an offense. . . . This flexible,
  commonsense approach does not require that the officer's belief be correct or even more likely true than
  false, so long as it is reasonable. . . . Moreover, this is
  an ex ante test: the fact that the officer later discovers
  additional evidence unknown to her at the time of the
  arrest is irrelevant to whether probable cause existed
  at the crucial time." *Qian v. Kautz*, 168 F.3d 949,
  953–54 (7th Cir. 1999).

Eighth Circuit

- "Where officers work together on an investigation, we
  have used the so-called 'collective knowledge' theory to
  impute the knowledge of one officer to others. We
  impute information if there has been some degree of

communication between the officers. This requirement
distinguishes officers functioning as a team from officers acting as independent actors who merely happen
to be investigating the same subject." *U.S. v. Terry*, 400
F.3d 575 (8th Cir. 2005).

- "[B]ecause the totality of circumstances determines the
existence of probable cause, evidence that tends to negate the possibility that a suspect has committed a
crime is relevant to whether the officer has probable
cause. An officer contemplating an arrest is not free to
disregard plainly exculpatory evidence, even if substantial inculpatory evidence (standing by itself) suggests
that probable cause exists. . . . In this sense, the
Fourth Amendment requires that we analyze the weight
of all the evidence—not merely the sufficiency of the incriminating evidence. . . ." *Kuehl v. Burtis*, 173 F.3d
646, 650 (8th Cir. 1999).

- "[O]fficers did not have probable cause to arrest
[Defendant] in a bus station when he appeared to be in
a hurry, carried a new bag, arrived from a source city
for narcotics, and had observable bulges under his shirt.
. . . . [T]he presence of the bulges could have been
bandages, a money belt, or any number of non-
contraband items. . . . [E]ven after the officer felt a
bulge and determined it was not a part of the defendant's anatomy, we held the officer did not have probable cause to arrest." *U.S. v. Eustaquio*, 198 F.3d 1068,
1071 (8th Cir. 1999).

Ninth Circuit

- "Where no specific criminal statute validly applies to
the facts at hand, an arrest is not supported by probable cause." *Santopietro v. Howell*, 857 F.3d 980, 987
(9th Cir. 2017).

- "Taking the facts in the light most favorable to the
plaintiffs, the officers did not have probable cause to arrest the three teenagers. The defendants attempt to
justify the arrest on the basis of the fact that G.S. was
initially holding what appeared to be a weapon. We
may assume that the officers were justified in initiating
an investigatory stop of the teenagers after they spotted
what they believed to be a gun in G.S.'s hand. The police determined almost immediately after approaching

G.S., however, that the gun was, in fact, a toy, and at that point any suspicion that the teenagers were engaged in a crime dissipated. Not only did none of the teenagers possess a gun, but none of them in any way matched the apartment manager's description of the suspects. They were three Samoan teenagers, not two black adults, and none of the boys was wearing either a brown shirt or a hooded long-sleeved T-shirt. Nevertheless, the officers handcuffed all three and placed them in the back of a police car *after* learning that the item in G.S.'s hand was a toy. At a minimum, then, the officers violated the Fourth Amendment by continuing the seizure beyond the point at which they determined that G.S. had not in fact had a weapon in his hand." *Sialoi v. City of San Diego*, 823 F.3d 1223, 1232–33 (9th Cir. 2016).

- "An individual's temporary refusal to comply with an officer's commands is not in itself a valid basis for an arrest. Nor is an individual's peaceful, verbal challenge to police action a valid basis." *Sialoi v. City of San Diego*, 823 F.3d 1223, 1234 (9th Cir. 2016) (citations omitted).
- "As with the three teenagers, the background circumstances on which the defendants rely to establish qualified immunity (the officers presence in a high-crime area) do not make it even 'reasonably arguable' that probable cause existed to arrest Sialoi Sialoi Jr." *Sialoi v. City of San Diego*, 823 F.3d 1223, 1234 (9th Cir. 2016).
- "As we have recognized, '[b]ecause the excessive force and false arrest factual inquiries are distinct, establishing a lack of probable cause to make an arrest does not establish an excessive force claim, and vice-versa.' Just proving lack of probable cause for the arrest, for instance, does not establish that the police used excessive force, or, indeed, any force. And force used by an officer to effectuate an arrest, 'regardless of whether [the officer] had probable cause to [make the] arrest,' may still be reasonable, for instance to overcome the arrestee's forcible resistance. Nevertheless, *Graham* counsels that the facts that gave rise to an unlawful detention or arrest can factor into the determination whether the force used to make the arrest was excessive." *Velazquez v. City of Long Beach*, 793 F.3d 1010, 1024 (9th Cir. 2015) (citations omitted).

- "[A] person's mere presence or mere propinquity to criminal activity alone does not support probable cause to search or arrest that person." *U.S. v. Buckner*, 179 F.3d 834, 838 (9th Cir. 1999).

Tenth Circuit

- "Probable cause doesn't require proof that something is more likely true than false. It requires only a 'fair probability,' a standard understood to mean something more than a 'bare suspicion' but less than a preponderance of the evidence at hand." *U.S. v. Denson*, 775 F.3d 1214, 1217 (10th Cir. 2014), cert. denied, 135 S. Ct. 2064, 191 L. Ed. 2d 967 (2015).
- "If the police learn information that destroys their probable cause to arrest a defendant, the arrest may become illegal." *U.S. v. Edwards*, 632 F.3d 633, 640 (10th Cir. 2001).

Eleventh Circuit

- "A warrantless arrest without probable cause violates the Constitution and provides a basis for a section 1983 claim but the existence of probable cause at the time of arrest constitutes an absolute bar to a section 1983 action for false arrest. If no constitutional right would have been violated were the allegations established, there is no necessity for further inquiries concerning qualified immunity. Probable cause to arrest exists when law enforcement officials have facts and circumstances within their knowledge sufficient to warrant a reasonable belief that the suspect had committed or was committing a crime. If a constitutional violation occurred because the officer lacked probable cause, it must be determined whether arguable probable cause existed. Arguable probable cause exists where reasonable officers in the same circumstances and possessing the same knowledge as the Defendant could have believed that probable cause existed to arrest." *Case v. Eslinger*, 555 F.3d 1317 (11th Cir. 2009).

D.C. Circuit

- "Having concluded that Hall's detention was an arrest, not a mere investigatory stop, we consider whether Officer Lee acted with the requisite probable cause.

Whether an officer acted with probable cause is an objective inquiry, dependent on whether the officer acted on the basis of 'reasonably trustworthy information . . . sufficient to warrant a prudent [person] in believing that the [suspect] had committed or was committing an offense.' The precise point at which probable cause arises is 'fluid,' and requires a 'totality-of-the-circumstances analysis.' . . . Probable cause to arrest requires at least some evidence supporting each element of the offense. The complaint alleges Officer Lee told Hall she was being detained for committing '[t]heft of services.' Prima facie evidence of theft of services is evidence that 'a person obtained services that he or she knew or had reason to believe were available to him or her only for compensation,' but the person 'departed from the place where the services were obtained knowing or having reason to believe that no payment had been made for the services rendered.' According to the complaint, the officers acted on the basis of a phone call from Cities accusing Hall of theft of services. The complaint alleges the call was placed after Cities had already charged Hall's bill to her card and received approval from the credit card company. The facts as alleged thus do not support the reported theft of services. There are no allegations, moreover, that officers took even the simplest steps to verify the details of the ostensible payment refusal. Taking the allegations of the complaint in the light most favorable to Hall and in the absence of information to corroborate Cities' assertions that Hall abandoned her bill, the district court could not conclude as a matter of law that the police had probable cause to conclude that Hall had committed or was committing theft of services. . . . A phone call from a member of the public lodging a complaint is not alone probable cause when the caller is not known to the police as reliable and when the complaint could readily be verified but is not (as here, where the police failed to ask Hall whether she in fact refused to pay)—at least in a circumstance such as the complaint Cities lodged here, which did not implicate an emergency situation, threatening conduct, a matter of public safety, or similar urgent concerns. If it were otherwise, members of the public could routinely call the police and, on the caller's word alone, get their enemies locked up." *Hall v. District of Columbia*, 867 F.3d 138, 154 (D.C. Cir. 2017) (citations omitted).

§ 4:3 Arrests in public places: A warrant is not required to arrest in a public place, even if it were feasible to obtain one

Supreme Court

- "An arrest is reasonable, for Fourth Amendment purposes, when an officer has probable cause to believe that arrestee committed even a minor crime in officer's presence. In such situation, warrantless arrests are reasonable under the Fourth Amendment, and while states are free to regulate such arrests however they desire, state restrictions do not alter the Fourth Amendment protections." *Virginia v. Moore*, 553 U.S. 164, 128 S. Ct. 1598, 170 L. Ed. 2d 559 (2008).

- "[A]lthough a warrant presumptively is required for a felony arrest in a suspect's home, the Fourth Amendment permits warrantless arrests in public places where an officer has probable cause to believe that a felony has occurred. . . . In explaining this rule, we have drawn upon the established distinction between a warrantless seizure in an open area and such a seizure on private premises." *Florida v. White*, 526 U.S. 559, 565–66, 119 S. Ct. 1555, 143 L. Ed. 2d 748 (1999).

- "[I]f probable cause exists, no warrant is required to apprehend a suspected felon in a public place." *Steagald v. U.S.*, 451 U.S. 204, 221, 101 S. Ct. 1642, 68 L. Ed. 2d 38 (1981).

- "[A] warrantless arrest in a public place is valid if the arresting officer had probable cause to believe the suspect is a felon." *Payton v. New York*, 445 U.S. 573, 590, 100 S. Ct. 1371, 63 L. Ed. 2d 639 (1980).

- "Law enforcement officers may find it wise to seek arrest warrants where practicable to do so, and their judgments about probable cause may be more readily accepted where backed by a warrant issued by a magistrate. But we decline to transform this judicial preference into a constitutional rule when the judgment of the Nation and Congress has for so long been to authorize warrantless public arrests on probable cause."

U.S. v. Watson, 423 U.S. 411, 423, 96 S. Ct. 820, 46 L. Ed. 2d 598 (1976).

First Circuit

- "The Supreme Court has refused to attach significance to the fact that the government had ample time to obtain a warrant but declined to procure one. Specifically, the Court stated that [t]he necessary inquiry [is] not whether there was a warrant or whether there was time to get one, but whether there was probable cause at the time of the arrest. Indeed, the government in *Watson* conceded that it had more than sufficient time to have obtained a warrant prior to the arrest. The Constitution does not require a warrant to effect an arrest in a public place. Moreover, law enforcement agents need only possess reasonable suspicion that a criminal activity is occurring in order to stop a moving automobile to investigate. Here, it is undisputed that the FBI agents had probable cause to stop the green van when it entered the Port Plaza Shopping Center. The arrests of [the Defendants] were effected in a public place, the middle of the shopping center parking lot. Accordingly, no arrest warrant was required, and whether or not the FBI agents could have obtained one prior to making the arrests is irrelevant." *U.S. v. DeMasi,* 40 F.3d 1306, 1312 (1st Cir. 1994).

Second Circuit

- "No reasonable expectation of privacy inheres in what is left visible to the naked eye. . . .Thus the Fourth Amendment does not require a police officer to obtain a warrant before making a felony arrest in a public place. . . ." *U.S. v. Gori,* 230 F.3d 44, 50 (2d Cir. 2000).

Third Circuit

- "Although police may make a warrantless arrest in a public place if they have probable cause to believe the suspect is a felon, the Fourth Amendment has drawn a firm line at the entrance to the house. Absent exigent circumstances, that threshold may not reasonably be crossed without a warrant." *Sharrar v. Felsing,* 128 F.3d 810, 819 (3d Cir. 1997).

Fifth Circuit

- "We have long known that law enforcement officials may arrest an individual in a public place without a warrant if they have probable cause to believe that the individual committed a felony. . . . Probable cause for a warrantless arrest exists when the totality of facts and circumstances within a police officer's knowledge at the moment of arrest are sufficient for a reasonable person to conclude that the suspect had committed or was committing an offense. . . . When considering what a reasonable person would have concluded, we take into account the expertise and experience of the law enforcement officials." *U.S. v. Garcia*, 179 F.3d 265, 268 (5th Cir. 1999).

- "In order to make a warrantless arrest in a public place, the arresting officers must have probable cause to believe that the suspect has committed, is committing, or is about to commit a crime." *Fontenot v. Cormier*, 56 F.3d 669, 674 (5th Cir. 1995).

- "In the second analytical step, we consider whether the official's actions were objectively reasonable. Objective reasonableness is assessed in light of legal rules clearly established at the time of the incident. For warrantless arrests, the test for whether the police officer ha[d] probable cause to arrest [is] if, at the time of the arrest, he had knowledge that would warrant a prudent person's belief that the person arrested had already committed or was committing a crime." *Mangieri v. Clifton*, 29 F.3d 1012, 1016, 30 Fed. R. Serv. 3d 229 (5th Cir. 1994).

Sixth Circuit

- "A police officer is permitted to make an arrest without a warrant for a misdemeanor committed in his presence. However, this requirement that a misdemeanor must have occurred in the officer's presence to justify a warrantless arrest is not mandated by the Fourth Amendment; it is merely a rule of the common law." *U.S. v. Smith*, 73 F.3d 1414, 1416, 1996 FED App. 0027P (6th Cir. 1996).

- "[T]he Fourth Amendment permits a duly authorized law enforcement officer to make a warrantless arrest in a public place even though he had adequate opportunity to procure a warrant after developing probable cause for arrest." *U.S. v. Wright*, 16 F.3d 1429, 1438, 40 Fed.

R. Evid. Serv. 281, 1994 FED App. 0049P (6th Cir.
1994).

Seventh Circuit

- "No authorities cited by either of the parties to this appeal, nor any that we have found, expressly require the
  police to obtain an arrest warrant before lawfully arresting a subject whom they have probable cause to
  believe has committed an offense in any instance other
  than an arrest in a suspect's home." *Woods v. City of
  Chicago*, 234 F.3d 979, 992, 55 Fed. R. Evid. Serv. 912
  (7th Cir. 2000).

Eighth Circuit

- "[W]e advance to a closer issue: whether Council was in
  a public place when the officers initiated the arrest, and
  if so, whether he was there voluntarily. The district
  court found, as a factual matter, Council was 'at the
  doorway' of the camper when Deputy Foley seized his
  arm and ordered him down the stairs. . . . Council
  acknowledges '[a] doorway of a person's home can
  become a public place,' but claims the situation here 'is
  not factually identical to *Santana*' and is instead more
  analogous to our decisions in *Duncan v. Storie*. . . and
  Mitchell v. Shearrer. . . . Council's attempt to invoke
  our reasoning in *Duncan* and *Mitchell* is akin to trying
  to fit a square peg in a round hole. That is, those cases
  came to us as interlocutory appeals in 42 U.S.C. § 1983
  cases so we decided all factual disputes in favor of the
  plaintiff; on the other hand, here the district court has
  made the critical factual findings—Council was 'in the
  doorway' and had not yet pulled back when Deputy
  Foley first seized his arm to arrest him. These findings
  were not clearly erroneous. Deputy Foley testified
  Council was '[d]ead even with the doorway' such that
  he was 'halfway in, halfway out.' Deputy Blehm stated
  Council was in the 'threshold' of the door. Council offered no conflicting account of his own. Lest we become
  too 'preoccupied with the exact location of the individual in relation to the doorway,' we make clear our general conclusion that Council forfeited any 'reasonable
  expectation of privacy' during the exchange. When
  Council appeared at his doorway, he was 'not merely

visible to the public, but was as exposed to public view, speech, hearing, and touch as if [ ]he had been standing completely outside [his] house.' This is supported by Deputy Blehm's testimony that he could still see and hear Council even though this deputy 'pretty much stayed out of view' at the side of the camper and was not involved in the initial interaction. Council was in a public place when Deputy Foley began to arrest him. But that is not enough to end our second inquiry— Council must have come to that public place voluntarily, without coercion or deceit. The district court found the evidence did not 'support [ ] a finding that the defendant came to be at his doorway as a result of either coercion or deceit on the part of the deputies,' and thus concluded Council 'voluntarily came to his doorway.' This is a factual determination we review for clear error based on the totality of the circumstances. We see no clear error. . . . To begin, our analytical starting place is different because in this case, unlike in *Conner*, the district court found Council did come to the door voluntarily. This is an important legal distinction. And, although there are some factual similarities, there are also significant dissimilarities. In this case only two officers approached Council's residence during normal waking hours to conduct a 'knock and talk,' a common information gathering method. They conveyed no intent to apprehend Council on the spot. Deputy Foley knocked twice, identifying himself as a police officer and saying 'come to the door' only after being asked who was there. Only one deputy was visible to Council. There is no indication this back-and-forth took several minutes to unfold or was extraordinarily loud, or that the officers ever unholstered their firearms in a display of force. Council could have ignored the request to come to the door or told the officers to go away, just as he later withheld consent to a search. . . . No doubt there is a line where officers' actions are coercive enough that compliance can no longer be deemed voluntary, yet we are not convinced that line was crossed here. The district court found Council came to stand in the doorway of his trailer residence voluntarily, and we cannot say this factual determination was clearly erroneous. Therefore, Council's Fourth Amendment rights were not violated when the officers first sought to arrest him." *United States v. Council*, 860 F.3d 604, 609–12 (8th Cir. 2017) (citations and text omitted).

§ 4:4 Houses: An individual has a high expectation of privacy in a residence

<u>Supreme Court</u>

- "It is axiomatic that the physical entry of the home is the chief evil against which the wording of the Fourth Amendment is directed. And a principal protection against unnecessary intrusions into private dwellings is the warrant requirement imposed by the Fourth Amendment on agents of the government who seek to enter the home for purposes of search or arrest." *Welsh v. Wisconsin*, 466 U.S. 740, 748, 104 S. Ct. 2091, 80 L. Ed. 2d 732 (1984).

- "[T]he Fourth Amendment prohibits the police from making a warrantless and nonconsensual entry into a suspect's home to make a routine felony arrest." *U.S. v. Johnson*, 457 U.S. 537, 538–39, 102 S. Ct. 2579, 73 L. Ed. 2d 202 (1982).

- "In the absence of exigent circumstances, we have consistently held that judicially untested determinations are not reliable enough to justify an entry into a person's home to arrest him without a warrant, or a search of a home for objects in the absence of a search warrant. We see no reason to depart from this settled course when the search of a home is for a person rather than an object. A contrary conclusion—that the police, acting alone and in the absence of exigent circumstances, may decide when there is sufficient justification for searching the home of a third party for the subject of an arrest warrant—would create a significant potential for abuse." *Steagald v. U.S.*, 451 U.S. 204, 213–15, 101 S. Ct. 1642, 68 L. Ed. 2d 38 (1981).

- "[T]he Fourth Amendment to the United States Constitution. . . .prohibits the police from making a warrantless and nonconsensual entry into a suspect's home in order to make a routine felony arrest. [T]he Fourth Amendment has drawn a firm line at the entrance to the house. Absent exigent circumstances, that threshold may not reasonably be crossed without a warrant."

Payton v. New York, 445 U.S. 573, 576, 100 S. Ct. 1371, 63 L. Ed. 2d 639 (1980).

First Circuit

- "We hold, therefore, that if the police have gained lawful entry to an individual's home based on a valid search warrant, they may arrest the individual before commencing the search, provided that they have probable cause to do so." *U.S. v. Winchenbach*, 197 F.3d 548, 554, 53 Fed. R. Evid. Serv. 18 (1st Cir. 1999).

Second Circuit

- "The Fourth Amendment looks with favor on 'overnight guests' not because there is something talismanic about a person's intent to stay in a dwelling on a particular night, but because a host's willingness to take in a guest to sleep—slumber being a vulnerable state during which privacy is cherished—indicates that the guest has been accepted into the private sphere of the household. Construing the record in the light most favorable to Samuel, we conclude that ('overnight guest' or not) he enjoyed a degree of acceptance into his mother's home sufficient to trigger Fourth Amendment protection. Indeed, each factor mentioned in *Carter* weighs strongly in Samuel's favor. His visit was social in nature. He had, in the past, spent a great deal of time at the apartment, sleeping there nearly as frequently as he slept at his own dwelling. He had a close relationship—indeed, a familial one—with the apartment's tenant. We have found no case denying Fourth Amendment standing on similar facts, and have found a number of cases finding Fourth Amendment standing on less convincing facts." *Figueroa v. Mazza*, 825 F.3d 89, 110–11 (2d Cir. 2016) (citations omitted).
- "The principle discussed in *Payton*, allowing officers to enter the residence of the suspect named in the arrest warrant, does not authorize entry into a residence in which the officers do not believe the suspect is residing but believe he is merely visiting. . . . *Steagald* did not, however, prohibit entry into a residence reasonably believed to belong to the person named in the arrest warrant." *U.S. v. Lovelock*, 170 F.3d 339, 344 (2d Cir. 1999).

Third Circuit

- "Although warrantless arrests in public places are valid, entry into a dwelling, even for purposes of an arrest for a serious crime, stands on an altogether different footing. A greater burden is placed on officials who enter a home or dwelling without consent. Freedom from intrusion into the home or dwelling is the archetype of the privacy protection secured by the Fourth Amendment." *Parkhurst v. Trapp*, 77 F.3d 707, 710–11 (3d Cir. 1996).

Sixth Circuit

- "As the Supreme Court has observed, the zone of privacy protected by the Fourth Amendment is most clearly defined when bounded by the unambiguous physical dimensions of an individual's home. . . . Indeed, the Fourth Amendment has drawn a firm line at the entrance to the house, a threshold which police officers generally may not cross without a warrant." *Ingram v. City of Columbus*, 185 F.3d 579, 586–87, 1999 FED App. 0258P (6th Cir. 1999).

Seventh Circuit

- "A warrantless entry into a residence to effect an arrest is presumptively unreasonable under the Fourth Amendment. . . .Where, however, someone with authority to do so consents to the entry, the entry is reasonable and the Fourth Amendment is not violated." *U.S. v. Walls*, 225 F.3d 858, 862 (7th Cir. 2000).
- "The Fourth Amendment prohibits the police from making a warrantless nonconsensual entry into a suspect's home in order to make a routine felony arrest or to conduct a search. This protection of the home against warrantless entries has been extended to hotel rooms." *U.S. v. Cotnam*, 88 F.3d 487, 495 (7th Cir. 1996).

Eighth Circuit

- "[Defendant] contends that he had a reasonable expectation of privacy in the property because it was owned by family and in a remote location. [Defendant] had no legitimate expectation of privacy in the property, because he had no ownership or possessory interest. The fact it belonged to his father is irrelevant; defendants have no expectation of privacy in a parent's home when they do not live there. While the remoteness of an area from a home may be relevant to the reasonableness of a search, the remoteness of the home itself is not. Further, [Defendant's] father expressly permitted police to search the property." *U.S. v. Skoda*, 705 F.3d 834 (8th Cir. 2013) (citations omitted).

- "[I]t is now clearly established that the Fourth Amendment prohibits a warrantless entry into a suspect's home to make a routine felony arrest absent consent or exigent circumstances." *Rogers v. Carter*, 133 F.3d 1114, 1118 (8th Cir. 1998).

Ninth Circuit

- "It does not matter that the officers did not actually enter the house to make the arrest. As this court has stated, 'it is the location of the arrested person, and not the arresting agents, that determines whether an arrest occurs within a home.' Because [defendant, who could open the front door of his trailer from his bed] did not take himself outside the physical zone of privacy of the house by going to the threshold of his house or to any other public place, the officers could not make a lawful warrantless arrest." *U.S. v. Quaempts*, 411 F.3d 1046 (9th Cir. 2005).

- "The Supreme Court and our court have made crystal clear that, in the absence of exigent circumstances, the police must obtain an arrest warrant before entering a person's home to arrest him." *U.S. v. Oaxaca*, 233 F.3d 1154, 1156–57 (9th Cir. 2000).

- "We note that this dispute is not controlled by *Welsh v. Wisconsin. . . .*where state officers in pursuit of a traffic violator entered the suspect's house, and the entry was held to violate the Fourth Amendment. Here, the pursuit, and ensuing altercation, took place on the porch, a public place for Fourth Amendment purposes under *United States v. Santana. . . .*" *U.S. v. Patch*, 114 F.3d 131, 134 (9th Cir. 1997).

Tenth Circuit

- "The district court did not err in holding that the arrest at the doorway was not invalid as in *U.S. v. Santana* the suspect was visible, standing in the threshold of his doorway, open to public view. He was in a place sufficiently public that he had no legitimate expectation of privacy. The officers had knocked, identified themselves, neither displayed nor threatened violence, and petitioner had opened the door. He had acknowledged their authority by asking if he could dress. *Payton* contains language that describes the Fourth Amendment as drawing a firm line at the entrance to one's house, but, on its facts, it has no application to a doorway arrest made in the circumstances of the present case." *McKinnon v. Carr*, 103 F.3d 934, 935–36 (10th Cir. 1996).

Eleventh Circuit

- " '[A]n arrest warrant founded on probable cause implicitly carries with it the limited authority to enter a dwelling in which the suspect lives . . . when there is reason to believe the suspect is within.' " *U.S. v. Hollis*, 780 F.3d 1064, 1068 (11th Cir. 2015), cert. denied, 136 S. Ct. 274, 193 L. Ed. 2d 200 (2015) (citation omitted).

- "[W]hen a police officer effectuates an arrest warrant in a third-party's abode, the officer may violate the Fourth Amendment rights of the third-party. But we agree with our sister circuits that the subject of an arrest warrant cannot challenge the execution of that warrant and the later discovery of evidence in a third-party's home." *U.S. v. Hollis*, 780 F.3d 1064, 1068–69 (11th Cir. 2015), cert. denied, 136 S. Ct. 274, 193 L. Ed. 2d 200 (2015) (citation omitted).

§ 4:5 Arrest warrants: An arrest warrant, issued upon probable cause, authorizes a search of the dwelling of the suspect when the police reasonably believe the suspect to be present

Supreme Court

- "[T]he Fourth Amendment has drawn a firm line at the entrance to the house. Absent exigent circumstances, that threshold may not reasonably be crossed without a warrant." *Payton v. New York*, 445 U.S. 573, 590, 100 S. Ct. 1371, 63 L. Ed. 2d 639 (1980).

First Circuit

- "The government itself stated at oral argument before

the district court that the arrest warrant did not give
the officers the authority to enter the house. Nonetheless, the court concluded that 'a reasonable officer in
the same position could have formed an objectively reasonable belief that [the subject of the arrest warrant]
lived at the premises and was present at the time of
entry.' . . . As a threshold matter, [the defendant]
argues that the court's use of the 'reasonable belief'
standard was incorrect, and that the officers instead
needed to demonstrate that they had probable cause to
believe that [the subject of the arrest warrant] lived in
the Menlo Street house and was home on the morning
of November 10. Although most circuits to have considered the issue have adopted the 'reasonable belief' standard, and treat it as less stringent than probable cause,
the Ninth Circuit requires probable cause. We have not
explicitly made a choice, but have implicitly accepted
the majority view." *U.S. v. Werra*, 638 F.3d 326 (1st Cir.
2011) (citations omitted).

- "Although 'actual viewing of the suspect on the premises
  is not required,' the officers must point to at least some
  evidence suggesting that the individual named in the
  arrest warrant is present." *U.S. v. Werra*, 638 F.3d 326
  (1st Cir. 2011) (citations omitted).
- "It is clearly established that a search warrant is
  ordinarily required to enter the home of a third person
  to arrest an individual who is believed to be inside the
  home. . . . This rule applies regardless of the existence
  of an arrest warrant." *Fletcher v. Town of Clinton*, 196
  F.3d 41, 49 (1st Cir. 1999).
- "When the police enter the home of the person they
  wish to arrest, the arrest warrant suffices for entry if
  there is reason to believe the suspect is within. . . .
  But even when armed with an arrest warrant, police
  must generally have a search warrant to enter lawfully
  a third person's home. . . . However, a third person's
  house may be lawfully entered without a search warrant if exigent circumstances exist. . . .and exigent circumstances include hot pursuit." *Joyce v. Town of
  Tewksbury, Mass.*, 112 F.3d 19, 21–22 (1st Cir. 1997).

Second Circuit

- "[I]n order to authorize entry into a person's home to

execute a warrant for his arrest, the officers' belief that
the residence to be entered is the home of the person
named in the warrant need not be supported by probable cause. Rather, the proper inquiry is whether there
is a reasonable belief that the suspect resides at the
place to be entered to execute the warrant, and whether
the officers have reason to believe that the suspect is
present. . . . Nor need the officers' belief, if reasonable,
be correct." *U.S. v. Lovelock*, 170 F.3d 339, 343 (2d Cir.
1999).

- "Generally, the police do not need a search warrant to
enter a suspect's home when they have an arrest warrant for the suspect. As the Supreme Court has observed, once an arrest warrant for a particular suspect
has issued, it is constitutionally reasonable to require
him to open his doors to the officers of the law. Agents
may enter a suspect's residence, or what they have reason to believe is his residence, in order to effectuate an
arrest that the suspect is present. [T]he proper inquiry
is whether there is a reasonable brief that the suspect
resides at the place to be entered to execute an arrest
warrant, and whether the officers have reason to believe
that the suspect is present." *U.S. v. Lauter*, 57 F.3d
212, 214–15 (2d Cir. 1995).

Fourth Circuit

- "[A]n 'all persons' warrant can pass constitutional
muster if the affidavit and information provided to the
magistrate supply enough detailed information to establish probable cause to believe that all persons on the
premises at the time of the search are involved in the
criminal activity. In our view, the inclusion of 'all
persons' language in a warrant presents probable cause
issues rather than particularity problems. 'A search
warrant authorization to search all persons found
within a specifically described place is not lacking
particularity in the sense that the executing officer will
be unable readily to determine to whom the warrant
applies.' . . .Thus, as long as there is good reason to
suspect or believe that anyone present at the anticipated
scene will probably be a participant in the criminal
activity occurring there, presence becomes the descriptive fact satisfying the aim of the Fourth Amendment."

Owens ex rel. Owens v. Lott, 372 F.3d 267 (4th Cir. 2004).

Fifth Circuit

- "If a court order under [state child protection law] suffices to meet the Fourth Amendment warrant requirement for a seizure, we see no reason that it should not also meet the warrant requirement in the context of a search of a child's home to locate the child. . . . Under the Fourth Amendment, we find it reasonable and permissible for state workers in possession of a facially valid temporary custody order, with a duty under state law to take care of the child, to enter the child's home to look for the child." *Wernecke v. Garcia*, 591 F.3d 386 (5th Cir. 2009).

- "In this case, the deputies had a warrant for the arrest of (plaintiff's) son. . .who resided at 16449 County Road 15. While *Summers* and *Anderson* would authorize the deputies to detain anyone found at that address during the execution of their arrest warrant for (her son), nothing in either of those cases provides authority for the proposition that the deputies could detain (plaintiff) outside of her own home, 16447 County Road 15, while they inquired about (her son's) whereabouts. Because (plaintiff) was at her own home when she was detained, and because the deputies had no right to search *(her home)* based on their arrest warrant for (her son). . .the detention cannot be justified . . . ." *Freeman v. Gore*, 483 F.3d 404 (5th Cir. 2007).

- "A valid arrest warrant carries with it the implicit but limited authority to enter the residence of the person named in the warrant in order to execute the warrant, where there is reason to believe that the suspect is within. As distinct from the probable cause standard that governs the initial issuance of the arrest warrant and that must be determined by a magistrate, we have defined previously the reason to believe standard to allow the officer, who has already been to the magistrate to secure an arrest warrant, to determine that the suspect is probably within certain premises without an additional trip to the magistrate and without exigent circumstances." *U.S. v. Route*, 104 F.3d 59, 62, 46 Fed. R. Evid. Serv. 442 (5th Cir. 1997).

Sixth Circuit

- "The *Payton* Court held that "an arrest warrant founded on probable cause implicitly carries with it the limited authority to enter a dwelling in which the suspect lives when there is reason to believe the suspect is within" . . . (T)he rule is sufficient to protect the suspect's Fourth Amendment rights even when the arrest warrant is executed in a third party's home in which the suspect may have a reasonable expectation of privacy . . . (T)he government argues that "reason to believe" is something less than probable cause and more akin to "reasonable suspicion." The majority adopts this view, and seven circuit courts of appeal have refused to apply the "probable cause" moniker to the "reason to believe" standard and instead have applied the "reason to believe" standard in a literal fashion." *U.S. v. Pruitt*, 458 F.3d 477, 2006 FED App. 0293P (6th Cir. 2006).

Eighth Circuit

- "A valid arrest warrant carries with it the authority to enter the residence of the person named in the warrant in order to execute the warrant so long as the police have a reasonable belief that the suspect resides at the place to be entered and that he is currently present in the dwelling." *U.S. v. Clayton*, 210 F.3d 841, 843 (8th Cir. 2000).
- "It is clearly established Fourth Amendment law that an arrest warrant founded on probable cause implicitly carries with it the limited authority to enter a dwelling in which the suspect lives when there is reason to believe the suspect is within. . . . Once inside, the law enforcement authorities may then lawfully search anywhere in the house that the suspect might be found." *Lyles v. City of Barling*, 181 F.3d 914, 917 (8th Cir. 1999).
- "Under *Payton*, officers executing an arrest warrant must have a reasonable belief that the suspect resides at the place to be entered and have reason to believe that the suspect is present at the time the warrant is executed. As indicated, the officers' assessment need not in fact be correct; rather, they need only reasonably believe that the suspect resides at the dwelling to be searched and is currently present at the dwelling." *U.S. v. Risse*, 83 F.3d 212, 216 (8th Cir. 1996).

- "A valid arrest warrant carries with it the implicit but limited authority to enter the residence of the person named in the warrant in order to execute that warrant. However, absent exigent circumstances or consent, an arrest warrant does not justify entry into a third person's home to search for the subject of the arrest warrant. Thus, if the suspect is just a guest of the third party, then the police must obtain a search warrant for the third party's dwelling in order to use evidence found against the third party. However, if the suspect is a co-resident of the third party, then *Steagald* does not apply, and *Payton* allows both arrest of the subject of the arrest warrant and use of evidence found against the third party." *U.S. v. Risse*, 83 F.3d 212, 215–16 (8th Cir. 1996).

Tenth Circuit

- "In a *Payton* analysis, this court recognizes a two-prong test: officers must have a reasonable belief the arrestee (1) lived in the residence, and (2) is within the residence at the time of entry." *U.S. v. Gay*, 240 F.3d 1222, 1226 (10th Cir. 2001).
- "The majority of circuits which have addressed the issue have agreed that, under Payton, police officers entering a residence pursuant to an arrest warrant must demonstrate a reasonable belief that the arrestee lived in the residence, and a reasonable belief that the arrestee could be found within the residence at the time of the entry." *Valdez v. McPheters*, 172 F.3d 1220, 1224 (10th Cir. 1999).

Eleventh Circuit

- "We have since held that *Payton* requires a two-part inquiry to determine if entry pursuant to an arrest warrant complies with the Fourth Amendment's proscription of unreasonable searches. . . .In particular, we have held that first, there must be a reasonable belief that the location to be searched is the suspect's dwelling, and second, the police must have reason to believe that the suspect is within the dwelling. . . .Furthermore, in evaluating this on the spot determination, as to the second *Payton prong*, courts must be sensitive to common sense factors indicating a resident's presence. . . .We believe such common sense factors must also guide courts in evaluating the first Payton prong." *U.S. v. Bervaldi*, 226 F.3d 1256, 1263 (11th Cir. 2000).

- "[F]or Fourth Amendment purposes, an arrest warrant founded on probable cause implicitly carries with it the limited authority to enter a dwelling in which the suspect lives when there is reason to believe the suspect is within. *Payton* thus requires a two-part inquiry: first, there must be a reasonable belief that the location to be searched is the suspect's dwelling, and second, the police must have reason to believe that the suspect is within the dwelling." *U.S. v. Magluta*, 44 F.3d 1530, 1533 (11th Cir. 1995).

§ 4:6 Exigent circumstances: Hot pursuit of fleeing suspects or other exigent circumstances may justify warrantless arrests in homes

Supreme Court

- "[A] search or seizure carried out on a suspect's premises without a warrant is *per se* unreasonable, unless the police can show the presence of exigent circumstances. [T]he court decided in *Payton v. New York* that warrantless felony arrests in the home are prohibited by the Fourth Amendment, absent probable cause and exigent circumstances. Before agents of the government may invade the sanctity of the home, the burden is on the government to demonstrate exigent circumstances that overcome the presumption of unreasonableness that attaches to all warrantless home entries." *Welsh v. Wisconsin*, 466 U.S. 740, 749, 750, 104 S. Ct. 2091, 80 L. Ed. 2d 732 (1984).

- "[H]ot pursuit means some sort of a chase, but it need not be an extended hue and cry in and about [the] public streets. The fact that the pursuit here ended almost as soon as it began did not render it any the less a hot pursuit sufficient to justify the warrantless entry into [Defendant's] house. Once [Defendant] saw the police, there was likewise a realistic expectation that any delay would result in destruction of evidence. [A] suspect may not defeat an arrest which has been set in motion in a public place by the expedient of escaping to a private place." *U.S. v. Santana*, 427 U.S. 38, 43, 96 S. Ct. 2406, 49 L. Ed. 2d 300 (1976).

- "[There is] no element of hot pursuit in the arrest of one who was not in flight, was completely surrounded by agents before she knew of their presence, who claims without denial that she was in bed at the time, and who made no attempt to escape." *Johnson v. U.S.*, 333 U.S. 10, 16 n.7, 68 S. Ct. 367, 92 L. Ed. 436 (1948).

First Circuit

- "As subsequent cases demonstrate. . . . *Payton* does not purport to declare an absolute rule. One recognized exception involves exigent circumstances. . . . Another applies to parolees and persons on probation. . . . A third, the precise scope of which is here at issue, permits the police to arrest an individual in his home, without an arrest warrant, as long as they are lawfully on the premises (by reason, say, of a search warrant) and probable cause exists. . . . In these cases, the police discovered the evidence that gave rise to probable cause during a lawful search of the premises and then arrested the occupant." *U.S. v. Winchenbach*, 197 F.3d 548, 553, 53 Fed. R. Evid. Serv. 18 (1st Cir. 1999).

- "The Constitution requires that police normally obtain a warrant before entering a person's home to make an arrest. In determining whether an exigency justifies a warrantless search and seizure, the test is whether there is such a compelling necessity for immediate action as will not brook the delay of obtaining a warrant. Exigency determinations are generally fact-intensive and thus must be made on a case-by-case basis." *U.S. v. Wihbey*, 75 F.3d 761, 766 (1st Cir. 1996).

- "To determine whether there is an exigency sufficient to justify a warrantless search and seizure, the test is whether there is such a compelling necessity for immediate action as will not brook the delay of obtaining a warrant. This necessarily fact-based inquiry requires that we consider factors including the gravity of the underlying offense, whether a delay would pose a threat to police or the public safety, and whether there is a great likelihood that evidence will be destroyed if the search is delayed until a warrant can be obtained." *U.S. v. Bartelho*, 71 F.3d 436, 442, 43 Fed. R. Evid. Serv. 501 (1st Cir. 1995).

Second Circuit

- "Though genuinely held, the officers' concerns about getting illegal guns off of the streets of Hartford are not pertinent to an exigency analysis. This is because testimony about how fast 'guns move' in Hartford, or about the violent gangs in that part of the city, are not specific facts or evidence particular to this case. Rather, they are generalized facts about the city and about the nature of gun trafficking. Such general knowledge, without more, cannot support a finding of exigency. The exigency inquiry 'turns on the district court's examination of the totality of circumstances confronting law enforcement agents *in the particular case.*'" *Harris v. O'Hare*, 770 F.3d 224, 235 (2d Cir. 2014), cert. denied, 136 S. Ct. 792, 193 L. Ed. 2d 709 (2016) (citations omitted).

Third Circuit

- "Before agents of the government may invade the sanctity of the home, the burden is on the government to demonstrate exigent circumstances that overcome the presumption of unreasonableness that attaches to all warrantless home entries." *Sharrar v. Felsing*, 128 F.3d 810, 820 (3d Cir. 1997).

Sixth Circuit

- "*Morgan* specifically enumerates three situations that justify abandonment of the warrant procedure under the exigent circumstances rubric: hot pursuit of a fleeing suspect; where a suspect represents an immediate threat to the arresting officers or the public; or where immediate police action is needed to prevent the destruction of vital evidence or to thwart the escape of known criminals." *U.S. v. Haddix*, 239 F.3d 766, 767, 2001 FED App. 0039P (6th Cir. 2001).

Seventh Circuit

- "*United States v. Santana*. . .holds that police who espy a suspect in the frame of a front door have found the suspect in a public place and therefore may follow the suspect into the interior of the house as part of hot pursuit even without a warrant." *U.S. v. Jones*, 149 F.3d 715, 716 (7th Cir. 1998).

- "Exigent circumstances exist when there is a compelling need for official action and no time to secure a warrant, such as when the police officers are in hot pursuit of the suspect." *Mason v. Godinez*, 47 F.3d 852, 856 (7th Cir. 1995).

- "Justice White made clear in *Buie* that the same considerations that justify the exceptions in *Terry* and *Long* animate the exception for the protective sweep. Law enforcement officers have an interest in ensuring their safety when they lawfully enter a house to effect an arrest. That interest justifies their ensuring that the dwelling does not harbor another person who is dangerous and who unexpectedly could launch an attack." *U.S. v. Burrows*, 48 F.3d 1011, 1015–16 (7th Cir. 1995).

- "The Fourth Amendment to the United States Constitution protects a person's right to be free from warrantless intrusions into his home. The Fourth Amendment protection also applies to warrantless intrusions into motel rooms when occupied as a temporary abode. The police may, however, enter a residence or motel room without a warrant if the intrusion falls within one of the established and well-delineated exceptions to the warrant requirement. One such exception is the exigent circumstances doctrine. Exigent circumstances are defined as a compelling need for official action and no time to secure a warrant. We determine the validity of a warrantless entry by objectively examining the reasonableness of a police officer's belief that he faced exigent circumstances and, therefore, lacked sufficient time to obtain a warrant." *U.S. v. Foxworth*, 8 F.3d 540, 544 (7th Cir. 1993).

Ninth Circuit

- "Although there is a presumption of invalidity attaching to warrantless entry of a residence, 'for Fourth Amendment purposes, an arrest warrant founded on probable cause implicitly carries with it the limited authority to enter a dwelling in which the suspect lives when there is reason to believe the suspect is within.' [citations omitted] . . . [We have] not previously had occasion to decide whether a misdemeanor bench warrant for failure to appear—as opposed to a felony arrest warrant—is sufficient to permit entry into a residence.

. . . The Second Circuit, however, in *United States v.
Spencer*, persuasively reasoned that the [U.S. Supreme]
Court's decision in *Payton [v. New York]* permits entry
into a residence to effectuate a valid arrest warrant,
regardless of the precise nature of the underlying
warrant. [citations omitted] . . . . [T]he [*Spencer* court]
. . . explained [that] 'the decision of the New York City
Criminal Court Judge to issue a bench warrant constituted a finding made by a neutral magistrate that [the
defendant] had failed to appear in a pending criminal
matter. . . . [T]he police, armed with the warrant, had
authority to find and seize [the defendant] anywhere
they could find him[, and d]efendant's rights under the
Fourth Amendment require no more.' [citations omit-
ted] . . . The holding in Spencer . . . has been followed
in similar cases with near uniformity by the federal
courts. [citations omitted] We find the reasoning of
Spencer persuasive, and affirm the district court's denial
of [defendant]'s motion to suppress. We hold that a valid
arrest warrant issued by a neutral magistrate judge,
including a properly issued bench warrant for failure to
appear, carries with it the limited authority to enter a
residence in order to effectuate the arrest as provided
for under *Payton* (footnote and citation omitted). . . .
The Fourth Amendment presumption against warrantless entries into the home is designed to protect privacy
interests against uncabined police discretion. [citation
omitted] Those interests are sufficiently safeguarded
when an entry is premised on the execution of a valid
arrest warrant issued by a judge or magistrate, regardless of whether that warrant is for a felony, a misdemeanor, or simply a bench warrant for failure to appear.
Here, the police held a valid warrant for [defendant]'s
arrest, a warrant that bore the confirmed address of the
residence police entered after following [defendant].
The entry and subsequent search for [defendant] were
reasonable and permissible under *Payton* and the
Fourth Amendment. . . . Th[us, th]e district court's decision to deny [defendant]'s motion to suppress was not
in error . . ." *U.S. v. Gooch*, 506 F.3d 1156, 1158–1160
(9th Cir. 2007).

Tenth Circuit

- "In addition to insuring that evidence will not be destroyed, officers may also make a warrantless arrest or conduct a warrantless search if they believe that their own lives or the lives of others are at risk. We have observed that, where fear that evidence will be destroyed provides the exigency, the existence of the exigency must be supported by clearly defined indications of exigency that are not subject to police manipulation or abuse and it is available only for serious crimes." *U.S. v. Wicks*, 995 F.2d 964, 970, 38 Fed. R. Evid. Serv. 1424 (10th Cir. 1993).

Eleventh Circuit

- "A warrantless search is allowed, however, where both probable cause and exigent circumstances exist. The test for whether or not exigent circumstances exist is whether the facts would lead a reasonable, experienced agent to believe that evidence might be destroyed or removed before a warrant could be secured. Recognized situations in which exigent circumstances exist include: danger of flight or escape; danger of harm to police officers or the general public; risk of loss, destruction, removal, or concealment of evidence; and hot pursuit of a fleeing suspect. This court has held that the need to invoke the exigent circumstances exception to the warrant requirement is particularly compelling in narcotics cases because narcotics can be so easily and quickly destroyed." *U.S. v. Reid*, 69 F.3d 1109, 1113 (11th Cir. 1995).

§ 4:7   Entering homes after arrests: Police may accompany an arrested person into his home after a lawful arrest

Supreme Court

- "[I]t is not unreasonable under the Fourth Amendment for a police officer, as a matter of routine, to monitor the movements of an arrested person, as his judgment dictates, following the arrest. The officer's need to ensure his own safety—as well as the integrity of the arrest—is compelling." *Washington v. Chrisman*, 455 U.S. 1, 7, 102 S. Ct. 812, 70 L. Ed. 2d 778, 1 Ed. Law Rep. 1087 (1982).

- "Here, the officer had placed [Defendant] under lawful arrest, and therefore was authorized to accompany him to his room for the purpose of obtaining identification." *Washington v. Chrisman*, 455 U.S. 1, 6, 102 S. Ct. 812, 70 L. Ed. 2d 778, 1 Ed. Law Rep. 1087 (1982).

Fourth Circuit

- "[A]n officer is authorized to take reasonable steps to address the safety of the arrestee and that the arrestee's partially clothed status may constitute an exigency justifying the officer's temporary reentry into the arrestee's home to retrieve clothes reasonably calculated to lessen the risk of injury to the defendant." *U.S. v. Gwinn*, 219 F.3d 326, 333 (4th Cir. 2000).

Sixth Circuit

- "In *Buie*, the Supreme Court weighed the need to ensure officer safety against an individual's reasonable expectation of privacy in the home, noting that the risk of danger in the context of an arrest in the home is as great as, if not greater than, it is in an on-the-street or roadside investigatory encounter. We believe that, in some circumstances, an arrest taking place just outside a home may pose an equally serious threat to the arresting officers. In our view, the fact that the arrest takes place outside rather than inside the home affects only the inquiry into whether the officers have a reasonable articulable suspicion that a protective sweep is necessary by reason of a safety threat. We decline to adopt a bright-line rule that prohibits police officers from conducting a protective sweep of a home every time they arrest a defendant outside that home, regardless of the potential danger from other persons inside." *U.S. v. Colbert*, 76 F.3d 773, 776–77, 1996 FED App. 0063P (6th Cir. 1996).

- "[Defendant] was already in custody and outside the house. Not only did he pose little or no threat to the arresting officers at that time, but, as we have already explained, [Defendant]'s dangerousness is not germane to the inquiry into whether the police may conduct a protective sweep in response to a reasonable suspicion of a threat from some other person inside the home. If district courts are allowed to justify protective sweeps based on the dangerousness of the arrestee, nearly every arrest taking place in or near a home will include a protective sweep." *U.S. v. Colbert*, 76 F.3d 773, 777, 1996 FED App. 0063P (6th Cir. 1996).

- "In order to find the protective sweep constitutional under *Buie*, the officers must articulate why it was reasonable for them to undertake a warrantless search of a motel room 20-75 feet from the arrest site once they had the defendant under their control. It is undisputed that [Defendant] had an expectation of privacy in his hotel room. In this case, the officers based the need for the search on several articulable factors that would lead a reasonably prudent officer to believe that the officers might be in danger from someone in the motel room. First, the officers had received information that another person would be meeting defendant at the motel room. Although the officers never saw anyone enter the room during the surveillance period, they did not know if someone was already in the room when they arrived. Second, defendant left the motel room door open so that anyone present in the room had a clear view of the officers, thereby threatening their safety from an unknown person present in the room. Third, the officers were familiar with defendant and knew that he had been arrested on two previous occasions in the presence of someone in possession of a firearm. In addition to these reasons, the officers did not act unreasonably in accompanying a shoeless, shirtless man about to be transported to jail back to his motel room. The door to the room was standing open. The defendant had clothes and other personal items to be retrieved. It was only natural, as a matter of common sense, for the officers to go with the defendant back into the room to retrieve his possessions. The law does not require officers to leave common sense at the door." *U.S. v. Biggs*, 70 F.3d 913, 916, 1995 FED App. 0345P (6th Cir. 1995).

Seventh Circuit

- "When the police assert from outside the home their authority to arrest a person, the y have not breached the person's privacy interest in the home. If the person recognizes and submits to that authority, the arrestee, in effect, has forfeited the privacy of his home to a certain extent. At that point, it is not unreasonable for the police to enter the home to the extent necessary to complete the arrest. A person who has submitted to the police's authority and stands waiting for the police to take him away can hardly complain when the police enter his home briefly to complete the arrest." *U.S. v. Berkowitz*, 927 F.2d 1376, 1387 (7th Cir. 1991).

Tenth Circuit

- "Several courts have indicated that, even without an express invitation as in *Chrisman*, police may conduct a limited entry into an area for the purpose of protecting the health or safety of an arrestee. This in no way creates a blank check for intrusion upon the privacy of the sloppily dressed. [E]ntry into the defendant's residence cannot be effected, in the absence of consent or exigent circumstances, solely upon the desire of law enforcement officers to complete the arrestee's wardrobe. What separates the present case from the impermissible seizure in *Anthon* is the presence of a legitimate and significant threat to the health and safety of the arrestee. There is no evidence in the present record that the concern for the arrestee's health and safety are pretextual. To the contrary, the record is clear that taking [Defendant] to the officers' vehicles would have posed a serious risk to his health." *U.S. v. Butler*, 980 F.2d 619, 621–22 (10th Cir. 1992).

D.C. Circuit

- "Although *Buie* concerned an arrest made in the home, the principles enunciated by the Supreme Court are fully applicable where, as here, the arrest takes place just outside the residence. That the police arrested the defendant outside rather than inside his dwelling is relevant to the question of whether they could reasonably fear an attack by someone within it. The officers' exact location, however, does not change the nature of the appropriate inquiry: Did articulable facts exist that would lead a reasonably prudent officer to believe a sweep was required to protect the safety of those on the arrest scene?" *U.S. v. Henry*, 48 F.3d 1282, 1284 (D.C. Cir. 1995).

§ 4:8 Pretext arrests: In determining whether an arrest is lawful, the court must apply an objective test, and not examine the officer's subjective intent

Supreme Court

- "It is alleged that federal officials had no intention of calling [the defendant] as [a witness], and that [he was] detained, at [Attorney General John Ashcroft's] direction, because federal officials suspected [him] of supporting terrorism but lacked sufficient evidence to charge [him] with a crime. . . . A warrant issued by a neutral Magistrate Judge authorized [the defendant's] arrest [pursuant to a federal material-witness statute which authorizes judges to 'order the arrest of [a] person' whose testimony 'is material in a criminal proceeding. . .if it is shown that it may become impracticable to secure the presence of the person by subpoena']. The affidavit accompanying the warrant application (as [the defendant] concedes) gave individualized reasons to believe that he was a material witness and that he would soon disappear. . . . In *Whren,* we declined to probe the motives behind seizures supported by probable cause but lacking a warrant approved by a detached magistrate. *Terry v. Ohio* and *Knights,* applied an objective standard to warrantless searches justified by a lesser showing of reasonable suspicion. We review even some suspicionless searches for objective reasonableness. If concerns about improper motives and pretext do not justify subjective inquiries in those less protective contexts, we see no reason to adopt that inquiry here. . . . [T]o say that ulterior motives do *not* invalidate a search that is legitimate because of probable cause to believe a crime has occurred is not to say that it *does* invalidate all searches that are legitimate for other reasons. '[O]nly an undiscerning reader,' would think otherwise. We referred to probable cause to believe that a violation of law had occurred because that was the legitimating factor in the case at hand. But the analysis of our opinion swept broadly to reject inquiries into motive generally. . . . Because [the defendant] concedes that individualized suspicion supported the issuance of the material-witness arrest warrant; and does not assert that his arrest would have been unconstitutional absent the alleged pretextual use of the warrant; we find no Fourth Amendment violation. Efficient and evenhanded application of the law demands that we look to whether the arrest is objectively justified, rather than to the motive of the arresting officer." *Ashcroft v. al-Kidd*, 563 U.S. 731, 131 S. Ct. 2074, 2079, 2082–83, 179 L. Ed. 2d 1149 (2011) (citations omitted).

- "The Arkansas Supreme Court's holding. . .cannot be squared with our decision in *Whren*, in which we noted our unwillingness to entertain Fourth Amendment challenges based on the actual motivations of individual officers, and held unanimously that subjective intentions play no role in ordinary, probable-cause Fourth Amendment analysis. . . .The judgment of the Arkansas Supreme Court is reversed. . . ." *Arkansas v. Sullivan*, 532 U.S. 769, 121 S. Ct. 1876, 1878, 149 L. Ed. 2d 994 (2001).

- "[There is no] principle that ulterior motives can invalidate police conduct that is justifiable on the basis of probable cause to believe that a violation of law has occurred. Not only have we never held, outside the context of inventory search or administrative inspection (discussed above), that an officer's motive invalidates objectively justifiable behavior under the Fourth Amendment; but we have repeatedly held and asserted the contrary." *Whren v. U.S.*, 517 U.S. 806, 811–12, 116 S. Ct. 1769, 135 L. Ed. 2d 89 (1996).

- "[T]he Constitution prohibits selective enforcement of the law based on considerations such as race. But the constitutional basis for objecting to intentionally discriminatory application of laws is the Equal Protection Clause, not the Fourth Amendment. Subjective intentions play no role in ordinary, probable-cause Fourth Amendment analysis." *Whren v. U.S.*, 517 U.S. 806, 813, 116 S. Ct. 1769, 135 L. Ed. 2d 89 (1996).

- "[T]he fact that the officer does not have the state of mind which is hypothecated by the reasons which provide the legal justification for the officer's action does not invalidate the action taken as long as the circumstances, viewed objectively, justify that action." *Scott v. U.S.*, 436 U.S. 128, 136, 98 S. Ct. 1717, 56 L. Ed. 2d 168 (1978).

First Circuit

- "How far *Whren* would extend in the face of dubious motives or other constitutional concerns is a more difficult question, and one not entirely avoidable here. Actual motive sometimes does play a role in section 1983 actions. But in evaluating arrests, the Supreme Court has given primacy to the Fourth Amendment's own objective standards, even where other constitutional bases might be invoked. This does not mean that probable cause forecloses every possible challenge to an arrest. *Whren* itself strongly implies that an equal protection challenge to an arrest, despite probable cause existing, might yet be entertained, although the court does not say what facts would be needed to support such a challenge. An objective showing that (for example) only blacks or Asians were ever arrested for a specific, widely committed offense would pose a different case than *Whren*." *Holland v. City of Portland*, 102 F.3d 6, 10–11 (1st Cir. 1996).

Second Circuit

- "The Supreme Court has held that whether a Fourth Amendment violation has occurred turns on an objective assessment of the officer's actions in light of the facts and circumstances confronting him at the time and not on the officer's actual state of mind at the time the challenged action was taken. . . . When analyzing issues surrounding the constitutionality of searches and seizures under the Fourth Amendment, we have adopted a wholly objective authorization test, which states that so long as the police are doing no more than they are legally permitted and objectively authorized to do, their actions are constitutional. . . . The fact that the officer does not have the state of mind which is hypothecated by the reasons which provide the legal justification for the officer's action does not invalidate the action taken as long as the circumstances, viewed objectively, justify that action." *Simms v. Village of Albion, N.Y.*, 115 F.3d 1098, 1108 (2d Cir. 1997).

Fifth Circuit

- "[W]hile we do not applaud what appears to be a common practice of some law enforcement officers to use technical violations as a cover for exploring more serious violations, we may look no further than the court's finding that the officer had a legitimate basis for stopping the vehicle." *U.S. v. Flores*, 63 F.3d 1342, 1362, 42 Fed. R. Evid. Serv. 1365 (5th Cir. 1995).

Seventh Circuit

- "If an arrest or a traffic stop is used merely as a pretext to search for evidence, that search constitutes a violation of the Fourth Amendment. *United States v. Trigg* case requires an objective analysis of the circumstances; if there was probable cause to make the stop, and if the stopping officer was acting with authority, the stop was not pretextual. So long as the police are doing no more than they are legally permitted and objectively authorized to do, an arrest is constitutional. Once we determine that the stop was based on a reasonable suspicion or probable cause, and that the officer was authorized by law to make the stop, the stop is constitutionally valid." *U.S. v. Willis*, 61 F.3d 526, 530 (7th Cir. 1995).

Eighth Circuit

- "[W]hether a Fourth Amendment violation has occurred turns on an objective assessment of the officer's actions in light of the facts and circumstances confronting him at the time. . .and not on the officer's actual state of mind at the time the challenged action was taken." *U.S. v. Clayton*, 210 F.3d 841, 844 (8th Cir. 2000).

- "Although *Whren* specifically concerned a traffic stop, we believe that its principle is applicable to all police activities for which probable cause is required. In analyzing [Defendant]'s arrest under the fourth amendment, we therefore ignore the officers' subjective intentions and focus solely on the objective question of whether probable cause existed." *U.S. v. Clarke*, 110 F.3d 612, 613–14 (8th Cir. 1997).

- "A pretextual traffic stop violates the Fourth Amendment. It is well established, however, that any traffic violation, no matter how minor, provides a police officer with probable cause to stop the driver of the vehicle. To determine whether a stop was based on probable cause or was merely pretextual, we apply a standard of objective reasonableness. So long as the officer is doing nothing more than he is legally permitted and objectively authorized to do, his actual state of mind is irrelevant for purposes of determining the lawfulness of the stop. Exceeding the speed limit is a legitimate basis for conducting a traffic stop. No further inquiry is required." *U.S. v. Pereira-Munoz*, 59 F.3d 788, 790–91 (8th Cir. 1995).

Ninth Circuit

- "That the officer lied about seeing Magallon–Lopez make an illegal lane change does not call into question the legality of the stop. The standard for determining whether probable cause or reasonable suspicion exists is an objective one; it does not turn either on the subjective thought processes of the officer or on whether the officer is truthful about the reason for the stop. If, for example, the facts provide probable cause or reasonable suspicion to justify a traffic stop, the stop is lawful even if the officer made the stop only because he wished to investigate a more serious offense. Likewise, if the facts support probable cause to arrest for one offense, the arrest is lawful even if the officer invoked, as the basis for the arrest, a different offense as to which probable cause was lacking. The Court in *Devenpeck* emphasized that the objective facts are what matter in situations like these:

  While it is assuredly good police practice to inform a person of the reason for his arrest at the time he is taken into custody, we have never held that to be constitutionally required. Hence, the predictable consequence of a rule limiting the probable-cause inquiry to offenses closely related to (and supported by the same facts as) those identified by the arresting officer is not . . . that officers will cease making sham arrests on the hope that such arrests will later be validated, but rather that officers will cease providing reasons for arrest. And even if this option were to be foreclosed by adoption of a statutory or constitutional requirement, officers would simply give every reason for which probable cause could conceivably exist.

  The same principle—that the objective facts are controlling in this context, not what the officer said or was thinking—applies here. So long as the facts known to the officer establish reasonable suspicion to justify an investigatory stop, the stop is lawful even if the officer

234

falsely cites as the basis for the stop a ground that is not supported by reasonable suspicion. We emphasize, however, that although our focus is on the objectively reasonable basis for the stop, not the officers' subjective intentions or beliefs, the facts justifying the stop must be known to officers at the time of the stop." *U.S. v. Magallon-Lopez*, 817 F.3d 671, 675 (9th Cir. 2016) (citations omitted).

- "[S]ubjective intentions play no role in ordinary, probable-cause Fourth Amendment analysis. The validity of an arrest depends upon the objective facts and circumstances of the arrest, not upon the arresting officer's subjective intent." *U.S. v. Sayetsitty*, 107 F.3d 1405, 1414, 46 Fed. R. Evid. Serv. 760 (9th Cir. 1997).

- "It is a well-settled principle that an arrest may not be used as a pretext to search for evidence without a search warrant where one would ordinarily be required under the Fourth Amendment. In deciding the standard we must apply to determine whether an arrest is pretextual, we note that the various standards reflected in our past decisions appear to have been superseded by the Supreme Court's recent decision in *Whren v. United States*. We acknowledge that *Whren* involved a somewhat different context from that involved here: Whereas *Whren* set forth the standard for determining whether a traffic stop is pretextual, we are confronted here with a defendant's allegation that his arrest was pretextual. In our view, however, the *Whren* analysis governs this case." *U.S. v. Hudson*, 100 F.3d 1409, 1414–15 (9th Cir. 1996).

§ 4:9 Deadly or excessive force: The unreasonable use of deadly or excessive force to effect an arrest is forbidden by the Fourth Amendment

Supreme Court

- "If law enforcement officers make a 'seizure' of a person using force that is judged to be reasonable based on a consideration of the circumstances relevant to that determination, may the officers nevertheless be held liable for injuries caused by the seizure on the ground that they committed a separate Fourth Amendment violation that contributed to their need to use force?

The Ninth Circuit has adopted a 'provocation rule' that imposes liability in such a situation. . . . We hold that the Fourth Amendment provides no basis for such a rule. A different Fourth Amendment violation cannot transform a later, reasonable use of force into an unreasonable seizure." *County of Los Angeles, Calif. v. Mendez*, 137 S. Ct. 1539, 1543–44, 198 L. Ed. 2d 52 (2017).

- "The reasonableness of the use of force is evaluated under an 'objective' inquiry that pays 'careful attention to the facts and circumstances of each particular case.' And '[t]he "reasonableness" of a particular use of force must be judged from the perspective of a reasonable officer on the scene, rather than with the 20/20 vision of hindsight.' 'Excessive force claims . . . are evaluated for objective reasonableness based upon the information the officers had when the conduct occurred.' That inquiry is dispositive: When an officer carries out a seizure that is reasonable, taking into account all relevant circumstances, there is no valid excessive force claim. . . . The basic problem with the provocation rule is that it fails to stop there. Instead, the rule provides a novel and unsupported path to liability in cases in which the use of force was reasonable. Specifically, it instructs courts to look back in time to see if there was a different Fourth Amendment violation that is somehow tied to the eventual use of force. That distinct violation, rather than the forceful seizure itself, may then serve as the foundation of the plaintiff's excessive force claim. . . . This approach mistakenly conflates distinct Fourth Amendment claims. Contrary to this approach, the objective reasonableness analysis must be conducted separately for each search or seizure that is alleged to be unconstitutional. An excessive force claim is a claim that a law enforcement officer carried out an unreasonable seizure through a use of force that was not justified under the relevant circumstances. It is not a claim that an officer used reasonable force after committing a distinct Fourth Amendment violation such as an unreasonable entry. . . . By conflating excessive force claims with other Fourth Amendment claims, the provocation rule permits excessive force claims that cannot succeed on their own terms. That is precisely how the rule operated in this case. The District Court found (and the

Ninth Circuit did not dispute) that the use of force by the deputies was reasonable under *Graham*. However, respondents were still able to recover damages because the deputies committed a separate constitutional violation (the warrantless entry into the shack) that in some sense set the table for the use of force. That is wrong. The framework for analyzing excessive force claims is set out in Graham. If there is no excessive force claim under Graham, there is no excessive force claim at all. To the extent that a plaintiff has other Fourth Amendment claims, they should be analyzed separately." *County of Los Angeles, Calif. v. Mendez*, 137 S. Ct. 1539, 1546–47, 198 L. Ed. 2d 52 (2017) (citations omitted).

• "The Court of Appeals also held that 'even without relying on [the] provocation theory, the deputies are liable for the shooting under basic notions of proximate cause.' In other words, the court apparently concluded that the shooting was proximately caused by the deputies' warrantless entry of the shack. Proper analysis of this proximate cause question required consideration of the 'foreseeability or the scope of the risk created by the predicate conduct,' and required the court to conclude that there was 'some direct relation between the injury asserted and the injurious conduct alleged.' . . . Unfortunately, the Court of Appeals' proximate cause analysis appears to have been tainted by the same errors that cause us to reject the provocation rule. The court reasoned that when officers make a 'startling entry' by 'barg [ing] into' a home 'unannounced,' it is reasonably foreseeable that violence may result. But this appears to focus solely on the risks foreseeably associated with the failure to knock and announce, which could not serve as the basis for liability since the Court of Appeals concluded that the officers had qualified immunity on that claim. By contrast, the Court of Appeals did not identify the foreseeable risks associated with the relevant constitutional violation (the warrantless entry); nor did it explain how, on these facts, respondents' injuries were proximately caused by the warrantless entry. In other words, the Court of Appeals' proximate cause analysis, like the provocation rule, conflated distinct Fourth Amendment claims and required only a murky causal link between the warrantless entry and the injuries attributed to it." *County of Los Angeles, Calif. v. Mendez*, 137 S. Ct. 1539, 1548-, 198 L. Ed. 2d 52 (2017).

- "[W]e simply decide whether the officers' failure to accommodate Sheehan's illness violated clearly established law. . . . . Under Ninth Circuit law, an entry that otherwise complies with the Fourth Amendment is not rendered unreasonable because it provokes a violent reaction. Under this rule, qualified immunity necessarily applies here because, as explained above, competent officers could have believed that the second entry was justified under both continuous search and exigent circumstance rationales. Indeed, even if Reynolds and Holder misjudged the situation, Sheehan cannot 'establish a Fourth Amendment violation based merely on bad tactics that result in a deadly confrontation that could have been avoided.' Courts must not judge officers with 'the 20/20 vision of hindsight.' . . . . The panel majority concluded that these three cases 'would have placed any reasonable, competent officer on notice that it is unreasonable to forcibly enter the home of an armed, mentally ill suspect who had been acting irrationally and had threatened anyone who entered when there was no objective need for immediate entry.' But even assuming that is true, *no precedent clearly established that there was not 'an objective need for immediate entry' here.* No matter how carefully a reasonable officer read *Graham, Deorle,* and *Alexander* beforehand, that officer could not know that reopening Sheehan's door to prevent her from escaping or gathering more weapons would violate the Ninth Circuit's test, even if all the disputed facts are viewed in respondent's favor." *City and County of San Francisco, Calif. v. Sheehan*, 135 S. Ct. 1765, 1775, 1776–77, 191 L. Ed. 2d 856 (2015) (inner citations omitted).

- "We have repeatedly told courts . . . not to define clearly established law at a high level of generality. The dispositive question is whether the violative nature of *particular* conduct is clearly established. This inquiry must be undertaken in light of the specific context of the case, not as a broad general proposition. Such specificity is especially important in the Fourth Amendment context, where the Court has recognized that it is sometimes difficult for an officer to determine how the relevant legal doctrine, here excessive force, will apply to the factual situation the officer confronts." *Mullenix v. Luna*, 136 S. Ct. 305, 308, 193 L. Ed. 2d 255 (2015) (inner quotations and citations omitted).

- "[The chase in this case exceeded 100 miles per hour and lasted over five minutes. During that chase, Rickard passed more than two dozen other vehicles, several of which were forced to alter course. Rickard's outrageously reckless driving posed a grave public safety risk. And while it is true that Rickard's car eventually collided with a police car and came temporarily to a near standstill, that did not end the chase. Less than three seconds later, Rickard resumed maneuvering his car. Just before the shots were fired, when the front bumper of his car was flush with that of one of the police cruisers, Rickard was obviously pushing down on the accelerator because the car's wheels were spinning, and then Rickard threw the car into reverse 'in an attempt to escape.' Thus, the record conclusively disproves respondent's claim that the chase in the present case was already over when petitioners began shooting. Under the circumstances at the moment when the shots were fired, all that a reasonable police officer could have concluded was that Rickard was intent on resuming his flight and that, if he was allowed to do so, he would once again pose a deadly threat for others on the road. Rickard's conduct even after the shots were fired—as noted, he managed to drive away despite the efforts of the police to block his path—underscores the point. In light of the circumstances we have discussed, it is beyond serious dispute that Rickard's flight posed a grave public safety risk, and here, as in *Scott*, the police acted reasonably in using deadly force to end that risk." *Plumhoff v. Rickard*, 134 S. Ct. 2012, 2021-22, 188 L. Ed. 2d 1056 (2014).

- "[I]f police officers are justified in firing at a suspect in order to end a severe threat to public safety, the officers need not stop shooting until the threat has ended. As petitioners noted below, 'if lethal force is justified, officers are taught to keep shooting until the threat is over.'" *Plumhoff v. Rickard*, 134 S. Ct. 2012, 2022, 188 L. Ed. 2d 1056 (2014) (citation omitted).

- "I disagree with the Court insofar as it articulates a *per se* rule. The majority states: 'A police officer's attempt to terminate a dangerous high-speed car chase that threatens the lives of innocent bystanders does not violate the Fourth Amendment, even when it places the fleeing motorist at risk of serious injury or death' . . . This statement is too absolute. As Justice Ginsburg points out. . .whether a high-speed chase violates the Fourth Amendment may well depend upon more circumstances than the majority's rule reflects. With these qualifications, I join the Court's opinion." *Scott v. Harris*, 550 U.S. 372, 127 S. Ct. 1769, 167 L. Ed. 2d 686 (2007).
- "In *Graham*, we held that claims of excessive force in the context of arrests or investigatory stops should be analyzed under the Fourth Amendment's objective reasonableness standard, not under substantive due process principles." *Saucier v. Katz*, 533 U.S. 194, 121 S. Ct. 2151, 2158, 150 L. Ed. 2d 272 (2001).
- "Where, as here, the excessive force claim arises in the context of an arrest or investigatory stop of a free citizen, it is most properly characterized as one invoking the protections of the Fourth Amendment, which guarantees citizens the right to be secure in their persons against unreasonable seizures of the person." *Graham v. Connor*, 490 U.S. 386, 394, 109 S. Ct. 1865, 104 L. Ed. 2d 443 (1989).
- "Determining whether the force used to effect a particular seizure is reasonable under the Fourth Amendment requires a careful balancing of the nature and quality of the intrusion on the individual's Fourth Amendment interests against the countervailing governmental interests at stake." *Graham v. Connor*, 490 U.S. 386, 396, 109 S. Ct. 1865, 104 L. Ed. 2d 443 (1989).
- "The use of deadly force to prevent the escape of all felony suspects, whatever the circumstances, is constitutionally unreasonable. Where the suspect poses no immediate threat to the officer and no threat to others, the harm resulting from failing to apprehend him does not justify the use of deadly force to do so. . . . A police officer may not seize an unarmed, nondangerous suspect by shooting him dead." *Tennessee v. Garner*, 471 U.S. 1, 11, 105 S. Ct. 1694, 85 L. Ed. 2d 1 (1985).

Second Circuit

- "At least two circuits and one decision from the District of Connecticut have suggested that the decision to employ a tactical team may violate the Fourth Amendment's prohibition on excessive force. . . . In November 2012—after the district court's decision in this case, but before the appeal was briefed—a panel of this Court determined that there was no clearly established right in this Circuit to be free from the deployment of a police SWAT team." *Terebesi v. Torreso*, 764 F.3d 217, 232 (2d Cir. 2014), cert. denied, 135 S. Ct. 1842, 191 L. Ed. 2d 723 (2015) (inner quotations and citations omitted).

- "A claim that excessive force was used in the course of a seizure is subject to an objective test of reasonableness under the totality of the circumstances, which requires consideration of the specific facts in each case, including the severity of the crime at issue, whether the suspect posed an immediate threat to the safety of others and whether he is actively resisting arrest. . . .The fact that a person whom a police officer attempts to arrest resists, threatens, or assaults the officer no doubt justifies the officer's use of some degree of force, but it does not give the officer license to use force without limit." *Sullivan v. Gagnier*, 225 F.3d 161, 165–66 (2d Cir. 2000).

Third Circuit

- "[T]he Supreme Court emphasized that the test is whether the officers' action are objectively reasonable in light of the facts and circumstances confronting them, without regard to their underlying intent or motivations. . . . Objective reasonableness, the Court made clear, has two important implications: First, if the shooting was not objectively reasonable under the circumstances, it is irrelevant that the officer was acting in good faith. Second, if the shooting was objectively reasonable, by contrast, then any bad faith motivating the officer would not matter for the purposes of the Fourth Amendment." *Abraham v. Raso*, 183 F.3d 279, 289 (3d Cir. 1999).

Fourth Circuit

- "The better approach in a case such as the one before us is to view the reasonableness of the force 'in full context, with an eye toward the proportionality of the force' in light of the totality of the circumstances. . . . Our analysis of the *Graham* factors when measured against the level of force used by Terry against Yates leads us to conclude that such force was not objectively reasonable in light of the totality of the circumstances in this case. Terry was ordered out of his car and subsequently tased three times over not having his driver's license. We have explained that '[d]eploying a taser is a serious use of force,' that is designed to 'inflict[ ] a painful and frightening blow.' For these reasons, it 'may only be deployed when a police officer is confronted with an exigency that creates an immediate safety risk and that is reasonably likely to be cured by using the taser.' As we held in *Estate of Armstrong*, '[t]he subject of a seizure does not create such a risk simply because he is doing something that can be characterized as resistance-even when that resistance includes physically preventing an officer's manipulations of his body.' The objective facts, when viewed in the light most favorable to Yates, as we must do at this point in the proceedings, show that he was neither a dangerous felon, a flight risk, nor an immediate threat to Terry or anyone else. Yates has thus established that Terry's use of his taser constituted excessive force in violation of Yates' Fourth Amendment rights." *Yates v. Terry*, 817 F.3d 877, 883, 886 (4th Cir. 2016) (citations omitted).

- "An attack by an unreasonably deployed police dog in the course of a seizure is a Fourth Amendment excessive force violation." *Vathekan v. Prince George's County*, 154 F.3d 173, 178 (4th Cir. 1998).

Fifth Circuit

- "[E]ven if Trammel's decision to pull his arm away from the officers can be characterized as some degree of resistance that would justify an officer's use of force, the quickness with which the officers resorted to tackling Trammel to the ground militates against a finding of reasonableness. This Court has several times found that the speed with which an officer resorts to force is relevant in determining whether that force was excessive to the need. Given that only three seconds elapsed between Officer Fruge's initial request that Trammel place his hands behind his back and when Officers Fruge, Garza, and Neveu tackled Trammel, we find that a reasonable jury could infer that the officers used very little, if any, negotiation before resorting to physical violence, and that the officers' conduct did not constitute the required 'measured and ascending' actions calibrated to Trammel's conduct. Accordingly, we hold that a reasonable jury could find that Trammel's pulling his arms away from the officers, along with the other circumstances of Trammel's arrest, did not justify the officers' decision to tackle Trammel to the ground. Thus, there is a genuine dispute of material fact as to whether the officers' use of force was objectively unreasonable. Similarly, we find that Trammel has independently presented a question of material fact as to whether the force used to gain control of his arms was excessive to the need. Viewing the facts in the light most favorable to Trammel, after the officers tackled him, they pummeled Trammel with their knees and fists in an attempt to get him to put his arms behind his back. Trammel contends the officers continued to do so even after he shouted that his arm was fused. Because Trammel's yelling about his arm can clearly be made out from the dash cam footage, a jury could reasonably infer that the officers heard Trammel's plea but nevertheless continued to beat him without consideration for his limited mobility and strength. Since Officer Fruge testified that Trammel never exhibited a desire to harm any of the officers, a reasonable jury could determine that, under the circumstances, the officers' decision to continue using force was objectively unreasonable. Thus, we hold that Trammel has presented sufficient facts to allege a violation of his constitutional right to be free from excessive force against Officers Fruge, Garza, and Nevue." *Trammell v. Fruge,* 2017 WL 3528437, * 6-7 (5th Cir. 2017) (citations omitted).

- "Application of the *Graham* factors shows that Brown's [use of force with a K9 unit] was objectively unreasonable. DUI is a serious offense, so that factor favors Brown. But the other factors push heavily for Cooper. No reasonable officer could conclude that Cooper posed an immediate threat to Brown or others. Cooper was not suspected of committing a violent offense, and Brown testified that Pressgrove, when calling for backup, had not warned that Cooper might be violent. Moreover, Brown could see Cooper's hands and knew he had no weapon. Indeed, Brown's own expert testified that there was no evidence that would have led a reasonable officer to believe that Cooper was a threat. Thus, this factor weighs strongly for Cooper. On the third factor, Cooper was not actively resisting arrest or attempting to flee or to strike Sunny. The only act of 'resistance' that Brown identifies is Cooper's failure to show his hands because, although they were on Sunny's head and visible to Brown, Brown wanted Cooper to raise his hands. Given that Sunny was still latched onto Cooper's calf at the time, the failure to raise his hands can hardly be characterized as 'active resistance.' But even if it was, any 'resistance' ended quickly. Brown ordered Cooper to roll onto his stomach, and Cooper complied with that order. At that point, no reasonable officer could believe that Cooper was actively resisting arrest; to the contrary, he was actively *complying*. And yet Brown still did not command Sunny to release the bite. Moreover, Brown was required to 'assess not only the need for force, but also "the relationship between the need and the amount of force used." ' Brown subjected Cooper to a lengthy dog attack that inflicted serious injuries, even though he had no reason to believe that Cooper posed a threat, and without first attempting to negotiate. And he continued applying force even after Cooper was actively complying with his orders. Brown's own expert conceded that there was no reason for Brown to permit Sunny to continue attacking once Cooper was on his stomach. . . . The undisputed facts establish that Brown's use of force was objectively unreasonable. To be clear, we do not say that *any* application of force to a compliant arrestee is *per se* unreasonable, and we do not opine on the line of reasonableness. Instead, we state only the obvious: Under the facts in this record, permitting a dog to continue biting a compliant and non-threatening arrestee is objectively unreasonable." *Cooper v. Brown*, 844 F.3d 517, 522–24 (5th Cir. 2016) (citations omitted).

- "[T]he question here is not, as plaintiffs assert, whether an officer violates the Fourth Amendment by shooting a suspect who is running away. Rather, it is whether an officer violates the Fourth Amendment by shooting a suspect who just fought the officer at length; disarmed him of his baton; prevented him from using his radio to call for backup; potentially attempted to obtain his gun; concussed and disoriented him; and broke free of his grasp; at the precise moment the officer's vision is impaired and he fears losing consciousness—and the evidence indicates that it was not apparent to Poitevent that Mendez was running away. In our view, using deadly force in such circumstances does not violate the Fourth Amendment." *Mendez v. Poitevent*, 823 F.3d 326, 333 (5th Cir. 2016).

- "When deadly force is used, it is clear that the severity and immediacy of the threat of harm to officers or others are paramount to the reasonableness analysis. With regard to high-speed chases, the Supreme Court has held that '[a] police officer's attempt to terminate a dangerous high-speed car chase that threatens the lives of innocent bystanders does not violate the Fourth Amendment, even when it places the fleeing motorist at risk of serious injury or death.' . . . These cases, however, do not establish a bright-line rule; 'a suspect that is fleeing in a motor vehicle is not so inherently dangerous that an officer's use of deadly force is *per se* reasonable.' Instead, *Scott, Plumhoff* and *Thompson* are simply applications of the Fourth Amendment's reasonableness requirement to particular facts. 'Nearly any suspect fleeing in a motor vehicle poses some threat of harm to the public. As the cases addressing this all-too-common scenario evince, the real inquiry is whether the fleeing suspect posed such a threat that the use of deadly force was justifiable.' " *Luna v. Mullenix*, 773 F.3d 712, 719–20 (5th Cir. 2014) (citations omitted).

- "The plaintiffs also point to evidence showing that Mullenix heard the warning that Leija had said he had a gun six minutes before the shooting, and went to the bridge and waited three minutes for Leija's car to approach. During this period Mullenix had time to consider his approach, including time to ask for his supervisor's opinion, inform Rodriguez of his intentions, and discuss the feasibility of shooting the car with Shipman. Plaintiffs argue that this is not the type of 'split-second judgment' that officers must make when faced with an imminent risk of harm to themselves or others. . . . Based on the evidence in the record, a jury could find that a reasonable officer would have concluded that the risk Leija posed was not sufficiently immediate so as to justify deadly force, and that the non-lethal methods already in place could stop the chase without the need for deadly force. We thus cannot conclude that Mullenix's actions were objectively reasonable as a matter of law." *Luna v. Mullenix*, 765 F.3d 531, 542 (5th Cir. 2014) (citations omitted).

Sixth Circuit

- "While the ultimate determination of reasonableness must be based on the totality of the circumstances, this court has repeatedly found three factors to be helpful in excessive force cases: '(1) the severity of the crime at issue; (2) whether the suspect poses an immediate threat to the safety of the officers or others; and (3) whether the suspect is actively resisting arrest or attempting to evade arrest by flight.' We are admonished not to assess those factors from a distance, but rather to consider that 'police officers are often forced to make split-second judgments—in circumstances that are tense, uncertain, and rapidly evolving—about the amount of force that is necessary in a particular situation.'" *Mitchell v. Schlabach*, 864 F.3d 416, 421 (6th Cir. 2017) (citations omitted).

- "As a matter of law, therefore, the defendants' use of force was not excessive under the Fourth Amendment. But that does not mean the dynamic entry, in particular, was wise. The warrant here concerned evidence only of a misdemeanor; and yet the defendants chose a course of action that, though constitutional, unavoidably jeopardized the officers' lives along with Moore's. In the end Moore was shot, though it just as easily could have been Penny—as the defendants themselves emphasize here. Meanwhile, the officers plainly had available to them other options that did not involve an immediate physical confrontation. The officers would have done well to consider them more seriously than they apparently did." *Moore v. City of Memphis*, 853 F.3d 866, 870-72 (6th Cir. 2017).

- "We have held that 'excessively forceful or unduly tight handcuffing is a constitutional violation under the Fourth Amendment' and that 'freedom from excessively forceful or unduly tight handcuffing is a clearly established right for purposes of qualified immunity.' To plead successfully a claim of excessively forceful handcuffing, the plaintiff must allege physical injury from the handcuffing. '[W]hen there is no allegation of physical injury, the handcuffing of an individual incident to a lawful arrest is insufficient as a matter of law to state a claim of excessive force under the Fourth Amendment.' " The extent of the physical injury suffered by the plaintiff need not be severe in order to sustain the excessive-force claim." *Courtright v. City of Battle Creek*, 839 F.3d 513, 518–19 (6th Cir. 2016) (citations omitted).

- "The heart of her argument is that, given the minor nature of the crime for which she was arrested, i.e., obstructing official business, the force exerted was disproportionate and unreasonable. Smith complains that the officers gripped her too tightly when grabbing her hand and guiding her to the patrol car. She claims to have suffered 'severe' bruises that 'lasted over a week' and 'emotional distress.' Under some circumstances, bruising alone can be sufficient to create a genuine issue of material fact that there was an injury sufficient to support an excessive force claim. Here, however, Smith's own deposition, even charitably construed, shows that the officers were not excessive in the amount of pressure they used[.]" *Smith v. City of Wyoming*, 821 F.3d 697, 717–18 (6th Cir. 2016) (citations omitted).

- "Even if Officer Jones had the right to use deadly force in self-defense, [the claimant] questions the use of so much force—twenty rounds in all. But, so far as the record shows, the number of rounds fired by the officer flows from the reasonable decision to engage the automatic-trigger function on his gun before entering the room. And no evidence shows that Officer Jones continued firing after he knew that he had already incapacitated Krause or that Krause had given up. '[I]f police officers are justified in firing at a suspect in order to end a severe threat to public safety, the officers need not stop shooting until the threat has ended.' " *Krause v. Jones*, 765 F.3d 675, 681 (6th Cir. 2014) (citation omitted).

Seventh Circuit

- "Of course, that also means that we are not holding the 'bite and hold' technique is *per se* deadly force. Rather, whether a 'bite and hold' technique constitutes deadly force 'depends on how [the dog] is trained to behave when confronting a suspect.' " *Becker v. Elfreich*, 821 F.3d 920, 926 (7th Cir. 2016) (citations omitted).

- "The exclusionary rule is used in only a subset of all constitutional violations—and excessive force in making an arrest or seizure is not a basis for the exclusion of evidence." *Evans v. Poskon*, 603 F.3d 362 (7th Cir. 2010).

- "Factors to consider in making a determination of whether the amount of force used to effectuate a seizure is reasonable include the severity of the crime at issue, whether the suspect poses an immediate threat to the safety of the officers or others, and whether he actively is resisting arrest or attempting to evade arrest by flight. (citation omitted) Other factors include whether the individual was under arrest or suspected of committing a crime, was armed, or was interfering or attempting to interfere with the officer's execution of his or her duties." *Estate of Escobedo v. Bender*, 600 F.3d 770 (7th Cir. 2010).

- "That an unnecessary killing of a person's pet offended search and seizure protections was clearly established at time of officers' shooting and killing of pet owner's dog, for purposes of officers' claim of qualified immunity from owner's § 1983 suit." *Viilo v. Eyre*, 547 F.3d 707 (7th Cir. 2008).

- "[T]he Officers' use of force in this case did not rise to the level of a constitutional violation. . . . [T]he relevant inquiry is 'whether the officers' actions [were] objectively reasonable in light of the facts and circumstances confronting them.' The amount of permissible force depends upon the specific situation, including 'the severity of the crime at issue, whether the suspect poses an immediate threat to the safety of the officers or others, and whether he is actively resisting arrest or attempting to evade arrest by flight.' When police officers face what is essentially a fluid situation, they are entitled to graduate their response to meet the demands of the circumstances confronting them." *Smith v. Ball State Univ.*, 295 F.3d 763 (7th Cir. 2002).

- "Whether an officer used excessive force during an arrest is determined under the objective reasonableness standard. We assess whether an officer's actions were objectively reasonable in light of the facts and circumstances confronting them, without regard to their underlying intent or motivation. . . .We consider the severity of the crime at issue, whether the suspect posed an immediate threat to the safety of the officers or others, and whether he was actively resisting arrest or attempting to evade arrest by flight. . . .We balance the amount of force used in relation to the danger posed to the community or to the arresting officers." *Smith v. City of Chicago*, 242 F.3d 737, 743, 56 Fed. R. Evid. Serv. 761 (7th Cir. 2001).

Eighth Circuit

- "Vester contends that Hallock infringed his Fourth Amendment right to be free from unreasonable seizures by using excessive force in arresting him. In evaluating this sort of constitutional claim, 'the test is whether the amount of force used was objectively reasonable under the particular circumstances.' 'The "reasonableness" of a particular use of force must be judged from the perspective of a reasonable officer on the scene, rather than with the 20/20 vision of hindsight.' For example, we have considered as relevant 'the severity of the crime at issue, whether the suspect poses an immediate threat to the safety of the officers or others, and whether he is actively resisting arrest or attempting to evade arrest by flight.' Based on the circumstances Hallock confronted upon arriving at the 101 Bar & Grill, his use of the arm-bar technique fell short of the level of force required to constitute a constitutional violation. Although Vester neither visibly possessed a weapon nor attempted to resist arrest prior to the takedown, a variety of factors suggest that the amount of force Hallock employed was reasonable under the circumstances. Particularly relevant are the severity of Vester's criminal conduct of threatening to stab various individuals, his refusal to comply with Hallock's repeated commands, the very real possibility that he still had a concealed knife on his person after exiting the vehicle, the resulting potential threat to Hallock's safety, and the fact that Hallock was making the arrest without any backup." *Vester v. Hallock*, 864 F.3d 884, 887 (8th Cir. 2017).

- "Here, by the undisputed facts, Robinson informed Tatum he was a police officer, told him he was under arrest, told him to put his hands on a clothes rack, warned him he would use pepper spray if he did not calm down, and then pepper sprayed him. Tatum was given an opportunity to comply. He did not, instead arguing angrily with Robinson. It was reasonable for Robinson to use *some* force. But it was not reasonable to immediately use significant force. In addition to the lack of justification from the three *Graham* factors, other facts and circumstances indicate only limited force was reasonable. Robinson was not alone—another security officer was close by, as were at least two Dillard's employees. Robinson was off-duty and in plain clothes. . . . It was not reasonable for Robinson to immediately use pepper spray. Pepper spray can cause more than temporary pain. Robinson presents no evidence he attempted to use other force to secure compliance—no evidence he tried to grab Tatum's hands and place them on the clothes rack, for example. Instead, he proceeded to pepper spray Tatum 14 seconds after he encountered him, and necessarily fewer seconds after Tatum failed to comply with his command." *Tatum v. Robinson*, 858 F.3d 544, 550 (8th Cir. 2017) (citations omitted).

- "Under the Fourth Amendment, police officers are liable for excessive force that is not objectively reasonable under the circumstances. Officers are 'justified in using force to remove a driver, whom they believed to be impaired, from his vehicle after he refused to comply with their order to exit it.' Here, it was objectively reasonable for Heady to believe that Boude's reach for the gearshift was an attempt to shift the car to drive and to flee. Heady knew about Boude's huffing the day before, so he had reason to believe she was intoxicated and a potential threat to public safety. When the brake lights to the SUV turned on—consistent with shifting gears— Heady said 'no, no, no,' reached into the car, and turned off the ignition. After Boude refused to comply with Heady's order to exit, he was 'justified in using force to remove [Boude], whom [Heady] believed to be impaired.' True, as the district court found, the dash-cam video does not 'blatantly contradict' Boude's allegation that she 'reached for the gear shift to make sure her vehicle was in park before she made any move to comply with Defendant's order that she turn the vehicle off.' However, qualified immunity does not depend on whether Boude was in fact attempting to flee when she reached for the gearshift; rather, the key is Heady's objectively reasonable beliefs under the circumstances. Here, assuming Boude's reach for the gearshift was innocent, Heady could still have an objectively reasonable belief that her movement was a non-compliant attempt to shift the car to drive and to flee. Boude contends that Heady's use of force was objectively unreasonable because when he removed her from the SUV, he had already taken the keys, eliminating any risk she might flee. Even after the car was off, it was reasonable for Heady to believe that Boude—intoxicated, and moments earlier non-compliant with his order to turn off the car—would continue to be non-compliant or attempt to flee on foot. Officers are 'justified in using force to remove a driver, whom they believed to be impaired, from his vehicle after he refused to comply with their order to exit.' Moments 'after [Boude] refused to comply' with Heady's order to turn off the car, he was 'justified in using force to remove' her. Boude relies on *Brown*, where this court found a fact dispute whether an officer held an objectively reasonable belief that force was necessary under the circumstances. There, the suspect's husband had been pulled over for allegedly driving under the influence. After he was handcuffed, the suspect—in the front passenger seat—became frightened and dialed 911. An officer told her to hang up. She refused. The officer then entered the car and tased her. Reversing a grant of qualified immunity, this court said, 'Whether [the officer] reasonably interpreted her refusal as a realistic threat to his personal safety or whether it constituted nothing more than an affront to his command authority is a matter for a jury to decide.' The facts here differ from *Brown* in two critical ways. First, the suspect in *Brown* was in the passenger seat; Boude was in the driver seat. Second, the suspect in *Brown* did not make any movement that could be reasonably interpreted as an attempt to flee. Here, it was objectively reasonable for Heady to believe that, when Boude—a suspected intoxicated driver—reached for the gearshift after he told her to exit the SUV, she was attempting to flee. Because Heady's use of force was objectively reasonable under the circumstances, he did not violate Boude's Fourth Amendment right to be free from excessive force. . . ." *Boude v. City of Raymore, Missouri*, 855 F.3d 930, 933–34 (8th Cir. 2017) (citations omitted).

• "At the time [police] acted, it was clear to a reasonable officer that knocking a *non-resisting* suspect to the ground after he had been forcibly removed from his home without cause violated his clearly established Fourth Amendment rights." *Smith v. Kansas City, Missouri Police Dept.*, 586 F.3d 576 (8th Cir. 2009) (emphasis in original).

• "A Fourth Amendment seizure requires an intentional act by an officer, and does not address accidental effects of otherwise lawful government conduct. We previously held [the arresting officer's] act of drawing his gun was objectively reasonable, and the accidental discharge did not constitute an unreasonable seizure violating [plaintiff's] constitutional rights. Therefore, the City cannot be held liable on either an unconstitutional policy or custom theory or on a failure to train or supervise theory." *McCoy v. City of Monticello*, 411 F.3d 920 (8th Cir. 2005).

• "Although there can be no question that the Fourth Amendment prohibits unreasonable seizures of the person, it is also well established that not every push or shove violates the Fourth Amendment. . . .The applicable test is whether the force used to effect a particular seizure is reasonable. . .In the context of a claim of excessive force, the reasonableness inquiry must be an objective one in that the court must only evaluate whether the officers' actions are objectively reasonable in light of the facts and circumstances confronting them, without regard to their underlying intent or motivation." *Lawson v. Hulm*, 223 F.3d 831, 834 (8th Cir. 2000).

Ninth Circuit

- "Although Lowry has not sued the individual police officers, her Monell claim against the City first requires her to establish that the force used against her was unconstitutionally excessive. In assessing the objective reasonableness of a particular use of force, we consider: (1) 'the severity of the intrusion on the individual's Fourth Amendment rights by evaluating the type and amount of force inflicted,' (2) 'the government's interest in the use of force,' and (3) the balance between 'the gravity of the intrusion on the individual' and 'the government's need for that intrusion.' This inquiry must be viewed 'from the perspective of a reasonable officer on the scene, rather than with the 20/20 vision of hindsight.' An officer's use of force cannot be deemed excessive based on facts that he reasonably would not have known or anticipated." *Lowry v. City of San Diego*, 858 F.3d 1248, 1256 (9th Cir. 2017) (en banc) (citations omitted).

- "The first step of the excessive force inquiry requires us to 'assess the severity of the intrusion on the individual's Fourth Amendment rights by evaluating "the type and amount of force inflicted."' We must undertake a case-by-case analysis. Our precedent establishes that characterizing the quantum of force with regard to the use of a police dog depends on the specific factual circumstances . . . . Here, the district court properly concluded that the use of force was 'moderate.' Unlike in Chew, where the police dog was 'beyond the reach of a countermanding order' when the dog found the plaintiff, dragged him up to ten feet, and 'nearly severed' his arm, in this case, Sergeant Nulton closely followed Bak and called her off very quickly after the initial contact with Lowry. In part because of Nulton's close proximity to Bak, the encounter between Lowry and Bak was so brief that Nulton did not even know if contact had occurred. Thus, the risk of harm posed by this particular use of force, and the actual harm caused, was moderate. The district court properly determined that the use of force in this instance was not severe." *Lowry v. City of San Diego*, 858 F.3d 1248, 1256–57 (9th Cir. 2017) (citations and text omitted).

- "The second step of the excessive force analysis under the Fourth Amendment is to 'evaluate the government's

interest in the use of force.' That interest is assessed by
considering three primary factors: '(1) the severity of
the crime at issue, (2) whether the suspect posed an immediate threat to the safety of the officers or others,
and (3) whether the suspect was actively resisting arrest or attempting to evade arrest by flight.' These factors, set forth in *Graham v. Connor*, are not exclusive,
however, and we examine the totality of the circumstances, considering other factors when appropriate.
The first *Graham* factor, the severity of the crime at issue, weighs in the City's favor. Because the building's
burglar alarm had been triggered late at night, the door
to the office suite had been left ajar, and no one
responded to Sergeant Nulton's warnings, the officers
reasonably concluded that a burglary might be in
progress. '[B]urglary and attempted burglary are
considered to carry an inherent risk of violence.' The
Supreme Court has stated that '[b]urglary is dangerous
because it can end in confrontation leading to violence.'
Thus, the seriousness of the suspected crime weighs in
favor of the City. The second *Graham* factor, 'whether
the suspect pose[d] an immediate threat to the safety of
the officers or others,' is 'the most important single element of the three specified factors.' When viewing the
facts from the perspective of the officers, it is apparent
that a reasonable officer could have concluded that if
there was someone committing a burglary in the building, that person might be armed and could pose an immediate threat to the safety of the officers. The officers
knew that they had been dispatched to respond to a
burglar alarm, that they arrived quickly to find a dark
commercial building and an open door, and that no one
responded to their warnings. In Miller, we concluded
that the officer was entitled to assume that the suspect
posed an immediate threat because he was hiding, the
officer did not know whether he was armed, and he had
ignored the officer's warning that a police dog would be
released. Similarly 'objectively menacing circumstances'
existed here. Moreover, when confronted with signs of a
burglary, investigating officers are entitled to protect
their own safety. We have previously observed that
'when officers suspect a burglary in progress, they have
no idea who might be inside and may reasonably as-

sume that the suspects will, if confronted, flee or offer armed resistance.' Thus, '[s]o long as the officers have established probable cause for a burglary, "in such exigent circumstances, the police are entitled to enter immediately using all appropriate force."' This factor weighs in favor of the City in this case. The third factor, whether Lowry was resisting or attempting to evade arrest, does not weigh substantially either way here. That factor can be important when an officer is facing a suspect and can observe whether that suspect is complying or resisting. In this case, though, nobody responded to the warnings shouted by Sergeant Nulton, so the officers did not know anything specific about whomever might have been inside the building. The district court concluded that because Lowry did not respond to Nulton's commands, 'the officers could [have] reasonably believe[d] that the suspect was ignoring their commands, thereby evading arrest.' Although we have acknowledged that '[e]ven purely passive resistance can support the use of some force,' we have explained that 'the level of force an individual's resistance will support is dependent on the factual circumstances underlying that resistance.' Our cases suggest that where the suspect passively resists arrest, a lesser degree of force is justified compared to situations in which the suspect actively resists arrest. In the end, this factor does not weigh either way in this case. In assessing the City's interest in the use of force, other relevant factors we have identified include 'whether proper warnings were given' and 'the availability of less intrusive alternatives to the force employed.' We have held that an important consideration in evaluating the City's interest in the use of force is 'whether officers gave a warning before employing the force.' All three officers testified that Sergeant Nulton issued a warning and repeated it before entering the suite with Bak. Although Lowry did not hear the warnings, the officers did not know and had no reason to know that someone would be in a nonresidential building late at night and sleeping so deeply that she would be unable to hear a warning or to be awakened by the officers' calls. The circumstances were not at all like those in Nelson, where we held that the officers had failed to give sufficient warning despite their attempts to do so because they were 45 to 150 feet from the group, in a party of 1,000 people, and it was 'undisputed that they lacked any means with which to amplify their voices so that they could be heard over the din of the crowd.' Here, the officers' issuance of warnings outside the door of the suite weighs in favor of the City. We also consider 'whether there were less intrusive means of force that might have been used before officers resorted' to releasing Bak. In assessing alternatives, however, we must not forget that 'officers "are not required to use the least intrusive degree of force possible."' As *Graham* cautioned, courts must allow 'for the fact that police officers are often forced to make split-second judgments—in circumstances that are tense, uncertain, and rapidly evolving—about the amount of force that is necessary in a particular situation.' The practice of allowing dogs to inspect areas off-lead is in place to protect officers' safety. Lowry suggests that the police dog could have been kept on her leash, albeit without any evidence in support of the effectiveness of that alternative technique. If that approach had been followed, Sergeant Nulton would have been required to expose himself to what the officers reasonably suspected was a burglar, lurking in the dark office, possibly armed. The conceivable alternatives to SDPD's policy do not weigh against the City's interest in the use of force under these particular circumstances.. . . The final step of the excessive force inquiry requires us to balance the gravity of the intrusion on Lowry's Fourth Amendment rights against the City's need for that intrusion. Here, the force used was not severe, and the officers had a compelling interest in protecting themselves against foreseeable danger in an uncertain situation, which they reasonably suspected to be an ongoing burglary. We conclude that the use of Bak under these circumstances did not violate Lowry's rights under the Fourth Amendment." *Lowry v. City of San Diego*, 858 F.3d 1248, 1257 (9th Cir. 2017) (citations omitted).

- "As we have recognized, '[b]ecause the excessive force and false arrest factual inquiries are distinct, establishing a lack of probable cause to make an arrest does not establish an excessive force claim, and vice-versa.' Just proving lack of probable cause for the arrest, for instance, does not establish that the police used excessive force, or, indeed, any force. And force used by an officer to effectuate an arrest, 'regardless of whether [the officer] had probable cause to [make the] arrest,' may still be reasonable, for instance to overcome the arrestee's forcible resistance. Nevertheless, *Graham* counsels that the facts that gave rise to an unlawful detention or arrest can factor into the determination whether the force used to make the arrest was excessive." *Velazquez v. City of Long Beach*, 793 F.3d 1010, 1024 (9th Cir. 2015) (citations omitted).

• "To decide this case a jury would have to answer just one simple question: Did the police see Cruz reach for his waistband? If they did, they were entitled to shoot; if they didn't, they weren't. But for a judge ruling on the officers' motion for summary judgment, this translates to a different question: Could any reasonable jury find it more likely than not that Cruz *didn't* reach for his waistband? In ruling for the officers, the district court answered this question 'No.' The evidence it relied on in reaching this conclusion—indeed, the only evidence that suggests this is what happened—is the testimony of the officers, four of whom say they saw Cruz make the fateful reach. But in the deadly force context, we cannot 'simply accept what may be a self-serving account by the police officer.' Because the person most likely to rebut the officers' version of events—the one killed—can't testify . . . In this case, there's circumstantial evidence that could give a reasonable jury pause. Most obvious is the fact that Cruz didn't have a gun on him, so why would he have reached for his waistband? Cruz probably saw that he was surrounded by officers with guns drawn. In that circumstance, it would have been foolish—but not wholly implausible—for him to have tried to fast-draw his weapon in an attempt to shoot his way out. But for him to make such a gesture when *no* gun is there makes no sense whatsoever. A jury may doubt that Cruz did this. Of course, a jury could reach the opposite conclusion. It might believe that Cruz *thought* he had the gun there, or maybe he had a death wish, or perhaps his pants were falling down at the worst possible moment. But the jury could also reasonably conclude that the officers lied. In reaching that conclusion, the jury might find relevant the uncontroverted evidence that Officer Linn, one of Cruz's shooters, recited the exact same explanation when he shot and killed another unarmed man, David Raya, two years later under very similar circumstances. Like Cruz, Raya was tracked down after a confidential informant told police that he had a gun and that he 'wasn't going back to prison,' and, as with Cruz, the tip led to an altercation with Anaheim police that ended with an unarmed Raya biting the dust. Perhaps the most curious similarity: According to the officers who shot the two unarmed men, both reached for their waistbands while the police had their guns trained on them. (One noteworthy difference: Raya was shot in the back because he was running away from Officer Linn when Linn saw him reach for his waistband.) 'They both reached for the gun' might be a plausible defense from officers in the line of duty. 'They both reached for no gun' sounds more like a song-and-dance. A jury might find implausible other aspects of the officers' story. For starters, *four* of the officers said they saw Cruz reach for his waistband. A jury might be skeptical that four pairs of eyes had a line of sight to Cruz's hand as he stood between the open car door and the SUV. There is also the fact that Cruz was left-handed, yet two officers attested that they saw Cruz reach for his waistband with his right hand. A reasonable jury could doubt that Cruz would have reached for a non-existent weapon with his off hand. Then there is the officers' claim that Cruz had 'exited' the Suburban, and 'stood in the doorway,' but after he was killed they had to cut him free from his seat belt because he was 'suspended' by it. How does a man who has 'emerged fully' from a vehicle, and 'turn[ed] to face forward,' end up hanging from his seat belt after he's shot? Maybe it's possible. But it's also possible that the officers didn't wait for Cruz to exit his car—or reach for his waistband—and simply opened fire on a man who was trying to comply with their instructions to '[g]et down on the ground.' The testimony of the only non-police eyewitness, Norman Harms, indicates that Cruz's feet indeed made it out of the car, but that Cruz was 'slipping on the ground, like kind of falling down,' as if he were 'tripping.' This paints a different picture than the officers' testimony that Cruz had fully emerged from his SUV and was poised to attack. Based on Harms's testimony, a jury might find that Cruz was trying to get out of the car (as he was ordered to do multiple times after he opened his door) but got caught in his seat belt. Were a jury to believe this version of events—which seems no less likely than a man shot while standing next to a vehicle becoming suspended by a seat belt—this would certainly cast doubt on the officers' credibility and lead the jury to find for plaintiffs." *Cruz v. City of Anaheim*, 765 F.3d 1076, 1079–80 (9th Cir. 2014).

- "No reasonable officer could have believed that [defendant]'s action in shooting. . .with the 'less lethal' lead-filled beanbag round was appropriate or lawful. To the contrary, 'it would be clear to a reasonable officer that [defendant's] conduct was unlawful.' . . . Given all the circumstances, the error in judgment, such as it was, does not constitute a 'reasonable mistake' of fact or law on [defendant]'s part. Viewing the facts in the light most favorable to the plaintiff, [defendant] was not entitled to qualified immunity for his use of excessive force." *Deorle v. Rutherford*, 272 F.3d 1272, 1275 (9th Cir. 2001).

- "Under the Fourth Amendment, police may use only such force as is objectively reasonable under the circumstances. . . .Determining whether force used in making an arrest is excessive or reasonable requires careful attention to the facts and circumstances of each particular case, including the severity of the crime at issue, whether the suspect poses an immediate threat to the safety of the officers or others, and whether he is actively resisting arrest or attempting to evade arrest by flight." *Cunningham v. Gates*, 229 F.3d 1271, 1288 (9th Cir. 2000), as amended, (Oct. 31, 2000).

Eleventh Circuit

- "In considering an excessive-force case, a court should determine whether an officer's conduct in making an arrest is objectively reasonable or if it is an over-reactive, disproportionate action for the situation relative to the response of the apprehended person. The lat-

ter is the sort of unconstitutional conduct that deprives
an officer of qualified-immunity protection in an obvious-
clarity case. Under the plaintiff's version of the alleged
excessive-force occurrence, an obvious-clarity case is
presented, when 'no factually particularized, preexisting case law [i]s necessary for it to be very obvious to
every objectively reasonable officer' confronting the
same situation that the officer's conduct 'violated [the
plaintiff's] constitutional right to be free of the excessive use of force,' precluding qualified-immunity
protection. '[I]n an excessive force case, qualified immunity applies *unless application of the standard would
inevitably lead every reasonable officer to conclude the
force was unlawful.*' 'A genuine "excessive force" claim
relates to the *manner in which an arrest was carried
out*, independent of whether law enforcement had the
power to arrest.' Courts must examine 'the fact pattern
from the perspective of a reasonable officer on the scene
with knowledge of the attendant circumstances and
facts, and balance the risk of bodily [or psychological]
harm to the suspect against the gravity of the threat
the officer sought to eliminate.' Consequently, 'the
words of a federal statute or federal constitutional provision may be *so clear* and the conduct *so bad* that *case
law is not needed to establish that the conduct cannot be
lawful.*' In an obvious-clarity case, where the officer's
conduct is plainly objectively unreasonable, a court does
not need prior case law to determine the force used by
the officer was excessive and unlawful, because it was
disproportionate. . . . There is no evidence Stephens
attempted to resist Deputy DeGiovanni's investigation
ending in his arrest or to evade his arrest by fleeing. To
the contrary, Stephens answered Deputy DeGiovanni's
questions, despite Deputy DeGiovanni's harsh, threatening questioning and his forcefully hitting Stephens in
his chest multiple times, ultimately causing his head to
strike the door jamb, resulting in permanent injury as
well as twisting Stephens's right hand and three fingers
backward, supporting his full body weight. Through it
all, Stephens was compliant, even when Deputy DeGiovanni arrested and handcuffed him. Stephens never attempted to flee the scene of his arrest. Consequently,
none of the *Graham* factors applies to Stephens's

encounter with and seizure by Deputy DeGiovanni as to Stephens's actions resulting in his seizure and arrest by Deputy DeGiovanni. '[Q]ualified immunity is not appropriate when the *Graham* analysis yields an answer that is clear beyond all doubt,' as in this case." *Stephens v. DeGiovanni*, 852 F.3d 1298, 1317–18, 1322–24 (11th Cir. 2017) (citations omitted).

- "There is substantial case authority in the Supreme Court and this Circuit clearly establishing that harming a suspect after that suspect is compliant, cooperative, under control, or otherwise subdued is gratuitous and, therefore, constitutionally excessive. The three cases Merricks cites establish nothing more than that. On the other hand, there is little, if any, authority dealing with the force an officer can use when he has the undisputed right to search a vehicle, and the driver obstructs the search. For that reason, in analyzing excessive force cases, it is important to understand not only what force was applied but when it was applied. If gratuitous force was applied after the suspect was subdued or otherwise cooperating, qualified immunity will likely not apply, unless the force is *de minimis*. If, on the other hand, the force was applied when the officer was trying to take control of the suspect or the situation confronting him, the officer can make a much better claim to the qualified immunity defense." *Merricks v. Adkisson*, 785 F.3d 553, 563 (11th Cir. 2015) (citations omitted).

- "But as we have pointed out, 'the typical arrest involves some force and injury.' When more force is required to effect an arrest without endangering officer safety, the suspect will likely suffer more severe injury, but that alone does not make the use of that amount of force unreasonable. (If it did, deadly force could never be used no matter what the circumstances were.) Even assuming, as we must at the summary judgment stage, that Mobley's alleged injuries did not occur when he wrecked his truck, the injuries he suffered were not disproportionate to the force that the officers reasonably could have believed was required to subdue him." *Mobley v. Palm Beach County Sheriff Dept.*, 783 F.3d 1347, 1355–56 (11th Cir. 2015).

- "[E]ven if the complaint could be read to allege that Mr.

Saunders disobeyed an order by lifting his head off the hot pavement, that minor transgression does not mean that the force allegedly used was a constitutionally permissible response, or that the agents are entitled to qualified immunity. The agents did not, by Mr. Saunders' account, merely exert some pressure to guide his head downward. Instead, they 'slammed' his head against the pavement with 'extreme force,' and, not surprisingly, this resulted in significant injuries to Mr. Saunders. The human skull is a relatively hearty vessel for the brain, but it will generally not fare well in a contest with hardened cement." *Saunders v. Duke*, 766 F.3d 1262, 1269 (11th Cir. 2014) (citations omitted).

- "Fourth Amendment jurisprudence has staked no bright line for identifying force as excessive. . .the hazy border between permissible and forbidden force is marked by a multifactored, case-by-case balancing test, and the test requires weighing of all the circumstances." *Jackson v. Sauls*, 206 F.3d 1156, 1170 (11th Cir. 2000).

- "The Supreme Court, in *Tennessee v. Garner*. . .held that the use of deadly force is warranted only if the suspect takes action to present an immediate risk of serious harm to others or the officer. This Court held that the decision in Garner provided a bright line that established when an officer may use deadly force in apprehending a suspect. . . . Where the suspect is not a fleeing felon and poses no immediate threat to the officer or others, the use of deadly force is a violation of the suspect's Fourth Amendment Rights and, therefore, unconstitutional." *Wood v. City of Lakeland, FL*, 203 F.3d 1288, 1292 (11th Cir. 2000).

§ 4:10 Forcible abduction: The trial court does not lose jurisdiction to try a defendant whose presence was secured by forcible abduction

Supreme Court

- "Respondent and his *amici* may be correct that respondent's abduction was shocking, and that it may be in violation of general international law principles. Mexico has protested the abduction of respondent through diplomatic notes, and the decision of whether respondent should be returned to Mexico, as a matter outside of the Treaty, is a matter for the Executive Branch. We conclude, however, that respondent's abduction was not in violation of the Extradition Treaty between the United States and Mexico, and therefore the rule of *Ker v. Illinois* is fully applicable to this case. The fact of respondent's forcible abduction does not therefore prohibit his trial in a court in the United States for violations of the criminal laws of the United States." *U.S. v. Alvarez-Machain*, 504 U.S. 655, 669–70, 112 S. Ct. 2188, 119 L. Ed. 2d 441 (1992).

- "This Court has never departed from the rule announced in *Ker* that the power of a court to try a person for crime is not impaired by the fact that he had been brought within the court's jurisdiction by reason of a forcible abduction. No persuasive reasons are now presented to justify overruling this line of cases. They rest on the sound basis that due process of law is satisfied when one present in court is convicted of crime after having been fairly apprized of the charges against him and after a fair trial in accordance with constitutional procedural safeguards. There is nothing in the Constitution that requires a court to permit a guilty person rightfully convicted to escape justice because he was brought to trial against his will." *Frisbie v. Collins*, 342 U.S. 519, 522, 72 S. Ct. 509, 96 L. Ed. 541 (1952).

- "[F]orcible abduction is no sufficient reason why the party should not answer when brought within the jurisdiction of the court which has the right to try him for such an offence, and presents no valid objection to his trial in such court." *Ker v. People of State of Illinois*, 119 U.S. 436, 444, 7 S. Ct. 225, 30 L. Ed. 421 (1886).

Fifth Circuit

- "A criminal defendant abducted to the United States from a nation with which it has an extradition treaty does not acquire a defense to the jurisdiction of this country's courts. The language of this country's treaty with Mexico does not support the proposition that abductions are prohibited outside its terms. Furthermore, the treaty only prohibits gaining a defendant's presence by means other than those set forth in the treaty when the nation from which the defendant was abducted objects." *U.S. v. Chapa-Garza*, 62 F.3d 118, 120 (5th Cir. 1995).

Seventh Circuit

- "For the past 100 years, the Supreme Court has consistently held that the manner in which a defendant is brought to trial does not affect the ability of the government to try him. The *Key-Frisbie* doctrine, as this rule has come to be known, states that the power of a court to try a person for a crime is not impaired by the fact that he has been brought within the court's jurisdiction by reason of a forcible abduction." *Matta-Ballesteros v. Henman*, 896 F.2d 255, 260 (7th Cir. 1990).

Eleventh Circuit

- "In *Alvarez-Machain*, the Court considered the issue of whether a criminal defendant, abducted to the United States from a nation with which it has an extradition treaty, thereby acquires a defense to the jurisdiction of this country's courts. . . . In answer, the Court stated: We hold that he does not, and that he may be tried in federal district court for violations of the criminal law of the United States." *U.S. v. Noriega*, 117 F.3d 1206, 1213, 47 Fed. R. Evid. Serv. 786 (11th Cir. 1997).
- "[Defendant]'s due process claim falls squarely within the Supreme Court's *Ker-Frisbie* doctrine, which holds that a defendant cannot defeat personal jurisdiction by asserting the illegality of the procurement of his presence." *U.S. v. Noriega*, 117 F.3d 1206, 1214, 47 Fed. R. Evid. Serv. 786 (11th Cir. 1997).

Chapter 5

Search Warrant Requirements

Research References

West's Key Number Digest

Criminal Law ⚖394, 1158; Customs Duties ⚖126; Searches and Seizures ⚖7, 23, 40, 101, 104 to 105, 111 to 117, 122 to 125, 141 to 147, 193, 200

KeyCite®: Cases and other legal materials listed in KeyCite Scope can be researched through the KeyCite service on Westlaw®. Use KeyCite to check citations for form, parallel references, prior and later history, and comprehensive citator information, including citations to other decisions and secondary materials.

---

§ 5:1   Issuance: The warrant must be issued by a disinterested magistrate

<u>Supreme Court</u>

- "A magistrate failing to manifest that neutrality and detachment demanded of a judicial officer when presented with a warrant application and who acts instead as an adjunct law enforcement officer cannot provide valid authorization for an otherwise unconstitutional search." *U.S. v. Leon*, 468 U.S. 897, 914, 104 S. Ct. 3405, 82 L. Ed. 2d 677 (1984).

- "[T]he participation of a detached magistrate in the probable-cause determination is an essential element of a reasonable search or seizure." *Steagald v. U.S.*, 451 U.S. 204, 216, 101 S. Ct. 1642, 68 L. Ed. 2d 38 (1981).

- "[T]he Town Justice did not manifest that neutrality and detachment demanded of a judicial officer when presented with a warrant application for a search and seizure. [H]e was not acting as a judicial officer but as an adjunct law-enforcement officer." *Lo-Ji Sales, Inc. v. New York*, 442 U.S. 319, 326–27, 99 S. Ct. 2319, 60 L. Ed. 2d 920, 5 Media L. Rep. (BNA) 1177 (1979).

- "The justice is not salaried. He is paid, so far as search warrants are concerned. . .for his issuance of the warrants and he receives nothing for denial of the warrant. [T]he issuance of the search warrant by the justice of the peace effected a violation of the Fourth and Fourteenth Amendments." *Connally v. Georgia*, 429 U.S. 245, 250–51, 97 S. Ct. 546, 50 L. Ed. 2d 444 (1977).

- "Inherent in the concept of a warrant is its issuance by a neutral and detached magistrate. [T]he Fourth Amendment does not contemplate the executive officers of Government as neutral and disinterested magistrates." *U.S. v. U.S. Dist. Court for Eastern Dist. of Mich., Southern Division*, 407 U.S. 297, 316–17, 92 S. Ct. 2125, 32 L. Ed. 2d 752 (1972).

- "[T]he state official who was the chief investigator and prosecutor in this case was not the neutral and detached magistrate required by the Constitution." *Coolidge v. New Hampshire*, 403 U.S. 443, 453, 91 S. Ct. 2022, 29 L. Ed. 2d 564 (1971).

- "[I]nferences [must] be drawn by a neutral and detached magistrate instead of being judged by the officer engaged in the often competitive enterprise of ferreting out crime." *Johnson v. U.S.*, 333 U.S. 10, 14, 68 S. Ct. 367, 92 L. Ed. 436 (1948).

Fifth Circuit

- "A determination by a neutral magistrate is a prerequisite to the sufficiency of an application for a warrant." *U.S. v. Alvarez*, 127 F.3d 372, 374 (5th Cir. 1997).

267

Sixth Circuit

- "[The duties of the person who signed the warrant] were similar to those of an administrative assistant. The court further found that [the signer] served at the pleasure of a law enforcement agent, as the Ohio County Jailer hired and could fire her. The court determined that [the signer's] job responsibilities included the following: handling the purchase orders for all jail bills; assisting the jailer with the yearly budget; keeping track of expenditures for the jail; billing surrounding counties for housing their inmates; maintaining the records of the jail's commissary account; handling the jailer's correspondence; and purchasing jail supplies. [She] additionally handled inmates' work release requests by obtaining information from the prisoners and completing work release forms. She assisted inmates with their child support obligations, helped inmates obtain legal representation, and facilitated inmates' drug rehabilitation placements. Unlike the county's deputy jailers, [the signer] did not carry a weapon; nor did she wear a badge or uniform. She never arrested anyone, did not participate in the ongoing training required of deputy jailers, and was not on the regular rotation of duties for monitoring prisoners. . . . Based on these factual findings, which this court finds the record supports, we conclude that [the signer] was not sufficiently disengaged from activities of law enforcement to satisfy the Fourth Amendment's neutral and detached requirement." *U.S. v. Parker*, 373 F.3d 770, 64 Fed. R. Evid. Serv. 635, 2004 FED App. 0197P (6th Cir. 2004).

- "The warrant at issue in this case was issued under state law by a Shelby County Judicial Commissioner. Essentially, [defendant] contends that Shelby County Judicial Commissioners are not neutral and detached in that they are appointed by a local legislative authority, the Shelby County Commission. Under Tennessee law, the legislative body of a county having a population in excess of 700,000 may appoint one or more judicial commissioners who are authorized to issue search warrants upon a finding of probable cause. . . . Appellant contends that these provisions of Tennessee law impermissibly place a legislative body, the Shelby

County Commission, in ultimate control of the judicial commissioners. . . . [Defendant] essentially contends that a judicial commissioner appointed by a legislative body of a county who is not a judge or even an attorney may not lawfully issue a search warrant or act as a neutral magistrate for purposes of the Fourth Amendment. The caselaw clearly rejects this position... [A] number of other courts have found that no constitutional violation occurs when a search warrant is issued by a non-lawyer." *U.S. v. Pennington*, 328 F.3d 215, 2003 FED App. 0129A (6th Cir. 2003).

- "Yet, the magistrate must perform his neutral and detached function and not serve merely as a rubber stamp for police. . . .To that end, deference to the issuing magistrate . . .is not boundless." *U.S. v. King*, 227 F.3d 732, 739, 2000 FED App. 0284P (6th Cir. 2000).

- "In *Coolidge*, the Supreme Court held that a state's Attorney General could not properly issue a search warrant. . . . [the Clerk]'s position as a circuit clerk is not similar to that of a state attorney general, the chief law enforcement agent of the state. Unlike an attorney general faced with issuing a search warrant, she is not confronted with the dual and conflicting responsibility of both ferreting out crime and prosecuting crime. . . . Similarly, this case is distinguishable from that in *Lo-Ji*, where the Supreme Court invalidated a search warrant issued by a judicial officer who also participated in the execution of the warrant. . . . Unlike the justice in *Lo-Ji*, [the Clerk] did not participate in the execution of the search warrant; she did not accompany police officers to the scene, nor did she direct them as to which items should be seized." *U.S. v. Bennett*, 170 F.3d 632, 637, 1999 FED App. 0105P (6th Cir. 1999).

- "There is. . .no evidence that [the] Magistrate. . .failed to act in a neutral and detached manner or was acting as a mere rubber stamp. There is no evidence to suggest that he was somehow involved in the competitive enterprise of ferreting out crime. . .or that he was blindly and automatically approving the warrant." *U.S. v. Chaar*, 137 F.3d 359, 364, 1998 FED App. 0052P (6th Cir. 1998).

- "The Fourth Amendment does not require prosecutorial review for a warrant to issue nor is there any other federal requirement for a prosecuting attorney to review the facts of a case and make a probable cause determination prior to review by a judicial officer." *Gibson v. McMurray*, 159 F.3d 230, 232, 1998 FED App. 0315P (6th Cir. 1998).

Eighth Circuit

- "We have held that a magistrate judge is neutral and detached if his or her impartiality cannot reasonably be questioned." *U.S. v. Mathison*, 157 F.3d 541, 548 (8th Cir. 1998).

Tenth Circuit

- "The Fourth Amendment may be violated when the judge abandons the judicial role and acts as an adjunct law enforcement officer." *J.B. v. Washington County*, 127 F.3d 919, 930, 121 Ed. Law Rep. 926 (10th Cir. 1997).

§ 5:2 Standard: The magistrate must find probable cause to believe that the place to be searched contains items connected with criminal activity

Supreme Court

- "A search warrant is issued upon a showing of probable cause to believe that the legitimate object of a search is located in a particular place, and therefore safeguards an individual's interest in the privacy of his home and possessions against the unjustified intrusion of the police." *Steagald v. U.S.*, 451 U.S. 204, 213, 101 S. Ct. 1642, 68 L. Ed. 2d 38 (1981).

- "[T]he grounds for a search must satisfy objective standards which ensure that the invasion of personal privacy is justified by legitimate governmental interests. The governmental interests to be served in the detection or prevention of crime are subject to traditional standards of probable cause to believe that incriminating evidence will be found." *Torres v. Com. of Puerto Rico*, 442 U.S. 465, 471, 99 S. Ct. 2425, 61 L. Ed. 2d 1 (1979).

- "[A]n officer may not properly issue a warrant to search. . .unless he can find probable cause therefor from facts or circumstances presented to him under oath or affirmation." *Nathanson v. U.S.*, 290 U.S. 41, 47, 54 S. Ct. 11, 78 L. Ed. 159 (1933).

First Circuit

- "It is a rare case in which every jot and tittle in an affidavit filed in support of an application for a search warrant will argue persuasively for a finding of probable cause. More often, there will be some facts and circumstances that paint the picture not in black and white, but in varying shades of gray. The task of the issuing magistrate is to make certain that she focuses on the forest—not on the individual trees. The ultimate question is not whether there is some doubt but, rather, whether the totality of the facts and circumstances described in the affidavit, viewed objectively, gives rise to a fair probability that a crime has been committed and that the search, if allowed, will reveal evidence of it." *U.S. v. Clark*, 685 F.3d 72, 78 (1st Cir. 2012) (citations omitted).

- "Probable cause, in the context of granting a search warrant, requires no more than the existence of a fair probability that evidence of a crime will be found." *U.S. v. Vega-Figueroa*, 234 F.3d 744, 755 (1st Cir. 2000).

Third Circuit

- "Generally, for a search to be reasonable, a government agent must establish probable cause to believe that evidence will be found on the person to be searched and obtain permission to conduct the search from a neutral and detached magistrate. An essential purpose of a warrant requirement is to protect privacy interests by assuring citizens subject to a search. . .that such intrusions are not the random or arbitrary acts of government agents." *U.S. v. Ward*, 131 F.3d 335, 340 (3d Cir. 1997).

Sixth Circuit

- "It is well established in this Circuit that drug paraphernalia recovered from a trash pull establishes probable cause to search a home when combined with other evidence of the resident's involvement in drug crimes. We have not previously considered, however, whether and under what circumstances trash pull evidence, standing alone, can establish probable cause to search a home. . . . 'The argument depends on an inference that "an individual arrested outside his residence with drugs in his pocket is likely to have stored drugs and related paraphernalia in that same residence." This inference can be drawn permissibly in some cases. But in all those cases, the affidavits contained an additional fact that permitted the magistrate to draw the inference that evidence of wrongdoing would be found in the defendants' homes—namely, the independently corroborated fact that the defendants were known drug dealers at the time the police sought to search their homes. That fact was absent from the affidavit in this case. McPhearson was not a known drug dealer: his prior convictions were for property crimes, and the warrant on which the police arrested him was for simple assault. In the absence of any facts connecting McPhearson to drug trafficking, the affidavit in this case cannot support the inference that evidence of wrongdoing would be found in McPhearson's home because drugs were found on his person.' . . . After a thorough review of the record and relevant case law, we agree with Defendant that the evidence recovered from the trash pull here did not create a fair probability that drugs would be found in Defendant's home." *United States v. Abernathy*, 843 F.3d 243, 251–53, 254 (6th Cir. 2016) (citations omitted).

- "The Fourth Amendment conditions warrants on probable cause and prohibits unreasonable seizures. A police officer violates those restrictions only when his deliberate or reckless falsehoods result in arrest and prosecution without probable cause. The resulting claim, what might be called an 'unreasonable prosecutorial seizure' claim, is traditionally known as a 'malicious prosecution' claim." *Newman v. Township of Hamburg*, 773 F.3d 769, 771–72 (6th Cir. 2014) (citations omitted).

Seventh Circuit

- "[T]he age of inculpatory information is only one factor that magistrates should consider in determining whether probable cause exists, and if other factors indicate that the information is reliable. . .the magistrate should not hesitate to issue the warrant." *U.S. v. Spry*, 190 F.3d 829, 836 (7th Cir. 1999).

- "In issuing a search warrant, a magistrate is given license to draw reasonable inferences concerning where the evidence referred to in the affidavit is likely to be kept, taking into account the nature of the evidence and the offense." *U.S. v. Singleton*, 125 F.3d 1097, 1102, 47 Fed. R. Evid. Serv. 1128 (7th Cir. 1997).

Eighth Circuit

- "Probable cause to issue a search warrant exists when an affidavit sets forth sufficient facts to justify a prudent person in the belief that contraband will be found in a particular place. . . . Courts should apply a common-sense approach and, considering all the relevant circumstances, determine whether probable cause exists." *U.S. v. Buchanan*, 167 F.3d 1207, 1211 (8th Cir. 1999).

Tenth Circuit

- "Probable cause doesn't require proof that something is more likely true than false. It requires only a 'fair probability,' a standard understood to mean something more than a 'bare suspicion' but less than a preponderance of the evidence at hand." *U.S. v. Denson*, 775 F.3d 1214, 1217 (10th Cir. 2014), cert. denied, 135 S. Ct. 2064, 191 L. Ed. 2d 967 (2015).

- "[A]ny investigation conducted by defense counsel fell well short of the mark of reasonableness. All of the eleven affiants were obvious and easily available sources of mitigation evidence family members and close acquaintances—and all indicate they were not contacted by defense counsel." *Mayes v. Gibson*, 210 F.3d 1284, 1289 (10th Cir. 2000).

- "The affidavit in this case failed to allege facts sufficient to establish probable cause. The affidavit contains repetitive statements regarding the physical description of the. . .residence and the identity of the occupants. Further, the affidavit contains statements about the criminal histories. . . .The affidavit does not reveal, however, the informant's basis of knowledge or adequately verify the informant's most serious allegation. . . .An affidavit replete with repetitive and tenuous facts does not provide a magistrate with a sufficient basis for drawing a reasonable inference that a search would uncover evidence of criminal activity." *U.S. v. Danhauer*, 229 F.3d 1002, 1006 (10th Cir. 2000).

- "When reviewing a magistrate's finding of probable cause for the issuance of a search warrant, we must consider the totality of the circumstances and determine whether the affidavit established the probability that evidence of criminal activity would be located in the desired search area." *U.S. v. Le*, 173 F.3d 1258, 1265 (10th Cir. 1999).
- "A nexus between the objects to be seized and the place to be searched for them is established when the circumstances set out in the affidavit would warrant a person of reasonable caution to believe that the articles sought would be found at the place to be searched. . . . There need not be direct evidence or personal knowledge that the items sought are located at the place to be searched, and we have recognized that courts often rely on the opinion of police officers as to where contraband may be kept." *U.S. v. Hargus*, 128 F.3d 1358, 1362 (10th Cir. 1997).

D.C. Circuit

- "[C]ounsel repeatedly argued that a particular circumstance did not 'necessarily' show or 'establish' that a drug transaction had occurred or that there would be drugs in the house . . .. Indeed, that is true even when we take all the relevant circumstances together. The affidavit and the confidential informant's tip on which it was based do not rule out innocent scenarios. It is surely possible that the 'unwitting informant' had it in for Washington and used his or her own supply of drugs to fake the supposed transaction. And it is possible that Washington did not generally follow the modus operandi that [Officer] Katz believed was prevalent in the drug market. But the probable cause test doesn't require that the facts assure certainty that contraband or evidence of a crime will be found—only a 'fair probability.' " *U.S. v. Washington*, 775 F.3d 405, 409 (D.C. Cir. 2014), cert. denied, 135 S. Ct. 2849, 192 L. Ed. 2d 884 (2015) (citations omitted).

§ 5:3 Probable cause defined: Probable cause is supplied by evidence which would lead a reasonable person to believe that an offense has been or is being committed or that the items to which a search warrant is directed are located in the area described

Supreme Court

- "We have described reasonable suspicion simply as a particularized and objective basis for suspecting the person stopped of criminal activity and probable cause to search as existing where the known facts and circumstances are sufficient to warrant a man of reasonable prudence in the belief that contraband or evidence of a crime will be found. We have cautioned that these two legal principles are not finely-tuned standards, comparable to the standards of proof beyond a reasonable doubt or of proof by a preponderance of the evidence. They are instead fluid concepts that take their substantive content from the particular contexts in which the standards are being assessed." *Ornelas v. U.S.*, 517 U.S. 690, 696, 116 S. Ct. 1657, 134 L. Ed. 2d 911 (1996).

- "[P]robable cause is a flexible, common-sense standard. It merely requires that the facts available to the officer would warrant a man of reasonable caution in the belief that certain items may be contraband or stolen property or useful as evidence of a crime; it does not demand any showing that such belief be correct or more likely true than false. A practical, nontechnical probability that incriminating evidence is involved is all that is required." *Texas v. Brown*, 460 U.S. 730, 742, 103 S. Ct. 1535, 75 L. Ed. 2d 502 (1983).

- "[P]robable cause is a fluid concept—turning on the assessment of probabilities in particular factual contexts—not readily, or even usefully, reduced to a neat set of legal rules. . . . While an effort to fix some general, numerically precise degree of certainty corresponding to probable cause may be helpful, it is clear that only the probability, and not a prima facie showing, of criminal activity is the standard of probable cause." *Illinois v. Gates*, 462 U.S. 213, 232, 235, 103 S. Ct. 2317, 76 L. Ed. 2d 527 (1983).

- "[Probable cause] mean[s] more than bare suspicion:

Probable cause exists where the facts and circumstances within their [the Officers'] knowledge and of which they had reasonably trustworthy information [are] sufficient in themselves to warrant a man of reasonable caution in the belief that an offense has been or is being committed." *Brinegar v. U.S.*, 338 U.S. 160, 175, 69 S. Ct. 1302, 93 L. Ed. 1879 (1949).

- "If the facts and circumstances before the officer are such as to warrant a man of prudence and caution in believing that the offense has been committed, it is sufficient." *Stacey v. Emery*, 97 U.S. 642, 645, 24 L. Ed. 1035, 1878 WL 18332 (1878).

First Circuit

- "Probable cause exists whenever the circumstances alleged in a supporting affidavit, viewed as a whole and from an objective vantage, suggest a 'fair probability' that evidence of a crime will be found in the place to be searched. Probable cause does not require either certainty or an unusually high degree of assurance. All that is needed is a 'reasonable likelihood' that incriminating evidence will turn up during a proposed search." *U.S. v. Clark*, 685 F.3d 72, 76 (1st Cir. 2012) (citations omitted).

- "A warrant application must demonstrate probable cause to believe that (1) a crime has been committed— the commission element, and (2) enumerated evidence of the offense will be found at the place to be searched— the so-called nexus element. . . . In order to establish probable cause, the facts presented to the magistrate need only warrant a man of reasonable caution to believe that evidence of a crime will be found. . . . The probable cause standard does not demand showing that such a belief be correct or more likely true than false." *U.S. v. Feliz*, 182 F.3d 82, 86 (1st Cir. 1999).

Second Circuit

- "[W]e have no difficulty concluding that the corrected affidavit established probable cause. The affidavit included evidence that an occupant of [defendant's] house, Joeym@optonline.net, was a member of the girls12-16 e-group, whose raison d'tre, or primary reason for existence, was the trading and collection of child pornography—a wholly illegal endeavor. It is common sense that an individual who joins such a site would more than likely download and possess such material. . . . While the affidavit does not explicitly state that [defendant] accessed child pornography, it ties the girls12-16 website to an individual living in [defendant's] home, and states child pornography was available to all who joined and was being distributed to some of the group's members, as shown by the agent's receipt of e-mails containing illegal child pornography and his downloading other such material from the website." *U.S. v. Martin*, 426 F.3d 68 (2d Cir. 2005).

Fifth Circuit

- "(T)he new information acquired by the police was that (defendant's) house contained two other residences in addition to his own. Because the IP address in question was registered in (defendant's) name, and because the two other individuals living in (defendant's) house maintained separate residences, there was still a fair probability that (defendant) was the party responsible for the illegal transmissions . . . Accordingly, we find that even in light of the new information regarding (defendant's) housemates, probable cause still existed for the search of (defendant's) premises. As a result, the district court did not err by refusing to suppress the fruits of the officers' search of (defendant's) premises." *U.S. v. Perez*, 484 F.3d 735 (5th Cir. 2007).

Sixth Circuit

- "It is well established in this Circuit that drug paraphernalia recovered from a trash pull establishes probable cause to search a home when combined with other evidence of the resident's involvement in drug crimes. We have not previously considered, however, whether and under what circumstances trash pull evidence, standing alone, can establish probable cause to search a home. . . . 'The argument depends on an inference that "an individual arrested outside his residence with drugs in his pocket is likely to have stored drugs and related paraphernalia in that same residence." This inference can be drawn permissibly in some cases. But in all those cases, the affidavits contained an additional fact that permitted the magistrate to draw the inference that evidence of wrongdoing would be found in the defendants' homes—namely, the independently corroborated fact that the defendants were known drug dealers at the time the police sought to search their homes. That fact was absent from the affidavit in this case. McPhearson was not a known drug dealer: his prior convictions were for property crimes, and the warrant on which the police arrested him was for simple assault. In the absence of any facts connecting McPhearson to drug trafficking, the affidavit in this case cannot support the inference that evidence of wrongdoing would be found in McPhearson's home because drugs were found on his person.' . . . After a thorough review of the record and relevant case law, we agree with Defendant that the evidence recovered from the trash pull here did not create a fair probability that drugs would be found in Defendant's home." *United States v. Abernathy*, 843 F.3d 243, 251–53, 254 (6th Cir. 2016) (citations omitted).

- "[We give t]he magistrate judge's decision to issue the warrant. . .great deference,. . .determining whether the magistrate judge 'had a substantial basis for finding that the affidavit established' a ' 'fair probability,' given the totality of the circumstances, that contraband or evidence of a crime will be found in a particular place.' [citation omitted] . . . . This requires 'a nexus between the place to be searched and the evidence sought.' [citation omitted] . . . 'In other words, the affidavit must suggest 'that there is reasonable cause to believe that the specific 'things' to be searched for and seized are located on the property to which entry is sought' and not merely 'that the owner of property is suspected of crime.' ' [citation omitted] . . . In United States v. Miggins, [citation omitted] we held. . .that a sufficient nexus existed to search the residence of a known drug dealer after he had been arrested for possession of cocaine. . . . . [T]he inference that a drug dealer keeps evidence of wrongdoing in his residence can be drawn permissibly if. . .the affidavit had 'the independently corroborated fact that the defendants were known drug dealers at the time the police sought to search their homes.' [citation omitted] . . . . [Defendant] contends that [there was no probable cause to] support the search of his residence [because] . . . he was not a 'known drug dealer,' never having been arrested or convicted of a drug offense, and that he was never observed in drug trafficking. . . . There was substantial evidence, however, that [defendant] was engaged in manufacturing methamphetamine. He was arrested at the site of the methamphetamine lab and the location of a large quantity of methamphetamine and ingredients for its manufacture under circumstances suggesting he was responsible for the operation. The informant related that [defendant] was engaged in cooking methamphetamine and that he was associated with Kozma, who had supplied her with methamphetamine. The search at 530 North Coolidge Street corroborated much of her information, some of which was against her penal interest. [citation omitted] . . . That probable cause existed to believe that [defendant] was engaged in the manufacture of methamphetamine is beyond dispute. We think that the rationale underlying. . .Miggins . . . is not limited to defendants engaged in the immediate distribution of drugs. The manufacturer is only a step away from dealing in his product. Indeed, the prohibition against drug trafficking extends to manufacturing. [citations omitted] Moreover[,] a manufacturer's residence is as likely to contain drug paraphernalia such as recipes, ingredients, and records of sales as that of a dealer. We conclude that the search of [defendant]'s residence was valid. *U.S. v. Kenny*, 505 F.3d 458 (6th Cir. 2007).

- "In *Schultz*, two search warrants were issued, one for the defendant's home and one for a safety deposit box the defendant maintained at a financial institution. . . . This Court determined that there was sufficient probable cause for a search warrant of the defendant's home to issue because there was evidence to establish both that the defendant was selling narcotics and that there might be evidence of that activity at the defendant's home. . . . But, we also found that there was no evidence tying the defendant's purported drug activities to the safety deposit box. . . . A police officer learned of the box while conducting a credit check of the defendant; thus, the officer had little more than a hunch that contraband or evidence of a crime would be found in the box. . . . For that reason, we decided that the search warrant for the safety deposit box should not have issued." *U.S. v. Bennett*, 170 F.3d 632, 638, 1999 FED App. 0105P (6th Cir. 1999).

Seventh Circuit

- "We have consistently held that probable cause to search one apartment in a multi-unit building does not support a warrant authorizing a search of the entire building. Rather, when a building is divided into more than one residential unit, a distinct probable cause determination must be made for each unit. . . .A warrant authorizing the search of an entire multi-unit building is fatally defective when the warrant authorizes the search of an entire structure and the officers do not know which unit contains the evidence of illegal conduct." *Jacobs v. City of Chicago*, 215 F.3d 758, 767, 46 Fed. R. Serv. 3d 832 (7th Cir. 2000).

- "In *United States v. Hinton* we held that when a building is divided into more than one residential unit, a distinct probable cause determination must be made for each unit. The general rule is that a warrant which describes an entire building when cause is shown for searching only one apartment is void. There is an exception to the *Hinton* rule, however, where although appearing to be a building of several apartments, the entire building is actually being used as a single unit. When this is the case, a finding of probable cause as to a portion of the premises is sufficient to support a search of the entire structure. We have found the used as a single unit exception to apply in cases where the target of the investigation or warrant exercised dominion and control over the entire building or had access to the entire structure." *U.S. v. Butler*, 71 F.3d 243, 249, 43 Fed. R. Evid. Serv. 460 (7th Cir. 1995).

Eighth Circuit

- "Probable cause to issue a search warrant exits if there is 'a fair probability that contraband or evidence of a crime will be found in a particular place.' 'Anticipatory warrants are. . .no different in principle from ordinary warrants. They require the magistrate to determine (1) that it is *now probable* that (2) contraband, evidence of a crime, or a fugitive will be on the described premises (3) when the warrant is executed.'" *U.S. v. Donnell*, 726 F.3d 1054 (8th Cir. 2013) (citations omitted).

- "The source and credibility of evidence in support of a warrant request is considered in the totality of the circumstances analysis, and a warrant is proper so long as the evidence as a whole creates a reasonable probability that the search will lead to the discovery of evidence." *U.S. v. Horn*, 187 F.3d 781, 786 (8th Cir. 1999).
- "The source and credibility of evidence in support of a warrant request is considered in the totality of the circumstances analysis, and a warrant is proper so long as the evidence as a whole creates a reasonable probability that the search will lead to the discovery of evidence." *U.S. v. Humphrey*, 140 F.3d 762, 764 (8th Cir. 1998).

Ninth Circuit

- "Under the totality of the circumstances, a search warrant issued to search a suspect's home computer and electronic equipment lacks probable cause when (1) no evidence of possession or attempt to possess child pornography was submitted to the issuing magistrate; (2) no evidence was submitted to the magistrate regarding computer or electronics use by the suspect; and (3) the only evidence linking the suspect's attempted child molestation to possession of child pornography is the experience of the requesting police officer, with no further explanation." *Dougherty v. City of Covina*, 654 F.3d 892, 895 (9th Cir. 2011).

Tenth Circuit

- "Probable cause doesn't require proof that something is more likely true than false. It requires only a 'fair probability,' a standard understood to mean something more than a 'bare suspicion' but less than a preponderance of the evidence at hand." *U.S. v. Denson*, 775 F.3d 1214, 1217 (10th Cir. 2014), cert. denied, 135 S. Ct. 2064, 191 L. Ed. 2d 967 (2015).
- "In determining whether an affidavit contains sufficient information to support a finding of probable cause for the issuance of a search warrant, this court, like the issuing judge or magistrate, must consider the totality of the circumstances and determine whether the affidavit

established the probability that evidence of criminal activity would be located in the desired search area." *U.S. v. Wittgenstein*, 163 F.3d 1164, 1171 (10th Cir. 1998).

Eleventh Circuit

- "Probable cause to support a search warrant exists when the totality of the circumstances allow a conclusion that there is a fair probability of finding contraband or evidence at a particular location." *U.S. v. Brundidge*, 170 F.3d 1350, 1352 (11th Cir. 1999).

D.C. Circuit

- "In light of the distinctness of the inquiries, probable cause to arrest a person will not itself justify a warrant to search his property. Regardless of whether an individual is validly suspected of committing a crime, an application for a search warrant concerning his property or possessions must demonstrate cause to believe that 'evidence is likely to be found at the place to be searched.' Moreover, '[t]here must, of course, be a nexus . . . . between the item to be seized and criminal behavior.' Those concerns about the distinct requirements for a search warrant are particularly salient in this case, for two reasons. First, the warrant application sought authorization to search a home, which stands at 'the very core' of the Fourth Amendment's protections. Second, the scope of a permissible search depends on the specific spaces in which the object of the search might be found. Authorization to search for an item fitting in the palm of a hand, like a cell phone, thus can entail an intrusive inspection of all corners of a home. (And here, as explained below, officers sought and obtained authorization to continue their search until they found every cell phone and electronic device in the apartment.) This case, in short, involves the prospect of an especially invasive search of an especially protected place. . . . Although the warrant application sought authorization to search for items other than a cell phone, those additional items have no bearing on our assessment of probable cause to search the home. The application, for instance, encompassed the seizure of any documents, newspaper articles, photographs, or other information relating to the crime. The affiant, however, suggested no reason whatsoever to expect the presence of incriminating documents, newspaper articles, or photographs in the apartment. The affidavit in fact contained no mention of those items apart from a final sentence summarily seeking authorization to seize any of them officers might happen to discover. The government thus understandably makes no argument that there was probable cause to search the apartment due to a belief that incriminating documents, articles, or photographs would be found there. The application also referenced electronic devices apart from cell phones, including computers, tablets, and personal digital assistants. Again, though, the affidavit provided no reason to suppose that Griffith possessed any of those devices or that any would be found in the apartment. And although we give a 'commonsense' rather than 'hypertechnical' reading to a warrant application, there is no commonsense reason simply to presume that individuals own a computer or tablet. Those sorts of devices do not approach cellphones in their ubiquity: whereas the Supreme Court, around the time of the warrant application in this case, observed that 'more than 90% of American adults . . . own a cell phone,' the same organization cited by the Court for that measure estimated the contemporaneous incidence of tablet ownership among adults at roughly 30% (2013), and of computer ownership at roughly 75% (2015), see Technology Device Ownership: 2015, Pew Research Center (Oct. 29, 2015), http://www.pewinternet.org/2015/10/29/technology-device-ownership-2015. . . . That brings us back to the warrant application's reliance on cell phones—in particular, on the possibility that Griffith owned a cell phone, and that his phone would be found in the home and would contain evidence of his suspected offense. With regard to his ownership of a cell phone, it is true that, as the Supreme Court recently said, cell phones are now 'such a pervasive and insistent part of daily life that the proverbial visitor from Mars might conclude they were an important feature of human anatomy.' We do not doubt that most people today own a cell phone. But the affidavit in this case conveyed no reason to think that Griffith, in par-

283

ticular, owned a cell phone. There was no observation of Griffith's using a cell phone, no information about anyone having received a cell phone call or text message from him, no record of officers recovering any cell phone in his possession at the time of his previous arrest (and confinement) on unrelated charges, and no indication otherwise of his ownership of a cell phone at any time. To the contrary, the circumstances suggested Griffith might have been less likely than others to own a phone around the time of the search: he had recently completed a ten-month period of confinement, during which he of course had no ongoing access to a cell phone; and at least one person in his circle—his potential co-conspirator, Carl Oliphant—was known not to have a cell phone. We are aware of no case, and the government identifies none, in which police obtained authorization to search a suspect's home for a cell phone without any particularized information that he owned one. In the typical case, officers will have already come into possession of a suspect's phone after seizing it on his person incident to his arrest. Officers also might receive reliable indication of a suspect's possession of a cell phone. There was no such information here about Griffith." *United States v. Griffith*, 2017 WL 3568288, *4-5 (D.C. Cir. 2017) (citations omitted).

§ 5:4   Description: The warrant must describe the person or the place to be searched, the items to be seized with particularity, and the time during which the search may be conducted

Supreme Court

- "The warrant was plainly invalid. . . . Indeed, petitioner concedes that the warrant was deficient in particularity because it provided no description of the type of evidence sought. The fact that the application adequately described the 'things to be seized' does not save the warrant from its facial invalidity. The Fourth Amendment by its terms requires particularity in the warrant, not in the supporting documents. . . . We do not say that the Fourth Amendment forbids a warrant from cross-referencing other documents. Indeed, most Courts of Appeals have held that a court may construe a warrant with reference to a supporting application or affidavit if the warrant uses appropriate words of incorporation, and if the supporting document accompanies the warrant. But in this case the warrant did not incorporate other documents by reference, nor did either the affidavit or the application (which had been placed under seal) accompany the warrant." *Groh v. Ramirez*, 540 U.S. 551, 124 S. Ct. 1284, 157 L. Ed. 2d 1068 (2004).

- "[W]arrants must particularly describe the things to be seized, as well as the place to be searched." *Dalia v. U.S.*, 441 U.S. 238, 255, 99 S. Ct. 1682, 60 L. Ed. 2d 177 (1979).
- "Where the standard is probable cause, a search or seizure of a person must be supported by probable cause particularized with respect to that person." *Ybarra v. Illinois*, 444 U.S. 85, 91, 100 S. Ct. 338, 62 L. Ed. 2d 238 (1979).
- "[T]he warrant left it entirely to the discretion of the officials conducting the search to decide what items were likely obscene and to accomplish their seizure. The Fourth Amendment does not permit such action. Nor does the Fourth Amendment countenance open-ended warrants, to be completed while a search is being conducted and items seized or after the seizure has been carried out." *Lo-Ji Sales, Inc. v. New York*, 442 U.S. 319, 325, 99 S. Ct. 2319, 60 L. Ed. 2d 920, 5 Media L. Rep. (BNA) 1177 (1979).
- "The warrant [requires] a particular description of things to be seized." *Coolidge v. New Hampshire*, 403 U.S. 443, 467, 91 S. Ct. 2022, 29 L. Ed. 2d 564 (1971).
- "The requirement that warrants shall particularly describe the things to be seized prevents the seizure of one thing under a warrant describing another. As to what is to be taken, nothing is left to the discretion of the officer executing the warrant." *Marron v. U.S.*, 275 U.S. 192, 196, 48 S. Ct. 74, 72 L. Ed. 231 (1927).

Third Circuit

- "To find probable cause to search, there needs to be a 'fair probability that contraband or evidence of a crime will be found in a particular place.' Because this inquiry focuses on the relation of criminal conduct to a particular location and not on the activities of any particular person, 'probable cause to arrest does not automatically provide probable cause to search the arrestee's home.' That is not to say that those facts establishing probable cause to arrest are irrelevant to probable cause to search the arrestee's house. 'If there is probable cause to believe that someone committed a crime, then the likelihood that that person's residence contains evidence of the crime increases.' [D]irect evidence linking the residence to criminal activity is not required to establish probable cause. . . . Instead, probable cause to search can be based on an accumulation of circumstantial evidence that together indicates a fair probability of the presence of contraband at the home of the arrested. [P]robable cause 'can be, and often is, inferred by considering the type of crime, the nature of the items sought, the suspect's opportunity for concealment and normal inferences about where a criminal might hide stolen property.'" *U.S. v. Burton*, 288 F.3d 91 (3d Cir. 2002).

Fourth Circuit

- "Our nation's historic aversion to the warrantless searches of dwelling houses and residences reaches its zenith when such searches are conducted at night. Nighttime searches have long been recognized as more intrusive than searches conducted during the day. In fact, the Supreme Court has deemed it 'difficult to imagine a more severe invasion of privacy than the nighttime intrusion into a private home.' That proposition is valid because, during the nighttime hours, searches of dwellings by government agents tend to involve 'rousing the residents out of their beds, and forcing them to stand by in indignity in their night clothes,' all of which 'smack[s] of a police state lacking in the respect for' individual privacy rights. Thus, warrantless nighttime searches of homes were characterized by the second Justice Harlan as creating 'a grave constitutional question.' Rule 41 of the Federal Rules of Criminal Procedure implements the Fourth Amendment's protections against warrantless searches. It provides that a judicial officer must issue a search warrant if a federal law enforcement officer or an attorney for the government presents an affidavit or other information showing probable cause to search a property. Additionally, Rule 41 sets forth procedures controlling the time at which a warrant may be executed, reflecting that 'increasingly severe standards of probable cause are necessary to justify increasingly intrusive searches.' Once issued, a warrant can normally be executed solely 'in the daytime,' between 6:00 a.m. and 10:00 p.m., 'unless the judge for good cause expressly authorizes execution' during the night. Good cause for a nighttime warrant might exist, for example, where necessary to prevent the destruction of evidence. Because of the separate, heightened burden of proof required for issuance of a nighttime warrant, the existence of a daytime warrant ordinarily does not justify a nighttime search. . . . Following the persuasive decisions of the Third and Tenth Circuits, as well as the Supreme Court's decision in *Jones* where the Court accepted that the government's concession that a nighttime search conducted pursuant to a daytime warrant violated the Fourth Amendment, we hold that the nighttime execution of a daytime warrant violates the Fourth Amendment, absent consent or exigent circumstances. Applying the foregoing principles to Yanez's Fourth Amendment timing claim reveals that the 5:00 a.m. search of the Premises violated the Fourth Amendment. . . . At bottom, Yanez's suppression motion implicates a simple rule: a daytime warrant does not authorize a nighttime search. The government implies that 5:00 a.m. essentially is 'close enough' to 6:00 a.m. in the eyes of the Fourth Amendment. Notably, however, as John Adams observed in successfully defending British soldiers charged in the Boston Massacre, '[f]acts are stubborn things.' And the stubbornest fact here is that 5:00 a.m. is not 6:00 a.m. At 6:00 a.m., the warrant sanctioned the ICE agents to enter into the Premises. At 5:00 a.m., the warrant did not permit such an entry. Because the nighttime execution of the daytime warrant violated Yanez's Fourth Amendment rights, as it was executed without consent or exigent circumstances, we must turn to the question of whether the agents egregiously violated Yanez's Fourth Amendment rights." *Yanez-Marquez v. Lynch*, 789 F.3d 434, 465–69 (4th Cir. 2015) (citations omitted).

- "[L]aw enforcement officers may seize an item pursuant to a warrant even if the warrant does not expressly mention and painstakingly describe it. (citation omitted) A warrant need not—and in most cases, cannot—scrupulously list and delineate each and every item to be seized. Frequently, it is simply impossible for law enforcement officers to know in advance exactly what business records the defendant maintains or how the case against him will unfold." *U.S. v. Phillips*, 588 F.3d 218 (4th Cir. 2009).
- "[E]ven where a warrant contains a technical inaccuracy, a sufficient description of the premises, especially where the executing officer had knowledge of the particular place to be searched, will meet the Fourth Amendment's particularity requirement." *U.S. v. Watts*, 352 Fed. Appx. 784 (4th Cir. 2009).
- "Search warrant's erroneous description of dwelling to be searched as single-family home, rather than as multi-unit dwelling, did not violate Fourth Amendment's particularity requirement, even though there were two mailboxes, one black and one white, affixed to the residence and two doorbells on doorframe, where the investigation of the residence occurred from a distance late at night following the suspect's arrest, the black mailbox was camouflaged by the house's dark coloring, the doorbells were small, the troopers focused their search on the first floor where the suspect resided, and all evidence seized came from that area." *U.S. v. Brooks*, 294 Fed. Appx. 71 (4th Cir. 2008).
- "Documents seized from the defendant's residence satisfied the search warrant's requirement that they may constitute evidence that health care fraud had been committed, given that the search warrant affidavit demonstrated probable cause that the defendant's medical practice had submitted fraudulent claims to health care benefit programs from the defendant's residence, and that the documents seized, such as financial records reflecting the defendant's income from medical practice, could serve as pieces of fraud puzzle in the investigation of a fraudulent scheme, particularly given the possibility that the evidence regarding possession and transfer of large sums of money could be a strong indicia of fraud." *U.S. v. Srivastava*, 540 F.3d 277, 102 A.F.T.R.2d 2008-6088 (4th Cir. 2008).

SEARCH WARRANT REQUIREMENTS

- "We recognize that a majority of our sister Circuit Courts of Appeals appear to require the satisfaction of both conditions before allowing a separate document to be read as part of the search warrant . . . In this circuit, however, it is sufficient *either* for the warrant to incorporate the supporting document by reference *or* for the supporting document to be attached to the warrant itself . . . We conclude that the search warrant properly cross-referenced the Attachment which, in turn, supplied the requisite particularity to the search warrant, regardless of whether the Attachment accompanied or was appended to the search warrant at the time it was executed." *U.S. v. Hurwitz*, 459 F.3d 463 (4th Cir. 2006).
- "[A]n 'all persons' warrant can pass constitutional muster if the affidavit and information provided to the magistrate supply enough detailed information to establish probable cause to believe that all persons on the premises at the time of the search are involved in the criminal activity. In our view, the inclusion of 'all persons' language in a warrant presents probable cause issues rather than particularity problems. . . . [A]s long as there is good reason to suspect or believe that anyone present at the anticipated scene will probably be a participant in the criminal activity occurring there, presence becomes the descriptive fact satisfying the aim of the Fourth Amendment." *Owens ex rel. Owens v. Lott*, 372 F.3d 267 (4th Cir. 2004).

Fifth Circuit

- "The Fourth Amendment requires that warrants 'particularly describ[e] the place to be searched, and the persons or things to be seized.' Some interpretation is unavoidable. Officers are 'not obliged to interpret [the warrant] narrowly.' Reasonable specificity is required, not 'elaborate detail.' . . . To avoid fatal generality, the place and items to be seized must 'be described with sufficient particularity so as to leave nothing to the discretion of the officer executing the warrant.'" *U.S. v. Triplett*, 684 F.3d 500, 504–05 (5th Cir. 2012) (citations omitted).
- "Search warrant stated with sufficient particularity the things and places to be searched where the warrant cited the statute criminalizing tax evasion and included

limiting language, itemizing what records could be
seized, and, in the list of items to be seized, the warrant
listed patient account statements, receivable reports,
invoice sales books, and account overdue letters." *U.S.
v. Van Meter*, 280 Fed. Appx. 394, 2008-1 U.S. Tax Cas.
(CCH) P 50373, 101 A.F.T.R.2d 2008-2482 (5th Cir.
2008).

Sixth Circuit

• "Consistent with the language of the Warrant Clause
and the historical purposes behind it, a search conducted in accordance with a valid warrant does not
become warrantless, and therefore "presumptively unreasonable," due to the manner in which the officers
conducted the search. As the Court has "[r]ecogniz[ed],"
"the specificity required by the [Warrant Clause of the]
Fourth Amendment does not generally extend to the
means by which warrants are executed" . . . While the
decision of officers not to present an incorporated affidavit to the occupant upon request may be a relevant
factor in determining the reasonableness of a search, it
does not make a warrant-supported search a warrantless one." *Baranski v. Fifteen Unknown Agents of
Bureau of Alcohol, Tobacco and Firearms*, 452 F.3d 433,
2006 FED App. 0225P (6th Cir. 2006).

• "In this case, law enforcement sought business and
financial records in connection with bank fraud. In a
business fraud case, the authorization to search for general business records is not overbroad. . . . [T]he warrant was specific in terms of the items to be seized; for
example, it listed 'logs or ledgers that reflect the recording of banking activity,' 'all bank statements, deposit
slips, withdrawal slips, official checks, money orders,
cancelled checks, wire transfers and other documents
for any and all bank accounts,' and other specific forms
of records. Moreover, . . . the law enforcement agents in
this case could not have known the precise documents
and records Defendants utilized in the check kiting
scheme. The items listed in the warrant were items
likely to provide information about Defendants' check
kiting scheme. A more specific alternative did not exist
to the search warrant's list of items to be seized." *U.S.
v. Abboud*, 438 F.3d 554, 97 A.F.T.R.2d 2006-1142, 2006
FED App. 0066P (6th Cir. 2006).

- "It is clear that the incorrect address in the warrant and the affidavit does not itself invalidate the search warrant. . . . In determining whether the warrant describes with sufficient particularity the place to be searched, we consider: (1) whether the place to be searched is described with sufficient particularity as to enable the executing officers to locate and identify the premises with reasonable effort; and (2) whether there is reasonable probability that some other premises may be mistakenly searched. An error in description does not, however, automatically invalidate a search warrant. . . . We have repeatedly upheld warrants like the one at issue where one part of the description is inaccurate, but the description has other accurate information to identify the place to be searched with particularity. . . . In the present case, the warrant and supporting affidavit specified that the place to be searched was 'Kimberly Beauty College, 937 28th St. S.W., Wyoming, MI 49509. Specifically a portioned off storage room in the lower level.' It is undisputed that two out of the three references in the warrant to the place to be searched were accurate. Kimberly Beauty College was, in fact, located on 28th Street S.W. in the 900 block, and there was a portioned-off storage room in the lower level of that building. Thus, even though the street address was inaccurate, the executing officers could still locate and identify Kimberly Beauty College with reasonable effort. Moreover, . . . [t]he executing officer. . . was also the warrant's affiant and the principal investigator of the fire at Kimberly Beauty College. At the time he filled out the affidavit, [officer] had already been to Kimberly Beauty College and had accompanied members of the fire department into the College's basement. Thus, the description in the warrant to search Kimberly Beauty College was sufficiently particular despite the inaccuracies." *U.S. v. Hang Le-Thy Tran*, 433 F.3d 472 (6th Cir. 2006).

- "[Defendant] does not argue that there is an inaccuracy in the description of the mobile home. Rather, he suggests its address 'is in all likelihood 1412 Mae Collins Road, Lot # 3.' However, this descriptive language is not included in the warrant, nor is it necessary. Here, the particularity requirement is met as the description includes specific directions from an identifiable point to the mobile home park at 1418 Mae Collins Road in Hamblen County, Tennessee. Once inside the park, the warrant describes the particular trailer by color, by a certain exterior trim, and by a wooden deck. In addition, the warrant includes an unusual feature of the trailer, the number 954 displayed under a window air conditioner on the right end of the trailer. Moreover, [the officer applying for the warrant] had attached a photograph of the trailer to the affidavit incorporated into the search warrant. Thus, even if [defendant's] speculation on the actual address is accurate, such conjecture is immaterial to the officers identifying the mobile home with reasonable effort." *U.S. v. Pelayo-Landero*, 285 F.3d 491, 2002 FED App. 0106P, 103 A.L.R.5th 761 (6th Cir. 2002).

- "The government concedes the two descriptive errors in the warrant, but contends that these are not fatal. . . . The test for determining whether a search warrant describes the premises to be searched with sufficient particularity is not whether the description is technically accurate in every detail. . .but rather whether the description is sufficient to enable the executing officer to locate and identify the premises with reasonable effort, and whether there is any reasonable probability that another premises might be mistakenly searched." *U.S. v. Durk*, 149 F.3d 464, 465, 1998 FED App. 0213P (6th Cir. 1998).

Seventh Circuit

- "Fifer alternatively argues that the evidence obtained from his electronic devices should be suppressed because the state search warrant didn't authorize the initial on-site search of the phones and tablet conducted at the apartment. Fifer's argument rests on a semantic distinction: the warrant identifies the apartment as the place 'to be searched,' and the electronic devices (and other objects) as the items 'to be seized.' According to Fifer, this distinction means that the warrant authorized only the seizure, but not the search, of the electronic devices found in the apartment. This argument fails for three reasons. First, by explicitly authorizing the police to seize the electronic devices found in

Fifer's apartment, the warrant implicitly authorized them to search those devices as well. At least, that's the most reasonable interpretation. After all, the whole point of a search warrant is to authorize police to search for evidence of a crime. And it seems inescapable that if there's probable cause to seize an object because it might contain evidence of a crime, then there's also probable cause to search the object for the evidence it might contain. Why, then, would the issuing judge order the police to seize an item—such as a computer, a phone, or even a safe (all listed in the warrant)—only to have them reapply for an essentially identical warrant to search the item seized? Why, when the same probable cause that justified the seizure also justifies the search? We think it generally makes more sense to read a search warrant's command to seize an electronic device as including a concomitant directive to search that device's digital contents. That's certainly the case here, where the basis for the seizure of Fifer's electronic devices was to search them for digital data. That's also how courts read federal search warrants. And in the absence of any contrary authority, there's no reason to read Illinois' search warrants any differently." *United States v. Fifer*, 863 F.3d 759, 766 (7th Cir. 2017) (citations omitted).

- "[T]here is nothing in the Supreme Court's case law (or the Ninth Circuit's for that matter) counseling the complete abandonment of the plain view doctrine in digital evidence cases. . . . Instead, we simply counsel officers and others involved in searches of digital media to exercise caution to ensure that warrants describe with particularity the things to be seized and that searches are narrowly tailored to uncover only those things described." *U.S. v. Mann*, 592 F.3d 779 (7th Cir. 2010).

- "[Plaintiffs] argued to the district court that the warrant fell far short of [the] particularity requirement because it did not catalogue the individual movie and game titles allegedly stolen from [the victim video store]. On appeal, plaintiffs contend that the warrant is insufficiently particular because it would not enable an officer reading it to differentiate between those items subject to the warrant and property lawfully possessed by [the plaintiffs]. They also assert that it placed no meaningful limits on the category of documents that might be seized. None of these arguments are meritorious. . . . The police had reason to believe that [plaintiffs] had stolen hundreds of videos and games. Under the circumstances, it would have been impractical to list each title individually. The warrant accommodated this reality by specifying that 'Video tapes' and 'Nintendo games' be seized. And because the universe of movies and games is so large, it was impractical to list the titles *not* suspected of being stolen. The warrant gave the officers as much guidance as was feasible." *Russell v. Harms*, 397 F.3d 458 (7th Cir. 2005).

- "Even if there were no constitutional requirement of particular description, or if seizure were so narrowly defined as to be irrelevant to most searches, a valid warrant would have to specify the object of the search, and that specification would operate to particularize the scope of the search. For the object determines the reasonable scope of the search, and all searches, to pass muster under the Fourth Amendment, must be reasonable. If you are looking for an adult elephant, searching for it in a chest of drawers is not reasonable. The principle that this example illustrates is that a search for a given type of evidence or contraband implies a limitation of the parts of the premises that may be searched." *Platteville Area Apartment Ass'n v. City of Platteville*, 179 F.3d 574, 579 (7th Cir. 1999).

Eighth Circuit

- "In determining the validity of a search warrant, it is sufficient that the description of the premises in the warrant is such that the officer can, with reasonable effort, ascertain and identify the place intended, and avoid mistakenly searching the wrong premises. Innocent mistakes or negligence alone are insufficient to void a search warrant. A search warrant's description of a residence to be searched may be adequate, even though the warrant provides an incorrect first name for the defendant as the owner of the residence where the incorrect first name was the name of the defendant's brother, was a negligible error, and the residence that the officers intended to be searched was searched." *U.S. v. Palega*, 556 F.3d 709 (8th Cir. 2009).

SEARCH WARRANT REQUIREMENTS

- "For local officers who know the roads within their jurisdiction and where there is no ambiguous geography in play (such as various roads by the same name), there is no need for the warrant to list the county and state in order for the [particularity] requirement to be met." *U.S. v. Carter*, 413 F.3d 712 (8th Cir. 2005).

- "A search warrant must state with sufficient particularity the property to be seized. The degree of specificity, however, depends on the circumstances and the types of items. In a scheme to defraud, a search warrant is sufficiently particular in its description of the items to be seized if it is as specific as the circumstances and nature of activity under investigation permit." *U.S. v. Henderson*, 416 F.3d 686, Unempl. Ins. Rep. (CCH) P 17700B (8th Cir. 2005).

- "To satisfy the particularity requirement of the fourth amendment, the warrant must be sufficiently definite to enable the searching officers to identify the property authorized to be seized. . . .The degree of specificity required will depend on the circumstances of the case and on the type of items involved. . . . A warrant naming only a generic class of items may suffice if the individual goods to be seized cannot be more precisely identified at the time that the warrant is issued. . . . We have upheld warrants authorizing the seizure of certain books and records. . .relating to the extortionate credit transaction business. . .and of any and all chemicals. . .books, records, chemical equipment, and personal papers relating to the manufacture and distribution of methamphetamine and the purchase of component chemicals and equipment which are contraband and fruits and instrumentalities of the commission of a crime which is in violation of a certain statute, identified by section and subsections." *U.S. v. Horn*, 187 F.3d 781, 788 (8th Cir. 1999).

Ninth Circuit

- "A search warrant authorizing the seizure of items of personal property which tended to identify the person in control, possession, and ownership of the listed property, including mail, photographs, diaries, and passports, and authorizing search only for the bunk space, cupboard, drawer, and two storage spaces which the ship's crew had told the special agents belonged to the foreign national defendant, described items to be seized with sufficient particularity, as required for probable cause to seize the defendant's incriminating mail from the bunk area, since the mail could identify the defendant as the person in control of the bunk area, the warrant was limited to exclude property containing no identifying information, and the agents lacked additional information which would have allowed a more specific description of items to be seized." *U.S. v. Shi*, 525 F.3d 709, 2008 A.M.C. 1077 (9th Cir. 2008).

• "The purpose of having a particularized, as opposed to general, warrant is to assure the individual whose property is searched or seized of the lawful authority of the executing officer, his need to search, and the limits of his power to search. In other words, a search warrant gives an officer the power to seize the items specified in the warrant. While an officer generally does not have the power to seize anything not specified in the warrant, he retains discretion over the execution of the search and, as is implicit in the word 'power,' can exercise discretion to leave items that may arguably come within the literal terms of the search warrant." *San Jose Charter of Hells Angels Motorcycle Club v. City of San Jose*, 402 F.3d 962 (9th Cir. 2005).

• "In determining whether a description is sufficiently precise, we have concentrated on one or more of the following: (1) whether probable cause exists to seize all items of a particular type described in the warrant, (2) whether the warrant sets out objective standards by which executing officers can differentiate items subject to seizure from those which are not, and (3) whether the government was able to describe the items more particularly in light of the information available to it at the time the warrant was issued." *U.S. v. Mann*, 389 F.3d 869 (9th Cir. 2004).

• "Police officers' authority to search premises that are described in a warrant is not unlimited. If, during the search, the officers become aware that the warrant describes multiple residences, the officers must confine their search to the residence of the suspect. . . .To determine whether the officers should have realized they were searching the wrong residence, the *Garrison* court set forth the following standard: The validity of the search of respondent's apartment pursuant to a warrant authorizing the search of the entire third floor depends on whether the officers' failure to realize the overbreadth of the warrant was objectively understandable and reasonable." *Mena v. City of Simi Valley*, 226 F.3d 1031, 1038 (9th Cir. 2000).

Tenth Circuit

- "An anticipatory search warrant, such as the warrant in this case, is valid 'when the warrant application indicates there will be a government-controlled delivery of contraband to the place to be searched, probable cause for a search is established and. . . provided the warrant's execution is conditioned on the contraband's delivery to, or receipt at, the designated place.' . . . [T]he probable cause requirement is satisfied by reference to a controlled delivery of contraband in the supporting affidavit. By adequately stating the conditions precedent to the warrant's execution (particularly the cooperation of an informant) in the affidavit, the warrant is valid despite the lack of a physical description of the premises. . . . The test for determining the adequacy of the description of the location to be searched is whether the description is sufficient 'to enable the executing officer to locate and identify the premises with reasonable effort, and whether there is any reasonable probability that another premise might be mistakenly searched.' . . . [A] clerical error as to the number of the house to be searched does not entail an error as to which house would, in fact be searched. '[P]ractical accuracy rather than technical precision controls the determination of whether a search warrant adequately describes the premises to be searched.' A technically wrong address does not invalidate a warrant if it otherwise describes the premises with sufficient particularity so that the police can ascertain and identify the place to be searched. 'The requisite specificity of the description. . . depends heavily on the facts of each case.' . . . Here we have the correct street, an address off by one digit, and an informant identifying the mistake; it is perfectly appropriate in such circumstances to cure the problem with the officer's knowledge. *U.S. v. Lora-Solano*, 330 F.3d 1288 (10th Cir. 2003).

- "[O]ur opinion in *Carey* notes several important limitations on the scope of computer searches of which the parties should be aware. In particular, we observed that the storage capacity of computers may require law enforcement officers to take a special approach. . . .Computers often contain intermingled documents (i.e., documents containing both relevant and irrelevant information). . . .When law enforcement officers confront such documents a more particularized inquiry may be required: Law enforcement must engage in the intermediate step of sorting various types of documents and then only search the ones specified in a warrant. Where officers come across relevant documents so intermingled with irrelevant documents that they cannot feasibly be sorted at the site, the officers may seal or hold the documents pending approval by a magistrate of the conditions and limitations on a further search through the documents. The magistrate should then require officers to specify in a warrant which type of files are sought." *U.S. v. Campos*, 221 F.3d 1143, 1148, 55 Fed. R. Evid. Serv. 226 (10th Cir. 2000).

D.C. Circuit

- "[Defendant] contends that the warrants issued in this case violated the particularity requirement because of the catch-all phrase that came at the end of each warrant's list of specific items to be seized: '[A] green card and driver's license [in] the name of Osman Dainkeh, cash money in the amount of approximately $500, a white gold chain, a dark blue police uniform, and any other evidence of a violation of Title 18 U.S.C. Sec. 242.' [Defendant] argues that the phrase 'any other evidence of a violation of Title 18 U.S.C. Sec. 242' is simply too broad to be regarded as particularly describing the things to be seized. We have no doubt that had the warrants merely authorized the seizure of 'evidence of a violation of Title 18 U.S.C. Sec. 242' they would indeed have been impermissibly broad. But that phrase did not stand alone, and instead came in the same sentence as, and at the conclusion of, a quite specific list of items to be seized. That list constrained the interpretation of the last phrase, making it reasonably clear that the warrants did not authorize the seizure of evidence of just any violation of Section 242, but rather of evidence relating to such a violation in connection with Osman Dainkeh. . . .[A] warrant's catch-all phrase must be read in light of the items that precede it, a principle further supported by the canon of construction known as ejusdem generis ('of the same kind or class'). Reading the warrants in accordance with that principle, we conclude that they were sufficiently particular to satisfy the strictures of the Fourth Amendment." *U.S. v. Pindell*, 336 F.3d 1049 (D.C. Cir. 2003).

§ 5:5 Description: Incorporation of affidavit's particular descriptions into warrant

Third Circuit

- "[F]or an affidavit to cure a warrant's lack of particularity, the words of incorporation in the warrant must make clear that the section lacking particularity is to be read in conjunction with the attached affidavit. Merely referencing the attached affidavit somewhere in the warrant without expressly incorporating it does not suffice." *U.S. v. Tracey*, 597 F.3d 140 (3d Cir. 2010).

Fifth Circuit

- "The law permits an affidavit incorporated by reference to amplify particularity, notwithstanding that, by its terms, the Fourth Amendment 'requires particularity in the warrant, not in the supporting documents.' When viewed alongside the affidavit, the warrant's list of items to be seized is reasonably focused. The underlying facts discuss how [the defendant] changed 'bed sheets'; the words hard drive and computer connect with the warrant's reference to 'electronic memory device'; 'cell phone' is reasonably related to knowledge about [the victim's] last use of her phone; 'digging tools' pertains to [the defendant's] travel to Alabama with an ax and shovel; and 'utility vehicles' aligns with knowledge that [the defendant] reported using a four-wheel vehicle in Alabama. Based on this nexus between the facts and circumstances and the items to be seized, we conclude that a reasonably well-trained officer could have concluded that the warrant satisfied Fourth Amendment particularity." *U.S. v. Triplett*, 684 F.3d 500, 505 (5th Cir. 2012) (citations omitted).

Eighth Circuit

- "The Warrant Clause's particularity requirement can be satisfied by including the items to be seized in an affidavit or attachment that is adequately referenced in the search warrant." *U.S. v. Hamilton*, 591 F.3d 1017 (8th Cir. 2010).

- "The problem with the warrant here is not a wholesale failure to incorporate the affidavit, but whether the warrant used 'appropriate words of incorporation' sufficient to incorporate the list of items to be seized. (citation omitted) Given our caselaw approving the use of incorporated documents to satisfy the particularity requirement, it was objectively reasonable for an officer with [the investigator]'s knowledge and involvement in the warrant application process to rely on the warrant as incorporating the list of items to be seized from the affidavit, even if we were now to conclude that the words of incorporation were less than clear." *U.S. v. Hamilton*, 591 F.3d 1017 (8th Cir. 2010).

§ 5:6   Showing: The affidavit must contain more than mere conclusions to enable the magistrate to make an independent evaluation of probable cause

Supreme Court

- "An affidavit must provide the magistrate with a substantial basis for determining the existence of probable cause, and [a] wholly conclusory statement fail[s] to meet this requirement. Sufficient information must be presented to the magistrate to allow that official to determine probable cause; his action cannot be a mere ratification of the bare conclusions of others." *Illinois v. Gates*, 462 U.S. 213, 239, 103 S. Ct. 2317, 76 L. Ed. 2d 527 (1983).

- "This is not to say that probable cause can be made out by affidavits which are purely conclusory, stating only the affiant's or an informer's belief that probable cause exists without detailing any of the underlying circumstances upon which that belief is based." *U.S. v. Ventresca*, 1965-2 C.B. 517, 380 U.S. 102, 108–09, 85 S. Ct. 741, 13 L. Ed. 2d 684, 16 A.F.T.R.2d 5787 (1965).

- "The Commissioner must judge for himself the persuasiveness of the facts relied on by a complaining officer to show probable cause. He should not accept without question the complainant's mere conclusion that the person whose arrest is sought has committed a crime. The complaint contains no affirmative allegation that the affiant spoke with personal knowledge of the matters contained therein; it does not indicate any sources for the complainant's belief; and it does not set forth any other sufficient basis upon which a finding of probable cause could be made." *Giordenello v. U.S.*, 357 U.S. 480, 486, 78 S. Ct. 1245, 2 L. Ed. 2d 1503 (1958).

- "Under the Fourth Amendment, an officer may not properly issue a warrant to search a private dwelling unless he can find probable cause therefor from facts or circumstances presented to him under oath or affirmation. Mere affirmance of belief or suspicion is not enough." *Nathanson v. U.S.*, 290 U.S. 41, 47, 54 S. Ct. 11, 78 L. Ed. 159 (1933).

First Circuit

- "The best practice is for an applicant seeking a warrant based on images of alleged child pornography to append the images or provide a sufficiently specific description of the images to enable the magistrate judge to determine independently whether they probably depict real children. An officer who fails to follow this approach without good reason faces a substantial risk that the application for a warrant will not establish probable cause." *U.S. v. Syphers*, 426 F.3d 461 (1st Cir. 2005).

Third Circuit

- "The point of the Fourth Amendment, which often is not grasped by zealous officers, is not that it denies law enforcement the support of the usual inferences which reasonable men draw from evidence. Its protection consists in requiring that those inferences be drawn by a neutral and detached magistrate instead of being judged by the officer engaged in the often competitive enterprise of ferreting out crime. . . .It follows that a police officer cannot make unilateral decisions about the materiality of information, or, after satisfying him or herself that probable cause exists, merely inform the magistrate or judge of inculpatory evidence." *Wilson v. Russo*, 212 F.3d 781, 787 (3d Cir. 2000).

Fourth Circuit

- "The affidavit in this case did not adequately support the magistrate's finding of probable cause. It depended on information from an unnamed informant, and provided no indication of that informant's truthfulness or reliability. [The Officer] included conclusory descriptions apparently designed to establish the informant's trustworthiness. We are particularly concerned with [the Officer]'s statements that the informant was a concerned citizen, and a mature person with personal connections with the suspects, who projected a truthful [sic] demeanor. We conclude that this affidavit fell far short of providing probable cause for a search warrant. Upholding this warrant would ratify police use of an unknown, unproven informant—with little or no corroboration—to justify searching someone's home." *U.S. v. Wilhelm*, 80 F.3d 116, 120 (4th Cir. 1996).

Sixth Circuit

- "In order to be able to properly determine whether probable cause exists sufficient to issue a warrant, the magistrate must be presented with an affidavit containing adequate supporting facts about the underlying circumstances, either from the direct knowledge and observations of the affiant or from reliable hearsay information; bare conclusions are not enough." *U.S. v. Robinson*, 352 Fed. Appx. 27 (6th Cir. 2009).

- "The affidavit is judged on the adequacy of what it does contain, not on what it lacks, or on what a critic might say should have been added. It is the totality of the circumstances that persuade us that the affidavit in the instant case was, in fact, not merely conclusory and bare bones. . . ." *U.S. v. Allen*, 211 F.3d 970, 975, 2000 FED App. 0157P (6th Cir. 2000).

- "Thus, a bare bones affidavit is similar to, if not the same as, a conclusory affidavit. It is one which states only the affiant's belief that probable cause existed." *U.S. v. Williams*, 224 F.3d 530, 533, 2000 FED App. 0272P (6th Cir. 2000).

- "In order for a magistrate to be able to perform his official function, the affidavit must contain adequate supporting facts about the underlying circumstances to show that probable cause exists for the issuance of the warrant." *U.S. v. Smith*, 182 F.3d 473, 477, 1999 FED App. 0237P (6th Cir. 1999).

Seventh Circuit

- "In determining whether probable cause supported the issuance of a search warrant in this case, we must determine whether there was a substantial basis for the magistrate's finding of probable cause. . . The magistrate's task is 'to make a practical, common-sense decision,' given the totality of the circumstances. . . The magistrate is entitled to rely upon the law enforcement officer's training and experience when evaluating the information related to him in the determination of probable cause." *U.S. v. Johnson*, 289 F.3d 1034 (7th Cir. 2002).

- "Our prior cases have recognized that, in issuing a search warrant, a magistrate is entitled to draw reasonable inferences about where the evidence is likely to be kept, based on the nature of the evidence and the type of offense, and that in the case of drug dealers evidence is likely to be found where the dealers live." *U.S. v. McClellan*, 165 F.3d 535, 546, 50 Fed. R. Evid. Serv. 1503 (7th Cir. 1999).

- "[S]ome of the factors which suggest that an informant's information is sufficiently reliable to support the issuance of a warrant include: (1) firsthand observation by the informant; (2) degree of detail provided; (3) corroboration of the informant's information by an officer's independent investigation and (4) the fact that the informant testified at the probable cause hearing." *U.S. v. Reddrick*, 90 F.3d 1276, 1280 (7th Cir. 1996).

Eighth Circuit

- "We agree with the District Court that (the affiant), by virtue of his experience as a computer repairman, was 'uniquely able, and properly motivated, to distinguish between child pornography and lawful images' . . . (T)he images. . . .that (the affiant) stated that he had observed on the (defendants') computer were disturbing and unlike any pornographic images (he) had observed on computers in the past. (He) distinguished between "adult" and "child" pornography and specifically characterized the images on the (defendants') computer as child pornography . . . . (The officer's) affidavit in support of the search warrant related each of these facts to (the judge), and we conclude that the affidavit was sufficient to establish probable cause for the issuance of the search warrant." *U.S. v. Grant*, 490 F.3d 627 (8th Cir. 2007).

- "An affidavit supporting a warrant must show that there is a fair probability that contraband or evidence of a crime will be found in a particular place. . . . The requisite nexus between a particular location and contraband is determined by the nature of the crime and the reasonable, logical likelihood of finding useful evidence." *U.S. v. Etheridge*, 165 F.3d 655, 657 (8th Cir. 1999).

Tenth Circuit

- "As a general rule, a search warrant based on a narcotics canine alert will be sufficient on its face if the affidavit states that the dog is trained and certified to detect narcotics. . . . We decline to encumber the affidavit process by requiring affiants to include a complete history of a drug dog's reliability beyond the statement that the dog has been trained and certified to detect drugs." *U.S. v. Kennedy*, 131 F.3d 1371, 1376–77 (10th Cir. 1997).

§ 5:7 **Informants: A warrant may issue based on affidavits containing only hearsay when the totality of the circumstances presented to the magistrate constitutes probable cause. The reliability of the informant and the factual basis of the information are factors to be considered in the totality of the circumstances for finding probable cause**

Supreme Court

- "In the absence of a statement detailing the manner in which the information was gathered, it is especially important that the [informant] describe the accused's criminal activity in sufficient detail that the magistrate may know that he is relying on something more substantial than a casual rumor." *Spinelli v. U.S.*, 393 U.S. 410, 416, 89 S. Ct. 584, 21 L. Ed. 2d 637 (1969) (abrogated on other grounds by, Illinois v. Gates, 462 U.S. 213, 103 S. Ct. 2317, 76 L. Ed. 2d 527 (1983)).

- "In *Gates*, we did not merely refine or qualify the two-pronged test. We rejected it as hypertechnical and divorced from the factual and practical considerations of everyday life on which reasonable and prudent men, not legal technicians, act." *Massachusetts v. Upton*, 466 U.S. 727, 732, 104 S. Ct. 2085, 80 L. Ed. 2d 721 (1984).
- "[W]e conclude that it is wiser to abandon the two-pronged test established by our decisions in *Aguilar*[1] and *Spinelli*.[2] In its place we reaffirm the totality of the circumstances analysis that traditionally has informed probable cause determinations. The task of the issuing magistrate is simply to make a practical, common-sense decision whether, given all the circumstances set forth in the affidavit before him, including the veracity and basis of knowledge of persons supplying hearsay information, there is a fair probability that contraband or evidence of a crime will be found in a particular place. And the duty of a reviewing court is simply to ensure that the magistrate had a substantial basis for conclud-[ing] that probable cause existed." *Illinois v. Gates*, 462 U.S. 213, 238–39, 103 S. Ct. 2317, 76 L. Ed. 2d 527 (1983).
- "Moreover, the two-pronged test directs analysis into two largely independent channels—the informant's veracity or reliability and his basis of knowledge. There are persuasive arguments against according these two

---

[Section 5:7]

[1]"[T]he magistrate must be informed of some of the underlying circumstances from which the informant concluded that the [seizable items] were where he claimed they were, and from which the officer concluded that the informant was credible or his information reliable." *Aguilar v. State of Tex.*, 378 U.S. 108, 114, 84 S. Ct. 1509, 12 L. Ed. 2d 723 (1964) (abrogated on other grounds by, Illinois v. Gates, 462 U.S. 213, 103 S. Ct. 2317, 76 L. Ed. 2d 527 (1983)).

[2]"In the absence of a statement detailing the manner in which the information was gathered, it is especially important that the [informant] describe the accused's criminal activity in sufficient detail that the magistrate may know that he is relying on something more substantial than a casual rumor." *Spinelli v. U.S.*, 393 U.S. 410, 416, 89 S. Ct. 584, 21 L. Ed. 2d 637 (1969) (abrogated on other grounds by, Illinois v. Gates, 462 U.S. 213, 103 S. Ct. 2317, 76 L. Ed. 2d 527 (1983)).

elements such independent status. Instead they are better understood as relevant considerations in the totality of circumstances analysis that traditionally has guided probable cause determinations: a deficiency in one may be compensated for, in determining the overall reliability of a tip, by a strong showing as to the other, or by some other indicia of reliability." *Illinois v. Gates*, 462 U.S. 213, 233, 103 S. Ct. 2317, 76 L. Ed. 2d 527 (1983).

• "It is enough, for purposes of assessing probable cause, that corroboration through other sources of information reduced the chances of a reckless or prevaricating tale, thus providing a substantial basis for crediting the hearsay." *Illinois v. Gates*, 462 U.S. 213, 244–45, 103 S. Ct. 2317, 76 L. Ed. 2d 527 (1983).

First Circuit

• "Where, as here, the police act on information from a confidential informant, 'law enforcement must provide some information from which a court can credit the informant's credibility.' In assessing an informant's credibility, we consider factors such as '(1) the probable veracity and basis of knowledge of the informant; (2) whether an informant's statements reflect first-hand knowledge; (3) whether some or all of the informant's factual statements were corroborated wherever reasonable and practicable; and (4) whether a law enforcement officer assessed, from his professional standpoint, experience, and expertise, the probable significance of the informant's information.' Applying those factors, CI-1 had a track record of supplying reliable information to police—as we noted earlier, three times before the February 2012 search CI-1 had proven reliable. Accordingly, when CI-1 tipped police off to Joshua and Shaw's planned trip to the New Bedford area about three weeks later, this track record gave police reason to believe CI-1's newest tip was probably reliable, too. Further, notwithstanding Joshua's unsubstantiated claim to the contrary, the record shows that CI-1 had first-hand knowledge of Joshua and Shaw's operation that bolstered CI-1's credibility. Specifically, CI-1 admitted to buying oxycodone from Joshua and Shaw many times, so the CI knew when their supply was low and when they needed to restock. Moreover, the tip included details of Joshua and Shaw's future activities 'ordinarily not easily predicted,' and almost all of these details were corroborated by police surveillance before Joshua's car was stopped. Police spotted Joshua's Cadillac (the vehicle identified by CI-1) on the highway heading out of town at 4:50 pm (shortly after CI-1 said Joshua and Shaw planned to leave) and followed it to a house in Acushnet (CI-1 said they would be driving to the New Bedford area, and Acushnet abuts New Bedford). The Cadillac parked next to a white Infiniti that belonged to John Doe 4 (the dealer identified by CI-1). After the Cadillac parked, Joshua and Shaw got out of the car (CI-1 said the two of them were making the trip). . . . Finally, police assessed and understood the significance of CI-1's information before making the stop. Police had independent knowledge of the brothers' prior drug-trafficking activity through the Willis investigation—including information from two Willis couriers caught bringing pills from Florida up to Massachusetts for the Gonsalves brothers. Furthermore, sources other than CI-1 developed during and after the Willis investigation told police that Joshua and Stanley were continuing to sell oxycodone sourced from other suppliers after Willis' arrest. If more were needed, the task force officer leading the Gonsalves investigation (and who told the officer who stopped Joshua that police already had probable cause) had specialized training and experience in drug investigations. In short, law enforcement assessed CI-1's tip in the context of the overall Willis and Gonsalves investigations and in light of their expertise . . . . But hold on. Before we find probable cause, Joshua says, we must consider indicia of an informant's unreliability, too—and Joshua thinks that CI-1's tip was so inaccurate that it could not support a finding of probable cause. Specifically, Joshua points out that (1) he drove to Acushnet, but CI-1 said he was headed to New Bedford; (2) CI-1 didn't mention that Shaw's friend would be with Joshua and Shaw; and (3) police only found 280 pills, not the promised 2,000. But none of these facts undermine our belief that police had probable cause to stop and search the car that night. First, although the task force officer's affidavit said Joshua was going to New Bedford, the officer testified at the suppression hearing that the CI said Joshua was going to the 'New Bedford area,' and the district court's findings of fact listed the destination as the 'New Bedford area.' Joshua does not challenge that finding of fact as clearly erroneous on appeal, so we adopt it here. Acushnet and New Bedford are adjoining towns, so CI-1's claim that Joshua was heading to the 'New Bedford area' was accurate. The same goes for his second point—that CI-1 didn't tell police that Tavares would be along for the ride—because the omission of the fact does not make CI-1's tip inaccurate as to the presence of Joshua and Shaw. But even if it did, we assess probable cause under the totality of the circumstances, and given the other factors we described above, this point does little to undermine the government's probable-cause argument or our probable-cause finding. Joshua's third argument—that Shaw was only carrying a fraction of the drugs that CI-1 predicted—doesn't help his case, either. We measure probable cause at the time the officers effectuate the search. That means the mid-search discovery of a smaller-than-anticipated pill stash does not change whether the officers had probable cause to begin with. All things considered, we find the police had probable cause to stop Joshua and search his car." *United States v. Gonsalves*, 859 F.3d 95, 103–05 (1st Cir. 2017) (citations omitted).

- "The affidavit provided numerous facts from which a magistrate could have easily concluded that the CI who advised Ross of Dixon's illegal drug sales was credible. First, Ross met with the informant in person on several occasions. . . . This sort of face-to-face contact between the agent and informant supports the informant's reliability. Second, the CI had given Ross fruitful tips in the past. Third, because of Ross's extensive contact with the CI, Ross would have been able to hold the CI responsible had he provided false information, which created an incentive for the CI to tell the truth. Fourth, the CI, in describing his purchases from Dixon, provided [a] specific, first-hand account of possible criminal activity—a hallmark of a credible tip—and in doing so implicated himself in the wrongdoing. Fifth, Ross independently corroborated facts that he had learned from the CI. [C]orroboration of even innocent activity reported in the tip may support a finding of probable cause. . . . Finally, Ross was highly experienced in the drug trafficking field, having participated in over 1000 drug investigations during his sixteen-year tenure in the Boston police Department. [T]he issuing judge making a probable cause determination may credit the experience and pertinent expertise of a law enforcement affiant in evaluating the authenticity of the informant's description of the target's modus operandi." *U.S. v. Dixon*, 787 F.3d 55, 59–60 (1st Cir. 2015), cert. denied, 136 S. Ct. 280, 193 L. Ed. 2d 204 (2015) (inner quotations and citations omitted).

- "Where the primary basis for a probable cause determination is information provided by a confidential informant, the affidavit must provide some information from which a magistrate can credit the informant's credibility. '[A] probable cause finding may be based on an informant's tip so long as the probability of a lying or inaccurate informer has been sufficiently reduced.' We apply a 'nonexhaustive list of factors' to examine the affidavit's probable cause showing, which include, among others: (1) whether the affidavit establishes the probable veracity and basis of knowledge of persons supplying hearsay information; (2) whether an informant's statements reflect first-hand knowledge; (3) whether some or all of the informant's factual statements were corroborated wherever reasonable or practicable (e.g., through police surveillance); and (4) whether a law enforcement affiant assessed, from his professional standpoint, experience, and expertise, the probable significance of the informant's provided information." *U.S. v. Gifford*, 727 F.3d 92 (1st Cir. 2013) (citations omitted).

- "An affidavit supporting a warrant application may rely upon information provided by a third-party source as long as the affiant gives the issuing magistrate a sufficient basis for crediting that source. In evaluating whether a particular affidavit crosses this threshold, we may consider, among other things, whether the affidavit establishes the source's veracity, whether the source's statement derives from firsthand knowledge, and whether all or any portion of the source's state-

ment is corroborated. We also may consider 'whether a
law enforcement affiant assessed, from his professional
standpoint, experience, and expertise, the probable significance of the informant's provided information.' None
of these factors is singularly dispositive, and a stronger
showing on one may offset a weaker showing on
another." *U.S. v. Clark*, 685 F.3d 72, 76–77 (1st Cir.
2012) (citations omitted).

• "The government contends that the hearsay tip in this
case was more reliable than the anonymous tip analyzed
in [*Florida v. J.L.*, 529 U.S. 266, 120 S. Ct. 1375, 146 L.
Ed. 2d 254 (2000)] because of the police officers' interactions with [informant], and because [informant] was
able to report a crime supposedly witnessed by his unnamed relative. . . . Contrary to the government's suggestion, however, the tip in this case bears some
important badges of unreliability not present in the
cases relied upon by the government. First, there is the
hearsay problem. While the police or a 911 operator
often can make some rough judgments about the age,
cognitive ability, and motivations of an anonymous
informant based on her tone of voice (if the tip occurs
via the telephone), or appearance and demeanor (if the
tip is delivered in person even by a complete stranger),
the police here had no way of knowing the state of mind
of [informant's] relative when she gave her information,
or whether she was a person who could be relied on to
relate events accurately. . . . Second, there was a higher
risk of fabrication here. The *J.L.* Court deemed anonymous tips inherently unreliable largely because such
tips carry with them a risk of fabrication by the
informant. . . . There is no indication in any of the cases
cited by the government that either a hearsay informant
or a party relaying a hearsay tip to the police had so
obvious a motive to lie as existed in this case. Finally,
crucially, and unlike in *J.L.*, the police had specific
reasons to doubt the tip by the time they made their
stop. . . . Here, the investigation the police had conducted actually undermined the tip's reliability. . . .
[A]s in *J.L.*, even with the minimally corroborative factors cited by the government, the police had uncovered
nothing of importance that could indicate the reliability
of the hearsay tip. To the contrary, the initial police

investigation did more to discredit the hearsay tip than to corroborate it. For these reasons, we conclude that the tip standing by itself was insufficient to provide reasonable suspicion for the March 31st vehicle stop." *U.S. v. Monteiro*, 447 F.3d 39 (1st Cir. 2006).

Second Circuit

- "In *Illinois v. Gates*, the Supreme Court abandoned its earlier two-pronged *Aguilar-Spinelli* test for assessing whether testimony by an informant could establish probable cause and instead reaffirmed the totality of the circumstances analysis that traditionally has informed probable cause determinations. In performing this examination of the 'totality of the circumstances,' however, the court may consider some of the same factors as were identified in *Aguilar* and *Spinelli*, including an informant's veracity, reliability and basis of knowledge, and the extent to which an informant's statements—even about a suspect's innocent activities—are independently corroborated. . . . In assessing the veracity of an informant's statements, it is improper to discount the information provided simply because the informant has no proven record of truthfulness or accuracy. There is, in particular, no need to show past reliability when the informant is in fact a participant in the very crime at issue. However, although other circuits have recognized that criminals caught red-handed may be reliable sources of information because the informant's interest in obtaining leniency creates a strong motive to supply accurate information, we have also cautioned that a criminal informer is less reliable than an innocent bystander with no apparent motive to falsify. Whether or not the informant speaks to an officer in person or through the mediation of an anonymous means of communication may also bear upon the reliability of the information he provides; thus, a face-to-face informant must be thought more reliable than an anonymous telephone tipster, for the former runs the greater risk that he may be held accountable if his information proves false. In addition to considering an informant's veracity, reliability, and basis of knowledge, in assessing the totality of the circumstances we also evaluate whether the information an informant provides

311

is corroborated by independent police investigation, because an informant who is right about some facts is more likely to be right about others. We consider such corroboration in evaluating the existence of probable cause even if only an informant's account of anticipated innocent activities is confirmed." *U.S. v. Gagnon*, 373 F.3d 230 (2d Cir. 2004).

- "Although discredited as a rigid two-pronged test, an informant's basis of knowledge and veracity remain important factors in a totality of the circumstances analysis." *U.S. v. Canfield*, 212 F.3d 713, 718 (2d Cir. 2000).

Third Circuit

- "Even if we were to conclude that Chief Detzel was reckless in excluding [from the warrant affidavit] the facts that no money exchanged hands during the silencer transaction and that policy officers conducted a preliminary search of the vehicle, we agree with the District Court that neither omission was material to the establishment of probable cause. It may well be true, as Johnson argues, that 'a judge would want to know' that Johnson failed to pay the C.I. at the time of the delivery. But not including that fact did not undermine the probable cause showing here. The simultaneous payment of money in exchange for goods may be proof of an illegal transaction, but the lack of a simultaneous exchange does not necessarily imply the absence of illegality. The C.I.'s communications with the police, as relayed in Chief Detzel's affidavit, amply demonstrated probable cause. Likewise, although the affidavit should have included language explaining that policy briefly looked in the driver's side of the vehicle, there is no evidence that the search was anything more than a cursory look that did not affect the probable cause determination. A 'quick visual check' of the floorboards, is a fact that does not change the outcome here." *U.S. v. Johnson*, 578 Fed. Appx. 150, 155 (3d Cir. 2014) (citations omitted).

Fourth Circuit

- "It is well settled that probable cause may be founded upon hearsay and information received from informants.

However, there is no bright-line rule as to when such information may establish probable cause. . . . Generally, when an effort is made to establish probable cause for the issuance of a search warrant based on hearsay from an informant, it is necessary to consider all the circumstances set forth in the affidavit, including the veracity and basis of knowledge of persons supplying hearsay information. The degree to which an informant's story is corroborated may also be an important factor. However, there is no set requirement that all tips be corroborated by subsequent police investigation in order to be considered credible. Whether subsequent corroboration is necessary must be determined in the light of the totality of the circumstances presented by the particular set of facts." *U.S. v. DeQuasie*, 373 F.3d 509 (4th Cir. 2004).

- "Unlike the anonymous tipster, a witness who directly approaches a police officer can also be held accountable for false statements. As the Supreme Court has observed, citizens who personally report crimes to the police thereby make themselves accountable for lodging false complaints. . . .Here the informant provided her home address to the officers. In doing so, the informant exposed herself to the repercussions of misleading or deceiving the police." *U.S. v. Christmas*, 222 F.3d 141, 144 (4th Cir. 2000).

Fifth Circuit

- "The temporal aspect for the test of probable cause is whether the anonymous information is reliable under the totality of the circumstances. . . . The totality of the circumstances test includes four factors: (1) the nature of the information; (2) whether there has been an opportunity for the police to see or hear the matter reported; (3) the veracity and the basis of the knowledge of the informant; (4) whether there has been any independent verification of the matters reported through police investigation." *U.S. v. Morales*, 171 F.3d 978, 981–82 (5th Cir. 1999).

Sixth Circuit

- "While adopting a presumption of reliability for eyewitness allegations, those cases also contain an important

313

limiting factor: Probable cause is created only by eye-witness allegations that are *'reasonably trustworthy,'* (emphasis added), and thus probable cause does *not* exist where 'there is an apparent reason for the officer to believe that the eyewitness was lying, did not accurately describe what he had seen, or was in some fashion mistaken regarding his recollection.' Put another way, the presumption of veracity applies only where the witness is 'someone with respect to whom there is *no* apparent reason to question the person's reliability.' " *Wesley v. Campbell*, 779 F.3d 421, 429–30 (6th Cir. 2015) (citations omitted).

- "Although it is true that an eyewitness's allegations need not be perfectly consistent in order to establish probable cause, we conclude that J.S.'s inconsistent stories should have suggested to [Officer] Rigney that he was unreliable." *Wesley v. Campbell*, 779 F.3d 421, 432 (6th Cir. 2015) (citation omitted).

- "In short, where an affidavit substantially relies on hearsay statements provided by a confidential informant, probable cause for a warrant to issue depends on whether the reliability of the informant or sufficient independent police corroboration of the informant's statements can be found within the four corners of the affidavit. Our precedent suggests that, in determining the reliability of statements provided by an informant under the totality of the circumstances, no single measure of reliability is required for a magistrate to find a confidential informant's statements reliable. Instead, we must balance all potential indicia of reliability present in the affidavit. This Court has repeatedly held that an affidavit that furnishes details of an informant's track record of providing reliable tips to the affiant can substantiate the informant's credibility, such that other indicia of reliability may not be required when relying on the informant's statements. However, where the affidavit does not aver facts showing the relationship between the affiant and the informant, or detail the affiant's knowledge regarding the informant providing prior reliable tips that relate to the same type of crimes as the current tip concerns, this Court has generally found that other indicia of reliability must be present to substantiate the informant's statements. The necessity of the affiant providing further indicia of reliability of his or her informant has been found even in cases where the informant's identity was disclosed to the magistrate and the statements amounted to an admission of criminal conduct." *U.S. v. Neal*, 577 Fed. Appx. 434, 440–41 (6th Cir. 2014) (citations omitted).

- "*United States v. Allen* does not invariably require an affiant to provide corroboration for a confidential informant's statements contained in an affidavit supporting a search-warrant application. In *Allen,* we held that, if a confidential informant—personally known by the affiant to be reliable—alleged direct, personal observation of criminal activity, then the affiant would not have to include in the affidavit further corroboration of the informant's allegations. We reasoned that a requirement that the police further corroborate such information from a confidential informant would aid lawbreakers, 'as detectives tried to conduct surveillance in crack-ridden neighborhoods without themselves being detected and their suspects alerted.' Moreover, we added, 'the additional time thus added to the process by mandating an independent police investigation, following a [confidential informant's] contact would provide a further advantage to drug dealers' already highly mobile, hit-and-run operations.' We declined 'to handicap the state in that way.' " *U.S. v. Brown*, 732 F.3d 569, 574 (6th Cir. 2013) (citations omitted).

- "Where, as here, the bulk of the information in the affidavit comes from a confidential source, a court must consider the veracity, reliability, and the basis of knowledge for that information as part of the totality of the circumstances analysis. While independent corroboration of a confidential informant's story is not a *sine qua non* to a finding of probable cause, in the absence of any indicia of the informants' reliability, courts insist that the affidavit contain substantial independent police corroboration. As long as the issuing judge can conclude independently that the informant is reliable, an affidavit based on the informant's tip will support a finding of probable cause. An affidavit is sufficient where a known person, named to the magistrate, to whose reliability an officer attests with some detail, states that he has seen a particular crime and particular evidence, in the recent past, such that a neutral and detached magistrate *may* believe that evidence of a crime will be found. . . . In sum, an affidavit that supplies little information concerning an informant's reliability may support a finding of probable cause, under the totality of the circumstances, if it includes sufficient corroborating information." *U.S. v. Coffee*, 434 F.3d 887, 2006 FED App. 0030P (6th Cir. 2006).

• "The additional evidence substantiating an informant's reliability need not be obtained from a source unrelated to the confidential informant—e.g., an independent police investigation or a second confidential informant—but may be any set of facts that support the accuracy of the information supplied by the informant." *U.S. v. May*, 399 F.3d 817, 2005 FED App. 0089P (6th Cir. 2005).

• "We hold that where a known person, named to the magistrate, to whose reliability an officer attests with some detail, states that he has seen a particular crime and particular evidence, in the recent past, a neutral and detached magistrate may believe that evidence of a crime will be found. There is, of course, no guarantee that the evidence will still be there, but the magistrate may determine that such a probability exists. This holding requires evidence sufficient to provide a basis for that judgment." *U.S. v. Allen*, 211 F.3d 970, 976, 2000 FED App. 0157P (6th Cir. 2000).

• "In applying the totality of the circumstances test, we will evaluate the reliability or veracity of the informant, the sufficiency of the subsequent corroboration of the tip, and the sufficiency of the affidavit's statement about the underlying circumstances from which the informant concluded illegal weapons would be found in defendant's home (basis of knowledge)." *U.S. v. Smith*, 182 F.3d 473, 478, 1999 FED App. 0237P (6th Cir. 1999).

• "To conclude, we believe the district court erred in finding that the affidavit lacked sufficient detail or corroboration to establish probable cause. Corroboration and an explicit and detailed description of wrongdoing are not automatic requirements for establishing probable cause, but are only two factors to be considered under the Gates totality of the circumstances test, which requires a balanced assessment of the relative weights of all the various indicia of reliability. . . . Although either richness of detail or a heightened level of corroboration may be required where information is provided by an anonymous informant of unknown veracity. . .information supplied by an informant of proven reliability may be sufficient, standing alone, to demonstrate probable cause. . . . In other words, if the prior track record of an informant adequately substantiates his credibility, other indicia of reliability are not necessarily required." *U.S. v. Smith*, 182 F.3d 473, 483, 1999 FED App. 0237P (6th Cir. 1999).

Seventh Circuit

- "When an affidavit is the only evidence presented to a judge in support of a search warrant, 'the validity of the warrant rests solely on the strength of the affidavit.' And when an informant serves as the source of information in an affidavit, the probable-cause determination turns on the informant's credibility. To evaluate an informant's credibility, we consider 'the level of detail, the extent of firsthand observation, the degree of corroboration, the time between the events reported and the warrant application, and whether the informant appeared or testified before the magistrate.' . . .To start, Agent Murphy corroborated more of Walker's story than Hansmeier is willing to admit. For instance, Walker told the officers that he had bought methamphetamine from Hansmeier at Hansmeier's house. Walker then successfully directed the officers to where Hansmeier lived. This did not verify Walker's claim that Hansmeier was dealing drugs, but it is important in gauging Walker's overall credibility as an informant. . . .Agent Murphy also corroborated Walker's story in three other ways. First, Agent Murphy stated that he was familiar with Hansmeier from previous investigations. Second, Agent Murphy's background check on Hansmeier uncovered that Hansmeier had been convicted of at least one drug-distribution-related offense in the past; although the record check does not corroborate Walker's story alone, 'it does retain some corroborative value.' And third, Agent Murphy included in the affidavit a detailed recollection of Hansmeier's drug dealing from an unnamed confidential informant, which counts as 'slight' corroboration. . . . Admittedly, those facts are

317

not enough alone to find Walker credible. But they are, to an extent, indicators of credibility. And any additional steps that Agent Murphy could have taken to corroborate Walker's story do 'not in any way detract from what was done.' . . . In any event, Hansmeier's emphasis on corroboration alone is misplaced: no one factor is determinative in weighing an informant's credibility. A weakness in one may be offset by the strength of others. . . . And here, the other factors strongly support Walker's credibility. Walker's information was detailed: he knew the type of drugs that Hansmeier dealt, the quantity that he could get from Hansmeier, and the price that Hansmeier charged. Walker's information was based on firsthand knowledge. And Walker's information was based on recent observation: he had seen drugs and drug money in Hansmeier's house and bought methamphetamine from Hansmeier just a few days before he spoke with Agent Murphy (to say nothing of the fact that Walker bought drugs from Hansmeier weekly, who always had a supply). . . . Still more facts bolster Walker's credibility. His statements were unimmunized and against his penal interest: he admitted buying 4 ounces of methamphetamine twice a week from Hansmeier, far more than the sixty-eight grams that police caught him with. And although Walker was a newly arrested informant, which subjects him to greater scrutiny, the issuing judge was entitled to conclude that Walker's recent arrest gave him an incentive to supply the police with accurate information in hopes of receiving lenient punishment for his own crimes. Finally, the issuing judge was aware that the officers knew who Walker was (that is, he was a confidential informant as opposed to an anonymous tipster), meaning that the officers could find him and hold him responsible if he gave misleading information—yet another check on credibility. . . .The only factor that doesn't favor Walker's credibility is that he didn't appear before the issuing judge. But that is the absence of just one of many factors used to evaluate an informant's credibility; the others all tend to favor Walker. . . . Thus, substantial evidence in the record supports the issuing judge's probable-cause determination." *United States v. Hansmeier*, 867 F.3d 807, 811–12 (7th Cir. 2017) (citations omitted).

- "Where the affidavit is supported by information from an informant, we employ a totality-of-the-circumstances inquiry to determine whether that information establishes probable cause for the search. This inquiry encompasses several factors, including: 'the level of detail, the extent of firsthand observation, the degree of corroboration, the time between the events reported and the warrant application, and whether the informant appeared or testified before the magistrate.' No one factor is dispositive; a deficiency in one factor may be compensated by a stronger showing in others. We give 'great deference' to the issuing judge's conclusion that there is probable cause." *United States v. Johnson*, 867 F.3d 737, 741 (7th Cir. 2017) (citations omitted).

- "While it is true that the testimony of a single, impartial eyewitness is sufficient to support probable cause, there is no corresponding rule to account for identifications obtained from persons who were not eyewitnesses to an event but viewed video footage afterwards." *Bailey v. City of Chicago*, 779 F.3d 689, 694 (7th Cir. 2015), cert. denied, 136 S. Ct. 200, 193 L. Ed. 2d 129 (2015) (citation omitted).

- "In applying for search warrants, however, police are not limited to relying only on informants with proven track records of providing truthful information. Past performance is one way of establishing the veracity or reliability of an informant, but it is not the only way." *U.S. v. Mitten*, 592 F.3d 767 (7th Cir. 2010).

- "A few unreliable informants are not much better than one. . . . . If an officer cannot demonstrate that an informant is reliable, then citing additional anonymous informants of unknown reliability does little to establish the factual foundation[s] that we[re] found lacking in *Koerth*. Nonetheless . . . . [under the instant] circumstances, [the investigating officer]'s failure to recognize that the warrant did not establish probable cause does not amount to a lack of good faith and the exclusionary rule is not the appropriate remedy." *U.S. v. Bell*, 585 F.3d 1045 (7th Cir. 2009).

- "[Informant] was not just an informant, but a newly-arrested informant, and as such merits a greater dose of skepticism when assessing his credibility." *U.S. v. Olson*, 408 F.3d 366 (7th Cir. 2005).

- "We have noted some factors that can help determine whether a lower court (state or federal) had sufficient information in the record before it to issue a warrant: 1. Whether the informant made firsthand observations; 2. The degree of detail the informant provided; 3. Whether police corroborated the informant's story with independent investigation; 4. Whether the informant testified at the probable cause hearing. . . . This is by no means an exhaustive list; these are merely factors we have found useful in the past." *U.S. v. McKinney*, 143 F.3d 325, 328–29 (7th Cir. 1998).

Eighth Circuit

- "In analyzing the totality of the circumstances to determine whether there was probable cause for a search warrant, an informant's veracity, reliability, and basis of knowledge are all relevant and important factors. A disclosure in an affidavit that the informant was an admitted participant in the crime and therefore an eyewitness to most of the acts constituting the crime as described in the affidavit is one manner to determine the credibility and reliability of an informant." *U.S. v. Palega*, 556 F.3d 709 (8th Cir. 2009).

- "Probable cause supported document search warrant for drug conspiracy defendant's residence, given affiant's handwritten notation on search warrant affidavit indicating that confidential informant had provided information that detailed drug ledgers were being kept at residence, that affidavit indicated that same informant had informed law enforcement that defendant was distributing methamphetamine from different residence, which was corroborated by two other informants, and that same informant had previously provided names and telephone numbers of persons involved in distribution of narcotics, which were independently corroborated and led to seizures of narcotics." *U.S. v. Guzman-Tlaseca*, 546 F.3d 571 (8th Cir. 2008).

- "When a confidential informant provides information in support of a search warrant, the issuing magistrate considers the informant's reliability and the basis of his knowledge. The totality of the circumstances analysis, however, does not mandate that both factors be present before a warrant may issue. Instead, a strong showing of one may compensate for a deficiency in the other. For example, if an informant is known for the unusual reliability of his predictions of certain types of criminal activities in a locality, his failure, in a particular case, to thoroughly set forth the basis of his knowledge surely should not serve as an absolute bar to a finding of probable cause. The information from [an informant] is sufficiently reliable if it is corroborated by other evidence, or if the informant has a history of providing reliable information." *U.S. v. Lucca*, 377 F.3d 927 (8th Cir. 2004).

- "The core question in assessing probable cause based upon information supplied by an informant is whether the information is reliable. . . .Information may be sufficiently reliable to support a probable cause finding if the person providing the information has a track record of supplying reliable information, or if it is corroborated by independent evidence." *U.S. v. Morales*, 238 F.3d 952, 953 (8th Cir. 2001).

Ninth Circuit

- "Under the totality of the circumstances, a search warrant issued to search a suspect's home computer and electronic equipment lacks probable cause when (1) no evidence of possession or attempt to possess child pornography was submitted to the issuing magistrate; (2) no evidence was submitted to the magistrate regarding computer or electronics use by the suspect; and (3) the only evidence linking the suspect's attempted child molestation to possession of child pornography is the experience of the requesting police officer, with no further explanation." *Dougherty v. City of Covina*, 654 F.3d 892, 895 (9th Cir. 2011).

- "When a search warrant is based solely on an informant's tip, as in this case, the proper analysis is whether probable cause exists from the totality of the circumstances to determine a sufficient level of reliability and basis of knowledge for the tip. ... Any crime involving dishonesty necessarily has an adverse effect on an informant's credibility. Therefore, when an informant's criminal history includes crimes of dishonesty, additional evidence must be included in the affidavit to bolster the informant's credibility or the reliability of the tip. Otherwise, an informant's criminal past involving dishonesty is fatal to the reliability of the informant's information, and his/her testimony cannot support probable cause." *U.S. v. Elliott*, 322 F.3d 710 (9th Cir. 2003).

Tenth Circuit

- "Generally, to be sufficient to support an inference of credibility and reliability, the corroborated information must be 'predictive' in nature. Predictive information is defined broadly as knowledge that the informant could not acquire from any source but the suspect, whether directly or indirectly, providing reason to believe that the informant has inside information—a special familiarity with the suspect's affairs, and is not just a member of the general public. . . . Reliance on an anonymous tip is justified when the tip contains a range of details relating not just to easily obtained facts and conditions existing at the time of the tip, but to future actions of third parties ordinarily not easily predicted. Even if the facts corroborated are themselves innocent, . . . they may show the informant to be a reliable source of information not available to the public or the police, not merely a neighbor with ulterior motives or an active imagination." *U.S. v. Hauk*, 412 F.3d 1179 (10th Cir. 2005).

- "[H]earsay evidence may form the basis for a probable cause determination. Moreover, we have previously recognized that multiple layers of hearsay may support a finding of probable cause for a search warrant. Despite this clear precedent, [defendant] insists that in this case the affiant. . . was not sufficiently proximate to the investigation to effectively corroborate the hearsay evidence to which he attested. [Defendant] reasons that because [affiant] had not independently verified the information provided by law enforcement agents, and because he did not personally obtain the tips from the cooperating witnesses, he could not personally be aware of, or accountable for, the accuracy of the information contained in his sworn affidavit. . . . *Jones* did not require an officer to corroborate information received from an informant through personal observation as [defendant] would have us hold. Rather, an officer simply must have knowledge of other matters that reasonably corroborate the informant's statements." *U.S. v. Mathis*, 357 F.3d 1200, 63 Fed. R. Evid. Serv. 692 (10th Cir. 2004).

§ 5:8   Staleness: An affidavit for a search warrant must present timely information, and the warrant must be promptly executed

Supreme Court

- "While the statute does not fix the time within which proof of probable cause must be taken by the judge or commissioner, it is manifest that the proof must be of facts so closely related to the time of the issue of the warrant as to justify a finding of probable cause at that time. Whether the proof meets this test must be determined by the circumstances of each case. It is in the light of the requirement that probable cause must properly appear when the warrant issues that we must read the provision which in explicit terms makes a warrant void unless executed within ten days after its date. That period marks the permitted duration of the proceeding in which the warrant is issued. There is no provision which authorizes the commissioner to extend its life or to revive it." *Sgro v. U.S.*, 287 U.S. 206, 210–11, 53 S. Ct. 138, 77 L. Ed. 260, 85 A.L.R. 108 (1932).

First Circuit

- "[C]ourts confronting suppression motions do not measure the timeliness of collected information mechanistically, merely counting the number of days elapsed. Rather, a number of integers must be factored into the calculus—e.g., the nature of the information, the nature and characteristics of the supposed criminal activity, the nature and characteristics of the place to be searched, the nature of the items delineated in the warrant—and the likely endurance of the information must be gauged on that basis. The longer the expected duration of the criminal activity and the longer the expected life of the items attendant to it, the more likely that a datum from the seemingly distant past will be relevant to a current investigation." *U.S. v. Schaefer*, 87 F.3d 562, 568 (1st Cir. 1996).

Second Circuit

- "In the Second Circuit, the principal factors in assessing whether or not the supporting facts have become stale are the age of those facts and the nature of the conduct alleged to have violated the law. . . . In general, the determination of whether information presented in support of an application is sufficiently current to support a finding of probable cause is one that must be made on the basis of the facts of each case. . . ." *Diamondstone v. Macaluso*, 148 F.3d 113, 124 (2d Cir. 1998).

Third Circuit

- "The age of the information supporting a warrant application is a factor that must be considered in determining probable cause. . . . If information is too old, it may have little value in showing that contraband or evidence is still likely to be found in the place for which the warrant is sought. . . . Age alone, however, does not determine staleness. The likelihood that the evidence sought is still at the place to be searched depends on a number of variables, such as the nature of the crime, of the criminal, of the thing to be seized, and of the place to be searched. . . . When an activity is of a protracted and continuous nature, the passage of time becomes less significant." *U.S. v. Williams*, 124 F.3d 411, 420 (3d Cir. 1997).

Fourth Circuit

- "A valid search warrant may issue only upon allegations of facts so closely related to the time of issue of the warrant as to justify a finding of probable cause at that time. Whether the proof meets this test must be determined by the circumstances of each case. . . . A critical issue regarding staleness is whether there was probable cause at the time of issuance of the search warrant to believe that the evidence was then located at the premises named in the warrant." *U.S. v. Rhynes*, 206 F.3d 349, 375–76 (4th Cir. 1999).

Sixth Circuit

- "Even though Lt. Drewery did not specify in his affidavit the dates on which he observed particular transactions, and while 'stale information cannot be used in a probable cause determination,' Lt. Drewery's observations were not stale for two reasons. First, Lt. Drewery did state that his observations occurred between October 15 and December 3—two to fifty-one days before the probable-cause determination. While 'drugs are usually sold and consumed in a prompt fashion,' the evidence of drug sales two to fifty-one days before is recent enough here to suggest that there may be further evidence of illegality in that place. In United States v. Greene, for instance, we held that 23–month–old evidence of drug sales was not stale when paired with information regarding a drug delivery in the prior month. Second, Lt. Drewery's observations of heavy car and foot traffic, repeated transactions, and one particular transaction in which an unknown man from apartment four took out a packet of marijuana from a bigger bag, all suggested that apartment four was home to an ongoing drug business of some size. We have recognized a 'general principle that when "the affidavit properly recites facts indicating activity of a protracted and continuous nature, a course of conduct, the passage of time becomes less significant."' It would certainly have been preferable for Lt. Drewery to have indicated the specific dates, but the fact that all of the multiple and repeated activities were observed within a defined period of less than seven weeks just prior to the date of the affidavit was sufficient to support probable cause. Perry argues that the lack of specific dates precludes either a conclusion that the activities were recent, or the existence of a protracted and continuous course of conduct. This attempt to play two ends against the middle is not persuasive in the context of this case. '[T]he function of a staleness test in the search warrant context is not to create an arbitrary time limitation within which discovered facts must be presented to a magistrate.' The relative recency of a set of actions and their relative closeness in time to each other combine to demonstrate probable cause, especially given the limited nature of our review of the probable-cause determination. Such review is limited to 'whether the magistrate had a substantial basis for finding that the affidavit established probable cause to believe that the evidence would be found at the place cited,' giving 'great deference to a magistrate's determination of probable cause.' On the merits, probable cause exists under the Fourth Amendment 'when there is a fair probability, given the totality of the circumstances, that contraband or evidence of a crime will be found in a particular place.' Also without merit is Perry's argument that the district court relied on information outside Lt. Drewery's affidavit in upholding the probable-cause determination of the Tennessee magistrate. The district court explicitly disavowed reliance on such information. After a federal magistrate judge referred to evidence outside of Lt. Drewery's affidavit without relying on it, the district court granted Perry's objection to disregard such evidence and stated: 'The Court will limit its factual findings to those described in the affidavit.' The district court then concluded in particular that 'there is substantial evidence within the four corners of the affidavit that a continuous and ongoing drug operation was being conducted' in apartment four." *United States v. Perry*, 864 F.3d 412, 414–416 (6th Cir. 2017) (citations omitted).

- "The point of the expiration of probable cause is determined by the nature of the crime and the circumstances of that case. Rather than focusing on the timeline of the evidence, we look to four factors to measure staleness:

  (1) the character of the crime (chance encounter in the night or regenerating conspiracy?), (2) the criminal (nomadic or entrenched?), (3) the thing to be seized (perishable and easily transferrable or of enduring utility to its holder?), and (4) the place to be searched (mere criminal forum of convenience or secure operational base?).

  Under these factors, the information in the affidavit was not stale." *U.S. v. Elbe*, 774 F.3d 885, 890 (6th Cir. 2014), cert. denied, 135 S. Ct. 1573, 191 L. Ed. 2d 656 (2015) (citations omitted).

- "The crime at issue in this case—the sale of drugs out of a residence—is not inherently ongoing. Rather, it exists upon a continuum ranging from an individual who effectuates the occasional sale from his or her personal holdings of drugs to known acquaintances, to an organized group operating an established and notorious drug den. The inclusion of outdated information has been insufficient to render an entire affidavit stale when the affidavit as a whole establishes that the criminal activity in question is ongoing and continuous, or closer to the 'drug den' end of the continuum. . . . [Here,] the investigation consisted solely of one modified controlled buy, in which a confidential informant gave pre-recorded buy money to an unidentified female, who was followed to the address in question, observed entering and leaving, and who later delivered a baggie of crack cocaine to the confidential informant. . . . More importantly, the affidavit offers no clue as to when this single controlled buy took place. Because probable cause has a durational aspect, at least some temporal reference point is necessary to ascertain its existence. . . . In this instance, without a date or even a reference to recent activity, etc., there is absolutely no way to begin measuring the continued existence of probable cause. This deficiency alone is sufficient to render the warrant invalid, without considering any of the affidavit's other weaknesses. Thus, we agree with the district court's finding that the warrant was invalid on staleness grounds." *U.S. v. Hython*, 443 F.3d 480, 13 A.L.R. Fed. 2d 719 (6th Cir. 2006).

- "[Defendant] contends that the warrant was stale at the time it was obtained. This court [has] stated that in determining whether evidence is stale, 'the length of time between the events listed in the affidavit and the application of the warrant, while clearly salient, is not controlling.' . . . Even if a significant period of time elapsed, it is possible the magistrate judge may infer that 'a search would uncover evidence of wrongdoing.' Here, the controlled purchase by the confidential informant took place on or about August 16, 1999. On August 19, 1999, the warrant was issued and executed. It is reasonable that three days after the drug purchase that police would find narcotics, related paraphernalia, and/or the marked money in the residence. Therefore, the warrant was not stale." *U.S. v. Pinson*, 321 F.3d 558, 2003 FED App. 0064P (6th Cir. 2003).

- "[T]he question of staleness depends on the inherent nature of the crime. . . . Instead of measuring staleness solely by counting the days on a calendar, courts must also concern themselves with the following variables: the character of the crime (chance encounter in the night or regenerating conspiracy?), the criminal (nomadic or entrenched?), the thing to be seized (perishable and easily transferable or of enduring utility to its holder?), the place to be searched (mere criminal forum of convenience or secure operational base. . . ." *U.S. v. Spikes*, 158 F.3d 913, 923, 49 Fed. R. Evid. Serv. 1564, 1998 FED App. 0273P (6th Cir. 1998).

- "[T]he function of a staleness test in the search warrant context is not to create an arbitrary time limitation within which discovered facts must be presented to a magistrate. Rather, the existence of probable cause is a function of the inherent nature of the crime. [I]f an affidavit recites activity indicating protracted or continuous conduct, time is of less significance. Moreover, although a significant period of time may have elapsed since a defendant's last reported criminal activity, it may be properly inferred that indicia of criminal activity will be kept for some period of time." *U.S. v. Canan*, 48 F.3d 954, 959, 41 Fed. R. Evid. Serv. 543, 1995 FED App. 0077P (6th Cir. 1995).

Seventh Circuit

- "[Defendant] focuses much of his appeal on staleness. He argues that the one to ten day period between the time the CI [confidential informant] witnessed [Defendant] in the apartment with cocaine and the execution of the search warrant is enough to render the warrant stale. . . . [Defendant] points out that the government has not cited any case where a warrant has been substantiated on the basis of a single occurrence of criminal activity outside a 72—hour window. [Defendant] may be correct in his assertion, but the absence of such precedent does not create a 72—hour rule. Indeed, there is no bright line rule for determining staleness. Instead of setting a time limit for staleness, we consider the age of the CI's information in conjunction with the rest of the factors. To the extent that ten days is a lengthier interval than usual, it is not so long as to completely dispel any belief that a search would be fruitful—particularly in light of the fact that the CI had previously provided reliable information to law enforcement resulting in arrest and seizure of drugs. [Defendant] also argues that the warrant was impermissibly stale because the supporting affidavits did not establish regularity of drug use or sale. While evidence of regularity may be helpful to determine how long a CI's information will remain useful, it is not a legal requirement. Instead, the affidavits must provide enough information to lead a reasonably prudent person to believe a search would be fruitful. Because the circumstances point toward probable cause, this staleness argument fails as well." *U.S. v. Sutton*, 742 F.3d 770 (7th Cir. 2014).

Eighth Circuit

- "Ortiz-Cervantes argues the information connecting him and the residence to the conspiracy to sell methamphetamine was stale. 'There is no bright-line test for determining when information in a warrant is stale.' 'A warrant becomes stale if the information supporting the warrant is not "sufficiently close in time to the issuance of the warrant and the subsequent search conducted so that probable cause can be said to exist as of the time of the search."' The first controlled buy that connected Ortiz-Cervantes to the conspiracy occurred on September 24, 2013—almost eight months before the search warrant was issued and the search was conducted—and the proffer interview in November 2013 identified Ortiz-Cervantes as selling methamphetamine more than a year before the search. However, just before the tenth and final controlled buy—which occurred the same day agents applied for and executed the search warrant— Orellana stopped at the 3308 Santa Rita Court residence on his way to Gonzalez's residence, immediately before Gonzalez met the undercover officer. . . . '"In investigations of ongoing narcotics operations, intervals of weeks or months between the last described act and the application for a warrant [do] not necessarily make the information stale,"' and a 'lapse of time is least important when the suspected criminal activity is continuing in nature and when the property is not likely to be destroyed or dissipated,' . . . .. Though drugs '"can be easily concealed and moved about,"' the facts here demonstrate 'a continuing pattern of behavior' sufficient to establish probable cause even with months-old information, ... A series of controlled buys spanning from months to hours before the application for a search warrant supported the agents' inference that Gonzalez, Orellana, and Ortiz-Cervantes had an ongoing conspiracy to sell methamphetamine and at least some transactions occurred at the 3308 Santa Rita Court residence. . . .The evidence tying 3308 Santa Rita Court to the conspiracy was not the strongest—communications with Ortiz-Cervantes before some controlled buys, but not all of them, visits to the residence Ortiz-Cervantes shared with Orellana's brother's family, and a statement Ortiz-Cervantes sold methamphetamine from the residence more than a year before the search—but was sufficient to create 'a fair probability that contraband or evidence of a crime [would] be found in a particular place.' '[W]e accord "substantial deference" to the judicial officer's finding,' and the district court was correct in denying Ortiz-Cervantes's motion to suppress the evidence for lack of probable cause." *United States v. Ortiz-Cervantes*, 2017 WL 3584041, *2-3 (8th Cir. 2017) (citations omitted).

• " 'A warrant becomes stale if the information supporting the warrant is not sufficiently close in time to the issuance of the warrant and the subsequent search conducted so that probable cause can be said to exist as of the time of the search.' 'We have no fixed formula for deciding when information has become stale, but we consider the nature of the crime being investigated and the property to be searched.' 'In investigations of ongoing narcotic operations, intervals of weeks or months between the last described act and the application for a warrant [does] not necessarily make the information stale.' 'A "lapse of time is least important when the suspected criminal activity is continuing in nature and when the property is not likely to be destroyed or dissipated."' . . . As detailed in the warrant application, the officers had reason to believe that Davis had continually sold methamphetamine for over a year. The warrant application also detailed multiple instances of confirmed drug-related activity at the residence between August 27, 2014, and September 29, 2014. The warrant issued on October 3, 2014, and the search occurred on October 9, 2014. Because the underlying criminal activity was continuing in nature, probable cause did not dissipate during the ten-day period between the last identified drug-related activity and execution of the warrant. Thus, the information contained in the warrant was not fatally stale." *United States v. Davis*, 867 F.3d 1021, 1028 (8th Cir. 2017) (citations omitted).

- "[The defendant] next argues that the warrantless search of his laptop, and the one-year delay from its seizure to the subsequent search, violated his Fourth Amendment rights. The warrant authorized the seizure of 'financial records. . .and all computers on the property.' The district court concluded: 'A search warrant which specifically authorized the seizure of a computer and a search for financial records clearly contemplates at least a limited search of the computer's contents' without the need of a second warrant. We agree. Searching the computer for records related to eBay sales was contemplated and therefore permitted by the warrant. [The defendant's] contention that the delay in searching the laptop was unreasonable, requiring suppression of evidence obtained by the search, is without merit. To the extent he complains of interference with his possessory interest in the laptop, Rule 41(g) of the Federal Rules of Criminal Procedure provided a remedy he did not invoke." *U.S. v. Gregoire*, 638 F.3d 962 (8th Cir. 2011).

- "There is no bright-line test for determining when information is stale. . . .and the vitality of probable cause cannot be quantified by simply counting the number of days between the occurrence of the facts supplied and the issuance of the affidavit. . . . Rather, time factors must be examined in the context of a specific case and the nature of the crime under investigation." *U.S. v. McNeil*, 184 F.3d 770, 775 (8th Cir. 1999).

- "The timeliness of the information supplied in an affidavit depends on the circumstances of the case, including the nature of the crime under investigation; the lapse of time is least important when the suspected criminal activity is continuing in nature and when the property is not likely to be destroyed or dissipated. . . . [I]nformation four months old, or even three years old, may supply probable cause for a warrant to search the home of someone suspected of illegal possession of a firearm, because possession is a continuing offense and because firearm enthusiasts tend to keep their weapons for long periods of time." *U.S. v. Horn*, 187 F.3d 781, 786 (8th Cir. 1999).

- "[T]here is no bright-line test for determining when information is stale. . .and the vitality of probable cause cannot be quantified by simply counting the number of days between the occurrence of the facts supplied and the issuance of the affidavit. . . . Time factors must be examined in the context of a specific case and the nature of the crime under investigation. . . . In addition, where continuing criminal activity is suspected, the passage of time is less significant." *U.S. v. Formaro*, 152 F.3d 768, 771 (8th Cir. 1998).

- "There is no bright-line test for determining when information is stale. Whether the averments in an affidavit are sufficiently timely to establish probable cause depends on the particular circumstances of the case, and the vitality of probable cause cannot be quantified by simply counting the number of days between the occurrence of the facts supplied and the issuance of the affidavit. Time factors must be examined in the context of a specific case and the nature of the crime under investigation." *U.S. v. LaMorie*, 100 F.3d 547, 554 (8th Cir. 1996).

Ninth Circuit

- "By its terms, the Fourth Amendment's Warrant Clause sets forth a number of items a warrant must contain to be valid, but a date on which the warrant is to be executed is not one of them. (citation omitted) Thus, in determining whether a search conducted after a warrant has expired complies with the Fourth Amendment, we look to ensure that probable cause to search continued to exist, and that the misdating of the warrant was inadvertent rather than intentional." *U.S. v. Butts*, 357 Fed. Appx. 850 (9th Cir. 2009).

- "The information in the affidavit was not stale. An affidavit must be based on facts so closely related to the time of the issue of the warrant as to justify a finding of probable cause at that time. . . . We held in *Durham* that probable cause was not established by an affidavit relying on events that occurred four months earlier.

. . . . The information relied on in this case was ten months old. However, the mere lapse of substantial amounts of time is not controlling in a question of staleness. . . . We evaluate staleness in light of the particular facts of the case and the nature of the criminal activity and property sought. . . . The information offered in support of the application for a search warrant is not stale if there is sufficient basis to believe, based on a continuing pattern or other good reasons, that the items to be seized are still on the premises." *U.S. v. Lacy*, 119 F.3d 742, 745–46 (9th Cir. 1997).

Tenth Circuit

- "Prior to its amendment in 1972, Federal Rule of Criminal Procedure 41 required the execution of search warrants within 10 days from the time of issuance and required search warrants to include a command to officers to perform the search 'forthwith.' See Fed.R.Crim.P. 41 advisory committee's note. Historically, most federal courts interpreted both components as substantively significant; they interpreted the 10-day time-limit as an outside limit and the term 'forthwith' as a requirement for officers to execute the search as soon as they reasonably could. But, now, Rule 41 (like its New Mexico counterpart) has abandoned the 'forthwith' requirement, leaving only the fixed time-period. See Fed.R.Crim.P. 41(e)(2)(A)(i); Fed.R.Crim.P. 41 advisory committee's note. The change was intended to eliminate any overlap or tension between the fixed time-limit and the 'forthwith' command. Fed.R.Crim.P. 41 advisory committee's note. . . . Treating the term as an anachronism, we do not read this warrant, merely incorporating form language, as commanding special haste. Even assuming the officers failed to abide the warrant's instruction to execute it 'forthwith,' the failure adds almost nothing to our assessment of the reasonableness of the search. The only colorable time constraint, aside from the requirement of continuing probable cause, was the 10-day limit in Rule 41. Fed.R.Crim.P. 41(e)(2)(A)(i). The nine-day delay here did not exceed this limit or run afoul of the staleness concerns that animate it. [Defendant] is not entitled to exclusion of the fruits of the search." *U.S. v. Garcia*, 707 F.3d 1190 (10th Cir. 2013) (citations omitted).

- "Other circuits have held that more recent events in an affidavit can refresh otherwise dated information. . . . We find this to be a sensible approach to the problem presented by an affidavit which describes both dated and recent facts." *U.S. v. Jardine*, 364 F.3d 1200 (10th Cir. 2004), cert. granted, judgment vacated on other grounds, 543 U.S. 1102, 125 S. Ct. 1024, 160 L. Ed. 2d 1008 (2005) (judgment vacated, and case remanded for further consideration in light of *U.S. v. Booker*, 543 U.S. 220, 125 S. Ct. 738, 160 L. Ed. 2d 621 (2005)).

- "Probable cause for a search warrant cannot be based on stale information that no longer suggests that the items sought will be found in the place to be searched. The determination of timeliness, however, does not depend on simply the number of days that have elapsed between the facts relied on and the issuance of the warrant. Instead, whether the information is too stale to establish probable cause depends on the nature of the criminal activity, the length of the activity, and the nature of the property to be seized. Where the offense in question is ongoing and continuing, the passage of time is not of critical importance." *U.S. v. Harris*, 369 F.3d 1157 (10th Cir. 2004).

- "The determination of whether information is stale depends on the nature of the crime and the length of criminal activity, not simply the number of days that have elapsed between the facts relied upon and the issuance of the warrant. The information regarding [defendant's] state of mind concerning returning to jail, his violent and paranoid tendencies, and his possession of a firearm all related to his involvement in the drug trade. This information was not stale as it was not likely to have changed over the eight-month period of time since [defendant] was still involved in the drug trade. Certainly, [defendant's] criminal history of violence was not affected by the passage of time. The district court did not err in failing to suppress the evidence based upon the presence of stale information in the affidavit." *U.S. v. Basham*, 268 F.3d 1199 (10th Cir. 2001).

Eleventh Circuit

- "We have developed a staleness doctrine in the context of probable cause which requires that the information supporting the government's application for a warrant must show that probable cause exists at the time the warrant issues." *U.S. v. Bervaldi*, 226 F.3d 1256, 1264 (11th Cir. 2000).

- "Information must be timely for probable cause to exist, for probable cause must exist at the time the magistrate judge issues the search warrant. Stale information is not fatal where the government's affidavit updates, substantiates, or corroborates the stale material." *U.S. v. Butler*, 102 F.3d 1191, 1198, 45 Fed. R. Evid. Serv. 1203 (11th Cir. 1997).

§ 5:9 Staleness: The staleness of a search for child pornography rests more on a pattern of continuing criminal activity than the passage of time

Second Circuit

- "Where the affidavit 'establishes a pattern of continuing criminal activity,' such that 'there is reason to believe that the cited activity was probably not a one-time occurrence,' the passage of time between the last alleged event and the warrant application is less significant." *U.S. v. Raymonda*, 780 F.3d 105, 114 (2d Cir. 2015).

- "We have recognized that the determination of staleness in investigations involving child pornography is 'unique.' Because 'it is well known that images of child pornography are likely to be hoarded by persons interested in those materials in the privacy of their homes[.]' . . . . Crucially, however, the value of that inference in any given case depends on the preliminary finding that the suspect is a person 'interested in' images of child pornography. The 'alleged "proclivities" of collectors of child pornography,' that is, 'are only relevant if there is probable cause to believe that [a given defendant] *is* such a collector.' . . . In all of these cases, the inference that the suspect was a collector of child pornography did not proceed merely from evidence of his access to child pornography at a single time in the past. Rather, it proceeded from circumstances suggesting that he had accessed those images willfully and deliberately, actively seeking them out to satisfy a preexisting predilection. Such circumstances tend to ne-

gate the possibility that a suspect's brush with child
pornography was a purely negligent or inadvertent
encounter, the residue of which was long ago expunged.
They suggest that the suspect accessed those images
because he was specifically interested in child pornography, and thus—as is common among persons interested
in child pornography—likely hoarded the images he
found. As the Sixth Circuit has observed, '[i]t is not
likely that . . . someone who was innocently surfing
the internet . . . accidentally paid $79.95 for a subscrip-
tion to [a child pornography] web site.' " *U.S. v.
Raymonda*, 780 F.3d 105, 114–15 (2d Cir. 2015) (citations omitted).

Sixth Circuit
- "The point of the expiration of probable cause is
  determined by the nature of the crime and the circumstances of that case. Rather than focusing on the
  timeline of the evidence, we look to four factors to measure staleness:

  (1) the character of the crime (chance encounter in the
  night or regenerating conspiracy?), (2) the criminal
  (nomadic or entrenched?), (3) the thing to be seized
  (perishable and easily transferrable or of enduring utility
  to its holder?), and (4) the place to be searched (mere
  criminal forum of convenience or secure operational
  base?).

  Under these factors, the information in the affidavit
  was not stale. For the first factor, we have held that
  'child pornography is not a fleeting crime' and it is a
  crime that is 'generally carried out in the secrecy of the
  home and over a long period.' As a result, the time limitations applied to more fleeting crimes do not control.
  . . . . Our 'relaxed approach' towards these temporal
  requirements in child pornography cases comports with
  the practice of other circuits. For the second factor, the
  defendant may be considered nomadic when the person
  moves 'from place to place, so as to decrease the probability of finding evidence at a given location.' . . . For
  the third factor, child pornography has a potentially in-
  finite life span because files 'can be easily duplicated
  and kept indefinitely even if they are sold or traded.'
  And, as the search warrant recognized, child pornography can be uncovered on a hard drive even if those im-

ages have been deleted. Finally, for the fourth factor, the place to be searched in this case was Elbe's residence, a 'secure operational base.' Given the nature of child pornography, the evidence of ongoing criminal activity, and our precedent upholding similar delays, the information in the affidavit was not stale." *U.S. v. Elbe*, 774 F.3d 885, 890–91 (6th Cir. 2014), cert. denied, 135 S. Ct. 1573, 191 L. Ed. 2d 656 (2015) (citations omitted).

Eighth Circuit

- "[P]olice did not apply for the warrant until 75 days after identifying [the defendant's] IP address and 51 days after associating it with him[, however, p]eriods much longer than 75 or 51 days have not rendered information stale in computer-based child-pornography cases. The affidavit in support of the search warrant attested that collectors of child pornography tend to retain images and that computer programs that download these images 'often leave[ ] files, logs or file remnants which would tend to show the exchange, transfer, distribution, possession or origin of the files.' The affidavit established a fair probability of finding evidence on Morgan's computers." *United States v. Morgan*, 842 F.3d 1070, 1074 (8th Cir. 2016), cert. denied, 137 S. Ct. 2176, 198 L. Ed. 2d 244 (2017) (citations omitted).

- "This Court, and others, have held that evidence developed within several months of an application for a search warrant for a child pornography collection and related evidence is not stale. . . . Given the circumstances of the case and the nature of the crime, the execution of the warrant five months after the development of the information did not render the warrant deficient in any respect based on stale information." *U.S. v. Estey*, 595 F.3d 836, 840 (8th Cir. 2010) (citations omitted).

Tenth Circuit

- "Although the amount of time between the most recent email and the search gives us some pause, the 'passage of time alone' cannot demonstrate staleness. In child pornography cases, the nature of the criminal activity and the nature of the property to be seized are especially relevant factors." *U.S. v. Burkhart*, 602 F.3d 1202, 1206 (10th Cir. 2010) (citation omitted).

§ 5:10   Scope: In executing a warrant, officers may not exceed its scope

Supreme Court

- "The Warrant Clause of the Fourth Amendment categorically prohibits the issuance of any warrant except one particularly describing the place to be searched and the persons or things to be seized. The manifest purpose of this particularity requirement was to prevent general searches. By limiting the authorization to search to the specific areas and things for which there is probable cause to search, the requirement ensures that the search will be carefully tailored to its justifications, and will not take on the character of the wide-ranging exploratory searches the Framers intended to prohibit." *Maryland v. Garrison*, 480 U.S. 79, 84, 107 S. Ct. 1013, 94 L. Ed. 2d 72 (1987).

First Circuit

- "In general, if the scope of a search exceeds that permitted by the terms of a valid warrant, the subsequent seizure is unconstitutional. . . . In certain limited circumstances, however, the plain view doctrine permits law enforcement agents to seize evidence in plain view during a lawful search even though the items seized are not included within the warrant's scope." *U.S. v. Hamie*, 165 F.3d 80, 82 (1st Cir. 1999).

- "[Defendant]'s second major claim of error is that the recovery of previously deleted information on the hard drive and diskettes was outside the scope of the warrant. . . . [M]ore serious branch of the argument is a challenge to the recovery of deleted material. . . . The seizure of unlawful images is within the plain language of the warrant; their recovery, after attempted destruction, is no different than decoding a coded message lawfully seized or pasting together scraps of a torn-up ransom note." *U.S. v. Upham*, 168 F.3d 532, 536–37, 84 A.L.R.5th 709 (1st Cir. 1999).

Second Circuit

- "Plaintiffs allege that the search, even incident to the warrant, was unreasonable because their property was destroyed during the course of the search. In particular, Plaintiffs allege that the Officers 'completely ransacked' the apartment, 'destroying much of [their] property,' and that the Officers left 'without performing any repairs.' 'Excessive or unnecessary destruction of property in the course of a search may violate the Fourth Amendment . . . ..' 'However, it is well recognized that officers executing search warrants on occasion must damage property in order to perform their duty,' and 'before any due process liability can be imposed for property damage occurring in a lawful search, it must be established that the police acted unreasonably or maliciously in bringing about the damage.' Moreover, there must be allegations that 'more than ordinary disarray and damage incident to the execution of the warrant occurred.' " *Green v. City of Mount Vernon*, 96 F. Supp. 3d 263, 290 (S.D. N.Y. 2015) (inner citations omitted).

Fourth Circuit

- "Whether seized evidence falls within the scope of a warrant's authorization must be assessed solely in light of the relation between the evidence and the terms of the warrant's authorization. In this case, because the scope of the search authorized by the warrant included the authority to open and cursorily view each file, the observation of child pornography within several of these files did not involve an intrusion on [defendant]'s protected privacy interests beyond that already authorized by the warrant, regardless of the officer's subjective motivations." *U.S. v. Williams*, 592 F.3d 511 (4th Cir. 2010).

- "At bottom, we conclude that the sheer amount of information contained on a computer does not distinguish the authorized search of the computer from an analogous search of a file cabinet containing a large number of documents." *U.S. v. Williams*, 592 F.3d 511 (4th Cir. 2010).

- "Courts have never held that a search is overbroad merely because it results in additional criminal charges. (citation omitted) Often, a single piece of evidence will

be probative of multiple crimes, especially in
cases. . .which involve intricate, interweaving, and
extensive financial fraud schemes." *U.S. v. Phillips*, 588
F.3d 218 (4th Cir. 2009).

Sixth Circuit

- "Although it seems troubling that Deputy Wagester
  stated in his deposition that he believed the search warrant only permitted testing for alcohol, and that
  Wagester ordered the blood retested for controlled substances despite never previously indicating he believed
  [Defendant] was under the influence of controlled substances, the search warrant on its face clearly authorizes samples to be tested for alcohol, or controlled substances, or both. Thus, we affirm the grant of summary
  judgment [for Wagester] for this claim." *Miller v.
  Sanilac County*, 606 F.3d 240, 251 (6th Cir. 2010).
- "In the case at hand, the officer's actions were not reasonable inasmuch as the area was not common area for
  purposes of being included within the parameters of the
  search of Defendant's unit. . .and the nature of the location of the basement in this two-unit dwelling should
  have put the agents on notice that the search warrant
  did not include this area." *U.S. v. King*, 227 F.3d 732,
  751, 2000 FED App. 0284P (6th Cir. 2000).
- "In this case the agents were executing a valid search
  warrant that required them to seize certain documentary evidence. Unless they were to seize every scrap of
  paper in the apartment, the agents had to examine such
  documents as they came across—and the seized documents were obviously in plain view of the agents
  responsible for examining them." *U.S. v. Calloway*, 116
  F.3d 1129, 1133, 1997 FED App. 0184P (6th Cir. 1997).
- "It is well established that those who execute lawful
  search warrants must do so in a reasonable manner.
  Officers in unquestioned command of a dwelling may
  exceed the scope of the authority implicitly granted
  them by their warrant when they permit unauthorized
  invasions of privacy by third parties who have no connection to the search warrant or the officers' purposes
  for being on the premises." *Stack v. Killian*, 96 F.3d
  159, 162, 1996 FED App. 0305P (6th Cir. 1996).

Seventh Circuit

- "[T]here is nothing in the Supreme Court's case law (or the Ninth Circuit's for that matter) counseling the complete abandonment of the plain view doctrine in digital evidence cases. . . . Instead, we simply counsel officers and others involved in searches of digital media to exercise caution to ensure that warrants describe with particularity the things to be seized and that searches are narrowly tailored to uncover only those things described." *U.S. v. Mann*, 592 F.3d 779 (7th Cir. 2010).

Eighth Circuit

- "A lawful search extends to all areas and containers in which the object of the search may be found. However, the manner in which a warrant is executed is always subject to judicial review to ensure that it does not traverse the general Fourth Amendment proscription against unreasonableness." *U.S. v. Weinbender*, 109 F.3d 1327, 1329 (8th Cir. 1997).
- "The warrant, fairly construed does not authorize a search of [Defendant]'s residence. It authorizes the search of the property. . .located by traveling to a certain place in a certain carefully described way. It specifically mentions a mobile home, an A-frame house, and a school bus, and thus authorizes a search of these structures and, by implication any other vehicles, structures, or property not noticeably separate from them. But as we have already said, [Defendant]'s camper trailer was distinctly separated from the property described in the warrant. The relevant cases do not support an interpretation of this warrant that would authorize the officers to extend their search into the well-demarcated bounds of a neighboring curtilage." *U.S. v. Schroeder*, 129 F.3d 439, 441–42 (8th Cir. 1997).

Ninth Circuit

- "As the defendants urge, the warrant arguably might have provided for a 'less invasive search of (defendant's) [email] 'inbox' and 'outbox' for the addressees specifically cited in the warrant, as opposed to the wholesale search of the contents of all emails purportedly looking for evidence 'reflecting' communications with those individuals.' Avoiding that kind of specificity and limitation was not unreasonable under the circumstances here, however. To require such a pinpointed computer search, restricting the search to an email program or to specific search terms, would likely have failed to cast a sufficiently wide net to capture the evidence sought. . . . Computer files are easy to disguise or rename, and were we to limit the warrant to such a specific search protocol, much evidence could escape discovery simply because of (the) labeling of the files documenting (the) criminal activity." *U.S. v. Adjani*, 452 F.3d 1140 (9th Cir. 2006).

- "The Constitution limits lawful search warrants to those particularly describing the place to be searched, and the person or things to be seized. General warrants are unconstitutional. The plain view doctrine, applied in the context of a search pursuant to a warrant, does not allow the use of a properly limited search warrant as a pretext to search for anything else. This is not to say that anytime the search turns up evidence outside the scope of the warrant, the additional evidence must be suppressed. Where the search pursuant to the warrant is a part of a serious valid, investigation and not a pretense fabricated to mask the federal officers' lack of probable cause to search for evidence of crimes other than that specified in the warrant, the plain view evidence is admissible." *U.S. v. Ewain*, 88 F.3d 689, 693 (9th Cir. 1996).

Tenth Circuit

- "[Defendant] also argues that in opening a [video] file while conducting a search for records of drug transactions, [a law enforcement officer] exceeded the scope of the warrant. For that reason, [defendant] contends the district court erred when it denied his motion to suppress evidence of the June 6 search of his computer. . . Analogies to other physical objects, such as dressers or file cabinets, do not often inform the situations we now face as judges when applying search and seizure law [to computer searches]. This does not, of course, mean that the Fourth Amendment does not apply to computers and cyberspace. Rather, we must acknowledge the key differences and proceed accordingly. . . [W]hen officers come across relevant computer files intermingled with irrelevant computer files, they may seal or hold the computer pending approval by a magistrate of the conditions and limitations on a further search of the computer. Officers must be clear as to what it is they are seeking on the computer and conduct the search in a way that avoids searching files of types not identified in the warrant. . . . Had [the officer] conducted a more extensive search than he did here by rummaging in folders and files beyond those he searched, he might well have exceeded the bounds of the warrant and the requirements of *Carey*. The fact of the matter, however, is that no such wholesale searching occurred here. [The officer] showed restraint by returning to the magistrate for a new warrant before commencing a new search for evidence of child pornography." *U.S. v. Walser*, 275 F.3d 981 (10th Cir. 2001).

- "The Supreme Court has instructed, the plain view doctrine may not be used to extend a general exploratory search from one object to another until something incriminating at last emerges. . . . The warrant obtained for the specific purpose of searching defendant's computers permitted only the search of the computer files for names, telephone numbers, ledgers, receipts, addresses, and other documentary evidence pertaining to the sale and distribution of controlled substances. The scope of the search was thus circumscribed to evidence pertaining to drug trafficking. The government's argument the files were in plain view is unavailing because it is the contents of the files and not the files themselves which were seized. . . . Although the question of what constitutes plain view in the context of computer files is intriguing and appears to be an issue of first impression for this court, and many others, we do not need to reach it here. Judging this case only by its own facts, we conclude the items seized were not authorized by the warrant. Further, they were in closed files and thus not in plain view." *U.S. v. Carey*, 172 F.3d 1268, 1272–73 (10th Cir. 1999).

- "Our general rule is that a description is sufficient if it enables the officers to ascertain the place to be searched with reasonable effort. . . . Here, the warrant identified the Nomad trailer by brand, color, and serial number. To call this rather particular warrant insufficient would be to ignore the admonition that practical accuracy rather than technical precision controls the determination of whether a search warrant adequately describes the place to be searched. . . . Furthermore, this court takes into account the executing officers' knowledge of the place to be searched in determining the adequacy of a warrant's descriptions. . . . The affidavit accompanying the warrant request stated that the officers had observed the Nomad the previous evening." *U.S. v. Hutchings*, 127 F.3d 1255, 1259–60 (10th Cir. 1997).

- "Under the law of this circuit, even evidence which is properly seized pursuant to a warrant must be suppressed if the officers executing the warrant exhibit flagrant disregard for its terms. The basis for blanket suppression when a search warrant is executed with flagrant disregard for its terms is found in our traditional repugnance to general searches which were conducted in the colonies pursuant to writs of assistance. To protect against invasive and arbitrary general searches, the Fourth Amendment mandates that search warrants particularly describe the place to be searched and the persons or things to be seized. Therefore, *Medlin II* establishes that when law enforcement officers grossly exceed the scope of a search warrant in seizing property, the particularity requirement is undermined and a valid warrant is transformed into a general warrant thereby requiring suppression of all evidence seized under that warrant." *U.S. v. Foster*, 100 F.3d 846, 849–50 (10th Cir. 1996).

- "The Fourth Amendment's requirement that a warrant particularly describe the things to be seized prevents a general, exploratory rummaging in a person's belongings and makes general searches impossible and prevents the seizure of one thing under a warrant describing another. As to what is to be taken, nothing is left to the discretion of the officer executing the warrant. The particularity requirement also ensures that a search is confined in scope to particularly described evidence relating to a specific crime for which there is demonstrated probable cause." *U.S. v. Janus Industries*, 48 F.3d 1548, 1553–54 (10th Cir. 1995).

Eleventh Circuit

- "A valid search warrant authorizing the search of vehicles on the subject property permits the search of vehicles arriving on that property during the course of the search, so long as those vehicles could reasonably contain items the officers are searching for." *U.S. v. Tamari*, 454 F.3d 1259 (11th Cir. 2006).

- "If a search exceeds the scope of terms of a warrant, any subsequent seizure is unconstitutional. However, a search may be extensive as reasonably necessary as required to locate the items described in the warrant and is generally not limited by the possibility that separate acts of entry or opening may be required to complete the search. This court has held that a warrant to search a specific area for a certain class of things authorizes government agents to break open locked containers which may contain the objects of the search." *U.S. v. Jackson*, 120 F.3d 1226, 1228–29 (11th Cir. 1997).

D.C. Circuit

- "This is an appeal from the denial of a motion, filed pursuant to Rule 41(g) of the Federal Rules of Criminal Procedure, seeking the return of all materials seized by the Executive upon executing a search warrant for non-legislative materials in the congressional office of a sitting Member of Congress. The question on appeal is whether the procedures under which the search was conducted were sufficiently protective of the legislative privilege created by the Speech or Debate Clause, Article I, Section 6, Clause 1 of the United States Constitution. Our precedent establishes that the testimonial privilege under the Clause extends to non-disclosure of written legislative materials. [citation omitted] Given the Department of Justice's voluntary freeze of its review of the seized materials and the procedures mandated on remand by this court in granting the Congressman's motion for emergency relief pending appeal, the imaging and keyword search of the Congressman's computer hard drives and electronic media exposed no legislative material to the Executive, and therefore did not violate the Speech or Debate Clause[. B]ut the review of the Congressman's paper files when the search was executed exposed legislative

material to the Executive and accordingly violated the
Clause. Whether the violation requires. . .the return of
all seized items, privileged as well as non-privileged,
depends upon a determination of which documents are
privileged and then, as to the non-privileged documents,
a balancing of the separation of powers underlying the
Speech or Debate Clause and the Executive's Article II,
Section 3 law enforcement interest in the seized
materials. The question of whether the seized evidence
must be suppressed under the Fourth Amendment is
not before us. . . . We hold that the compelled disclosure
of privileged material to the Executive during execution
of the search warrant for Rayburn House Office Building Room 2113 violated the Speech or Debate Clause
and that the Congressman is entitled to the return of
documents that the court determines to be privileged
under the Clause. We do not, however, hold, in the
absence of a claim by the Congressman that the operations of his office have been disrupted as a result of not
having the original versions of the non-privileged documents, that remedying the violation also requires the
return of the non-privileged documents. The Congressman has suggested no other reason why return of such
documents is required pursuant to Rule 41(g) and, in
any event, it is doubtful that the court has jurisdiction
to entertain such arguments following the return of the
indictment against him while this appeal was pending."
*U.S. v. Rayburn House Office Building, Room 2113,
Washington, D.C. 20515*, 497 F.3d 654, 655–656 (D.C.
Cir. 2007).

§ 5:11 Anticipatory warrants: A warrant issued before the contraband arrives at the property is valid in carefully controlled circumstances

Supreme Court

- "Most anticipatory warrants subject their execution to
  some condition precedent other than the mere passage
  of time—a so-called 'triggering condition.' . . . If the
  government were to execute an anticipatory warrant
  before the triggering condition occurred, there would be
  no reason to believe the item described in the warrant
  could be found at the searched location; by definition,

the triggering condition which establishes probable cause has not yet been satisfied when the warrant is issued. [Defendant] argues that for this reason anticipatory warrants contravene the Fourth Amendment's provision that 'no Warrants shall issue, but upon probable cause.' . . . We reject this view, as has every Court of Appeals to confront the issue. . . . Because the probable-cause requirement looks to whether evidence will be found *when the search is conducted,* all warrants are, in a sense, 'anticipatory.' . . . Thus, when an anticipatory warrant is issued, the fact that the contraband is not presently located at the place described in the warrant is immaterial, so long as there is probable cause to believe that it will be there when the search warrant is executed. . . . The Ninth Circuit invalidated the anticipatory search warrant at issue here because the warrant failed to specify the triggering condition. The Fourth Amendment's particularity requirement, it held, applies with full force to the conditions precedent to an anticipatory search warrant. The Fourth Amendment, however, does not set forth some general 'particularity requirement.' It specifies only two matters that must be 'particularly describ[ed]' in the warrant: 'the place to be searched' and 'the persons or things to be seized.' . . . The language of the Fourth Amendment is likewise decisive here; its particularity requirement does not include the conditions precedent to execution of the warrant." *U.S. v. Grubbs*, 547 U.S. 90, 126 S. Ct. 1494, 164 L. Ed. 2d 195, 31 A.L.R. Fed. 2d 635 (2006).

Second Circuit

- "In order to lay any perceived ambiguity in *Garcia* to rest, we here clarify that an anticipatory warrant whose perfection requires no more than the delivery of a package to, or in the presence of, the suspect, is not invalidated because the parcel is taken off the premises after delivery. The package's relevance to such a warrant is that it suggests a relationship between drug dealers and a suspect's premises. The warrant remains contingent until delivery because some uncertainty exists as to whether the suspect will give further credence to that relationship by accepting the package. When the suspect accepts the parcel, that uncertainty is resolved.

At that point, the package becomes irrelevant. Predicating the validity of the warrant on the continued presence of the package makes much ado out of something whose significance has in fact been exhausted." *U.S. v. Becerra*, 97 F.3d 669, 671 (2d Cir. 1996).

- "[A]n anticipatory warrant is valid even though it does not state on its face the conditions precedent for its execution, when (1) clear, explicit, and narrowly drawn conditions for the execution of the warrant are contained in the affidavit that applies for the warrant application, and (2) those conditions are actually satisfied before the warrant is executed." *U.S. v. Moetamedi*, 46 F.3d 225, 229 (2d Cir. 1995).

- "If read literally, the fourth amendment would forbid a warrant that specifies no particular place for the search and leaves the location to be determined at a future time. The Supreme Court, however, has refused to apply the fourth amendment literally, preferring instead a flexible approach designed to keep pace with a technologically advancing society. It has not simply frozen into constitutional law those law enforcement practices that existed at the time of the fourth amendment's passage. In short, the fourth amendment's prohibition against unreasonable searches and seizures must be interpreted in light of contemporary norms and conditions. Under its flexible interpretation, the Supreme Court in numerous cases has rejected the narrow shackles that might otherwise flow from a literal reading of the fourth amendment." *U.S. v. Bianco*, 998 F.2d 1112, 1122–23 (2d Cir. 1993).

Third Circuit

- "We agree with the other circuits that the simple fact that a warrant is anticipatory. . .does not invalidate a warrant or make it somehow suspect or legally disfavored. . . . We hold, therefore, that anticipatory warrants which meet the probable cause requirement and specifically identify the triggering event are not per se unconstitutional. . . . [W]hen presented with an application for an anticipatory warrant, the magistrate judge cannot rely on police assurances that the search will not be conducted until probable cause exists. . . . Instead, the magistrate judge must find, based on facts existing when the warrant is issued, that there is probable cause to believe the contraband, which is not yet at the place to be searched, will be there when the warrant is executed." *U.S. v. Loy*, 191 F.3d 360, 364–65 (3d Cir. 1999).

Seventh Circuit

- "An anticipatory warrant must be supported by probable cause to believe that contraband will be located at the premises to be searched after certain events transpire." *U.S. v. Brack*, 188 F.3d 748, 755 (7th Cir. 1999).

- "[P]robable cause to uphold an anticipatory search warrant exists when a government official presents independent evidence indicating that delivery of contraband will, or is likely to, occur and when the magistrate conditions the warrant on that delivery. . . . In *Garcia*, a seminal case on anticipatory warrants, the court also recognized that warrants conditioned on future events present some potential for abuse. As such, the court cautioned that a magistrate issuing an anticipatory warrant should protect against premature execution by listing in the warrant the conditions governing the execution which are explicit, clear, and narrowly drawn so as to avoid misunderstanding or manipulation by government agents." *U.S. v. Dennis*, 115 F.3d 524, 528 (7th Cir. 1997).

- "As stated earlier, we find no cases from this circuit requiring (as a matter of constitutional law) anticipatory warrants to explicitly state that the expected delivery must occur prior to execution of the warrant. Hence, we do not believe that an anticipatory search warrant's constitutionality is doomed by the absence of such language even though other circuit courts in reviewing similar challenges to anticipatory warrants have significantly focused on the presence or absence of such conditioning language. While *Garcia* and its progeny may support a preference that anticipatory search warrants contain such language, we are not compelled by the Constitution to require it since all that is constitutionally required is that the search warrant be supported by probable cause." *U.S. v. Leidner*, 99 F.3d 1423, 1427 (7th Cir. 1996).

Eighth Circuit
- "[Defendant] contends the search warrant for her residence was not supported by probable cause because it failed to describe with particularity the places to be searched or the items to be seized. ... An anticipatory search warrant should be upheld if independent evidence shows the delivery of contraband will or is likely to occur and the warrant is conditioned on that delivery. ... The affidavit in support of the search warrant averred that an Express Mail package had been intercepted and was addressed to the location that was the subject of the search warrant. The affidavit stated that the package was opened pursuant to a search warrant and found to contain over one kilogram of cocaine. The affiant explained that he had reason to believe that items such as drugs, weapons, and drug paraphernalia would be present at the address, as well as other evidence relating to identification of the residents. The affidavit also stated the officers' intent to make a controlled delivery of the package before executing the search warrant. . . . The information contained in the affidavit, along with [the officer's] averment based upon his experience that drug traffickers often keep in their residences records of their illicit activity, large amounts of cash, assets purchased with the proceeds of drug transactions, and guns to protect their drugs and cash, provided the issuing judge with a substantial basis for finding probable cause to search [the defendant's] residence. The quantity of drugs in the package indicated a distribution amount. Based on the officer's experience, it was reasonable to conclude the apartment may contain guns, money, and pagers, and thus it was appropriate to include those items in the list of items to be seized. It was also appropriate to include documents that might identify the owner or renter of the apartment to establish constructive possession of the Express Mail package. Accordingly, the anticipatory search warrant was supported by probable cause." *U.S. v. Walker*, 324 F.3d 1032 (8th Cir. 2003).
- "The court found that the anticipatory warrant was invalid because there was no evidence of a nexus between the defendant's home and the receipt of the pornography at the post office. . . .We agree, of course, that there

must be evidence of a nexus between the contraband and the place to be searched before a warrant may properly issue. . . ." *U.S. v. Tellez*, 217 F.3d 547, 550 (8th Cir. 2000).

- "Anticipatory search warrants may be issued even absent exigent circumstances. An anticipatory search warrant should be upheld if independent evidence shows the delivery of contraband will or is likely to occur and the warrant is conditioned on that delivery." *U.S. v. Bieri*, 21 F.3d 811, 814 (8th Cir. 1994).

Ninth Circuit

- "Because the Fourth Amendment commands that warrants be drafted with particularity, we have held that the conditions precedent to any search must be stated in [an anticipatory] warrant. Requiring the warrant to set forth the conditions precedent to the search serves two important purposes: it (1) limits the discretion of the officers executing the warrant, and (2) informs the property owner or resident of the proper scope of the search. It is important to emphasize that we have not held that the condition precedent must be stated within the four corners of the warrant itself. The Fourth Amendment's particularity requirement is satisfied if (1) an affidavit setting forth the triggering event for the search accompanies the warrant at the time of the search, and (2) the warrant sufficiently incorporates that accompanying affidavit. . . . [T]he affidavit must accompany the warrant and be incorporated by reference in order to be considered in conjunction with the warrant." *U.S. v. Vesikuru*, 314 F.3d 1116, 1119 (9th Cir. 2002).

- "The First Circuit rule is that anticipatory search warrants must set forth the conditions to be met and that those conditions must be explicit, clear, and narrowly drawn. . . . We conclude that the First Circuit's view that, when a warrant's execution is dependent on the occurrence of one or more conditions, the warrant itself must state the conditions precedent to its execution and these conditions must be clear, explicit, and narrow, is more consistent with our prior precedent than the law of some of the other circuits. . . . Our holding is consistent with our long line of cases requiring that warrants be drafted with particularity." *U.S. v. Hotal*, 143 F.3d 1223, 1226–27 (9th Cir. 1998).

- "An affidavit in support of an anticipatory search warrant must show that the property sought is on a sure course to the destination targeted for the search. A controlled delivery pursuant to a warrant issued earlier is permissible." *U.S. v. Ruddell*, 71 F.3d 331, 333 (9th Cir. 1995).

Tenth Circuit

- "This Court has rejected any suggestion that an affidavit in support of an anticipatory warrant must be subjected to closer scrutiny than an affidavit seeking the issuance of a warrant which would be effective immediately. Nonetheless, our cases have stressed that the warrant or affidavit should express conditions permitting the search to be conducted only after the anticipated events have taken place. The articulation of the triggering event serves two important purposes. First, it ensures that the warrant will not be executed prematurely, before there is probable cause. Second, and more importantly, it maintains judicial control over the probable cause determination and over the circumstances of the warrant's execution. If the triggering event were articulated in terms of an exercise of the officer's unfettered discretionary judgment—for example, when events occur that establish probable cause—this would transfer control over probable cause determinations from the magistrate to the law enforcement officer, and thus undermine the purpose of the warrant requirement. Accordingly, an anticipatory warrant is valid only if the conditions precedent to execution are clearly set forth in the warrant or in the affidavit in support. *U.S. v. Hernandez-Rodriguez*, 352 F.3d 1325 (10th Cir. 2003).

- "Anticipatory warrants differ from traditional search warrants in that at the time of issuance they are not supported by probable cause to believe that contraband is currently located at the place to be searched. . . . In fact, a court issues an anticipatory warrant with the knowledge that the contraband does not presently exist at the location to be searched. . . . This does not mean, however, that anticipatory warrants need not be supported by probable cause. Instead, before issuing an anticipatory warrant the magistrate must determine, based on the information presented in the warrant application, that there is probable cause to believe the items to be seized will be at the designated place when the search is to take place. . . . Probable cause for anticipatory warrants is contingent on the occurrence of certain expected or triggering events, typically the future delivery, sale, or purchase of contraband. Therefore, in making the probable cause determination, the magistrate must take into account the likelihood that the triggering events will occur on schedule and as predicted. . . . If the triggering events do not occur, the anticipatory warrant is void." *U.S. v. Rowland*, 145 F.3d 1194, 1201 (10th Cir. 1998).

- "Many, if not most, search warrants are effective upon issuance and may be executed immediately thereafter. However, an anticipatory search warrant, i.e., a warrant which only becomes effective upon the happening of a future event, is not unconstitutional *per se* and is, indeed, no stranger to the law. Such warrants have repeatedly been upheld, assuming probable cause and so long as the conditions precedent to execution are clearly set forth in the warrant or in the affidavit in support of the anticipatory warrant." *U.S. v. Hugoboom*, 112 F.3d 1081, 1085 (10th Cir. 1997).

Eleventh Circuit

- "Anticipatory search warrants, i.e., warrants that become effective upon the happening of a future event, have repeatedly been upheld where they are supported by probable cause and the conditions precedent to the search are clearly set forth in the warrant or supporting affidavit. . . .Indeed, every circuit to have addressed the question has held that anticipatory search warrants are not categorically unconstitutional." *U.S. v. Santa*, 236 F.3d 662, 671 (11th Cir. 2000).

§ 5:12 Execution: To execute a warrant, a lawful entry is required

Supreme Court

- "The deputies needed a moment to secure the room and

353

ensure that other persons were not close by or did not present a danger. Deputies were not required to turn their backs to allow (the occupants) to retrieve clothing or to cover themselves with the sheets. . . . Officers executing search warrants on occasion enter a house when residents are engaged in private activity; and the resulting frustration, embarrassment, and humiliation may be real, as was true here. When officers execute a valid warrant and act in a reasonable manner to protect themselves from harm, however, the Fourth Amendment is not violated." *Los Angeles County, California v. Rettele*, 550 U.S. 609, 127 S. Ct. 1989, 167 L. Ed. 2d 974 (2007).

- "The issue here is remedy . . . What the knock-and-announce rule has never protected. . .is one's interest in preventing the government from seeing or taking evidence described in a warrant. Since the interests that *were* violated in this case have nothing to do with the seizure of the evidence, the exclusionary rule is inapplicable . . . In sum, the social costs of applying the exclusionary rule to knock-and-announce violations are considerable; the incentive to such violations is minimal to begin with, and the extant deterrences against them are substantial-incomparably greater than the factors deterring warrantless entries when *Mapp* was decided. Resort to the massive remedy of suppressing evidence of guilt is unjustified." *Hudson v. Michigan*, 547 U.S. 586, 126 S. Ct. 2159, 165 L. Ed. 2d 56, 23 A.L.R. Fed. 2d 823 (2006).

- "[T]he issue comes down to whether it was reasonable to suspect imminent loss of evidence after the 15 to 20 seconds the officers waited prior to forcing their way. Though. . . this call is a close one, we think that after 15 or 20 seconds without a response, police could fairly suspect that cocaine would be gone if they were reticent any longer. . . . [T]he fact that [defendant] was actually in the shower and did not hear the officers is not to the point, and the same is true of the claim that it might have taken him longer than 20 seconds if he had heard the knock and headed straight for the door. As for the shower, it is enough to say that the facts known to the police are what count in judging reasonable waiting time, and there is no indication that the police knew that [defendant] was in the shower and thus unaware of an impending search that he would otherwise have tried to frustrate. And the argument that 15 to 20 seconds was too short for [defendant] to have come to the door ignores the very risk that justified prompt entry. True, if the officers were to justify their timing here by claiming that [defendant's] failure to admit them fairly suggested a refusal to let them in, [defendant] could at least argue that no such suspicion can arise until an occupant has had time to get to the door, a time that will vary with the size of the establishment, perhaps five seconds to open a motel room door, or several minutes to move through a townhouse. In this case, however, the police claim exigent need to enter, and the crucial fact in examining their actions is not time to reach the door but the particular exigency claimed. On the record here, what matters is the opportunity to get rid of cocaine, which a prudent dealer will keep near a commode or kitchen sink. The significant circumstances include the arrival of the police during the day, when anyone inside would probably have been up and around, and the sufficiency of 15 to 20 seconds for getting to the bathroom or the kitchen to start flushing cocaine down the drain. That is, when circumstances are exigent because a pusher may be near the point of putting his drugs beyond reach, it is imminent disposal, not travel time to the entrance, that governs when the police may reasonably enter; since the bathroom and kitchen are usually in the interior of a dwelling, not the front hall, there is no reason generally to peg the travel time to the location of the door, and no reliable basis for giving the proprietor of a mansion a longer wait than the resident of a bungalow, or an apartment like [defendant's]. And 15 to 20 seconds does not seem an unrealistic guess about the time someone would need to get in a position to rid his quarters of cocaine. Once the exigency had matured, of course, the officers were not bound to learn anything more or wait any longer before going in, even though their entry entailed some harm to the building." *U.S. v. Banks*, 540 U.S. 31, 124 S. Ct. 521, 157 L. Ed. 2d 343 (2003).

- "[T]he Fourth Amendment does require that police actions in execution of a warrant be related to the objec-

tives of the authorized intrusion. . . . Certainly the
presence of reporters inside the home was not related to
the objectives of the authorized intrusion. . . . We hold
that it is a violation of the Fourth Amendment for police to bring members of the media or other third parties into a home during the execution of a warrant when
the presence of the third parties in the home was not in
aid of the execution of the warrant." *Wilson v. Layne*,
526 U.S. 603, 611–14, 119 S. Ct. 1692, 143 L. Ed. 2d
818, 27 Media L. Rep. (BNA) 1705 (1999).

- "In order to justify a no-knock entry, the police must
  have a reasonable suspicion that knocking and announcing their presence, under the particular circumstances, would be dangerous or futile, or that it would
  inhibit the effective investigation of the crime by, for
  example, allowing the destruction of evidence. This
  standard—as opposed to a probable cause requirement—strikes the appropriate balance between the legitimate law enforcement concerns at issue in the execution of search warrants and the individual privacy
  interests affected by no-knock entries. This showing is
  not high, but the police should be required to make it
  whenever the reasonableness of a no-knock entry is
  challenged." *Richards v. Wisconsin*, 520 U.S. 385,
  394–95, 117 S. Ct. 1416, 137 L. Ed. 2d 615 (1997).

- "Our own cases have acknowledged that the common-
  law principle of announcement is embedded in Anglo-
  American law, but we have never squarely held that
  this principle is an element of the reasonableness inquiry under the Fourth Amendment. Given the longstanding common-law endorsement of the practice of
  announcement, we have little doubt that the Framers
  of the Fourth Amendment thought that the method of
  an officer's entry into a dwelling was among the factors
  to be considered in assessing the reasonableness of a
  search or seizure." *Wilson v. Arkansas*, 514 U.S. 927,
  934, 115 S. Ct. 1914, 131 L. Ed. 2d 976 (1995).

- "[L]aw officers constitutionally may break and enter to
  execute a search warrant where such entry is the only
  means by which the warrant effectively may be
  executed." *Dalia v. U.S.*, 441 U.S. 238, 247, 99 S. Ct.
  1682, 60 L. Ed. 2d 177 (1979).

- "An unannounced intrusion into a dwelling—what [18

U.S.C.] § 3109 basically proscribes—is no less an unannounced intrusion whether officers break down a door, force open a chain lock on a partially open door, open a locked door by use of a passkey, or, as here, open a closed but unlocked door. The protection afforded by, and the values inherent in, § 3109 must be governed by something more than the fortuitous circumstance of an unlocked door." *Sabbath v. U.S.*, 391 U.S. 585, 590, 88 S. Ct. 1755, 20 L. Ed. 2d 828 (1968).

First Circuit

- "The key precedent is *Hudson*. There, the Supreme Court squarely addressed whether a violation of the knock-and-announce rule might justify the exclusion of evidence seized. Noting that exclusion of evidence 'has always been [a] last resort, not [a] first impulse,' the Court held the exclusionary rule inapplicable to knock-and-announce violations. In taking this position, the Court noted two independent requirements for applying the exclusionary rule and explained why a knock-and-announce violation could never meet those requirements. To begin, the Court deemed but-for causation 'a necessary. . .condition for suppression.' In other words, there must be a causal link between the constitutional violation alleged and the discovery of the evidence seized. In the Court's view, a violation of the knock-and-announce rule could never achieve this benchmark; whether the officers knocked or not, the evidence would inevitably be discovered during the subsequent (valid) search. The *Hudson* Court set out a second condition for applying the exclusionary rule: that the beneficial effects of exclusion outweigh its social costs. In explaining why application of the exclusionary rule to knock-and-announce violations would be costly, the Court worried about a possible flurry of knock-and-announce litigation from prisoners seeking a 'get-out-of-jail-free card,' the potential for increased violence against officers hesitant to enter unannounced for fear that gathered evidence would be suppressed, and the potential for the destruction of evidence by those inside the dwelling. As against these substantial costs, the only benefit from exclusion would be the deterrence of police misconduct. Because the costs of using the

exclusionary rule to remedy knock-and-announce violations would so clearly outweigh any corresponding
benefits, the Court found this second requirement
unmet." *U.S. v. Garcia-Hernandez*, 659 F.3d 108, 112
(1st Cir. 2011) (citations omitted).

- "We hasten to add that we are not suggesting that officers who unlawfully enter a home must subject
themselves to the risk of being harmed by a resident
whom they believe is armed and dangerous. They are
certainly entitled to take reasonable actions to defend
themselves. But the reasonableness of the officers'
interaction with such an individual for that protective
purpose does not determine the Fourth Amendment
suppression issue generated by the unlawful entry. In
this case, because [the defendant] had a reasonable
expectation of privacy in the foyer and the officers
entered the house unlawfully, the officers' encounter
with [the defendant] and the discovery of the gun were
both results of the officers' unconstitutional conduct.
[The defendant] was thus entitled to suppression of the
gun." *U.S. v. Werra*, 638 F.3d 326 (1st Cir. 2011).

- "[Defendant's] second argument on the motion to suppress is that the police should have either sought a no-
knock warrant or informed the judge issuing the warrant that they intended to conduct a no-knock entry
because they knew in advance of seeking the warrant
that they would conduct a no-knock entry. The Supreme
Court has stated that the rule of announcement falls
under the Fourth Amendment's reasonableness clause,
as opposed to its warrant clause. The Court has also
made clear that the reasonableness of a police officer's
decision to conduct a no-knock entry 'must be evaluated
as of the time they [conduct the entry].' We see no reason why a no-knock entry that is reasonable at the time
it is conducted would suddenly become unreasonable
because the officers intended to conduct a no-knock
entry when they got the warrant but did not inform the
issuing judge of their intention. . . . Further, in the
instant case, it would have been futile for the police to
seek a no-knock warrant, because the issuing judge had
a policy of leaving it up to the police to determine
whether a no-knock entry was necessary." *U.S. v.
Boulanger*, 444 F.3d 76 (1st Cir. 2006).

- "Federal constitutional law does not proscribe the use of civilians in searches. In fact, Congress has explicitly authorized the practice. . . . and courts have repeatedly upheld the practice. Courts have articulated guidelines for evaluating police involvement of citizens in searches under the Fourth Amendment's reasonableness standard. The civilian must have been serving a legitimate investigative function. . . . Also, the officers must have some demonstrable need for the presence of the civilian. . . . The district court cited no authority for its conclusion that the failure to obtain prior judicial approval for civilian assistance violates federal constitutional law. Appellants cite no authority on appeal. We have found none in our own research. In the absence of any authority, we will not improvise a rule that seems unnecessary in light of the overarching requirement that the use of civilians in the execution of a search must still meet the constitutional standard of reasonableness." *Bellville v. Town of Northboro*, 375 F.3d 25 (1st Cir. 2004).

Second Circuit

- "The government and [defendant] dispute the propriety of [federal] agents' actions [while executing arrest and search warrants at defendant's apartment] under the Fourth Amendment and 18 U.S.C. § 3109. . . . Section 3109 authorizes federal officers to break open doors or windows for entry or exit in certain circumstances. . . . [citations omitted] 'From earliest days, the common law drastically limited the authority of law officers to break the door of a house to effect an arrest.' [citation and footnote omitted]. By enacting § 3109, Congress codified this common law tradition . . .' [citation omitted] The Fourth Amendment, the scope of which is established, at least in part, by reference to the traditional protections afforded by the common law, likewise incorporates this principle: '. . . the method of an officer's entry into a dwelling [i]s among the factors to be considered in assessing the reasonableness of a search or seizure.' [citation omitted] Accordingly, under the Fourth Amendment and § 3109, ...[l]aw enforcement officers who execute a search warrant at a residence generally must give notice of their authority and provide the occupant a reasonable opportunity to respond before entering. [citation omitted] . . . Although [the Supreme Court's decision in *Hudson v. Michigan*] forecloses [defendant]'s argument that the Fourth Amendment requires suppression of the evidence obtained during the search of his apartment, [defendant] suggests suppression is warranted on an independent ground, namely § 3109. . . . We find that the reasoning in *Hudson* applies with equal force to § 3109, and thus hold that an alleged violation of the statutory knock-and-announce rule cannot form the basis for suppression of the evidence discovered in the ensuing search. . . . Given the common law origins of § 3109 and the Fourth Amendment's knock-and-announce principle, it is unsurprising that they overlap to a considerable extent. Indeed, we have often observed that the contours of § 3109 coincide with the reasonableness inquiry of the Fourth Amendment. [citations omitted] Because § 3109 'codifies the common law in this area,' while 'the common law in turn informs the Fourth Amendment,' Fourth Amendment cases necessarily 'serve as guideposts in construing the statute.' [citations omitted] . . . Because of this crossfertilization, both § 3109 and the Fourth Amendment knock-and-announce principle have been held subject to the same exceptions and found to protect similar interests. Three circumstances may justify a no-knock entrance, permitting officers to disregard the knock and announce rule altogether: (1) when law enforcement officers reasonably fear violence may result if they were to announce their presence; (2) when officers have reason to believe evidence may be destroyed if they were to provide notice before entry; or (3) when an announcement by officers would be futile, as may occur when the circumstances indicate that the inhabitants are well aware of the officers' presence. [citations omitted] And like the Fourth Amendment, § 3109 serves three principal interests: '(1) the reduction of potential for violence to both the police officer and the occupants of the house into which entry is sought; (2) the needless destruction of private property; and (3) a recognition of the individual's right of privacy in his house.' [citations omitted] But the knock-and-announce rule, either under the Fourth Amendment or § 3109, has never prevented 'the government from seeing or taking evidence described in a warrant.' [citation omitted] . . . [Defendant, however,] suggests the lack of a civil remedy for violations of § 3109 requires application of the exclusionary rule to adequately deter federal officers from violating the knock-and-announce rule. . . . One would think that the facts underlying an alleged violation of § 3109 would form the basis for attacking the propriety of the search as also violative of the Fourth Amendment. [citation omitted] If such is the case, a cause of action for damages may lie against the federal officer under *Bivens v. Six Unknown Named Agents of Federal Bureau of Narcotics* [citation omitted]. [Thus, t]he possibility of a *Bivens* claim. . .provides an adequate incentive for federal officers to stay within the bounds of the knock-and-announce rule when executing search warrants. [citation omitted] . . . [Additionally, w]e . . . agree with the D.C. Circuit and the Fifth Circuit that no direct precedent from the Supreme Court prevents us from holding the exclusionary rule inapplicable to § 3109. [citations omitted] It is true that, '[i]f a precedent of [the Supreme] Court has direct application in a case, yet appears to rest on reasons rejected in some other line of decisions, the Court[s] of Appeals should follow the case which directly controls, leaving to this Court the prerogative of overruling its own decisions.' [citation omitted] . . . Just as no Supreme Court precedent stands in the way of our holding, no previous [Second Circuit] decision. . .has held that a § 3109 violation requires suppression. . . . [Therefore,] we hold that alleged violations of § 3109 do not trigger the exclusionary rule. . . . In sum, a claim by a defendant that federal officers violated the knock-and-announce rule under either the Fourth Amendment or 18 U.S.C. § 3109 cannot form the basis for suppression of the evidence obtained in the ensuing search. . . ." *U.S. v. Acosta*, 502 F.3d 54 (2d Cir. 2007).

- "The question we must address, in light of the rule's purposes and history, is whether law enforcement officers' gaining entry into a house by ruse, as here, by misstating their identity to effect an arrest, is a breaking, which would render the entry illegal and taint the fruits thereof. . . . We. . . conclude that [the officer's] successful ruse does not render the law enforcement officers' entry into [defendant's] apartment a breaking within the meaning of section 3109. ... Because [the officer's] ruse did not violate section 3109, and because we have been given, and ourselves can find, no independent basis for concluding on the facts of this case that the entry at issue separately violated the Fourth Amendment, we conclude that there was no such constitutional violation." *U.S. v. Alejandro*, 368 F.3d 130 (2d Cir. 2004), opinion supplemented, 100 Fed. Appx. 846 (2d Cir. 2004).

Fourth Circuit

- "[Defendant], in his dwelling and free from any coercion or duress, heard a knock at the door and unequivocally stated, 'the door is open; come on in.' By his statement, [defendant] gave consent to enter to whoever was standing at his door. The persons knocking at the door could have been pollsters, salesmen, or, as in this case, officers of the law. . . . Thus, when the deputies opened [defendant's] unlocked door, they had been authorized to do so. . . . They did not forcibly enter [defendant]s] dwelling. By its terms, the knock-and-announce rule applies when law enforcement officers attempt a forcible entry into a dwelling. [Defendant's] consent, transmitted to [the officers] through his statement that 'the door is open; come on in,' made the deputies' entrance into [defendant's] dwelling a permissible one. . . . We conclude that [defendant's] statement to the deputies was voluntary and amounted to an invitation to them to enter his dwelling regardless of the fact that [defendant] did not know who was knocking at his door. [Defendant's] consent renders the deputies' entrance into his dwelling a permissible one, and the knock-and-announce rule does not apply to bar the introduction into evidence of the .40 caliber H & K pistol obtained in this reasonable unannounced entry. . . . Finally, we explain that we do not create an exception to the knock-and-announce rule. Our warrant does not extend so far. . . . We are of opinion and hold that the unannounced entry in this case was reasonable and not in violation of the Fourth Amendment." *U.S. v. Hatfield*, 365 F.3d 332 (4th Cir. 2004).

- "[T]he requirements of the knock and announce rule were met here. In this case, [defendant], having been arrested and questioned by the police outside his home, clearly had notice of the authority and purpose of the officers executing the search warrant. Although [defendant's] knowledge of the presence of the police did not come from a knock and announce at his door, he nevertheless had the functional equivalent of notice of authority and purpose as required by the statute. The officers twice asked [defendant] for a key to the door or if anyone was inside and received no response. In addition to having received the notice to which he was entitled under the statute, [defendant] effectively refused entry to the police by declining, through his silence, to provide a key to the front door when asked." *U.S. v. Dunnock*, 295 F.3d 431 (4th Cir. 2002).

Fifth Circuit

- "[T]he common-law knock-and-announce principle forms a part of the Fourth Amendment reasonableness inquiry, which applies with equal force to state and federal law enforcement officers alike. . . . However, the Fourth Amendment's reasonableness requirement is flexible and does not ignore valid law enforcement interests. . . . The notion that the common-law knock-and-announce principle is part of the reasonableness inquiry is relatively new in Fourth Amendment jurisprudence. Hence, no case from the Supreme Court or this Court has yet specifically addressed how long officers must wait before entering a residence after knocking and announcing their presence. There are cases in other circuits dealing with the amount of time required under the federal knock-and-announce statute. Generally, a delay of five-seconds or less after knocking and announcing has been held a violation. . . ." *U.S. v. Jones*, 133 F.3d 358, 361 (5th Cir. 1998).

Sixth Circuit

- "Most of the federal courts of appeals to have considered the question, including the Sixth Circuit, have held that a single search warrant may authorize more than one entry into the premises identified in the warrant, as long as the second entry is a reasonable continuation of the original search. . . . [This possibility,] however, does not permit the police unlimited access to the premises identified in a warrant throughout the life of the warrant. Courts have long recognized the dangers of official abuse that inhere in such a rule. ... [A] warrant authorizes only one search[, but]. . .under certain circumstances, police may temporarily suspend the initial execution of a search warrant and continue the search at another time. Two aspects of the reasonable continuation rule must therefore be observed. First, the subsequent entry must indeed be a continuation of the original search, and not a new and separate search. . . . Second, the decision to conduct a second entry to continue the search must be reasonable under the totality of the circumstances." *U.S. v. Keszthelyi*, 308 F.3d 557, 2002 FED App. 0362P (6th Cir. 2002).

Seventh Circuit

- "In this case, however, the appropriate inquiry is not whether [officer] waited a reasonable time before ordering the forcible entry into the apartment. Rather, the question is whether the sound of footsteps moving laterally in relation to the entry door was sufficient to excuse the task force from waiting a reasonable period of time. In other words, did exigent circumstances exist that justified disregarding the knock and announce requirement? This court has held that exigent circumstances exist when a suspect's awareness of the search would increase the danger to police officers or others, or when an officer must act quickly to prevent the destruction of evidence. Whether such exigent circumstances exist must be viewed from the totality of circumstances known to the officers at the time of the forcible entry. . . . Taking into consideration only those facts known to [officer] at the time he ordered the forcible entry, the sound of footsteps coming from inside the apartment and not moving closer to the entry door was sufficient for [officer] to order the forcible entry and disregard the knock and announce requirement. The search warrant was for drugs, specifically cocaine. Of course, drugs, particularly cocaine, are the quintessential form of evidence that may be easily destroyed. [Officer] testified that he was familiar with the layout of the apartment and knew that the bathroom, the likely scene of any attempt at destroying evidence, was located to one side of the entry door. Given this, the movement in the apartment, from one side of the apartment to the other, could have indicated an attempt to destroy evidence. The fact that [officer's] fears were not realized, that the footsteps were those of a 13-year-old girl, is immaterial. [Officer] could not have known who was moving in the apartment. Given the layout of the apartment and the evidence that was the subject of the warrant, [officer] was justified in believing that someone might be attempting to destroy evidence. He was, therefore, justified in ordering the forcible entry into the apartment." *U.S. v. Gillaum*, 372 F.3d 848 (7th Cir. 2004).

- "Police had little reason to apply a battering ram to a door that was already ajar, and using the concussion grenade created a risk that people close to the detonation point would be injured. Children are especially vulnerable, and the officers knew that one was in the apartment. Although they peeked inside the living room, planning not to use the device if they saw the child, they could have missed someone in a corner or behind the furniture. A child who hears the door being broken down is likely to hide." *U.S. v. Jones*, 214 F.3d 836, 838 (7th Cir. 2000).

<u>Eighth Circuit</u>

- "In *Wilson v. Layne*, the Supreme Court noted: 'Where the police enter a home under the authority of a warrant to search for stolen property, the presence of third parties for the purpose of identifying the stolen property has long been approved by this Court and our common-law tradition.' That is precisely what happened in this case. Citing no supporting authority, [the defendant] argues the principle should not apply because the [third parties'] presence was not needed to identify the specific items named in the warrant. But this is not a constitutional prerequisite. When the police entered [the defendant's] home to execute the warrant, they discovered a massive cache of items that appeared to fall within the universe of the suspected thefts. It was objectively reasonable for the officers to turn to the [third parties], owners and managers of [the

store], a theft victim, for help in confirming which items
there was probable cause to believe had been stolen.
'The general touchstone of reasonableness which
governs Fourth Amendment analysis. . .governs the
method of execution of the warrant.' The execution of
the warrant to search [the defendant's] home was
constitutionally reasonable." *U.S. v. Gregoire*, 638 F.3d
962 (8th Cir. 2011).

- "When law-enforcement officers have searched a residence without knocking and announcing their presence,
and when federal agents played some role in that
search, we have typically begun our inquiry by asking
what law applies. Generally, our inquiry has focused on
whether the search implicates the federal 'no-knock
statute,' 18 U.S.C. Sec. 3109. While section 3109 does
not apply to searches conducted entirely by state officers pursuant to a state warrant, section 3109 does
apply when federal officers are a significant part of a
search. Recent Supreme Court precedent convinces us
that this significant-part-of-the-search question is now
irrelevant in most situations. . . . After [*Wilson v.
Arkansas*, 514 U.S. 927, 930, 115 S. Ct. 1914, 131 L.
Ed. 2d 976 (1995)], even if a state chooses not to
regulate in the area, it is clear that the Fourth Amendment requires an inquiry into the reasonableness of a
no-knock search even if there is no federal involvement
triggering section 3109. Next, after *Wilson*, it was
unclear whether section 3109's scope was broader than
the Fourth Amendment's. *Wilson* taught that a no-
knock search always implicated the Fourth Amendment's reasonableness requirement. But if section 3109
provided a broader protection against no-knock
searches, courts still had to ask whether the search
triggered section 3109 to determine the appropriate
standard. This inquiry is no longer material because
the Court soon clarified that both section 3109 and the
Fourth Amendment codified the same common-law
knock-and-announce principle, and that both are subject
to the same exceptions. After these cases, we know that
a defendant need not show federal involvement to
invoke protections against unreasonable no-knock
searches. And we know that showing federal involvement does not entitle a defendant to greater protections

than does the Fourth Amendment." *U.S. v. Scroggins*, 361 F.3d 1075 (8th Cir. 2004).

- [Defendant] next urges that the District Court erred when it declined to suppress the evidence found in his home because the search was conducted at night, without a showing of necessity, and therefore violated the Fourth Amendment. We disagree. . . . The District Court properly held that [defendant] failed to demonstrate that the nighttime search of his home was unreasonable. Moreover, even if [defendant] were to have shown that the search was unreasonable, a court does not automatically suppress evidence gathered pursuant to a warrant, but instead considers whether the defendant was prejudiced or whether there was a reckless disregard of applicable procedure, both of which are absent here. Finally, even had [defendant] shown prejudice or a reckless disregard of procedures, an invalid warrant does not compel suppression of the evidence if the police officers acted based on a good-faith belief in the validity of the warrant, as they did here. In this case, St. Louis police conducted surveillance on [defendant's] home for several days (including the day of the search) during daytime hours and at night. Based on this surveillance and based on information from a confidential informant, the officers concluded that [defendant] was likely dealing crack cocaine and heroin. On the day of the search, the officers sought a search warrant from a state circuit judge, who issued a warrant at approximately 7:45 p.m. The warrant provided that the search should be conducted 'within 10 days after the issuance of this warrant by day or night.' The officers executed the warrant later that evening at approximately 10:00 p.m. after additional support arrived. In these circumstances, the District Court did not err when it ruled that the search did not violate the Fourth Amendment merely because it occurred at night." *U.S. v. Harris*, 324 F.3d 602 (8th Cir. 2003).
- "The Fourth Amendment does not require notice to an absent homeowner before execution of a search for which a warrant has issued." *U.S. v. DeBuse*, 289 F.3d 1072 (8th Cir. 2002).

Ninth Circuit

- "In granting (defendant's) motion to suppress, the district court concluded that (defendant's) Fourth Amendment rights were violated because the police officers failed to provide him with a copy of the search warrant. On its face, the Fourth Amendment does not require that a copy of the warrant be served on the person whose premises are being searched . . . Here, as in *Hudson*, given that a valid search warrant entitled the officers to retrieve drugs and firearms in the apartment, '[r]esort to the massive remedy of suppressing evidence of guilt is unjustified' . . . In light of the rationale of the exclusionary rule and the considerations set out by the Supreme Court in *Hudson*, we conclude that suppression was not an appropriate remedy in this case." *U.S. v. Hector*, 474 F.3d 1150 (9th Cir. 2007).

- "We . . . hold that the law enforcement officers did not act unreasonably in delaying service in light of the totality of the circumstances facing them. . . . The officers tried to serve the warrant in good faith, were unable to do so on account of a language barrier, and promptly called for interpretive assistance. They served the warrant as soon as was practicable—while the search was ongoing and forty minutes to an hour after it began." *U.S. v. Martinez-Garcia*, 397 F.3d 1205 (9th Cir. 2005).

- "Although our decision that the entry was lawful primarily hinges on the officers' knowledge that [defendant] was armed, we stress that our holding does not depart from the principle explicitly recognized by other jurisdictions that the presence of a gun, standing alone, is insufficient to justify noncompliance with the knock and announce rule. There is a clear distinction between a scenario where an armed suspect poses a perceived threat and one where a firearm is merely known to be present in a residence. To lawfully dispense with the knock and announce requirement, the government must demonstrate that the presence of firearms raised a legitimate concern for officer safety. In other words, our holding in this case merely confirms the proposition that the presence of a firearm coupled with evidence that a suspect is willing and able to use the weapon will often justify noncompliance with the knock and announce requirement. [Defendant's] unusual and threatening behavior with his pistol distinguishes this case from those where officers reasonably suspect only the presence of a firearm in the targeted residence." *U.S. v. Bynum*, 362 F.3d 574 (9th Cir. 2004).

- "It is not disputed that [a DEA agent] served [defendant] with the face sheet of the warrant and all the attachments incorporated into the warrant and necessary to satisfy the requirements of the Fourth Amendment. We conclude that this is all that is required under Rule 41 [, which] provides that the 'officer executing the warrant must: (A) give a copy of the warrant and a receipt for the property taken to the person from whom, or from whose premises, the property was taken; or (B) leave a copy of the warrant and receipt at the place where the officer took the property.' We have held clearly that Rule 41 must be interpreted in the light of the policies that underlie the warrant requirement: providing the property owner assurance of the lawful authority of the executing officer, his need to search, and the limits of his power to search. To comport with Rule 41, the government must serve a complete copy of the warrant at the outset of the search. . . . Here, the important policies that underlie the warrant requirement were satisfied by the elements of the warrant that [the agent] served on [defendant] during the search. The face sheet and attachments provided sufficient indicia of the agents' lawful authority to conduct the search, what and where they legally could search, and the crimes for which evidence was sought: The face sheet of the warrant clearly stated that a magistrate judge had found probable cause for the search, thus indicating the agents' legal authority. The limits of that authority were set out by Attachment A and Attachment B that stated, with particularity, where the agents could search and what they could seize. The attachments also provided [defendant] with adequate notice of the purpose of the search by specifying the federal crimes that were suspected and for evidence of which the search was conducted. . . . [I]f the face sheet and attachments clearly state that the agents have lawful authority to conduct the search and specify the location to be searched and the items sought, the affidavit supporting the probable cause determination need not be served at the time of the search." *U.S. v. Celestine*, 324 F.3d 1095 (9th Cir. 2003).

Eleventh Circuit

- " '[A]n arrest warrant founded on probable cause implicitly carries with it the limited authority to enter a dwelling in which the suspect lives . . . when there is reason to believe the suspect is within.' " *U.S. v. Hollis*, 780 F.3d 1064, 1068 (11th Cir. 2015), cert. denied, 136 S. Ct. 274, 193 L. Ed. 2d 200 (2015) (citation omitted).
- "[W]hen a police officer effectuates an arrest warrant in a third-party's abode, the officer may violate the Fourth Amendment rights of the third-party. But we agree with our sister circuits that the subject of an arrest warrant cannot challenge the execution of that warrant and the later discovery of evidence in a third-party's home." *U.S. v. Hollis*, 780 F.3d 1064, 1068–69 (11th Cir. 2015), cert. denied, 136 S. Ct. 274, 193 L. Ed. 2d 200 (2015) (citation omitted).

§ 5:13 Execution: Police may not use excessive force when executing a search warrant

Second Circuit

- " 'Absent special circumstances, the police of course have the authority to detain occupants of premises while an authorized search is in progress, regardless of individualized suspicion.' Thus, generally, Defendants would be acting lawfully if they detained Green incident to a valid search valid warrant or would be shielded by qualified immunity if they acted with good faith reliance on the apparently valid warrant. However, if Defendants knew they were in the wrong location, the search was no longer constitutional, and thus the continued confinement of Green during that unconstitutional search was no longer constitutional, nor could a reasonable officer think otherwise." *Green v. City of Mount Vernon*, 96 F. Supp. 3d 263, 294 (S.D. N.Y. 2015) (inner citation omitted).
- "When considering whether handcuffing constitutes excessive force, a court 'is to consider evidence that: 1) the handcuffs were unreasonably tight; 2) the defendants ignored the arrestee's pleas that the handcuffs were too tight; and 3) the degree of injury to the wrists.' Additionally, 'there is a consensus among courts in [the Second Circuit] that tight handcuffing does not consti-

tute excessive force unless it causes some injury beyond temporary discomfort.' 'These injuries need not be severe or permanent, but must be more than merely de minimis.'" *Green v. City of Mount Vernon*, 96 F. Supp. 3d 263, 295–96 (S.D. N.Y. 2015) (citations omitted).

- "Under case law in this District, '[i]n executing a search warrant for drugs, as in this case, it is reasonable for police officers to enter a residence with guns drawn to secure the area and prevent harm to themselves or others.' Though it is less clear whether pointing guns at children when effecting a search warrant related to narcotics constitutes excessive force[.]" *Green v. City of Mount Vernon*, 96 F. Supp. 3d 263, 296 (S.D. N.Y. 2015) (citations omitted).

Sixth Circuit

- "The use of excessive force in the execution of a search warrant constitutes a Fourth Amendment violation. (citations omitted) To determine whether a constitutional violation based on excessive force has occurred, this Court applies 'the objective-reasonableness standard, which depends on the facts and circumstances of each case viewed from the perspective of a reasonable officer on the scene and not with 20/20 hindsight.'" *Binay v. Bettendorf*, 601 F.3d 640 (6th Cir. 2010).

Seventh Circuit

- "The exclusionary rule is used in only a subset of all constitutional violations—and excessive force in making an arrest or seizure is not a basis for the exclusion of evidence." *Evans v. Poskon*, 603 F.3d 362 (7th Cir. 2010).

§ 5:14   Standard of review: The decision of the magistrate to issue a warrant must be examined with great deference

Supreme Court

- "Just as the discovery of contraband cannot validate a warrant invalid when issued, so is it equally clear that the discovery of facts demonstrating that a valid warrant was unnecessarily broad does not retroactively invalidate the warrant. The validity of the warrant must be assessed on the basis of the information that the officers disclosed, or had a duty to discover and to disclose, to the issuing magistrate. While the purpose justifying a police search strictly limit the permissible extent of the search, the Court has also recognized the need to allow some latitude for honest mistakes that are made by officers in the dangerous and difficult process of making arrests and executing search warrants." *Maryland v. Garrison*, 480 U.S. 79, 85–87, 107 S. Ct. 1013, 94 L. Ed. 2d 72 (1987).

- "[A] reviewing court is not to conduct a *de novo* determination of probable cause, but only to determine whether there is substantial evidence in the record supporting the magistrate's decision to issue the warrant." *Massachusetts v. Upton*, 466 U.S. 727, 728, 104 S. Ct. 2085, 80 L. Ed. 2d 721 (1984).

- "Deference to the magistrate, however, is not boundless. It is clear, first, that the deference accorded to a magistrate's finding of probable cause does not preclude inquiry into the knowing or reckless falsity of the affidavit on which that determination was based."*U.S. v. Leon*, 468 U.S. 897, 914, 104 S. Ct. 3405, 82 L. Ed. 2d 677 (1984).

- "Even if the warrant application was supported by more than a bare bones affidavit, a reviewing court may properly conclude that, notwithstanding the deference that magistrates deserve, the warrant was invalid because the magistrate's probable cause determination reflected an improper analysis of the totality of the circumstances or because the form of the warrant was improper in some respect." *U.S. v. Leon*, 468 U.S. 897, 915, 104 S. Ct. 3405, 82 L. Ed. 2d 677 (1984).

- "[A]fter-the-fact scrutiny by courts of the sufficiency of an affidavit should not take the form of *de novo* review. A magistrate's determination of probable cause should be paid great deference by reviewing courts. [S]o long as a magistrate had a substantial basis for conclud[ing] that a search would uncover evidence of wrongdoing, the Fourth Amendment requires no more." *Illinois v. Gates*, 462 U.S. 213, 236, 103 S. Ct. 2317, 76 L. Ed. 2d 527 (1983).

- "[A]ffidavits for search warrants must be tested and interpreted by magistrates and courts in a commonsense and realistic fashion. A grudging or negative attitude by reviewing courts toward warrants will tend to discourage police officers from submitting their evidence to a judicial officer before acting. [W]hen a magistrate has found probable cause, the courts should not invalidate the warrant by interpreting the affidavit in a hypertechnical, rather than a commonsense, manner. Although in a particular case it may not be easy to determine when an affidavit demonstrates the existence of probable cause, the resolution of doubtful or marginal cases in this area should be largely determined by the preference to be accorded to warrants." *U.S. v. Ventresca*, 1965-2 C.B. 517, 380 U.S. 102, 108–09, 85 S. Ct. 741, 13 L. Ed. 2d 684, 16 A.F.T.R.2d 5787 (1965).

First Circuit

• "[W]here the defendant makes a substantial preliminary showing that a false statement knowingly and intentionally, or with reckless disregard for the truth, was included by the affiant in the warrant affidavit, and if the allegedly false statement is necessary to the finding of probable cause, the Fourth Amendment requires that a hearing be held at the defendant's request. A material omission of information may also trigger a *Franks* hearing. . . . We note an important difference between the 'necessary' inquiries when the challenge is to the omission of an allegedly material fact rather than to the inclusion of an allegedly false material statement. With an omission, the inquiry is whether its inclusion in an affidavit would have led to a *negative* finding by the magistrate on probable cause. If a false statement is in the affidavit, the inquiry is whether its inclusion was necessary for a *positive* finding by the magistrate on probable cause." *U.S. v. Castillo*, 287 F.3d 21 (1st Cir. 2002).

Second Circuit

• "A magistrate's determination of probable cause should be paid great deference by reviewing courts. . . . A reviewing court should not interpret supporting affidavits in a hypertechnical, rather than a commonsense manner. . . . The resolution of doubtful cases. . .should be largely determined by the preference to be accorded to warrants." *U.S. v. Martin*, 157 F.3d 46, 52 (2d Cir. 1998).

Third Circuit

- "The Supreme Court has instructed that a reviewing court may not conduct a de novo review of a probable cause determination. Even if a reviewing court would not have found probable cause in a particular case, it must nevertheless uphold a warrant so long as the issuing magistrate's determination was made consistent with the minimal substantial basis standard. This standard does not mean that reviewing courts should simply rubber stamp a magistrate's conclusions. Nevertheless, the role of the reviewing court is quite limited. The Supreme Court has directed that although in a particular case it may not be easy to determine when an affidavit demonstrates the existence of probable cause, the resolution of doubtful or marginal cases in this area should be largely determined by the preference to be accorded to warrants." *U.S. v. Conley*, 4 F.3d 1200, 1205 (3d Cir. 1993).

Fourth Circuit

- "[T]he case law plainly establishes that an appellate court must accord great deference to a magistrate's finding of probable cause. Indeed, the Supreme Court has held that [r]easonable minds frequently may differ on the question whether a particular affidavit establishes probable cause, and we have thus concluded that the preference for warrants is most appropriately effectuated by according great deference to a magistrate's determination. Thus, the magistrate's determination should be overturned in this case only if there is no substantial basis for concluding that probable cause existed." *Simmons v. Poe*, 47 F.3d 1370, 1380, 31 Fed. R. Serv. 3d 451 (4th Cir. 1995).

Sixth Circuit

- "[W]e must give great deference to a magistrate's determination of probable cause. Consequently, we may only reverse a magistrate's decision to grant a search warrant if the magistrate arbitrarily exercised his or her authority. We review the probable-cause sufficiency of an affidavit to ascertain whether the magistrate had a substantial basis for finding that the affidavit established probable cause to believe that the evidence would be found at the place cited. Probable cause exists when there is a fair probability, given the totality of the circumstances, that contraband or evidence of a crime will be found in a particular place. In reviewing whether the affidavit supports the magistrate's probable-cause determination, we must review the affidavit in a commonsense, rather than a hypertechnical, manner. This means that we must review the affidavit based on a totality of the circumstances determination, rather than a line-by-line scrutiny." *U.S. v. Brown*, 732 F.3d 569, 573 (6th Cir. 2013) (inner quotations and citations omitted).

- "This court pays great deference to a magistrate's findings, which should not be set aside unless arbitrarily exercised." *U.S. v. King*, 227 F.3d 732, 739, 2000 FED App. 0284P (6th Cir. 2000).

Seventh Circuit

- "A magistrate's determination of probable cause is to be given considerable weight and should be overruled only when the supporting affidavit, read as a whole in a realistic and common sense manner, does not allege specific facts and circumstances from which the magistrate could reasonably conclude that the items sought to be seized are associated with the crime and located in the place indicated." *U.S. v. Quintanilla*, 218 F.3d 674, 677 (7th Cir. 2000).

Eighth Circuit

- "The Supreme Court has recognized that, because of the Constitution's strong preference for searches conducted pursuant to a warrant, an issuing judge's determination of probable cause should be paid great deference by reviewing courts. . . . Accordingly, if we are satisfied that the issuing judge had a substantial basis to conclude that the search would uncover evidence of criminal activity, we will find that the warrant was valid and that the search was conducted in accordance with the standards of the Fourth Amendment." *U.S. v. Wright*, 145 F.3d 972, 975 (8th Cir. 1998).

Tenth Circuit

- "We review the reasonableness of a warrant to determine whether the issuing magistrate. . .had a substantial basis for finding probable cause, giving great deference to the issuing magistrate judge's decision." *U.S. v. Kennedy*, 131 F.3d 1371, 1375 (10th Cir. 1997).

§ 5:15   Standard of review: What law governs in cases of joint state-federal investigations?

Fourth Circuit

- "[T]he question of what law governs the application for a warrant cannot be resolved solely on the basis of the *investigation's* character, but instead turns on the nature of the *judicial proceeding* undertaken during the course of the investigation, such as a proceeding initiated by the application for a search warrant. Therefore, when a member of a joint task force initiates a proceeding in state court to obtain a search warrant in furtherance of the joint investigation, it is not only relevant to understand the role of federal officers in obtaining the warrant and conducting the search, but it is also *necessary* to review the details of the proceeding itself to determine what law the warrant will serve and the scope of the warrant." *U.S. v. Claridy*, 601 F.3d 276 (4th Cir. 2010) (emphasis in original).

§ 5:16   False affidavits: The defendant is entitled to a hearing when he makes specific allegations of deliberate or reckless material false statements in the affidavits upon which a search warrant was issued

Supreme Court

- "Suppression remains an appropriate remedy if the magistrate or judge in issuing a warrant was misled by information in an affidavit that the affiant knew was false or would have known was false except for his reckless disregard of the truth." *U.S. v. Leon*, 468 U.S. 897, 923, 104 S. Ct. 3405, 82 L. Ed. 2d 677 (1984).
- "[W]here the defendant makes a substantial preliminary showing that a false statement knowingly and intentionally, or with reckless disregard for the truth, was included by the affiant in the warrant affidavit, and if the allegedly false statement is necessary to the

finding of probable cause, the Fourth Amendment requires that a hearing be held at the defendant's request." *Franks v. Delaware*, 438 U.S. 154, 155–56, 98 S. Ct. 2674, 57 L. Ed. 2d 667 (1978).

- "[W]hen the Fourth Amendment demands a factual showing sufficient to comprise probable cause, the obvious assumption is that there will be a truthful showing. This does not mean truthful in the sense that every fact recited in the warrant affidavit is necessarily correct, for probable cause may be founded upon hearsay and upon information received from informants, as well as upon information within the affiant's own knowledge that sometimes must be garnered hastily. But surely it is to be truthful in the sense that the information put forth is believed or appropriately accepted by the affiant as true." *Franks v. Delaware*, 438 U.S. 154, 164–65, 98 S. Ct. 2674, 57 L. Ed. 2d 667 (1978).

First Circuit

- "Material omissions from a warrant affidavit also may furnish the basis for a successful *Franks* challenge. The required showing is two-fold: first, the omission must have been either intentional or reckless; and second, the omitted information, if incorporated into the affidavit, must be sufficient to vitiate probable cause. Because there is no requirement that every shred of known information be included in a warrant affidavit, the omission of a particular detail, without more, is not enough to satisfy the mens rea element of the *Franks* test. Rather, an omission triggers the exclusionary rule only if it is 'designed to mislead, or . . . made in reckless disregard of whether [it] would mislead, the magistrate' in his appraisal of the affidavit. Recklessness may be inferred directly from the fact of omission only if 'the omitted information was *critical* to the probable cause determination.' Negligent omissions—even negligent omissions of highly probative information—do not satisfy this strict standard." *U.S. v. Tanguay*, 787 F.3d 44, 49 (1st Cir. 2015) (citations omitted).

- "Ordinarily, this makes good sense: when the affiant has no substantial reason to doubt the veracity or completeness of the information included in her affidavit, a failure either to verify the accuracy of that information or to go in search of contrary information is not reckless. But this general rule—like virtually every general rule—admits of at least one exception. To understand the operation of this exception, some background is necessary. The *Franks* Court established that a defendant is entitled to an evidentiary hearing to test the veracity of a warrant affidavit if he can make a substantial showing that the affiant, with reckless disregard for the truth, included a materially false statement in the affidavit. We have previously held that a material omission from a warrant affidavit, no less than the inclusion of a materially false statement, may furnish the basis for a successful *Franks* challenge when that omission was made with similar recklessness. . . . [W]hen proffering the warrant application, Nolet 'understood full well that [Wiggin's] credibility was at issue, based on his [altered prescription] conviction, if nothing else.' . . . In addition, Nolet knew that Wiggin's history included the altered prescription conviction and that he had experienced other 'scrapes' with the law. Given that *Nolet's* case for probable cause depended entirely on Wiggin's account, we think that this web of circumstantial evidence sent up a red flag— and that red flag may have been sufficient to create a duty of further inquiry. To sum up, our holding is that the district court erred in ruling as a matter of law that an affiant never has a duty to make further inquiry before presenting a warrant application to a magistrate. Because the court below, erroneously relying on its categorical disavowal of any duty of further inquiry, did not pose any of the further questions that had to be asked, we must regard its order denying the appellant's motion to suppress as without force pending the completion of the further proceedings described below." *U.S. v. Tanguay*, 787 F.3d 44, 52–53 (1st Cir. 2015) (citations omitted).

- "Information supporting probable cause for a warrant is often set forth in an affidavit provided by a law enforcement officer, as happened here. An affidavit supporting a search warrant is presumptively valid. But if a defendant makes a 'substantial preliminary showing that a false statement . . . with reckless disregard for the truth[ ] was included by the affiant in the warrant affidavit, and if the allegedly false statement is necessary to the finding of probable cause, the Fourth Amendment requires that a hearing be held at the defendant's request.' For a warrant to be voided and the fruits of a search excluded, the defendant must: (1) show that the affiant in fact made a false statement or omission 'knowingly and intentionally, or with reckless disregard for the truth,' (2) make this showing by a preponderance of the evidence, and (3) show that, with the recklessly omitted information added to the affidavit, the reformed affidavit fails to establish probable cause. An allegation is made with 'reckless disregard for the truth' if the affiant 'in fact entertained serious doubts as to the truth of the allegations or where circumstances evinced obvious reasons to doubt the veracity of the allegations in the application.' 'In the case of allegedly material omissions, recklessness may be inferred where the omitted information was critical to the probable cause determination.' " *U.S. v. Gifford*, 727 F.3d 92 (1st Cir. 2013) (citations omitted).

- "[W]e conclude, as did the district court, that the omitted and allegedly false statements in the affidavit in support of the warrant were not material to the issuance of the warrant. There was ample probable cause to search the warehouse and no basis to suppress. As the district court pointed out, the warrant was supported by information from two other CIs [confidential informants] who were not [James 'Whitey'] Bulger and who offered more detailed information about a large-scale marijuana conspiracy. There was no basis for any insinuation that the CIs fabricated this information. Further, the warrant affidavit included eyewitness observations by multiple agents about the unusual behavior of individuals and vehicles on April 5 and 6, 1983, which eventually led to the agents observing two vehicles leaving the warehouse and discovering that those vehicles contained bales of marijuana. The surveillance combined with the marijuana in the vehicles gave the agents probable cause to believe that the warehouse contained additional marijuana and evidence of trafficking. From these facts, the district court concluded that even if Bulger had been identified as the third CI (and thus the information linked to him been rendered unreliable), and even if [an FBI agent's] purportedly false story about discovering the warehouse had been omitted, the remainder of the affidavit readily established probable cause. We agree. And because the allegedly withheld information was not material, it cannot be the basis for a finding of fundamental error." *Murray v. U.S.*, 704 F.3d 23 (1st Cir. 2013).

- "[I]nformation supporting probable cause may be set out in an affidavit submitted with the application for a search warrant. Although '[t]here is. . .a presumption of validity with respect to the affidavit supporting the search warrant,' that presumption may be refuted during a so-called *Franks* hearing. However, to get a *Franks* hearing, a party must first make two 'substantial preliminary showings': (1) that a false statement or omission in the affidavit was made knowingly and intentionally or with reckless disregard for the truth; and (2) the falsehood or omission was necessary to the finding of probable cause. Failure to make a showing on either element dooms a party's hearing request. In the event that a hearing is granted and 'at that hearing the allegation of perjury or reckless disregard is established by the defendant by a preponderance of the evidence, and, with the affidavit's false material set to one side [or the omitted material included], the affidavit's. . .content is insufficient to establish probable cause, the search warrant must be voided and the fruits of the search excluded to the same extent as if probable cause was lacking on the face of the affidavit.' " *U.S. v. Rigaud*, 684 F.3d 169, 173 (1st Cir. 2012) (citations omitted).

- "In such cases, where the defendant challenges the accuracy of the affidavit but has failed to make the substantial preliminary showing required by *Franks*, the court may conduct an in camera interview of the officer-affiant, and, if necessary, of the informant. A district court is not required to do so, however; the decision whether an in camera proceeding is needed to test the officer-affiant's credibility rests entirely with the district court." *U.S. v. Manning*, 79 F.3d 212, 220, 44 Fed. R. Evid. Serv. 204 (1st Cir. 1996).

Third Circuit
- "Even if we were to conclude that Chief Detzel was reck-

less in excluding [from the warrant affidavit] the facts that no money exchanged hands during the silencer transaction and that policy officers conducted a preliminary search of the vehicle, we agree with the District Court that neither omission was material to the establishment of probable cause. It may well be true, as Johnson argues, that 'a judge would want to know' that Johnson failed to pay the C.I. at the time of the delivery. But not including that fact did not undermine the probable cause showing here. The simultaneous payment of money in exchange for goods may be proof of an illegal transaction, but the lack of a simultaneous exchange does not necessarily imply the absence of illegality. The C.I.'s communications with the police, as relayed in Chief Detzel's affidavit, amply demonstrated probable cause. Likewise, although the affidavit should have included language explaining that policy briefly looked in the driver's side of the vehicle, there is no evidence that the search was anything more than a cursory look that did not affect the probable cause determination. A 'quick visual check' of the floorboards, is a fact that does not change the outcome here." *U.S. v. Johnson*, 578 Fed. Appx. 150, 155 (3d Cir. 2014) (citations omitted).

Fourth Circuit

- "A defendant may obtain a hearing concerning the validity of an affidavit supporting a search warrant by making a substantial preliminary showing that the affiant omitted material facts with the intent to make, or in reckless disregard of whether [he] thereby made, the affidavit misleading. This showing requires a detailed offer of proof, and [a]llegations of negligence or innocent mistake are insufficient. The defendant must also show that the omitted material was necessary to the finding of probable cause, i.e., that the omitted material was such that its inclusion in the affidavit would defeat probable cause. Upon making this two-part preliminary showing, a defendant is entitled to a hearing, at which he bears the burden of proving the allegations by a preponderance of the evidence." *U.S. v. Shorter*, 328 F.3d 167 (4th Cir. 2003).

Fifth Circuit

- "(I)t is clear that *Franks* itself was confined to providing a mechanism for challenging a search warrant that was not supported by probable cause but that, due to the inclusion of deliberately falsified allegations in the warrant affidavit, appeared to be supported by probable cause. The principles of *Franks* have never been applied to facially invalid warrants, and we decline to so extend *Franks* today. Because we have found that there was insufficient evidence to establish probable cause on the face of (the officer's) warrant affidavit, we conclude that *Franks* is inapplicable. Accordingly, the district court did not err in granting summary judgment to (the officer) on (defendant's) *Franks* claim." *Kohler v. Englade*, 470 F.3d 1104 (5th Cir. 2006).

- "The good-faith exception to the exclusionary rule does not apply if the warrant affidavit contains a false statement that was made intentionally or with reckless disregard for its truth. If an allegation of intentional falsity or a reckless disregard for the truth is 'established by the defendant by a preponderance of the evidence,' the we must then excise the offensive language from the affidavit and determine whether the remaining portion would have established the necessary probable cause. Note that the initial burden here is upon the defendant to prove that false information was given intentionally or recklessly. If the defendant fails to meet his burden, or if the affidavit would have sufficiently provided probable cause without the false information, the warrant did not violate the Fourth Amendment and the evidence should not have been excluded." *U.S. v. Cavazos*, 288 F.3d 706 (5th Cir. 2002).

Sixth Circuit

- "Dunning argues that because probable cause did not support the search warrant the district court erred by denying his motion to suppress. He claims that conclusions in the detective's affidavit were wholly conclusory because the detective had relied on computer software results to identify child pornography files. Although wholly conclusory statements would fail to meet the probable cause requirement, the detective's statements in this case were not wholly conclusory. The detective in this case submitted an affidavit to a state circuit

judge in support of his application for a warrant to
search Dunning's home. In the affidavit, the detective
set out his training and experience as well as his use of
'law enforcement systems to query IP addresses in Kentucky that had been seen sharing child sexual exploitation files.' Dunning claims that because the detective
did not have the source code for the computer program,
'it [was] not possible to authenticate the function of the
application or validate its "calibration"' and that 'statements contained within his search warrant affidavit
[were] therefore "wholly conclusory," because he did not
have enough information to substantiate his claims
without the source code.' A defendant who challenges
the factual assertions in an affidavit supporting a
search warrant is entitled to an evidentiary hearing if

> (1) the defendant makes a substantial preliminary show-
> ing that the affiant engaged in deliberate falsehood or
> reckless disregard for the truth in omitting information
> from the affidavit, and (2) a finding of probable cause
> would not be supported by the affidavit if the omitted
> material were considered to be a part of it.

This court has joined the First Circuit in rejecting the
argument that a higher degree of certainty is required
when the government uses software to locate IP
addresses. *See United States v. Schumacher*, which held
that the defendant failed to establish any way in which
omission of certain information in the search warrant
affidavit was material to a finding of probable cause. As
in *Schumacher*, the omission of information regarding
the reliability of the CPS software does not call into
question the reliability of this software and does not
provide grounds for an evidentiary hearing. Furthermore, it is arguable that such information would have
only strengthened the affidavit by showing that the
software was reliable. As the district court held, the
detective was trained to use, and had previously used,
software to investigate child pornography crimes, and
he identified and confirmed that the files containing
child pornography had been shared by Dunning's IP address on various dates. Moreover, Dunning failed to
make even a preliminary showing that the detective
knowingly, intentionally, or recklessly made false statements in his affidavit. Dunning also argues that the
detective's use of the software to find his IP address is

similar to the use of the drug-sniffing dog in *Florida v. Harris*, and that he should have had the same opportunity to challenge the software's reliability as the defendant had in *Harris* 'to challenge such evidence of a dog's reliability, whether by cross-examining the testifying officer or by introducing his own fact or expert witnesses.' But the analogy falls far short. The CPS software merely combs through large amounts of data and takes note of when and what IP address downloaded suspect material. As the Second Circuit explained in United States v. Thomas,

> [t]raditionally, law enforcement officers seek to detect child pornography offenses by manually sending out search queries for illicit material over P2P [peer to peer] networks, one-by-one. CPS automates this process by canvassing these public P2P networks, identifying files that contain child pornography, cataloguing this information, and providing law enforcement officers with a list of the online users who are sharing these files over P2P networks.

Unlike a drug-sniffing dog, whose potential errors law enforcement might not be able to detect without more invasive search, CPS merely records information it finds on public peer-to-peer networks, thus automating law enforcement's task of combing through those public networks, a task that law enforcement could do in real time using publicly available tools." *United States v. Dunning*, 857 F.3d 342, 346–48 (6th Cir. 2017) (citations omitted).

- "To deserve a *Franks* hearing to challenge the validity of a search warrant, a defendant must make a substantial preliminary showing of two elements: first, a defendant must show that the affiant included—either knowingly and intentionally or with reckless disregard for the truth—a false statement in the affidavit. . . . [The second requirement requires the defendant to] show that the probable-cause finding required the allegedly false statement. For even if material that is the subject of the alleged falsity or reckless disregard is set to one side, as long as there remains sufficient content in the warrant affidavit to support a finding of probable cause, no hearing is required. An affidavit, with the false part excised, will still establish probable cause if it provide[s] the magistrate judge with a basis for finding there was a fair probability that contraband or evidence of a crime would be found at' the stated location." *U.S. v. Brown*, 732 F.3d 569, 575 (6th Cir. 2013) (inner quotations and citations omitted).

- "In *Franks v. Delaware*. . . .the Supreme Court held that a search based on a warrant that contains deliberately or recklessly false allegations is invalid unless the remaining portions of the affidavit provide probable cause. Thus, a court considering whether to suppress evidence based on an allegation that the underlying affidavit contained false statements must apply a two-part test: (1) whether the defendant has proven by a preponderance of the evidence that the affidavit contains deliberately or recklessly false statements and (2) whether the affidavit, without the false statements, provides the requisite probable cause to sustain the warrant." *U.S. v. Charles*, 138 F.3d 257, 263, 1998 FED App. 0074P (6th Cir. 1998).

- "Although material omissions are not immune from inquiry under *Franks*, we have recognized that an affidavit which omits potentially exculpatory information is less likely to present a question of impermissible official conduct than one which affirmatively includes false information. This is so because an allegation of omission potentially opens officers to endless conjecture about investigative leads, fragments of information, or other matter than might, if included, have redounded to defendant's benefit." *U.S. v. Atkin*, 107 F.3d 1213, 1217, 79 A.F.T.R.2d 97-1301, 1997 FED App. 0085P (6th Cir. 1997).

Seventh Circuit

- "Officers do not act reasonably if they intentionally or recklessly provide false information to obtain a warrant." *Olson v. Champaign County, Ill.*, 784 F.3d 1093, 1100 (7th Cir. 2015).

- "In order to obtain a *Franks* hearing, [defendant] needed to make a 'substantial preliminary showing' that the affiant had intentionally or recklessly included a false statement in the affidavit, and that the false statement was material, in the sense that it was necessary to find probable cause. (citation omitted) The standard is not whether the affidavit contains a false statement, but whether the affiant knew or should have known that a statement was false." *U.S. v. Schultz*, 586 F.3d 526 (7th Cir. 2009).

- "To obtain a. . .*Franks* hearing. . .[Defendant] had to establish by a substantial preliminary showing that: (1) the affidavit contained a false material statement; (2) the affiant made the false statement intentionally, or with reckless disregard to the truth; and (3) the false statement is necessary to support the finding of probable cause. . . .These elements are hard to prove, and thus *Franks* hearings are rarely held." *U.S. v. Swanson*, 210 F.3d 788, 789–90 (7th Cir. 2000).

Eighth Circuit

- "Under our decisions, the Fourth Amendment requires a hearing where the defendant makes a substantial preliminary showing that (1) the affiant omitted facts with the intent to mislead the issuing judge, or omitted the facts in reckless disregard of the fact that the omissions would mislead, and (2) the affidavit, if supplemented by the omitted information, could not support a finding of probable cause. Gater focuses exclusively on Sullivan's alleged omission of information about the second confidential source. Gater argues that Sullivan recklessly omitted that the source had a history of drug use, had recently used drugs, and was paid for information about Gater. . . . The district court found 'no evidence to support that TFO Sullivan intended to omit facts to make the affidavit misleading, or that he did so in reckless disregard of making the affidavit misleading.' We see no error in this conclusion. Sullivan informed the issuing judge that the source had provided information for three years about persons selling narcotics, had participated in controlled purchases of drugs for law enforcement, and had visited Gater's residence several times with others while they purchased drugs. Sullivan presumably thought the issuing judge naturally would infer that a confidential source with that background must have a history of involvement with illegal drugs. As the district court observed, 'it is often people involved in criminal activities themselves that have the most knowledge about other criminal activities, [so] it is no surprise that most confidential informants are engaged in some sort of criminal activity.' " *United States v. Gater*, 2017 WL 3528239, *2 (8th Cir. 2017) (citations omitted).

- "A showing of negligence or innocent mistake is not enough to establish a *Franks* violation." *U.S. v. Butler*, 594 F.3d 955 (8th Cir. 2010).

- "[T]here was sufficient evidence to support the district court's finding that [the officer applying for a search warrant] intended to be under oath. Almost all of the apposite cases indicate that this is the relevant inquiry because a person who manifests an intention to be under oath is in fact under oath. We also observe that [the officer's] evident state of mind when he signed the affidavit and application for a warrant ensured that the purpose of the fourth amendment's 'Oath or affirmation' requirement was fulfilled. An oath or affirmation 'is designed to ensure that the truth will be told by insuring that the witness or affiant will be impressed with the solemnity and importance of his words. The theory is that those who have been impressed with the moral, religious or legal significance of formally undertaking to tell the truth are more likely to do so than those who have not made such an undertaking or been so impressed.' We believe that the circumstances that caused [the officer] to believe that he was signing under oath would also have impressed upon him the 'importance of his words.' We think that the better practice is for an affiant orally to affirm or swear before a person authorized to administer oaths. But in this case we believe that the facts support a conclusion that [the officer] was under oath when he made the application for the warrant because he intended to undertake and did undertake that obligation by the statements that he made in his affidavit and by his attendant conduct. In other words, a person may be under oath even though that person has not formally taken an oath by raising a hand and reciting formulaic words." *U.S. v. Brooks*, 285 F.3d 1102 (8th Cir. 2002).

- "*Franks* is limited to cases of perjurious or recklessly false statements or omissions made by a police officer in support of a warrant; the rule does not apply to negligent misrepresentations or omissions." *U.S. v. Schmitz*, 181 F.3d 981, 986 (8th Cir. 1999).

- "The requirement of a substantial preliminary showing

is not lightly met. . . . A mere allegation standing alone, without an offer of proof in the form of a sworn affidavit of a witness or some other reliable corroboration, is insufficient to make the difficult preliminary showing. . . . When no proof is offered that an affiant deliberately lied or recklessly disregarded the truth, a *Franks* hearing is not required." *U.S. v. Mathison*, 157 F.3d 541, 548 (8th Cir. 1998).

- "In determining whether statements were made with a reckless disregard for the truth, we have applied the standard used in First Amendment cases. That standard being, whether the affiant in fact entertained serious doubts as to the truth of the affidavits or had obvious reasons to doubt the accuracy of the information contained therein." *U.S. v. Johnson*, 78 F.3d 1258, 1262 (8th Cir. 1996).

Ninth Circuit

- "Perkins argues that Agent Ensley intentionally or recklessly omitted material information from the warrant application and that, had that information been included, the application would not have supported probable cause. Under *Franks*, a criminal defendant has the right to challenge the veracity of statements made in support of an application for a search warrant. To prevail on a *Franks* challenge, the defendant must establish two things by a preponderance of the evidence: first, that 'the affiant officer intentionally or recklessly made false or misleading statements or omissions in support of the warrant[,]' and second, that the false or misleading statement or omission was material, i.e., 'necessary to finding probable cause.' If both requirements are met, 'the search warrant must be voided and the fruits of the search excluded . . . .' Because we conclude that Perkins has established both prongs under *Franks*, we hold that the district court erred in denying his motion to suppress." *United States v. Perkins*, 850 F.3d 1109, 1116 (9th Cir. 2017) (citations omitted).

- "Second, even if the misstatements in the warrant affidavit were inserted intentionally or recklessly, the remainder of the affidavit contains sufficient evidence to support a finding of probable cause. The Court in *Franks* held that if material that is the subject of the alleged falsity or reckless disregard is set to one side, and there remains sufficient content in the warrant affidavit to support a finding of probable cause, no hearing is required." *U.S. v. Hammett*, 236 F.3d 1054, 1059 (9th Cir. 2001).

- "A defendant is entitled to an evidentiary hearing on the validity of the affidavit underlying a search warrant if the defendant can make a substantial preliminary showing that (1) the affidavit contains intentionally or recklessly false statements or misleading omissions, and (2) the affidavit cannot support a finding of probable cause without the allegedly false information. . . .If an informant's history of criminal acts involving dishonesty renders his/her statements unworthy of belief, probable cause must be analyzed without those statements." *U.S. v. Reeves*, 210 F.3d 1041, 1044 (9th Cir. 2000).

- "The threshold determination in a *Franks* hearing is whether erroneous statements or omissions in an affidavit supporting a search warrant were made knowingly and intentionally, or with reckless disregard for the truth. . . . If such a finding is made, the court then determines whether with the affidavit's false material set to one side, the affidavit's remaining content is insufficient to establish probable cause." *U.S. v. Senchenko*, 133 F.3d 1153, 1158, 48 Fed. R. Evid. Serv. 746, 28 Envtl. L. Rep. 20506 (9th Cir. 1998).

Tenth Circuit

- "An affidavit does not provide probable cause to support a search warrant if the affiant intentionally or recklessly asserted material falsehoods. . . . But [the defendant] has never asserted, before this court or in the district court, that the affiant intentionally or recklessly made false statements. Thus, a *Franks* hearing would have been improper." *U.S. v. Lewis*, 594 F.3d 1270, 81 Fed. R. Evid. Serv. 592 (10th Cir. 2010).

Eleventh Circuit

- "We need not address the statements Special Agent Zdrojewski allegedly omitted from the affidavit. The heart of Barsoum's argument is that a *Franks* hearing would have allowed him to show that the information

was deliberately omitted. This argument misunder-
stands the *Franks* standard. *Franks* requires that a
defendant make a substantial *preliminary* showing that
statements or omissions are intentionally false or recklessly misleading, and that those statements or omissions altered the probable cause showing. The allegations of deliberate omission 'must be more than
conclusory and must be supported by more than a mere
desire to cross-examine.' " *U.S. v. Barsoum*, 763 F.3d
1321 (11th Cir. 2014), petition for certiorari filed, 135 S.
Ct. 1883, 191 L. Ed. 2d 753 (2015) (citations omitted).

- "If a defendant demonstrates by a preponderance of the
  evidence that an affidavit used to obtain a search warrant contains intentionally or recklessly made false
  statements or omissions that were essential to a finding
  of probable cause, the district court must void the
  search warrant and exclude the fruits of the search."
  U.S. v. Sailor, 355 Fed. Appx. 359 (11th Cir. 2009).

- "If a defendant demonstrates by a preponderance of the
  evidence that an affidavit used to procure a search warrant contains intentionally or recklessly false statements and that, the false statements aside, the affidavit is insufficient to establish probable cause, the
  district court must void the search warrant and exclude
  the fruits of the search." *U.S. v. Anderton*, 136 F.3d
  747, 749 (11th Cir. 1998).

D.C. Circuit

- "A movant seeking to obtain a *Franks* hearing 'must
  show that (1) the affidavit contained false statements;
  (2) the statements were material to the issue of probable cause; and (3) the false statements were made
  knowingly and intentionally, or with reckless disregard
  for the truth.' (citation omitted) 'To mandate an evidentiary hearing,' the movant's attack on the affidavit supporting the warrant 'must be more than conclusory.' "
  U.S. v. Becton, 601 F.3d 588, 81 Fed. R. Evid. Serv.
  1253 (D.C. Cir. 2010).

§ 5:17 Suppression: If the officers unreasonably rely on a warrant, the evidence may be suppressed

Supreme Court

- "In the absence of an allegation that the magistrate abandoned his detached and neutral role, suppression is appropriate only if the officers were dishonest or reckless in preparing their affidavit or could not have harbored an objectively reasonable belief in the existence of probable cause." *U.S. v. Leon*, 468 U.S. 897, 926, 104 S. Ct. 3405, 82 L. Ed. 2d 677 (1984).

- "[A] warrant may be so facially deficient—i.e., in failing to particularize the place to be searched or the things to be seized—that the executing officers cannot reasonably presume it to be valid." *U.S. v. Leon*, 468 U.S. 897, 923, 104 S. Ct. 3405, 82 L. Ed. 2d 677 (1984).

- "The exception will also not apply in cases where the issuing magistrate wholly abandoned his judicial role in the manner condemned in *Lo-Ji Sales*; in such circumstances, no reasonably well-trained officer should rely on the warrant. Nor would an officer manifest objective good faith in relying on a warrant based on an affidavit 'so lacking in indicia of probable cause as to render official belief in its existence entirely unreasonable.'" *U.S. v. Leon*, 468 U.S. 897, 923, 104 S. Ct. 3405, 82 L. Ed. 2d 677 (1984).

Second Circuit

- "There are four circumstances in which the good-faith exception does not apply: (1) where the issuing [judge] has been knowingly misled; (2) where the issuing [judge] wholly abandoned his or her judicial role; (3) where the application is so lacking in indicia of probable cause as to render reliance upon it unreasonable; and (4) where the warrant is so facially deficient [such as by failing to particularize the place to be searched or the things to be seized] that reliance upon it is unreasonable. In such circumstances, reliance on the legal judgment of the issuing judge would not be objectively reasonable." *U.S. v. Falso*, 544 F.3d 110 (2d Cir. 2008), for additional opinion, see, 293 Fed. Appx. 838 (2d Cir. 2008).

- "Generally, the way a defendant demonstrates that statements in an affidavit intentionally or recklessly misled a district court is through a *Franks* hearing. The Fourth Amendment entitles a defendant to a hearing if he or she makes a substantial preliminary showing that a deliberate falsehood or statement made with reckless disregard for the truth was included in the warrant affidavit and the statement was necessary to the judge's finding of probable cause. To avoid fishing expeditions into affidavits that are otherwise presumed truthful, to mandate an evidentiary hearing: [T]he challenger's attack must be more than conclusory and must be supported by more than a mere desire to cross-examine. There must be allegations of deliberate falsehood or of reckless disregard for the truth, and those allegations must be accompanied by an offer of proof. They should point out specifically the portion of the warrant affidavit that is claimed to be false; and they should be accompanied by a statement of supporting reasons. Affidavits or sworn or otherwise reliable statements of witnesses should be furnished, or their absence satisfactorily explained. Allegations of negligence or innocent mistake are insufficient." *U.S. v. Falso*, 544 F.3d 110 (2d Cir. 2008), for additional opinion, see, 293 Fed. Appx. 838 (2d Cir. 2008).

- "The rationale for blanket suppression is that a search that greatly exceeds the bounds of a warrant and is not conducted in good faith is essentially indistinguishable from a general search." *U.S. v. Shi Yan Liu*, 239 F.3d 138, 141 (2d Cir. 2000).

Third Circuit

- "[W]e cannot say that Nardinger acted deliberately, recklessly, or with gross negligence in executing the warrant. Nardinger should have shown the attachment to [the defendant], but that misstep—stemming from his inexperience and misunderstanding of the magistrate judge's order—does not mean that he deliberately violated [the defendant]'s Fourth Amendment rights. In short, application of the exclusionary rule would provide little deterrent effect and would not justify the costs of suppression." *U.S. v. Franz*, 772 F.3d 134, 149 (3d Cir. 2014).

- "The fact that an officer executes a search pursuant to a warrant typically suffices to prove that an officer conducted a search in good faith and justifies application of the good faith exception. Nevertheless, we have identified four narrow situations in which an officer's reliance on a warrant is not reasonable:

(1) when the magistrate judge issued the warrant in reliance on a deliberately or recklessly false affidavit;

(2) when the magistrate judge abandoned his judicial role and failed to perform his neutral and detached function;

(3) when the warrant was based on an affidavit so lacking in indicia of probable cause as to render official belief in its existence entirely unreasonable; or

(4) when the warrant was so facially deficient that it failed to particularize the place to be searched or the things to be seized."

U.S. v. Ninety-Two Thousand Four Hundred Twenty-Two Dollars and Fifty-Seven Cents ($92,422.57), 307 F.3d 137 (3d Cir. 2002).

Fourth Circuit

● "A search is not invalidated in its entirety merely because some seized items were not identified in the warrant. Rather, invalidation of an entire search based on a seizure of items not named in the warrant is an extraordinary remedy that should be used only when the violations of the warrant's requirements are so extreme that the search is essentially transformed into an impermissible general search. Put another way, searching officers may be said to have flagrantly disregarded the terms of a warrant when they engage in indiscriminate fishing for evidence. . . We conclude that the extraordinary remedy of blanket suppression is not warranted here. . . In many cases, items that were not identified in the warrant were seized because they were part of a larger item of evidentiary value. For example, a grocery list was seized because it was found inside a date book containing names and addresses; [co-defendant] does not dispute that the date book was an item within the scope of the warrant. Similarly, a page of Spanish homework was seized not for the evidentiary value of the homework, but rather because the back of the page contained notations and telephone numbers relevant to the investigation. Furthermore, we note that the officers suspended the search and obtained a second warrant before seizing an item found above the ceiling tiles in [codefendant's] bedroom. Such scrupulous regard for the protections afforded by the Fourth Amendment belies any intent to disregard the terms of the warrant. We therefore affirm the denial of blanket suppression." *U.S. v. Robinson*, 275 F.3d 371, 58 Fed. R. Evid. Serv. 211 (4th Cir. 2001).

Fifth Circuit

- "An officer's reliance on a warrant is not objectively reasonable and therefore not entitled to the good-faith exception to the exclusionary rule if the underlying affidavit is 'bare bones,' i.e., so lacking in indicia of probable cause as to render official belief in its existence entirely unreasonable." *U.S. v. McCray*, 354 Fed. Appx. 205 (5th Cir. 2009).

- "Although we presume validity with respect to the affidavit supporting the search warrant, [d]eference to the magistrate, is not boundless. [T]he deference accorded to the magistrate's finding of probable cause does not preclude inquiry into the knowing or reckless falsity of the affidavit on which that determination was based. If the defendant successfully makes this showing, and if the defect in the affidavit is material, the evidence obtained pursuant to the faulty affidavit is inadmissible." *U.S. v. Tomblin*, 46 F.3d 1369, 1376–77, 41 Fed. R. Evid. Serv. 964 (5th Cir. 1995).

Sixth Circuit

- "If probable cause is found to be lacking in a search warrant, the good-faith exception will apply to uphold the search unless the evidence is so lacking in indicia of probable cause as to render official belief in its existence entirely unreasonable." *U.S. v. Watkins*, 179 F.3d 489, 494, 1999 FED App. 0213P (6th Cir. 1999).

Seventh Circuit

- "Officers do not act reasonably if they intentionally or recklessly provide false information to obtain a warrant." *Olson v. Champaign County, Ill.*, 784 F.3d 1093, 1100 (7th Cir. 2015).

- "The prosecutor in *Kalina* was performing essentially the same function as police officers who obtain a warrant by swearing to false information, and police officers can be sued for such actions under *Malley v. Briggs*. Employing the functional approach and applying the teachings of *Kalina* here, we conclude that [the prosecutor] is not entitled to absolute immunity. He performed the same function as a police officer witness when he swore to facts. A police officer witness would not be entitled to absolute immunity for swearing to false information, so neither is [the prosecutor]. His signature is below the following statement: 'The undersigned, being duly sworn, states upon information and belief that the facts set forth in the foregoing information are true." It is irrelevant that his affidavit was not on a separate piece of paper. In signing that he stated "upon information and belief that the facts set forth' were true, [the prosecutor] converted that part of the information into his own affidavit. . . . [W]hen a prosecutor goes beyond signing the information to initiate the suit by swearing to the facts it contains, the attorney is no longer absolutely immune from suit." *Olson v. Champaign County, Ill.*, 784 F.3d 1093, 1102–03 (7th Cir. 2015).

• "Provision of criminal procedure rule, authorizing district court to issue warrant to search for and seize person or property located within district, concerned substantive judicial authority, not procedures, precluding application of provision to statute requiring district court issuing out-of-district warrant for seizure of electronic communications to use procedures described in federal rules, and thus, defendant's electronic communications seized pursuant to out-of-district warrant, during investigation of his failure to pay over $145,000 in child support, were not subject to suppression as warrant was not rendered invalid by alleged violation of rule's procedures." *U.S. v. Berkos*, 543 F.3d 392 (7th Cir. 2008).

• "The exclusionary rule has. . . a deterrent effect when, by punishing behavior which violates a citizen's Fourth Amendment rights and removing the incentive for its repetition, it alters the behavior of individual law-enforcement officers or the policies of their departments. The exclusionary rule should not be applied, therefore, when its application will not result in appreciable deterrence. . . .[E]vidence should not be suppressed if

an officer acted with objective good faith, obtained the
search warrant from a neutral and detached magistrate,
and acted within its scope, since the exclusion of evidence could have no affect on police conduct. In other
words, under those circumstances, because there is
nothing to deter, the good-faith exception to the
exclusionary rule applies." *U.S. v. Merritt*, 361 F.3d
1005 (7th Cir. 2004), cert. granted, judgment vacated
on other grounds, 543 U.S. 1099, 125 S. Ct. 1024, 160
L. Ed. 2d 995 (2005) (judgment vacated, and case
remanded for further consideration in light of *U.S. v.
Booker*, 543 U.S. 220, 125 S. Ct. 738, 160 L. Ed. 2d 621
(2005)).

Eighth Circuit

- "Invalidating a search warrant because the magistrate
  was affected in some minor way by tainted information,
  when the warrant would have been granted even
  without the tainted information, would work against
  the principle that the fruit of the poisonous tree doctrine not be used to place the government in a worse
  position than it would have been in absent its illegal
  conduct." *U.S. v. Swope*, 542 F.3d 609 (8th Cir. 2008).

- "Situations in which an officer's reliance on a warrant
  would be unreasonable are when: (1) the officer included
  information in the affidavit he knew was false or would
  have known was false except for his reckless disregard
  of the truth; (2) the affidavit is so lacking in probable
  cause that it is objectively unreasonable for the officer
  to rely on it; (3) the judge failed to act in a neutral and
  detached manner; or (4) the warrant is so facially
  deficient that the officer cannot reasonably presume the
  warrant to be valid." *U.S. v. Phillips*, 88 F.3d 582, 586
  (8th Cir. 1996).

- "The *Leon* decision does not extend to the instant case,
  where there is no indication that the officers' conduct
  was objectively reasonable. Rather, there was a clear
  violation of the knock and announce rule, without the
  presence of exigent circumstances. The Fourth Amendment limitations are designed to deter precisely this
  kind of conduct. The incentive for officers to operate
  within those limitations in the future is provided by our
  application of the exclusionary rule." *U.S. v. Marts*, 986
  F.2d 1216, 1219 (8th Cir. 1993).

- "[E]ven if the violation of *Franks* could be protected under *Leon*, we could not find that the officers acted reasonably when they executed this warrant. At the time the warrant was executed, not only did the officers know that Turbo had failed to alert to the package, they were also aware that a second dog called in to verify this conclusion had not even shown the amount of interest that Turbo exhibited. Nevertheless, the officers executed the warrant, ignoring the obvious negative finding obtained during the second sniff. This is indefensible. Not only was the warrant deficient under *Franks*, this further information should have alerted the officers that they lacked probable cause to examine the package. Furthermore, we think the officers had a duty to provide the magistrate judge with any information which would undercut the warrant's validity." *U.S. v. Jacobs*, 986 F.2d 1231, 1235 (8th Cir. 1993).

Ninth Circuit

- "Because the warrant in this case was facially invalid, no reasonable agent could have relied on it absent some exceptional circumstance. The mere fact that the warrant was reviewed by two AUSA's and signed by a magistrate does not amount to exceptional circumstances. [W]hen a warrant is facially overbroad, absent specific assurances from an impartial judge or magistrate that the defective warrant is valid despite its overbreadth, a reasonable reliance argument fails." *U.S. v. Kow*, 58 F.3d 423, 428–29 (9th Cir. 1995).

- "Ordinarily, only evidence that is obtained in violation of a warrant is suppressed. However, in cases where there is a flagrant disregard for the terms of the warrant, the district court may suppress all of the evidence, including evidence that was not tainted by the violation. This extraordinary remedy should be used only when the violations of the warrant's requirements are so extreme that the search is essentially transformed into an impermissible general search." *U.S. v. Mittelman*, 999 F.2d 440, 444 (9th Cir. 1993).

Tenth Circuit

- "Under the severability doctrine, '[t]he infirmity of part of a warrant requires the suppression of evidence seized pursuant to that part of the warrant, but does not require the suppression of anything described in the valid portions of the warrant (or lawfully seized-on plain view grounds, for example-during. . .execution [of the valid portions])' . . . . We apply a multiple-step analysis to determine whether severability is applicable: First, we divide the warrant in a commonsense, practical manner into individual clauses, portions, paragraphs, or categories. We then evaluate the constitutionality of each individual part to determine whether some portion of the warrant satisfies the probable cause and particularity requirements of the Fourth Amendment. If no part of the warrant particularly describes items to be seized for which there is probable cause, then severance does not apply, and all items seized by such a warrant should be suppressed. If, however, at least a part of the warrant is sufficiently particularized and supported by probable cause, then we proceed to determine whether the requirements set out in *Naugle* have been satisfied. In doing so, we first determine whether the valid portions are distinguishable from the invalid portions. If the parts may be meaningfully severed, then we next look to the warrant on its face to determine whether the valid portions make up "the greater part of the warrant," by examining both the quantitative and qualitative aspects of the valid portions relative to the invalid portion . . . If the valid portions make up "the greater part of the warrant," then we sever those portions, suppress the evidence seized pursuant to the portions that fail to meet the Fourth Amendment's warrant requirement, and admit all evidence seized pursuant to the valid portions or lawfully seized during execution of the valid portions . . . ." *U.S. v. Sells*, 463 F.3d 1148 (10th Cir. 2006).

- "Officers [seeking a no-knock warrant] must demonstrate that they have an objectively reasonable concern that exigent circumstances exist. The warrant in this case is lacking in a sufficient indicia of reasonable suspicion that exigent circumstances exist as to [defendant's] potential for violence or as to the threat posed by his past history of possessing firearms. As we have already discussed, the affidavit in support of the no-knock search warrant presented facts that established past possession of firearms and small amounts of marijuana, and present evidence of the same. Officers failed to present any evidence of past violent behavior that would indicate a potential for present violence or futility, or any other evidence that would provide a reason to believe [defendant] would be violent. In light of our clear precedent providing that mere allegations of the presence of a firearm are insufficient to support a no-knock entry, we cannot say that law enforcement officers' reliance on the state judge's authorization was objectively reasonable. Therefore we conclude that law enforcement officers are not entitled to a good-faith exception to suppression of evidence in this case." *U.S. v. Nielson*, 415 F.3d 1195 (10th Cir. 2005).

§ 5:18 Good faith exception: Where an officer reasonably relies on a warrant which is subsequently determined to be invalid, the evidence seized will not be suppressed

Supreme Court

- "The exclusionary rule operates as a judicially created remedy designed to safeguard against future violations of Fourth Amendment rights through the rule's general deterrent effect. As with any remedial device, the rule's application has been restricted to those instances where its remedial objectives are thought most efficaciously served." *Arizona v. Evans*, 514 U.S. 1, 10–11, 115 S. Ct. 1185, 131 L. Ed. 2d 34 (1995).

- "[T]he practice of denying criminal defendants an exclusionary remedy from Fourth Amendment violations when those errors occur despite the good faith of the Government actors does not require the affirmance of petitioner's conviction in this case. Finding the deterrent remedy of suppression not compelled by the Fourth Amendment that case specifically relied on the objectionable collateral consequence of the interference with the criminal justice system's truth-finding function in requiring a blanket exclusionary remedy for all violations and the relative ineffectiveness of such remedy to deter future Fourth Amendment violations in particular cases." *Ryder v. U.S.*, 515 U.S. 177, 185–86, 115 S. Ct. 2031, 132 L. Ed. 2d 136 (1995).

- "The application of the exclusionary rule to suppress evidence obtained by an officer acting in objectively reasonable reliance on a statute would have as little deterrent effect on the officer's actions as would the exclusion of evidence when an officer acts in objectively reasonable reliance on a warrant. Unless a statute is clearly unconstitutional, an officer cannot be expected to question the judgment of the legislature that passed the law. . . . Penalizing the officer for the [legislature's] error, rather than his own, cannot logically contribute to the deterrence of Fourth Amendment violations." *Illinois v. Krull*, 480 U.S. 340, 349–50, 107 S. Ct. 1160, 94 L. Ed. 2d 364 (1987).
- "[T]he Fourth Amendment exclusionary rule should be modified so as not to bar the use in the prosecution's case-in-chief of evidence obtained by officers acting in reasonable reliance on a search warrant issued by a detached and neutral magistrate but ultimately found to be unsupported by probable cause." *U.S. v. Leon*, 468 U.S. 897, 900, 104 S. Ct. 3405, 82 L. Ed. 2d 677 (1984).
- "[T]he exclusionary rule is designed to deter police misconduct rather than to punish the errors of judges and magistrates. [T]here exists no evidence suggesting that judges and magistrates are inclined to ignore or subvert the Fourth Amendment or that lawlessness among these actors requires application of the extreme sanction of exclusion." *U.S. v. Leon*, 468 U.S. 897, 916, 104 S. Ct. 3405, 82 L. Ed. 2d 677 (1984).

First Circuit

- "Ordinarily, this makes good sense: when the affiant has no substantial reason to doubt the veracity or completeness of the information included in her affidavit, a failure either to verify the accuracy of that information or to go in search of contrary information is not reckless. But this general rule—like virtually every general rule—admits of at least one exception. To understand the operation of this exception, some background is necessary. The *Franks* Court established that a defendant is entitled to an evidentiary hearing to test the veracity of a warrant affidavit if he can make a substantial showing that the affiant, with reckless disregard for the truth, included a materially false statement in the affidavit. We have previously held that a material omission from a warrant affidavit, no less than the inclusion of a materially false statement, may furnish the basis for a successful *Franks* challenge when that omission was made with similar recklessness. . . . [W]hen proffering the warrant application, Nolet 'understood full well that [Wiggin's] credibility was at issue, based on his [altered prescription] conviction, if nothing else.' . . . In addition, Nolet knew that Wiggin's history included the altered prescription conviction and that he had experienced other 'scrapes' with the law. Given that Nolet's case for probable cause depended entirely on Wiggin's account, we think that this web of circumstantial evidence sent up a red flag—and that red flag may have been sufficient to create a duty of further inquiry. To sum up, our holding is that the district court erred in ruling as a matter of law that an affiant never has a duty to make further inquiry before presenting a warrant application to a magistrate. Because the court below, erroneously relying on its categorical disavowal of any duty of further inquiry, did not pose any of the further questions that had to be asked, we must regard its order denying the appellant's motion to suppress as without force pending the completion of the further proceedings described below." *U.S. v. Tanguay*, 787 F.3d 44, 52–53 (1st Cir. 2015) (citations omitted).

Third Circuit

- "[W]e cannot say that Nardinger acted deliberately, recklessly, or with gross negligence in executing the warrant. Nardinger should have shown the attachment to [the defendant], but that misstep—stemming from his inexperience and misunderstanding of the magistrate judge's order—does not mean that he deliberately violated [the defendant]'s Fourth Amendment rights. In short, application of the exclusionary rule would provide little deterrent effect and would not justify the costs of suppression." *U.S. v. Franz*, 772 F.3d 134, 149 (3d Cir. 2014).

Fourth Circuit

- "Reasonableness does not, by definition, entail

401

perfection. Rather, the reasonableness inquiry acknowledges the ambiguous and often dangerous circumstances confronting officers in the process of executing
search warrants and therefore affords officers 'some
latitude for honest mistakes.' " *U.S. v. Phillips*, 588
F.3d 218 (4th Cir. 2009).

Fifth Circuit

- "The good-faith exception requires answering the question of 'whether a reasonably well-trained officer would
have known that the search was illegal despite the
magistrate's authorization.' We have held there is no
good faith if one of four circumstances exists:

  (1) If the issuing magistrate/judge was misled by information in an affidavit that the affiant knew was false or
  would have known except for reckless disregard of the
  truth; (2) where the issuing magistrate/judge wholly
  abandoned his or her judicial role; (3) where the warrant
  is based on an affidavit so lacking in indicia of probable
  cause as to render official belief in its existence entirely
  unreasonable; and (4) where the warrant is so facially
  deficient in failing to particularize the place to be
  searched or the things to be seized that the executing officers cannot reasonably presume it to be valid."
  U.S. v. Triplett, 684 F.3d 500, 504 (5th Cir. 2012).

- "The hurdle for obtaining suppression on that basis is 'a
high one.' Officers are not ordinarily expected to question a magistrate's judgment as to probable cause. This
is so because magistrates are considered more qualified
than law enforcement in making that assessment.
Courts will not suppress evidence even when the affidavit fails to establish probable cause, unless it is obvious
that no reasonably competent officer would have
concluded that the warrant should issue. This will occur when a magistrate has not only acted mistakenly in
authorizing the warrant, but has fallen outside the
range of professional competence." *U.S. v. Triplett*, 684
F.3d 500, 506 (5th Cir. 2012) (quotations and citations
omitted).

Sixth Circuit

- "In *United States v. Laughton,* we explained that good-
faith reliance on a subsequently invalidated warrant is
impossible in four situations:

(1) when the warrant is issued on the basis of an affidavit that the affiant knows (or is reckless in not knowing) contains false information;

(2) when the issuing magistrate abandons his neutral and detached role and serves as a rubber stamp for police activities;

(3) when the affidavit is so lacking in indicia of probable cause that a belief in its existence is objectively unreasonable; and

(4) when the warrant is so facially deficient that it cannot reasonably be presumed to be valid.

. . . Here, Silvey argues only that the third situation exists, contending that the affidavit was so barren of detail that a reasonable officer would have known that the warrant did not meet constitutional standards. Thus, the question becomes 'whether the officers in the instant case had a reasonable basis to believe that the information that was submitted [to the magistrate] supported the issuance of a warrant.' . . . To answer that question, we must consider the definition of probable cause. As the Supreme Court explained in *Gates,* probable cause exists when there is a fair probability, given the totality of the circumstances, that agents will find contraband or evidence of a crime in a particular place. For this standard to be met, there must be a nexus between the place to be searched and the evidence sought. In addition, the information relied upon to establish probable cause cannot be stale; there must be some indication that the evidence sought will be found at the time of the search." *U.S. v. Silvey,* 393 Fed. Appx. 301, 305 (6th Cir. 2010) (citations omitted).

- "However, when it comes to probable cause, the name says it all; certainty is never required, only a fair probability. When the issue is one of good-faith reliance, even less is necessary." *U.S. v. Silvey,* 393 Fed. Appx. 301, 306 (6th Cir. 2010).

- "The language and legislative history of Title III strongly militate against engrafting the good-faith exception into Title III warrants . . . . (T)he language in Title III provides that exclusion is the exclusive remedy for an illegally obtained warrant. In contrast to the law governing probable cause under the Fourth Amendment, the law governing electronic surveillance via wiretap is codified in a comprehensive statutory scheme providing explicit requirements, procedures, and protections . . . (T)he district court did not err in suppressing the fruits of the wiretap. . .because there is no good-faith exception for warrants improperly issued under Title III." *U.S. v. Rice*, 478 F.3d 704, 2007 FED App. 0088P (6th Cir. 2007).

- "Consequently, this Court concludes that, although the search warrant itself did not describe the second house with particularity or contain probable cause to search the second house, and although the affidavit was not properly incorporated into the warrant and did not, at any rate, contain probable cause to search the second house, the evidence seized during the search was nevertheless admissible pursuant to the good-faith exception in Leon. . . . Under the facts of this case, we conclude that the affidavit was not so lacking in indicia of probable cause as to render official belief in its existence entirely unreasonable." *U.S. v. Watkins*, 179 F.3d 489, 499, 1999 FED App. 0213P (6th Cir. 1999).

Seventh Circuit

- "A few unreliable informants are not much better than one. . . . If an officer cannot demonstrate that an informant is reliable, then citing additional anonymous informants of unknown reliability does little to establish the factual foundation[s] that we[re] found lacking in *Koerth*. Nonetheless . . . [under the instant] circumstances, [the investigating officer]'s failure to recognize that the warrant did not establish probable cause does not amount to a lack of good faith and the exclusionary rule is not the appropriate remedy." *U.S. v. Bell*, 585 F.3d 1045 (7th Cir. 2009).

- "Under the good faith doctrine, evidence recovered during the execution of a facially-valid search warrant that is later invalidated by the courts is not always subject to suppression. . . . Suppression is appropriate only if the officers were dishonest or reckless in preparing their affidavit or could not have harbored an objectively reasonable belief in the existence of probable cause." *U.S. v. Spry*, 190 F.3d 829, 834 (7th Cir. 1999).

- "Although *Whren* was decided in the context of a traffic stop, we think it is instructive here. . . . [T]he subjective intentions of the Drug Task Force officer played no role in the probable cause analysis in this case. The officer was rightfully on the scene pursuant to a valid warrant allowing a search for evidence of hunting violations. That the Drug Task Force officer might have hoped to find evidence relating to cocaine trafficking is irrelevant to the Fourth Amendment analysis under *Whren*, because once probable cause exists, and a valid warrant has been issued, the officer's subjective intent in conducting the search is irrelevant." *U.S. v. Van Dreel*, 155 F.3d 902, 904–05 (7th Cir. 1998).

Eighth Circuit

- "Since the application of the test is fact driven, we review the facts here. The flash drive and computer were originally seized in May 2007 under a valid search warrant. The equipment then remained in the custody of law enforcement until agent Weidman was faced with disposing property in January 2008. Before reviewing any of the evidence Weidman went to the county attorney's office for instructions on the correct way to dispose of property. The county attorney's office told him to apply to a state court judge for a disposal of property order. Weidman went to the state court and provided it with a list of the property seized from Koch's home under the original warrant. A state court judge then issued an order for the disposal of property, leaving to agent discretion which means of disposal was appropriate for particular evidence. It was only after the order was obtained from the state court that agent Weidman and those assisting him reviewed any of the evidence they were considering for disposal or for training use. When they came to the flash drive, they believed it was necessary to view its contents to make sure that it did not contain gambling information and could therefore be returned to Koch . . . We conclude that Weidman and the other agents were acting in good faith when they opened the flash drive and unexpectedly discovered child pornography. Before looking into any equipment they had not simply relied on the original warrant, but sought legal advice from the county attorney's office which they then followed by applying for a court order. It was while they were in the process of following the court's directions about disposal of the property seized under that warrant and checking for any gambling material on the flash drive that they came across the pornographic pictures involving young girls. They did not prolong the viewing but closed the drive within just a few minutes . . . . Whether or not the state court should have done more in response to agent Weidman's request for a disposal order, instructed him to obtain a new warrant, or tailored the order more specifically is immaterial in terms of the exclusionary rule. That was illustrated in *Leon*. There, a magistrate judge was found to have erred in finding probable cause for a warrant which police officers used to conduct a search. The Supreme Court concluded that the Fourth Amendment exclusionary rule should not be applied under those circumstances, for the rule is 'designed to deter police misconduct rather than to punish the errors of judges and magistrates.' Since the officers had acted in good faith, the evidence should not have been suppressed." *U.S. v. Koch*, 625 F.3d 470, 477-78 (8th Cir. 2010).

- "Even if the warrant application were deficient, the search was lawful under the good-faith exception of *United States v. Leon* . . . Under this exception, absent allegations that the magistrate was not neutral, suppression is appropriate only if the officers were dishonest or reckless in preparing their affidavit or could not have harbored an objectively reasonable belief in the existence of probable cause." *U.S. v. Etheridge*, 165 F.3d 655, 658 (8th Cir. 1999).

- "[W]hen assessing the objective good faith of police officers executing a warrant, we must look to the totality of the circumstances, including any information known to the officers but not presented to the issuing judge." *U.S. v. Weeks*, 160 F.3d 1210, 1212 (8th Cir. 1998).

Ninth Circuit

- "Although we reject the *Freedman* court's specific formulation of the good faith test, we agree that the test of good faith reliance under § 2707(e) should contain both an objective and subjective element. Accordingly, we now hold that the good faith defense under 18 U.S.C. § 2707(e) is met when the defendant complies with a subpoena (or other process detailed in § 2707(e) of the SCA) that appears valid on its face, in the absence of any indication of irregularity sufficient to put the defendant on notice that the subpoena may be invalid or contrary to applicable law. A defendant may not benefit from the good faith defense, however, if the defendant actually knew that the subpoena (or other process) was invalid under the applicable law. Thus, whether a particular defendant satisfies the requirements to establish 'good faith reliance' is a mixed question of law and fact. Whether the defendant actually knew that a subpoena was invalid is a question of fact. Whether the defendant's belief in the subpoena's validity was objectively reasonable is itself a mixed question of law and fact. If there are disputed issues of material fact as to the 'historical facts of what the [defendant] knew or what he did, it is clear that these are questions of fact for the jury to determine.' Whether those 'historical facts' support an objective belief that the defendant acted reasonably, however, is a question of law to be decided by the court." *Sams v. Yahoo! Inc.*, 713 F.3d 1175, 1180-81 (9th Cir. 2013) (citations omitted).

Tenth Circuit

- "Under the *Leon* exception, improperly obtained evidence remains admissible when the executing agents 'act with an objectively "reasonable good-faith belief" that their conduct is lawful or when their conduct involves only simple, "isolated" negligence . . . .' The Supreme Court has identified five situations where the exception does not apply:
  1. the affiant obtains the warrant by recklessly or intentionally supplying false information to the judge,
  2. the judge abandons his or her judicial role,
  3. the executing officers cannot reasonably believe that probable cause existed,
  4. the warrant is facially deficient, and
  5. the warrant is based on a '"bare bones" affidavit' and the officers 'then rely on colleagues who are ignorant of the circumstances under which the warrant was obtained to conduct the search.' "

United States v. Workman, 863 F.3d 1313, 1317–18 (10th Cir. 2017) (citations omitted).

- "An executing officer is generally presumed to be acting in good-faith reliance upon a warrant. However, this presumption is not absolute. There are four situations in which the presumption of good faith and, consequently, the good-faith exception to the exclusionary rule do not apply: (1) when the issuing magistrate was misled by an affidavit containing false information or information that the affiant would have known was false if not for his reckless disregard of the truth; (2) when the issuing magistrate wholly abandon[s her] judicial role; (3) when the affidavit in support of the warrant is so lacking in indicia of probable cause as to render official belief in its existence entirely unreasonable; and (4) when a warrant is so facially deficient that the executing officer could not reasonably believe it was valid." *U.S. v. Augustine*, 742 F.3d 1258 (10th Cir. 2014) (inner quotations and citations omitted).

- "Before delving into *Leon,* we note that we do not decide whether the good-faith exception applies in the Title III context, a question unresolved in our circuit and on which other circuits are split. We need not wade in these murky waters because, as the parties conceded and as we agree, there is no Title III suppression mechanism for GPS data. Our analysis starts and ends with *Leon.* Under *Leon,* we presume good-faith when an officer acts pursuant to a warrant unless one of 'four contexts' apply. Mr. Barajas claims that one such context applies here—the 'affidavit [was] so lacking in indicia of probable cause as to render official belief in its existence entirely unreasonable.' He argues that the affidavit is 'devoid of facts' as to why 'communications between the suspects' might be found in the GPS data. The stumbling block to Mr. Barajas's argument is that he construes the affidavit too technically, focusing on what the affidavit *literally* requests and where the government *literally* searched. But, as noted above, 'the Fourth Amendment's commands. . .are practical and not abstract.' We cannot limit our analysis to what the affidavit requests. Rather, we must ask whether the affidavit as a whole 'establishes a minimally sufficient nexus between the illegal activity and the place to be searched.' [W]e impose a lower standard in good-faith determinations than we do with probable cause, only requiring 'a minimal nexus' as compared to 'a substantial nexus.' . . . . However, even if the affidavit is not 'devoid of facts,' the good-faith exception will not apply when an officer 'knows or should have known that a search warrant was invalid.' We presume that law enforcement officials have a reasonable knowledge of the law. Mr. Barajas suggests the agents knew or should have known the order was invalid because they knew (1) that GPS data is not typically intercepted pursuant to a wiretap order; and (2) that the affidavit did not request GPS data. We disagree. First, we have no reason to believe the government cannot obtain GPS data through a wiretap order. Assuming pinging is a search, the burden to obtain GPS data would be no greater than a wiretap—probable cause. But even if Mr. Barajas is correct, he cannot show the agents were on notice of this fact because the law on electronic surveillance is very much unsettled. The agents' knowledge of the gap between the affidavit and the order gives us more pause, but we cannot say this gap was intentional." *U.S. v. Barajas*, 710 F.3d 1102, 1110–11 (10th Cir. 2013) (citations omitted).

- "With respect to the mismatched description and address of the place to be searched, [Defendant] emphasizes the officers' knowledge of the inaccuracy well before the search and their considered choice not to obtain an accurate warrant. Obtaining a corrected warrant may have been the better choice, particularly since there was ample time to do so, but the error does not warrant suppression of the evidence. Regardless of the error concerning the address, the issuing judge clearly intended for the officers to search the residence described and depicted in the warrant application. There was never any doubt about which residence police should search; this practical reality outweighs the technical error in the warrant. . . . . The photograph and description of [Defendant's] home in the affidavit, combined with the knowledge of the agents involved, enabled the executing officers to locate the premises without difficulty or confusion and virtually eliminated the possibility of searching the wrong residence. The district court did not err in denying *Garcia*'s motion to suppress." *U.S. v. Garcia*, 707 F.3d 1190 (10th Cir. 2013).

- "Because the *Leon* exception cannot be applied when execution of the warrant was not limited to things for which probable cause to search had been shown, proper execution of an invalid warrant is a pre-condition: if the pre-condition exists, then the court should apply the objective good faith test to the warrant, asking whether a reasonably trained officer could have believed that the search was authorized in spite of the defect in the warrant.. . .*Leon* does not apply if the execution of the warrant was improper." *U.S. v. Potts*, 586 F.3d 823 (10th Cir. 2009).

- "Although we have determined that the supporting affidavit did not establish probable cause, we cannot say it was so facially insufficient under the state of law at the time he obtained the warrant that [the] Agent. . .should have known the search was illegal despite the magistrate's authorization." *U.S. v. Tuter*, 240 F.3d 1292, 1300, 178 A.L.R. Fed. 675 (10th Cir. 2001).

- "This court concludes the search warrant failed to establish probable cause because the nexus between the alleged criminal activity and [Defendant]'s residence was insufficient. Nonetheless, the district court did not err in refusing to suppress the evidence seized because the officer acted in objectively reasonable, good-faith reliance on the warrant." *U.S. v. Danhauer*, 229 F.3d 1002, 1007–08 (10th Cir. 2000).

- "Application of the good-faith exception in this case is. . .consistent with the exception's rationale. As the Court stated in *Leon*, the exclusionary rule should only be applied in those unusual cases when its purpose, to deter police misconduct, will be furthered. . . . As indicated, the officers' reliance in this case on the magistrate's determination of probable cause was not objectively unreasonable, and there is no indication in the record that the officers were involved in any misconduct in executing the warrant. Penalizing the officers for a mistake not their own cannot logically contribute to the deterrence of Fourth Amendment violations. . . . Consequently, the evidence seized at [Defendant]'s home pursuant to the warrant need not be suppressed." *U.S. v. Rowland*, 145 F.3d 1194, 1208 (10th Cir. 1998).

Eleventh Circuit

- "[First, t]he deterrent purpose of the exclusionary rule necessarily assumes that the police have engaged in willful, or at the very least negligent, conduct which has deprived the defendant of some right." [citation omitted] The conduct in question in this case is the failure of someone inside the Dale County Sheriff's Department to record in that department's records the fact that the arrest warrant for [defendant] had been recalled or rescinded by the court or by the clerk's office. That failure to bring the records up to date is 'at the very least negligent.' [citation omitted] We will assume for present purposes that the negligent actor, who is unidentified in the record, is an adjunct to law enforcement in Dale County and is to be treated for purposes of the exclusionary rule as a police officer. [citation omitted] . . . [S]econd[,] . . . applying the exclusionary rule to these circumstances. . .will not deter bad record-keeping to any appreciable extent, if at all. There are several reasons for this. For one thing, the conduct in question is a negligent failure to act, not a deliberate or tactical choice to act. There is no reason to believe that anyone in the Dale County Sheriff's Department weighed the possible ramifications of being negligent and decided to be careless in record-keeping. Deterrents work best where the targeted conduct results from conscious decision making, because only if the decision maker considers the possible results of her actions can she be deterred. . . . Another reason that excluding evidence resulting from the negligent failure to update records is unlikely to reduce to any significant extent that type of negligence is that there are already abundant incentives for keeping records current. . . . There is also the unique circumstance here that the exclusionary sanction would be levied not in a case brought by officers of the department that was guilty of the negligent record keeping, but instead it would scuttle a case brought by officers of a different department in another county, one whose officers and personnel were entirely innocent of any wrongdoing or carelessness. We do not mean to suggest that Dale County law enforcement agencies are not interested in the successful prosecution of crime throughout the state, but their primary responsibility and interest lies in their own cases. Hop-

ing to gain a beneficial deterrent effect on Dale County
personnel by excluding evidence in a case brought by
Coffee County officers would be like telling a student
that if he skips school one of his classmates will be
punished. The student may not exactly relish the prospect of causing another to suffer, but human nature being what it is, he is unlikely to fear that prospect as
much as he would his own suffering. For all of these
reasons, we are convinced that this is one of those situations where '[a]ny incremental deterrent effect which
might be achieved by extending the rule. . .is uncertain at best,' [citation omitted] where the benefits of
suppression would be 'marginal or nonexistent,' [cita-
tion omitted] and where the exclusionary rule would
not 'pay its way by deterring official lawlessness.' [cita-
tion omitted] [A]ny minimal deterrence that might
result from applying the exclusionary rule in these circumstances would not outweigh the heavy cost of
excluding otherwise admissible and highly probative
evidence. [citation omitted] . . . [W]e note. . .that the
test for reasonable police conduct is objective. [citation
omitted] The district court found that 'there [was] no
credible evidence of routine problems with disposing of
recalled warrants' and updating records in Dale County,
and [defendant] does not contest that finding. If faulty
record-keeping were to become endemic in that county,
however, officers in Coffee County might have a difficult time establishing that their reliance on records
from their neighboring county was objectively
reasonable. The good faith exception to the exclusionary
rule does not shelter evidence that was obtained in an
unconstitutional arrest or search that was based on
objectively unreliable information." *U.S. v. Herring*, 492
F.3d 1212, 1214–1219 (11th Cir. 2007), judgment aff'd,
555 U.S. 135, 129 S. Ct. 695, 172 L. Ed. 2d 496 (2009).

- "[T]he warrant in this case, even if subsequently
determined by the district court to be overly broad, was
not so facially deficient—i.e., failing to particularize the
place to be searched or the things to be seized—that the
executing officers could not have reasonably presumed
it to be valid. . . .The application of the good faith
exception to the exclusionary rule, therefore, is not
precluded in this case by a warrant that no reasonable

officer could have relied upon." *U.S. v. Travers*, 233 F.3d 1327, 1330 (11th Cir. 2000).

Chapter 6

Warrantless Searches

§ 6:1   Presumption: A warrantless search is presumed to
be unreasonable

§ 6:2   Burden of proof: The prosecution must establish
the validity of a warrantless search

§ 6:3   Exceptions: Many exceptions to the warrant
requirement have been recognized. Their
elements are set forth in subsequent chapters

Research References

West's Key Number Digest
Arrest ⊕68; Searches and Seizures ⊕23 to 24, 42, 47, 58, 192

KeyCite®: Cases and other legal materials listed in KeyCite Scope can be
researched through the KeyCite service on Westlaw®. Use KeyCite to
check citations for form, parallel references, prior and later history, and
comprehensive citator information, including citations to other decisions
and secondary materials.

---

§ 6:1   Presumption: A warrantless search is presumed to be unreasonable

Supreme Court

- "A warrantless search by the police is invalid unless it
  falls within one of the narrow and well-delineated
  exceptions to the warrant requirement." *Flippo v. West
  Virginia*, 528 U.S. 11, 13, 120 S. Ct. 7, 145 L. Ed. 2d 16
  (1999).

- "Time and again, this Court has observed that searches
  and seizures conducted outside the judicial process,
  without prior approval by judge or magistrate, are *per
  se* unreasonable under the Fourth Amendment—subject
  only to a few specifically established and well delineated
  exceptions." *Minnesota v. Dickerson*, 508 U.S. 366, 372,
  113 S. Ct. 2130, 124 L. Ed. 2d 334 (1993).

- "Although the homicide investigators in this case may

well have had probable cause to search the premises, it is undisputed that they did not obtain a warrant. Therefore, for the search to be valid, it must fall within one of the narrow and specifically delineated exceptions to the warrant requirement. In *Mincey v. Arizona*, we unanimously rejected the contention that one of the exceptions to the warrant clause is a murder scene exception. Although we noted that police may make warrantless entries on premises where they reasonably believe that a person within is in need of immediate aid, and that they may make a prompt warrantless search of the area to see if there are other victims or if a killer is still on the premises, we held that the murder scene exception is inconsistent with the Fourth and Fourteenth Amendments." *Thompson v. Louisiana*, 469 U.S. 17, 20–21, 105 S. Ct. 409, 83 L. Ed. 2d 246 (1984).

- "It is a first principle of Fourth Amendment jurisprudence that the police may not conduct a search unless they first convince a neutral magistrate that there is probable cause to do so." *New York v. Belton*, 453 U.S. 454, 457, 101 S. Ct. 2860, 69 L. Ed. 2d 768 (1981).

- "The search without a warrant can survive constitutional inhibition only upon a showing that the surrounding facts brought it within one of the exceptions to the rule that a search must rest upon a search warrant." *Stoner v. State of Cal.*, 376 U.S. 483, 486, 84 S. Ct. 889, 11 L. Ed. 2d 856 (1964).

- "Any assumption that evidence sufficient to support a magistrate's disinterested determination to issue a search warrant will justify the officers in making a search without a warrant would reduce the [Fourth] Amendment to a nullity and leave the people's homes secure only in the discretion of police officers." *Johnson v. U.S.*, 333 U.S. 10, 14, 68 S. Ct. 367, 92 L. Ed. 436 (1948).

First Circuit

- "As was the case here, police often rely on tips from confidential informants to underlie probable cause. But the principle is long-standing that '[e]ven where a search warrant is obtained, the police must show a basis for the search beyond the mere fact of an assertion by an informer.' It follows then that '[a]t least as much is required to support a search without a warrant.' Therefore, when, as here, 'the primary basis for a probable cause determination is information provided by a confidential informant,' law enforcement must 'provide some information from which a [court] can credit the informant's credibility.' In other words, a 'probable cause finding may be based on an informant's tip so long as the probability of a lying or inaccurate informer has been sufficiently reduced.' Applying these factors to the instant case, we find that there is simply no indication on this record that the police explored the Informant's basis of knowledge for the information he relayed, or that the police bothered to corroborate any of the information that actually suggested that criminal activity was afoot at Cruz–Ramos's home. Even if we were to agree with the district court that the information the Informant provided was detailed, we find that because the police did not sufficiently test the reliability of the detailed information, the denial of the motion to suppress cannot stand." *U.S. v. Ramirez-Rivera*, 800 F.3d 1, 27–28 (1st Cir. 2015) (citations omitted).

Third Circuit

- "[A] warrantless search of a closed wallet is an unreasonable search under the Fourth Amendment unless it is justified by one of the recognized exceptions to the warrant requirement. . . . [A] 'billfold offered no immediately apparent evidence of an inculpatory nature. It was only after the billfold itself had been searched that the large denomination currency was revealed.' " *U.S. v. Rivera-Padilla*, 365 Fed. Appx. 343 (3d Cir. 2010).

- "To search a person's home and belongings, police officers ordinarily must first seek a warrant based on probable cause supported by oath or affirmation. Warrantless searches are presumptively unreasonable under the Fourth Amendment." *Parkhurst v. Trapp*, 77 F.3d 707, 711 (3d Cir. 1996).

Fifth Circuit

- "[Defendant] argues that the district court erred in focusing on whether he had a valid privacy interest in his clothing at the time the police seized them [from a

417

hospital], because the existence of a privacy interest is relevant to the constitutionality of a search, not a seizure. He urges that an illegal seizure can take place even in the absence of a valid privacy interest in the seized item as long as the defendant establishes that the seizure interfered with his constitutionally protected possessory interests in the property. Moreover, he argues, even if an officer would be justified in a brief temporary search or seizure of property based on the theory that a defendant does not have a reasonable expectation of privacy in the property, a permanent seizure such as occurred in this case is not allowed without a warrant or without proof by the Government that an exception to the warrant requirement existed. We find [defendant's] arguments meritorious. The Government's contentions that [defendant] had no valid possessory interest in the clothing because he abandoned that interest and that the hospital was a joint possessor of the clothing are unavailing. Numerous courts have held that an emergency room patient does not forfeit his possessory rights to clothing simply by walking (or in many cases being carried) through the hospital door. We agree with other jurisdictions that have addressed the issue. [Defendant] did not forfeit his possessory interest in his clothing by entering [the hospital] and that the officers presumptively violated his Fourth Amendment rights in retrieving the clothes from the hospital. The Government presented no evidence indicating that Neely had done anything to suggest he had given up the possessory interest in his clothes, and the hospital's policy of placing the clothing in a bag and putting it in a locker in the clothing storage room suggested that it was holding the clothes for him until he recovered. . . .Therefore we find that [defendant] retained a sufficient possessory interest in the clothes to complain of this seizure and that, absent application of an exception to the warrant requirement, we must hold the seizure unreasonable under the Fourth Amendment." *U.S. v. Neely*, 345 F.3d 366 (5th Cir. 2003).

Sixth Circuit

- "The Fourth Amendment provides that the right of the

people to be secure in their persons, houses papers and effects, against unreasonable searches and seizures, shall not be violated. This principle generally prohibits the warrantless entry of law enforcement personnel into a person's home." *U.S. v. Ivy*, 165 F.3d 397, 401, 1998 FED App. 0381P (6th Cir. 1998).

- "The Fourth Amendment generally requires police officers to obtain a warrant before searching or seizing persons, houses, papers, and effects. This constitutional protection also applies to hotel rooms." *U.S. v. Allen*, 106 F.3d 695, 698, 1997 FED App. 0049P (6th Cir. 1997).

Seventh Circuit

- "A search is generally considered unreasonable unless the government obtains a warrant issued upon probable cause." *U.S. v. Basinski*, 226 F.3d 829, 833 (7th Cir. 2000).

- "Under the Fourth Amendment, a search usually is not reasonable unless the government obtains a warrant issued upon probable cause; there are, however, certain limited exceptions. . . .To be a reasonable search without a warrant and probable cause, the government must show a special need, beyond the normal need for law enforcement, that makes the warrant and probable cause requirement impracticable." *Joy v. Penn-Harris-Madison School Corp.*, 212 F.3d 1052, 1058, 144 Ed. Law Rep. 866 (7th Cir. 2000).

Eighth Circuit

- "The Fourth Amendment to the United States Constitution provides a right to be free from unreasonable searches and seizures, a right that generally—though not always—translates into a warrant requirement." *Brayman v. U.S.*, 96 F.3d 1061, 1065 (8th Cir. 1996).

- "The Fourth Amendment does not require that a warrant be obtained in every case. Nevertheless, one governing principle, justified by history and by current experience, has consistently been followed: except in certain carefully defined classes of cases, a search of private property without proper consent is unreasonable unless it has been authorized by a valid search warrant." *U.S. v. Boettger*, 71 F.3d 1410, 1413 (8th Cir. 1995).

419

Ninth Circuit
- "The presumption of unconstitutionality that accompanies the warrantless entry into a home to conduct a search or make an arrest may be overcome only by showing consent or exigent circumstances." *Lopez-Rodriguez v. Mukasey*, 536 F.3d 1012, 40 A.L.R. Fed. 2d 767 (9th Cir. 2008).
- "The search warrant requirement arose from the Founder's understanding that power is a heady thing; and history shows that the police acting on their own cannot be trusted." *U.S. v. Gantt*, 194 F.3d 987, 991 (9th Cir. 1999) (overruled on other grounds by, U.S. v. W.R. Grace, 526 F.3d 499 (9th Cir. 2008)).

§ 6:2   Burden of proof: The prosecution must establish the validity of a warrantless search

Supreme Court
- "[T]he burden is on those seeking the exemption to show the need for it." *U.S. v. Jeffers*, 342 U.S. 48, 51, 72 S. Ct. 93, 96 L. Ed. 59, 41 A.F.T.R. (P-H) P 130 (1951).
- "We are not dealing with formalities. The presence of a search warrant serves a high function. Absent some grave emergency, the Fourth Amendment has interposed a magistrate between the citizen and the police. This was done not to shield criminals nor to make the home a safe haven for illegal activities. It was done so that an objective mind might weigh the need to invade that privacy in order to enforce the law. The right of privacy was deemed too precious to entrust to the discretion of those whose job is the detection of crime and the arrest of criminals. Power is a heady thing; and history shows that the police acting on their own cannot be trusted. And so the Constitution requires a magistrate to pass on the desires of the police before they violate the privacy of the home. We cannot be true to that constitutional requirement and excuse the absence of a search warrant without a showing by those who seek exemption from the constitutional mandate that the exigencies of the situation made that course imperative." *McDonald v. U.S.*, 335 U.S. 451, 455–56, 69 S. Ct. 191, 93 L. Ed. 153 (1948).

First Circuit

- "A warrantless search of a private residence is presumptively unreasonable under the Fourth Amendment. The government therefore must prove that the initial search came within some recognized exception to the Fourth Amendment warrant requirement. Generally speaking, absent probable cause and exigent circumstances the Fourth Amendment bars warrantless, nonconsensual entries of private residences." *U.S. v. Tibolt*, 72 F.3d 965, 968–69 (1st Cir. 1995).

Second Circuit

- "If it is established that the place or object subjected to the warrantless search is one in which the plaintiff has a reasonable expectation of privacy, the [Prosecution] has the burden of showing that the search was valid because it fell within one of the exceptions to the warrant requirement." *McCardle v. Haddad*, 131 F.3d 43, 48 (2d Cir. 1997).

Third Circuit

- "However, certain circumstances can excuse the warrant requirement. Among these are an inventory search incident to a lawful arrest objects in plain view of the officers and exigent circumstances. To excuse the absence of a warrant, the burden rests on the State to show the existence of these exceptional situations." *Parkhurst v. Trapp*, 77 F.3d 707, 711 (3d Cir. 1996).

Fifth Circuit

- "When a warrantless search or seizure is conducted, the burden shifts to the government to justify the warrantless search." *U.S. v. Jones*, 234 F.3d 234, 239 (5th Cir. 2000).
- "The government bears the ultimate burden of proof when it searches without a warrant." *U.S. v. Rivas*, 157 F.3d 364, 368 (5th Cir. 1998).

Sixth Circuit

- "In the absence of a warrant authorizing the officers' entry into Defendant's home, the Government must overcome the presumption that this entry was unreasonable." *U.S. v. Rohrig*, 98 F.3d 1506, 1515, 1996 FED App. 0346P (6th Cir. 1996).

Seventh Circuit

- "Where the government obtains evidence in a search conducted pursuant to one of these exceptions, it bears the burden of establishing that the exception applies." *U.S. v. Basinski*, 226 F.3d 829, 833 (7th Cir. 2000).

Eighth Circuit

- "Because the search in this case was conducted without a warrant, the burden is on the government, as the district court recognized, to prove that the search comported with the requirements of the Fourth Amendment. That is to say, the warrantless search of luggage is presumptively unreasonable and thus presumptively unconstitutional." *U.S. v. Rouse*, 148 F.3d 1040, 1041 (8th Cir. 1998) (rejected on other grounds by, U.S. v. Runyan, 275 F.3d 449 (5th Cir. 2001)).

Tenth Circuit

- "The government has the burden of proving that an exception to the warrant requirement applies." *U.S. v. Edwards*, 242 F.3d 928, 937 (10th Cir. 2001), superseded, 632 F.3d 633 (10th Cir. 2001).
- "The government bears the burden of proving exigency. . . . In assessing whether the burden was met, we are guided by the realities of the situation presented by the record. We should evaluate the circumstances as they would have appeared to prudent, cautious, and trained officers. . . . There is no absolute test for determining whether exigent circumstances are present because such a determination ultimately depends on the unique facts of each controversy. . . . [W]e should remember that, as an exception to the warrant requirement, exigent circumstances must be jealously and carefully drawn." *U.S. v. Anderson*, 154 F.3d 1225, 1233 (10th Cir. 1998).
- "It is a basic principle of Fourth Amendment law that searches and seizures inside a home without a warrant are presumptively unreasonable. Therefore, absent consent or exigent circumstances, police may not enter a citizen's residence without a warrant. When the police do seek to enter a home without a warrant, the government bears the burden of proving that sufficient

exigency exists." *U.S. v. Scroger*, 98 F.3d 1256, 1259 (10th Cir. 1996).

§ 6:3 Exceptions: Many exceptions to the warrant requirement have been recognized. Their elements are set forth in subsequent chapters

Supreme Court

- "The rule legitimizing warrantless searches that are conducted incident to a suspect's arrest covers searches that are incident to any lawful arrest, with constitutional law providing the reference point by which to judge the lawfulness of the arrest. [W]hile States are free to regulate such arrests however they desire, state restrictions do not alter the Fourth Amendment's protections. A custodial arrest of a suspect based on probable cause is a reasonable intrusion under the Fourth Amendment; and because that intrusion is lawful, a search incident to that arrest requires no additional justification. Interests justifying a search incident to an arrest, are the protection of the arresting officer and the safeguarding of evidence, which are present whenever an officer makes an arrest." *Virginia v. Moore*, 553 U.S. 164, 128 S. Ct. 1598, 170 L. Ed. 2d 559 (2008).

- "We. . .have made it clear that there are exceptions to the warrant requirement. When faced with special law enforcement needs, diminished expectations of privacy, minimal intrusions, or the like, the Court has found that certain general, or individual, circumstances may render a warrantless search or seizure reasonable." *Illinois v. McArthur*, 531 U.S. 326, 121 S. Ct. 946, 949, 148 L. Ed. 2d 838 (2001).

- "Since warrantless searches of a home are impermissible absent consent or exigent circumstances, we conclude that the instant search violated the Fourth Amendment." *Steagald v. U.S.*, 451 U.S. 204, 216, 101 S. Ct. 1642, 68 L. Ed. 2d 38 (1981).

- "[O]ur past decisions make clear that only in a few specifically established and well-delineated situations. . .may a warrantless search of a dwelling withstand constitutional scrutiny, even though the authorities have probable cause to conduct it. There is no suggestion that anyone consented to the search. The officers were not responding to an emergency. . . . They were not in hot pursuit of a fleeing felon. The goods ultimately seized were not in the process of destruction. Nor were they about to be removed from the jurisdiction." *Vale v. Louisiana*, 399 U.S. 30, 34–35, 90 S. Ct. 1969, 26 L. Ed. 2d 409 (1970).

First Circuit

- "As was the case here, police often rely on tips from confidential informants to underlie probable cause. But the principle is long-standing that '[e]ven where a search warrant is obtained, the police must show a basis for the search beyond the mere fact of an assertion by an informer.' It follows then that '[a]t least as much is required to support a search without a warrant.' Therefore, when, as here, 'the primary basis for a probable cause determination is information provided by a confidential informant,' law enforcement must 'provide some information from which a [court] can credit the informant's credibility.' In other words, a 'probable cause finding may be based on an informant's tip so long as the probability of a lying or inaccurate informer has been sufficiently reduced.' Applying these factors to the instant case, we find that there is simply no indication on this record that the police explored the Informant's basis of knowledge for the information he relayed, or that the police bothered to corroborate any of the information that actually suggested that criminal activity was afoot at Cruz–Ramos's home. Even if we were to agree with the district court that the information the Informant provided was detailed, we find that because the police did not sufficiently test the reliability of the detailed information, the denial of the motion to suppress cannot stand." *U.S. v. Ramirez-Rivera*, 800 F.3d 1, 27–28 (1st Cir. 2015) (citations omitted).
- "The Supreme Court has recognized a general rule that warrantless searches are presumptively unreasonable. . .while simultaneously acknowledging a few specifically established and well-delineated exceptions to this rule. . . ." *U.S. v. Jones*, 187 F.3d 210, 219 (1st Cir. 1999).

Second Circuit

- "When law enforcement officials take a vehicle into custody, they may search the vehicle and make an inventory of its contents without the need for a search warrant and without regard to whether there is probable cause to suspect that the vehicle contains contraband or evidence of criminal conduct. Separate itemization of every single object found in an automobile is not required for an inventory search to conform with the Fourth Amendment." *U.S. v. Lopez*, 547 F.3d 364 (2d Cir. 2008).

- "Where police officers were lawfully present in defendant's room by virtue of defendant's consent, the computer was in plain view, and, based on the information known to them at the time, the officers had probable cause to seize the computer." *U.S. v. O'Brien*, 303 Fed. Appx. 948 (2d Cir. 2008).

- "A warrantless search is per se unreasonable under the Fourth Amendment—subject only to a few specifically established and well-delineated exceptions. . . . Under the security check exception, when law enforcement officers have lawfully entered premises in connection with an arrest, they are entitled to make a quick and limited security check of the premises to be sure there are no persons or objects on the premises to pose a safety threat to the officers." *U.S. v. Kiyuyung*, 171 F.3d 78, 83 (2d Cir. 1999).

Third Circuit

- "The general rule is that warrantless searches are presumptively unreasonable. . . .The courts have, however, fashioned exceptions to the general rule, recognizing that in certain limited situations the government's interest in conducting a search without a warrant outweighs the individual's privacy interest." *U.S. v. Ubiles*, 224 F.3d 213, 216–17 (3d Cir. 2000), as amended, (Sept. 28, 2000).

Sixth Circuit

- "Where exceptions do exist to the general rule that warrantless searches of a home's curtilage violate the Fourth Amendment, they exist only in those exceptional circumstances in which special needs, beyond the normal need for law enforcement, make the warrant and probable-cause requirement impracticable." *Jacob v. Township of West Bloomfield*, 531 F.3d 385 (6th Cir. 2008).

- "It is axiomatic that the Fourth Amendment protects people from unreasonable government intrusions into their legitimate expectations of privacy. . . .and that absent some exception, police may not conduct a warrantless search of an individual's home. . . . One exception allows police to enter a residence without a warrant if there is probable cause to believe that there is a burglary in progress. . . . Another exception, of course, is a consensual search. . . . Both of these exceptions are circumscribed, however, by the object of the search. . . ." *U.S. v. Reed*, 141 F.3d 644, 648–49, 1998 FED App. 0110P (6th Cir. 1998).

- "Under the automobile exception to the warrant requirement, law enforcement officers may search a readily mobile vehicle without a warrant if they have probable cause to believe that the vehicle contains evidence of a crime." *U.S. v. Lumpkin*, 159 F.3d 983, 986, 1998 FED App. 0330P (6th Cir. 1998).

Seventh Circuit

- "Although the Fourth Amendment generally prohibits searches and seizures performed without a warrant, there is an exception when someone with actual or apparent authority consents to the search or seizure." *U.S. v. Aghedo*, 159 F.3d 308, 310 (7th Cir. 1998).

Eighth Circuit

- "Under the plain view doctrine, evidence may be seized without a warrant if the following three conditions are met: (1) the officer did not violate the Fourth Amendment in arriving at the place from which the evidence could be plainly viewed; (2) the object's incriminating character is immediately apparent; and (3) the officer has a lawful right of access to the object itself." *U.S. v. Armstrong*, 554 F.3d 1159 (8th Cir. 2009).

- "The plain view doctrine allows law enforcement officers to seize evidence without a warrant when the initial intrusion is lawful, the discovery of the evidence is inadvertent, and the incriminating nature of the evidence is immediately apparent." *U.S. v. Raines*, 243 F.3d 419, 422 (8th Cir. 2001).

- "Warrantless searches incident to a custodial arrest are justified by the reasonableness of searching for weapons, instruments of escape, and evidence of crime when a person is taken into official custody and lawfully detained." *Curd v. City Court of Judsonia, Arkansas*, 141 F.3d 839, 842 (8th Cir. 1998).

Ninth Circuit

- "[A] public employee has a reasonable expectation of privacy in her workplace office. However, such an expectation may be unreasonable if the 'intrusion is by a supervisor rather than a law enforcement official.' The [Supreme] Court [has] held that a warrantless search of an employee's office by a public employer for work-related, non-investigatory reasons or pursuant to an investigation of work-related employee misconduct, was not subject to review under the probable cause standard, but rather the less rigorous standard of 'reasonableness under all the circumstances.' The Court's less heightened standard of review for public employer searches has its origins in the 'realities of the workplace' that frequently require employers 'to enter the offices and desks of their employees for legitimate work-related reasons wholly unrelated to illegal conduct' in order to 'complete the government agency's work in a prompt and efficient manner.' Thus, a work-related search requires no warrant." *U.S. v. Jones*, 286 F.3d 1146 (9th Cir. 2002).

Tenth Circuit

- "An inventory search conducted as part of regular procedures, and for administrative rather than investigatory purposes, does not require a warrant." *U.S. v. Edwards*, 242 F.3d 928, 938 (10th Cir. 2001), superseded, 632 F.3d 633 (10th Cir. 2001).

Chapter 7

Searches Incident to Arrest

§ 7:1   Scope: A search incident to a lawful arrest is
        permissible when it is limited in scope
§ 7:2   Nature: A search incident to a lawful arrest must
        be contemporaneous in time and place
§ 7:3   Arrests in vehicles: If a person is arrested after a
        vehicle stop, the passenger compartment of the
        vehicle, including containers, may be searched
        incident to the arrest under limited circumstances
§ 7:4   Booking searches: A jailhouse search of an arrested
        person's possessions may be justified as a delayed
        search incident to arrest
§ 7:5   Search of modern cell phones: officers must
        generally secure a warrant before conducting
        such a search

Research References

West's Key Number Digest
Arrest ⚖71.1; Searches and Seizures ⚖52, 58

KeyCite®: Cases and other legal materials listed in KeyCite Scope can be
researched through the KeyCite service on Westlaw®. Use KeyCite to
check citations for form, parallel references, prior and later history, and
comprehensive citator information, including citations to other decisions
and secondary materials.

---

§ 7:1   Scope: A search incident to a lawful arrest is
permissible when it is limited in scope

Supreme Court

- "In *Robinson*.. . .we noted the two historical rationales
  for the search incident to arrest exception: (1) the need
  to disarm the suspect in order to take him into custody,
  and (2) the need to preserve evidence for later use at
  trial." *Knowles v. Iowa*, 525 U.S. 113, 116, 119 S. Ct.
  484, 142 L. Ed. 2d 492 (1998).

- "[I]mmediately upon arrest an officer may lawfully

search the person of an arrestee; he may also search
the area within the arrestee's immediate control." *Illinois
v. Lafayette*, 462 U.S. 640, 644, 103 S. Ct. 2605, 77 L.
Ed. 2d 65 (1983).

- "[I]t is not unreasonable under the Fourth Amendment
  for a police officer, as a matter of routine, to monitor
  the movements of an arrested person, as his judgment
  dictates, following the arrest. The officer's need to
  ensure his own safety—as well as the integrity of the
  arrest—is compelling. Such surveillance is not an
  impermissible invasion of the privacy or personal liberty of an individual who has been arrested. It is of no
  legal significance whether the officer was in the room,
  on the threshold, or in the hallway, since he had a right
  to be in any of these places as an incident of a valid
  arrest." *Washington v. Chrisman*, 455 U.S. 1, 7, 8, 102
  S. Ct. 812, 70 L. Ed. 2d 778, 1 Ed. Law Rep. 1087 (1982).

- "[W]hen a policeman has made a lawful custodial arrest
  of the occupant of an automobile, he may, as a contemporaneous incident of that arrest, search the passenger
  compartment of that automobile. It follows from this
  conclusion that the police may also examine the contents
  of any containers found within the passenger compartment, for if the passenger compartment is within reach
  of the arrestee, so also will containers in it be within
  his reach. Such a container may, of course, be searched
  whether it is open or closed, since the justification for
  the search is not that the arrestee has no privacy interest in the container, but that the lawful custodial arrest
  justifies the infringement of any privacy interest the arrestee may have." *New York v. Belton*, 453 U.S. 454,
  460–61, 101 S. Ct. 2860, 69 L. Ed. 2d 768 (1981).

- "The authority to search the person incident to a lawful
  custodial arrest, while based upon the need to disarm
  and to discover evidence, does not depend on what a
  court may later decide was the probability in a particular arrest situation that weapons or evidence would in
  fact be found upon the person of the suspect. A custodial
  arrest of a suspect based on probable cause is a reasonable intrusion under the Fourth Amendment; that
  intrusion being lawful, a search incident to the arrest
  requires no additional justification." *U.S. v. Robinson*,
  414 U.S. 218, 235, 94 S. Ct. 467, 38 L. Ed. 2d 427 (1973).

- "When an arrest is made, it is reasonable for the arresting officer to search the person arrested in order to remove any weapons that the latter might seek to use in order to resist arrest or effect his escape. Otherwise, the officer's safety might well be endangered, and the arrest itself frustrated. In addition, it is entirely reasonable for the arresting officer to search for and seize any evidence on the arrestee's person in order to prevent its concealment or destruction. And the area into which an arrestee might reach in order to grab a weapon or evidentiary items must, of course, be governed by a like rule. A gun on a table or in a drawer in front of one who is arrested can be as dangerous to the arresting officer as one concealed in the clothing of the person arrested. There is ample justification, therefore, for a search of the arrestee's person and the area within his immediate control—construing that phrase to mean the area from within which he might gain possession of a weapon or destructible evidence." *Chimel v. California*, 395 U.S. 752, 762–63, 89 S. Ct. 2034, 23 L. Ed. 2d 685 (1969).

- "[C]ontemporaneous searches [are] justified by the need to seize weapons and other things which might be used to assault an officer or effect an escape, as well as by the need to prevent the destruction of evidence of the crime—things which might easily happen where the weapon or evidence is on the accused's person or under his immediate control." *Preston v. U.S.*, 376 U.S. 364, 367, 84 S. Ct. 881, 11 L. Ed. 2d 777 (1964).

Fifth Circuit

- "(Defendant) concedes that the officers' post-arrest seizure of his cell phone from his pocket was lawful, but he argues that, since a cell phone is analogous to a closed container. . .the police had no authority to examine the phone's contents without a warrant . . . (H)owever. . .here no warrant was required since the search was conducted pursuant to a valid custodial arrest . . . (The officer) therefore (was) permitted to search (defendant's) cell phone pursuant to his arrest . . . The district court correctly denied (defendant's) motion to suppress. . .the call records and text messages retrieved from his cell phone." *U.S. v. Finley*, 477 F.3d 250, 72 Fed. R. Evid. Serv. 377 (5th Cir. 2007).

Seventh Circuit
- "As an incident to a lawful arrest, the police can search not only the person they have arrested to make sure he doesn't have a weapon but also and for the same purpose they can search the area within his immediate control—the area within grabbing distance—in which a weapon might be concealed that he could attempt to use against the officers or in which there might be evidence of his crime that he could destroy. There is no doubt that the police were entitled to open the cabinet in the entertainment center. The defendant had identified himself as a dangerous person by resisting arrest and reaching for a gun even though he knew the crowd of officers were indeed law enforcement officers and not rival gangsters. He had a gun in his waistband; he might have other guns in the apartment—perhaps in the entertainment center. The apartment was tiny, which meant not only that there were few other places in which to hide another gun or other guns but also that the defendant was within a few steps of the entertainment center. Handcuffed, lying face down on the floor, and surrounded by police, he was unlikely to be able to make a successful lunge for the entertainment center. But the police did not know how strong he was, and he seemed desperate. If the search is limited to the area under the defendant's control at the time of his arrest, the fact that it is no longer under his control at the time of the search does not invalidate the search." *U.S. v. Tejada*, 524 F.3d 809 (7th Cir. 2008).
- "Searches incident to arrests are valid in order to find weapons and to search for and seize any evidence on the arrestee's person in order to prevent concealment and to preserve evidence for trial." *U.S. v. Williams*, 209 F.3d 940, 943 (7th Cir. 2000).
- "It has long been the rule that law enforcement officers may conduct a full search of an arrestee in order to discover weapons the arrestee might be carrying and to preserve evidence that might be destroyed. . . .Such a search is permissible, however, only if the arrest was legal." *U.S. v. Sawyer*, 224 F.3d 675, 678 (7th Cir. 2000).

Ninth Circuit
- "Warrantless searches incident to a lawful arrest are

permitted under the Fourth Amendment for the purpose of finding weapons the arrestee might use or evidence the arrestee might conceal or destroy." *U.S. v. Johnson*, 357 Fed. Appx. 29 (9th Cir. 2009).

- "Searches incident to arrest are exempted from the warrant and probable cause requirements of the Fourth Amendment. Such searches are justified as a means to find weapons the arrestee might use or evidence the arrestee might conceal or destroy. Accordingly, the permissible scope of a search incident to arrest is limited to the area within the arrestee's immediate control—the area into which an arrestee might reach in order to grab a weapon or evidentiary item." *U.S. v. Caseres*, 533 F.3d 1064 (9th Cir. 2008).

- "A search incident to arrest is an exception to the general rule against warrantless searches. The justification for permitting a warrantless search is the need of law enforcement officers to seize weapons or other things which might be used to assault an officer or effect an escape, as well as the need to prevent the loss or destruction of evidence. A legitimate search incident to arrest is limited to the arrestee's person and to the area within his immediate control, meaning the area from within which he might gain possession of a weapon or destructible evidence. In determining whether a search is justified under the search incident to arrest exception, therefore, the critical inquiry is whether the search was properly limited to the area within the arrestee's immediate control at the time of his arrest. In evaluating the validity of such a search, courts are to weigh such factors as the number of persons being arrested, the number of officers present, their physical positioning with regard to the arrestee and the premises being searched, the display of guns by the officers, and the distance between the arrestee and the place searched." *U.S. v. Hudson*, 100 F.3d 1409, 1419 (9th Cir. 1996).

Tenth Circuit

- "Because searches incident to arrest are meant to discover hidden weapons and to prevent the suspect from destroying evidence. . .a search incident to arrest may extend only to the area within the suspect's immediate control, as that is the only area from which the suspect could draw a weapon or damage evidence." *U.S. v. Edwards*, 242 F.3d 928, 937 (10th Cir. 2001), superseded, 632 F.3d 633 (10th Cir. 2001).

- "In *Chimel v. California* . . . the Court established an exception to allow the contemporaneous search of a lawfully arrested person and the immediately surrounding area without a warrant in order to promote safety and prevent the concealment or destruction of evidence. . . . *Chimel* limited and defined the area of a permissible search incident to arrest to include the area from within which the arrestee might gain possession of a weapon or destructible evidence." *U.S. v. Olguin-Rivera*, 168 F.3d 1203, 1205 (10th Cir. 1999).

Eleventh Circuit

- "A law enforcement agent may search for weapons within the range of a person's immediate grasp, even when they are not in the process of conducting a lawful arrest, but only based on reasonable suspicion that the person poses a danger to the agent." *U.S. v. Bennett*, 555 F.3d 962 (11th Cir. 2009).

D.C. Circuit

- "A search incident to arrest is a well recognized exception to the Fourth Amendment's warrant requirement. As the Supreme Court held in *Chimel v. California*, when an arrest is made, it is reasonable for the arresting officer to search the person arrested in order to remove any weapons that the latter might seek to use in order to resist arrest or effect his escape." *U.S. v. Christian*, 187 F.3d 663, 666 (D.C. Cir. 1999).

- "In *Chimel v. United States*, the Supreme Court held that, incident to a lawful arrest, the police may properly search the area within the arrestee's immediate control. . . . A search of that area is permissible, regardless whether in the circumstances of a particular case it is probable that weapons or evidence would in fact be found there." *In re Sealed Case 96–3167*, 153 F.3d 759, 767 (D.C. Cir. 1998).

§ 7:2   Nature: A search incident to a lawful arrest must be contemporaneous in time and place

Supreme Court

- "Once petitioner admitted ownership of the sizable quantity of drugs the police clearly had probable cause to place the petitioner under arrest. Where the formal arrest followed quickly on the heels of the challenged search of petitioner's person, we do not believe it particularly important that the search preceded the arrest rather than vice versa." *Rawlings v. Kentucky*, 448 U.S. 98, 111, 100 S. Ct. 2556, 65 L. Ed. 2d 633 (1980).
- "[A] search can be incident to an arrest only if it is substantially contemporaneous with the arrest." *Shipley v. California*, 395 U.S. 818, 819, 89 S. Ct. 2053, 23 L. Ed. 2d 732 (1969).
- "[I]t is axiomatic that an incident search may not precede an arrest and serve as part of its justification." *Sibron v. New York*, 392 U.S. 40, 63, 88 S. Ct. 1889, 20 L. Ed. 2d 917 (1968).
- "Once an accused is under arrest and in custody, then a search made at another place, without a warrant, is simply not incident to the arrest." *Preston v. U.S.*, 376 U.S. 364, 367, 84 S. Ct. 881, 11 L. Ed. 2d 777 (1964).

First Circuit

- "A search incident to a lawful arrest is another traditional exception to the Fourth Amendment's warrant requirement. Some courts have held that a defendant's resistance to even an invalid *Terry* stop or arrest can be independent grounds for a new, independent arrest, and that evidence discovered in a search incident to that lawful arrest is admissible. We agree that [the defendant's] actions of shoving [the officer] and resisting arrest provided grounds for his arrest and a search incident to that arrest. But the validity of that search does not determine the suppression issue generated by the original unlawful seizure of [the defendant]. The gun at issue here was not discovered in a search subsequent to or incident to [the defendant's] arrest. While the district court correctly noted that '[t]he gun was seized only *after* [the defendant] shoved [the officer] and only *after* the officers succeeded in wrestling [the defendant] to the ground and placing him under arrest,' the district court failed to account for the fact that [the officer] conducted the frisk—the search that first discovered the gun—*before* [the defendant] shoved

435

him and *before* [the defendant] was arrested. The gun was not discovered by a search incident to his arrest, but rather by the frisk that *preceded* [the defendant's] subsequent actions of shoving [the officer] and resisting arrest. The temporal relationship between the discovery of the weapon and the unlawful acts distinguishes this case from *King,* which the government cites as support. In *King,* we assumed initial unlawful police conduct but denied suppression of a seized weapon against the passenger in a car because the driver of the car committed the intervening crime of shooting at the police officers before the officers discovered the passenger's weapon. 'At the moment the shot was fired, [the officer] had all the probable cause that was needed to search King.' In this case, [the officer] discovered the gun in a search conducted prior to [the defendant] committing any unlawful acts. [The defendant's] 'intervening' crimes were not, in fact, intervening and thus could not purge the taint of the prior illegal stop." *U.S. v. Camacho*, 661 F.3d 718, 730–31 (1st Cir. 2011) (citations omitted).

- "[E]vidence recovered after an arrest may not form the basis of probable cause for that arrest. However, whether a formal arrest occurred prior to or followed quickly on the heels of the challenged search does not affect the validity of the search so long as the probable cause existed prior to the search." *U.S. v. Bizier*, 111 F.3d 214, 217 (1st Cir. 1997).

Fourth Circuit

- "Officers may retrieve text messages and other information from cell phones and pagers seized incident to an arrest. The evidence establishes that the initial search of the cell phone occurred in Murphy's presence and at his direction, after he indicated to Trooper Chapman that the phone contained phone numbers for people who could corroborate his identity. Another search of the cell phone occurred at the Sheriff's Department during the course of the inventory search, when a supervising officer noted that the cell phone contained potentially incriminating information and directed Trooper Pruett to retain the cell phone as evidence in the case. Of course, once the cell phone was held for evidence, other officers and investigators were entitled to conduct a further review of its contents, as Agent Snedeker did, without seeking a warrant." *U.S. v. Murphy*, 552 F.3d 405 (4th Cir. 2009).

- "*Belton* stands for the proposition that justification for a search incident to arrest continues even after the likelihood of danger or destruction of evidence has subsided, but that *Chadwick* indicates that the justification does not continue indefinitely. . . . Hence, the determinative issue. . .is whether the time and distance between elimination of the danger and performance of the search is unreasonable." *U.S. v. Johnson*, 114 F.3d 435, 440, 47 Fed. R. Evid. Serv. 153 (4th Cir. 1997).

Sixth Circuit

- "It is well-settled that arrest warrants are not search warrants. (citation omitted) Thus, the Supreme Court has identified two types of warrantless protective sweeps of a residence that are constitutionally permissible immediately following an arrest. The first type allows officers to 'look in closets and other spaces immediately adjoining the place of arrest from which an attack could be immediately launched.' (citation omitted) The second type of sweep goes 'beyond' immediately adjoining areas but is confined to 'such a protective sweep, aimed at protecting the arresting officers[.]' " *U.S. v. Archibald*, 589 F.3d 289 (6th Cir. 2009).

Eighth Circuit

- "(Defendant's) property was seized by the FBI, turned over to local authorities, returned to the FBI, and then searched. Although (defendant) relies heavily on the date of transcription, December 16, (the agent) testified that he investigated the items on December 11 or 12, 2001, after receiving them from the local authorities . . . . Although a period of time elapsed between the arrest and the subsequent search of (defendant's) property, we conclude that the search was reasonable under the Fourth Amendment." *U.S. v. Johnson*, 450 F.3d 366 (8th Cir. 2006).
- "Under the *Belton* framework, we see merit in the view that the determination whether a search is a "contemporaneous" incident of an arrest involves more than simply a temporal analysis . . . . The precise context is

important to the reasonableness of the search, and it is significant that during the sixty minutes that (defendant) was in the patrol car, the officers were unsure whether he would be transported to the police station for booking, or released at the scene with only a citation. . . . It was only after (defendant) was deemed unable or unwilling to assist law enforcement that the trooper determined to make a "full custodial arrest" . . . . The search of (defendant's) truck certainly was contemporaneous with this decision to proceed with a full custodial arrest. Although an hour had elapsed since the initial detention, we think that it was still reasonable for police to consider (defendant) a "recent occupant" of the truck. The episode began with an encounter between the trooper and (defendant) at the vehicle, and the search was the culmination of a continuing series of events at the scene arising from the traffic stop." *U.S. v. Hrasky*, 453 F.3d 1099 (8th Cir. 2006).

Ninth Circuit

- "We must decide whether an automobile search that is commenced five minutes after a defendant has been arrested and removed from the scene qualifies as a search incident to arrest. . . . The government argues that the search was proper under *Belton's* bright-line rule that a police officer may search the passenger compartment of an automobile and its containers as a contemporaneous incident of a lawful arrest. . . . We agree because the search in this case occurred during a continuous series of events closely connected in time to the arrest." *U.S. v. McLaughlin*, 170 F.3d 889, 891 (9th Cir. 1999).
- "Concerning the temporal scope of the search, we have held that a search incident to arrest must be conducted at about the same time as the arrest. That search may be conducted shortly after the arrestee has been removed from the area, provided that (1) the search is restricted to the area that was within the arrestee's immediate control when he was arrested and (2) events occurring after the arrest but before the search incident to arrest did not render the search unreasonable. In *Turner*, for example, we held a search incident to arrest was not unreasonable where only a few minutes had passed between the arrest and the search, the defendant

was taken to the next room out of concern for the officers' safety, a gun was found in the room where the defendant had been arrested, and the defendant was held near the site of the arrest." *U.S. v. Hudson*, 100 F.3d 1409, 1419 (9th Cir. 1996).

Tenth Circuit

- "Courts have found that a search may be incident to an arrest in cases where the search and arrest were separated by times ranging from five to 60 minutes. An hour would seem to be at the outer limits of substantially contemporaneous, if not beyond. The hour delay resulted from the officers' pursuing their primary mission—executing the search warrant. To delay the formal announcement of an arrest while that effort is underway strikes us as eminently reasonable: the sooner the search is completed, the sooner the intrusion from the search will end; and the formality of the arrest accomplishes little when the person to be arrested is already being detained. [F]or search-incident-to-arrest purposes we may deem the arrest to have occurred before the formal announcement to a suspect that he is under arrest. To be sure, it appears that there can be no search incident to arrest unless the suspect is at some point formally placed under arrest. But the arrest itself, for constitutional purposes, may be said to have occurred well before that formality." *U.S. v. Sanchez*, 555 F.3d 910 (10th Cir. 2009).

- "The justification for allowing searches incident to arrest also places a temporal restriction upon the police's conduct. . . . .[O]nce the immediate rationale for conducting a search incident to arrest has passed, the police may not then engage in a search absent probable cause to do so." *U.S. v. Edwards*, 242 F.3d 928, 937 (10th Cir. 2001), superseded, 632 F.3d 633 (10th Cir. 2001).

- "A warrantless search preceding an arrest is a legitimate search incident to arrest as long as (1) a legitimate basis for the arrest existed before the search, and (2) the arrest followed shortly after the search." *U.S. v. McKissick*, 204 F.3d 1282, 1296 (10th Cir. 2000).

- "In order to be a legitimate search incident to arrest, the search need not take place after the arrest. A warrantless search preceding an arrest is a legitimate search incident to arrest as long as (1) a legitimate basis for the arrest existed before the search, and (2) the arrest followed shortly after the search. . . . Whether or not the officer intended to actually arrest the defendant at the time of the search is immaterial to this two-part inquiry." *U.S. v. Anchondo*, 156 F.3d 1043, 1045 (10th Cir. 1998).

D.C. Circuit

- "(Defendant) argues the search was unlawful because he "had no reason to believe he was being arrested at the time of the search" and the "search incident to arrest" exception to the warrant requirement of the Fourth Amendment to the Constitution of the United States does not apply to a search conducted prior either to the announcement of a formal arrest or to the suspect being taken into custody. . . . We reject that view . . . Indeed, every circuit that has considered the question-save one-has concluded that a search incident to arrest may precede the arrest . . . Powell acknowledges the officers had probable cause to arrest him and his companion for urinating in public before they searched his car . . . Therefore. . .because 'the police had probable cause to arrest [before the search], the search was valid as one incident to arrest.' " *U.S. v. Powell*, 483 F.3d 836 (D.C. Cir. 2007).

- "[T]he Chimel test is not whether an area was probably accessible to the suspect at the time of the search, but whether it was conceivably accessible. . . . Accordingly, we have upheld searches even when hindsight might suggest that the likelihood of the defendant reaching the area in question was slight. . . ." *U.S. v. Christian*, 187 F.3d 663, 671 (D.C. Cir. 1999).

- "As long as a search is contemporaneous with and an integral part of a lawful arrest. . .the police may search a container that was within reach when the arrest occurs, even if the officer has since seized it and gained exclusive control over it. . . . [T]he determination of immediate control must be made when the arrest occurs. . . . [A] search is incident to arrest only so long as it is an integral part of the arrest process. The relevant distinction turns upon whether the arrest and search are so separated in time or by intervening events that the latter cannot fairly be said to have been incident to the former." *In re Sealed Case 96–3167*, 153 F.3d 759, 768 (D.C. Cir. 1998).

§ 7:3 Arrests in vehicles: If a person is arrested after a vehicle stop, the passenger compartment of the vehicle, including containers, may be searched incident to the arrest under limited circumstances

Supreme Court

- "A breath test does not 'implicat[e] significant privacy concerns.' Blood tests are a different matter. . . . Blood tests are significantly more intrusive, and their reasonableness must be judged in light of the availability of the less invasive alternative of a breath test. . . . Breath tests have been in common use for many years. Their results are admissible in court and are widely credited by juries, and respondents do not dispute their accuracy or utility. What, then, is the justification for warrantless blood tests? One advantage of blood tests is their ability to detect not just alcohol but also other substances that can impair a driver's ability to operate a car safely. A breath test cannot do this, but police have other measures at their disposal when they have reason to believe that a motorist may be under the influence of some other substance (for example, if a breath test indicates that a clearly impaired motorist has little if any alcohol in his blood). Nothing prevents the police from seeking a warrant for a blood test when there is sufficient time to do so in the particular circumstances or from relying on the exigent circumstances exception to the warrant requirement when there is not. . . . Because breath tests are significantly less intrusive than blood tests and in most cases amply serve law enforcement interests, we conclude that a breath test, but not a blood test, may be administered as a search incident to a lawful arrest for drunk driving. As in all cases involving reasonable searches incident to arrest, a warrant is not needed in this situation." *Birchfield v. North Dakota*, 136 S. Ct. 2160, 2178, 2184, 2185, 195 L. Ed. 2d 560 (2016) (citation omitted).

- "If there is no possibility that an arrestee could reach into the area that law enforcement officers seek to search, both justifications for the search-incident-to-arrest exception are absent and the rule does not apply." *Arizona v. Gant*, 556 U.S. 332, 129 S. Ct. 1710, 173 L. Ed. 2d 485, 47 A.L.R. Fed. 2d 657 (2009).
- "[W]e reject [a broad] reading of *Belton* and hold that the *Chimel* rationale authorizes police to search a vehicle incident to a recent occupant's arrest only when the arrestee is unsecured and within reaching distance of the passenger compartment at the time of the search. . . . [Additionally], [a]lthough it does not follow from *Chimel*, we also conclude that circumstances unique to the vehicle context justify a search incident to a lawful arrest when it is 'reasonable to believe evidence relevant to the crime of arrest might be found in the vehicle.'" *Arizona v. Gant*, 556 U.S. 332, 129 S. Ct. 1710, 173 L. Ed. 2d 485, 47 A.L.R. Fed. 2d 657 (2009).
- "In many cases, as when a recent occupant is arrested for a traffic violation, there will be no reasonable basis to believe the vehicle contains relevant evidence. (citations omitted) But in others, including *Belton* and *Thornton*, the offense of arrest will supply a basis for searching the passenger compartment of an arrestee's vehicle and any containers therein." *Arizona v. Gant*, 556 U.S. 332, 129 S. Ct. 1710, 173 L. Ed. 2d 485, 47 A.L.R. Fed. 2d 657 (2009).
- "Under our view, *Belton* and *Thornton* permit an officer to conduct a vehicle search when an arrestee is within reaching distance of the vehicle or it is reasonable to believe the vehicle contains evidence of the offense of arrest. Other established exceptions to the warrant requirement authorize a vehicle search under additional circumstances when safety or evidentiary concerns demand." *Arizona v. Gant*, 556 U.S. 332, 129 S. Ct. 1710, 173 L. Ed. 2d 485, 47 A.L.R. Fed. 2d 657 (2009).
- "The threat to officer safety from issuing a traffic citation. . .is a good deal less than in the case of a custodial arrest. . . . A routine traffic stop. . .is a relatively brief encounter and is more analogous to a so-called *Terry* stop. . .than to a formal arrest. . . . In *Robinson*, we held that the authority to conduct a full field search as incident to an arrest was a bright-line

rule, which was based on the concern for officer safety and destruction or loss of evidence, but which did not depend in every case upon the existence of either concern. Here we are asked to extend that bright-line rule to a situation where the concern for officer safety is not present to the same extent and the concern for destruction or loss of evidence is not present at all. We decline to do so." *Knowles v. Iowa*, 525 U.S. 113, 117–19, 119 S. Ct. 484, 142 L. Ed. 2d 492 (1998).

- "[W]hen a policeman has made a lawful custodial arrest of the occupant of an automobile, he may, as a contemporaneous incident of that arrest, search the passenger compartment of that automobile. It follows from this conclusion that the police may also examine the contents of any containers found within the passenger compartment, for if the passenger compartment is within reach of the arrestee, so also will containers in it be within his reach. Such a container may, of course, be searched whether it is open or closed, since the justification for the search is not that the arrestee has no privacy interest in the container, but that the lawful custodial arrest justifies the infringement of any privacy interest the arrestee may have." *New York v. Belton*, 453 U.S. 454, 460–61, 101 S. Ct. 2860, 69 L. Ed. 2d 768 (1981).

Third Circuit

- "Though officers may lawfully search the passenger compartment of the car incident to arrest. . . .such a search incident to arrest does not extend to the trunk of the car. . . .Thus, in order for the search of the trunk to comport with the Fourth Amendment, it had to have been supported by the level of suspicion required under the Fourth Amendment." *U.S. v. Baker*, 221 F.3d 438, 443 (3d Cir. 2000), as amended, (Sept. 21, 2000).

Sixth Circuit

- "Recently, in *Knowles v. Iowa*. . . .a unanimous Supreme Court held that a full-blown search of an automobile and its driver, after an officer had elected to issue the driver a traffic citation rather than arresting the driver, violated the Fourth Amendment. Because neither the officer's safety nor the need to preserve evidence was implicated by the routine traffic stop, the Court held that once the driver was stopped for speeding and was issued a citation, all of the evidence necessary to prosecute him had been obtained and, without a reasonable suspicion that other criminal activity was afoot, the stop of the vehicle and issuance of a traffic citation did not justify a full search of the vehicle." *U.S. v. Hill*, 195 F.3d 258, 264, 1999 FED App. 0351P (6th Cir. 1999).

Seventh Circuit

- "The *Belton* rule is confined to searches of the interior of the passenger compartment of an automobile. . . . The passenger compartment is within the arrestee's immediate control—it is an area into which an arrestee might reach in order to grab a weapon or evidentiary item. . . . Logic dictates that if the passenger compartment is within reach of the arrestee, so also will containers in it be within his reach." *U.S. v. Richardson*, 121 F.3d 1051, 1056 (7th Cir. 1997).

- "[T]he validity of the search at issue here is governed by the general rule regarding searches incident to a lawful custodial arrest [which] allow police officers to search any area into which an arrestee might reach to remove a weapon or to conceal evidence. At the time he was approached and subsequently arrested [the] defendant was standing about three feet from the curb or about even with the middle of the trunk of the car. Unless the defendant possessed extraordinary abilities not revealed in the record, it would have been impossible for him to have reached anything in the passenger compartment. And since the front passenger seat of the Cadillac was not within the defendant's grab area the warrantless search of that area violated the Fourth Amendment." *U.S. v. Adams*, 26 F.3d 702, 705 (7th Cir. 1994).

Eighth Circuit

- "Under the search incident to arrest exception to the warrant requirement of the Fourth Amendment of the United States Constitution, officers may search a vehicle incident to an arrest only if (1) the arrestee is unrestrained and 'within reaching distance of the passenger compartment' when the search begins or (2) 'it is reasonable to believe the vehicle contains evidence of the offense of arrest.' The district court determined the warrantless search of Stegall's SUV was constitutionally reasonable under *Gant's* second exception because the officers had a reasonable basis to believe Stegall's SUV contained evidence relevant to the crime of his arrest. We agree. Under the second *Gant* exception, officers may conduct a warrantless search of a vehicle incident to arrest—even after the arrestee is restrained in the back of a patrol vehicle—when officers have a reasonable basis to believe the vehicle contains evidence related to the crime of arrest. Officers reasonably believed Stegall's vehicle might contain evidence relevant to Stegall's arrest for terroristic threatening because (1) Stegall confirmed he was the driver of the SUV and involved in an earlier road rage incident, (2) Stegall told the officers he 'probably' had a firearm in his vehicle, (3) the 911 caller positively identified Stegall as the driver who brandished a gun at him during the reported road rage incident, and (4) a witness observed Stegall concealing something in the rear hatch of his SUV. Because these facts created a reasonable basis for the officers to believe Stegall's SUV contained evidence relevant to the terroristic threat charge—the gun, we affirm the district court's ruling that the officers' warrantless search of Stegall's SUV was reasonable." *United States v. Stegall*, 850 F.3d 981, 984 (8th Cir. 2017).

- "The search incident to arrest in this case involved the area immediately inside the rubber window seal, where [officer] placed his pen light. That area is reachable by an occupant without exiting the vehicle, and an occupant could conceal contraband, evidence, and certain weapons inside the window seal. Small packages of drugs, drug paraphernalia such as syringes or razors, documentary evidence, and potential weapons such as small knives or letter openers could fit inside that area. While seated in the driver's seat, one could easily part the rubber strips with two fingers, just as [officer] did, to hide or retrieve such objects. Accordingly, we hold that the deputy's parting of the window seal and intrusion into the area immediately below the seal falls within the scope of a lawful search incident to arrest." *U.S. v. Barnes*, 374 F.3d 601 (8th Cir. 2004).

Tenth Circuit

- "[I]f the police arrest the occupant of a car they may also search the passenger compartment of the vehicle, but they may not search other areas that are outside the suspect's immediate control or grab space." *U.S. v. Edwards*, 242 F.3d 928, 937 (10th Cir. 2001), superseded, 632 F.3d 633 (10th Cir. 2001).

- "Under *New York v. Belton*. . .officers may search any containers, open or closed, in the passenger compartment of a vehicle incident to a lawful arrest of an occupant of the vehicle. . . . The Court in *Knowles* instead held that the Fourth Amendment does not permit a search incident to citation, while leaving the rule of *Belton* intact." *U.S. v. Humphrey*, 208 F.3d 1190, 1201–02 (10th Cir. 2000).

- "The district court applied the rules from *Belton* and its progeny to invalidate the search in this instance because it determined any evidence or weapons contained in the covered cargo area of the vehicle were beyond the defendants' reasonable ability to access, thereby making the covered cargo area more like a trunk than part of the passenger compartment. However, we disagree with the court's conclusion and find where, as here, the vehicle contains no trunk, the entire inside of the vehicle constitutes the passenger compartment and may be lawfully searched. . .regardless of the imposition of an easily-retractable vinyl covering or its ostensible effect on the defendants' ability to reach the area." *U.S. v. Olguin-Rivera*, 168 F.3d 1203, 1205 (10th Cir. 1999).

Eleventh Circuit

- "When an occupant of an automobile is the subject of a lawful arrest, the Fourth Amendment permits the arresting officers to contemporaneously conduct a warrantless search not only of the occupant himself but also of the passenger compartment of the automobile, as well as any closed (or open) containers found in this area of the automobile. Containers, in this context, refer to any object capable of holding another object and thus include an automobile's glove compartment (whether locked or unlocked), as well as any containers found therein, such as the zipped leather bag that was discovered in this case." *U.S. v. Gonzalez*, 71 F.3d 819, 825–26 (11th Cir. 1996).

D.C. Circuit

- "Presumably, the 'reasonable to believe' standard requires less than probable cause, because otherwise *Gant*'s evidentiary rationale would merely duplicate the 'automobile exception,' which the Court specifically identified as a distinct exception to the warrant requirement. . . . Rather, the 'reasonable to believe' standard probably is akin to the 'reasonable suspicion' standard required to justify a *Terry* search. . . . Accordingly, the officer's assessment of the likelihood that there will be relevant evidence inside the car must be based on more than 'a mere hunch,' but 'falls considerably short of [needing to] satisfy[ ] a preponderance of the evidence standard.' " *U.S. v. Vinton*, 594 F.3d 14 (D.C. Cir. 2010).

- "To the extent that *Belton* might be thought to apply only to automobiles, however, we have already rejected that interpretation. In *Brown* the contents of a zippered pouch were admitted into evidence even though by the time it was searched the pouch had been moved beyond the reach of the defendant, who was being detained on a street corner." *U.S. v. Abdul-Saboor*, 85 F.3d 664, 668 (D.C. Cir. 1996).

§ 7:4 Booking searches: A jailhouse search of an arrested person's possessions may be justified as a delayed search incident to arrest

Supreme Court

- "An arrested person is not invariably taken to a police station or confined; if an arrestee is taken to the police station, that is no more than a continuation of the custody inherent in the arrest status. Nonetheless, the factors justifying a search of the person and personal effects of an arrestee upon reaching a police station but prior to being placed in confinement are somewhat different from the factors justifying an immediate search at the time and place of arrest." *Illinois v. Lafayette*, 462 U.S. 640, 645, 103 S. Ct. 2605, 77 L. Ed. 2d 65 (1983).

- "[O]nce the accused is lawfully arrested and is in custody, the effects in his possession at the place of detention that were subject to search at the time and

447

place of his arrest may lawfully be searched and seized without a warrant even though a substantial period of time has elapsed between the arrest and subsequent administrative processing, on the one hand, and the taking of the property for use as evidence, on the other. This is true where the clothing or effects are immediately seized upon arrival at the jail, held under the defendant's name in the property room of the jail, and at a later time searched and taken for use at the subsequent criminal trial." *U.S. v. Edwards*, 415 U.S. 800, 807, 94 S. Ct. 1234, 39 L. Ed. 2d 771 (1974).

- "The property was subject to search at the place of arrest. We do not think it significantly different, when the accused decides to take the property with him, for the search of it to occur instead at the first place of detention when the accused arrives there, especially as the search of property carried by an accused to the place of detention has additional justifications, similar to those which justify a search of the person of one who is arrested." *Abel v. U.S.*, 362 U.S. 217, 239, 80 S. Ct. 683, 4 L. Ed. 2d 668 (1960).

First Circuit

- "In the case of a lawful custodial arrest a full search of the person is not only an exception to the warrant requirement of the Fourth Amendment, but is also a reasonable search under that amendment. . . . Thus, under *Robinson*, if the arrest was lawful, a searching officer does not need to have any further justification for performing a full body search of an arrestee. . . . Moreover, a search incident to arrest need not occur at the scene of the arrest, but may legally be conducted later when the accused arrives at the place of detention." *Swain v. Spinney*, 117 F.3d 1, 5–6 (1st Cir. 1997).

Fifth Circuit

- "A person lawfully arrested has no reasonable expectation of privacy with respect to property properly taken from his person for inventory by the police. Later examination of that property by another law-enforcement officer is, therefore, not an unreasonable search within the meaning of the Fourth Amendment." *U.S. v. Thompson*, 837 F.2d 673, 674, 24 Fed. R. Evid. Serv. 731 (5th Cir. 1988).

- "Examining all the items removed from the arrestee's person or possession and listing or inventorying them is a reasonable administrative procedure." *U.S. v. Loaiza-Marin*, 832 F.2d 867, 868 (5th Cir. 1987).

Seventh Circuit

- "In [Appellant's] case, on the other hand, the arresting officer had a reasonable suspicion that [he] had hidden some type of contraband in his pants. Therefore, for purposes of jail security, it was necessary to conduct a more intrusive search to either dispel or confirm that suspicion. Where an arrestee is wearing blue jeans or another heavy material, even the most thorough pat-down search will not necessarily turn up small items such as several hits of LSD on postage stamps, a small rock of crack cocaine, or a razor blade. Accordingly, it is not unreasonable to conduct a limited strip search, as [the Trooper] performed on [the prisoner], when an officer is trying to recover suspected contraband." *Kraushaar v. Flanigan*, 45 F.3d 1040, 1046 (7th Cir. 1995).
- "[S]earches and seizures that could be made on the spot at the time of arrest may legally be conducted later when the accused arrives at the place of detention. The courts of appeals have followed this same rule, holding that both the person and the property in his immediate possession may be searched at the station house after the arrest has occurred at another place and if evidence of crime is discovered, it may be seized and admitted into evidence." *U.S. v. Rodriguez*, 995 F.2d 776, 778 (7th Cir. 1993).

Eighth Circuit

- "(Plaintiff) filed this action pursuant to 42 U.S.C. § 1983, 'individually and behalf of all other persons similarly situated,' alleging, among other things, that the policy of the Minnehaha, South Dakota, County Juvenile Detention Center ("JDC") to "strip search[ ] minors without probable cause" was unconstitutional . . . (W)e conclude that after weighing the special needs for the search against the invasion of personal rights involved, the balance tips in favor of reasonableness. We thus conclude that (Defendants) did not violate (Plaintiff's) constitutional rights." *Smook v. Minnehaha County*, 457 F.3d 806 (8th Cir. 2006).

- "The search took place at the station house about fifteen minutes after [Defendant] was arrested. This delay could be fatal if, for example, a large piece of luggage were opened and inspected without a warrant. . . . The timeliness requirement for luggage or other personal property not immediately associated with the person of the arrestee is, in other words, constitutionally fairly strict. . . . On the other hand, searches of the person and articles immediately associated with the person of the arrestee, are measured with a different, more flexible constitutional time clock. . . . Searches of the person and those articles immediately associated with the person may be made either at the time of arrest or when the accused arrives at the place of detention." *Curd v. City Court of Judsonia, Arkansas*, 141 F.3d 839, 843 (8th Cir. 1998).

Tenth Circuit

- "We are convinced, based on the record before us, that probable cause to believe further contraband would be found in the bag did not exist at the time [the] sergeant first opened the bag at the bus station. Therefore, his search was in accordance with departmental policy directing him to open locked containers before booking. While Defendant argues the location of the search (at the bus station rather than the police station) mandates a finding that its purpose was merely a ruse for general rummaging, we find this argument without merit." *U.S. v. Evans*, 937 F.2d 1534, 1538 (10th Cir. 1991).

§ 7:5 Search of modern cell phones: officers must generally secure a warrant before conducting such a search

Supreme Court

- "The fact that an arrestee has diminished privacy interests does not mean that the Fourth Amendment falls out of the picture entirely. Not every search 'is acceptable solely because a person is in custody.' . . . Modern cell phones, as a category, implicate privacy concerns far beyond those implicated by the search of a cigarette pack, a wallet, or a purse. A conclusion that inspecting the contents of an arrestee's pockets works no substantial additional intrusion on privacy beyond the arrest itself may make sense as applied to physical items, but any extension of that reasoning to digital data has to rest on its own bottom." *Riley v. California*, 134 S. Ct. 2473, 2488-89, 189 L. Ed. 2d 430, 42 Media L. Rep. (BNA) 1925 (2014).

- "[T]he proverbial visitor from Mars might conclude [that modern cell phones] were an important feature of human anatomy. . . . Cell phones, however, place vast quantities of personal information literally in the hands of individuals. . . . We therefore decline to extend *Robinson* to searches of data on cell phones, and hold instead that officers must generally secure a warrant before conducting such a search." *Riley v. California*, 134 S. Ct. 2473, 2484-85, 189 L. Ed. 2d 430, 42 Media L. Rep. (BNA) 1925 (2014).

- "[U]nknown physical objects may always pose risks, no matter how slight, during the tense atmosphere of a custodial arrest. . . . No such unknowns exist with respect to digital data. As the First Circuit explained, the officers who searched Wurie's cell phone 'knew exactly what they would find therein: data. They also knew that the data could not harm them.' " *Riley v. California*, 134 S. Ct. 2473, 2485, 189 L. Ed. 2d 430, 42 Media L. Rep. (BNA) 1925 (2014) (citations omitted).

- "[O]nce law enforcement officers have secured a cell phone, there is no longer any risk that the arrestee himself will be able to delete incriminating data from the phone. . . . To the extent that law enforcement still has specific concerns about the potential loss of evidence in a particular case, there remain more targeted ways to address those concerns. If the police are truly confronted with a now or never situation,—for example, circumstances suggesting that a defendant's phone will be the target of an imminent remote-wipe attempt—they may be able to rely on exigent circumstances to search the phone immediately. Or, if officers happen to seize a phone in an unlocked state, they may be able to disable a phone's automatic-lock feature in order to prevent the phone from locking and encrypting data. Such a preventive measure could be analyzed under the principles set forth in our decision in *McArthur*, 531 U.S. 326, 121 S.Ct. 946, which approved officers' rea-

sonable steps to secure a scene to preserve evidence
while they awaited a warrant." *Riley v. California*, 134
S. Ct. 2473, 2486, 189 L. Ed. 2d 430, 42 Media L. Rep.
(BNA) 1925 (2014) (citations and inner quotations
omitted).

Chapter 8

Exigent Circumstances

§ 8:1   Justification: A warrantless search is permitted
        when both probable cause and exigent
        circumstances exist
§ 8:2   Definition: Examples of exigent circumstances
        include hot pursuit, a fleeing suspect, destruction
        of evidence, or other situations in which speed is
        essential
§ 8:3   Protective sweeps: A limited search for other
        persons on the premises requires probable cause
        and exigent circumstances
§ 8:4   Police-created exigent circumstances vitiates the
        "exigent circumstances" exception to the warrant
        requirement

Research References

West's Key Number Digest
Arrest ☞68, 71 to 71.1; Searches and Seizures ☞25, 25.1, 53, 54

> **KeyCite®:** Cases and other legal materials listed in KeyCite Scope can be
> researched through the KeyCite service on Westlaw®. Use KeyCite to
> check citations for form, parallel references, prior and later history, and
> comprehensive citator information, including citations to other decisions
> and secondary materials.

§ 8:1   Justification: A warrantless search is permitted when both probable cause and exigent circumstances exist

Supreme Court

- "[I]n the absence of hot pursuit there must be at least
  probable cause to believe that one or more of the other
  [exigent circumstances] factors justifying the entry were
  present and that in assessing the risk of danger, the
  gravity of the crime and likelihood that the suspect is
  armed should be considered." *Minnesota v. Olson*, 495
  U.S. 91, 100, 110 S. Ct. 1684, 109 L. Ed. 2d 85 (1990).

- "[A] search or seizure carried out on a suspect's premises without a warrant is *per se* unreasonable, unless the police can show the presence of exigent circumstances. [T]he court decided in *Payton v. New York* that warrantless felony arrests in the home are prohibited by the Fourth Amendment, absent probable cause and exigent circumstances. Before agents of the government may invade the sanctity of the home, the burden is on the government to demonstrate exigent circumstances that overcome the presumption of unreasonableness that attaches to all warrantless home entries." *Welsh v. Wisconsin*, 466 U.S. 740, 749, 750, 104 S. Ct. 2091, 80 L. Ed. 2d 732 (1984).

- "[A]n important factor to be considered when determining whether any exigency exists is the gravity of the underlying offense for which the arrest is being made. Moreover, although no exigency is created simply because there is probable cause to believe that a serious crime has been committed, application of the exigent circumstances exception in the context of a home entry should rarely be sanctioned when there is probable cause to believe that only a minor offense, such as the kind at issue in this case, has been committed." *Welsh v. Wisconsin*, 466 U.S. 740, 753, 104 S. Ct. 2091, 80 L. Ed. 2d 732 (1984).

- "The Fourth Amendment does not require police officers to delay in the course of an investigation if to do so would gravely endanger their lives or the lives of others." *Warden, Md. Penitentiary v. Hayden*, 387 U.S. 294, 298–99, 87 S. Ct. 1642, 18 L. Ed. 2d 782 (1967).

First Circuit

- "An imminent threat to the life or safety of members of the public, the police officers, or a person located within the residence, may qualify as an exigent circumstance that renders a warrantless entry reasonable." *Estate of Bennett v. Wainwright*, 548 F.3d 155 (1st Cir. 2008).

Second Circuit

- "Though genuinely held, the officers' concerns about getting illegal guns off of the streets of Hartford are not pertinent to an exigency analysis. This is because testimony about how fast 'guns move' in Hartford, or about the violent gangs in that part of the city, are not specific facts or evidence particular to this case. Rather, they are generalized facts about the city and about the nature of gun trafficking. Such general knowledge, without more, cannot support a finding of exigency. The exigency inquiry 'turns on the district court's examination of the totality of circumstances confronting law enforcement agents *in the particular case.*' "*Harris v. O'Hare*, 770 F.3d 224, 235 (2d Cir. 2014), cert. denied, 136 S. Ct. 792, 193 L. Ed. 2d 709 (2016) (citations omitted).

Third Circuit

• "In. . . limited situations, the need for effective law enforcement trumps the right of privacy and the requirement of a search warrant, thereby excusing an otherwise unconstitutional intrusion. Exigent circumstances, however, do not meet Fourth Amendment standards if the government deliberately creates them. . . .The District Court found that exigent circumstances—the possibility of evidence being destroyed—existed *after* the officers knocked on the hotel room door and demanded entry. . . . [I[n order to determine whether the police impermissibly manufacture or create exigent circumstances, we must look to the reasonableness and propriety of their actions and investigative tactics *preceding* their warrantless entry. . . . As the record plainly indicates, the officers decided to enter room 511 without a warrant. It was that decision to conduct a warrantless entry and search of the room, without any urgent need to do so, that impermissibly created the very exigency relied upon by the government in this case. . . . There is no indication in the record that [defendant] was aware of the surveillance prior to the officers' decision to gain entry. Consequently, the police here could have maintained their surveillance until a search warrant had been secured." *U.S. v. Coles*, 437 F.3d 361 (3d Cir. 2006).

Fifth Circuit

• "The first question is whether the officers acted with probable cause and under exigent circumstances when they initially raided and searched (defendant's) home.

However, we need not determine whether the officers acted with probable cause because we conclude that the exigent circumstances arose because of the conduct of the officers . . . (T)he next question is whether (defendant's) consent to conduct the second search of the residence. . .was valid . . . Here, we do not decide whether (defendant's) consent was voluntary because even if it were, her consent was not an independent act of free will, given the closeness in time between the initial unconstitutional raid and the consent she gave, the absence of intervening circumstances, and the "flagrancy" of the initial unconstitutional raid into and the search of her home . . . Because the officers impermissibly created the exigent circumstances and because (defendant's) consent was not an independent act of free will, we hold that the searches of (defendant's) residence were unreasonable under the Fourth Amendment." *U.S. v. Gomez-Moreno*, 479 F.3d 350 (5th Cir. 2007).

- "[Lessee] was arrested after having exited his apartment wearing only boxer shorts. ... The officers sought to provide clothing against the possibility of personal injury to their charge. [Lessee] may not have been surrounded by broken glass in a trailer park, but the hazards of public sidewalks and streets pose a threat of injury to the feet and other exposed areas of the body. Even without considering any issue of 'common decency' in transporting a person in underwear to a jailhouse or police station, we hold that in a situation such as this, the potential of a personal safety hazard to the arrestee places a duty on law enforcement officers to obtain appropriate clothing. For that reason, we hold that exigent circumstances existed for the officers to enter [lessee's] apartment without a warrant to obtain clothing for him." *U.S. v. Wilson*, 306 F.3d 231 (5th Cir. 2002).

- "The police here believed the suspects to be armed and in possession of easily-disposed-of illicit drugs. Yet, without justification, they abandoned their secure surveillance positions and took action they believed might give the suspects cause and opportunity to retrieve the weapons or dispose of the drugs. Their decision to take this action was not justified by an absence of time to secure a warrant or by any other reasonable

predicate. The record is devoid of evidence that an
exigency was created by the suspects' awareness of police surveillance, or that the suspects were attempting
to leave the premises with drugs, or otherwise seeking
to dispose of same. No exigency was an otherwise natural occurrence during the course of the police
investigation. The police may not now rely on these circumstances of their own making to support the proposition that the warrant requirement should be excused."
U.S. v. Vega, 221 F.3d 789, 799–800, 54 Fed. R. Evid.
Serv. 1502 (5th Cir. 2000).

Sixth Circuit

- "The risk of danger exigency most frequently justifies
  warrantless entries in cases where the Government is
  acting in something other than a traditional law
  enforcement capacity. Because we find that [the law
  enforcement officer] was neither faced with any true
  immediacy, nor confronted by any real danger that serious consequences would certainly occur to the police or
  others if he did not enter the. . . residence, we conclude
  that exigent circumstances, in particular, the risk of
  danger exigency cannot justify [the officer's] warrantless entry. First, it is clear that time was not of the essence in attending to the possible water leak at the. . .
  residence. . . . Second, any risk of danger to the police
  or others was created by the agents when they permitted [defendant's landlady] to reenter the. . . residence. .
  . . Third, other than the danger created by the agents,
  there was no risk of danger as that term is used in
  Fourth Amendment jurisprudence because the potential
  danger was merely the risk of damage to property and
  such risk was, at best, speculative. . . . Moreover, it is
  clear that securing a warrant in this case would not
  have presented any significant problem. . . .We find it
  clear that the entry into the Bluegrass residence was
  not justified by exigent circumstances." *U.S. v. Williams*,
  354 F.3d 497, 2003 FED App. 0456A (6th Cir. 2003).

Seventh Circuit

- "Police may not search a person's home without a warrant unless there is an emergency . . . [or] what in
  legal jargon. . .are called 'exigent circumstances' (cita-

tions omitted). . . . [In this case,] we are left with a
group of people appearing at [defendant's] door, several
in police uniform, and a person in the house observing
unsurprisingly that 'the police are at the door,' together
with a sound of movement, not further defined—unless
someone was standing right inside the door when the
police knocked, there would have had to be movement
within before the door could be opened. No doubt at
some point, knowing there were people in the house,
knowing it was a drug house, the officers would be reasonable in inferring from the failure to answer the door
that the persons inside were busy destroying evidence,
or perhaps even arming themselves to resist entry by
the police violently (citations omitted). The Supreme
Court has suggested that the police need not hold off
for more than 15 or 20 seconds (citation omitted). . . .
[However,] there is no purpose in knocking if the occupant isn't given a chance to answer the door. . . .
The government has presented no evidence that, like
mink devouring their young when they hear a loud
noise, criminals always (or at least in the vast majority
of cases) set about to destroy evidence whenever the police knock on the door. Doubtless it is a common reaction, but how common we are not told. . . . Many cases
say that law-enforcement officers cannot be allowed to
manufacture an emergency and then use the emergency
to justify dispensing with the procedures ordinarily
required to search a home (citations omitted). . . . But
the 'manufacturing' metaphor is misleading. . . . [I]n
the present case, . . . the officers had time to obtain a
warrant and no reason to think before they arrived at
[defendant's] door that anyone inside the house knew
the police were approaching. They had time at least to
initiate the process of obtaining a warrant by phone or
email, and if something happened before the warrant
was issued to create a grave concern about the possible
destruction of evidence they could have moved in at
once. But nothing happened; and it is the fact that nothing happened, rather than the 'manufacture of exigent
circumstances,' that undermines the government's
position. For there is a sense in which any time police
knock and announce their presence and the occupants
respond in a suspicious manner (such as the "running

feet" not heard in this case), the police can be regarded as the "manufacturers" of the emergency that then justifies their barging in and searching the house and arresting the occupants. That would not justify suppression of the evidence found in the search (citation omitted). . . . The government argues that the police waited 30 or even 45 seconds before breaking down [defendant's] door. The judge, however, as the government fails to acknowledge, found only that it was more than 20 seconds. . . . Even 20 seconds may be a long time to answer a knock on the door by the police when someone is heard within acknowledging that the police are at the door. But the government does not argue that a 20-second interval is long enough to justify entering the house forcibly. It does not argue for a 30-second or a 20-second or a 15-second rule, though the case law we cited might well be thought to justify such a rule when there is probable cause to believe that a house contains drugs and occupants. . . . The district judge did not find that the police had heard [occupants of the house] 'yell' or that what they did hear could be interpreted as a warning [that police are here and to destroy the drugs]. . . . In short, if police hear a crime being committed within a house (and spoliation of evidence is a crime), then they can enter immediately, without knocking; if they do not hear a crime (more precisely, if they do not have probable cause to believe a crime is in progress), they have to get a warrant. The government has failed to show that in this case the police had probable cause to believe that evidence was being, or was about to be, destroyed when they entered. . . ." *U.S. v. Collins*, 510 F.3d 697 (7th Cir. 2007).

- "Police received a 911 emergency call of an assault, possibly in progress. Such calls, by themselves, 'can be enough to support warrantless searches under the exigent circumstances exception, particularly where... the caller identified himself.' [The 911 caller] identified herself when reporting the assault. Additionally, [the arresting officer] found the front door open in the middle of the night and heard a noise from inside the house that sounded like a person standing up and falling down. Based on those circumstances, a reasonable officer would have feared for the safety of someone inside.

Accordingly, because exigent circumstances justified [the officer's] entry, we uphold the district court's denial of [defendant's] motion to suppress. *U.S. v. Jenkins*, 329 F.3d 579 (7th Cir. 2003).

- "In the context of removing a child from his home and family, a seizure is reasonable if it is pursuant to a court order, if it is supported by probable cause, or if it is justified by exigent circumstances, meaning that state officers have reason to believe that life or limb is in immediate jeopardy." *Brokaw v. Mercer County*, 235 F.3d 1000, 1010 (7th Cir. 2000).

- "When determining whether exigent circumstances exist, the court must analyze the situation from the perspective of the officers at the scene. Accordingly, we ask not what the police could have done but rather whether they had, at the time, a reasonable belief that there was a compelling need to act and no time to procure a search warrant." *U.S. v. Marshall*, 157 F.3d 477, 482 (7th Cir. 1998).

Eighth Circuit

- "We have held in a number of cases that police officers are justified in making an exigent-circumstances entry when, after going to a residence with evidence that an individual was involved in a drug transaction, they knock and identify themselves and then witness an individual retreat or conduct himself in a way that suggests the destruction of evidence." *U.S. v. Cisneros-Gutierrez*, 598 F.3d 997 (8th Cir. 2010).

Ninth Circuit

- "[Defendant] argues that the Government failed to show that a telephonic warrant was either unavailable or impracticable under the circumstances. . . . This burden, however, is not part of the emergency doctrine. . . nor has this showing been required in our precedent applying the doctrine." *U.S. v. Stafford*, 416 F.3d 1068 (9th Cir. 2005).

- "The emergency doctrine is derived from police officers' community caretaking function. ... The appropriateness of the emergency doctrine is best understood in light of the particular facts of a case in which it is invoked. The officers here knew that Christopher's mother [,who had been arrested,] was not caring for him, and they could not locate him in the places she said he was. They were also unaware of the safety conditions inside the house. The possibility of a nine-year-old child in a house in the middle of the night without the supervision of any responsible adult is a situation requiring immediate police assistance. Further, the district court's determination that the officers acted out of a genuine concern for Christopher's welfare is supported by the record. [The investigating officer] specifically testified that he entered the house to determine if Christopher was being supervised by a responsible adult. Additionally, before the officers entered the house, they took several other steps. They knocked at the front door first, asked [the mother] again where Christopher was, and went across the street to wake up a neighbor and ask him about the boy. This evidence supports the district court's finding that the officers' entry was motivated by a concern for Christopher's welfare. Thus, we agree with the district court that [the officers'] entry was lawful. ... [T]he record reflects that the officers lawfully walked through the house in order to assist Christopher in dressing. All of the evidence described in the search warrant to establish probable cause for the subsequent search was in plain view. Thus, the use of the evidence was lawful." *U.S. v. Bradley,* 321 F.3d 1212 (9th Cir. 2003).

- "The Fourth Amendment prohibits police officers from making a warrantless entry into a person's home, unless the officers have probable cause and are presented with exigent circumstances." *LaLonde v. County of Riverside,* 204 F.3d 947, 954 (9th Cir. 2000).

Tenth Circuit

- "[T]he exigent circumstances exception permits warrantless home entries when officers reasonably believe that some actor or object in a house may *immediately* cause harm to persons or property not in or near the house." *Armijo ex rel. Armijo Sanchez v. Peterson,* 601 F.3d 1065 (10th Cir. 2010) (emphasis in original).

- "[J]ust as exigent circumstances permit a warrantless home entry, emergencies may justify a warrantless seizure in the home." *Armijo ex rel. Armijo Sanchez v. Peterson,* 601 F.3d 1065 (10th Cir. 2010).

- "The Fourth Amendment does not require officers to use the least restrictive means to investigate a threat." *Armijo ex rel. Armijo Sanchez v. Peterson*, 601 F.3d 1065 (10th Cir. 2010).

- "In risk of personal danger cases, the basic aspects of the exigent circumstances exception are (1) the officers must have reasonable grounds to believe that there is an immediate need to protect the lives or safety of themselves or others; (2) the search must not be motivated by an intent to arrest or seize evidence; and (3) there must be some reasonable basis, approaching probable cause, to associate the emergency with the place to be searched." *U.S. v. Thomas*, 372 F.3d 1173 (10th Cir. 2004).

- "There are four requirements for a permissible warrantless entry when the police fear the imminent destruction of evidence. Such an entry must be (1) pursuant to clear evidence of probable cause, (2) available only for serious crimes and in circumstances where the destruction of evidence is likely, (3) limited in scope to the minimum intrusion necessary, and (4) supported by clearly defined indicators of exigency that are not subject to police manipulation or abuse." *U.S. v. Carter*, 360 F.3d 1235 (10th Cir. 2004).

- "After examining the record, we conclude that it contains no evidence that could lead a reasonable state actor to conclude that there were exigent circumstances [justifying the removal of a child from his home]. Although defendants at times assert that a delay to obtain a warrant might have cost [the child] his life, the evidence shows otherwise. Defendants were aware that various doctors had suspected that [the child] was a victim of [Munchausen's Syndrome By Proxy] for quite some time, and the record indicates that there was nothing particularly unusual about [his] condition at the time he was removed. [The child's] attending physician stated on the phone that it would be a mistake to remove him from the home. Because no evidence indicates that [the child] was in immediate threat of death or severe physical harm—indeed, the evidence points to the opposite conclusion—we do not find sufficient exigent circumstances to relieve the state actors here of the burden of obtaining a warrant." *Roska ex rel. Roska v. Peterson*, 328 F.3d 1230 (10th Cir. 2003).

- "The government bears the burden of proving exigency. . . . In assessing whether the burden was met, we are guided by the realities of the situation presented by the record. We should evaluate the circumstances as they would have appeared to prudent, cautious, and trained officers. . . . There is no absolute test for determining whether exigent circumstances are present because such a determination ultimately depends on the unique facts of each controversy. . . . [W]e should remember that, as an exception to the warrant requirement, exigent circumstances must be jealously and carefully drawn." *U.S. v. Anderson*, 154 F.3d 1225, 1233 (10th Cir. 1998).

Eleventh Circuit

- "In light of the relevant circumstances in this case, we conclude there is no question but that there was an objectively imminent danger to the Doe children so as to justify [social worker's] temporary removal of the children without prior court authorization. ... Appellants also contend that [the statute under which the children were removed] and [social worker's] application of it violated their Fourth Amendment right to be free from unreasonable searches and seizures. ... [T]he seizure of the children was not unconstitutional if supported by exigent circumstances." *Doe v. Kearney*, 329 F.3d 1286 (11th Cir. 2003).

- "This case presents an issue of first impression to this Circuit concerning whether law enforcement officials may conduct a warrantless search of a private residence in response to an emergency situation reported by an anonymous 911 caller. We conclude that when exigent circumstances demand an immediate response, particularly where there is danger to human life, protection of the public becomes paramount and can justify a limited, warrantless intrusion into the home. . . [B]ased on the information conveyed by the 911 caller and the personal observations of the officers, there was probable cause to believe a person located at the residence was in danger. Under the exigent circumstances exception to the Fourth Amendment, the officers were not required to obtain a warrant before entering Appellant's home. . . [T]he warrantless search of Appellant's residence was

463

based largely on information provided by an anonymous caller. However, the information given by the caller involved a serious threat to human life. Furthermore, the information concerned an on-going emergency requiring immediate action. . . Because the police had no reason to doubt the veracity of the 911 call, particularly in light of the personal observations of the officers once they arrived on the scene, their warrantless search for victims was constitutional." *U.S. v. Holloway*, 290 F.3d 1331 (11th Cir. 2002).

• "If we were to condone the warrantless entry of [the] apartment under the circumstances presented here, we would effectively allow officers to create exigencies by failing to procure a warrant while there was time to do so. Every situation would become an eventual emergency; the practice of obtaining a warrant would soon fall by the wayside, and the exception would swallow the rule. Thus, we hold that in circumstances such as those presented here, where law enforcement agents have ample time and information to secure an anticipatory search warrant, lack of time to obtain a warrant after delivery of the contraband is insufficient to justify a warrantless search." *U.S. v. Santa*, 236 F.3d 662, 674 (11th Cir. 2000).

§ 8:2   Definition: Examples of exigent circumstances include hot pursuit, a fleeing suspect, destruction of evidence, or other situations in which speed is essential

<u>Supreme Court</u>

• "We do not express any view on whether [the officer's] entry into [the home owner's] yard in pursuit of [the suspect] was constitutional. But whether or not the constitutional rule applied by the court below was correct, it was not 'beyond debate.' There is no suggestion in this case that [the officer] knowingly violated the Constitution; the question is whether, in light of precedent existing at the time, he was 'plainly incompetent' in entering [the home owner's] yard to pursue the fleeing [suspect]. The Ninth Circuit concluded that he was. It did so despite the fact that federal and state courts nationwide are sharply divided on the question whether an officer with probable cause to arrest a suspect for a misdemeanor may enter a home without a warrant while in hot pursuit of that suspect. . . . To summarize the law at the time [the officer] made his split-second decision to enter [the home owner's] yard: Two opinions of this Court were equivocal on the lawfulness of his entry; two opinions of the State Court of Appeal affirmatively authorized that entry; the most relevant opinion of the Ninth Circuit was readily distinguishable; two Federal District Courts in the Ninth Circuit had granted qualified immunity in the wake of that opinion; and the federal and state courts of last resort around the Nation were sharply divided. Stanton may have been mistaken in believing his actions were justified, but he was not 'plainly incompetent.' " *Stanton v. Sims*, 134 S. Ct. 3, 187 L. Ed. 2d 341 (2013) (42 U.S.C.A. § 1983 action by home owner who alleged that when officer kicked open fence gate, which she had been standing behind, her forehead was cut and her shoulder was injured; remanded for consideration of officer's claim to qualified immunity).

- "The question presented here is whether the natural metabolization of alcohol in the bloodstream presents a *per se* exigency that justifies an exception to the Fourth Amendment's warrant requirement for nonconsensual blood testing in all drunk-driving cases. We conclude that it does not, and we hold, consistent with general Fourth Amendment principles, that exigency in this context must be determined case by case based on the totality of the circumstances. . . . The State properly recognizes that the reasonableness of a warrantless search under the exigency exception to the warrant requirement must be evaluated based on the totality of the circumstances. But the State nevertheless seeks a *per se* rule for blood testing in drunk-driving cases. . . . It is true that as a result of the human body's natural metabolic processes, the alcohol level in a person's blood begins to dissipate once the alcohol is fully absorbed and continues to decline until the alcohol is eliminated. . . . This fact was essential to our holding in *Schmerber*, as we recognized that, under the circumstances, further delay in order to secure a warrant after the time spent investigating the scene of the accident and transporting the injured suspect to the hospital to receive treatment would have threatened the destruction of evidence. But it does not follow that we should depart from careful case-by-case assessment of exigency and adopt the categorical rule proposed by the State and its *amici*. In those drunk-driving investigations where police officers can reasonably obtain a warrant before a blood sample can be drawn without significantly undermining the efficacy of the search, the Fourth Amendment mandates that they do so. We do not doubt that some circumstances will make obtaining a warrant impractical such that the dissipation of alcohol from the bloodstream will support an exigency justifying a properly conducted warrantless blood test. That, however, is a reason to decide each case on its facts, as we did in *Schmerber,* not to accept the considerable overgeneralization that a *per se* rule would reflect. The context of blood testing is different in critical respects from other destruction-of-evidence cases in which the police are truly confronted with a now or never situation. . . . The State's proposed *per se* rule also fails to account for advances in the 47 years since *Schmerber* was decided that allow for the more expeditious processing of warrant applications, particularly in contexts like drunk-driving investigations where the evidence offered to establish probable cause is simple. The Federal Rules of Criminal Procedure were amended in 1977 to permit federal magistrate judges to issue a warrant based on sworn testimony communicated by telephone. As amended, the law now allows a federal magistrate judge to consider "information communicated by telephone or other reliable electronic means." States have also innovated. Well over a majority of States allow police officers or prosecutors to apply for search warrants remotely through various means, including telephonic or radio communication, electronic communication such as e-mail, and video conferencing. And in addition to technology-based developments, jurisdictions have found other ways to streamline the warrant process, such as by using standard-form warrant applications for drunk-driving investigations. We by no means claim that telecommunications innovations have, will, or should eliminate all delay from the warrant-application process. Warrants inevitably take some time for police officers or prosecutors to complete and for magistrate judges to review. Telephonic and electronic warrants may still require officers to follow time-consuming formalities designed to create an adequate record, such as preparing a duplicate warrant before calling the magistrate judge. And improvements in communications technology do not guarantee that a magistrate judge will be available when an officer needs a warrant after making a late-night arrest. But technological developments that enable police officers to secure warrants more quickly, and do so without undermining the neutral magistrate judge's essential role as a check on police discretion, are relevant to an assessment of exigency. That is particularly so in this context, where BAC evidence is lost gradually and relatively predictably. Of course, there are important countervailing concerns. While experts can work backwards from the BAC at the time the sample was taken to determine the BAC at the time of the alleged offense, longer intervals may raise questions about the accuracy of the calculation. For that reason, exigent circumstances justifying a warrantless blood sample may arise in the regular course of law enforcement due to delays from the warrant application process. But adopting the State's *per se* approach would improperly ignore the current and future technological developments in warrant procedures, and might well diminish the incentive for jurisdictions to pursue progressive approaches to warrant acquisition that preserve the protections afforded by the warrant while meeting the legitimate interests of law enforcement. In short, while the natural dissipation of alcohol in the blood may support a finding of exigency in a specific case, as it did in *Schmerber*, it does not do so categorically. Whether a warrantless blood test of a drunk-driving suspect is reasonable must be determined case by case based on the totality of the circumstances." *Missouri v. McNeely*, 133 S. Ct. 1552, 1556, 1560–63, 185 L. Ed. 2d 696 (2013) (inner quotations and citations omitted).

- "Officers do not need ironclad proof of 'a likely serious, life-threatening' injury to invoke the emergency aid exception. . . . [T]he test, as we have said, is not what [the police officer] believed, but whether there was 'an objectively reasonable basis for believing' that medical assistance was needed, or persons were in danger." *Michigan v. Fisher*, 558 U.S. 45, 130 S. Ct. 546, 175 L. Ed. 2d 410, 58 A.L.R.6th 839 (2009).

- "Only when an apparent threat has become an actual harm can officers rule out innocuous explanations for ominous circumstances. But '[t]he role of a peace officer includes preventing violence and restoring order, not simply rendering first aid to casualties.' (citation omitted) It sufficed to invoke the emergency aid exception that it was reasonable to believe that [defendant] had hurt himself (albeit nonfatally) and needed treatment that in his rage he was unable to provide, or that [defendant] was about to hurt, or had already hurt, someone else." *Michigan v. Fisher*, 558 U.S. 45, 130 S. Ct. 546, 175 L. Ed. 2d 410, 58 A.L.R.6th 839 (2009).

- "A warrantless search by the police is invalid unless it falls within one of the narrow and well-delineated exceptions to the warrant requirement. . . . [I]n. . .*Mincy v. Arizona*. . .we rejected the contention that there is a murder scene exception to the Warrant Clause of the Fourth Amendment. We noted that police may make warrantless entries onto premises if they reasonably believe a person in in need of immediate aid and may make prompt warrantless searches of a homicide scene for possible other victims or a killer on the premises. . .but we rejected any general murder scene exception as inconsistent with the Fourth and Foureenth Amendments—. . . ." *Flippo v. West Virginia*, 528 U.S. 11, 13–14, 120 S. Ct. 7, 145 L. Ed. 2d 16 (1999).

- "Except for the fact that the offense under investigation was a homicide, there were no exigent circumstances in this case. . . . There was no indication that evidence would be lost, destroyed, or removed during the time required to obtain a search warrant. Indeed, the police guard at the apartment minimized that possibility. And there is no suggestion that a search warrant could not easily and conveniently have been obtained. We decline to hold that the seriousness of the offense under investigation itself creates exigent circumstances of the kind that under the Fourth Amendment justify a warrantless search." *Mincey v. Arizona*, 437 U.S. 385, 394, 98 S. Ct. 2408, 57 L. Ed. 2d 290 (1978).

- "[The Officers] saw [the suspect] standing in the doorway of the house with a brown paper bag in her hand. They pulled up to within 15 feet of [the suspect] and got out of their van, shouting 'police' and displaying their identification. As the officers approached, [the suspect] retreated into the vestibule of her house. . . . The. . .question is whether her act of retreating into her house could thwart an otherwise proper arrest. We hold that it could not." *U.S. v. Santana*, 427 U.S. 38, 40, 96 S. Ct. 2406, 49 L. Ed. 2d 300 (1976).

- "The police were informed that an armed robbery had taken place, and that the suspect had entered [the house] less than five minutes before they reached it. They acted reasonably when they entered the house and began to search for a man of the description they had been given and for weapons which he had used in the robbery or might use against them. Speed here was essential, and only a thorough search of the house for persons and weapons could have insured that [the suspect] was the only man present and that the police had control of all weapons which could be used against them or to effect an escape." *Warden, Md. Penitentiary v. Hayden*, 387 U.S. 294, 298–99, 87 S. Ct. 1642, 18 L. Ed. 2d 782 (1967).

First Circuit

- "The appellant also challenges the district court's related finding that the situation the agents encountered at the Cedar Street apartment constituted exigent circumstances. The facts, as supportably found by the district court, are straightforward. As soon as the agents knocked on the front door of the apartment and identified themselves, they heard someone inside the apartment running away from the door. They noticed that the door was sealed shut. Given the totality of what they knew and what they reasonably suspected, the agents had reason to think—as the district court found—that the unseen individual was trying to destroy evidence. The agents knew that drugs can be flushed down a toilet or washed down a drain in the blink of an eye. Furthermore, the fact that the front door was sealed shut was itself suspicious. Weighing these facts, the district court found that the agents were confronted by exigent circumstances. Moreover, the agents 'did not create the exigency by engaging or threatening to engage in conduct that violates the Fourth Amendment.' Thus, the court reasoned, the exigency—combined with the existence of probable cause—justified the agents' warrantless entry into the apartment. We agree: when entry into private premises is reasonably necessary to head off the imminent loss of evidence, a law enforcement officer armed with probable cause normally may enter the premises without a warrant. In an effort to blunt the force of this reasoning, the appellant suggests that what the agents heard was equally consistent with the sounds made by someone moving toward the front door to admit the agents. But this is whistling past the graveyard: the front door was sealed shut and, given the circumstances that obtained, a law enforcement officer might well have distinguished whether the footsteps of a person inside the apartment were moving toward his location or away from it. The sockdolager, of course, is that the district court credited the agents' impressions that the noises they heard sounded like someone running away from the front door. That was a finding of fact, and it was not clearly erroneous. In sum, the record solidly supports the district court's determination that probable cause and exigent circumstances coalesced to justify the agents' warrantless entry into the Cedar Street apartment. Consequently, the evidence found in plain sight at the time of that entry, together with the evidence gathered as a result of the ensuing warrant-backed search, was admissible at trial. It follows inexorably, as night follows day, that the district court did not err in denying the appellant's motion to suppress." *United States v. Almonte-Báez*, 857 F.3d 27, 31–34 (1st Cir. 2017) (citations omitted).

- "This appeal poses the question of whether police officers, responding to a call from a citizen concerned that the door to her absent neighbor's home is standing wide open, have a right to enter the home in pursuance of their community caretaking function. While the answer to this question is freighted with uncertainty, that uncertainty points the way to the proper disposition of the case: because there is no clearly established law that would deter reasonable police officers from effecting such an entry, the individual defendants are entitled to qualified immunity. Consequently, we affirm the district court's dismissal of the action." *MacDonald v. Town of Eastham*, 745 F.3d 8 (1st Cir. 2014).

- "Exigent circumstances exist where there is such a compelling necessity for immediate action as will not brook the delay of obtaining a warrant. . . . There are four recognized categories of exigent circumstance: (1) hot pursuit of a fleeing felon; (2) threatened destruction of evidence inside a residence before a warrant can be obtained; (3) a risk that the suspect may escape from the residence undetected; or (4) a threat, posed by a suspect, to the lives or safety of the public, the police officers, or to herself." *Fletcher v. Town of Clinton*, 196 F.3d 41, 49 (1st Cir. 1999).

Third Circuit

- "[C]ritical to *Hayden's* reasoning was the fact that 'the seizures occurred *prior to or immediately contemporaneous with* Hayden's arrest, as part of an effort to find a[n armed] suspected felon.' This case differs from *Hayden* because the gun was not found 'prior to or contemporaneous with' Mallory's arrest, but *after* the premises had been secured, Mallory had been located and handcuffed, and as he was being led out the front door by multiple officers. . . . From *Hayden, Ford, Goree,* and *Lopez* we can discern factors that will be useful for determining whether the search in this case was justified by a reasonable belief that it was necessary to protect officer safety. These factors may include, but are not limited to: how soon after the alleged offense the search occurred; whether the alleged offense was violent in nature; whether the search occurred prior to or contemporaneous with Mallory's apprehension; whether the premises as a whole had been secured, or whether it was possible that unknown individuals remained in the house; whether Mallory or any of his family members had acted in an aggressive or threatening manner toward the police; whether other members of the family were free to move about the house unsupervised by an officer; how easily Mallory or a family member could have obtained and used the firearm; and the degree of

471

intrusiveness of the search. In light of these considerations, we agree with the District Court that any
exigency justifying a warrantless search had dissipated
by the time Officer Hough recovered the gun, and
therefore suppression was warranted." *U.S. v. Mallory*,
765 F.3d 373, 384, 386 (3d Cir. 2014) (citations omitted).

- "Warrantless seizure of defendant's shoes following his
  interview with police was lawful under exigent circumstances; although there was a coercive element in the
  police officer's statement that defendant would have to
  remain at the police station while he applied for a warrant, where such coercion was minimal given that
  exigent circumstances, or the possibility that evidence
  may have been removed or destroyed, justified a warrantless seizure of defendant's shoes." *U.S. v. Tyree*,
  292 Fed. Appx. 207 (3d Cir. 2008).

Fifth Circuit

- "The government cannot rely on exigent circumstances
  to excuse a warrantless entry if it created the exigent
  circumstances through its own actions. We distinguish
  between cases where the exigent circumstances arise
  naturally during a delay in obtaining a warrant and
  those where officers have deliberately created the
  exigent circumstances. When determining whether the
  government created the exigent circumstances, this
  Court considers not just the motivation of the officers,
  but also the reasonableness and propriety of the
  investigative tactics that created the exigency." *U.S. v.
  Hearn*, 563 F.3d 95 (5th Cir. 2009).

- "The possibility that evidence will be removed or
  destroyed, the pursuit of a suspect, and immediate
  safety risks to officers and others are exigent circumstances that may excuse an otherwise unconstitutional
  intrusion into a residence. . . .Because it is essentially
  a factual determination, there is no set formula for
  determining when exigent circumstances may justify a
  warrantless entry." *U.S. v. Jones*, 239 F.3d 716, 720
  (5th Cir. 2001).

- "In addition to the problem of a lack of probable cause,
  the officers also did not have exigent circumstances.
  The government bears the burden of proving that an
  exigency existed. . . . In this case, the officers did not

face any serious concerns regarding exigency. The record reflects no evidence that the contraband was about to be removed or destroyed. The officers could have waited while a search warrant was obtained with little or no danger to the officers guarding the warehouse. Further, the suspects did not know that the officers were present outside the warehouse. These facts and circumstances do not support the district court's finding of exigency, and therefore, without probable cause and exigent circumstances, the warrantless entry was unreasonable." *U.S. v. Morales*, 171 F.3d 978, 982 (5th Cir. 1999).

Sixth Circuit

- "On appeal, Lewis limits his challenge to the opening of the door. But the Fourth Amendment does not preclude the mere opening of the vehicle door in the context of these facts. The police here engaged in a function that was entirely divorced from a criminal investigation, such that the 'community caretaker' exception to the Fourth Amendment applied. Therefore, because '[t]he standard of probable cause is peculiarly related to criminal investigations, not routine, noncriminal procedures,' Officers Turner and Cloyd did not need a warrant or probable cause for their limited intrusion on Lewis's privacy. . . . First, the local officers' action here fits within the community-caretaker exception. Officers Turner and Cloyd responded to reports that a woman was intoxicated in a Wal-Mart; observed that she was, in fact, intoxicated to the point of 'nodding off'; and tried to get her out of the store without arresting her by finding her a safe ride home. This case is similar to other cases in which this court has applied the community-caretaker exception. Most notably, in *Rohrig*, local police officers responded to complaints of loud music blaring from a private home in the middle of the night and entered the home without a warrant 'for the limited purpose of locating and abating [the] nuisance'—an action that this court deemed to fall within the community-caretaker function. Similarly, in this case, local police officers Turner and Cloyd responded to reports of a visibly intoxicated woman in a Wal-Mart, and approached her boyfriend Lewis solely to determine

whether he would be able to drive her home. . . .
Second, there is no evidence that the officers' action
was taken with any traditional law-enforcement purpose
that would make the community-caretaker exception
inapplicable. The community-caretaking exception applies most clearly when the action of the police is 'totally
divorced from the detection, investigation, or acquisition of evidence relating to the violation of a criminal
statute,' . . .. Here, the district court found that the officers' 'sole purpose was to find Lakes a safe ride home,'
from which the district court concluded that the officers
'were not investigating a crime.' In the context of a motion to suppress, such a finding can be overturned only
if clearly erroneous. There was no clear error here: Officer Turner testified as to his and Officer Cloyd's
purpose, which the district court clearly found credible;
furthermore, there is no evidence in the record to rebut
this account of the officers' purpose. Accordingly, this
case is similar to Brown, in which this court reasoned
that the community-caretaker exception would apply to
a police officer's stopping a vehicle because the officer
was not seeking to investigate a crime but only to question the driver as to the whereabouts of a missing
minor. Furthermore, this case is distinguishable from
United States v. Williams, where this court refused to
apply the community-caretaking exception for officers
who entered a home, ostensibly to investigate claims of
a water leak, but also because they had grounds to
suspect the home was being used to grow marijuana.
. . . Third, given the community-caretaking nature of
the officers' action, any limited intrusion on Lewis's
privacy from simply opening the door was reasonable.
Lewis was in his car, not his home, which weighs in
favor of the reasonableness of any search. As the
Supreme Court noted in the case that gave rise to the
community-caretaker exception, 'for the purposes of the
Fourth Amendment there is a constitutional difference
between houses and cars,' because of the 'ambulatory
character' of cars and the fact that 'extensive, and often
noncriminal contact with automobiles will bring local
officials in "plain view" of evidence, fruits, or instrumentalities of a crime, or contraband.' Accordingly, as this
circuit has noted, 'the community caretaking function

articulated in [Dombrowski] has been principally applied to the warrantless searches of automobiles.' The fact that Lewis was in his car also distinguishes this case from the two cases that he cites in arguing that the community-caretaker exception should not apply. In both cases, the court held that the community-caretaker exception did not apply because whatever interest the community had in the intrusion could not overcome the significant privacy interests in the home—a concern that is not present in this case. . . . . Furthermore, the officers' intrusion into Lewis's car was minimal, which also weighs in favor of the reasonableness of any search. This is not a case where the police officers conducted a search of the vehicle looking for drugs—for example, by looking in the glove compartment, looking under the seats, opening the trunk, or opening containers in the car. Rather, the officers merely opened the door to check on the apparently sleeping Lewis, which prompted Lewis to throw the baggie containing pills onto the back floorboard of his truck, catching Officer Turner's attention. True, the officers apparently did not knock on the truck window or attempt to speak with Lewis before opening the door, which might have been more respectful of Lewis's privacy. However, as the Fourth Circuit has reasoned, 'the community-caretaking exception is not limited to the least intrusive means of protecting the public.' Given that the officers' opening of Lewis's door was minimally intrusive, any failure to knock or attempt to speak does not make the officers' actions here unreasonable." *United States v. Lewis*, 2017 WL 3668439, *2-3 (6th Cir. 2017) (citations omitted).

- "We agree. . .that the activation of an alarm in conjunction with additional information supporting the possibility of a break-in is sufficient to support police officers' determination that an exigency exists. The very purpose for a home security alarm is to signal that something may be amiss . . . . While this court by no means suggests that the police have license to enter a private residence every time an alarm is activated, they do have a duty to investigate, and, when the facts and circumstances suggest reasonable suspicion that an exigency exists, to enter the home." *U.S. v. Brown*, 449 F.3d 741, 2006 FED App. 0184P (6th Cir. 2006).

- "The Appellant emphasizes that the police admitted that exigent circumstances were not present before they arrived at the [decedent's] home, and that the police never saw a crime being committed and did not hear [decedent] threaten anyone. As the district court correctly observed, however, the fact that exigent circumstances did not exist at some earlier point in time is irrelevant, since our inquiry is limited to whether exigent circumstances existed at the moment the police entered the residence. Moreover, this court has never held that the police must witness a crime for exigent circumstances to be present. Where, as here, an armed and volatile individual poses an obvious threat to another, we do not believe the Fourth Amendment requires the police to stand idly by until they actually observe a criminal act." *Ewolski v. City of Brunswick*, 287 F.3d 492, 2002 FED App. 0133P (6th Cir. 2002).
- "The police must have an objectively reasonable basis for their belief that evidence will be lost or destroyed— the mere possibility of the loss or destruction of evidence is an insufficient basis for the warrantless entry of a house to prevent the destruction of evidence." *U.S. v. Ukomadu*, 236 F.3d 333, 337, 2001 FED App. 0006P (6th Cir. 2001).
- "[A] warrantless entry to prevent the destruction of evidence is justified if the government demonstrates: 1) a reasonable belief that third parties are inside the dwelling; and 2) a reasonable belief that these third parties may soon become aware the police are on their trail, so that the destruction of evidence would be in order." *U.S. v. Lewis*, 231 F.3d 238, 241, 2000 FED App. 0383P (6th Cir. 2000).
- "This Court has traditionally found the presence of exigent circumstances excusing the warrant requirement for entry into a home where (1) the officers involved were in hot pursuit of a fleeing suspect; (2) the suspect posed an immediate threat to arresting officers or to the public; and (3) immediate police action was necessary to prevent the destruction of vital evidence or to prevent the escape of a known criminal." *Ingram v. City of Columbus*, 185 F.3d 579, 587, 1999 FED App. 0258P (6th Cir. 1999).
- "This Circuit has adopted a two-pronged test to deter-

mine when the possibility of the destruction of evidence might constitute exigent circumstances sufficient to justify a warrantless entry into a home. Warrantless entry to prevent the destruction of evidence is justified if the government demonstrates: (1) a reasonable belief that third parties are inside the dwelling; and (2) a reasonable belief that the loss or destruction of evidence is imminent." *U.S. v. Gaitan-Acevedo*, 148 F.3d 577, 585, 49 Fed. R. Evid. Serv. 590, 1998 FED App. 0143P (6th Cir. 1998).

- "[E]xigent circumstances permitted the officers to conduct a warrantless examination of a vehicle that was unlocked and running in an area where a crowd had gathered. In only a matter of seconds, an individual could have taken the car or the car could have injured any member of the crowd or a police officer had it slipped out of gear. . . . Under the community caretaking function enunciated by the Supreme Court in *Cady v. Dombrowski*. . .we conclude that officers were entitled to enter the car without a warrant in order to protect themselves and the public from the danger created by the manner in which plaintiff's car was left unattended." *Smith v. Thornburg*, 136 F.3d 1070, 1075, 1998 FED App. 0056P (6th Cir. 1998).

Seventh Circuit

- "One such exception is the exigent circumstances exception, which allows for a warrantless entry into a home 'when there is a pressing need for the police to enter' but insufficient time to secure a warrant. A subset of this exception is the emergency aid doctrine, which 'recognizes that a warrantless entry into the home may be appropriate when police enter for an urgent purpose other than to arrest a suspect or to look for evidence of a crime.' Pursuant to the doctrine, warrantless entry is permitted 'to render emergency assistance to an injured occupant or to protect an occupant from imminent injury.' The burden rests with the government to establish that the emergency aid doctrine applies. An objective test applies and requires the court to determine whether the officer, given the facts that were known to him or her at the time, reasonably believed it was necessary to enter the home 'to render assistance or

prevent harm to persons or property within.' Because
this is an objective test, the officer's subjective intent
and the seriousness of the crime being investigated are
irrelevant to whether the doctrine applies. Rather, the
defining characteristic of the doctrine is urgency." *United
States v. Tepiew*, 859 F.3d 452, 456–57 (7th Cir. 2017).

• "The. . .question. . .is whether the government can
bear the burden of demonstrating that the police faced
exigent circumstances when they searched the safe [in
defendant's hotel room]. [citation omitted] Exigent circumstances exist if a[n] officer had an objectively 'reasonable belief that there was a compelling need to act
and no time to obtain a warrant.' [citation omitted]
[Defendant] argues first that any exigencies dissolved
once the police arrived and realized that the kidnapping victim, Colon, was not and never had been in the
room. . . . The question as to whether exigent circumstances exist is viewed through the eyes of a reasonable
police officer. [citation omitted] When the officers arrived, they did indeed conclude that Colon was not in
[defendant's] room and never had been there. That
conclusion, however, did not eviscerate the exigency.
. . . [At that point (1:30 a.m.)], Colon was still missing
and the ransom was four hours late. The kidnappers,
who had already threatened to kill Colon, had called
the victim's family again demanding to know why the
ransom had not yet been paid. Police officers also knew
that the kidnappers were conducting counter-
surveillance and that they probably knew that [defen-
dant] had been arrested. . . . [Defendant] argues that
because Colon himself could not have been hidden in
the small safe there were no exigencies that permitted
a search of the safe. [However], there was a great deal
of evidence to suggest that [defendant] had been in the
room and the officers had compelling reasons to suspect
that [defendant] was involved in the kidnapping. They
did not believe that the kidnappers would have trusted
a complete stranger to pick up $100,000 in ransom, and
the force with which [defendant] resisted arrest made
the officers believe that he knew he was on the hook for
a serious crime. By the time they found the safe, the officers knew that [defendant] had lied about being home-
less (they knew that, at a minimum, he had been rent-

ing a hotel room for a long time and paying in cash), that he lied about having checked out of the [hotel], and that he had tried to conceal the location of the [hotel] in which he had been staying. Of course Colon himself could not have been concealed in the safe, but it could have contained phone numbers to reach accomplices, maps to a hide-out location, notes about the kidnapping plan, or Mr. Colon's wallet or car keys or other personal effects that would have confirmed [defendant]'s knowledge of Colon's whereabouts. . . . [I]n *[Brigham City v.] Stuart* [citation omitted], the Supreme Court explored the magnitude of urgency required before officers may conduct a warrantless search. . . . According to the Court, [since] the officers [in that case] had an objectively reasonable belief that the injured adult might need help and that the violence was just beginning[,] . . . [t]hey were not required to wait until the violence escalated and a 'blow rendered someone unconscious.' [citation omitted] In the case before us, the exigencies were even greater. The police knew that Colon could be killed at any time and that [defendant] might be holding the literal or proverbial key to his whereabouts. . . . [Defendant, however,] argues that the prosecution has not demonstrated that obtaining a warrant would have been impossible or impracticable during the four hours between [defendant]'s arrest and the search of his [hotel] room. [Defendant], however, is focused on the wrong time frame. Since the warrantless search of the [hotel] room is not at issue, we need only look to see whether there was adequate time to obtain a warrant to search the [hotel room] safe. [Defendant] argues that the clock begins to tick at the moment the officers had the right to obtain a warrant. . . . [T]he officers had no idea that they would need a warrant to search the safe until they arrived at the room and found[:] first, that there was a safe in the room[;] second, that the safe was locked[;] and third, that the girlfriend who had consented to the search of the room could not legally consent to a search of the safe. Prior to the search of the hotel room, the officers simply had no reason to know they would need a warrant to search the safe. The clock began to tick, therefore, at the moment the officers discovered a locked safe. . . . [Defendant] makes much of the fact that no one asked [him] about the key cards until two hours after his arrest, and argues that had they done so immediately, they could have sought a warrant shortly after 9:30 p.m. But a court may not second guess how the police structure their priorities in an investigation. In this case, the police and agents initially focused their efforts on the area surrounding the Logan Square subway station, hoping that because [defendant] had a low powered walkie talkie, the kidnappers might be in the vicinity. [Defendant] initially told the officers that he had checked out of the hotel, so the officers did not prioritize a search for the hotel room. Only after they ran out of leads did the officers circle back to review [defendant]'s personal effects and re-prioritize investigation of the key. . . . Within minutes of discovering a locked safe, the officers sought and received access to the safe from the hotel manager. [footnote omitted] . . . [B]ased on the paraphernalia [they found] in the room, the officers may have believed that the safe contained drugs . . . [and/or] clues to the whereabouts of. . .Colon. In any event, their subjective suspicions about the contents of the safe are irrelevant. [citation omitted] If a reasonable officer might have believed. . .the safe contained information that would lead to the safe recovery of. . .Colon, the. . .officers were justified in searching the safe immediately rather than waiting for a warrant, even if they also believed they might find evidence of a drug crime. [citation omitted] . . . [Therefore], the district court correctly determined that exigent circumstances justified the warrantless search. . . ." *U.S. v. Bell*, 500 F.3d 609, 613–615 (7th Cir. 2007).

• "The district court found the following facts:

— The detectives knew that [defendant] was a suspect in the robbery of the Midwest America Federal Credit Union earlier that morning and that his car may have been involved.

— The detectives knew a 'wad of bills' was found in [defendant's] car.

— The detectives had seen 'flames and smoke coming from a grill in the back of [defendant's] house.

— They had rung the doorbell and had been told by [defendant] that no one was home at his house.

— [Defendant] was asked if he wanted the fire to be put out, to which he responded, 'No, just don't worry about it, let it go.'

— While [detective] was on top of the fence, with his hands on the railing of the balcony, he could observe that paper was being burned on the grill.

— After climbing on the balcony to get a closer look, [detective] could see that the papers being burned were money wrappers.

The district court did not commit clear error in making these factual findings. Each finding was well-supported by testimonial evidence. A reasonable officer, given this situation, would have had probable cause to believe evidence would be destroyed before a warrant could be obtained if the officers on the scene did not intervene. . . . In this case, the evidence was literally burning. The warrant requirement does not compel police officers to stand idly by while evidence is destroyed in front of them. The exigent circumstances exception was created to avoid just such a scenario." *U.S. v. Andrews*, 442 F.3d 996 (7th Cir. 2006).

- "[A] police officer's subjective belief that exigent circumstances exist is insufficient to make a warrantless search. Instead, as is normally the case for Fourth Amendment inquiries, the test is objective: the government must establish that the circumstances as they appeared at the moment of entry would lead a reasonable, experienced law enforcement officer to believe that someone inside the house, apartment, or hotel room required immediate assistance." *U.S. v. Richardson*, 208 F.3d 626, 629 (7th Cir. 2000).

- "Where law enforcement officers have probable cause to believe that illegal activity is being conducted in a particular place and exigent circumstances exist, a warrantless search may be valid. . . .Exigent circumstances may include the probability that evidence will be destroyed before a valid search warrant can be obtained from a neutral magistrate. . . .However, the bare fact that officers are executing a warrant to search for illegal narcotics is not sufficient to constitute exigent circumstances. Specific facts indicating that evidence is likely to be destroyed must be present in order for exigent circumstances to exist." *Jacobs v. City of Chicago*, 215 F.3d 758, 769–70, 46 Fed. R. Serv. 3d 832 (7th Cir. 2000).

Eighth Circuit

- "[T]he district court's instruction correctly recited the Supreme Court's description of an 'emergency,' as the instruction directly quoted the 'immediate aid' language used in *Fisher*. In that case, the Court explained that the 'emergency aid exception' 'requires only an objectively reasonable basis for believing that a person within the house is in need of immediate aid.' Furthermore, contrary to the 'danger to life or limb' instruction that the Ders requested, the Court stated that '[o]fficers do not need ironclad proof of "a likely serious, life-threatening" injury to invoke the emergency aid exception.' " *Der v. Connolly*, 666 F.3d 1120, 1129–30 (8th Cir. 2012) (citations omitted).

Ninth Circuit

- "True, the officers saw Nora in possession of a handgun. But Nora never aimed the weapon at the officers or anyone else, and the officers had no evidence that he had used or threatened to use it. The officers had no reason to believe that illegal weapons such as explosives were present inside Nora's home, or that anyone else to whom Nora may have posed a danger was inside. Nor had Nora given any other indication that he was in 'an agitated and violent state.' Finally, the officers had no reason to believe Nora might pose a danger to the public by attempting to flee, since they had the house completely surrounded and could monitor all exit points. Our conclusion that no exigency existed is buttressed by the fact that the offense involved here was a misdemeanor." *U.S. v. Nora*, 765 F.3d 1049, 1054–55 (9th Cir. 2014) (citations omitted).
- "Finally, the fact that the agents waited for backup before entering [defendant's apartment] does not negate their reliance on an emergency justification." *U.S. v. Reyes-Bosque*, 596 F.3d 1017 (9th Cir. 2010).
- "We are aware of no authority establishing the need to approve or preauthorize tactical decisions made by police during an armed standoff, whether or not

residential. . . . [I]mposing an ongoing warrant requirement upon officers engaged in an armed standoff creates an unprecedented hurdle to apprehending armed
suspects and resolving an existing dangerous situation.
. . . [I]t would impede swift resolution of dangerous circumstances by erecting an unreasonable legal obstacle
of questionable value that only encourages the kind of
judicial second-guessing the Supreme Court has repeatedly condemned. Reasonableness remains the touchstone under the Fourth Amendment. . . . The calculus
of reasonableness must embody allowance for the fact
that police officers are often forced to make split-second
judgments—in circumstances that are tense, uncertain,
and rapidly evolving. Once exigent circumstances were
established to justify warrantless action, the passage of
time as defendant obstinately rebuffed officers' efforts
to effectuate his full arrest did not rejuvenate the warrant requirement." *Fisher v. City of San Jose*, 558 F.3d
1069 (9th Cir. 2009).

Tenth Circuit

- "Although we have never directly addressed the issue,
  our sister circuits appear to unanimously agree, and
  reasonably so in our view, 'that an officer may lawfully
  enter a residence without a warrant under the exigent
  circumstances exception when the officer reasonably
  believes a burglary is in progress' . . . (W)e conclude
  that (the officer) had a particularized and objective basis
  for concluding that there was 'a probability or substantial chance' that a burglary was in progress. . .and that
  (defendants) were involved in that burglary . . . (I)n
  addition to having probable cause to believe a burglary
  was in progress, the circumstances provided (the officer) with a reasonable basis for concluding that the
  warrant requirement was impractical. Had she left the
  scene to obtain a warrant, (the officer) clearly risked allowing a potential burglary to continue, thereby placing
  the contents of the residence. . .at issue, and likely allowing the two obvious burglary suspects to flee." *U.S.
  v. McCullough*, 457 F.3d 1150 (10th Cir. 2006).

- "The basic aspects of the 'exigent circumstances' exception are that (1) the law enforcement officers must have
  reasonable grounds to believe that there is immediate

need to protect their lives or others or their property or that of others, (2) the search must not be motivated by an intent to arrest and seize evidence, and (3) there must be some reasonable basis, approaching probable cause, to associate an emergency with the area or place to be searched. . . . [G]ranting unfettered permission to officers to enter homes, based only upon a general assumption domestic calls are *always* dangerous, would violate the Fourth Amendment." *U.S. v. Davis*, 290 F.3d 1239 (10th Cir. 2002).

Eleventh Circuit

- "[T]here are several well-established exceptions to the warrant requirement. One such exception permits warrantless entry when 'exigent circumstances' create a compelling need for official action and [there is] no time to secure a warrant. In such a case, the exigencies of the situation make the needs of law enforcement so compelling that the warrantless search is objectively reasonable under the Fourth Amendment. The most urgent of these exigencies is the need to protect or preserve life in an emergency situation. This is known as the 'emergency aid' exception. Under the emergency aid exception, officers may enter a home without a warrant to render emergency assistance to an injured occupant or to protect an occupant from imminent injury. In order for the exception to apply, officers must have an objectively reasonable belief that someone inside is seriously injured or threatened with such injury, and is in need of immediate aid. The officer's subjective motivation is irrelevant. The government bears the burden of demonstrating that the exception applies." *U.S. v. Timmann*, 741 F.3d 1170 (11th Cir. 2013) (internal citations omitted).

- "Courts have held police officers' belief that someone inside a home needs immediate assistance objectively reasonable under various circumstances. However, these circumstances have in common the indicia of an urgent, ongoing emergency, in which officers have received emergency reports of an ongoing disturbance, arrived to find a chaotic scene, and observed violent behavior, or at least evidence of violent behavior. . . . Where the emergency aid exception is marshaled to justify warrantless entry in case of a possible suicide attempt, we have found a belief that the victim was in danger and in need of immediate aid reasonable under circumstances that similarly indicate an urgent, ongoing emergency." *U.S. v. Timmann*, 741 F.3d 1170 (11th Cir. 2013) (internal citations omitted).

- "Nor was the Fourth Amendment violated when [two officers] pursued [the defendant] into the rooming house and attempted to subdue him. [The defendant's] striking of [the first officer] gave the law enforcement officers probable cause to arrest him for the state offenses of resisting arrest with violence or battery of a law enforcement officer. Because the officers had probable cause to arrest [the defendant], they were entitled to pursue him into the rooming house. We have previously recognized that law enforcement officers may enter a dwelling without a search warrant when they do so while in "hot pursuit" of a suspect." *U.S. v. Williams*, 731 F.3d 1222 (11th Cir. 2013) (internal citations omitted).

D.C. Circuit

- "[Defendant] maintains the anticipated presence of a firearm on the premises to be searched cannot by itself excuse the officers' failure fully to comply with Section 3109. . . . [W]e have no occasion to decide whether the anticipated presence of a gun could be sufficient by itself to create an exigency excusing less than full compliance with the requirements of the knock and announce statute and of the Fourth Amendment. Again there is something more involved than a mere gun. A rocket launcher (a/k/a bazooka), is a high-powered weapon designed for use against hardened targets—such as armored tanks—with which the MPD presumably has little, if any, experience. The MPD was reasonably apprehensive enough to send more than 20 members of the ERT to execute the warrant specifically because of the danger created by the potential of the rocket launcher being in the house. . . . The unconventional nature of the weapon and the speed with which it could be loaded sufficed to create an exigency that ripened almost immediately after the officers knocked and announced their presence and purpose." *U.S. v. Crippen*, 371 F.3d 842 (D.C. Cir. 2004).

§ 8:3   Protective sweeps: A limited search for other persons on the premises requires probable cause and exigent circumstances

Supreme Court

- "The Fourth Amendment permits a properly limited protective sweep in conjunction with an in-home arrest when the searching officer possesses a reasonable belief based on specific and articulable facts that the area to be swept harbors an individual posing a danger to those on the arrest scene." *Maryland v. Buie*, 494 U.S. 325, 337, 110 S. Ct. 1093, 108 L. Ed. 2d 276 (1990).

- "We emphasize that such a protective sweep, aimed at protecting the arresting officers, if justified by the circumstances, is nevertheless not a full search of the premises, but may extend only to a cursory inspection of those spaces where a person may be found. The sweep lasts no longer than is necessary to dispel the reasonable suspicion of danger and in any event no longer than it takes to complete the arrest and depart the premises." *Maryland v. Buie*, 494 U.S. 325, 335–36, 110 S. Ct. 1093, 108 L. Ed. 2d 276 (1990).

- "We hold that as incident to the arrest the officers could, as a precautionary matter and without probable cause or reasonable suspicion, look in closets and other spaces immediately adjoining the place of arrest from which an attack could be immediately launched. Beyond that, however, we hold that there must be articulable facts which, taken together with the rational inferences from those facts, would warrant a reasonably prudent officer in believing that the area to be swept harbors an individual posing a danger to those on the arrest scene." *Maryland v. Buie*, 494 U.S. 325, 334, 110 S. Ct. 1093, 108 L. Ed. 2d 276 (1990).

First Circuit

- "In sum, there were not articulable facts—even when considered as a whole—supporting the presence of another individual in Delgado's residence. To be sure, the government did not know for certain that no one else would be in Delgado's residence who might pose a danger. But '[l]ack of information cannot provide an articulable basis upon which to justify a protective

sweep.' For while 'there could always be a dangerous
person concealed within a structure[,] . . . that in itself
cannot justify a protective sweep, unless such sweeps
are simply to be permitted as a matter of course, a
result hardly indicated by the Supreme Court in *Buie*.' "
United States v. Delgado-Pérez, 867 F.3d 244, 256 (1st
Cir. 2017) (citations omitted).

- "When police encounter and arrest a partially clothed
individual in his home, the need to dress him may constitute an exigency justifying the officers in entering
another room in order to obtain needed clothing . . .
The evidence at the suppression hearing indicated that,
as a matter of policy, Boston police officers in similar
situations allowed arrestees to select the clothes that
they wished to wear. The arrestee, however, typically
would not be given direct access to the closet. Thus, the
question reduces to whether a cabinet eight to ten feet
away from an unrestrained suspect can be said to be
within the suspect's immediate control . . . The officers
were arresting a person whom they knew to have been
charged with a crime of violence. Law enforcement officers who embark on perilous duties are not expected
to ignore the need for commonsense precautions. And
here. . .the officers targeted their search to the closet,
which was about to become the locus of activity. The
district court found as a fact that the closet was readily
accessible to (defendant). That finding was not clearly
erroneous . . . Accordingly, we uphold the district
court's ultimate conclusion that the scope of the search
was within permissible limits." *U.S. v. Nascimento*, 491
F.3d 25 (1st Cir. 2007).

Second Circuit

- "Adapting [the *MacDonald*] test to the present case—
since we are concerned with (a) the Officers' remaining
in the apartment beyond the time when the arrest of
Accilien had been accomplished, and (b) a reentry,
rather than an initial entry (the Officers having lawfully entered the apartment pursuant to the arrest warrant), into a room in which there were no longer any
potentially threatening persons (the protective sweep
having been lawfully completed and all adult males
having been secured in the kitchen)—we conclude that

most of the *MacDonald* factors, along with other
important considerations, based on substantiated facts
found by the district court, lead to the conclusion that
exigent circumstances justified the Officers' warrantless
return to the second bedroom.. . . We begin with fact
that the Officers, having lawfully entered the apartment with a warrant to arrest Accilien, fortuitously saw
drugs and a gun, with a chambered round, in plain view
during their lawful protective sweep of the bedroom.
Drug trafficking is plainly a serious crime, one often accompanied by violence, ... There was a clear need for
the Officers to remain in the apartment long enough to
ensure, inter alia, that persons engaged in drug trafficking were not released. There were four adult males
in the small apartment when the Officers arrived
around 6:00 a.m. The living room, equipped with a mattress on the floor or a pull-out couch, was occupied by
the woman and children. The bedroom in which the
drugs and gun were found contained not only a bed but
an inflatable mattress. There was thus probable cause
to believe that the drugs and gun were owned by one of
the four men; whoever owned those items was subject
to immediate arrest; all four men were suspects. Although at the time of the Officers' reentry into the by-
then-empty bedroom there was no reason to believe that
any of the suspects were armed, it was objectively reasonable to fear that if the owner of the drugs and gun
were not identified and were allowed to depart he would
likely attempt to escape apprehension or further
detection. In the interest of protecting the public, it was
the responsibility of law enforcement not only to seize
the drugs and the gun, but also to determine who owned
or possessed them and to place that person under
arrest. No doubt the Officers could have sought (and
obtained) a search warrant for the apartment; but a
search would likely not tell the Officers who owned the
drugs and gun. The purpose of their reentry into the
bedroom was not to search for additional items that
might be found there—a task that could have been
performed without bringing Accilien or any of the other
suspects into the room—but rather to seek information
as to who owned the drugs and the gun. Thus, the Officers reasonably sought to determine expeditiously

whom, if anyone other than Accilien, they should arrest.
Perhaps, instead of questioning Accilien as to the identities of the other three men and as to who owned the
drugs and gun, the Officers could have taken all four
men to the police station for questioning. But mere presence at a place in which there are illegal drugs is not a
crime. Certainly it was less intrusive for the Officers to
attempt to find out immediately whom, other than Accilien, to arrest and whom not to. Further, given the
possibility that the drugs and gun did not belong to Accilien, it was reasonable for the Officers to attempt to
have him name the owner outside of the presence of the
other men, in order to facilitate Accilien's candor and
reduce the possibility of intimidation by the owner. But
in order to interview Accilien beyond the hearing of the
other three men, the Officers were forced to go somewhere other than the kitchen. The apartment was very
small, about 500 square feet in total, consisting of the
living room occupied by the woman and children, the
kitchen, the bathroom, and the bedroom. There was no
door between the kitchen entrance to the apartment
and the landing at the top of the stairs; there was no
anteroom, or any hallway, in which the Officers could
question Accilien privately. In these circumstances,
given the need to determine which of the other men in
the apartment—if any of them—should be arrested, the
Officers' decision to return to the bedroom, the only unoccupied room other than the bathroom, in order simply
to question Accilien, or to question any of the other men
individually, in order to determine whom to arrest for
possession of the drugs and the gun, was objectively
reasonable. After Accilien identified Delva and stated
that those items belonged to Delva, the Officers arrested
Delva. In sum, the law enforcement interest in promptly
questioning Accilien in private while the other three
men were still being detained was strong, and the
return to the empty bedroom for that purpose was a
reasonable and minimal intrusion into the residents'
privacy. Although the government did not argue exigent
circumstances in the district court, we conclude that
the facts found by the district court, and substantiated
by the evidence, provide ample basis for application of
the exigent circumstances exception to the Officers'

reentry into the bedroom. In these circumstances, as we see no error in the district court's finding that the cellphone and letters were observed in that room in plain view, we conclude that the record required the denial of Delva's motions to suppress the cellphone and the letters." *United States v. Delva*, 858 F.3d 135, 154–56 (2d Cir. 2017) (citations omitted).

- "Protective search is permissible whether or not carrying a concealed weapon violates any applicable state law." *U.S. v. Padilla*, 548 F.3d 179 (2d Cir. 2008).

- "In the instant case—unlike when officers enter a suspect's home in order to execute an arrest warrant or under exigent circumstances—there was no need for the police officers to enter [defendant's] home in the first place. They were there for their own convenience (and perhaps for his) while taking his statement. Indeed, the entrance or hallway of the building, or their own police vehicle, would have fulfilled their stated purposes: getting out of the rain, separating [defendant] and the building superintendent from each other, and obtaining a measure of privacy. . . . There was also nothing preventing the officers from making explicit any concern they may have had about the presence of others in [defendant's] apartment and seeking his express permission for a search of other rooms. . . . The search of the apartment was unconstitutional. . . because the police lacked specific, articulable facts to justify their warrantless search. . . . Officers must point to facts that give rise to an individualized suspicion and cannot rely solely on generalizations that suspects are usually accompanied by dangerous third parties. As we have noted, in finding 'articulable facts' to justify the protective sweep of [defendant's] apartment, the district court pointed to: 1) the officers' knowledge that [defendant] had recently emerged from a heated argument; 2) the police radio call which informed them that [defendant] might have a gun; 3) the fact that [defendant] stated he did not have a gun prior to being questioned about it; and 4) the fact that the officers had not recovered the gun during their pat-down frisk of him. Even if these facts support a reasonable inference that [defendant] was hiding a gun in the apartment, we do not see how they support the inference that there was a person hiding in the apartment who might use it. Any concern that [defendant] himself might be dangerous was fully and permissibly addressed by the officers by frisking [defendant], and by a search within his 'grab area' . . . The search of an adjoining room to which [defendant] had no ready access was unnecessary for this purpose. The government, moreover, has pointed to nothing in the record from which a reasonable police officer could have inferred that there was a specific danger of unknown third-parties hiding in [defendant's] apartment. . . . Lack of information cannot provide an articulable basis upon which to justify a protective sweep." *U.S. v. Gandia*, 424 F.3d 255 (2d Cir. 2005).

- "A warrantless search is per se unreasonable under the Fourth Amendment—subject only to a few specifically established and well-delineated exceptions. . . . Under the security check exception, when law enforcement officers have lawfully entered premises in connection with an arrest, they are entitled to make a quick and limited security check of the premises to be sure there are no persons or objects on the premises to pose a safety threat to the officers." *U.S. v. Kiyuyung*, 171 F.3d 78, 83 (2d Cir. 1999).

Third Circuit

- "Although this court has never ruled on the circumstances in which a protective sweep of a home, as defined in *Buie*, would be permissible as incident to an arrest occurring just outside the home, those circuits that have addressed the issue have uniformly held that the reasoning of *Buie* is also applicable and that under those circumstances, protective sweeps of the home in such situations are not per se unreasonable. . . . Those courts also agree that a sweep incident to an arrest occurring just outside the home must be analyzed under the second prong of the *Buie* analysis requiring articulable facts which, taken together with the rational inferences from those facts, would warrant a reasonably prudent officer in believing that the area to be swept harbors an individual posing a danger to those on the arrest scene." *Sharrar v. Felsing*, 128 F.3d 810, 823–24 (3d Cir. 1997).

Fifth Circuit

- "To be constitutionally valid, (1) 'the police must not have entered (or remained in) the home illegally and their presence within it must be for a legitimate law enforcement purpose'; (2) 'the protective sweep must be supported by a reasonable, articulable suspicion. . .that the area to be swept harbors an individual posing a danger to those on the scene'; (3) 'the legitimate protective sweep may not be a full search but may be no more than a cursory inspection of those spaces where a person may be found'; and (4) the protective sweep 'may last. . .no longer than is necessary to dispel the reasonable suspicion of danger, and. . .no longer than the police are justified in remaining on the premises.' " *U.S. v. Roberts*, 612 F.3d 306, 311 (5th Cir. 2010) (citations and internal quotations omitted).
- "In light of the presence of a firearm at the scene of a domestic altercation, the officers acted reasonably in securing the scene by sweeping the trailer to determine whether other persons were present who might access that firearm." *U.S. v. Rodriguez*, 601 F.3d 402 (5th Cir. 2010).
- "Both *Terry* and the protective sweep doctrine of *Gould* depend on a reasonableness inquiry that evolves with new information. . . . If officers gain new information relevant to safety or criminal conduct, the scope of their permissible investigation may expand. For example, reasonable suspicion may 'ripen' or 'develop' into probable cause for an arrest if a *Terry* stop reveals further evidence of criminal conduct. . . . The justification for a protective sweep likewise is circumscribed by the evolving facts. The protective sweep must cover no more than those spaces where police reasonably suspect a person posing danger could be found, and must last no longer than necessary to dispel the suspicion and no longer than the police are otherwise constitutionally justified in remaining on the premises." *U.S. v. Scroggins*, 599 F.3d 433 (5th Cir. 2010).
- "Articulable facts and inferences existing at time of defendant's arrest, from which reasonable police officer could have believed that defendant's apartment harbored another dangerous individual, justified protective sweep of defendant's apartment where, while being escorted inside the apartment to dress following his ar-

rest on a parole violation warrant, the defendant suddenly closed an interior door, such action was inconsistent with the defendant's demeanor to that point, the police saw a firearm in plain view, the defendant began violently resisting arrest, resulting in injuries to two officers, and the defendant called for help during the fight with police in the street, even though no one else was in the street." *U.S. v. James*, 291 Fed. Appx. 676 (5th Cir. 2008).

- "Any arrest may be accompanied by a search 'incident to the arrest' of the immediate vicinity, limited to areas in which weapons might be found, regardless of probable cause or reasonable suspicion. The immediate vicinity may include even closed closets and other spaces. Further, aside from the search incident to arrest, police may conduct a protective sweep of the relevant premises, provided the police possess a reasonable suspicion, based on specific and articulable facts, that another person may be on the premises and pose a danger to the police. Such a protective sweep may be no more than a cursory inspection of those spaces where a person may be found and may last no longer than is necessary to dispel the reasonable suspicion of danger[,] nor longer than the police are justified in remaining on the premises. The protective sweep may even occur *after* the suspect is arrested." *U.S. v. Virgil*, 444 F.3d 447 (5th Cir. 2006).

- "[A]rrest is not always, or per se, an indispensable element of an in-home protective sweep, and. . . although arrest may be highly relevant, particularly as tending to show the requisite potential of danger to the officers, that danger may also be established by other circumstances. *U.S. v. Gould*, 364 F.3d 578 (5th Cir. 2004) (abrogated on other grounds by, Kentucky v. King, 563 U.S. 452, 131 S. Ct. 1849, 179 L. Ed. 2d 865 (2011)).

Sixth Circuit

- "It is well-settled that arrest warrants are not search warrants. (citation omitted) Thus, the Supreme Court has identified two types of warrantless protective sweeps of a residence that are constitutionally permissible immediately following an arrest. The first type al-

lows officers to 'look in closets and other spaces immediately adjoining the place of arrest from which an
attack could be immediately launched.' (citation omitted) The second type of sweep goes 'beyond' immediately
adjoining areas but is confined to 'such a protective
sweep, aimed at protecting the arresting officers[.]' "
U.S. v. Archibald, 589 F.3d 289 (6th Cir. 2009).

- "Defendant. . .argues. . .that because of the remoteness of the crawl space and the size of the door, the officers nevertheless exceeded their authority to conduct
a protective sweep. These arguments are without merit
. . . (T)here is no requirement that the area searched
be immediately adjacent to the area where the defendant was arrested . . . . It is undisputed that the crawl
space could hold a person. A small, out-of-the-way space
makes a good hiding place for a dangerous individual; it
is implausible to think that the persons who are the
object of the protective sweep would limit themselves to
large, open areas where they could be easily spotted.
We therefore conclude that the district court properly
denied. . .(defendant's) motion to suppress." *U.S. v.
Stover*, 474 F.3d 904, 72 Fed. R. Evid. Serv. 388, 2007
FED App. 0046P (6th Cir. 2007).

Seventh Circuit

- "[T]he protective sweep described in *Buie* is conducted
pursuant to an arrest for which there was a warrant.
The police had properly established probable cause with
respect to the targeted individual and the area he
occupied. That critical fact is missing here, as there was
no warrant to search apartment 7. These are not
unimportant limitations on the *Buie* rule; at the very
least, it would be a significant expansion of *Buie* to hold
that it applies to a seizure and subsequent search of a
person for whom there is no arrest warrant, at the
threshold of a dwelling for which there is no search
warrant." *U.S. v. Johnson*, 170 F.3d 708, 716 (7th Cir.
1999).

Eighth Circuit

- " '[S]earches conducted outside the judicial process,
without prior approval by judge or magistrate, are per
se unreasonable under the Fourth Amendment—subject

only to a few specifically established and well-delineated exceptions.' One such exception is the 'protective sweep.' 'A "protective sweep" is a quick and limited search of premises, incident to an arrest and conducted to protect the safety of police officers or others. It is narrowly confined to a cursory visual inspection of those places in which a person might be hiding.' 'The government bears the burden of proving that [the protective sweep] exception to the search warrant requirement applies.' The Fourth Amendment permits 'the protective sweep . . . if the searching officer possesse[d] a reasonable belief based on specific and articulable facts which, taken together with the rational inferences from those facts, reasonably warrant[ed] the officer in believing that the area swept harbored an individual posing a danger to the officer or others.' '*Buie* authorizes protective sweeps for unknown individuals in a house who may pose a threat to officers as they effectuate an arrest; *Buie* does not allow a protective sweep for weapons or contraband.' " *United States v. Alatorre*, 863 F.3d 8110, 813–14 (8th Cir. 2017) (citations omitted).

- "Under *Maryland v. Buie*. . . .a protective sweep is justified in connection with an in-home arrest if an officer reasonably believes that the area to be swept harbors an individual posing a danger to those at the arrest scene." *U.S. v. Boyd*, 180 F.3d 967, 975 (8th Cir. 1999).

Ninth Circuit

- "Warrantless search of upstairs of defendant's home was not within the scope of a lawful protective sweep, absent articulable facts which would have warranted a belief that the upstairs area harbored an individual posing a danger to those on the arrest scene." *U.S. v. Deeks*, 303 Fed. Appx. 507 (9th Cir. 2008).
- "[A] protective sweep may last no longer than it takes to complete the arrest and depart the premises. . . .Additionally, the government did not point to any facts that demonstrated that a reasonably prudent officer would have believed that the apartment would have believed that the apartment harbored an individual posing a danger to those on the arrest scene." *U.S. v. Reid*, 226 F.3d 1020, 1027 (9th Cir. 2000).
- "Once the agents had probable cause to enter the resi-

dence, they were entitled to do so if they merely were
conducting a protective sweep to ensure that no potentially dangerous persons were hiding inside the
residence." *U.S. v. Meza-Corrales*, 183 F.3d 1116, 1124
(9th Cir. 1999).

<u>Tenth Circuit</u>

- "On appeal, Nelson argues that the district court erred
  in relying on Prong Two to deny his motion because the
  deputies had no reason to believe that a dangerous third
  person was hiding in the residence. The government
  defends the district court's reasoning and asserts three
  alternative grounds for affirming: (1) under Prong One,
  the deputies lawfully searched the first level because
  that area immediately adjoins the place of Nelson's arrest; (2) the good-faith exception to the exclusionary
  rule applies; and (3) Bradley consented to a search of
  the entire residence. In reviewing these arguments and
  the district court's denial of Nelson's motion, we examine the district court's factual findings for clear error
  and its application of the relevant legal standards de
  novo. The district court concluded that Deputy Owens
  lawfully conducted a protective sweep of the first level
  because, under Prong Two, the deputies could have reasonably believed that 'someone else [aside from Nelson]
  was in the house who could pose a danger to the [depu-
  ties] or others.' We disagree. The district court relied on
  three facts in reaching its conclusion: (1) Allie attempted to shut the front door on the deputies; (2) Allie
  incorrectly informed the deputies that Nelson was
  upstairs, on the fourth level, when in fact he was on the
  first level; and (3) Nelson failed to immediately show
  himself to the deputies when they instructed him to do
  so. But these facts don't create an inference that someone other than Nelson was hiding in the house, whether
  the three facts are taken separately or together. Nor
  does the government explain how these facts create the
  necessary inference. Instead, the government resorts to
  a fallback position—that 'the officers had no way of
  knowing if anyone else was in the residence.' But for
  the following reasons, that argument turns Prong Two
  on its head. Under Prong Two, the government is
  required to articulate specific facts giving rise to the

inference of a dangerous third person's presence. As we've previously explained, 'there could always be a dangerous person concealed within a structure. But that in itself cannot justify a protective sweep, unless such sweeps are simply to be permitted as a matter of course . . . .' In short, '"[n]o information' cannot be an articulable basis for a sweep that requires information to justify it in the first place."' Accordingly, if the deputies had no knowledge regarding the potential presence of a third person, then the government is per se unable to make the affirmative showing that *Buie* requires." *United States v. Nelson*, 2017 WL 3526570, *2-3 (10th Cir. 2017) (citations omitted).

- "Even under our precedent, however, a search may precede an arrest and still be incident to that arrest. . . We have followed *Rawlings* to allow searches of vehicles and persons prior to an arrest. . . In such cases, there must be a legitimate basis for the arrest prior to the search, and the arrest must follow quickly thereafter . . . . There is no reason why the same rule should not apply to protective sweeps of a residence. Protective sweeps, wherever they occur, may precede an arrest, and still be incident to that arrest, so long as the arrest follows quickly." *U.S. v. Torres-Castro*, 470 F.3d 992 (10th Cir. 2006).

- "A protective sweep is a brief search of premises during an arrest to ensure the safety of those on the scene. The Fourth Amendment allows a protective sweep if police have a reasonable belief based on specific and articulable facts which, taken together with the rational inferences from those facts, reasonably warrants the officer in believing that the area swept harbors an individual posing a danger to the officer or others. . . . The limited intrusion is justified by the interest of the officers in taking steps to assure themselves that the house in which a suspect is being, or has just been, arrested is not harboring other persons who are dangerous and who could unexpectedly launch an attack. . . . The search must be narrowly confined to a cursory visual inspection of those places in which a person might be hiding. . . .and may last no longer than is necessary to dispel the reasonable suspicion of danger and in any event no longer than it takes to complete the arrest and depart the premises. . . ." *U.S. v. Smith*, 131 F.3d 1392, 1396 (10th Cir. 1997).

- "[T]he district court found that the officers were in the trailer for less than one minute and that the purpose of the entry was to conduct a quick sweep of the trailer to secure the trailer and ensure the safety of the officers. The Fourth Amendment does not require a warrant for brief protective sweeps like this one." *U.S. v. Hutchings*, 127 F.3d 1255, 1259 (10th Cir. 1997).

Eleventh Circuit

- "A 'protective sweep' is a quick and limited search of premises, incident to an arrest and conducted to protect the safety of police officers or others. A protective sweep may also be undertaken without an arrest warrant, so long as the officers are lawfully within the premises due to, for example, the existence of exigent circumstances. In order to conduct a protective sweep, an officer must possesses a reasonable belief based on specific and articulable facts that the area to be swept harbors an individual posing a danger to those on the arrest scene." *U.S. v. Timmann*, 741 F.3d 1170 (11th Cir. 2013) (internal citations omitted).

- "Officers cannot move a detained person into an area that they wish to search purely to bring that area into the person's grab area and to permit protective sweep thereof; however, when their movement of the detained person is not pretextual, the search of new grab area is lawful." *U.S. v. Bennett*, 555 F.3d 962 (11th Cir. 2009).

- "Here, the government's own action undermines any claim that the entry had a protective purpose. It is undisputed that the sweep in this case did not immediately follow the arrest. . . . During the interim period, approximately forty-five minutes, the officers simply sat in their cars outside the warehouse. The agents, thus, saw no immediate need to enter the warehouse to protect themselves or other persons in the area. *Buie* requires officers to have a reasonable basis for believing that their search will reduce the danger of harm to themselves or of violent interference with their mission. . . ." *U.S. v. Chaves*, 169 F.3d 687, 692 (11th Cir. 1999).

D.C. Circuit

- "The safety of the officers, not the percentage of the home searched, is the relevant criterion. If an apartment is small enough that all of it immediately adjoins the place of arrest and all of it constitutes a space or spaces from which an attack could be immediately launched, then the entire apartment is subject to a limited sweep of spaces where a person may be found." *U.S. v. Thomas*, 429 F.3d 282 (D.C. Cir. 2005), on reh'g in part, 179 Fed. Appx. 60 (D.C. Cir. 2006).

- "As with a search incident to arrest, we analyze a protective sweep from the vantage point of the time of the arrest and ask whether the place searched was one immediately adjoining the place of arrest from which an attack could be immediately launched. . . . The district court found that the small bedroom was only a few feet from the larger bedroom door and only a few feet from the top of the stairs, and was a space from which an attack could be immediately launched." *In re Sealed Case 96-3167*, 153 F.3d 759, 770 (D.C. Cir. 1998).

§ 8:4 Police-created exigent circumstances vitiates the "exigent circumstances" exception to the warrant requirement

Supreme Court

- "Under Ninth Circuit law, an entry that otherwise complies with the Fourth Amendment is not rendered unreasonable because it provokes a violent reaction. Under this rule, qualified immunity necessarily applies here because, as explained above, competent officers could have believed that the second entry was justified under both continuous search and exigent circumstance rationales. Indeed, even if Reynolds and Holder misjudged the situation, Sheehan cannot 'establish a Fourth Amendment violation based merely on bad tactics that result in a deadly confrontation that could have been avoided.' Courts must not judge officers with 'the 20/20 vision of hindsight.' " *City and County of San Francisco, Calif. v. Sheehan*, 135 S. Ct. 1765, 1776–77, 191 L. Ed. 2d 856 (2015) (inner citations omitted).

- "[W]arrantless searches are allowed when the circumstances make it reasonable, within the meaning of the Fourth Amendment, to dispense with the warrant requirement. Therefore, the answer to the question before us is that the exigent circumstances rule justifies a warrantless search when the conduct of the police preceding the exigency is reasonable in the same sense. Where, as here, the police did not create the exigency by engaging or threatening to engage in conduct that violates the Fourth Amendment, warrantless entry to prevent the destruction of evidence is reasonable and thus allowed. . . . When law enforcement officers who are not armed with a warrant knock on a door, they do no more than any private citizen might do. And whether the person who knocks on the door and requests the opportunity to speak is a police officer or a private citizen, the occupant has no obligation to open the door or to speak. When the police knock on a door but the occupants choose not to respond or to speak, 'the investigation will have reached a conspicuously low point,' and the occupants 'will have the kind of warning that even the most elaborate security system cannot provide.' And even if an occupant chooses to open the door and speak with the officers, the occupant need not allow the officers to enter the premises and may refuse to answer any questions at any time. Occupants who choose not to stand on their constitutional rights but instead elect to attempt to destroy evidence have only themselves to blame for the warrantless exigent-circumstances search that may ensue." *Kentucky v. King*, 563 U.S. 452, 131 S. Ct. 1849, 1858, 1862, 179 L. Ed. 2d 865 (2011) (citations omitted).

• "Absent some grave emergency, the Fourth Amendment has interposed a magistrate between the citizen and the police. This was done not to shield criminals nor to make the home a safe haven for illegal activities. It was done so that an objective mind might weigh the need to invade that privacy in order to enforce the law. The right of privacy was deemed too precious to entrust to the discretion of those whose job is the detection of crime and the arrest of criminals. Power is a heady thing; and history shows that the police acting on their own cannot be trusted. And so the Constitution requires a magistrate to pass on the desires of the police before they violate the privacy of the home. We cannot be true to that constitutional requirement and excuse the absence of a search warrant without a showing by those who seek exemption from the constitutional mandate that the exigencies of the situation made that course imperative." *McDonald v. U.S.*, 335 U.S. 451, 455–56, 69 S. Ct. 191, 193, 93 L. Ed. 153 (1948).

Fifth Circuit

- "Our 'manufactured exigency' cases have recognized a distinction between law enforcement actions that inadvertently set in motion a chain of events that create exigent circumstances, and cases where the police should have foreseen that their actions would create exigent circumstances." *U.S. v. Timoteo*, 353 Fed. Appx. 968 (5th Cir. 2009).

- "The government cannot rely on exigent circumstances to excuse a warrantless entry if it created the exigent circumstances through its own actions. . . . When determining whether the government created the exigent circumstances, this Court considers not just the motivation of the officers, but also the reasonableness and propriety of the investigative tactics that created the exigency." *U.S. v. Hearn*, 563 F.3d 95, 106 (5th Cir. 2009).

- "To determine whether law enforcement officials have manufactured an exigency, we look to whether (1) there was sufficient time to secure a warrant, and (2) whether the exigency was created by unreasonable law enforcement tactics. . . . It is well settled that exigencies deliberately manufactured by the Government violate the Fourth Amendment, especially if the Government's actions are intentionally taken to avoid the warrant requirement. (citations omitted) But we have not gone so far as to hold that *only* deliberately manufactured exigencies rise to the level of a Fourth Amendment violation. Rather, we have held that bad faith on the part of law enforcement officers is not required. (citations omitted) Indeed, on a number of occasions, we have found exigencies were manufactured despite the absence of evidence showing specific intent to subvert the warrant requirement. For example, we have held that when the Government controls the timing of an investigation, exigent circumstances arising out of law enforcement actions consistent with that timing are

§ 8:4   SEARCH AND SEIZURE CHECKLISTS

deemed manufactured." *U.S. v. Howard*, 106 F.3d 70, 78 (5th Cir. 1997) (emphasis in original).

- "Just as exigent circumstances are an exception to the warrant requirement, a police-manufactured exigency is an exception to an exception." *U.S. v. Rico*, 51 F.3d 495, 502 (5th Cir. 1995).

502

Chapter 9

Stop and Frisk

Research References

West's Key Number Digest

Arrest ⟶53, 58, 63.4 to 63.5; Criminal Law ⟶394.4; Searches and
Seizures ⟶13, 23 to 24, 47.1, 49, 67, 120 to 123

KeyCite®: Cases and other legal materials listed in KeyCite Scope can be
researched through the KeyCite service on Westlaw®. Use KeyCite to
check citations for form, parallel references, prior and later history, and
comprehensive citator information, including citations to other decisions
and secondary materials.

---

§ 9:1   Nature of stop: A forcible stop of an individual
constitutes a seizure; thus the Fourth
Amendment is implicated

Supreme Court

• "The reasonableness of the officer's decision to stop a

suspect does not turn on the availability of less intrusive investigatory techniques. Such a rule would unduly hamper the police's ability to make swift on-the-spot decisions—here, respondent was about to get into a taxicab—and it would require courts to indulge in unrealistic second-guessing." *U.S. v. Sokolow*, 490 U.S. 1, 11, 109 S. Ct. 1581, 104 L. Ed. 2d 1 (1989).

- "While the very presence of a police car driving parallel to a running pedestrian could be somewhat intimidating, this kind of police presence does not, standing alone, constitute a seizure. Without more, the police conduct here—a brief acceleration to catch up with respondent, followed by a short drive alongside him—was not so intimidating that respondent could reasonably have believed that he was not free to disregard the police presence and go about his business." *Michigan v. Chesternut*, 486 U.S. 567, 575, 108 S. Ct. 1975, 100 L. Ed. 2d 565 (1988).

- "[T]he officer may ask the detainee a moderate number of questions to determine his identity and to try to obtain information confirming or dispelling the officer's suspicions. But the detainee is not obliged to respond. And, unless the detainee's answers provide the officer with probable cause to arrest him, he must then be released." *Berkemer v. McCarty*, 468 U.S. 420, 439–40, 104 S. Ct. 3138, 82 L. Ed. 2d 317 (1984).

- "If there is no detention—no seizure within the meaning of the Fourth Amendment—then no constitutional rights have been infringed." *Florida v. Royer*, 460 U.S. 491, 498, 103 S. Ct. 1319, 75 L. Ed. 2d 229 (1983).

- "We must balance the nature and quality of the intrusion of the individual's Fourth Amendment interests against the importance of the governmental interests alleged to justify the intrusion. When the nature and extent of the detention are minimally intrusive of the individual's Fourth Amendment interests, the opposing law enforcement interests can support a seizure based on less than probable cause." *U.S. v. Place*, 462 U.S. 696, 703, 103 S. Ct. 2637, 77 L. Ed. 2d 110 (1983).

- "We conclude that a person has been seized within the meaning of the Fourth Amendment only if, in view of all the circumstances surrounding the incident, a reasonable person would have believed that he was not free to leave. Examples of circumstances that might indicate a seizure, even where the person did not attempt to leave, would be the threatening presence of several officers, the display of a weapon by an officer, some physical touching of the person of the citizen, or the use of language or tone of voice indicating that compliance with the officer's request might be compelled. In the absence of some such evidence, otherwise inoffensive contact between a member of the public and the police cannot, as a matter of law, amount to a seizure of that person." *U.S. v. Mendenhall*, 446 U.S. 544, 554–55, 100 S. Ct. 1870, 64 L. Ed. 2d 497 (1980).

- "[D]etention of the respondent against his will constituted a seizure of his person, and the Fourth Amendment guarantee of freedom from unreasonable searches and seizures is clearly implicated." *Cupp v. Murphy*, 412 U.S. 291, 294, 93 S. Ct. 2000, 36 L. Ed. 2d 900 (1973).

- "It must be recognized that whenever a police officer accosts an individual and restrains his freedom to walk away, he has seized that person." *Terry v. Ohio*, 392 U.S. 1, 16, 88 S. Ct. 1868, 20 L. Ed. 2d 889 (1968).

- "Obviously, not all personal intercourse between policemen and citizens involves seizures of persons. Only when the officer, by means of physical force or show of authority, has in some way restrained the liberty of a citizen may we conclude that a seizure has occurred." *Terry v. Ohio*, 392 U.S. 1, 19 n.16, 88 S. Ct. 1868, 20 L. Ed. 2d 889 (1968).

Third Circuit

- "In *Terry v. Ohio*. . .the Supreme Court held that a police officer may conduct a warrantless stop and frisk if specific and articulable facts, together with all rational inferences, suggest that the suspect was involved in criminal activity. This investigatory stop is short of an arrest and can be justified by less than the probable cause necessary for an arrest. . . . However, a mere hunch or inchoate and unparticularized suspicion cannot justify a stop and frisk under *Terry*." *U.S. v. Brown*, 159 F.3d 147, 149 (3d Cir. 1998).

Sixth Circuit

- "We do not believe that [officer] overstepped the permissible bounds of the *Terry* doctrine by handcuffing [defendant]. First, it was [defendant] who made the request to be returned to his vehicle because he was cold. [Officer], considering this and knowing that people on PCP can become extremely violent, handcuffed [defendant] not only to conduct the pat-down but also to be able to place [defendant] in his car and out of the cold, without having to worry about the possible weapons in [defendant's] car that he could reach. Second, in light of the situation, it appears that [officer] made a quick call in a threatening situation, to ensure the safety not only of himself but also his fellow officers. . . . In addition, as regards the use of the handcuffs specifically, this Circuit has previously held that the use of handcuffs does not exceed the bounds of a *Terry* stop, so long as the circumstances warrant that precaution. In this case, it seems reasonable that [officer] believed that handcuffing [defendant] was the only way to secure the situation. Accordingly, the district court did not err when it concluded that this was a legitimate *Terry* stop." *U.S. v. Foster*, 376 F.3d 577, 65 Fed. R. Evid. Serv. 1, 2004 FED App. 0230P (6th Cir. 2004).

Seventh Circuit

- "[T]he police officer must be justified in his or her initial detention of the individual. In the absence of probable cause for arrest, a police officer may stop and briefly detain a person for investigative purposes, so long as the officer has a reasonable suspicion supported by articulable facts that criminal activity may be afoot. . . . The officer's reasonable suspicion should be based on the totality of the circumstances—the whole picture." *U.S. v. Johnson*, 170 F.3d 708, 713 (7th Cir. 1999).

- "As Fourth Amendment seizures, traffic stops. . .are governed by the principles applied by the Supreme Court to investigative detentions in *Terry v. Ohio*. . . . In addition to being justified at its inception, then, a traffic stop also must be reasonably related in scope to the circumstances which justified the interference in the first place. . . . As we observed in *Finke*, the detention caused by the traffic stop must be temporary and last no longer than is necessary to effectuate the purpose of the stop." *Valance v. Wisel*, 110 F.3d 1269, 1276, 46 Fed. R. Evid. Serv. 1127 (7th Cir. 1997).

Eighth Circuit

- "For driving behavior to support a reasonable suspicion of criminal activity justifying investigatory stop, it need not have violated some traffic law." *U.S. v. Walker*, 555 F.3d 716 (8th Cir. 2009).

Ninth Circuit

- "Like probable cause determinations, the reasonable suspicion analysis is not readily, or even usefully, reduced to a neat set of legal rules and, also like probable cause, takes into account the totality of the circumstances. . . . Although the level of suspicion required for a brief investigatory stop is less demanding than that for probable cause, the Fourth Amendment nevertheless requires an objective justification for such a stop." *U.S. v. Montero-Camargo*, 208 F.3d 1122, 1129 (9th Cir. 2000).

Tenth Circuit

- "An investigative stop that was neither consensual nor the result of probable cause must fulfill two requirements: (1) the stop must be justified at its inception, and (2) the resulting detention must be reasonably related in scope to the circumstances which justified the interference in the first place." *U.S. v. Salzano*, 158 F.3d 1107, 1111 (10th Cir. 1998).

§ 9:2 Grounds for stop: To stop an individual lawfully, the police officer must have a reasonable suspicion that the person stopped is involved in criminal activity

Supreme Court

- "[R]easonable men make mistakes of law, too, and such mistakes are no less compatible with the concept of reasonable suspicion. Reasonable suspicion arises from the combination of an officer's understanding of the facts and his understanding of the relevant law. The officer may be reasonably mistaken on either ground. Whether the facts turn out to be not what was thought, or the law turns out to be not what was thought, the result is the same: the facts are outside the scope of the law. There is no reason, under the text of the Fourth Amendment or our precedents, why this same result should be acceptable when reached by way of a reasonable mistake of fact, but not when reached by way of a similarly reasonable mistake of law. . . . But just because mistakes of law cannot justify either the imposition or the avoidance of criminal liability, it does not follow that they cannot justify an investigatory stop." *Heien v. North Carolina*, 135 S. Ct. 530, 536, 540, 190 L. Ed. 2d 475 (2014).

- "I am not sure that the Fourth Amendment requires such independent corroboration before the police can act, at least in the special context of anonymous tips reporting drunk driving. This is an important question that is not answered by our past decisions, and that has deeply divided federal and state courts. The Court should grant the petition for certiorari to answer the question and resolve the conflict . . . . On the one hand, our cases allow police to conduct investigative stops based on reasonable suspicion, viewed under the totality of the circumstances. In *Florida v. J.L.*, however, we explained that anonymous tips, in the absence of additional corroboration, typically lack the 'indicia of reliability' needed to justify a stop under the reasonable suspicion standard . . . . This Court has in fact recognized that the dangers posed by drunk drivers are unique, frequently upholding anti-drunk-driving policies that might be constitutionally problematic in other, less exigent circumstances . . . . In the absence of controlling precedent on point, a sharp disagreement has emerged among federal and state courts over how to apply the Fourth Amendment in this context. The majority of courts examining the question have upheld investigative stops of allegedly drunk or erratic drivers, even when the police did not personally witness any traffic violations before conducting the stops . . . . The conflict is clear and the stakes are high. The effect of the rule below will be to grant drunk drivers 'one free swerve' before they can legally be pulled over by police. It will be difficult for an officer to explain to the family of a motorist killed by that swerve that the police had a tip that the driver of the other car was drunk, but that they were powerless to pull him over, even for a quick check." *Virginia v. Harris*, 558 U.S. 978, 130 S. Ct. 10, 175 L. Ed. 2d 322 (2009) (Chief Justice ROBERTS, with whom Justice SCALIA joins, dissenting from denial of certiorari) (citations omitted).

- "An individual's presence in an area of expected criminal activity, standing alone, is not enough to support a reasonable, particularized suspicion that the person is committing a crime. . . . But officers are not required to ignore the relevant characteristics of a location in determining whether the circumstances are sufficiently suspicious to warrant further investigation. Accordingly, we have previously noted the fact that the stop occurred in a high crime area among the relevant contextual considerations in a *Terry* analysis. . . . Our cases have also recognized that nervous, evasive behavior is a pertinent factor in determining reasonable suspicion. . . . Headlong flight—wherever it occurs—is the consummate act of evasion: it is not necessarily indicative of wrongdoing, but it is certainly suggestive of such." *Illinois v. Wardlow*, 528 U.S. 119, 124, 120 S. Ct. 673, 145 L. Ed. 2d 570 (2000).

- "Unlike a tip from a known informant whose reputation can be assessed and who can be held responsible if her allegations turn out to be fabricated. . . .an anonymous tip alone seldom demonstrates the informant's basis of knowledge or veracity. . . .As we have recognized, however, there are situations in which an anonymous tip, suitably corroborated, exhibits sufficient indicia of reliability to provide reasonable suspicion to make the investigatory stop." *Florida v. J.L.*, 529 U.S. 266, 270, 120 S. Ct. 1375, 146 L. Ed. 2d 254 (2000).

- "We have described reasonable suspicion simply as a particularized and objective basis for suspecting the person stopped of criminal activity and probable cause to search as existing where the known facts and circumstances are sufficient to warrant a man of reasonable prudence in the belief that contraband or evidence of a crime will be found. We have cautioned that these two legal principles are not finely-tuned standards, comparable to the standards of proof beyond a reasonable doubt or of proof by a preponderance of the evidence. They are instead fluid concepts that take their substantive content from the particular contexts in which the standards are being assessed." *Ornelas v. U.S.*, 517 U.S. 690, 696, 116 S. Ct. 1657, 134 L. Ed. 2d 911 (1996).

● "The Fourth Amendment requires some minimal level of objective justification for making the stop That level of suspicion is considerably less than proof of wrongdoing by a preponderance of the evidence. We have held that probable cause means a fair probability that contraband or evidence of a crime will be found, and the level of suspicion required for a *Terry* stop is obviously less demanding than that for probable cause." *U.S. v. Sokolow*, 490 U.S. 1, 7, 109 S. Ct. 1581, 104 L. Ed. 2d 1 (1989).

● "[I]f police have a reasonable suspicion, grounded in specific and articulable facts, that a person they encounter was involved in or is wanted in connection with a completed felony, then a *Terry* stop may be made to investigate that suspicion. Assuming the police make a *Terry* stop in objective reliance on a flyer or bulletin, we hold that the evidence uncovered in the course of the stop is admissible if the police who issued the flyer or bulletin possessed a reasonable suspicion justifying a stop, and if the stop that in fact occurred was not significantly more intrusive than would have been permitted the issuing department." *U.S. v. Hensley*, 469 U.S. 221, 228, 105 S. Ct. 675, 83 L. Ed. 2d 604 (1985).

● "[T]he Court acknowledge[s] the authority of the police to make a forcible stop of a person when the officer has reasonable, articulable suspicion that the person has been, is, or is about to be engaged in criminal activity." *U.S. v. Place*, 462 U.S. 696, 702, 103 S. Ct. 2637, 77 L. Ed. 2d 110 (1983).

● "[A person] may not be detained even momentarily without reasonable, objective grounds for doing so; and his refusal to listen or answer does not, without more, furnish those grounds. [N]ot all seizures of the person must be justified by probable cause to arrest for a crime. [C]ertain seizures are justifiable under the Fourth Amendment if there is articulable suspicion that a person has committed or is about to commit a crime." *Florida v. Royer*, 460 U.S. 491, 498, 103 S. Ct. 1319, 75 L. Ed. 2d 229 (1983).

- "[A]ny curtailment of a person's liberty by the police must be supported at least by a reasonable and articulable suspicion that the person seized is engaged in criminal activity." *Reid v. Georgia*, 448 U.S. 438, 440, 100 S. Ct. 2752, 65 L. Ed. 2d 890 (1980).
- "[E]ven assuming that purpose [to prevent crime] is served to some degree by stopping and demanding identification from an individual without any specific basis for believing he is involved in criminal activity, the guarantees of the Fourth Amendment do not allow it. When such a stop is not based on objective criteria, the risk of arbitrary and abusive police practices exceeds tolerable limits." *Brown v. Texas*, 443 U.S. 47, 52, 99 S. Ct. 2637, 61 L. Ed. 2d 357 (1979).
- "[A] police officer may in appropriate circumstances and in an appropriate manner approach a person for purposes of investigating possible criminal behavior even though there is no probable cause to make an arrest." *Terry v. Ohio*, 392 U.S. 1, 22, 88 S. Ct. 1868, 20 L. Ed. 2d 889 (1968).

First Circuit

- "The officer's suspicion must be both particular, in that it is 'grounded in specific and articulable facts,' and objective, such that a reasonable officer in similar circumstances also would harbor suspicion. An inquiry into reasonableness requires a reviewing court to consider the totality of the surrounding circumstances, 'tak[ing] care not to evaluate facts in splendid isolation' but 'apprais[ing] [them] in the context in which they occurred.' The Supreme Court has held that a defendant's apprehensive, evasive behavior may further heighten reasonable suspicion and that flight from law enforcement is a clear act of evasion. We have described flight as unprovoked running upon recognizing the police and have concluded that acts like warily looking over one's shoulder contribute to an officer's reasonable suspicion. An officer may stop an individual in order to 'resolve the ambiguity' in conduct that is lawful but oblique and unusual." *U.S. v. Hart*, 674 F.3d 33, 38-39 (1st Cir. 2012) (citations omitted).

Third Circuit

- "When an encounter is consensual, no reasonable suspicion is required." *U.S. v. Crandell*, 554 F.3d 79 (3d Cir. 2009).
- "It is well settled that the smell of marijuana alone, if articulable and particularized, may establish not merely reasonable suspicion, but probable cause. . . . The question of what constitutes 'particularized' for the purposes of a reasonable suspicion inquiry does not reduce to a rigid definition precisely because reasonable suspicion is itself a flexible standard. In the abstract, the defendants may be correct that, at some point, a broadly diffuse and undistinguished marijuana odor will not automatically provide the necessary particularity to establish reasonable suspicion. . . . Here, it is undisputed that the officers drove in-between the two vehicles that were parked next to each other. As the officers drove by, coming to within three or four feet of defendants' car, they smelled an identifiable marijuana odor. Officer Huertas also testified that the both the defendants' car window (facing the officers' SUV) and the officers' own window were open. While it is true that no officer testified directly as to *which* car the odor had come from, relying on their skill and experience, it would have been reasonable for the officers to conclude that the odor was coming from one, the other, or both vehicles. For the purposes of reasonable suspicion, that probability establishes the odor as sufficiently particularized." *U.S. v. Ramos*, 47 V.I. 755, 443 F.3d 304 (3d Cir. 2006).

Fourth Circuit

- "Before an officer can stop and frisk a citizen, she must have 'reasonable and articulable suspicion that the person seized is engaged in criminal activity.' We recently warned against the Government's proffering 'whatever facts are present, no matter how innocent, as indicia of suspicious activity' and noted that we were 'deeply troubled by the way in which the Government attempts to spin. . . .mundane acts into a web of deception.' This concern is only heightened when the 'mundane acts' emerge from the refusal to consent to a voluntary search. If the important limitations on the 'stop and frisk' regime crafted by *Terry v. Ohio,* are not to become dead letters, refusing to consent to a search cannot itself justify a nonconsensual search." *U.S. v. Massenburg*, 654 F.3d 480, 482 (4th Cir. 2011) (citations omitted).

- "The anonymous tip in this case, like the one in *J.L.*, lacks sufficient indicia of reliability. In fact, the tip here was so barren of detail about the alleged culprits' physical descriptions that it was even less reliable than the deficient tip in *J.L.* The 911 caller told the Union police dispatcher that several black males were drinking and causing a disturbance at a certain intersection. The caller said nothing else. Specifically, he did not identify himself, did not give his location or vantage point, and did not explain how he knew about the disturbance. The tipster did not say exactly how many men were present, and apart from mentioning their race, gave no information about their appearance. The caller did not mention whether the men were residents of the neighborhood or outsiders. Finally, he did not say whether the men were in an automobile or whether they had access to one." *U.S. v. Jones*, 242 F.3d 215, 218 (4th Cir. 2001).

Fifth Circuit

- "It did not matter that there was no direct evidence that suggested the occupants were carrying contraband. The facts suggested that something *illegal* was afoot, so the police were entitled, as long they acted with reasonable diligence, to pursue several plausible theories in attempting to resolve the suspicion that reasonably had been created by the absence of the authorized driver, the inconsistent stories, the nervousness, and the presentation of a fake identification card. . . . Requiring police to have particularized facts that support a finding that 'criminal activity may be afoot' is different from requiring the police to articulate particularized facts that support a finding that a particular specific crime is afoot. We think the latter approach, as in *Dortch*'s, referenced 'particularized suspicion' requirement, goes beyond reasonable suspicion by in substance virtually requiring direct evidence or the substantial equivalent thereof and imposes a requirement that is too close to probable cause." *U.S. v. Pack*, 612 F.3d 341, 355-356 (5th Cir. 2010), opinion modified on denial of reh'g, U.S. v. Pack, 622 F.3d 383 (5th Cir. 2010) (citations omitted).

Sixth Circuit

- "It is undisputed that the officers lacked reasonable suspicion to seize Johnson when they called for him to stop and that Johnson was entitled to keep walking. Nonetheless, the government insisted at oral argument that ignoring an unconstitutional order contributes to reasonable suspicion. We seriously doubt the wisdom of labeling reasonably suspicious the proper exercise of one's constitutional rights." *U.S. v. Johnson*, 620 F.3d 685, 694 (6th Cir. 2010).

- "[T]here is an ongoing debate about the circumstances under which a person responding to the arrival of police will raise suspicion of wrongdoing. *This case,* however, does not present even a close question. Johnson did not change course or otherwise react suspiciously to the police. He did not react *at all.* Instead, his trajectory remained constant: he continued walking in the manner he had been walking (according to the district court, 'at a normal pace,') and in the direction he had been walking when the officers first observed him. Upon reaching the white car, he opened the passenger-side door and put his bag inside, undoubtedly what he had intended to do even before the police arrived. Johnson's conduct was the quintessential example of 'going about one's business'-protected, unsuspicious conduct that the Supreme Court has characterized as 'the opposite' of flight." *U.S. v. Johnson*, 620 F.3d 685, 695 (6th Cir. 2010).

- "Although the reasonable-suspicion calculation for holding a suspect beyond the time reasonably required to fulfill the purposes of the initial stop examines the totality of the circumstances, even where the government points to several factors that the Court of Appeals has recognized as valid considerations, they may not together provide reasonable suspicion if they are all relatively minor and subject to significant qualification, particularly where the case lacks any of the stronger indicators of criminal conduct that have accompanied these minor factors in other cases." *U.S. v. Bell*, 555 F.3d 535 (6th Cir. 2009).

- "This Court evaluates the legitimacy of the investigatory stop by making a two-part assessment of its reasonableness. First, the Court must determine whether there was a proper basis to stop the individual based upon the officer's 'aware[ness] of specific and articulable facts which gave rise to a reasonable suspicion.'. . . Second, the Court must evaluate 'whether the degree of intrusion into the suspect's personal security was reasonably related in scope to the situation at hand, which is judged by examining the reasonableness of the officials' conduct given their suspicions and the surrounding circumstances.'. . . The fact that a given locale is well known for criminal activity will not *by itself* justify a *Terry* stop; but it is among the various factors that officers may take into account. The officers testified that they believed that [arrestee] was engaged in the offense of loitering for prostitution because: (1) her dress and attire were typical of prostitutes; (2) she was in an area known for prostitution activity; (3) they recognized her as a woman who had been convicted of prostitution crimes in the past; and (4) she waved in a manner that they identified as being characteristic of a prostitute's means of soliciting customers. This Court finds that the combination the above observations, when considered from the perspective of officers with specialized training and familiarity with the behavior of prostitutes, provide reasonable suspicion to justify a stop." *U.S. v. Martin*, 289 F.3d 392, 2002 FED App. 0156P (6th Cir. 2002).

Seventh Circuit

- "A mere suspicion of illegal activity at a particular place is not enough to transfer that suspicion to anyone who leaves that property. The Fourth Amendment allows officers to "stop and briefly detain a person for investigative purposes if the officer has a reasonable suspicion supported by articulable facts that criminal activity "may be afoot."" This reasonableness standard typically requires a set of facts that we can measure against an objective standard such as 'probable cause or a less stringent test' such as reasonable suspicion. In those circumstances where we do not insist on 'some quantum of individualized suspicion,' we rely on other safeguards to assure that the reasonable expectation of privacy is not 'subject to the discretion of the official in the field.' For instance, an officer with a warrant to search a place may stop anyone leaving that place without additional individualized suspicion, but a mere suspicion of illegal activity about a place, without more, is not enough to justify stopping everyone emerging from that property. . . . The government's attempt to justify the stop based on reasonable suspicion despite the lack of *particular* suspicion about the car actually stopped ignores that the Supreme Court has only allowed such stops in narrow circumstances. Namely, when the police have a warrant to search a house, the detention of individuals found leaving that house is constitutionally reasonable because of 'the nature of the articulable and individualized suspicion on which the police base the detention of the occupant of a home subject to a search warrant.' . . . [T]he purported basis of the stop—a suspicion about a place and some surprising behavior a few minutes earlier—would essentially allow the government to set up checkpoint stops outside suspected drug production or distribution sites to detect 'ordinary criminal wrongdoing.' " *U.S. v. Bohman*, 683 F.3d 861, 864–66 (7th Cir. 2012) (citations omitted).

- "While we recognize that officer safety is important, under the law, officers are not free to pat down citizens at will." *Gentry v. Sevier*, 597 F.3d 838 (7th Cir. 2010).

Eighth Circuit

- "In conducting investigation following a *Terry* stop, an officer may engage in brief questioning on matters even unrelated to the original offense if the initial detention is not prolonged by the questions. When a suspect's response to an investigatory question following a *Terry* stop raises suspicion unrelated to the original offense, the officer may expand his inquiry to satisfy the suspicion." *U.S. v. Banks*, 553 F.3d 1101, 78 Fed. R. Evid. Serv. 734 (8th Cir. 2009).

Ninth Circuit

- "In assessing the totality of the circumstances, relevant considerations may include: observing a visible bulge in a person's clothing that could indicate the presence of a weapon; seeing a weapon in an area the suspect controls, such as a car; 'sudden movements' suggesting a potential assault or 'attempts to reach for an object

that was not immediately visible'; 'evasive and deceptive responses' to an officer's questions about what an
individual was up to; unnatural hand postures that suggest an effort to conceal a firearm; and whether the officer observes anything during an encounter with the
suspect that would dispel the officer's suspicions regarding the suspect's potential involvement in a crime or
likelihood of being armed. This last point is especially
important. Even where certain facts might support reasonable suspicion a suspect is armed and dangerous
when viewed initially or in isolation, a frisk is not justified when additional or subsequent facts dispel or negate the suspicion. Just as a suspicion must be reasonable and individualized, it must be based on the *totality*
of the circumstances known to the officer. Officers may
not cherry pick facts to justify the serious Fourth
Amendment intrusion a frisk imposes." *Thomas v.
Dillard*, 818 F.3d 864, 877 (9th Cir. 2016), as amended,
(May 5, 2016) (citations omitted).

- "We are aware that the reasonable suspicion calculus
  takes into consideration the totality of the
  circumstances. . . . We are also aware that in certain
  circumstances conduct that is wholly lawful may nevertheless support a finding of reasonable suspicion. . . .
  As we have discussed, the government argues that three
  factors justified the investigatory stop: (1) a wholly
  conjectural and unsupported FBI tip; (2) a police
  detective's observation of two vehicles leaving the house,
  one in the early morning, the other in the early afternoon, with the stop of the second driver and the search
  of his bag revealing no marijuana or other contraband;
  and (3) the detective's extraordinary statement, inconsistent with his other testimony in the case, that he
  heard the distinctive sound of marijuana packages being loaded into a third vehicle. None of the three,
  considered separately, provides any basis for reasonable
  suspicion. Viewing them in their totality, they still add
  up to zero." *U.S. v. Thomas*, 211 F.3d 1186, 1192 (9th
  Cir. 2000).

Tenth Circuit

- " 'A confidential tip may justify an investigatory stop if
  under the totality of the circumstances the tip furnishes

both sufficient indicia of reliability and sufficient information to provide reasonable suspicion that criminal conduct is, has, or is about to occur.' The determination of '[w]hether a tip provides reasonable suspicion to make a traffic stop is case-specific,' and no single factor is dispositive. [R]elevant factors include: (1) whether the informant lacked 'true anonymity' (i.e., whether the police knew some details about the informant or had means to discover them); (2) whether the informant reported contemporaneous, firsthand knowledge; (3) whether the informant provided detailed information about the events observed; (4) the informant's stated motivation for reporting the information; and (5) whether the police were able to corroborate information provided by the informant. Turning to the first of these factors, '[u]nlike a tip from a known informant whose reputation can be assessed and who can be held responsible if her allegations turn out to be fabricated, an anonymous tip alone seldom demonstrates the informant's basis of knowledge or veracity.' In *United States v. Johnson,* we further explained that '[a] tipster who refuses to identify himself may simply be making up the story, perhaps trying to use the police to harass another citizen.' On the other hand, jeopardizing one's anonymity creates 'disincentive for making false allegations.' . . . . To assess the reliability of a tip, however, we must examine 'the totality of the circumstances—the whole picture' and 'no single factor is dispositive.' A 911 caller who offers only 'minimal' identifying information—that he was at or in front of an address across the street from where shots were fired—is not 'completely unidentifiable;' giving the address was at least an 'indicium of reliability.' Here, the 911 operator never asked the caller for his name or other identifying information and there is no reason to believe he would not have provided this information if requested. And there is no indication the caller was 'making up the story, perhaps trying to use the police to harass another citizen.' " *U.S. v. Madrid,* 713 F.3d 1251, 1258–60 (10th Cir. 2013) (citations omitted).

D.C. Circuit

- "When determining whether a *Terry* stop was supported

by reasonable suspicion, this Court does not separately scrutinize each factor relied upon by the officer conducting the search. . . . An officer on the beat does not encounter discrete, hermetically sealed facts. Rather, as we repeatedly have cautioned, the question of whether reasonable suspicion existed can only be answered by considering the totality of the circumstances as the officer on the scene experienced them." *U.S. v. Edmonds*, 240 F.3d 55, 59 (D.C. Cir. 2001).

§ 9:3 Arrests: An overly intrusive investigatory stop may be viewed as an arrest requiring probable cause

Supreme Court

- "Admittedly, *Terry*, *Dunaway*, *Royer*, and *Place* considered together, may in some instances create difficult line-drawing problems in distinguishing an investigative stop from a *de facto* arrest. Obviously, if an investigative stop continues indefinitely, at some point it can no longer be justified as an investigative stop. But our cases impose no rigid time limitation on *Terry* stops. In assessing whether a detention is too long to be justified as an investigative stop, we consider it appropriate to examine whether the police diligently pursued a means of investigation that was likely to confirm or dispel their suspicions quickly, during which time it was necessary to detain the defendant. . . . We reject the contention that a 20-minute stop is unreasonable when the police have acted diligently and a suspect's actions contribute to the added delay about which he complains." *U.S. v. Sharpe*, 470 U.S. 675, 685, 105 S. Ct. 1568, 84 L. Ed. 2d 605 (1985).

- "There is no doubt that at some point in the investigative process, police procedures can qualitatively and quantitatively be so intrusive with respect to a suspect's freedom of movement and privacy interests as to trigger the full protection of the Fourth and Fourteenth Amendments. And our view continues to be that the line is crossed when the police, without probable cause of a warrant, forcibly remove a person from his home or other place in which he is entitled to be and transport him to the police station, where he is detained, although briefly, for investigative purposes. We adhere to the view that such seizures, at least where not under judicial supervision, are sufficiently like arrests to invoke the traditional rule that arrests may constitutionally be made only on probable cause." *Hayes v. Florida*, 470 U.S. 811, 816, 105 S. Ct. 1643, 84 L. Ed. 2d 705 (1985).

- "Detentions may be investigative yet violative of the Fourth Amendment absent probable cause. In the name of investigating a person who is no more than suspected of criminal activity, the police may not carry out a full search of the person or of his automobile or other effects. Nor may the police seek to verify their suspicions by means that approach the conditions of arrest." *Florida v. Royer*, 460 U.S. 491, 499, 103 S. Ct. 1319, 75 L. Ed. 2d 229 (1983).

First Circuit

- "[N]either the use of handcuffs nor the drawing of a weapon necessarily transforms a valid *Terry* stop into a de facto arrest." *U.S. v. Fornia-Castillo*, 408 F.3d 52 (1st Cir. 2005).
- "There is no scientifically precise formula that enables courts to distinguish between investigatory stops. . .and. . .de facto arrests. . . . The ultimate inquiry, however, is whether there was a formal arrest or restraint on freedom of movement of the degree associated with a formal arrest. . . . In assessing whether there was a restraint on freedom of movement, a court must examine all the circumstances surrounding the interrogation." *U.S. v. Trueber*, 238 F.3d 79, 93 (1st Cir. 2001).
- "There is no litmus-paper test. . .to determine whether any particular mode of detention amounted to a de facto arrest. . . . It is often said that an investigatory stop constitutes a de facto arrest when a reasonable man in the suspect's position would have understood his situation, in the circumstances then obtaining, to be tantamount to being under arrest. . . . [W]here the detention is distinguishable from, yet has some features normally associated with, an arrest—the analysis must revert to an examination of whether the particular arrest-like measures implemented can nevertheless be

reconciled with the limited nature of a *Terry*-type stop." *U.S. v. Acosta-Colon*, 157 F.3d 9, 14–15 (1st Cir. 1998).

- "Factors that can elevate a non-arrest seizure to a *de facto* arrest requiring probable cause include extending an investigative stop beyond the time necessary to confirm or dispel reasonable suspicion, and physically blocking the suspect's exit such that a reasonable person would not feel free to leave. The use of guns and the presence of more than one police officer, however, do not necessarily convert an investigative stop into an arrest. Above all else, our cases in this area evince the fact specific nature of the inquiry." *U.S. v. Young*, 105 F.3d 1, 7–8, 46 Fed. R. Evid. Serv. 307 (1st Cir. 1997).

Fifth Circuit

- "Lengthy detentions following *Terry* stops are often problematic, because they serve to escalate an investigatory stop, which can be initiated with only reasonable suspicion, into an arrest, which requires probable cause." *U.S. v. Webster*, 162 F.3d 308, 332 (5th Cir. 1998).

Sixth Circuit

- "An investigative *Terry* stop may indeed ripen into an arrest through the passage of time or the use of force. . . . When this occurs, the continued detention of suspects must be based upon probable cause. . . . Although there is no bright line that distinguishes an investigative stop from a de facto arrest. . .the length and manner of an investigative stop should be reasonably related to the basis for the initial intrusion." *Houston v. Clark County Sheriff Deputy John Does 1-5*, 174 F.3d 809, 814, 1999 FED App. 0150P (6th Cir. 1999).

Seventh Circuit

- "We have held that '[a] person has the right to be free from an officer's knowing use of handcuffs in a way that would inflict *unnecessary* pain or injury, *if* that person presents little or no risk of flight or threat of injury.' We also have recognized a limited set of circumstances in which handcuffs are appropriate without converting a *Terry* stop into a full arrest. Chief among them is officer safety and the possibility of the presence of a weapon.

. . .The absence of a firearm on Mr. Howell's person
was not the only danger that Officer Smith had to
consider. The officer had received a report of an armed
road rage incident involving the discharge of a firearm.
Residual anger and, indeed, irrationality often accompany such episodes, and Officer Smith had to
protect himself and the public from such a contingency.
The show-up encounter between the victim and Mr.
Howell at the scene of the stop also was a relevant factor for Officer Smith to consider in determining how to
secure Mr. Howell. Ensuring the security of the alleged
perpetrator and the safety of the victim in such a
circumstance is an obvious consideration in an officer's
decision making. Indeed, during this show-up, the
victim affirmatively identified Mr. Howell as the
perpetrator to the police, thus justifying a more prolonged investigation while the officers thoroughly
searched Mr. Howell's vehicle for a firearm. . . .The
threat presented by the present situation was far more
substantial and concrete [than the case being
distinguished]. Moreover, Officer Smith had minimal
and nonspecific information about the extent to which
the handcuffs were causing distress and injury. Although the record is replete with evidence of Mr.
Howell's earlier difficulties with his shoulder and of his
difficulties after this encounter, we must focus on what
Officer Smith knew at the time of the incident. During
the arrest, and while placed in handcuffs, Mr. Howell
at most told Officer Smith that he recently had surgery
that limited the mobility of his arm; he never stated
explicitly that he was in pain or actively suffering in
any way. We further note that Mr. Howell also concedes
that Officer Smith was not overly forceful when placing
him in handcuffs. . . . The crux of the matter is that,
from Officer Smith's perspective, he was dealing with an
individual suspected of committing a felony involving
the discharge of a firearm on the public way. Although
'[a] person has the right to be free from an officer's
knowing use of handcuffs in a way that would inflict
unnecessary pain or injury,' that right is tempered by
the attendant 'risk of flight or threat of injury.' Here,
although Officer Smith had a duty to *consider* the information that Mr. Howell had given him about his condi-

tion, he had very little information to evaluate. That information, moreover, clearly did not outweigh the very concrete information about the crime and the circumstances under which it was allegedly committed. Officer Smith's decision did not violate the Fourth Amendment." *Howell v. Smith*, 853 F.3d 892, 898-900 (7th Cir. 2017) (citations and footnotes omitted).

- "Not only were [the police officers] outnumbered, they were approaching a moving vehicle containing individuals who had been with Salazar just moments beforehand. Given the possibility that Salazar was hidden inside the vehicle, their clear disadvantage attempting on foot to stop a moving vehicle, and the possibility, given the nature of Salazar's suspected crimes, that individuals in the car may have been armed, it was not unreasonable to draw weapons to safely effect the stop. These same reasons support the officers' decision to detain Matz with handcuffs, frisk him, and search the car to verify that Salazar was not inside. Matz and everyone else in the vicinity had already made it patently clear that they did not intend to remain where they were and speak to the police, and so Klotka and Zuberbier could reasonably have believed handcuffing the occupants of the car was the most safe and efficient way to ascertain Salazar's whereabouts and any pertinent information about his suspected crimes. It was also a reasonable approach to deal with the rapidly evolving situation and prevent things from turning violent. Klotka and Zuberbier called for backup almost immediately." *Matz v. Klotka*, 769 F.3d 517, 526-27 (7th Cir. 2014), petition for certiorari filed, 135 S. Ct. 1901, 191 L. Ed. 2d 765 (2015) (inner citations omitted).

- "Though it would seem anomalous, we have previously held that where safety is at issue handcuffing is not a per se arrest for purposes of the Fourth Amendment. Handcuffing and placing in a squad car, as happened here, would seem to be a step beyond that." *U.S. v. Brown*, 79 F.3d 1499, 1510 (7th Cir. 1996).

Eighth Circuit

- "We recognize that an officer who has a reasonable suspicion that crime is afoot, but not probable cause to arrest a person, may conduct an investigative stop, and

that this may include questioning and other efforts to
identify the person in question. . . . If a stop lasts too
long, however, or if it is too intrusive, then the stop is
converted into an arrest. . . . In determining whether
an officer's conduct goes beyond what is permissible in
an investigative stop, we are bound to consider the
degree of fear and humiliation that the police conduct
engenders." *Pace v. City of Des Moines*, 201 F.3d 1050,
1054 (8th Cir. 2000).

Ninth Circuit

- "Taking the facts in the light most favorable to the
  plaintiffs, the officers did not have probable cause to arrest the three teenagers. The defendants attempt to
  justify the arrest on the basis of the fact that G.S. was
  initially holding what appeared to be a weapon. We
  may assume that the officers were justified in initiating
  an investigatory stop of the teenagers after they spotted
  what they believed to be a gun in G.S.'s hand. The police determined almost immediately after approaching
  G.S., however, that the gun was, in fact, a toy, and at
  that point any suspicion that the teenagers were
  engaged in a crime dissipated. Not only did none of the
  teenagers possess a gun, but none of them in any way
  matched the apartment manager's description of the
  suspects. They were three Samoan teenagers, not two
  black adults, and none of the boys was wearing either a
  brown shirt or a hooded long-sleeved T-shirt. Nevertheless, the officers handcuffed all three and placed them
  in the back of a police car *after* learning that the item
  in G.S.'s hand was a toy. At a minimum, then, the officers violated the Fourth Amendment by continuing
  the seizure beyond the point at which they determined
  that G.S. had not in fact had a weapon in his hand."
  Sialoi v. City of San Diego, 823 F.3d 1223, 1232–33 (9th
  Cir. 2016).
- "As with the three teenagers, the background circumstances on which the defendants rely to establish qualified immunity (the officers presence in a high-crime
  area) do not make it even 'reasonably arguable' that
  probable cause existed to arrest Sialoi Sialoi Jr." *Sialoi
  v. City of San Diego*, 823 F.3d 1223, 1234 (9th Cir. 2016).
- "There is clearly no mechanical checklist to distinguish

between *Terry* stops and formal arrest or the equivalent of arrest. Our review. . .turns on the particular facts and circumstances of each case. When officers make a stop supported by reasonable suspicion, they are authorized to take such steps as are reasonably necessary to protect their personal safety and to maintain the status quo during the course of the stop. A brief but complete restriction of liberty, if not excessive under the circumstances, is permissible during a *Terry* stop and does not necessarily convert the stop into an arrest." *U.S. v. $109,179 in U.S. Currency*, 228 F.3d 1080, 1084 (9th Cir. 2000).

- "We held in *Allen v. City of Los Angeles*. . .that pointing a weapon at a suspect, ordering him to lie on the ground, handcuffing him, and placing him in a vehicle for questioning for a brief period does not automatically convert an investigatory detention into an arrest requiring probable cause. Whether the stop becomes an arrest depends on the circumstances. Police officers are entitled to employ reasonable methods to protect themselves and others in potentially dangerous situations. . . . The forceful 24 minute detention in *Allen* was, as a matter of law, not an arrest because it was reasonable in the circumstances as a means for the police to determine whether there was a reason to arrest Allen. Likewise, we held in *Alexander v. County of Los Angeles*. . .that qualified immunity applied to a stop for 45 minutes to an hour, with the suspects handcuffed and held in a patrol car while awaiting arrival of a robbery victim to identify them. This is not to suggest a rule generally immunizing police for stops of up to an hour, or with handcuffs or weapons." *Halvorsen v. Baird*, 146 F.3d 680, 684, 50 Fed. R. Evid. Serv. 338 (9th Cir. 1998).

Tenth Circuit

- "An officer detaining a pedestrian has an equally strong interest in knowing whether that individual has a violent past or is currently wanted on outstanding warrants. The citizen's interest, on the other hand, is no more robust merely because a short detention occurs while traversing on foot. Moreover, permitting a warrants check during a *Terry* stop on the street also "promotes the strong government interest in solving crimes and bringing offenders to justice" . . . . Thus, we hold that (defendant's) Fourth Amendment rights were neither violated when his identity was obtained during a valid *Terry* stop nor when his identity was shortly thereafter used to run a warrants check." *U.S. v. Villagrana-Flores*, 467 F.3d 1269 (10th Cir. 2006).

- "[S]everal factors. . . guide our determination of whether a person was, in fact, seized. They include: 1) the threatening presence of several officers; 2) the brandishing of a weapon by an officer; 3) some physical touching by an officer; 4) use of aggressive language or tone of voice indicating that compliance with an officer's request is compulsory; 5) prolonged retention of a person's personal effects; 6) a request to accompany the officer to the station; 7) interaction in a nonpublic place or a small, enclosed place; 8) and absence of other members of the public. We have refused to treat any of the factors cited above as dispositive. Nor are these factors exclusive. Rather, we base our Fourth Amendment analysis on the totality of the circumstances. When viewing the totality of the circumstances, it may be that the strong presence of two or three factors demonstrates that a reasonable person would have believed that he was not free to terminate an encounter with government officials." *Jones v. Hunt*, 410 F.3d 1221 (10th Cir. 2005).

- "Our next inquiry then, is whether the officers detained the men longer than necessary to confirm or dispel their suspicions regarding drug activity. . . . . The men were detained for approximately twenty minutes while the officers searched the area, patted them down, and asked for identification. This length of time was not unreasonable. . . . . There is no evidence that the police took more time than was necessary to investigate the suspected drug activity; they diligently pursued a means of investigation that was likely to confirm or dispel their suspicions quickly." *U.S. v. Soto-Cervantes*, 138 F.3d 1319, 1323 (10th Cir. 1998).

- "It is well settled that a police-citizen encounter which goes beyond the limits of a *Terry* stop is an arrest that must be supported by probable cause or consent to be valid. . . . . However, a *Terry* stop does not automati-

cally elevate into an arrest where police officers use
handcuffs on a suspect or place him on the ground. . . .
Police officers are authorized to take such steps as are
reasonably necessary to protect their personal safety
and to maintain the status quo during the course of a
Terry stop. . . . At least nine courts of appeals, including this circuit, have determined the use of intrusive
precautionary measures (such as handcuffs or placing a
suspect on the ground) during a *Terry* stop do not necessarily turn a lawful *Terry* stop into an arrest under
the Fourth Amendment. . . . The hallmark of the
Fourth Amendment is reasonableness. As long as the
precautionary measures employed by officers during a
Terry stop are reasonable, they will be permitted
without a showing of probable cause." *Gallegos v. City
of Colorado Springs*, 114 F.3d 1024, 1030 (10th Cir.
1997).

§ 9:4   Grounds for frisk: To frisk an individual lawfully, the police officer must have a reasonable belief that the person stopped is armed and dangerous

Supreme Court

- "A stop and frisk may be conducted without violating
  the Fourth Amendment's ban on unreasonable searches
  and seizures if two conditions are met. First, the
  investigatory stop (temporary detention) must be lawful, a requirement met in an on-the-street encounter
  when a police officer reasonably suspects that the
  person apprehended is committing or has committed a
  crime. Second, to proceed from a stop to a frisk (patdown
  for weapons), the officer must reasonably suspect that
  the person stopped is armed and dangerous. For the
  duration of a traffic stop, the Court recently confirmed,
  a police officer effectively seizes everyone in the vehicle,
  the driver and all passengers." *Arizona v. Johnson*, 555
  U.S. 323, 129 S. Ct. 781, 172 L. Ed. 2d 694 (2009).
- "[W]e hold that an anonymous tip lacking indicia of
  reliability of the kind contemplated in *Adams* and *White*
  does not justify a stop and frisk whenever and however
  it alleges the illegal possession of a firearm." *Florida v.
  J.L.*, 529 U.S. 266, 274, 120 S. Ct. 1375, 146 L. Ed. 2d
  254 (2000).

- "[A] law enforcement officer, for his own protection and safety, may conduct a patdown to find weapons that he reasonably believes or suspects are then in the possession of the person he has accosted." *Ybarra v. Illinois*, 444 U.S. 85, 93, 100 S. Ct. 338, 62 L. Ed. 2d 238 (1979).
- "The officer need not be absolutely certain that the individual is armed; the issue is whether a reasonably prudent man in the circumstances would be warranted in the belief that his safety or that of others was in danger." *Terry v. Ohio*, 392 U.S. 1, 27, 88 S. Ct. 1868, 20 L. Ed. 2d 889 (1968).
- "The police officer is not entitled to seize and search every person whom he sees on the street or of whom he makes inquiries. Before he places a hand on the person of a citizen in search of anything, he must have constitutionally adequate, reasonable grounds for doing so. In the case of the self-protective search for weapons, he must be able to point to particular facts from which he reasonably inferred that the individual was armed and dangerous." *Peters v. New York*, 392 U.S. 40, 64, 88 S. Ct. 1912, 20 L. Ed. 2d 917 (1968) *Peters v. New York*, 392 U.S. 40, 64, 88 S. Ct. 1912, 20 L. Ed. 2d 917 (1968).

First Circuit

- Sometimes, however, the reasonable suspicion of a crime that justifies a stop will also justify a frisk because the very nature of the crime poses a sufficient risk that the stopped individual is armed and dangerous. Pointing to Justice Harlan's concurrence in *Terry*, we have observed that "[w]hen the officer suspects a crime of violence, the same information that will support an investigatory stop will without more support a frisk." Our holding in *United States v. Pontoo*, provided an easy vehicle for finding such an association. The officer conducting the *Terry* stop reasonably suspected the defendant of a very recent murder. That was enough, we held, to warrant a pat-down for weapons as well. "In cases in which the individual stopped is suspected of having just committed a murder, it is reasonable for an officer to conclude that [the individual] may be armed and dangerous." . . . We have also extended this type of reasoning to certain crimes that we pronounce are "associated with" violence . . . . And we have applied this reasoning to suspected cases of street-dealer-level transactions, at least where the suspect also appeared unusually anxious at the time of the stop. As justification, we noted that "[t]he connection between drugs and violence is . . . legendary." At the other end of the spectrum, we have found that suspected fraud in the form of passing a bad check is not the type of crime that, without much more, will generate sufficient grounds for a frisk. . . . Here, the suspected crime purportedly justifying the stop was the unlawful possession of a firearm. In deciding whether a particular crime is sufficiently associated with a risk of violence to justify a frisk, we would ideally have access to empirical data to measure the extent of the association. Rarely, though, do courts seem to receive such information. We therefore rely on our (largely unscientific) observations and experiences and on comparisons with our (also non-empirical) classifications of other crimes. Although such an approach might seem dubious in many circumstances, in the instance of this particular crime—illegal possession of an instrument designed precisely to cause serious harm—we can be reasonably confident in our conclusion. Simply put, if an officer reasonably suspects a lawfully stopped, unusually nervous individual of unlawfully possessing a firearm, the officer need not simply hope that the firearm will not be used. Rather, to be unusually nervous and reasonably suspected of being armed unlawfully when stopped is to be reasonably viewed as dangerous enough to justify a frisk. This conclusion means that, in this case, the lawfulness of the frisk and the lawfulness of the stop turn on the answer to a single question: Did the facts leading up to the simultaneous stop-and-frisk make it "reasonabl[e] to conclude" that Belin was both unusually nervous and in possession of a firearm? . . . Although the issue is close and we are not free of doubt, we find that the facts support such a conclusion. *United States v. Belin*, 2017 WL 3599066, *4-5 (1st Cir. 2017) (citations and footnotes omitted).

<u>Second Circuit</u>

- "The officers, after initiating the stop, twice ordered that [defendant] remove his hands from his pockets, which he refused to do. The report of an assault in progress, the matching description, and the additional factors that supported the stop provided the officers with reason to believe that [defendant] was armed and dangerous, and that the refusal to remove his hands was an effort to conceal a weapon. Accordingly, the officer conducting the patdown search was warranted in the belief that his safety or that of others was in danger." *U.S. v. Simmons*, 560 F.3d 98 (2d Cir. 2009).

• "(T)he question we must answer is whether a suspect may be frisked in certain circumstances as part of a *Terry* stop without officers' relying on a reasonable suspicion that he is armed . . . Our holding in this case is a narrow one. We are not holding that the police are entitled to pat down a person, absent reasonable suspicion that he is armed, simply because they have stopped that person pursuant to a lawful *Terry* stop. However, in cases where the police may lawfully transport a suspect to the scene of the crime in the rear of a police car, the police may carry out a departmental policy, imposed for reasons of officer safety, by patting down that person. Because the police must have a legitimate law-enforcement reason to transport a suspect, we see little danger that policies such as these might be used as a pretext for a suspicionless frisk." *U.S. v. McCargo*, 464 F.3d 192 (2d Cir. 2006).

• "*Terry* confirms that an investigatory stop entails more than the governmental interest in investigating crime; there is also the more immediate interest of the neutralization of danger to the policeman in the investigative circumstance." *U.S. v. Gori*, 230 F.3d 44, 56 (2d Cir. 2000).

• "Under *Terry*, to determine whether police officers were justified in frisking a temporarily detained person to see if he is carrying weapons, we apply an objective standard: would the facts available to the officer at the moment of the seizure or the search warrant an officer of reasonable caution in the belief that the action taken was appropriate?" *U.S. v. Rahman*, 189 F.3d 88, 120, 52 Fed. R. Evid. Serv. 425 (2d Cir. 1999).

Third Circuit

• "In *Terry [v. Ohio,]* the Supreme Court held that a warrantless seizure based on less than probable cause could be constitutionally permissible. . . . In outlining the contours of a permissible 'Terry stop,' the Court noted that '[t]he officer need not be absolutely certain that the individual is armed; the issue is whether a reasonably prudent man in the circumstances would be warranted in the belief that his safety or that of others was in danger. . . . The police officer must be able to point to specific and articulable facts which, taken together with rational inferences from those facts, reasonably warrant the intrusion (citations omitted).' . . . Consistent with these statements, we have ruled that when 'determining whether a stop is justified, the court must view the circumstances surrounding the stop in their entirety, giving due weight to the experience of the officers (citation omitted).' . . . In this case, the entirety of the circumstances, as described by [the testimony of the police officer who stopped defendant] (found by the District Court to be credible), justified the Terry stop of [defendant]. First, the U-Haul in which [defendant] sat was parked in an odd and obstructive manner. Second, as [the officer] approached the U-Haul he observed the driver. . .holding an open pocket knife. Third, he also noticed 'quick and furtive movements' by the passengers, [defendant and another male passenger]. And fourth, upon having his dispatcher run a check on [the driver]'s license, [the officer] was informed that [the driver] had an outstanding arrest warrant. This report later proved to be in error, but [the officer] was not unreasonable in relying on it (citation omitted). . . . Given these facts, [the officer] was 'justified in believing that the individual whose suspicious behavior he [wa]s investigating at close range [defendant] [wa]s armed and presently dangerous to the officer or to others' (citation omitted). As [the officer] testified, '[t]he pat-down was for officer safety. I already had one knife. I knew there was a weapon in the car, and a lot of times we as police officers like to add plus one. Where there's one weapon, there's likely another weapon. There were three of them at one point. . .and there was myself and my partner[, who arrived at the scene shortly before [defendant]'s pat-down]. So we're outnumbered. It was for officer safety. . . . We already had one wanted person. . . . . The fast movements of the hands going from the dash and then being concealed underneath them and what appeared to be in the pockets was also an issue. . . . The fact that [the driver] could not provide any answers to simple questions that I had asked him also raised my suspicion of some possible criminal activity.' This testimony—again, found by the District Court to be credible—reveals the 'specific and articulable facts which, taken together, with rational inferences from those facts, reasonably warrant[ed]' subjecting defendant to a pat-down search [citation omitted]. The stop, therefore, was justified under *U.S. v. Yamba*, 506 F.3d 251 (3d Cir. 2007).

- "[Defendant] argues that the police had no reason to believe he was armed and dangerous, and thus could not lawfully conduct a *Terry* protective pat down. We find no error in the district court's conclusion that [the] Officer had reason to believe that he could be facing armed and dangerous felons. That this fraud occurred at a bank in broad daylight could lead one to believe that the perpetrators might have armed themselves to facilitate their escape if confronted. Although the radio bulletin did not describe this response as a bank robbery, it is reasonable to conclude that the suspects might use force and be armed." *U.S. v. Edwards*, 53 F.3d 616, 618 (3d Cir. 1995).

Fourth Circuit

- "Before an officer can stop and frisk a citizen, she must have 'reasonable and articulable suspicion that the person seized is engaged in criminal activity.' We recently warned against the Government's proffering 'whatever facts are present, no matter how innocent, as indicia of suspicious activity' and noted that we were 'deeply troubled by the way in which the Government attempts to spin. . .mundane acts into a web of deception.' This concern is only heightened when the 'mundane acts' emerge from the refusal to consent to a voluntary search. If the important limitations on the 'stop and frisk' regime crafted by *Terry v. Ohio,* are not to become dead letters, refusing to consent to a search cannot itself justify a nonconsensual search." *U.S. v. Massenburg*, 654 F.3d 480, 482 (4th Cir. 2011) (citations omitted).

- "Once an officer has a basis to make a lawful investigatory stop, he may protect himself during that stop by conducting a search for weapons if he has reason to believe that the suspect is armed and dangerous. . . . But an officer may not conduct this protective search for purposes of safety until he has a reasonable suspicion that supports the investigatory stop. . . . In short, an officer may encounter citizens and attempt to question them without implicating the Fourth Amendment. But during such police-citizen encounters, an officer is not entitled, without additional justification, to conduct a protective search. To conduct such a protective search, an officer must first have reasonable suspicion supported by articulable facts that criminal activity may be afoot." *U.S. v. Burton*, 228 F.3d 524, 528 (4th Cir. 2000).
- "Police may conduct a patdown search without a warrant if, under the totality of the circumstances, the officer has an articulable, reasonable suspicion that a person is involved in criminal activity and that he is armed. . . . The reasonableness of the search is measured objectively. If a reasonably prudent person would believe that his safety, or the safety of others, is endangered, he may conduct a limited search of outer clothing to discover any weapons." *U.S. v. Raymond*, 152 F.3d 309, 312 (4th Cir. 1998).

Fifth Circuit

- "First, the officers knew they were in a crime-ridden neighborhood and were on the property of an apartment complex, which was suffering from gang-related activity and had enlisted local police to monitor the area. 'An individual's presence in an area of expected criminal activity, standing alone, is not enough to support a reasonable, particularized suspicion that the person is committing a crime. But officers are not required to ignore the relevant characteristics of a location in determining whether the circumstances are sufficiently suspicious to warrant further investigation.' . . . Second, Ponder knew Miranda, having previously arrested him, and also knew of both Miranda's recent criminal record and gang activity. This information, coupled with Ponder's experiential knowledge concerning the La Primera gang and its violent proclivities

(including its tendency to carry weapons), supports the
suspicion that Miranda may have been armed and
dangerous . . . . In sum, the circumstances here led
Ponder to reasonably suspect that Miranda was trespassing on La Promenade's property and that he may
have been armed and dangerous: Miranda was a known
felon, a gang member in a violent gang, wearing gang
colors, and trespassing at an apartment complex, which
was suffering from gang-related crime. Indeed, we have
recognized that 'when someone engages in suspicious
activity in a high crime area, where weapons and
violence abound, police officers must be particularly
cautious in approaching and questioning him.' We agree
with the district court that a 'reasonably prudent
[person]' in Ponder's (and Dominguez's) position would
be warranted in believing that his safety was endangered, and that reasonable suspicion supported the frisk
of Miranda." *U.S. v. Miranda*, 393 Fed. Appx. 243,
245-246 (5th Cir. 2010).

Sixth Circuit

- "[In *Noble*], we were critical of nervousness as an indicator of dangerousness, noting that, because many law-
abiding citizens are nervous during traffic stops, it is
unreliable. . . . [W]hile we have cautioned against relying too heavily on nervousness as indicia of dangerousness, Pacheco's nervousness is another factor in the
totality-of-the-circumstances analysis that supports a
reasonable-suspicion finding. While '[n]ervous behavior,
standing alone, is not enough to justify a *Terry* search,'
nervousness is still relevant to the reasonable-suspicion
calculus. And we have found reasonable suspicion in
other cases based, in part, on the suspect's extraordinary nervousness that increased as the traffic stop
progressed. In *Noble*, there was no testimony that the
suspect became increasingly nervous. Here, in contrast,
Trivette testified that Pacheco was 'extremely nervous,'
and that as the stop progressed, Pacheco began glancing around the vehicle and rummaging through the
glove box. Additionally, Noble did not avoid all eye
contact with the officers, fidget with his pockets, or
otherwise act as if he was concealing something. In
contrast, Trivette testified that Pacheco 'wouldn't even

make eye contact with [him]' and that 'he was fidgeting around' as he opened up the glove box and shuffled papers back and forth, removing nothing. Further, Trivette testified that Pacheco was looking down at the floorboard and over at the area between the console and his seat. Trivette claimed that, in his experience, this is an area where firearms are often concealed. He went on to say that Pacheco disregarded his presence and that 'it was like he was looking for like an avenue of escape almost.' The absence of these factors weighed against reasonable suspicion in *Noble*; their presence weighs in favor here." *United States v. Pacheco*, 841 F.3d 384, 391, 393 (6th Cir. 2016) (citations omitted).

- "Defendant was a passenger in a vehicle that was pulled over for driving with a broken taillight. When asked for identification, the driver immediately admitted that he did not have a valid license—a misdemeanor criminal offense. The driver was arrested and locked in the back of the patrol car. At that point, officers returned to the vehicle to 'make contact' with Defendant, who was still seated in the passenger seat. The officers did not have any reason to suspect that Defendant was engaged in any criminal activity or that Defendant was armed and dangerous. Nevertheless, the officers ordered Defendant out of the vehicle and told him to put his hands on his head with his fingers interlaced. Officers then began to escort Defendant to the patrol car to search him for weapons and/or drugs. While Defendant was being escorted to the patrol car for a 'pat down' search, he broke free and ran away. The officers pursued Defendant, but did not make any audible commands for him to stop. After Defendant was chased and apprehended by officers, he was searched and found to be carrying a pistol and two bags of hashish, a derivative of marijuana. . . . We agree with the district court that the firearm and the hashish recovered during the search are inadmissible because they were recovered in violation of Defendant's Fourth Amendment rights. The district court correctly determined that the purpose of the traffic stop had been accomplished after the driver was arrested, and Defendant was unlawfully detained after the traffic stop was completed. We further agree with the district court's finding that the officers lacked

reasonable suspicion to justify prolonging the traffic
stop. Under the circumstances, the officers should have
advised Defendant that the vehicle was being impounded and informed Defendant that he was free to
go." *U.S. v. Cheatham*, 577 Fed. Appx. 500, 501–20 (6th
Cir. 2014) (citations omitted).

- "We agree with the district court that, as a matter of
  law, the search began when the officer physically
  positioned Defendant on the hood of a police car by grabbing his shirt, instructed him to spread his legs, and
  then physically touched him on his side, presumably in
  an attempt to uncover contraband or a weapon. [The officer's] intent to search was apparent, and the physical
  contact clearly indicates that the search had begun.
  'Before [an officer] places a hand on the person of a citizen in search of anything, he must have constitutionally adequate, reasonable grounds for doing so.' . . ."
  U.S. v. Moore, 390 Fed. Appx. 503, 509 (6th Cir. 2010).

- "Supreme Court case law is clear that the standard for
  searching a car is very different than that of searching
  a passenger of a car. . . . The search of the car was
  permissible because [the driver] consented to the
  search, but the government never received consent to
  search Defendant's person and did not attempt to
  conduct a timely *Terry* search following the traffic stop;
  it certainly did not have the probable cause necessary
  to overcome 'the unique, significantly heightened protection afforded against searches of one's person.' " *U.S. v.
  Moore*, 390 Fed. Appx. 503, 507 (6th Cir. 2010).

Seventh Circuit

- "[T]the area in which the incident occurred gave police
  officers particular reason to be concerned about the possibility of gun-related violence. The neighborhood was
  known as a high-crime area of the city; but more
  importantly, there were indications of gang activity,
  recent reports of shots fired, and the occurrence of a
  drive-by shooting with two victims two days earlier and
  one block away from the location where the men were
  discovered drinking. These specific and recent indicia of
  violence, including gun-related violence, increased the
  odds that an individual detained at this location for apparent criminal activity (even a petty offense like the

one at issue here) might be armed. The incidence of crime in the area would not by itself legally justify a protective pat-down. But it is one factor which, in conjunction with the other circumstances we discuss, contributed to a reasonable suspicion that [Defendant] might be armed." *U.S. v. Patton*, 705 F.3d 734 (7th Cir. 2013) (citations omitted).

- "When conducting a protective pat-down during a *Terry* stop, the officer must be able to point to specific and articulable facts that the individual is armed and presents a risk of harm to the officer or to others. . . . [T]he inquiry is objective: would a reasonably prudent person believe in the circumstances that the individual he is dealing with is armed and dangerous?" *U.S. v. Brown*, 232 F.3d 589, 592 (7th Cir. 2000).

Eighth Circuit

- "To recapitulate, the short stretch of street where Officer Sundermeier encountered Dortch had a more specific and direct connection to guns (with recent reports of gunshots) than the neighborhood-wide '"hot spot"' at issue in *Jones*; Dortch's heavy coat was markedly more unseasonable in June, and thus unusual and suspicious, than the *Jones* defendant's sweatshirt in September; Dortch's apparent association with the two illegally stopped vehicles, which resembled those in which guns had been found in the same location not long before, had no analogue in *Jones*; and Dortch's movements, suggestive of concealment and preparation for action, were more threatening than the protective 'clutching' the police observed in *Jones*. To hold that a police officer's concern for safety was reasonable in the one case but not the other is not to make the law 'unknowable' or 'unworkable,' as Dortch warns. Rather, 'it is the nature of the totality[-of-the-circumstances] rule.'" *United States v. Dortch*, 2017 WL 3567825, *5 (8th Cir. 2017) (citations omitted).
- "At the time he performed the protective search, [the officer] was aware that [the defendant] had a prior incident involving assault with a weapon, and, as explained above, [the officer] had a reasonable suspicion that [the defendant] was involved with drug manufacturing. These factors support the reasonable-

ness of [the officer]'s decision to perform a protective
search. Furthermore, [the officer] observed a bulge in
[the defendant]'s coat pockets, and that bulge could
have indicated the presence of a weapon. Considering
these facts in combination, the protective search did not
run afoul of the Fourth Amendment." *U.S. v. Chartier*,
772 F.3d 539, 544–45 (8th Cir. 2014) (citations omitted).

- "A pat-down search. . . .protects the officer's personal
safety while dealing with a person he reasonably
believes may be armed and presently dangerous. To be
constitutionally reasonable, a protective frisk must also
be based upon reasonable suspicion that criminal activity is afoot, and therefore pat-down searches normally
occur during investigative stops of persons suspected of
criminal activity." *U.S. v. Davis*, 202 F.3d 1060, 1062
(8th Cir. 2000).

- "The United States Supreme Court has held a warrantless pat-down search for weapons is permissible when
there are specific and articulable facts which, taken
together with rational inferences from those facts,
would lead a police officer reasonably to believe the
suspect is armed and presently dangerous to the officer
or to others. . . . To decide whether there is a reasonable, articulable suspicion that a suspect is armed and
presently dangerous, we consider the totality of circumstances known to the officer at the time of the search.
. . . An officer's decision to place a traffic offender in
the back of a patrol car does not create a reasonable,
articulable suspicion to justify a pat-down search that
the circumstances would not otherwise allow." *U.S. v.
Glenn*, 152 F.3d 1047, 1048–49 (8th Cir. 1998).

Ninth Circuit

- "The only fact Dillard seriously presses for suspecting
Thomas was armed at the time he demanded to frisk is
the perceived domestic violence nature of the crime he
was investigating. It is true, of course, that the type of
crime a person is suspected of committing may be highly
relevant to the existence of reasonable suspicion for a
weapons frisk. In *Terry*, the officer's suspicion that
Terry was armed was premised largely on his substantiated suspicion that Terry was planning a daytime store
robbery and that such robberies are likely to involve

the use of weapons.' Similarly, we have held it is reasonable for an officer to assume a suspected narcotics trafficker is likely armed. The same is true for a suspected bank robber, someone suspected of involvement in a large-scale marijuana growing operation, and a suspect in certain nighttime burglaries. On the other hand, when a person is being investigated for a crime that is neither 'likely to involve the use of weapons,' nor 'frequently associated with weapons,' suspicion of such a crime does not provide reason to suspect a person is armed. We have not previously addressed whether domestic violence is the type of crime that is likely to involve weapons, such that the nature of the crime itself may provide suspicion a suspect is armed. We address that issue now, and hold domestic violence is not a crime such as bank robbery or trafficking in large quantities of drugs that is, as a general matter, likely to involve the use of weapons. Thus, officers may not rely solely on the domestic violence nature of a call to establish reasonable suspicion for a frisk." *Thomas v. Dillard*, 818 F.3d 864, 878 (9th Cir. 2016), as amended, (May 5, 2016) (citations omitted).

Tenth Circuit

- "It was reasonable for the Task Force to conduct a pat down search because they legitimately believed [Defendant] was a suspect in two armed robberies and a robbery/murder. It was reasonable for the Task Force to believe he and his traveling companion, who himself was a potential accomplice in the robberies, might be armed and dangerous. The Task Force's decision to conduct a pat down search was reasonable to protect the agents' personal safety." *U.S. v. Lang*, 81 F.3d 955, 966 (10th Cir. 1996).

D.C. Circuit

- "Even a lawfully possessed weapon may pose a threat, and because the purpose of a *Terry* search is not to discover evidence of crime, but to allow the officer to pursue his investigation without fear of violence, the lawfulness of defendant's possession is irrelevant to this aspect of the *Terry* analysis." *U.S. v. Christian*, 187 F.3d 663, 669 (D.C. Cir. 1999).

§ 9:5 Nature of frisk: The search for weapons must be a limited intrusion

Supreme Court

- "If the protective search goes beyond what is necessary to determine if the suspect is armed, it is no longer valid under *Terry* and its fruits will be suppressed." *Minnesota v. Dickerson*, 508 U.S. 366, 376, 113 S. Ct. 2130, 124 L. Ed. 2d 334 (1993).
- "Nothing in *Terry* can be understood to allow a generalized cursory search for weapons or, indeed, any search whatever for anything but weapons." *Ybarra v. Illinois*, 444 U.S. 85, 93–94, 100 S. Ct. 338, 62 L. Ed. 2d 238 (1979).
- "The purpose of this limited search is not to discover evidence of crime, but to allow the officer to pursue his investigation without fear of violence, and thus the frisk for weapons must be equally necessary and reasonable." *Adams v. Williams*, 407 U.S. 143, 146, 92 S. Ct. 1921, 32 L. Ed. 2d 612 (1972).
- "[The pat-down seeking concealed weapons] must be confined in scope to an intrusion reasonably designed to discover guns, knives, clubs, or other hidden instruments for the assault of the police officer. . . . [In this case, the Officer] confined his search strictly to what was minimally necessary to learn whether the men were armed and to disarm them once he discovered the weapons. He did not conduct a general exploratory search for whatever evidence of criminal activity he might find. Such a search is a reasonable search under the Fourth Amendment." *Terry v. Ohio*, 392 U.S. 1, 29–31, 88 S. Ct. 1868, 20 L. Ed. 2d 889 (1968).
- "[The Officer] was looking for narcotics and he found them. The search was not reasonably limited in scope to the accomplishment of the only goal which might conceivably have justified its inception—the protection of the officer by disarming a potentially dangerous man." *Peters v. New York*, 392 U.S. 40, 65, 88 S. Ct. 1912, 20 L. Ed. 2d 917 (1968).

First Circuit

- "Defendant argues [arresting officer's] concern about a weapon hidden in his shoe was unreasonable and did not justify extending the search beyond a pat-down of his outer clothing. According to Defendant, his weapon posed no danger to the officers because it was not 'readily accessible.' To be sure, [the officer] acknowledged at the suppression hearing that Defendant would have had to remove his shoe to access the weapon. The problem with Defendant's argument is that when [the officer] placed his finger into the instep of Defendant's mid-top sneaker, he did not know the weapon was 'inaccessible.' What [the officer] did know based upon the surrounding facts and circumstances, and the inferences to be drawn therefrom, was that Defendant might well be armed. [The officer's] belief was objectively reasonable. . . . We hold under the totality of the circumstances of this case that [the officer's] insertion of his index finger into the instep of the Defendant's mid-top sneaker did not exceed the proper scope of his protective search." *U.S. v. Barboza*, 412 F.3d 15 (1st Cir. 2005).

- "We agree with appellant and the district court, however, that the pat-down search conducted by the officers exceeded the permissible scope of a *Terry* detention. . . .The officer who frisked appellant. . .acknowledged. . .that he made no attempt to distinguish between bulging items that could be weapons and other types of concealed objects, reaching into appellant's pockets whenever he felt a protrusion and emptying all items onto the floor. If this indiscriminate removal of items embraced objects that were readily identifiable by touch as non-weapons, then the further invasion of appellant's privacy occasioned by removing them from his pockets was unnecessary and thus unlawful." *U.S. v. Campa*, 234 F.3d 733, 739 (1st Cir. 2000).

Third Circuit

- "[A]n excessively intrusive *Terry* stop is not unconstitutional because its overly broad scope necessarily places a suspect under *de facto* arrest without probable cause, as [defendant] suggests here. Rather, an improperly executed *Terry* stop violates the Fourth Amendment because its scope is generally unreasonable under all of the circumstances." *U.S. v. Johnson*, 592 F.3d 442 (3d Cir. 2010).

- "That [the police officer] was entitled to stop [defendant] under *Terry [v. Ohio]* still leaves the question of whether the pat-down search was properly conducted. For if it was not, there would be a ripple effect on the criminal case against him, ending in the exclusion of the papers with allegedly stolen credit card numbers as 'fruit[s] of the poisonous tree' [citations omitted]. . . . Those papers, of course, were found in a routine (and legal) inventory search upon [defendant]'s booking at the police station,. . .which took place after his arrest—an arrest made possible only by the discovery of marijuana during the *Terry* search [citation and footnote omitted]. . . . In *Terry*, the Supreme Court said that '[t]he scope of the search must be strictly tied to and justified by the circumstances which rendered its initiation permissible' [citation omitted]. . . . The proper scope of a search becomes critical when police discover something suspicious they were not expecting or intending to find. And in such a case the 'plain view' doctrine often governs whether their discovery can be admitted against a defendant [citation omitted]." *U.S. v. Yamba*, 506 F.3d 251 (3d Cir. 2007).

- "We agree with the district court that [the] Officer was within the bounds of *Terry* in opening the envelope because he was justifiably concerned that it concealed a small-caliber handgun. The four-by-six inch envelope was packed full of nineteen hard plastic cards—whether credit cards or drivers' licenses—which the record demonstrates created the feel of a hard, bulky object. Moreover, the government presented the district court with tangible evidence that a small-caliber handgun, in its holster, fits inside the envelope and has roughly the same feel inside the envelope as did the credit cards it contained. In the hasty examination necessitated by a protective search, [the] Officer could reasonably have confused the square, bulky mass of credit cards and drivers' licenses for a small handgun sheathed in a square, leather holster that masked its outlines." *U.S. v. Edwards*, 53 F.3d 616, 619 (3d Cir. 1995).

Fourth Circuit

- "Once an officer has patted down a suspect for weapons and determined that he is not armed, that officer exceeds the permissible scope of a *Terry* frisk if he continues to search the suspect. . . . An officer's squeezing, sliding and otherwise manipulating the contents of a defendant's pocket, if the officer knows the pocket contains no weapon, is prohibited. . . . Having detected the presence of an unknown, potentially dangerous object on a suspect during a frisk, the test for whether an officer may search farther and seize the item is an objective one. . . . [T]he only question is whether a reasonably prudent man in the circumstances would have been warranted in the belief that his safety or that of others was in danger. . . . That is, would a reasonable officer in those circumstances have believed that the item could likely be a weapon?" *U.S. v. Swann*, 149 F.3d 271, 274–75 (4th Cir. 1998).

- "Directing that he raise his shirt required little movement by [Defendant] and allowed [the] Officer to immediately determine whether [Defendant] was armed without having to come in close contact with him. And, it minimized the risk that he could draw his weapon before [the] Officer could attempt to neutralize the potential threat. In comparison, complying with this direction involved a limited intrusion upon [Defendant]'s personal security. Indeed, this act was less intrusive than the patdown frisk sanctioned in *Terry*. The officer avoided the serious intrusion upon the sanctity of the person necessitated by the patdown frisk, which requires the officer to feel with sensitive fingers every portion of the prisoner's body." *U.S. v. Baker*, 78 F.3d 135, 138 (4th Cir. 1996).

Sixth Circuit

- "During a *Terry* stop, a police officer may conduct a limited search for concealed weapons, if the officer believes that a suspect may be dangerous. . . . Because the search must be strictly circumscribed by the exigencies which justify its initiation. . .the search must be limited to that which is necessary for the discovery of weapons which might be used to harm the officer." *U.S. v. Walker*, 181 F.3d 774, 778, 1999 FED App. 0228P (6th Cir. 1999).

Seventh Circuit

- "During a *Terry* stop, an officer with reason to believe he is dealing with an armed and dangerous individual may conduct a non-invasive pat-down search of a detainee to ensure for his own safety and that of others nearby that the detainee does not possess a weapon. . . . A search for weapons in the absence of probable cause to arrest, however, must, like any other search, be strictly circumscribed by the exigencies which justify its initiation." *U.S. v. Rivers*, 121 F.3d 1043, 1045 (7th Cir. 1997).

Eighth Circuit

- "Once an investigative stop has been initiated, a police officer who has reason to believe that the person stopped may be armed and dangerous may conduct a pat-down search for weapons to protect officer safety." *U.S. v. Williams*, 139 F.3d 628, 630 (8th Cir. 1998).
- "During an investigative stop, officers may check for weapons and may take any additional steps reasonably necessary to protect their personal safety and to maintain the status quo during the course of the stop." *U.S. v. Beck*, 140 F.3d 1129, 1134 (8th Cir. 1998).

Tenth Circuit

- "A pat-down protective search or seizure is permissible if the police reasonably believe that a suspect is presently armed and dangerous. . . . Police officers are authorized to take reasonable steps necessary to secure their safety and maintain the status quo during a stop. . . . However, the use of firearms, handcuffs, and other forceful techniques are justified only by probable cause or when the circumstances reasonably warrant such measures." *U.S. v. Gama-Bastidas*, 142 F.3d 1233, 1240 (10th Cir. 1998).

D.C. Circuit

- "A frisk may after all be conducted even when a suspect's clothing exhibits no visible bulges. The limitation imposed by *Dickerson* is that once the officer finds an object on the person of a suspect, he may not palpate it more than is necessary to determine whether it is a weapon." *U.S. v. Johnson*, 212 F.3d 1313, 1317 (D.C. Cir. 2000).

§ 9:6   Search after frisk: Feeling an object that might be contraband may justify a more extensive intrusion to seize the contraband

Supreme Court

- "If a police officer lawfully pats down a suspect's outer clothing and feels an object whose contour or mass makes its identity immediately apparent, there has been no invasion of the suspect's privacy beyond that already authorized by the officer's search for weapons; if the object is contraband, its warrantless seizure would be justified by the same practical considerations that inhere in the plain view context." *Minnesota v. Dickerson*, 508 U.S. 366, 375, 113 S. Ct. 2130, 124 L. Ed. 2d 334 (1993).

- "*Terry* itself demonstrates that the sense of touch is capable of revealing the nature of an object with sufficient reliability to support a seizure. The very premise of *Terry*, after all, is that officers will be able to detect the presence of weapons through the sense of touch and *Terry* upheld precisely such a seizure. Even if it were true that the sense of touch is generally less reliable than the sense of sight, that only suggests that officers will less often be able to justify seizures of unseen contraband. Regardless of whether the officer detects the contraband by sight or by touch the Fourth Amendment's requirement that the officers have probable cause to believe that the item is contraband before seizing it ensures against excessively speculative seizures." *Minnesota v. Dickerson*, 508 U.S. 366, 376, 113 S. Ct. 2130, 124 L. Ed. 2d 334 (1993).

First Circuit

- "The Supreme Court repeatedly has recognized that officers have a right of access to contraband that they discover while acting within the bounds of a lawful *Terry* investigation." *U.S. v. Jones*, 187 F.3d 210, 221 (1st Cir. 1999).

Third Circuit

- "In *Minnesota v. Dickerson*, the [U.S. Supreme] Court took up the issue of 'whether police officers may seize nonthreatening contraband detected during a protective patdown search of the sort permitted by *Terry[v. Ohio],*' and decided that 'the answer clearly is that they may, so long as the officers' search stays within the bounds marked by *Terry*' [citation omitted]. Since *Dickerson*, many courts have focused on exactly how 'immediately' an officer must know that something felt during a *Terry* search is contraband or precisely how much a clothed object can be manipulated before a search becomes illegal. [citations omitted] And in the course of admitting in evidence certain contraband that was discovered in a *Terry* search, courts have credited testimony by some police officers that suggests remarkable sensory powers. [citation omitted] Even the officer in this case testified—credibly, according to the district court—that after feeling through a 'middle medium weight jacket' for what '[p]robably wasn't even a half second,' he nevertheless 'could tell right away' that the lump in defendant's pocket was marijuana. . . . We reject a narrow focus on how quickly and certainly the nature of an object felt during a *Terry* search is known and on how much manipulation of a person's clothing is acceptable. . . . Such searches necessarily involve a certain amount of 'squeezing, sliding and otherwise manipulating' of a suspect's outer clothing [citation omitted] in an attempt to discern whether weapons are hidden underneath. . . . The proper question under *Dickerson*. . . . is not the immediacy and certainty with which an officer knows an object to be contraband or the amount of manipulation required to acquire that knowledge, but rather what the officer believes the object is by the time he concludes that it is not a weapon. That is, a *Terry* search cannot purposely be used to discover contraband, but it is permissible that contraband be confiscated if spontaneously discovered during a properly executed *Terry* search. Moreover, when determining whether the scope of a particular *Terry* search was proper, the areas of focus should be whether the officer had probable cause to believe an object was contraband before he knew it not to be a weapon and whether he acquired that knowledge in a manner consistent with a routine frisk. [citations omitted] Assuming that an officer is authorized to conduct a *Terry* search at all, he is authorized to assure himself that a suspect has no weapons. He is allowed to slide or manipulate an object in a suspect's pocket, consistent with a routine frisk, until the officer is able reasonably to eliminate the possibility that the object is a weapon. If, before that point, the officer develops probable cause to believe, given his training and experience, that an object is contraband, he may lawfully perform a more intrusive search. If, indeed, he discovers contraband, the officer may seize it, and it will be admissible against the suspect. If, however, the officer 'goes beyond what is necessary to determine if the suspect is armed, it is no longer valid under *Terry* and its fruits will be suppressed.' [citation omitted]. . . . In our case, [the officer] 'felt around' or otherwise 'manipulated' the contents of [defendant]'s pocket in the process of checking for weapons when he came across what in his experience could be contraband. It is not key whether [the officer] was certain that the object in [defendant]'s pocket was contraband by the time he knew it not to be a weapon; what is key is whether [the officer] had probable cause to believe that it was and this occurred at the same moment or before he determined that [defendant] had no gun on his person. . . . The record demonstrates that probable cause indeed existed before [the officer]'s search went beyond the bounds of *Terry*. [The officer] testified that, when he felt [defendant]'s pocket, he could feel a plastic bag containing a 'soft[,] spongy-like substance.' . . . [Although] '[lawn] grass. . . or oregano' might feel similarly soft or spongy, people do not normally go around with those substances in their pockets [footnote omitted]. Moreover, [the officer] also felt 'small buds and seeds' along with the contents of the plastic bag. This detail is more consistent with marijuana than lawn grass or oregano. Based on [the officer]'s experience, he reasonably suspected that [defendant] had marijuana in his pocket. His belief was reached quickly and upon minimal manipulation of [defendant]'s pocket from the outside, consistent with a routine frisk allowed by *Terry*. And though [the officer] admitted to manipulating the object even after forming the belief that it was not a weapon, he only did so to 'mak[e] sure it was what [he] knew it to be.' In other words, by that point [the officer] already had probable cause to conduct a more intrusive search than that au-

thorized by *Terry* alone. . . . [T]he veracity of [the of-
ficer]'s testimony. . . was credited by the district court[,
and]. . . we cannot say that the court's finding was
clearly erroneous. Nevertheless, consistent with the
legal standard set out above, we purposely do not rely
on the precision of [the officer]'s testimony that he
reached his conclusion within 'a half second.' However
long it took [the officer] to form that belief, the record
indicates that he did so within the bounds of *Terry*, as
there is nothing to suggest that he conducted anything
beyond a routine frisk until after there was probable
cause to search more intrusively. . . . For these reasons,
the *Terry* search that revealed marijuana in [defen-
dant]'s coat pocket was conducted within the bounds set
by the Supreme Court. We therefore affirm the district
court's denial of [defendant]'s motion to suppress the
later-discovered slips of paper and, consequently, his
convictions for wire fraud. . . ." *U.S. v. Yamba*, 506
F.3d 251 (3d Cir. 2007).

Fourth Circuit

- "*Minnesota v. Dickerson*. . . .set forth the plain feel doctrine, which holds that contraband discovered during a
  lawful *Terry* stop is admissible so long as the search
  does not exceed the bounds permitted by *Terry*. . . .
  Thus, if the contour or mass of the object makes its
  identity immediately apparent, the officer may lawfully
  seize it. . . . Once an officer has determined that the
  object is not a weapon, however, and if its shape or size
  does not indicate its contraband matters, the search
  must stop." *U.S. v. Raymond*, 152 F.3d 309, 312 (4th
  Cir. 1998).

Fifth Circuit

- "Both *Terry* and the protective sweep doctrine of *Gould*
  depend on a reasonableness inquiry that evolves with
  new information. . . . If officers gain new information
  relevant to safety or criminal conduct, the scope of their
  permissible investigation may expand. For example,
  reasonable suspicion may 'ripen' or 'develop' into probable cause for an arrest if a *Terry* stop reveals further
  evidence of criminal conduct. . . . The justification for a
  protective sweep likewise is circumscribed by the evolv-

ing facts. The protective sweep must cover no more than those spaces where police reasonably suspect a person posing danger could be found, and must last no longer than necessary to dispel the suspicion and no longer than the police are otherwise constitutionally justified in remaining on the premises." *U.S. v. Scroggins*, 599 F.3d 433 (5th Cir. 2010).

- "The primary issue at hand is the reasonableness of the patdown. Under *Terry [v. Ohio]*, a law-enforcement officer may briefly detain and frisk an individual, as long as the officer has a reasonable, articulable suspicion of criminal activity. [citation omitted] 'The officer need not be absolutely certain that the individual is armed; the issue is whether a *reasonably prudent man in the circumstances* would be warranted in the *belief* that his safety or that of others was in danger' (emphasis added). [citation omitted] Accordingly, for determining reasonable-suspicion vel non, a court must consider the totality of the circumstances. [citation omitted] 'This process allows officers to draw on their own experience and specialized training to make inferences from and deductions about the cumulative information available to them that might well elude an untrained person.' [citation omitted]. . . In granting the suppression motion, the district court relied on *Ybarra v. Illinois* [citation omitted] for the proposition that [defendant] and Aycock's presence in the home where a narcotics search was to take place, without more, did not provide individualized suspicion that [defendant] was either involved in drug trafficking or armed and dangerous. . . . The circumstances at hand are markedly different [than those in *Ybarra*]. We are mindful that 'person's mere propinquity to others independently suspected of criminal activity does not, without more, give rise to *probable cause* to search that person' (emphasis added). [citations omitted]. . . In contrast, occupants of a house generally have a closer relationship, and it is not unreasonable to think their relationship might extend to involvement in illegal activities. (Although it was later determined that [defendant] did not reside at the house, the Officers did not know that previous to the patdown.) Along that line, the Officers had been conducting surveillance of the house and had just arrested Fitzger-

ald, who, a short time before, had exited the house carrying a large quantity of drugs and a loaded handgun.
Based on these factors, reasonable officers could believe
that [defendant] and Aycock could also have been
involved in drug trafficking and were therefore possibly
armed as well. [citations omitted] The patdown was
reasonable. . . ." *U.S. v. Darensbourg*, 236 Fed. Appx.
991 (5th Cir. 2007) (Not selected for publication in the
Federal Reporter, NO. 06-30726).

- "[Defendant] argues that the removal of his pocket's
  contents was unreasonable because the frisk revealed
  nothing that could be taken for a weapon by an experienced officer under any stretch of the imagination. ...
  [The Officer] testified that he thought the large bulge in
  [Defendant]'s pocket was some type of weapon. The
  combination of change, over $1,400 of currency, and a
  cardboard box containing a gold chain was no mere
  bump. ... In the light most favorable to the government,
  [the Officer] had not ruled out the possibility that the
  large bulge was a weapon, and his removal of the
  pocket's contents was not beyond the scope of a permissible *Terry* frisk." *U.S. v. Campbell*, 178 F.3d 345, 349
  (5th Cir. 1999).

- "[I]f, during a *Terry* weapons search, a police officer
  feels an object whose contour or mass makes its identity
  [as contraband] immediately apparent, its seizure is
  lawful. [T]he purpose of a *Terry* search is to eliminate
  the threat of violence to an investigating officer, and is
  therefore limited to that which is necessary for the
  discovery of weapons which might be used to harm the
  officer or others nearby." *U.S. v. Maldonado*, 42 F.3d
  906, 909 (5th Cir. 1995).

Sixth Circuit

- "In *Minnesota v. Dickerson*. . .the Supreme Court held
  that police may seize non-threatening contraband
  detected by touch during a protective pat-down search
  if the search stays within the bounds marked by *Terry*.
  . . ." *U.S. v. Walker*, 181 F.3d 774, 778, 1999 FED App.
  0228P (6th Cir. 1999).

Seventh Circuit

- "This court has not had occasion to consider a case so

factually analogous to *Dickerson*, but other courts have upheld the admission of evidence discovered through non-intrusive pat-down searches during which the incriminating nature of the contraband is ascertained immediately. In *United States v. Hughes*. . .for example, an officer performing a valid *Terry* pat-down search felt lumps of crack cocaine in defendant's pants pocket. Because his first impression was that the lumps were contraband and no further manipulation was necessary the court upheld the seizure of the cocaine. . . . In contrast, seizures considered unconstitutional resulted from investigative overreaching not present here." *U.S. v. Rivers*, 121 F.3d 1043, 1046–47 (7th Cir. 1997).

Eighth Circuit

- "When an officer discovers contraband during the course of a legitimate *Terry* search, the Fourth Amendment does not require its suppression. . . . Typically, such discoveries are made when contraband comes into plain view of the officer conducting a protective search. But the principle is not limited to what can be seen. If a police officer lawfully pats down a suspect's outer clothing and feels an object whose contour or mass makes its identity immediately apparent, there has been no invasion of the suspect's privacy beyond that already authorized by the officer's search for weapons." *U.S. v. Williams*, 139 F.3d 628, 630 (8th Cir. 1998).

Ninth Circuit

- "Had the officer continued to manipulate the object beyond what was necessary to ascertain that it posed no threat, he would have run afoul of the Supreme Court's holding in *Minnesota v. Dickerson*. . . .The district court, however, believed. . .that he did not seek to manipulate the object, but was nevertheless alerted immediately to the presence of drugs by the familiar sensation of plastic sliding against a granular substance. Once the presence of the drugs became known in this manner, they could be seized without the defendant's consent pursuant to a tactile variation on the plain-view rule." *U.S. v. Mattarolo*, 209 F.3d 1153, 1158 (9th Cir. 2000).

§ 9:7   Plain-feel doctrine

Supreme Court

- "The plain view doctrine has an obvious application by
  analogy to cases in which an officer discovers contraband through the sense of touch during an otherwise
  lawful search. The rationale of the plain-view doctrine
  is that if contraband is left in open view and is observed
  by a police officer from a lawful vantage point, there
  has been no invasion of a legitimate expectation of
  privacy and thus no search within the meaning of the
  Fourth Amendment-or at least no search independent
  of the initial intrusion that gave the officers their
  vantage point. . . . The warrantless seizure of contraband that presents itself in this manner is deemed justified by the realization that resort to a neutral magistrate under such circumstances would often be
  impracticable and would do little to promote the objectives of the Fourth Amendment. . . . The same can be
  said of tactile discoveries of contraband. If a police officer lawfully pats down a suspect's outer clothing and
  feels an object whose contour or mass makes its identity
  immediately apparent, there has been no invasion of
  the suspect's privacy beyond that already authorized by
  the officer's search for weapons; if the object is contraband, its warrantless seizure would be justified by the
  same practical considerations that inhere in the plain-
  view context." *Minnesota v. Dickerson*, 508 U.S. 366,
  113 S. Ct. 2130, 124 L. Ed. 2d 334 (1993).

Third Circuit

- "The proper question under the plain feel doctrine is
  not the immediacy and certainty with which an officer
  knows an object to be contraband or the amount of
  manipulation required to acquire that knowledge, but
  rather what the officer believes the object is by the time
  he concludes that it is not a weapon. Under the plain
  feel doctrine, assuming that an officer is authorized to
  conduct a *Terry* search at all, he is authorized to assure
  himself that a suspect has no weapons, and is allowed
  to slide or manipulate an object in a suspect's pocket,
  consistent with a routine frisk, until the officer is able
  reasonably to eliminate the possibility that the object is

a weapon. If, before the officer is able reasonably to eliminate the possibility that the object in question is a weapon, the officer develops probable cause to believe, given his training and experience, that an object is contraband, he may lawfully perform a more intrusive search; if he discovers contraband, the officer may seize it, and it will be admissible against the suspect, but if the officer goes beyond what is necessary to determine if the suspect is armed, it is no longer valid under *Terry* and its fruits will be suppressed." *U.S. v. Yamba*, 506 F.3d 251 (3d Cir. 2007).

Fourth Circuit

- "Officer who conducted lawful pat-down search of defendant's person was authorized to remove contraband from the defendant's pocket under the plain feel doctrine where, after feeling the object, the officer grabbed it to immobilize it, once he secured it, officer realized that the object was not a weapon, but instead a large, hard, irregular object, roughly the size and shape of a hockey puck, wrapped in a plastic bag, at which point officer removed the object, believing it to be a controlled dangerous substance." *U.S. v. Jones*, 289 Fed. Appx. 593 (4th Cir. 2008).

Sixth Circuit

- "The plain view doctrine. . .is best understood not as an independent exception to the warrant clause, but simply as an extension of whatever the prior justification for an officer's access to an object may be. So understood, courts have logically extended this concept to permit the admission of evidence discovered with other sensory faculties—plain smell and plain hearing. The US Supreme Court has put its imprimatur on plain feel. The Supreme Court has held that police officers may seize nonthreatening contraband detected during a protective patdown search of the sort permitted by *Terry*, so long as the officers' search stays within the bounds marked by *Terry*. . . . The proper question. . .is not the immediacy and certainty with which an officer knows an object to be contraband or the amount of manipulation required to acquire that knowledge, but rather what the officer believes the object is by the time he concludes that it is not a weapon. That is, a *Terry* search cannot purposely be used to discover contraband, but it is permissible that contraband be confiscated if spontaneously discovered during a properly executed *Terry* search. Moreover, when determining whether the scope of a particular *Terry* search was proper, the areas of focus should be whether the officer had probable cause to believe an object was contraband before he knew it not to be a weapon and whether he acquired that knowledge in a manner consistent with a routine frisk. Assuming that an officer is authorized to conduct a *Terry* search at all, he is authorized to assure himself that a suspect has no weapons. He is allowed to slide or manipulate an object in a suspect's pocket, consistent with a routine frisk, until the officer is able reasonably to eliminate the possibility that the object is a weapon. If, before that point, the officer develops probable cause to believe, given his training and experience, that an object is contraband, he may lawfully perform a more intrusive search. If, indeed, he discovers contraband, the officer may seize it, and it will be admissible against the suspect. If, however, the officer goes beyond what is necessary to determine if the suspect is armed, it is no longer valid under *Terry* and its fruits will be suppressed." *U.S. v. Campbell*, 549 F.3d 364 (6th Cir. 2008).

Chapter 10

Vehicle Stops

Research References

West's Key Number Digest

Aliens ⬥4; Arrest ⬥63.5(6), 68, 71.1; Automobiles ⬥61, 349;
    Constitutional Law ⬥319.5; Searches and Seizures ⬥60 to 61,
    69

KeyCite®: Cases and other legal materials listed in KeyCite Scope can be researched through the KeyCite service on Westlaw®. Use KeyCite to check citations for form, parallel references, prior and later history, and comprehensive citator information, including citations to other decisions and secondary materials.

---

§ 10:1 Significance of stop: A seizure occurs whenever a vehicle is stopped; therefore the Fourth Amendment applies

Supreme Court

- "A traffic stop of a car communicates to a reasonable passenger that he or she is not free to terminate the encounter with the police and move about at will." *Arizona v. Johnson*, 555 U.S. 323, 129 S. Ct. 781, 172 L. Ed. 2d 694 (2009).

- "For the duration of a traffic stop, a police officer effectively seizes everyone in the vehicle, the driver and all passengers. Accordingly, in a traffic-stop setting, the first *Terry* condition—a lawful investigatory stop-is met whenever it is lawful for police to detain an automobile and its occupants pending inquiry into a vehicular violation. The police need not have, in addition, cause to believe any occupant of the vehicle is involved in criminal activity." *Arizona v. Johnson*, 555 U.S. 323, 129 S. Ct. 781, 172 L. Ed. 2d 694 (2009).

- "A traffic stop necessarily curtails the travel a passenger has chosen just as much as it halts the driver, diverting both from the stream of traffic to the side of the road, and the police activity that normally amounts to intrusion on "privacy and personal security" does not normally (and did not here) distinguish between passenger and driver . . . An officer who orders one particular car to pull over acts with an implicit claim of right based on fault of some sort, and a sensible person would not expect a police officer to allow people to come and go freely from the physical focal point of an investigation into faulty behavior or wrongdoing. If the likely wrongdoing is not the driving, the passenger will reasonably feel subject to suspicion owing to close association; but even when the wrongdoing is only bad driving, the passenger will expect to be subject to some scrutiny, and his attempt to leave the scene would be so obvi-

ously likely to prompt an objection from the officer that
no passenger would feel free to leave in the first place
. . . Holding that the passenger in a private car is not
(without more) seized in a traffic stop would invite police officers to stop cars with passengers regardless of
probable cause or reasonable suspicion of anything illegal . . . . The fact that evidence uncovered as a result of
an arbitrary traffic stop would still be admissible
against any passengers would be a powerful incentive
to run the kind of "roving patrols" that would still
violate the driver's Fourth Amendment right." *Brendlin
v. California*, 551 U.S. 249, 127 S. Ct. 2400, 168 L. Ed.
2d 132 (2007).

- "Temporary detention of individuals during the stop of
  an automobile by the police, even if only for a brief period and for a limited purpose, constitutes a seizure of
  persons within the meaning of this provision." *Whren v.
  U.S.*, 517 U.S. 806, 809–10, 116 S. Ct. 1769, 135 L. Ed.
  2d 89 (1996).

- "A [F]ourth Amendment seizure occurs when a vehicle
  is stopped at a checkpoint The question thus becomes
  whether such seizures are reasonable under the Fourth
  Amendment." *Michigan Dept. of State Police v. Sitz*,
  496 U.S. 444, 450, 110 S. Ct. 2481, 110 L. Ed. 2d 412
  (1990).

- "The Fourth Amendment applies to seizures of the
  person, including brief investigatory stops such as the
  stop of the vehicle here." *U.S. v. Cortez*, 449 U.S. 411,
  417, 101 S. Ct. 690, 66 L. Ed. 2d 621 (1981).

- "The Fourth and Fourteenth Amendments are implicated in this case because stopping an automobile and
  detaining its occupants constitute a seizure within the
  meaning of those Amendments, even though the purpose
  of the stop is limited and the resulting detention quite
  brief." *Delaware v. Prouse*, 440 U.S. 648, 653, 99 S. Ct.
  1391, 59 L. Ed. 2d 660 (1979).

- "It is agreed that checkpoint stops are seizures within
  the meaning of the Fourth Amendment." *U.S. v.
  Martinez-Fuerte*, 428 U.S. 543, 556, 96 S. Ct. 3074, 49
  L. Ed. 2d 1116 (1976).

First Circuit

- "It is doctrinal bedrock that a police stop of a moving

vehicle constitutes a seizure of the vehicle's occupants and therefore comes within the purview of the Fourth Amendment. . . . This principle applies equally to drivers and passengers. . . . Hence, each occupant of a car has a right to challenge the propriety of a traffic stop under the Fourth Amendment. Although courts occasionally use the term standing as a shorthand for this status, the real implication is that the individual's Fourth Amendment interests were affected by official actions." *U.S. v. Woodrum*, 202 F.3d 1, 5–6 (1st Cir. 2000).

Third Circuit

- "In light of the 'automobile exception' to the usual search warrant requirement, it is difficult to pick a worse place to conceal evidence of a crime than an automobile. The Supreme Court has interpreted—and reinterpreted—the automobile exception so expansively that the Court essentially has obviated the requirement that the government obtain a warrant to search a vehicle provided it has probable cause to believe that the vehicle contains evidence of a crime. . . . Even though it is clear that the government had the opportunity to seek a warrant before searching the Mustang, we hold that the automobile exception to the warrant requirement obviated its need to do so as the government had probable cause for the search of the Mustang and its contents. Inasmuch as the automobile exception was applicable, there were virtually no temporal, physical, or numerical limitations on the search's scope. Thus, the government could make a broad search of the Mustang including its contents, even if contained in packages—and could repeat the search as long as it remained in continuous control of the Mustang. The government took advantage of this broad authority and, in making its search lawfully uncovered evidence that Donahue had committed weapons-related offenses. Consequently, the District Court should not have suppressed the evidence the government seized in the search. Accordingly, we will reverse the order suppressing the evidence seized in the search of the Mustang and its contents and we will remand the case to the District Court for further proceedings." *U.S. v. Donahue*, 764 F.3d 293, 295–96 (3d Cir. 2014).

Fourth Circuit

- "Because an automobile stop is a seizure of a person, the stop must comply with the Fourth Amendment's requirement that it not be unreasonable under the circumstances. . . . As a result, such a stop must be justified by probable cause or a reasonable suspicion, based on specific and articulable facts, of unlawful conduct." *U.S. v. Wilson*, 205 F.3d 720, 722–23 (4th Cir. 2000).

Sixth Circuit

- " 'The Fourth Amendment forbids law enforcement officers from making unreasonable searches and seizures, "and its protections extend to brief investigatory stops of. . .vehicles that fall short of traditional arrest.' " In order to effect a traffic stop, an officer must possess either probable cause of a civil infraction or reasonable suspicion of criminal activity. We primarily enforce these standards through the exclusionary rule, which requires the suppression of any evidence seized during a vehicle search premised on an illegal traffic stop." *U.S. v. Lyons*, 687 F.3d 754, 762–763 (6th Cir. 2012).

Eighth Circuit

- "Blocking a vehicle so its occupant is unable to leave during the course of an investigatory stop is reasonable to maintain the status quo while completing the purpose of the stop. . . . . We conclude that blocking [Defendant]'s truck with the squad car resulted in a Fourth Amendment seizure. The seizure, however, was based on a reasonably articulable suspicion and satisfies the first prong of *Terry* that the initial stop be justified." *U.S. v. Tuley*, 161 F.3d 513, 515 (8th Cir. 1998).

Ninth Circuit

- "The Fourth Amendment entitles a person to drive down a road without being stopped by the government, unless the law enforcement officer who stops him has a reasonable suspicion based on articulable facts of criminal activity." *U.S. v. Tiong*, 224 F.3d 1136, 1139 (9th Cir. 2000).
- "The Fourth Amendment prohibits an officer from stopping a vehicle without a reasonable or well-founded

suspicion of criminal conduct at the time of the stop."
U.S. v. Olafson, 213 F.3d 435, 439 (9th Cir. 2000).

- "An automobile stop by police is a seizure within the
  meaning of the Fourth Amendment. . . . Such a stop is
  subject to the constitutional requirement that it not be
  unreasonable. . . . If the officer had probable cause to
  believe that a traffic violation had occurred, the seizure
  is reasonable." *U.S. v. Garcia*, 205 F.3d 1182, 1186–87
  (9th Cir. 2000).

Tenth Circuit

- "[T]he 'touchstone of the Fourth Amendment is reasonableness, not individualized suspicion.' Accordingly, the
  Supreme Court has carved out exceptions to the general
  rule where the primary purpose of a group seizure went
  beyond ordinary crime control. For example, the Court
  has upheld a border patrol roadblock designed to
  intercept illegal aliens. And it has upheld a sobriety
  checkpoint aimed at removing drunk drivers from the
  road to protect public safety. In those situations, the
  Court has not required individualized reasonable
  suspicion, instead favoring a group-level balance of
  interests, weighing the public interest against intrusions on individuals' liberty." *U.S. v. Paetsch*, 782 F.3d
  1162, 1169 (10th Cir. 2015), cert. denied, 136 S. Ct. 195,
  193 L. Ed. 2d 153 (2015) (citations omitted).

- "A routine traffic stop is indisputably a seizure within
  the meaning of the Fourth Amendment. (citation omitted) However, because a traffic stop is 'necessarily [a]
  swift action predicated upon the on-the-spot observations of the officer on the beat,' an officer need only reasonably suspect that a crime is in the offing to justify
  such a detention. . . . [Nevertheless,] [a]bsent some
  particularized, objective basis to believe the dealer plate
  [observed on the defendant's car by the officer] was actually not issued to this vehicle or that it was actually not
  authorized to display the plate, further detention [of
  defendant after initial stop to see that a license plate
  was attached] was unconstitutional." *U.S. v.
  Pena-Montes*, 589 F.3d 1048 (10th Cir. 2009).

- "It is undisputed that stopping an automobile and
  detaining its occupants constitutes a seizure within the
  meaning of the Fourth Amendment. . . . A warrantless

seizure of an automobile and its occupants may be reasonable if predicated on probable cause and exigent circumstances." *U.S. v. Gama-Bastidas*, 142 F.3d 1233, 1239 (10th Cir. 1998).

- "An investigative detention must be temporary, lasting no longer than necessary to effectuate the purpose of the stop, and the scope of the detention must be carefully tailored to its underlying justification. During a traffic stop for speeding, a police officer is permitted to ask such questions, examine such documentation, and run such computer verifications as necessary to determine that the driver has a valid license and is entitled to operate the vehicle. The officer may detain the driver and his vehicle as long as reasonably necessary to make these determinations and to issue a citation or warning. In appropriate circumstances, to ensure the officer's safety, the officer may obtain information regarding the detainee's criminal history. However, when the driver has produced a valid license and proof that he is entitled to operate the car, he must be allowed to proceed on his way, without being subject to further delay by police for additional questioning." *U.S. v. Wood*, 106 F.3d 942, 945 (10th Cir. 1997).

Eleventh Circuit

- "A traffic stop is a seizure within the meaning of the Fourth Amendment. . . . Because a routine traffic stop is only a limited form of seizure, it is more analogous to an investigative detention than a custodial arrest." *U.S. v. Purcell*, 236 F.3d 1274, 1277 (11th Cir. 2001).

§ 10:2 Grounds for stop: There must be reasonable suspicion to justify an investigatory stop of an individual vehicle

Supreme Court

- "An officer, in other words, may conduct certain unrelated checks during an otherwise lawful traffic stop. But contrary to Justice ALITO's suggestion, he may not do so in a way that prolongs the stop, absent the reasonable suspicion ordinarily demanded to justify detaining an individual. Beyond determining whether to issue a traffic ticket, an officer's mission includes 'ordinary

inquiries incident to [the traffic] stop.' Typically such
inquiries involve checking the driver's license, determining whether there are outstanding warrants against the
driver, and inspecting the automobile's registration and
proof of insurance. These checks serve the same objective as enforcement of the traffic code: ensuring that
vehicles on the road are operated safely and responsibly.
A dog sniff, by contrast, is a measure aimed at 'detect-
[ing] evidence of ordinary criminal wrongdoing.' Candidly, the Government acknowledged at oral argument
that a dog sniff, unlike the routine measures just
mentioned, is not an ordinary incident of a traffic stop.
Lacking the same close connection to roadway safety as
the ordinary inquiries, a dog sniff is not fairly characterized as part of the officer's traffic mission. . . . The
Government argues that an officer may 'incremental[ly]'
prolong a stop to conduct a dog sniff so long as the officer is reasonably diligent in pursuing the traffic-
related purpose of the stop, and the overall duration of
the stop remains reasonable in relation to the duration
of other traffic stops involving similar circumstances.
The Government's argument, in effect, is that by
completing all traffic-related tasks expeditiously, an officer can earn bonus time to pursue an unrelated criminal investigation. The reasonableness of a seizure,
however, depends on what the police in fact do. In this
regard, the Government acknowledges that 'an officer
always has to be reasonably diligent.' How could diligence be gauged other than by noting what the officer
actually did and how he did it? If an officer can complete
traffic-based inquiries expeditiously, then that is the
amount of 'time reasonably required to complete [the
stop's] mission.' As we said in *Caballes* and reiterate
today, a traffic stop 'prolonged beyond' that point is
'unlawful.' The critical question, then, is not whether
the dog sniff occurs before or after the officer issues a
ticket, but whether conducting the sniff 'prolongs'—*i.e.*,
adds time to—'the stop.'" *Rodriguez v. U.S.*, 135 S. Ct.
1609, 1615–16, 191 L. Ed. 2d 492 (2015) (citations
omitted).

- "[O]nce a motor vehicle has been lawfully detained for a
traffic violation, the police officers may order the driver
to get out of the vehicle without violating the Fourth

Amendment's proscription of unreasonable searches and seizures. An officer making a traffic stop may order passengers to get out of the car pending completion of the stop as well. The government's legitimate and weighty interest in officer safety, the Court said, outweighs the de minimis additional intrusion of requiring a driver, already lawfully stopped, to exit the vehicle." *Arizona v. Johnson*, 555 U.S. 323, 129 S. Ct. 781, 172 L. Ed. 2d 694 (2009).

- "Based upon that whole picture the detaining officers must have a particularized and objective basis for suspecting the particular person stopped of criminal activity. First, the assessment must be based upon all of the circumstances. The analysis proceeds with various objective observations, information from police reports, if such are available, and consideration of the modes or patterns of operation of certain kinds of lawbreakers. . . . The second element contained in the idea that an assessment of the whole picture must yield a particularized suspicion is the concept that the process just described must raise a suspicion that the particular individual being stopped is engaged in wrongdoing." *U.S. v. Cortez*, 449 U.S. 411, 417–18, 101 S. Ct. 690, 66 L. Ed. 2d 621 (1981).

- "The marginal contribution to roadway safety possibly resulting from a system of spot checks cannot justify subjecting every occupant of every vehicle on the roads to a seizure—limited in magnitude compared to other intrusions but nonetheless constitutionally cognizable—at the unbridled discretion of law enforcement officials. To insist neither upon an appropriate factual basis for suspicion directed at a particular automobile nor upon some other substantial and objective standard or rule to govern the exercise of discretion would invite intrusions upon constitutionally guaranteed rights based on nothing more substantial than inarticulate hunches. [E]xcept in those situations in which there is at least articulable and reasonable suspicion that a motorist is unlicensed or that an automobile is not registered, or that either the vehicle or an occupant is otherwise subject to seizure for violation of law, stopping an automobile and detaining the driver in order to check his driver's license and the registration of the

automobile are unreasonable under the Fourth
Amendment." *Delaware v. Prouse*, 440 U.S. 648, 661,
663, 99 S. Ct. 1391, 59 L. Ed. 2d 660 (1979).

Second Circuit

- "We share these courts' concern regarding the intrusiveness of successive investigations based on the same reasonable suspicion and conclude that where the same
suspicion justifies successive investigations, and the officer conducting the subsequent investigation is aware
of the prior investigation and the suspicion that supported it, the investigations' duration and scope must
be both individually and collectively reasonable under
the Fourth Amendment. . . . Everyone agrees that it
was constitutionally permissible for both Trooper
Loiselle and Sergeant Albright to stop Foreste's vehicle,
regardless of their subjective motives, because both officers had probable cause to believe that a traffic infraction had occurred. At issue, however, is not the reasonableness of the stops themselves or even the
reasonableness of the officers' decisions to extend the
stops for further investigation. The question is whether
the reasonableness of the investigations' scope and
duration should be evaluated individually or in
combination. . . . [T]hat question depends not on the
officers' subjective motivations but on whether the
investigatory detentions were based on the same or independent reasonable suspicion. Ordinarily, of course,
stops for separate traffic infractions are unrelated, and
any extensions of those stops for investigation are unrelated as well. But looking only to whether independent
traffic violations support successive traffic stops would
create a rule subject to the same gamesmanship
highlighted by the Eighth Circuit in *Ilazi*. One officer
could stop a vehicle for a traffic infraction on a common
drug corridor, become suspicious of the driver's nervousness or explanation for his trip, and then detain the vehicle while a drug-sniffing dog is called to the scene. If
the dog took too long to arrive (or, upon arriving, failed
to detect any drugs), the officer could telephone a second
officer down the road and apprise him of the situation.
The second officer could then follow the vehicle until
spotting a second traffic infraction, stop the vehicle,

and, based on the suspicions relayed by the first officer, detain the vehicle a second time to again wait for a dog. Through combination, successive stops could be extended to an unreasonably intrusive length even if each stop were supported by independent probable cause and each investigative detention itself were sufficiently limited in duration." *U.S. v. Foreste*, 780 F.3d 518, 525–26 (2d Cir. 2015).

- "[A] traffic stop may not be based on the suspicion that, if stopped, a motorist may subsequently do something that violates the law. Thus, a police officer may not stop a pedestrian simply because she suspects that the pedestrian will react to her questioning by behaving in a disorderly manner. And a citizen is not subject to arrest based on the suspicion that he might respond by resisting arrest. A fortiori, a stop may not be based on the belief that the suspect, if stopped, may react by doing something that is itself no more than evidence of a violation of the law." *Diamondstone v. Macaluso*, 148 F.3d 113, 125 (2d Cir. 1998).

Third Circuit

- "Observations by law enforcement officers created a reasonable suspicion that the defendant was using a car to conduct illegal activity and that it contained drugs, thus providing a sufficient basis for the temporary seizure of the vehicle to allow a trained dog to sniff it for a possible alert to drugs where the officers had observed the defendant driving the car on the day of his arrest on drug and weapons charges, he was standing by the car with the ignition on when the agents arrested him, they had observed him conduct two apparent drug transactions from the car five days earlier, and he had run away from the car prior to his arrest on a previous occasion." *U.S. v. Ferrell*, 293 Fed. Appx. 934 (3d Cir. 2008).

- "At the outset, we must address the question whether reasonable suspicion or the higher standard of probable cause is required to support an investigatory traffic stop under the Fourth Amendment . . . . (W)e find persuasive the Ninth Circuit's reasoning in *Lopez-Soto*. As discussed in that opinion, there is little in *Whren* to suggest that the Court meant to create a new probable

cause standard in the context of investigatory traffic
stops. Instead, the Court in *Whren* was responding to
the situation before it-one in which the officer obviously
possessed probable cause . . . . (W)e now join our sister
circuits in holding that the *Terry* reasonable suspicion
standard applies to routine traffic stops." *U.S. v. Delfin-
Colina*, 464 F.3d 392 (3d Cir. 2006).

Fourth Circuit

- "Important to the court's decision was its belief that
  [the officer] could not see the crack from the rear seat of
  the police vehicle, past the two officers in the front seat,
  across an intersection, through the tinted rear window
  of the Crown Victoria as the Crown Victoria turned
  right, away from the officer. For the same reasons, the
  court declined to credit the testimony of [the other of-
  ficers] that they also saw the crack in the Crown Victoria's windshield. Thus, the court determined, the
  Government failed to establish that the traffic stop was
  based on reasonable and articulable suspicion of unlawful conduct." *U.S. v. Gaines*, 668 F.3d 170 (4th Cir.
  2012).

- "As with an individual who encounters police on foot,
  headlong flight or other nervous, evasive behavior in response to a roadblock may contribute to reasonable
  suspicion that the driver is engaged in criminal activity.
  Such evasive behavior is not going about one's business,
  but instead suggests that the driver is avoiding the
  roadblock for other than innocent reasons. Indeed, we
  have repeatedly recognized that evasive reactions to the
  presence of police may be considered in determining
  whether reasonable suspicion exists for an investigatory stop." *U.S. v. Smith*, 396 F.3d 579 (4th Cir. 2005).

- "An objective assessment of the facts and circumstances
  of this stop compels the conclusion that the officer
  lacked any articulable, reasonable suspicion that a
  violation had occurred. Simply put, he saw nothing
  wrong, and he suspected nothing. Upholding a stop on
  these facts would permit the police to make a random,
  suspicionless stop of any car with a temporary tag. The
  Fourth Amendment does not afford the police such
  unbridled discretion." *U.S. v. Wilson*, 205 F.3d 720, 724
  (4th Cir. 2000).

Fifth Circuit

- "A state computer database indication of insurance
status may establish reasonable suspicion when the officer is familiar with the database and the system itself
is reliable. If that is the case, a seemingly inconclusive
report such as 'unconfirmed' will be a specific and
articulable fact that supports a traffic stop. Viewed in
the light most favorable to the government, Officer
Leal's testimony provides sufficient support for the reliability of the database. Officer Leal explained the process for inputting license plate information, described
how records in the database are kept, and noted that he
was familiar with these records. He explained that 'with
the knowledge and experience of working,' he knows
the vehicle is uninsured when an 'unconfirmed' status
appears because the computer system will either return
an 'insurance confirmed' or 'unconfirmed' response.
When Broca-Martinez's attorney questioned the system's reliability, Officer Leal confirmed that it was usually accurate. ('Q: So, in other words, he could have or
not have insurance, correct? A: No.') ('Q: You asked him
for his insurance? A: Not that I recall. I already knew
that the vehicle wasn't insured.') ('Q: I mean reports are
sometimes inaccurate, right? A: For the most part, no.').
. . .Even if Officer Leal was not positive Broca-Martinez
was uninsured, he cleared the bar for reasonable
suspicion. An officer does not have to be certain a violation has occurred. 'This would raise the standard for
reasonable suspicion far above probable cause or even a
preponderance of the evidence, in contravention of the
Supreme Court's instructions.'" *United States v. Broca-
Martinez*, 855 F.3d 675, 680–81 (5th Cir. 2017) (citations omitted).
- "Reasonable suspicion can rest on a mistake of law or
fact if the mistake is objectively reasonable. . . .Henry
contends that the initial stop was not justified. He does
not contest the district court's finding that his license-
plate frame obstructed the view of the expiration date
on his registration sticker. Instead, he asserts that [La.
Stat. Ann. § 32:53(A)(3)] does not cover obstructed
registration stickers. He maintains that the statute,
which provides that '[e]very permanent registration
license plate . . . shall be maintained free from foreign

materials and in a condition to be clearly legible,' requires only that the letters and numbers on the plate itself be clearly legible. The government disagrees, asserting that Section 32:53 prohibits obstruction of attached registration stickers by a license-plate frame, which the government categorizes as a 'foreign material[ ]' . . . We need not opine on the proper interpretation of Section 32:53, because Louisiana caselaw establishes that the officers' interpretation, even if mistaken, was objectively reasonable. In *State v. Pena*. . ., the court considered whether an officer had reasonable suspicion to stop a vehicle based on, among other things, improper display of a license plate. 'The photographs introduced into evidence revealed that although the numbers and letters on the license plate were clearly visible, the top and bottom portions of the plate were partially obscured by a license plate frame.' After citing [the predecessor to Section 32:53(A)(3)], the court concluded that the officer 'had reasonable suspicion that a traffic violation had occurred' because, in part, 'the photographs introduced into evidence revealed that the license plate was partially obscured . . . .' Given *Pena*, [the officers'] belief that Section 32:53(A)(3) prohibited an obscured registration sticker was objectively reasonable. *Pena* directly rejects Henry's position that Section 32:53 applies only to the lettering and numbering on the plate itself. To the contrary, the court held that a license-plate frame that obscured part of the plate violated the statute, even though the lettering and numbering on the plate was 'clearly visible.' Though *Pena* does not specifically address obscured registration stickers, its broad construction of the statute can reasonably be construed to apply to them. . . .In sum, we take no position on the correct interpretation of Section 32:53(A)(3). We conclude only that, given *Pena*, the officers' belief that Henry's obstructed registration sticker violated Section 32:53, even if mistaken, was objectively reasonable. Thus, they had reasonable suspicion, which justified the traffic stop." *United States v. Henry*, 853 F.3d 754, 757–58 (5th Cir. 2017) (citations and footnotes omitted).

Sixth Circuit

- "[A]n officer may conduct a stop based on information obtained from fellow officers. This is known as the 'collective-knowledge doctrine.' When an officer executes a stop based in part on information obtained from another law-enforcement official, the doctrine imputes to the officer conducting the stop the knowledge of those with whom he communicated. '[I]f a flyer or bulletin has been issued on the basis of articulable facts supporting a reasonable suspicion that the wanted person has committed an offense, then reliance on that flyer or bulletin justifies a stop to check identification, to pose questions to the person, or to detain the person briefly while attempting to obtain further information.' However, 'if the flyer has been issued in the absence of a reasonable suspicion, then a stop in the objective reliance upon it violates the Fourth Amendment.' Furthermore, 'the stop that in fact occurred [must not be] significantly more intrusive than would have been permitted' based on the reasonable suspicion." *Brown v. Lewis*, 779 F.3d 401, 412–13 (6th Cir. 2015) (citations omitted).

- "Strict application of the collective-knowledge doctrine would result in a determination that the officers did not have reasonable suspicion to stop Brown. The 911 operator did overhear certain statements made by an intoxicated male which could potentially establish reasonable suspicion, namely his statements about hiding from the police and about wanting to 'kill that bitch.' But no one in the room took the statement seriously; all of the other voices on the call dispute, criticize or laugh at these statements. The statements could therefore support, at most, reasonable suspicion to stop the intoxicated male but no other individual in the house. The 911 operator, moreover, could hear the same intoxicated male voice, still within the house, after the officers saw Brown's car pull away from the house. Because the 911 operator knew that the intoxicated male—the sole individual for whom the police had reasonable suspicion—could not be in the car, the police did not have reasonable suspicion to stop the car." *Brown v. Lewis*, 779 F.3d 401, 413 (6th Cir. 2015)).

- "[T]he pertinent Fourth Amendment framework for the initial stop is therefore the reasonable suspicion standard. The reasonableness of a traffic stop is measured by the same standards set forth for investigatory stops in *Terry v. Ohio* and its progeny. . . . Provided that reasonable suspicion exists to support the initial stop, the principles that define the scope of reasonable police conduct under *Terry* also circumscribe any subsequent detention or search resulting therefrom. The degree of a traffic stop's intrusion must be reasonably related in scope to the situation at hand, as judged by examining the reasonableness of the officer's conduct given his suspicions and the surrounding circumstances. Accordingly, an officer may make inquiries unrelated to the traffic stop so long as those questions do not measurably extend the detention and the individual's responses are voluntary. Reasonable suspicion supporting a traffic stop may ripen into probable cause to search a vehicle based on the officer's interactions with the car's occupants. Probable cause to search a vehicle is defined as 'reasonable grounds for belief, supported by less than *prima facie* proof but more than mere suspicion.' Probable cause exists when there is a 'fair probability that contraband or evidence of a crime will be found in a particular place.' " *U.S. v. Lyons*, 687 F.3d 754, 763–764 (6th Cir. 2012) (citations omitted).

● "An investigative detention is reasonable in scope if the detention was sufficiently limited in time and the investigative means used by the officers involve the least intrusive means reasonably available. When the initial traffic stop has concluded, we have adopted a bright-line rule that any subsequent prolonging, even de minimis, is an unreasonable extension of an otherwise lawful stop. Because a crafty officer, knowing this rule, may simply delay writing a ticket for the initial traffic violation until after she has satisfied herself that all of her hunches were unfounded, we also treat the unreasonable extension of a not-yet-completed traffic stop as a seizure. Unreasonable, however, does not include de minimis extensions." *U.S. v. Stepp*, 680 F.3d 651, 661–62 (6th Cir. 2012) (citations omitted).

● "The officers seized [defendant]'s luggage tag and bundles of money pursuant to a properly executed search warrant for the [GMC] Suburban [vehicle]. Therefore, in order to suppress this evidence, [defendant] must show that the warrant was obtained as a result of a prior illegality. [Defendant] contends that his arrest during [an investigatory] stop of the Suburban is the prior illegality that tainted the subsequent search warrant for the Suburban. . . . [He argues that] because the illegal arrest allowed the officers to execute a canine narcotics sniff and. . . .the results of the canine sniff were included in the supporting affidavit, the search warrant is a fruit of his illegal arrest. . . . [Defendant]'s argument erroneously equates the investigatory stop of the Suburban with his allegedly illegal arrest. Even assuming he was illegally arrested at the time the Suburban was stopped, it was the investigatory stop—and not the illegal arrest—that produced the canine narcotics sniff and the resulting search warrant. So long as the officers acted properly in stopping the vehicle and executing the canine sniff, the resulting search warrant was not tainted by a prior illegality. [In Brendlin v. California, t]he Supreme Court. . .recognized that a passenger of a stopped vehicle, like [defendant], 'is seized within the meaning of the Fourth Amendment' and 'so may challenge the constitutionality of the stop.' . . . We conclude that the stop of the Suburban was lawful. An officer may conduct an investigatory stop if it is supported by a 'reasonable suspicion' of criminal activity. 'Reasonable suspicion' requires the officer to have ' 'a particularized and objective basis for suspecting the particular person. . .of criminal activity' based on 'specific and articulable facts[.]' ' [Defendant] does not challenge the stop of the Suburban for investigatory purposes, and we find that the officers indeed had reasonable suspicion to support the stop. The officers had been monitoring, following, and listening to Ovalle—the driver of the Suburban—for at least two days. During this time[,] they had heard Ovalle and his companions discuss guns, kilos, and large sums of money. They also knew that Ovalle had left the Sheraton after complaining of 'too many people asking too many questions' and that he had later returned to transport two individuals who claimed to work for him. These 'specific and articulable facts' provided 'reasonable suspicion' for an investigatory stop of the Suburban. . . . We turn next to whether the canine narcotics sniff exceeded the permissible scope or duration of the investigatory stop. '[A]n investigative detention must be temporary and last no longer than is necessary to effectuate the purpose of the stop.' The scope of activities conducted during an investigatory stop 'must reasonably be related to the circumstances that initially justified the stop.' The officers reasonably suspected the Suburban's occupants of illegal drug trafficking, and the canine narcotics sniff is directly related to investigating this suspicion. Moreover, the duration of the stop was reasonable; the canine sniff was performed within a half hour of the stop, and we have previously upheld an investigatory stop that included a thirty-five minute wait for the canine unit. Thus the canine narcotics sniff was lawfully conducted as part of the investigatory stop. . . . [Defendant] provides no evidence that his allegedly illegal arrest contributed to or in any way tainted the search warrant for the Suburban. Consequently, we need not determine the precise timing of [defendant]'s arrest or whether it was supported by probable cause. Because we find that the officers did not act unlawfully in stopping the Suburban or executing a canine narcotics sniff, and because [defendant] has failed to show that the search warrant was the fruit of a prior illegality, we affirm the district court's refusal to suppress the evidence seized from the Suburban." *U.S. v. Garcia*, 496 F.3d 495 (6th Cir. 2007) (citations omitted).

Seventh Circuit

• "In isolation, each of Ruiz's actions might be more susceptible to an innocent explanation than the not-so-innocent explanation ascribed to it by the officers. We doubt that any one of Ruiz's actions, as witnessed by the officers, would alone give rise to the suspicion necessary to justify a *Terry* stop—including his parking-lot meeting with a suspected drug dealer and taking actions consistent with the operation of a trap. But when all of Ruiz's actions are viewed in concert and through the lens of experienced law enforcement officers, the innocent explanations begin to look less likely and the not-so-innocent explanations begin to look more likely." *U.S. v. Ruiz*, 785 F.3d 1134, 1142 (7th Cir. 2015) (citations omitted).

- "[Defendant's] motion to suppress presents an issue of first impression in this circuit and, apparently, in the federal courts: whether a discrepancy between the observed color of a car and the color listed on its registration alone is sufficient to give rise to reasonable suspicion of criminal activity. Where our sister circuits have considered color discrepancies, they have relied on the discrepancy as only one of several factors establishing reasonable suspicion. . . . Our review of the totality of the circumstances here leads us to conclude that no reasonable suspicion of vehicle theft attaches to a completely lawful color discrepancy in the absence of any evidence suggesting otherwise. In light of that conclusion, [the officer's] decision to stop [Defendant's] vehicle lacked reasonable suspicion that the vehicle was stolen." *U.S. v. Uribe*, 709 F.3d 646 (7th Cir. 2013).
- "[S]o long as the circumstances confronting a police officer support the reasonable belief that a driver has committed even a minor traffic offense, the officer has probable cause to stop the driver." *U.S. v. Cashman*, 216 F.3d 582, 586 (7th Cir. 2000).

Eighth Circuit

- "[The officer] observed two apparent rental vehicles with license plates from the same state [Texas] traveling in tandem [in Arkansas], and he then discovered a large quantity of marijuana in one of them. Accordingly, we conclude that the information possessed by the officers constituted 'specific and articulable facts which, taken together with rational inferences from those facts, reasonably warrant[ed]' the stop of the [other vehicle] driven by [Defendant]." *U.S. v. Allen*, 705 F.3d 367 (8th Cir. 2013).
- "Whether a seizure was reasonable is a question of law." *U.S. v. Farnell*, 701 F.3d 256, 261 (8th Cir. 2012).
- "Here, [the officer] was aware of the February 26 bulletins—which included multiple photos of a white van with a single door on the driver's side—and the April 29 dispatch, which described the bank robbery suspect's vehicle as a white van. [The officer] was also aware of description of the suspect as a heavy-set, white male. Additionally, when [Defendant] drove past him, [the officer] observed [Defendant] shielding his face with one

hand. The location and timing of [the officer's] interception of [Defendant] are also consistent with what [the officer] knew about the bank robbery: [The officer] positioned himself at an intersection along a known travel route from Cuba to the interstate highway and observed [Defendant's] van approaching him approximately one hour after the dispatch regarding the robbery. In view of the above, we are satisfied that [the officer] had, at a minimum, a 'reasonable suspicion' that [Defendant] was engaged in criminal activity when he turned on his lights and siren and stopped [Defendant's] van." *U.S. v. Farnell*, 701 F.3d 256, 262 (8th Cir. 2012).

• "Although a *suspicionless* seizure of a motorist whose primary purpose was to detect evidence of ordinary criminal wrongdoing is not permissible under a 'special needs' analysis, the seizure of [defendant] was not suspicionless. Because the seizure was not at a random checkpoint, but instead arose out of a lawful traffic stop, the general rule of balancing for reasonableness should be applied." *U.S. v. Mohamed*, 600 F.3d 1000 (8th Cir. 2010).

• "[N]either mistake of law nor mistake of fact renders a traffic stop illegal so long as the officer's actions were objectively reasonable in the circumstances. We conclude that the officers' actions were reasonable under these circumstances. We credit the district court's finding that the officers could not see the temporary registration affixed to the vehicle's windshield until after they had stopped the vehicle. Because a lack of license plates or a temporary registration would have constituted a violation of state law, the officers had reasonable suspicion to stop the vehicle. [Defendant] also argues that the officers illegally ordered him out of his vehicle. Once a vehicle has been stopped for a traffic violation, a police officer may order the driver out of the vehicle without violating the Fourth Amendment. . . ." *U.S. v. Bueno*, 443 F.3d 1017 (8th Cir. 2006).

• "An investigative stop does not violate the Fourth Amendment if the police have reasonable suspicion that the vehicle or its occupants are involved in criminal activity. The level of suspicion required for a *Terry* stop is obviously less demanding than that for probable cause." *U.S. v. Bell*, 183 F.3d 746, 749 (8th Cir. 1999).

Ninth Circuit

- "That the officer lied about seeing Magallon–Lopez make an illegal lane change does not call into question the legality of the stop. The standard for determining whether probable cause or reasonable suspicion exists is an objective one; it does not turn either on the subjective thought processes of the officer or on whether the officer is truthful about the reason for the stop. If, for example, the facts provide probable cause or reasonable suspicion to justify a traffic stop, the stop is lawful even if the officer made the stop only because he wished to investigate a more serious offense. Likewise, if the facts support probable cause to arrest for one offense, the arrest is lawful even if the officer invoked, as the basis for the arrest, a different offense as to which probable cause was lacking. The Court in *Devenpeck* emphasized that the objective facts are what matter in situations like these:

  > While it is assuredly good police practice to inform a person of the reason for his arrest at the time he is taken into custody, we have never held that to be constitutionally required. Hence, the predictable consequence of a rule limiting the probable-cause inquiry to offenses closely related to (and supported by the same facts as) those identified by the arresting officer is not . . . that officers will cease making sham arrests on the hope that such arrests will later be validated, but rather that officers will cease providing reasons for arrest. And even if this option were to be foreclosed by adoption of a statutory or constitutional requirement, officers would simply give every reason for which probable cause could conceivably exist.

  The same principle—that the objective facts are controlling in this context, not what the officer said or was thinking—applies here. So long as the facts known to the officer establish reasonable suspicion to justify an investigatory stop, the stop is lawful even if the officer falsely cites as the basis for the stop a ground that is not supported by reasonable suspicion. We emphasize, however, that although our focus is on the objectively reasonable basis for the stop, not the officers' subjective intentions or beliefs, the facts justifying the stop must be known to officers at the time of the stop." *U.S. v. Magallon-Lopez*, 817 F.3d 671, 675 (9th Cir. 2016) (citations omitted).

- "[T]he notoriety of a road as an alien smuggling route has long been held by numerous courts, including the Supreme Court, as a relevant factor supporting reasonable suspicion." *U.S. v. Palos-Marquez*, 591 F.3d 1272 (9th Cir. 2010).
- "We are satisfied that the collective knowledge doctrine includes no requirement regarding the content of the communication that one officer must make to another. Where one officer knows facts constituting reasonable suspicion or probable cause (sufficient to justify action under an exception to the warrant requirement), and he communicates an appropriate order or request, another officer may conduct a warrantless stop, search, or arrest without violating the Fourth Amendment." *U.S. v. Ramirez*, 473 F.3d 1026 (9th Cir. 2007).
- "[L]aw enforcement officers may briefly stop a moving automobile to investigate a reasonable suspicion that its occupants are involved in criminal activity. However, the governmental interest in investigating possible criminal conduct based on an officer's reasonable suspicion may be outweighed by the Fourth Amendment interest of the driver in remaining secure from the intrusion. . . . [In *U.S. v.*] *Hensley*, the United States Supreme Court held that 'if police have a reasonable suspicion, grounded in specific and articulable facts, that a person they encounter was involved in or is wanted in connection with a *completed* felony, then a *Terry* stop may be made to investigate that suspicion.' The *Hensley* court explicitly confined its analysis to the felony context, leaving open the question whether the rule could be extended to 'all past crimes, however serious,' i.e., misdemeanors. . . . [W]e recognize that the police have a manifest interest in identifying the perpetrators of crime, whether the offense be minor or major. Finding the violator of even a humble noise ordinance has some value to society and certainly would have rewarded the persistent concern of the complaining neighbor Harmel [in this case]. But giving satisfaction to Mr. Harmel and locating the source of annoyingly loud music are not all that guide us. There is a traditional and constitutionally preserved interest in personal security from governmental intrusion, which fuels the requirements that the police obtain warrants

before making an arrest and that police have reasonable suspicion that criminal activity is afoot before making a *Terry* stop. The matter, in our view, stands on different footing with regard to a completed crime that is a misdemeanor that does not endanger the public. . . . Directly pulling over the driver of the Cougar was indeed the most efficient approach to investigating Harmel's complaint. But simple efficiency and expediency of law enforcement efforts do not automatically override the other crucial element of the Hensley balancing test—personal security from governmental intrusion in the operation of one's vehicle. Moreover, the reasonableness of an investigative stop is to a degree undermined, where, as here, the police have not pursued alternate available opportunities to gather information about the driver. That [defendant] was leaving the area might have warranted an immediate *Terry* stop at the expense of alternative investigative methods in circumstances involving an offense that threatened public safety, but the noise violation here created no such exigency. To validate the investigative stop under these circumstances would invite the erosion of the Fourth Amendment rights of [defendant] and others. . . . We hold that under the balancing test set forth in Hensley, a court reviewing the reasonableness of a stop to investigate a past misdemeanor (or other minor infraction) must assess the potential risk to public safety associated with the nature of the offense. Under the circumstances here, it was unreasonable for the Nampa police to pull over [defendant] on suspicion of having played his music too loudly where they did not duly consider the lack of any threat to public safety, especially given the untested alternative means of ascertaining [defendant]'s identity. The motion to suppress was erroneously denied." *U.S. v. Grigg*, 498 F.3d 1070, 1074–1083 (9th Cir. 2007) (citations omitted).

- "Whether *Wren* applies to *parking* violations under California's civil-administrative enforcement scheme is a matter of first impression in this court. We conclude that it does and that, here, the parking violation justified the investigatory stop of (the) vehicle. In so holding, we note that our conclusion is consistent with the decisions of our sister circuits that have considered

Wren's application to parking violations." *U.S. v. Choud-hry,* 461 F.3d 1097 (9th Cir. 2006).

- "As the list of factors set out in *Brignoni-Ponce* suggests, sometimes conduct that may be entirely innocuous when viewed in isolation may properly be considered in arriving at a determination that reasonable suspicion exists. . . . At the same time, however, innocuous conduct does not justify an investigatory stop unless there is other information or surrounding circumstances of which the police are aware, which, when considered along with the otherwise innocuous conduct, tend to indicate criminal activity has occurred or is about to take place." *U.S. v. Montero-Camargo,* 208 F.3d 1122, 1130 (9th Cir. 2000).

- "A suspicion based on such a mistaken view of the law cannot be the reasonable suspicion required for the Fourth Amendment, because the legal justification for a traffic stop] must be objectively grounded. . . .In other words, if an officer makes a traffic stop based on a mistake of law, the stop violates the Fourth Amendment." *U.S. v. Twilley,* 222 F.3d 1092, 1096 (9th Cir. 2000).

- "*United States v. Rodriguez,* was a driving-while-Hispanic case in which we held that reasonable suspicion could not be premised on a profile that could certainly fit hundreds of thousands of law abiding daily users of the highways of Southern California." *U.S. v. Osborn,* 203 F.3d 1176, 1182 (9th Cir. 2000).

- "As in the Fifth Circuit cases of *Lopez-Valdez* and *Miller,* the traffic stop in the case before us was not objectively grounded in the governing law. What [the] Officer. . .reasonably suspected, namely that [Defendant] had not affixed a registration sticker to his rear window, simply was not a violation of Baja California law. This cannot justify the stop under the Fourth Amendment." *U.S. v. Lopez-Soto,* 205 F.3d 1101, 1106 (9th Cir. 2000).

Tenth Circuit

- "Though we analyze these facts under the totality of the circumstances, we first note which factors have less weight in our analysis. We start with the most troubling justification: Vasquez's status as a resident of Colorado.

The Officers rely heavily on Vasquez's residency because Colorado is 'known to be home to medical marijuana dispensaries.' But we find this justification, in isolation or in tandem with other considerations, unconvincing. As we have said previously, 'that the defendant[ ] [was] traveling from a drug source city—or . . . a drug source state—does little to add to the overall calculus of suspicion.' Such a factor is 'so broad as to be indicative of almost nothing.' Moreover, our fellow circuits have concluded the state of residence of a detained motorist is an 'extremely weak factor, at best' in the reasonable suspicion calculus because 'interstate motorists have a better than equal chance of traveling from a source state to a demand state.' Currently, twenty-five states permit marijuana use for medical purposes, with Colorado, Alaska, Oregon, Washington, and Washington, D.C. permitting some recreational use under state law. Thus, the Officer's reasoning would justify the search and seizure of the citizens of more than half of the states in our country. It is wholly improper to assume that an individual is more likely to be engaged in criminal conduct because of his state of residence, and thus any fact that would inculpate every resident of a state cannot support reasonable suspicion. Accordingly, it is time to abandon the pretense that state citizenship is a permissible basis upon which to justify the detention and search of out-of-state motorists, and time to stop the practice of detention of motorists for nothing more than an out-of-state license plate." *Vasquez v. Lewis*, 834 F.3d 1132, 1137-38 (10th Cir. 2016), cert. denied, 137 S. Ct. 1580, 197 L. Ed. 2d 705 (2017) (citations omitted).

- "[T]he 'touchstone of the Fourth Amendment is reasonableness, not individualized suspicion.' Accordingly, the Supreme Court has carved out exceptions to the general rule where the primary purpose of a group seizure went beyond ordinary crime control. For example, the Court has upheld a border patrol roadblock designed to intercept illegal aliens. And it has upheld a sobriety checkpoint aimed at removing drunk drivers from the road to protect public safety. In those situations, the Court has not required individualized reasonable suspicion, instead favoring a group-level balance of interests, weighing the public interest against intrusions on individuals' liberty." *U.S. v. Paetsch*, 782 F.3d 1162, 1169 (10th Cir. 2015), cert. denied, 136 S. Ct. 195, 193 L. Ed. 2d 153 (2015) (citations omitted).

- "Finally, Mr. Madrid claims the district court erred both in determining that the anonymous 911 call was reliable and in finding that the tip gave rise to reasonable suspicion to stop his vehicle. 'A confidential tip may justify an investigatory stop if under the totality of the circumstances the tip furnishes both sufficient indicia of reliability and sufficient information to provide reasonable suspicion that criminal conduct is, has, or is about to occur.' The determination of '[w]hether a tip provides reasonable suspicion to make a traffic stop is case-specific,' and no single factor is dispositive. [R]elevant factors include: (1) whether the informant lacked 'true anonymity' (i.e., whether the police knew some details about the informant or had means to discover them); (2) whether the informant reported contemporaneous, firsthand knowledge; (3) whether the informant provided detailed information about the events observed; (4) the informant's stated motivation for reporting the information; and (5) whether the police were able to corroborate information provided by the informant. Turning to the first of these factors, '[u]nlike a tip from a known informant whose reputation can be assessed and who can be held responsible if her allegations turn out to be fabricated, an anonymous tip alone seldom demonstrates the informant's basis of knowledge or veracity.' In *United States v. Johnson,* we further explained that '[a] tipster who refuses to identify himself may simply be making up the story, perhaps trying to use the police to harass another citizen.' On the other hand, jeopardizing one's anonymity creates 'disincentive for making false allegations.' . . . To assess the reliability of a tip, however, we must examine 'the totality of the circumstances—the whole picture,' and 'no single factor is dispositive.' A 911 caller who offers only 'minimal' identifying information—that he was at or in front of an address across the street from where shots were fired—is not 'completely unidentifiable;' giving the address was at least an 'indicium of reliability.' Here, the 911 operator never asked the caller for his name or other identifying information and there is no reason to believe he would not have provided this information if requested. And there is no indication the caller was 'making up the story, perhaps trying to use the police to harass another citizen.' " *U.S. v. Madrid*, 713 F.3d 1251, 1258–60 (10th Cir. 2013) (citations omitted).

- "A traffic stop is a seizure within the meaning of the Fourth Amendment, even though the purpose of the stop is limited and the resulting detention quite brief. . . . A routine traffic stop, however, is more analogous to an investigative detention than a custodial arrest. . . . We therefore analyze such stops under the principles developed for investigative detentions set forth in *Terry v. Ohio*. . . . To determine the reasonableness of an investigative detention, we make a dual inquiry, asking first whether the officer's action was justified at its inception, and second whether it was reasonably related in scope to the circumstances which justified the interference in the first place." *U.S. v. Hunnicutt*, 135 F.3d 1345, 1348 (10th Cir. 1998).

- "We conclude in reviewing the aggregate facts, based on the extensive findings of the district court, that the mantra totality of the circumstances cannot metamorphose these facts into reasonable suspicion. . . . [T]he three factors that support the agent's conclusion that [Defendant] was evading him, the lack of eye contact, the abrupt exit, and the gas station activity, become so innocent or susceptible to varying interpretations as to be innocuous. . . . Under the totality of the circumstances, we hold the remaining factors in the aggregate do not amount to a reasonable suspicion to stop [Defendant]." *U.S. v. De la Cruz-Tapia*, 162 F.3d 1275, 1280 (10th Cir. 1998).

Eleventh Circuit

- "Given that the smell of marijuana alone may provide a basis for reasonable suspicion for further investigation of possible criminal conduct, the initial stop was valid." *U.S. v. White*, 593 F.3d 1199 (11th Cir. 2010).

- "Under the Fourth Amendment, a decision to stop an automobile is reasonable where the police have probable cause to believe that a traffic violation occurred. . . .and an officer's motive in making the traffic stop does not invalidate what is otherwise objectively justifiable behavior under the Fourth Amendment. . . ." *U.S. v. Simmons*, 172 F.3d 775, 778 (11th Cir. 1999).

§ 10:3 Further questioning: Additional questioning that goes beyond the original purpose of the stop must be supported by additional reasonable suspicion

Supreme Court

- "An officer, in other words, may conduct certain unrelated checks during an otherwise lawful traffic stop. But contrary to Justice ALITO's suggestion, he may not do so in a way that prolongs the stop, absent the reasonable suspicion ordinarily demanded to justify detaining an individual. Beyond determining whether to issue a traffic ticket, an officer's mission includes 'ordinary inquiries incident to [the traffic] stop.' Typically such inquiries involve checking the driver's license, determining whether there are outstanding warrants against the driver, and inspecting the automobile's registration and proof of insurance. These checks serve the same objective as enforcement of the traffic code: ensuring that vehicles on the road are operated safely and responsibly. A dog sniff, by contrast, is a measure aimed at 'detect[ing] evidence of ordinary criminal wrongdoing.' Candidly, the Government acknowledged at oral argument that a dog sniff, unlike the routine measures just mentioned, is not an ordinary incident of a traffic stop. Lacking the same close connection to roadway safety as the ordinary inquiries, a dog sniff is not fairly characterized as part of the officer's traffic mission. . . . The Government argues that an officer may 'incremental[ly]' prolong a stop to conduct a dog sniff so long as the officer is reasonably diligent in pursuing the traffic-related purpose of the stop, and the overall duration of the stop remains reasonable in relation to the duration of other traffic stops involving similar circumstances. The Government's argument, in effect, is that by completing all traffic-related tasks expeditiously, an officer can earn bonus time to pursue an unrelated criminal investigation. The reasonableness of a seizure, however, depends on what the police in fact do. In this regard, the Government acknowledges that 'an officer always has to be reasonably diligent.' How could diligence be gauged other than by noting what the officer actually did and how he did it? If an officer can complete traffic-based inquiries expeditiously, then that is the amount of 'time reasonably required to complete [the stop's] mission.' As we said in *Caballes* and reiterate today, a traffic stop 'prolonged beyond' that point is 'unlawful.' The critical question, then, is not whether the dog sniff occurs before or after the officer issues a ticket, but whether conducting the sniff 'prolongs'—*i.e.,* adds time to—'the stop.' " *Rodriguez v. U.S.*, 135 S. Ct. 1609, 1615–16, 191 L. Ed. 2d 492 (2015) (citations omitted).

- "An officer's inquiries into matters unrelated to the justification for the traffic stop. . .do not convert the encounter into something other than a lawful seizure, so long as those inquiries do not measurably extend the duration of the stop." *Arizona v. Johnson,* 555 U.S. 323, 129 S. Ct. 781, 172 L. Ed. 2d 694 (2009).

- "A seizure that is justified solely by the interest in issuing a warning ticket to the driver can become unlawful if it is prolonged beyond the time reasonably required to complete that mission." *Illinois v. Caballes,* 543 U.S. 405, 125 S. Ct. 834, 160 L. Ed. 2d 842 (2005).

Fourth Circuit

- "[T]he question presented is a narrow one: Once the officer learned that there were no outstanding warrants, and having been provided an LPR card by the defendant as identification, was he permitted to then call [Immigration and Customs Enforcement (ICE)]—a call that took some portion of 'a few minutes'—to verify the validity of the LPR card? . . . . When a police officer lawfully detains a vehicle, 'police diligence involves requesting a driver's license and vehicle registration, running a computer check, and issuing a ticket.' The officer may also, 'in the interest of personal safety,' request that the passengers in the vehicle provide identification, at least so long as the request does not prolong the seizure. Similarly, the officer may 'inquir[e] into matters unrelated to the justification for the traffic stop,' and may take other actions that do not constitute 'searches' within the meaning of the Fourth Amendment, such as conducting a dog-sniff of the vehicle, but again only 'so long as those inquiries [or other actions] do not measurably extend the duration of the stop.' Strictly speaking, the scope and duration inquiries under *Terry's* second prong are distinct. They become intertwined, however, in cases where, as here, the actions a defendant argues exceeded the scope of the stop necessarily also extended its duration. This raises the following question: Under what circumstances, if ever, may an officer prolong a traffic stop to investigate matters unrelated to the justification for the stop and without reasonable suspicion, whether through questioning or other means? . . . If 'the totality of the circumstances, viewed objectively, establishes that the officer, without reasonable suspicion, definitively abandoned the prosecution of the traffic stop and embarked on another sustained course of investigation, this would surely bespeak a lack of diligence.' This standard incorporates both the duration and scope components of *Terry's* second prong. . . . In cases where, as here, the questioning does extend the seizure, the scope of an officer's unrelated investigation could be relevant to whether the officer 'definitively abandoned the prosecution of the traffic stop and embarked on another sustained course of investigation.' . . . We believe the 'diligently pursue' standard applies nonetheless, because either questioning a person directly or pursuing other means of investigation may, in the context of a particular traffic stop, be relevant to whether an officer diligently pursued the investigation of the justification for the stop. . . . Although the officer's call to ICE was unrelated to the justification for the stop and extended the time (if only for a portion of 'a few minutes') during which the officer kept the vehicle at the side of the highway, the totality of the circumstances demonstrates that [the officer] 'diligently pursue[d] the investigation of the justification for the stop,' and was not otherwise 'dilatory in [his] investigation.' " *U.S. v. Guijon-Ortiz*, 660 F.3d 757, 763–70 (4th Cir. 2011) (citations omitted).

Fifth Circuit

- "We do not find it unreasonable that an officer who has stopped a driver based on code violations and safety concerns involving a trailer would ask the driver to exit the vehicle to look at the trailer and discuss the problems. Furthermore, we agree that [the officer's] question asking where [Defendant] was driving from occurred before [the officer] had finished dealing with the traffic offenses and did not extend the scope or duration of the stop. [Defendant's] untruthful answer created further suspicion justifying continued detention, and his subsequent answers created even further suspicion. Based on this reasonable suspicion, [the officer] continued to investigate, ultimately requesting and receiving permission to search the truck. Because [the officer's] continued search and seizure beyond the scope of the initial traffic stop were justified by additional reasonable suspicion, the district court did not err in concluding that the scope of the stop was reasonable." *U.S. v. Andres*, 703 F.3d 828 (5th Cir. 2013).

- "After *Brigham,* we do not find that a detention during a valid traffic stop violates the detainees' Fourth Amendment rights where it exceeds the amount of time needed to investigate the traffic infraction that initially caused the stop, so long as (1) the facts that emerge during the police officer's investigation of the original offense create reasonable suspicion that additional criminal activity warranting additional present investigation is afoot, (2) the length of the entire detention is reasonable in light of the suspicious facts, and (3) the scope of the additional investigation is reasonable in light of the suspicious facts, meaning that it is reasonable to believe that each crime investigated, if established, would likely explain the suspicious facts that gave rise to the reasonable suspicion of criminal activity." *U.S. v. Pack*, 612 F.3d 341, 357-58 (5th Cir. 2010), opinion modified on denial of reh'g, U.S. v. Pack, 622 F.3d 383 (5th Cir. 2010).

- "[Defendant] argues that even if the initial stop was lawful, [the officer] did not have reasonable suspicion to continue detaining [defendant] after clearing his driver's license and registration. . . . 'Once the purpose of a valid traffic stop has been completed and an officer's initial suspicions have been verified or dispelled, the detention must end unless there is additional reasonable suspicion supported by articulable facts.' [citation

omitted] 'Officers must base their reasonable suspicion
on 'specific and articulable facts,' not merely 'inarticulate hunches' of wrongdoing.' [citation omitted] However, 'courts must allow law enforcement officers to
draw on their own experience and specialized training
to make inferences from and deductions about the
cumulative information available to them that might
well elude an untrained person.' [citation and internal
quotation marks omitted] . . . Here, the district court
did not err in determining that [the officer] had reasonable suspicion to continue his questioning, given the
discrepancies in [defendant]'s story and the FBI drug
alert. [The officer] testified that in his experience drug
traffickers often tell stories that 'just don't add up' and
often purchase vehicles for 'mules' to use in drug trafficking, thus explaining the insurance card and registration date discrepancies. Additionally, [the officer] correctly relied on the drug alert. The FBI's wire taps and
surveillance during June, July, and August of 2004 gave
the FBI agents reasonable suspicion to believe that the
Durango contained drugs. Under the 'collective knowledge' doctrine, [the officer] could rely on the FBI's drug
alert, even though he did not have personal knowledge
of the evidence uncovered by the FBI, to establish his
reasonable suspicion that the Durango contained drugs.
[citation omitted] It is immaterial to the length of the
detention in this case that [the officer] actually stopped
the Durango based on the missing front license plate.
[citation omitted] The FBI drug alert distinguishes this
case from cases in which the detaining officers did not
possess reliable information that the detainees were
presently engaged in drug trafficking. [citations omit-
ted] . . . Nor did the district court err in concluding
that [the officer]'s subsequent search of the vehicle was
reasonably related to dispelling his justifiable suspicion.
[The officer] became particularly suspicious when
observing the fresh tool marks on the back seat's bolts
and fresh glue on carpet of a different color. In [the of-
ficer]'s experience, this evidence suggested a hidden
compartment, which warranted a trip to the mechanic's
shop to resolve his suspicion. [The officer]'s actions were
reasonable." *U.S. v. Khanalizadeh*, 493 F.3d 479 (5th
Cir. 2007).

- "After the computer checks were finished, any delay that occurred with respect to the warning citation being meted out was due to the officers' action or inaction. The basis for the stop was essentially completed when the dispatcher notified the officers about the defendants' clean records, three minutes before the officers sought consent to search the vehicle. Accordingly, the officers should have ended the detention and allowed the defendants to leave. And the failure to release the defendants violated the Fourth Amendment." *U.S. v. Jones*, 234 F.3d 234, 241 (5th Cir. 2000).

Sixth Circuit

- "It also is well-established that, during a traffic stop, an officer may order passengers out of the vehicle pending the completion of the stop. The officers do not need independent justification to remove the driver or passengers from the vehicle. This is so, in large part, because traffic stops are 'fraught with danger' for police officers." *United States v. Pacheco*, 841 F.3d 384, 390 (6th Cir. 2016) (citations omitted).

- "Defendant was a passenger in a vehicle that was pulled over for driving with a broken taillight. When asked for identification, the driver immediately admitted that he did not have a valid license—a misdemeanor criminal offense. The driver was arrested and locked in the back of the patrol car. At that point, officers returned to the vehicle to 'make contact' with Defendant, who was still seated in the passenger seat. The officers did not have any reason to suspect that Defendant was engaged in any criminal activity or that Defendant was armed and dangerous. Nevertheless, the officers ordered Defendant out of the vehicle and told him to put his hands on his head with his fingers interlaced. Officers then began to escort Defendant to the patrol car to search him for weapons and/or drugs. While Defendant was being escorted to the patrol car for a 'pat down' search, he broke free and ran away. The officers pursued Defendant, but did not make any audible commands for him to stop. After Defendant was chased and apprehended by officers, he was searched and found to be carrying a pistol and two bags of hashish, a derivative of marijuana. . . . . We agree with the district court that

587

the firearm and the hashish recovered during the search are inadmissible because they were recovered in violation of Defendant's Fourth Amendment rights. The district court correctly determined that the purpose of the traffic stop had been accomplished after the driver was arrested, and Defendant was unlawfully detained after the traffic stop was completed. We further agree with the district court's finding that the officers lacked reasonable suspicion to justify prolonging the traffic stop. Under the circumstances, the officers should have advised Defendant that the vehicle was being impounded and informed Defendant that he was free to go." *U.S. v. Cheatham*, 577 Fed. Appx. 500, 501–02 (6th Cir. 2014) (citations omitted).

- "An investigative detention is reasonable in scope if the detention was sufficiently limited in time and the investigative means used by the officers involve the least intrusive means reasonably available. When the initial traffic stop has concluded, we have adopted a bright-line rule that any subsequent prolonging, even de minimis, is an unreasonable extension of an otherwise lawful stop. Because a crafty officer, knowing this rule, may simply delay writing a ticket for the initial traffic violation until after she has satisfied herself that all of her hunches were unfounded, we also treat the unreasonable extension of a not-yet-completed traffic stop as a seizure. Unreasonable, however, does not include de minimis extensions." *U.S. v. Stepp*, 680 F.3d 651, 661–62 (6th Cir. 2012) (citations omitted).

- "(L)ocal law enforcement and the FBI conducted the same investigation and search of Plaintiffs. Although the record does not clearly indicate whether the detention occurred at the direction of the FBI or of local law enforcement, or merely arose from confusion and miscommunication, it makes little difference. To delay Plaintiffs for the purpose of enabling the FBI to arrive at the scene to conduct effectively the same investigation when the initial investigation conducted by local law enforcement had dispelled their suspicions similarly "served no investigatory purpose" . . . The investigation conducted by local law enforcement allowed "the police to test the validity of their suspicions," and in the end, did not reveal a basis for probable cause . . . Thus,

we find that Defendants violated Plaintiffs' Fourth
Amendment rights by subjecting them to an unreason-
able seizure of their persons." *Center for Bio-Ethical
Reform, Inc. v. City of Springboro*, 477 F.3d 807 (6th
Cir. 2007).

- "[T]he police had reasonable suspicion to detain [defen-
dant] for the additional approximately thirty to forty-
five minutes it took for the police to bring the first drug-
sniffing dog to the scene and have the dog check the
vehicle for the presence of narcotics. . . . The use of the
first drug-sniffing dog was a minimally intrusive means
of investigating whether the officers' suspicions that
[defendant's] vehicle contained narcotics were valid.
The use of the first drug-sniffing dog, by itself, did not
encroach upon [defendant's] reasonable expectation of
privacy. There is also no evidence in the record that the
additional approximately thirty-minute delay of [defen-
dant] and his vehicle while the first drug-sniffing dog
was located and procured was unreasonable in light of
the officers' reasonable suspicions. . . . Given that the
police had no reason to continue to suspect that
[defendant] possessed narcotics, delaying [defendant's]
vehicle an additional hour in order to permit a second
examination of the vehicle by another drug-sniffing dog
was unreasonable." *U.S. v. Davis*, 430 F.3d 345, 2005
FED App. 0449P (6th Cir. 2005).

- "A traffic stop is analogous to a *Terry* stop in that, following the initial stop, the subsequent detention cannot
be excessively instrusive and must be reasonably
realted in time to the investigation." *U.S. v. Wellman*,
185 F.3d 651, 656, 1999 FED App. 0291P (6th Cir. 1999).

- "An ordinary traffic stop. . .is more akin to an investigative detention rather than a custodial arrest, and the
principles announced in *Terry v. Ohio*. . .apply to
define the scope of reasonable police conduct. . . . Reasonable police conduct under such circumstances is such
that any subsequent detention after the initial stop
must not be excessively intrusive in that the officer's
actions must be reasonably related in scope to circumstances justifying the initial interference. . . . Once the
purpose of the traffic stop is completed, a motorist cannot be further detained unless something that occurred
during the stop caused the officer to have a reasonable

and articulable suspicion that criminal activity was afoot." *U.S. v. Hill*, 195 F.3d 258, 264, 1999 FED App. 0351P (6th Cir. 1999).

Seventh Circuit

- "With respect to the duration of the stop, there is no rigid time limit placed on *Terry* stops. And a defendant's actions can contribute to a permissible extension of the stop. . . . Likewise, assuming reasonable suspicion exists (as it did here), a reasonable delay attributable to arranging for a canine unit to conduct a sniff may permissibly extend the duration of a stop. At the outset of the stop, Ruiz gave answers which increased rather than allayed the officers' suspicions. Ruiz claimed to be parked in the driveway because he was interested in renting the house, but, as the district court noted, his "backing out of that driveway [after] the police car passed him . . . is inconsistent with looking at a house he might want to rent." Also suspicious was Ruiz's claim that he was at the mall to visit a furniture store, when he did not park within view of any furniture store and, unbeknownst to Ruiz, the officers had witnessed Ruiz meet with the subject of their narcotics investigation in the parking lot. The officers' suspicions were increased further by Ruiz's Texas driver's license, combined with his car being registered in Wisconsin and containing no personal items. In short, the first few minutes of the stop only served to increase the officers' reasonable suspicion that Ruiz was operating a trap car, and this justified further investigation by the officers. The remainder of the time in the driveway was devoted to Tapia's search of Ruiz's car and the officers' attempt to summon a canine unit for assistance. The district court found that Ruiz voluntarily consented to the search of his car. This finding is not challenged by Ruiz, and the finding was not clearly erroneous. In the words of the district court, Ruiz's voluntary consent to the search was 'consistent with the entire modus operandi . . . of the officers . . . mak[ing] this defendant feel as comfortable as possible while they were talking to him.' " *U.S. v. Ruiz*, 785 F.3d 1134, 1143–44 (7th Cir. 2015) (citations omitted).
- "Although [Defendant] challenges the entirety of the

stop after the issuance of the written warning, we view the traffic stop as having three distinct phases. The first phase began with [the officer's] initiation of the stop and lasted through the issuance of the written warning. This phase lasted approximately 11 minutes, and as mentioned above, was reasonable based on [the officer's] observation of the van exceeding the speed limit. In the next phase of the stop, which lasted about eight to nine minutes, [the officer] left [Defendant] in the squad car, questioned [the passenger] about the packages, requested the shipping papers, and received [the passenger's] consent to search the van, resulting in the positive dog alert. In the final phase of the stop, [the officer] and other law enforcement agents searched the van, recovered brick-shaped objects wrapped in plastic, to which the dog again alerted for the presence of narcotics, and handcuffed [Defendant]. This phase lasted approximately 20 minutes. . . . [T]he entirety of [Defendant's] detention caused by the traffic stop was justified, and the district court correctly denied his motion to suppress." *U.S. v. Bueno*, 703 F.3d 1053 (7th Cir. 2013), cert. granted, judgment vacated on other grounds, 133 S. Ct. 2830, 186 L. Ed. 2d 881 (2013).

- "[T]here is some support for the argument that requesting a criminal history check is a reasonable, constitutional part of all or most traffic stops. We find such a bright line rule troubling, however, because often criminal history checks take longer to process than the usual license and warrant requests, and after a certain point meaningful additional time could, we believe, constitute an unreasonable detention of the average traveler. Unless technology permits criminal record requests to be conducted reasonably contemporaneously with the license and warrant checks normally solicited, we are reluctant to say such checks are always reasonable or justified in the average traffic stop." *U.S. v. Finke*, 85 F.3d 1275, 1280 (7th Cir. 1996).

Eighth Circuit

- "[Investigating officer] was accompanied at the scene by a drug dog, and his deployment of the dog to sniff the exterior of the vehicle, only six minutes into the encounter, did not impermissibly expand the scope of the traffic stop." *U.S. v. Hernandez-Mendoza*, 600 F.3d 971 (8th Cir. 2010), as amended, in No. 08-3898(July 7, 2010) and opinion amended on denial of reh'g, 611 F.3d 418 (8th Cir. 2010).

- "In order to protect an individual's interest in liberty, the Fourth Amendment limits a detention or search conducted subsequent to a lawful traffic stop. (citation omitted) A lawful traffic stop that is extended in order to execute a canine sniff does not become an unconstitutional seizure where the stop is reasonably prolonged and constitutes only de minimis intrusions on a defendant's liberty. (citation omitted) For example, in *Alexander*, 448 F.3d at 1017, the canine sniff was a de minimis intrusion when it occurred four minutes after the completion of a lawful traffic stop. In *Martin*, 411 F.3d at 1002, a canine sniff that occurred two minutes after the conclusion of the traffic stop was considered a de minimis intrusion." *U.S. v. Mohamed*, 600 F.3d 1000 (8th Cir. 2010).

- "After a lawful traffic stop, an officer may complete routine tasks, which may include asking a passenger for identification and running a computer check if the passenger consents to the request for identification." *U.S. v. Cloud*, 594 F.3d 1042 (8th Cir. 2010).

- "A reasonable investigation following a justifiable traffic stop may include asking for the driver's license and registration, asking the driver to sit in the patrol car, and asking about the driver's destination and purpose. . . . . If an officer's suspicions are aroused in the course of such an investigation, the officer is entitled to expand the scope of the stop to ask questions unrelated to the original traffic offense, and consent given in the course of such questioning is valid so long as it is voluntary." *U.S. v. Allegree*, 175 F.3d 648, 650 (8th Cir. 1999).

- "If during a traffic stop, an officer develops a reasonable, articulable suspicion that a vehicle is carrying contraband, he has justification for a greater intrusion unrelated to the traffic offense. When [Officer] responded to [Defendant's] failure to consent to a search of the boxes by detaining the truck and calling for a drug dog, he had a reasonable suspicion that [Defendant] was transporting drugs. [Officer] had observed that [Defendant] was extremely nervous, that he claimed to be transporting blankets for P & E Rug Company, but could not state the address to which he was to deliver the blankets, did not have a bill of lading or permit for transporting the blankets, had rented the truck in his own name for cash, had a laser detector, radar detector and ham radio in the cab, and was traveling from El Paso and Albuquerque, known source cities for drugs. Although there is a possible innocent explanation for each of the factors, as a totality they created a reasonable suspicion justifying further investigation reasonable in scope." *U.S. v. White*, 42 F.3d 457, 460 (8th Cir. 1994).

Ninth Circuit

- "(Defendant's) primary argument, that the officers lacked reasonable suspicion to support their questioning, is 'premised on the assumption that the officers were required to have independent reasonable suspicion in order to question [him]. . .because the questioning constituted a discrete Fourth Amendment event.' *Muehler v. Mena*, 544 U.S. 93, 100-01, 125 S. Ct. 1465, 161 L. Ed. 2d 299 (2005). In making this claim, (defendant) understandably relied on our precedent holding that, during a traffic stop, a police officer may only 'ask questions that are reasonably related in scope to the justification for his initiation of contact' and may expand the scope of questioning beyond the initial purpose of the stop only if he 'articulate[s] suspicious factors that are particularized and objective' . . . . The Supreme Court, however, recently decided in *Muehler*, that 'mere police questioning does not constitute a seizure' unless it prolongs the detention of the individual, and, thus, no reasonable suspicion is required to justify questioning that does not prolong the stop . . . Although *Muehler* involved an interrogation during a search of a building, and made no mention of our precedent regarding questioning during traffic stops, its reasoning is equally applicable in the traffic stop context . . . To the extent that *Chavez-Valenzuela, Murillo*, and *Perez* hold that such questioning must be supported by separate reasonable suspicion, they have been overruled by *Muehler*." . . . . We hold that the officers' questioning of (defendant) did not extend the duration of a lawful stop.

For this reason, we also hold that the expanded questioning need not have been supported by separate reasonable suspicion." *U.S. v. Mendez*, 476 F.3d 1077 (9th Cir. 2007).

- "The Supreme Court established the basic requirements for detaining a driver after a traffic stop in its decisions in *United States v. Brignoni-Ponce*. . .holding that any questioning must relate to the purpose of the stop, and in *Florida v. Royer*. . .holding that the detention must be temporary and unintrusive." *U.S. v. Rojas-Millan*, 234 F.3d 464, 469–70 (9th Cir. 2000).

Tenth Circuit

- "A traffic stop must be justified at its inception and, in general, the officer's actions during the stop must be reasonably related in scope to 'the mission of the stop itself.' In particular, questioning on matters unrelated to that mission is improper if it 'measurably extend[s] the duration of the stop.' Defendant contends on appeal that the officer's questions about his criminal history and travel plans were unrelated to the mission of the traffic stop and measurably extended its duration. . . . Maher asked Defendant whether he had 'ever been in trouble before,' whether he had 'been to prison before,' and 'for what' he had been convicted. Defendant argues that these questions had no direct relation to his broken tag light. But an officer's mission during a traffic stop is not limited to determining whether to issue a ticket. The Supreme Court has declared that this mission 'includes ordinary inquiries incident to the traffic stop.' And recognizing that '[t]raffic stops are especially fraught with danger to police officers,' the Court has included among such inquiries 'negligibly burdensome' inquiries that an officer needs to make 'in order to complete his mission safely,'. . .. As the Court stated, '[T]he government's officer safety interest stems from the mission of the stop itself.'. . ... If running a computer check of a driver's criminal history is justifiable as a 'negligibly burdensome' inquiry useful for officer safety, we fail to see how asking the driver about that history could be unreasonable under the Fourth Amendment. The information requested by Maher did not exceed the scope of what a computer check would reveal. A driver's answer may not be as reliable as a computer check but the time involved is much shorter. And just 'allowing the officer to ask the question may provide important clues pertaining to safety,' such as nervous or evasive responses. A recent decision of this court further supports the propriety of asking questions that serve the purpose of officer safety. In *United States v. Morgan*, the defendant argued that an officer's request for identification exceeded the permissible scope of a bicycle traffic stop because state law did not require a license for bicycling. In upholding the officer's request, we pointed out that '[c]ourts have long recognized that questions concerning a suspect's identity are a routine and accepted part of police investigations.' The justification for this, we said, was that '"[k]nowledge of identity may inform an officer that a suspect is wanted for another offense, or has a record of violence or mental disorder."' If asking for a person's identity is justified because it may help to discover 'a record of violence,' surely there is nothing wrong with the more directly relevant (and efficient) inquiry concerning criminal history. We conclude that the criminal-history questions were not unreasonable under the Fourth Amendment. *United States v. Cone*, 2017 WL 3623921, *2-3 (10th Cir. 2017) (citations omitted).

- "There remains the challenge to Maher's asking Defendant something like 'What are you doing here?' or 'Who are you visiting here?' Defendant's contention is hardly frivolous. In *Holt* we explained that '[t]ravel plans typically are related to the purpose of a traffic stop because the motorist is traveling at the time of the stop.' As Defendant points out, however, '[i]nquiring into the Defendant's reason for being at the hotel was not related to the [broken tag light] or vehicular travel, because the Defendant . . . . had reached his destination.' But we need not address the merits of this argument because Defendant fails to show that suppression of the evidence would be appropriate even assuming a Fourth Amendment violation. . . . Defendant fails to show a factual nexus between the travel-plan question and the discovery of drugs within his vehicle. The chain of events after Maher's questioning of Defendant was as follows: Maher asked Defendant to

step out of his vehicle while he ran a background check.
Upon Defendant's compliance, the pistol was in plain
view. The pistol was seized because Defendant, as a
felon, could not lawfully possess it. And the securing of
the pistol led to the detection of the drugs. Thus, the
causal chain flows naturally from the request that
Defendant exit his vehicle to the discovery of the drugs.
The Supreme Court has upheld the routine traffic-stop
practices of asking drivers to exit their vehicles and
running warrant checks on them. The only causation
question, then, is whether Maher would have decided to
run a background check and ask Defendant to exit his
car if Maher had not previously asked Defendant about
the purpose of his travel. The answer is clearly yes.
Maher testified that he typically asked drivers to step
out of their vehicles while he ran a warrant check. And
the district court found that Defendant was asked to
exit the vehicle because of officer-safety concerns.
Defendant does not challenge this factual finding, nor
does he argue that the travel-plan question led to safety
concerns. Indeed, there is no evidence in the record
regarding how Defendant answered the question. In
short, the necessary but-for causal connection between
the travel-plan question and the discovery of the evidence is absent." *United States v. Cone, No. 16-5125,*
2017 WL 3623921, at *3–4 (10th Cir. Aug. 24, 2017)
(citations omitted).

"Morgan argues that Officer Barnhart exceeded the scope
of the traffic stop by ordering him to get off his bicycle.
At the outset, we note one significant difference between
Morgan and the defendants in the cases he cites. In
Pennsylvania v. Mimms, and *Wilson*, the defendants
complied with the officers' orders to get out of the car,
resulting in an incremental increase in their seizures. In
contrast, Morgan disobeyed Officer Barnhart's order to
get off his bicycle. Morgan cites no cases concluding that
officers violate the Fourth Amendment during an
otherwise-lawful seizure when they order a suspect to do
something, and the suspect does not comply. Further,
even had Morgan complied and stepped off his bicycle,
he still could not show that Officer Barnhart violated his
Fourth Amendment rights. 'The touchstone of our analysis under the Fourth Amendment is always "the reason-

ableness in all the circumstances of the particular governmental invasion of a citizen's personal security.'" Reasonableness depends 'on a balance between the public interest and the individual's right to personal security free from arbitrary interference by law officers.' . . .. Here, we see little difference between Officer Barnhart's ordering Morgan off his bicycle and an officer's asking a driver to step out of an automobile. In fact, in our view, stepping off a bicycle is less intrusive than stepping out of a car. Morgan argues that Officer Barnhart was unjustified in ordering him off the bicycle because Officer Barnhart could already see him. But consistent with *Mimms*, Officer Barnhart's ordering Morgan off his bicycle was 'at most a mere inconvenience.' And we conclude that public-interest concerns outweighed any personal-liberty intrusion or inconvenience. After all, Officer Barnhart had reason to believe Morgan posed a flight risk on his bicycle. We cannot fault the police for trying to minimize flight risks and the safety concerns that flight and pursuit would entail. Thus, we conclude that after lawfully stopping Morgan, Officer Barnhart did not violate the Fourth Amendment by ordering him to get off the bicycle." *United States v. Morgan*, 855 F.3d 1122, 1126–27 (10th Cir. 2017) (citations and text omitted).

- "A routine traffic stop is indisputably a seizure within the meaning of the Fourth Amendment. (citation omitted) However, because a traffic stop is 'necessarily [a] swift action predicated upon the on-the-spot observations of the officer on the beat,' an officer need only reasonably suspect that a crime is in the offing to justify such a detention. . . . [Nevertheless,] [a]bsent some particularized, objective basis to believe the dealer plate [observed on the defendant's car by the officer] was actually not issued to this vehicle or that it was actually not authorized to display the plate, further detention [of defendant after initial stop to see that a license plate was attached] was unconstitutional." *U.S. v. Pena-Montes*, 589 F.3d 1048 (10th Cir. 2009).

- "Officers with reasonable suspicion to believe that the occupants of a vehicle are engaged in the unlawful transportation of contraband may detain the vehicle for a reasonable time to obtain a properly trained dog to sniff for contraband. Given the distance between the scene of the detention and the nearest handler, as well as (the officer's) diligence in promptly calling the dog handler and the handler's speedy arrival, a 40-minute detention was reasonable." *U.S. v. Mendoza*, 468 F.3d 1256 (10th Cir. 2006).

- "(A) traffic stop may become a consensual encounter, requiring no reasonable suspicion, if the officer returns the license and registration and asks questions without further constraining the driver by an "overbearing show of authority" . . . Once the officer has returned the driver's documents, further questioning amounts to an unlawful detention only if the driver has objectively reasonable cause to believe that he is not free to leave . . . We have held that the return of documents is not sufficient to transform a detention into a consensual encounter if the totality of the circumstances gives the driver an objectively reasonable basis to believe he is not free to go . . . Such a reasonable belief may be supported by the presence of more than one officer, the display of a weapon, the physical touching of the detainee, the officer's use of a commanding tone of voice, and the officer's use of intimidating body language." *U.S. v. Chavira*, 467 F.3d 1286 (10th Cir. 2006).

- "A driver must be permitted to proceed after a routine traffic stop if a license and registration check reveal no reason to detain the driver unless the officer has reasonable articulable suspicion of other crimes or the driver voluntarily consents to further questioning." *U.S. v. West*, 219 F.3d 1171, 1176 (10th Cir. 2000).

- "When a driver has produced a valid license and proof of entitlement to operate the vehicle, an officer may issue a citation, but then usually must allow the driver to proceed without further delay or questioning. . . . Two exceptions to this general rule exist however. An officer may question the driver further if (1) the officer has an objectively reasonable and articulable suspicion that the driver is engaged in illegal activity, or (2) the driver voluntarily consents to further questioning." *U.S. v. Patten*, 183 F.3d 1190, 1193 (10th Cir. 1999).

- "[T]he officer may detain the driver for questioning unrelated to the initial stop if he has an objectively reasonable and articulable suspicion illegal activity has oc-

curred or is occurring. . . . .A variety of factors may
contribute to the formation of an objectively reasonable
suspicion of illegal activity. Among those factors that
have justified further questioning are having no proof of
ownership of the vehicle, having no proof of authority to
operate the vehicle, and inconsistent statements about
destination. . . . Also among those are driving with a
suspended license. . .and reluctance to stop. . . . In
particular, the inability to offer proof of ownership or
authorization to operate the vehicle has figured promi-
nently in many of our cases upholding further
questioning." *U.S. v. Hunnicutt*, 135 F.3d 1345, 1349
(10th Cir. 1998).

• "A law enforcement officer conducting a routine traffic
stop may request a driver's license and vehicle registration, run a computer check, and issue a citation. When
the driver has produced a valid license and proof of
entitlement to operate the car, the driver must be allowed to proceed without further delay for additional
questioning. Further questioning is permissible, however, if (1) during the course of the traffic stop the officer acquires an objectively reasonable and articulable
suspicion that the driver is engaged in illegal activity;
or (2) the driver voluntarily consents to the officer's additional questioning. Under the first set of circumstances, a Fourth Amendment seizure has taken place,
but it is reasonable and consequently constitutional.
Under the second set of circumstances, there is no
seizure, and hence the Fourth Amendment's strictures
are not implicated. However, if the officer continues to
question the driver in the absence of either set of circumstances, any evidence derived from that questioning (or a resulting search) is impermissibly tainted in
Fourth Amendment terms." *U.S. v. Elliott*, 107 F.3d
810, 813 (10th Cir. 1997).

• "Several specific, articulable facts, taken together with
rational inferences from them, reasonably supported
[the officer's] continued detention of Defendant. First,
[the officer] did not find it plausible that Defendant
would drive from California to North Carolina merely
to take a very dilapidated sofa to some friends. Second,
[officer] found suspicious Defendant's reference to
Shreveport and his uncertainty as to where in North

Carolina he was going. Third, [officer] noted that
Defendant's story was not consistent with [the passenger's] in that Defendant said they intended to return
to California after Christmas but [the passenger] said
they intended to return before Christmas, within a few
days of December 14." *U.S. v. Kopp*, 45 F.3d 1450,
1453–54 (10th Cir. 1995).

Eleventh Circuit

- "(W)e conclude that a reasonable person in (defendant's)
  circumstances would have felt free to terminate the
  encounter and to decline (the officers) request for further information. This conclusion is based not only on
  the fact that (defendant) had received all of his documentation and thus had everything he needed to
  proceed on his way, but also that his follow-up discussion with (the officer) appears. . .to have been fully cooperative and non-coercive. The fact that (defendant)
  opted to answer (the officer's) follow-up question, rather
  than voluntarily terminating the encounter, does not
  change our conclusion that the exchange had converted
  from a traffic stop into a consensual encounter. (A)s a
  result, (defendant) was not detained at the time he offered to have his car searched. . .(and his) Fourth
  Amendment rights were not implicated by this
  encounter." *U.S. v. Ramirez*, 476 F.3d 1231 (11th Cir.
  2007).
- "[W]e have consistently held that once an officer has
  briefly stopped a motor vehicle operator for the purpose
  of issuing a traffic violation (i.e., a ticket), the officer's
  continuing detention of the vehicle's occupants is authorized under the Fourth Amendment only if the officer
  can point to specific and articulable facts which, taken
  together with rational inferences from those facts, reasonably warrant the intrusion." *U.S. v. Pruitt*, 174 F.3d
  1215, 1219 (11th Cir. 1999).

§ 10:4 Expectation of privacy: An automobile affords a lesser expectation of privacy than a house for Fourth Amendment purposes

Supreme Court

- "The legitimate expectation that information about

perfectly lawful activity will remain private is categorically distinguishable from respondent's hopes or expectations concerning the nondetection of contraband in the trunk of his car. A dog sniff conducted during a concededly lawful traffic stop that reveals no information other than the location of a substance that no individual has any right to possess does not violate the Fourth Amendment." *Illinois v. Caballes*, 543 U.S. 405, 125 S. Ct. 834, 160 L. Ed. 2d 842 (2005).

- "Our first cases establishing the automobile exception to the Fourth Amendment's warrant requirement were based on the automobile's ready mobility, an exigency sufficient to excuse failure to obtain a search warrant once probable cause to conduct the search is clear. More recent cases provide a further justification: the individual's reduced expectation of privacy in an automobile, owing to its pervasive regulation. If a car is readily mobile and probable cause exists to believe it contains contraband, the Fourth Amendment thus permits police to search the vehicle without more." *Pennsylvania v. Labron*, 518 U.S. 938, 940, 116 S. Ct. 2485, 135 L. Ed. 2d 1031 (1996).

- "When a vehicle is being used on the highways, or if it is readily capable of such use and is found stationary in a place not regularly used for residential purposes—temporary or otherwise—the two justifications for the vehicle exception come into play. First, the vehicle is obviously readily mobile by the turn of an ignition key, if not actually moving. Second, there is a reduced expectation of privacy stemming from its use as a licensed motor vehicle subject to a range of police regulation inapplicable to a fixed dwelling. While it is true that respondent's vehicle possessed some, if not many of the attributes of a home, it is equally clear that the vehicle falls clearly within the scope of the exception laid down in *Carroll*. Like the automobile in *Carroll*, respondent's motor home was readily mobile. Furthermore, the vehicle was licensed to operate on public streets; [was] serviced in public places; and [was] subject to extensive regulation and inspection. And the vehicle was so situated that an objective observer would conclude that it was being used not as a residence, but as a vehicle." *California v. Carney*, 471 U.S. 386, 392–93, 105 S. Ct. 2066, 85 L. Ed. 2d 406 (1985).

- "It is unnecessary for us to decide here whether the same expectations of privacy are warranted in a car as would be justified in a dwelling place in analogous circumstances. We have on numerous occasions pointed out that cars are not to be treated identically with houses or apartments for Fourth Amendment purposes." *Rakas v. Illinois*, 439 U.S. 128, 148, 99 S. Ct. 421, 58 L. Ed. 2d 387 (1978).

- "This Court has traditionally drawn a distinction between automobiles and homes or offices in relation to the Fourth Amendment. [T]he inherent mobility of automobiles creates circumstances of such exigency that, as a practical necessity, rigorous enforcement of the warrant requirement is impossible. Besides the element of mobility, less rigorous warrant requirements govern because the expectation of privacy with respect to one's automobile is significantly less than that relating to one's home or office. Automobiles, unlike homes, are subjected to pervasive and continuing governmental regulation and controls, including periodic inspection and licensing requirements. The expectation of privacy as to automobiles is further diminished by the obviously public nature of automobile travel." *South Dakota v. Opperman*, 428 U.S. 364, 367–68, 96 S. Ct. 3092, 49 L. Ed. 2d 1000 (1976).

Fourth Circuit

- "It is axiomatic, of course, that one has a lesser expectation of privacy in a motor vehicle, in part because its function is transportation and it seldom serves as one's residence or as the repository of personal effects. Because of this, and the fact that vehicular travel is, of necessity, highly regulated, individuals traveling in vehicles must expect that the State, in enforcing its regulations, will intrude to some extent on their privacy." *U.S. v. Stanfield*, 109 F.3d 976, 982 (4th Cir. 1997).

Seventh Circuit

- "While it is always preferable that a warrant be obtained before a search is made. . .there are circumstances in which the warrant requirement does not apply. . . . The search of an automobile is often such a circumstance. . . . Because of the inherent mobility of vehicles, and the lessened expectation of privacy the Supreme Court has recognized in them, the search of a vehicle is sometimes permissible even in the absence of a warrant." *U.S. v. Faison*, 195 F.3d 890, 893 (7th Cir. 1999).

- "[I]t is generally recognized that the privacy interests of people who are in transit on public thoroughfares are substantially less than those that attach to fixed dwellings." *U.S. v. Rem*, 984 F.2d 806, 812 (7th Cir. 1993).

- "Two considerations justify the automobile exception: the lessened privacy expectation a person has in a car, as opposed to his home, and the ready mobility of a car. These two justifications come into play [w]hen a vehicle is being used on the highways, or if it is readily capable of such use and is found stationary in a place not regularly used for residential purposes—temporary or otherwise." *U.S. v. Foxworth*, 8 F.3d 540, 545 (7th Cir. 1993).

Ninth Circuit

- "Expectation of privacy in an automobile is significantly different from the expectation of privacy within a home." *U.S. v. Ordaz*, 145 F.3d 1111, 1112 (9th Cir. 1998).

Tenth Circuit

- "[A] person has a lesser expectation of privacy in a motor vehicle because its function is transportation and it seldom serves as one's residence or as the repository of personal effects. A car has little capacity for escaping public scrutiny." *U.S. v. Eylicio-Montoya*, 18 F.3d 845, 850 (10th Cir. 1994).

- "Although the appellants point out that they took turns sleeping in the car during the return leg of their trip, we do not believe that the Supreme Court intended that any time an accused takes a long distance road trip in a car, the car is to be treated like a home for Fourth Amendment purposes. The point remains that regardless of whether it is driven across town or across the country, a car does not envelop its occupants in a house-like cloak of Fourth Amendment protection." *U.S. v.*

Jefferson, 925 F.2d 1242, 1251, 32 Fed. R. Evid. Serv.
916 (10th Cir. 1991).

- "[N]otwithstanding the Supreme Court's recognition
  that an individual operating an automobile upon the
  highway may have a lesser expectation of privacy than
  does an individual in a residence, the person operating
  a car does not lose all reasonable expectation of privacy
  simply because the automobile and its use are subject
  to governmental regulation. We think that the detention of a motorist stopped for speeding to question him
  about what he has in his car that is not subject to public view and whether he is carrying large amounts of
  cash clearly impacts to some extent upon legitimate
  Fourth Amendment interests in privacy and security.
  This is clearly something more than a mere inconvenience and cannot be justified under the rationale of
  Pennsylvania v. Mimms. We therefore reaffirm our
  initial conclusion that the detention of the defendant
  constituted an unreasonable seizure under the Fourth
  Amendment." *U.S. v. Walker*, 941 F.2d 1086, 1089–90
  (10th Cir. 1991).

D.C. Circuit

- "A passenger on a commercial bus certainly has no property interest in the crevice between the seats or for that
  matter in the rack above the seats, the area beneath
  the seats, or anywhere else that personal effects may be
  stowed. Nor are we aware of any socially recognized
  expectation of privacy in the interior of a bus. The
  Supreme Court has consistently affirmed that a traveler on a public thoroughfare has a lesser privacy interest than does the occupant of a fixed dwelling. In particular, we note that passengers on a commercial bus
  come and go with every stop, may move freely about the
  vehicle while on board, and are at liberty to stow their
  personal articles wherever space permits. Of course, a
  bus passenger might maintain physical control over
  property stowed in close proximity to his person if he is
  quick to intercede in order to prevent another from
  disturbing it; but that he might well have to assert
  himself in order to ward off others only highlights the
  lack of any societal understanding that he may expect
  privacy in such a place. The appellant could not reason-

ably expect privacy in a clear plastic bag merely because he put it out of sight in a recess in the interior of a public bus." *U.S. v. Ramos*, 960 F.2d 1065, 1068 (D.C. Cir. 1992).

§ 10:5 Vehicle roadblocks: Vehicles may also be stopped at general roadblocks which serve legitimate governmental purposes

Supreme Court

- "[W]e have almost uniformly rejected invitations to probe subjective intent [motivating relevant officials, in order to determine the reasonableness of a search]. There is one category of exception. . . . In *Edmond,* we held that the Fourth Amendment could not condone suspicionless vehicle checkpoints set up for the purpose of detecting illegal narcotics. Although we had previously approved vehicle checkpoints set up for the purpose of keeping off the road unlicensed drivers, or alcohol-impaired drivers, and for the purpose of interdicting those who illegally cross the border, we found the drug-detection purpose in *Edmond* invalidating because it was 'ultimately indistinguishable from the general interest in crime control.' . . . It was not the absence of probable cause that triggered the invalidating-purpose inquiry in *Edmond.* To the contrary, *Edmond* explicitly said that it would approve checkpoint stops for 'general crime control purposes' that were based upon merely 'some quantum of individualized suspicion.' Purpose was relevant in *Edmond* because 'programmatic purposes may be relevant to the validity of Fourth Amendment intrusions undertaken *pursuant to a general scheme without individualized suspicion,*' (emphasis added)." *Ashcroft v. al-Kidd*, 563 U.S. 731, 131 S. Ct. 2074, 2081, 179 L. Ed. 2d 1149 (2011) (citations omitted).

- "The checkpoint stop here differs significantly from that in *Edmond.* The stop's primary law enforcement purpose was not to determine whether a vehicle's occupants were committing a crime, but to ask vehicle occupants, as members of the public, for their help in providing information about a crime in all likelihood committed by others. The police expected the information elicited to help them apprehend, not the vehicle's occupants, but other individuals. . . . Neither do we believe, *Edmond* aside, that the Fourth Amendment would have us apply an *Edmond*-type rule of automatic unconstitutionality to brief, information-seeking highway stops of the kind now before us. For one thing, the fact that such stops normally lack individualized suspicion cannot by itself determine the constitutional outcome. As in *Edmond*, the stop here at issue involves a motorist. The Fourth Amendment does not treat a motorist's car as his castle. And special law enforcement concerns will sometimes justify highway stops without individualized suspicion. Moreover, unlike *Edmond*, the context here (seeking information from the public) is one in which, by definition, the concept of individualized suspicion has little role to play. Like certain other forms of police activity, say, crowd control or public safety, an information-seeking stop is not the kind of event that involves suspicion, or lack of suspicion, of the relevant individual. For another thing, information-seeking highway stops are less likely to provoke anxiety or to prove intrusive. The stops are likely brief. The police are not likely to ask questions designed to elicit self-incriminating information. And citizens will often react positively when police simply ask for their help as 'responsible citizen[s]' to give whatever information they may have to aid in law enforcement. Further, the law ordinarily permits police to seek the voluntary cooperation of members of the public in the investigation of a crime. . . . The importance of soliciting the public's assistance is offset to some degree by the need to stop a motorist to obtain that help—a need less likely present where a pedestrian, not a motorist, is involved. The difference is significant in light of our determinations that such an involuntary stop amounts to a 'seizure' in Fourth Amendment terms. That difference, however, is not important enough to justify an *Edmond*-type rule here. After all, as we have said, the motorist stop will likely be brief. Any accompanying traffic delay should prove no more onerous than many that typically accompany normal traffic congestion. And the resulting voluntary questioning of a motorist is as likely to prove important for police investigation as is the questioning of a pedestrian. Given these considerations, it would seem anomalous were the law (1) ordinarily to allow police freely to seek the voluntary cooperation of pedestrians but (2) ordinarily to forbid police to seek similar voluntary cooperation from motorists. Finally, we do not believe that an *Edmond*-type rule is needed to prevent an unreasonable proliferation of police checkpoints. Practical considerations—namely, limited police resources and community hostility to related traffic tie-ups—seem likely to inhibit any such proliferation. And, of course, the Fourth Amendment's normal insistence that the stop be reasonable in context will still provide an important legal limitation on police use of this kind of information-seeking checkpoint." *Illinois v. Lidster*, 540 U.S. 419, 124 S. Ct. 885, 157 L. Ed. 2d 843 (2004).

- "[O]ur holding today does nothing to alter the constitutional status of the sobriety and border checkpoints that we approved in *Sitz* and *Martinez-Fuerte*, or of the type of traffic checkpoint that we suggested would be lawful in *Prouse*. The constitutionality of such checkpoint programs still depends on a balancing of the competing interests at stake and the effectiveness of the program. . . .When law enforcement authorities pursue primarily general crime control purposes at checkpoints such as here, however, stops can only be justified by some quantum of individualized suspicion." *City of Indianapolis v. Edmond*, 531 U.S. 32, 47, 121 S. Ct. 447, 148 L. Ed. 2d 333 (2000).

- "The primary purpose of the Indianapolis narcotics checkpoints is in the end to advance the general interest in crime control. . . .We decline to suspend the usual requirement of individualized suspicion where the police seek to employ a checkpoint primarily for the ordinary enterprise of investigating crimes. We cannot sanction stops justified only by the generalized and ever-present possibility that interrogation and inspection may reveal that any given motorist has committed some crime." *City of Indianapolis v. Edmond*, 531 U.S. 32, 44, 121 S. Ct. 447, 148 L. Ed. 2d 333 (2000).

- "The Fourth Amendment requires government to respect the right of the people to be secure in their persons against unreasonable searches and seizures. This restraint on government conduct generally bars officials from undertaking a search or seizure absent individualized suspicion. Searches conducted without grounds for suspicion of particular individuals have been upheld, however, in certain limited circumstances. These circumstances include brief stops for questioning or observation at a fixed Border Patrol checkpoint or at a sobriety checkpoint and administrative inspections in closely regulated businesses." *Chandler v. Miller*, 520 U.S. 305, 308, 117 S. Ct. 1295, 137 L. Ed. 2d 513, 12 I.E.R. Cas. (BNA) 1233, 145 A.L.R. Fed. 657 (1997).

- "This case poses the question whether a State's use of highway sobriety checkpoints violates the Fourth and Fourteenth Amendments to the United States Constitution. We hold that it does not. In sum, the balance of the State's interest in preventing drunken driving, the extent to which this system can reasonably be said to advance that interest, and the degree of intrusion upon individual motorists who are briefly stopped, weighs in favor of the state program. We therefore hold that it is consistent with the Fourth Amendment." *Michigan Dept. of State Police v. Sitz*, 496 U.S. 444, 447, 455, 110 S. Ct. 2481, 110 L. Ed. 2d 412 (1990).

- "In marked contrast to a police car pursuing with flashing lights, or to a policeman in the road signaling an oncoming car to halt, a roadblock is not just a significant show of authority to induce a voluntary stop, but is designed to produce a stop by physical impact if voluntary compliance does not occur." *Brower v. County of Inyo*, 489 U.S. 593, 598, 109 S. Ct. 1378, 103 L. Ed. 2d 628 (1989).

- "This holding does not preclude the States from developing methods for spot checks that involve less intrusion or that do not involve the unconstrained exercise of discretion. Questioning of all oncoming traffic at roadblock-type stops is one possible alternative." *Delaware v. Prouse*, 440 U.S. 648, 663, 99 S. Ct. 1391, 59 L. Ed. 2d 660 (1979).

- "[S]tops for brief questioning routinely conducted at permanent checkpoints are consistent with the Fourth Amendment and need not be authorized by warrant." *U.S. v. Martinez-Fuerte*, 428 U.S. 543, 566, 96 S. Ct. 3074, 49 L. Ed. 2d 1116 (1976).

First Circuit

- "The threshold requirement under *Sitz* and *Edmond*—
  that sobriety concerns be the primary purpose of the
  checkpoint—is met in this case. . . . In the present case,
  Sitz establishes the 'gravity of the public concerns' with
  the death and injury toll taken by drunken drivers and
  the fact that sobriety checkpoints can 'advance the public interest' sufficiently to make such a checkpoint
  reasonable. . . . But in *Sitz,* Chief Justice Rehnquist
  went out of his way to say that whether and where to
  establish a stop is primarily a judgment for state or local officials." *U.S. v. William*, 603 F.3d 66 (1st Cir. 2010).

Second Circuit

- "The duration of the stop was not significantly increased
  by the fact that the MDTs search multiple databases,
  including law enforcement databases. Although our decision in *United States v. Harrison,* related to traffic
  stops instead of checkpoints, it applies with equal force
  in this context, where the initial stop is not challenged.
  In *Harrison,* we wrote that 'an officer's inquiries into
  matters unrelated to the justification for the traffic
  stop. . .do not convert the encounter into something
  other than a lawful seizure, so long as those inquiries
  do not measurably extend the duration of the stop.'
  Finally, we note that Bernacet does not argue that the
  checkpoint was illegal in itself or that the stated
  purpose of protecting traffic safety in an accident prone
  location was pretextual. He argues, instead, that it was
  improper for the police, at a lawfully conducted traffic
  safety checkpoint, to search for parole status in addition to DMV records. If he were able to establish that
  the checkpoint was actually conducted for basic crime
  control purposes and not for vehicle safety reasons, then
  we would likely find the checkpoint unconstitutional."
  U.S. v. Bernacet, 724 F.3d 269 (2d Cir. 2013) (citations
  omitted).

Fifth Circuit

- "A checkpoint does not violate the Fourth and Fourteenth Amendments to the United States Constitution
  so long as the balance of the State's interest, the extent
  to which the checkpoint can reasonably advance that
  interest, and the degree of intrusion upon individual

motorists who are briefly stopped, tilts in favor of the checkpoint program. The Supreme Court has found two such checkpoints to be reasonable: (1) a temporary checkpoint intended to deter and detect drunk drivers and set up pursuant to a detailed committee plan and (2) a permanent checkpoint set up to detect illegal aliens. The Court has also recognized that a state has a substantial interest in enforcing licensing and registration laws, though that interest is not substantial enough to justify roving patrol stops as an enforcement mechanism." *U.S. v. Ramirez-Gonzalez*, 87 F.3d 712, 714 (5th Cir. 1996).

Sixth Circuit

- "The Supreme Court has made it clear that persons stopped for any purpose at motorist checkpoints set up by government officials on public highways have been seized for Fourth Amendment purposes. . . . In order for a checkpoint seizure to satisfy the constitutional requirements of the Fourth Amendment, it must be reasonable under the circumstances. . . . Whether a particular checkpoint seizure is reasonable is determined by the balancing test established in *Brown v. Texas*. . . . The test weighs the gravity of the public concerns served by the seizure, the degree to which the seizure advances the public interest, and the severity of the interference with individual liberty. . . . In considering the severity of the intrusion on individual liberty, the court must consider both the objective intrusion of the seizure—the duration of the stop and the intensity of any brief questioning and visual inspection that might attend it—and its subjective intrusion—its potential for generating fear and surprise to law-abiding motorists." *U.S. v. Huguenin*, 154 F.3d 547, 551–52, 1998 FED App. 0256P (6th Cir. 1998).

Seventh Circuit

- "Stopping a car at a roadblock is a seizure within the meaning of the Fourth Amendment. . . .even though the sequel—the peering into the car windows and the sniffing of the car by the dog outside—does not rise to the level of a search as that term of the amendment has been interpreted by the Supreme Court." *Edmond v.*

Goldsmith, 183 F.3d 659, 661; 82 A.L.R.5th 699 (7th Cir. 1999), judgment aff'd, 531 U.S. 32, 121 S. Ct. 447, 148 L. Ed. 2d 333 (2000).

- "In *Sitz*, the state of Michigan set up various checkpoints to detect drunk drivers at selected sites on state roads. According to the guidelines setting up the checkpoint program, all vehicles traveling through this checkpoint were briefly detained while uniformed officers asked the drivers a few questions and looked for signs of intoxication. [T]he Court found that the level of subjective intrusion brought about by this sobriety checkpoint, through which all incoming motorists were required to pass, was, for constitutional purposes, indistinguishable from the checkpoint upheld in *Martinez-Fuerte*. Thus, what was dispositive in *Sitz* was that pursuant to neutral guidelines uniformed officers conducting the checkpoint stopped every incoming vehicle, and were not at liberty to randomly decide which motorists would be stopped and which would not. In this manner incoming motorists could observe that the stop was official, and that it was being applied to everyone so that a reasonable motorist would have no reason to believe that he or she was a target of unbridled police discretion." *U.S. v. Trevino*, 60 F.3d 333, 337 (7th Cir. 1995).

Eighth Circuit

- "The Sugar Tree Road checkpoint program, as it was operated in the present case, ... violated the Fourth Amendment insofar as its primary purpose was the interdiction of drug trafficking (which the government concedes) and the officers operating the Sugar Tree Road checkpoint were under instructions to stop *every* vehicle that took the Sugar Tree Road exit. While the checkpoint at issue in the present case differs from the checkpoint at issue in [a previous roadblock case] in that the [police] used signs to suggest to drivers that taking the Sugar Tree Road exit was a way to *avoid* a police checkpoint, the mere fact that some vehicles took the exit under such circumstances does not, in our opinion, create individualized reasonable suspicion of illegal activity as to every one of them. Indeed, as the government's evidence indicated, while some drivers may have wanted to avoid being caught for drug trafficking, many more took the exit for wholly innocent reasons—such as wanting to avoid the inconvenience and delay of being stopped or because it was part of their intended route. General profiles that fit large numbers of innocent people do not establish reasonable suspicion. Without first stopping the vehicles and questioning the drivers, the police had no way to determine why any particular vehicles were exiting at the Sugar Tree Road ramp. Finding a quantum of individualized suspicion only *after* a stop occurs cannot justify the stop itself." *U.S. v. Yousif*, 308 F.3d 820 (8th Cir. 2002).

Tenth Circuit

- "The individualized suspicion toward Paetsch distinguishes our case from other roadblock cases, such as *Martinez–Fuerte* and *Sitz*. In those cases, the Supreme Court analyzed programmatic checkpoints against intrusions on innocent motorists detained. Those cases did not reach the situation presented here—how to analyze a Fourth Amendment claim when officers develop individualized suspicion toward a particular person after the initial checkpoint encounter. The Court itself made this distinction. . . . Paetsch cites no case like ours where police developed individualized reasonable suspicion of a defendant midway through a group seizure. In our view, once individualized reasonable suspicion develops, a defendant may complain about the underlying checkpoint or barricade only for what happened up to that time. Once police develop individualized suspicion of a person seized as part of a group, that person may not rely on later intrusions on others detained by the barricade. To allow Paetsch to do so would violate the principle that 'Fourth Amendment rights are personal rights that may not be asserted vicariously.' " *U.S. v. Paetsch*, 782 F.3d 1162, 1173 (10th Cir. 2015), cert. denied, 136 S. Ct. 195, 193 L. Ed. 2d 153 (2015) (citations omitted).
- "The Fourth Amendment protects against unreasonable searches and seizures. Generally, a seizure made without individualized suspicion of wrongdoing is unreasonable. A traffic stop is a 'seizure within the

meaning of the Fourth Amendment.' Because roadblocks and checkpoints seize people without individualized reasonable suspicion, they would violate the Fourth Amendment if subject to that general rule. And, even here, where police had GPS information showing that the tracker (and likely the bank robber) were in one of the 20 cars, police initially lacked reasonable, articulable suspicion of any *particular* person. But the 'touchstone of the Fourth Amendment is reasonableness, not individualized suspicion.' Accordingly, the Supreme Court has carved out exceptions to the general rule where the primary purpose of a group seizure went beyond ordinary crime control. For example, the Court has upheld a border patrol roadblock designed to intercept illegal aliens. And it has upheld a sobriety checkpoint aimed at removing drunk drivers from the road to protect public safety. In those situations, the Court has not required individualized reasonable suspicion, instead favoring a group-level balance of interests, weighing the public interest against intrusions on individuals' liberty." *U.S. v. Paetsch*, 782 F.3d 1162, 1168–69 (10th Cir. 2015), cert. denied, 136 S. Ct. 195, 193 L. Ed. 2d 153 (2015) (citations omitted).

- "Here, the police knew far more than that an armed bank robber was fleeing on a 'likely route': they knew that the stolen money (and likely the armed criminal who stole it) sat in a car idling at that very intersection. And, because the police barricaded only the 20 cars possibly containing the bank robber, their barricade was appropriately tailored to achieve its constitutional purpose—'to catch a dangerous criminal who is likely to flee by way of a particular route.' As such, the barricade's group seizure did not violate the Fourth Amendment simply because it lacked individualized suspicion of a particular motorist. But that does not entirely resolve whether the barricade comported with the Fourth Amendment. We still must examine whether it was reasonable under the totality of the circumstances. . . . Officers at the roadway intersection knew that Paetsch was fleeing a bank robbery, and they knew he had brandished a firearm. These circumstances represent a 'substantial' public threat. . . . When reviewing programmatic checkpoints, the Supreme Court has mea-

613

sured the second *Brown* factor based on what percentage of the total seizures uncovered wrongdoing. Officers here detained 20 cars, and one contained a bank robber. This 5% 'hit' rate is higher than the hit rate of other roadblocks that the Supreme Court has found effective. . . . In an emergency situation, the hit-rate analysis does not fully capture the substantial weight of the second *Brown* factor in our case. . . . . An emergency barricade, by contrast, addresses a specific concern—here, the threat posed by an armed, fleeing bank robber. In this context, a 'hit' resolves the concern completely. . . . . In light of these factual circumstances and the Supreme Court's admonition not to 'indulge in unrealistic second-guessing,' we conclude that the decision to barricade the 20 cars reasonably advanced the public interest. The roadblock cases instruct us to weigh the first two *Brown* factors against the third—the severity of the interference with individual liberty. Here, police seized 29 people. When officers developed individualized suspicion of Paetsch, they had detained the innocent people in their cars for 29 minutes. While we sympathize with the innocent motorists caught in the barricade resulting from Paetsch's armed bank robbery, we conclude that these intrusions on individual liberty do not tip the scale in Paetsch's favor." *U.S. v. Paetsch*, 782 F.3d 1162, 1170–72 (10th Cir. 2015), cert. denied, 136 S. Ct. 195, 193 L. Ed. 2d 153 (2015) (citations omitted).

- "[A] brief stop at a highway roadblock for the limited purpose of verifying a driver's license, registration, and proof of insurance is a reasonable intrusion into the lives of drivers and their passengers even in the absence of reasonable suspicion that an individual passenger or motorist is engaged in illegal activity." *U.S. v. Galindo-Gonzales*, 142 F.3d 1217, 1221 (10th Cir. 1998).

- "The stop of a vehicle at a roadblock on a public thoroughfare is clearly a seizure within the meaning of the Fourth Amendment. But the Fourth Amendment forbids only those seizures that are unreasonable. In determining whether the stop of plaintiff's vehicle was unreasonable, we must evaluate the circumstances of the stop and the relevant interests at stake. Our analysis is guided by the three-part test articulated by the

Supreme Court in *Brown v. Texas.* Under *Brown*, the constitutionality of a stop depends on the gravity of the public concerns served by the seizure, the degree to which the seizure advances the public interest, and the severity of the interference with individual liberty." *Romo v. Champion*, 46 F.3d 1013, 1016 (10th Cir. 1995).

Eleventh Circuit

- "In summary, the balance of the state's interest in enforcing its license and registration requirements, the extent to which the roadblocks furthered that interest, and the degree of intrusion on individual motorists who experienced only slight delays weigh in favor of the state program. We therefore hold that the operation, as planned, did not violate the Constitution. And, in the case of most motorists, the roadblocks were in reality conducted consistently with the Fourth and Fourteenth Amendments. But, in the limited instances of motorists who were delayed for significantly more than the brief time it took to conduct the license check and who were told they could not turn around and leave the line before reaching the roadblock, the roadblocks could constitute an unreasonable seizure." *Merrett v. Moore*, 58 F.3d 1547, 1553 (11th Cir. 1995).

§ 10:6 Initial intrusion: The police may take reasonable actions to protect themselves after a lawful stop of a motor vehicle

Supreme Court

- "Unlike a general interest in criminal enforcement, however, the government's officer safety interest stems from the mission of the stop itself. Traffic stops are 'especially fraught with danger to police officers,' so an officer may need to take certain negligibly burdensome precautions in order to complete his mission safely. On-scene investigation into other crimes, however, detours from that mission. So too do safety precautions taken in order to facilitate such detours. Thus, even assuming that the imposition here was no more intrusive than the exit order in *Mimms,* the dog sniff could not be justified on the same basis. Highway and officer safety are interests different in kind from the Government's endeavor to detect crime in general or drug trafficking in particular." *Rodriguez v. U.S.*, 135 S. Ct. 1609, 1616, 191 L. Ed. 2d 492 (2015) (citations omitted).

- "We must therefore now decide whether the rule of *Mimms* applies to passengers as well as to drivers. On the public interest side of the balance, the same weighty interest in officer safety is present regardless of whether the occupant of the stopped car is a driver or passenger. Regrettably, traffic stops may be dangerous encounters. In 1994 alone, there were 5,762 officer assaults and 11 officers killed during traffic pursuits and stops. In the case of passengers, the danger of the officer's standing in the path of oncoming traffic would not be present except in the case of a passenger in the left rear seat, but the fact that there is more than one occupant of the vehicle increases the possible sources of harm to the officer. On the personal liberty side of the balance, the case for the passengers is in one sense stronger than that for the driver. There is probable cause to believe that the driver has committed a minor vehicular offense, but there is no such reason to stop or detain the passengers. But as a practical matter, the passengers are already stopped by virtue of the stop of the vehicle. The only change in their circumstances which will result from ordering them out of the car is that they will be outside of, rather than inside of, the stopped car. Outside the car, the passengers will be denied access to any possible weapon that might be concealed in the interior of the passenger compartment. It would seem that the possibility of a violent encounter stems not from the ordinary reaction of a motorist stopped for a speeding violation, but from the fact that evidence of a more serious crime might be uncovered during the stop. And the motivation of a passenger to employ violence to prevent apprehension of such a crime is every bit as great as that of the driver. In summary, danger to an officer from a traffic stop is likely to be greater when there are passengers in addition to the driver in the stopped car. While there is not the same basis for ordering the passengers out of the car as there is for ordering the driver out, the additional intrusion on the passenger is minimal. We therefore hold that an officer making a traffic stop may order passengers to get out of the car pending completion of the stop." *Maryland v. Wilson*, 519 U.S. 408, 413–15, 117 S. Ct. 882, 137 L. Ed. 2d 41 (1997).

- "[O]nce a motor vehicle has been lawfully detained for a traffic violation, the police officers may order the driver to get out of the vehicle without violating the Fourth Amendment's proscription of unreasonable searches and seizures." *Pennsylvania v. Mimms*, 434 U.S. 106, 111 n.6, 98 S. Ct. 330, 54 L. Ed. 2d 331 (1977).

- "Certainly it would be unreasonable to require that police officers take unnecessary risks in the performance of their duties." *Terry v. Ohio*, 392 U.S. 1, 23, 88 S. Ct. 1868, 20 L. Ed. 2d 889 (1968).

First Circuit

- "We first look to whether the officer acted properly in ordering appellant to step outside his vehicle upon being stopped. The district court in effect concluded that the officer's suspicions were justifiably heightened, not only by the abrupt manner in which appellant's vehicle pulled over and came to a stop, but by the exaggerated level of movement of the occupants of the car as it came to a stop, particularly those of the passenger in the right front seat. Given these findings, which are fully supported by the record, the officer's request that appellant step outside his automobile was justified." *U.S. v. Cruz*, 156 F.3d 22, 26, 50 Fed. R. Evid. Serv. 212 (1st Cir. 1998).

Second Circuit

- "[W]here there has been a *Terry* stop of an automobile, the officer may take steps to assure himself that the person with whom he is dealing is not armed with a weapon that could unexpectedly and fatally be used against him. . .provided that the officer has a reasonable belief that the individual whose suspicious behavior he is investigating at close range is armed and presently dangerous to the officer or to others. . . . Such a search, however, must be limited in scope to this protective purpose." *McCardle v. Haddad*, 131 F.3d 43, 48 (2d Cir. 1997).

Fourth Circuit

- "Long before its holding in *Gant*. . . .the Supreme Court held that an officer conducting a lawful traffic stop may, as a safety measure, order any passenger to exit the vehicle as a matter of course. (citations omitted) Nothing in *Gant,* which limits permissible searches incident to arrest, undermines the bright-line rule established in *Wilson.*" *U.S. v. Rumley,* 588 F.3d 202 (4th Cir. 2009).

- "In *Wilson,* the Court held that police officers may, as a matter of course, order passengers to exit a vehicle during a routine traffic stop pending completion of the stop. The Court adopted this bright line rule after weighing the public's strong interest in officer safety against the minimal intrusion on a car passenger's private interests." *U.S. v. Raymond,* 152 F.3d 309, 311 (4th Cir. 1998).

- "[I]n *Maryland v. Wilson,* the Supreme Court, relying again on the same public interest in police safety, held that police officers making lawful traffic stops could require passengers to step out of the vehicle as a matter of course. . . . Explaining its extension of *Mimms* to passengers, the Court stated that danger to an officer from a traffic stop is likely to be greater when there are passengers in addition to the driver in the stopped car." *U.S. v. Sakyi,* 160 F.3d 164, 168 (4th Cir. 1998).

- "An officer is authorized to take such steps as [are] reasonably necessary to protect [his] personal safety and to maintain the status quo during the course of [a *Terry*] stop. Where, as here, an officer has been informed by a radio dispatcher that the owner of a vehicle is an armed and dangerous Rambo type and that he should approach the vehicle with caution, it unquestionably is reasonable for the officer to draw his weapon when approaching the vehicle to question its driver." *Foote v. Dunagan,* 33 F.3d 445, 448 (4th Cir. 1994).

Fifth Circuit

- "The Fourth Amendment permits law enforcement officers who have lawfully detained a motor vehicle to order the driver and any passengers to step out, and neither probable cause nor reasonable suspicion is required. The Supreme Court has blessed this practice as not unreasonable under the Fourth Amendment, because concerns for officer safety outweigh the minimal intrusion on the privacy of drivers and passengers. The same safety concerns, as well as the lack of any feasible, less intrusive alternative, support permitting a law enforcement officer, who orders an occupant to exit a vehicle and is met with the occupant's claim of being physically unable to do so, to open that occupant's door and conduct a minimally necessary visual inspection of just his person. If this in turn should produce articulable facts that lead the officer to form a reasonable suspicion that the occupant is armed and dangerous or is concealing contraband, the officer may then conduct a pat down to the same extent that he could have following an occupant's exit from the vehicle on his own." *U.S. v. Meredith*, 480 F.3d 366 (5th Cir. 2007).

- "It is settled that officers conducting a lawful *Terry* stop of a vehicle may order both the driver and the passengers to exit the vehicle pending completion of the stop. . . . The touchstone of *Mimms* and *Wilson* is that officer safety is potentially threatened whenever officers stop a vehicle. . . . Rarely are concerns for officer safety more paramount than during the stop of a vehicle suspected of transporting drugs." *U.S. v. Ibarra-Sanchez*, 199 F.3d 753, 761 (5th Cir. 1999).

Sixth Circuit

- "It also is well-established that, during a traffic stop, an officer may order passengers out of the vehicle pending the completion of the stop. The officers do not need independent justification to remove the driver or passengers from the vehicle. This is so, in large part, because traffic stops are 'fraught with danger' for police officers." *United States v. Pacheco*, 841 F.3d 384, 390 (6th Cir. 2016) (citations omitted).

- "The general test for the allowable scope of law enforcement activity during a *Terry* stop is whether the surrounding circumstances give rise to a justifiable fear for personal safety. Courts have generally upheld law enforcement actions taken during investigatory stops, including making such stops with weapons drawn[,] when those actions are reasonably necessary for the protection of the officers. In a situation where the officers have reason to believe the occupants of a vehicle are armed and dangerous, officers certainly may order occupants out of a car." *U.S. v. Garza*, 10 F.3d 1241, 1246 (6th Cir. 1993).

Seventh Circuit

- "*Mimms* held that the police may order the driver out of her car after a lawful vehicle stop, even in the absence of reasonable suspicion that the driver is armed. Just as a *Buie* protective sweep accompanies a lawful arrest, the *Mimms* removal of a driver from her car is conducted pursuant to a lawful stop. As the Supreme Court explained, coming on top of the vehicle stop, this invasion is de minimis." *U.S. v. Johnson*, 170 F.3d 708, 716 (7th Cir. 1999).

Eighth Circuit

- "Once a vehicle has been lawfully stopped, an officer is authorized to take necessary measures to determine whether the person is in fact carrying a weapon and to neutralize the threat of physical harm. . . . Such measures may include a pat-down search for weapons if the officer reasonably believes that the person is armed and dangerous. . . . It is reasonable for an officer to believe that an individual may be armed and dangerous when that individual is suspected of being involved in a drug transaction because weapons and violence are frequently associated with drug transactions." *U.S. v. Robinson*, 119 F.3d 663, 667 (8th Cir. 1997).

Ninth Circuit

- "The primary basis behind the legitimate and weighty governmental interest in *Mimms* was the danger to police officers when confronting a driver seated in an automobile. That danger is equally grave when a police officer confronts passengers; indeed, it may be more dangerous to have the driver outside the vehicle while one or more other passengers are left inside. One or more passengers may be seated in the back seat of a car, or the back of a sport utility vehicle, making it difficult, if not impossible, for the officer to keep a close watch on these passengers. Having all occupants step out of the vehicle protects the safety of the officer while the officer is dealing with the driver regarding the traffic violation. We believe that the governmental interest weighs strongly in favor of permitting a police officer to order all occupants out of a vehicle. Although we recognize that the driver, not the passengers, was the cause of the traffic stop, that fact does not alter the balance of interests. The weighty interest in officer safety is not dependent on the danger from the driver as a result of being stopped for a traffic violation, it is dependent on the inherent danger from approaching seated people in a vehicle, whether driver or passenger. Because we conclude that it is reasonable under the Fourth Amendment for police officers to direct all occupants of a vehicle to step out of their vehicle following a valid traffic stop, the officers' conduct challenged on appeal in this case was per se reasonable." *Ruvalcaba v. City of Los Angeles*, 64 F.3d 1323, 1327–28 (9th Cir. 1995).

Tenth Circuit

- "Maher asked Defendant whether he had 'ever been in trouble before,' whether he had 'been to prison before,' and 'for what' he had been convicted. Defendant argues that these questions had no direct relation to his broken tag light. But an officer's mission during a traffic stop is not limited to determining whether to issue a ticket. The Supreme Court has declared that this mission 'includes ordinary inquiries incident to the traffic stop.' And recognizing that '[t]raffic stops are especially fraught with danger to police officers,' the Court has included among such inquiries 'negligibly burdensome' inquiries that an officer needs to make 'in order to complete his mission safely,' As the Court stated, '[T]he government's officer safety interest stems from the mission of the stop itself.' Notable for our purposes, the one case cited by the Court as providing an example of a proper inquiry was this court's en banc decision in United States v. Holt. . .. As described in Rodriguez, our Holt decision 'recogniz[ed] [an] officer safety justification for criminal record and outstanding warrant checks.' If running a computer check of a driver's criminal history is justifiable as a 'negligibly burdensome' inquiry useful for officer safety, we fail to see how asking the driver about that history could be unreasonable under the Fourth Amendment. The information requested by Maher did not exceed the scope of what a computer check would reveal. A driver's answer may not be as reliable as a computer check but the time involved is much shorter. And just 'allowing the officer to ask the question may provide important clues pertaining to safety,' such as nervous or evasive responses." *United States v. Cone*, 2017 WL 3623921, *2-3 (10th Cir. 2017) (citations omitted).

- "In *Pennsylvania v. Mimms*, the Supreme Court held that when an officer lawfully stops a vehicle for a traffic violation, the officer may order the driver out of the vehicle without violating the Fourth Amendment. It is not apparent to us why a passenger should be treated differently from the driver of the vehicle for this analysis because the risk to the officer and the intrusion upon the privacy of the suspect will be similar whether the suspect is a driver or a passenger. Thus, we apply *Pennsylvania v. Mimms* to the situation where the passenger is a suspect." *U.S. v. Hill*, 60 F.3d 672, 681–82, 42 Fed. R. Evid. Serv. 227 (10th Cir. 1995).

§ 10:7 Further intrusion: If the police officer has a reasonable belief that the person stopped is presently armed and dangerous, he or she may conduct a limited protective frisk of the person stopped. The vehicle may also be detained briefly for a limited investigation

Supreme Court

- "To justify a patdown of the driver or a passenger during a traffic stop, however, just as in the case of a pedestrian reasonably suspected of criminal activity, the police must harbor reasonable suspicion that the person subjected to the frisk is armed and dangerous." *Arizona v. Johnson*, 555 U.S. 323, 129 S. Ct. 781, 172 L. Ed. 2d 694 (2009).

- "The question remains, however, as to whether the officers could not only effect the seizure of respondent necessary to detain him briefly outside the vehicle, but also effect a search for the VIN that may have been necessary only because of that detention. The pistol beneath the seat did not, of course, disappear when respondent closed the car door behind him. To have returned respondent immediately to the automobile would have placed the officers in the same situation that the holding in *Mimms* allows officers to avoid—permitting an individual being detained to have possible access to a dangerous weapon and the benefit of the partial concealment provided by the car's exterior. In light of the danger to the officers' safety that would have been presented by returning respondent immediately to the car, we think the search to obtain the VIN was not prohibited by the Fourth Amendment." *New York v. Class*, 475 U.S. 106, 116, 106 S. Ct. 960, 89 L. Ed. 2d 81 (1986).

- "[T]he officer [was] justified in conducting a limited search for weapons once he had reasonably concluded that the person whom he had legitimately stopped might be armed and presently dangerous." *Pennsylvania v. Mimms*, 434 U.S. 106, 111–12, 98 S. Ct. 330, 54 L. Ed. 2d 331 (1977).

- "When [Defendant] rolled down his window, rather than complying with the policeman's request to step out of the car so that his movements could more easily be seen, the revolver allegedly at [Defendant's] waist became an even greater threat. Under these circumstances the policeman's action in reaching to the spot where the gun was thought to be hidden constituted a limited intrusion designed to insure his safety, and we conclude that it was reasonable." *Adams v. Williams*, 407 U.S. 143, 148, 92 S. Ct. 1921, 32 L. Ed. 2d 612 (1972).

- "[The pat-down seeking concealed weapons] must be confined in scope to an intrusion reasonably designed to discover guns, knives, clubs, or other hidden instruments for the assault of the police officer." *Terry v. Ohio*, 392 U.S. 1, 29, 88 S. Ct. 1868, 20 L. Ed. 2d 889 (1968).

First Circuit

- "The circumstances of this stop are such that the officer would have been foolhardy not to have frisked appellant for weapons. . . . In particular, the time of day and location of the incident, the excessive speed at which the vehicle was driven, the manner in which it came to a stop, and the unexplained commotion among its occupants who outnumbered the police officer five to one, was sufficient cause to conduct the initial limited patdown of appellant's front pants pockets, in which contraband was in fact discovered." *U.S. v. Cruz*, 156 F.3d 22, 26, 50 Fed. R. Evid. Serv. 212 (1st Cir. 1998).

Second Circuit

- "We share these courts' concern regarding the intrusiveness of successive investigations based on the same reasonable suspicion and conclude that where the same suspicion justifies successive investigations, and the officer conducting the subsequent investigation is aware of the prior investigation and the suspicion that supported it, the investigations' duration and scope must be both individually and collectively reasonable under the Fourth Amendment. . . . Everyone agrees that it was constitutionally permissible for both Trooper Loiselle and Sergeant Albright to stop Foreste's vehicle, regardless of their subjective motives, because both officers had probable cause to believe that a traffic infraction had occurred. At issue, however, is not the reasonableness of the stops themselves or even the reasonableness of the officers' decisions to extend the stops for further investigation. The question is whether the reasonableness of the investigations' scope and duration should be evaluated individually or in combination. . . . [T]hat question depends not on the officers' subjective motivations but on whether the investigatory detentions were based on the same or independent reasonable suspicion. Ordinarily, of course, stops for separate traffic infractions are unrelated, and any extensions of those stops for investigation are unrelated as well. But looking only to whether independent traffic violations support successive traffic stops would create a rule subject to the same gamesmanship highlighted by the Eighth Circuit in *Ilazi*. One officer could stop a vehicle for a traffic infraction on a common drug corridor, become suspicious of the driver's nervousness or explanation for his trip, and then detain the vehicle while a drug-sniffing dog is called to the scene. If the dog took too long to arrive (or, upon arriving, failed to detect any drugs), the officer could telephone a second officer down the road and apprise him of the situation. The second officer could then follow the vehicle until spotting a second traffic infraction, stop the vehicle, and, based on the suspicions relayed by the first officer, detain the vehicle a second time to again wait for a dog. Through combination, successive stops could be extended to an unreasonably intrusive length even if each stop were supported by independent probable cause and each investigative detention itself were sufficiently limited in duration." *U.S. v. Foreste*, 780 F.3d 518, 525–26 (2d Cir. 2015).

- "We consider here whether officers who reasonably believe that they have valid grounds for pulling over a vehicle, but then realize once the vehicle is stopped that they acted on the basis of a mistake of fact, violate the Fourth Amendment rights of the occupants of the vehicle simply by walking up to the vehicle. We conclude that in such circumstances the officers do not violate the Fourth Amendment rights of the occupants because it is reasonable for the officers to approach the vehicle to explain the situation and to inform the occupants that they are free to go. If, immediately upon coming near the vehicle, the officers learn new facts that give rise to a reasonable belief that the occupants are engaged in criminal activity, the officers may continue the detention to investigate further." *U.S. v. Jenkins*, 452 F.3d 207 (2d Cir. 2006).

- "[The Officer] was conducting a lawful protective patdown search. . .when he felt the heavy object in [Defendant]'s coat pocket. He manipulated the object for a few seconds to determine what it was, and felt a hard object and then a softer object. At that point, [the Officer] was not yet able to exclude the possibility that there was a weapon in the pocket, so that the search was still within the bounds of *Terry*, and [the Officer] had become fairly certain the pocket contained drugs. That belief, combined with [Defendant]'s evasive and suspicious conduct, gave the officers probable cause to search [Defendant]'s pocket for contraband. The police were therefore permitted to remove and open the rolled-up paper bag." *U.S. v. Rogers*, 129 F.3d 76, 79 (2d Cir. 1997).

Third Circuit

- "[P]olice can conduct a limited weapons pat-down of a passenger of a lawfully stopped car so long as the constitutional requirements of *Terry* are met. . . .[A]n officer need not be absolutely certain that the individual is armed so long as the officer's concern was objectively reasonable. . . .Thus, a police officer can, as a matter of course, order the driver. . .and the passengers. . .out of a lawfully stopped car." *U.S. v. Kithcart*, 218 F.3d 213, 219 (3d Cir. 2000), as amended, (Aug. 31, 2000).

Fourth Circuit

- "[W]e hold that in connection with a lawful traffic stop of an automobile, when the officer has a reasonable suspicion that illegal drugs are in the vehicle, the officer may, in the absence of factors allaying his safety concerns, order the occupants out of the vehicle and pat them down briefly for weapons to ensure the officer's safety and the safety of others." *U.S. v. Sakyi*, 160 F.3d 164, 169 (4th Cir. 1998).

- "[W]e believe that the Court's decisions in *Mimms* and *Wilson* in particular would support a holding that whenever, during a lawful traffic stop, officers are required to approach a vehicle with windows so heavily tinted that they are unable to view the interior of the stopped vehicle, they may, when it appears in their experienced judgment prudent to do so, open at least one of the vehicle's doors and, without crossing the plane of the vehicle, visually inspect its interior in order to ascertain whether the driver is armed, whether he has access to weapons, or whether there are other occupants of the vehicle who might pose a danger to the officers. Indeed, it seems to us that a contrary holding would not only be irreconcilable with, but arguably undermine altogether, the caselaw from the Supreme Court that was developed specifically for the purpose of protecting officer safety during what are, in today's society, frighteningly perilous encounters." *U.S. v. Stanfield*, 109 F.3d 976, 981 (4th Cir. 1997).

Sixth Circuit

- "[In *Noble*], we were critical of nervousness as an indicator of dangerousness, noting that, because many law-abiding citizens are nervous during traffic stops, it is unreliable. . . . [W]hile we have cautioned against relying too heavily on nervousness as indicia of dangerousness, Pacheco's nervousness is another factor in the totality-of-the-circumstances analysis that supports a reasonable-suspicion finding. While '[n]ervous behavior, standing alone, is not enough to justify a *Terry* search,' nervousness is still relevant to the reasonable-suspicion calculus. And we have found reasonable suspicion in other cases based, in part, on the suspect's extraordinary nervousness that increased as the traffic stop progressed. In *Noble*, there was no testimony that the suspect became increasingly nervous. Here, in contrast, Trivette testified that Pacheco was 'extremely nervous,' and that as the stop progressed, Pacheco began glancing around the vehicle and rummaging through the glove box. Additionally, Noble did not avoid all eye contact with the officers, fidget with his pockets, or otherwise act as if he was concealing something. In contrast, Trivette testified that Pacheco 'wouldn't even make eye contact with [him]' and that 'he was fidgeting around' as he opened up the glove box and shuffled papers back and forth, removing nothing. Further, Trivette testified that Pacheco was looking down at the floorboard and over at the area between the console and his seat. Trivette claimed that, in his experience, this is an area where firearms are often concealed. He went on to say that Pacheco disregarded his presence and that 'it was like he was looking for like an avenue of escape almost.' The absence of these factors weighed against reasonable suspicion in *Noble*; their presence weighs in favor here." *United States v. Pacheco*, 841 F.3d 384, 391, 393 (6th Cir. 2016) (citations omitted).

- "The Supreme Court has declined to hold that reasonable suspicion can never be created by an anonymous tip, and has further held that where 'an informant is shown to be right about some things, he is probably right about other facts that he has alleged, including the claim that the object of the tip is engaged in criminal activity.' As the night's events unfolded, the source's predictions continued to come true. Though not dispositive of reasonable suspicion that Pacheco was armed, the informant's corroborated tip adds support to Trivette's decision to perform a pat-down search." *United States v. Pacheco*, 841 F.3d 384, 392–93 (6th Cir. 2016).
- "Defendant was a passenger in a vehicle that was pulled

over for driving with a broken taillight. When asked for identification, the driver immediately admitted that he did not have a valid license—a misdemeanor criminal offense. The driver was arrested and locked in the back of the patrol car. At that point, officers returned to the vehicle to 'make contact' with Defendant, who was still seated in the passenger seat. The officers did not have any reason to suspect that Defendant was engaged in any criminal activity or that Defendant was armed and dangerous. Nevertheless, the officers ordered Defendant out of the vehicle and told him to put his hands on his head with his fingers interlaced. Officers then began to escort Defendant to the patrol car to search him for weapons and/or drugs. While Defendant was being escorted to the patrol car for a 'pat down' search, he broke free and ran away. The officers pursued Defendant, but did not make any audible commands for him to stop. After Defendant was chased and apprehended by officers, he was searched and found to be carrying a pistol and two bags of hashish, a derivative of marijuana. . . . We agree with the district court that the firearm and the hashish recovered during the search are inadmissible because they were recovered in violation of Defendant's Fourth Amendment rights. The district court correctly determined that the purpose of the traffic stop had been accomplished after the driver was arrested, and Defendant was unlawfully detained after the traffic stop was completed. We further agree with the district court's finding that the officers lacked reasonable suspicion to justify prolonging the traffic stop. Under the circumstances, the officers should have advised Defendant that the vehicle was being impounded and informed Defendant that he was free to go." *U.S. v. Cheatham*, 577 Fed. Appx. 500, 501–02 (6th Cir. 2014) (citations omitted).

- "[W]hen police officers reasonably fear that suspects are armed and dangerous, they may order the suspects out of a car and may draw their weapons when those steps are reasonably necessary for the protection of the officers. . . . Further, detention in a police cruiser does not automatically transform a *Terry* stop into an arrest. . . . Nor does the use of handcuffs exceed the bounds of a *Terry* stop, so long as the circumstances warrant that precaution. . . . [B]ased upon the facts known to the officers at the time of the stop, their use of handcuffs and their detention of the men in the cruisers were both reasonably necessary to protect the officers' safety during the investigation. These precautions were therefore reasonably related to the investigation that warranted the initial stop." *Houston v. Clark County Sheriff Deputy John Does 1-5*, 174 F.3d 809, 814–15, 1999 FED App. 0150P (6th Cir. 1999).

Ninth Circuit

- "Under the rule of *Terry v. Ohio*. . . .an officer may always order the driver and passenger out of a vehicle during a traffic stop . . . and may even handcuff and move both if he reasonably fears for his safety. . . ." *Rohde v. City of Roseburg*, 137 F.3d 1142, 1144 (9th Cir. 1998).
- "Once [Defendant] was validly stopped, [the Officer] properly asked [him] to exit his car. [Defendant] was stopped late at night in a secluded area known for drug trafficking. He was a suspected cocaine dealer. [The Officer] reasonably performed a pat-down search for his own protection. Asking [Defendant] to sit in the back of the patrol car during the computer check was similarly a reasonable precautionary measure, whether or not it constituted an arrest." *U.S. v. Cannon*, 29 F.3d 472, 476–77 (9th Cir. 1994).

Tenth Circuit

- "Under *Terry v. Ohio* an officer may frisk a suspect for weapons if he has a reasonable articulable suspicion that his safety or that of others is in danger. The facts available to [the] Officer here (he was alone on an isolated stretch of highway, he was about to engage in a search of a car, and he had just been warned to approach [Defendant] with extreme caution) would warrant a man of reasonable caution to believe that a frisk would be necessary to protect himself." *U.S. v. McRae*, 81 F.3d 1528, 1536 (10th Cir. 1996).
- "Notwithstanding our reluctance to indulge in unrealistic second-guessing of police officers in determining whether a seizure was reasonably related in scope to its jurisdiction we hold that [the] Officer's failure to use

less intrusive means to ensure her safety while advising [Defendant] to cease honking was unreasonable. The traffic hazard [Defendant] presented, which was the basis for the detention, was alleviated when [Defendant] ceased honking and explained himself prior to [the] Officer's observation of the pistol; nonetheless, [the] Officer had the right to explain the situation to [Defendant] and ensure that he would not continue to present a traffic hazard. Once she saw the gun, [the] Officer could separate Defendants from the gun for her own safety by ordering Defendants out of the car. However, [the] Officer's conduct, as noted above, went far beyond what was necessary to ensure her safety while advising Defendants of the hazardous traffic conditions. [The] Officer initiated what was essentially an arrest procedure and went far beyond what was necessary to protect her safety. Accordingly, the seizure of Defendants was unreasonable in violation of the Fourth Amendment." *U.S. v. King*, 990 F.2d 1552, 1563 (10th Cir. 1993).

§ 10:8 Arrests: An overly intrusive vehicle stop may constitute an arrest requiring probable cause

Supreme Court

- "In assessing whether a detention is too long in duration to be justified as an investigative stop, we consider it appropriate to examine whether the police diligently used a means of investigation that was likely to confirm or dispel their suspicions quickly, during which time it was necessary to detain the defendant. We reject the contention that a 20-minute stop is unreasonable when the police have acted diligently and a suspect's actions contribute to the added delay about which he complains." *U.S. v. Sharpe*, 470 U.S. 675, 686, 688, 105 S. Ct. 1568, 84 L. Ed. 2d 605 (1985).

First Circuit

- "Remember that '[a] *Terry* stop is not necessarily a snapshot of events frozen in time and place,' but rather more closely resembles an ongoing process. 'For that reason, "[t]he propriety of an officer's actions after an initial stop depends on what the officer knows (or has reason to believe) and how events unfold.'" "'[I]f an officer undertakes an investigation pursuant to a *Terry* stop, his ensuing actions must be 'fairly responsive to the emerging tableau.'" We have explained that, as an investigation unfolds, an officer's focus can shift, and he can 'increase the scope of his investigation by degrees' when his suspicions grow during the stop. Indeed, 'the police are in need of an escalating set of flexible responses, graduated in relation to the amount of information they possess.' . . .. Back to our case. Let's travel back: Blake was suspicious '[f]rom the very start' of the traffic stop. Dion's truck bore Colorado plates, but Dion had an Arizona license with a P.O. box; Dion oddly offered on multiple occasions during the stop for Blake to search the truck; Dion's 'extreme nervousness' persisted throughout the stop; his reasoning for traveling—a long car trip from Arizona to Pennsylvania to consult his CPA—didn't add up; his travel route was off; the stretch of highway was a drug-trafficking corridor; and he concealed aspects of his drug-trafficking history. Any one of those facts, standing alone, might not support reasonable suspicion. Seizing on this observation, Dion tackles these facts one by one, arguing that each is not a basis for reasonable suspicion. Dion contends that: (1) his initial offer to Blake to search the truck was not 'odd' or suspicious, and neither the government nor Blake articulated any reason why it was; (2) the nervousness Blake observed is not an important factor in the reasonable-suspicion calculus and, regardless, the video of the traffic stop shows that Dion was not 'particularly nervous'; (3) Dion's travel plans and route—though 'off' in Blake's view—were not implausible, and so do not support reasonable suspicion; and (4) Blake did not learn of Dion's history of drug trafficking until after the stop was impermissibly extended, and Dion's twenty-five-year-old conviction was too old to support anything more than a hunch. But the Supreme Court has flatly rejected just this sort of 'divide-and-conquer analysis' because it is inconsistent with the requirement that courts examine the totality of the circumstances. Indeed, 'a fact that is innocuous in itself may in combination with other innocuous facts take on added significance.' That is what we have here: 'taking in the whole picture,' these facts are sufficient to support a reasonable suspicion that criminal activity was afoot, specifically that Dion was involved in drug-related activities. Addressing each of Dion's points, but mindful of the totality of the circumstances, we briefly explain. As Dion concedes, our case law allows an officer carrying out a routine traffic stop to request identification from the driver and to inquire into the driver's itinerary. That's how this traffic stop began. Dion, who was driving a vehicle with Colorado plates, produced an Arizona license, and he described his travel itinerary as a return trip from a cross-country road trip to visit a CPA in Pennsylvania. A drive of that distance for that purpose is reasonably viewed as odd, to say the least, and that odd answer to a concededly appropriate question about travel itinerary both prompted and warranted Blake's follow-up questions in the cruiser on that subject, as well as his Google Maps search, which revealed that the route Dion was traveling was 'off' for his stated journey. We need not dwell on Dion's argument that this questionably odd explanation for the trip 'was not implausible or deceptive' because the explanation for the trip was hardly the only suspicious occurrence during this traffic stop. After Blake asked Dion to accompany him back to his cruiser while Blake issued the citation, Dion volunteered an entirely unprompted offer for Blake to search his truck. Contrary to Dion's contention on appeal, Blake explained why this spontaneous offer to search struck him as 'odd' and 'suspicious': in his experience, it was odd and uncommon for someone to offer to have the officer search a vehicle. And, as we explained, we afford 'a measurable degree of deference to the perceptions of experienced law enforcement officers.' Moreover, the offer to search was not an isolated, one-time occurrence. Instead, during the time he spent in Blake's cruiser, Dion made multiple unsolicited offers to Blake to search his vehicle. Furthermore, Blake stopped Dion on a known drug-trafficking thoroughfare, and he observed Dion to be nervous from the get-go—two factors that, while not indicative of criminal activity standing on their own, can (and should) be thrown into the reasonable-suspicion mix under our case law. Citing *United States v. McKoy*, Dion tries to minimize the role to be played by his nervousness in the reasonable-suspicion calculus. But *McKoy* is quite different from Dion's case. The *McKoy* defendant's nervousness—which was limited to appearing nervous and avoiding eye contact with two police officers as they approached his vehicle—was easily explained as 'a common and entirely natural reaction to police presence.' That pales in comparison to Dion's sustained nervousness throughout the entire stop. Blake characterized Dion as 'extremely nervous,' and his observations of Dion's pounding carotid artery and 'pulse in the area of his stomach underneath his shirt' confirm this assessment. In fact, Blake elaborated that Dion's nervousness was unlike the nervousness commonly shown by stopped drivers (the 'common and entirely natural reaction to police presence' we discussed in McKoy) when pulled over because it was so persistent, even after Dion was reassured that only a warning citation would issue. Dion also complains that Blake's questions relating to Dion's criminal history had nothing to do with the purpose of the traffic stop for speeding. This contention may be true, but it ignores how the events were playing out, i.e. the emerging tableau of what Blake knew. Blake already had concluded the route of Dion's journey seemed 'off,' Dion's offer to search the truck was odd, Dion was extremely and persistently nervous, and the encounter was playing out on a known drug-trafficking thoroughfare. In these circumstances, Blake was justified in asking Dion about his criminal history." *United States v. Dion*, 859 F.3d 114, 124–27 (1st Cir. 2017) (citations omitted).

- "The fifty-minute detention was indeed a lengthy one, and in other circumstances would perhaps weigh in favor of finding a de facto arrest. A long duration however, does not by itself transform an otherwise valid stop into an arrest. . . . Here, the period of detention was justified. . . . In responding to the circumstances, the officers diligently pursued a means of investigation that would dispel their suspicions. They initiated a number of computer checks on the car and its occupants and reasonably awaited the results." *U.S. v. Owens*, 167 F.3d 739, 749 (1st Cir. 1999).

<u>Second Circuit</u>

- "The various elements of the plaintiffs' detention, especially when viewed collectively, would not permit a reasonable juror to conclude that the plaintiffs were merely subjected to a *Terry* stop: (a) the plaintiffs were boxed-in by six police vehicles and outnumbered two-to-one by officers with their guns drawn or at the ready, the plaintiffs were forcefully ordered from their vehicle, harshly handled, and kept in handcuffs for the duration of the detention, the plaintiffs were placed in separate police cruisers and questioned, and at least one plaintiff was read *Miranda* rights, and (d) the defendants extensively searched the plaintiffs, their vehicle, and the contents of a bag found inside the vehicle." *Oliveira v. Mayer*, 23 F.3d 642, 646 (2d Cir. 1994).

Third Circuit

- "Under the *Terry* cases, the reasonableness of the intrusion is the touchstone, balancing the need of law enforcement officials against the burden on the affected citizens and considering the relation of the policeman's actions to his reason for stopping the suspect. The vast majority of courts have held that police actions in blocking a suspect's vehicle and approaching with weapons ready, and even drawn, does not constitute an arrest per se." *U.S. v. Edwards*, 53 F.3d 616, 619 (3d Cir. 1995).

Fifth Circuit

- "Those purposes were served when the computer check came back negative, and [Defendant] should have been free to leave in his car at that point. Once he was not permitted to drive away, the extended detention became an unreasonable seizure, because it was not supported by probable cause. To hold other wise would endorse police seizures that are not limited to the scope of the officers' reasonable suspicion and that extend beyond a reasonable duration." *U.S. v. Dortch*, 199 F.3d 193, 199–200 (5th Cir. 1999), opinion corrected on denial of reh'g, 203 F.3d 883 (5th Cir. 2000).

Sixth Circuit

- "If 'the length and manner' of the stop, including any force used, are not 'reasonably related to the basis for the initial intrusion,' then the stop ripens into an arrest, for which the officers must show probable cause." *Brown v. Lewis*, 779 F.3d 401, 412 (6th Cir. 2015) (citation omitted).

- "Defendant was a passenger in a vehicle that was pulled over for driving with a broken taillight. When asked for identification, the driver immediately admitted that he did not have a valid license—a misdemeanor criminal offense. The driver was arrested and locked in the back of the patrol car. At that point, officers returned to the vehicle to 'make contact' with Defendant, who was still seated in the passenger seat. The officers did not have any reason to suspect that Defendant was engaged in any criminal activity or that Defendant was armed and dangerous. Nevertheless, the officers ordered Defendant out of the vehicle and told him to put his hands on his head with his fingers interlaced. Officers then began to escort Defendant to the patrol car to search him for weapons and/or drugs. While Defendant was being escorted to the patrol car for a 'pat down' search, he broke free and ran away. The officers pursued Defendant, but did not make any audible commands for him to stop. After Defendant was chased and apprehended by officers, he was searched and found to be carrying a pistol and two bags of hashish, a derivative of marijuana. . . . We agree with the district court that the firearm and the hashish recovered during the search are inadmissible because they were recovered in violation of Defendant's Fourth Amendment rights. The district court correctly determined that the purpose of the traffic stop had been accomplished after the driver was arrested, and Defendant was unlawfully detained after the traffic stop was completed. We further agree with the district court's finding that the officers lacked reasonable suspicion to justify prolonging the traffic stop. Under the circumstances, the officers should have advised Defendant that the vehicle was being impounded and informed Defendant that he was free to go." *U.S. v. Cheatham*, 577 Fed. Appx. 500, 501–02 (6th Cir. 2014) (citations omitted).

Seventh Circuit

- "A *Terry* investigative stop is a brief detention which gives officers a chance to verify (or dispel) well-founded

635

suspicions that a person has been, is, or is about to be engaged in criminal activities. Nevertheless, we have over the years witnessed a multifaceted expansion of *Terry*. For better or for worse, the trend has led to the permitting of the use of handcuffs, the placing of weapons and other measures of force more traditionally associated with arrest than with investigatory detention. Unfortunately, the line between a lawful *Terry* stop and an unlawful arrest is not bright. In fact, stops too intrusive to be justified by suspicion under *Terry*, but short of custodial arrest, are reasonable when the degree of suspicion is adequate in light of the degree and the duration of the restraint. Thus the crux of our inquiry is whether the nature of the restraint imposed meets the Fourth Amendment's standard of objective reasonableness." *U.S. v. Vega*, 72 F.3d 507, 515 (7th Cir. 1995).

Eighth Circuit

- "[A]n officer does not seize a person by asking for license and registration if he does not 'convey a message that compliance with [his] request is required.' " *U.S. v. Lopez-Mendoza*, 601 F.3d 861 (8th Cir. 2010).
- "A *Terry* stop may turn into an arrest if the stop lasts for an unreasonably long time or if officers use unreasonable force. . . . The limits of a *Terry* stop were. . .not exceeded when the defendant was handcuffed and placed in a police car while the officers searched the truck. There were two suspects and only two officers at the scene at the time of the initial stop. . . . In light of the dangerous nature of the suspected crime of drug trafficking and the good possibility that the driver or passenger had a weapon, the defendant's confinement with handcuffs in the back of a police car during the search of the truck was reasonably necessary to maintain the status quo, protect the officers, and allow them to conduct the search of the truck immediately and without interference." *U.S. v. Navarrete-Barron*, 192 F.3d 786, 790–91 (8th Cir. 1999).
- "[I]n determining whether a detention following a lawful stop of a vehicle is reasonable, we have held that a court must consider both the length of the detention and law enforcement officers' efforts to conduct their

investigation in a quick and unintrusive manner." *U.S. v. Beck*, 140 F.3d 1129, 1134 (8th Cir. 1998).

- "[A] twenty-minute detention was reasonable when the police acted diligently and defendant contributed to the delay. [A] ninety-minute detention of defendant's luggage was unreasonable when agents did not act diligently to minimize the delay. When police need the assistance of a drug dog in roadside *Terry* stops, it will in general take time to obtain one; local government police forces and the state highway patrol cannot be expected to have drug dogs immediately available to all officers in the field at all times. Courts must consider the law enforcement purposes to be served by the stop as well as the time reasonably needed to effectuate those purposes. The one-hour period between the time [the Officer] pulled [Defendant] over and the time [the Officer] arrested [Defendant] was not an unreasonable period to wait for a drug dog to verify [Officer's] suspicion. The length of the detention was reasonable, and Roberts acted diligently to minimize the detention period." *U.S. v. Bloomfield*, 40 F.3d 910, 917 (8th Cir. 1994).

Ninth Circuit

- "Use of a tire deflation device to stop a vehicle, near an international border, whose driver is reasonably suspected of criminal activity, does not convert a stop into an arrest." *U.S. v. Zaccagnini*, 357 Fed. Appx. 132 (9th Cir. 2009).
- "The length and scope of detention must be justified by the circumstances authorizing its initiation. Thus, when an officer has obtained sufficient information to issue a citation, a continued detention without probable cause to arrest for a crime is unreasonable." *Pierce v. Multnomah County, Or.*, 76 F.3d 1032, 1038 (9th Cir. 1996).

Tenth Circuit

- "The officers had already frisked the defendants for weapons, and knew that none of them was armed. The officers had conducted sweeps of the passenger compartments of the vehicles, and had discovered no weapons. The officers on the scene, who did have weapons, outnumbered the defendants. The use of handcuffs was justified until all six defendants were secured, and for a reasonable time thereafter, while the officers conducted protective sweeps of the cars and assessed the situation. The officers were justified in keeping defendant who they still suspected was a wanted felon, in handcuffs, while they attempted to investigate his identity. It is not unreasonable to fear that a wanted felon will attempt to flee, and may jeopardize the safety of officers in such an attempt. The level of force, therefore, did not transform the legitimate detention into an arrest." *U.S. v. Shareef*, 100 F.3d 1491, 1507 (10th Cir. 1996).

- "[W]e conclude that [Defendant] was illegally arrested during the approximately thirty minutes between the time when the police completed their *Terry* search of his person and vehicle, and the time when the discovery of the drug processing station at 1001 Revere Street gave rise to probable cause for [Defendant]'s arrest." *U.S. v. Edwards*, 103 F.3d 90, 94 (10th Cir. 1996).

D.C. Circuit

- "[N]one of appellant's specific objections to the investigatory stop demonstrate that it was not reasonable or that it crossed the line into an illegal arrest. First, we know of no case that has held it unreasonable for seven or eight officers to aid in the stop of a car carrying four passengers when there is no showing of any threat or exertion of unlawful force by those officers. Second, although the government concedes that appellant was not free to leave the scene during the stop, that fact alone does not convert the stop into an arrest." *U.S. v. Mangum*, 100 F.3d 164, 169 (D.C. Cir. 1996).

§ 10:9 Pretext stops: When an officer has probable cause to stop a vehicle, the officer's subjective intent is irrelevant

Supreme Court

- "In *Whren*, we held that an individual officer's subjective intentions are irrelevant to the Fourth Amendment validity of a traffic stop that is justified objectively by probable cause to believe that a traffic violation has occurred." *City of Indianapolis v. Edmond*, 531 U.S. 32, 45, 121 S. Ct. 447, 148 L. Ed. 2d 333 (2000).

- "[There is no] principle that ulterior motives can

invalidate police conduct that is justifiable on the basis
of probable cause to believe that a violation of law has
occurred. Not only have we never held, outside the
context of inventory search or administrative inspection
that an officer's motive invalidates objectively justifiable behavior under the Fourth Amendment; but we
have repeatedly held and asserted the contrary." *Whren
v. U.S.*, 517 U.S. 806, 811–12, 116 S. Ct. 1769, 135 L.
Ed. 2d 89 (1996).

Second Circuit

- "We share these courts' concern regarding the intrusiveness of successive investigations based on the same reasonable suspicion and conclude that where the same
  suspicion justifies successive investigations, and the officer conducting the subsequent investigation is aware
  of the prior investigation and the suspicion that supported it, the investigations' duration and scope must
  be both individually and collectively reasonable under
  the Fourth Amendment. . . . Everyone agrees that it
  was constitutionally permissible for both Trooper
  Loiselle and Sergeant Albright to stop Foreste's vehicle,
  regardless of their subjective motives, because both officers had probable cause to believe that a traffic infraction had occurred. At issue, however, is not the reasonableness of the stops themselves or even the
  reasonableness of the officers' decisions to extend the
  stops for further investigation. The question is whether
  the reasonableness of the investigations' scope and
  duration should be evaluated individually or in
  combination. . . . [T]hat question depends not on the
  officers' subjective motivations but on whether the
  investigatory detentions were based on the same or independent reasonable suspicion. Ordinarily, of course,
  stops for separate traffic infractions are unrelated, and
  any extensions of those stops for investigation are unrelated as well. But looking only to whether independent
  traffic violations support successive traffic stops would
  create a rule subject to the same gamesmanship
  highlighted by the Eighth Circuit in *Ilazi*. One officer
  could stop a vehicle for a traffic infraction on a common
  drug corridor, become suspicious of the driver's nervousness or explanation for his trip, and then detain the ve-

hicle while a drug-sniffing dog is called to the scene. If
the dog took too long to arrive (or, upon arriving, failed
to detect any drugs), the officer could telephone a second
officer down the road and apprise him of the situation.
The second officer could then follow the vehicle until
spotting a second traffic infraction, stop the vehicle,
and, based on the suspicions relayed by the first officer,
detain the vehicle a second time to again wait for a dog.
Through combination, successive stops could be extended to an unreasonably intrusive length even if each
stop were supported by independent probable cause and
each investigative detention itself were sufficiently
limited in duration." *U.S. v. Foreste*, 780 F.3d 518,
525–26 (2d Cir. 2015).

- "The Fourth Amendment's concern with reasonableness
  allows certain actions to be taken in certain circumstances, whatever the subjective intent. . . . Therefore,
  a police officer who observes a traffic violation may stop
  a car without regard to what a reasonable officer would
  do under the circumstances and without regard to the
  officer's own subjective intent. . . . In other words, an
  officer's use of a traffic violation as a pretext to stop a
  car in order to obtain evidence for some more serious
  crime is of no constitutional significance. . . . A fair
  reading of *Whren* and other car stop cases leads to the
  conclusion that an observed traffic violation legitimates
  a stop even if the detectives do not rely on the traffic
  violation." *U.S. v. Dhinsa*, 171 F.3d 721, 724–25 (2d
  Cir. 1998).

Fifth Circuit

- "The traffic stop may have been pretextual. But under
  Whren v. United States, a traffic stop, even if pretextual,
  does not violate the Fourth Amendment if the officer
  making the stop has probable cause to believe that a
  traffic violation has occurred. This is an objective test
  based on the facts known to the officer at the time of
  the stop, not on the motivations of the officer in making
  the stop. On the other hand, if it is clear that what the
  police observed did not constitute a violation of the cited
  traffic law, there is no objective basis for the stop, and
  the stop is illegal." *U.S. v. Escalante*, 239 F.3d 678,
  680–81 (5th Cir. 2001).

Sixth Circuit

- "Although Pacheco does not outright challenge the traffic stop, he suggests throughout his briefing that the officers' true motive for stopping the vehicle was 'to pursue a narcotics investigation.' However, '[s]ubjective intentions play no role in ordinary, probable-cause Fourth Amendment analysis.' Thus, the two traffic infractions justified Phalen and Trivette in stopping the Aviator." *United States v. Pacheco*, 841 F.3d 384, 390 (6th Cir. 2016) (citations omitted).

- "In *Whren*, the Supreme Court set the standard that governs this case: As a general matter, the decision to stop an automobile is reasonable where the police have probable cause to believe that a traffic violation has occurred." *U.S. v. Johnson*, 242 F.3d 707, 709, 2001 FED App. 0067P (6th Cir. 2001).

- "[A]n officer who has probable cause to believe a civil traffic violation has occurred may generally stop the vehicle regardless of his or her subjective motivation for doing so." *U.S. v. Akram*, 165 F.3d 452, 455, 1999 FED App. 0012P (6th Cir. 1999).

- "In *Whren v. United States*. . .the Supreme Court held that as long as law enforcement officers have probable cause to believe that a traffic violation has occurred, the resulting stop is lawful and does not violate the Fourth Amendment irrespective of the subjective motive of the officers. The *Whren* court stated that a traffic stop is reasonable if there was probable cause for the traffic stop, and it is irrelevant what else the officer intended to investigate at the time of the stop." *U.S. v. Wellman*, 185 F.3d 651, 655, 1999 FED App. 0291P (6th Cir. 1999).

- "We share in the concern that police officers are using the state of the law in this Circuit as carte blanche permission to stop and search target or profile vehicles for drugs. Of course, the Supreme Court in *Whren* confirmed that a police officer is legally allowed to stop a vehicle for a traffic violation when there is probable cause for the traffic stop, without regard for the officer's subjective motivation. . . . As with the concern that the courts must be particularly careful in scrutinizing a police officer's purpose for initially stopping a target vehicle, we believe that the courts must also carefully scrutinize a police officer's conduct during the course of such a stop to insure that it is limited to effectuating the purpose of the stop. Likewise, the courts must carefully scrutinize an officer's stated reasons for detaining the individual beyond the purpose of the stop to insure that the reasons rise to the level of reasonable suspicion, so that the officer does not abuse his authority under Whren." *U.S. v. Hill,* 195 F.3d 258, 267, 1999 FED App. 0351P (6th Cir. 1999).

Seventh Circuit

- "A police officer's decision to stop an automobile will be considered reasonable, however, if the officer had probable cause to believe a traffic violation occurred. . . . That is the case even if it can be shown that the officer actually made the stop for some other reason—for example, a hunch that the vehicle's driver was engaged in drug trafficking. . . . After *Whren,* the officer's subjective intentions play no role in our probable cause inquiry." *Valance v. Wisel,* 110 F.3d 1269, 1275, 46 Fed. R. Evid. Serv. 1127 (7th Cir. 1997).

- "We underscored last year that the argument that ulterior motives invalidate a police stop for a traffic violation is a tired argument in this circuit and this country. The repetition of this argument may be due, in part, to the judicial adherence to the term pretextual in the face of a Supreme Court sanctioned test that has abandoned the every-day use of the term. Post *Whren,* pretext is devoid of its traditional sense; what remains is to look for the absence of an objective rationale for a search. And lest counsel be tempted to quibble with the reasonableness of an objective rationale in the context of a moving violation, we also point out that our objective analysis is indifferent to the relatively minor nature of the traffic offense." *U.S. v. Williams,* 106 F.3d 1362, 1365, 46 Fed. R. Evid. Serv. 686 (7th Cir. 1997).

Eighth Circuit

- "We disagree that Coleman lacked probable cause merely because he relied on the wrong statute. The Supreme Court has repeatedly held that an officer's state of mind or subjective motivation is irrelevant to the probable-cause analysis. '[T]he Fourth Amendment's concern with "reasonableness" allows certain actions to be taken in certain circumstances, *whatever* the subjective intent.' The district court suggested that Coleman's affirmative reliance on the wrong statute during the suppression hearing makes this case distinguishable from *Guevara*. But an officer's subjective motivation—whether revealed at the time of the traffic stop or at the time of a suppression hearing—is irrelevant to the probable-cause inquiry. Even though Coleman testified that Section 103 was the subjective basis for the traffic stop, Section 302 could still provide the objective legal justification needed to support probable cause for the stop." *U.S. v. Demilia*, 771 F.3d 1051, 1054–55 (8th Cir. 2014) (citations omitted).

- "A valid traffic stop may not be challenged on the ground that it was a pretext for other investigation." *U.S. v. $404,905.00 in U.S. Currency*, 182 F.3d 643, 646 (8th Cir. 1999).
- "While a pretextual traffic stop is constitutionally impermissible . . . [i]t is well established. . .that any traffic violation, no matter how minor, provides a police officer with probable cause to stop the driver of the vehicle. . . . In deciding whether a stop was pretextual or based on probable cause, the district court applies an objectively reasonable standard. . . . Under this objective test, so long as police have probable cause to believe that a traffic violation has occurred, the stop is valid even if the police would have ignored the traffic violation but for their suspicion that greater crimes are afoot. . . . The Supreme Court has made it clear that the subjective motivations of an officer in making a traffic stop are irrelevant to the determination of whether that stop was appropriate." *U.S. v. Chatman*, 119 F.3d 1335, 1339–40 (8th Cir. 1997).

Ninth Circuit

- "We emphasize that the presence of a criminal investigatory motive, by itself, does not render an administrative stop pretextual. Nor does a dual motive—one valid, and one impermissible. 'More is involved than the mere expectation that incriminating evidence might be found; the pretext arises out of the fact that the evidence is found in a search which would not have occurred at all . . . .' Thus, '[w]e apply an objective test to determine

643

whether a stop made for an ostensibly legal reason is a
pretext for what is, in reality, an impermissible reason.'
More specifically, 'we ask whether the officer would
have made the stop in the absence of the invalid
purpose. Thus, in order to prove that a stop is unreasonably pretextual, a defendant must show that the stop
would not have occurred in the absence of an impermissible reason.' Orozco has met his burden of making such
a showing here . . .. The objective evidence clearly
establishes that the only reason for the stop was the officers' belief that Orozco could possibly be hauling
marijuana or methamphetamine in his tractor-trailer.
We focus on two such sources of evidence. First, the
manner in which the stop itself was conducted strongly
suggests that it was wholly pretextual. Briefly, as
discussed above, after receiving a tip about the location
of Orozco's truck, Sergeant Brewer 'immediately'
contacted Trooper Zehr to 'advise[ ] him of the vehicle
and its location.' After this conversation, the troopers
drove out to Mile Post 37 in White Pine County, to 'be
on the lookout for' Orozco's truck. Thus, but for the tip,
the officers would not even have been in position to stop
the truck. When the truck arrived, Zehr had to pull out
behind a different commercial truck and drive past it in
order to pull over Orozco's truck. Indeed, arrangements
had apparently been made for a drug-sniffing dog to be
stationed less than a mile away. Second, we find significant Trooper Boynton's testimony regarding the use of
administrative inspections as a pretext to investigate
criminal activity, and more specifically, his testimony
regarding 'common knowledge.' We disagree with the
district court's suggestion that it was common knowledge only that Troopers Zehr and Boynton, as opposed
to Nevada troopers in general, understood that they
could use administrative inspections to investigate criminal activity. That reading simply cannot be reconciled
with the language Boynton used: when law enforcement
officers testify that it is 'common knowledge that you
can do that,' they are obviously referring to knowledge
of practices possessed by those officers charged with
enforcing the administrative scheme." *United States v.
Orozco*, 858 F.3d 1204, 1213–14 (9th Cir. 2017) (citations omitted).

- "In *Whren v. United States.* . .a case involving a pretextual traffic stop, the U.S. Supreme Court held that the constitutionality of a traffic stop does not depend on the subjective motivation or intent of the officers. . . .The fact that the alleged traffic violation is a pretext for the stop is irrelevant, so long as the objective circumstances justify the stop." *U.S. v. Wallace*, 213 F.3d 1216, 1219 (9th Cir. 2000), as amended, (July 7, 2000).

Eleventh Circuit

- "In *Whren*, the Court held that where there is a finding that the police had probable cause to believe that the defendant had committed a traffic code violation, that renders the stop reasonable under the Fourth Amendment. In reiterating the traditional common-law rule that probable cause justifies search and seizure the Court rejected an analysis based on an inquiry into the subjective state-of-mind of the individual police officer to determine whether the stop was pretextual; instead, the Court looked solely to the objective factor of whether the district court had found probable cause to justify a detention based on a traffic violation. In this case, the defendants do not dispute the district court's finding that they were travelling at seventy miles per hour in a sixty-five-miles-per-hour zone." *U.S. v. Griffin*, 109 F.3d 706, 707 (11th Cir. 1997).

Chapter 11

Vehicle Searches

Research References

West's Key Number Digest

Arrest ⬤➞63.5, 71.1; Automobiles ⬤➞349.5(10); Searches and Seizures ⬤➞59 to 65

§ 11:1 Expectation of privacy: A person has a lesser expectation of privacy in a vehicle than he does in a residence or luggage

Supreme Court

- "Although we have recognized that a motorist's privacy interest in his vehicle is less substantial than in his home, the former interest is nevertheless important and deserving of constitutional protection." *Arizona v. Gant,* 556 U.S. 332, 129 S. Ct. 1710, 173 L. Ed. 2d 485, 47 A.L.R. Fed. 2d 657 (2009).

- "[N]either *Ross* itself nor the historical evidence it relied upon admits of a distinction among packages or containers based on ownership. When there is probable cause to search for contraband in a car, it is reasonable for police officers—like customs officials in the Founding era—to examine packages and containers without a showing of individualized probable cause for each one. A passenger's personal belongings, just like the driver's belongings or containers attached to the car like a glove compartment, are in the car, and the officer has probable cause to search for contraband in the car. . . . Passengers, no less than drivers, possess a reduced expectation of privacy with regard to the property that they transport in cars, which trave [l] public thoroughfares. . .seldom serve as. . .the repository of personal effects. . .are subjected to police stop and examination to enforce pervasive governmental controls as an everyday occurrence. . .and, finally, are exposed to traffic accidents that may render all their contents open to public scrutiny." *Wyoming v. Houghton,* 526 U.S. 295, 302–03, 119 S. Ct. 1297, 143 L. Ed. 2d 408 (1999).

- "Our first cases establishing the automobile exception to the Fourth Amendment's warrant requirement were based on the automobile's ready mobility, an exigency sufficient to excuse failure to obtain a search warrant once probable cause to conduct the search is clear. More recent cases provide a further justification: the individual's reduced expectation of privacy in an automobile, owing to its pervasive regulation. If a car is readily mobile and probable cause exists to believe it contains contraband, the Fourth Amendment thus permits police to search the vehicle without more." *Pennsylvania v. Labron*, 518 U.S. 938, 940, 116 S. Ct. 2485, 135 L. Ed. 2d 1031 (1996).

- "The factors that generally diminish the reasonable expectation of privacy in automobiles are applicable *a fortiori* to the VIN. As we have discussed above, the VIN plays an important part in the pervasive regulation by the government of the automobile. A motorist must surely expect that such regulation will on occasion require the State to determine the VIN of his or her vehicle, and the individual's reasonable expectation of privacy in the VIN is thereby diminished. This is especially true in the case of a driver who has committed a traffic violation. In addition, it is unreasonable to have an expectation of privacy in an object required by law to be located in a place ordinarily in plain view from the exterior of the automobile. The VIN's mandated visibility makes it more similar to the exterior of the car than to the trunk or glove compartment. The exterior of a car, of course, is thrust into the public eye, and thus to examine it does not constitute a search." *New York v. Class*, 475 U.S. 106, 116, 106 S. Ct. 960, 89 L. Ed. 2d 81 (1986).

- "[T]here is a reduced expectation of privacy stemming from [a vehicle's] use as a licensed motor vehicle subject to a range of police regulation inapplicable to a fixed dwelling." *California v. Carney*, 471 U.S. 386, 393, 105 S. Ct. 2066, 85 L. Ed. 2d 406 (1985).

- "A person travelling in an automobile on public thoroughfares has no reasonable expectation of privacy in his movements from one place to another." *U.S. v. Knotts*, 460 U.S. 276, 281, 103 S. Ct. 1081, 75 L. Ed. 2d 55 (1983).

Second Circuit

- "[C]itizens' reasonable expectations of privacy in their vehicles are reduced by the far-reaching web of state and federal regulations that covers not only vehicles but also our nation's roadways. As a result, warrantless searches of readily mobile vehicles, when based on probable cause, are reasonable under the Fourth Amendment." *U.S. v. Navas*, 597 F.3d 492 (2d Cir. 2010).

- "The district court's finding that the defendants' temporary, voluntary presence in the police barracks for questioning pursuant to the ruse meant that the vehicles were not readily mobile, and that searches of them were therefore not within the automobile exception, was in error . . . . Whether a vehicle is "readily mobile" within the meaning of the automobile exception has more to do with the inherent mobility of the vehicle than with the potential for the vehicle to be moved from the jurisdiction, thereby precluding a search . . . . In this case, the police could not lawfully have detained the defendants in the police station had they not consented to remain there. Furthermore, the possibility existed that confederates in another car, of whom the police were unaware, might have observed the police intervention and might drive the car away . . . . Thus even if the vehicles searched in the case at bar were not "readily mobile" within the meaning of the automobile exception, a warrantless search of them would be justified based on the diminished expectation of privacy enjoyed by the drivers and passenger while traveling on the Thruway." *U.S. v. Howard*, 489 F.3d 484 (2d Cir. 2007).

Fourth Circuit

- "Defendant abandoned the vehicle he was driving and thus lost any reasonable expectation of privacy in the contents of vehicle, rendering police search of trunk of vehicle permissible; after being pursued by police during a dangerous high-speed chase, defendant jumped out of the still-moving vehicle and fled on foot, as the car drifted down the road into oncoming traffic before coming to a stop on the median." *U.S. v. Kirlew*, 291 Fed. Appx. 536 (4th Cir. 2008).
- "It is axiomatic, of course, that one has a lesser expectation of privacy in a motor vehicle, in part because its function is transportation and it seldom serves as one's

residence or as the repository of personal effects. Because of this, and the fact that vehicular travel is, of necessity, highly regulated, individuals traveling in vehicles must expect that the State, in enforcing its regulations, will intrude to some extent on their privacy." *U.S. v. Stanfield*, 109 F.3d 976, 982 (4th Cir. 1997).

Sixth Circuit

- "A motorist has no legitimate expectation of privacy shielding that portion of the interior of an automobile which may be viewed from outside the vehicle by either inquisitive passersby or diligent police officers." *U.S. v. Campbell*, 549 F.3d 364 (6th Cir. 2008).

- "Defendant's vehicles were validly seized and subject to forfeiture as to permit warrantless searches, upon reasonable finding by police that vehicles were connected to drug trafficking activity; defendant's name appeared on ledger of drug trafficking organization, and police later learned that defendant owned the expensive vehicles despite no reported income." *U.S. v. Musick*, 291 Fed. Appx. 706 (6th Cir. 2008).

- "[A] search of an automobile may be conducted without a warrant even if it is not readily mobile. Even in cases where an automobile was not immediately mobile, the lesser expectation of privacy resulting from its use as a readily mobile vehicle justified application of the vehicular exception. The lesser expectation of privacy derives from the pervasive regulation of vehicles capable of traveling on the public highways. In short, the pervasive schemes of regulation, which necessarily lead to reduced expectations of privacy, and the exigencies attendant to ready mobility justify searches without prior recourse to the authority of a magistrate so long as the overriding standard of probable cause is met." *U.S. v. Haynes*, 301 F.3d 669, 2002 FED App. 0279P (6th Cir. 2002).

Seventh Circuit

- "The expectation of privacy with respect to one's automobile is significantly less than that relating to one's home or office. As a result, when an inventory search is carried out in accordance with standard procedures in the local police department, it tends to ensure that the intrusion is limited to the extent necessary to carry out the caretaking function." *U.S. v. Lozano*, 171 F.3d 1129, 1131 (7th Cir. 1999).

- "While it is always preferable that a warrant be obtained before a search is made. . .there are circumstances in which the warrant requirement does not apply. . . . The search of an automobile is often such a circumstance. . . . Because of the inherent mobility of vehicles, and the lessened expectation of privacy the Supreme Court has recognized in them, the search of a vehicle is sometimes permissible even in the absence of a warrant." *U.S. v. Faison*, 195 F.3d 890, 893 (7th Cir. 1999).

- "Although it is well-established that citizens have a reasonable, albeit diminished, expectation of privacy in their automobiles, one may argue that any expectation of privacy is not reasonable once a person has subjected the automobile to search. The protections associated with the Fourth Amendment, however, are tied to objective reasonableness and merely lowering one's subjective expectations does not cause the constitutional protections to disappear." *McGann v. Northeast Illinois Regional Commuter R.R. Corp.*, 8 F.3d 1174, 1182, 8 I.E.R. Cas. (BNA) 1697, 9 I.E.R. Cas. (BNA) 827 (7th Cir. 1993).

Eighth Circuit

- "A person has no reasonable expectation of privacy in an automobile belonging to another." *U.S. v. Spotted Elk*, 548 F.3d 641 (8th Cir. 2008).

Ninth Circuit

- "Expectation of privacy in an automobile is significantly different from the expectation of privacy within a home." *U.S. v. Ordaz*, 145 F.3d 1111, 1112 (9th Cir. 1998).

- "Law enforcement officers are entitled to search an automobile without first obtaining a warrant in those cases where the police have probable cause to believe that an automobile contains evidence of a crime. This vehicle exception to the warrant requirement is founded on two basic principles. First, automobiles are mobile and can be moved quickly outside the jurisdiction of the magistrate from whom the warrant must be sought. Second, the expectation of privacy in one's vehicle is reduced by the pervasive regulations governing vehicles capable of traveling upon public roads." *U.S. v. Hatley*, 15 F.3d 856, 858 (9th Cir. 1994).

Tenth Circuit

- "The Supreme Court has held that 'police officers who have probable cause to believe there is contraband inside an automobile that has been stopped on the road may search it without obtaining a warrant. . . . If this justification for searching a vehicle exists, it does not vanish simply because the vehicle has been immobilized. . . Nor does it require a reviewing court to determine that the vehicle might have been driven away, or its contents tampered with, during the period required to obtain a search warrant. . . .' [T]he 'plain view doctrine'. . .allows a police officer to properly seize evidence of a crime without a warrant if: '(1) the officer was lawfully in a position from which to view the object seized in plain view; (2) the object's incriminating character was immediately apparent—i.e., the officer had probable cause to believe the object was contraband or evidence of a crime; and (3) the officer had a lawful right of access to the object itself.' Reviewing courts have sometimes utilized both of these exceptions in combination in upholding warrantless vehicle searches. More specifically, if an officer has lawfully observed an object of incriminating character in plain view in a vehicle, that observation, either alone or in combination with additional facts, has been held sufficient to allow the officer to conduct a probable cause search of the vehicle. . . [B]ecause [defendant] left the driver's side door of his truck open, he had 'no legitimate expectation of privacy shielding that portion of the interior of' his truck which could have been 'viewed from outside the vehicle by either inquisitive passersby or diligent police officers.' The fact that [the officer's] observation occurred after [defendant] had been arrested does not affect the legality of the observation." *U.S. v. Sparks*, 291 F.3d 683 (10th Cir. 2002).

§ 11:2 Exigent circumstances: The mobility of motor vehicles often constitutes exigent circumstances justifying a warrantless search

Supreme Court

- "Recognition of the need to seize readily movable contraband before it is spirited away undoubtedly underlies the early federal laws relied upon in Carroll. . . . This need is equally weighty when the automobile, as opposed to its contents, is the contraband that the police seek to secure." *Florida v. White*, 526 U.S. 559, 565, 119 S. Ct. 1555, 143 L. Ed. 2d 748 (1999).

- "Our first cases establishing the automobile exception to the Fourth Amendment's warrant requirement were based on the automobile's ready mobility, an exigency sufficient to excuse failure to obtain a search warrant once probable cause to conduct the search is clear. More recent cases provide a further justification: the individual's reduced expectation of privacy in an automobile, owing to its pervasive regulation. If a car is readily mobile and probable cause exists to believe it contains contraband, the Fourth Amendment thus permits police to search the vehicle without more." *Pennsylvania v. Labron*, 518 U.S. 938, 940, 116 S. Ct. 2485, 135 L. Ed. 2d 1031 (1996).

- "Like the automobile in *Carroll*, respondent's motor home was readily mobile. Absent the prompt search and seizure, it could readily have been moved beyond the reach of the police." *California v. Carney*, 471 U.S. 386, 393, 105 S. Ct. 2066, 85 L. Ed. 2d 406 (1985).

- "[S]ince its earliest days Congress had recognized the impracticability of securing a warrant in cases involving the transportation of contraband goods. Given the nature of an automobile in transit, the Court recognized that an immediate intrusion is necessary if police officers are to secure the illicit substance. In this class of cases, the Court held that a warrantless search of an automobile is not unreasonable." *U.S. v. Ross*, 456 U.S. 798, 806–07, 102 S. Ct. 2157, 72 L. Ed. 2d 572 (1982).

- "Exigent circumstances with regard to vehicles are not limited to situations where probable cause is unforeseeable and arises only at the time of arrest. The exigency may arise at any time, and the fact that the police might have obtained a warrant earlier does not negate the possibility of a current situation's necessitating prompt police action." *Cardwell v. Lewis*, 417 U.S. 583, 595–96, 94 S. Ct. 2464, 41 L. Ed. 2d 325 (1974).

- "The word automobile is not a talisman in whose presence the Fourth Amendment fades away and disappears. And surely there is nothing in this case to invoke the meaning and purpose of the rule of *Carroll v. United States*—no alerted criminal bent on flight, no fleeting opportunity on an open highway after a hazardous chase, no contraband or stolen goods or weapons, no confederates waiting to move the evidence, not even the inconvenience of a special police detail to guard the immobilized automobile." *Coolidge v. New Hampshire*, 403 U.S. 443, 461–62, 91 S. Ct. 2022, 29 L. Ed. 2d 564 (1971).

- "[T]he circumstances that furnish probable cause to search a particular auto for particular articles are most often unforeseeable; moreover, the opportunity to search is fleeting since a car is readily moveable. [T]he occupants are alerted, and the car's contents may never be found again if a warrant must be obtained." *Chambers v. Maroney*, 399 U.S. 42, 50–51, 90 S. Ct. 1975, 26 L. Ed. 2d 419 (1970).

First Circuit

- "The Supreme Court has held that in light of the exigency arising out of the likely disappearance of a vehicle, warrantless searches of a vehicle do not contravene the Warrant Clause of the Fourth Amendment when such searches are based upon probable cause to believe that the vehicle contains evidence of a crime. In *Acevdo*, the Supreme Court extended this exception to containers found within a moveable vehicle. The Court held that where police had probable cause to search a container, the Fourth Amendment did not require the police to obtain a warrant to open the sack in a movable vehicle simply because they lack probable cause to search the entire car." *U.S. v. Schiavo*, 29 F.3d 6, 9 (1st Cir. 1994).

- "Under the automobile exception, the only essential predicate for a valid warrantless search of a motor vehicle by law enforcement officers is probable cause to believe that the [vehicle] contains contraband or other evidence of criminal activity. The inherent mobility of motor vehicles and the reduced expectation of privacy associated with them justify application of the vehicular exception [e]ven in cases where an automobile [is] not immediately mobile." *U.S. v. McCoy*, 977 F.2d 706, 710 (1st Cir. 1992).

Second Circuit

- "[T]he fact that the trailer was 'detached from a. . .cab with its legs dropped,' (citation omitted) did not eliminate its inherent mobility. . . . In sum, the trailer in this case was: (1) affixed with at least one axle and a set of wheels; and (2) capable of being attached to a cab and driven away. Therefore, we conclude that the trailer was inherently mobile at the time of the search, notwithstanding the fact that it was unhitched from the cab that initially transported it to the warehouse. Accordingly, we hold that the mobility rationale militates in favor of the conclusion that the search of the trailer was lawful under the automobile exception." *U.S. v. Navas*, 597 F.3d 492 (2d Cir. 2010).

Fourth Circuit

- "[W]hether the police exercise control over an automobile sufficient to eliminate any exigencies may turn on a number of imponderable factors. Were the applicability of the automobile exception to turn on such factors, it would be hard for courts to administer the exception in a coherent and predictable manner. The result would be a series of finely spun legal distinctions that would render the exception difficult for police to follow in quickly developing situations." *U.S. v. Kelly*, 592 F.3d 586 (4th Cir. 2010).

Fifth Circuit

- "Because the officers had probable cause to believe that the van—which was in operational condition and was parked in the mall parking lot which was open to the public (at least those shopping at the mall) though not publicly owned—contained narcotics, they were legally authorized to search it without a warrant, even if the circumstances were not exigent. The district court hence erred in granting the motion to suppress." *U.S. v. Sinisterra*, 77 F.3d 101, 105 (5th Cir. 1996).

- "The word automobile is not a talisman in whose presence the Fourth Amendment fades away and disappears. And surely there is nothing in this case to invoke the meaning and purpose of the rule of *Carroll v. United States*—no alerted criminal bent on flight, no fleeting opportunity on an open highway after a hazardous chase, no contraband or stolen goods or weapons, no confederates waiting to move the evidence, not even the inconvenience of a special police detail to guard the immobilized automobile." *U.S. v. Reed*, 26 F.3d 523, 529 (5th Cir. 1994).

Sixth Circuit

- "Under the automobile exception to the warrant requirement, law enforcement officers may search a readily mobile vehicle without a warrant if they have probable cause to believe that the vehicle contains evidence of a crime." *U.S. v. Lumpkin*, 159 F.3d 983, 986, 1998 FED App. 0330P (6th Cir. 1998).

Seventh Circuit

- "While it is always preferable that a warrant be obtained before a search is made. . .there are circumstances in which the warrant requirement does not apply. . . . The search of an automobile is often such a circumstance. . . . Because of the inherent mobility of vehicles, and the lessened expectation of privacy the Supreme Court has recognized in them, the search of a vehicle is sometimes permissible even in the absence of a warrant." *U.S. v. Faison*, 195 F.3d 890, 893 (7th Cir. 1999).

Eighth Circuit

- "[The trooper] had probable cause to search the truck. The truck was towing a trailer for which [Defendant] did not provide registration information, that lacked a visible license plate, and that had been reported stolen. The trailer, moreover, contained a license plate registered to another trailer that had been reported stolen. Furthermore, the truck and the trailer had just left a residence where the police suspected the presence of stolen trailers—a fact known to [the trooper] at the time of the search. In light of these facts and considering the totality of the circumstances, [the trooper] had probable cause to search the truck. Based upon the truck's nexus to both [Defendant] and the trailers, there was a fair probability that the truck contained evidence related to the ownership status and the theft of the trailers. Accordingly, pursuant to the automobile exception, [the trooper] did not need a warrant to search the truck. This probable cause allowed [the trooper] to search inside the metal work booklet and inside the truck's console as well, both of which could have contained information related to the ownership status and the theft of the trailers. We therefore affirm the denial of [Defendant's] motion to suppress." *U.S. v. Vore*, 743 F.3d 1175 (8th Cir. 2014), as corrected, (June 4, 2014).

Ninth Circuit

- "Because [the automobile] exception is justified by the exigency created by the inherent mobility of vehicles as well as the relatively minimal expectation of privacy that exists with respect to automobiles, . . . the applicability of the automobile exception does not turn on whether the car's owner or driver has already been taken into custody or the risk of mobility has otherwise been eliminated." *U.S. v. Scott*, 705 F.3d 410 (9th Cir. 2012).

§ 11:3 Standard: To search a vehicle based upon exigent circumstances the police must have probable cause to believe that it contains seizable items

Supreme Court

- "The Fourth Amendment generally requires police to secure a warrant before conducting a search. . . . As we recognized nearly 75 years ago in *Carroll v. United States*. . . there is an exception to this requirement for searches of vehicles. And under our established precedent, the automobile exception has no separate exigency requirement. . . . In this case, the Court of Special Appeals found that there was abundant probable cause that the car contained contraband. This finding alone satisfies the automobile exception to the Fourth Amendment's warrant requirement. . . . The holding of the Court of Special Appeals that the automobile exception requires a separate finding of exigency in addition to a finding of probable cause is squarely contrary to our holdings in *Ross* and *Labron*. We therefore grant the petition for writ of certiorari and reverse the judgment of the Court of Special Appeals." *Maryland v. Dyson*, 527 U.S. 465, 466–68, 119 S. Ct. 2013, 144 L. Ed. 2d 442 (1999).

- "*Ross* summarized its holding as follows: If probable cause justifies the search of a lawfully stopped vehicle, it justifies the search of every part of the vehicle and its contents that may conceal the object of the search. . . . And our later cases describing *Ross* have characterized it as applying broadly to all containers within a car, without qualification as to ownership." *Wyoming v. Houghton*, 526 U.S. 295, 301, 119 S. Ct. 1297, 143 L. Ed. 2d 408 (1999).

- "[T]he exception to the warrant requirement established in *Carroll* applies only to searches of vehicles that are supported by probable cause. In this class of cases, a search is not unreasonable if based on facts that would justify the issuance of a warrant, even though a warrant has not actually been obtained." *U.S. v. Ross*, 456 U.S. 798, 809, 102 S. Ct. 2157, 72 L. Ed. 2d 572 (1982).

- "[I]f the search and seizure without a warrant are made upon probable cause, that is, upon a belief, reasonably arising out of circumstances known to the seizing officer, that an automobile or other vehicle contains that which by law is subject to seizure the search and seizure are valid." *Carroll v. U.S.*, 267 U.S. 132, 149, 45 S. Ct. 280, 69 L. Ed. 543, 39 A.L.R. 790 (1925).

Second Circuit

- "[C]itizens' reasonable expectations of privacy in their vehicles are reduced by the far-reaching web of state and federal regulations that covers not only vehicles but also our nation's roadways. As a result, warrantless searches of readily mobile vehicles, when based on probable cause, are reasonable under the Fourth Amendment." *U.S. v. Navas*, 597 F.3d 492 (2d Cir. 2010).

Fourth Circuit

- "[W]hether the police exercise control over an automobile sufficient to eliminate any exigencies may turn on a number of imponderable factors. Were the applicability of the automobile exception to turn on such factors, it would be hard for courts to administer the exception in a coherent and predictable manner. The result would be a series of finely spun legal distinctions that would render the exception difficult for police to follow in quickly developing situations." *U.S. v. Kelly*, 592 F.3d 586 (4th Cir. 2010).

- "Probable cause is simply not so exacting a standard that it requires a dog to be able to pinpoint the location of drugs within a foot or two. Instead, it is a 'commonsense' conception that deals with 'the factual and practical considerations of everyday life.'" *U.S. v. Kelly*, 592 F.3d 586 (4th Cir. 2010).

- "This court has held that the odor of marijuana, without more, may provide requisite probable cause to support the warrantless search of a vehicle and baggage contained in that vehicle." *U.S. v. Lesane*, 361 Fed. Appx. 537 (4th Cir. 2010).

Sixth Circuit

- "One of the exceptions to the requirement that the government obtain a warrant before searching private property is the automobile exception, which excuses the police from obtaining a warrant when they have probable cause to believe that a vehicle they have stopped contains evidence of a crime." *U.S. v. Hill*, 195 F.3d 258, 273, 1999 FED App. 0351P (6th Cir. 1999).

- "Pursuant to the automobile exception to the warrant requirement, an officer may search a readily mobile vehicle without a warrant if he has probable cause to believe that the vehicle contains evidence of a crime. . . . We define probable cause as reasonable grounds for belief, supported by less than prima facie proof but more than mere suspicion." *Smith v. Thornburg*, 136 F.3d 1070, 1074, 1998 FED App. 0056P (6th Cir. 1998).

Seventh Circuit

- "A police officer who smells marijuana coming from a car has probable cause to search that car. Further, a police officer's use of a drug-sniffing dog around the exterior of a car is not an illegal search." *U.S. v. Franklin*, 547 F.3d 726 (7th Cir. 2008).

- "A bank robber's threat to shoot the teller, the presence of a wrapper in plain view in the car, and the defendant's ownership of the car were enough to supply probable cause to believe that it contained evidence of a bank robbery, and thus the warrantless search of the car did not violate the defendant's Fourth Amendment rights, where the defendant's mother and his ex-wife had told police that he had robbed the bank." *U.S. v. Templeton*, 543 F.3d 378 (7th Cir. 2008).

- "[A] police officer may search an automobile without a warrant, so long as the search is supported by probable cause. . . . Probable cause to search exists if, given the totality of the circumstances, there is a fair probability that contraband or evidence of a crime will be found in a particular place. . . . An automobile search justified by probable cause may extend to any part of the vehicle in which evidence or contraband might be concealed, including, of course, the trunk of the car." *U.S. v. Ledford*, 218 F.3d 684, 688 (7th Cir. 2000).

- "Automobiles may be searched without a warrant if there is probable cause that the car contains evidence the officers are entitled to seize." *U.S. v. Thornton*, 197 F.3d 241, 249, 53 Fed. R. Evid. Serv. 569 (7th Cir. 1999).

Eighth Circuit

- "Wright complains that the officers lacked probable cause to search his vehicle in the parking lot, but the smell of burnt marijuana and the presence of a marijuana cigar in plain view through the window were sufficient to justify a search for drugs. No warrant was required for search of the vehicle and because the police had probable cause to look for drugs, they properly could search the glove compartment as a place that could conceal the object of their search." *United States v. Wright*, 844 F.3d 759, 763 (8th Cir. 2016), cert. denied, 137 S. Ct. 2279 (2017) (citations omitted).

- "The circumstances here indicated a fair probability that contraband or evidence of a crime would be found in the Trailblazer. It was late at night in a remote area and the suspiciousness of [a co-defendant's] presence was compounded by his story about [Defendant] calling for help and then walking away. Implements of meth production lay near the cars, including a lithium battery shell casing, pliers, lithium strips, tinfoil, and a gas can with a plastic tube coming out of it. Police saw a red tablet that looked like pseudoephedrine in the car, along with a bag containing pseudoephedrine boxes on the floorboard. Further, the other implements of meth production found in [the co-defendant's] van increased the probability that contraband or evidence of a crime was in [Defendant's] Trailblazer." *U.S. v. Skoda*, 705 F.3d 834 (8th Cir. 2013) (citations omitted).

- "As long as the law enforcement officials have probable cause, they may search an automobile without a warrant under the automobile exception. . . .Probable cause exists when, given the totality of the circumstances, a reasonable person could believe there is a fair probability that contraband or evidence of a crime would be found in a particular place." *U.S. v. Fladten*, 230 F.3d 1083, 1085 (8th Cir. 2000).

- "Police may search a car without a warrant if they have probable cause to believe that the car contains contraband or evidence. . . . Probable cause requires only a probability or substantial chance of criminal activity, not an actual showing of such activity." *U.S. v. Neumann*, 183 F.3d 753, 756 (8th Cir. 1999).

- "[T]he Supreme Court has recognized that the odor of an illegal drug can be highly probative in establishing probable cause for a search. . . . Many lower courts have relied primarily on the odor of marijuana in determining that probable cause existed for a warrantless automobile search." *U.S. v. Gipp*, 147 F.3d 680, 685 (8th Cir. 1998).

Ninth Circuit

- "Because the dog alerted to both the trunk area and the glove box, probable cause existed to believe that both those areas contained narcotics. Police officers who have stopped an automobile legitimately and who have probable cause to believe that contraband is concealed somewhere within it may conduct a warrantless search of the vehicle." *U.S. v. Garcia*, 205 F.3d 1182, 1187 (9th Cir. 2000).

Tenth Circuit

- "Probable cause doesn't require proof that something is more likely true than false. It requires only a 'fair probability,' a standard understood to mean something more than a 'bare suspicion' but less than a preponderance of the evidence at hand." *U.S. v. Denson*, 775 F.3d 1214, 1217 (10th Cir. 2014), cert. denied, 135 S. Ct. 2064, 191 L. Ed. 2d 967 (2015).

- "Under the automobile exception to the Fourth Amendment's warrant requirement, police officers who have probable cause to believe there is contraband inside an automobile that has been stopped on the road may search it without obtaining a warrant. Once officers' suspicions of contraband inside a motor vehicle rise to the level of probable cause, they are empowered to search the entire vehicle, including the trunk and all containers therein that might contain contraband." *U.S. v. Vazquez*, 555 F.3d 923 (10th Cir. 2009).

- "Here, the officers had an independent legal basis upon which to proceed because the dog's positive alert to the presence of drugs in the van provided probable cause. (citation omitted) As a result, it is immaterial whether [defendant] consented to cutting open the seat. Once the officers had probable cause to search the seat, his consent was no longer necessary." *U.S. v. Carbajal-Iriarte*, 586 F.3d 795 (10th Cir. 2009).

- "The... car was not immobile as the result of a justifiable police stop but simply because it was having mechanical problems. Regardless, Appellant's car had not lost its *inherent* mobility. Additionally, the repair shop was open all night and the mechanic had indicated that the van would be operable again before morning. The shop was open to the public, including to the Appellant, all night. We are of the view that mere temporary immobility due to a readily repairable problem while at an open public repair shop does not remove the vehicle from the category of 'readily mobile.' " *U.S. v. Mercado*, 307 F.3d 1226 (10th Cir. 2002).

- "In *United States v. Ross*, the Supreme Court determined that the permissible scope of a warrantless automobile search is defined by the object of the search and the places in which there is probable cause to believe it may be found. . . .Relying on this principle, this court has held that although the smell of burnt marijuana emanating from a vehicle provides probable cause to search the passenger compartment of that vehicle, if that search fails to uncover corroborating evidence of contraband, probable cause to search the trunk of the vehicle does not exist. . . .This rule is premised on the common-sense proposition that the smell of burnt marijuana is indicative of drug usage, rather than drug trafficking, and because it is unreasonable to believe people smoke marijuana in the trunks of cars, the mere smell of burnt marijuana does not create the fair probability that the trunk contains marijuana." *U.S. v. Wald*, 216 F.3d 1222, 1226 (10th Cir. 2000).

- "Probable cause to search a vehicle is established if, under the totality of the circumstances, there is a fair probability that the car contains contraband or evidence. . . . In a case involving raw marijuana, this court has held that the odor of marijuana alone can satisfy the probable cause requirement to search a vehicle or baggage. . . . [T]his court has established a commonsense distinction between the smells of burnt and raw marijuana based on the imperative that the scope of a warrantless search is defined by the object of the search and the places in which there is probable cause to believe that it may be found. . . . [T]he smell of burnt marijuana is generally consistent with personal use of marijuana in the passenger compartment of an automobile. In such a case, therefore, there is no fair probability that the trunk of the car contains marijuana and an officer must limit the search to the passenger compartment absent corroborating evidence of contraband. . . . When, on the other hand, an officer encounters, as was the case here, the overpowering smell of raw marijuana, there is a fair probability that the car is being used to transport large quantities of marijuana and that the marijuana has been secreted in placed other than the passenger compartment. Accordingly, in such circumstances, a search of the trunk is appropriate." *U.S. v. Downs*, 151 F.3d 1301, 1303, 188 A.L.R. Fed. 763 (10th Cir. 1998).

§ 11:4 Time and place of search: If probable cause and exigent circumstances existed originally, the police may search the vehicle at a later time without securing a warrant

Supreme Court

- "Inasmuch as the Government was entitled to seize the packages and could have searched them immediately without a warrant, we conclude that the warrantless search three days after the packages were placed in the DEA warehouse was reasonable and consistent with our precedent involving searches of impounded vehicles." *U.S. v. Johns*, 469 U.S. 478, 486, 105 S. Ct. 881, 83 L. Ed. 2d 890 (1985).

- "[I]f an immediate search on the street is permissible without a warrant, a search soon thereafter at the police station is permissible if the vehicle is impounded." *U.S. v. Ross*, 456 U.S. 798, 807 n.9, 102 S. Ct. 2157, 72 L. Ed. 2d 572 (1982).

- "[P]olice officers with probable cause to search an automobile at the scene where it was stopped could constitutionally do so later at the station house without first obtaining a warrant. . . . [T]he probable-cause factor that developed at the scene still obtained at the station house." *Texas v. White*, 423 U.S. 67, 68, 96 S. Ct. 304, 46 L. Ed. 2d 209 (1975).

- "[W]here the police may stop and search an automobile under *Carroll*, they may also seize it and search it later at the police station." *Coolidge v. New Hampshire*, 403 U.S. 443, 463, 91 S. Ct. 2022, 29 L. Ed. 2d 564 (1971).

Fourth Circuit

- "Not a single published federal case speaks of a temporal limit to the automobile exception. The Supreme Court has repeatedly stated that a warrantless search of a car (1) need not occur contemporaneously with the car's lawful seizure and (2) need not be justified by the existence of exigent circumstances that might have made it impractical to secure a warrant prior to the search." *U.S. v. Gastiaburo*, 16 F.3d 582, 587 (4th Cir. 1994).

- "[T]he justification to conduct a warrantless search under the automobile exception does not disappear merely because the car has been immobilized and impounded. Under the Supreme Court's precedents, the fact that impoundment may have made it virtually impossible for anyone to drive the car away or to tamper with its contents is irrelevant to the constitutionality of a warrantless search under the circumstances of the present case." *U.S. v. Gastiaburo*, 16 F.3d 582, 586 (4th Cir. 1994).

Fifth Circuit

- "There is no constitutional difference between seizing and holding a car before presenting the probable cause issue to a magistrate and on the other hand carrying out an immediate search without a warrant. Given probable cause to search, either course is reasonable under the Fourth Amendment." *U.S. v. Sinisterra*, 77 F.3d 101, 104 (5th Cir. 1996).
- "[T]here being both probable cause to arrest and probable cause to believe that the vehicle contained contraband extant at the time of the roadside search, the later search of the truck at the state troopers' headquarters passes constitutional muster." *U.S. v. Kye Soo Lee*, 962 F.2d 430, 439 (5th Cir. 1992).

Sixth Circuit

- "It is well established that police may search an automobile and the containers within it where they have probable cause to believe contraband or evidence is contained. . . . . If police officers have probable cause, they may conduct a warrantless search of the vehicle, even after it has been impounded and is in police custody." *U.S. v. Kincaide*, 145 F.3d 771, 779, 49 Fed. R. Evid. Serv. 655, 1998 FED App. 0151P (6th Cir. 1998).

Eighth Circuit

- "Having the truck used in the abduction in custody and the victim's statement that [Appellant] had placed his gun in the truck's air filter, [Officer] would reasonably look in the air filter for the gun. Contrary to [Appellant]'s argument, the officer did not conduct a generalized search for evidence of other crimes, but merely conducted a search related to the reason [Appellant] was arrested, the reason his [truck] had been impounded, and the reason [the truck] was being retained. Like the warrantless seizure of [Appellant]'s truck, the warrantless search of the truck for more evidence of the kidnapping did not violate the Fourth Amendment, and thus, the district court properly granted summary judgment to [the Officers]." *Capraro v. Bunt*, 44 F.3d 690, 691 (8th Cir. 1995).

• "Once the officers discovered the three packages of drugs in the passenger compartment, they had probable cause to search the remainder of the automobile. This probable cause allowed them to search every part of the vehicle and any containers therein that could have concealed the object of the officer's search, namely, more drugs. Because the safe in the trunk certainly was large enough to contain more drugs, the officers could have immediately opened it during their search. They also could have opened it later at the station, as they indeed did." *U.S. v. Riedesel*, 987 F.2d 1383, 1391–92 (8th Cir. 1993).

Ninth Circuit

• "Thus, the totality of the circumstances provided probable cause to believe the car contained evidence of the robberies. . . .Because the agents had probable cause to search the car, and the automobile exception to the warrant requirement applies, the search was valid. . . .This authority did not evanesce simply because the officers decided to impound the car and search it later." *U.S. v. Henderson*, 241 F.3d 638, 648–49 (9th Cir. 2000), as amended, (Mar. 5, 2001).

Tenth Circuit

• "The Supreme Court has held that police officers who have probable cause to believe there is contraband inside an automobile that has been stopped on the road may search it without obtaining a warrant. . . . Although the automobile exception to the Fourth Amendment's warrant requirement is based in part on the ready mobility of automobiles, the justification to conduct such a warrantless search does not vanish once the car has been immobilized; nor does it depend upon a reviewing court's assessment of the likelihood in each particular case that the car would have been driven away, or that its contents would have been tampered with, during the period required for the police to obtain a warrant." *U.S. v. Anderson*, 114 F.3d 1059, 1065–66 (10th Cir. 1997).

D.C. Circuit

- "Authorities may conduct a warrantless search of a motor vehicle if they have probable cause to believe it contains contraband or evidence of a crime. If authorities have probable cause, they may either conduct an immediate search or remove the vehicle to a police station and search it at some later time." *U.S. v. Lawson*, 410 F.3d 735, 67 Fed. R. Evid. Serv. 574 (D.C. Cir. 2005).

§ 11:5   Containers in vehicles: A vehicle search based on probable cause and exigent circumstances may encompass any container in which contraband might be located

Supreme Court

- "We hold that police officers with probable cause to search a car may inspect passengers' belongings found in the car that are capable of concealing the object of the search." *Wyoming v. Houghton*, 526 U.S. 295, 307, 119 S. Ct. 1297, 143 L. Ed. 2d 408 (1999).

- "In light of the minimal protection to privacy afforded by the *Chadwick-Sanders* rule, and our serious doubt whether that rule substantially serves privacy interests, we now hold that the Fourth Amendment does not compel separate treatment for an automobile search that extends only to a container within the vehicle." *California v. Acevedo*, 500 U.S. 565, 576, 111 S. Ct. 1982, 114 L. Ed. 2d 619 (1991).

- "The line between probable cause to search a vehicle and probable cause to search a package in that vehicle is not always clear, and separate rules that govern the two objects to be searched may enable the police to broaden their power to make warrantless searches and disserve privacy interests. At the moment when officers stop an automobile, it may be less than clear whether they suspect with a high degree of certainty that the vehicle contains drugs in a bag or simply contains drugs. If the police know that they may open a bag only if they are actually searching the entire car, they may search more extensively than they otherwise would in order to establish the general probable cause required by *Ross*." *California v. Acevedo*, 500 U.S. 565, 574, 111 S. Ct. 1982, 114 L. Ed. 2d 619 (1991).

- "The interpretation of the *Carroll* doctrine set forth in *Ross* now applies to all searches of containers found in an automobile. In other words, the police may search without a warrant if their search is supported by probable cause." *California v. Acevedo*, 500 U.S. 565, 579, 111 S. Ct. 1982, 114 L. Ed. 2d 619 (1991).

- "Because the Customs officers had probable cause to believe that the pickup trucks contained contraband, any expectation of privacy in the vehicles or their contents was subject to the authority of the officers to conduct a warrantless search. The warrantless search of the packages was not unreasonable merely because the Customs officers returned to Tucson and placed the packages in a DEA warehouse rather than immediately opening them. . . . . Inasmuch as the Government was entitled to seize the packages and could have searched them immediately without a warrant, we conclude that the warrantless search three days after the packages were placed in the DEA warehouse was reasonable and consistent with our precedent involving searches of impounded vehicles." *U.S. v. Johns*, 469 U.S. 478, 486, 105 S. Ct. 881, 83 L. Ed. 2d 890 (1985).

- "If probable cause justifies the search of a lawfully stopped vehicle, it justifies the search of every part of the vehicle and its contents that may conceal the object of the search." *U.S. v. Ross*, 456 U.S. 798, 825, 102 S. Ct. 2157, 72 L. Ed. 2d 572 (1982).

- "The scope of a warrantless [automobile] search based on probable cause is no narrower—and no broader— than the scope of a search authorized by a warrant supported by probable cause. Only the prior approval of the magistrate is waived; the search otherwise is as the magistrate could authorize. The scope of a warrantless search of an automobile thus is not defined by the nature of the container in which the contraband is secreted. Rather, it is defined by the object of the search and the places in which there is probable cause to believe that it may be found. Just as probable cause to believe that a stolen lawnmower may be found in a garage will not support a warrant to search an upstairs bedroom, probable cause to believe that undocumented aliens are being transported in a van will not justify a warrantless search of a suitcase." *U.S. v. Ross*, 456 U.S. 798, 823–24, 102 S. Ct. 2157, 72 L. Ed. 2d 572 (1982).

Fourth Circuit

- "This court has held that the odor of marijuana, without more, may provide requisite probable cause to support the warrantless search of a vehicle and baggage contained in that vehicle." *U.S. v. Lesane*, 361 Fed. Appx. 537 (4th Cir. 2010).

- "The police may search an automobile and the containers within it where they have probable cause to believe contraband or evidence is contained. Probable cause exists where, given all the facts at the time of the search, there is a fair probability that contraband or evidence of a crime will be found in a particular place." *U.S. v. Ford*, 88 F.3d 1350, 1358, 45 Fed. R. Evid. Serv. 174 (4th Cir. 1996).

Fifth Circuit

- "The automobile exception permits the authorities to search a vehicle at the police station without a warrant provided the search is supported by probable cause. If supported by probable cause, every part of a vehicle which may conceal the object of the search may be searched. The scope of a warrantless search based on probable cause is no narrower—and no broader—than the scope of a search authorized by a warrant supported by probable cause. Only the prior approval of a magistrate is waived; the search otherwise is as the magistrate could authorize. In this case the government had probable cause to search the vehicle and was authorized to examine behind the wall after the drug dog alerted at that location." *U.S. v. Zucco*, 71 F.3d 188, 191–92 (5th Cir. 1995).

- "It is well settled that, in a case such as this, the detection of the odor of marihuana justifies a search of the entire vehicle. As the Supreme Court stated in *Ross*, [i]f probable cause justifies the search of a lawfully stopped vehicle, it justifies the search of every part of the vehicle and its contents that may conceal the object of the search. The Court further observed that, if there is probable cause to suspect that the vehicle contains contraband, then the search may extend not only to closed containers, but also to a car's trunk or glove compartment. The same reasoning applies to the area under the hood, where drugs may also be concealed." *U.S. v. McSween*, 53 F.3d 684, 687 (5th Cir. 1995).

Seventh Circuit

- "Under the automobile exception to the warrant requirement of the Fourth Amendment, law enforcement officers may search an automobile without a warrant when they have probable cause to believe that the vehicle contains contraband or evidence of criminality. The scope of the search may extend to all parts of the vehicle in which contraband or evidence could be concealed, including closed compartments and trunks." *U.S. v. Ortiz*, 84 F.3d 977, 983 (7th Cir. 1996).

Eighth Circuit

- "Police may search a car without a warrant if they have probable cause to believe that the car contains contraband or evidence. . . . In such circumstances, the police may search every part of the car and its contents that may conceal the object of the search. . . . If probable cause exists to believe a container in the trunk of a car contains contraband, the container may be searched without a warrant." *U.S. v. Payne*, 119 F.3d 637, 642 (8th Cir. 1997).

Tenth Circuit

- "In the context of vehicle searches, a warrantless search is permissible if there is probable cause to believe that the vehicle contains contraband. . . .In addition, if there is probable cause to search a vehicle, the police are allowed to search any package within the vehicle that is capable of concealing the object of the search." *U.S. v. Edwards*, 632 F.3d 633, 645 (10th Cir. 2001).

§ 11:6 Arrest of occupant: If a person is arrested after a vehicle stop, the passenger compartment of the vehicle may be searched incident to the arrest

Supreme Court

- "If there is no possibility that an arrestee could reach into the area that law enforcement officers seek to search, both justifications for the search-incident-to-arrest exception are absent and the rule does not apply." *Arizona v. Gant*, 556 U.S. 332, 129 S. Ct. 1710, 173 L. Ed. 2d 485, 47 A.L.R. Fed. 2d 657 (2009).

- "[W]e reject [a broad] reading of *Belton* and hold that the *Chimel* rationale authorizes police to search a vehicle incident to a recent occupant's arrest only when the arrestee is unsecured and within reaching distance of the passenger compartment at the time of the search. . . . . [Additionally], [a]lthough it does not follow from *Chimel,* we also conclude that circumstances unique to the vehicle context justify a search incident to a lawful arrest when it is 'reasonable to believe evidence relevant to the crime of arrest might be found in the vehicle.' " *Arizona v. Gant*, 556 U.S. 332, 129 S. Ct. 1710, 173 L. Ed. 2d 485, 47 A.L.R. Fed. 2d 657 (2009).

- "In many cases, as when a recent occupant is arrested for a traffic violation, there will be no reasonable basis to believe the vehicle contains relevant evidence. (citations omitted) But in others, including *Belton* and *Thornton,* the offense of arrest will supply a basis for searching the passenger compartment of an arrestee's vehicle and any containers therein." *Arizona v. Gant*, 556 U.S. 332, 129 S. Ct. 1710, 173 L. Ed. 2d 485, 47 A.L.R. Fed. 2d 657 (2009).

- "Under our view, *Belton* and *Thornton* permit an officer to conduct a vehicle search when an arrestee is within reaching distance of the vehicle or it is reasonable to believe the vehicle contains evidence of the offense of arrest. Other established exceptions to the warrant requirement authorize a vehicle search under additional circumstances when safety or evidentiary concerns demand." *Arizona v. Gant*, 556 U.S. 332, 129 S. Ct. 1710, 173 L. Ed. 2d 485, 47 A.L.R. Fed. 2d 657 (2009).

- "The threat to officer safety from issuing a traffic citation . . . is a good deal less than in the case of a custodial arrest. . . . A routine traffic stop . . . is a relatively brief encounter and is more analogous to a so-called *Terry* stop . . . than to a formal arrest. . . . In *Robinson*, we held that the authority to conduct a full field search as incident to an arrest was a bright-line rule, which was based on the concern for officer safety and destruction or loss of evidence, but which did not depend in every case upon the existence of either concern. Here we are asked to extend that bright-line rule to a situation where the concern for officer safety is not present to the same extent and the concern for destruction or loss of evidence is not present at all. We decline to do so." *Knowles v. Iowa*, 525 U.S. 113, 117–19, 119 S. Ct. 484, 142 L. Ed. 2d 492 (1998).

- "[W]hen a policeman has made a lawful custodial arrest of the occupant of an automobile, he may, as a contemporaneous incident of that arrest, search the passenger compartment of that automobile. It follows from this conclusion that the police may also examine the contents of any containers found within the passenger compartment, for if the passenger compartment is within reach of the arrestee, so also will containers in it be within his reach. Such a container may, of course, be searched whether it is open or closed, since the justification for the search is not that the arrestee has no privacy interest in the container, but that the lawful custodial arrest justifies the infringement of any privacy interest the arrestee may have." *New York v. Belton*, 453 U.S. 454, 460–61, 101 S. Ct. 2860, 69 L. Ed. 2d 768 (1981).

First Circuit

- "The vehicle at issue here, an Isuzu Rodeo, is a medium-size sport utility vehicle and does not have a discrete trunk compartment. Instead, it is equipped with a rear storage area that is clearly reachable without exiting the vehicle. Consequently, because it is an 'area into which an arrestee might reach in order to grab a weapon or evidentiary item,' the search of this portion of the vehicle was valid incident to (defendant's) arrest." *U.S. v. Allen*, 469 F.3d 11 (1st Cir. 2006).

Second Circuit

- "In *Knowles*, the Supreme Court considered whether officers who had probable cause to arrest an individual for a traffic violation but instead issued a citation could conduct a search of the individual's car without probable cause. . . . Although the Supreme Court previously had held that an officer can conduct a search incident-to-arrest without probable cause, it determined that an officer who issues a citation for a traffic violation cannot conduct a search without probable cause even if the officer could have arrested the driver for the traffic violation." *U.S. v. Dhinsa*, 171 F.3d 721, 726 (2d Cir. 1998).

Sixth Circuit

- "Recently, in *Knowles v. Iowa*. . .a unanimous Supreme Court held that a full-blown search of an automobile and its driver, after an officer had elected to issue the driver a traffic citation rather than arresting the driver, violated the Fourth Amendment. Because neither the officer's safety nor the need to preserve evidence was implicated by the routine traffic stop, the Court held that once the driver was stopped for speeding and was issued a citation, all of the evidence necessary to prosecute him had been obtained and, without a reasonable suspicion that other criminal activity was afoot, the stop of the vehicle and issuance of a traffic citation did not justify a full search of the vehicle." *U.S. v. Hill*, 195 F.3d 258, 264, 1999 FED App. 0351P (6th Cir. 1999).

Seventh Circuit

- "More analogous to our case is the Supreme Court's recent pronouncement in *Knowles*, where the Court refused to extend the auto search cases to a situation in which an officer who issued a traffic citation conducted a full search of the person's car." *U.S. v. Johnson*, 170 F.3d 708, 716 (7th Cir. 1999).

Ninth Circuit

- "In *New York v. Belton*, the U.S. Supreme Court attempted to set forth a workable rule for arrests of vehicle occupants. 453 U.S. at 460, 101 S.Ct. 2860. The Court held that, because the vehicle's entire passenger compartment is in fact generally, even if not inevitably, within the arrestee's immediate control, a search of the entire passenger compartment is justified in all such cases. However, if the defendant was not arrested while still inside the vehicle, then he must be a recent occupant of the vehicle for a search of the vehicle incident to his arrest to be constitutional. Issues of spatial proximity are important to determining whether the arrestee can be considered a recent occupant of the vehicle. Federal and state courts have been sharply divided over what distance constitutes sufficient spatial proximity between the arrestee and the vehicle for the arrestee to be considered a recent occupant, thereby making the vehicular search incident to arrest constitutional. [W]e cannot grant the police an automatic entitlement to search an arrestee's vehicle regardless of its distance from the place of the arrest. Permitting police to conduct broad investigative or rummaging searches following an arrest, irrespective of the exigencies, effectively makes the Fourth Amendment dead letter." *U.S. v. Caseres*, 533 F.3d 1064 (9th Cir. 2008).

Tenth Circuit

- "[I]f the police arrest the occupant of a car they may also search the passenger compartment of the vehicle, but they may not search other areas that are outside the suspect's immediate control or grab space." *U.S. v. Edwards*, 632 F.3d 633, 643 (10th Cir. 2001).

- "Under *New York v. Belton*. . . .officers may search any containers, open or closed, in the passenger compartment of a vehicle incident to a lawful arrest of an occupant of the vehicle. . . . The Court in *Knowles* instead held that the Fourth Amendment does not permit a search incident to citation, while leaving the rule of *Belton* intact." *U.S. v. Humphrey*, 208 F.3d 1190, 1201–02 (10th Cir. 2000).

- "The district court applied the rules from *Belton* and its progeny to invalidate the search in this instance because it determined any evidence or weapons contained in the covered cargo area of the vehicle were beyond the defendants' reasonable ability to access, thereby making the covered cargo area more like a trunk than part of the passenger compartment. However, we disagree with the court's conclusion and find where, as here, the vehicle contains no trunk, the entire inside of the vehicle constitutes the passenger compartment and may be lawfully searched . . . regardless of the imposition of an easily-retractable vinyl covering or its ostensible effect on the defendants' ability to reach the area." *U.S. v. Olguin-Rivera*, 168 F.3d 1203, 1205 (10th Cir. 1999).

Eleventh Circuit

- "When an occupant of an automobile is the subject of a lawful arrest, the Fourth Amendment permits the arresting officers to contemporaneously conduct a warrantless search not only of the occupant himself but also of the passenger compartment of the automobile, as well as any closed (or open) containers found in this area of the automobile. Containers, in this context, refer to any object capable of holding another object and thus include an automobile's glove compartment (whether locked or unlocked), as well as any containers found therein, such as the zipped leather bag that was discovered in this case." *U.S. v. Gonzalez*, 71 F.3d 819, 825–26 (11th Cir. 1996).

§ 11:7   Protective searches of vehicles: When police have lawfully stopped a vehicle and have a reasonable suspicion that it contains weapons that may be dangerous to the officers, they may conduct a protective search of the passenger compartment

Supreme Court

- "In *New York v. Belton*, 453 U.S. 454, 101 S. Ct. 2860, 69 L. Ed. 2d 768 (1981), we held that when a police officer has made a lawful custodial arrest of an occupant of an automobile, the Fourth Amendment allows the officer to search the passenger compartment of that vehicle as a contemporaneous incident of arrest. . . . *Belton* governs even when an officer does not make contact until the person arrested has left the vehicle." *Thornton v. U.S.*, 541 U.S. 615, 124 S. Ct. 2127, 158 L. Ed. 2d 905 (2004).

- "In *Terry v. Ohio*, 392 U.S. 1, 88 S. Ct. 1868, 20 L. Ed. 2d 889 (1968), we upheld the validity of a protective search for weapons in the absence of probable cause to arrest because it is unreasonable to deny a police officer the right to neutralize the threat of physical harm when he possesses an articulable suspicion that an individual is armed and dangerous. We did not, however, expressly address whether such a protective search for weapons could extend to an area beyond the person in the absence of probable cause to arrest. [T]he police searched the passenger compartment because they had reason to believe that the vehicle contained weapons potentially dangerous to the officers. We hold that the protective search of the passenger compartment was reasonable under the principles articulated in *Terry* and other decisions of this Court." *Michigan v. Long*, 463 U.S. 1032, 1034–35, 103 S. Ct. 3469, 77 L. Ed. 2d 1201 (1983).

- "Our past cases indicate then that protection of police and others can justify protective searches when police have a reasonable belief that the suspect poses a danger, that roadside encounters between police and suspects are especially hazardous, and that danger may arise from the possible presence of weapons in the area surrounding a suspect. These principles compel our conclusion that the search of the passenger compartment of an automobile, limited to those areas in which a weapon may be placed or hidden, is permissible if the police officer possesses a reasonable belief based on specific and articulable facts which, taken together with the rational inferences from those facts, reasonably warrant the officers in believing that the suspect is dangerous and the suspect may gain immediate control of weapons." *Michigan v. Long*, 463 U.S. 1032, 1049, 103 S. Ct. 3469, 77 L. Ed. 2d 1201 (1983).

- "Therefore, the balancing required by *Terry* clearly weighs in favor of allowing the police to conduct an area search of the passenger compartment to uncover weapons, as long as they possess an articulable and objectively reasonable belief that the suspect is potentially dangerous." *Michigan v. Long*, 463 U.S. 1032, 1051, 103 S. Ct. 3469, 77 L. Ed. 2d 1201 (1983).

- "If, while conducting a legitimate *Terry* search of the interior of the automobile, the officer should, as here, discover contraband other than weapons, he clearly cannot be required to ignore the contraband, and the Fourth Amendment does not require its suppression in such circumstances." *Michigan v. Long*, 463 U.S. 1032, 1050, 103 S. Ct. 3469, 77 L. Ed. 2d 1201 (1983).

Fourth Circuit

- "[W]hether the police exercise control over an automobile sufficient to eliminate any exigencies may turn on a number of imponderable factors. Were the applicability of the automobile exception to turn on such factors, it would be hard for courts to administer the exception in a coherent and predictable manner. The result would be a series of finely spun legal distinctions that would render the exception difficult for police to follow in quickly developing situations." *U.S. v. Kelly*, 592 F.3d 586 (4th Cir. 2010).

- "The same officer-safety considerations that were applied in *Terry* and *Mimms* prompted the Court in *Michigan v. Long* . . . to hold that when a police officer lawfully stops a vehicle and possesses a reasonable belief based on specific and articulable facts . . . that the suspect is dangerous and . . . may gain immediate control of weapons, the officer may search the areas of the passenger compartment of the automobile where a weapon may be placed or hidden. . . . The Court based its reasoning in part on the reality that such stops involve an investigation at close range when the officer remains particularly vulnerable in part because a full custodial arrest has not been effected, and the officer must make a quick decision as to how to protect himself and others from possible danger. . . . Thus, in the context of a lawful automobile stop when the officer is presented with an objectively suspicious and potentially dangerous circumstance, the officer may conduct what amounts to a frisk of an automobile for weapons." *U.S. v. Sakyi*, 160 F.3d 164, 167–68 (4th Cir. 1998).

Fifth Circuit

- "We have recognized that [e]ach case involving the reasonableness of a *Terry* stop and frisk turns on its own facts. Several facts in the instant case demonstrate that the officers' search of the passenger compartment of [Defendant]'s car was reasonable under *Terry* and

Long. First, [The Officer] testified that [Defendant] and his wife both appeared extremely nervous and gave inconsistent explanations for their trip. Second, [The Officer] noticed a box of .9 millimeter bullets on the front floorboard of [Defendant]'s car. Finally, when [The Officer] asked [Defendant]'s wife where the gun was, she stated that she did not know, a remark [The Officer] interpreted to mean that there was a gun in the car. Based on these facts known to the officers at the time of the search, we hold that their conduct in searching the passenger compartment of [Defendant]'s vehicle for weapons was reasonable under the objective standard of *Terry* and *Long*." *U.S. v. Baker*, 47 F.3d 691, 694–95 (5th Cir. 1995).

Sixth Circuit

- "A court will determine if law enforcement officers had a reasonable, articulable suspicion of danger to justify a search of the areas of a motor vehicle that are immediately accessible to the driver based upon an examination of the individual factors, taken as a whole, and whether they give rise to reasonable suspicion, even if each individual factor is entirely consistent with innocent behavior when examined separately." *U.S. v. Shank*, 543 F.3d 309 (6th Cir. 2008).

Seventh Circuit

- "Under *Michigan v. Long* and its progeny, the dashboard of [Defendant]'s Mercedes fell within the area into which an arrestee might reach in order to grab a weapon. . .and thus the search was constitutional." *U.S. v. Mancillas*, 183 F.3d 682, 700, 52 Fed. R. Evid. Serv. 694 (7th Cir. 1999).

- "The approach of *Terry* was later applied to the context of a n officer's encounter with a motorist in which the officer has a reasonable belief, based on articulable suspicions, that the motorist is dangerous and may gain immediate control of weapons. In this context also, a search of the passenger compartment limited to those areas in which a weapon might be placed is permissible." *U.S. v. Burrows*, 48 F.3d 1011, 1015 (7th Cir. 1995).

Eighth Circuit

- "We also find that the search of the truck by the officers during the *Terry* stop passes constitutional muster. It is well established that once reasonable suspicion is established, a search of a vehicle's interior is permissible regardless of whether police officers have removed the occupants of the vehicle." *U.S. v. Navarrete-Barron*, 192 F.3d 786, 791 (8th Cir. 1999).

- "[T]he search of the passenger compartment of an automobile, limited to those areas in which a weapon may be placed or hidden, is permissible if the police officer possesses a reasonable belief based on specific and articulable facts, which taken together with the rational inferences from those facts, reasonably warrant the officer in believing that the suspect is dangerous and the suspect may gain immediate control of weapons." *U.S. v. Gleason*, 25 F.3d 605, 608 (8th Cir. 1994).

Tenth Circuit

- "Here, the officers reasonably concluded that the defendants were traveling together. In *Ybarra*, the officers were looking for drugs. Here the police suspected that one of the defendants was armed and dangerous. The defendants' conduct in failing to produce licenses or to pull over when signaled by the police gave the officers individualized suspicion of the other defendants. Perhaps most important, the police confronted the defendants in their cars, at night. Unlike the officers in *Ybarra*, the officers here could not tell whether the defendants had weapons on their persons or within reach. Although the officers had not been informed that the other defendants were dangerous, we believe that in this case a reasonably prudent man in the circumstances would be warranted in the belief that his safety was in danger. The reasonable belief that the defendants posed a danger justified the procedures in this case. The officers were entitled to display their weapons, to separate defendants from their vehicles, to conduct a pat down search, and to restrain the defendants with handcuffs until the officers had completed securing all the defendants." *U.S. v. Shareef*, 100 F.3d 1491, 1506 (10th Cir. 1996).

Eleventh Circuit

- "It is well established that officers conducting a traffic stop may take such steps as are reasonably necessary to protect their personal safety. . . .This includes conducting a protective search of the driver. . . .the passengers. . . .and the vehicle. . . . .The officer may seize any contraband, including weapons, in plain view. . . . .The officer may use a flash light to illuminate a vehicle's dark interior. . . .The officer may also prolong the detention to investigate the driver's license and the vehicle registration. . . .and may do so by requesting a computer check." *U.S. v. Purcell*, 236 F.3d 1274, 1277–78 (11th Cir. 2001).

- "A warrantless weapons search of a suspect and his car, pursuant to a limited detention, does not violate the Fourth Amendment if the police have reasonable articulable suspicion to justify such a limited detention. A *Terry* stop can also be used to investigate those suspected of being in the commission of a crime. Pursuant to a *Terry* stop, the police are entitled to search the passenger compartment of the detainee's vehicle for weapons." *Riley v. City of Montgomery, Ala.*, 104 F.3d 1247, 1250–51 (11th Cir. 1997).

§ 11:8 Global positioning systems (GPS): Attaching an electronic monitoring device to a vehicle constitutes a search under the Fourth Amendment

Supreme Court

- "The Fourth Amendment provides in relevant part that '[t]he right of the people to be secure in their persons, houses, papers, and effects, against unreasonable searches and seizures, shall not be violated.' It is beyond dispute that a vehicle is an 'effect' as that term is used in the Amendment. We hold that the Government's installation of a GPS device on a target's vehicle, and its use of that device to monitor the vehicle's movements, constitutes a 'search.' It is important to be clear about what occurred in this case: The Government physically occupied private property for the purpose of obtaining information." *U.S. v. Jones*, 565 U.S. 400, 132 S. Ct. 945, 949, 181 L. Ed. 2d 911 (2012) (citation omitted).

- "[T]he *Katz* reasonable-expectation-of-privacy test has been *added to,* not *substituted for,* the common-law trespassory test. . . . [W]e do not make trespass the exclusive test. Situations involving merely the transmission of electronic signals without trespass would *remain* subject to *Katz* analysis." *U.S. v. Jones,* 565 U.S. 400, 132 S. Ct. 945, 952–53, 181 L. Ed. 2d 911 (2012).

First Circuit

- "After the district court denied the motion to suppress [in this case], the Supreme Court decided *United States v. Jones,* which held that the Government's installation of a GPS device on a target's vehicle, and its use of that device to monitor the vehicle's movements, constitutes a search for Fourth Amendment purposes. The Justices all agreed that a search had occurred, but differed as to why. The five-Justice majority held that a search occurred because [t]he Government physically occupied private property for the purpose of obtaining information. The majority opinion emphasized that the government had committed a common-law trespass by installing the tracker on the defendant's car. Justice Sotomayor provided the fifth vote for that position because she agreed that a search occurs at a minimum where the government obtains information via physical intrusion, but wrote separately to caution that physical intrusion is now unnecessary to many forms of surveillance, and to suggest that some unique attributes of GPS surveillance . . . will require particular attention in future cases. Finally, Justice Alito, joined by Justices Ginsburg, Breyer, and Kagan, took issue with the majority's trespass-based approach but nevertheless found that a search had occurred under the reasonable-expectation-of-privacy test articulated in *Katz v. United States*. *Jones* thus establishes that the district court's reason for denying the suppression motion in this case— that the placement of the GPS device on the vehicle cannot be considered a search—is no longer sound. Consequently, this appeal turns on two questions that remain open after *Jones:* whether the kind of search recognized in *Jones* and conducted here requires a warrant (instead of mere probable cause or reasonable suspicion), and, if so, whether the resulting evidence can nevertheless avoid suppression under the good-faith exception to the exclusionary rule articulated in *Davis v. United States*. Here, we need not decide whether the government can show that GPS tracking is exempt from the basic rule that warrantless searches are per se unreasonable, because we agree with the government's alternative argument: even if the agents' use of the GPS tracker in this case was unconstitutional, their conduct fits within the good-faith exception to the exclusionary rule. Under that exception, as recently explicated in *Davis*, searches conducted in objectively reasonable reliance on binding appellate precedent are not subject to the exclusionary rule. In this case, suppression would be inappropriate because the agents' attachment and monitoring of the GPS tracker was authorized by settled, binding circuit precedent." *U.S. v. Sparks*, 711 F.3d 58, 61–63 (1st Cir. 2013) (inner quotations and citations omitted).

Fifth Circuit

- "[Defendant] argues that the warrantless placement and use of the GPS device to monitor the truck he was driving violated the Fourth Amendment. [Defendant] further argues that because this illegal GPS search directly led to the discovery of the drugs in his truck, the drugs must be suppressed under the 'fruit of the poisonous tree' doctrine. . . . We need not decide whether warrantless GPS searches are per se unreasonable. Furthermore, we need not decide whether the agents in this case acted without a warrant or whether the drug evidence is derived from the GPS search. Even assuming that a Fourth Amendment violation occurred and that suppression would otherwise be appropriate, the evidence should not be suppressed in this case because the officers acted in reasonable reliance on circuit precedent. . . . In December 2009, it was objectively reasonable for agents operating within the Fifth Circuit to believe that warrantless GPS tracking was permissible under circuit precedent. In United States v. Michael, 645 F.2d 252, 257 (5th Cir.1981) (en banc), this court held that 'reasonable suspicion is adequate to support warrantless beeper installation' on a

suspect's vehicle parked in a public place. . . . Despite
any possible technological differences between a 1981
'beeper' and the GPS device used in this case, the
functionality is sufficiently similar that the agents' reliance on Michael to install a GPS device on the truck, in
light of the reasonable suspicion of drug trafficking,
was objectively reasonable." *U.S. v. Andres*, 703 F.3d
828 (5th Cir. 2013).

Chapter 12

Container and Luggage Searches

Research References

West's Key Number Digest

Arrest ⟊71.1; Searches and Seizures ⟊13, 25 to 29, 50, 57 to 59,
62, 65

KeyCite®: Cases and other legal materials listed in KeyCite Scope can be
researched through the KeyCite service on Westlaw®. Use KeyCite to
check citations for form, parallel references, prior and later history, and
comprehensive citator information, including citations to other decisions
and secondary materials.

---

§ 12:1   Nonseizure: Some touching or moving of
containers does not constitute a seizure

Supreme Court

- "When a bus passenger places a bag in an overhead bin, he expects that other passengers or bus employees may move it for one reason or another. Thus, a bus passenger clearly expects that his bag may be handled. He does not expect that other passengers or bus employees will, as a matter of course, feel the bag in an exploratory manner. But this is exactly what the agent did here. We therefore hold that the agent's physical manipulation of petitioner's bag violated the Fourth Amendment." *Bond v. U.S.*, 529 U.S. 334, 338–39, 120 S. Ct. 1462, 146 L. Ed. 2d 365 (2000).

Sixth Circuit

- "[N]o seizure occurred here because the facts of the case reveal that there was no meaningful interference with defendant's possessory interest in his bag. The bag was moved only a short distance (from an open overhead compartment to the seat below), for a short time (just long enough for the dog to walk up and down the aisle), and the movement occurred at a time when defendant had left the bag unattended, so his access to it was never impaired. Finally, had the dog not indicated that the bag contained drugs, defendant would have been able to travel uninterrupted to the next stop with his bag. Because there was no meaningful interference with defendant's possessory interest in his bag, there was no seizure." *U.S. v. Gant*, 112 F.3d 239, 242, 1997 FED App. 0140P (6th Cir. 1997).
- "A number of cases have held that a passenger on a common carrier has no reasonable expectation of privacy in the exterior of his luggage or the airspace surrounding it. Because we conclude that defendant had no reasonable expectation of privacy in the exterior of his bag when it was on the open luggage rack of a commercial bus, we hold that [the Officer]'s initial touch of the exterior of defendant's bag was not an unreasonable search in violation of the Fourth Amendment." *U.S. v. Guzman*, 75 F.3d 1090, 1093, 1095, 1996 FED App. 0055P (6th Cir. 1996).

Seventh Circuit

- "As *Place* makes clear, a canine sniff does not expose non-contraband items within a bag to public view;

consequently such an inspection does not constitute a search within the meaning of the Fourth Amendment when the bag is in a public place." *U.S. v. Ward*, 144 F.3d 1024, 1031 (7th Cir. 1998).

- "Given the unfortunate realities of today's world, where law enforcement authorities must combat a steady influx of illicit drugs, as well as guard against possible terrorist incidents accomplished with devices ranging from simple handguns to sophisticated bombs, it is not surprising that over the last few decades our society has accepted increased security measures (e.g., hand-held metal detectors used to scan one's torso) at many locations such as airports, courthouses, hospitals, and even schools. In light of these realities, we agree with other courts of appeal that have held that the reasonable expectation of privacy inherent in the contents of luggage is not compromised by a police officer's physical touching of the exterior of luggage left exposed in the overhead rack of a bus." *U.S. v. McDonald*, 100 F.3d 1320, 1325 (7th Cir. 1996).

- "The Supreme Court has affirmed that a person possesses a privacy interest in the contents of personal luggage that is protected by the Fourth Amendment. However, it is generally recognized that the privacy interest of people who are in transit [i.e., on a bus, train, or airplane] on public thoroughfares is substantially less than those that attach to a fixed dwelling. Moreover, what one knowingly exposes to the public is not a subject of Fourth Amendment protection." *U.S. v. McDonald*, 100 F.3d 1320, 1324–25 (7th Cir. 1996).

Eighth Circuit

- "[E]xamining the outside of the package and then subjecting the package to a dog sniff as it sat at the rear of a delivery truck did not constitute a detention requiring a reasonable, articulable suspicion because, at that point, the officers had not delayed or otherwise interfered with the normal processing of the package. . . . [T]he detention occurred when the officers removed the package from the stream of mail in response to the dog's alert." *U.S. v. Vasquez*, 213 F.3d 425, 426–27, 55 Fed. R. Evid. Serv. 218 (8th Cir. 2000).

- "Individuals possess a privacy interest in the contents

of their personal luggage that is protected by the Fourth Amendment. . . . Of course, not every intrusion with an individual's luggage constitutes a search within the meaning of the Fourth Amendment. For example, a canine sniff of an individual's luggage does not constitute a search. . . . Similarly, no search occurs when an officer briefly moves luggage from the overhead compartment of a bus to the aisle in order to facilitate a canine sniff." *U.S. v. Gwinn*, 191 F.3d 874, 878 (8th Cir. 1999).

- "[T]he removal of the baggage from the overhead compartment was completely related to the lawful purpose for which the detective boarded the bus. After boarding the bus and seeing Jupp alert, the detective clearly had reasonable suspicion to conclude that narcotics were located somewhere in the overhead compartment. Passengers have no objective, reasonable expectation that their baggage will never be moved once placed in an overhead compartment. It is not uncommon for the bus driver or a fellow passenger to rearrange the baggage in the overhead compartment or to temporarily remove the baggage and place it in a seat or in the aisle in order to rearrange and maximize the use of limited compartment space." *U.S. v. Harvey*, 961 F.2d 1361, 1364 (8th Cir. 1992).

Ninth Circuit

- "Here [Defendant's] only interest was that the airline, as his bailee, would place his luggage on the next plane, which was to leave about two hours after his plane. The entire process of removing the luggage from the cart, taking it from one office to the other, and having the dog sniff it, was completed prior to the time the luggage would have been placed on the airplane. The airline did not give up custody of the luggage to the narcotics officers until after the dog had indicated the presence of narcotics. The appellant does not claim any constitutional violation on account of the actions of the officers after the dog indicated the presence of narcotics. Because nothing that the officers did interfered with the appellant's possessory interests in his luggage prior to the dog sniffing, there was no seizure of the luggage." *U.S. v. Johnson*, 990 F.2d 1129, 1132 (9th Cir. 1993).

Tenth Circuit

- "Travelers have a legitimate expectation of privacy in their personal luggage, which the Fourth Amendment protects. . . . That expectation of privacy, however, is not unlimited. . . . Not every investigative technique which reveals something about the contents of a traveler's luggage constitutes a search within the meaning of the Fourth Amendment. For example, a visual inspection of that which is in plain view does not constitute a search. . . . A dog sniff, which is so limited both in the manner in which the information is obtained and in the content of the information revealed by the procedure, is not a search. . . . Nor does a search occur where officials detect the odor of illegal drugs by using their own sense of smell. . . . Official actions, such as sniffs and field tests, which reveal only whether an illegal substance may be present and little else, compromise no legitimate expectation of privacy." *U.S. v. Nicholson*, 144 F.3d 632, 636 (10th Cir. 1998).

§ 12:2 Seizure: Reasonable suspicion that a container holds seizable items will justify a warrantless seizure of the container, which must be limited in scope

Supreme Court

- "The Fourth Amendment provides that the right of the people to be secure in their persons, houses, papers, and effects, against unreasonable searches and seizures, shall not be violated. . . . A traveler's personal luggage is clearly an effect protected by the Amendment." *Bond v. U.S.*, 529 U.S. 334, 336, 120 S. Ct. 1462, 146 L. Ed. 2d 365 (2000).

- "[T]he Government asks us to recognize the reasonableness under the Fourth Amendment of warrantless seizures of personal luggage from the custody of the owner on the basis of less than probable cause, for the purpose of pursuing a limited course of investigation, short of opening the luggage, that would quickly confirm or dispel the authorities' suspicion. Specifically, we are asked to apply the principles of *Terry v. Ohio* to permit such seizures on the basis of reasonable, articulable suspicion, premised on objective facts, that the luggage contains contraband or evidence of a crime. In our view, such application is appropriate." *U.S. v. Place*, 462 U.S. 696, 702, 103 S. Ct. 2637, 77 L. Ed. 2d 110 (1983).

- "[W]hen the police seize luggage from the suspect's custody, we think the limitations applicable to investigative detentions of the person should define the permissible scope of an investigative detention of the person's luggage on less than probable cause. Under this standard, it is clear that the police conduct here exceeded the permissible limits of a *Terry*-type investigative stop. The length of the detention of respondent's luggage alone precludes the conclusion that the seizure was reasonable in the absence of probable cause." *U.S. v. Place*, 462 U.S. 696, 708–09, 103 S. Ct. 2637, 77 L. Ed. 2d 110 (1983).

First Circuit

- "In determining whether it is reasonable to search a particular container for an object, search warrants and affidavits should be considered in a common sense manner, and hypertechnical readings should be avoided." *U.S. v. Rogers*, 521 F.3d 5 (1st Cir. 2008).

Sixth Circuit

- "Probable cause . . . can support the detention of property without a warrant, if the exigencies demand it or some other recognized exception to the warrant requirement is present. . . . In *Place*, the court applied the *Terry* stop exception to the warrant requirement, permitting seizures of personal luggage from the custody of the owner for the purpose of pursuing a limited course of investigation, based not on probable cause, but upon a reasonable, articulable suspicion, premised on objective facts, that the luggage contains contraband or evidence of a crime. . . . The Fourth Amendment, therefore, requires officers to have reasonable suspicion of criminal activity to detain temporarily for investigation either an individual or his belongings." *U.S. v. Avery*, 137 F.3d 343, 349, 1998 FED App. 0059A (6th Cir. 1997).

- "*Place* does not give blanket authority to base all seizures on no more than reasonable articulable suspicions; rather, *Place* allows courts to evaluate individual circumstances and decide whether reasonable articulable suspicions are all that is required to justify the seizure at issue." *U.S. v. Fifty-Three Thousand Eighty-Two Dollars in U.S. Currency, $53,082.00*, 985 F.2d 245, 249 (6th Cir. 1993).

- "The facts of *Place* present a substantially different type of privacy interest than is presently involved. In *Place*, government agents seized the defendant's luggage; whereas, in this case, the agents seized cash which claimants carried on their persons. Luggage is routinely subject to airport scrutiny unlike items carried on one's person. Obviously, the privacy interests in luggage are of a different order than the privacy interests in personal effects carried on the person. First, luggage is routinely x-rayed as part of airport security. Second, with respect to the luggage itself, as opposed to its contents, the person's possession of the luggage is open and public. One need only observe a person to determine whether he is in custody of luggage. Personal effects, however, are concealed on the possessor's person." *U.S. v. Fifty-Three Thousand Eighty-Two Dollars in U.S. Currency, $53,082.00*, 985 F.2d 245, 249 (6th Cir. 1993).

Seventh Circuit

- "Police officer's smelling of marijuana as he stood next to validly stopped vehicle alone was enough to give rise to probable cause to search entire vehicle, including closed garbage bag belonging to defendant, who was passenger in vehicle." *U.S. v. Mosby*, 541 F.3d 764 (7th Cir. 2008).

- "The Supreme Court has held that when the police seize luggage from the suspect's custody . . . the limitations applicable to investigative detentions of the person should define the permissible scope of an investigative detention of the person's luggage on less than probable cause. . . . Thus, the detention of a traveler's luggage must be supported by a reasonable belief, based on specific and articulable facts, that it contains contraband. . . . The detention itself must also be reasonable . . . an assessment that turns on the diligence of the authorities, the length of the detention, and the information conveyed to the suspect. . . ." *U.S. v. Ward*, 144 F.3d 1024, 1030 (7th Cir. 1998).

- "The officers' decision to detain [Defendant's] tote bag for a canine sniff was likewise justified. A narcotics detection dog would have quickly confirmed or dispelled the officers' suspicion that the bag contained narcotics without causing undue embarrassment or disturbing its other contents. Moreover, the proposed detention would have lasted no more than approximately fifteen minutes. Where the scope of the detention and the investigative technique employed is so carefully tailored to its underlying justification, there is no Fourth Amendment violation." *U.S. v. McCarthur*, 6 F.3d 1270, 1277–78, 39 Fed. R. Evid. Serv. 1126 (7th Cir. 1993).

Eighth Circuit

- "[I]f law enforcement's detention of checked luggage delays a passenger's travel or significantly impacts the passenger's freedom of movement, the Seizure Clause is implicated. . . . [A] commercial bus passenger has less possessory interest in checked luggage than he has in carry-on luggage in his immediate possession. . . . As long as law enforcement officers do not deprive the commercial carrier of its custody of the checked luggage, no meaningful interference with the passenger's checked luggage occurs. Boiling these principles down, we believe courts must focus on three factors when considering whether law enforcement's interference with checked luggage constitutes a seizure. First, did law enforcement's detention of the checked luggage delay a passenger's travel or significantly impact the passenger's freedom of movement? Second, did law enforcement's detention of the checked luggage delay its timely delivery? Third, did law enforcement's detention of the checked luggage deprive the carrier of its custody of the checked luggage? If none of these factors is satisfied, then no Fourth Amendment seizure has occurred. Conversely, if even a single factor is satisfied, then a Fourth Amendment seizure has occurred." *U.S. v. Va Lerie*, 424 F.3d 694 (8th Cir. 2005).
- "We agree with the line drawn by the Tenth Circuit. While a passenger can expect that others will perhaps push aside or briefly touch his bag in an attempt to accommodate their own luggage or to maximize storage space, we think that the majority of the traveling public

would not expect their luggage, even those pieces placed in an overhead compartment, to be subject to a calculated and thorough squeezing and manipulation of their exteriors. Unlike a canine sniff or the incidental touching that accompanies the moving of luggage from the overhead, the feeling and manipulation of a bag's exterior involves a much more intrusive and prolonged contact with the piece." *U.S. v. Gwinn*, 191 F.3d 874, 879 (8th Cir. 1999).

- "We begin by evaluating the issue of seizure. A seizure occurs when, in the totality of the circumstances surrounding the encounter, a reasonable person would believe that she is not free to leave. . . . Seizing luggage without asking consent, or in spite of a suspect's refusal to consent, or compelling a suspect to go to an interdiction room constitutes a show of authority and creates a reasonable belief that the suspect is not free to leave." *U.S. v. Pena-Saiz*, 161 F.3d 1175, 1177 (8th Cir. 1998).

- "Police officers must have either the owner's consent or a reasonable suspicion supported by articulable objective facts that the luggage contains drugs in order to detain a person's luggage for a sniff search." *U.S. v. Tillman*, 81 F.3d 773, 775 (8th Cir. 1996).

Ninth Circuit

- "The seizure of luggage from a traveler's possession intrudes on both the suspect's possessory interest in his luggage as well as his liberty interest in proceeding with his itinerary. Every minute that the detention continues exacerbates the intrusion on the luggage owner's liberty. Even if government agents were perfectly diligent, then, a seizure without probable cause could still last too long to pass muster under the Fourth Amendment. On the other hand, some detentions are clearly short enough that, so long as the government acts with diligence, no Fourth Amendment violation exists." *U.S. v. $191,910.00 in U.S. Currency*, 16 F.3d 1051, 1060 (9th Cir. 1994).

Tenth Circuit

- "The seizure of his briefcase, for the purpose of arranging its exposure to a narcotics detection dog, was permissible only if the officers at that time had reasonable articulable suspicion that the briefcase contained narcotics. A reasonable suspicion requires more than an inchoate and unparticularized suspicion or hunch. Whether officers had a reasonable suspicion justifying their action must be evaluated under the totality of the circumstances." *U.S. v. Carhee*, 27 F.3d 1493, 1497 (10th Cir. 1994).

§ 12:3   Search: Searches of closed containers normally require a warrant based upon probable cause

Supreme Court

- "The Fourth Amendment provides that the right of the people to be secure in their persons, houses, papers, and effects, against unreasonable searches and seizures, shall not be violated. . . . . A traveler's personal luggage is clearly an effect protected by the Amendment." *Bond v. U.S.*, 529 U.S. 334, 336, 120 S. Ct. 1462, 146 L. Ed. 2d 365 (2000).

- "Where law enforcement authorities have probable cause to believe that a container holds contraband or evidence of a crime, but have not secured a warrant, the Court has interpreted the [Fourth] Amendment to permit seizure of the property, pending issuance of a warrant to examine its contents, if the exigencies of the circumstances demand it or some other recognized exception to the warrant requirement is present." *U.S. v. Place*, 462 U.S. 696, 701, 103 S. Ct. 2637, 77 L. Ed. 2d 110 (1983).

- "[T]he general principle [is] that closed packages and containers may not be searched without a warrant." *U.S. v. Ross*, 456 U.S. 798, 812, 102 S. Ct. 2157, 72 L. Ed. 2d 572 (1982).

First Circuit

- "Although probable cause, as well as exigent circumstances, may support the warrantless seizure of an enclosed opaque container the same probable-cause showing is not necessarily sufficient to justify its subsequent warrantless search. These discrete treatments stem from the recognition that seizure temporarily deprives the defendant of a possessory interest only, whereas a search entails an intrusion upon privacy interests as well. Normally, therefore, once an exigency ends, as by an arrest or the seizure and custodial retention of a container by the police, a neutral judicial officer must authorize any subsequent search on a showing of probable cause." *U.S. v. Doe*, 61 F.3d 107, 111 (1st Cir. 1995).

- "The Customs agents did not act reasonably (hence they acted unconstitutionally) in taking x-rays of the luggage, rather than simply obtaining a search warrant." *U.S. v. Maldonado-Espinosa*, 968 F.2d 101, 103 (1st Cir. 1992).

Second Circuit

- "Under Fourth Amendment law a container need not be locked or fastened shut for there to be a legitimate expectation of privacy in its contents, though those facts are emphasized when they exist. The Supreme Court has rejected a constitutional distinction between worthy and unworthy containers and has noted that the Fourth Amendment provides protection to the owner of every container that conceals its contents from plain view. The often-stated requirement that a container need only be closed reflects the standard that for there to be a reasonable expectation of privacy, the contents of a container should not be apparent without opening. So long as the opaque file folders were closed or were in closed boxes, and did not reveal their contents, then a reasonable expectation of privacy continued even after they were stolen from defendants office." *U.S. v. Knoll*, 16 F.3d 1313, 1321 (2d Cir. 1994).

Third Circuit

- "The length of the detention of respondent's luggage alone precludes the conclusion that the seizure was reasonable in the absence of probable cause. Although we have recognized the reasonableness of seizures longer than momentary ones, the brevity of the invasion of the individual's Fourth Amendment interests is an important factor in determining whether the seizure is so minimally intrusive as to be justifiable on reasonable suspicion. Moreover, in assessing the effect of the length of the detention, we take into account whether the police diligently pursue their investigation. Thus, although we decline to adopt any outside time limitation for a permissible *Terry* stop, we have never approved a seizure of the person for the prolonged 90-minute period involved here and cannot do so on the facts presented by this case. Although the 90-minute detention of respondent's luggage is sufficient to render the seizure unreasonable, the violation was exacerbated by the failure of the agents to accurately inform respondent of the place to which they were transporting his luggage, of the length of time he might be dispossessed, and of what arrangements would be made for return of the luggage if the investigation dispelled the suspicion. In short, we hold that the detention of respondent's luggage in this case went beyond the narrow authority possessed by police to detain briefly luggage reasonably suspected to contain narcotics." *U.S. v. Frost*, 999 F.2d 737, 741–42 (3d Cir. 1993).

Fourth Circuit

- "We hold that when a container is within the immediate control of the defendant at the beginning of an encounter with law enforcement officers, and when the officers search the container at the scene of the arrest, the Fourth Amendment does not prohibit a reasonable delay, such as the one in this case, between the elimination of danger and the search." *U.S. v. Johnson*, 114 F.3d 435, 440, 47 Fed. R. Evid. Serv. 153 (4th Cir. 1997).

Fifth Circuit

- "Nor is this a case where the searching officers had reason to believe that the container contained a dangerous instrumentality such that opening the container was imperative for safety reasons. The drums were labeled as phosphoric acid, but the record does not indicate that they posed a hazard to anyone's safety. They were properly sealed and had been handled without mishap. The customs agents opened one of the drums to confirm their suspicions that drugs were inside. This was a search for evidence of a crime, not an effort to protect the safety of the officers and the SMT employees at the Brownsville terminal." *U.S. v. Villarreal*, 963 F.2d 770, 775 (5th Cir. 1992).

Eighth Circuit

- "The search took place at the station house about fifteen minutes after [Defendant] was arrested. This delay could be fatal if, for example, a large piece of luggage were opened and inspected without a warrant. . . . The timeliness requirement for luggage or other personal property not immediately associated with the person of the arrestee is, in other words, constitutionally fairly strict. . . . On the other hand, searches of the person and articles immediately associated with the person of the arrestee, are measured with a different, more flexible constitutional time clock. . . . Searches of the person and those articles immediately associated with the person may be made either at the time of arrest or when the accused arrives at the place of detention." *Curd v. City Court of Judsonia, Arkansas*, 141 F.3d 839, 843 (8th Cir. 1998).

Ninth Circuit

- "The fact that [defendant] stored his [gym bag, in which a shotgun was discovered during a search to which the defendant did not consent] under a bed, even though the bed was not exclusively under his control, strongly supports our conclusion that his expectation of privacy in the bag was reasonable... Quite simply, by placing his gym bag under the bed, [defendant] 'manifested an expectation that the contents would remain free from public examination.' ... We find that his expectation was reasonable. If the Fourth Amendment does not protect [defendant's] expectation of privacy in the contents of his bag, stored under the bed in an apartment where he sleeps and keeps his belongings, we find it difficult to imagine what the Fourth Amendment does protect." *U.S. v. Davis*, 332 F.3d 1163 (9th Cir. 2003).

- "A person has an expectation of privacy in his or her private, closed containers. . . . A person does not forfeit that expectation of privacy merely because the container is located in a place that is not controlled exclusively by the container's owner. . . . Thus, in *Welch*, we held that a person retained her expectations of privacy in her purse even though the purse was in a trunk of a car over which she and someone else both had control." *U.S. v. Fultz*, 146 F.3d 1102, 1105 (9th Cir. 1998).

Tenth Circuit

- "In *Florida v. Royer* . . . the United States Supreme Court addressed a situation where a defendant was requested to take his luggage from an airport concourse to an examination room approximately 40 feet away for the purposes of a drug inspection. In that case, unlike here, the officers had articulable suspicion to approach that particular defendant because he satisfied a drug courier profile. In the examination area, the defendant consented to a request to open his suitcase, at which time drugs were discovered. There, like here, the state neglected to get a search warrant first. The Court held that this was an illegal search, and it rejected the government's argument that the consent was voluntary because it had been induced by the government's conduct that was violative of the defendant's Fourth Amendment rights. . . . In short, a citizen's peaceful refusal to comply win an unlawful order cannot be used to justify the subsequent search." *U.S. v. Garzon*, 119 F.3d 1446, 1451 (10th Cir. 1997).

D.C. Circuit

- "First, the plastic bag was transparent. Second, he hid the bag in the passenger area of a commercial bus. Because [Defendant's] luggage was transparent, he could have no expectation of privacy in the bag itself. While a traveler who carries a toothbrush and a few articles of clothing in a paper bag or knotted scarf may claim an equal right to conceal his possessions from official inspection as the sophisticated executive with the locked attache case, the fourth amendment provides protection to the owner of only a container that conceals its contents from plain view." *U.S. v. Ramos*, 960 F.2d 1065, 1067 (D.C. Cir. 1992).

§ 12:4 **Automobiles: The automobile exception will justify a warrantless search of containers in automobiles if the evidence for which there is probable cause to search the vehicle might be secreted in such containers**

Supreme Court

- "In many cases, as when a recent occupant is arrested

for a traffic violation, there will be no reasonable basis
to believe the vehicle contains relevant evidence. (citations omitted) But in others, including *Belton* and
Thornton, the offense of arrest will supply a basis for
searching the passenger compartment of an arrestee's
vehicle and any containers therein." *Arizona v. Gant,*
556 U.S. 332, 129 S. Ct. 1710, 173 L. Ed. 2d 485, 47
A.L.R. Fed. 2d 657 (2009).

- "[N]either *Ross* itself nor the historical evidence it relied
upon admits of a distinction among packages or containers based on ownership. When there is probable cause
to search for contraband in a car, it is reasonable for
police officers—like customs officials in the Founding
era—to examine packages and containers without a
showing of individualized probable cause for each one.
A passenger's personal belongings, just like the driver's
belongings or containers attached to the car like a glove
compartment, are in the car, and the officer has probable cause to search for contraband in the car. . . . Passengers, no less than drivers, possess a reduced expectation of privacy with regard to the property that they
transport in cars, which trave[l] public thoroughfares
. . . seldom serve as . . . the repository of personal effects . . . are subjected to police stop and examination
to enforce pervasive governmental controls as an everyday occurrence . . . and, finally, are exposed to traffic
accidents that may render all their contents open to
public scrutiny." *Wyoming v. Houghton,* 526 U.S. 295,
302–03, 119 S. Ct. 1297, 143 L. Ed. 2d 408 (1999).

- "[T]he *Sanders* majority stressed the heightened privacy
expectation in personal luggage and concluded that the
presence of luggage in an automobile did not diminish
the owner's expectation of privacy in his personal items.
[T]his Court in *Ross* took the critical step of saying that
closed containers in cars could be searched without a
warrant because of their presence within the
automobile. Despite the protection that *Sanders* purported to extend to closed containers, the privacy interest in those closed containers yielded to the broad scope
of an automobile search." *California v. Acevedo,* 500
U.S. 565, 572, 111 S. Ct. 1982, 114 L. Ed. 2d 619 (1991).

- "Because the Customs officers had probable cause to
believe that the pickup trucks contained contraband,

any expectation of privacy in the vehicles or their contents was subject to the authority of the officers to conduct a warrantless search. The warrantless search of the packages was not unreasonable merely because the Customs officers returned to Tucson and placed the packages in a DEA warehouse rather than immediately opening them. . . . Inasmuch as the Government was entitled to seize the packages and could have searched them immediately without a warrant, we conclude that the warrantless search three days after the packages were placed in the DEA warehouse was reasonable and consistent with our precedent involving searches of impounded vehicles." *U.S. v. Johns*, 469 U.S. 478, 486–88, 105 S. Ct. 881, 83 L. Ed. 2d 890 (1985).

- "If probable cause justifies the search of a lawfully stopped vehicle, it justifies the search of every part of the vehicle and its contents that may conceal the object of the search." *U.S. v. Ross*, 456 U.S. 798, 825, 102 S. Ct. 2157, 72 L. Ed. 2d 572 (1982).

- "The scope of a warrantless [automobile] search based on probable cause is no narrower—and no broader—than the scope of a search authorized by a warrant supported by probable cause. Only the prior approval of the magistrate is waived; the search otherwise is as the magistrate could authorize. The scope of a warrantless search of an automobile thus is not defined by the nature of the container in which the contraband is secreted. Rather, it is defined by the object of the search and the places in which there is probable cause to believe that it may be found. Just as probable cause to believe that a stolen lawnmower may be found in a garage will not support a warrant to search an upstairs bedroom, probable cause to believe that undocumented aliens are being transported in a van will not justify a warrantless search of a suitcase." *U.S. v. Ross*, 456 U.S. 798, 823–24, 102 S. Ct. 2157, 72 L. Ed. 2d 572 (1982).

Fourth Circuit

- "This court has held that the odor of marijuana, without more, may provide requisite probable cause to support the warrantless search of a vehicle and baggage contained in that vehicle." *U.S. v. Lesane*, 361 Fed. Appx. 537 (4th Cir. 2010).

- "The police may search an automobile and the containers within it where they have probable cause to believe contraband or evidence is contained. Probable cause exists where, given all the facts at the time of the search, there is a fair probability that contraband or evidence of a crime will be found in a particular place." *U.S. v. Ford*, 88 F.3d 1350, 1358, 45 Fed. R. Evid. Serv. 174 (4th Cir. 1996).

Fifth Circuit

- "Finally, the officers were justified in opening the liquor box containing cocaine, due to their probable cause to believe that drugs were located in the car, which extended to the entire vehicle and all containers found therein." *U.S. v. Seals*, 987 F.2d 1102, 1107 (5th Cir. 1993).

Seventh Circuit

- "Under the automobile exception to the warrant requirement of the Fourth Amendment, law enforcement officers may search an automobile without a warrant when they have probable cause to believe that the vehicle contains contraband or evidence of criminality. The scope of the search may extend to all parts of the vehicle in which contraband or evidence could be concealed, including closed compartments and trunks." *U.S. v. Ortiz*, 84 F.3d 977, 983 (7th Cir. 1996).

Eighth Circuit

- "A warrantless search of an automobile for contraband is allowed under the Fourth Amendment if an officer has probable cause to justify the search, or if the officer has obtained voluntary consent, provided that the search is limited to the scope of the consent, ... Observations made by an officer during a consensual search of a vehicle may provide the officer with probable cause to expand the scope of the search under the automobile exception. 'Probable cause exists when, given the totality of the circumstances, a reasonable person could believe there is a fair probability that contraband or evidence of a crime would be found in a particular place.' Probable cause is a 'practical and common-sensical standard' that is based on 'the totality of the circumstances' and requires only 'the kind of fair probability on which reasonable and prudent people, not legal technicians, act.' Moreover, '[i]f probable cause justifies the search of a lawfully stopped vehicle, it justifies the search of every part of the vehicle and its contents that may conceal the object of the search,' . . .. In determining whether probable cause exists, an officer 'may draw inferences based on his own experience.' . . .Allen began his search pursuant to Arredondo's voluntary consent, which entitled Allen to search all areas of the truck, including the passenger compartment where the air compressor was located. Allen's detection of the odor of fresh paint, his unimpeded observation of fresh paint on the air compressor's tank and the rough, jagged, non-factory welds on the motor-attaching bracket and on the air tank itself, gave him probable cause to believe 'that contraband or evidence of a crime [was] present.' . . .The totality of the circumstances—coupled with Allen's training and experience in 'hundreds' of drug investigations—provided 'a fair probability' from the moment Allen observed the air compressor that the truck held 'contraband or evidence of a crime.' . . . Accordingly, under the automobile exception to the warrant requirement, Allen was permitted to search 'every part of the vehicle and its contents' that could conceal drug-related contraband, including the air compressor." *United States v. Murillo-Salgado*, 854 F.3d 407, 417–18 (8th Cir. 2017), petition for certiorari filed (U.S. July 19, 2017) (citations omitted).

- "Prior to entering the van, [the officer] asked [Defendant] if any items that he had described to [Defendant] as being connected to the robbery—a blue button-down shirt, a ball cap, a large amount of money, and a weapon—were in the van. [Defendant] told him that there was a gun in the center console. . . . [The officer's] search of the closed green bag where he found the black baseball cap, black t-shirt, blue denim long-sleeved t-shirt, and $4562.00 was proper for at least the reason that the green bag was in the van when [the officer] conducted the second search [of the van]." *U.S. v. Farnell*, 701 F.3d 256, 264 (8th Cir. 2012).

- "The law is clear that officers may search the passenger

compartment of an automobile and examine the contents of any containers found within the passenger compartment when they have made a lawful custodial arrest of the occupant of an automobile." *U.S. v. Williams*, 165 F.3d 1193, 1195 (8th Cir. 1999).

- "Once the officers discovered the three packages of drugs in the passenger compartment, they had probable cause to search the remainder of the automobile. This probable cause allowed them to search every part of the vehicle and any containers therein that could have concealed the object of the officer's search, namely, more drugs. Because the safe in the trunk certainly was large enough to contain more drugs, the officers could have immediately opened it during their search. They also could have opened it later at the station, as they indeed did." *U.S. v. Riedesel*, 987 F.2d 1383, 1391–92 (8th Cir. 1993).

Ninth Circuit

- "The Supreme Court in *United States v. Johns* . . . refused to hold that police must immediately search all containers and packages discovered during a warrantless vehicle search. This result would be of little benefit to the person whose property is searched, and where police officers are entitled to seize the container and continue to have probable cause to believe that it contains contraband, we do not think that delay in the execution of the warrantless search is necessarily unreasonable. . . . . Whereas the contents of most containers can be examined with relative ease at the scene, videotapes and film require specialized equipment and often take many hours to view. The justification for postponing examination is thus stronger for tapes and film than for ordinary closed containers. When there is probable cause to suspect that videotapes and film contain evidence of a crime, they need not be viewed at the scene of the search. As *Johns* also held, however, the delay must be reasonable in light of all the circumstances." *U.S. v. Albers*, 136 F.3d 670, 674, 1998 A.M.C. 1017 (9th Cir. 1998), as amended on denial of reh'g, (Mar. 20, 1998).

Tenth Circuit

- "In the context of vehicle searches, a warrantless search is permissible if there is probable cause to believe that the vehicle contains contraband. . . .In addition, if there is probable cause to search a vehicle, the police are allowed to search any package within the vehicle that is capable of concealing the object of the search." *U.S. v. Edwards*, 242 F.3d 928, 939 (10th Cir. 2001), superseded, 632 F.3d 633 (10th Cir. 2001).

- "[W]here an officer legitimately stops a car, and has probable cause to believe drugs are concealed in that car, he may conduct a warrantless search of the car and the containers within it that could conceal the object of the search. Similarly, the Tenth Circuit stated that [o]nce probable cause exists for a search, the police have authority to search the entire vehicle. Furthermore, the United States Supreme Court has stated that, [i]f probable cause justifies the search of a lawfully stopped vehicle, it justifies the search of every part of the vehicle and its contents that may conceal the object of the search. Accordingly, the Tenth Circuit and the United States Supreme Court have made it clear that [w]hen a legitimate search is underway nice distinctions between glove compartments, upholstered seats, trunks, and wrapped packages must give way to the interest in the prompt and efficient completion of the task at hand." *U.S. v. Nielsen*, 9 F.3d 1487, 1489 (10th Cir. 1993).

§ 12:5 Other exceptions: The search incident to arrest, exigent circumstances and plain view doctrines may obviate the need to secure a warrant to search containers

Supreme Court

- "[T]he protection afforded by the [Fourth] Amendment varies in different settings. The luggage carried by a traveler entering the country may be searched at random by a customs officer; the luggage may be searched no matter how great the traveler's desire to conceal the contents may be. A container carried at the time of arrest often may be searched without a warrant and even without any specific suspicion concerning its contents." *U.S. v. Ross*, 456 U.S. 798, 823, 102 S. Ct. 2157, 72 L. Ed. 2d 572 (1982).

- "[W]hen a policeman has made a lawful custodial arrest of the occupant of an automobile, he may, as a contemporaneous incident of that arrest, search the passenger compartment of that automobile. It follows from this conclusion that the police may also examine the contents of any containers found within the passenger compartment, for if the passenger compartment is within reach of the arrestee, so also will containers in it be within his reach. Such a container may, of course, be searched whether it is open or closed, since the justification for the search is not that the arrestee has no privacy interest in the container, but that the lawful custodial arrest justifies the infringement of any privacy interest the arrestee may have." *New York v. Belton*, 453 U.S. 454, 460–61, 101 S. Ct. 2860, 69 L. Ed. 2d 768 (1981).

First Circuit

- "Marine enforcement officers acted reasonably in searching containers on vessel, based on consent given by owner of vessel, where containers were not locked, nor were they identified as anyone else's personal property, and no one advised officers at the time of the search that the containers were not the property of the vessel owner." *U.S. v. Carrasco*, 540 F.3d 43 (1st Cir. 2008).

Second Circuit

- "We consider whether the government may employ random, suspicionless container searches in order to safeguard mass transportation facilities from terrorist attack. The precise issue before us is whether one such search regime, implemented on the New York City subway system, satisfies the special needs exception to the Fourth Amendment's usual requirement of individualized suspicion. We hold that it does . . . . (W)e expressly hold that the special needs doctrine does not require, as a threshold matter, that the subject of the search possess a reduced privacy interest. Instead, once the government establishes a special need, the nature of the privacy interest is a factor to be weighed in the balance . . . Where, as here, a search program is designed and implemented to seek out concealed explosives in order to safeguard a means of mass transportation from terrorist attack, it serves a special need . . . (T)he Program is reasonable, and therefore constitutional, because (1) preventing a terrorist attack on the subway is a special need; (2) that need is weighty; (3) the Program is a reasonably effective deterrent; and (4) even though the searches intrude on a full privacy interest, they do so to a minimal degree." *MacWade v. Kelly*, 460 F.3d 260 (2d Cir. 2006).

- "That the defendant did not—and probably could not— know what the officer was looking for does not change our view of his consent. It is self-evident that a police officer seeking general permission to search a vehicle is looking for evidence of illegal activity. It is just as obvious that such evidence might be hidden in closed containers. If the consent to search is entirely open-ended, a reasonable person would have no cause to believe that the search will be limited in some way." *U.S. v. Snow*, 44 F.3d 133, 135 (2d Cir. 1995).

Third Circuit

- "Defendant voluntarily abandoned any interest in his bedroom safe through his repeated denials of ownership of it, and thus, agents did not need a search warrant or consent to validly search it where agents received consent to search the defendant's bedroom from defendant's." *U.S. v. Anderson*, 284 Fed. Appx. 977 (3d Cir. 2008).

Fourth Circuit

- "The *Edwards* Court held that, once the justification for a search incident to arrest is established, a delay before the search does not render the search invalid: In *Edwards'* wake, this and other courts of appeals consistently upheld container searches even if they occurred after delays and the suspects no longer could reach the containers' contents." *U.S. v. Han*, 74 F.3d 537, 542 (4th Cir. 1996).
- "Courts have drawn a distinction between the plain view seizure of a container and the subsequent search of that container, because its seizure under the plain view doctrine does not compromise the interest in preserving the privacy of its contents, while its search does. As a consequence, to protect the privacy interest

of the contents of a container, courts will allow a search of a container following its plain view seizure only where the contents of a seized container are a foregone conclusion. The court in *Corral* reasoned that when a container is not closed, or transparent, or when its distinctive configuration proclaims its contents, the container supports no reasonable expectation of privacy and the contents can be said to be in plain view. In determining whether the contents of a container are a foregone conclusion, the circumstances under which an officer finds the container may add to the apparent nature of its contents." *U.S. v. Williams*, 41 F.3d 192, 197 (4th Cir. 1994).

Fifth Circuit

- "The Supreme Court has offered gun cases and burglar kits as examples of containers the distinctive characteristics of which proclaim their contents. We have been careful to construe this exception narrowly, however, so as not to embroil ourselves in the task of categorizing containers on the basis of what they typically contain. We have said that camera bags and hunting boxes fall beyond the scope of the exception, since their contents cannot be inferred simply by looking at them." *U.S. v. Villarreal*, 963 F.2d 770, 776 (5th Cir. 1992).

Seventh Circuit

- "A person may possess a privacy interest in the contents of personal luggage. However, that privacy interest can be forfeited where the person abandons the luggage. Fourth Amendment protection does not extend to abandoned property." *U.S. v. Rem*, 984 F.2d 806, 810 (7th Cir. 1993).

Eighth Circuit

- "Morgan had no reasonable expectation of privacy when he voluntarily displayed his cell-phone screen in the presence of the detectives. . . . Morgan believes that the plain-view doctrine applies only if: (1) the officer is in a lawful position to view the evidence, (2) the officer discovers the incriminating evidence inadvertently, and (3) the incriminating nature of the evidence is immediately apparent. Morgan contends the last two conditions are not satisfied. This contention conflates the plain-view doctrine for seizures with the plain-view doctrine for searches. An officer does not violate the Fourth Amendment by viewing evidence from a position he lawfully occupies, remembering it, and using it later. Observing what is in plain sight does not implicate the additional requirements for a seizure; being in a lawful position to observe evidence is sufficient." *United States v. Morgan*, 842 F.3d 1070, 1074 (8th Cir. 2016), cert. denied, 137 S. Ct. 2176, 198 L. Ed. 2d 244 (2017) (citations omitted).

- "Defendant relinquished his reasonable expectation of privacy over handgun by abandoning it under a tree." *U.S. v. Richardson*, 537 F.3d 951 (8th Cir. 2008).
- "The warrantless search of abandoned property does not constitute an unreasonable search and does not violate the Fourth Amendment." *U.S. v. James*, 534 F.3d 868 (8th Cir. 2008).
- "The warrantless search of an automobile, predicated on consent, may be expanded beyond the scope of the consent when it yields a basis for a reasonable articulable suspicion that additional contraband may be found in parts of the car not included in the consent." *U.S. v. Alverez*, 235 F.3d 1086, 1089 (8th Cir. 2000).
- "The search took place at the station house about fifteen minutes after [Defendant] was arrested. This delay could be fatal if, for example, a large piece of luggage were opened and inspected without a warrant. . . . The timeliness requirement for luggage or other personal property not immediately associated with the person of the arrestee is, in other words, constitutionally fairly strict. . . . On the other hand, searches of the person and articles immediately associated with the person of the arrestee, are measured with a different, more flexible constitutional time clock. . . . Searches of the person and those articles immediately associated with the person may be made either at the time of arrest or when the accused arrives at the place of detention." *Curd v. City Court of Judsonia, Arkansas*, 141 F.3d 839, 843 (8th Cir. 1998).

Ninth Circuit

- "With respect to the physical scope of the search, we

have held that a search incident to arrest may encompass a room from which the arrestee has been removed. We have also held that a search incident to arrest may justify the opening of containers found within the physical area covered by the search. The rationale for searches of open or closed containers is not that the arrestee has no privacy interest in the container, but that the lawful custodial arrest justifies the infringement of any privacy interest the arrestee may have." *U.S. v. Hudson*, 100 F.3d 1409, 1419–20 (9th Cir. 1996).

- "There can be no reasonable expectation of privacy in a container if its contents can be discerned from its outward appearance." *U.S. v. Huffhines*, 967 F.2d 314, 319 (9th Cir. 1992).

Eleventh Circuit

- "A briefcase is often the repository for more than business documents. Rather, it is the extension of one's own clothing because it serves as a larger pocket in which such items as wallets and credit cards, address books, personal calendar/diaries, correspondence, and reading glasses often are carried. Few places outside one's home justify a greater expectation of privacy than does the briefcase. Nonetheless, as with other property subject to Fourth Amendment protection, a briefcase can be abandoned, causing a forfeiture of such rights." *U.S. v. Ramos*, 12 F.3d 1019, 1024 (11th Cir. 1994).

D.C. Circuit

- "[A]s a rule, even when officers may lawfully seize a package, they must obtain a warrant before examining its contents. [citations omitted] However, [in *Arkansas v. Sanders*,] the Supreme Court . . . suggested an important exception [to that rule by noting that] . . . 'some containers (for example[,] a kit of burglar tools or a *gun case*) by their very nature cannot support any reasonable expectation of privacy because their contents can be inferred from their outward appearance.' [citation omitted; emphasis added in court's opinion] . . . *Sanders* decided which of two principles took precedence: the requirement that officers obtain a warrant before opening a package, as described in *United States v. Chadwick* [citation omitted], or the 'automobile

exception' to the warrant requirement, as described in
Carroll v. United States [citation omitted]. . . . . [T]he
Sanders majority suggested that with some packages,
the precedence question would be moot, as there would
be no reasonable expectation of privacy as to the
contents in the first place. Addressing only those packages that sufficiently concealed their contents, *Sanders*
held that the *Chadwick* rule took precedence. The Court
later reversed course in *California v. Acevedo*, overturn-
ing *Sanders* with regard to the precedence order of the
two rules[;] . . . *Acevedo*[, however,] did not address
the . . . proposed exception [noted by the Court in
Sanders]. [citation omitted] . . . This court . . . adopted
the *Sanders* dictum as the law of the circuit in *United
States v. Ross* [citation omitted] (*Ross I*). . . . Foreshad-
owing *Acevedo*, the Supreme Court[, in '*Ross II*',]
overturned *Ross I*, holding that where an officer has
probable cause to search a closed container in an
automobile, the officer may open the container even
without a warrant. [citation omitted] However, *Ross II*
in no way undercut the *Sanders* dictum; indeed, the
Court recited that rule in a footnote [citation omitted]
and based much of its analysis on the plurality opinion
in *Robbins v. California*, which was limited to 'container[s] that conceal [their] contents from plain view.' [cita-
tion omitted] . . . Thus, the *Sanders* exception remains
the law in this circuit, *Ross II* notwithstanding. We accordingly reaffirm that gun cases and similar containers support no reasonable expectation of privacy if their
contents can be inferred from their outward appearance.
Applying this rule, we reject [defendant]'s argument
regarding the gun case and hence affirm the district
court's order denying his motion to suppress the gun."
U.S. v. Taylor, 497 F.3d 673, 679–681 (D.C. Cir. 2007).

• "Because [Defendant's] luggage was transparent, he
could have no expectation of privacy in the bag itself.
While a traveler who carries a toothbrush and a few
articles of clothing in a paper bag or knotted scarf [may]
claim an equal right to conceal his possessions from official inspection as the sophisticated executive with the
locked attache case, the fourth amendment provides
protection to the owner of only a container that conceals
its contents from plain view. Therefore, unless some at-

tribute of the crevice into which [Defendant] stuffed the plastic bag made it reasonable for him to expect that it would remain private, he had no fourth amendment protection against the search that brought it to light." *U.S. v. Ramos*, 960 F.2d 1065, 1067 (D.C. Cir. 1992).

§ 12:6 Inventory: When a vehicle is impounded, closed containers may be opened under the rationale of inventory searches. Closed containers may be searched under the rationale of inventory searches when an arrestee is booked into jail

Supreme Court

• "The Court today holds that police officers may open closed containers while conducting a routine inventory search of an impounded vehicle. I join the Court's opinion, but write separately to underscore the importance of having such inventories conducted only pursuant to standardized police procedures." *Colorado v. Bertine*, 479 U.S. 367, 376, 107 S. Ct. 738, 93 L. Ed. 2d 739 (1987).

• "At the stationhouse, it is entirely proper for police to remove and list or inventory property found on the person or in the possession of an arrested person who is to be jailed. A range of governmental interests support an inventory process. A standardized procedure for making a list or inventory as soon as reasonable after reaching the stationhouse not only deters false claims but also inhibits theft or careless handling of articles taken from the arrested person. Arrested persons have also been known to injure themselves—or others—with belts, knives, drugs or other items on their person while being detained. Dangerous instrumentalities—such as razor blades, bombs, or weapons—can be concealed in innocent-looking articles taken from the arrestee's possession. Finally, inspection of an arrestee's personal property may assist the police in ascertaining or verifying his identity. Applying these principles, we hold that it is not unreasonable for police, as part of the routine procedure incident to incarcerating an arrested person, to search any container or article in his possession, in accordance with established inventory procedures."

711

Illinois v. Lafayette, 462 U.S. 640, 646, 103 S. Ct. 2605, 77 L. Ed. 2d 65 (1983).

Second Circuit

- "[W]hen the authorities have come into possession of a container lawfully, it is reasonable, within the meaning of the Fourth Amendment, for them to conduct an inventory search of the container. . . . Lost property found by the police or found property turned over to the police is in the lawful possession of the police. . . ." *Gudema v. Nassau County*, 163 F.3d 717, 722 (2d Cir. 1998).

- "The police thus had authority to inventory [Defendant's] possessions for safe-keeping while he was in custody. Our inquiry is not over, however, because the right to inventory a suspect's belongings does not carry in its wake unlimited discretion. Instead, the inventory must be conducted pursuant to established inventory procedures. Particularly when closed containers are involved, the police are required to have an established policy regarding the containers, so that the inventory does not become a ruse for a general rummaging in order to discover incriminating evidence. Although the policy need not be in writing, there must be a standardized procedure." *U.S. v. Griffiths*, 47 F.3d 74, 78 (2d Cir. 1995).

- "[L]aw enforcement officials may open closed containers as part of an inventory search so long as they act in good faith pursuant to standardized criteria or established routine. The existence of such a valid procedure may be proven by reference to either written rules and regulations, or testimony regarding standard practices. Although the procedure must not be a pretext for a general rummaging in order to discover incriminating evidence, it may allow the searching officers sufficient discretion in deciding whether or not to open a specific container." *U.S. v. Thompson*, 29 F.3d 62, 65–66 (2d Cir. 1994).

Third Circuit

- "A decision to impound a vehicle contrary to a standardized procedure or even in the absence of a standardized procedure is not a per se violation of the

Fourth Amendment." *U.S. v. Smith*, 522 F.3d 305 (3d Cir. 2008).

Fourth Circuit

- "To be valid, inventory search must be conducted according to standardized criteria, such as uniform police department policy. For inventory search of vehicle to be lawful, the vehicle searched must be in lawful custody of police. If a motor vehicle is in lawful custody, the police may inventory the vehicle, if such inventories are routine and conducted pursuant to standard police procedures, as long as the purpose of the inventory is to secure the vehicle or its contents and not to gather incriminating evidence against the owner." *U.S. v. Murphy*, 552 F.3d 405 (4th Cir. 2009).

Fifth Circuit

- "In *Wells* the majority observed that it would be permissible to allow the opening of closed containers whose contents officers determine they are unable to ascertain from examining the containers' exteriors. The allowance of the exercise of judgment based on concerns related to the purposes of an inventory search does not violate the Fourth Amendment." *U.S. v. Andrews*, 22 F.3d 1328, 1336 (5th Cir. 1994).

Sixth Circuit

- "It is settled law that the police may conduct an inventory search of an automobile that is being impounded without running afoul of the Fourth Amendment. 'In order to be deemed valid, an inventory search may not be undertaken for purposes of investigation, and it must be conducted according to standard police procedures.' A general written inventory policy does not grant officers carte blanche when conducting a search; rather, it must be sufficiently tailored to only produce an inventory. Thus, '[i]n conducting an inventory search, officers do not enjoy their accustomed discretion; they simply follow the applicable policy.' 'Nonetheless, officers may exercise some judgment based on concerns related to the purposes of an inventory search; for example, they may decide to open particular containers if they cannot determine the contents.' 'When a legitimate search is underway, and when its purpose and its limits have been precisely defined, nice distinctions between closets, drawers, and containers, in the case of a home, or between glove compartments, upholstered seats, trunks, and wrapped packages, in the case of a vehicle, must give way to the interest in the prompt and efficient completion of the task at hand.' " *U.S. v. Jackson*, 682 F.3d 448, 455 (6th Cir. 2012) (citations omitted).

Seventh Circuit

- "[W]ithin the constraints of the policy/procedure, officers may exercise discretion in deciding whether or not to open a particular container. . . . A police officer may be allowed sufficient latitude to determine whether a particular container should or should not be opened in light of the nature of the search and characteristics of the container itself. Thus, while policies of opening all containers or of opening no containers are unquestionably permissible, it would be equally permissible, for example, to allow the opening of closed containers whose contents officers determine they are unable to ascertain from examining the containers' exteriors. The allowance of the exercise of judgment based on concerns related to the purposes of an inventory search does not violate the Fourth Amendment." *U.S. v. Lozano*, 171 F.3d 1129, 1132 (7th Cir. 1999).

- "Inventory searches serve to protect an owner's property while it is in the custody of the police, to insure against claims of lost, stolen, or vandalized property, and to guard the police from danger. . . . Generally, reasonable police regulations relating to inventory procedures administered in good faith satisfy the Fourth Amendment. . . . As for closed containers, so long as standardized criteria or established routines exist regarding the opening of closed containers, searching such containers is permissible. . . . The existence of a police policy, however, does not necessarily eviscerate officers' discretion in deciding whether to search a particular container." *U.S. v. Richardson*, 121 F.3d 1051, 1055 (7th Cir. 1997).

- "[P]olice may search the contents of a vehicle so long as standardized criteria or established routine exist regarding the opening of containers. The procedure should direct officers to inventory the contents of an impounded item and should not be a disguise for general rummaging in order to discover incriminating evidence. However, within the constraints of the policy/procedure, officers may exercise discretion in deciding whether or not to open a particular container." *U.S. v. Wilson*, 938 F.2d 785, 788 (7th Cir. 1991).

Eighth Circuit

- "Inventory searches may be conducted without a warrant or probable cause to search, so long as they are reasonable under the totality of the circumstances. An inventory search protects an owner's property while in police custody as well as protecting the police from danger and from subsequent claims about stolen property. Officers have broad authority to conduct inventory searches of items 'found on the person or in the possession of an arrested person who is to be jailed.' Examining 'all the items removed from the arrestee's person or possession and listing or inventorying them is an entirely reasonable administrative procedure.'" *U.S. v. Allen*, 713 F.3d 382, 387-88 (8th Cir. 2013) (citations omitted).

Ninth Circuit

- "Whether an impoundment of a vehicle is warranted under the community caretaking doctrine depends on the location of the vehicle and the police officer's duty to prevent it from creating a hazard to other drivers or from being a target for vandalism or theft." *U.S. v. Caseres*, 533 F.3d 1064 (9th Cir. 2008).

Chapter 13

Inventory Searches

Research References

West's Key Number Digest
Arrest ⬤⇒71.1; Searches and Seizures ⬤⇒58, 66

KeyCite®: Cases and other legal materials listed in KeyCite Scope can be
researched through the KeyCite service on Westlaw®. Use KeyCite to
check citations for form, parallel references, prior and later history, and
comprehensive citator information, including citations to other decisions
and secondary materials.

---

§ 13:1   Seizure of vehicles: For an inventory of a vehicle to be legal, police custody of the vehicle must be lawful

Supreme Court

- "In the interests of public safety and as part of what
  the Court has called community caretaking functions
  automobiles are frequently taken into police custody.
  Vehicle accidents present one such occasion. Police will
  also frequently remove and impound automobiles which
  violate parking ordinances and which thereby jeopardize
  both the public safety and the efficient movement of

717

vehicular traffic. The authority of police to seize and remove from the streets vehicles impeding traffic or threatening public safety and convenience is beyond challenge." *South Dakota v. Opperman*, 428 U.S. 364, 368–69, 96 S. Ct. 3092, 49 L. Ed. 2d 1000 (1976).

- "[T]he car was lawfully in police custody, and the police were responsible for protecting the car; while engaged in the performance of their duty to protect the car they came across incriminating evidence." *Harris v. U.S.*, 390 U.S. 234, 237, 88 S. Ct. 992, 19 L. Ed. 2d 1067 (1968).

- "Just as a search authorized by state law may be an unreasonable one under [the Fourth] Amendment, so may a search not expressly authorized by state law be justified as a constitutionally reasonable one. While it is true that lawful custody of an automobile does not of itself dispense with constitutional requirements of searches thereafter made of it the reason for and nature of the custody may constitutionally justify the search." *Cooper v. State of Cal.*, 386 U.S. 58, 61, 87 S. Ct. 788, 17 L. Ed. 2d 730 (1967).

First Circuit

- "Courts have regularly upheld warrantless vehicle impoundments when police are acting not as investigators but as community caretakers, responsible for protecting public safety and preventing hazards by removing vehicles that impede traffic, risk vandalism, or create inconvenience." *U.S. v. Sanchez*, 612 F.3d 1, 7 (1st Cir. 2010). Lynch, concurring.

- [L]aw enforcement officials are not required to give arrestees the opportunity to make arrangements for their vehicles when deciding whether impoundment is appropriate. But law enforcement officials are required to have a non-investigatory reason for seizing an arrestee's car in the first place. Case law supports the view that where a driver is arrested and there is no one immediately on hand to take possession, the officials have a legitimate non-investigatory reason for impounding the car." *Vega-Encarnacion v. Babilonia*, 344 F.3d 37 (1st Cir. 2003).

- "[W]hen a driver is lawfully arrested and thus disabled from continuing his journey, the Constitution permits the police to carry out a routine inventory examination incident to impounding the vehicle." *U.S. v. Staula*, 80 F.3d 596, 603 (1st Cir. 1996).

• "[T]he Supreme Court in *Bertine* seemed specifically to hold that the Constitution permits arresting officers to impound, pursuant to standard procedures, an arrested person's automobile that might otherwise be left abandoned. This result, the Court said, reflects the government's legitimate interest in reducing automobile theft and damage, the individual's diminished expectation of privacy in an automobile, and the tendency of clear, standard rules to control police abuses." *U.S. v. Ramos-Morales*, 981 F.2d 625, 627 (1st Cir. 1992).

Second Circuit

• [W]hen a car is properly seized by the police pursuant to a forfeiture statute, the government has a greater possessory interest in the car than the owner, permitting law enforcement officers to search the seized vehicle without a warrant. . . . [I]n U.S. v. Lasanta, 978 F.2d 1300, 1306, 36 Fed. R. Evid. Serv. 1404 (2d Cir. 1992) (we indicated that a warrant was necessary to effect a proper civil forfeiture seizure, but in *Florida v. White*, 526 U.S. 559, 119 S. Ct. 1555, 143 L. Ed. 2d 748 (1999), the Supreme Court specifically rejected *Lasanta*, at least as it pertains to motor vehicles seized in public places. The Court ruled that law enforcement officers may seize forfeitable vehicles from public places without a warrant if they have probable cause to believe that the vehicle is, in fact, subject to forfeiture. Thus, . . . law enforcement officers who have probable cause to believe an automobile is subject to forfeiture may both seize the vehicle from a public place and search it without a warrant." *U.S. v. Gaskin*, 364 F.3d 438 (2d Cir. 2004).

Fifth Circuit

• "The police may impound vehicles for public safety and community caretaking." *U.S. v. Hope*, 102 F.3d 114, 116 (5th Cir. 1996).

• "[Defendant] asserts that the truck should not have been impounded because it did not fall under the types of vehicles that may be impounded under *Opperman*. The Court in *Opperman* listed a few examples of when impoundment of vehicles is warranted. Essentially, [Defendant] argues that since the *Opperman* court did not make a specific reference to impoundment of vehicles in public parking lots, the impoundment in this case must be unlawful. This argument assumes that the *Opperman* court intended to make an exhaustive list of appropriate impoundment scenarios—an assumption that the opinion in *Opperman* does not support. We agree with the government that the impoundment in this case falls within police officers' community caretaking functions. By impounding [Defendant's] brother-in-law's truck, [the officer] ensured that the truck was not left in a public parking lot where it could have become a nuisance, and where it could have been damaged or stolen." *U.S. v. Ponce*, 8 F.3d 989, 996, 39 Fed. R. Evid. Serv. 1373 (5th Cir. 1993).

Sixth Circuit

- "It is well-established that law enforcement officers may make a warrantless search of a legitimately seized vehicle provided the inventory is conducted according to standardized criteria or established routine." *U.S. v. Hurst*, 228 F.3d 751, 758, 2000 FED App. 0333P (6th Cir. 2000).

Seventh Circuit

- "Warrantless inventory searches of cars in police custody are . . . proper as long as the police lawfully have custody of the vehicles." *U.S. v. Jensen*, 169 F.3d 1044, 1048 (7th Cir. 1999).
- "If the arrest was legal, so was the search of the van, not only because the van had been abandoned but also because the police were entitled to impound it when they found it (since the renter was in jail) and to conduct an inventory search of it. But if the arrest was illegal, evidence obtained by the discovery of the key hidden by the arrested persons in the police car and the ensuing discovery, impoundment, and search of the van would be inadmissible, all that being a fruit of the unlawful arrest." *U.S. v. Ienco*, 92 F.3d 564, 568, 45 Fed. R. Evid. Serv. 415 (7th Cir. 1996).
- "The Alton police did not articulate a constitutionally legitimate rationale for impounding [Defendant]'s car.

While protection of the arrestee's property and municipal liability are both valid reasons to conduct an inventory after a legal impoundment, they do not establish the a priori legitimacy of the seizure. The suggestion that the police were obliged to impound the vehicle to protect it from theft or vandalism, strikes us as making up new police obligations after the fact where none existed before. The police do not owe a duty to the general public to remove vulnerable automobiles from high-crime neighborhoods. The touchstone of Fourth Amendment analysis is reasonableness. The policy of impounding the car without regard to whether the defendant can provide for its removal is patently unreasonable if the ostensible purpose for impoundment is for the caretaking of the streets. The decision to impound an automobile, unless it is supported by probable cause of criminal activity, is only valid if the arrestee is otherwise unable to provide for the speedy and efficient removal of the car from public thoroughfares or parking lots." *U.S. v. Duguay*, 93 F.3d 346, 352–53 (7th Cir. 1996).

Eighth Circuit

- "The police may impound vehicles in the interests of public safety and as part of what the Court has called 'community caretaking functions.' Officers are permitted to exercise their discretion in deciding whether to impound a vehicle, so long as that discretion is exercised according to standard criteria and on the basis of something other than suspicion of evidence of criminal activity." *U.S. v. Kanatzar*, 370 F.3d 810 (8th Cir. 2004), cert. granted, judgment vacated on other grounds, 543 U.S. 1107, 125 S. Ct. 1010, 160 L. Ed. 2d 1029 (2005) and opinion reinstated, 139 Fed. Appx. 760 (8th Cir. 2005).

Ninth Circuit

- "A police officer's incomplete inventory list for items found in the defendant's vehicle following his arrest did not establish that the inventory search was subterfuge for an unconstitutional investigatory search where, pursuant to police department policy, an inventory would have been taken of the defendant's vehicle following his arrest even if the arresting officer had acquiesced in the defendant's request and released the vehicle to the defendant's girlfriend, rather than impounding the vehicle, and, therefore, suppression of the firearm found during the inventory search was not warranted on the grounds that the inventory search was subterfuge for a warrantless investigatory search." *U.S. v. Kindle*, 293 Fed. Appx. 497 (9th Cir. 2008).

- "Whether an impoundment is warranted under the community caretaking doctrine depends on the location of the vehicle and the police officer's duty to prevent it from creating a hazard to other drivers or from being a target for vandalism or theft. [E]ven if preventing future unlawful operation were a sufficient community caretaking function in and of itself, it would obviously not apply to cases . . ., where the unlicensed driver was taken into custody." *U.S. v. Caseres*, 533 F.3d 1064 (9th Cir. 2008).

- "An impoundment may be proper under the community caretaking doctrine if the driver's violation of a vehicle regulation prevents the driver from lawfully operating the vehicle, and also if it is necessary to remove the vehicle from an exposed or public location. The violation of a traffic regulation justifies impoundment of a vehicle if the driver is unable to remove the vehicle from a public location without continuing its illegal operation. On the other hand, a decision to impound a vehicle that is not consistent with the police's role as 'caretaker' of the streets may be unreasonable. . . . [T]he decision to impound a vehicle after the driver has violated a vehicle regulation must consider the location of the vehicle, and whether the vehicle was actually impeding traffic or threatening public safety and convenience on the streets, such that impoundment was warranted. While [officer] may not have believed that the [plaintiffs] would comply with all regulations in the future, when he issued citations and called for the vehicle to be impounded, the vehicle was already parked in the [plaintiffs'] home driveway. [Plaintiff husband] was licensed to drive the car. Under these circumstances, the [plaintiffs'] car was not creating any impediment to traffic or threatening public safety. An officer cannot reasonably order an impoundment in situations where

the location of the vehicle does not create any need for
the police to protect the vehicle or to avoid a hazard to
other drivers. Defendants have argued that the impoundment satisfied the 'caretaking' function by deterring the [plaintiffs] from repeating this illegal activity
[husband teaching unlicensed wife how to drive] in the
future. . . . While the Supreme Court has accepted a
deterrence rationale for civil forfeitures of vehicles that
were used for criminal activity, the deterrence rationale
is incompatible with the principles of the community
caretaking doctrine. Unlike in civil forfeitures, where
the seizure of property penalizes someone who has been
convicted of a crime, the purpose of the community
caretaking function is to remove vehicles that are presently impeding traffic or creating a hazard. The need to
deter a driver's unlawful conduct is by itself insufficient
to justify a tow under the 'caretaker' rationale. The
deterrence rationale is also not a sufficient justification
here because of the negligible deterrent effect in this
case. . . . The City has not demonstrated in law or logic
that deterrence is a sufficient purpose to justify the particular impoundment that occurred here." *Miranda v.
City of Cornelius*, 429 F.3d 858 (9th Cir. 2005).

Tenth Circuit

• "[I]mpoundment of [the] vehicle was reasonable. The
driver of the car and one of the passengers were placed
under arrest. Neither could prove ownership of the vehicle nor provide proof of registration. The license plates
affixed to the car matched a different vehicle. Under
these conditions, the car could not be lawfully operated
on Utah's roads. Although the record indicates a third
person occupied the vehicle, under the circumstances
she could not have taken immediate custody of the car.
The vehicle, of necessity, had to be impounded." *U.S. v.
Haro-Salcedo*, 107 F.3d 769, 771 (10th Cir. 1997).

Eleventh Circuit

• "*Opperman* might be read to extend only to impoundments of vehicle which present a hazard. In *Bertine* the
Court addressed the question of whether the police
violated the Fourth Amendment by impounding the vehicle rather than permitting [the Owner] to make

723

alternative arrangements for its disposition. [and] declined to adopt such a view." *Sammons v. Taylor*, 967 F.2d 1533, 1539 (11th Cir. 1992).

§ 13:2   Justification: The inventory search may be conducted only to protect the owner's property and to protect the police against claims and dangers

Supreme Court

- "When vehicles are impounded, local police departments generally follow a routine practice of securing and inventorying the automobiles' contents. These procedures developed in response to three distinct needs: [1] the protection of the owner's property . . . [2] the protection of the police against claims or disputes over lost or stolen property and [3] the protection of the police from potential danger." *South Dakota v. Opperman*, 428 U.S. 364, 369, 96 S. Ct. 3092, 49 L. Ed. 2d 1000 (1976).

First Circuit

- "[Defendant], a retired U.S. Air Force officer, was in the midst of a difficult divorce in Pennsylvania in 2001. A Pennsylvania family court had issued a domestic restraining order against [defendant, which] forbade him from abusing, harassing, or threatening his wife or children, and from 'possessing, transferring or acquiring any weapons' for one year from the date of the order. . . . [A]t the second session [with a psychiatrist], [defendant] stated that he might plan a bombing or disperse anthrax; that he was capable of such things based on his military experience; that [psychiatrist] would read about his actions in the papers; that he would go after President Bush; and that he had been previously caught with firearms in his car in Maryland in violation of a judge's order. [Psychiatrist] was sufficiently troubled by [defendant's] comments that she called the FBI before the third session. . . . [W]hile the officers and agents met with [defendant], [psychiatrist] prepared a 'pink paper', i.e., an order from a medical professional providing for the involuntary commitment and psychiatric evaluation of an individual thought to be a danger to himself or others. . . . After [defendant] was taken away, [an inventory search] revealed several double-edged knives, a replica pistol, and a rifle case. At this point, [officers' obtained a search warrant. After obtaining the warrant, the officers opened [defendant's] rifle case, which contained an assault rifle and approximately 1300 rounds of ammunition. . . . [Defendant] was indicted on one count of violating 18 U.S.C. § 922(g)(8), which outlaws possession of a firearm by anyone subject to a domestic restraining order. He moved to suppress the firearm on the ground that the decision by the Wellesley police officer to impound his vehicle violated his Fourth Amendment rights. . . . [T]he community caretaking function encompasses law enforcement's authority to remove vehicles that impede traffic or threaten public safety and convenience. [Defendant] argues that the community caretaking exception does not apply to the impoundment of his car because the government failed to establish that the car was towed from [psychiatrist's] property pursuant to standard operating procedures. . . .Courts, including this one, have frequently held that impoundments of vehicles for community caretaking purposes are consonant with the Fourth Amendment so long as the impoundment decision was reasonable under the circumstances. . . . We have explained previously that it is inappropriate for the existence of (and adherence to) standard procedures to be the sine qua non of a reasonable impound decision[.]. . . Accordingly, the impoundment of [defendant's] car did not violate the Fourth Amendment merely because there was no evidence that the impoundment was done pursuant to pre-existing police protocols. . . . For several reasons, the decision to tow [defendant's] car from [psychiatrist's] property was reasonable. First, [defendant] was being removed from [psychiatrist's] property in an ambulance for a psychiatric evaluation, and there is no claim that the decision to evaluate [defendant] was pretextual. Because [defendant] would be indisposed for an indeterminate, and potentially lengthy, period, the officers properly made arrangements for the safekeeping of the vehicle, which was packed with his personal belongings. Because [defendant's] car was filled with many of his belongings, it was a possible target for theft or vandalism. Second, towing the vehicle reduced the risk of a future confrontation between [defendant] and [psychiatrist]. . . . Third, [defendant's] comments to [psychiatrist] led to a concern that [defendant's] car might contain items constituting a threat to public safety, such as explosive material, chemicals or biological agents. . . . Finally, there was no obvious alternative means for removing the car other than impoundment. . . . That [police officer] may have favored impounding the car, in part, because she wished to search its contents is not dispositive. A search or seizure undertaken pursuant to the community caretaking exception is not infirm merely because it may also have been motivated by a desire to investigate crime." *U.S. v. Coccia*, 446 F.3d 233 (1st Cir. 2006).

Second Circuit

- "[Inventory] searches are constitutional under the Fourth Amendment because they 'serve to protect an owner's property while it is in the custody of the police, to insure against claims of lost, stolen, or vandalized property, and to guard the police from danger.' Today, 'the inventory search constitutes a well-defined exception to the warrant requirement.' Although inventory searches typically occur at a police station or an impoundment facility, rather than at the time of the arrest, ... the Fourth Amendment does not require that police conduct inventory searches at any particular location. Of course, 'the right to [make an] inventory... does not carry in its wake unlimited discretion.' Under the inventory search doctrine, we have held that law enforcement officials may open closed containers as part of an inventory search so long as they act in good faith pursuant to standardized criteria or established routine. The existence of such a valid procedure may be proven by reference to either written rules and regulations or testimony regarding standard practices. A valid inventory search routine may allow the searching officers 'sufficient latitude to determine whether a particular container should or should not be opened,' but '[t]he individual police officer must not be allowed so much latitude that inventory searches are turned into 'a purposeful and general means of discovering evidence of crime.' In short, '[t]he policy or practice governing inventory searches should be designed to produce an inventory.' " *U.S. v. Mendez*, 315 F.3d 132 (2d Cir. 2002).

Third Circuit

• "Inventory searches are excepted from the general warrant requirement for several reasons: to protect the owner's property while it remains in police custody, to protect the police from claims or disputes over lost property, and to protect the police from potential danger." *U.S. v. Silveus*, 50 V.I. 1101, 542 F.3d 993 (3d Cir. 2008).

Fifth Circuit

• "Thus, an inventory search of a seized vehicle is reasonable and not violative of the Fourth Amendment if it is conducted pursuant to standardized regulations and procedures that are consistent with (1) protecting the property of the vehicle's owner, (2) protecting the police against claims or disputes over lost or stolen property, and (3) protecting the police from danger." *U.S. v. Lage*, 183 F.3d 374, 380 (5th Cir. 1999).

• "The record does not support the conclusion that [the Officer] exceeded the scope of an inventory search or failed to follow standardized procedures when he searched the truck's ashtray. The Police Department had standardized, written procedures for impoundment and inventory of cars. The police department procedures included a policy authorizing an officer to inventory the contents of the vehicle in unlocked compartments. The ashtray of the truck was an unlocked compartment and [the Officer] had no way of knowing whether the owner of the truck used the ashtray to store personal items. Since the ashtray was accessible to the wrecker company that later towed the truck, [the Officer's] search complied with the police department's standardized procedures and was consistent with legitimate purposes for inventory searches, which include the protection of the owner's property and avoidance of police liability for loss. Since [Defendant] has failed to show that the police, who were following standardized procedures, acted in bad faith or for the sole purpose of investigation, the search was reasonable under the Fourth Amendment." *U.S. v. Ponce*, 8 F.3d 989, 995, 39 Fed. R. Evid. Serv. 1373 (5th Cir. 1993).

Sixth Circuit

- "After lawfully taking custody of a vehicle, officers may conduct a warrantless inventory search. Such inventory searches serve to protect an owner's property while it is in the custody of the police, to insure against claims of lost, stolen, or vandalized property, and to guard the police from danger." *U.S. v. Lumpkin*, 159 F.3d 983, 987, 1998 FED App. 0330P (6th Cir. 1998).

Seventh Circuit

- "Warrantless inventory searches of automobiles in police custody do not violate the Fourth Amendment. The inventory search exception to the warrant requirement is premised on an individual's diminished expectation of privacy in an automobile and three important governmental interests in inventorying an automobile: to protect an owner's property while the automobile is in police custody, to ensure against claims of lost, stolen, or damaged property, and to guard the police from danger." *U.S. v. Lomeli*, 76 F.3d 146, 148, 43 Fed. R. Evid. Serv. 1005 (7th Cir. 1996).

Eighth Circuit

- "[W]hen taking custody of property such as a suspect's vehicle, law enforcement officers may conduct a warrantless search and inventory of the contents of the vehicle in order to protect the owner's property, to protect the police against claims of lost or stolen property, and to protect the police from potential danger. The central inquiry in determining whether such an inventory search is reasonable is a consideration of the totality of the circumstances." *U.S. v. Baldenegro-Valdez*, 703 F.3d 1117 (8th Cir. 2013) (citations omitted).

- "Impoundment of a vehicle for the safety of the property and the public is a valid 'community caretaking' function of the police. Police may take protective custody of a vehicle when they have arrested its occupants, even if it is lawfully parked and poses no public safety hazard." *U.S. v. Petty*, 367 F.3d 1009 (8th Cir. 2004).

- "[Defendant] also argues in his brief that even though the police department had a written policy directing a content inventory of all vehicles being towed, [the arresting officer] clearly had an investigative motive to

search [defendant's] vehicle because he testified that he
believed [defendant] was attempting to conceal his
identity. We conclude, however, that after the decision
was made to impound the vehicle, the law permitted an
inventory search consistent with police procedures to
protect [defendant's] property and to protect the police
against claims of lost or stolen property and from
potential danger. Even if the officer had another motive, the presence of an investigative motive does not
invalidate an otherwise valid inventory search." *U.S. v.
Kanatzar*, 370 F.3d 810 (8th Cir. 2004), cert. granted,
judgment vacated on other grounds, 543 U.S. 1107; 125
S. Ct. 1010, 160 L. Ed. 2d 1029 (2005) and opinion
reinstated, 139 Fed. Appx. 760 (8th Cir. 2005).

- "Law enforcement may search a lawfully impounded vehicle to compile an inventory list of the vehicle's
contents without violating the Fourth Amendment. To
do so, officers need neither search warrant nor probable
cause, for they are not investigating a crime; instead,
they are performing an administrative or care-taking
function. In performing this function, officers may
legitimately be protecting the owner's property while it
remains in custody. They may be protecting themselves
from claims of lost or damaged property or from any
potential danger posed by the unknown contents of the
vehicle. The only limit on such searches is they must be
reasonable under the circumstances. Inventory searches
are reasonable if conducted according to standardized
police procedures, which vitiate concerns of an investigatory motive or excessive discretion." *U.S. v. Rowland*,
341 F.3d 774 (8th Cir. 2003).

- "The presence of an investigative motive does not
invalidate an otherwise valid inventory search. . . . In
this case, the police possessed valid reasons to impound
the vehicle, which under the St. Paul impound policy,
required an inventory search prior to impoundment.
These reasons included: the vehicle was in a no parking
zone on a busy street, it was worth more than $15,000,
it was in a high-crime area, and the City of St. Paul
was responsible for its protection. The fact that the officers also suspected appellant was involved in drug
trafficking and might have evidence of such activity in
the vehicle does not invalidate the officers' decision or

demonstrate they acted in bad faith." *U.S. v. Garner*, 181 F.3d 988, 991–92 (8th Cir. 1999).

- "After lawfully taking custody of an automobile, police may search the automobile without a warrant to produce an inventory of the automobile's contents. . . . The intrusion is justified by governmental interests in protecting the owner's property while it remains in police custody, in protecting the police against claims or disputes over lost or stolen property, and in protecting the police from potential danger. . . . The Fourth Amendment is not offended if, considering the totality of the circumstances, the inventory search is reasonable." *U.S. v. Mayfield*, 161 F.3d 1143, 1145 (8th Cir. 1998).

- "A warrantless inventory search must be done pursuant to standard police procedures and for the purpose of protecting the car and its contents. . . . The Tenth Circuit concluded in a case similar to the present case that. . . . searching behind the door panel of a vehicle does not qualify as standard police procedure, and does not serve the purpose of protecting the car and its contents under any normal construction of those terms, at least on the evidence in this record." *U.S. v. Best*, 135 F.3d 1223, 1225 (8th Cir. 1998).

- "It is well-settled that a police officer, after lawfully taking custody of an automobile, may conduct a warrantless inventory search of the property to secure and protect vehicles and their contents within police custody." *U.S. v. Rehkop*, 96 F.3d 301, 305 (8th Cir. 1996).

- "We also reject [Defendant's] contention that the officers went beyond the scope of a permissible inventory search when they searched the van's engine compartment. Because [Defendant] had a bag of cocaine in his shirt pocket when he was arrested, the officers had ample justification to search all areas of the van where personal property might be found, to protect the public from persons who might find contraband drugs in the van." *U.S. v. Lewis*, 3 F.3d 252, 254 (8th Cir. 1993).

- "In this case, there are many factors that support the reasonableness of the search. First, one of the reasons for an inventory search is to protect the public and the police from potential danger. In the interest of public safety, police must often play a caretaking role. [Defendant's] car was parked in a public lot and a crowd had gathered at the site of the arrest. The experienced police officers at the scene later testified that there was a high likelihood that additional drugs and/or firearms would be in [Defendant's] vehicle. The police made an informed and reasonable decision to search the car and exercise their custodial duty immediately under the circumstances. It was entirely appropriate and reasonable for the police to conduct an inventory search of the car to ensure that any dangerous instrumentalities did not fall into another person's hands." *U.S. v. Mays*, 982 F.2d 319, 321 (8th Cir. 1993).

Ninth Circuit

• "Under California Vehicle Code § 22651(h)(1), the police may impound a vehicle [w]hen an officer arrests any person driving or in control of a vehicle for an alleged offense and takes that person into custody. A lawfully impounded vehicle may be searched for the purpose of determining its condition and contents at the time of impounding. Anything observed in the vehicle during the inventory search is admissible against the defendant. Such warrantless inventory searches of vehicles are lawful only if conducted pursuant to standard police procedures that are aimed at protecting the owner's property and at protecting the police from the owner charging them with having stolen, lost, or damaged his property. Additionally, a vehicle can be impounded under § 22651(h)(1) only if impoundment serves some community caretaking function. [T]he police lacked the authority to impound and conduct an inventory search of Caseres' car—which was lawfully parked on the street two houses away from his residence—because doing so did not serve any community caretaking purpose." *U.S. v. Caseres*, 533 F.3d 1064 (9th Cir. 2008).

Tenth Circuit

• "It is common practice for the police to conduct an inventory of the contents of vehicles they have taken into their custody or are about to impound. Such inventories are now a well-defined exception to the warrant requirement of the Fourth Amendment. They are not treated as investigative searches because they serve three administrative purposes: the protection of the owner's property while it remains in police custody, the protection of the police against claims or disputes over lost or stolen property, and the protection of the police from potential danger. Although inventory searches need not be supported by a warrant or probable cause, they are restricted in other ways. First, they are reasonable only if conducted according to standardized procedures. Second, the policy or practice governing inventory searches should be designed to produce an inventory; in other words, an inventory search must be justified by the administrative purposes of such searches. An inventory search must not be a ruse for a general rummaging in order to discover incriminating evidence." *U.S. v. Tueller*, 349 F.3d 1239 (10th Cir. 2003).

- "An inventory search is a well-defined exception to the warrant requirement of the Fourth Amendment designed to effect three purposes: protection of the owner's property, protection of the police against claims of lost or stolen property, and protection of the police from potential danger. However, inventory searches are reasonable only if conducted according to standardized procedures. An inventory search must not be a ruse for a general rummaging in order to discover incriminating evidence, but rather an administrative procedure designed to produce an inventory." *U.S. v. Haro-Salcedo*, 107 F.3d 769, 772–73 (10th Cir. 1997).

§ 13:3 Nature of search: The inventory search must be a normal part of standard police procedure and not a pretext for an investigatory search

Supreme Court

- "[I]n *Florida v. Wells* we stated that an inventory search must not be used as a ruse for a general rummaging in order to discover incriminating evidence; [in] *Colorado v. Bertine* in approving an inventory search, we apparently thought it significant that there had been no showing that the police, who were following standard procedures, acted in bad faith or for the sole purpose of investigation; [in] *New York v. Burger* we observed, in upholding the constitutionality of a warrantless administrative inspection, that the search did not appear to be a pretext for obtaining evidence of violation of penal laws." *Whren v. U.S.*, 517 U.S. 806, 811, 116 S. Ct. 1769, 135 L. Ed. 2d 89 (1996).

- "Our view that standardized criteria or established routine must regulate the opening of containers found during inventory searches is based on the principle that an inventory search must not be a ruse for a general rummaging in order to discover incriminating evidence. The policy or practice governing inventory searches should be designed to produce an inventory. The individual police officer must not be allowed so much latitude that inventory searches are turned into a purposeful and general means of discovering evidence of crime." *Florida v. Wells*, 495 U.S. 1, 4, 110 S. Ct. 1632, 109 L. Ed. 2d 1 (1990).

- "[I]n forbidding uncanalized discretion to police officers conducting inventory searches, there is no reason to insist that they be conducted in a totally mechanical all or nothing fashion. [I]nventory procedures serve to protect an owner's property while it is in the custody of the police, to insure against claims of lost, stolen, or vandalized property, and to guard the police from danger. A police officer may be allowed sufficient latitude to determine whether a particular container should or should not be opened in light of the nature of the search and characteristics of the container itself. Thus, while policies of opening all containers or of opening no containers are unquestionably permissible, it would be equally permissible, for example, to allow the opening of closed containers whose contents officers determine they are unable to ascertain from examining the containers' exteriors. The allowance of the exercise of judgment based on concerns related to the purposes of an inventory search does not violate the Fourth Amendment." *Florida v. Wells*, 495 U.S. 1, 4, 110 S. Ct. 1632, 109 L. Ed. 2d 1 (1990).

- "[P]olice officers may open closed containers while conducting a routine inventory search of an impounded vehicle. [S]uch inventorys [sic] [must be] conducted only pursuant to standardized police procedures." *Colorado v. Bertine*, 479 U.S. 367, 384, 107 S. Ct. 738, 93 L. Ed. 2d 739 (1987).

• "[T]here is no suggestion whatever that this standard [inventory] procedure, essentially like that followed throughout the country, was a pretext concealing an investigatory police motive." *South Dakota v. Opperman*, 428 U.S. 364, 376, 96 S. Ct. 3092, 49 L. Ed. 2d 1000 (1976).

• "The Court's previous recognition of the distinction between motor vehicles and dwelling places leads us to conclude that the type of caretaking search conducted here of a vehicle that was neither in the custody nor on the premises of its owner, and that had been placed where it was by virtue of lawful police action, was not unreasonable solely because a warrant had not been obtained. . . . Where, as here, the trunk of an automobile, which the officer reasonably believed to contain a gun, was vulnerable to intrusion by vandals, we hold that the search was not unreasonable within the meaning of the Fourth and Fourteenth Amendments." *Cady v. Dombrowski*, 413 U.S. 433, 447–48, 93 S. Ct. 2523, 37 L. Ed. 2d 706 (1973).

Second Circuit

• "Every detail of a search procedure is not required to be governed by a standardized policy in order for a warrantless inventory search to be conducted pursuant to a standardized policy in conformance with the Fourth Amendment." *U.S. v. Lopez*, 547 F.3d 364 (2d Cir. 2008).

• "The Fourth Amendment does not permit police officers to disguise warrantless, investigative searches as inventory searches. The fact that an officer is motivated in part by criminal investigative objectives does not disqualify an inventory search that is performed under standardized procedures for legitimate custodial purposes." *U.S. v. Lopez*, 547 F.3d 364 (2d Cir. 2008).

Fourth Circuit

• "Proper inventory search is merely an incidental administrative step following arrest and preceding incarceration, conducted to protect arrestee from theft of his possessions, to protect police from false accusations of theft, and to remove dangerous items from arrestee prior to his jailing. Lawfulness of inventory search of motor vehicle's contents, after officer had stopped vehicle on side of busy roadway and arrested its occupants, was not affected by fact that search was not completed on side of roadway, and that officers, after opening some containers on scene, removed the rest of the unopened containers from vehicle in order to complete inventory search at Sheriff's Department." *U.S. v. Murphy*, 552 F.3d 405 (4th Cir. 2009).

- "The lawfulness of an inventory search of a motor vehicle's contents, after an officer stops a vehicle on the side of a busy roadway and arrests its occupants, is not affected by the fact that the search was not completed on the side of roadway, and that the officers, after opening some containers on the scene, removed the rest of the unopened containers from vehicle in order to complete the inventory search at the Sheriff's Department." *U.S. v. Murphy*, 552 F.3d 405 (4th Cir. 2009).

- "For the inventory search exception to apply, the search must have 'be[en] conducted according to standardized criteria,' such as a uniform police department policy, and performed in good faith, ... A police department's policy on inventory searches does not have to specifically use the phrase 'closed containers' to permit the search and seizure of such items. . . . However, within the constraints of the policy, officers may exercise discretion in deciding whether or not to open a particular container. . . . Here, by requiring that searching officers perform a 'complete inventory' in order to 'to prevent any loss or theft,' the Department's policy gives officers the discretion to determine whether a valuable may be located within a container so as to require that container's opening." *U.S. v. Matthews*, 591 F.3d 230 (4th Cir. 2009).

Fifth Circuit

- "Under the Fourth Amendment, warrantless searches are presumptively unreasonable. . . . There is, however, an exception to the warrant requirement when a law enforcement officer conducts an inventory of seized property if that inventory is part of a bona fide police routine administrative caretaking function. . . . Under these circumstances, the Fourth Amendment requires only that an inventory not be a ruse for a general rummaging in order to discover incriminating evidence." *U.S. v. Lage*, 183 F.3d 374, 380 (5th Cir. 1999).

- "The record is devoid of any evidence that standard inventory procedures were in place and were, in fact, followed by the Memphis police when they searched the Honda. The searching officer turned over the evidence found to the Texas officers and did not bag and tag same as the search procedures prescribed. It is beyond serious debate that the prosecution bears the burden of establishing that any evidence submitted, which resulted from an inventory search, was the result of a search conducted in accordance with known, established police procedures. That did not occur herein and the evidence found in the search of the Honda should not have been admitted in evidence." *U.S. v. Hope*, 102 F.3d 114, 117 (5th Cir. 1996).

Sixth Circuit

- "It is settled law that the police may conduct an inventory search of an automobile that is being impounded without running afoul of the Fourth Amendment. 'In order to be deemed valid, an inventory search may not be undertaken for purposes of investigation, and it must be conducted according to standard police procedures.' A general written inventory policy does not grant officers carte blanche when conducting a search; rather, it must be sufficiently tailored to only produce an inventory. Thus, '[i]n conducting an inventory search, officers do not enjoy their accustomed discretion; they simply follow the applicable policy.' 'Nonetheless, officers may exercise some judgment based on concerns related to the purposes of an inventory search; for example, they may decide to open particular containers if they cannot determine the contents.' 'When a legitimate search is underway, and when its purpose and its limits have been precisely defined, nice distinctions between closets, drawers, and containers, in the case of a home, or between glove compartments, upholstered seats, trunks, and wrapped packages, in the case of a vehicle, must give way to the interest in the prompt and efficient completion of the task at hand.' " *U.S. v.*

Jackson, 682 F.3d 448, 455 (6th Cir. 2012) (citations omitted).

- "One recognized exception to the warrant requirement permits law enforcement officers to conduct inventory searches, including the contents of closed containers, so long as they do so pursuant to standardized procedures . . . This exception recognizes that in addition to investigating crime, officers have an established care-taking role vis-a-vis the public . . . Inventory searches further legitimate goals of protecting property from theft or damage, preventing property disputes between the owner and police, and mitigating safety risks inherent in taking possession of unknown items . . . But officers must conduct a permissible inventory search in good faith, not as a pretext for criminal investigation . . . In conducting an inventory search, officers do not enjoy their accustomed discretion; they simply follow the applicable policy . . . Whether a police department maintains a written policy is not determinative, where testimony establishes the existence and contours of the policy . . . The large backpack in this case is not akin to a "repository of personal effects," such as a purse . . . (Defendant) contends that in removing the bag from the car and carrying it with him to the truck, he manifested his privacy interest in the bag. But (the officer) testified that although (defendant) removed the bag from his car, he eventually left it on the road, where it could have been damaged, lost, or stolen. Although (defendant) may have had a greater privacy expectation for the backpack than for other items in plain sight in his car, he never gave the police any clear signal asserting his privacy." *U.S. v. Tackett*, 486 F.3d 230 (6th Cir. 2007).

- "Although this circuit has not previously dealt directly with the question of an inventory search under the hood of a vehicle, other circuits have. . . . We agree with the position taken by the Eighth and Tenth Circuits and, therefore, hold that a valid inventory search conducted by law enforcement officers according to standard procedure may include the engine compartment of a vehicle." *U.S. v. Lumpkin*, 159 F.3d 983, 988, 1998 FED App. 0330P (6th Cir. 1998).

Seventh Circuit

- "[W]ithin the constraints of the policy/procedure, officers may exercise discretion in deciding whether or not to open a particular container. . . . A police officer may be allowed sufficient latitude to determine whether a particular container should or should not be opened in light of the nature of the search and characteristics of the container itself. Thus, while policies of opening all containers or of opening no containers are unquestionably permissible, it would be equally permissible, for example, to allow the opening of closed containers whose contents officers determine they are unable to ascertain from examining the containers' exteriors. The allowance of the exercise of judgment based on concerns related to the purposes of an inventory search does not violate the Fourth Amendment." *U.S. v. Lozano*, 171 F.3d 1129, 1132 (7th Cir. 1999).
- "The police do not have free rein; rather, inventory search procedures must be sufficiently regulated to satisfy the Fourth Amendment and evidence will be suppressed if uncovered during an inventory search that is not regulated by any police policy. Requiring sufficient regulation of inventory searches ensures that a police procedure is not merely a pretext for concealing an investigatory police motive. But the fact that an inventory search may also have had an investigatory motive does not invalidate it." *U.S. v. Lomeli*, 76 F.3d 146, 148, 43 Fed. R. Evid. Serv. 1005 (7th Cir. 1996).

Eighth Circuit
- "Law enforcement officers may conduct a warrantless search and inventory in order to protect the owner's property, to protect the police against claims of lost or stolen property, and to protect the police from potential danger. Officers may not raise the inventory-search banner in an after-the-fact attempt to justify what was purely and simply a search for incriminating evidence, but they are permitted to keep their eyes open for potentially incriminating items that they might discover in the course of an inventory search, as long as their sole purpose is not to investigate a crime. . . . [Defendant] argues that the search of the vehicle was impermissible because it was performed for investigatory purposes only. Since the registered owner had arrived

at the scene of the stop and was ready and willing to
take the vehicle, he asserts that there was no need for
officers to impound the car and inventory its contents. .
. . Here, the officers followed the Cedar Rapids Police
Department policy governing inventory searches when
it performed the search, and there is no indication that
the policy permits officers to perform inventory searches
in an unconstitutional manner. [Defendant] had been
alone in the vehicle at the time of his arrest, and the
police could not have been sure that it was safe for
[owner] to take possession of it." *U.S. v. Beal*, 430 F.3d
950, 68 Fed. R. Evid. Serv. 1242 (8th Cir. 2005).

- "Adherence to standardized procedures is necessary to
ensure that the search is not merely a ruse for general
rummaging in order to discover incriminating evidence,
since inventory searches are often conducted in the
absence of the safeguards of a warrant and probable
cause. Requiring an officer to conduct an inventory
search pursuant to standardized criteria or an established routine does not mean that the search must be
made in a totally mechanical fashion. Indeed, police
may keep their eyes open for potentially incriminating
items that they might discover in the course of an inventory search, as long as their sole purpose is not to
investigate a crime. However, the Constitution does not
permit police to 'aise the inventory-search banner in an
after-the-fact attempt to justify what was purely and
simply a search for incriminating evidence. . . . The
department's inventory search procedures require an
inventory of the impounded vehicle's contents. In addition, 'if there is personal property of value not permanently affixed in a vehicle, the officer shall list the
contents on the tow sheet.' The policy also requires an
inventory of the contents of the trunk and the glove box
after making 'every reasonable attempt to open these
areas.' If these areas are locked and no key is available,
the officer 'shall not do damage to the vehicle in an attempt to open these areas,' but if an officer has 'probable cause to believe there is evidence of a crime in
these locked areas, they should place a 'hold' on the vehicle until a search warrant can be obtained.' The policy
also provides that 'objects such as boxes, briefcases, or
other closed containers should be opened and the

contents inventoried.' Once again, if the container is locked, officers may attempt to open the container without doing damage, but if the container cannot be opened the officer 'must determine if they have probable cause to obtain a search warrant for the container.' . . . All the Government established at the suppression hearing is that procedures were in place. It failed to establish compliance with those procedures. . . . Absent such evidence, the Government has failed to demonstrate that the officer conducted the search in compliance with the department's inventory search policy, and thereby failed to demonstrate that the inventory search exception applies." *U.S. v. Kennedy*, 427 F.3d 1136 (8th Cir. 2005).

- "Inventory searches are reasonable when they are conducted according to standardized police procedures. . . . Compliance with procedures merely tends to ensure the intrusion is limited to carrying out the government's caretaking function. . . . This does not mean that inventory searches are always unreasonable when standard procedures are not followed, however." *U.S. v. Mayfield*, 161 F.3d 1143, 1145 (8th Cir. 1998).

Ninth Circuit

- "Police officer's incomplete inventory list for items found in defendant's vehicle following his arrest did not establish that inventory search was subterfuge for unconstitutional investigatory search." *U.S. v. Kindle*, 293 Fed. Appx. 497 (9th Cir. 2008).
- "We are satisfied that [the] Officer. . .was acting in accordance with City and Police policy to conduct a complete inventory, and that he had no discretion. In context, the instructions authorizing an officer to permit removal of personal property from an impounded vehicle allow the exercise of discretion only after the inventory has been completed and before the vehicle is towed." *U.S. v. Penn*, 233 F.3d 1111, 1117 (9th Cir. 2000).

Tenth Circuit

- "The district court found the DEA search, conducted for investigatory rather than administrative purposes, could not properly be characterized as an inventory

search. Thus, the warrantless search of [the] vehicle
was unreasonable, and the evidence seized could not be
admissible under an administrative search theory." *U.S.
v. Haro-Salcedo*, 107 F.3d 769, 773 (10th Cir. 1997).

D.C. Circuit

- "The Fourth Amendment requires, again, that an inventory search be reasonable and, if a standard procedure
for conducting an inventory search is in effect, it must
be followed . . . Adherence to a standard procedure
ensures that an inventory search is 'not . . . a ruse for
a general rummaging in order to discover incriminating
evidence' . . . More than a single officer's *ad hoc* description of a new practice is required to decide that a
thirty-year-old inventory search procedure-in-writing-
has been altered by "necessity" . . . Because the officers failed to follow . . . standard procedure, the
impoundment of (defendant's) vehicle was unreasonable
and thus violated the Fourth Amendment. Likewise, 'if
the seizure of the car was unconstitutional, the materials later recovered during the inventory search [are]
excluded.' " *U.S. v. Proctor*, 489 F.3d 1348 (D.C. Cir.
2007).

§ 13:4 Booking searches: A custodial search of an arrestee's personal effects may be justified as an inventory procedure

Supreme Court

- "[I]t is not unreasonable for police, as part of the routine procedure incident to incarcerating an arrested
person, to search any container or article in his possession, in accordance with established inventory
procedures." *Illinois v. Lafayette*, 462 U.S. 640, 648, 103
S. Ct. 2605, 77 L. Ed. 2d 65 (1983).
- "A range of governmental interests support an inventory process. A standardized procedure for making a
list or inventory as soon as reasonable after reaching
the stationhouse not only deters false claims but also
inhibits theft or careless handling of articles taken from
the arrested person. Arrested persons have also been
known to injure themselves—or others—with belts,
knives, drugs or other items on their person while being

detained. Dangerous instrumentalities—such as razor blades, bombs, or weapons—can be concealed in innocent-looking articles taken from the arrestee's possession. Examining all the items removed from the arrestee's person or possession and listing or inventorying them is an entirely reasonable administrative procedure. It is immaterial whether the police actually fear any particular package or container; the need to protect against such risks arises independent of a particular officer's subjective concerns. Finally, inspection of an arrestee's personal property may assist the police in ascertaining or verifying his identity." *Illinois v. Lafayette*, 462 U.S. 640, 646, 103 S. Ct. 2605, 77 L. Ed. 2d 65 (1983).

- "[O]nce the accused is lawfully arrested and is in custody, the effects in his possession at the place of detention that were subject to search at the time and place of his arrest may lawfully be searched and seized without a warrant even though a substantial period of time has elapsed between the arrest and subsequent administrative processing, on the one hand, and the taking of the property for use as evidence, on the other hand. This is true where the clothing or effects are immediately seized upon arrival at the jail, held under the defendant's name in the property room of the jail, and at a later time searched and taken for use at the subsequent criminal trial." *U.S. v. Edwards*, 415 U.S. 800, 807, 94 S. Ct. 1234, 39 L. Ed. 2d 771 (1974).

First Circuit

- "A warrantless search is permitted under the Fourth Amendment if it is carried out pursuant to a standardized inventory policy. Such a standardized inventory policy may be unwritten." *U.S. v. Hawkins*, 279 F.3d 83 (1st Cir. 2002).

Second Circuit

- "After such an arrest and seizure, an inventory search of the property seized is justified by the government's interests in averting any danger the property might pose, in protecting the property from unauthorized interference, and in protecting itself against claims of theft or negligent treatment of the property. Thus, if there has been a lawful arrest and an immediately ensuing search is not justifiable as incident to the arrest, a motion to suppress the proceeds of the immediate search may nonetheless be denied if the contents would inevitably have been discovered in a permissible inventory search." *U.S. v. Perea*, 986 F.2d 633, 644 (2d Cir. 1993).

Sixth Circuit

- "As the Supreme Court has noted, the rationale justifying an inventory search differs somewhat from that of a search incident to arrest, although it, too, falls outside the warrant requirement. The rationale of *Lafayette* focuses upon protection of both the arrestee and police during the period a suspect is detained at the station house." *U.S. v. McCroy*, 102 F.3d 239, 240–41, 1996 FED App. 0381P (6th Cir. 1996).
- "The Supreme Court has found that inventory searches of automobiles as well as an inventory search of the personal effects of an arrestee at a police station were permissible under the Fourth Amendment." *U.S. v. Thomas*, 11 F.3d 620, 628 (6th Cir. 1993).

Seventh Circuit

- "[A] warrantless inventory search is constitutionally permissible if (1) the individual whose possession is to be searched has been lawfully arrested, and (2) the search satisfies the fourth amendment standard of reasonableness, i.e., it is conducted as part of the routine procedure incident to incarcerating an arrested person and in accordance with established inventory procedures." *U.S. v. Richardson*, 121 F.3d 1051, 1055 (7th Cir. 1997).

Eighth Circuit

- "[A]nother exemption from the fourth amendment warrant requirement is that recognized for inventory searches of containers or articles in the possession of an arrested person. A warrantless inventory search is constitutionally permissible if (1) the individual whose possession is to be searched has been lawfully arrested, and (2) the search satisfies the fourth amendment standard of reasonableness, that is, if it is conducted as part

743

of the routine procedure incident to incarcerating an arrested person and in accordance with established inventory procedures." *U.S. v. Caves*, 890 F.2d 87, 93 (8th Cir. 1989).

- "[R]equiring the police to formally book arrestees before inventorying their belongings would benefit no one. It is reasonable, in light of the underlying rationales of inventory searches, namely, safety, deterrence of theft, and the prevention of false claims against the police, that the arrestee's belongings be inventoried at the first place the processing begins, whether or not the arrestee is ultimately booked or incarcerated there. No particular stationhouse setting is crucial to the validity of an inventory search." *U.S. v. Woolbright*, 831 F.2d 1390, 1394, 23 Fed. R. Evid. Serv. 1277 (8th Cir. 1987).

Chapter 14

Plain View

§ 14:1   Location of police: The police officer must be at a
         location where he has a legal right to be in order
         to seize an item in his plain view
§ 14:2   Nature of discovery: The discovery of the seized
         item need not be inadvertent
§ 14:3   Nature of evidence: It must be immediately
         apparent that the seized item is incriminating,
         and officers must have probable cause to believe
         that it is incriminating
§ 14:4   Scope of plain view: Where officials enter a
         private property to fight a fire, the scope of the
         warrantless search plain view doctrine is limited
         to that reasonably necessary to extinguish the
         blaze
§ 14:5   Scope of plain view exception: computer files

Research References

West's Key Number Digest
Automobile ☞349.5; Searches and Seizures ☞16, 47 to 51, 63

KeyCite®: Cases and other legal materials listed in KeyCite Scope can be
researched through the KeyCite service on Westlaw®. Use KeyCite to
check citations for form, parallel references, prior and later history, and
comprehensive citator information, including citations to other decisions
and secondary materials.

---

§ 14:1   Location of police: The police officer must be at a location where he has a legal right to be in order to seize an item in his plain view

<u>Supreme Court</u>

- "The rationale of the plain view doctrine is that if
  contraband is left in open view and is observed by a police officer from a lawful vantage point, there has been
  no invasion of a legitimate expectation of privacy and
  thus no search within the meaning of the Fourth

745

Amendment—or at least no search independent of the initial intrusion that gave the officers their vantage point." *Minnesota v. Dickerson*, 508 U.S. 366, 375, 113 S. Ct. 2130, 124 L. Ed. 2d 334 (1993).

- "[I]f police are lawfully in a position from which they view an object, if its incriminating character is immediately apparent, and if the officers have a lawful right of access to the object, they may seize it without a warrant." *Minnesota v. Dickerson*, 508 U.S. 366, 375, 113 S. Ct. 2130, 124 L. Ed. 2d 334 (1993).

- "It is, of course, an essential predicate to any valid warrantless seizure of incriminating evidence that the officer did not violate the Fourth Amendment in arriving at the place from which the evidence could be plainly viewed." *Horton v. California*, 496 U.S. 128, 136, 110 S. Ct. 2301, 110 L. Ed. 2d 112 (1990).

- "[N]ot only must the officer be lawfully located in a place from which the object can be plainly seen, but he or she must also have a lawful right of access to the object itself." *Horton v. California*, 496 U.S. 128, 137, 110 S. Ct. 2301, 110 L. Ed. 2d 112 (1990).

- "The plain view doctrine is grounded on the proposition that once police are lawfully in a position to observe an item first-hand, its owner's privacy interest in that item is lost; the owner may retain the incidents of title and possession but not privacy." *Illinois v. Andreas*, 463 U.S. 765, 771, 103 S. Ct. 3319, 77 L. Ed. 2d 1003 (1983).

- "[T]he police officer must lawfully make an initial intrusion or otherwise properly be in a position from which he can view a particular area. [P]lain view provides grounds for seizure of an item when an officer's access to an object has some prior justification under the Fourth Amendment." *Texas v. Brown*, 460 U.S. 730, 737, 103 S. Ct. 1535, 75 L. Ed. 2d 502 (1983).

- "[T]he police officer [must have] had a prior justification for an intrusion in the course of which he came inadvertently across a piece of evidence incriminating the accused. [T]his initial intrusion is justified by a warrant or by an exception such as hot pursuit or search incident to a lawful arrest, or by an extraneous valid reason for the officer's presence." *Coolidge v. New Hampshire*, 403 U.S. 443, 466–67, 91 S. Ct. 2022, 29 L. Ed. 2d 564 (1971).

First Circuit

- "The court below found that '[t]he officers were admitted to the residence with [the appellant's] voluntary consent.' The appellant does not seriously contest this finding. Nor could he: he has admitted that upon the officers' arrival, he opened his front door and affirmatively signaled for the officers to enter. Two other considerations cinch the matter: the record is barren of any evidence that might support an inference that this gesture was induced through force, pressure, or deception; and the consensual entry took place *before* the state court orders were served. . . . Still, consent to enter a home does not, by itself, give law enforcement officers carte blanche to rummage through the premises and perform a general search. After all, a warrantless search may not exceed the scope of the consent obtained. Here, however, once the officers were lawfully present in the appellant's apartment, another exception to the Fourth Amendment's warrant requirement came into play. We refer, of course, to the plain view doctrine. . . . As we have explained, the plain view doctrine permits the warrantless seizure of an item if the officer is lawfully present in a position from which the item is clearly visible, there is probable cause to seize the item, and the officer has a lawful right of access to the item itself." *U.S. v. Gamache*, 792 F.3d 194, 198–99 (1st Cir. 2015) (citations omitted).
- "Although a person generally has an expectation of privacy in items he places in a closed container, some containers so betray their contents as to abrogate any such expectation. The contents of such containers are treated as being in plain view." *U.S. v. Meada*, 408 F.3d 14 (1st Cir. 2005).
- "[A]n essential predicate to the seizure of evidence not within a warrant's purview is that the officer did not violate the Fourth Amendment in arriving at the place from which the evidence could be plainly viewed." *U.S. v. Hamie*, 165 F.3d 80, 82 (1st Cir. 1999).
- "First, the officer must lawfully have reached the position from which he plainly could view the seized object." *U.S. v. Jones*, 187 F.3d 210, 219 (1st Cir. 1999).

Second Circuit
- "The 'plain view' exception to the Fourth Amendment's

warrant requirement is well-established. Under the plain view doctrine, a law enforcement officer may seize evidence without a warrant if (1) the officer is 'lawfully in a position from which [the officer] view[s] an object,' (2) the object's 'incriminating character is immediately apparent,' and (3) the officer has 'a lawful right of access to the object.' When an officer, during a justified intrusion, encounters incriminating evidence, [t]he doctrine serves to supplement the prior justification—whether it be a warrant for another object, hot pursuit, search incident to lawful arrest, or some other legitimate reason for being present unconnected with a search directed against the accused—and permits the warrantless seizure." *United States v. Babilonia*, 854 F.3d 163, 179–80 (2d Cir. 2017) (citations omitted).

Fifth Circuit

- "Law enforcement officers may seize anything they find in plain view without a search warrant. . . . An object falls within plain view if law enforcement officers are lawfully in a position from which they view it, if its incriminating character is immediately apparent, and if the officers have a lawful right of access to it." *U.S. v. Munoz*, 150 F.3d 401, 411 (5th Cir. 1998).

- "The final requirement for a plain view seizure is that the officer have a rightful access to the evidence. One Circuit has stated that this prong of *Horton* is best understood as emphasizing that even though contraband plainly can be seen and identified from outside the premises, a warrantless entry into those premises to seize the contraband would not be justified. . . . This factor, therefore, is ordinarily implicated in situations such as when an officer on the street sees an object through the window of a house, or when officers make observations via aerial photography or long-range surveillance. In those cases, the officers cannot use the plain view doctrine to justify a warrantless seizure, because to do so would require a warrantless entry upon private premises." *U.S. v. Paige*, 136 F.3d 1012, 1024 (5th Cir. 1998).

- "One situation falling within the plain view doctrine involves the seizure of contraband while searching the home of a suspect subject to a valid arrest warrant.

". . . In this case, the law enforcement officers go into
the residence based on a reasonable belief that the
suspect is there and an arrest warrant founded on probable cause. . . . After entering, they begin to search for
the suspect. This effort sometimes necessitates looking
in places where the suspect might be hiding. . . . In the
process, they come across an obviously incriminating
object—that is, an object they have probable cause to
believe is either evidence of a crime or contraband. . . .
Since the arrest warrant places them in a lawful position to view the incriminating object—by authorizing
their presence in the residence—and the search for the
suspect in places where he might be hiding establishes
their lawful right of access to it, they can seize it
without a search warrant." *U.S. v. Munoz*, 150 F.3d
401, 411 (5th Cir. 1998).

Sixth Circuit

- "An officer at the scene of an automobile stop, who can
  see the butt of a handgun under the passenger seat
  while standing outside the vehicle, can confiscate the
  gun under the plain-view exception to warrant
  requirement." *U.S. v. Campbell*, 549 F.3d 364 (6th Cir.
  2008).

- "Oxymoronic and unfortunate as it may seem, (defendant) appears to have been done in by a burning
  waterbed. The fire on the waterbed led to the bed being
  punctured, which in turn led to potential electrical
  dangers throughout much of the house due to the seep-
  age of excess water into the rooms below. This exigency
  justified local fire officials' warrantless search of many
  of the rooms of the house-including the furnace room in
  which the explosives were found in plain view-to ensure
  that the water was cleaned up and no such damage had
  occurred. We therefore affirm the district court's denial
  of (defendant's) motion to suppress the explosives." *U.S.
  v. Buckmaster*, 485 F.3d 873 (6th Cir. 2007).

Eighth Circuit

- "Morgan had no reasonable expectation of privacy when
  he voluntarily displayed his cell-phone screen in the
  presence of the detectives. . . . Morgan believes that
  the plain-view doctrine applies only if: (1) the officer is

749

in a lawful position to view the evidence, (2) the officer discovers the incriminating evidence inadvertently, and (3) the incriminating nature of the evidence is immediately apparent. Morgan contends the last two conditions are not satisfied. This contention conflates the plain-view doctrine for seizures with the plain-view doctrine for searches. An officer does not violate the Fourth Amendment by viewing evidence from a position he lawfully occupies, remembering it, and using it later. Observing what is in plain sight does not implicate the additional requirements for a seizure; being in a lawful position to observe evidence is sufficient." *United States v. Morgan*, 842 F.3d 1070, 1075 (8th Cir. 2016), cert. denied, 137 S. Ct. 2176, 198 L. Ed. 2d 244 (2017) (citations omitted).

Ninth Circuit

- "[T]his circuit and other circuits have recognized that officers must sometimes move away from the front door when they are attempting to contact the occupants of a residence. Generally, the subsequent discovery of evidence in plain view does not violate the Fourth Amendment." *U.S. v. Hammett*, 236 F.3d 1054, 1060 (9th Cir. 2001).
- "[T]he Supreme Court has limited warrantless seizures under the plain view doctrine to situations where the officer had a legal right to be at the location from which the object was plainly viewed." *U.S. v. Bulacan*, 156 F.3d 963, 968 (9th Cir. 1998), as amended, (Nov. 16, 1998).

§ 14:2 Nature of discovery: The discovery of the seized item need not be inadvertent

Supreme Court

- "[In *Coolidge*] Justice Stewart concluded that the inadvertence requirement was necessary to avoid a violation of the express constitutional requirement that a valid warrant must particularly describe the things to be seized. We find two flaws in this reasoning. First, evenhanded law enforcement is best achieved by the application of objective standards of conduct, rather than standards that depend upon the subjective state of mind of the officer. Second, the suggestion that the inadvertence requirement is necessary to prevent the police from conducting general searches, or from converting specific warrants into general warrants, is not persuasive because that interest is already served by the requirements that no warrant issue unless it particularly describ[es] the place to be searched and the persons or things to be seized." *Horton v. California*, 496 U.S. 128, 137–38, 110 S. Ct. 2301, 110 L. Ed. 2d 112 (1990).

First Circuit

- "In a feeble effort to contest this element, the appellant notes that the officers did not actually see the sawed-off shotgun until after the appellant pointed it out. That is true as far as it goes—but it does not take the appellant anywhere near his desired destination. The Fourth Amendment is concerned only with infringements upon reasonable expectations of privacy, and 'persons cannot reasonably maintain an expectation of privacy in that which they display openly.' It follows, we think, that an individual cannot frustrate the application of the plain view doctrine by the simple expedient of pointing out openly visible contraband before the police have a chance to note the presence of the contraband. What controls here is the undisputed fact that the sawed-off shotgun was clearly visible from the officers' lawful vantage point." *U.S. v. Gamache*, 792 F.3d 194, 199 (1st Cir. 2015) (citations omitted).

Second Circuit

- "The Supreme Court stated that the fourth amendment plain view doctrine did not require that the items be found inadvertently, as long as the search is confined in area and duration by the terms of a warrant or a valid exception to the warrant requirement." *U.S. v. Scopo*, 19 F.3d 777, 783 (2d Cir. 1994).

Fifth Circuit

- "The Court held that the warrantless seizure of the weapons found in plain view during the lawful search for the stolen property was permissible even though the discovery of the weapons was not inadvertent. The

Court rejected the plurality opinion in *Coolidge v. New Hampshire*, that the plain view exception only has application if the discovery of the evidence is inadvertent." *U.S. v. Hill*, 19 F.3d 984, 989 (5th Cir. 1994).

Sixth Circuit

- "The U.S. Supreme Court has articulated two requirements for a valid plain view search: (1) the incriminating nature of the item in plain view must be immediately apparent, and (2) the officer must be lawfully located in a position from which he or she can plainly see the item and have lawful access to it. The officer need not come across the seized item inadvertently." *U.S. v. Bradshaw*, 102 F.3d 204, 211, 1996 FED App. 0374P (6th Cir. 1996).

Ninth Circuit

- "Since the police were lawfully searching for evidence of murder in the graphics files, that they had legitimately accessed [pursuant to a valid search warrant] and where the incriminating child pornography was located, the evidence was properly admitted under the plain view doctrine." *U.S. v. Wong*, 334 F.3d 831 (9th Cir. 2003).

- "Once the police are lawfully searching in a place for one thing, they may seize another that is in plain view, if its incriminating nature is immediately apparent. After the plurality opinion in *Coolidge v. New Hampshire* it had been thought that the discovery of the thing not described in the warrant had to be inadvertent, but *Horton* holds that inadvertence is not required. If a police officer has a valid warrant for one item, and fully expects to find another, based on a suspicion whether or not it amounts to probable cause, the suspicion or expectation does not defeat the lawfulness of the seizure." *U.S. v. Ewain*, 88 F.3d 689, 693 (9th Cir. 1996).

- "The primary effect of *Horton* was to dispose of any inadvertence requirement to the plain view exception. The question of whether the discovery of evidence in plain view must be inadvertent had been litigated with differing results in federal and state courts. In deciding this question, the Court delineated three requirements which must be present in order for the plain view exception to apply. First, the Court recognized that the doctrine can only be applied if the officer did not violate the Fourth Amendment in arriving at the place from which the evidence could be plainly viewed. Second, the Court noted that the incriminating character of the evidence must also be immediately apparent. Third, the Court stated that the officer must also have a lawful right of access to the object itself." *G & G Jewelry, Inc. v. City of Oakland*, 989 F.2d 1093, 1099 (9th Cir. 1993).

Tenth Circuit

- "In 1990, a majority of the Court. . .held that inadvertence is not a necessary condition of legitimate plain-view seizures. . . . The Court stated that the fact that an officer is interested in an item of evidence and fully expects to find it in the course of a search should not invalidate its seizure if the search is confined in area and duration by the terms of a warrant or a valid exception to the warrant requirement." *U.S. v. Le*, 173 F.3d 1258, 1268 (10th Cir. 1999).

Eleventh Circuit

- "Just because a police officer is glad to have the opportunity to see that which is apparent at the scene of a valid arrest—when it is his duty to make the arrest—does not make his seeing these things invalid. Just because the police officers were glad that they could capitalize on the opportunity by incidentally seeing what was in plain view is of no moment. Whether or not a Fourth Amendment violation has occurred depends upon objective reasonableness in light of the facts and circumstances." *U.S. v. Hromada*, 49 F.3d 685, 691 (11th Cir. 1995).

§ 14:3 Nature of evidence: It must be immediately apparent that the seized item is incriminating, and officers must have probable cause to believe that it is incriminating

Supreme Court

- "If the police lack probable cause to believe that an object in plain view is contraband without conducting some further search of the object—i.e., if its incriminating character [is not] immediately apparent the plain-view doctrine cannot justify its seizure." *Minnesota v. Dickerson*, 508 U.S. 366, 375, 113 S. Ct. 2130, 124 L. Ed. 2d 334 (1993).

- "In *Arizona v. Hicks* this Court held invalid the seizure of stolen stereo equipment found by police while executing a valid search warrant for other evidence. Although the police were lawfully on the premises pursuant to the search warrant, they obtained probable cause to believe that the stereo equipment was contraband only after moving the equipment to permit officers to read its serial numbers. The subsequent seizure of the equipment could not be justified by the plain-view doctrine, this Court explained, because the incriminating character of the stereo equipment was not immediately apparent; rather, probable cause to believe that the equipment was stolen arose only as a result of a further search—the moving of the equipment—that was not authorized by the search warrant or by any exception to the warrant requirement." *Minnesota v. Dickerson*, 508 U.S. 366, 378, 113 S. Ct. 2130, 124 L. Ed. 2d 334 (1993).

- "[The plain-view doctrine] has an obvious application by analogy to cases in which an officer discovers contraband through the sense of touch during an otherwise lawful search. . . . If a police officer lawfully pats down a suspect's outer clothing and feels an object whose contour or mass makes its identity immediately apparent, there has been no invasion of the suspect's privacy beyond that already authorized by the officer's search for weapons; if the object is contraband, its warrantless seizure would be justified by the same practical considerations that inhere in the plain-view context." *Minnesota v. Dickerson*, 508 U.S. 366, 113 S. Ct. 2130, 124 L. Ed. 2d 334 (1993).

- "Not only must the item be in plain view, its incriminating character must also be immediately apparent. In this case the items seized from petitioner's home were discovered during a lawful search authorized by a valid warrant. When they were discovered, it was immediately apparent to the officer that they constituted incriminating evidence. He had probable cause, not only to obtain a warrant to search for the stolen property, but also to believe that the weapons and handguns had been used in the crime he was investigating. The search was authorized by the warrant, the seizure was authorized by the plain view doctrine." *Horton v. California*, 496 U.S. 128, 136, 142, 110 S. Ct. 2301, 110 L. Ed. 2d 112 (1990).

- "We have not ruled on the question whether probable cause is required in order to invoke the plain view doctrine. We now hold that probable cause is required. Dispensing with the need for a warrant is worlds apart from permitting a lesser standard of cause for the seizure than a warrant would require, i.e., the standard of probable cause. No reason is apparent why an object should routinely be seizable on lesser grounds, during an unrelated search and seizure, than would have been needed to obtain a warrant for that same object if it had been known to be on the premises." *Arizona v. Hicks*, 480 U.S. 321, 327, 107 S. Ct. 1149, 94 L. Ed. 2d 347 (1987).

- "The plain view doctrine authorizes seizure of illegal or evidentiary items visible to a police officer whose access to the object has some prior Fourth Amendment justification and who has probable cause to suspect that the item is connected with criminal activity." *Illinois v. Andreas*, 463 U.S. 765, 771, 103 S. Ct. 3319, 77 L. Ed. 2d 1003 (1983).

- "[I]t must be immediately apparent to the police that the items they observe may be evidence of a crime, contraband, or otherwise subject to seizure." *Texas v. Brown*, 460 U.S. 730, 737, 103 S. Ct. 1535, 75 L. Ed. 2d 502 (1983).

- "The plain view exception to the Fourth Amendment warrant requirement permits a law enforcement officer to seize what clearly is incriminating evidence or contraband when it is discovered in a place where the officer has a right to be." *Washington v. Chrisman*, 455 U.S. 1, 5–6, 102 S. Ct. 812, 70 L. Ed. 2d 778, 1 Ed. Law Rep. 1087 (1982).

- "[T]he extension of the original justification is legitimate only where it is immediately apparent to the police that they have evidence before them." *Coolidge v. New Hampshire*, 403 U.S. 443, 466, 91 S. Ct. 2022, 29 L. Ed. 2d 564 (1971).

First Circuit

- "[T]he plain view doctrine . . . permits the seizure of items located in plain view if '(1) the seizing officer has a prior justification for being in a position to see the item in plain view and (2) the evidentiary value of the item is immediately apparent.' . . . Evidentiary value is 'immediately apparent' if there are 'enough facts' for a reasonable person to believe that the items in plain view may be contraband or evidence of a crime. . . . The search was conducted pursuant to an investigation of a loansharking conspiracy that used violence to enforce repayment obligations. The officers had reason to believe that the weapons could have evidentiary value in connection with their investigation, as [defendant] could have used the weapons to collect debts or to protect his cash. It makes no difference that the weapons were not used to commit the crimes for which Perrotta was convicted; the Fourth Amendment requires simply that the investigators, at the time of the seizure, had reasonable grounds to believe that the items 'may [have been] contraband or evidence of a crime.'" *U.S. v. Perrotta*, 289 F.3d 155, 58 Fed. R. Evid. Serv. 1391 (1st Cir. 2002).

- "[T]he doctrine requires that the evidence's incriminating character be immediately apparent to the officer. . . . The term immediately apparent has been defined as sufficient to constitute probable cause to believe it is evidence of criminal activity. . . . This standard requires there must be enough facts for a reasonable person to believe that the items in plain view may be contraband or evidence of a crime. A practical, nontechnical probability that incriminating evidence is involved is all that is required." *U.S. v. Hamie*, 165 F.3d 80, 82–83 (1st Cir. 1999).

Second Circuit

- "As long as the scope of that initial search comported with the Fourth Amendment—i.e., was no more intrusive than necessary to accomplish its purpose of detecting weapons or explosives—then it is of no constitutional moment that the object found was not what was sought." *U.S. v. $557,933.89, More or Less, in U.S. Funds*, 287 F.3d 66 (2d Cir. 2002).

Third Circuit

- "[A] warrantless search of a closed wallet is an unreasonable search under the Fourth Amendment unless it is justified by one of the recognized exceptions to the warrant requirement. . . . [A] 'billfold offered no immediately apparent evidence of an inculpatory nature. It was only after the billfold itself had been searched that the large denomination currency was revealed.' " *U.S. v. Rivera-Padilla*, 365 Fed. Appx. 343 (3d Cir. 2010).

Fifth Circuit

- "[T]he governing standard demands not that items be 'inherently incriminating,' but that their incriminating nature be 'immediately apparent.' 'The incriminating nature of an item is "immediately apparent" if the officers have "probable cause" to believe that the item is either evidence of a crime or contraband.' " *U.S. v. Conlan*, 786 F.3d 380, 388 (5th Cir. 2015) (citations omitted).

- "The incriminating nature of an item is 'immediately apparent' if the officers have 'probable cause' to believe that the item is either evidence of a crime or contraband. . . . It appears that at the time of seizure, the officers did not have probable cause to believe that the shotgun was shorter than legally allowed or that the serial number was obliterated, because the officers could only see the weapon's handle. Further, the officers did not have probable cause to believe that [defendant] was a felon, which could have made his possession of the firearm illegal. Nor did the officers have any basis to believe that the shotgun was used in the domestic altercation with [defendant's girlfriend] such that it would qualify as evidence of a crime. . . . Nonetheless, we think the police were justified in temporarily seizing the shotgun under these circumstances . . . on a temporary basis to secure it so that the officers could investigate the domestic disturbance call. Once seized for this purpose, the incriminating nature of the weapon became apparent and it was then subject to permanent seizure as contraband." *U.S. v. Rodriguez*, 601 F.3d 402 (5th Cir. 2010).

- "In other contexts, this Court has held that the probable cause determinations may be based upon the collective knowledge of the police officers at the scene, as long as there is some general communication between the officers. This Court has also relied upon the collective knowledge doctrine when assessing whether reasonable suspicion (a lower standard than probable cause) existed. Although this Court has not applied the collective knowledge doctrine in the specific context of a seizure justified by the plain view doctrine, the Courts of Appeals for other circuits have done so. . . . [Under the circumstances of this case,] application of the collective knowledge doctrine supports the finding that the officers had probable cause to believe that [firearms found in plain view] were incriminating." *U.S. v. Waldrop*, 404 F.3d 365 (5th Cir. 2005).

Sixth Circuit

- "[In a case where police officers conducted a valid traffic stop of a car in which the defendant was a passenger and the officer had a tip of suspected drug trafficking], there was a strong nexus between the suspected narcotics trafficking and the cocaine and currency seized." *United States v. Pacheco*, 841 F.3d 384, 395 (6th Cir. 2016)

- "Officers may not manipulate an object to determine whether it is contraband; instead, it must be immediately apparent that the object is contraband." *U.S. v. Stanley*, 351 Fed. Appx. 69 (6th Cir. 2009).

- "The seizure of an item in plain view 'is legitimate only where it is immediately apparent to the police that they have evidence before them.' [citation omitted] Even though the officers in this case were authorized to search only for cocaine, they took over a hundred documents from [defendant]'s house, claiming that the plain view doctrine permitted their seizure. At trial[, the officer] testified that it was necessary to look through [defendant]'s papers and envelopes to ensure that they did not contain small packets of cocaine, but he acknowledged that it was unnecessary to read the documents in executing the search for cocaine. [The federal agent], however, expressly testified that he read and reviewed every document that he thought might contribute to his federal investigation of [defendant]. . . . The precise issue we must address here is whether a document, even though in plain view, is within the plain view exception if it must be read in order for its incriminating nature to be determined. We hold that it is not. . . . The 'immediately apparent' requirement is a vital constraint on the plain view doctrine exception to the Fourth Amendment warrant requirement. The Fourth Amendment requires that warrants must 'particularly describ[e] . . . [the] things to be seized.' [citation omitted] Requiring particular descriptions in search warrants prevents police officers from engaging in general exploratory searches—an evil experienced and abhorred by our nation's founders. [citation omitted] Because the plain view doctrine supplants the need for a particularized warrant, the 'immediately apparent' requirement is necessary to prevent officers from using the plain view doctrine as a means to extend a particularized search authorized by Fourth Amendment principles into an unlawful exploratory search. [citations and internal quotations omitted] An overbroad reading of the immediately apparent requirement subverts and jeopardizes fundamental Fourth Amendment principles. . . . In [*U.S. v.*]*McLevain* [citation omitted], we said that in determining whether an object's incriminating nature is 'immediately apparent,' we look to three factors, none of which is necessary but each of which is instructive: (1) 'a nexus between the seized object and the items particularized in the search warrant'; (2) 'whether the 'intrinsic nature' or appearance of the seized object gives probable cause to believe that it is associated with criminal activity'; and (3) whether 'the executing officers can at the time of discovery of the object on the facts then available to them determine probable cause of the object's incriminating nature.' [citation omitted] [Additionally,] . . . we have specifically held that an object's incriminating nature is not immediately apparent if it 'appears suspicious to an officer but further investigation is required to establish probable cause as to its association with criminal activity[.]' [citation omitted] Moreover, the officer must recognize the incriminating nature of an object as a result of his 'immediate' or 'instantaneous sensory perception.' [citations and internal quotation omitted] . . . We conclude that the criminal nature of most of the documents seized by [the

officer] and [the federal agent] was not immediately
apparent. Neither the intrinsic nature nor the appearance of most of the documents gave the officers probable cause to believe that they were associated with
criminal activity. Further, the officers did not, as a
result of their 'instantaneous sensory perception,' recognize the incriminating nature of most of those
documents. Receipts, financial records, and invoices, in
and of themselves, are lawful and innocuous items, and
the testimony of [the officer] and [the federal agent]
made it clear that in order to establish an association
between these documents and any criminal activity,
they had to undertake 'further investigation.' [The
federal agent] expressly admitted that he read and
reviewed every document that he thought might assist
in [defendant]'s prosecution. These documents therefore
did not come within the scope of the plain view exception to the warrant requirement." *U.S. v. Garcia*, 496
F.3d 495, 510–511 (6th Cir. 2007).

- "[The 'immediately apparent' requirement] ... limits the
use of the 'plain view' exception in two important ways.
Requiring that evidence be 'immediate' and 'apparent'
constrains the expansion of the limited search authorized by the warrant into a generalized search, and it
prevents officers from having an opportunity to create a
reason to expand the search. This Court has long
deliberated what 'immediately apparent' means. We
[have] summarized the factors used in many of our prior
cases[, and have] found that while none of these factors
is necessary, they are instructive as to what this court
has used to find that the criminality of a piece of evidence was 'immediately apparent.' The factors include
1) a nexus between the seized object and the items
particularized in the search warrant, 2) whether the
'intrinsic nature' or appearance of the seized object gives
probable cause to believe that it is associated with criminal activity, and 3) whether the executing officers can
at the time of discovery of the object on the facts then
available to them determine probable cause of the
object's incriminating nature. ... [T]he Supreme Court
does not require that officers *know* that evidence is
contraband. Instead, probable cause is a flexible,
common-sense standard. It merely requires that the

facts available to the officer would warrant a man of
reasonable caution in the belief that certain items may
be contraband or stolen property or useful as evidence
of a crime." *U.S. v. McLevain*, 310 F.3d 434, 2002 FED
App. 0390P (6th Cir. 2002).

- "If . . . the incriminating nature of the evidence is not
  immediately apparent, then the plain-view doctrine
  would not support the seizure. . . . But, if an article of
  obvious contraband is already in plain view, neither its
  observation nor its seizure would involve any invasion
  of privacy." *U.S. v. Reed*, 141 F.3d 644, 649, 1998 FED
  App. 0110P (6th Cir. 1998).

Seventh Circuit

- "Here, there was no crime being investigated, and thus
  no probable cause to believe that the weapons were
  linked to criminal activity. Accordingly, the plain view
  exception is inapplicable. . . ." *Perry v. Sheahan*, 222
  F.3d 309, 317 (7th Cir. 2000).

Eighth Circuit

- "The immediately apparent requirement means that officers must have probable cause to associate the property with criminal activity. Probable cause demands not
  that an officer be sure or certain but only that the facts
  available to a reasonably cautious man would warrant
  a belief that certain items may be contraband or stolen
  property or useful as evidence of a crime." *U.S. v.
  Weinbender*, 109 F.3d 1327, 1330 (8th Cir. 1997).

Ninth Circuit

- "The determination of whether the officers had probable
  cause to believe that the items seized were illegal,
  unlawful, or associated with criminal activity is objective, but we apply it to the 'actual and/or perceived
  belief of the law enforcement officer as he engages in
  search and seizure.' This standard does not require the
  officers to know that the item seized is illegal." *U.S. v.
  Stafford*, 416 F.3d 1068 (9th Cir. 2005).
- "Evidence may be seized without a warrant. . .when it
  is within plain view. The plain view exception requires:
  (1) that the initial intrusion must be lawful; and (2)
  that the incriminatory nature of the evidence must be

immediately apparent to the officer." *U.S. v. Garcia*, 205 F.3d 1182, 1187 (9th Cir. 2000).

Tenth Circuit

- "Probable cause doesn't require proof that something is more likely true than false. It requires only a 'fair probability,' a standard understood to mean something more than a 'bare suspicion' but less than a preponderance of the evidence at hand." *U.S. v. Denson*, 775 F.3d 1214, 1217 (10th Cir. 2014), cert. denied, 135 S. Ct. 2064, 191 L. Ed. 2d 967 (2015).

- "The 'plain smell' doctrine. . . is simply a logical extension of the 'plain view' doctrine. Here, the district court found, and [defendant] does not dispute, that the officers executing the search warrant (1) were lawfully in the. . . house, (2) had lawful authority to conduct a protective sweep of the entire premises, including the garage and basement, (3) smelled a strong odor of raw marijuana coming from duffle bags in the basement and garage, all of which were in plain sight, and (4) observed residue of marijuana on the duffle bags in the basement. We conclude these circumstances, considered together, clearly justified the seizure of the duffle bags." *U.S. v. Angelos*, 433 F.3d 738 (10th Cir. 2006).

Eleventh Circuit

- "Fingerprint evidence observed on vessel that was suspected to have been used in alien smuggling operation was subject to seizure, even absent mention of evidence in warrant to search vessel, as evidence was observed in plain view by officers who had probable cause to believe that fingerprints were evidence of a crime." *U.S. v. Zaldivar*, 292 Fed. Appx. 868 (11th Cir. 2008).

- "Police officers were justified in seizing bag under plain view doctrine; while executing arrest warrant in apartment, agent noticed bag lying under broken window through which bank robbery suspect had just escaped, female in bedroom told agent that bag belonged to suspect, and bag looked identical to one in photos of robbed banks." *U.S. v. Johnson*, 295 Fed. Appx. 342 (11th Cir. 2008).

§ 14:4 Scope of plain view: Where officials enter a private property to fight a fire, the scope of the warrantless search plain view doctrine is limited to that reasonably necessary to extinguish the blaze

Second Circuit

- "Where officials enter private property to fight a fire, the scope of the warrantless search is limited to that reasonably necessary to extinguish the blaze, determine the cause and origin of a fire, and ensure against rekindling; however, any contraband or other evidence of a crime seen in plain view during such a circumscribed search may be used to establish probable cause to obtain a warrant to conduct a broader search." *U.S. v. Klump*, 536 F.3d 113 (2d Cir. 2008).

Eighth Circuit

- "Although search warrant for defendant's convenience store was directed solely toward the purportedly stolen goods defendant had purchased from undercover officer, officers properly seized firearms from store's office pursuant to plain view doctrine where the officers were allowed to be in the office and were permitted to look in places where the purportedly stolen items might have been concealed, given that warrant allowed the officers to search the store's office for the purportedly stolen goods." *U.S. v. Abumayyaleh*, 530 F.3d 641 (8th Cir. 2008).

§ 14:5 Scope of plain view exception: computer files

Seventh Circuit

- "[T]here is nothing in the Supreme Court's case law (or the Ninth Circuit's for that matter) counseling the complete abandonment of the plain view doctrine in digital evidence cases. . . . Instead, we simply counsel officers and others involved in searches of digital media to exercise caution to ensure that warrants describe with particularity the things to be seized and that searches are narrowly tailored to uncover only those things described." *U.S. v. Mann*, 592 F.3d 779 (7th Cir. 2010).

2010.

Chapter 15

Abandonment

§ 15:1   Act: Abandonment is a voluntary relinquishment
         of control of property
§ 15:2   Consequence: An individual who abandons
         property does not retain a constitutionally
         protected expectation of privacy in the property
§ 15:3   Exception: a police officer's reasonable mistake of
         fact that the property was abandoned does not
         violate the Fourth Amendment

Research References

West's Key Number Digest

Drugs and Narcotics ☞185.10; Searches and Seizures ☞28

KeyCite®: Cases and other legal materials listed in KeyCite Scope can be researched through the KeyCite service on Westlaw®. Use KeyCite to check citations for form, parallel references, prior and later history, and comprehensive citator information, including citations to other decisions and secondary materials.

---

§ 15:1   Act: Abandonment is a voluntary relinquishment of control of property

Supreme Court

- "We observed in *Tyler* that reasonable privacy expectations may remain in fire-damaged premises. 'People may go on living in their homes or working in their offices after a fire. Even when that is impossible, private effects often remain on the fire-damaged premises.' Privacy expectations will vary with the type of property, the amount of fire damage, the prior and continued use of the premises, and in some cases the owner's efforts to secure it against intruders. Some fires may be so devastating that no reasonable privacy interests remain in the ash and ruins, regardless of the owner's subjective expectations. The test essentially is an objective one: whether 'the expectation [is] one that society is prepared to recognize as "reasonable." If reasonable privacy interests remain in the fire-damaged property, the warrant requirement applies, and any official entry must be made pursuant to a warrant in the absence of consent or exigent circumstances. . . . A burning building of course creates an exigency that justifies a warrantless entry by fire officials to fight the blaze. Moreover, in *Tyler* we held that once in the building, officials need no warrant to *remain* for 'a reasonable time to investigate the cause of the blaze after it has been extinguished.' Where, however, reasonable expectations of privacy remain in the fire-damaged property, additional investigations begun after the fire has been extinguished and fire and police officials have left the scene, generally must be made pursuant to a warrant or the identification of some new exigency. The aftermath of a fire often presents exigencies that will not tolerate the delay necessary to obtain a warrant or to secure the owner's consent to inspect fire-damaged premises. Because determining the cause and origin of a fire serves a compelling public interest, the warrant requirement does not apply in such cases. If a warrant is necessary, the object of the search determines the type of warrant required. If the primary object is to determine the cause and origin of a recent fire, an administrative warrant will suffice. To obtain such a warrant, fire officials need show only that a fire of undetermined origin has occurred on the premises, that the scope of the proposed search is reasonable and will not intrude unnecessarily on the fire victim's privacy, and that the search will be executed at a reasonable and convenient time. If the primary object of the search is to gather evidence of criminal activity, a criminal search warrant may be obtained only on a showing of probable cause to believe that relevant evidence will be found in the place to be searched. If evidence of criminal activity is discovered during the course of a valid administrative search, it may be seized under the 'plain view' doctrine. This evidence then may be used to establish probable cause to obtain a criminal search warrant. Fire officials may not, however, rely on this evidence to expand the scope of their administrative search without first making a successful showing of probable cause to an independent judicial officer. The object of the search is important even if exigent circumstances exist. Circumstances that justify a warrantless search for the cause of a fire may not justify a search to gather evidence of criminal activity once that cause has been determined. If, for example, the administrative search is justified by the immediate need to ensure against rekindling, the scope of the search may be no broader than reasonably necessary to achieve its end. A search to gather evidence of criminal activity not in plain view must be made pursuant to a criminal warrant upon a traditional showing of probable cause. . . . As the State conceded at oral argument, this case is distinguishable for several reasons. First, the challenged search was not a continuation of an earlier search. Between the time the firefighters had extinguished the blaze and left the scene and the arson investigators first arrived about 1:00 p.m. to begin their investigation, the Cliffords had taken steps to secure the privacy interests that remained in their residence against further intrusion. These efforts separate the entry made to extinguish the blaze from that made later by different officers to investigate its origin. Second, the privacy interests in the residence-particularly after the Cliffords had acted-were significantly greater than those in the fire-damaged furniture store, making the delay between the fire and the mid-day search unreasonable absent a warrant, consent, or exigent circumstances. We frequently have noted that privacy interests are especially strong in a private residence. These facts-the interim efforts to secure the burned-out premises and the heightened privacy interests in the home-distinguish this case from *Tyler*. At least where a homeowner has made a reasonable effort to secure his fire-damaged home after the blaze has been extinguished and the fire and police units have left the scene, we hold that a subsequent post-fire search must be conducted pursuant to a warrant, consent, or the identification of some new exigency. So long as the primary purpose is to ascertain the cause of the fire, an administrative warrant will suffice." *Michigan v. Clifford*, 464 U.S. 287, 292–95, 104 S. Ct. 641, 646–49, 78 L. Ed. 2d 477 (1984) (citations omitted).

- "[Items] were found in the room's wastepaper basket, where petitioner had put them while packing his belongings and preparing to leave. He had thrown them away. . . . There can be nothing unlawful in the Government's appropriation of such abandoned property." *Abel v. U.S.*, 362 U.S. 217, 241, 80 S. Ct. 683, 4 L. Ed. 2d 668 (1960).

- "The defendant's own acts, and those of his associates, disclosed the jug, the jar and the bottle—and there was no seizure in the sense of the law when the officers examined the contents of each after it had been abandoned." *Hester v. U.S.*, 265 U.S. 57, 58, 44 S. Ct. 445, 68 L. Ed. 898 (1924).

Third Circuit

- "A warrantless search of property is permissible under the Fourth Amendment where the owner has abandoned his reasonable expectation of privacy in that property. This determination must be made from an objective viewpoint, and proof of intent to abandon must be established by clear and unequivocal evidence. We look at the totality of the facts and circumstances in making such a determination. In most cases, disclaiming ownership or physically relinquishing the property is sufficient to establish abandonment. We note that, 'abandonment for purposes of the Fourth Amendment differs from abandonment in property law; here the analysis examines the individual's reasonable expectation of privacy, not his property interest in the item.' Thus, our holding will not turn on whether the house was abandoned under the common law of property. 'Indeed, there is a real difference between property-law and constitutional abandonment, for courts have repeatedly found abandonment for constitutional purposes in situations that might not support a finding of abandonment in the common-law understanding.' Therefore, the fact that for common law purposes real property cannot be abandoned is not dispositive. Rather, it will inform our inquiry. As such, what the common law property rules suggest is that abandonment of real property under the Fourth Amendment is difficult, but not impossible, to establish. . . . [A] person can, as he can with any other property, sufficiently manifest an intent to abandon his house. . . . A person can, through his own acts or omissions, manifest an intent to relinquish his legitimate expectation of privacy in his real property, as the same test applies regardless of the nature of the property. This is, however, a difficult standard to meet, and one that requires a careful analysis of all the facts and circumstances of a particular case. Before the government may cross the threshold of a home without a warrant, there must be clear, unequivocal and unmistakable evidence that the property has been abandoned. Only then will such a search be permitted." *U.S. v. Harrison*, 689 F.3d 301, 306–09, 99 A.L.R.6th 795 (3d Cir. 2012) (citations omitted).

- "Although a person has a privacy interest in the contents of his personal luggage, he forfeits that interest when he abandons his property. Abandonment for purposes of the Fourth Amendment differs from abandonment in property law; here the analysis examines the individual's reasonable expectation of privacy, not his property interest in the item. A court must determine from an objective viewpoint whether property has been abandoned. Proof of intent to abandon property must be established by clear and unequivocal evidence." *U.S. v. Fulani*, 368 F.3d 351 (3d Cir. 2004).

Fourth Circuit

- "When a person voluntarily abandons his privacy interest in property, his subjective expectation of privacy becomes unreasonable, and he is precluded from seeking to suppress evidence seized from it. The proper test for abandonment is not whether all formal property rights have been relinquished, but whether the complaining party retains a reasonable expectation of privacy in the property alleged to be abandoned. In making that determination, however, it is still relevant to consider a defendant's property interest." *U.S. v. Stevenson*, 396 F.3d 538 (4th Cir. 2005).

Seventh Circuit

- "To demonstrate abandonment, the government must prove by a preponderance of the evidence that the defendant's voluntary words or actions would lead a reasonable person in the searching officer's position to believe that the defendant relinquished his property interests in the item to be searched. This is an objective test and the defendant's subjective desire to later reclaim an item is irrelevant. We look solely to the external manifestations of the defendant's intent as judged by a reasonable person possessing the same knowledge available to the government agents involved in the search. . . . The defendants' subjective desire to maintain control of the package is irrelevant. . . in light of the external manifestations of their intent. At the time the warrant was issued, [defendant 1] had expressly disavowed the package. He refused to accept its delivery and he was the only resident of the home to whom the package was addressed. The postal inspectors were obviously not aware of his later-expressed intent to receive the package. A reasonable person in the postal inspector's position would believe that [defendant 1] relinquished his property interests in the parcel. [Defendant 1] therefore abandoned the package and his Fourth Amendment claim fails. The case for [defendant 2] is only a little more difficult. He launched the package into the stream of mail without any legitimate way of retrieving it. Because he sent it via Express Mail and used a false return address, he acknowledges he would have been required to produce a copy of the mailing label and proper identification in the name of the sender in order to retrieve the package. His counsel conceded at oral argument that [defendant 2] did not have proper identification in the name [in which the package was mailed]. Because [defendant 2] could not retrieve the package and [defendant 1] refused to accept it, the parcel was abandoned. *U.S. v. Pitts*, 322 F.3d 449 (7th Cir. 2003).

- "To demonstrate abandonment, the government must establish by a preponderance of the evidence that the defendant's voluntary words or conduct would lead a reasonable person in the searching officer's position to believe that the defendant relinquished his property interests in the item searched or seized. . . .Because this is an objective test, it does not matter whether the defendant harbors a desire to later reclaim an item; we look solely to the external manifestations of his intent as judged by a reasonable person possessing the same knowledge available to the government agents. . . .We look at the totality of the circumstances, but pay particular attention to explicit denials of ownership and to any physical relinquishment of the property." *U.S. v. Basinski*, 226 F.3d 829, 836–37 (7th Cir. 2000).

- "There are three general types of abandonment cases, which are based on these two indicia of abandonment. The first type is characterized by the presence of a fleeing defendant who relinquishes an object to make his flight easier or because discarding the item might make it easier for him to later claim that he never possessed it. . . .The second type of case is closely related to the first, for in so-called garbage cases the defendant places material in or near a refuse receptacle that is readily accessible to the public, and in which he usually places other discarded materials. . . .In the third type of case, the defendant is usually caught red-handed with or near a container of contraband, whereupon he denies that the container or its contents are his." *U.S. v. Basinski*, 226 F.3d 829, 837 (7th Cir. 2000).

- "In determining whether a person has abandoned property, we can infer from words spoken, acts done, and other objective facts whether he voluntarily discarded, left behind, or otherwise relinquished his interest in the property in question." *Bond v. U.S.*, 77 F.3d 1009, 1013 (7th Cir. 1996).

- "In *California v. Greenwood* the Supreme Court held that the Fourth Amendment does not prohibit the warrantless search and seizure of garbage left for collection outside the curtilage of the home. The garbage containers in *Greenwood* were located at the curb in place for collection at a fixed time. As in this case, the evidence which was collected from *Greenwood*'s garbage was found inside sealed, opaque bags. The Court held that any expectation of privacy in the garbage was not objectively reasonable because of the extent to which the garbage was exposed to the public. Specifically, the Court noted that it is common knowledge that plastic garbage bags left on or at the side of a public street are readily accessible to animals, children, scavengers, snoops, and other members of the public. Moreover, the garbage was placed at the curb for the express purpose of conveying it to a third party, the trash collector, who might himself have sorted through respondents' trash or permitted others, such as the police, to do so." *U.S. v. Shanks*, 97 F.3d 977, 979 (7th Cir. 1996).

- "An abandonment that results from police misconduct is not valid. In examining the voluntariness of a person's response to a police officer's inquiry, a court should inquire as to whether a reasonable person (i.e. a person who was not carrying contraband) would feel free to refuse to comply with the officer's request. Moreover, an abandonment that occurs in response to proper police activity has not been coerced in violation of the Fourth Amendment." *U.S. v. McDonald*, 100 F.3d 1320, 1328 (7th Cir. 1996).

Eighth Circuit

- "We conclude that the entry into the home did not violate Barnes's clearly established constitutional rights. It was reasonable for the officers to believe that their obligation to knock and announce their presence, or to ascertain the arrestee's presence, does not apply to an abandoned property. A search of abandoned property 'does not implicate the Fourth Amendment, for any expectation of privacy in the item searched is forfeited upon its abandonment.' Even though it turned out that Barnes had not actually abandoned the house, officers do not violate the Fourth Amendment if they act upon a mistake of fact that is objectively reasonable, and they are also entitled to qualified immunity if a mistake about abandonment was objectively reasonable. . . . McKenney also argues that even if the officers could reasonably have believed that the house was abandoned at the time they entered, they should have known otherwise when they heard the fan upstairs. But because a reasonable officer could have concluded that the house was abandoned, a reasonable officer also could have concluded that anyone in the house was a trespasser who has no privacy interest under the Fourth Amendment." *McKenney v. Harrison*, 635 F.3d 354 (8th Cir. 2011).

- "In determining whether property has been abandoned for Fourth Amendment purposes, the court must look to the totality of the circumstances, noting in particular two factors: whether the suspect denied ownership of the property and whether he physically relinquished the property. . . . Further, whether an abandonment has occurred is determined on the basis of the objective facts available to the investigating officers, not on the basis of the owner's subjective intent." *U.S. v. Liu*, 180 F.3d 957, 960 (8th Cir. 1999).

- "When a person voluntarily abandons property, he forfeits any expectation of privacy that he might otherwise have had in it. . . . Here, [Defendant] denied that he owned the black bag only after he had been seized and handcuffed by the officers. Given this scenario, [Defendant]'s actions can hardly be characterized as a voluntary act." *U.S. v. Gwinn*, 191 F.3d 874, 877 (8th Cir. 1999).

- "Whether an abandonment has occurred is determined on the basis of objective facts available to the investigating officers, not on the basis of the owner's subjective intent. . . . When considering whether the circumstances support a finding of abandonment, two important factors are denial of ownership and physical relinquishment of the property." *U.S. v. Landry*, 154 F.3d 897, 899 (8th Cir. 1998).

- "[Defendant]'s statements to the officers that he did not own the bag were sufficient to constitute abandonment. . . . When [Defendant] disclaimed ownership, he surrendered any legitimate expectation of privacy he had in the bag. The fact that he forfeited his Fourth Amendment guarantee of privacy was enough to discharge the officers' Fourth Amendment obligation to obtain a search warrant. The Fourth Amendment only protects privacy. It does not immunize people who, finding themselves in a compromising situation, voluntarily trade their interest in privacy for a chance to escape incrimination, no matter how unwise the decision may seem in retrospect." *U.S. v. Sanders*, 130 F.3d 1316, 1317–18 (8th Cir. 1997).

Ninth Circuit

- "To find that a person has abandoned property, a district court need only conclude whether the person so relinquished his interest in the property that he no longer retained a reasonable expectation of privacy at the time of the search. Here, prior to police entry into the

773

residence in search of medical information, [the defendant] told aid personnel that the house was not his, and that the contents of the house belonged to McAlpin. [The defendant] had also produced identification which listed his address as being in another city, and informed police that the address listed on the identification was his correct address. Finally, when released by police, [the defendant] got into his car and drove away. Because [the defendant's] actions are not consistent with any reasonable expectation of privacy, the district court's determination that [the defendant] had abandoned the residence was not clearly erroneous." *U.S. v. Ferguson*, 33 Fed. Appx. 849, 850 (9th Cir. 2002) (citations omitted).

- "A defendant who voluntarily abandons property has no standing to contest its search and seizure. . . . But abandonment is a question of intent. . . . An abandonment must be voluntary, and an abandonment that results from Fourth Amendment violation cannot be voluntary." *U.S. v. Stephens*, 206 F.3d 914, 917 (9th Cir. 2000).

Tenth Circuit

- "Tubens contends his abandoning the carry-on was not voluntary, and thus that suppression is required, because his disclaimer of ownership was precipitated by a violation of his Fourth Amendment rights. Although he separately challenges as unconstitutional most of the component parts of the officers' investigation, the unifying theme throughout his brief is that the officers lacked the legal justification necessary to investigate as they did. We disagree: even assuming, as the district court did, that the officers' investigation of Tubens escalated from a consensual encounter, requiring no justification, to an investigative detention, requiring reasonable suspicion of criminal activity, that standard was more than satisfied under the circumstances of this case, where two drug dogs independently alerted to Tubens' checked suitcase, and he responded to the officers' subsequent investigation in an evasive and inconsistent manner. Under the strictures of *Terry v. Ohio*, in other words, no Fourth Amendment violation precipitated Tubens' abandonment of the suspect carry-on because the officers' investigation was both justified at its inception and reasonably related in scope to the circumstances which justified the interference in the first place." *U.S. v. Tubens*, 765 F.3d 1251, 1254 (10th Cir. 2014) (inner quotations and citations omitted).

- "Every case in which we have found abandonment involved a situation where the defendant either (1) explicitly disclaimed an interest in the object, or (2) unambiguously engaged in physical conduct that constituted abandonment. For example, in *United States v. Austin* . . . the defendant entrusted his luggage to a total stranger at the airport. The stranger, concerned that it might contain a bomb, turned it over to airport security. We held that releasing luggage to a total stranger constitutes abandonment, at least until such time as it is recovered. In *United States v. Jones* . . . the defendant threw away a knapsack while being chased by the police. We held that the physical act of discarding the knapsack on to public property where it could be picked up by anyone constituted abandonment." *U.S. v. Garzon*, 119 F.3d 1446, 1452 (10th Cir. 1997).

Eleventh Circuit

- "We readily affirm the district court's denial of the motion to suppress the evidence recovered from trash left at the curb in front of [defendant's] house. . . . Having placed the garbage near the curb for the purpose of conveying it to third parties, the trash collector, or other members of the public, we cannot find that appellant had a reasonable expectation of privacy in the inculpatory items discarded. Whether there was a reasonable expectation of privacy in the trash left at the left side of the residence near the garage is a closer question, the obvious distinction being that trash left near the curb is more exposed to the public than is trash left closer to the house. [Defendant] urges that the trash near the garage was within the curtilage (generally the land or yard adjoining a house) of his home and therefore well within the protections of the Fourth Amendment. The district court never made a specific finding that the trash near the garage was inside or outside the curtilage, and we find it unnecessary to decide that question on appeal. [We must] consider the extent to which the garbage was exposed to the public, and that analysis does not require a 'curtilage' determination. . . .We believe that the proper focus. . . is whether the garbage was readily accessible to the public so as to render any expectation of privacy objectively unreasonable. . . . We agree that placing trash in a location where it is *routinely* removed by trash collectors, on the day designated for trash collection, lessens the reasonableness of a homeowner's expectation of privacy. . . . Although a member of the public would have had to access [defendant's] property to gain access to the trash, that fact alone does not provide him with a reasonable expectation of privacy. . . . Even though the trash was located on [defendant's] property, near his garage, there was no reasonable expectation of privacy because the trash was sufficiently exposed to the public. . . . Unfortunately, we can offer no bright-line rule to fit all future garbage suppression cases. These inquiries are highly fact-intensive, and we simply find that on the particular facts of this case, [defendant] had no reasonable expectation of privacy in either the trash near the curb or the trash near his house." *U.S. v. Segura-Baltazar*, 448 F.3d 1281 (11th Cir. 2006).

§ 15:2 Consequence: An individual who abandons property does not retain a constitutionally protected expectation of privacy in the property

Supreme Court

- "The warrantless search and seizure of the garbage bags left at the curb outside the [Defendant's] house would violate the Fourth Amendment only if respondents manifested a subjective expectation of privacy in their garbage that society accepts as objectively reasonable. It may be that respondents did not expect that the contents of their garbage bags would become known to the police or other members of the public. An expectation of privacy does not give rise to Fourth Amendment protection, however, unless society is prepared to accept that expectation as objectively reasonable. Accordingly, having deposited their garbage in an area particularly suited for public inspection and, in a manner of speaking, public consumption, for the express purpose of having strangers take it. respondents could have had no reasonable expectation of privacy in the inculpatory items that they discarded." *California v. Greenwood*, 486 U.S. 35, 39, 108 S. Ct. 1625, 100 L. Ed. 2d 30 (1988).

First Circuit

- "Defendant had no reasonable expectation of privacy with respect to the crack cocaine and the firearm he allegedly threw away while being pursued by police, as required to be able to challenge their seizure under the Fourth Amendment; defendant actively disowned any interest in the items." *U.S. v. Lipscomb*, 539 F.3d 32 (1st Cir. 2008).

- "When a defendant abandons property before a seizure occurs, the Fourth Amendment is not implicated because the property is not the fruit of an illegal search and seizure. An arrest requires either physical force or, where that is absent, submission to the assertion of authority. The police have made an assertion of authority only if their words and actions would have caused an average citizen to believe he was not free to leave. In *Hodari*, a police officer was chasing the defendant and, moments before the officer tackled him, the defendant tossed a rock of cocaine from his person. The Court held that, assuming that [the Officer's] pursuit constituted a show of authority enjoining [the Defendant] to halt, since [he] did not comply with that injunction he was not seized until he was tackled. Thus, the cocaine abandoned during the course of the chase was not the fruit of a seizure." *U.S. v. Lewis*, 40 F.3d 1325, 1334, 41 Fed. R. Evid. Serv. 661 (1st Cir. 1994).

Second Circuit

- "[T]he Fourth Amendment's prohibition against unreasonable searches is designed to protect an individual's reasonable expectation of privacy. . . . However, mere ownership of property does not establish a legitimate expectation of privacy unless the owner vigilantly protects the right to exclude others. . . . Thus, even in the absence of a warrant and probable cause, a search of property that has been abandoned, for example, does not violate a privacy interest. . . . And although an owner retains some privacy interest in property that is merely lost or stolen, rather than intentionally abandoned, that interest is outweighed by the interest of law enforcement officials in identifying and returning such property to the owner." *Gudema v. Nassau County*, 163 F.3d 717, 722 (2d Cir. 1998).

Third Circuit

- "Defendant voluntarily abandoned any interest in his bedroom safe through his repeated denials of ownership of it, and thus, agents did not need a search warrant or consent to validly search it; agents received consent to search defendant's bedroom from defendant's aunt, and although agents did not initially have authority to search the safe, defendant repeatedly denied ownership of safe, even after he was administered *Miranda* warnings." *U.S. v. Anderson*, 284 Fed. Appx. 977 (3d Cir. 2008).

Fourth Circuit

- "Defendant abandoned the vehicle he was driving and thus lost any reasonable expectation of privacy in the contents of vehicle, rendering police search of trunk of vehicle permissible; after being pursued by police during a dangerous high-speed chase, defendant jumped out of the still-moving vehicle and fled on foot, as the car drifted down the road into oncoming traffic before coming to a stop on the median." *U.S. v. Kirlew*, 291 Fed. Appx. 536 (4th Cir. 2008).
- "[A] person who voluntarily abandons property loses any reasonable expectation of privacy in the property and is consequently precluded from seeking to suppress evidence seized from the property. Denial of ownership constitutes abandonment." *U.S. v. Han*, 74 F.3d 537, 543 (4th Cir. 1996).

Seventh Circuit

- "Abandoned property is not subject to Fourth Amendment protection. . . .This is because Fourth Amendment protection only extends to places and items for which a person has a reasonable expectation of privacy, and no person can have a reasonable expectation of privacy in an item that he has abandoned." *U.S. v. Basinski*, 226 F.3d 829, 836 (7th Cir. 2000).

- "Because the garbage cans in this case were readily accessible and visible from a public thoroughfare, the alley, and because it is common for scavengers to snoop through garbage cans found in such alleys, we agree that [Defendant] could harbor no reasonable expectation of privacy since the garbage was essentially exposed to the public." *U.S. v. Shanks*, 97 F.3d 977, 980 (7th Cir. 1996).

Eighth Circuit

- "Police may search trash left outside the curtilage of the house to be picked up by garbage collectors, because the owners of the trash have abandoned it." *U.S. v. Spotted Elk*, 548 F.3d 641 (8th Cir. 2008).
- "Defendant relinquished his reasonable expectation of privacy over handgun by abandoning it under a tree." *U.S. v. Richardson*, 537 F.3d 951 (8th Cir. 2008).
- "A warrantless search of abandoned property is constitutional because any expectation of privacy in the item searched is forfeited upon its abandonment. . . . In determining whether property has been abandoned for Fourth Amendment purposes, the court must look to the totality of the circumstances, noting in particular two factors: whether the suspect denied ownership of the property and whether he physically relinquished the property." *U.S. v. Chandler*, 197 F.3d 1198, 1200, 53 Fed. R. Evid. Serv. 879 (8th Cir. 1999).
- "When a person abandons his luggage, his expectation of privacy in the property is so eroded that he no longer has standing to challenge a search of the luggage on Fourth Amendment grounds." *U.S. v. Liu*, 180 F.3d 957, 960 (8th Cir. 1999).
- "We are of the view . . . that the search of the interior of his bag did not violate [Defendant]'s Fourth Amendment rights because he voluntarily abandoned it prior to that search. When a person voluntarily abandons property, he or she forfeits any expectation of privacy that he or she might otherwise have had in it." *U.S. v. Washington*, 146 F.3d 536, 537 (8th Cir. 1998).
- "The Fourth Amendment's protection extends only to those who have a legitimate expectation of privacy in

the property at the time it is searched. . . . It is therefore firmly established that a warrantless search of abandoned property is not unreasonable and does not violate the Constitution." *U.S. v. Sanders*, 130 F.3d 1316, 1317 (8th Cir. 1997).

- "A warrantless search of abandoned property does not implicate the Fourth Amendment, for any expectation of privacy in the item searched is forfeited upon its abandonment. . . . The issue is not abandonment in the strict property right sense, but rather, whether the defendant in leaving the property has relinquished her reasonable expectation of privacy so that the search and seizure is valid. . . . Whether an abandonment has occurred is determined on the basis of the objective facts available to the investigating officers, not on the basis of the owner's subjective intent. . . . This determination is to be made in light of the totality of the circumstances, and two important factors are denial of ownership and physical relinquishment of the property." *U.S. v. Tugwell*, 125 F.3d 600, 602 (8th Cir. 1997).

- "The warrantless seizure of abandoned property does not violate the Fourth Amendment. This is because [w]hen individuals voluntarily abandon property, they forfeit any expectation of privacy in it that they might have had. The existence of police pursuit or investigation at the time of abandonment does not itself render the abandonment involuntary. An expectation of privacy is a question of intent, which may be inferred from words spoken, acts done and other objective facts. However, abandonment cannot be the product of unlawful police conduct. The evidence showed that, when confronted by police officers, [Defendant] dropped the package, backed away from the apartment door and attempted to flee. In the present case [Defendant] was not seized until after he dropped the package. The police officer's order to drop to the ground constituted the requisite show of authority but, like the defendant in *Hodari D.*, [Defendant] did not comply with that injunction. Instead, he dropped everything he was carrying, including the package, backed away from the door and ran down the hall. He was not seized until he was apprehended by the police." *U.S. v. Segars*, 31 F.3d 655, 658 (8th Cir. 1994).

Tenth Circuit

- "In garbage cases, Fourth Amendment reasonableness turns on public accessibility to the trash. . . . Society does not recognize a reasonable expectation of privacy in trash left for collection in an area accessible to the public." *U.S. v. Long*, 176 F.3d 1304, 1308 (10th Cir. 1999).

Eleventh Circuit

- "Generally, an individual enjoys a reasonable expectation of privacy in personal luggage. However, an individual who abandons or denies ownership of personal property may not contest the constitutionality of its subsequent acquisition by the police. In determining whether there has been abandonment, the critical inquiry is whether the person prejudiced by the search voluntarily discarded, left behind, or otherwise relinquished his interest in the property in question so that he could no longer retain a reasonable expectation of privacy with regard to it at the time of the search. Whether abandonment has occurred is a question of intent that may be inferred from acts, words and other objective facts. While the individual whose property was searched bears the burden of proving a legitimate expectation of privacy in the items searched, the burden of proving abandonment is on the government." *U.S. v. Cofield*, 272 F.3d 1303 (11th Cir. 2001).

- "In *California v. Greenwood*, the Supreme Court held that a warrantless search and seizure of garbage left in a plastic bag on the curb in front of, but outside the curtilage of, a private house did not violate the Fourth Amendment. The Court held that such a search would only violate the Fourth Amendment if the persons discarding the garbage manifested a subjective expectation of privacy in their garbage that society accepts as objectively reasonable." *U.S. v. Hall*, 47 F.3d 1091, 1094 (11th Cir. 1995).

§ 15:3 Exception: a police officer's reasonable mistake of fact that the property was abandoned does not violate the Fourth Amendment

Third Circuit

- "In this case, it is undisputed that the house was not actually abandoned and that [the defendant], as a renter, possessed a reasonable expectation of privacy in the property. Therefore, the only issue before us is whether the police officers' belief that the house was abandoned justified their warrantless entry. The law does not require that police officers always be factually correct; it does demand, however, that they always be reasonable. 'Consequently, a reasonable mistake of fact does not violate the Fourth Amendment.' In deciding what is reasonable, a court is to apply an objective standard, looking at whether 'the facts available to the officer at the moment . . . warrant a man of reasonable caution in the belief' that the search was permissible. . . . It is unreasonable to assume that a poorly maintained home is an abandoned home. A one-time look at 2114 North Franklin Street in its dilapidated condition would not justify the police entering it without a warrant because a reasonably cautious officer would only assume that the person who occupied the home did not maintain it as they should, not that they had clearly manifested an intent to relinquish their expectation of privacy in the house. There simply is no 'trashy house exception' to the warrant requirement. . . . It is one thing to infer that a person has abandoned his expectation of privacy in his home based on a one-time observation. It is quite another to observe that same property in that same dilapidated condition with a front door that is 'always open' over the course of several months. Over time, the inference that the property has been 'thrown away' becomes significantly stronger. Given the combination of the rundown exterior, the 'always open' door, the trashed interior, and the extended observations over time, the police officers were reasonable in their mistaken belief that the house was abandoned. Based on the totality of the circumstances, the warrantless search was permitted under the Fourth Amendment and the District Court did not err when it denied *Harrison*'s motion to suppress." *U.S. v. Harrison*, 689 F.3d 301, 309–12, 99 A.L.R.6th 795 (3d Cir. 2012) (citations omitted).

Eight Circuit

- "We conclude that the entry into the home did not violate Barnes's clearly established constitutional rights. It was reasonable for the officers to believe that their obligation to knock and announce their presence, or to ascertain the arrestee's presence, does not apply to an abandoned property. A search of abandoned property 'does not implicate the Fourth Amendment, for any expectation of privacy in the item searched is forfeited upon its abandonment.' Even though it turned out that Barnes had not actually abandoned the house, officers do not violate the Fourth Amendment if they act upon a mistake of fact that is objectively reasonable, and they are also entitled to qualified immunity if a mistake about abandonment was objectively reasonable. The totality of the circumstances supported an objectively reasonable belief by the officers that the house was abandoned. The officers found the house in disrepair, with an unkempt yard and a fence that was incomplete and falling apart. There were no vehicles parked in the driveway. No one responded when the officers knocked on the front door, and the back door was open three or four inches. Through the open door, the officers could see into the kitchen, where the cabinets were open and empty, the refrigerator was open, empty, and pulled away from the wall, and there was no furniture or personal effects. There were no lights on, sounds from appliances, or other indications that the house had electrical power. In light of these facts, it was reasonable for [the officers] to conclude that the house was abandoned." *McKenney v. Harrison*, 635 F.3d 354, 358–59 (8th Cir. 2011) (citations omitted).

Chapter 16

Curtilage

Research References

West's Key Number Digest
Searches and Seizures ⊙26 to 27

KeyCite®: Cases and other legal materials listed in KeyCite Scope can be researched through the KeyCite service on Westlaw®. Use KeyCite to check citations for form, parallel references, prior and later history, and comprehensive citator information, including citations to other decisions and secondary materials.

---

§ 16:1   Curtilage doctrine: The curtilage is afforded the same Fourth Amendment protections as is the home

Supreme Court

- "We do not express any view on whether [the officer's] entry into [the home owner's] yard in pursuit of [the suspect] was constitutional. But whether or not the constitutional rule applied by the court below was cor-

785

rect, it was not 'beyond debate.' There is no suggestion in this case that [the officer] knowingly violated the Constitution; the question is whether, in light of precedent existing at the time, he was 'plainly incompetent' in entering [the home owner's] yard to pursue the fleeing [suspect]. The Ninth Circuit concluded that he was. It did so despite the fact that federal and state courts nationwide are sharply divided on the question whether an officer with probable cause to arrest a suspect for a misdemeanor may enter a home without a warrant while in hot pursuit of that suspect. . . . To summarize the law at the time [the officer] made his split-second decision to enter [the home owner's] yard: Two opinions of this Court were equivocal on the lawfulness of his entry; two opinions of the State Court of Appeal affirmatively authorized that entry; the most relevant opinion of the Ninth Circuit was readily distinguishable; two Federal District Courts in the Ninth Circuit had granted qualified immunity in the wake of that opinion; and the federal and state courts of last resort around the Nation were sharply divided. Stanton may have been mistaken in believing his actions were justified, but he was not 'plainly incompetent.' " *Stanton v. Sims*, 134 S. Ct. 3, 187 L. Ed. 2d 341 (2013) (42 U.S.C.A. § 1983 action by home owner who alleged that when officer kicked open a fence gate, which she had been standing behind, her forehead was cut and her shoulder was injured; remanded for consideration of officer's claim to qualified immunity).

- "[T]he *Katz* reasonable-expectation-of-privacy test has been *added to,* not *substituted for,* the common-law trespassory test." *U.S. v. Jones*, 565 U.S. 400, 132 S. Ct. 945, 952, 181 L. Ed. 2d 911 (2012).
- "[W]e believe that curtilage questions should be resolved with particular reference to four factors: the proximity of the area claimed to be curtilage to the home, whether the area is included within an enclosure surrounding the home, the nature of the uses to which the area is put, and the steps taken by the resident to protect the area from observation by people passing by. We do not suggest that combining these factors produces a finely tuned formula that, when mechanically applied, yields a correct answer to all extent-of-curtilage questions.

Rather, these factors are useful analytical tools only to the degree that, in any given case, they bear upon the centrally relevant consideration—whether the area in question is so intimately tied to the home itself that it should be placed under the home's 'umbrella' of Fourth Amendment protection." *U.S. v. Dunn*, 480 U.S. 294, 301, 107 S. Ct. 1134, 94 L. Ed. 2d 326 (1987).

- "The protection afforded the curtilage is essentially a protection of families and personal privacy in an area intimately linked to the home, both physically and psychologically, where privacy expectations are most heightened. The claimed area here was immediately adjacent to a suburban home, surrounded by high double fences. This close nexus to the home would appear to encompass this small area within the curtilage." *California v. Ciraolo*, 476 U.S. 207, 212–13, 106 S. Ct. 1809, 90 L. Ed. 2d 210 (1986).

- "[O]nly the curtilage, not the neighboring open fields, warrants the Fourth Amendment protections that attach to the home. At common law, the curtilage is the area to which extends the intimate activity associated with the sanctity of a man's home and the privacies of life, and therefore has been considered part of home itself for Fourth Amendment purposes. Thus, courts have extended Fourth Amendment protection to the curtilage; and they have defined the curtilage, as did the common law, by reference to the factors that determine whether an individual reasonably may expect that an area immediately adjacent to the home will remain private." *Oliver v. U.S.*, 466 U.S. 170, 180, 104 S. Ct. 1735, 80 L. Ed. 2d 214 (1984).

First Circuit

- "The curtilage of one's home encompasses 'the area immediately surrounding and associated with the home,' and it is regarded as part of the home for purposes of the Fourth Amendment . . . .. Pérez argues that the agents violated the Fourth Amendment by trespassing on the curtilage of his home by entering through the back gate. We need not here resolve whether the area between the back gate and the front door is curtilage, because the officers did not use force to enter it, and they did not search the area—they only passed through it in order to knock on Pérez's front door. In *Jardines*, the Supreme Court found that officers had violated the Fourth Amendment by searching (using a drug-sniffing dog) the curtilage of the defendant's home; the Supreme Court also considered it 'an unsurprising proposition' that the officers could have passed through the defendant's curtilage and 'lawfully approached his home to knock on the front door in hopes of speaking with him.' This is so, because an 'implicit license typically permits the visitor to approach the home by the front path, knock promptly. . . . Complying with the terms of that traditional invitation . . . is generally managed without incident by the Nation's Girl Scouts and trick-or-treaters.' The FBI agents therefore did not violate the curtilage of Pérez's home by opening the back gate or by merely walking from the back gate to the front door. *United States v. Perez-Diaz*, 848 F.3d 33, 39 (1st Cir. 2017) (citations omitted).

Second Circuit

- "In determining whether an area is within the curtilage of a home and entitled to the same privacy protections under the Fourth Amendment as the home, the court should examine: (1) the area's proximity to the main residence; (2) any enclosure of the property or area; (3) use of the property or area; and (4) steps taken to protect the property or area from view." *U.S. v. Hayes*, 551 F.3d 138 (2d Cir. 2008).

- "Path taken by the police canine to the east of the house and through the backyard to sniff scrub brush located 65 feet from the back door of the house and on the border of the neighbor's property, which revealed a black bag containing narcotics in the brush, did not invade the curtilage of the home for Fourth Amendment purposes. While there was an alternative path to the backyard along the driveway in full view of the street which was plainly outside the curtilage, the narcotic smell was so strong it could be smelled from 65 feet away, and if the canine had taken an alternate path he would have led the officer to the bag." *U.S. v. Hayes*, 551 F.3d 138 (2d Cir. 2008).

- "The initial warrantless entry onto the suspect's property to search a shed did not violate the suspect's Fourth

Amendment rights, where the area searched was not within the curtilage of the suspect's home; any trees, bushes, or stumps on the property's perimeter did not significantly limit access to or the visibility of the shed from neighboring properties, the shed was clearly a structure meant for dogs and not for intimate human activity, overflowing "poop pit" near shed suggested area would be unattractive to private home activities, and area was relatively open to exposure from neighbors and the public at large." *Simko v. Town of Highlands*, 276 Fed. Appx. 39 (2d Cir. 2008).

Fourth Circuit

- "Though we conclude the officers' conduct comported with the Fourth Amendment, we reiterate that the area within the curtilage of the home typically is afforded the most stringent Fourth Amendment protection. . . . It was not unreasonable, however, for officers responding to a 911 call to enter the backyard when circumstances indicated they might find the homeowner there. Thus, the officers did not violate the Fourth Amendment. . . ." *Alvarez v. Montgomery County*, 147 F.3d 354, 359 (4th Cir. 1998).

Fifth Circuit

- "The Fourth Amendment extends to protect the curtilage of a home from unconstitutional searches. . . . The curtilage constitutes the area within which a person reasonably may expect that the area in question should be treated as the home itself. . . . In determining whether an area outside the home is curtilage, we must consider four factors: the proximity of the area to the home, whether it is within an enclosure surrounding the home, the nature of the uses to which the area is put, and the steps taken by the resident to protect the area from outside observation." *U.S. v. Thomas*, 120 F.3d 564, 571 (5th Cir. 1997).

Sixth Circuit

- "Therefore, we hold that where knocking at the front door is unsuccessful in spite of indications that someone is in or around the house, an officer may take reasonable steps to speak with the person being sought out even where such steps require an intrusion into the curtilage. In this case, there were indications that someone was present within the . . . home, knocking at the front door proved unsuccessful, proceeding around the house and onto the back deck was a reasonable step, and that step was directed towards initiating a conversation with the person or persons in the house. Therefore, the . . . officers' entry into the curtilage in order to effectuate the knock and talk investigative technique did not violate Plaintiffs' Fourth Amendment rights." *Hardesty v. Hamburg Tp.*, 461 F.3d 646 (6th Cir. 2006).

- "The Supreme Court has noted that, for most homes, the boundaries of the curtilage will be clearly marked; and the conception defining the curtilage—as the area around the home to which the activity of home life extends—is a familiar one easily understood from our daily experience. . . . Unfortunately this test endorses a we know it when we see it approach that provides little guidance to courts attempting to determine whether a particular area falls within a home's curtilage. . . . In an effort to clarify the law in this area, the Supreme Court in *United States v. Dunn* . . . outlined four factors to employ as analytic tools in determining whether a particular area constitutes curtilage." *Daughenbaugh v. City of Tiffin*, 150 F.3d 594, 598, 1998 FED App. 0232P (6th Cir. 1998).

- "The concept of curtilage, unfortunately, evades precise definition. In *Oliver* . . . the Supreme Court explained that at common law curtilage was defined to include those areas to which extends the intimate activity associated with the sanctity of a man's home and the privacies of life. Therefore, the federal courts have historically defined curtilage by reference to the factors that determine whether an individual reasonably may expect that an area immediately adjacent to the home will remain private." *U.S. v. Jenkins*, 124 F.3d 768, 772, 1997 FED App. 0263P (6th Cir. 1997).

Seventh Circuit

- "[The protection of the Fourth Amendment] is not limited to the four walls of one's home, but extends to the curtilage of the home as well. The home's curtilage encompasses 'the area outside the home itself but so close to and intimately connected with the home and the activities that normally go on there that it can reasonably be considered part of the home.' [citation omitted]. . . . A curtilage line is not necessarily the property line, nor can it be located merely by measuring the distance separating the home and the area searched. [citation omitted] Instead, a home's 'curtilage' is the area outside the home itself but so close to and intimately connected with the home and the activities that normally go on there that it can reasonably be considered part of the home. . . . Thus whether an area is within a house's curtilage depends not only on proximity to the house but also on the use of the area and efforts to shield it from public view and access as well as the nature for which it is used." *U.S. v. French*, 291 F.3d 945 (7th Cir. 2002).

Eighth Circuit

- "We resolve curtilage questions with particular reference to four factors: the proximity of the garage to the farmhouse, whether the farmhouse and garage are within the same enclosure, the nature and uses of the garage, and the steps [defendant] took to protect the garage from being seen by others. Every curtilage determination is distinctive and stands or falls on its own unique set of facts. . . . Applying these four factors to [defendant's] farmstead and the area immediately surrounding it, the district court's finding that the garage lay outside the curtilage of the farmhouse was not clearly erroneous. First, the record does not contain evidence of the distance from [defendant's] house to his garage. Neither party included in its brief the proximity of the garage to the farmhouse. However, [officer] testified that the farmhouse and garage are in close proximity. The distance alone, however, is not determinative that the garage should be treated as an adjunct of the house. Second, [defendant's] garage did not lie within the fence surrounding the farmhouse. However [defendant] urges that the natural enclosure of trees surrounding both the farmhouse and the garage mark the home's enclosure and that the land within it is protected by the home's curtilage. Specifically, [defendant] argues that this wooded vegetation surrounding the farmhouse and the garage, enclosing both into the same wooded area, mark the farmhouse's curtilage. . . . The fact that one's view from the road of the garage is obscured by the trees does not itself establish that the garage should be included within the farmhouse's Fourth Amendment protection. . . . Third, [defendant] contends that the parking of his car and motorcycle in the garage are evidence that his garage was used for activities and privacies of domestic life requiring Fourth Amendment protection. Contrary to [defendant's] testimony about his use of the garage, [officer] testified the garage appeared to only be used to store junk and grow marijuana. However, [officer] did not have this evidence concerning [defendant's] use of the garage before he climbed the ladder. Objective data does not include that found only after officers have invaded the area in question. We believe that reasonable officers would expect that the garage was likely to be used for private activities. The garage's doors were locked, electricity was wired to the garage, and it was close to the farmhouse, which are typical signs of private activities. The third *Dunn* factor weighs in favor of finding that [defendant's] garage was protected. However, these factors are not applied mechanically or in isolation; therefore, this factor alone does not require us to conclude that Gerard's garage was intimately tied to the farmhouse. Fourth, [defendant] contends that he took steps to prevent casual onlookers standing in open fields from viewing inside the garage. The garage was set back from the road, situated so that it did not face the road. [Defendant] attempted to prevent public access to his garage by placing locks on all three of the doors to the garage. In addition, [defendant] secreted the interior of the garage by placing plastic and cardboard in the windows. Also, the contents of the garage were not visible from aerial surveillance. However, the evidence also shows [defendant's] driveway led from the road directly to the garage. No internal fences prevented persons from approaching the garage. Also, [defendant] posted no signs excluding strangers from access to the garage. [Defendant] did nothing to cover the marijuana odor escaping from the vent of the garage. Lastly, the garage was not completely blocked

from view of members of the public driving down the
street. Based upon the evidence in this case, we cannot
say the district court clearly erred in finding that
[defendant's] garage was not within the farmstead's
curtilage." *U.S. v. Gerard*, 362 F.3d 484 (8th Cir. 2004).

• "In contrast, we believe that the officers in this case did
not act reasonably when they assumed that [Defen-
dant]'s property was the same as that described in the
warrant, because the distinction between the property
described in the warrant and [Defendant]'s curtilage
was abundantly apparent. As the Court has admonished, the mistakes must be those of reasonable men,
acting on facts leading sensibly to their conclusions.
. . . But here, though the boundaries of curtilage are
naturally and necessarily imprecise, the officers undertook a search that caused them to invade what they
could not fail to have known was potentially another's
curtilage." *U.S. v. Schroeder*, 129 F.3d 439, 443 (8th
Cir. 1997).

Ninth Circuit

• "Curtilage comes to us by way of Middle English and
traces its roots to the Old French *courtillage,* roughly
meaning court or little yard. In modern times it has
come to mean those portions of a homeowner's property
so closely associated with the home as to be considered
part of it. The walkway leading from the street to the
house is probably part of the curtilage, and the stairs
from the walkway to the porch almost certainly are, as
is the porch where grandma sits and rocks most
afternoons and watches strangers pass by. The attached
garage on the side of the house is part of the curtilage,
and so is the detached shed where dad keeps his shop
equipment and mom her gardening tools-so long as it's
not too far from the house itself. The front lawn is part
of the curtilage, and the driveway and the backyard-if
it's not too big, and is properly separated from the open
fields beyond the house . . . . Whether some portion of
property-the porch, the stairs, the shed, the yard, the
chicken coop-is part of the curtilage is sometimes a
disputed question. But once it is determined that
something is part of the curtilage, it's entitled to
precisely the same Fourth Amendment protections as

the home itself. How do we know? Because the Supreme
Court has said so repeatedly." *U.S. v. Pineda-Moreno*,
617 F.3d 1120 (9th Cir. 2010). Kozinski, dissent.

- "The panel's rationale for concluding that Pineda-
Moreno had no reasonable expectation of privacy is even
more worrisome than its disregard of Supreme Court
precedent: According to the panel, Pineda-Moreno's
driveway was open to the public in that strangers wishing to reach the door of his trailer 'to deliver the
newspaper or to visit someone would have to go through
the driveway to get to the house.' But there are many
parts of a person's property that are accessible to
strangers for limited purposes: the mailman is entitled
to open the gate and deposit mail in the front door slot;
the gas man may come into the yard, go into the basement or look under the house to read the meter; the
gardener goes all over the property, climbs trees, opens
sheds, turns on the sprinkler and taps into the electrical outlets; the pool man, the cable guy, the telephone
repair man, the garbage collector, the newspaper
delivery boy (we should be so lucky) come onto the property to deliver their wares, perform maintenance or
make repairs. This doesn't mean that we invite neighbors to use the pool, strangers to camp out on the lawn
or police to snoop in the garage." *U.S. v. Pineda-Moreno*,
617 F.3d 1120 (9th Cir. 2010). Kozinski, dissent.

- "The panel authorizes police to do not only what invited
strangers could, but also uninvited children-in this case
crawl under the car to retrieve a ball and tinker with
the undercarriage. But there's no limit to what neighborhood kids will do, given half a chance: They'll jump
the fence, crawl under the porch, pick fruit from the
trees, set fire to the cat and micturate on the azaleas.
To say that the police may do on your property what
urchins might do spells the end of Fourth Amendment
protections for most people's curtilage . . . . The very
rich will still be able to protect their privacy with the
aid of electric gates, tall fences, security booths, remote
cameras, motion sensors and roving patrols, but the
vast majority of the 60 million people living in the Ninth
Circuit will see their privacy materially diminished by
the panel's ruling. Open driveways, unenclosed porches,
basement doors left unlocked, back doors left ajar, yard

gates left unlatched, garage doors that don't quite close, ladders propped up under an open window will all be considered invitations for police to sneak in on the theory that a neighborhood child might, in which case, the homeowner 'would have no grounds to complain.' . . . There's been much talk about diversity on the bench, but there's one kind of diversity that doesn't exist: No truly poor people are appointed as federal judges, or as state judges for that matter. Judges, regardless of race, ethnicity or sex, are selected from the class of people who don't live in trailers or urban ghettos. The everyday problems of people who live in poverty are not close to our hearts and minds because that's not how we and our friends live. Yet poor people are entitled to privacy, even if they can't afford all the gadgets of the wealthy for ensuring it. Whatever else one may say about Pineda-Moreno, it's perfectly clear that he did not expect-and certainly did not consent-to have strangers prowl his property in the middle of the night and attach electronic tracking devices to the underside of his car. No one does." *U.S. v. Pineda-Moreno*, 617 F.3d 1120 (9th Cir. 2010). Kozinski, dissent.

- "There is no fixed distance at which home's curtilage ends, for Fourth Amendment purposes and, while not conclusive, fencing configurations are important factors in defining home's curtilage, for purposes of Fourth Amendment." *U.S. v. Davis*, 530 F.3d 1069 (9th Cir. 2008).

- "The Government does not suggest that [Border Patrol agent's] search is covered by any of the traditional justifications for a warrantless search, but instead relies entirely on a statute, 8 U.S.C. Sec. 1357(a)(3), for the proposition that the search was authorized by law. That statute gives Border Patrol agents the power, without warrant, 'within a distance of twenty-five miles from any... external boundary [of the United States] to have access to private lands, but not dwellings, for the purpose of patrolling the border to prevent the illegal entry of aliens into the United States.' The Government argues that the curtilage is not a 'dwelling,' and therefore falls within the ambit of this statute, which creates an exception to the warrant requirement. [Defendant] contends that the residential curtilage does fall within the definition of a 'dwelling,' and that the statutory search authority therefore does not apply. . . . [T]here are good reasons to eschew the plain meaning interpretation here, because it would indeed work an absurd result. Excluding only dwellings, in the most restricted literal sense, from the Border Patrol's warrantless search authority would provide its agents the unchecked ability to enter every backyard in metropolitan San Diego, Detroit, Buffalo, and El Paso, all of which are well within twenty-five miles of external borders of the United States. Aside from the obvious constitutional implications of such an interpretation, we seriously doubt that Congress intended to give the Border Patrol such unique and sweeping powers. . . . Congress's intent was only to allow warrantless searches—in other words, searches without probable cause—of areas to which the Fourth Amendment does not reach. Because the Fourth Amendment's protections do reach the curtilage, we conclude that Congress intended to exempt the residential curtilage from the Border Patrol's warrantless search authority." *U.S. v. Romero-Bustamente*, 337 F.3d 1104 (9th Cir. 2003).

- "Nowhere is the protective force of the fourth amendment more powerful than it is when the sanctity of the home is involved. . . .The Supreme Court has extended the protections afforded by the Fourth Amendment to the curtilage of a house, which is defined as the area to which extends the intimate activity associated with the sanctity of a man's home and the privacies of life." *U.S. v. Hammett*, 236 F.3d 1054, 1059 (9th Cir. 2001).

- "While a liberal reading of the warrant is required, when law enforcement wishes to search two houses or two apartments, it must establish probable cause as to each. . . In the evidentiary hearing, the district court found that before executing the warrant . . ., the DEA agent reasonably believed the rear building to be a garage. When the officers entered the rental unit, however, they realized that it was a place where someone lived. While the living room of the rental unit contained storage boxes, the second room contained appliances associated with a separate dwelling, including a woodburning stove, cooking stove, refrigerator, and sink. The unit also had its own bathroom. The rental unit was clearly a separate dwelling for which a separate warrant was required. It cannot be viewed as an extension of the main house. . . Similarly, a search of a guest room in a single family home which is rented or used by a third party, and, to the extent that the third party acquires a reasonable expectation of privacy, requires a warrant. . . [Tenant] possessed a reasonable expectation of privacy in the interior spaces of the rear accessory building where he was a tenant. Neither did the search warrant . . . describe [tenant's] rental unit as a place to be searched, nor did the affidavit establish probable cause to search [tenant's] rooms. Hence, the rooms in the rear building where [tenant] lived were not within the scope of the warrant . . . Any marijuana discovered there would not have been admissible evidence. . . However, the rear building's storage rooms where the agents discovered marijuana are another matter. Defendant . . . argues that because the storage rooms were not specifically described in the warrant, they, like [tenant's] rental unit, were outside the warrant's scope. It follows, [defendant] asserts, that evidence found inside them must be suppressed. [Defendant's] argument fails. The storage rooms were not part of the rental unit; rather, they are curtilage of the main house and within the embrace of the warrant." *U.S. v. Cannon*, 264 F.3d 875, 104 A.L.R.5th 649 (9th Cir. 2001).

- "We can conceive of no reason to distinguish a garage, where people spend time, work, and store their possessions, from a den or a kitchen, where people spend time, work, and store their possessions. Simply put, a person's garage is as much a part of his castle as the rest of his home." *U.S. v. Oaxaca*, 233 F.3d 1154, 1157 (9th Cir. 2000).

<u>Tenth Circuit</u>

- "The sideyard was immediately adjacent to the house. Thus, the proximity factor suggests this area is curtilage. The sideyard was enclosed on three sides: (1) on the east by an exterior wall of the house; (2) on the north by the gate door; and (3) on the west by a fence. As such, the sideyard is partially, though not completely, enclosed. . . . [T]he unenclosed side is the expected path one would take to get to the sideyard, and it is a paved sidewalk. . . . Thus, this factor weighs against a finding of curtilage. There is some evidence in the record that a portion of the sideyard area was used as a garden for melons. Gardening is an activity often associated with the curtilage of a home. . . . Whatever intimate character a few melon plants might add to the sideyard, we cannot conclude that gardening was a primary or even significant use of this area. Indeed, the presence of the electric meter and paved walkway belie any claim that the sideyard was intended as a private space for gardening. Thus, this factor also weighs against a finding of curtilage. . . . [T]he utility meter and gate were visible from the street and that the sideyard was connected to the driveway by a paved walkway that was accessible to any and all persons wishing to enter upon it. . . . Allowing meter readers on the premises is not necessarily dispositive, but here the fact that the area was accessed by a walkway and was not enclosed, coupled with the fact that the Defendants knew the area was frequented by a meter reader who might be expected to report observed illegal activity, leads to a conclusion that this fourth factor also weighs against a finding of curtilage. As a result of the above analysis, we conclude that the district court did not commit clear error in finding that Defendants' sideyard did not fall within the curtilage of their home. As a result, law enforcement presence in this area did not violate the Fourth Amendment." *U.S. v. Tolase-Cousins*, 440 F.3d 1237 (10th Cir. 2006), opinion amended and superseded on reh'g, 455 F.3d 1116 (10th Cir. 2006).

Eleventh Circuit

- "We hold, however, that, under the totality of the circumstances, the Deputies' entry into the [plaintiffs'] garage was a violation of the Fourth Amendment. The garage here is attached to the home itself, putting it in closer proximity to the home than an unattached garage. In contrast with a carport, the attached garage has walls on three sides and has the capability, if the outside door is rolled down, of being closed to maintain privacy. [Plaintiff] also attempted to exercise her Fourth Amendment rights. In her first conversation with [the officer], she explained that her husband might need a while before he would be able to come to the door. [The officer] expressed his willingness to wait, and [plaintiff], by closing and locking the front door, indicated that she was maintaining her privacy in the meantime. Following this encounter, when [plaintiff] noticed [the officer] walking up to her window through her bushes, she screamed at him to get out of her bushes and off her property and threatened to call the police. Finally, and most significantly, when [the officers] remained on the property, [plaintiff] attempted to close the garage door in order to maintain privacy in that area as well. Under these circumstances and in light of [plaintiff's] indications that she intended to maintain privacy, we hold that entering the garage as [plaintiff] attempted to close it was a violation of the Fourth Amendment." *Coffin v. Brandau*, 642 F.3d 999, 1012–13 (11th Cir. 2011).

- "Police officers had probable cause to search defendant's residence; although warrant failed to describe guesthouse, the warrant authorized officers to search "all outbuildings and vehicles located on the curtilage," which necessarily included the guesthouse." *U.S. v. Johnson*, 281 Fed. Appx. 909 (11th Cir. 2008).

§ 16:2 Open field doctrine: Fourth Amendment protections do not extend to the 'open fields' surrounding the curtilage and the home

Supreme Court

- "It is clear, however, that the term open fields may include any unoccupied or undeveloped area outside of the curtilage. An open field need be neither open nor a field as those terms are used in common speech." *Oliver v. U.S.*, 466 U.S. 170, 180 n.11, 104 S. Ct. 1735, 80 L. Ed. 2d 214 (1984).

- "[T]he special protection accorded by the Fourth Amendment to the people in their persons, houses, papers, and effects, is not extended to the open fields. The distinction between the latter and the house is as old as the common law." *Hester v. U.S.*, 265 U.S. 57, 59, 44 S. Ct. 445, 68 L. Ed. 898 (1924).

Fourth Circuit

- "[Defendant] ... maintains that the aerial surveillance of his property violated his Fourth Amendment rights because the surveillance constituted a warrantless search of the curtilage of his home. Because an individual ordinarily possesses the highest expectation of privacy within the curtilage of his home, that area typically is afforded the most stringent Fourth Amendment protection. Nevertheless, what a person knowingly exposes to the public, even in his own home or office, is not a subject of Fourth Amendment protection. Thus, a law enforcement officer's observations from a public vantage point where he has a right to be and from which the activities or objects he observes are clearly visible do not constitute a search within the meaning of the Fourth Amendment. ... [Defendant's] argument... rests almost entirely on the factual assertion that the helicopter violated FAA regulations by flying as low as 35 feet over his property. The district court rejected [defendant's] testimony and found that the helicopter fully complied with applicable regulations regarding proper altitude. Additionally, testimony from law enforcement officers established that such flights were a regular occurrence in the area where [defendant's] farm was located. We therefore conclude that the aerial observation of [defendant's] property did not violate his Fourth Amendment rights." *U.S. v. Breza*, 308 F.3d 430 (4th Cir. 2002).

Fifth Circuit

- "[T]he officers in this case were entitled to observe the steel building either by air or on foot because the building, like the barn in *Pace*, stood in an open field. And, as we have already discussed, the fact that the officers enhanced their observations with a thermal imager does not require a different conclusion. The device, when used in an open field, does not offend the Fourth Amendment because it is passive and non-intrusive. The sanctity of one's home or business is undisturbed. We therefore conclude that the DEA's warrantless use of a thermal imager in this case was not an unconstitutional search." *U.S. v. Ishmael*, 48 F.3d 850, 857 (5th Cir. 1995).
- "In *Dow Chemical*, the Court reaffirmed that there is

an expectation of privacy in commercial structures which society is prepared to accept as reasonable, thus bringing the interiors of such structures within the protections of the Fourth Amendment. Whatever *Dow Chemical* may have left open concerning the concept of a curtilage surrounding a business or commercial establishment, *Dunn* indicates that there is no business curtilage surrounding a barn lying within an open field. Thus, there was no constitutional violation when the officers crossed the fence and looked into the [Defendant's] barn." *U.S. v. Pace*, 955 F.2d 270, 276 (5th Cir. 1992).

Sixth Circuit

- "The open fields doctrine, as enunciated by the Supreme Court in *Hester v. United States* . . . and reaffirmed in *Oliver v. United States* . . . holds that the government's intrusion onto open fields without a search warrant is not one of those unreasonable searches proscribed by the text of the Fourth Amendment. . . . The doctrine stems from the Supreme Court's observation that the Fourth Amendment refers only to persons, houses, papers, and effects (and not to fields) and the Court's belief that society is not prepared to recognize as reasonable an individual's subjective expectation of privacy in an open field. . . . The Supreme Court, moreover, has made clear that the application of this doctrine does not turn on the nuances of particular cases and that trial courts should not adopt an ad hoc approach to evaluating whether an individual has a reasonable expectation of privacy in a particular open field. The rather typical presence of fences, closed or locked gates, and No Trespassing signs on an otherwise open field therefore has no constitutional import." *U.S. v. Rapanos*, 115 F.3d 367, 372, 44 Env't. Rep. Cas. (BNA) 2097, 27 Envtl. L. Rep. 20961, 1997 FED App. 0165P (6th Cir. 1997).

- "The picnic site clearly falls within the definition of open fields which was set forth in *Oliver*. It was located in a publicly accessible, wooded area and was on 214 acres of land. The picnic site was not located near defendant's parents' home. Defendant's parents did not even attempt to create privacy in the area, such as erect fences or signs. Moreover, the picnic site contained no

residential dwellings. There was a tent on the site, but
there was no indication that the tent was like a home
or even a temporary habitation. Therefore, the area
surrounding the tent was not like the area immediately
surrounding a home, in which an individual does have
a legitimate privacy interest." *U.S. v. Rigsby*, 943 F.2d
631, 636, 33 Fed. R. Evid. Serv. 1417 (6th Cir. 1991).

Eighth Circuit

• "In assessing whether a particular area is curtilage, we
determine 'whether the area in question is so intimately
tied to the home itself' that we should extend the Fourth
Amendment's protection to it. We consider 'factors that
bear on whether an individual reasonably may expect
that the area in question should be treated as the home
itself.' These factors are 'the proximity of the area
claimed to be curtilage to the home, whether the area is
included within an enclosure surrounding the home,
the nature of the uses to which the area is put, and the
steps taken by the resident to protect the area from
observation by people passing by.' The Supreme Court
'identified the central component of this inquiry as
whether the area harbors the intimate activity associated with the sanctity of a man's home and the privacies of life.' " *U.S. v. Mathias*, 721 F.3d 952, 956 (8th
Cir. 2013) (citations omitted).

Ninth Circuit

• "At common law, curtilage was the area outside the
walls of a home from which theft at night amounted to
burglary. More recently, the curtilage of a home
sometimes has been used to define the area in which it
is not necessary to retreat before using deadly force in
self-defense. Curtilage has also been defined as the area
to which extends the intimate activity associated with
the sanctity of a man's home and the privacies of life.
For the purposes of the Fourth Amendment, curtilage is
important because it extends to a larger area the right
to privacy a person enjoys inside the home: An individual may not legitimately demand privacy for activities
conducted out of doors in fields, except in the area immediately surrounding the home." *U.S. v. Gorman*, 104
F.3d 272, 274 (9th Cir. 1996).

- "[Defendant] did not have a constitutionally protected
right to maintain privacy in open fields, outside his
home and curtilage. The place where the officers stood,
outside the fence, was open fields, outside his curtilage.
Curtilage is an ancient English law term used to mark
off an area outside the walls of the home as being within
the geographic area in which theft at night amounts to
burglary. The protection of houses in the Fourth
Amendment extends to curtilage, which means the land
immediately surrounding and associated with the home
to which extends the intimate activity associated with
the sanctity of a man's home and the privacies of life.
The greenhouses were fenced off, not just from the public, but also from the residential portion of [Defendant]'s
property, and were entirely separate from the places of
intimate activity associated with the home. The unfortunate use of the term open fields in this body of law
causes misunderstanding and confusion, and should be
replaced by a term which means what is says, such as
unprotected area. In this case, the observation was
made from open fields, outside the curtilage, and the
area observed was outside the curtilage, so under
Traynor, the Fourth Amendment did not entitle [Defen-
dant] to privacy from the observation." *U.S. v. Van
Damme*, 48 F.3d 461, 464–65 (9th Cir. 1995).

Tenth Circuit

- "[T]he use of silent video surveillance must still comply
with the Fourth Amendment. . . .Whether [Defendant]
can claim the FBI violated her Fourth Amendment
rights by using these video cameras to observe the activity occurring outside the houses depends on whether
[Defendant] had a reasonable expectation of privacy in
the area viewed by the cameras. . . .The use of video
equipment and cameras to record activity visible to the
naked eye does not ordinarily violate the Fourth
Amendment." *U.S. v. Jackson*, 213 F.3d 1269, 1280
(10th Cir. 2000), cert. granted, judgment vacated on
other grounds, 531 U.S. 1033, 121 S. Ct. 621, 148 L. Ed.
2d 531 (2000).

Eleventh Circuit

- "[A] significant factor in the Court's Fourth Amendment

analysis is the intimacy of detail and activity that a
surveillance technique reveals in a particular case. In
Oliver, for example, the Court reaffirmed the open fields
doctrine, first established in *Hester v. United States*,
and held that individuals had no reasonable expectation of privacy in open fields. The Court distinguished
such areas from enclaves [that] should be free from
arbitrary government interference, reasoning that open
fields do not provide the setting for those intimate
activities that the Amendment is intended to shelter
from government interference or surveillance." *U.S. v.
Ford*, 34 F.3d 992, 996 (11th Cir. 1994).

§ 16:3 Legitimate expectation of privacy: The determination of whether the Fourth Amendment was violated depends upon whether the person challenging the search has a legitimate expectation of privacy in the place that was searched

Supreme Court

- "[T]he *Katz* reasonable-expectation-of-privacy test has
  been *added to,* not *substituted for,* the common-law
  trespassory test." *U.S. v. Jones*, 565 U.S. 400, 132 S. Ct.
  945, 952, 181 L. Ed. 2d 911 (2012).
- "[This case addresses] the following question: Whether
  surveillance of the interior of a partially covered
  greenhouse i n a residential backyard from the vantage
  point of a helicopter located 400 feet above the greenhouse constitutes a search for which a warrant is
  required under the Fourth Amendment. Any member of
  the public could legally have been flying over [Defen-
  dant's] property in a helicopter at the altitude of 400
  feet and could have observed [Defendant's] greenhouse.
  The police officer did no more. This is not to say that an
  inspection of the curtilage of a house from an aircraft
  will always pass muster under the Fourth Amendment
  simply because the plan is within the navigable airspace provided by law. But it is of obvious importance
  that the helicopter in this case was not violating the
  law, and there is nothing in the record or before us to
  suggest that helicopters flying at 400 feet are sufficiently rare in this country to lend substance to the re-

spondent's claim that he reasonably anticipated that his greenhouse would not be subject to observation from that altitude." *Florida v. Riley*, 488 U.S. 445, 451, 109 S. Ct. 693, 102 L. Ed. 2d 835 (1989).

- "That the area is within the curtilage does not itself bar all police observation. The Fourth Amendment protection of the home has never been extended to require law enforcement officers to shield their eyes when passing by a home on public thoroughfares. Nor does the mere fact that an individual has taken measures to restrict some views of his activities preclude an officer's observations from a public vantage point where he has a right to be and which renders the activities clearly visible. What a person knowingly exposes to the public, even in his own home or office, is not a subject of Fourth Amendment protection. Any member of the public flying in this airspace who glanced down could have seen everything that these officers observed. On this record, we readily conclude that respondent's expectation that his garden was protected from such observation is unreasonable and is not an expectation that society is prepared to honor." *California v. Ciraolo*, 476 U.S. 207, 213–14, 106 S. Ct. 1809, 90 L. Ed. 2d 210 (1986).

- "[A]n individual may not legitimately demand privacy for activities conducted out of doors in fields, except in the area immediately surrounding the home. [O]pen fields do not provide the setting for those intimate activities that the Amendment is intended to shelter from government interference or surveillance." *Oliver v. U.S.*, 466 U.S. 170, 178–79, 104 S. Ct. 1735, 80 L. Ed. 2d 214 (1984).

- "[N]o expectation of privacy extended to movements of objects such as the drum of chloroform outside the cabin in the open fields." *U.S. v. Knotts*, 460 U.S. 276, 282, 103 S. Ct. 1081, 75 L. Ed. 2d 55 (1983).

- "[B]y focusing on legitimate expectations of privacy in Fourth Amendment jurisprudence, the Court has not altogether abandoned use of property concepts in determining the presence or absence of the privacy interest protected by that Amendment. On the other hand, even a property interest in premises may not be sufficient to establish a legitimate expectation of privacy with respect to particular items located on the premises

or activity conducted thereon." *Rakas v. Illinois*, 439
U.S. 128, 144 n.12, 99 S. Ct. 421, 58 L. Ed. 2d 387
(1978).

Second Circuit

- "The touchstone of the inquiry into whether an area is
  within the curtilage of a home and entitled to the same
  privacy protections under the Fourth Amendment as
  the home is whether the defendant had a reasonable
  expectation of privacy in the area near the home that
  he claims to be protected by the Fourth Amendment.
  Scrub brush located 65 feet from the back door of the
  house and on the border of the neighbor's property was
  not within the curtilage of the home where the scrub
  brush served as a border and was located at the fringe
  of the property in relation to the home, the yard was
  not fenced off from street, the scrub was at edge of
  mowed area of yard, simple care and maintenance of
  the lawn did not transform area into curtilage, and general scrub area was visible from street." *U.S. v. Hayes*,
  551 F.3d 138 (2d Cir. 2008).

- "In sum, although the defendants could easily have
  shielded their activities from public view, they failed to
  take the simple and obvious steps necessary to do so.
  By exposing their illicit cocaine activities to the side
  yard—a place where they should have anticipated that
  other persons might have a right to be—defendants
  failed to exhibit a subjective expectation that they
  intended their dealings in the bedroom to be private.
  Hence, the police observations did not violate defendants' Fourth Amendment rights." *U.S. v. Fields*, 113
  F.3d 313, 322 (2d Cir. 1997).

Fourth Circuit

- "Because individuals ordinarily possess the highest
  expectation of privacy within the curtilage of their
  home, that area typically is afforded the most stringent
  Fourth Amendment protection. However, what a person
  knowingly exposes to the public, even in his own home
  is not subject of Fourth Amendment protection. Thus, a
  law enforcement officer's observations from a public
  vantage point where he has a right to be and from which
  the activities or objects he observes are clearly visible

do not constitute a search within the meaning of the
Fourth Amendment." *U.S. v. Taylor*, 90 F.3d 903, 908
(4th Cir. 1996).

Fifth Circuit

- "In regard to the first two factors, the proximity to the
  home and whether the area was within an enclosure
  surrounding the home, there was testimony that a fence
  surrounded the apartment and that it was approximately three feet away from the door of the apartment.
  Those two factors weigh in favor of the appellants. The
  next two factors, the nature of the uses to which the
  area is put and the steps taken by the resident to
  protect the area from outside observation, strongly
  indicate that the area is not curtilage. As found by the
  district court, the gate was left hanging open, and the
  resident had not taken any steps to indicate that the
  gate was an entry to a place that permission had to be
  given to enter." *U.S. v. Thomas*, 120 F.3d 564, 571 (5th
  Cir. 1997).

Sixth Circuit

- "While the Supreme Court has never required that law
  enforcement officers . . . shield their eyes when passing by a home on public thoroughfares . . . the officers
  still must observe the area being searched from a lawful vantage point. . . . The officers in the case at bar
  made the incriminating observations of the unattached
  garage while standing in a constitutionally protected
  area—the backyard." *Daughenbaugh v. City of Tiffin*,
  150 F.3d 594, 601, 1998 FED App. 0232P (6th Cir. 1998).

Eighth Circuit

- "[Defendant] next argues that the marijuana plants
  seized outside the house should have been suppressed.
  He contends that they were seized as a result of the aerial observation by [officer], and that because the
  helicopter was operating below normal cruising altitude
  in a manner not permissible for the general public, [of-
  ficer's] observations constituted a search for which a
  warrant was required. [Officer] testified that the
  helicopter's typical cruising altitude for spotting
  marijuana is 500 feet, but that investigators sometimes

fly lower-in this case, down to 200 or 300 feet-to confirm a marijuana sighting. The parties dispute whether the plants observed were within the curtilage of the home or on land akin to 'open fields.' Aerial surveillance of even the curtilage of a home from publicly navigable airspace, at an altitude generally used by the public and conducted with the naked eye, is not a 'search' within the meaning of the Fourth Amendment, because there is no reasonable expectation of privacy in areas visible to the public. . . . While the police dropped to an altitude of 200 or 300 hundred feet to observe [defendant's] property, this altitude would have been legally permissible for any member of the public, and there is no evidence that the helicopter interfered with the respondent's normal use of the curtilage, observed any intimate details connected with the use of the home or curtilage, or created undue noise, wind, dust, or threat of injury, or that such flights are so rare as to violate a reasonable expectation of privacy. In these circumstances, there was no search, and the police were not required to obtain a warrant to conduct a helicopter flyover of the property." *U.S. v. Warford*, 439 F.3d 836 (8th Cir. 2006).

Ninth Circuit

- "The Supreme Court has explained that the role of reasonable expectation analysis in evaluating the constitutionality of searches of the curtilage is only in determining the scope of the curtilage, and not the propriety of the intrusion." *U.S. v. Perea-Rey*, 680 F.3d 1179, 1186 (9th Cir. 2012).
- "Assuming arguendo that the officers committed a trespass in walking into [Defendant]'s open driveway, he has failed to demonstrate that he had a legitimate expectation of privacy cognizable under the Fourth Amendment in this portion of his property." *U.S. v. McIver*, 186 F.3d 1119, 1126 (9th Cir. 1999).

Tenth Circuit

- "In *Oliver*, the Court held that even when fields are protected by fences or No Trespassing signs, they do not provide the setting for those intimate activities that the Fourth Amendment is intended to shelter from government interference or surveillance." *U.S. v. Lewis*, 240 F.3d 866, 871 (10th Cir. 2001).

Eleventh Circuit

- "[T]he only issue before us is whether tenants in a large, high-rise apartment building, the front door of which has an undependable lock that was inoperable on the day in question, have a reasonable expectation of privacy in the common areas of their building. Our answer is no. On the day of the search, the lobby of this apartment building and the hallways and other common areas of it were open and accessible not only to all the many tenants and their visitors, to the landlord and all its employees, to workers of various types, and to delivery people of all kinds, but also to the public at large. There was nothing to prevent anyone and everyone who wanted to do so from walking in the unlocked door and wandering freely about the premises. Under these circumstances, any expectation of privacy in the common areas of the building was not only unreasonable, but foolhardy." *U.S. v. Miravalles*, 280 F.3d 1328 (11th Cir. 2002).

- "[T]he Supreme Court has consistently stated that a commercial proprietor has a reasonable expectation of privacy only in those areas where affirmative steps have been taken to exclude the public. This failure to exclude the public takes on increased significance when the asserted expectation of privacy is in discarded garbage. The common knowledge that garbage left on the side of a public street is readily accessible to animals, children, scavengers, snoops and other members of the public renders an expectation of Fourth Amendment protection unjustified. A commercial proprietor incurs a similarly diminished expectation of privacy when garbage is placed in a dumpster which is located in a parking lot that the business shares with other businesses, and no steps are taken to limit the public's access to the dumpster. It is common knowledge that commercial dumpsters have long been a source of fruitful exploration for scavengers." *U.S. v. Hall*, 47 F.3d 1091, 1096 (11th Cir. 1995).

- "[T]he Court's precedents regarding waste disposal suggest that [Defendant's] expectation of privacy in his vented heat is not one that society is prepared to accept as objectively reasonable. In *California v. Greenwood*, the Supreme Court held that a homeowner did not have an objective expectation of privacy in garbage left for collection outside the curtilage of his home. The Court stated that it was common knowledge that garbage left at the curbside is readily accessible to the public, most obviously the trash collectors for whom the garbage was deposited. The heat that [Defendant] intentionally vented from his mobile home was a waste byproduct of his marijuana cultivation and is analogous to the inculpatory items that the respondents in *Greenwood* discarded in their trash." *U.S. v. Ford*, 34 F.3d 992, 997 (11th Cir. 1994).

§ 16:4   Garbage left outside curtilage of house

Third Circuit

- "In Greenwood [California v. Greenwood, 486 U.S. 35, 108 S. Ct. 1625, 100 L. Ed. 2d 30 (1988)], the Supreme Court held that the Fourth Amendment does not prohibit the warrantless seizure and search of garbage left for collection on a curb outside of the curtilage of the home. In Greenwood, the Court employed the two-part analysis set forth by Katz v. U.S., 389 U.S. 347, 88 S. Ct. 507, 19 L. Ed. 2d 576 (1967). The Court concluded that even though the Greenwood defendants had a subjective expectation of privacy in their garbage, society was not prepared to accept that expectation as objectively reasonable. The Court found that the defendants had exposed their garbage to the public sufficiently to defeat their claim to Fourth Amendment protection. [The present defendant] concedes that Greenwood is still the controlling authority for Fourth Amendment protections of garbage bags left on the curb outside the curtilage of the home for pick up by a third party. Furthermore, he has not attempted to factually distinguish his case from Greenwood. Greenwood compels the conclusion that when [defendant] placed his garbage on the curb outside of the curtilage of his home, he sufficiently exposed it to the public to defeat his claim that the garbage was protected by the Fourth Amendment. Third Circuit precedent, cited approvingly by the Supreme Court in Greenwood, also compels this conclusion." *U.S. v. McKenzie*, 283 Fed. Appx. 13 (3d Cir. 2008).

<u>Eighth Circuit</u>

- "Police may search trash left outside the curtilage of the house to be picked up by garbage collectors, because the owners of the trash have abandoned it." *U.S. v. Spotted Elk*, 548 F.3d 641 (8th Cir. 2008).

§ 16:5 Knock and talk: A knock-and-talk inquiry is a permissible means of obtaining information regarding alleged criminal activity

<u>Supreme Court</u>

- "*Marasco* held that an unsuccessful 'knock and talk' at the front door does not automatically allow officers to go onto other parts of the property. It did not hold, however, that knocking on the front door is *required* before officers go onto other parts of the property that are open to visitors. . . . . In *Marasco*, the Third Circuit noted that '[o]fficers are allowed to knock on a residence's door or otherwise approach the residence seeking to speak to the inhabitants just as any private citizen may.' The court also said that, '"when the police come on to private property . . . and restrict their movements to places visitors could be expected to go (*e.g.*, walkways, driveways, porches), observations made from such vantage points are not covered by the Fourth Amendment."' Had Carroll read those statements before going to the Carmans' house, he may have concluded—quite reasonably—that he was allowed to knock on any door that was open to visitors." *Carroll v. Carman*, 135 S. Ct. 348, 351, 190 L. Ed. 2d 311 (2014) (citations omitted).

<u>First Circuit</u>

- "A police officer may approach and knock on a citizen's front door, and request the opportunity to speak to the citizen, in what is known as a knock-and-talk. The citizen does not have to answer or speak to the police officers, and if he does speak to the officers, he does not have to allow them into their homes. 'Consensual searches are a recognized exception to the Fourth Amendment's warrant requirement, but the government bears the burden to prove by a preponderance of the evidence that defendant or an authorized third party gave the consent voluntarily.' Whether the consent was given voluntarily is a question of fact that 'turns on the district court's comprehensive assessment of the totality of the circumstances attending the interaction between defendant/third party and the searching officers.' Factors to be weighed in making this comprehensive assessment include, but are not limited to, '(i) the consenter's age, education, past experiences, and intelligence; (ii) whether law enforcement officials advised the consenter of his constitutional right to refuse consent; (iii) the length and conditions of the consenter's detention and/or questioning; and (iv) law enforcement officials' use of any inherently coercive tactics.' In considering the totality of the circumstances, we are especially swayed by the fact that Pérez is an experienced police officer. An experienced police officer understands that when FBI agents turn up on his doorstep, he has no obligation to speak to them. He knows that he does not have to let them in. If he should choose to speak to the agents or to invite them in, he also understands that he is free not to answer any questions. Yet Pérez chose to speak to the agents through the door for two minutes. He chose to step aside so as to let them enter. He chose to answer a number of questions. He chose to show them the hard drive he had hidden away. And when the officers asked him for something he did not wish to provide—access to his laptop—he withdrew his consent. Once the consent was withdrawn, the officers promptly ceased the search, and Agent Ortiz went to secure a search warrant. The entire interaction lasted only an estimated thirty to forty-five minutes, and took place in surroundings that were familiar to Pérez—his own home. The FBI agents did not use any inherently coercive tactics; they asked Pérez straightforward questions, which he willingly answered. Pérez makes much of the fact that the knock-and-talk took place at 8:30 a.m., after he had returned from a late shift the previous night, and that he was therefore tired. However, even if we accept Pérez's testimony that he returned from work at 3:00 a.m., 8:30 a.m. is hardly unreasonable. In addition, Pérez himself testified that he was expecting a visit from his landlord that morning. He could not therefore have been entirely surprised to receive a knock on his door, or been entirely unprepared to have visitors in his home." *United States v. Perez-Diaz*, 848 F.3d 33, 39–40 (1st Cir. 2017) (citations omitted).

Fourth Circuit

- "Under [the knock-and-talk] exception, 'a police officer not armed with a warrant may approach a home and knock, precisely because that is "no more than any private citizen might do."' . . . . An officer may also bypass the front door (or another entry point usually used by visitors) when circumstances reasonably indicate that the officer might find the homeowner elsewhere on the property. Critically, however, the right to knock and talk does not entail a right to conduct a general investigation on a home's curtilage." *Covey v. Assessor of Ohio County*, 777 F.3d 186, 192–93 (4th Cir. 2015) (citations omitted).

Fifth Circuit

- "Three key principles reveal themselves in the above discussion of the knock-and-announce rule generally and the futility justification specifically. First, the rule is not dependent on the officer's authority to search the home; otherwise, we would not have had the Supreme Court's decision in *Wilson,* which involved the execution of a warrant. The officer's authority to enter the home—by virtue of a warrant or other exigent circumstances—is separate and apart from the 'method of an officer's entry.' Second, any no-knock entry, regardless of the officer's authority to enter the home, must be justified by a reasonable suspicion, under the circumstances, that knocking and announcing would be dangerous or futile or that it would inhibit effective investigation of the crime. Third, the rule contemplates that all of the occupants of a home possess the same constitutional rights—i.e., all of the occupants are entitled to be free from no-knock entries. The suspect is not the only one who is protected in his home, his "'castle of defense and asylum.'" Those who live in the home enjoy that same protection. 'Futility' therefore justifies a no-knock entry only when the officer has a reasonable suspicion that the *occupants* of the residence to be searched are already aware of the officer's presence. The officer must be able to articulate this reasonable suspicion." *Trent v. Wade*, 776 F.3d 368, 380–81 (5th Cir. 2015) (citations omitted).

- "The purpose of a knock-and-talk investigation is 'to make investigatory inquiry, or, if officers reasonably suspect criminal activity, to gain the occupants' consent to search.' 'The purpose . . . is not to create a show of force, nor to make demands on occupants, nor to raid a residence.'" *U.S. v. Hernandez*, 392 Fed. Appx. 350, 352 (5th Cir. 2010) (citations omitted).

- "When officers demand entry into a home without a warrant, they have gone beyond the reasonable 'knock and talk' strategy of investigation. To have conducted a valid, reasonable 'knock and talk,' the officers could have knocked on the front door . . . and awaited a response; they might have then knocked on the back door . . . . When no one answered, the officers should have ended the 'knock and talk' and changed their strategy by retreating cautiously, seeking a search warrant, or conducting further surveillance." *U.S. v. Gomez-Moreno*, 479 F.3d 350, 356 (5th Cir. 2007).

Ninth Circuit

- "The Supreme Court's rejection of good faith, subjective intent tests to gauge Fourth Amendment violations implicitly overrules some of the reasoning of cases like *Davis* and *Hammett*, which turned in part on the officer's subjective intent. Accordingly, we can no longer rely on the good faith belief of law enforcement officers in our analysis of whether an incursion into the curtilage for a knock and talk violates the Fourth Amendment. To be clear, it remains permissible for officers to approach a home to contact the inhabitants. The constitutionality of such entries into the curtilage hinges on whether the officer's actions are consistent with an attempt to initiate consensual contact with the occupants of the home." *U.S. v. Perea-Rey*, 680 F.3d 1179, 1187–88 (9th Cir. 2012) (citations omitted).

- "Officers conducting a knock and talk also need not approach only a specific door if there are multiple doors accessible to the public. [T]he law does not require an officer to determine which door most closely approximates the Platonic form of main entrance and then, after successfully completing this metaphysical inquiry, approach only that door. An officer [initiating] a knock and talk visit may approach any part of the building . . . where uninvited visitors could be expected. However, once an attempt to initiate a consensual encounter with the occupants of a home fails, the officers should end the knock and talk and change their strategy by retreating cautiously, seeking a search warrant, or conducting further surveillance." *U.S. v. Perea-Rey*, 680 F.3d 1179, 1188 (9th Cir. 2012) (quotations and citations omitted).

Eleventh Circuit

- "[The officer] acted lawfully when he knocked on the door of the rooming house on Grand Avenue and engaged [the defendant] in conversation. As this Court has explained, '[t]he Fourth Amendment, which prohibits unreasonable searches and seizures by the government, is not implicated by entry upon private land to knock on a citizen's door for legitimate police purposes unconnected with a search of the premises.' United States v. Taylor, 458 F.3d 1201, 1204 (11th Cir.2006). [The officer] performed such a 'knock and talk' in this case. He and [a second officer] learned of criminal activity occurring at the rooming house. To investigate these reports, the officers went to the rooming house. There, [the first officer] knocked on the front door and asked the occupant of the house questions. These actions were for 'legitimate police purposes unconnected with a search of the [rooming house].' " *U.S. v. Williams*, 731 F.3d 1222 (11th Cir. 2013).

Chapter 17

Consent

Research References

§ 17:1 Voluntariness: The prosecutor has the burden of proving that a defendant's consent to a warrantless search was given freely and voluntarily

Supreme Court

- "Consent that is the product of official intimidation or harassment is not consent at all. Citizens do not forfeit their constitutional rights when they are coerced to comply with a request that they would prefer to refuse." *Florida v. Bostick*, 501 U.S. 429, 438, 111 S. Ct. 2382, 115 L. Ed. 2d 389 (1991).

- "[W]here the validity of a search rests on consent, the State has the burden of proving that the necessary consent was obtained and that it was freely and voluntarily given, a burden that is not satisfied by showing a mere submission to a claim of lawful authority." *Florida v. Royer*, 460 U.S. 491, 497, 103 S. Ct. 1319, 75 L. Ed. 2d 229 (1983).

- "The question whether the respondent's consent to accompany the agents was in fact voluntary or was the product of duress or coercion, express or implied, is to be determined by the totality of all the circumstances and is a matter which the government has the burden of proving." *U.S. v. Mendenhall*, 446 U.S. 544, 557, 100 S. Ct. 1870, 64 L. Ed. 2d 497 (1980).

- "The prosecutor has the burden of proving that the consent was, in fact, freely and voluntarily given." *Bumper v. North Carolina*, 391 U.S. 543, 548, 88 S. Ct. 1788, 20 L. Ed. 2d 797 (1968).

First Circuit

- "Consent must be voluntary to be valid. Whether consent is voluntary is to be determined by examining the totality of the circumstances, including the interaction between the police and the person alleged to have given consent. The heart of the government's argument is that [an apartment lessee] voluntarily consented to the search when she responded 'Okay' to [a law enforcement officer's] statement, 'I'm going to look in here.' The government argues that the totality of the circumstances demonstrate [the lessee's] 'Okay' was voluntary consent. These circumstances include the fact that [the

lessee] was sitting in a chair in her living room; that
[the lessee] was a 'cop nut' and was fascinated by the
police; the fact that [the lessee] had met [the officer] on
a prior occasion; the fact that [the lessee's] demeanor
was low-key; and the fact that [the lessee] did not
protest when [another officer] told the other officers to
search the house for weapons. The Magistrate Judge
examined the totality of the circumstances and found
that [the lessee] did not voluntarily consent to the
search of her home. ... We rule that the evidence fairly
supports the Magistrate Judge's finding. ... Absent voluntary consent, this search violated the Fourth
Amendment." *U.S. v. Weidul*, 325 F.3d 50 (1st Cir.
2003).

- "It is the prosecution's burden to establish, by a
preponderance of the evidence, that consent was freely
and voluntarily given; there must be more than mere
acquiescence in the face of an unfounded claim of present lawful authority." *U.S. v. Perez-Montanez*, 202 F.3d
434, 438, 53 Fed. R. Evid. Serv. 400 (1st Cir. 2000).

- "To establish applicability of the consent exception, the
government must prove valid consent by a preponderance of the evidence." *U.S. v. Forbes*, 181 F.3d 1, 5 (1st
Cir. 1999).

Second Circuit

- "With respect to consent to enter the house, the evidence at the hearing tended to show that [defendant]
was arrested outside his house by five or six officers,
that he was handcuffed, that he was read his *Miranda*
rights, and that the officers then asked him whether he
would like to give them his 'pedigree' information
outside or inside his house. [Defendant] agreed to give
the information inside the house. This record supports
the District Court's finding that the consent given to
enter the house was voluntary. The fact that police drew
their guns to effectuate the arrest does not necessarily
establish coercion, neither does the fact that [defendant]
was handcuffed. The fact that [defendant] was not
informed that there were places other than his front
yard or his house where the questioning could take
place also does not make his consent involuntary.
Finally, even considering all these events together—the

'totality of the circumstances'—we see little, if anything, to support the conclusion that [defendant] was coerced into allowing the officers to enter his house." *U.S. v. Ansaldi*, 372 F.3d 118 (2d Cir. 2004).

Third Circuit

- "Fact that officers may have had reasonable suspicion does not prevent them from relying on a citizen's consent to search. Furthermore, officers are not required to inform citizens of their right not to cooperate when seeking permission to conduct a warrantless consent search." *U.S. v. Crandell*, 554 F.3d 79 (3d Cir. 2009).
- "[P]olice officers conducting a routine, suspicionless drug interdiction need not inform bus passengers that they have the right to refuse consent to searches." *U.S. v. Fulani*, 368 F.3d 351 (3d Cir. 2004).

Fifth Circuit

- "When a request for consent is preceded by an illegal search or seizure, a different analysis applies. '[I]f an individual gives consent [to search] after being subject to an initial unconstitutional search, the consent is valid only if it was an independent act of free will, breaking the causal chain between the consent and the constitutional violation.' " *U.S. v. Gomez-Moreno*, 479 F.3d 350, 357 (5th Cir. 2007).
- "A search conducted pursuant to consent is another exception to the Fourth Amendment's warrant requirement. . . . The government must prove, by a preponderance of the evidence, that consent was freely and voluntarily given." *U.S. v. Morales*, 171 F.3d 978, 982 (5th Cir. 1999).
- "A consensual search is a well-settled exception to the search warrant requirement. In determining whether a search based upon consent is valid, the government must prove that the search was voluntary and that the defendant consented to the search or consent was obtained from a third party with the ability to give valid consent." *U.S. v. Navarro*, 169 F.3d 228, 231, 51 Fed. R. Evid. Serv. 757 (5th Cir. 1999).

Sixth Circuit

- "Because the government often asserts that a defendant

consented in cases where the police have some evidence
of illicit activity, but lack probable cause to arrest or
search. . .we carefully examine the government's claim
that a defendant consented. Moreover, we note that not
any type of consent will suffice, but instead, only
consent that is unequivocally, specifically, and intelligently given, uncontaminated by any duress and
coercion." *U.S. v. Worley*, 193 F.3d 380, 386, 1999 FED
App. 0346P (6th Cir. 1999).

- "The government bears the burden of proving, through
clear and positive testimony that the consent to search
was given voluntarily. . . . Consent is voluntary when
it is unequivocal, specific and intelligently given,
uncontaminated by any duress or coercion." *U.S. v. Ivy*,
165 F.3d 397, 402, 1998 FED App. 0381P (6th Cir. 1998).

- "The question of whether a consent to search is voluntary and knowing is a question of fact to be determined
from the totality of all the circumstances. . . . Moreover, the burden of establishing the validity of the
consent is upon the government." *U.S. v. Abdullah*, 162
F.3d 897, 902, 1998 FED App. 0348P (6th Cir. 1998).

Seventh Circuit

- "[Defendant's] mother could give consent to the police
to enter her home, but she didn't—not effective consent,
at any rate. For her consent was conditioned on the police having a warrant, and they didn't; that at least is
the natural interpretation of the facts as we have
recited them. Often it is irrelevant to the question of
consent whether there was a warrant or not. A valid
warrant is an independent basis for arrest, making
consent irrelevant. Indeed, if there is a warrant, it will
normally provide the only basis for the arrest because it
will make consent, if given, involuntary; [defendant's]
mother could not refuse to allow the police to execute a
warrant—could not, in short, withhold her consent. . .
.But if as in. . . this case. . . there is no warrant or no
valid or applicable warrant (the warrant might not be
broad enough to cover what the police wanted to search
for or seize), consent is vitiated: vitiated not only by the
claim of the police to have a warrant—as long as
[defendant's] mother believed the claim, and there is no
reason to doubt that she did, her consent to the search

was involuntary and does not bar a challenge to the lawfulness of the arrest—but also by fraud. Although the law permits the police to pressure and cajole, conceal material facts, and actively mislead, it draws the line at outright fraud, as where police extract a confession in exchange for a false promise to set the defendant free. The consent of [defendant's] mother was procured by an outright and material lie, and was therefore ineffectual." *Hadley v. Williams*, 368 F.3d 747 (7th Cir. 2004).

Eighth Circuit

- "To the extent the government argues that (defendant's) actions constituted implied consent to (the officer's) entry, we disagree. We examine the totality of the circumstances to determine whether consent was voluntary or coerced . . . . Although a person who opens a door in response to a simple knock by officers knowingly exposes to the public that which can be seen through the door . . . we have held that one who does so in response to a demand under color of authority does not open the door voluntarily . . . (defendant) opened the door following over ten minutes of persistent knocks and requests by (the officer), officers were stationed at both doors of the duplex and (an officer) had commanded (defendant) to open the door. A reasonable person in (defendant's) situation would have concluded that he had no choice but to acquiesce and open the door." *U.S. v. Poe*, 462 F.3d 997 (8th Cir. 2006).

- "[A] person can render a search legal by behaving in a way that would cause a reasonable person to believe that he or she has knowingly and voluntarily consented, whether or not the person actually intends to consent. Thus, the Fourth Amendment requires only that the police reasonably believe the search to be consensual. Consequently, [defendant's] actual subjective state of mind at the time that he allegedly gave his consent is not determinative; our focus, rather, is on how a reasonable person could have perceived his state of mind at that time." *U.S. v. Cedano-Medina*, 366 F.3d 682 (8th Cir. 2004).

Ninth Circuit

- "We agree with [Defendant] that [the] Officer['s] . . . request for permission to search the truck with one hand resting on his gun was implicitly coercive. An officer's keeping his hand on his weapon throughout a colloquy with a suspect is clearly distinguishable from our decisions finding voluntary consent where an officer simply possessed a weapon. . . . Combined with the fact that the incident took place on a desert highway, with nobody else in sight, [the] Officer['s] . . . actions would have been viewed by a reasonable person essentially as a command to allow a search of the truck. . . . A person's obedience to a show of authority is by itself insufficient to establish voluntary consent. . . . Although consent can be inferred from nonverbal actions, the government must show that consent was unequivocal and specific and freely and intelligently given." *U.S. v. Chan-Jimenez*, 125 F.3d 1324, 1327–28 (9th Cir. 1997) (rejected on other grounds by, U.S. v. Al Nasser, 555 F.3d 722 (9th Cir. 2009)).
- "The existence of consent to a search is not lightly to be inferred and the government always bears the burden of proof to establish the existence of effective consent." *U.S. v. Reid*, 226 F.3d 1020, 1025 (9th Cir. 2000).

Tenth Circuit

- "As part of a consensual encounter, an officer may approach an individual, ask a few questions, ask to examine the individual's identification, and even ask for consent to search 'as long as the police do not convey a message that compliance with their requests is required.' 'So long as a reasonable person would feel free to disregard the police and go about his business, the encounter is consensual and no reasonable suspicion is required.' " *U.S. v. Madden*, 682 F.3d 920, 925 (10th Cir. 2012) (citations omitted).

Eleventh Circuit

- "Police officers, possessing neither reasonable suspicion nor probable cause, may still search a person without a warrant as long as they first obtain the voluntary consent of the person in question. (citation omitted) Whether consent is voluntary is a question of fact to be determined by the totality of the circumstances; and the government bears the burden of proving both (1) the existence of consent and (2) that the consent was voluntary and not an acquiescence to a claim of lawful authority." *U.S. v. Duncan*, 356 Fed. Appx. 250 (11th Cir. 2009).

- "Defendant, a government postal employee, consented to search of her purse, by virtue of her voluntary employment and her decision to bring her purse on postal property." *U.S. v. Esser*, 284 Fed. Appx. 757 (11th Cir. 2008).

- "While the government's burden of proving the voluntariness of consent is not satisfied by showing a mere submission to a claim of lawful authority. . . .the government need not establish [Defendant]'s knowledge of the right to refuse consent as the sine qua non of an effective consent. . . . [Defendant]'s consent was voluntary as long as it was the product of an essentially free and unconstrained choice." *U.S. v. Zapata*, 180 F.3d 1237, 1241 (11th Cir. 1999).

§ 17:2   Test: The voluntariness of a person's consent is determined by the totality of the circumstances

Supreme Court

- "And just as it would be thoroughly impractical to impose on the normal consent search the detailed requirements of an effective warning so too would it be unrealistic to require police officers to always inform detainees that they are free to go before a consent to search may be deemed voluntary. The Fourth Amendment test for a valid consent to search is that the consent be voluntary, and voluntariness is a question of fact to be determined from all the circumstances." *Ohio v. Robinette*, 519 U.S. 33, 39–40, 117 S. Ct. 417, 136 L. Ed. 2d 347, 148 A.L.R. Fed. 739 (1996).

- "The Fourth Amendment proscribes unreasonable searches and seizures; it does not proscribe voluntary cooperation. The cramped confines of a bus are one relevant factor that should be considered in evaluating whether a passenger's consent is voluntary." *Florida v. Bostick*, 501 U.S. 429, 439, 111 S. Ct. 2382, 115 L. Ed. 2d 389 (1991).

- "[W]e have long approved consensual searches because it is no doubt reasonable for the police to conduct a search once they have been permitted to do so. The standard for measuring the scope of a suspect's consent under the Fourth Amendment is that of objective reasonableness—what would the typical reasonable person have understood by the exchange between the officer and the suspect?" *Florida v. Jimeno*, 500 U.S. 248, 250–51, 111 S. Ct. 1801, 114 L. Ed. 2d 297 (1991).

- "Although the Constitution does not require proof of knowledge of a right to refuse as the *sine qua non* of an effective consent to a search, such knowledge was highly relevant to the determination that there had been consent." *U.S. v. Mendenhall*, 446 U.S. 544, 558–59, 100 S. Ct. 1870, 64 L. Ed. 2d 497 (1980).

- "[T]he question whether a consent to a search was in fact voluntary or was a product of duress or coercion, express or implied, is a question of fact to be determined from the totality of all the circumstances." *Schneckloth v. Bustamonte*, 412 U.S. 218, 227, 93 S. Ct. 2041, 36 L. Ed. 2d 854 (1973).

First Circuit

- "The validity of a defendant's consent must be gauged under the totality of the circumstances. When evaluating the totality of the circumstances, an inquiring court must look for evidence of coercion, duress, confusion, and the like. A consenting party's mental frailties may have a bearing upon this analysis. But such frailties are entitled to little weight in the abstract. For weight to attach, there must be evidence of some nexus between, say, the individual's mental condition and the giving of consent, or some evidence that officers obtained consent by exploiting a known vulnerability. When the evidence shows that the consenting party was 'responsive, lucid, and cooperative with the police officers,' post hoc claims of incompetency inspire suspicion . . . .. In the case at hand, the appellant acknowledges that he read and signed a consent form authorizing the search of his residence. That form, among other things, specifically advised him that he had a right not to consent to the search. He nonetheless maintains that his consent was not voluntarily given. He says that he had just

825

been thrown to the ground and arrested, and suggests that he was intimidated and under intense stress. The record, however, undermines this suggestion: Moulton (whose testimony was credited by the district court) stated that more than twenty minutes elapsed between the appellant's arrest and his consent to the search. The appellant appeared cooperative and lucid throughout, even if a bit 'nerved up.' What is more, no officer's weapon was drawn and no threats were uttered. . . . The appellant also argues that his history of mental illness—anxiety, depression, and bipolar disorder—vitiated his consent. But the record contains nothing in the way of persuasive evidence that might show a nexus between the appellant's psychiatric history and the giving of consent. Importantly, the officers who testified observed no evidence of mental incapacity during their interactions with the appellant. Overall, he seemed calm, albeit nervous, and was 'able to carry on a conversation.' In the last analysis, the voluntariness of the appellant's consent presented an issue of fact for the district court. We have said before that '[w]here the evidence supports two plausible but conflicting inferences, the factfinder's choice between them cannot be clearly erroneous.' So it is here: there was ample record support for the district court's conclusion that the appellant, even given his afflictions, was not so stressed by the circumstances that his consent could be regarded as either coerced or otherwise involuntary. We therefore uphold the denial of the appellant's fourth motion to suppress." *United States v. Coombs*, 857 F.3d 439, 449 (1st Cir. 2017) (citations omitted).

● "Consensual searches are a recognized exception to the Fourth Amendment's warrant requirement, but the government bears the burden to prove by a preponderance of the evidence that defendant or an authorized third party gave the consent voluntarily. If under all the circumstances it has appeared that the consent to search was not given voluntarily—that it was coerced by threats or force, or granted only in submission to a claim of lawful authority—then the consent invalid and the search unreasonable. In determining the voluntariness of a consent to search, besides evidence of police coercion or intimidation, the totality-of-the-circumstances test requires consideration of any evidence that law enforcement officers' fraud, deceit, trickery or misrepresentation prompted defendant's acquiescence to the search." *U.S. v. Vanvliet*, 542 F.3d 259 (1st Cir. 2008).

- "Valid consent renders a warrantless search constitutionally permissible, and while consent must be voluntary to be valid, there is no requirement that the person who gave consent must have been explicitly advised of the right to withhold it." *U.S. v. Perez-Montanez*, 202 F.3d 434, 438, 53 Fed. R. Evid. Serv. 400 (1st Cir. 2000).

Third Circuit

- "There is no talismanic definition of voluntariness, mechanically applicable to the host of situations where the question has arisen. Instead, we determine the voluntariness of a consent by examining the totality of the circumstances." *U.S. v. Price*, 558 F.3d 270 (3d Cir. 2009).

Fourth Circuit

- "The Fourth Amendment protects against 'unreasonable searches and seizures.' Searches without probable cause are presumptively unreasonable, but if an individual consents to a search, probable cause is unnecessary. We review for clear error a district court's determination that a search is consensual under the Fourth Amendment. We apply a subjective test to analyze whether consent was given, looking to the totality of the circumstances. The government has the burden of proving consent. Relevant factors include the officer's conduct, the number of officers present, the time of the encounter, and characteristics of the individual who was searched, such as age and education. Whether the individual searched was informed of his right to decline the search is a 'highly relevant' factor." *U.S. v. Robertson*, 736 F.3d 677 (4th Cir. 2013).

Fifth Circuit

- "The inquiry is not a subjective one; it does not hinge on whether the defendant knew of his right to refuse entry, or even upon whether the defendant actually believed himself to be consenting. Rather, the test is objective. We must ask whether the totality of the circumstances establishes that the defendant permitted the police inside his home. Though the defendant's subjective understanding of his constitutional right is one factor in the analysis, we will also consider the defendant's personal characteristics, the length and nature of the police-citizen interaction, and the use of police coercion, subtle or otherwise." *U.S. v. Holland*, 522 Fed. Appx. 265 (6th Cir. 2013) (citations omitted).

- "[T]his court has established a six-factor inquiry for determining whether consent was voluntarily given, such factors including: 1) the voluntariness of the defendant's custodial status; 2) the presence of coercive police procedures; 3) the extent and level of the defendant's cooperation with the police; 4) the defendant's awareness of his right to refuse consent; 5) the defendant's education and intelligence; and 6) the defendant's belief that no incriminating evidence will be found. No single factor in this analysis is dispositive." *U.S. v. Williams*, 365 F.3d 399 (5th Cir. 2004).

- "In order to give valid consent, the person consenting to the recording of his conversations must be mentally competent to understand the nature of his act. . . . Further, the act of consent must be the consensual act of one who knew what he was doing and had a reasonable appreciation of the nature and significance of his actions." *U.S. v. Dukes*, 139 F.3d 469, 472 (5th Cir. 1998).

Sixth Circuit

- "Consent must be proved by clear and positive testimony, and, to be voluntary it must be unequivocal, specific, and intelligently given, uncontaminated by any duress or coercion. . . . The defendant's knowledge of his right to refuse to consent is a factor, but the government need not prove that the defendant had such knowledge to establish that consent was voluntary." *U.S. v. Erwin*, 155 F.3d 818, 823, 1998 FED App. 0291P (6th Cir. 1998).

- "After an hour and a half of this situation—of police threats to arrest [Defendant's Girlfriend] and take the child, of [Defendant's Girlfriend] being shackled to a table, of the child being taken from his mother's arms, of repeated police solicitations for consent—[Defendant] finally acquiesced and signed the consent to search form. Perhaps this was a form of coerced chivalry on [Defendant]'s behalf. Perhaps his will was overcome by the time, the threats, the police handling his child, and the sight of his girlfriend chained to a table. One thing is certain: [Defendant]'s consent was not voluntarily imparted; his will was indeed overcome. Given the totality of the circumstances, it is plain that the government did not meet its burden of proving by clear and positive testimony that [Defendant] gave his consent freely and voluntarily, untainted by any duress or coercion. This Court is left with the definite and firm conviction that a mistake has been committed. . . . We therefore find that the district court committed clear error when it held that [Defendant]'s consent was voluntarily given and allowed into evidence the fruits of this unlawful search." *U.S. v. Ivy*, 165 F.3d 397, 404, 1998 FED App. 0381P (6th Cir. 1998).

Seventh Circuit

- "Consent can come in many forms, but it must always be given voluntarily. As the district court noted, [the defendant] does not challenge McCune's entry on the grounds that [the defendant's] nonverbal response was involuntary, nor does he offer any evidence of duress or coercion. Rather, [the defendant] only argues that he never consented to McCune entering his residence. As such, the crux of this appeal is whether [the defendant's] nonverbal response constituted implied consent for McCune to enter [the defendant's] residence. Whether [the defendant] impliedly consented to McCune's entry is a question of fact to be determined under the totality of the circumstances, and the trial court's determination will be reversed only if it is clearly erroneous." *U.S. v. Sabo*, 724 F.3d 891, 893 (7th Cir. 2013) (citations omitted).

- "Under the totality of the circumstances, the consent to a search of a residence provided by defendant's girlfriend, who was co-occupant of residence with defendant, was freely given. Although girlfriend initially resisted a search, telling officer that the police should get a warrant, and officer continued talking to her for between five and 20 minutes before she finally told officer to go ahead, she was not detained or under arrest, there was never any physical coercion, and she was a 22-year-old adult, with four children, who was employed as an officer manager." *U.S. v. Hicks*, 539 F.3d 566 (7th Cir. 2008).

• "The defendant argues that upon learning that he was the owner of the bag, the officer to whom he had told this, who was standing with him at the rear of the car, should have told the officer searching the duffel bag to stop; and he could easily have done this before she found the cocaine, because he was only a few steps away from her and in any event well within shouting distance. This is not a preposterous argument but the defendant couples it with the preposterous argument that the officer's knowledge that the defendant was the owner of the bag should be *automatically* imputed to the officer searching the duffel bag, as if all the police officers in Springfield, Illinois (where the stop occurred) share a single brain. ... But the question on which the lawfulness of the seizure of the cocaine turns is not whether [defendant] owned the duffel bag. It is whether he revoked the driver's consent to search the entire car, necessarily including the bag. By his silence in the face of her consent he forfeited any right to claim that her consent was ineffective to authorize the search because the bag was his. His silence was confirmation or ratification of her authority to consent." *U.S. v. West*, 321 F.3d 649 (7th Cir. 2003).

Eighth Circuit

• "Gerald argues the district court clearly erred when it found that he voluntarily consented to the searches of the hotel room and car. 'The government bears the burden of proving voluntary consent to a search by a preponderance of the evidence and we review a district court's finding of voluntary consent under a clear error standard.' . . . . First, Gerald challenges the district court's finding that he consented to the searches of the hotel room and car at all. Gerald points out that during the suppression hearing, his handwriting expert, Wendy Carlson, opined that the signature on the consent form for the search of the hotel room was not Gerald's, and that it was highly probable Tolsma had forged it. Gerald contends that the district court improperly rejected Carlson's opinion because she, unlike the government's handwriting expert, was not an FBI employee. He also contends that there is no evidence he consented to the search of the car. . . . In finding that Gerald signed the consent form, the district court noted that the government's handwriting expert called Carlson's methodology into question, that the government impeached Carlson's qualifications, that Tolsma and Sheridan both testified that Gerald signed the form, and that Gerald verbally confirmed on the audio recording that he signed the form. The district court further noted that although Gerald did not sign a separate consent form for the search of the car, Tolsma and Sheridan testified that Gerald verbally consented to the search of the car, Gerald's verbal consent to the search of the car was captured on the audio recording, and Gerald subsequently stated in a recorded telephone call from jail that he consented to the search of the car. . . . Under these circumstances, we cannot say the district court committed clear error in finding Gerald consented to the searches of the hotel room and car. The court's written order explains that it discounted Carlson's testimony not because she was not an FBI employee, but because her testimony was inconsistent with the other evidence presented, including the testimony of Tolsma and Sheridan. It was not clear error for the court to credit this evidence over Carlson's expert opinion. Additionally, Gerald's own contemporaneous and subsequent statements provide evidentiary support for the court's conclusion that he consented to the searches. Accordingly, the court did not err in finding Gerald consented to the searches of his hotel room and car." *United States v. LeBeau*, 867 F.3d 960, 970–71 (8th Cir. 2017) (citations omitted).

• "That police were present and told [the defendant's wife] Debra about efforts to obtain a search warrant does not dictate a finding that later-given consent was the product of coercion or duress. We do not think restrictions on [*the defendant's*] movement undermine the district court's finding about *Debra's* free will. Under the totality of the circumstances, there was no clear error in

finding voluntary consent. To vitiate the unlawfulness
of an entry, consent to a search must be both voluntary
and 'an intervening independent act of a free will' sufficient 'to purge the primary taint of the unlawful
invasion.' Whether consent sufficiently disperses the
taint of an unlawful entry is determined by reference to
'temporal proximity' between the entry and the consent,
'the presence of intervening circumstances, and, particularly, the purpose and flagrancy of the official
misconduct.' Observance of the *Miranda* rule is also relevant where applicable." *U.S. v. Brandwein*, 796 F.3d
980, 985 (8th Cir. 2015), petition for certiorari filed, 136
S. Ct. 1214, 194 L. Ed. 2d 216 (2016).

- "Whether a person voluntarily consents to a search is a
question of fact." *U.S. v. Farnell*, 701 F.3d 256 (8th Cir.
2012).
- "The question whether [the defendant] voluntarily
consented to a search of his person is a question of fact.
. . . . The Fourth Amendment 'is not triggered by a
consensual encounter between an officer and a private
citizen.' An encounter which is initially consensual,
however, can become non-consensual and therefore
'implicat[e] the Fourth Amendment when, considering
the totality of the circumstances, the questioning is so
intimidating, threatening, or coercive that a reasonable
person would not have believed himself free to leave' or
to end the encounter. We consider seven non-exclusive
factors when examining the totality of the circumstances, which are:

    [O]fficers positioning themselves in a way to limit the
    person's freedom of movement, the presence of several of-
    ficers, the display of weapons by officers, physical touch-
    ing, the use of language or intonation indicating compli-
    ance is necessary, the officer's retention of the person's
    property, or an officer's indication the person is the focus
    of a particular investigation.

    . . . This case turns not on [the defendant's] last act
    before being handcuffed, but rather [the officer's] first
    act after placing [the defendant] in handcuffs, which was
    to lift [the defendant's] pant leg to reveal the concealed
    bulge. Under the circumstances involved in this case,
    [the officer] violated the Fourth Amendment when he
    searched underneath an article of [the defendant's] cloth-
    ing without his consent and without probable cause to do

so, instead of performing a pat down to confirm whether the concealed bulge was a weapon. . . . [A]n officer's observation of a concealed bulge, standing alone, does not amount to probable cause to support an arrest." *U.S. v. Aquino*, 674 F.3d 918, 922–23 (8th Cir. 2012) (citations omitted).

- " 'Whether or not the suspect has actually consented to a search, the Fourth Amendment requires only that the police reasonably believe the search to be consensual.' (citation omitted) 'The focus is not whether [the defendant] subjectively consented, but rather, whether a reasonable officer would believe consent was given and can be inferred from words, gestures, or other conduct.' " *U.S. v. Pena-Ponce*, 588 F.3d 579 (8th Cir. 2009).

- "The custodial status of the consenting party is not determinative of voluntariness." *U.S. v. Fleck*, 413 F.3d 883, 67 Fed. R. Evid. Serv. 738 (8th Cir. 2005).

- "Factors we consider when determining if consent was freely and voluntarily given. . . include 1) age, 2) general intelligence and education, 3) whether the individual was under the influence of drugs or alcohol, 4) whether she was informed of the *Miranda* rights, and 5) whether she had experienced prior arrests and was thus aware of the protections the legal system affords suspected criminals. Additionally, the environment in which the alleged consent was secured is also relevant. Accordingly, we consider 1) the length of time one was detained, 2) whether the police threatened, physically intimidated, or punished the suspect, 3) whether the police made promises or misrepresentations, 4) whether the suspect was in custody or under arrest when the consent was given, 5) whether the consent occurred in a public or a secluded place, and 6) whether the suspect stood by silently as the search occurred. We also consider whether the defendant's contemporaneous reaction to the search was consistent with consent. The factors should not be applied mechanically, and no single factor is dispositive or controlling." *U.S. v. Escobar*, 389 F.3d 781 (8th Cir. 2004).

- "[T]he mere presence of some police officers in a confined space does not necessarily exert coercion of a constitutionally-defective nature. . . .The relevant inquiry. . .is whether the officers did anything to af-

firmatively communicate to the defendant that she was
not free to terminate the encounter or to refuse the
consent request. . . .Only when officers so indicate, by
explicit or implicit means, by implied threat or covert
force, does consent become involuntary." *U.S. v.
Zamoran-Coronel*, 231 F.3d 466, 469 (8th Cir. 2000).

Ninth Circuit

- "Here, the STING officers advised passengers that they
  were free to leave the bus. They did not tell passengers
  that they were free to remain on the bus and terminate
  the encounter by declining to answer their questions.
  The instructions given over the Greyhound public address system conveyed to passengers that they had two
  choices: stay on the bus and consent to the search, or
  get off the bus. This was a Hobson's choice because by
  getting off the bus, a passenger ran the risk of giving
  the STING officers reasonable suspicion to stop him."
  U.S. v. Stephens, 206 F.3d 914, 917 (9th Cir. 2000).

Tenth Circuit

- "When law enforcement officers ask to search a home,
  there will generally be factors surrounding the request
  that have coercive effect. For example, in this case there
  were a number of officers present; the officers warned
  [occupant] that harboring a fugitive was against the
  law; [occupant] was on medication; and [occupant] was
  arguably physically uncomfortable because it was cold
  outside and, as he had evidently been sleeping, he was
  clad in boxer shorts." *U.S. v. McKinney*, 363 Fed. Appx.
  665 (10th Cir. 2010).

- "The Supreme Court has held that a defendant's consent
  to a search may be voluntary even when the consenting
  party was not informed he could refuse. (citation omitted) Thus, the mere fact Agent Small did not specifically tell [defendant] that he was allowed to decline the
  request does not render the consent involuntary." *U.S.
  v. Carbajal-Iriarte*, 586 F.3d 795 (10th Cir. 2009).

- "[T]he district court was correct in this case to conclude
  the encounter was consensual. [Defendant] admits that
  the agents asked for permission to enter his home and
  that he invited them inside. The agents' request for
  permission to enter is not the same thing as an explicit

advisement that [defendant] had the right to terminate the encounter or refuse consent. An explicit advisement, however, is not a requirement; it is merely a factor to be considered in the totality of the circumstances. . . . The district court found that the agents were dressed in plain clothes and did not display their weapons at any time, that their tone and demeanor were professional, and that there was no evidence that they raised their voices or physically touched or restrained [defendant]. The court further found that the encounter occurred at a reasonable hour, and that the agents did not take possession of [defendant's] identification or other belongings, except for the evidence seized, for any measurable period of time. . . . In this case, the presence of more than one agent does not outweigh the multiple other factors indicating a purely consensual encounter." *U.S. v. Spence*, 397 F.3d 1280 (10th Cir. 2005).

- "[T]he most troubling issue is whether, given [defendant's] mental condition, his consent was nonetheless the product of a rational intellect and a free will and made with a mental awareness so that the act of consent was that of one who knew what he was doing. This requires both understanding and judgment. However, our cases have never required perfect mental ability to find a consent to search was voluntary. Although the record in this case suggests that [frontotemporal dementia] is a degenerative disorder that could ultimately affect [defendant's] judgment, [defendant] has not pointed this court to any specific evidence of the extent of his impairment at the time of his consent to search. Indeed, the officers testified that no aspect of [defendant's] dysfunction was apparent to them, and [defendant's] co-workers also testified they were not aware of [defendant's] illness prior to his arrest. Indeed, [defendant] was cognizant enough to ask for an attorney before he made any statement to the police. Moreover, the district court found no evidence that the police had attempted to exploit any of his vulnerabilities. Based on this evidence, we see no reason to conclude the district court's finding that [defendant] gave voluntary consent was clearly erroneous." *U.S. v. Sims*, 428 F.3d 945 (10th Cir. 2005).

Eleventh Circuit

- "Police officers, possessing neither reasonable suspicion
  nor probable cause, may still search a person without a
  warrant as long as they first obtain the voluntary
  consent of the person in question. (citation omitted)
  Whether consent is voluntary is a question of fact to be
  determined by the totality of the circumstances; and
  the government bears the burden of proving both (1)
  the existence of consent and (2) that the consent was
  voluntary and not an acquiescence to a claim of lawful
  authority." *U.S. v. Duncan*, 356 Fed. Appx. 250 (11th
  Cir. 2009).

- "In *Schneckloth*, the Supreme Court held that the
  voluntariness-of-consent analysis is conducted with reference to the totality of the circumstances and set forth
  a number of factors for a court to consider in conducting
  its inquiry: the person's youth, his lack of education, evidence of the person's low intelligence, the existence of
  advice as to the nature of the constitutional right
  implicated, the length of detention preceding the
  request to consent, the nature of prior questioning, the
  environment, and whether any physical punishment
  was involved." *U.S. v. Zapata*, 180 F.3d 1237, 1241
  (11th Cir. 1999).

**§ 17:3   Consent after detention: If the consenting
           party is in custody, the voluntariness of the
           consent is still measured by the totality of the
           circumstances, although courts will often
           analyze the relevant factors more critically**

Supreme Court

- "And just as it would be thoroughly impractical to
  impose on the normal consent search the detailed
  requirements of an effective warning so too would it be
  unrealistic to require police officers to always inform
  detainees that they are free to go before a consent to
  search may be deemed voluntary. The Fourth Amendment test for a valid consent to search is that the
  consent be voluntary, and voluntariness is a question of
  fact to be determined from all the circumstances." *Ohio
  v. Robinette*, 519 U.S. 33, 39–40, 117 S. Ct. 417, 136 L.
  Ed. 2d 347, 148 A.L.R. Fed. 739 (1996).

- "[T]he fact of custody alone has never been enough in itself to demonstrate a coerced confession or consent to search. Similarly, the absence of proof that [Defendant] knew he could withhold his consent, though it may be a factor in the overall judgment, is not to be given controlling significance." *U.S. v. Watson*, 423 U.S. 411, 424, 96 S. Ct. 820, 46 L. Ed. 2d 598 (1976).

First Circuit

- "Although sensitivity to the heightened possibility of coercion is appropriate when a defendant's consent is obtained during custody. . .custody alone has never been enough in itself to demonstrate. . .coerced. . .consent to search." *U.S. v. Collazo-Aponte*, 216 F.3d 163, 187, 54 Fed. R. Evid. Serv. 1311 (1st Cir. 2000), cert. granted in part, judgment vacated on other grounds, 532 U.S. 1036, 121 S. Ct. 1996, 149 L. Ed. 2d 1000 (2001).

Second Circuit

- "[Defendant] submits that, in light of the forcible entry into [homeowner's] apartment, her subsequent consent to search could not reasonably be deemed voluntary. . . . [T]he question of whether a person's statement has been purged of the taint of prior official illegality does not hinge on a simple 'but for' analysis, but rather must be answered on the facts of each case. . . .Only a half hour elapsed between the entry into [homeowner's] apartment and her consent to search. Viewed in isolation, this might appear insufficient time to dissipate any taint from a forced entry. Nevertheless. . .intervening events, even within a brief time, can sometimes sever the causal connection between an illegal entry and a subsequent consent to search, thereby permitting a court to conclude that the consent fairly reflects an act of free will. . . . [B]efore [homeowner's] consent to search was sought, the entering SWAT team left her apartment, [defendant] was arrested and removed from the premises, [homeowner's] own liberty was restored, and she was allowed to call her sister to come help with the care of her young child. Together, these intervening events effectively replaced the fearful atmosphere of the initial forcible entry with relative calm. This complete

change in circumstances explains [homeowner's] perception of the entry as having occurred 'way, way before'
her consent to search. [Homeowner] testified that the
officers who remained on the premises treated her 'with
respect' in explaining the situation leading to the entry
and in seeking her consent to search. Moreover, she
stated that she then knew that she was not required to
consent to any search. In short, because the intervening
circumstances successfully dissipated any taint from
the initial entry, we can confidently conclude that
[homeowner's] consent represented an independent act
of her free will." *U.S. v. Snype*, 441 F.3d 119, 69 Fed. R.
Evid. Serv. 817 (2d Cir. 2006).

Fifth Circuit

- "The facts surrounding Agent Garcia's search establish
  an implied limit to Escamilla's consent. Just as Escamilla's directly handing Agent Garcia the phone initiated
  the consensual search, a reasonable person would
  understand that Agent Garcia's directly handing the
  phone back to Escamilla ended it. Agent Garcia's search
  during the stop was one, complete search, and Agent
  Antonelli's search at the station was a second, distinct
  search requiring a warrant, its own consent, or some
  other exception to the warrant requirement. When the
  facts and circumstances surrounding a person's consent
  suggest a natural end to the consensual exchange with
  law enforcement, officers should not view the earlier
  consent as 'authorizing a second search at some future
  time if the first search is not fruitful.' Because it is
  undisputed that Agent Antonelli did not have a warrant and the Government does not offer any other exception to the Fourth Amendment's usual warrant requirement to justify his search, we find that Agent Antonelli's
  post-arrest manual search of the phone at the Border
  Patrol station was unconstitutional, and the district
  court should have suppressed the evidence linked to
  this search." *United States v. Escamilla*, 852 F.3d 474,
  485 (5th Cir. 2017) (citations omitted).
- "The district court should have acknowledged that the
  officers' knock-and-talk conduct was an unreasonable
  search. Had it done so, the court then would have
  proceeded not to the six-factor voluntariness analysis of

Hernandez's consent, but instead to the alternative analysis of whether her consent was an independent act of free will, breaking the chain of causation between the constitutional violation and the consent. Courts consider that question by weighing three factors: (1) the temporal proximity of the illegal conduct and the consent; (2) the presence of intervening circumstances; and (3) the purpose and flagrancy of the initial misconduct." *U.S. v. Hernandez*, 392 Fed. Appx. 350, 353 (5th Cir. 2010) (citations omitted).

Sixth Circuit

- "It is well-established that a warrantless search by law enforcement officials will be upheld if a detainee has voluntarily consented to the search. . . . . The government has the burden of demonstrating that consent was freely and voluntarily given, and was not the result of coercion, duress, or submission to a claim of authority." *U.S. v. Van Shutters*, 163 F.3d 331, 335, 1998 FED App. 0361P (6th Cir. 1998).

- "In *United States v. Watson* the Supreme Court applied *Bustamonte* to a defendant who consented to a search while in custody. Specifically stating that the fact of custody alone has never been enough in itself to demonstrate a coerced confession or consent to search the *Watson* Court identified a number of factors that led to a finding of voluntary consent, including the absence of any overt act or threat of force against the defendant; the absence of any promises to the defendant or any indication of more subtle forms of coercion that might flaw his judgment; the defendant's giving his post-arrest consent on a public street and not in the confines of the police station; the absence of any indication that the defendant was a newcomer to the law, mentally deficient, or unable in the face of custodial arrest to exercise a free choice; and the defendant's receiving *Miranda* warnings and notification that the results of the search could be used against him." *U.S. v. Crowder*, 62 F.3d 782, 787, 1995 FED App. 0241P (6th Cir. 1995).

Seventh Circuit

- "When the officers handcuffed [defendant], they asked him for consent to search the house and he gave it. He argues that his consent was given involuntarily, that it was a product of intimidating circumstances. The government ripostes that since he had been 'caught red-handed' he 'had a choice and at that instant, he decided to try to help himself by cooperating with the investigation,' and thus his consent was voluntary. That misses the point. He was 'caught red-handed' only because the police had barged in and were searching the house. The jig was up. But it was up because of the officers' unlawful act, and they cannot use their unlawful act as the basis for an inference of consent (citations omitted), just as a robber cannot defend by reference to the eagerness with which his victim chose to surrender his money rather than his life. Suppose the police had accosted [defendant] on the street and asked him for consent to search his home. It is doubtful that he would have given it, and the government does not bother even to argue that he would have. He consented to the choice at a time when he had no real choice, and he had no real choice because of police misconduct. . . ." *U.S. v. Collins*, 510 F.3d 697 (7th Cir. 2007).

- "Consent given during an illegal detention is presumptively invalid. Although the consent may nevertheless be valid provided that it is sufficiently attenuated from the illegal police action to dissipate the taint, the government here has not established that [defendant's girlfriend's] consent was attenuated from her illegal arrest. In assessing whether the taint of an illegal seizure was dissipated before consent was given, we consider the time that elapsed between the illegal act and the subsequent acquisition of evidence; the presence of intervening factors; and the purpose and flagrancy of the official misconduct. When consent to search is given by a person who remains illegally detained, the government is unlikely to meet its burden of showing that the consent was sufficiently attenuated from the illegality. Here, [the girlfriend's] consent was given while she was still in custody because of the illegal arrest and there was no intervening event of significance. Under these circumstances, we conclude that her consent to search the Buick was tainted by her illegal arrest and was therefore invalid." *U.S. v. Cellitti*, 387 F.3d 618 (7th Cir. 2004).

Eighth Circuit

- "[ ] Gerald argues that even if he did consent to the searches, his consent was not voluntary because he was handcuffed and in custody at the time of consent and had not been given Miranda warnings. 'The question of voluntariness requires a broad factual inquiry; there is no bright-line rule to determine when an "essentially free and unconstrained choice," becomes one that is "the result of duress or coercion."' Rather, we consider whether consent is voluntary based on the totality of the circumstances, 'including a defendant's age, intelligence, and education; whether he cooperates with police; his knowledge of his right to refuse consent; and his familiarity with arrests and the legal system.' 'Also relevant is the environment in which consent was given and whether the police threatened, intimidated, punished, or falsely promised something to the defendant; whether the defendant was in custody or under arrest when consent was given and, if so, how long he had been detained; and whether consent occurred in a public or secluded area.' . . . We conclude the district court did not err in finding that Gerald's consent to the searches was voluntary. Although the facts that Gerald was handcuffed and was not given Miranda warnings weigh in Gerald's favor, other facts support the court's finding of voluntariness: The agents did not threaten or intimidate Gerald, the agents told Gerald that he was not under arrest and that they wanted to ask him questions about the woman in his room, the agents informed Gerald that he did not have to speak with them, Gerald was cooperative with the agents and engaged them in conversation, and Gerald had prior experience with the legal system. Based on the totality of the circumstances, we cannot say the district court clearly erred in finding Gerald's consent was voluntary." *United States v. LeBeau*, 867 F.3d 960, 971 (8th Cir. 2017) (citations omitted).
- "That police were present and told [the defendant's wife] Debra about efforts to obtain a search warrant does not dictate a finding that later-given consent was the product of coercion or duress. We do not think restrictions on [*the defendant's*] movement undermine the district court's finding about *Debra's* free will. Under the total-

ity of the circumstances, there was no clear error in finding voluntary consent. To vitiate the unlawfulness of an entry, consent to a search must be both voluntary and 'an intervening independent act of a free will' sufficient 'to purge the primary taint of the unlawful invasion.' Whether consent sufficiently disperses the taint of an unlawful entry is determined by reference to 'temporal proximity' between the entry and the consent, 'the presence of intervening circumstances, and, particularly, the purpose and flagrancy of the official misconduct.' Observance of the *Miranda* rule is also relevant where applicable." *U.S. v. Brandwein*, 796 F.3d 980, 985 (8th Cir. 2015), petition for certiorari filed, 136 S. Ct. 1214, 194 L. Ed. 2d 216 (2016).

- "Here, [the officer's] discovery of the gun, along with the circumstances of his encounter with [Defendant] and his knowledge of the bank robbery suspect, . . . amount to probable cause to believe that additional evidence of the bank robbery would be found inside the van. . . . [The officer] thus did not need to obtain [Defendant's] consent, or a warrant, when he searched the van for a second time [after Defendant had been handcuffed but before his arrest]." *U.S. v. Farnell*, 701 F.3d 256, 264 (8th Cir. 2012).

- "Consent is not voluntary when it is the product of duress or coercion, either express or implied. . . . The record shows that [Defendant] believed that she was under arrest and that she had to submit to the patdown search. The officers did nothing to allay her fears but, rather, told her the opposite, informing [Defendant] that This is what we do. We talk to people, we search people's bags, we pat search people. This is what we do everyday. . . . The officers persisted in their requests, and did not tell [Defendant] that she was free to leave. Thus, the record supports the district court's finding that, under the totality of the circumstances, [Defendant] did not voluntarily consent to the pat-down search, and that the search resulted from an unlawful investigatory stop." *U.S. v. Pena-Saiz*, 161 F.3d 1175, 1177–78 (8th Cir. 1998).

- "In assessing the legality of a consent to search, the voluntariness of the criminal suspect's consent is the key. In determining voluntariness, all circumstances of the consent must be examined. The reading of *Miranda* rights in some circumstances tends to show that any subsequent consent to search by the person in custody is voluntary. In a similar vein, the Fifth Amendment's protection against self-incriminating statements may limit further interrogation once a person in custody invokes his right to counsel, but there is no similar prohibition on securing a voluntary consent to search for physical evidence." *U.S. v. Knight*, 58 F.3d 393, 397 (8th Cir. 1995).

Ninth Circuit

- "When an individual gives consent to search after an arrest made without probable cause, that consent to search, like a confession, may be tainted by the illegal arrest and so invalid and suppressible. Consent may be tainted even though it is 'voluntary' within the meaning of the Fifth Amendment. The relevant factors in determining whether a consent to search is tainted are: (1) whether *Miranda* warnings were administered prior to the consent; (2) the temporal proximity of the arrest to the [consent]; (3) the presence of intervening circumstances, and (4) the purpose and flagrancy of the official misconduct. The government bears the burden of showing admissibility." *U.S. v. Patzer*, 277 F.3d 1080 (9th Cir. 2002).

- "This Court considers the following five factors in determining whether a person has freely consented to a search: (1) whether defendant was in custody; (2) whether the arresting officers had their guns drawn; (3) whether *Miranda* warnings were given; (4) whether the defendant was told he had the right not to consent; and (5) whether the defendant was told that a search warrant could be obtained." *U.S. v. Cormier*, 220 F.3d 1103, 1112 (9th Cir. 2000).

Tenth Circuit

- "We recognize that arresting and handcuffing are coercive acts. But the consent of a handcuffed arrestee may well be voluntary." *U.S. v. Silva-Arzeta*, 602 F.3d 1208 (10th Cir. 2010).

- "[C]onsent to search may be voluntary even though the consenting party is being detained at the time consent is given. . . .and law enforcement agents fail to advise him of his *Miranda* rights. . . . The proper inquiry centers on whether the defendant suffered, inter alia, physical mistreatment, use of violence or threats of violence, promises or inducements, deception or trickery." *U.S. v. Dozal*, 173 F.3d 787, 796, 51 Fed. R. Evid. Serv. 712 (10th Cir. 1999).

- "Whether or not a party has voluntarily consented to a search is a question of fact that the district court must evaluate in view of the totality of the circumstances. . . . Consent to search may be voluntary even though the consenting party is being detained at the time consent is given." *U.S. v. Doyle*, 129 F.3d 1372, 1377 (10th Cir. 1997).

- "There was no evidence of any duress or coercion by [the Officer]. To the contrary, the district court found that [the Officer] told [Defendant] he was free to go and returned his documents before inquiring if he could ask some questions. There was no evidence of physical mistreatment, violence, threats, promises or inducements, deception or trickery, display of a weapon, use of a commanding manner or tone of voice, or the presence of more than one officer. A consent to search is not invalid merely because it is given by a person detained in a police car. Nor is a consent given inside a police car when the person is not detained invalid." *U.S. v. Hernandez*, 93 F.3d 1493, 1500 (10th Cir. 1996).

- "[T]he government must show that there was no duress or coercion, express or implied, that the consent was unequivocal and specific, and that it was freely and intelligently given. The fact of defendant's detention is a factor to be considered in determining voluntariness, but it is not dispositive. Valid consent may be given by a person being detained." *U.S. v. Nicholson*, 983 F.2d 983, 988, 37 Fed. R. Evid. Serv. 721 (10th Cir. 1993).

- "Mere submission to lawful authority does not equate to consent, rather valid consent must be unequivocal and specific, and freely and intelligently given. Merely because a person is detained or in custody does not preclude voluntary consent." *U.S. v. Manuel*, 992 F.2d 272, 275 (10th Cir. 1993).

§ 17:4 Third-party consent: Consent to a warrantless search may be given by a third party who reasonably appears to share control of the premises or items to be searched

Supreme Court

- "Our cases firmly establish that police officers may search jointly occupied premises if one of the occupants consents. In Georgia v. Randolph, 547 U.S. 103, 126 S.Ct. 1515, 164 L.Ed.2d 208 (2006), we recognized a narrow exception to this rule, holding that the consent of one occupant is insufficient when another occupant is present and objects to the search. In this case, we consider whether *Randolph* applies if the objecting occupant is absent when another occupant consents. Our opinion in *Randolph* took great pains to emphasize that its holding was limited to situations in which the objecting occupant is physically present. We therefore refuse to extend *Randolph* to the very different situation in this case, where consent was provided by an abused woman well after her male partner had been removed from the apartment they shared." *Fernandez v. California*, 134 S. Ct. 1126, 188 L. Ed. 2d 25 (2014).

- "The Fourth Amendment recognizes a valid warrantless entry and search of premises when police obtain the voluntary consent of an occupant who shares, or is reasonably believed to share, authority over the area in common with a co-occupant who later objects to the use of evidence so obtained. The question here is whether such an evidentiary seizure is likewise lawful with the permission of one occupant when the other, who later seeks to suppress the evidence, is present at the scene and expressly refuses to consent. We hold that, in the circumstances here at issue, a physically present co-occupant's stated refusal to permit entry prevails, rendering the warrantless search unreasonable and invalid as to him." *Georgia v. Randolph*, 547 U.S. 103, 126 S. Ct. 1515, 164 L. Ed. 2d 208 (2006).

- "[C]ommon authority rests on mutual use of the property by persons generally having joint access or control for most purposes. The burden of establishing that common authority rests upon the State. On the basis of this record, it is clear that burden was not sustained." *Illinois v. Rodriguez*, 497 U.S. 177, 181, 110 S. Ct. 2793, 111 L. Ed. 2d 148 (1990).

- "[W]hat is at issue when a claim of apparent consent is raised is not whether the right to be free of searches has been waived, but whether the right to be free of unreasonable searches has been violated. As with other factual determinations bearing upon search and seizure, determination of consent to enter must be judged against an objective standard: would the facts available to the officer at the moment warrant a man of reasonable caution in the belief that the consenting party had authority over the premises. If not, then warrantless entry without further inquiry is unlawful unless authority actually exists. But if so, the search is valid." *Illinois v. Rodriguez*, 497 U.S. 177, 183–84, 110 S. Ct. 2793, 111 L. Ed. 2d 148 (1990).

- "[T]he prosecution is not limited to proof that consent was given by the defendant, but may show that permission to search was obtained from a third party who possessed common authority over or other sufficient relationship to the premises or effects sought to be inspected." *U.S. v. Matlock*, 415 U.S. 164, 171, 94 S. Ct. 988, 39 L. Ed. 2d 242 (1974).

- "Common authority rests on mutual use of the property by persons generally having joint access or control for most purposes, so that it is reasonable to recognize that any of the co-inhabitants has the right to permit the inspection in his own right and that the others have assumed the risk that one of their number might permit the common areas to be searched." *U.S. v. Matlock*, 415 U.S. 164, 171 n.7, 94 S. Ct. 988, 39 L. Ed. 2d 242 (1974).

- "No less than a tenant of a house, or the occupant of a room in a boarding house, a guest in a hotel room is entitled to constitutional protection against unreasonable searches and seizures. That protection would disappear if it were left to depend upon the unfettered discretion of an employee of the hotel. It follows that this search without a warrant was unlawful." *Stoner v. State of Cal.*, 376 U.S. 483, 490, 84 S. Ct. 889, 11 L. Ed. 2d 856 (1964).

First Circuit
- "Marine enforcement officers acted reasonably in

searching containers on vessel, based on consent given
by owner of vessel, where containers were not locked,
nor were they identified as anyone else's personal property, and no one advised officers at the time of the
search that the containers were not the property of the
vessel owner." *U.S. v. Carrasco*, 540 F.3d 43 (1st Cir.
2008).

• "[Lessee] characterized [defendant's] bedroom as 'his
space.' She did not enter the room as a regular matter,
and she told police before they entered that she was not
supposed to enter the room. [Lessee] did not even have
a key to go into the room and instead had to use a but-
ter knife to pry the door open. We find, therefore, that
[lessee's] consent to the search of the house could not
extend to the search of the room [defendant] was using.
The fact that the agents smelled the scent of burning
marihuana emanating from the room when they reached
the second floor does not cure the problem. Odors alone
do not authorize a search without a warrant. Where the
odor of a forbidden substance is identified by someone
found qualified to know the odor, there may well be
probable cause to justify issuance of a search warrant,
but it is not sufficient to justify a warrantless search."
U.S. v. Jimenez, 419 F.3d 34 (1st Cir. 2005).

• "Even if [defendant's landlady] did not have actual
authority to authorize the search, the evidence need not
be suppressed because [the searching officer] had a reasonable basis for believing that [the landlady] had common authority over the stairway. . . . [T]he Fourth
Amendment is not violated when an officer enters
without a warrant because he reasonably, though erroneously, believed that the person who consented to his
entry is authorized to do so. An officer's reliance on a
person's apparent authority must be judged against an
objective standard: whether a person of reasonable caution with the facts available to him or her would believe
the consenting party had authority over the premises.
At the time of the search, [the landlady] told Officer
Hutchins that she rented the two upstairs bedrooms to
[the defendant and his girlfriend]. She did not inform
him that she considered the stairway and landing part
of [defendant's] rented space. When [the landlady]
asked [the officer] to search the upstairs bedrooms, he

told her that he could not conduct a search without a warrant because Marshall and Jones had an expectation of privacy; nevertheless, [the landlady] then asked him to search the stairwell. Because [the officer] had just explained the limitation on his ability to conduct a search, he could reasonably assume that [the landlady] would not have thereafter asked him to search [defendant's] private space. Thus, [the landlady's] request for him to walk up the staircase, under these circumstances, would have given a reasonable person the impression that she had common authority over this area." *U.S. v. Marshall*, 348 F.3d 281 (1st Cir. 2003).

Second Circuit

- "Passengers, no less than drivers, possess a reduced expectation of privacy with regard to the property that they transport in cars, passengers may nonetheless retain an actual, reasonable, socially recognized expectation of privacy in their luggage, even when it is transported in a vehicle driven by or shared with others. The Government can legitimate the warrantless search of a passenger's luggage by showing that it was made pursuant to a valid consent. To do this, the Government must show by a preponderance of the evidence that the party consenting to the search had the requisite authority to consent to the full scope of the search conducted. The requisite authority can be either actual or apparent." *U.S. v. Sparks*, 287 Fed. Appx. 918 (2d Cir. 2008).

Fourth Circuit

- "Whether the officers reasonably believed that (the wife) had authority to consent to a search of all the contents of the computer's hard drive, however, depends on viewing these facts in light of the totality of the circumstances known to the officers at the time of the search . . . (T)he officers did not have any indication from (the wife), or any of the attendant circumstances, that any files were password-protected . . . Despite (the wife's) suggestion that she lacked deep familiarity with the computer, the totality of the circumstances provided the officers with the basis for an objectively reasonable belief that (the wife) had authority to consent to a search of the computer's hard drive. Therefore, the police were justified in relying on (the wife's) consent to search the computer and all of its files, such that no search warrant was required." *U.S. v. Buckner*, 473 F.3d 551 (4th Cir. 2007).

Fifth Circuit

- "Ranch owner, who informed police officers that he had originally hired arrestee as a laborer and was allowing arrestee and another individual to reside in trailer located on his property without paying any rent, and that he owned all furniture in trailer, enjoyed unlimited and unrestricted access, and had in fact entered trailer unannounced and without obtaining prior consent on several occasions, had apparent authority to consent to search of trailer." *Morales v. Boyd*, 304 Fed. Appx. 315 (5th Cir. 2008).

Sixth Circuit

- "Even with the consent of a person with common authority, however, the police generally may not enter when another occupant of the home is physically present and expressly refuses to permit entry. . . . The Supreme Court has consistently validated the right to retreat into one's home and avoid contact with the police. Any reasonable officer would have understood that to enter a private home after being expressly told the occupant could not speak with him, in the course of a routine child welfare check, flies in the face of this clearly established law." *Smith v. City of Wyoming*, 821 F.3d 697, 709–11 (6th Cir. 2016) (citations omitted).

- "The apparent-authority doctrine excuses otherwise impermissible searches where the officers conducting the search 'reasonably (though erroneously) believe that the person who has consented' to the search had the authority to do so. . . . [However,] [a]lthough many items that belong to a houseguest like [defendant] might also be used by the dwelling's resident (such as books, compact discs, magazines, or a portable stereo), a shoebox that is surrounded by the guest's clothes and that sits in the corner of a closet in a little-used room is not likely to be such an item." *U.S. v. Taylor*, 600 F.3d 678 (6th Cir. 2010).

- " "(C)onsent once removed" . . . requires that an 'undercover agent or informant 1) enter . . . at the express invitation of someone with authority to consent; 2) at that point established the existence of probable cause to effectuate an arrest or search; 3) immediately summoned help from other officers' . . . (T)he doctrine of "consent once removed" (applies) to a situation in which the initial consent was given only to a civilian informant . . . . All three components of the doctrine of "consent once removed" were present here . . . . (The) undercover officer entered the hotel room (by) express invitation . . . , and there was probable cause to arrest both men at the time that they were seized. Upon seeing the second person in the room, whose hands were hidden from view, (the undercover officer) immediately summoned help from the backup officers watching from across the hall. '[T]he back-up officers were acting within constitutional limits when they entered to assist . . . (him) since no further invasion of privacy was involved once the undercover officer made the initial entry' . . . . The officers' entry into the hotel room did not violate the Fourth Amendment." *U.S. v. Romero*, 452 F.3d 610, 2006 FED App. 0219P (6th Cir. 2006).

- "Common authority is not to be implied from a mere property interest that a third party has in the property, but from mutual use by persons generally having joint access or control for most purposes. The burden of establishing that a third party possesses common authority to consent to a search rests with the state. Even if a third party does not possess actual common authority over the area that was searched, the Fourth Amendment is not violated if the police relied in good faith on a third party's apparent authority to consent to the search. Apparent authority is judged by an objective standard. A search consented to by a third party without actual authority over the premises is nonetheless valid if the officers reasonably could conclude from the facts available that the third party had authority to consent to the search." *U.S. v. Gillis*, 358 F.3d 386, 2004 FED App. 0047P (6th Cir. 2004).

- "In *U.S. v. Roark*, 36 F.3d 14, 1994 FED App. 0347P (6th Cir. 1994), defendant lived in a home owned by his sister, who lived in the primary residence located on the same property, but who testified that she lacked authorization to enter her brother's home without his permission. After defendant's sister consented to a search of the home in which defendant was living, police found substantial amounts of marijuana and defendant was arrested. Defendant pled guilty to illegal drug and firearm possession, but reserved his right to appeal the district court's denial of his motion to suppress. On appeal, this court first addressed whether, as an initial matter, defendant's sister possessed the authority to consent to a search of the home of which she was the owner but in which defendant resided. The court held that defendant's sister was so authorized. . . Although we hold that the sheriff's deputies [who, in the instant case, accompanied the administratrix of an estate to the decedent's house, in which her brother lived, so that she could inventory the contents] are entitled to qualified immunity in light of *Roark*, this is not to say we are in agreement that *Roark* was correctly decided. . . If *Roark* were generally applied, then, for example, an absentee landlord would have the ability to consent to the search of a tenant's residence. That is not the law. . . Because the issue before us is qualified immunity, rather than a direct challenge to *Roark* we have no need to explore the matter any further in this case." *Wilhelm v. Boggs*, 290 F.3d 822, 2002 FED App. 0182P (6th Cir. 2002).

Seventh Circuit

- "Factors in determining whether a person has actual or apparent authority to consent to a warrantless search, so as to render the search reasonable under the Fourth Amendment, include: (1) possession of a key to premises; (2) person's admission that she lives at the residence; (3) possession of a driver's license listing the residence as the driver's legal address; (4) receiving mail and bills at that residence; (5) keeping clothing at the residence; (6) having one's children reside at that address; (7) keeping personal belongings such as a diary or pet at that residence; (8) performing household chores at home; (9) being on lease for premises and/or paying rent; and (10) being allowed into home when owner is not present." *U.S. v. Groves*, 530 F.3d 506 (7th Cir. 2008).

- "Resident's refusal of consent for warrantless search of home was no longer effective to bar voluntary consent of co-resident, once objecting resident was validly arrested and removed from home; objecting resident was no longer both present and objecting." *U.S. v. Henderson*, 536 F.3d 776 (7th Cir. 2008).
- "Persons with authority to consent to warrantless search of residence, so as to render search reasonable under Fourth Amendment, include occupant of home or premises, and any third parties who have common authority over or other sufficient relationship to premises or effects sought to be inspected." *U.S. v. Henderson*, 536 F.3d 776 (7th Cir. 2008).
- "Although a third party generally cannot consent to a warrantless search of another's home, there is an exception when the government can show by a preponderance of the evidence that the third party possessed common authority over, or other sufficient relationship to, the premises or effects sought to be inspected. Apparent authority to consent exists when the facts available to an officer at the time of a search would allow a person of reasonable caution to believe that the consenting party had authority over the premises." *U.S. v. Ryerson*, 545 F.3d 483 (7th Cir. 2008).
- "[W]here a defendant allows a third party to exercise actual or apparent authority over the defendant's property, he is considered to have assumed the risk that the third party might permit access to others, including government agents. . . .Third-party consent to a search can legitimately be given whether the premises to be searched are as expansive as a house or as minute as a briefcase. The key to consent is actual or apparent authority over the area to be searched." *U.S. v. Basinski*, 226 F.3d 829, 834 (7th Cir. 2000).
- "[T]he foundation of third party consent is assumption of risk. . . . For example, a person who shares a car with another person understands that the partner may invite strangers into it, and that the privacy right of one is not absolute but contingent in large measure on the decisions of the other. . . . Decisions of either person define the extent of the privacy involved, a principle that does not depend on whether the stranger welcomed into the car turns out to be a police officer or

another party to the crime." *U.S. v. Jensen*, 169 F.3d
1044, 1049 (7th Cir. 1999).

Eighth Circuit

- "That police were present and told [the defendant's wife]
  Debra about efforts to obtain a search warrant does not
  dictate a finding that later-given consent was the product of coercion or duress. We do not think restrictions
  on [*the defendant's*] movement undermine the district
  court's finding about *Debra's* free will. Under the totality of the circumstances, there was no clear error in
  finding voluntary consent. To vitiate the unlawfulness
  of an entry, consent to a search must be both voluntary
  and 'an intervening independent act of a free will' sufficient 'to purge the primary taint of the unlawful
  invasion.' Whether consent sufficiently disperses the
  taint of an unlawful entry is determined by reference to
  'temporal proximity' between the entry and the consent,
  'the presence of intervening circumstances, and, particularly, the purpose and flagrancy of the official
  misconduct.' Observance of the *Miranda* rule is also relevant where applicable." *U.S. v. Brandwein*, 796 F.3d
  980, 985 (8th Cir. 2015), petition for certiorari filed, 136
  S. Ct. 1214, 194 L. Ed. 2d 216 (2016).

- "As a legal matter, consent to search, a valid exception
  to the warrant requirement, may be given either by the
  suspect or by some other person who has common
  authority over, or sufficient relationship to, the item to
  be searched. The district court correctly concluded that
  the search of the Jaguar did not violate the Fourth
  Amendment if [defendant's girlfriend] had common
  authority over the car. As a factual matter, the district
  court did not clearly err in finding [defendant's girl-
  friend] had common authority over the Jaguar based on
  'mutual use, joint access, and control.' [She] not only
  drove the Jaguar, but explained to the officers that she
  was the Jaguar's only licensed driver ([the defendant's]
  license was suspended). [Defendant's girlfriend] had the
  only key to the car, and earlier that day [the defendant]
  expressly told [her] she could drive the car home from
  work. Even if [the defendant] is correct that he gave
  [her] only narrow permission to drive the car home from
  work because it was raining, [defendant's girlfriend]

described for the officers her control over the car in broad terms sufficient to give a reasonable appearance of authority. Given that [defendant's girlfriend] testified she freely 'said yes' and unlocked the car herself, the district court did not err in finding her consent voluntary." *U.S. v. Scott*, 732 F.3d 910 (8th Cir. 2013).

- "In recent years, whether a third party validly consented to search of a shared computer has been a recurring Fourth Amendment issue, particularly in child pornography prosecutions. . . . When determining whether a third party exercised actual or apparent common authority over the contents of a computer, courts typically examine several factors—whether the consenting third party in fact used the computer, whether it was located in a common area accessible to other occupants of the premises, and—often most importantly—whether the defendant's files were password protected. . . . In this case, [Defendant] was in jail on January 22. A temporary seizure of the computers while the officers applied for a search warrant did not meaningfully interfere with his possessory interests. [Defendant's father], who was in actual possession of the computers in his home, consented to their seizure, indeed, he asked the officers to take them from the home. Viewed from this perspective, no Fourth Amendment 'seizure' occurred. . . . [T]he officers' limited purpose in temporarily seizing the computers—to avoid the destruction of evidence while they applied for a search warrant—is relevant to the validity of [Defendant's father's] third party consent. . . . [T]he officers reasonably relied on [Defendant's father's] actual or apparent authority to consent to a temporary seizure, without inquiring as to whether he 'used or had electronic access to the computers.' " *U.S. v. Clutter*, 674 F.3d 980, 984-85 (8th Cir. 2012).

- "The principle 'does not rest upon the law of property . . . but rests rather on mutual use of the property by persons generally having joint access or control for most purposes, so that it is reasonable to recognize that any of the co-inhabitants has the right to permit the inspection in his own right and that the others have assumed the risk that one of their number might permit the common area to be searched.' Even when a third party lacks actual authority to consent to search or seizure of shared property or premises, the Fourth Amendment is not violated if the officers reasonably relied on the third party's apparent authority to consent, because the Amendment's reasonableness requirement demands of government agents 'not that they always be correct, but that they always be reasonable.' . . . . In recent years, whether a third party validly consented to search of a shared computer has been a recurring Fourth Amendment issue, particularly in child pornography prosecutions. It is a sensitive issue because, '[f]or most people, their computers are their most private spaces.' When determining whether a third party exercised actual or apparent common authority over the contents of a computer, courts typically examine several factors— whether the consenting third party in fact used the computer, whether it was located in a common area accessible to other occupants of the premises, and—often most importantly—whether the defendant's files were password protected. . . . . [T]he only Fourth Amendment issue with any factual support is whether the three computers were validly *seized* at the Clutter home on January 22. There is no evidence that the officers *searched* the computers before obtaining an unchallenged warrant authorizing the search. The distinction, though often overlooked, is important:

> Although our Fourth Amendment cases sometimes refer indiscriminately to searches and seizures, there are important differences between the two . . . . The Amendment protects two different interests of the citizen—the interest in retaining possession of property and the interest in maintaining personal privacy. A seizure threatens the former, a search the latter. As a matter of timing, a seizure is usually preceded by a search, but when a container is involved the converse is often true. Significantly, the two protected interests are not always present to the same extent; for example, the seizure of a locked suitcase does not necessarily compromise the secrecy of its contents, and the search of a stopped vehicle does not necessarily deprive its owner of possession."

U.S. v. Clutter, 674 F.3d 980, 983-85 (8th Cir. 2012) (citations omitted).

- "Even if the police make a mistake of fact about a third party's authority over the premises, a search of the premises will be legal if the circumstances lead the police reasonably to believe that they have the consent of a third party with common authority. The police may rely on a third party's consent to search throughout the house, so long as the consent appeared to extend so far. If part of a dwelling is appropriated for the exclusive use of one occupant, other inmates of the house have no right to consent to police entry of the space from which they themselves are excluded." *U.S. v. Almeida-Perez*, 549 F.3d 1162 (8th Cir. 2008).

- "We agree with the district court that [officer] reasonably believed that [tenant] had the authority to consent to the search. The cabinet was found in a common closet. When asked, [tenant] retrieved the key from a common key rack and handed it to [officer] without warning that the cabinet or its contents belonged to someone else. [Defendant] remained silent, giving the officers no reason to believe that he had a superior privacy interest in the cabinet. . . . [Defendant argues that [officer] used [tenant's] consent to 'intentionally bypass' [defendant's] superior privacy interest. As the district court noted, we have acknowledged (but never invoked) intentional bypass as a narrow exception to the Supreme Court's third party consent principles, explaining that 'police may not rely on a third party's consent to intentionally bypass a person who is present, has a superior privacy interest in the premises, *and actively objects to the search.*' Here, of course, [defendant] was present and did not object to the search. . . . When as in this case a third party with apparent authority gives unequivocal consent, and the defendant is present and fails to disclose a superior privacy interest and object to the search, there is no intentional bypass." *U.S. v. Elam*, 441 F.3d 601 (8th Cir. 2006).
- "The Fourth Amendment's general prohibition against warrantless searches does not apply when officers obtain voluntary consent from the person whose property is searched or from a third party with common authority over the property. . . . [B]ut police may not rely on a third party's consent to intentionally bypass a person who is present, has a superior privacy interest in the premises, and actively objects to the search. . . ." *U.S. v. Esparza*, 162 F.3d 978, 980 (8th Cir. 1998).

<u>Ninth Circuit</u>

- "Regarding implied consent, only in narrow circumstances may consent be implied by actions and in most
implied consent cases it is the suspect himself who takes
an action which implies consent. (citations omitted) It is
'a most uncommon situation' where the court is asked
to infer consent from a third party's actions." *Espinosa
v. City and County of San Francisco*, 598 F.3d 528 (9th
Cir. 2010).
- "That the police did not ask the defendant for his
consent to search the home does not invalidate his wife's
consent because the defendant was 'justifiably absent
from the search colloquy' and did not voice any objection on his own." *U.S. v. Salas De La Rosa*, 366 Fed.
Appx. 757 (9th Cir. 2010).
- "Although (defendant) retained a legitimate expectation
of privacy in his workplace office, (his employer)
retained the ability to consent to a search of (defendant's) office and his business computer. And because
valid third party consent to search the office and computer located therein was given by his employer, the
district court's order denying suppression of the evidence of child pornography existing on (defendant's)
computer is affirmed." *U.S. v. Ziegler*, 474 F.3d 1184,
153 Lab. Cas. (CCH) P 60340 (9th Cir. 2007).
- "Like private telephone conversations, either party to a
chat room exchange has the power to surrender each
other's privacy interest to a third party. The nature of
consent illustrates a reality of the Internet, namely,
that a person initiating an Internet-based conversation
does not control the recipient." *U.S. v. Meek*, 366 F.3d
705 (9th Cir. 2004).
- "The government argues that even if [defendant] had a
reasonable expectation of privacy in his [gym bag, which
he kept under his bed], the search was legal because
[lessee] validly consented to a search of the apartment
and, as an occupant and lessee, she had authority to
give consent to search anywhere on the premises...
Because the record here... does not in any way intimate
that [lessee] had mutual use and joint access to or
shared control over [defendant's] gym bag, it is clear
that [lessee] lacked actual authority to consent to a
search of the bag... [Lessee] indicated to the officers
which bedroom was occupied by [defendant and his

girlfriend] and stated that [defendant] occasionally
stayed there. Although Officer Dyer testified that [les-
see] told them the bedroom was a 'spare' room, he also
testified that [lessee] informed them that [defendant's]
belongings were in the room. Because the officers were
aware that [defendant's] belongings were in a specific
area separate from [lessee's] belongings, they could not
reasonably believe that she had control over them...
Thus, the officers were aware of the actual facts that
established [lessee's] lack of authority to consent to the
search of [defendant's] bag." *U.S. v. Davis*, 332 F.3d
1163 (9th Cir. 2003).

- "The government contends that. . .had apparent
  authority to consent because he answered the front door
  and appeared to be alone in the apartment. This evidence, however, is insufficient because the mere fact of
  access, without more, does not indicate that the access
  was authorized." *U.S. v. Reid*, 226 F.3d 1020, 1025 (9th
  Cir. 2000).

- "[A] co-tenant's consent to the search of a residence [is]
  effective even if the other co-tenant protested. . . ."
  U.S. v. Flores, 172 F.3d 695, 698 (9th Cir. 1999).

- "The existence of apparent authority entails a three-
  part analysis. First, did the searching officer believe
  some untrue fact that was then used to assess the
  consent-giver's use of and access to or control over the
  area searched? Second, was it under the circumstances
  objectively reasonable to believe that the fact was true?
  Finally, assuming the truth of the reasonably believed
  but untrue fact, would the consent-giver have had
  actual authority?" *U.S. v. Fiorillo*, 186 F.3d 1136, 1144,
  48 Env't. Rep. Cas. (BNA) 1993, 29 Envtl. L. Rep. 21396
  (9th Cir. 1999), as amended on denial of reh'g and reh'g
  en banc, (Sept. 10, 1999).

Tenth Circuit

- "Ms. Austin had joint access to and control over the
  shop. The record indicates that Ms. Austin, at the
  request of Plaintiff, had obtained a bond in order to sell
  cars for Plaintiff. The record also shows that she would
  sometimes help Mr. Austin with his vehicle repair work.
  The fact that Ms. Austin's name did not appear on the
  lease does not diminish her authority to consent to a

search based on her access to and control over the shop. Thus, Ms. Austin had actual authority to consent to a search of the shop. At the very least, both Mr. and Ms. Austin had apparent authority to consent to the search. A police officer who is called to come to a business by the business owner's spouse and then invited inside by the caller, in the presence of the owner of the business and with no objections made, is justified in acting upon the invitation without further inquiry." *Patel v. Hall*, 849 F.3d 970, 981 (10th Cir. 2017).

- "Defendant's wife did not have actual authority to consent to the search of a hotel room where a sawed-off shotgun was found where the defendant and his wife were estranged, she spent a total of 20 minutes in the room with the defendant, she did not have a key, did not leave any personal belongings in the room, and did not plan to spend the night there." *U.S. v. Arrington*, 296 Fed. Appx. 646 (10th Cir. 2008).

- "(Defendant) contends that ambiguities in the situation facing the officers at (his) residence required the officers to ask further questions concerning (his 91 year old father's) authority to consent to a computer search prior to commencing the search . . . . Valid third party consent can arise either through the third party's actual authority or the third party's apparent authority. A third party has actual authority to consent to a search "if that third party has either (1) mutual use of the property by virtue of joint access, or (2) control for most purposes" . . . When the property to be searched is an object or container, the relevant inquiry must address the third party's relationship to the object . . . . This court has not previously considered expectations of privacy associated with a home computer in a third party consent situation . . . . Given the pervasiveness of computers in American homes, this court must reach some, at least tentative, conclusion about the category into which personal computers fall. A personal computer is often a repository for private information the computer's owner does not intend to share with others . . . . A critical issue in assessing a third party's apparent authority to consent to the search of a home computer . . . is whether law enforcement knows or should reasonably suspect because of surrounding circumstances that the computer is password protected . . . In addition to password protection, courts also consider the location of the computer within the house and other indicia of household members' access to the computer in assessing third party authority. Third party apparent authority to consent to a search has generally been upheld when the computer is located in a common area of the home that is accessible to other family members under circumstances indicating the other family members were not excluded from using the computer . . . Viewed under the requisite totality-of-the-circumstances analysis, the facts known to the officers at the time the computer search commenced created an objectively reasonable perception that (defendant's father) was, at least, *one* user of the computer. That objectively reasonable belief would have been enough to give (him) apparent authority to consent to a search." *U.S. v. Andrus*, 483 F.3d 711 (10th Cir. 2007), decision clarified on denial of reh'g, 499 F.3d 1162 (10th Cir. 2007).

- "The officers also ask this court to adopt the "consent-once-removed" doctrine based on policy considerations. They argue that without this doctrine law enforcement will be severely hampered in its pursuit of drug traffickers because the use of informants is vital, and requiring officers to obtain a warrant whenever an informant was in a home would jeopardize personal safety and cause delays. This argument fails for two reasons. First, this contradicts the nature of the exceptions based on exigent circumstances requiring that the police may not manipulate or abuse the circumstances creating the exigency . . . Second, as recently restated by the Supreme Court in *Georgia v. Randolph*, "[a] generalized interest in expedient law enforcement cannot, without more, justify a warrantless search" . . . Thus, while our case law would support a holding that the Fourth Amendment allows an undercover officer to summon backup officers within a home after that officer has been invited with consent, neither the case law nor a rational extension of the case law would support including officers summoned by an informant within a home. Based on this, we hold that entering (defendant's) home based on the invitation of an informant and without a warrant, direct consent, or other exigent circumstances, the task force officers violated (defendant's) constitutional rights under the Fourth Amendment." *Callahan v. Millard County*, 494 F.3d 891 (10th Cir. 2007), rev'd on other grounds, 555 U.S. 223, 129 S. Ct. 808, 172 L. Ed. 2d 565 (2009).

- "Consensual searches constitute one exception to the warrant requirement. [citations omitted] Consent may be obtained from the individual whose property is searched, or in certain instances, from a third party who possesses either actual authority or apparent authority to consent to the search. [citations omitted] . . . The Supreme Court's decision in [*U.S. v.*] *Matlock* sets forth the test for actual authority. [citation omitted] . . . Under Matlock, 'common authority' is . . . based on . . . 'mutual use of the property by persons generally having joint access or control for most purposes, so that it is reasonable to recognize that any of the cohabitants has the right to permit inspection in his own right and that the others have assumed the risk that one of their number might permit the common area to be searched.' [citation omitted] . . . [W]e have read *Matlock* to establish the following standards for assessing actual authority to consent to a search of a residence: '(1) mutual use of the property by virtue of joint access, or (2) control for most purposes over it.' [citation and emphasis omitted] The first of these standards—mutual use by virtue of joint access—is 'a fact-intensive inquiry.' [citation omitted] We require the government to show that 'the third party entered the premises or room at will, without the consent of the subject of the search.' [citation omitted] . . . In contrast, the second standard—control for most purposes over the property—is a 'normative inquiry dependent upon whether the relationship between the defendant and the third party is the type which creates a presumption of control for most purposes over the property by the third party.' [citation omitted] If the presumption of control is not rebutted, then the third party has actual authority to consent to a search of the defendant's property. [citation omitted] Parent-child and husband-wife relationships trigger this presumption, but 'a simple co-tenant relationship does not create a presumption of control and actual access would have to be

shown.' [citation omitted] . . . In applying these
principles of actual authority, we must be mindful of
the Supreme Court's recent observation [in *Georgia v.
Randolph*] that . . . '[t]he constant element in the assessing reasonableness in the consent cases . . . is the
great significance given to widely shared social expectations, which are naturally enough influenced by the law
of property, but not controlled by its rules.' [citation
omitted] Thus, whether the defendant's reasonable
expectation of privacy was infringed by the third party's
consent to the search is a paramount concern. [citation
omittted]" *U.S. v. Cos*, 498 F.3d 1115 (10th Cir. 2007).

• "A person who resides with the defendant and engages
  in mutual use of the property may authorize a warrantless search." *U.S. v. Dozal*, 173 F.3d 787, 792, 51 Fed.
  R. Evid. Serv. 712 (10th Cir. 1999).

• "[A] third party has authority to consent to a search of
  property if that third party has either (1) mutual use of
  the property by virtue of joint access, or (2) control for
  most purposes over it. Mutual use of property by virtue
  of joint access is a fact-intensive inquiry which requires
  findings by a court that the third party entered the
  premises or room at will, without the consent of the
  subject of the search. . . . Unlike the fact-intensive inquiry of mutual use, control for most purposes of property is a normative inquiry dependent upon whether
  the relationship between the defendant and the third
  party is the type which creates a presumption of control
  for most purposes over the property by the third party.
  If a relationship creates such a presumption of control
  and is unrebutted, the third party has authority to
  consent to a search of the property. Relationships which
  give rise to a presumption of control of property include
  parent-child relationships and husband-wife
  relationships." *U.S. v. Rith*, 164 F.3d 1323, 1329–30, 51
  Fed. R. Evid. Serv. 197 (10th Cir. 1999).

• "The two federal circuit courts that have addressed the
  issue of the capacity of minors to consent to searches
  have reached similar conclusions. The Eleventh Circuit
  held that, as a matter of law, a minor child can give
  third-party consent to the entry of law enforcement
  officers. . . . The Sixth Circuit held that minors have
  the capacity to consent to search the family residence

when the minors otherwise satisfy the requirements for third-party consent under the *Matlock* test. . . . We agree that minority does not, per se, bar a finding of actual authority to grant third-party consent to entry." *U.S. v. Gutierrez-Hermosillo*, 142 F.3d 1225, 1230–31, 152 A.L.R. Fed. 757 (10th Cir. 1998).

Eleventh Circuit

- "The Supreme Court crafted the *Randolph* rule in the context of the search of a residence. Both Thomas and the government acknowledge that it is an open question whether *Randolph* applies to searches of personal effects, such as computers. Indeed, federal appeals courts have split on this issue. We need not settle the issue here, though. . . . When the police obtained Olausen's consent to search the HP computer and undertook the forensic scan, they knew that: (1) the computer was easily accessible and located in an unlocked room in the Thomas's shared residence; (2) Olausen had access to the computer and had used it that morning; and (3) Olausen and Thomas shared the password to access the computer. Based on this information, it appeared that Olausen had control and authority over the HP computer, and could consent to a forensic search. The fact that Thomas was the primary user of the computer, worked from home, and typically deleted his Internet history, used pop-up-ware and spam filters, and usually fully shut down the HP computer (although he did not on the night in question) were insufficient to show that Olausen lacked the requisite common authority to provide consent. Despite Thomas's security measures, Olausen had 'joint access or control [over the computer] for most purposes,' and Thomas did not isolate his Internet use in a manner that prevented Olausen from accessing it all together." *U.S. v. Thomas*, 818 F.3d 1230, 1240–41 (11th Cir. 2016), cert. denied, 137 S. Ct. 171, 196 L. Ed. 2d 142 (2016) (citations omitted).

- "Consent to search may be provided by a third party who possesses common authority over the premises for most purposes, so that it is reasonable to recognize that the third party has the right to permit inspection and others have assumed the risk that the third party might allow the area to be searched." *U.S. v. Smith*, 353 Fed. Appx. 229 (11th Cir. 2009).

- "A defendant can knowingly and voluntarily contractually agree to allow third parties to enter a space where the defendant has an expectation of privacy." *U.S. v. Smith*, 353 Fed. Appx. 229 (11th Cir. 2009).
- "Generally, hotel employee does not have authority to consent to warrantless search of room rented to guest." *U.S. v. Mercer*, 541 F.3d 1070 (11th Cir. 2008).
- "As part of the contract, and on the reverse side of each and every Federal Express airbill utilized by defendants we find the following notice: 'We may, at our option, open and inspect your packages prior to or after you give them to us to deliver.'. . .[T]his bold, unqualified 'right to inspect' renders our factual scenario here irreconcilably different from *Jacobsen*.. . . No reasonable person would expect to retain his or her privacy interest in a packaged shipment after signing an airbill containing an explicit, written warning that the carrier is authorized to act in direct contravention to that interest. Federal Express told its customers two things: (1) do not ship cash, and (2) we may open and inspect your packages at our option. As a matter of law, this simply eliminates any expectation of privacy. We affirm the district court's finding that [defendant] did not have any legitimate expectation of privacy in the packages x-rayed by the IRS agents. As an alternative basis for affirming the denial of the motion to suppress, we also find a consent to search through the bailment relationship. Just as the 'right to inspect' notice defeated [defendant's] privacy interest, we believe it also served to defeat [defendant's] Fourth Amendment challenge because it authorized Federal Express, as a bailee of the packages, to consent to a search." *U.S. v. Young*, 350 F.3d 1302, 92 A.F.T.R.2d 2003-7085 (11th Cir. 2003).

§ 17:5　Scope of consent: A consent search may not exceed the terms of the consent; once given, consent to search may be withdrawn

Supreme Court

- "A suspect may of course delimit as he chooses the scope of the search to which he consents. But if his consent would reasonably be understood to extend to a particular container, the Fourth Amendment provides no grounds for requiring a more explicit authorization." *Florida v. Jimeno*, 500 U.S. 248, 252, 111 S. Ct. 1801, 114 L. Ed. 2d 297 (1991).

- "We think that it was objectively reasonable for the police to conclude that the general consent to search respondent's car included consent to search containers within that car which might bear drugs. A reasonable person may be expected to know that narcotics are generally carried in some form of a container. Contraband goods rarely are strewn across the trunk or floor of a car. The authorization to search in this case, therefore, extended beyond the surfaces of the car's interior to the paper bag lying on the car's floor." *Florida v. Jimeno*, 500 U.S. 248, 251, 111 S. Ct. 1801, 114 L. Ed. 2d 297 (1991).

- "When an official search is properly authorized—whether by consent or by the issuance of a valid warrant—the scope of the search is limited by the terms of its authorization. Consent to search a garage would not implicitly authorize a search of an adjoining house." *Walter v. U.S.*, 447 U.S. 649, 656–57, 100 S. Ct. 2395, 65 L. Ed. 2d 410 (1980).

First Circuit
- "The appellant submits that, despite his ready relinquishment of his sawed-off shotgun, his cooperation with the police was actually coerced. In his view, he was given a Hobson's choice: either comply with the served orders (thereby turning over evidence of a known violation of federal law) or refuse to comply with the orders (thereby risking prosecution under state law). Caught between Scylla and Charybdis, his thesis runs, he cannot be deemed to have voluntarily consented to the seizure of the shotgun. Under the circumstances, his surrender of it amounted to compelled self-incrimination in violation of the Fifth Amendment and, thus, the act of relinquishment, to the extent that it demonstrated his possession of the illegal weapon, could not be used against him in a criminal case. . . . The appellant's argument raises a number of potentially interesting legal questions concerning the use of incriminating evidence seized without a warrant but under

the auspices of a court order. But we are mindful that '[c]ourts should strive to avoid gratuitous journeys through forbidding constitutional terrain,' and the appellant's intricate web of constitutional claims need not be addressed today. Here, there is a valid and independent legal theory upon which the admission of the sawed-off shotgun against the appellant can be grounded. Accordingly, its exclusion is not required." *U.S. v. Gamache*, 792 F.3d 194, 197–98 (1st Cir. 2015) (citations omitted).

- "The court below found that '[t]he officers were admitted to the residence with [the appellant's] voluntary consent.' The appellant does not seriously contest this finding. Nor could he: he has admitted that upon the officers' arrival, he opened his front door and affirmatively signaled for the officers to enter. Two other considerations cinch the matter: the record is barren of any evidence that might support an inference that this gesture was induced through force, pressure, or deception; and the consensual entry took place *before* the state court orders were served. . . . Still, consent to enter a home does not, by itself, give law enforcement officers carte blanche to rummage through the premises and perform a general search. After all, a warrantless search may not exceed the scope of the consent obtained. Here, however, once the officers were lawfully present in the appellant's apartment, another exception to the Fourth Amendment's warrant requirement came into play. We refer, of course, to the plain view doctrine. . . . As we have explained, the plain view doctrine permits the warrantless seizure of an item if the officer is lawfully present in a position from which the item is clearly visible, there is probable cause to seize the item, and the officer has a lawful right of access to the item itself." *U.S. v. Gamache*, 792 F.3d 194, 198–99 (1st Cir. 2015) (citations omitted).

- "A general consent to search subsumes the specific consent to search any easily accessible containers that may be located within the designated search area." *U.S. v. Stierhoff*, 549 F.3d 19, 2009-1 U.S. Tax Cas. (CCH) P 50103, 102 A.F.T.R.2d 2008-7111 (1st Cir. 2008).

- "Since it comes within an established exception to the Fourth Amendment warrant requirement, a consensual search may not exceed the scope of the consent given. . . . The standard for measuring the scope of a suspect's consent under the Fourth Amendment is that of objective reasonableness—what would the typical reasonable person have understood by the exchange between the officer and the suspect? . . . We therefore look beyond the language of the consent itself, to the overall context, which necessarily encompasses contemporaneous police statements and actions." *U.S. v. Turner*, 169 F.3d 84, 87 (1st Cir. 1999).

Fourth Circuit

- "[T]he giver of consent . . . controls the scope of consent. It is perfectly within a homeowner's rights to give a limited consent to search." *U.S. v. Coleman*, 588 F.3d 816 (4th Cir. 2009).
- "[D]eterminations about the objective reasonableness of a search are made as of the time when the search takes place, based on the information available to officers *at that time*. . . . Just as facts uncovered at a later date cannot justify an unreasonable search, so also they cannot undermine a reasonable one." *U.S. v. Coleman*, 588 F.3d 816 (4th Cir. 2009) (emphasis in original).
- "The suspect may impose limits on the items or areas subject to the consent search, just as he may refuse to allow any search whatsoever in the absence of a warrant. But, when a suspect gives his general and unqualified consent for an officer to search a particular area, the officer does not need to return to ask for fresh consent to search a closed container located within that area. [Defendant] argues that locked containers are different from closed containers and do not fall within the scope of a suspect's general consent to search a larger area. He is correct that a suspect's general, blanket consent to search a given area or item, by itself, would not likely permit officers to break into a locked container located within the area being searched. However, the scope of a consent search is not limited only to those areas or items for which specific verbal permission is granted. Consent may be supplied by non-verbal conduct as well. Thus, a suspect's failure to object (or withdraw his consent) when an officer exceeds limits allegedly set by the suspect is a strong indicator that the

search was within the proper bounds of the consent search." *U.S. v. Jones*, 356 F.3d 529, 63 Fed. R. Evid. Serv. 474 (4th Cir. 2004).

Fifth Circuit

- "The facts surrounding Agent Garcia's search establish an implied limit to Escamilla's consent. Just as Escamilla's directly handing Agent Garcia the phone initiated the consensual search, a reasonable person would understand that Agent Garcia's directly handing the phone back to Escamilla ended it. Agent Garcia's search during the stop was one, complete search, and Agent Antonelli's search at the station was a second, distinct search requiring a warrant, its own consent, or some other exception to the warrant requirement. When the facts and circumstances surrounding a person's consent suggest a natural end to the consensual exchange with law enforcement, officers should not view the earlier consent as 'authorizing a second search at some future time if the first search is not fruitful.' Because it is undisputed that Agent Antonelli did not have a warrant and the Government does not offer any other exception to the Fourth Amendment's usual warrant requirement to justify his search, we find that Agent Antonelli's post-arrest manual search of the phone at the Border Patrol station was unconstitutional, and the district court should have suppressed the evidence linked to this search." *United States v. Escamilla*, 852 F.3d 474, 485 (5th Cir. 2017) (citations omitted).

- "The Deputies themselves comprehended the unreasonableness of the notion that Iraheta's consent extended to the duffle bag in the trunk. Deputy Cox stated that he did not know how many bags were in the trunk, who the bags belonged to at the time, and never inquired into their ownership. . . . Although Defendants did not object to the search nor claim ownership of the luggage searched, we conclude that that is not decisive under these facts. It is undisputed that both Gonzalez and Meraz–Garcia did not hear Iraheta give consent to the search nor were they ever informed of Iraheta's consent by the officers. Under these circumstances, the onus was on the officers to act reasonably. All of the facts indicated a likelihood that the bag did not belong to

Iraheta, and therefore, it was unreasonable to rely on Iraheta's consent alone in searching the bag." *U.S. v. Iraheta*, 764 F.3d 455, 464–65 (5th Cir. 2014) (citations omitted).

- "[W]here, as here, an officer does not express the object of the search, the searched party, who knows the contents of the vehicle, has the responsibility explicitly to limit the scope of the search. (citation omitted) Otherwise, an affirmative response to a general request is evidence of general consent to search. (citation omitted) [Defendant] did not qualify his consent to the officers, who therefore had general consent to search the truck." *U.S. v. Garcia*, 604 F.3d 186 (5th Cir. 2010).

- "The district court found, over disputed testimony, that [defendant] gave [immigration agent] consent to enter his house. [Defendant] contends, however, that because his consent did not extend to the other agents present at the scene, the other agents' entrance into his house violated his Fourth Amendment rights. [The agent] explained his objective—a search for illegal aliens—before entering the house. A reasonable person observing the exchange between [the agent] and [defendant] would conclude that [defendant] authorized a search of his house for people who might be illegal aliens, and that is exactly what transpired. . . . Although the agents characterized their action as a protective sweep, the actions they took to perform the sweep were within the scope of [defendant's] original consent. . . . At no point during the thirty to forty-five minutes the agents were in the house did they search for physical evidence. . . . [Defendant's] argument that the initial consent he gave [agent] to enter and search his home was specific to [agent], and was not meant to extend to the other agents present at the scene, is inconsistent with [defendant's] actions during the search. It is the defendant's responsibility to limit the scope of the search if he so intends. Accordingly, a failure to object to the breadth of the search is properly considered an indication that the search was within the scope of the initial consent. In the instant case, [defendant] made no attempt to limit the scope of his consent and never objected to the additional agents entering his house. From this it can be inferred that the aid given [agent] by the additional agents was within the scope of [defendant's] consent. . . . [Defendant] also asserts that, after [agent left the house and read him his *Miranda* rights, the consent to search was automatically withdrawn without his having to do or say anything to that effect. This court has never adopted a rule declaring that consent is automatically terminated upon arrest. Rather, consent is a fact-sensitive inquiry dependent on the totality of the circumstances. . . . .[T]he fact that a person is formally placed under arrest sometime after the first consent does not work as an automatic withdrawal of the consent previously given." *U.S. v. Mendez*, 431 F.3d 420 (5th Cir. 2005).

- "Law enforcement officials are not required to separately request permission to search each container within a vehicle for which they have received consent to search. [Defendant] chose not to place any explicit limitations in his response to their general request, which, in this Circuit, is evidence of general consent. At the time [defendant] consented to a search of the trailer, he knew that the brown cardboard boxes contained marijuana. ... The fact that [defendant] did not object when [the investigating officer] actually began to open the box provides additional evidence that the agent's actions were within the scope of initial consent. ... [Defendant's] expectation of privacy with regard to the brown cardboard boxes did not rise to the level of that evidenced by a locked container. Locked containers require specific knowledge of a combination, possession of a key, or a demonstration of significant force to open. The boxes at issue in this case were located inside the trailer of a commercial vehicle and could be easily opened by removing or cutting through a single piece of tape. A single piece of tape is commonly used on a cardboard box not to send any particular message of privacy, but rather to keep the stiff side flaps closed to prevent the contents from spilling out and being damaged during transit. The box was not marked with the word 'private,' placed underneath two pieces of heavy luggage, or otherwise sent out a message to curious eyes that its owner placed particular importance upon the privacy of its contents. An objective appraisal of all of the circumstances surrounding the search of the cardboard box indicates that [defendant's] apparent expectation of privacy regarding its contents did not rise to the level of making its search unreasonable under the Fourth Amendment. *U.S. v. Mendoza-Gonzalez*, 318 F.3d 663 (5th Cir. 2003).

Sixth Circuit

- "Defendant appeals the district court's denial of his suppression motion on the ground that the search of defendant's gas tank exceeded the reasonable scope of defendant's consent. When law enforcement officers rely upon consent as the basis for a warrantless search, the scope of the consent given determines the permissible scope of the search. The standard for measuring the scope of a suspect's consent under the Fourth Amendment is that of objective reasonableness. The proper question is what would the typical reasonable person have understood by the exchange between the officer and the suspect. A reasonable person likely would have understood his consent to exclude a search that would damage his property. Generally, the expressed object of the search defines the scope of that search. . . . Before [officer] obtained defendant's consent to search the vehicle, he had asked defendant whether he possessed any illegal contraband, such as drugs or stolen goods. In so asking, [officer] thereby had informed defendant that those widely-varied items would be the object of any search. Defendant, per the consent-to-search form that he executed, consented to a search of the vehicle without expressly limiting the scope of that search. It was objectively reasonable for [officers] to have concluded that this general consent to search the vehicle included consent to search any container within that vehicle that might have held illegal contraband. As [officer] testified, it was well-known that the model vehicle that defendant was driving had an easily accessible gas tank in which to hide narcotics. Moreover, the accessing and search of the gas tank caused no damage to either the vehicle, in general, or the gas tank, in particular. Therefore, it was objectively reasonable for [officers] to have believed that defendant's general consent to search the vehicle encompassed consent to search the vehicle's gas tank. The Fourth Amendment did not require either officer to obtain separate permission to search the gas tank. . . . We note that, although defendant had the opportunity to do so, he never objected to the officers' search of the gas tank and, thus, neither clarified that the scope of his sweeping consent excluded such a search nor revoked his consent. The district court did not clearly err in finding that the search of the gas tank fell within the reasonable scope of defendant's consent to search the vehicle." *U.S. v. Garrido-Santana*, 360 F.3d 565, 2004 FED App. 0052P (6th Cir. 2004).

- "The district court was also correct in finding that the opening of the box of Tide did not exceed the scope of defendant's consent. Ordinarily, general consent to a search permits the opening of closed but unlocked containers found in the place as to which consent was given. . . . This analysis is particularly applicable to luggage search cases, since the luggage of a typical traveler is likely to include numerous containers, such as those in which health and hygiene products are packaged. A reasonable person who consents to a search of one of his bags would not expect the officer to repeat his request for consent before examining each new item encountered in the bag. . . . That approach would be unduly burdensome, and inconsistent with the objective reasonableness standard established by the Supreme Court in *Jimeno*." *U.S. v. Gant*, 112 F.3d 239, 243, 1997 FED App. 0140P (6th Cir. 1997).

Seventh Circuit

- "[W]e conduct a fact-specific inquiry to decide whether someone had actual or apparent authority to consent to a search. . . . Where someone with actual or apparent authority consents to a general search, law enforcement may search anywhere within the general area where the sought-after item could be concealed." *U.S. v. Jackson*, 598 F.3d 340 (7th Cir. 2010).
- "Police use of a thermal imager during their search of the garage of defendant's residence did not negate the defendant's ex-wife's consent to the search of the garage, because she was present and did not object to its use." *U.S. v. Ryerson*, 545 F.3d 483 (7th Cir. 2008).
- "[T]he scope of a search is generally defined by its expressed object. . . . [A] general consent form does not

override a more explicit statement specifying the object of the search. . . . [G]overnment agents may not obtain consent to search on the representation that they intend to look only for certain specified items and subsequently use that consent as a license to conduct a general exploratory search. . . . [Defendant] signed a clearly-worded consent form that gave the police permission to search his entire apartment and vehicle. One of the officers even read the consent form verbatim to [defendant] prior to [defendant] signing it. Furthermore, . . . [officer] testified he told [defendant] they were searching for anything related to criminal activity, not just evidence related to guns. . . . [Defendant's] consent was also of a broad nature, as it (at a minimum) allowed the police to search for anything 'related to' guns. . . . [W]hen [defendant] consented to a search for guns 'or anything related to them,' he consented to a search of his private papers, which included notebooks and journals. . . . As for the notebooks, they may have uncovered relevant and useful information, such as receipts, completed forms, or a personal inventory of all of [defendant's] guns. It may have also revealed whether [defendant] possessed owner's manuals for the guns. Searching for this type of information was permissible because it was 'related to' the search for guns. In addition, there may have been other guns, either hidden or out of sight. A review of the notebooks could reasonably have revealed the possible presence or location of such guns. As a result, the police had the authority to look where such paperwork might be found, which included [defendant's] notebooks. . . . Given the unique circumstances of this case, the police could also look in [defendant's] journal not only for the appropriate paperwork, but also for information detailing how [defendant] intended to use his arsenal of weapons. This was a legitimate question and was within the scope of [defendant's] consent, given his discussion with the officers as well as the presence of the number and types of firearms, explosives, and other weapons in plain sight, along with the report that [defendant] had been acting strangely." *U.S. v. Breit*, 429 F.3d 725 (7th Cir. 2005).

- "Under the Fourth Amendment, the standard for

measuring the scope of an individual's consent is objective reasonableness: what would the typical reasonable
person have understood by the exchange between the
officer and the person giving consent?" *U.S. v. Wesela*,
223 F.3d 656, 661, 55 Fed. R. Evid. Serv. 552 (7th Cir.
2000).

- "[C]onsent to search premises cannot always extend to
  every closed container within them, because such a rule
  would imply that consent to search the United Airlines
  baggage facility at O'Hare Airport would justify searching everyone's luggage—a proposition we were not willing to endorse." *U.S. v. Melgar*, 227 F.3d 1038, 1041
  (7th Cir. 2000).

- "The scope of a consent to search is generally determined by the investigators' express object of the search,
  applying a standard of reasonableness to the parties'
  understanding of that object. . . . We apply a standard
  of objective reasonableness, asking how a reasonable
  person would have understood the conversation between
  the law enforcement officer and the person giving
  consent. . . . A lawful search of fixed premises generally extends to the entire areas in which the object of
  the search may be found and is not limited by the possibility that separate acts of entry or opening may be
  required to complete the search." *U.S. v. Aghedo*, 159
  F.3d 308, 311 (7th Cir. 1998).

- "The scope of a search is generally characterized by its
  expressed object. Moreover, the scope of consent is
  determined by how a reasonable person would have
  understood the conversation between the law enforcement officer and the criminal suspect. To be succinct,
  we use a standard of objective reasonableness. [B]efore
  [the Defendant] consented to the search of his luggage,
  the drug enforcement officers told him that they were
  looking for individuals traveling with large quantities
  of illegal drugs. Thus, the expressed object of the search
  was illegal drugs. When [the Defendant] gave the DEA
  agents his permission to search his luggage for drugs, a
  reasonable person would have understood [the Defen-
  dant]'s consent for the search of his luggage to include
  permission to search any items inside his luggage which
  might reasonably contain drugs." *U.S. v. Maldonado*,
  38 F.3d 936, 940, 40 Fed. R. Evid. Serv. 495 (7th Cir.
  1994).

Eighth Circuit

- "(Defendant) placed no qualifications or limitations upon his consent to (the officer's) search of the vehicle for drugs. During the search, (the officer) noticed the scarred screws and believed, based upon his experience, that they may have concealed a compartment where one could hide drugs. He opened the compartment in a minimally intrusive manner by removing the screws, and he did no damage to the vehicle in the process. At no time did (defendant) object or suggest that he wished to withdraw his consent to the search. Therefore, under our precedent, we cannot say that the search of the false compartment exceeded the scope of (defendant's) general consent to search the vehicle for drugs." *U.S. v. Ferrer-Montoya*, 483 F.3d 565 (8th Cir. 2007).

- "[Defendant] . . . argues that he was deprived of an opportunity to withdraw or limit the scope of his consent after the search began because [the officer] told him to sit in the squad car during the search. [citation omitted] . . . Even assuming that the searching officers had some independent duty to ensure [defendant] an opportunity to withdraw consent after the search began—and [defendant] offers no authority suggesting that such a duty exists—the facts here do not compel the conclusion that [defendant] lacked such an opportunity. The squad car was parked immediately behind [defendant]'s truck. [Defendant] was not handcuffed, and he sat in the front seat of the squad car for the duration of the search. If [defendant] wished to withdraw his consent, there is no evidence that he was unable to do so—particularly because [defendant] made no attempt to attract the attention of the officers once the search began. Under these facts, [defendant] was at least obligated to make some effort to communicate an intent to withdraw his consent. He did not, and therefore we find [defendant]'s argument on this issue to be without merit." *U.S. v. Gallardo*, 495 F.3d 982, 990 (8th Cir. 2007).

Ninth Circuit

- "(W)e . . . clarify the rule in this Circuit, that a request from a law enforcement agent to "look," in the proper context, is the same as a request to "search." . . . (The officer) did not exceed the scope of (defendant's) *general* consent by searching the trunk . . . (since) realizing that (the officer) was looking for weapons and narcotics, the reasonable person would expect him to search the trunk and look under loose carpet. Whether or not (defendants) were coerced into believing that they had no authority to withdraw their consent is a question of fact and must be decided by the district court in the first instance." *U.S. v. McWeeney*, 454 F.3d 1030 (9th Cir. 2006).

- "The standard for measuring the scope of a suspect's consent under the Fourth Amendment is that of objective reasonableness—what would the typical reasonable person have understood by the exchange between the officer and the suspect? The first search of the van, in which $3,360 was discovered in a child seat, was valid. Because [the owner of the van] placed no explicit limit on the scope of that search, and the child seat reasonably could contain contraband, the officers' search of the seat was not outside the scope of consent. Likewise, the district court properly refused to suppress the methamphetamine found behind the van's speaker. Although [the owner] did not explicitly give consent to search that particular area, he informed the officers that drugs could be found there and cannot seriously contend that it would have been unreasonable to expect the officers to act on that information, especially in light of his previous unqualified and unrestricted consent to search the van. When an individual gives general consent to search a vehicle, and thereafter volunteers that evidence may be found in a specific area inside it, he thereby indicates that a search for that evidence would be within the scope of the original consent." *U.S. v. Rodriguez-Preciado*, 399 F.3d 1118 (9th Cir. 2005), opinion amended, 416 F.3d 939 (9th Cir. 2005).

Tenth Circuit

- "That [defendant] repeatedly consented to these searches favors the conclusion that the duration of the search was reasonable." *U.S. v. Carbajal-Iriarte*, 586 F.3d 795 (10th Cir. 2009).
- "[Defendant] makes the related claim that the search prior to the canine alert exceeded the scope and duration of his consent. [Defendant] generally argues that

the extensiveness of the search exceeded the scope of
his consent, and specifically asserts that because [of-
ficers] assured him at several points that the search
would be brief or end shortly, he gave his consent with
the assumption that the search would be brief. Thus,
[defendant] argues, the two and one half hour detention
violated the durational limitations the Fourth Amendment imposes on investigative stops. . . . [T]here is no
absolute rule for determining how long an investigative
detention may continue before it becomes unreasonable
under the Fourth Amendment. Rather, the length of
the stop and the potential intrusion on an individual's
Fourth Amendment rights must be juxtaposed against
the need to consider the law enforcement purposes to be
served by the stop as well as the time reasonably needed
to effectuate those purposes. . . . A general grant of
permission to search an automobile typically extends to
the entire car, absent an objection or an explicit limitation by the grantee. Where a defendant's consent is
predicated explicitly on an understanding that the
search will be brief, an extended detention sometimes
exceeds the scope of the consent. . . . Although [defen-
dant] argues that the search of his vehicle was more
extensive than his consent permitted, the record reveals
that prior to the canine alert, [officer] requested and
received separate consent to search the trunk, look in
the bags, and look under the hood. [Defendant] objected
to the scope of the search only after the canine alert. As
to duration, we find nothing in the record that would
suggest that [defendant] objectively communicated a
request to limit the duration of the search prior to the
canine alert. . . . [Defendant's] consent in the instant
case was confined by neither time nor location. . . .
Moreover, the additional fact that the police asked for
and received [defendant's] consent at various intervals
throughout the detention also weighs strongly in favor
of concluding the duration of the detention was
reasonable. . . . Therefore, even if the detention arguably became more than an investigative detention,
[defendant's] repeated consents negated the need for a
warrant." *U.S. v. Rosborough*, 366 F.3d 1145 (10th Cir.
2004).

- "The search of a container does not exceed the scope of

Search and Seizure Checklists
header here

consent when, under the circumstances of the particular case, it was objectively reasonable for the officer to believe that the scope of the suspect's consent permitted him to open the container. A defendant's failure to limit the scope of a general authorization to search, and failure to object when the search exceeds what he later claims was a more limited consent, is an indication that the search was within the scope of consent." *U.S. v. Jackson*, 381 F.3d 984 (10th Cir. 2004).

- "The general rule is that where a suspect does not limit the scope of a search, and does not object when the search exceeds what he later claims was a more limited consent, an officer is justified in searching the entire vehicle." *U.S. v. West*, 219 F.3d 1171, 1177 (10th Cir. 2000).
- "We therefore hold that, before an officer may actually destroy or render completely useless a container which would otherwise be within the scope of a permissive search, the officer must obtain explicit authorization, or have some other, lawful, basis upon which to proceed." *U.S. v. Osage*, 235 F.3d 518, 522 (10th Cir. 2000).
- "In determining the scope of a defendant's consent, we ask what a reasonable person would have understood by the exchange between the defendant and police officer. . . . [A] defendant's failure to object when the search exceeds what he later claims was a more limited consent, is an indication the search was within the scope of consent." *U.S. v. Patten*, 183 F.3d 1190, 1194 (10th Cir. 1999).
- "The scope of a search is generally defined by its expressed object and is limited by the breadth of the consent given. The standard for measuring the scope of a suspect's consent under the Fourth Amendment is that of objective reasonableness—what would the typical reasonable person have understood by the exchange between the officer and the suspect. [I]n *McRae*, we concluded a defendant's consent to an officer's request to look in his car gave the officer authorization to search the car, including lifting up carpeting in the trunk of the car. Likewise, in *United States v. Espinosa* we concluded a defendant's consent to an officer's request to look through the defendant's automobile authorized the officer to conduct a thorough search of the vehicle." *U.S. v. Elliott*, 107 F.3d 810, 814–15 (10th Cir. 1997).

Eleventh Circuit

- "We see no error in the district court's finding that, in seeking a search warrant, Detective Monaghan relied on information obtained *before* Thomas even objected and attempted to revoke Olausen's consent to search the HP computer. Detective Monaghan did not continue searching after Thomas expressed uncertainty about signing the written consent form, so assuming that Olausen had the authority to consent to a search in the first place, the law enforcement officers complied with the *Randolph* rule. Therefore, whether the applicable rule for searching personal effects is the *Randolph* rule or the general principle that anyone with shared control over the property can consent to a search (regardless of the other party's objection), the only issue in this case is whether Olausen had actual or apparent authority to consent to a forensic search of the computer, even though Thomas had taken steps to prevent her from viewing his Internet history. We answer this question in the affirmative." *U.S. v. Thomas*, 818 F.3d 1230, 1241 (11th Cir. 2016), cert. denied, 137 S. Ct. 171, 196 L. Ed. 2d 142 (2016) (citations omitted).

- "Search of the suspect's motel room, including the movement of a towel found on the bed next to drugs and drug paraphernalia, was within the reasonable scope of the suspect's consent to search, where the consent was general in nature and the officer did not tell the suspect that he was looking for anything specific." *U.S. v. Gordon*, 294 Fed. Appx. 579 (11th Cir. 2008).

- "[A] search is impermissible when an officer does not conform to the limitations imposed by the person giving consent. . . . When an individual provides a general consent to search, without expressly limiting the terms of his consent, the search is constrained by the bounds of reasonableness: what a police officer could reasonably interpret the consent to encompass. . . . A general consent to search for specific items includes consent to search any compartment or container that might reasonably contain those items." *U.S. v. Zapata*, 180 F.3d 1237, 1242–43 (11th Cir. 1999).

§ 17:6   Implied consent: Consent may be implied where there is a warning of the possibility of a search as a condition to entry

First Circuit

- "The appellant submits that, despite his ready relinquishment of his sawed-off shotgun, his cooperation with the police was actually coerced. In his view, he was given a Hobson's choice: either comply with the served orders (thereby turning over evidence of a known violation of federal law) or refuse to comply with the orders (thereby risking prosecution under state law). Caught between Scylla and Charybdis, his thesis runs, he cannot be deemed to have voluntarily consented to the seizure of the shotgun. Under the circumstances, his surrender of it amounted to compelled self-incrimination in violation of the Fifth Amendment and, thus, the act of relinquishment, to the extent that it demonstrated his possession of the illegal weapon, could not be used against him in a criminal case. . . . The appellant's argument raises a number of potentially interesting legal questions concerning the use of incriminating evidence seized without a warrant but under the auspices of a court order. But we are mindful that '[c]ourts should strive to avoid gratuitous journeys through forbidding constitutional terrain,' and the appellant's intricate web of constitutional claims need not be addressed today. Here, there is a valid and independent legal theory upon which the admission of the sawed-off shotgun against the appellant can be grounded. Accordingly, its exclusion is not required." *U.S. v. Gamache*, 792 F.3d 194, 197–98 (1st Cir. 2015) (citations omitted).

Fourth Circuit

- "[T]he officers did not explicitly ask for, and [informant] did not explicitly give, consent to a search. . . . There is no question that consent to search can be implied from a person's words, gestures, or conduct. It is the Government's burden, however, to establish the existence of such consent. This burden is heavier where consent is not explicit, since consent is not lightly to be inferred. In determining whether consent to search was freely

and voluntarily given, the factfinder must examine the
totality of the circumstances surrounding the consent. .
. . [T]he denial of the motion to suppress was not error.
Testimony at the suppression hearing established that
[informant] had a close working relationship with law
enforcement and that he had allowed an undercover officer into his home to purchase drugs from [defendant].
Moreover, [informant] testified that the officers were
'welcome' to enter his home even though they did not
ask his permission to do so." *U.S. v. Moreland*, 437 F.3d
424, 69 Fed. R. Evid. Serv. 627 (4th Cir. 2006).

Seventh Circuit

- "Consent can come in many forms, but it must always
  be given voluntarily. As the district court noted, [the
  defendant] does not challenge McCune's entry on the
  grounds that [the defendant's] nonverbal response was
  involuntary, nor does he offer any evidence of duress or
  coercion. Rather, [the defendant] only argues that he
  never consented to McCune entering his residence. As
  such, the crux of this appeal is whether [the defendant's]
  nonverbal response constituted implied consent for Mc-
  Cune to enter [the defendant's] residence. Whether [the
  defendant] impliedly consented to McCune's entry is a
  question of fact to be determined under the totality of
  the circumstances, and the trial court's determination
  will be reversed only if it is clearly erroneous." *U.S. v.
  Sabo*, 724 F.3d 891, 893 (7th Cir. 2013) (citations
  omitted).

Eighth Circuit

- "When a person permits an officer to enter the person's
  home, the officer does not have free reign to wander
  around the home and search any area of the house,
  without further consent. Defendant who had allowed
  police officers to enter his residence did not impliedly
  consent to officer's entry into his bedroom when he kind
  of flipped his hand in that direction after officer asked
  him for identification; officers had initially failed to
  obtain defendant's consent to search at a traffic stop
  and did not push the issue because defendant appeared
  to be too intoxicated, and after defendant was transported back to his residence, he refused to consent to

search when officers told him they did not have a
warrant." *U.S. v. Castellanos*, 518 F.3d 965 (8th Cir.
2008).

- "[A] person can render a search legal by behaving in a
  way that would cause a reasonable person to believe
  that he or she has knowingly and voluntarily consented,
  whether or not the person actually intends to consent.
  Thus, the Fourth Amendment requires only that the
  police reasonably believe the search to be consensual.
  Consequently, [defendant's] actual subjective state of
  mind at the time that he allegedly gave his consent is
  not determinative; our focus, rather, is on how a reasonable person could have perceived his state of mind
  at that time." *U.S. v. Cedano-Medina*, 366 F.3d 682
  (8th Cir. 2004).

Ninth Circuit

- "Regarding implied consent, only in narrow circumstances may consent be implied by actions and in most
  implied consent cases it is the suspect himself who takes
  an action which implies consent. (citations omitted) It is
  'a most uncommon situation' where the court is asked
  to infer consent from a third party's actions." *Espinosa
  v. City and County of San Francisco*, 598 F.3d 528 (9th
  Cir. 2010).

- "As a matter of first impression in this Circuit, we must
  decide when a search conducted at the entry gate to a
  military base is reasonable. Because such installations
  often warn of the possibility of search as a condition to
  entry, a warrantless search of a person seeking to enter
  a military base may be deemed reasonable based on the
  implied consent of the person searched. We remand to
  the district court to allow the development of a more
  complete factual record to determine whether implied
  consent was present here." *Morgan v. U.S.*, 323 F.3d
  776 (9th Cir. 2003).

§ 17:7 Implied consent: Consent may be implied
where there is a warning of the possibility of a
search as a condition to entry—Exception:
Consent to a blood draw is not implied when
law imposes criminal penalties

Supreme Court

- "Having concluded that the search incident to arrest doctrine does not justify the warrantless taking of a blood sample, we must address respondents' alternative argument that such tests are justified based on the driver's legally implied consent to submit to them. It is well established that a search is reasonable when the subject consents and that sometimes consent to a search need not be express but may be fairly inferred from context. Our prior opinions have referred approvingly to the general concept of implied-consent laws that impose civil penalties and evidentiary consequences on motorists who refuse to comply. Petitioners do not question the constitutionality of those laws, and nothing we say here should be read to cast doubt on them. It is another matter, however, for a State not only to insist upon an intrusive blood test, but also to impose criminal penalties on the refusal to submit to such a test. There must be a limit to the consequences to which motorists may be deemed to have consented by virtue of a decision to drive on public roads. . . . Borrowing from our Fifth Amendment jurisprudence, the United States suggests that motorists could be deemed to have consented to only those conditions that are 'reasonable' in that they have a 'nexus' to the privilege of driving and entail penalties that are proportional to severity of the violation. But in the Fourth Amendment setting, this standard does not differ in substance from the one that we apply, since reasonableness is always the touchstone of Fourth Amendment analysis. And applying this standard, we conclude that motorists cannot be deemed to have consented to submit to a blood test on pain of committing a criminal offense." *Birchfield v. North Dakota*, 136 S. Ct. 2160, 2185–86, 195 L. Ed. 2d 560 (2016).

§ 17:8 Consent following agents' illegal entry: Purging the taint

<u>Eighth Circuit</u>

- "When an illegal entry precedes a defendant's grant of consent to search, the Government must show (1) that the defendant's consent was voluntary and (2) that 'the consent was an independent act of [the defendant's] free will that purged the taint of the Fourth Amendment violation.' To determine whether the defendant's consent purged the taint of the illegal entry, we consider '(1) the temporal proximity between the Fourth Amendment violation and the grant of consent to search; (2) the presence of any intervening circumstances; and (3) the purpose and flagrancy of the [agents'] Fourth Amendment violation.' We also consider 'the giving of Miranda warnings where applicable.' " *U.S. v. Whisenton*, 765 F.3d 938, 941 (8th Cir. 2014) (citations omitted).

- "Greer consented to the search of the home, both orally and in writing. The district court found, correctly in our view, that Greer's consent to search was voluntary, but voluntary consent alone is not sufficient to avoid suppression based on the unlawful entry. The government also must establish that the consent was an independent act of Greer's free will that purged the taint of the Fourth Amendment violation." *U.S. v. Greer*, 607 F.3d 559, 563-64 (8th Cir. 2010) (citations omitted).

- "Because the purported act of free will is the defendant's consent to search, the Government must prove by a preponderance of the evidence that the defendant's consent to search was voluntary and that the defendant's consent was an act of free will sufficient to purge the taint of the Fourth Amendment violation." *U.S. v. Barnum*, 564 F.3d 964, 969 (8th Cir. 2009) (citation omitted).

Chapter 18

Border and Immigration Stops and Searches

§ 18:12   Body cavity searches: Body cavity searches at
          the border must be based on a higher standard
          than strip searches

§ 18:13   Alimentary canal smugglers: Suspected
          alimentary canal smugglers may be detained
          for a reasonable period of time, may be placed
          under surveillance, and may be given laxatives

§ 18:14   Plain view applicable: Plain view exception
          applies to border stops and searches

Research References

West's Key Number Digest

Aliens, Immigration, and Citizenship ⬅440 to 449; Automobiles
⬅349; Customs Duties ⬅126; Searches and Seizures ⬅60.1,
73

KeyCite®: Cases and other legal materials listed in KeyCite Scope can be
researched through the KeyCite service on Westlaw®. Use KeyCite to
check citations for form, parallel references, prior and later history, and
comprehensive citator information, including citations to other decisions
and secondary materials.

---

§ 18:1   Standard: A reasonable search may be conducted of all persons and property at the international border without individualized suspicion and without a warrant

Supreme Court

- "Consistent with Congress' power to protect the Nation
  by stopping and examining persons entering this
  country, the Fourth Amendment's balance of reasonableness is qualitatively different at the international
  border than in the interior. Routine searches of the
  persons and effects of entrants are not subject to any
  requirement of reasonable suspicion, probable cause, or
  warrant, and first-class mail may be opened without a
  warrant on less than probable cause. Automotive travelers may be stopped at fixed check points near the border without individualized suspicion even if the stop is
  based largely on ethnicity . . . and boats on inland
  waters with ready access to the sea may be hailed and
  boarded with no suspicion whatever." *U.S. v. Montoya
  de Hernandez*, 473 U.S. 531, 538, 105 S. Ct. 3304, 87 L.
  Ed. 2d 381 (1985).

- "Under these circumstances, we conclude that the detention in this case [6 hours] was not unreasonably long. It occurred at the international border, where the Fourth Amendment balance of interests leans heavily to the Government. Respondent's detention was long, uncomfortable, indeed, humiliating; but both its length and its discomfort resulted solely from the method by which she chose to smuggle illicit drugs into this country." *U.S. v. Montoya de Hernandez*, 473 U.S. 531, 544, 105 S. Ct. 3304, 87 L. Ed. 2d 381 (1985).

- "The authority of the United States to search the baggage of arriving international travelers is based on its inherent sovereign authority to protect its territorial integrity. By reason of that authority, it is entitled to require that whoever seeks entry must establish the right to enter and to bring into the country whatever he may carry." *Torres v. Com. of Puerto Rico*, 442 U.S. 465, 472–73, 99 S. Ct. 2425, 61 L. Ed. 2d 1 (1979).

- "Border searches, . . . from before the adoption of the Fourth Amendment, have been considered to be reasonable by the single fact that the person or item in question had entered into our country from outside. This longstanding recognition that searches at our borders without probable cause and without a warrant are nonetheless reasonable has a history as old as the Fourth Amendment itself." *U.S. v. Ramsey*, 431 U.S. 606, 619, 97 S. Ct. 1972, 52 L. Ed. 2d 617 (1977).

- "Travellers may be . . . stopped in crossing an international boundary because of national self protection reasonably requiring one entering the country to identify himself as entitled to come in, and his belongings as effects which may be lawfully brought in." *Carroll v. U.S.*, 267 U.S. 132, 154, 45 S. Ct. 280, 69 L. Ed. 543, 39 A.L.R. 790 (1925).

First Circuit

- "It is well established that the Fourth Amendment's balance of reasonableness is qualitatively different at the international border than in the interior. . . . . Under the border search exception, routine searches of the persons and effects of entrants are not subject to any requirement of reasonable suspicion, probable cause, or warrant." *U.S. v. Beras*, 183 F.3d 22, 25–26, 164 A.L.R. Fed. 807 (1st Cir. 1999).

- "We join our sister circuits and conclude that the border search exception to the Fourth Amendment applies to outgoing travelers. In our view, there is a convincing policy justification for extending the exception." *U.S. v. Beras*, 183 F.3d 22, 26, 164 A.L.R. Fed. 807 (1st Cir. 1999).

- "The most significant circumstance is that this incident occurred in the course of a Customs inspection at our nation's border. In the context of Customs inspections, our assessment of whether an interrogation is custodial must take into account the strong governmental interest in controlling our borders. . . . Questions from Customs officials are especially understood to be a necessary and important routine for travelers arriving at American entry points. This understanding cuts against the potentially coercive aspect of the Customs inquiry, and lessens the need for *Miranda* warnings. . . . The Eleventh Circuit has stated, Events which might be enough to signal custody away from the border will not be enough to establish custody in the context of entry into the country." *U.S. v. Fernandez-Ventura*, 132 F.3d 844, 846–47 (1st Cir. 1998).

Third Circuit

- "The functional equivalent of a border includes the first port where a ship docks after arriving from a foreign country. Even at the border an individual is entitled to be free from unreasonable search and seizure, and his or her privacy interests must be balanced against the sovereign's interests. Border searches fall into two categories: routine searches that require no suspicion, and nonroutine searches that require reasonable suspicion. To ascertain whether a border search can be classified as routine, the degree to which the search intrudes on a traveler's privacy must be examined." *U.S. v. Whitted*, 50 V.I. 1081, 541 F.3d 480, 43 A.L.R. 6th 771 (3d Cir. 2008).

- "Search of private living quarters in a cabin aboard a ship at the functional equivalent of a border is a nonroutine border search and must be supported by reasonable suspicion of criminal conduct because a passenger cabin is more like an individual's home than an automobile, and thus, whereas the dignity and privacy interests of the person do not carry over to border searches of an automobile, the privacy interests of an individual in his living quarters are significantly greater and compel more rigorous Fourth Amendment protection." *U.S. v. Whitted*, 50 V.I. 1081, 541 F.3d 480, 43 A.L.R.6th 771 (3d Cir. 2008).

Fifth Circuit

- "An officer's conduct is reasonably related to the justification for the stop when the officer 'diligently pursue[s] a means of investigation that is likely to confirm or dispel [the officer's] suspicions quickly.' Officers unreasonably—hence, unconstitutionally— prolong a stop if they detain a person 'beyond the time needed to investigate the circumstances that caused the stop.' . . . After stopping Escamilla, the Border Patrol agents continued to amass suspicion that he was involved in smuggling. Although the Border Patrol dog's sniff did not indisputably confirm the agents' suspicion by revealing hidden contraband, neither did the sniff dispel suspicion, contrary to Escamilla's suggestion. The dog 'alert[ed]' in a way that led the agents to believe the F-150 had recently carried or been near contra- band—a fact consistent with their suspicion that it served as a 'scout' or 'disturbance' vehicle for another car, which still constitutes criminal activity. Further, the overall stop—justified by suspicion of smuggling, rather than a mere traffic violation—lasted no more than 24 minutes. Consequently, any delay between the agents' completing the dog sniff and arresting Escamilla after Border Patrol Agent Jennings found drugs in the F-250 was reasonable." *United States v. Escamilla*, 852 F.3d 474, 482–83 (5th Cir. 2017) (citations omitted).
- "Continuation of warrantless border search of defen- dant's vehicle for approximately two hours despite unsuccessful search results was not unreasonable under Fourth Amendment. Border patrol agents did not need to have reasonable suspicion of criminal activity to remove portion of dashboard of defendant's vehicle and use probe to locate cocaine, where such conduct did not result in serious damage to, or destruction of vehicle." *U.S. v. Cervantez-Valerio*, 275 Fed. Appx. 417 (5th Cir. 2008).

- "[Defendant] argues that even if the search was routine, the traditional border search exception should not be extended to outgoing searches. . . . [T]oday we join our sister circuits in holding that the border search exception applies for all outgoing searches at the border." *U.S. v. Odutayo*, 406 F.3d 386 (5th Cir. 2005).
- "Warrantless searches and seizures are unreasonable per se unless they fall within a few narrowly defined exceptions. . . . The border-search doctrine is one of those exceptions. . . . Under the border-search doctrine, government agents may conduct a routine search at the international border or its functional equivalent without probable cause, a warrant, or any suspicion to justify the search. . . . Routine searches are generally classified as those which do not seriously invade a traveler's privacy. . . . A stop and search that is not routine requires a reasonable suspicion of wrongdoing to pass constitutional muster. . . . Reasonable suspicion is defined as a particularized and objective basis for suspecting the particular person of smuggling contraband." *U.S. v. Rivas*, 157 F.3d 364, 367 (5th Cir. 1998).
- "This Circuit has never before confronted the issue of whether drilling into the body of a vehicle at a border checkpoint amounts to a routine or a nonroutine search. However, the First Circuit has held that drilling into a closed, metal cylinder was not a routine search because force was used to effect the search. . . . We agree with this analysis and conclude that drilling into [Defendant]'s trailer was a nonroutine search." *U.S. v. Rivas*, 157 F.3d 364, 367 (5th Cir. 1998).

Sixth Circuit

- "The border search exception generally provides that routine searches of the persons and effects of entrants are not subject to any requirement of reasonable suspicion, probable cause, or warrant. Such searches may be conducted at an international border checkpoint or its functional equivalent. Further, every circuit that has considered the question has concluded, at least with regard to the circumstances before it, that the border search exception applies to 'exit searches' as well as searches of incoming persons and materials. . . . We conclude that each of the above rationales supports the application of the *Ramsey* border search exception to the search of the outgoing cargo container here. While most cases that have dealt with this issue previously have involved the protection of the sovereign's interests in its currency, the United States's interest in preventing the export of weapons to other countries also implicates the sovereign's interest in protecting itself. Further, this interest also weighs heavily when balanced against the individual's Fourth Amendment interest in being free from the search at issue. The government's control and regulation of the export of weapons implicates significant government interests in the realms of national security and relations with other nations. On the other side of the scales, travellers (or exporters) undoubtedly have a lesser expectation of privacy when they (or their goods) leave the country if for no other reason than the departure from the United States is almost invariably followed by an entry into another country which will likely conduct its own border search. Thus, the warrantless search of the cargo container was permitted under the *Ramsey* border search exception." *U.S. v. Boumelhem*, 339 F.3d 414, 2003 FED App. 0281P (6th Cir. 2003).

Seventh Circuit

- "Searches made at the border are reasonable, under Fourth Amendment requirements, simply by virtue of the fact that they occur at the border." *Rahman v. Chertoff*, 530 F.3d 622, 70 Fed. R. Serv. 3d 1463 (7th Cir. 2008).

- "*Miranda*. . .is a mismatch for the immigration process, at least at the outset. No one believes that the Constitution requires the immigration inspector to greet new arrivals by saying: Welcome to the United States. You have a right to remain silent. Anything you say may be used against you. You have a right to counsel and, if you cannot afford a lawyer, one will be appointed for you. Now, please let me see your passport. A person seeking entry into the United States does not have a right to remain silent; the immigrant must honestly describe his identity, nationality, business, and claim of entitlement to enter, and must do this without the aid

of counsel. The United States is entitled to condition
entry on willingness to provide essential information.
No information, no entry. Refusing to extend the boon
of entry to those who remain silent can be seen as
compulsion in the sense that it is a (potentially steep)
price tag for remaining silent, yet the government's
right to insist on information as a condition of entry
cannot reasonably be denied. As a result, the fifth
amendment privilege no more applies to these questions than the fourth amendment blocks the inspection
of parcels at the border." *U.S. v. Gupta*, 183 F.3d 615,
617–18 (7th Cir. 1999).

Ninth Circuit

- "[I]t is the traveler who must demonstrate he is entitled
  to cross our borders and to bring with him whatever he
  may wish to carry." *U.S. v. Cotterman*, 637 F.3d 1068
  (9th Cir. 2011), on reh'g en banc, 709 F.3d 952 (9th Cir.
  2013) (citation omitted).
- "In determining whether a customs search comports
  with Fourth Amendment requirement of reasonableness, the court must consider the scope of the intrusion,
  the manner of the search's conduct, and the justification for the search's initiation. Customs inspectors'
  suspicionless opening of sealed envelope containing
  personal correspondence, enclosed in package to be
  shipped to the Philippines at functional equivalent of
  the border, was valid under Fourth Amendment, where
  Customs inspectors were conducting an outbound currency interdiction operation targeting packages bound
  for the Philippines to determine if the sender was
  exporting monetary instruments." *U.S. v. Seljan*, 547
  F.3d 993 (9th Cir. 2008).
- "The scope and manner of the Customs border inspection of the contents of a sealed envelope, enclosed in a
  package to be sent to the Philippines, was constrained
  and thus reasonable under the Fourth Amendment,
  where the inspector was authorized to open the package and scan the letter to determine whether the
  defendant had violated monetary instrument reporting
  requirements, and the inspector could ascertain by a
  glance that unmistakable evidence of pedophilia was
  present in the envelope." *U.S. v. Seljan*, 547 F.3d 993
  (9th Cir. 2008).

- "Search of defendant's computer hard drive at border, like searches of other property, did not require reasonable suspicion under Fourth Amendment." *U.S. v. Singh*, 295 Fed. Appx. 190 (9th Cir. 2008).
- " 'The border search doctrine is a narrow exception to the Fourth Amendment prohibition against warrantless searches without probable cause.' [citation omitted] Under this doctrine, customs officials routinely conduct searches at the international border to identify the illegal transportation of contraband or undeclared articles across the border. [citation omitted] Such border searches are grounded in the government's right to protect the United States' territorial integrity by examining persons and property entering and leaving the country [footnote omitted] and 'are reasonable simply by virtue of the fact that they occur at the border.' [citations omitted] As a consequence, searches at the international border require neither a warrant nor individualized suspicion. [citation omitted] . . . The border search standard applies equally to searches of persons or property leaving the United States as to those entering the country. [citation omitted] . . . Even at the border or its functional equivalent, however, the Fourth Amendment imposes some limits on governmental authority. Searches at the border must still be reasonable in scope and manner. [citation omitted] We evaluate reasonableness by examining three factors: '[t]he scope of the intrusion, the manner of its conduct, and the justification for its initiation.' [citation omitted]" *U.S. v. Seljan*, 497 F.3d 1035, 1040 (9th Cir. 2007), on reh'g en banc, 547 F.3d 993 (9th Cir. 2008).
- "(Defendant) argues he was not subject to a warrantless border search because he never *legally* crossed the U.S.-Canada border . . . There is no authority for the proposition that a person who fails to obtain legal entry at his destination may freely reenter the United States; to the contrary, he or she may be searched just like any other person crossing the border . . . Thus, the routine border search of (defendant's) laptop was reasonable, regardless whether (defendant) obtained foreign contraband in Canada or was under "official restraint."' *U.S. v. Romm*, 455 F.3d 990 (9th Cir. 2006).
- "Congress has conferred broad authority on customs of-

ficers to search all persons coming into the United States from foreign countries. A traveler crossing an international boundary may reasonably be required to identify himself as entitled to come in, and his belongings as effects which may be lawfully brought in. Thus, at the border one's expectation of privacy is less than in the interior and the Fourth Amendment balance between the government's interests and the traveler's privacy rights is struck more favorably to the Government. Such searches are deemed reasonable under the Fourth Amendment by the single fact that the person or item in question has entered into our country from outside." *U.S. v. Gonzalez-Rincon*, 36 F.3d 859, 864 (9th Cir. 1994).

Tenth Circuit

- "The Fourth Amendment protects against unreasonable searches and seizures. Generally, a seizure made without individualized suspicion of wrongdoing is unreasonable. A traffic stop is a 'seizure within the meaning of the Fourth Amendment.' Because roadblocks and checkpoints seize people without individualized reasonable suspicion, they would violate the Fourth Amendment if subject to that general rule. And, even here, where police had GPS information showing that the tracker (and likely the bank robber) were in one of the 20 cars, police initially lacked reasonable, articulable suspicion of any *particular* person. But the 'touchstone of the Fourth Amendment is reasonableness, not individualized suspicion.' Accordingly, the Supreme Court has carved out exceptions to the general rule where the primary purpose of a group seizure went beyond ordinary crime control. For example, the Court has upheld a border patrol roadblock designed to intercept illegal aliens. And it has upheld a sobriety checkpoint aimed at removing drunk drivers from the road to protect public safety. In those situations, the Court has not required individualized reasonable suspicion, instead favoring a group-level balance of interests, weighing the public interest against intrusions on individuals' liberty." *U.S. v. Paetsch*, 782 F.3d 1162, 1168–69 (10th Cir. 2015), cert. denied, 136 S. Ct. 195, 193 L. Ed. 2d 153 (2015) (citations omitted).

Eleventh Circuit

- "In general, there is no constitutional violation when customs officials first encounter an individual seeking entry into the United States, stop the person, and conduct a preliminary border search. (citations omitted) The officer may conduct routine questioning, check luggage, and conduct a pat-down search without any level of suspicion." *U.S. v. Glover*, 353 Fed. Appx. 314 (11th Cir. 2009).

- "[B]ecause of the sovereign's responsibility, some degree of questioning and of delay is necessary and is to be expected at entry points into the United States. Because of this expectation, questioning at the border must rise to a distinctly accusatory level before it can be said that a reasonable person would feel restraints on his ability to roam to the degree associated with formal arrest. We stress that events which might be enough often to signal custody away from the border will not be enough to establish custody in the context of entry into the country. This idea is consistent with cases involving facts similar to this one, which have indicated that a secondary interview is part of the border routine and does not require *Miranda* warnings." *U.S. v. Moya*, 74 F.3d 1117, 1120 (11th Cir. 1996).

D.C. Circuit

- "Courts have routinely rejected the notion that cooperation among federal agencies renders a border search unlawful . . . . Customs officials conducted a permissible border search and lawfully seized the documents. The district court's finding that there was "some evidence" of FBI involvement in the search, as a result of an FBI request to Customs to retain the financial documents, does not require a different conclusion . . . ." *U.S. v. Gurr*, 471 F.3d 144, 71 Fed. R. Evid. Serv. 1206 (D.C. Cir. 2006).

§ 18:2 Scope: Full contents of any package may be searched

Ninth Circuit

- "Customs officials conducting border search for illegal transportation of monetary instruments may search the full contents of any package, container or other object to be searched, even if that package, container or other object serves to enclose smaller envelopes or other wrapped or sealed objects; where personal correspondence or other documents indicate evidence of contraband or other criminal activity that is immediately apparent to the inspecting official, those items too may be searched even though such evidence may not relate to the interdiction of undeclared currency. Further, the scope and manner of Customs border inspection of the contents of the sealed envelope was constrained and thus reasonable under the Fourth Amendment, where the inspector was authorized to open package and scan the letter to determine whether the defendant had violated the monetary instrument reporting requirements, and the inspector could ascertain by a glance that unmistakable evidence of pedophilia was present in the envelope." *U.S. v. Seljan*, 547 F.3d 993 (9th Cir. 2008).

§ 18:3 Functional equivalents of borders: The border search exception is applicable to searches conducted at the functional equivalent of a border

Supreme Court

- "Whatever the permissible scope of intrusiveness of a routine border search might be, searches of this kind may in certain circumstances take place not only at the border itself, but at its functional equivalents as well. For example, searches at an established station near the border, at a point marking the confluence of two or more roads that extend from the border, might be functional equivalents of border searches. For another example, a search of the passengers and cargo of an airplane arriving at a St. Louis airport after a nonstop flight from Mexico City would clearly be the functional equivalent of a border search." *Almeida-Sanchez v. U.S.*, 413 U.S. 266, 272–73, 93 S. Ct. 2535, 37 L. Ed. 2d 596 (1973).

First Circuit

- "[Defendant] was patted down at the functional equivalent of an international border. . . .and the district court supportably found that the pat down was conducted pursuant to a routine border search. Thus, neither probable cause nor reasonable suspicion was required." *U.S. v. Beras*, 183 F.3d 22, 26, 164 A.L.R. Fed. 807 (1st Cir. 1999).

- "The sea boundary of United States territory is a marine league (three geographic miles) from shore, and comprises a border for fourth amendment purposes. Because it is not practical to set up checkpoints at the outer perimeter of a country's territorial waters, courts have consistently recognized the constitutionality of warrantless searches at the functional equivalent of the sea border." *U.S. v. Victoria-Peguero*, 920 F.2d 77, 80, 1993 A.M.C. 1520 (1st Cir. 1990).

Second Circuit

- "Different requirements govern vehicle stops at the international border or its functional equivalent because there '[t]he Government's interest in preventing the entry of unwanted persons and effects is at its zenith.'" *U.S. v. Wilson*, 699 F.3d 235, 242 (2d Cir. 2012).

Fifth Circuit

- "The border search doctrine is also applicable to stops and searches conducted at the functional equivalent of the border, i.e., the first point at which an entrant may practically be detained. For example, the functional equivalent of the border has been found to be the airport where an international flight lands, or the port where a ship docks after arriving from a foreign country. A search at the functional equivalent of the border is justified under the border search doctrine because it is in essence no different than a search conducted at the border; the reason for allowing such a search to take place other than at the actual physical border is the practical impossibility of requiring the subject searched to stop at the physical border. Thus, a routine search made at the border or its functional equivalent may be made without probable cause or any suspicion to justify the search." *U.S. v. Cardenas*, 9 F.3d 1139, 1147 (5th Cir. 1993).

Seventh Circuit

- "Under the 'functional equivalent' doctrine, routine border searches are constitutionally permissible at places other than actual borders where travelers frequently enter or exit the country. Thus even though Chicago is not an international border, searches at customs at O'Hare are permissible under the functional equivalent doctrine." *U.S. v. Yang*, 286 F.3d 940 (7th Cir. 2002).

Ninth Circuit

- "Today we examine a question of first impression in the Ninth Circuit: whether the search of a laptop computer that begins at the border and ends two days later in a Government forensic computer laboratory almost 170 miles away can still fall within the border search doctrine. The district court considered the issue to be a simple matter of time and space. It concluded that the search of property seized at an international border and moved 170 miles from that border for further search cannot be justified by the border search doctrine. We disagree . . . . We find no basis under the law to distinguish the border search power merely because logic and practicality may require some property presented for entry—and not yet admitted or released from the sovereign's control—to be transported to a secondary site for adequate inspection. The border search doctrine is not so rigid as to require the United States to equip every entry point—no matter how desolate or infrequently traveled—with inspectors and sophisticated forensic equipment capable of searching whatever property an individual may wish to bring within our borders or be otherwise precluded from exercising its right to protect our nation absent some heightened suspicion. . . . Rather, the Government made it abundantly clear to [the defendant] that his computers and cameras were not cleared for entry into the United States and that it had retained custody of that property until it could fully allay its concerns that they contained contraband. As a result, he never regained his normal expectation of privacy in his computer because he could only reasonably expect that it would be searched to alleviate the self-protection concerns of the sovereign. He never breathed that deep sigh of relief that follows from the realization that he had faced all the rigors of inspection and that nothing more lingered to impede his travels." *U.S. v. Cotterman*, 637 F.3d 1068 (9th Cir. 2011), on reh'g en banc, 709 F.3d 952 (9th Cir. 2013).

• "Searches of international passengers at American airports are considered border searches, and thus generally are reasonable, because they occur at the functional equivalent of a border. Reasonable suspicion is not needed for customs officials to search a laptop computer or other personal electronic storage devices at the border. Border search was not carried out in particularly offensive manner, so as to come under exception to government's broad border search powers, where Customs and Border Patrol officers simply had defendant boot up his laptop computer, and looked at its electronic contents." *U.S. v. Arnold*, 533 F.3d 1003, 45 A.L.R. Fed. 2d 715 (9th Cir. 2008).

• "Search of defendant's express package at regional sorting facility in Oakland, California took place at the functional equivalent of the United States border, and thus, customs officers did not need warrant or reasonable suspicion to search contents of the package." *U.S. v. Seljan*, 547 F.3d 993 (9th Cir. 2008).

• "Despite its name, a border search need not take place at the actual international border . . . . These searches may take place at the physical border or its "functional equivalent" . . . . This extension of the border search doctrine reflects '[t]he practical difficulty of getting to and searching every vehicle or carrier at the precise moment it crosses land or sea borders' . . . . We have also recognized another category of border search: the extended border search. Extended border searches are typically separated from the border by "a greater spatial and temporal distance" from the actual border than searches at the functional equivalent of the border . . . Because 'the delayed nature of an extended border search . . . necessarily entails a greater level of intrusion on legitimate expectations of privacy than an ordinary border search,' the government must justify an extended border search with reasonable suspicion that the search may uncover contraband or evidence of criminal activity . . . We have recognized that comparison of absolute time and spatial differences alone is not enough to distinguish between a search at the border's

functional equivalent and an extended border search.
Rather, we also look to whether the search . . . occurred
at the last practicable opportunity before its passage
over the international border . . . (W)e hold that the
search of (defendant's) UPS package at the Louisville
hub took place at the functional equivalent of the
border. The Louisville sorting hub represents the last
practicable opportunity for Customs officers to inspect
international packages before UPS places them into
sealed containers for departure from the United States.
Even if the airplanes briefly stop at another hub or
airport to refuel or redistribute cargo before departing
our country, it is unreasonable to require customs officials to wait until that last domestic stop to unload
the packages from the airplane, reopen the sealed
containers, and conduct an inspection before allowing
the airplane to proceed to its international destination."
U.S. v. Abbouchi, 502 F.3d 850 (9th Cir. 2007).

Tenth Circuit

- "At locations other than the actual border or its
  functional equivalent, border patrol officers may stop
  vehicles only if they are aware of specific articulable
  facts, together with rational inferences from those facts,
  that reasonably warrant suspicion that a crime has been
  committed." *U.S. v. Doyle*, 129 F.3d 1372, 1375 (10th
  Cir. 1997).

- "[I]n recognition of the government's power to exclude
  aliens and to effect that power by routine inspections
  and searches of individuals or conveyances seeking to
  cross our borders, the Court conceived the government's
  right to stop and search without probable cause at
  places that are the functional equivalent of the border.
  At the same time, however, the Court held a roving
  patrol 20 miles from the border was of a wholly different sort. Because that stop was not at the functional
  equivalent of the border, the Court applied Fourth
  Amendment considerations and determined it was
  unreasonable." *U.S. v. Venzor-Castillo*, 991 F.2d 634,
  637 (10th Cir. 1993).

Eleventh Circuit

- "To determine what constitutes a functional equivalent

of the border, this court has established a test which evaluates the circumstance of the search rather than merely its location. Because the crossing of the border is not as obvious at a functional equivalent of a border as it is at the actual border, this circuit requires three elements to demonstrate that a search was conducted at a functional equivalent: 1) reasonable certainty that the border was crossed; 2) no opportunity for the object of the search to have changed materially since the crossing; and 3) the search must have occurred at the earliest practicable point after the border to crossing." *U.S. v. Hill*, 939 F.2d 934, 937 (11th Cir. 1991).

- "This circuit has upheld suspicionless searches at international airports even though the passenger had left the Customs area, had proceeded to the baggage claim area, or had been moving about the airport for thirty minutes after leaving the plane and had checked into an adjacent hotel. In each of these cases it was possible for the Customs agents to have conducted their searches earlier, such as during the deplaning. The cases, however, held that such immediate searches w ere not necessary, because they found it reasonable for Customs agents to be permitted to conduct their searches when practicable in crowded or busy airports." *U.S. v. Hill*, 939 F.2d 934, 937 (11th Cir. 1991).

- "At the functional equivalent of the border, Customs agents may conduct suspicionless searches in certain circumstances. Searches conducted at the actual border of the country are permitted without any suspicion of illegality; they are reasonable under the fourth amendment based on the single fact that the person or item entered the country from outside. For the purpose of suspicionless Customs searches, the border is elastic. Because people can enter the country at points other than along the actual border, courts look to whether the point of entry is the functional equivalent of the border. Places such as international airports within the country and ports within the country's territorial waters exemplify such functional equivalents." *U.S. v. Hill*, 939 F.2d 934, 936 (11th Cir. 1991).

- "A dwelling, together with its surrounding curtilage, is not always a sanctuary from law enforcement activity, even if the police act without a warrant. The Supreme

Court has refused to permit a suspect to defeat a warrantless arrest that has been set in motion in a public place—and which is otherwise proper—by the expedient of escaping to a private place. We similarly refuse to allow [Defendant] to cross the border in an airplane and then to thwart Customs' lawful right to search that airplane at the first practicable point by his parking the plane in a private place. We hold that Customs' warrantless search of an airplane inside the curtilage of the suspect's home is a lawful search if all other requirements for a valid search of that plane at the functional equivalent of the border are satisfied, including the requirement that there has been no opportunity for the object of the search to have changed materially since the time of the border crossing." *U.S. v. Emmens*, 893 F.2d 1292, 1295 (11th Cir. 1990).

§ 18:4 Extended border area: The border search exception applies in the immediate vicinity of the border, but requires reasonable suspicion

Third Circuit

- "Under the reasonable suspicion standard, to conduct a search of a passenger cabin on a ship, customs officers must be able to articulate reasons that led to the search of the cabin that are indicative of behavior in which most innocent people do not engage." *U.S. v. Whitted*, 50 V.I. 1081, 541 F.3d 480, 43 A.L.R.6th 771 (3d Cir. 2008).

Fifth Circuit

- "[T]he border search doctrine has been extended to allow government officials to conduct a warrantless search and seizure beyond the border or its functional equivalent on the reasonable suspicion of criminal activity. The main difference between the functional equivalent of the border search and an extended border search is that the latter takes place after the first point in time when the entity might have been stopped within the country. An extended border search entails a greater intrusion on an entrant's legitimate expectations of privacy than does a search conducted at the border or its functional equivalent. Accordingly, this court has determined that three factors must be demonstrated before an extended border search is deemed reasonable and hence constitutionally permissible: (1) a showing of a reasonable certainty or a high degree of probability that a border crossing has occurred; (2) a showing of a reasonable certainty that no change in the condition of the person or vehicle being inspected occurred from the time of the border crossing until the search and that the contraband found was present when the person or vehicle crossed the border; and (3) a showing of a reasonable suspicion that criminal activity was occurring. This court has also determined that reasonable certainty is a standard which requires more than probable cause, but less than proof beyond a reasonable doubt. Further, in determining whether there is a reasonable suspicion that criminal activity was occurring, each case must turn on the totality of the particular circumstances." *U.S. v. Cardenas*, 9 F.3d 1139, 1147–48 (5th Cir. 1993).

- "Although reported cases concerning the extended border search doctrine involve the search of a vehicle, the doctrine was not formulated to apply only to vehicles that have crossed the border. The major impetus behind the extended border search doctrine is the government interest in stopping drug traffic. We explained the basic rationale for an extended border search in *United States v. Richards*, While the mere fact that a person or thing has once crossed the border does not sanction a search of it forever after, we have also recognized that the need to protect personality and property against warrantless invasion must be balanced against the myriad difficulties facing customs and immigration officials who are charged with the enforcement of smuggling and immigration laws. We have, therefore, recognized in the doctrine of extended border search, the government's power, under certain circumstances, to search without a warrant persons and things after they have entered the country." *U.S. v. Cardenas*, 9 F.3d 1139, 1149 (5th Cir. 1993).

- "We have at times focused our inquiry initially on the question of whether arresting agents could reasonably conclude a particular vehicle originated its journey at the border. Frequently, this issue is settled by an analysis of the road the vehicle was travelling on, the number of towns along the road, the number of intersecting roads and, finally, the number of miles away from the border the vehicle was at the point of the actual stop itself. Here, the vehicle was between 40 and 50 miles from the border. The road is a rural, two-lane highway with approximately 90% of its traffic consisting of ranch trucks and hunting jeeps. The vehicle, a mid-size passenger car, was travelling in an easterly direction, and the towns serviced by the western direction of the road are all on or very near the border. We hold that under these facts the agents had a reasonable suspicion to conclude the vehicle had originated its journey at the border." *U.S. v. Cardona*, 955 F.2d 976, 980 (5th Cir. 1992).

Seventh Circuit

- "The extended border doctrine provides that non-routine border searches that occur near the border are deemed constitutionally permissible if reasonable under the Fourth Amendment. To determine whether an extended border search is reasonable courts consider whether: (1) there is a reasonable certainty that a border crossing has occurred; (2) there is a reasonable certainty that no change in condition of the luggage has occurred since the border crossing; and (3) there is a reasonable suspicion that criminal activity has occurred." *U.S. v. Yang*, 286 F.3d 940 (7th Cir. 2002).

Ninth Circuit

- "When reviewing an officer's reasonable suspicion, we must look at the totality of the circumstances. . . . In the context of border patrol stops, the totality of the circumstances may include characteristics of the area, proximity to the border, usual patterns of traffic and time of day, previous alien or drug smuggling in the area, behavior of the driver, appearance or behavior of passengers, and the model and appearance of the vehicle. Not all of these factors must be present or highly probative in every case to justify reasonable suspicion. And the facts must be filtered through the lens of the agents' training and experience." *U.S. v. Valdes-Vega*, 738 F.3d 1074 (9th Cir. 2013) (citations and internal quotations omitted).

- "[T]he facts show that two experienced border patrol agents observed a truck with foreign plates driving in a suspicious manner in an area frequented by smugglers. The total circumstances garnered the attention of the agents. These circumstances align with factors that the Supreme Court has indicated may be significant in evaluating a roving border patrol stop, and we conclude that they are probative here. In light of the totality of the circumstances, giving due weight to the agents' experience and reasonable deductions, we hold that the agents had a reasonable, particularized basis for suspecting [Defendant] of smuggling contraband. The stop was supported by reasonable suspicion." *U.S. v. Valdes-Vega*, 738 F.3d 1074 (9th Cir. 2013) (citations and internal quotations omitted).

- "[V]iewing the facts in the totality of the circumstances and taking into account the agents' training and experience, we decline to second-guess the agents' decision to stop the truck for investigation. Even innocent, non-criminal acts can foster reasonable suspicion in the total context. There is no need for an officer to rule out an innocent explanation. This holds true even if it is far from certain that the suspect is actually engaged in illegal activity. A series of innocent acts may be enough for reasonable suspicion justifying an investigatory stop, even though the circumstances amount to far less than probable cause. We do not endorse stopping cars based on mere whim. But [Defendant's] behavior was not so innocuous as to suggest that he was merely plucked from a crowd at random." *U.S. v. Valdes-Vega*, 738 F.3d 1074 (9th Cir. 2013) (citations and internal quotations omitted).

- "The government has more latitude to detain people in a border-crossing context . . . but such detentions are acceptable only during the time of extended border searches." *U.S. v. Juvenile (RRA-A)*, 229 F.3d 737, 743 (9th Cir. 2000).

- "Extended border searches take place a greater spatial and temporal distance from the border than a search at the functional equivalent of the border and therefore require reasonable suspicion. Some searches, though not at the border, occur so spatially and temporally close to it that they are considered border searches. The fact that some search occurred at the time of the initial border crossing simply does not prevent later searches from coming under the rules of border searches." *U.S. v. Ogbuehi*, 18 F.3d 807, 812–13 (9th Cir. 1994).

- "The government has more latitude to detain people in a border-crossing context. . .but such detentions are acceptable only during the time of extended border searches." *U.S. v. Juvenile (RRA-A)*, 229 F.3d 737, 743 (9th Cir. 2000).

- "Extended border searches take place a greater spatial and temporal distance from the border than a search at the functional equivalent of the border and therefore require reasonable suspicion. Some searches, though not at the border, occur so spatially and temporally close to it that they are considered border searches. The fact that some search occurred at the time of the initial border crossing simply does not prevent later searches from coming under the rules of border searches." *U.S. v. Ogbuehi*, 18 F.3d 807, 812–13 (9th Cir. 1994).

Tenth Circuit

- "Because [the] Agent encountered [the Defendant] less than sixty miles from the United States-Mexico border, the proximity of the stop to the border also weighs in favor of the reasonableness of [the] Agent['s] suspicion that [Defendant] was en route from the border. Although we eschew any inflexible mile benchmark in considering the second *Brignoni-Ponce* factor, we find the federal regulations informative. In addition, there is a marked contrast in distances from the border between this case and *U.S. v. Venzor-Castillo* where we held that the agent lacked reasonable suspicion to conduct a stop 235 miles from border." *U.S. v. Lopez-Martinez*, 25 F.3d 1481, 1485 (10th Cir. 1994).

Eleventh Circuit

- "An extended border search, is a search that occurs beyond the functional equivalent of the border. An extended border search may not be conducted unless the officials have a reasonable suspicion of criminal activity. The critical distinction is that general border searches, including secondary customs searches, do not require any suspicion of illegal activity. In contrast, an extended border search requires a reasonable suspicion of illegal activities." *U.S. v. Santiago*, 837 F.2d 1545, 1548, 24 Fed. R. Evid. Serv. 1037 (11th Cir. 1988).

§ 18:5 International mail: Under the rationale justifying border searches, mail arriving from foreign countries may be searched

Supreme Court

- "[N]o different constitutional standard should apply simply because the envelopes were mailed, not carried. The critical fact is that the envelopes cross the border and enter this country, not that they are brought in by one mode of transportation rather than another." *U.S. v. Ramsey*, 431 U.S. 606, 620, 97 S. Ct. 1972, 52 L. Ed. 2d 617 (1977).

Fifth Circuit

- "There appears to be no sound reason to distinguish between incoming mail and other property that crosses our border. Affixing a postage stamp to a parcel should not grant it immunity that would not be accorded a package carried by a traveller." *U.S. v. Richards*, 638 F.2d 765, 772 (5th Cir. 1981).

- "Mail sorting rooms at a port of entry like New York are border areas. Thus, the instant search was reasonable simply because the package was searched at a border area after entering this country from Thailand." *U.S. v. Pringle*, 576 F.2d 1114, 1117 (5th Cir. 1978).

Ninth Circuit

- "Although it is undisputed that the officers did not follow the proper procedures for obtaining a mail cover, suppression is not the appropriate remedy for a failure to follow agency regulations. . . .In *Ani*, we held that the exclusionary rule was not triggered when a customs inspector searched a package sent via international mail without reasonable cause and contrary to postal regulations. Rather, we held that, because border searches of international mail to not require probable cause, the customs inspector's search did not violate a constitutional mandate." *U.S. v. Hinton*, 222 F.3d 664, 674 (9th Cir. 2000).

- "The Ninth Circuit has repeatedly addressed what constitutes reasonable cause for a border search of international mail. . . . We have established that the reasonable cause test is not exacting; it is considerably milder than probable cause. . . . Under this test, officials may conduct a search so long as they are aware of specific articulable facts, together with rational inferences from those facts, that reasonably warrant suspicion that the package contains illegal material. The reasons for the application of such a mild standard are clear—border searches of international mail intrude on neither a constitutional nor a statutory expectation of privacy." *U.S. v. Taghizadeh*, 87 F.3d 287, 289 (9th Cir. 1996), as amended, (Aug. 14, 1996).
- "Inspection of mail from abroad is a border search for which neither a search warrant nor probable cause is required. Such searches are considered reasonable under the Fourth Amendment simply by virtue of the fact that they occur at the border." *U.S. v. Most*, 789 F.2d 1411, 1414 (9th Cir. 1986).
- "There is no question that the initial opening of the package by customs agents was lawful. Customs officials are authorized to inspect incoming international mail when they have a reasonable cause to suspect that the mail contains contraband. 'Reasonable cause to suspect' is a considerably milder standard than probable cause." *U.S. v. Dubrofsky*, 581 F.2d 208, 211 (9th Cir. 1978).

D.C. Circuit

- "Defendant concedes that no warrant was required for the initial opening of the box, as it arrived at the border via international mail." *U.S. v. Gbemisola*, 225 F.3d 753, 758 (D.C. Cir. 2000).

§ 18:6   Controlled deliveries: When law enforcement agents lawfully learn that there is contraband in a container, they may reseal the container and deliver it to the intended recipients

Supreme Court

- "The lawful discovery by common carriers or customs officers of contraband in transit presents law enforcement authorities with an opportunity to identify and prosecute the person or persons responsible for the movement of the contraband. To accomplish this, the police, rather than simply seizing the contraband and destroying it, make a so-called controlled delivery of the container to its consignee, allowing the container to continue its journey to the destination contemplated by the parties. The person dealing in the contraband can then be identified upon taking possession of and asserting dominion over the container." *Illinois v. Andreas*, 463 U.S. 765, 769, 103 S. Ct. 3319, 77 L. Ed. 2d 1003 (1983).

- "The threshold question, then, is whether an individual has a legitimate expectation of privacy in the contents of a previously lawfully searched container. It is obvious that the privacy interest in the contents of a container diminishes with respect to a container that law enforcement authorities have already lawfully opened and found to contain illicit drugs. No protected privacy interest remains in contraband in a container once government officers lawfully have opened that container and identified its contents as illegal. The simple act of resealing the container to enable the police to make a controlled delivery does not operate to revive or restore the lawfully invaded privacy rights." *Illinois v. Andreas*, 463 U.S. 765, 771, 103 S. Ct. 3319, 77 L. Ed. 2d 1003 (1983).

- "The issue then becomes, at what point after an interruption of control or surveillance [should courts] recognize the individual's expectation of privacy in the container as a legitimate right protected by the Fourth Amendment proscription against unreasonable searches. In fashioning a standard, we must be mindful of three Fourth Amendment principles. First, the standard should be workable for application by rank and file, trained police officers. Second, it should be reasonable; for example, it would be absurd to recognize as legitimate an expectation of privacy where there is only a minimal probability that the contents of a particular container had been changed. Third, the standard should be objective, not dependent on the belief of individual police officers. A workable, objective standard that limits the risk of intrusion on legitimate privacy interests is whether there is a substantial likelihood that the contents of the container have been changed during the gap in surveillance. We hold that absent a substantial likelihood that the contents have been changed, there is no legitimate expectation of privacy in the contents of a container previously opened under lawful authority." *Illinois v. Andreas*, 463 U.S. 765, 772–73, 103 S. Ct. 3319, 77 L. Ed. 2d 1003 (1983).

Second Circuit

- "[I]n a typical controlled delivery case, the validity of the seizure is determined as of the time the drugs are first seized, not as of the time they are retaken. Having taken proper dominion over the drugs and kept them under close surveillance, the government is deemed to be in constructive possession of them, even though, for purpose of identification, they are delivered to another." *U.S. v. Singh*, 811 F.2d 758, 761 (2d Cir. 1987).

Seventh Circuit

- "Controlled deliveries of contraband apparently serve a useful function in law enforcement. They most ordinarily occur when a carrier, usually an airline, unexpectedly discovers what seems to be contraband while inspecting luggage to learn the identity of its owner, or when the contraband falls out of a broken or damaged piece of luggage, or when the carrier exercises its inspection privilege because some suspicious circumstance has caused it concern that it may unwittingly be transporting contraband. Frequently, after such a discovery, law enforcement agents restore the contraband to its container, then close or reseal the container, and authorize the carrier to deliver the container to its owner. When the owner appears to take delivery he is arrested and the container with the contraband is seized and then searched a second time for the contraband known to be there." *U.S. v. Bulgier*, 618 F.2d 472, 476 (7th Cir. 1980).

§ 18:7 Checkpoint stops: Border officials may stop vehicles routinely and question passengers at traffic or airport checkpoints

Supreme Court

- "In *Martinez-Fuerte*, we found that the balance tipped in favor of the Government's interests in policing the Nation's borders. . . .In so finding, we emphasized the difficulty of effectively containing illegal immigration at the border itself. . . .We also stressed the impracticality of the particularized study of a given car to discern whether it was transporting illegal aliens, as well as the relatively modest degree of intrusion entailed by the stops." *City of Indianapolis v. Edmond*, 531 U.S. 32, 38, 121 S. Ct. 447, 148 L. Ed. 2d 333 (2000).

- "The Fourth Amendment requires government to respect the right of the people to be secure in their persons against unreasonable searches and seizures. This restraint on government conduct generally bars officials from undertaking a search or seizure absent individualized suspicion. Searches conducted without grounds for suspicion of particular individuals have been upheld, however, in certain limited circumstances. These circumstances include brief stops for questioning or observation at a fixed Border Patrol checkpoint or at a sobriety checkpoint and administrative inspections in closely regulated businesses." *Chandler v. Miller*, 520 U.S. 305, 308, 117 S. Ct. 1295, 137 L. Ed. 2d 513, 12 I.E.R. Cas. (BNA) 1233, 145 A.L.R. Fed. 657 (1997).

- "[T]he Border Patrol [may] maintain permanent checkpoints at or near intersections of important roads leading away from the border at which a vehicle may be stopped for brief questioning of its occupants even though there is no reason to believe that the particular vehicle contains illegal aliens." *U.S. v. Villamonte-Marquez*, 462 U.S. 579, 587, 103 S. Ct. 2573, 77 L. Ed. 2d 22 (1983).

- "[A] requirement that stops on major routes inland always be based on reasonable suspicion would be impractical because the flow of traffic tends to be too heavy to allow the particularized study of a given car that would enable it to be identified as a possible carrier of illegal aliens. While the need to make routine checkpoint stops is great, the consequent intrusion on Fourth Amendment interests is quite limited. Accordingly, we hold that the stops and questioning at issue may be made in the absence of any individualized suspicion at reasonably located checkpoints." *U.S. v. Martinez-*

Fuerte, 428 U.S. 543, 557, 562, 96 S. Ct. 3074, 49 L. Ed. 2d 1116 (1976).

Fifth Circuit

- "The Supreme Court cases are predicated on the requirement that the trial court determine the purpose or purposes of a checkpoint before it undertakes any analysis of whether the checkpoint comports with the requirements of the Fourth Amendment. Arguably, in determining the purpose or purposes of any checkpoint, a distinction must be drawn between the law enforcement objective or objectives that the checkpoint was designed to advance, and incidental law enforcement benefits that may flow from the checkpoint stops." *U.S. v. Ramirez-Gonzalez*, 87 F.3d 712, 715 (5th Cir. 1996).
- "The constitutional rights of a traveler on our highways are simply not infringed by the mere requirement that he move his car out of the flow of traffic from the primary area of an immigration checkpoint several yards to the secondary area of that same checkpoint." *U.S. v. Dovali-Avila*, 895 F.2d 206, 207 (5th Cir. 1990).

Ninth Circuit

- "[A] stop conducted at a clearly visible temporary checkpoint pursuant to a routine inspection of all vehicles for illegal aliens is not unreasonable under the Fourth Amendment." *U.S. v. Soto-Camacho*, 58 F.3d 408, 411 (9th Cir. 1995).

Tenth Circuit

- "The stop of a vehicle at a fixed checkpoint constitutes a seizure to which the Fourth Amendment's requirement of reasonableness applies. . . . Even in the absence of individualized suspicion, a brief seizure at a checkpoint may be reasonable if conducted in a neutral manner for the purpose of effectuating important governmental purposes." *U.S. v. Galindo-Gonzales*, 142 F.3d 1217, 1221 (10th Cir. 1998).
- "Our concern is with the application of the Fourth Amendment to the routine stop of a vehicle at a permanent checkpoint operated by the Border Patrol at a place away from the international boundary, the scope of questioning following the stop, and the subsequent

search of the vehicle. These stops are made for the purpose of conducting routine and limited inquiry into residence status and customs matters. They are selectively made for the sole purpose of a routine and limited inquiry that cannot feasibly be made of every motorist. The intrusion is minimal. The stop is brief, and because of its public and relatively routine nature it should not be frightening or offensive. Initial questioning regarding citizenship and custom matters may be conducted at either the primary or secondary inspection areas without any individualized suspicion." *U.S. v. Ledesma-Dominguez*, 53 F.3d 1159, 1161 (10th Cir. 1995).

- "[I]f an agent observes suspicious circumstances during initial questioning, he may briefly question the motorist concerning those suspicions and ask the motorist to explain. While there is no single or narrow definition of a suspicious circumstance we have noted that a suspicious circumstance is not equivalent to the reasonable suspicion standard. We apply a common sense view of the totality of the circumstances to determine whether suspicious circumstances exist." *U.S. v. Massie*, 65 F.3d 843, 848 (10th Cir. 1995).

- "It is true that [a] routine checkpoint stop must be brief and unintrusive. We have held that a routine stop includes a cursory visual inspection of the vehicle, however, as well as brief questions concerning vehicle ownership, destination, and travel plans if reasonably related to the agent's duty to prevent the smuggling of contraband. Moreover, an agent may ask a motorist to explain suspicious circumstances which the agent has identified by relying on his training and experience. The presence of a suspicious circumstance allows a border patrol agent to ask a few additional questions concerning the suspicion during the course of a routine customs inspection. The questions that the agent asked [Defendant] during his two-minute detention at the primary inspection area clearly fall within the ambit of routine inquiry or were justified by the suspicious circumstances observed by the agent." *U.S. v. Sukiz-Grado*, 22 F.3d 1006, 1008–09 (10th Cir. 1994).

- "In conclusion, the border agents possessed broad discretion to refer Defendant to the secondary inspection area at the border checkpoint. Once at the secondary inspection area, the agents immediately obtained objective evidence that created a reasonable suspicion of wrongdoing. This justified the continued detention and more thorough questioning of Defendant. However, even if they had not immediately obtained such evidence, the agents could have lawfully asked Defendant more questions based on the suspicious circumstances as revealed by the totality of the circumstances. These circumstances included Defendant's responding to the border officer's question with a question of his own, indicating that the conversation would naturally continue a few moments longer. Given the undisputed fact that traffic was backing up, and that Defendant was being unresponsive, suspicious circumstances were present so that some further questioning was warranted." *U.S. v. Sanders*, 937 F.2d 1495, 1501–02 (10th Cir. 1991).

Eleventh Circuit

- "[T]he validity of a screening program does not 'turn[ ] on whether significant numbers of putative air pirates are actually discovered by the searches conducted under the program.' Instead, '[w]hen the Government's interest lies in deterring highly hazardous conduct, a low incidence of such conduct, far from impugning the validity of the scheme for implementing this interest, is more logically viewed as a hallmark of success.'" *Corbett v. Transportation Sec. Admin.*, 767 F.3d 1171, 1180–81 (11th Cir. 2014), cert. denied, 135 S. Ct. 2867, 192 L. Ed. 2d 897 (2015) (citations omitted).

- "The Fourth Amendment does not compel the Administration to employ the least invasive procedure or one fancied by Corbett. Airport screening is a permissible administrative search; security officers search all passengers, abuse is unlikely because of its public nature, and passengers elect to travel by air knowing that they must undergo a search. The 'jeopardy to hundreds of human lives and millions of dollars of property inherent in the pirating or blowing up of a large airplane' outweighs the slight intrusion of a generic body scan or, as a secondary measure, a pat-down." *Corbett v. Transportation Sec. Admin.*, 767 F.3d 1171, 1182 (11th Cir. 2014), cert. denied, 135 S. Ct. 2867, 192 L. Ed. 2d 897 (2015) (citations omitted).

§ 18:8   Traffic checkpoint searches: At traffic checkpoints, border officials may direct a vehicle to the side and conduct a search only if they have probable cause or a valid consent

Supreme Court

- "[S]tops for brief questioning routinely conducted at permanent checkpoints are consistent with the Fourth Amendment and need not be authorized by warrant. The principal protection of Fourth Amendment rights at checkpoints lies in appropriate limitations on the scope of the stop. [C]heckpoint searches are constitutional only if justified by consent or probable cause to search." *U.S. v. Martinez-Fuerte*, 428 U.S. 543, 566–67, 96 S. Ct. 3074, 49 L. Ed. 2d 1116 (1976).

- "[A]t traffic checkpoints removed from the border and its functional equivalents, officers may not search private vehicles without consent or probable cause." *U. S. v. Ortiz*, 422 U.S. 891, 896–97, 95 S. Ct. 2585, 45 L. Ed. 2d 623 (1975).

Fifth Circuit

- "Although only reasonable suspicion is needed to stop a vehicle for an immigration check, probable cause or consent is necessary in order to search a vehicle." *U.S. v. Inocencio*, 40 F.3d 716, 723 (5th Cir. 1994).

Ninth Circuit

- "In *United States v. Martinez-Fuerte* the Court approved stops at permanent border checkpoints in the absence of articulable individualized reasons for suspicion to ask about citizenship and immigration status. However, [n]either the vehicle nor its occupants are searched, and visual inspection of the vehicle is limited to what can be seen without a search. Any further search requires consent or probable cause." *U.S. v. Santa Maria*, 15 F.3d 879, 882 (9th Cir. 1994).

Tenth Circuit

- "The Supreme Court has spoken, in general terms, on the extent of nonverbal conduct permissible at a routine checkpoint stop. A routine checkpoint stop includes a visual inspection of the vehicle, but the inspection is limited to what can be seen without a search. In order to search a vehicle at a traffic checkpoint, agents must have probable cause or consent." *U.S. v. Rascon-Ortiz*, 994 F.2d 749, 754 (10th Cir. 1993).

- "Officers may not selectively search vehicles at a border unless they have probable cause or consent to justify the search." *U.S. v. Pinedo-Montoya*, 966 F.2d 591, 594 (10th Cir. 1992).

- "Border patrol agents may question individuals regarding suspicious circumstances, in addition to citizenship matters, when those individuals are stopped at a permanent checkpoint. But any further detention must be based on the individual's consent or probable cause, or upon a valid investigative detention. Detention and search beyond the routine customs inspection requires reasonable suspicion justified by a particularized and objective basis for suspecting the particular person of smuggling contraband." *U.S. v. Sanders*, 937 F.2d 1495, 1499 (10th Cir. 1991).

§ 18:9 Roving patrol stops: Border officials on roving patrol require a reasonable suspicion to stop a vehicle

Supreme Court

- "[S]tops by the Border Patrol may be justified under circumstances less than those constituting probable cause for arrest or search. [T]he test is . . . whether, based upon the whole picture, they, as experienced Border Patrol agents, could reasonably surmise that the particular vehicle they stopped was engaged in criminal activity." *U.S. v. Cortez*, 449 U.S. 411, 421, 101 S. Ct. 690, 66 L. Ed. 2d 621 (1981).

- "Except at the border and its functional equivalents, officers on roving patrol may stop vehicles only if they are aware of specific articulable facts, together with rational inferences from those facts, that reasonably warrant suspicion that the vehicles contain aliens who may be illegally in the country." *U.S. v. Brignoni-Ponce*, 422 U.S. 873, 884, 95 S. Ct. 2574, 45 L. Ed. 2d 607 (1975).

Fifth Circuit

- "When roving Border Patrol agents stop a vehicle in a

'border area,' rather than at an official checkpoint, we consider whether several factors (known as the *Brignoni-Ponce* factors) contribute to the agents' reasonable suspicion: (1) the area's proximity to the border; (2) the area's characteristics; (3) the usual traffic patterns on the road; (4) the agents' previous experience with criminal activity; (5) information about recent illegal trafficking in the area; (6) the appearance of the vehicle; (7) the driver's behavior; and (8) the passengers' number, appearance, and behavior. Because reasonable suspicion is a totality-of-the-circumstances analysis, we consider these factors collectively, not in isolation. Here, all of the factors weigh in favor of the Government. The OKM Ranch is only thirty miles from the Texas-Mexico border, 'where many smuggling trips originate.' The ranch is also a 'common corridor[ ]' for smugglers because it circumvents two Border Patrol checkpoints, and '[i]t is well established that a road's reputation as a smuggling route adds to the reasonableness of the agents' suspicion.' Relying on their years of Border Patrol experience, Agent Garcia and Agent Freed noticed several suspicious facts about the F-150 Escamilla was driving. To start, they were 'propelled into action by sensors designed to avoid routine ranch traffic' and discovered 'an unfamiliar and atypical-looking oil field vehicle.' 'Legitimate' ranch traffic usually arrives early in the morning, but at 6:30 a.m., the F-150 appeared to be leaving. The truck also lacked the usual markings of an oil company vehicle, was registered to a residence rather than a business, and had temporary 'paper tags,' which smugglers often use. Escamilla was also driving 'in tandem'—a manner of travel common among smugglers—with the F-250 in front of him for several minutes." *United States v. Escamilla*, 852 F.3d 474, 481 (5th Cir. 2017) (citations omitted).

- "Border Patrol officers on roving patrol may detain vehicles for investigation only if they are 'aware of specific, articulable facts, together with rational inferences from those facts, that reasonably warrant suspicion that the vehicle is involved in illegal activities.' In *U.S. v. Brignoni-Ponce,* the Supreme Court laid out a multi-factored analysis in deciding 'whether there is reasonable suspicion to stop a car in the border area.'

Factors that may be considered include: (1) the characteristics of the area in which the vehicle is encountered; (2) the arresting agent's previous experience with criminal activity; (3) the area's proximity to the border, (4) the usual traffic patterns on the road; (5) information about recent illegal trafficking in aliens or narcotics in the area; (6) the appearance of the vehicle; (7) the driver's behavior; and, (8) the passengers' number, appearance, and behavior. 'Not every *Brignoni-Ponce* factor need weigh in favor of reasonable suspicion for it to be present, nor does the Fourth Amendment require the law enforcement officer eliminate all reasonable possibility of innocent travel before conducting an investigatory stop.' The totality of the circumstances is taken into consideration when deciding whether Guerrero had reasonable suspicion to stop Garza's pickup truck." *U.S. v. Garza*, 727 F.3d 436 (5th Cir. 2013) (citations omitted).

- "None of the [*Brignoni-Ponce*] factors alone is dispositive, and courts must analyze them as a whole, rather than each in isolation." *U.S. v. Rico-Soto*, 690 F.3d 376, 380 (5th Cir. 2012).
- "Despite the lack of proximity to the border, examining the facts from the above analysis under the remaining *Brignoni—Ponce* factors demonstrates that Gill's stop was justified. First, he made the stop on Interstate 10, a major alien-smuggling corridor. Second, the van was traveling westbound through his location in the mid-morning, the main time, route, and direction Gill's past experience has shown smugglers pass by through the area. Third, Gill's extensive experience in the Lake Charles area and with the Border Patrol generally leaves him keenly able to aggregate subtle clues the rest of us miss. Fourth, intel reports showed 'Paisanos' vans had recently become active in transporting illegal aliens and, though not yet apprehended in the Lake Charles region, they had been caught transporting illegal aliens in other places. Fifth, the vehicle was a 15 passenger van, often used in smuggling aliens, and was registered to an individual woman in Houston rather than the company to whose fleet it was labeled as belonging. Finally, although the driver committed no traffic violation, the passengers were the expected

number and orientation for an alien smuggling operation's return trip." *U.S. v. Rico-Soto*, 690 F.3d 376, 380 (5th Cir. 2012).

- "A United States Border Patrol agent's temporary detention of an occupant of a vehicle for investigatory purposes while on roving patrol is constitutional if, at a minimum, the agent reasonably suspects that an occupant of the vehicle is involved in illegal activity." *U.S. v. Guerrero-Barajas*, 240 F.3d 428, 432 (5th Cir. 2001).
- "[P]roximity to the border, is a paramount factor in determining reasonable suspicion. . . .Although we do not adhere to a bright line test with regard to this factor, a car traveling more than fifty (50) miles from the border is usually viewed as being too far from the border to support an inference that it originated its journey there." *U.S. v. Zapata-Ibarra*, 212 F.3d 877, 881 (5th Cir. 2000).
- "The agents identified specific articulable facts to support their reasonable suspicion for the stop, most significantly the characteristics of the area of the stop, including the proximity to the Sarita checkpoint, the rigid suspension of the vehicle, the type of vehicle, the dirty appearance of the passengers, and the time of the stop. When viewed in the light most favorable to the government and in the context of the agents' previous knowledge and experience with alien smuggling cases in the area, these particular facts and inferences rationally drawn from them reasonably led the agents to suspect [Defendant] was transporting illegal aliens in his van." *U.S. v. Chavez-Chavez*, 205 F.3d 145, 150 (5th Cir. 2000).
- "Border Patrol agents on roving patrol may stop a vehicle when they are aware of specific articulable facts that, together with the rationale inferences that may be drawn from those facts, reasonably warrant suspicion that the particular vehicle is involved in illegal activities." *U.S. v. Gonzalez*, 190 F.3d 668, 671 (5th Cir. 1999).
- "Because proximity to the border cannot alone justify a stop, a finding of reasonable suspicion in this case would have to be based, in large part, upon the number of passengers in the car. As already discussed, however, Fifth

Circuit precedent indicates that the mere presence of numerous people in a car does not raise a reasonable suspicion. Nor are we willing in the instant case to assign some magic number at which point reasonable suspicion would arise. Thus, absent a showing by the Government that other *Brignoni-Ponce* factors weigh in its favor, we hold that a midsize sedan traveling on a road near the U.S.-Mexican border with as many as eight visible passengers does not give rise to reasonable suspicion of unlawful activity." *U.S. v. Lopez-Valdez*, 178 F.3d 282, 288 (5th Cir. 1999).

- "Any number of factors may be taken into account in deciding whether there is reasonable suspicion to stop a car in the border area. . . . Those factors include: (1) the characteristics of the area in which a vehicle is encountered; (2) proximity to the border; (3) the usual patterns of traffic on the particular road; (4) previous experience with alien traffic; (5) information about recent illegal border crossings in the area; (6) the driver's behavior, e.g., erratic driving or obvious attempts to evade officers; (7) aspects of the vehicle itself, e.g., suitability of the design for concealment and transport of aliens; (8) appearance of the vehicle, e.g., appears heavily loaded; (9) vehicle has an extraordinary number of passengers; (10) persons in the vehicle are observed attempting to hide; (11) appearance of the driver or passengers, e.g., certain aspects of dress and haircut, may indicate that the driver or passenger is from Mexico." *U.S. v. Jones*, 149 F.3d 364, 367 (5th Cir. 1998).

- "The totality of the circumstances does not support a reasonable suspicion of illegal activity. The fact that [Defendant], who was from Garland, Texas, and who [the] Agent . . . described as looking like a tourist, was driving northbound on Highway 118 approximately eighty (80) miles north of the Texas-Mexico border at 7:00 a.m., after sunrise, with his lights on in a Toyota 4 Runner with fresh mud on it with a blue tarp over something in the rear cargo area is far more consistent with [Defendant] being a tourist coming from Big Bend National Park than an alien smuggler or drug smuggler who crossed the Rio Grande before dawn that morning. The inoperative tail light and time period when [Defendant] came through the checkpoint south of Alpine do

not alter the inescapable conclusion that [the] Agent
. . . lacked reasonable suspicion to make an investigatory immigration stop." *U.S. v. Jones*, 149 F.3d 364, 371
(5th Cir. 1998).

Ninth Circuit

- "[T]he Fourth Amendment prohibits an officer on roving
  patrol near the border from stopping a vehicle in the
  absence of an objectively 'reasonable suspicion' that the
  'particular vehicle may contain aliens who are illegally
  in the country' or is involved in some other criminal
  conduct." *Chavez v. U.S.*, 683 F.3d 1102, 1111 (9th Cir.
  2012).

- "[D]iscovery of undocumented individuals in a vehicle
  does not excuse an initial lack of reasonable suspicion."
  Chavez v. U.S., 683 F.3d 1102, 1112 (9th Cir. 2012).

- "[T]he Fourth Amendment prohibits an officer on roving
  patrol near the border from stopping a vehicle in the
  absence of an objectively 'reasonable suspicion' that the
  'particular vehicle may contain aliens who are illegally
  in the country' or is involved in some other criminal
  conduct." *Chavez v. U.S.*, 683 F.3d 1102, 1111 (9th Cir.
  2012).

- "[D]iscovery of undocumented individuals in a vehicle
  does not excuse an initial lack of reasonable suspicion."
  Chavez v. U.S., 683 F.3d 1102, 1112 (9th Cir. 2012).

Tenth Circuit

- "In determining whether there is reasonable suspicion
  to stop a car in the border area, officers may consider
  any number of factors, including: (1) characteristics of
  the area in which the vehicle is encountered; (2) the
  proximity of the area to the border; (3) the usual patterns of traffic on the particular road; (4) the previous
  experience of the agent with alien traffic; (5) information about illegal border crossings in the area; (6) the
  driver's behavior, including any obvious attempts to
  evade officers; (7) aspects of the vehicle such as a station wagon with concealed compartments; and (8) the
  appearance that the vehicle is heavily loaded. . . . This
  test does not purport to provide outcome determinative
  criteria, nor does it require us to view any fact in
  isolation. Rather, our examination for reasonable

suspicion must take into account the totality of the circumstances surrounding the stop." *U.S. v. Doyle*, 129 F.3d 1372, 1375 (10th Cir. 1997).

- "Border patrol agents on roving patrol may stop vehicles only if they are aware of specific articulable facts, together with rational inferences from those facts, that reasonably warrant suspicion that those vehicles' occupants may be involved in criminal activity. Any number of factors might contribute to an agent's decision to stop a vehicle on reasonable suspicion. The law does not specify a minimum number of factors necessary to constitute reasonable suspicion or any outcome determinative criteria. Each case turns upon its own facts. In all instances, however, the agent is entitled to assess the facts in light of his experience in detecting criminal activity. Law enforcement officers may perceive meaning in actions that appear innocuous to the untrained observer. This is not to say that an agent may stop a vehicle on an unparticularized suspicion or hunch. While the necessary level of suspicion is considerably less than proof of wrongdoing by a preponderance of the evidence, the Fourth Amendment requires some minimal level of objective justification." *U.S. v. Cantu*, 87 F.3d 1118, 1121 (10th Cir. 1996).

- "[B]order patrol agents on roving patrol may stop vehicles only if they are aware of specific articulable facts, together with rational inferences from those facts, that reasonably warrant suspicion that the vehicles are involved in criminal activity. [E]ach fact must either be rationally suspicious in itself, or, despite being innocent on its face, must be rationally suspicious when viewed in context with the other articulable facts. [A] vehicle with out-of-state license plates is by definition not a local vehicle. Second, while out-of-state license plates may be a relevant consideration in some circumstances this factor in and of itself is not significantly probative of illegal activity and adds little to the reasonable suspicion equation Therefore, the only arguably significant articulable fact before us upon which the decision to stop the Thunderbird could rationally have been based was the interest shown by its occupant in the passing van and the border patrol vehicle. Even if we add the marginally significant fact that the Thunderbird

bore out-of-state license plates, the *Brignoni-Ponce* test
is not met. Consequently, [the] Agent lacked reasonable
suspicion to order the Thunderbird stopped, and the
stop therefore violated the Fourth Amendment." *U.S. v.
Martinez-Cigarroa*, 44 F.3d 908, 911 (10th Cir. 1995).

§ 18:10 Roving patrol searches: Border officials on roving patrol need probable cause or a valid consent to search a stopped vehicle

Supreme Court

- "[B]ecause of the importance of the governmental interest at stake, the minimal intrusion of a brief stop, and
  the absence of practical alternatives for policing the
  border, we hold that when an officer's observations lead
  him reasonably to suspect that a particular vehicle may
  contain aliens who are illegally in the country, he may
  stop the car briefly and investigate the circumstances
  that provoke suspicion. [T]he stop and inquiry must be
  reasonably related in scope to the justification for their
  initiation. [B]ut any further detention or search must
  be based on consent or probable cause." *U.S. v. Brignoni-
  Ponce*, 422 U.S. 873, 881–82, 95 S. Ct. 2574, 45 L. Ed.
  2d 607 (1975).
- "[T]he search of the [Defendant's] automobile by a roving patrol. [i]n the absence of probable cause of consent
  . . . violated the Fourth Amendment right to be free of
  unreasonable searches and seizures." *Almeida-Sanchez
  v. U.S.*, 413 U.S. 266, 273, 93 S. Ct. 2535, 37 L. Ed. 2d
  596 (1973).

Ninth Circuit

- "If after a valid investigatory stop probable cause arises,
  the search may then be made." *U.S. v. Bugarin-Casas*,
  484 F.2d 853, 854 (9th Cir. 1973).

§ 18:11 Border strip searches: Strip searches at a border may be conducted only pursuant to real or reasonable suspicion

Second Circuit

- "The light touching of appellant's back followed by a
  lifting of his shirt arguably straddles the line between

the two categories of border searches—searching more than personal belongings or effects such as a purse, wallet, or even outer jacket was involved; but the search was not nearly as intrusive as a body cavity or full strip search. Since the potential indignity resulting from a pat on the back followed by a lifting of one's shirt simply fails to compare with the much greater level of intrusion associated with a body cavity or full strip search, we decline to hold that reasonable suspicion was here required." *U.S. v. Charleus*, 871 F.2d 265, 268 (2d Cir. 1989).

- "[A]lthough anyone entering or leaving the country may expect to have his luggage and personal effects examined, he does not expect that his entry or departure, standing alone, will cause him to be subjected to a strip search. Before a border official may insist upon such an extensive invasion of privacy, he should have a suspicion of illegal concealment that is based upon something more than the border crossing, and the suspicion should be substantial enough to make the search a reasonable exercise of authority." *U.S. v. Asbury*, 586 F.2d 973, 975–76 (2d Cir. 1978).

Ninth Circuit

- "The Supreme Court has recognized three types of searches in which more is required than simple application of the border search doctrine. First, the Government must have reasonable suspicion to conduct 'highly intrusive searches of the person.' Second, the Court has recognized the possibility 'that some searches of property are so destructive as to require' particularized suspicion. Finally, the Court has left 'open the question whether, and under what circumstances, a border search might be deemed unreasonable because of the particularly offensive manner in which it is carried out.' " *U.S. v. Cotterman*, 637 F.3d 1068 (9th Cir. 2011), on reh'g en banc, 709 F.3d 952 (9th Cir. 2013) (citations and internal quotations omitted).

- "Strip searches and body-cavity searches are of course considered nonroutine, and, unlike luggage searches and patdowns, must be supported by reasonable suspicion. Once customs officials reasonably suspect that an international traveler is smuggling contraband, however, they may detain her and perform the searches necessary to either verify or dispel the suspicion that she will introduce a harmful agent into this country." *U.S. v. Gonzalez-Rincon*, 36 F.3d 859, 864 (9th Cir. 1994).

- "Real suspicion that the person to be searched is smuggling narcotics is required for a border strip search—a search involving visual inspection of body surfaces. Real suspicion is subjective suspicion supported by objective, articulable facts." *U.S. v. Aman*, 624 F.2d 911, 912 (9th Cir. 1980).

Eleventh Circuit

- "Border searches are not subject to the probable cause and warrant requirements of the Fourth Amendment; rather, they are simply subject to that amendment's more amorphous reasonableness standard. We have applied this reasonableness requirement by adopting a flexible test which adjusts the strength of suspicion required for a particular search to the intrusiveness of that search. In determining the level of intrusiveness of a search, extensiveness alone does not control. Rather, it is the personal indignity suffered by the individual searched that controls the level of suspicion required to make the search reasonable." *U.S. v. Villabona-Garnica*, 63 F.3d 1051, 1057 (11th Cir. 1995).

- "A more intrusive search, the strip search, requires a particularized 'reasonable suspicion'. This standard has been held to have been met if a person behaves in an articulably suspicious manner." *U.S. v. Vega-Barvo*, 729 F.2d 1341, 1345 (11th Cir. 1984).

§ 18:12 Body cavity searches: Body cavity searches at the border must be based on a higher standard than strip searches

Supreme Court

- "We hold that the detention of a traveler at the border, beyond the scope of a routine customs search and inspection, is justified at its inception if customs agents, considering all the facts surrounding the traveler and her trip, reasonably suspect that the traveler is smuggling contraband in her alimentary canal. . . . It is also important to note what we do *not* hold. Because the issues are not presented today we suggest no view on what level of suspicion, if any, is required for nonroutine border searches such as strip, body cavity, or involuntary x-ray searches." *U.S. v. Montoya de Hernandez*, 473 U.S. 531, 541, 105 S. Ct. 3304, 87 L. Ed. 2d 381 (1985).

Second Circuit

• "[T]he specific and objective facts articulated by [the Inspector] justified a substantial suspicion on his part that appellants were attempting to smuggle narcotics into the United States. [The Inspector] did not, however, rush appellants to the x-ray room. Instead, he proceeded from the less intrusive to the more intrusive. When a search of appellants' luggage turned up nothing, [the Inspector] obtained authorization from his supervisors to have female agents conduct a pat-down search and then a strip search. Since the internally secreted drugs could not be detected in either search, [the Inspector] was left with the choice of either verifying their presence by x-ray or letting nature take its course and supervising appellants during their periods of defection." *U.S. v. Reyes*, 821 F.2d 168, 170 (2d Cir. 1987).

Fifth Circuit

• "[T]he greater the intrusion, the greater must be the reason for conducting a search that results in such invasion. . . . Thus, what constitutes reasonable suspicion to justify a particular search may not suffice to justify a more intrusive or demeaning search." *U.S. v. Afanador*, 567 F.2d 1325, 1328 (5th Cir. 1978).

Ninth Circuit

• "Routine searches at a United States international border require no objective justification, probable cause or warrant. . . . Although routine border searches may proceed without probable cause or justification, reasonable suspicion is required for the detention of a traveler at the border beyond the scope of a routine customs search and inspection. . . . [T]he degree of intrusiveness is a critical factor in distinguishing between rou-

tine and non-routine searches. . . . Our past decisions
highlight types of border searches that are so intrusive
that they require at least reasonable suspicion. For
example. . .we held that a strip search at the border
requires real suspicion, and that a body cavity search at
the border requires a clear indication that the suspect
is carrying contraband in a body cavity. And, in *United
States v. Summerfield* we decided that an intrusion into
an individual's body requires a clear indication that
desired evidence will be found. These decisions are consistent with the Supreme Court's statement that strip
searches, body cavity searches, and involuntary x-ray
searches are examples of non-routine border searches.
. . . [A] border search goes beyond the routine only
when it reaches the degree of intrusiveness present in a
strip search or body cavity search. . . . Border searches
involving the removal of shoes do not entail the degree
of intrusiveness present in strip and body cavity
searches. . . . The search of [Defendant's] shoes and
baggage was a routine border search, and no reasonable
suspicion was necessary." *U.S. v. Ramos-Saenz*, 36 F.3d
59, 61–62 (9th Cir. 1994), as amended, (Oct. 14, 1994).

- "More, however, is required for a body cavity search at
a border, a search which involves an intrusion beyond
the body's surface. A clear indication or plain suggestion that the suspect is concealing contraband *in his
body cavity* is required for such a search." *U.S. v. Aman*,
624 F.2d 911, 912 (9th Cir. 1980).

- "We have found a violation of the Fourth Amendment
since the initiation of the intrusive body cavity search
was unjustified because of the lack of any clear indication or plain suggestion in the minds of Dr. Salerno and
his rectal invasion squad members, that [Defendant]
had any narcotics cached in his rectal cavity." *Huguez
v. U.S.*, 406 F.2d 366, 380 (9th Cir. 1968).

Tenth Circuit

- "It is necessary to show preliminarily that there is a
clear indication of the presence of narcotics." *Yanez v.
Romero*, 619 F.2d 851, 855 (10th Cir. 1980).

Eleventh Circuit

- "At the border, a customs inspector must have a rea-

927

sonable suspicion that a person is carrying contraband internally before a person's stomach may be searched either by x-ray or by detaining the person until he excretes his stomach's contents. The reasonable suspicion standard requires a showing of articulable facts which are particularized as to the person and as to the place that is to be searched." *U.S. v. Henao-Castano*, 729 F.2d 1364, 1366 (11th Cir. 1984).

§ 18:13 Alimentary canal smugglers: Suspected alimentary canal smugglers may be detained for a reasonable period of time, may be placed under surveillance, and may be given laxatives

Second Circuit

- "We have recently seen a significant increase in alimentary-canal drug smugglers who, by swallowing drug-filled condoms, use their bodies to shield illegal drugs from the eyes of customs inspectors. Because of this unusual practice, our courts have been faced with novel legal issues in guiding law enforcement officials who seek to discover and apprehend the smugglers." *U.S. v. Onumonu*, 967 F.2d 782, 783, 36 Fed. R. Evid. Serv. 273 (2d Cir. 1992).

- "[A] suspect may constitutionally be detained until their bodily processes dispel the suspicion that they will introduce a harmful agent into this country. Once reasonable suspicion was established, the governmental authorities could detain [Defendant] until he demonstrated, through his bowel movements, that the suspicion was either confirmed or unwarranted. We recognize [Defendant's] discomfort, but it is undeniably true that the length of his detention and of his discomfort resulted solely from the method by which [he] chose to smuggle illicit drugs into this country." *U.S. v. Onumonu*, 967 F.2d 782, 790, 36 Fed. R. Evid. Serv. 273 (2d Cir. 1992).

- "We hold that the detention of a traveler at the border, beyond the scope of a routine customs search and inspection, is justified at its inception if customs agents, considering all the fact surrounding the traveler and her trip, reasonably suspect that the traveler is smuggling contraband in her alimentary canal. The reasonable suspicion standard has been applied in a number of contexts and effects a needed balance between private and public interests when law enforcement officials must make a limited intrusion on less than probable cause. It thus fits well into the situations involving alimentary canal smuggling at the border: this type of smuggling gives no external signs and inspectors will rarely possess probable cause to arrest or search, yet governmental interests in stopping smuggling at the border are high indeed. Under this standard, officials at the border must have a particularized and objective basis for suspecting the particular person of alimentary canal smuggling." *U.S. v. Esieke*, 940 F.2d 29, 33 (2d Cir. 1991).

- "More recently, in *United States v. Odofin*, this Court rejected a claim that a five-day border detention without judicial authorization was so long as to violate the Fourth Amendment. In that case, appellant was detained by customs officials who suspected that he was an alimentary canal drug smuggler. After five days of detention without a bowel movement, a lawyer appeared before a Magistrate and argued that the continued detention was unreasonable. The magistrate disagreed and permitted the detention to continue. Ultimately, [Appellant] was held for a total of twenty-four days until he began to pass several balloons containing narcotics. On appeal, we found no violation of the Fourth Amendment." *U.S. v. Esieke*, 940 F.2d 29, 34 (2d Cir. 1991).

Fifth Circuit

- "If the fourth amendment is to have any meaning, it must require a judicial determination that there is a basis—under the applicable standard—for any extended restraint of liberty. We hold that under basic fourth amendment principles, the government, after detaining a suspected alimentary canal drug smuggler, must seek a judicial determination, within a reasonable period, that reasonable suspicion exists to support the detention. The fourth amendment does not require a formal adversary hearing for such a determination; informal presentation of the evidence supporting the customs agent's suspicion before a neutral and detached judicial officer satisfies the concerns underlying the fourth amendment. Failure to obtain such a judicial determination within 48 hours shifts the burden to the government to demonstrate a bona fide emergency or extraordinary circumstance justifying the lengthier delay." *U.S. v. Adekunle*, 2 F.3d 559, 562 (5th Cir. 1993).

Ninth Circuit

- "Detention for a monitored bowel movement is justified if customs officers have a particularized and objective basis for suspecting the particular person of alimentary canal smuggling. The customs inspectors based their suspicion on several factors they learned through interviewing her that we re not consistent with innocent travel. These factors include her nervous demeanor and her lies about the purpose of her trip and her occupation, which are not easily susceptible to rote profile recitations." *U.S. v. Gonzalez-Rincon*, 36 F.3d 859, 863 (9th Cir. 1994).

- "Even if we assume that [Defendant] had a subjective expectation of privacy in his hospital room, that expectation was not objectively reasonable. [Defendant] however, did not voluntarily admit himself into the hospital; he was admitted under police supervision following his arrest. Based on the x-rays and [Defendant's] condition, the police had probable cause to believe that [Defendant] had the balloons in his stomach and that the balloons contained illegal narcotics. The police thus were justified in arresting [Defendant]. Under these circumstances, it would be wholly unrealistic not to expect the police to place [Defendant] under surveillance. In addition, [t]he balloons certainly, or at least probably, contained contraband. They were subject to immediate confiscation. Any invasion of [Defendant's] privacy was necessitated entirely by the unsavory method by which he chose to smuggle the drugs into this country and the time it took for him to expel the balloons. We therefore conclude that the district court did not err in refusing to suppress the heroin seized by the police." *U.S. v. George*, 987 F.2d 1428, 1432 (9th Cir. 1993).

Eleventh Circuit

- "Once reasonable suspicion exists that a person entering the country is an internal drug smuggler, the government may detain the traveler until enough time has passed to allow the contents of the suspected smuggler's stomach to be excreted. The traveler-suspect often has some control over the length of his detention; for example, he could choose the usually speedier alternative of an x-ray examination. We accept that there may be limits on how long police can detain a suspected internal carrier (or how many bowel movements can be required); these limits, however, have not been approached in this case where the international traveler was held only ninety minutes and when only two bowel movements were involved." *U.S. v. Rodriguez*, 74 F.3d 1164, 1164–65 (11th Cir. 1996).

§ 18:14 Plain view applicable: Plain view exception applies to border stops and searches

Ninth Circuit

- "Plain view exception to search warrant requirement of Fourth Amendment applied to Customs inspectors' discovery of letter, enclosed in package to be sent to the Philippines, which contained apparent evidence of pedophilia, where inspectors were conducting outbound currency interdiction targeting packages bound for the Philippines to determine if the sender was exporting monetary instruments." *U.S. v. Seljan*, 547 F.3d 993 (9th Cir. 2008).

Chapter 19

Department of Homeland Security Searches and Seizures

§ 19:1   Seizures of persons: Fourth Amendment standards govern the stopping, interrogating, and arresting of suspected illegal aliens

§ 19:2   Searches of private premises: A warrant is required to search private premises for illegal aliens. Strict probable cause standards are required in criminal cases but not in civil administrative proceedings

§ 19:3   Suppression: Illegally seized evidence may be admitted in deportation hearings

Research References

West's Key Number Digest

Aliens, Immigration, and Citizenship ☞440 to 459; Arrest ☞68; Criminal Law ☞394; Searches and Seizures ☞73, 126, 129

KeyCite®: Cases and other legal materials listed in KeyCite Scope can be researched through the KeyCite service on Westlaw®. Use KeyCite to check citations for form, parallel references, prior and later history, and comprehensive citator information, including citations to other decisions and secondary materials.

---

§ 19:1   Seizures of persons: Fourth Amendment standards govern the stopping, interrogating, and arresting of suspected illegal aliens

<u>Supreme Court</u>

- "We reject the claim that the entire work forces of the two factories were seized for the duration of the surveys when the INS placed agents near the exits of the factory sites. . . . [W]orkers were not prevented by the agents from moving about the factories. The obvious purpose of the agents' presence at the factory doors was to insure that all persons in the factories were

questioned. If mere questioning does not constitute a
seizure when it occurs inside the factory, it is no more a
seizure when it occurs at the exits." *I.N.S. v. Delgado*,
466 U.S. 210, 218, 104 S. Ct. 1758, 80 L. Ed. 2d 247
(1984).

First Circuit
- "The fourth amendment permits immigration officers—
  whether at a factory in California or an airport in
  Puerto Rico—to ask questions about immigration status
  as long as those whom they question can freely disregard the questions and continue about their business."
  Lopez v. Garriga, 917 F.2d 63, 70 (1st Cir. 1990).

Fourth Circuit
- "[T]he question presented is a narrow one: Once the officer learned that there were no outstanding warrants,
  and having been provided an LPR card by the defendant
  as identification, was he permitted to then call [Im-
  migration and Customs Enforcement (ICE)]—a call that
  took some portion of 'a few minutes'—to verify the validity of the LPR card? . . . When a police officer lawfully detains a vehicle, 'police diligence involves requesting a driver's license and vehicle registration, running a
  computer check, and issuing a ticket.' The officer may
  also, 'in the interest of personal safety,' request that the
  passengers in the vehicle provide identification, at least
  so long as the request does not prolong the seizure.
  Similarly, the officer may 'inquir[e] into matters unrelated to the justification for the traffic stop,' and may
  take other actions that do not constitute 'searches'
  within the meaning of the Fourth Amendment, such as
  conducting a dog-sniff of the vehicle, but again only 'so
  long as those inquiries [or other actions] do not measurably extend the duration of the stop.' Strictly speaking,
  the scope and duration inquiries under *Terry's* second
  prong are distinct. They become intertwined, however,
  in cases where, as here, the actions a defendant argues
  exceeded the scope of the stop necessarily also extended
  its duration. This raises the following question: Under
  what circumstances, if ever, may an officer prolong a
  traffic stop to investigate matters unrelated to the
  justification for the stop and without reasonable

suspicion, whether through questioning or other means? . . . If 'the totality of the circumstances, viewed objectively, establishes that the officer, without reasonable suspicion, definitively abandoned the prosecution of the traffic stop and embarked on another sustained course of investigation, this would surely bespeak a lack of diligence.' This standard incorporates both the duration and scope components of *Terry's* second prong. . . . In cases where, as here, the questioning does extend the seizure, the scope of an officer's unrelated investigation could be relevant to whether the officer 'definitively abandoned the prosecution of the traffic stop and embarked on another sustained course of investigation.' . . . We believe the 'diligently pursue' standard applies nonetheless, because either questioning a person directly or pursuing other means of investigation may, in the context of a particular traffic stop, be relevant to whether an officer diligently pursued the investigation of the justification for the stop. . . . Although the officer's call to ICE was unrelated to the justification for the stop and extended the time (if only for a portion of 'a few minutes') during which the officer kept the vehicle at the side of the highway, the totality of the circumstances demonstrates that [the officer] 'diligently pursue[d] the investigation of the justification for the stop,' and was not otherwise 'dilatory in [his] investigation.' " *U.S. v. Guijon-Ortiz*, 660 F.3d 757, 763–70 (4th Cir. 2011) (citations omitted).

Ninth Circuit

- "A government agent may conduct a seizure of a person in order to investigate whether that person is an illegal alien. However, to justify the seizure the agent must articulate objective facts providing a reasonable suspicion that [the subject of the seizure] was an alien illegally in this country. The specific facts articulated by the agents must provide a rational basis for separating out the illegal aliens from American citizens and legal aliens. [W]e find that the sole basis for the seizure was the defendant's racial background or national origin, a basis that was itself unreasonable." *Orhorhaghe v. I.N.S.*, 38 F.3d 488, 497 (9th Cir. 1994).
- "Finally, allowing INS agents to seize and interrogate

an individual simply because of his foreign-sounding name or his foreign-looking appearance risks allowing race or national-origin to determine who will and who will not be investigated. The sound of one's name often serves as a proxy in many people's minds for one's race or national origin. In light of this deeply-entrenched association between surnames and particular racial or national groups, we conclude that INS targeting of individuals on the basis of their foreign-sounding names raises precisely the same concerns regarding racial discrimination that compelled our decision in *Gonzalez-Rivera*." *Orhorhaghe v. I.N.S.*, 38 F.3d 488, 498 (9th Cir. 1994).

- "A principal purpose of the *Miranda* warnings is to permit the suspect to make an intelligent decision as to whether to answer the government agent's questions. . . . In deportation proceedings, however—in light of the alien's burden of proof, the requirement that the alien answer nonincriminating questions, the potential adverse consequences to the alien of remaining silent, and the fact that an alien's statement is admissible in the deportation hearing despite his lack of counsel at the preliminary interrogation—*Miranda* warnings would be not only inappropriate but could also serve to mislead the alien." *U.S. v. Alderete-Deras*, 743 F.2d 645, 648 (9th Cir. 1984).

- "Section 28(a)(2) of Title 8 U.S.C. authorizes an INS officer to arrest without a warrant any alien in the United States, if he has reason to believe that the alien so arrested is in the United States in violation of any such law or regulation and is likely to escape before a warrant can be obtained for his arrest. . . . The phrase has reason to believe has been equated with the constitutional requirement of probable cause." *Tejeda-Mata v. Immigration and Naturalization Service*, 626 F.2d 721, 724–25 (9th Cir. 1980).

- "Appellant was not arrested until probable cause existed that he was an illegal alien. The informant's tip gave the agent a founded suspicion upon which he could briefly detain and question appellant. The agent's subsequent observation that appellant matched the informant's description and the detection of the altered I-151 card [make] it clear that when appellant was arrested this founded suspicion had ripened into probable cause." *U.S. v. Reyes-Oropesa*, 596 F.2d 399, 400 (9th Cir. 1979).

Tenth Circuit

- "One could imagine other circumstances where the flight of a passenger might create reasonable suspicion that the driver was also engaged in criminal activity. But this case does not present such circumstances. When the agents apprehended [the passenger], they discovered he was illegally in the United States. That is a status crime, which would not necessarily suggest that the driver of the vehicle from which he fled was also involved in criminal activity. One could further imagine other circumstances where the discovery that a fleeing passenger was in the United States illegally might engender reasonable suspicion that the driver and the rest of the vehicle's occupants might also be unlawfully in the country. That might be the case, for example, if the stop occurred close to the U.S.-Mexican border on a highway or road frequently used by illegal immigrants to enter the United States undetected and multiple people fled from a van. But those are not the circumstances presented here. . . . [W]e reject the general premise that once someone has been identified by authorities as unlawfully in the United States, anyone providing him with transportation for his daily activities is also reasonably suspected of criminal activity." *U.S. v. De La Cruz*, 703 F.3d 1193 (10th Cir. 2013).

D.C. Circuit

- "[T]he immigration officer may detain an individual, reasonably believed to be an alien, against his will for the purpose of questioning. We believe the statutory interrogation authority comprehends such detentions, but, because they are far greater intrusions upon personal privacy than the non-forcible approaches, and since aliens in this country are sheltered by the Fourth Amendment in common with citizens, such a reading of the Congressional mandate must be controlled by the constitutional standards governing similar detentions made by other law enforcement officials. We hold that immigration officers, in accordance with the Congressional grant of authority found in Section 287(a)(1) [of the Immigration and Nationality Act] may make forcible detentions of a temporary nature for the purposes of interrogation under circumstances created by reasonable suspicion, not arising to the level of probable cause to arrest, that the individual so detained is illegally in this country." *Au Yi Lau v. U.S. Immigration and Naturalization Service*, 445 F.2d 217, 223 (D.C. Cir. 1971).

§ 19:2   Searches of private premises: A warrant is required to search private premises for illegal aliens. Strict probable cause standards are required in criminal cases but not in civil administrative proceedings

Second Circuit

- "[A]fter [the] arrest, [INS agents] were required to do as best they could to maintain custody of the aliens lawfully arrested and surveillance of the house while a search warrant was being obtained. [T]he conviction must be reversed because of the . . . search of the house [without a warrant]." *U.S. v. Rodriguez*, 532 F.2d 834, 839 (2d Cir. 1976).

D.C. Circuit

- "First we think that Congress, in passing the Immigration and Nationality Act, contemplated a vigorous enforcement program that might include INS entries into private premises for the purpose of questioning any alien or person believed to be an alien, and of detaining those aliens believed to be in this country illegally. Second, since an INS search is conducted pursuant to a civil administrative mandate, the warrant issued to permit such a search may therefore be evaluated under a standard of probable cause different from that applied to criminal warrants. We agree that the District Court's stringent formulation of probable cause was inappropriate in the present situation. [The definition of probable cause called for should] . . . comport with the multiplicity of hybrid administrative law enforcement activities in a non-criminal context." *Blackie's House of Beef, Inc. v. Castillo*, 659 F.2d 1211, 1218–19 (D.C. Cir. 1981).

- "We conclude that the INS's right to enter commercial premises, with a proper warrant, for the purpose of searching out a suspected violation of the immigration laws derives from its general statutory power to seek out and question suspected illegal aliens. . . . [T]he court should have examined the warrant and supporting affidavits with an eye to whether the warrant [contained] sufficient specificity and reliability to prevent the exercise of unbridled discretion by law enforcement officials." *Blackie's House of Beef, Inc. v. Castillo*, 659 F.2d 1211, 1222 (D.C. Cir. 1981).

§ 19:3   Suppression: Illegally seized evidence may be admitted in deportation hearings

Supreme Court

- "At issue here is the exclusion of credible evidence gathered in connection with peaceful arrests by INS officers. We hold that evidence derived from such arrests need not be suppressed in an INS civil deportation hearing." *I.N.S. v. Lopez-Mendoza*, 468 U.S. 1032, 1051, 104 S. Ct. 3479, 82 L. Ed. 2d 778 (1984).

- "INS has already taken sensible and reasonable steps to deter Fourth Amendment violations by its officers, and this makes the likely additional deterrent value of the exclusionary rule small. The costs of applying the exclusionary rule in the context of civil deportation hearings are high. In particular, application of the exclusionary rule in cases such as Sandoval's would compel the courts to release from custody persons who would then immediately resume their commission of a crime through their continuing, unlawful presence in this country. There comes a point at which courts, consistent with their duty to administer the law, cannot continue to create barriers to law enforcement in the pursuit of a supervisory role that is properly the duty of the Executive and Legislative Branches." *I.N.S. v. Lopez-Mendoza*, 468 U.S. 1032, 1050, 104 S. Ct. 3479, 82 L. Ed. 2d 778 (1984).

Second Circuit

- "The exclusionary rule does not apply to civil deportation proceedings, in part because 'a deportation hearing is intended to provide a streamlined determination of eligibility to remain in this country, nothing more.' The Court left open whether exclusion might nevertheless be required for unspecified 'egregious violations of Fourth Amendment or other liberties that might transgress notions of fundamental fairness.' This Court has since answered the question left open in *Lopez-Mendoza* by holding that exclusion of evidence is appropriate if 'record evidence establishe[s] . . . . that an egregious violation that was fundamentally unfair had occurred.' *Almeida–Amaral* posited in dicta some features of egregious abuse: (1) 'if an individual is subjected to a seizure for *no* reason at all, that by itself may constitute an egregious violation, but only if the seizure is sufficiently severe'; and (2) 'even where the seizure is not especially severe, it may nevertheless qualify as an egregious violation if the stop was based on race (or some other grossly improper consideration).' No egregious violation occurred in that case because 'nothing in the record' suggested that the seizure was particularly 'severe'; and petitioner 'offer[ed] nothing other than his own intuition to show that race played a part in the arresting agent's decision.' The court, therefore, had no occasion to explore: (1) how severe an abuse must be to be egregious; (2) what it means for a stop to be 'based on race'; and (3) what 'other' considerations are 'grossly improper.' What is clear, however, is that 'egregious' by definition is very bad indeed, and that the Supreme Court contemplated only such abuses as 'transgress notions of fundamental fairness.' As we have explained, the test for egregiousness is *more* demanding than the test for overcoming qualified immunity. The standard is therefore stringent, entails a shock to the conscience, and is rarely satisfied." *Maldonado v. Holder*, 763 F.3d 155 (2d Cir. 2014) (citations omitted).

- "To warrant a hearing at which the petitioner can adduce evidence in support of suppression, he must do more than simply ask. In *Cotzojay,* we cited with approval the BIA's burden-shifting framework for adjudicating suppression motions in the deportation context: if the petitioner offers an affidavit that could support a basis for excluding the evidence in . . . question, it must then be supported by testimony. If the petitioner establishes a *prima facie* case, the burden of proof shifts to the Government to show why the evidence in question should be admitted. That is no simple matter: An affidavit cannot support a basis for exclusion unless, if taken as true, it makes out an egregious constitutional violation. The affidavit in *Cotzojay* satisfied this test, because it averred facts that were appalling under any standard: a deliberate, nighttime, warrantless entry into an individual's home, without consent and in the absence of exigent circumstances." *Maldonado v. Holder*, 763 F.3d 155 (2d Cir. 2014) (citations and inner quotations omitted).

Fourth Circuit

- "In our case, the IJ, the BIA, and the Attorney General all agree that the exclusionary rule applies in removal proceedings to egregious violations of the Fourth Amendment. Although we have not had occasion to consider the application of the exclusionary rule in removal proceedings in a published opinion, we are in agreement with those courts that have concluded that the rule applies to egregious violations of the Fourth Amendment. To hold otherwise would give no effect to the language used by the Supreme Court in *Lopez–Mendoza* expressing concern over fundamentally unfair methods of obtaining evidence and would ignore the fact that eight justices in *Lopez–Mendoza* seem to have agreed that the exclusionary rule applies in removal proceedings in some form. Moreover, even assuming the Court's limitation in *Lopez–Mendoza* could be construed as dicta, we simply cannot ignore the import of the language used by the Supreme Court in that case. Accordingly, we hold that the exclusionary rule applies in removal proceedings where the challenged evidence has been obtained by 'egregious violations of [the] Fourth Amendment . . . that might transgress notions of fundamental fairness and undermine the probative value of the evidence obtained.' Under this holding, an alien seeking the application of the exclusionary rule to a Fourth Amendment claim in a removal hearing faces two hurdles at the *prima facie* case stage. First, she must allege facts that state a violation of her rights under the Fourth Amendment. Second, the alien must show that the alleged violation of the Fourth Amendment was egregious. To get an evidentiary hearing, the alien must satisfy both prongs. If an evidentiary hearing is warranted, the alien will have the opportunity to present testimony and evidence in support of her Fourth Amendment claim. Upon the establishment of a *prima facie* case, the burden of proof shifts to the government to demonstrate why the IJ should admit the challenged evidence. A court reviewing the alien's claim may, but is not required to, address both the constitutional and egregiousness prongs. Like a § 1983 qualified immunity inquiry, the court can choose to decline to address whether a Fourth Amendment violation has occurred and first address whether the egregiousness prong has been satisfied. Thus, if the alien fails to allege facts sufficient to show that an immigration official has violated the Fourth Amendment, relief can be denied alone on that basis. Alternatively, relief can be denied where the alien fails to allege facts that an immigration official egregiously violated the Fourth Amendment. If there is an evidentiary hearing on the alien's claim, relief can be denied if the alien fails to meet her evidentiary burden on either prong." *Yanez-Marquez v. Lynch*, 789 F.3d 434, 450–51 (4th Cir. 2015) (citations omitted).

- "In our view, the sounder egregiousness approach is the totality of the circumstances standard as applied in the Second, Third, and Eighth Circuits. This standard is a flexible case-by-case standard, taking into account a variety of factors. It allows the court to examine all of the facts it deems relevant to the egregiousness inquiry and focuses on the unreasonableness of the conduct of the law enforcement officers. Factors a court may consider include: (1) whether the Fourth Amendment violation was intentional; (2) whether the violation was unreasonable in addition to being illegal; (3) whether there were threats, coercion, physical abuse, promises, or an unreasonable show of force by the law enforcement officers; (4) whether there was no articulable suspicion for the search or seizure whatsoever; (5) where, when, and how the search, seizure or questioning took place; (6) whether the search, seizure, or questioning was particularly lengthy; (7) whether the law enforcement officers procured an arrest or search warrant; (8) any unique characteristics of the alien involved; and (9) whether the violation was based on racial considerations. This list is not meant to be exhaustive, as there is 'no one-size-fits-all approach to determining whether a Fourth Amendment violation is egregious.' The facts of each case will dictate the relevant factors for consideration. Importantly, the alien's evidence, in its totality, must support a basis to suppress the challenged evidence under a finding of egregiousness, even at the *prima facie* case stage. Such evidence cannot be based on intuition or speculation, especially as it relates to the intent of law enforcement officers. Suppression hearings should be the exception, not the rule in removal proceedings, so the alien's evidentiary burden, even at the *prima facie* case stage, is high." *Yanez-Marquez v. Lynch*, 789 F.3d 434, 460–61 (4th Cir. 2015) (citations omitted).

Fifth Circuit

- "[I]mmigration and deportation records are not suppressible, even if officers on the scene become aware of a defendant's immigration status by means of a constitutional violation." *U.S. v. Scroggins*, 599 F.3d 433 (5th Cir. 2010).

Ninth Circuit

- "In *INS v. Lopez-Mendoza*, the Supreme Court applied the test articulated in *United States v. Janis*, to determine the applicability of the exclusionary rule to civil proceedings, specifically in the context of an immigration hearing. A majority of the Court concluded that, because the deterrent effect of applying the exclusionary rule in civil cases is minimal and its cost is significant, as a general rule, evidence obtained in an unlawful manner will not be excluded from civil proceedings. The *Lopez-Mendoza* Court, however, limited its holding to situations that do not involve egregious violations of Fourth Amendment or other liberties that might transgress notions of fundamental fairness and undermine the probative value of the evidence obtained." *Gonzalez-Rivera v. I.N.S.*, 22 F.3d 1441, 1448 (9th Cir. 1994).

- "[U]nder Ninth Circuit law, all bad faith violation[s] of an individual's fourth amendment rights are considered sufficiently egregious to require application of the exclusionary sanction in a civil proceeding. Under Ninth Circuit law, a bad faith constitutional violation occurs when evidence is obtained by deliberate violations of the fourth amendment, or by conduct a reasonable officer should have known is in violation of the Constitution." *Gonzalez-Rivera v. I.N.S.*, 22 F.3d 1441, 1449 (9th Cir. 1994).

- "In *Adamson*, we took up the Supreme Court's suggestion. We held that, even in administrative proceedings in which the test announced in *United States v. Janis*, eliminates the exclusionary rule, administrative tribunals are still required to exclude evidence that was obtained by deliberate violations of the fourth amendment or by conduct a reasonable officer should know is in violation of the Constitution." *Orhorhaghe v. I.N.S.*, 38 F.3d 488, 493 (9th Cir. 1994).

Chapter 20

Boat Stops and Searches

reasonable suspicion that the area contains
seizable items

Research References

West's Key Number Digest

Customs Duties ⚷126; Drugs and Narcotics ⚷183.10; International Law ⚷7; Searches and Seizures ⚷13, 25.1, 57, 59; Shipping ⚷9

KeyCite®: Cases and other legal materials listed in KeyCite Scope can be researched through the KeyCite service on Westlaw®. Use KeyCite to check citations for form, parallel references, prior and later history, and comprehensive citator information, including citations to other decisions and secondary materials.

---

§ 20:1 Standard: The Fourth Amendment applies to stops and searches conducted by governmental agents within the jurisdiction of the United States, on the high seas, and in foreign waters

Supreme Court

- "The Fourth Amendment not only protects all within our bounds; it also shelters our citizens wherever they may be in the world from unreasonable searches by our own government." *Reid v. Covert*, 354 U.S. 1, 5–6, 77 S. Ct. 1222, 1 L. Ed. 2d 1148 (1957).

First Circuit

- "[B]ecause of the circumstances and exigencies of the maritime setting, we have recognized that individuals have a diminished expectation of privacy on a vessel as opposed to that which can be claimed in their homes." *U.S. v. Cardona-Sandoval*, 6 F.3d 15, 21 (1st Cir. 1993).

Second Circuit

- "While plaintiffs enjoy undiminished privacy expectations in their carry-on baggage and we presume such undiminished expectation in the trunks of their vehicles, we find that the remaining two factors under the "special needs" doctrine weigh heavily in the government's favor. Indeed, given that both the intrusions on plaintiffs' privacy interests are minimal and the measures adopted by LCT are reasonably efficacious in serving the government's undisputedly important special need to protect ferry passengers and crew from terrorist acts, we find no constitutional violation." *Cassidy v. Chertoff*, 471 F.3d 67, 2006 A.M.C. 2863 (2d Cir. 2006).

Third Circuit

- "The sanctity of private dwellings, whether temporary or permanent, generally gives rise to the most stringent Fourth Amendment protection. Individuals have a reasonable and high expectation of privacy in their living and sleeping quarters aboard ships, even at national borders, which merits Fourth Amendment protection." *U.S. v. Whitted*, 50 V.I. 1081, 541 F.3d 480, 43 A.L.R. 6th 771 (3d Cir. 2008).

- "Just as a customs officer is entitled to rely on unconfirmed information relayed to him by his supervisor in order to look out for and search an individual at the border, so too is a customs officer permitted to rely on Treasury Enforcement Communications System (TECS) information entered by other customs officials to create reasonable suspicion for a search." *U.S. v. Whitted*, 50 V.I. 1081, 541 F.3d 480, 43 A.L.R.6th 771 (3d Cir. 2008).

- "[I]n general Fourth Amendment jurisprudence, searches of vessels fall within the exigent circumstances exception to the warrant requirement. In *Carroll v. United States* . . . the Supreme Court held that, practically since the beginning of the government, a warrant has not been required for searches of ships and automobiles because the vehicle can be quickly moved out of the locality or jurisdiction in which the warrant must be sought. . . . The seaworthiness of the Mona Queen gave rise to the risk of flight, meaning that the Coast Guard officers were justified by exigent circumstances in conducting a warrantless search of the vessel." *U.S. v. Boynes*, 149 F.3d 208, 212, 1999 A.M.C. 249, 28 Envtl. L. Rep. 21410 (3d Cir. 1998).

Fifth Circuit

- "[T]he mere existence of a statutory authority to make a search does not obviate the need for Fourth Amendment compliance." *U.S. v. Conroy*, 589 F.2d 1258, 1268 (5th Cir. 1979).

947

D.C. Circuit

- "When the Customs Service successfully stopped [the boat] by means of a flashing strobe light, it conducted a seizure that triggered the protections of the Fourth Amendment." *U.S. v. Gonzalez*, 875 F.2d 875, 877, 1990 A.M.C. 271 (D.C. Cir. 1989).

§ 20:2   Document stops in inland waters: Customs officials may stop a boat in inland waters without reasonable suspicion and board it to inspect its documentation

Supreme Court

- "[C]ustoms officials acting pursuant to [19 U.S.C. § 1581(a) (1976)] and without any suspicion of wrongdoing, [may] board for inspection of documents a vessel that is located in waters providing ready access to the sea." *U.S. v. Villamonte-Marquez*, 462 U.S. 579, 580–81, 103 S. Ct. 2573, 77 L. Ed. 2d 22 (1983).

- "In a lineal ancestor to the statute at issue here the First Congress clearly authorized the suspicionless boarding of vessels, reflecting its view that such boardings are not contrary to the Fourth Amendment; this gives the statute before us an impressive historical pedigree. Random stops without any articulable suspicion of vehicles away from the border are not permissible under the Fourth Amendment . . . but stops at fixed checkpoints or at roadblocks are. The nature of waterborne commerce in waters providing ready access to the open sea is sufficiently different from the nature of vehicular traffic on highways as to make possible alternatives to the sort of stop made in this case less likely to accomplish the obviously essential governmental purposes involved. The system of prescribed outward markings used by States for vehicle registration is also significantly different [from] the system of external markings on vessels, and the extent and type of documentation required by federal law is a good deal more variable and more complex than are the state vehicle registration laws. The nature of the governmental interest in assuring compliance with documentation requirements, particularly in waters where the need to deter or apprehend smugglers is great, are substantial.

All of these factors lead us to conclude that the action of
the Customs officers in stopping and boarding the *Henry
Morgan II* was reasonable, and was therefore consistent
with the Fourth Amendment." *U.S. v. Villamonte-
Marquez*, 462 U.S. 579, 592–93, 103 S. Ct. 2573, 77 L.
Ed. 2d 22 (1983).

First Circuit

- "[A] crew member cannot have an expectation of privacy
  in a space that the Coast Guard is free to inspect in the
  course of a document and safety check. Obviously,
  contraband that the Coast Guard observes within plain
  view (or detects by sensory perception) while searching
  the cargo hold is not within an area in which crew
  members could have a reasonable or legitimate privacy
  interest. This, of course, would apply to the captain as
  well." *U.S. v. Cardona-Sandoval*, 6 F.3d 15, 22 (1st Cir.
  1993).

Eleventh Circuit

- "Officer Bradley testified that Costa Rica is 'a source
  country' for narcotics and child exploitation. Williams
  traveled to Costa Rica alone, using his middle name,
  and had previously taken flights and cruises to Costa
  Rica. Two of Williams's prior flights to and from Costa
  Rica were shortly before he took cruises there, which
  Bradley had seen other cruise ship passengers do to arrange drug deals. Williams had a criminal history, and
  Bradley learned that when Williams traveled using his
  middle name, he was not stopped by Customs. Prior to
  searching Williams's cabin, Bradley had also learned
  that Williams declined to have his room cleaned the
  day he came back onto the ship from Costa Rica. These
  circumstances demonstrate that Williams traveled to 'a
  source country for narcotics and child exploitation' in a
  manner that drug traffickers had been known to use, he
  used the name which would allow him to pass Customs
  officers without being questioned about his criminal
  history, and he declined to have his room cleaned after
  returning from a drug source country. We find no error
  in the district court's conclusion that these seemingly
  innocuous acts nevertheless constituted reasonable
  suspicion to an officer trained in investigating the travel

patterns of cruise passengers." *U.S. v. Williams*, 419
Fed. Appx. 902 (11th Cir. 2011).

- "Customs officers may board a vessel in Customs waters
to check its documents even if the boarding serves
merely as a pretext for the officers' desire to look for
signs of contraband." *U.S. v. Albano*, 722 F.2d 690, 695
(11th Cir. 1984).

D.C. Circuit

- "[T]he Constitution does not impose even a reasonable
suspicion requirement on customs officials stopping a
boat that is capable of ocean travel and is located within
their jurisdiction." *U.S. v. Gonzalez*, 875 F.2d 875, 881,
1990 A.M.C. 271 (D.C. Cir. 1989).

§ 20:3 Investigatory stops in inland waters: Customs officials having a reasonable suspicion that illegal activity is occurring on a vessel in inland waters may make an investigatory stop of the vessel

Fifth Circuit

- "Customs officers may make an investigatory stop of a
vessel on inland waters adjacent to the open Gulf of
Mexico under 19 U.S.C.A. § 1581(a) on facts that justify
a reasonable suspicion of illegal activity. The evidence
need not support suspicion on a border crossing, but
only of the presence of contraband." *U. S. v. D'Antignac*,
628 F.2d 428, 434, 6 Fed. R. Evid. Serv. 1012 (5th Cir.
1980).

Ninth Circuit

- "We hold that the Coast Guard had reasonable suspicion
to believe that the *Myth* was importing drugs. The listing of the *Myth* as a boat suspected of smuggling, the
Myth's unusual location, its attempt to change course,
and its lowered position in the water, indicating that it
was carrying cargo, could reasonably lead a Coast
Guard officer to believe the *Myth* was smuggling
contraband." *U.S. v. Davis*, 905 F.2d 245, 250, 1990
A.M.C. 2289 (9th Cir. 1990).
- "With regard to the officers coming alongside the Red
Baron and immediately stepping onto the deck, [w]e are

persuaded that a boarding is a necessary element of many vessel investigatory stops, given the sound and motion of water, the often significant size differential between the government's boat and the investigated vessel, and the extreme mobility of water craft." *U.S. v. Maybusher*, 735 F.2d 366, 372 (9th Cir. 1984).

- "A stop and boarding after dark must be for cause, requiring at least a reasonable and articulable suspicion of noncompliance, or must be conducted after administrative standards so drafted that the decision to search is not left to the sole discretion of the Coast Guard officer." *U.S. v. Eagon*, 707 F.2d 362, 365 (9th Cir. 1982).

Eleventh Circuit

- "Record testimony reveals that the vessel sailed within striking distance of the Florida coast, was riding very low in the water, seemed to change course when approached, did not stop when requested, and smelled of marijuana prior to the Coast Guard's boarding. These factors, viewed together, were sufficient to induce a reasonable suspicion of violation of United States law." *U.S. v. Mena*, 863 F.2d 1522, 1528 (11th Cir. 1989).

- "Customs officers may make investigatory stops of vessels on inland waters on facts which justify a reasonable suspicion of illegal activity." *U.S. v. Kent*, 691 F.2d 1376, 1378 (11th Cir. 1982).

§ 20:4 Searches in inland waters: Warrantless searches in inland waters are permissible when probable cause and exigent circumstances exist

First Circuit

- "[T]he circumstances and exigencies of the maritime setting afford people on a vessel a lesser expectation of privacy than in their homes, obviating the usual Fourth Amendment requirements of a warrant." *U.S. v. Green*, 671 F.2d 46, 53, 1983 A.M.C. 1665 (1st Cir. 1982).

Third Circuit

- "[I]n general Fourth Amendment jurisprudence, searches of vessels fall within the exigent circumstances exception to the warrant requirement. In *Carroll v.*

United States . . . the Supreme Court held that, practically since the beginning of the government, a warrant has not been required for searches of ships and automobiles because the vehicle can be quickly moved out of the locality or jurisdiction in which the warrant must be sought. . . . The seaworthiness of the Mona Queen gave rise to the risk of flight, meaning that the Coast Guard officers were justified by exigent circumstances in conducting a warrantless search of the vessel." *U.S. v. Boynes*, 149 F.3d 208, 212, 1999 A.M.C. 249, 28 Envtl. L. Rep. 21410 (3d Cir. 1998).

Fifth Circuit

- "The inherent mobility of a vessel and the attendant possibility of flight or disposal of evidence certainly amount to exigent circumstances." *U. S. v. D'Antignac*, 628 F.2d 428, 434, 6 Fed. R. Evid. Serv. 1012 (5th Cir. 1980).

§ 20:5 Border searches: A search of a vessel that has crossed into the territory of the United States is subject to border search standards if the search takes place in an area contiguous to, or a functional equivalent of, the border

First Circuit

- "While it is uncertain what the geographic limits of a seagoing border search may be, the evidence must support a finding that the vessel crossed into territorial waters in order to uphold a governmental incursion as a border search." *U.S. v. Victoria-Peguero*, 920 F.2d 77, 80, 1993 A.M.C. 1520 (1st Cir. 1990).

Fifth Circuit

- "Our precedent establishes that a border crossing occurs whenever a vessel crosses from international waters into the United States, regardless of the defendant's departure point." *U.S. v. Pickett*, 598 F.3d 231 (5th Cir. 2010).

Ninth Circuit

- "The Supreme Court has indicated that the Fourth Amendment is weakened in the context of border searches. . . . Searches conducted at border checkpoints and searches of vessels in waters providing the open sea are analyzed in light of the proximity of the border." *U.S. v. Bulacan*, 156 F.3d 963, 972 (9th Cir. 1998), as amended, (Nov. 16, 1998).

- "[A] search in customs waters is a functional border search when the vessel has crossed from territorial waters of the United States and there is sufficient evidence to convince a fact finder, to a reasonable certainty, that any contraband which might be found at the time of the search was also aboard at the border crossing." *U.S. v. Stanley*, 545 F.2d 661, 667, 1980 A.M.C. 1195 (9th Cir. 1976).

- "[A] search without probable cause pursuant to 19 U.S.C. § 1581(a) of a vessel in a harbor may be valid under the Fourth Amendment as a border search at the functional equivalent of the border . . . where there are articulable facts to support a reasonably certain conclusion by the customs officers that a vessel had crossed the border and entered our territorial waters." *U.S. v. Tilton*, 534 F.2d 1363, 1366 (9th Cir. 1976).

Eleventh Circuit

- "Because of the United States' strong interest in national self-protection, '[r]outine searches of the persons and effects of entrants are not subject to any requirement of reasonable suspicion, probable cause, or warrant.' A person may be subjected to a pat-down search or frisk. A traveler's luggage may be inspected. Incoming international mail may be examined. Vehicles may be searched. All without any level of suspicion. Those searches are 'reasonable simply by virtue of the fact that they occur at the border.' . . . Even at the border, however, reasonable suspicion is required for highly intrusive searches of a person's body such as a strip search or an x-ray examination . . . . While [the defendant] was not subjected to a highly intrusive search of his body, his cabin was searched and that implicates significant Fourth Amendment principles. A cabin is a crew member's home-and a home 'receives the greatest Fourth Amendment protection.' . . . In none of those decisions discussing the Fourth Amendment protections afforded to the home was it at the border, and on that critical distinction this case turns. A home in a fixed location within the United States cannot be used as a means to transport into this country contraband or weapons of mass destruction that threaten national security. A crew member's cabin, like the rest of the ship on which it is located, can and does pose that threat . . . . That threat is the reason why 'the Fourth Amendment balance between the interests of the Government and the privacy right of the individual is . . . struck much more favorably to the Government at the border.' . . . The concern that contraband or worse will be smuggled into this country has special force in modern times. At the dawn of the atomic age, Churchill warned that '[t]he Dark Ages may return-the Stone Age may return on the gleaming wings of science; and what might now shower immeasurable material blessings upon mankind may even bring about its total destruction.'[ ] The gleaming wings of science have brought us readily transportable chemical and biological weapons, and there are reports of suitcase-size nuclear bombs, all of which could be used by terrorists to commit murder on an unimaginable scale and to inflict devastating economic injury. . . . Given the dangers we face, the paramount national interest in conducting border searches to protect this nation and its people makes it unreasonable to require any level of suspicion to search any part of a foreign cargo vessel coming into this country. Crew members' cabins are no exception because, like any other part of a vessel, they can be used to smuggle in weapons of mass destruction, illegal devices, or other contraband." *U.S. v. Alfaro-Moncada*, 607 F.3d 720, 728-30, 2010 A.M.C. 1680 (11th Cir. 2010) (citations omitted).

• "Given the practical difficulties in Maritime law enforcement and other considerations, we think it wise to consider the contiguous zone [3 to 12 miles from the shoreline] the functional equivalent of the border. The standard applied to searches in the contiguous zone will be prescribed by border search standards." *U.S. v. Hidalgo-Gato*, 703 F.2d 1267, 1273 (11th Cir. 1983).

§ 20:6 American vessels on the high seas: United States registered vessels on the high seas are subject to routine safety or documentation inspections

First Circuit

- "Beyond the three mile limit, Congress has designated the customs waters of the United States and authorized federal customs officers to search vessels within those waters, i.e., within twelve miles of shore." *U.S. v. Victoria-Peguero*, 920 F.2d 77, 80, 1993 A.M.C. 1520 (1st Cir. 1990).

- "The sea boundary of United States territory is a marine league (three geographic miles) from shore, and comprises a border for fourth amendment purposes. Because it is not practical to set up checkpoints at the outer perimeter of a country's territorial waters, courts have consistently recognized the constitutionality of warrantless searches at the functional equivalent of the sea border." *U.S. v. Victoria-Peguero*, 920 F.2d 77, 80, 1993 A.M.C. 1520 (1st Cir. 1990).

Fifth Circuit

- "The Coast Guard has plenary authority to board American vessels beyond the twelve mile limit with neither probable cause nor even particularized suspicion [under 14 U.S.C. § 89(a)]. After legally boarding the vessel, [the Officer] noticed the flooding and entered the cabin under his authority to conduct a safety inspection. The bales [of marijuana], in plain view, and the odor emanating from them clearly established probable cause sufficient to justify a full and complete search." *U.S. v. Hicks*, 624 F.2d 32, 33 (5th Cir. 1980).

- "14 U.S.C. § 89(a) confers on the Coast Guard plenary power to stop and board any American flag vessel anywhere on the high sea in the complete absence of suspicion of criminal activity, at least for the purpose of conducting an administrative inspection. . . . If the administrative inspection gives rise to a suspicion of criminal activity, a full search may be conducted. A search warrant is not necessary." *U.S. v. Robbins*, 623 F.2d 418, 420 (5th Cir. 1980).

Eleventh Circuit

955

- "This circuit has long recognized that the Coast Guard's routine stop, boarding and inspection of an American vessel on the high seas does not normally rise to the level of custodial detention thus requiring *Miranda* warnings." *U.S. v. Rioseco*, 845 F.2d 299, 302, 18 Envtl. L. Rep. 21106 (11th Cir. 1988).

§ 20:7 Foreign vessels on the high seas: The Coast Guard may stop and search a foreign vessel on the high seas if it has a reasonable suspicion that those aboard the vessel are involved in criminal activity

First Circuit

- "A foreign vessel can be constructively within customs waters, even though it is on the high seas, if there is a treaty or other arrangement between a foreign government and the United States enabling or permitting the authorities of the United States to board, examine, search, seize, or otherwise to enforce upon such vessel upon the high seas the laws of the United States." *U.S. v. Molinares Charris*, 822 F.2d 1213, 1216–17, 23 Fed. R. Evid. Serv. 498 (1st Cir. 1987).

- "[T]he Coast Guard's failure to obtain Honduras' consent to search a Honduran ship on the high seas did not require suppression of the evidence found. The purpose of international law's consent requirement is to protect nations, not individuals; and, if the nation does not care, the individual cannot raise lack of consent as a ground for suppression." *U.S. v. Kincaid*, 712 F.2d 1, 3 (1st Cir. 1983).

- "[A] Coast Guard helicopter had surprised the *Persistence* in a rendezvous with a fishing vessel. The ships had taken off in different directions. A different Coast Guard cutter had caught up with the *Persistence* later that day, boarded, and found a man who was the subject of a Drug Enforcement Administration warrant. Three days later, the Coast Guard had located the fishing vessel . . . with marijuana residue in the hold. [When sighted] the *Persistence* was riding sluggishly, low in the water, and heavy in the bow. [S]he did not respond until after two hours to the Coast Guard's efforts to hail her by radio. The response then . . . [was]

contradictory. These facts, when taken together, gave the officers a reasonable and articulable suspicion that the *Persistence* was carrying marijuana below deck." *U.S. v. Green*, 671 F.2d 46, 54, 1983 A.M.C. 1665 (1st Cir. 1982).

Second Circuit

• "[A]n officer having a reasonable suspicion, based on articulable, objective facts, that criminal activity is afoot may make an investigatory stop that is reasonable both in its duration and its intrusiveness on the individual's legitimate privacy expectations. [D]iffering expectations of privacy in various kinds of . . . vessels may result in differences in the balancing of the interests relevant in assessing the reasonableness of an investigatory stop, but they do not make inapplicable the principles which require that balancing be done." *U.S. v. Streifel*, 665 F.2d 414, 422–23, 1982 A.M.C. 1155 (2d Cir. 1981).

Fifth Circuit

• "[14 U.S.C.] section 89(a) authorizes the Coast Guard to seize a foreign vessel in international waters if the Coast Guard first has a reasonable suspicion that those aboard the vessel are engaged in a conspiracy to smuggle contraband into the United States." *U.S. v. Williams*, 617 F.2d 1063, 1074, 1980 A.M.C. 2550 (5th Cir. 1980).

Ninth Circuit

• "Here, the alleged unconstitutional delay took place outside of the United States in international waters, and there is no suggestion that (defendant) had any substantial connection to this country . . . Because (defendant) cannot show that he is one of the "People of the United States," . . . he is not entitled to protection under the Fourth Amendment." *U.S. v. Zakharov*, 468 F.3d 1171 (9th Cir. 2006).

• "Although the Ninth Circuit has not directly addressed the issue of the timing of consent, it is logical that the Coast Guard may seize a ship before it receives permission from the flag nation. Obtaining consent can be a lengthy process. If the Coast Guard could not hold a suspected ship while waiting, the ship would have an opportunity to escape or to destroy evidence. In this case, the Coast Guard secured the ship only to eliminate this chance of escape; it did not arrest the crew until St. Vincent consented to United States authority. For these reasons, we hold that the Coast Guard's boarding and searching of the LUCKY STAR, with the ship master's consent, before obtaining consent of the flag nation, did not deprive the United States of jurisdiction." *U.S. v. Khan*, 35 F.3d 426, 430, 1996 A.M.C. 1213 (9th Cir. 1994).

- "We hold that the protections of the fourth amendment do not extend to the search of the *Myth* on the high seas. Although *Verdugo-Urquidez* only held that the fourth amendment does not apply to searches and seizures of nonresident aliens in foreign countries, the analysis and language adopted by the Court creates no exception for searches of nonresident aliens on the high seas." *U.S. v. Davis*, 905 F.2d 245, 251, 1990 A.M.C. 2289 (9th Cir. 1990).

§ 20:8 American vessels in foreign waters: Unless the sovereign power involved objects, the Coast Guard has the authority to stop and search United States vessels in foreign waters on a showing of probable cause coupled with exigent circumstances

Fifth Circuit

- "The pattern of legislation . . . and the subsequent congressional action [of 14 U.S.C. § 89(a)] make it clear that, in the absence of objection by the sovereign power involved, Congress intended the Coast Guard to have authority to stop and search American vessels on foreign waters as well as on the high sea and in territorial waters." *U.S. v. Conroy*, 589 F.2d 1258, 1266–67 (5th Cir. 1979).

- "[The statute, 14 U.S.C. § 89(a), is] a grant of plenary authority to stop and board United States vessels on the high seas for either a safety-and-document inspection or to check for obvious customs and narcotics violations. Once aboard, if probable cause arises to suspect the presence of narcotics, a search can then be made of the vessel." *U.S. v. Conroy*, 589 F.2d 1258, 1268 (5th Cir. 1979).

§ 20:9 Scope of searches: The Coast Guard may not search a private area of a ship unless it has a reasonable suspicion that the area contains seizable items

First Circuit

- "In the maritime context, the relative intrusiveness of a search must be justified by a corresponding level of suspicion supported by specific facts gathered by investigating officials. We recognize that by allowing each inspection to provide the basis for a more intrusive search—document and safety inspection supplying reasonable suspicion which later supports a probable cause determination—we risk manipulation by government officials of the factual progression that provided the authority for ever more intrusive searches. More intrusive searches that yield no contraband can halt the forward progression evidence that would justify a full, destructive search. Thus, if a document and safety inspection causes a Coast Guard officer to have reasonable suspicion with respect to certain areas, and a search of those areas yields nothing, then a destructive search might not be justified. Ultimately, a full, stem to stern, destructive search may only be conducted on the basis of probable cause." *U.S. v. Cardona-Sandoval*, 6 F.3d 15, 23–24 (1st Cir. 1993).

- "Because of the special circumstances implicated by searches and seizures of vessels while at sea, we have recognized a diminished expectation of privacy. Nevertheless, we require that the Coast Guard possess reasonable and articulable grounds for suspecting that the vessel or those on board are engaging in criminal activities before conducting a thorough search beyond checking for compliance with safety regulations. The necessary reasonable suspicion may be formed on the basis of facts obtained during the safety and document inspection, and once reasonable suspicion exists the inspecting officers may drill into a suspicious area to search for contraband. Both the document and safety inspection, and a search pursuant to reasonable suspicion, must be confined to areas reasonably incident to the purpose of the inspection. Therefore, a reasonable suspicion search only authorizes a limited intrusion. For example, if a particular area of a vessel raises a reasonable suspicion, then that area may be investigated further. Neither authority provides carte blanche to destroy a vessel." *U.S. v. Cardona-Sandoval*, 6 F.3d 15, 23 (1st Cir. 1993).

Third Circuit

- "Under the reasonable suspicion standard, to conduct a search of a passenger cabin on a ship, customs officers must be able to articulate reasons that led to the search of the cabin that are indicative of behavior in which most innocent people do not engage. Reasonable suspicion is not a high standard that will prevent customs officers from detecting drug smugglers at our borders. Rather, it sets a relatively low threshold that will continue to permit the kind of cabin searches customs officers currently conduct." *U.S. v. Whitted*, 50 V.I. 1081, 541 F.3d 480, 43 A.L.R.6th 771 (3d Cir. 2008).

- "Individuals have a reasonable and high expectation of privacy in their living and sleeping quarters aboard ships, even at national borders, which merits Fourth Amendment protection. As a passenger of a cruise liner, Whitted had a reasonable expectation of privacy in his cabin: he excluded others from it, used it as his home, and slept and conducted his daily life therein. This expectation was eminently reasonable from an objective standpoint. As the Supreme Court has recognized, [w]e are at our most vulnerable when we are asleep because we cannot monitor our own safety or the security of our belongings. It is for this reason that, although we may spend all day in public places, when we cannot sleep in our own home we seek out another private place to sleep, whether it be a hotel room, or the home of a friend. Just as individuals seek privacy in hotel rooms or another's home to sleep, cruise ship passengers seek out privacy in their sleeping cabins and expect that they will not be opened or intruded upon without consent. A search of a individual's living quarters is among the most intrusive of searches-invading as it does a place where the individual expects not to be disturbed." *U.S. v. Whitted*, 50 V.I. 1081, 541 F.3d 480, 43 A.L.R.6th 771 (3d Cir. 2008).

Fifth Circuit

- "[T]he fourth amendment requires at least a reasonable suspicion that contraband or evidence of criminal activity will be found before the Coast Guard may, pursuant to section 89(a), search a private area of the hold of a vessel in international waters for the purpose of finding such items. It follows, of course, that, in the context of such searches, the fourth amendment does *not* require a search warrant." *U.S. v. Williams*, 617 F.2d 1063, 1087, 1980 A.M.C. 2550 (5th Cir. 1980).
- "The only limit upon the Coast Guard's authority to search vessels lawfully boarded is that it may not search private areas for the purpose of finding evidence of criminal activity without reason to suspect the existence there of such evidence." *U.S. v. Robbins*, 623 F.2d 418, 420 (5th Cir. 1980).

Eleventh Circuit

- "A secret compartment constructed within the confines of the hull of the ship is totally unlike a personal dufflebag or footlocker in terms of the uses to which it may be put, and the expectations of exclusive control to which it gives rise. We cannot imagine that society would recognize a reasonable expectation of privacy in the use of dead space in the hull of a ship, sealed with permanent fiberglass and painted to match the surrounding surfaces, for the legitimate storage of personal items." *U.S. v. Lopez*, 761 F.2d 632, 636 (11th Cir. 1985).

Chapter 21

Administrative Searches

§ 21:1   Rule: A search warrant is generally required to make a search or inspection to check compliance with regulatory requirements

§ 21:2   Standard: To obtain an administrative search warrant, the government must show that reasonable administrative standards for conducting inspections are being followed with respect to the premises to be searched

§ 21:3   Closely regulated industries: Industries with a long history of pervasive governmental regulation may be inspected without a warrant

§ 21:4   Emergencies: In emergency situations a warrant may not be required

§ 21:5   Vital government interest: Warrantless administrative searches which further vital governmental interests are reasonable if the public interest is great and the intrusion minor

§ 21:6   Scope: Statute providing for inspection outlines scope of administrative search

Research References

West's Key Number Digest

Fires ⊶9; Searches and Seizures ⊶12, 23, 26, 67, 79, 129

KeyCite®: Cases and other legal materials listed in KeyCite Scope can be researched through the KeyCite service on Westlaw®. Use KeyCite to check citations for form, parallel references, prior and later history, and comprehensive citator information, including citations to other decisions and secondary materials.

---

§ 21:1   Rule: A search warrant is generally required to make a search or inspection to check compliance with regulatory requirements

Supreme Court

• "A judicial warrant and probable cause are not needed

where the search or seizure is justified by 'special needs, beyond the normal need for law enforcement,' such as the need to deter drug use in public schools, or the need to assure that railroad employees engaged in train operations are not under the influence of drugs or alcohol, and where the search or seizure is in execution of an administrative warrant authorizing, for example, an inspection of fire-damaged premises to determine the cause, or an inspection of residential premises to assure compliance with a housing code. But those exceptions do not apply where the officer's purpose is not to attend to the special needs or to the investigation for which the administrative inspection is justified." *Ashcroft v. al-Kidd*, 563 U.S. 731, 131 S. Ct. 2074, 2081, 179 L. Ed. 2d 1149 (2011) (citations omitted).

- "A four-Justice plurality concluded that the correct analysis has two steps. First, because 'some [government] offices may be so open . . . that no expectation of privacy is reasonable,' a court must consider '[t]he operational realities of the workplace' to determine if an employee's constitutional rights are implicated. Second, where an employee has a legitimate privacy expectation, an employer's intrusion on that expectation 'for noninvestigatory, work-related purposes, as well as for investigations of work-related misconduct, should be judged by the standard of reasonableness under all the circumstances.' " *City of Ontario, Cal. v. Quon*, 560 U.S. 746, 130 S. Ct. 2619, 2622-23, 177 L. Ed. 2d 216, 30 I.E.R. Cas. (BNA) 1345, 93 Empl. Prac. Dec. (CCH) P 43907, 159 Lab. Cas. (CCH) P 61011 (2010).

- "We have. . .allowed searches for certain administrative purposes without particularized suspicion of misconduct, provided that those searches are appropriately limited." *City of Indianapolis v. Edmond*, 531 U.S. 32, 37, 121 S. Ct. 447, 148 L. Ed. 2d 333 (2000).

- "We hold, therefore, that public employer intrusions on the constitutionally protected privacy interests of government employees for noninvestigatory, work-related purposes, as well as for investigations of work-related misconduct, should be judged by the standard of reasonableness under all the circumstances. Under this reasonableness standard, both the inception and the scope of the intrusion must be reasonable. [There must be reasonable grounds for suspecting] that the employee is guilty of work-related misconduct, or that the search is necessary for a noninvestigatory work-related purpose such as to retrieve a needed file." *O'Connor v. Ortega*, 480 U.S. 709, 725, 107 S. Ct. 1492, 94 L. Ed. 2d 714, 1 I.E.R. Cas. (BNA) 1617, 42 Empl. Prac. Dec. (CCH) P 36891 (1987).

- "Searches for administrative purposes, like searches for evidence of crime, are encompassed by the Fourth Amendment. The officials may be health, fire, or building inspectors. Their purpose may be to locate and abate a suspected public nuisance, or simply to perform a routine periodic inspection. The privacy that is invaded may be sheltered by the walls of a warehouse or other commercial establishment not open to the public. These deviations from the typical police search are . . . clearly within the protection of the Fourth Amendment." *Michigan v. Tyler*, 436 U.S. 499, 504–06, 98 S. Ct. 1942, 56 L. Ed. 2d 486 (1978).

- "The Warrant Clause of the Fourth Amendment protects commercial buildings as well as private homes. To hold otherwise would belie the origin of that Amendment, and the American colonial experience." *Marshall v. Barlow's, Inc.*, 436 U.S. 307, 311, 98 S. Ct. 1816, 56 L. Ed. 2d 305, 6 O.S.H. Cas. (BNA) 1571, 1978 O.S.H. Dec. (CCH) P 22735, 8 Envtl. L. Rep. 20434 (1978).

- "The basic purpose of [the Fourth] Amendment . . . is to safeguard the privacy and security of individuals against arbitrary invasions by governmental officials. [O]ne governing principle, justified by history and by current experience, has consistently been followed: except in certain carefully defined classes of cases, a search of private property without a proper consent is unreasonable unless it has been authorized by a valid search warrant." *Camara v. Municipal Court of City and County of San Francisco*, 387 U.S. 523, 528–29, 87 S. Ct. 1727, 18 L. Ed. 2d 930 (1967).

- "[W]e see no justification for . . . relaxing Fourth Amendment safeguards where the official inspection is intended to aid enforcement of laws prescribing minimum physical standards for commercial premises. The businessman, like the occupant of a residence, has a constitutional right to go about his business free from unreasonable official entries upon his private commercial property. The businessman, too, has that right placed in jeopardy if the decision to enter and inspect for a violation of regulatory laws can be made and enforced by the inspector in the field without official authority evidenced by a warrant." *See v. City of Seattle*, 387 U.S. 541, 543, 87 S. Ct. 1737, 18 L. Ed. 2d 943 (1967).

First Circuit

- "The circumstances and exigencies of the maritime setting afford people on a vessel a lesser expectation of privacy than in their homes, obviating the usual fourth amendment requirements of a warrant." *U.S. v. Vilches-Navarrete*, 523 F.3d 1 (1st Cir. 2008).
- "[S]pecifically, our inquiry is whether a company has a reasonable expectation of privacy in industrial wastewater that is on a private street and underneath a 171-pound manhole cover but 300 feet away from and flowing irrevocably into the public sewer system. The EPA inspectors urge that we adopt a per se rule that there is never a reasonable expectation of privacy in wastewater. This we decline to do. Judgments about reasonable expectations of privacy are very fact-specific, and there may be fact situations where wastewater is entitled to constitutional protection. . . . Ultimately, we conclude that the controlling fact here is that the wastewater at Manhole 1 is irretrievably flowing into the public sewer, which is only 300 feet away. The wastewater will inevitably reach Manhole 2, where the public sewer begins, after only a short period of time, and once it reaches that point, any member of the public can take a sample. Wastewater at Manhole 1 under these circumstances is similar to trash left out on the curb for pick-up by the trash collector, which enjoys no reasonable expectation of privacy, even if left in opaque bags." *Riverdale Mills Corp. v. Pimpare*, 392 F.3d 55, 59 Env't. Rep. Cas. (BNA) 1801, 35 Envtl. L. Rep. 20004 (1st Cir. 2004).
- "An administrative subpoena is not self-executing and is therefore technically not a search. It is at most a constructive search, amounting to no more than a simple direction to produce documents, subject to

judicial review and enforcement. Thus, unlike the subject of an actual search, the subject of an administrative subpoena has an opportunity to challenge the subpoena before yielding the information. In the course of that resistance, the Fourth Amendment is available to the challenger as a defense against enforcement of the subpoena." *U.S. v. Sturm, Ruger & Co., Inc.*, 84 F.3d 1, 3, 17 O.S.H. Cas. (BNA) 1604, 1995-1997 O.S.H. Dec. (CCH) P 31189 (1st Cir. 1996).

Second Circuit

- "We hold, based on the particular facts of this case, that [plaintiff] had a reasonable expectation of privacy in the contents of his office computer. . . [Plaintiff] occupied a private office with a door. He had exclusive use of the desk, filing cabinet, and computer in his office. [Plaintiff] did not share use of his computer with other employees in the Accounting Bureau nor was there evidence that visitors or the public had access to his computer. We are aware that public employees' expectations of privacy in their offices, desks, and file cabinets, like similar expectations of employees in the private sector, may be reduced by virtue of actual office practices and procedures, or by legitimate regulation. Construing the evidence in favor of [plaintiff], as we must in reviewing this grant of summary judgment against him, we do not find that the [employer] either had a general practice of routinely conducting searches of office computers or had placed [plaintiff] on notice that he should have no expectation of privacy in the contents of his office computer. . . . Even though [plaintiff] had some expectation of privacy in the contents of his office computer, the investigatory searches by the [employer] did not violate his Fourth Amendment rights. An investigatory search for evidence of suspected work-related employee misfeasance will be constitutionally reasonable if it is justified at its inception and of appropriate scope. We agree with the district court that both of these requirements are satisfied here." *Leventhal v. Knapek*, 266 F.3d 64, 17 I.E.R. Cas. (BNA) 1697, 144 Lab. Cas. (CCH) P 59372 (2d Cir. 2001).
- "*O'Connor v. Ortega*, the Supreme Court held that the usual requirements of a warrant and probable cause for

government searches do not apply to a government's work-related investigation into the performance of its own employee. . . . A four-Justice plurality concluded that investigations of work-related misconduct should be judged by the standard of reasonableness under all the circumstances. . . . A fifth Justice stated that he would hold that government searches . . . to investigate violations of workplace rules—searches of the sort that are regarded as reasonable and normal in the private-employer context—do not violate the Fourth Amendment." *Gudema v. Nassau County*, 163 F.3d 717, 723 (2d Cir. 1998).

Fourth Circuit

- "The Toxic Substances Control Act (TSCA) provides the EPA with inspection authority. Specifically, for purposes of administering TSCA, the EPA may inspect any establishment, facility, or other premises in which substances regulated by the Act are manufactured, processed, stored, or held before or after their distribution in commerce. In addition, this inspection authority reaches any conveyance being used to transport a regulated substance in connection with distribution in commerce. EPA's inspection powers extend to all things within the premises or conveyance inspected that bear on whether the requirements of TSCA have been met with respect to regulated substances within such premises or conveyance. The EPA's inspection authority under TSCA carries with it the authority to obtain a warrant. When Congress invests an agency with enforcement and investigatory authority, it is not necessary for Congress to identify explicitly each and every technique that may be used in executing the statutory mission. . . . Instead, regulatory or enforcement authority generally carries with it all the modes of inquiry and investigation traditionally employed or useful to execute the authority granted. A federal regulatory agency is authorized to apply for a warrant to execute a statutory grant of inspection authority." *U.S. v. M/V SANCTUARY*, 540 F.3d 295, 67 Env't. Rep. Cas. (BNA) 1481, 2008 A.M.C. 2221 (4th Cir. 2008).
- "Probable cause for an administrative warrant may be based on (1) specific evidence of an existing violation, or

(2) a showing that reasonable legislative or administrative standards for conducting an inspection are satisfied with respect to a particular establishment." *U.S. v. M/V SANCTUARY*, 540 F.3d 295, 67 Env't. Rep. Cas. (BNA) 1481, 2008 A.M.C. 2221 (4th Cir. 2008).

- "One exception to the warrant requirement arises when the requirement is rendered impracticable by special needs, beyond the normal need for law enforcement. . . . In *O'Connor*, the Supreme Court held that a government employer's interest in the efficient and proper operation of the workplace may justify warrantless work-related searches. . . . In particular, the *O'Connor* Court held that when a government employer conducts a search pursuant to an investigation of work-related misconduct, the Fourth Amendment will be satisfied if the search is reasonable in its inception and its scope." *U.S. v. Simons*, 206 F.3d 392, 400 (4th Cir. 2000).

Fifth Circuit

- "In companion cases, the Court did extend a warrant requirement of a sort to administrative inspections of private homes and business properties, the purpose of which was to verify compliance with municipal health and safety codes. . . .Balancing the need for searches against the property owners' privacy, the Court concluded that warrants were necessary to check the unfettered discretion code enforcement officers had in the field." *Freeman v. City of Dallas*, 242 F.3d 642, 650 (5th Cir. 2001).

Sixth Circuit

- "Although the Fourth Amendment provides some protection against administrative or regulatory searches, such investigations are generally less intrusive than one which could potentially lead to criminal sanctions, and are accordingly more likely to be tolerated under the Fourth Amendment." *Jacob v. Township of West Bloomfield*, 531 F.3d 385 (6th Cir. 2008).

Seventh Circuit

- "[A] warrant or probable cause standard does not apply when a government employer conducts a search of its employees' offices, desks or files. . . . [T]he *O'Connor* plurality required only that such searches be 'reasonable.' To be considered legally valid under the plurality's reasoning, a search must be reasonable in both its inception and scope. A search will be justified in its inception when the search is necessary for a non-investigatory work-related purpose such as to receive a work-related file. A search is reasonable in scope when the search methods adopted are reasonably related to the objectives of the search and are not overly intrusive in light of the alleged misconduct. [T]he search conducted in the instant case was reasonable. . . . [T]he County Prosecutor had a policy of retrieving files from the offices of terminated employees (even before they have been afforded the opportunity to remove all of their personal effects) upon termination. The district court did not find that prosecutors initially entered [defendant's] office with knowledge of [defendant's] participation in a bribery scheme or in an effort to marshal evidence against him. In light of these facts, we agree with the district court's factual determination that the search of [defendant's] office lacked an investigatory pretext and find that it was reasonable in its inception. In addition, we find that the search was reasonable in its scope. Based upon the evidence presented, the prosecutors did not engage in overly intrusive or abusive tactics. Rather, . . . the prosecutors searched only those areas that were likely to contain work-related materials." *U.S. v. Fernandes*, 272 F.3d 938 (7th Cir. 2001).

- "The Supreme Court has, under carefully defined circumstances, upheld a variety of suspicionless (and warrantless) searches and seizures conducted as part of regulatory schemes. In these cases, however, the standards are different from those applied to searches and seizures conducted in the course of criminal investigations." *U.S. v. Johnson*, 170 F.3d 708, 717 (7th Cir. 1999).

- "Although *Camara* and the other decisions that allow the use of warrants for administrative or regulatory searches modify the conventional understanding of the Fourth Amendment's probable cause requirement for warrants, since it is the essence of such searches that there is no probable cause to believe that a particular search will yield evidence of a violation of law, the Supreme Court has not as yet held that the other requirements of the amendment's warrant clause—that the warrant be (1) under oath and describe with particularity (2) the place to be searched and (3) the persons or things to be seized—are to be bent for administrative warrants." *Platteville Area Apartment Ass'n v. City of Platteville*, 179 F.3d 574, 578 (7th Cir. 1999).

Ninth Circuit

- "It is well established that searches conducted as part of a general regulatory scheme, done in furtherance of administrative goals rather than to secure evidence of a crime, may be permissible under the Fourth Amendment without a particularized showing of probable cause." *U.S. v. Bulacan*, 156 F.3d 963, 967 (9th Cir. 1998), as amended, (Nov. 16, 1998).

§ 21:2 Standard: To obtain an administrative search warrant, the government must show that reasonable administrative standards for conducting inspections are being followed with respect to the premises to be searched

Supreme Court

- "[A local ordinance provides that a] hotel owner who refuses to give an officer access to his or her registry can be arrested on the spot. The Court has held that business owners cannot reasonably be put to this kind of choice. Absent an opportunity for precompliance review, the ordinance creates an intolerable risk that searches authorized by it will exceed statutory limits, or be used as a pretext to harass hotel operators and their guests. Even if a hotel has been searched 10 times a day, every day, for three months, without any violation being found, the operator can only refuse to comply with an officer's demand to turn over the registry at his or her own peril. To be clear, we hold only that a hotel owner must be afforded an *opportunity* to have a neutral decisionmaker review an officer's demand to search the registry before he or she faces penalties for failing to comply. Actual review need only occur in those rare instances where a hotel operator objects to turning over the registry. Moreover, this opportunity can be provided without imposing onerous burdens on those charged with an administrative scheme's enforcement. . . . Of course administrative subpoenas are only one way in which an opportunity for precompliance review can be made available. But whatever the precise form, the availability of precompliance review alters the dynamic between the officer and the hotel to be searched, and reduces the risk that officers will use these administrative searches as a pretext to harass business owners." *City of Los Angeles, Calif. v. Patel*, 135 S. Ct. 2443, 2452–53, 2454, 192 L. Ed. 2d 435 (2015).

- "Fourth Amendment reasonableness 'is predominantly an objective inquiry.' We ask whether 'the circumstances, viewed objectively, justify [the challenged] action.' If so, that action was reasonable '*whatever* the subjective intent' motivating the relevant officials. This approach recognizes that the Fourth Amendment regulates conduct rather than thoughts, and it promotes evenhanded, uniform enforcement of the law. Two 'limited exception[s]' to this rule are our special-needs and administrative-search cases, where 'actual motivations' do matter." *Ashcroft v. al-Kidd*, 563 U.S. 731, 131 S. Ct. 2074, 2080–81, 179 L. Ed. 2d 1149 (2011) (citations omitted).

- "While reasonableness under the Fourth Amendment is predominantly an objective inquiry, our special needs and administrative search cases demonstrate that purpose is often relevant when suspicionless intrusions pursuant to a general scheme are at issue." *City of Indianapolis v. Edmond*, 531 U.S. 32, 47, 121 S. Ct. 447, 148 L. Ed. 2d 333 (2000).

- "If the primary object is to determine the cause and origin of a recent fire, an administrative warrant will suffice. To obtain such a warrant, fire officials need show only that a fire of undetermined origin has occurred on the premises, that the scope of the proposed search is reasonable and will not intrude unnecessarily on the fire victim's privacy, and that the search will be executed at a reasonable and convenient time. If the primary object of the search is to gather evidence of criminal activity, a criminal search warrant may be obtained only on a showing of probable cause to believe that relevant evidence will be found in the place to be searched. If evidence of criminal activity is discovered during the course of a valid administrative search, it may be seized under the plain view doctrine." *Michigan v. Clifford*, 464 U.S. 287, 294, 104 S. Ct. 641, 78 L. Ed. 2d 477 (1984).

- "Whether the Secretary proceeds to secure a warrant or other process, with or without prior notice, [p]robable cause in the criminal law sense is not required. For purposes of an administrative search such as this, probable cause justifying the issuance of a warrant may be based not only on specific evidence of an existing violation but also on a showing that reasonable legislative or administrative standards for conducting an . . . inspection are satisfied with respect to a particular [establishment]." *Marshall v. Barlow's, Inc.*, 436 U.S. 307, 320, 98 S. Ct. 1816, 56 L. Ed. 2d 305, 6 O.S.H. Cas. (BNA) 1571, 1978 O.S.H. Dec. (CCH) P 22735, 8 Envtl. L. Rep. 20434 (1978).

- "The agency's particular demand for access will of course be measured, in terms of probable cause to issue a warrant, against a flexible standard of reasonableness that takes into account the public need for effective enforcement of the particular regulation involved." *See v. City of Seattle*, 387 U.S. 541, 545, 87 S. Ct. 1737, 18 L. Ed. 2d 943 (1967).

- "[W]e think that a number of persuasive factors combine to support the reasonableness of [administrative] inspection. First, such programs have a long history of judicial and public acceptance. . . . Second, the public interest demands that all dangerous conditions be prevented or abated, yet it is doubtful that any other canvassing technique would achieve acceptable results. Finally, because the inspections are neither personal in nature nor aimed at the discovery of evidence of crime, they involve a relatively limited invasion of the . . . citizen's privacy." *Camara v. Municipal Court of City and County of San Francisco*, 387 U.S. 523, 537, 87 S. Ct. 1727, 18 L. Ed. 2d 930 (1967).

First Circuit

- "The requirements for enforcement of an administrative

subpoena are not onerous. In order to obtain judicial backing the agency must prove that (1) the subpoena is issued for a congressionally authorized purpose, the information sought is (2) relevant to the authorized purpose and (3) adequately described, and (4) proper procedures have been employed in issuing the subpoena. As long as the agency satisfies these modest requirements, the subpoena is per se reasonable and Fourth Amendment concerns are deemed satisfied." *U.S. v. Sturm, Ruger & Co., Inc.*, 84 F.3d 1, 4, 17 O.S.H. Cas. (BNA) 1604, 1995-1997 O.S.H. Dec. (CCH) P 31189 (1st Cir. 1996).

Fifth Circuit

- "It is settled law that the Fourth Amendment applies not only to searches and seizures of private homes, but also to searches and seizures of commercial premises. Under certain circumstances, however, warrantless searches on commercial property may be reasonable within the meaning of the Fourth Amendment. Specifically, the Supreme Court has recognized an exception to the warrant requirement for searches of closely or pervasively regulated industries, provided three criteria are met: First, there must be a substantial government interest that informs the regulatory scheme pursuant to which the inspection is made. Second, the warrantless inspections must be necessary to further the regulatory scheme. Finally, the statute's inspection program, in terms of the certainty and regularity of its application, must provide a constitutionally adequate substitute for a warrant." *U.S. v. Blocker*, 104 F.3d 720, 726–27 (5th Cir. 1997).

- "The search will be reasonable if based either on (1) specific evidence of an existing violation, (2) a showing that reasonable legislative or administrative standards for conducting an inspection are satisfied with respect to a particular [establishment] or (3) a showing that the search is pursuant to an administrative plan containing specific neutral criteria." *U.S. v. Harris Methodist Fort Worth*, 970 F.2d 94, 101, 38 Soc. Sec. Rep. Serv. 207, 59 Empl. Prac. Dec. (CCH) P 41728 (5th Cir. 1992).

Seventh Circuit

- "When the Supreme Court authorized administrative searches of residential housing, it didn't grant state and local governments carte blanche. The requirement of reasonableness that the Fourth Amendment imposes on all searches, whether or not pursuant to warrant, entails the striking of a balance between the benefits of an administrative search in implementing valid governmental programs and its costs to the property and privacy interests of the persons whose homes. . .are searched." *Platteville Area Apartment Ass'n v. City of Platteville*, 179 F.3d 574, 581 (7th Cir. 1999).
- "[T]he Supreme Court, in *Marshall v. Barlow's, Inc.*, made clear that for nonconsensual OSHA inspections a warrant is necessary. Probable cause in the criminal law sense is not required. Probable cause may be based on (1) specific evidence of an existing violation or (2) on a showing that the inspection is part of a reasonable legislative or administrative plan. This court has stated that when an administrative search is predicated on an employee complaint, a warrant may issue upon a showing of the relaxed standard of administrative probable cause. A mere allegation of danger from an employee without sufficient documentation or supporting data is insufficient; in order to establish administrative probable cause, the warrant application must support a reasonable belief or lead to a reasonable suspicion that the OSHA Act or its regulations have been violated." *Matter of Establishment Inspection of Kelly-Springfield Tire Co.*, 13 F.3d 1160, 1166, 16 O.S.H. Cas. (BNA) 1561, 1994 O.S.H. Dec. (CCH) P 30314 (7th Cir. 1994).

Eighth Circuit

- "An administrative subpoena, unlike a warrant, does not need to be supported by probable cause and is analyzed under the Fourth Amendment's general reasonableness standard. 'The showing of reasonable cause required to support an application for enforcement of a subpoena duces tecum "is satisfied . . . by the court's determination that the investigation is authorized by Congress, is for a purpose Congress can order, and the documents sought are relevant to the inquiry."' It is well established that a 'subpoena is properly enforced if (1) issued pursuant to lawful authority, (2) for a lawful purpose, (3) requesting information relevant to the lawful purpose, and (4) the information sought is not unreasonable.' If an agency has satisfied these requirements for an administrative subpoena, the burden shifts to the respondent to show that judicial enforcement 'would amount to an abuse of the court's process.' . . . . Because the Government has satisfied the requirements for judicial enforcement of the subpoenas, Whispering Oaks bears the burden of showing enforcement would be an abuse of process. The court's process is abused when a subpoena is 'issued for an improper purpose, such as to harass the [respondent] or to put pressure on him to settle a collateral dispute, or for any other purpose reflecting on the good faith of the particular investigation.' " *U.S. v. Whispering Oaks Residential Care Facility, LLC*, 673 F.3d 813, 817 (8th Cir. 2012) (citations omitted).

Ninth Circuit

- "Instead of inspecting the Tarabochias' catch and commercial fishing records in the field, at a commercial fishing establishment, or through a fish and wildlife checkpoint—all of which, both parties agree, would have been authorized under Washington law—the WDFW officers decided to stop the Tarabochias as they traveled in their pickup truck on a highway. They effectuated this stop despite admittedly lacking any suspicion of unlawful behavior or statutory authority that would permit this search under the administrative search exception. We hold that, under these circumstances, this stop, and the search that followed, constituted a Fourth Amendment violation." *Tarabochia v. Adkins*, 766 F.3d 1115, 1125 (9th Cir. 2014).

- "Because these searches require no warrant or particularized suspicion, an administrative search scheme invests the Government with the power to intrude into the privacy of ordinary citizens. This power carries with it a vast potential for abuse. . . . Therefore, courts must take care to ensure that an administrative search is not subverted into a general search for evidence of crime. . . . While administrative searches are an exception to the Fourth Amendment's warrant requirement, they are not an exception to the Fourth Amendment's standard of reasonableness. . . . Because of the potential for abuse, courts have exercised care to see that these searches are not unduly extended. . . . To meet the test of reasonableness, an administrative screening search must be as limited in its intrusiveness as is consistent with satisfaction of the administrative need that justifies it." *U.S. v. Bulacan*, 156 F.3d 963, 967 (9th Cir. 1998), as amended, (Nov. 16, 1998).

- "This Court held that an unlawful secondary purpose invalidates an otherwise permissible administrative search scheme . . . The court . . . found that where the scope of the search was no longer for purely administrative purposes, but included criminal investigatory purposes, it could no longer be justified as an administrative search." *U.S. v. Bulacan*, 156 F.3d 963, 969 (9th Cir. 1998), as amended, (Nov. 16, 1998).

Eleventh Circuit

- "The Fourth Amendment does not compel the Administration to employ the least invasive procedure or one fancied by Corbett. Airport screening is a permissible administrative search; security officers search all passengers, abuse is unlikely because of its public nature, and passengers elect to travel by air knowing that they must undergo a search. The 'jeopardy to hundreds of human lives and millions of dollars of property inherent in the pirating or blowing up of a large airplane' outweighs the slight intrusion of a generic body scan or, as a secondary measure, a pat-down." *Corbett v. Transportation Sec. Admin.*, 767 F.3d 1171, 1182 (11th Cir. 2014), cert. denied, 135 S. Ct. 2867, 192 L. Ed. 2d 897 (2015) (citations omitted).

D.C. Circuit

- "To obtain a valid search warrant, OSHA must establish administrative probable cause in one of two ways. First, OSHA may demonstrate specific evidence of an existing violation. Alternatively, OSHA can show that reasonable legislative or administrative standards for conducting an inspection are satisfied with respect to a particular [establishment]." *Tri-State Steel Const., Inc. v. Occupational Safety & Health Review Com'n*, 26 F.3d 173, 177, 16 O.S.H. Cas. (BNA) 1845, 1994 O.S.H. Dec. (CCH) P 30449 (D.C. Cir. 1994).

§ 21:3 Closely regulated industries: Industries with a long history of pervasive governmental regulation may be inspected without a warrant

Supreme Court

- "Our cases recognize a limited exception to the Fourth Amendment's warrant requirement for searches of businesses in 'closely regulated industries.' The thinking is that, other things being equal, the 'expectation of privacy in commercial premises' is significantly less than the 'expectation in an individual's home.' And where a business operates in an industry with a 'long tradition of close government supervision'—liquor dealers and pawnbrokers are classic examples—the expectation of privacy becomes 'particularly attenuated.' In this case, a New Jersey appellate court applied this doctrine to uphold a warrantless search by a state environmental official of [Appellants'] backyard. The [Appellants'] residential property contains wetlands protected by a New Jersey environmental statute. According to the court below, the presence of these wetlands brought the [Appellants'] yard 'directly under the regulatory arm' of the State 'just as much' as if the yard had been involved in a 'regulated industry.' This Court has not suggested that a State, by imposing heavy regulations on the use of privately owned residential property, may escape the Fourth Amendment's warrant requirement. But because this case comes to us on review of a decision by a state intermediate appellate court, I agree that today's denial of certiorari is appropriate. It does bear mentioning, however, that 'denial of certiorari does not constitute an expression of any opinion on the merits.' " *Huber v. New Jersey Dept. of Environmental Protection*, 562 U.S. 1302, 131 S. Ct. 1308, 179 L. Ed. 2d 643 (2011) (citations omitted).
- "The Fourth Amendment requires government to respect the right of the people to be secure in their persons against unreasonable searches and seizures. This restraint on government conduct generally bars officials from undertaking a search or seizure absent individualized suspicion. Searches conducted without grounds for suspicion of particular individuals have been upheld,

however, in certain limited circumstances. These circumstances include brief stops for questioning or observation at a fixed Border Patrol checkpoint or at a sobriety checkpoint and administrative inspections in closely regulated businesses." *Chandler v. Miller*, 520 U.S. 305, 308, 117 S. Ct. 1295, 137 L. Ed. 2d 513, 12 I.E.R. Cas. (BNA) 1233, 145 A.L.R. Fed. 657 (1997).

- "An expectation of privacy in commercial premises, . . . is different from, and indeed less than, a similar expectation in an individual's home. This expectation is particularly attenuated in commercial property employed in closely regulated industries. . . . . [T]he doctrine is essentially defined by the pervasiveness and regularity of the federal regulation and the effect of such regulation upon an owner's expectation of privacy. [T]he duration of a particular regulatory scheme would remain an important factor in deciding whether a warrantless inspection pursuant to the scheme is permissible." *New York v. Burger*, 482 U.S. 691, 700–01, 107 S. Ct. 2636, 96 L. Ed. 2d 601 (1987).

- "This warrantless inspection, however, even in the context of a pervasively regulated business, will be deemed to be reasonable only so long as three criteria are met. First, there must be a substantial government interest that informs the regulatory scheme pursuant to which the inspection is made. Second, the warrantless inspections must be necessary to further [the] regulatory scheme. Finally, the statute's inspection program, in terms of the certainty and regularity of its application, [must] provid[e] a constitutionally adequate substitute for a warrant. In other words, the regulatory statute must perform the two basic functions of a warrant: it must advise the owner of the commercial premises that the search is being made pursuant to the law and has a properly defined scope, and it must limit the discretion of the inspecting officers." *New York v. Burger*, 482 U.S. 691, 702–03, 107 S. Ct. 2636, 96 L. Ed. 2d 601 (1987).

- "[A] warrant may not be constitutionally required when Congress has reasonably determined that warrantless searches are necessary to further a regulatory scheme and the federal regulatory presence is sufficiently comprehensive and defined that the owner of com-

mercial property cannot help but be aware that his
property will be subject to periodic inspections undertaken for specific purposes." *Donovan v. Dewey*, 452
U.S. 594, 600, 101 S. Ct. 2534, 69 L. Ed. 2d 262, 1981
O.S.H. Dec. (CCH) P 25458 (1981).

- "Certain industries have such a history of government
  oversight that no reasonable expectation of privacy
  could exist for a proprietor over the stock of such an
  enterprise. Liquor . . . and firearms . . . are industries
  of this type; when an entrepreneur embarks upon such
  a business, he has voluntarily chosen to subject himself
  to a full arsenal of governmental regulation." *Marshall
  v. Barlow's, Inc.*, 436 U.S. 307, 313, 98 S. Ct. 1816, 56
  L. Ed. 2d 305, 6 O.S.H. Cas. (BNA) 1571, 1978 O.S.H.
  Dec. (CCH) P 22735, 8 Envtl. L. Rep. 20434 (1978).

- "Federal regulation of the interstate traffic in firearms
  is not as deeply rooted in history as governmental
  control of the liquor industry, but close scrutiny of this
  traffic is undeniably of central importance to federal efforts to prevent violent crime. . . . It is also apparent
  that if [the Gun Control Act] is to be properly enforced
  and inspection made effective, inspections without warrant must be deemed reasonable official conduct under
  the Fourth Amendment. We have little difficulty in
  concluding that . . . the inspection may proceed without
  a warrant where specifically authorized by statute."
  U.S. v. Biswell, 406 U.S. 311, 315, 316, 317, 92 S. Ct.
  1593, 32 L. Ed. 2d 87 (1972).

- "We agree that Congress has broad power to design
  such powers of inspection under the liquor laws as it
  deems necessary to meet the evils at hand. The general
  rule that administrative entry, without consent, upon
  the portions of commercial premises which are not open
  to the public may only be compelled through prosecution or physical force within the framework of a warrant procedure, is therefore not applicable here." *Colon-
  nade Catering Corp. v. U.S.*, 1970-1 C.B. 333, 397 U.S.
  72, 76, 90 S. Ct. 774, 25 L. Ed. 2d 60 (1970).

First Circuit

- "Ordinarily, administrative searches are permitted in
  highly regulated industries where authorized by a
  statutory scheme and where, in addition, the scheme

furthers a substantial government interest, warrantless inspections are necessary to further this interest, and the scheme provides a constitutionally adequate substitute for a warrant in terms of notice to those regulated and restrictions on the administrator's discretion. . . . [Defendant's] first objection to [the] administrative search of his office is that the medical profession should not be treated as a highly regulated enterprise. Whatever the status of the profession in the abstract, the statute in this case permits administrative searches of 'establishments' where drugs are manufactured or stored, and the seizure at issue is solely of drugs reasonably believed to have been misbranded or adulterated. Our focus, therefore, is on the regulation of drugs—not the practice of medicine in general. In Rhode Island, as under federal law and in other states, drugs are heavily regulated in storage and dispensation and have been for many years. . . . The other three conditions for an administrative search are that the scheme serve a substantial government interest, that administrative (warrantless) searches be 'necessary,' and that the scheme impose alternative safeguards. The first is obviously satisfied and the second is adequately covered by case law explaining the need for random and surprise inspections. . . . [Defendant] claims that the third condition—the 'constitutionally adequate substitute for a warrant,'—is not satisfied because neither the statute nor regulations under it (there are none) limit [law enforcement officers'] discretion as to such searches. This overstates the matter: [officer's] authority was limited to entry 'at all reasonable hours' to determine whether 'any of the provisions of this chapter are being violated,' and to 'secure samples or specimens.' These are adequately specific limits on the timing and scope of the activity." *U.S. v. Gonsalves*, 435 F.3d 64 (1st Cir. 2006).

- "Commerce, by its very nature, often results in a heightened governmental interest in regulation. This increased interest necessarily results in a diminution of the privacy interests of those who operate commercial premises. That trend crests when an industry operates under pervasive regulation. In such circumstances, warrantless inspections of commercial sites may be constitutionally permissible. . . . [W]e see no meaningful distinction between commercial premises and commercial vehicles. Consequently, the threshold question in this case is whether interstate commercial trucking is regulated to the extent necessary to give rise to the administrative search exception. We conclude that it is. . . . We next must determine whether the regulatory scheme surrounding this industry satisfies the tripartite *Burger* standard. As to the first criterion, it cannot be gainsaid that the government has a significant interest in regulating the interstate trucking industry (e.g., to ensure traveler safety, hold costs in check, and restrict what commodities may be transported interstate). . . . As to the second criterion, we think it self-evident that warrantless inspections of commercial trucks are necessary to further the regulatory scheme. Because the industry is so mobile, surprise is an important component of an efficacious inspection regime. . . . And, finally, because violations of the regulatory scheme often are not apparent to a patrolling officer, inspections are sometimes the only way in which violations can be discovered. We conclude, therefore, that effective enforcement of the regulatory regime would be impossible in the absence of impromptu inspections. The regulatory scheme applicable to the interstate commercial trucking industry also satisfies the final *Burger* criterion. The carefully delineated scope of the federal regulations suitably cabins the discretion of the enforcing officer. Moreover, the regulations themselves give ample notice to interstate truckers that inspections will be made on a regular basis. To cinch matters, commercial drivers are required by law to be familiar with the applicable regulations, and [defendant] concedes that he was aware that his vehicle could be searched at the discretion of an inspecting officer. Since all three of the *Burger* criteria are satisfied, it follows inexorably that an administrative search of a commercial truck is constitutionally permissible." *U.S. v. Maldonado*, 356 F.3d 130 (1st Cir. 2004).

Second Circuit

- "Although the foundation for the administrative search exception to the warrant requirement is entirely distinct from the rationales underlying the automobile exception, the discussion of the applicable regulatory structures in this authority is instructive. Based on the nature and scope of the regulations relating to the commercial trucking industry, we are persuaded that defendants' reasonable expectations of privacy in the trailer were minimal. Therefore, the reduced-privacy rationale provides further support for our conclusion that the warrantless search of this inherently mobile trailer was reasonable under the Fourth Amendment." *U.S. v. Navas*, 597 F.3d 492 (2d Cir. 2010).

- "Under certain circumstances, . . . the Fourth Amendment permits warrantless administrative searches of commercial property. . . In closely regulated industries, for example, warrantless administrative searches of commercial premises conducted pursuant to a regulatory scheme are constitutionally permitted if they meet three criteria: First, there must be a 'substantial' government interest that informs the regulatory scheme pursuant to which the inspection is made. Second, the warrantless inspections must be necessary to further the regulatory scheme. Finally, the statute's inspection program, in terms of the certainty and regularity of its application, must provide a constitutionally adequate substitute for a warrant. In other words, the regulatory statute must perform the two basic functions of a warrant: it must advise the owner of the commercial premises that the search is being made pursuant to the law and has a properly defined scope, and it must limit the discretion of the inspecting officers. To perform this first function, the statute must be sufficiently comprehensive and defined that the owner of commercial property cannot help but be aware that his property will be subject to periodic inspections undertaken for specific purposes. In addition, in defining how a statute limits the discretion of the inspectors, we have observed that it must be carefully limited in time, place and scope." *Anobile v. Pelligrino*, 284 F.3d 104 (2d Cir. 2002), opinion amended and superseded, 303 F.3d 107 (2d Cir. 2002).

- "In *Burger*, the Supreme Court upheld a New York law allowing unannounced, warrantless, on-site inspections of vehicle dismantlers in light of the nexus between widespread automobile theft and the dismantling industry. The Court noted that the expectation of privacy is particularly attenuated in industries that are closely regulated. [T]he government interest in the regulation of nursing homes and the need for warrant-less searches is clearly of a different and higher order than is found in the vehicle dismantling industry. We believe that nursing homes' right of privacy with regard to matters related to their compliance with patient care rules and regulations is even less than attenuated. It is virtually non-existent." *Blue v. Koren*, 72 F.3d 1075, 1081, 49 Soc. Sec. Rep. Serv. 716 (2d Cir. 1995).

Third Circuit

- "Since we have no difficulty concluding that Pennsylvania's funeral industry is a 'closely regulated industry,' our[ ] *Burger* inquiry proceeds to determining if the searches authorized by the FDL are reasonable. That inquiry requires us to focus on three criteria:

  First, there must be a substantial government interest that informs the regulatory scheme pursuant to which the inspection is made . . . . Second, the warrantless inspections must be necessary to further the regulatory scheme . . . . Finally, the statute's inspection program . . . must provide a constitutionally adequate substitute for a warrant."

  Heffner v. Murphy, 745 F.3d 56 (3d Cir. 2014) (citations omitted).

- "Plaintiffs' *Burger* challenge also relies on the absence of appropriate temporal limitation on searches of funeral establishments. . . . Time limitations, along with those related to the scope and location of a search, are key to restricting inspectors' discretion. Accordingly, courts reviewing regulatory search schemes under *Burger* generally look to whether the statutes and regulations at issue place adequate temporal limits on government officers' ability to conduct searches of private property. . . . However, context matters and courts have consistently upheld statutes permitting administrative searches in the absence of time restrictions where such limitations would frustrate the underlying governmental interest. . . . Obviously, the concerns that lead to the regulation of funeral facilities do not disappear at the close of business, nor is the need for regulatory compliance restricted to business hours. . . . Therefore the state has a strong interest in ensuring that the funeral business complies with applicable regulations 24 hours a day, 7 days a week. Limiting regulatory inspections to business hours would not advance that interest. In mounting a facial challenge to the FDL, Plaintiffs must persuade us that 'there is no set of circumstances' under which the FDL's inspection scheme may be applied constitutionally. Plaintiffs have failed to do so. As we have just explained, the very fact that death is not restricted to normal business hours or workdays belies any suggestion that administrative searches of funeral parlors should be so restricted. Given the totality of the FDL's warrantless administrative inspection scheme, we hold that the statute adequately limits the discretion of government officers." *Heffner v. Murphy*, 745 F.3d 56 (3d Cir. 2014) (citations omitted).

- "Factors to consider when determining whether a particular industry is closely regulated include: duration of the regulation's existence, pervasiveness of the regulatory scheme, and regularity of the regulation's application." *Free Speech Coalition, Inc. v. Attorney General of U.S.*, 677 F.3d 519 (3d Cir. 2012).

Fourth Circuit

- "The city's administrative search of a billiard club was not a pretext for a purely criminal investigation, as would violate the Fourth Amendment, since the search served primarily, if not entirely, a regulatory purpose; local police officers observed alcohol violations prior to the administrative inspection, there was no evidence or allegation that the officers or officials searched for anything other than alcohol violations, and the alcohol violation was discovered during the subject search." *Ruttenberg v. Jones*, 283 Fed. Appx. 121 (4th Cir. 2008).

Sixth Circuit

- "*Burger* requires only that the statute advise the owner of the commercial premises that the search is being made pursuant to the law and that it limit the discretion of the inspecting officers. This means that the statute must be sufficiently comprehensive so that a commercial property owner cannot help but be aware that his property will be subject to periodic inspection undertaken for specific purposes. Although limitations on the number of searches is a factor in the analysis, it is not dispositive unless the statute, as a whole, inadequately limits the inspector's discretion." *U.S. v. Branson*, 21 F.3d 113, 117, 1994 FED App. 0114P (6th Cir. 1994).

Seventh Circuit

- "[A city ordinance which requires dealers in second-hand merchandise to obtain licenses, collect information about each person from whom they purchase goods, and] make their records available to the police for inspection on demand during business hours. ... The district court held that the obligation to admit the police for inspection does not violate the Fourth Amendment because it is reasonable in time (being limited to business hours, when anyone may walk in off the street and peruse the inventory) and scope (being limited to records that facilitate identification of stolen goods). The district judge observed that sellers of used merchandise long have been closely regulated to separate legitimate dealers from fences, and that decisions such as *New York v. Burger*, 482 U.S. 691, 107 S. Ct. 2636, 96 L. Ed. 2d 601 (1987), deem 'reasonable' searches of business premises designed to ensure compliance with regulatory requirements. This aspect of the district court's decision seems to us correct, for the reasons the district judge gave. If the City should implement these provisions in an unconstitutional manner (for example, by increasing the frequency of inspections of shops that carry disfavored recording), then both money damages and injunctive relief will be available. If applied as written, though, they comport with the Constitution." *Second City Music, Inc. v. City of Chicago, Ill.*, 333 F.3d 846 (7th Cir. 2003).
- "The test employed by the Court in reaching its holding has four steps. First it must be determined whether governmental regulation of the industry in question is pervasive. Governmental regulation is pervasive if the regulatory presence is so comprehensive and defined that the business owner cannot help but be aware that

his commercial property will be subject to periodic inspections undertaken for specific purposes. Nevertheless, even if this requirement is met, a warrantless inspection of a business in a pervasively regulated industry will not be considered reasonable unless three additional criteria are met. First, there must be a substantial governmental interest that informs the regulatory scheme pursuant to which the inspection is made. Second, the warrantless inspections must be necessary to further the regulatory scheme. And, finally, the statute's inspection program must perform the two basic functions of a warrant: it must advise the owner of the premises that the search is being conducted pursuant to the law and within a properly defined scope; and it must limit the discretion of the inspecting officers." *Lesser v. Espy*, 34 F.3d 1301, 1306 (7th Cir. 1994).

Eighth Circuit

- "[C]losely regulated industries may be subject to warrantless searches of property, if 'the rules governing the search offer an adequate substitute for the fourth amendment warrant requirement.' (citation omitted) To qualify as a valid substitute, the rules governing the search must first provide adequate notice by being 'sufficiently comprehensive and defined that the owner of commercial property cannot help but be aware that his property will be subject to periodic inspections undertaken for specific purposes.' (citation omitted) Second, the rules must limit the discretion of inspecting officers 'in time, place, and scope.' " *U.S. v. Parker*, 587 F.3d 871 (8th Cir. 2009).

Ninth Circuit

- "The administrative search exception is applicable to warrantless searches where the search promotes an important governmental interest, is authorized by statute, and the authorizing statute and its regulatory scheme provide specific limitations on the manner and place of the search so as to limit the possibility of abuse. Where an inspection is authorized by statute but there are 'no rules governing the procedure that inspectors must follow, the Fourth Amendment and its various restrictive rules apply.' An industry's long history of regulation is also relevant to this inquiry insofar as it limits an individual's reasonable expectation of privacy in things or places traditionally subject to search under the industry's regulatory scheme. It therefore comes as no surprise that the cases in which this exception has been applied involve warrantless searches conducted on the premises or within the milieu of the regulated business or industry. To justify the stop under this exception, the officers rely on the state's broad interest in protecting the fishery, the long history of regulation of the commercial fishing industry, and two Washington state statutory provisions. To be sure, protecting the fishery is an important governmental interest and '[c]ommercial fishing has a long history of being a closely regulated industry.' But a specific statute authorizing a particular type of warrantless search is required, and the existence of such a statute alone may not even be sufficient, for the administrative search exception to apply. The officers rely on two statutory provisions within Washington's Fish and Wildlife Enforcement Code as providing authority for the stop and search at issue. [The first] statute does not expressly authorize an *automobile* stop or define 'engaged in fishing,' and Defendants have pointed to no regulatory or other published authority applying this provision to a roving automobile stop of commercial fishers. Assuming, *arguendo,* that one could be 'engaged in fishing' while driving on a highway with salmon, given the statute's lack of definition and failure explicitly to authorize the stop and search of an automobile, a commercial fisher is unlikely to be aware that this provision could subject him or her to a stop and search while engaging in this conduct. This factor weighs against finding that [the statute] meets the demands of the administrative search exception, much less that it authorizes this type of stop in the first place." *Tarabochia v. Adkins,* 766 F.3d 1115 (9th Cir. 2014) (citations omitted).

- "Missouri statute authorizing inspection of commercial vehicles satisfied requirements for administrative search exception to warrant requirement; commercial trucking industry was a pervasively regulated industry." *U.S. v. Delgado,* 545 F.3d 1195 (9th Cir. 2008).

- "It is undisputed that Customs agents searched Intrigue's storage area within the Port Services FTZ [foreign trade zone] and seized twelve sample cartons of cigarettes without a warrant. We conclude, however, that this initial search and sampling was a constitutional administrative search . . . The United States Supreme Court . . . has carved out a limited number of contexts within which a warrant is not required. Administrative searches of "closely regulated" industries are one such exception and may be conducted without a warrant, so long as they meet certain standards of reasonableness. . . . Even though we conclude that the FTZ regulations clearly authorize inspections without warrants and that the storage of goods in FTZs is "closely regulated" commercial activity, to satisfy the Fourth Amendment, the administrative search must also be reasonable. . . . We therefore hold that the Customs Service searches authorized by the FTZ regulations are 'directly connected with the environment the Legislature seeks to regulate' . . . and the FTZ regulatory scheme provides a constitutionally adequate substitute for a warrant. The warrantless search of Intrigue's storage area and the initial sampling constituted a valid and reasonable administrative search." *U.S. v. 4,432 Mastercases of Cigarettes, More Or Less*, 448 F.3d 1168, 28 Int'l Trade Rep. (BNA) 1611 (9th Cir. 2006).

- "Whether a business is closely regulated is essentially defined by the pervasiveness and regularity of the regulation, and the effect of such regulation upon an owner's expectation of privacy. . . . [A] proper balancing of the factors, especially in the context of the purpose behind the closely regulated industry exception, indicates that abortion clinics are not a closely regulated industry." *Tucson Woman's Clinic v. Eden*, 379 F.3d 531 (9th Cir. 2004).

Tenth Circuit

- "Under *Burger*, a warrantless inspection made pursuant to a regulatory scheme governing a pervasively regulated business is reasonable if it meets three criteria. First, the regulatory scheme must be informed by a substantial government interest. Second, warrantless inspections must be necessary to further the regulatory scheme. Third, the inspection program must provide a constitutionally adequate substitute for a warrant in terms of the certainty and regularity of its application. The *Burger* criteria are applied generally to a statutory scheme, not to a given set of facts arising under that scheme." *U.S. v. Mitchell*, 518 F.3d 740, 69 Fed. R. Serv. 3d 1713 (10th Cir. 2008).

- "Because an automobile salvage business is in a closely regulated industry, it may be subject to warrantless administrative searches, conducted pursuant to statute." *U.S. v. Johnson*, 408 F.3d 1313 (10th Cir. 2005).

- "Because Defendant was operating a carrier that is closely regulated, he had a significantly reduced expectation of privacy in his trailer. . . . Defendant does not dispute that the regulatory scheme at issue in this case is validated by a state interest that outweighs the intrusiveness of the program of searches or seizures of commercial carriers." *U.S. v. Burch*, 153 F.3d 1140, 1142–43, 49 Fed. R. Evid. Serv. 1510 (10th Cir. 1998).

- "[Defendant], as the owner of a closely regulated business, was subject to regulatory inspections. Such warrantless inspections are deemed reasonable under the Fourth Amendment when performed pursuant to a plan which incorporates specific and neutral criteria. Although the government may address a problem in a regulated industry through administrative and penal sanctions, an administrative inspection may not be used as a pretext solely to gather evidence of criminal activity. Rather, a warrant issued on probable cause by a neutral magistrate is required." *U.S. v. Johnson*, 994 F.2d 740, 742 (10th Cir. 1993).

Eleventh Circuit

- "Where an act authorizing administrative inspections fails to tailor the scope and frequency of such administrative inspections to the particular governmental concern, and does not provide any standards to guide inspectors either in their selection of establishments to be searched or in the exercise of their authority to search, a search warrant will be required." *Swint v. City of Wadley, Ala.*, 51 F.3d 988, 998 (11th Cir. 1995).

§ 21:4 Emergencies: In emergency situations a warrant may not be required

Supreme Court

- "The object of the search is important even if exigent circumstances exist. Circumstances that justify a warrantless search for the cause of a fire may not justify a search to gather evidence of criminal activity once that cause has been determined." *Michigan v. Clifford*, 464 U.S. 287, 294, 104 S. Ct. 641, 78 L. Ed. 2d 477 (1984).
- "[I]n the regulatory field, our cases have recognized the importance of prompt inspections, even without a warrant, in emergency situations." *Michigan v. Tyler*, 436 U.S. 499, 509, 98 S. Ct. 1942, 56 L. Ed. 2d 486 (1978).
- "[A]n entry to fight a fire requires no warrant, and . . . once in the building, officials may remain there for a reasonable time to investigate the cause of the blaze. Thereafter, additional entries to investigate the cause of fire must be made pursuant to the warrant procedures governing administrative searches." *Michigan v. Tyler*, 436 U.S. 499, 511, 98 S. Ct. 1942, 56 L. Ed. 2d 486 (1978).
- "[P]rovision for a hearing before seizure and condemnation and destruction of food which is unwholesome and unfit for use is not necessary. The right to so seize is based upon the right and duty of the State to protect and guard, as far as possible, the lives and health of its inhabitants, and . . . it is proper to provide that food which is unfit for human consumption should be summarily seized and destroyed to prevent the danger which would arise from eating it." *North American Cold Storage Co. v. City of Chicago*, 211 U.S. 306, 315, 29 S. Ct. 101, 53 L. Ed. 195 (1908).

First Circuit

- "In *Clifford* the Court laid out three factors for analyzing the constitutionality of warrantless searches of fire-damaged premises: whether there are legitimate privacy interests in the fire-damaged property that are protected by the Fourth Amendment; whether exigent circumstances justify the government intrusion regardless of any reasonable expectation of privacy; and, whether the object of the search is to determine the cause of the fire or to gather evidence of criminal activity." *U.S. v. Mitchell*, 85 F.3d 800, 805–06, 44 Fed. R. Evid. Serv. 893 (1st Cir. 1996).

Seventh Circuit

- "*Tyler* adds that entries that occur during the initial firefighting efforts do not require warrants, even if officials conduct a criminal investigation. . . . [H]ere. . . . [C]riminal investigators came and went between about 2:00 A.M. and 7:00 A.M. on the morning of the fire, a briefer period than in *Tyler*, and the need for prompt investigation was more urgent because volatile liquids posed a risk of explosion. Firefighters remained throughout the investigation, as they had not done in *Tyler* (or *Clifford*, where the fact that firefighting efforts ended before the criminal investigation began led the Court to hold that a warrant was required)." *U.S. v. Loos*, 165 F.3d 504, 506 (7th Cir. 1998).

Tenth Circuit

- "[T]he Supreme Court in *Tyler* rejected the notion that the exigency justifying a warrantless entry to fight a fire ends with the dousing of the last flame. We think this view of the firefighting function is unrealistically narrow. . . . Fire officials are charged not only with extinguishing fires, but with finding their causes. Prompt determination of the fire's origin may be necessary to prevent its recurrence. . . . For this reason, fire officials need no warrant to enter and remain in a building for a reasonable time to investigate the cause of a blaze after it has been extinguished." *U.S. v. Finnigin*, 113 F.3d 1182, 1185 (10th Cir. 1997).

§ 21:5 Vital government interest: Warrantless administrative searches which further vital governmental interests are reasonable if the public interest is great and the intrusion minor

Supreme Court

- "In holding that workplace searches undertaken either for noninvestigatory work-related purposes or to investigate work-related misconduct may be predicated on reasonable suspicion rather than probable cause, the Court in *Ortega* defined the 'workplace' as 'those areas... that are related to work and are generally within the employer's control.' As an example, at a hospital, the hallways, cafeteria, offices, desks, and file cabinets, among other areas, are part of the workplace. However, personal possessions on workplace territory, such as closed personal luggage or a handbag, would not necessarily be considered part of the workplace context. [Defendant] contends that *Ortega* is inapplicable to this case because his car was like a closed briefcase or suitcase that under *Ortega* might not be in the workplace. We disagree. [Defendant's] car was parked in the Institution's parking lot, which was on agency property, adjacent to the Institution, and available to accommodate employees and visitors of the Institution. The agency maintained control over the parking lot, as evidenced by the notice posted at the entrance of the parking lot advising visitors and employees that '[a]ll persons entering upon these premises are subject to routine searches of their person, property (*including vehicles*), and packages' (emphasis added). Unlike a situation in which a public employee brings a closed suitcase to work without any expectation that it would be searched, [defendant] was on notice that his car could be searched. Therefore, [defendant's] car, as situated in the Institution's parking lot, was within the 'workplace' as set forth in *Ortega*." *Wiley v. Department of Justice*, 328 F.3d 1346 (Fed. Cir. 2003).

Second Circuit

- "The Supreme Court has applied the so-called special needs exception outside the criminal investigatory context. In these cases, a significant governmental interest, such as the maintenance of institutional security, public safety, and order, must prevail over a minimal intrusion on an individual's privacy rights to justify a search on less than individualized suspicion. For example, the Court has employed this exception to uphold the constitutionality of searches and seizures designed to maintain order and security in hospitals . . . in schools . . . in highly regulated industries . . . and in government agencies. . . . The special needs cases reaffirm the longstanding principle that neither a warrant nor probable cause, nor, indeed, any measure of individualized suspicion, is an indispensable component of reasonableness in every circumstance." *Roe v. Marcotte*, 193 F.3d 72, 78 (2d Cir. 1999).

Eighth Circuit

- "The location of a parking lot and the circumstances of inmate access are relevant to the 'interests of the correctional institution in maintaining security'; a lot outside the confines of the prison has greater potential to be a source of contraband when prisoners have unsupervised access to it. Randomly searching such a lot may be an efficient means of preventing the smuggling of contraband. Therefore, balancing a prison employee's privacy interests against 'the substantial government interests in the efficient and proper operation of the workplace,' specifically, the interests of the correctional institution in maintaining security, it is reasonable under all the circumstances to search, by 'systematic random selection,' employee vehicles in prison parking lots to which inmates have unsupervised access." *True v. Nebraska*, 612 F.3d 676, 682, 30 I.E.R. Cas. (BNA) 1537, 93 Empl. Prac. Dec. (CCH) P 43931, 159 Lab. Cas. (CCH) P 61021 (8th Cir. 2010).

Ninth Circuit

- "Instead of inspecting the Tarabochias' catch and commercial fishing records in the field, at a commercial fishing establishment, or through a fish and wildlife checkpoint—all of which, both parties agree, would have been authorized under Washington law—the WDFW officers decided to stop the Tarabochias as they traveled in their pickup truck on a highway. They effectuated this stop despite admittedly lacking any suspicion of unlawful behavior or statutory authority that would permit this search under the administrative search exception. We hold that, under these circumstances, this stop, and the search that followed, constituted a Fourth Amendment violation." *Tarabochia v. Adkins*, 766 F.3d 1115, 1125 (9th Cir. 2014).
- "The Government may search people entering sensitive facilities, such as government buildings, for explosives

and weapons. . . . Such a search, however, must be limited and no more intrusive than necessary to protect against the danger to be avoided. . . ." *U.S. v. Bulacan*, 156 F.3d 963, 973 (9th Cir. 1998), as amended, (Nov. 16, 1998).

- "The government's involvement in promulgating the Federal Aviation Administration guidelines to combat hijacking is so pervasive as to bring any search conducted pursuant to that program within the reach of the Fourth Amendment." *U.S. v. Ross*, 32 F.3d 1411, 1413 (9th Cir. 1994), as amended, (Nov. 22, 1994).

- "[C]ourthouse security procedures in the San Francisco Hall of Justice, including the use of a magnetometer, fell into the category of permissible administrative searches. Taking judicial notice of threats of violence directed at courthouses that had given rise to an urgent need for protective measures, we concluded that security measures that included a pat-down search as a secondary search procedure were reasonable under the fourth amendment." *Klarfeld v. U.S.*, 944 F.2d 583, 586 (9th Cir. 1991).

Tenth Circuit

- "Within the last thirty years, courts have increasingly recognized certain narrow circumstances that justify searches and seizures without reference to the Fourth Amendment's warrant clause or probable cause requirement. These are situations in which the requirement of a warrant based upon probable cause is ill-suited to achieving certain 'special needs' of government, such as enforcing school discipline, allowing administrative searches of the business premises of 'closely-regulated industries,' and taking inventory of seized items for 'caretaking' purposes. In all 'special needs' cases, the nature of the need addressed makes particularized suspicion impossible or otherwise renders the warrant requirement impractical... If a special need renders the warrant requirement impracticable, we then balance the nature of the privacy interest upon which the search intrudes and the degree of intrusion occasioned by the search against 'the nature and immediacy of the government concern at issue... and the efficacy of this means for meeting it. We find no special need that renders the warrant requirement impracticable when social workers *enter a home* to remove a child, absent exigent circumstances. First, we note that individualized suspicion is at the heart of a removal of a child from a home, distinguishing the instant case from the various drug testing cases that have been addressed by the Court. Second... (assuming that exigent circumstances are not present), there is no need for surprise or sudden action that renders obtaining a warrant counterproductive. Nor is this situation similar to the position of [a] probationer—the [parents] were not in the criminal justice system, there was no deterrent function being served by the threat of a sudden, warrantless search, and there was no immediate need for a quick response. Simply put, unless the child is in imminent danger, there is no reason that it is impracticable to obtain a warrant before social workers remove a child from the home." *Roska ex rel. Roska v. Peterson*, 328 F.3d 1230 (10th Cir. 2003).

Eleventh Circuit

- "Contrary to Corbett's assertion, the scanners effectively reduce the risk of air terrorism. Although this proposition is self-evident, Corbett disputes it on the ground that he has circumvented the scanners and speculates that the rates of failure and false-positives are high. But the Fourth Amendment does not require that a suspicionless search be fool-proof or yield exacting results. The Supreme Court has explained that the evaluation of effectiveness is 'not meant to transfer from politically accountable officials to the courts the decision as to which among reasonable alternative law enforcement techniques should be employed to deal with a serious public danger.' Choosing which technique best serves the government interest at stake should be left to those with 'a unique understanding of, and a responsibility for, limited public resources, including a finite number of police officers.' '[W]e need only determine whether the [scanner] is a reasonably effective means of addressing the government interest in deterring and detecting a terrorist attack' at airports. Common sense tells us that it is." *Corbett v. Transportation Sec. Admin.*, 767 F.3d 1171, 1181 (11th Cir. 2014), cert. denied, 135 S. Ct. 2867, 192 L. Ed. 2d 897 (2015) (citations omitted).

- "The Fourth Amendment does not compel the Administration to employ the least invasive procedure or one fancied by Corbett. Airport screening is a permissible administrative search; security officers search all passengers, abuse is unlikely because of its public nature, and passengers elect to travel by air knowing that they must undergo a search. The 'jeopardy to hundreds of human lives and millions of dollars of property inherent in the pirating or blowing up of a large airplane' outweighs the slight intrusion of a generic body scan or, as a secondary measure, a pat-down." *Corbett v. Transportation Sec. Admin.*, 767 F.3d 1171, 1182 (11th Cir. 2014), cert. denied, 135 S. Ct. 2867, 192 L. Ed. 2d 897 (2015) (citations omitted).

§ 21:6 Scope: Statute providing for inspection outlines scope of administrative search

Fourth Circuit

- "Search of billiard club operator's office, during administrative search of club for alcohol violations, did not exceed scope of officers' statutory authority, as would violate the Fourth Amendment; Virginia Administrative Code provisions allowing for searches for alcohol violations cast a wide net, and office was not a private residence." *Ruttenberg v. Jones*, 283 Fed. Appx. 121 (4th Cir. 2008).

Ninth Circuit

- "Instead of inspecting the Tarabochias' catch and commercial fishing records in the field, at a commercial fishing establishment, or through a fish and wildlife checkpoint—all of which, both parties agree, would have been authorized under Washington law—the WDFW officers decided to stop the Tarabochias as they traveled in their pickup truck on a highway. They effectuated this stop despite admittedly lacking any suspicion of unlawful behavior or statutory authority that would permit this search under the administrative search exception. We hold that, under these circumstances, this stop, and the search that followed, constituted a Fourth Amendment violation." *Tarabochia v. Adkins*, 766 F.3d 1115, 1124–25 (9th Cir. 2014).

Tenth Circuit

- "The New Mexico statute authorizes inspectors to inspect the vehicle and its contents to determine whether all laws and all rules and regulations of the departments of this state with respect to public safety, health, welfare and comfort have been fully complied with. In addition, the statute provides the person in charge of the port of entry may satisfy himself as to the contents of the cargo. An inspector may also inspect the vehicle's contents to ensure all excise taxes on fuel, alcohol, or other property have been paid. New Mexico's regulatory scheme clearly contemplates entrance into the trailer to inspect blocking and bracing, and also allows inspection of the contents of the vehicle. There is no meaningful distinction under this statutory scheme between inspection of the contents of a vehicle and inspection of a vehicle to confirm there are no contents. If an operator could escape inspection by giving a verbal statement that the trailer was empty, New Mexico's ability to conduct meaningful inspections would be seriously compromised. This is particularly true where, as here, the officer has reason to believe the operator has not provided accurate information. New Mexico's statutory scheme contemplates the inspection of trailers to confirm compliance with New Mexico's laws and this authorization extends to inspections to confirm an operator's assertion that he or she carries no cargo. However, an officer's order for defendant, a long haul truck driver, to unlock trailer in order to confirm defendant's assertion that he had no cargo did not exceed scope of permissible inspections under New Mexico's statutory scheme authorizing inspections of commercial trucks, especially given that officer had reason to believe that defendant had not provided accurate information concerning his cargo." *U.S. v. Mitchell*, 518 F.3d 740, 69 Fed. R. Serv. 3d 1713 (10th Cir. 2008).

Eleventh Circuit

- "Administrative searches are an exception to the Fourth Amendment's warrant requirement, but they are not an exception to the Fourth Amendment's requirement for reasonableness. As with any search, the scope and execution of an administrative inspection must be reasonable in order to be constitutional. Although a statute authorizing administrative searches may be constitutional, actual searches conducted under that authority may not. Even when warrantless administrative inspections are permitted, the Constitution requires that such inspections be appropriately limited. Nor may an authorizing statute commit the conduct of such an inspection to the unbridled discretion of the inspector. The statute must limit the discretion of the inspecting officers and the inspection must have a properly defined scope. There must be reasonable legislative or administrative standards for conducting an . . . inspection. Where a statute authorizes the inspection but makes no rules governing the procedures that inspectors must follow, the Fourth Amendment and its various restrictive rules apply. The fundamental function of these rules is to protect citizens from the unbridled discretion [of] executive and administrative officers." *Bruce v. Beary*, 498 F.3d 1232 (11th Cir. 2007).

Chapter 22

Airport Searches

Research References

West's Key Number Digest

Arrest ⚷63.4 to 63.5, 68; Criminal Law ⚷394, 412, 1224; Searches and Seizures ⚷13, 22 to 23, 37, 57, 179, 184, 194

KeyCite®: Cases and other legal materials listed in KeyCite Scope can be researched through the KeyCite service on Westlaw®. Use KeyCite to check citations for form, parallel references, prior and later history, and comprehensive citator information, including citations to other decisions and secondary materials.

---

§ 22:1   Seizure of the person: The Fourth Amendment applies to an airport stop only when a seizure occurs

Supreme Court

- "If there is no detention—no seizure within the meaning of the Fourth Amendment—then no constitutional rights have been infringed." *Florida v. Royer*, 460 U.S. 491, 498, 103 S. Ct. 1319, 75 L. Ed. 2d 229 (1983).
- "[I]t is submitted that the entire encounter was consensual and hence [Defendant] was not being held against his will at all. We find this submission untenable. Asking for and examining [Defendant's] ticket and his driver's license were no doubt permissible in themselves, but when the officers identified themselves as narcotics agents, told [him] that he was suspected of transporting narcotics, and asked him to accompany them to the police room, while retaining his ticket and driver's license and without indicating in any way that he was free to depart, [Defendant] was effectively seized for the purposes of the Fourth Amendment. These circumstances surely amount to a show of official authority such that a reasonable person would have believed he was not free to leave." *Florida v. Royer*, 460 U.S. 491, 501–02, 103 S. Ct. 1319, 75 L. Ed. 2d 229 (1983).
- "[A] person has been 'seized' within the meaning of the Fourth Amendment only if, in view of all of the circumstances surrounding the incident, a reasonable person would have believed that he was not free to leave. Examples of circumstances that might indicate a seizure, even where the person did not attempt to leave, would be the threatening presence of several officers, the display of a weapon by an officer, some physical touching of the person of the citizen, or the use of language or tone of voice indicating that compliance with the officer's request might be compelled. In the absence of some such evidence, otherwise inoffensive contact between a member of the public and the police cannot, as a matter of law, amount to a seizure of that person." *U.S. v. Mendenhall*, 446 U.S. 544, 554–55, 100 S. Ct. 1870, 64 L. Ed. 2d 497 (1980).

Second Circuit

- "[A] person has been seized within the meaning of the Fourth Amendment only if, in view of all of the circumstances surrounding the incident, a reasonable person would have believed that he was not free to leave. This objective test allows law enforcement officers to predict the ramifications of their conduct and ensures a uniform application of fourth amendment protection to similarly situated individuals. It calls for a contextual approach that takes into account the particular facts of each case to meet varying circumstances. The subjective intentions of the police officers during an encounter are relevant only to the extent that they are conveyed to the individual approached." *U.S. v. Hooper*, 935 F.2d 484, 491 (2d Cir. 1991).

Fourth Circuit

- "[Defendant] was not physically restrained by the police or by other factors from moving through the airport terminal, but the persistence of [the] officers would clearly convey to a reasonable person that he was not free to leave the questioning by the police. The fact that [Defendant] continued walking through the airport is not dispositive. Despite his best efforts, [Defendant] was unable to terminate the encounter, to ignore the police presence and go about his business, or to go on his way. The principle embodied by the phrase free to leave means the ability to ignore the police and to walk away from them." *U.S. v. Wilson*, 953 F.2d 116, 122 (4th Cir. 1991).

- "The courts have examined a number of factors when determining whether an officer did, in fact, display such a show of authority. The factors most frequently looked to by the courts include: (1) the number of police officers present, (2) whether the police officers were in uniform and whether they displayed their weapons (3) whether the officer touched the defendant or made any attempt to physically block his departure or restrain his movement (4) whether the officer's questioning was conversational rather than intimidating—i.e., did the officer raise his voice or threaten the defendant, (5) whether the officer informed the defendant that he positively suspected him of illegal activity rather than treating the encounter as routine in nature, and (6) whether, if the officer requested from the defendant either his plane ticket or some form of official identification, the officer promptly returned it." *U.S. v. Gray*, 883 F.2d 320, 322–23 (4th Cir. 1989).

Seventh Circuit

- "We apply an objective standard to determine whether an airport encounter between a citizen and police amounts to a seizure. The determination of whether an encounter is voluntary is made on the basis of all relevant circumstances and includes consideration of psychological factors. If a reasonable person would have felt free to disregard the police to go about his business the encounter is consensual. Our cases have made it clear that the police do not violate the Fourth Amendment merely by approaching a person in an airport and asking routine questions, including those relating to identification, airline ticket information, and the nature and length of recent air travel. Although the lengthy retention of documents such as identification and airline tickets is a factor in determining whether a stop has occurred the mere request for and voluntary production of driver's licenses and airplane tickets does not constitute a seizure, but rather falls into the category of a non-coercive police-citizen encounter. Nor can the mere request for consent to search a suspect's luggage be deemed a per se paralyzing communication that escalates every consensual encounter into a *Terry* stop." *U.S. v. Rodriguez*, 69 F.3d 136, 141–42 (7th Cir. 1995).

- "[W]e have repeatedly emphasized that there generally is no seizure when a law enforcement agent merely approaches an individual in an airport and, after identifying himself, begins to ask routine questions relating to the individual's identification, travel plans, and ticket information. Moreover, the agent's non-threatening request to search the individual's luggage generally will not convert a consensual interview into an investigatory stop requiring a reasonable suspicion that the person was or is engaged in criminal activity. It is clear, however, that a consensual encounter can develop into an investigatory stop through the conduct of the investigating officers." *U.S. v. Odum*, 72 F.3d 1279, 1283 (7th Cir. 1995).

- "While in *Borys* we stated that retaining airline tickets
  and driver's licenses has been a crucial factor in finding
  that a seizure has occurred, we held that, when an officer merely glances at a ticket, it does not amount to a
  seizure. In the instant case, the court found that the
  agents returned the ticket and identification immediately after looking at them. Appellant does not assert that the agent did anything but examine the documents before he returned them. While the fact that one
  agent took notes as the other agent read the information aloud may require this review of the identification
  to be more than the glance in *Borys*, it clearly does not
  rise to the level of the case where agents, while holding
  a plane ticket and a driver's license, asked defendants
  to follow them to another room. The instant case did
  not rise above the level of a consensual encounter. Appellant was not deprived of his ticket or identification
  for an unusual length of time, nor was he taken to an
  isolated area while the agents had his documents." *U.S.
  v. Soto-Lopez*, 995 F.2d 694, 698 (7th Cir. 1993).

Tenth Circuit

- "Here, the encounter occurred on a public curbside and
  the officers never surrounded or otherwise restrained
  [Defendant] from walking away. The officers were not
  wearing uniforms and did not brandish their weapons
  or otherwise threaten her. The officers promptly
  returned her airline ticket and identification to her after examining them. . . . The officers informed her on
  two separate occasions that she was not under arrest
  and that she was free to leave. . . . The officers never
  moved, touched, physically restrained, or otherwise
  prevented her from leaving or continuing along the
  curbside. . . . Accordingly, none of the usual factors
  indicating a person has been seized exist in this case."
  U.S. v. Torres-Guevara, 147 F.3d 1261, 1265 (10th Cir.
  1998).
- "[Defendant] would not reasonably have felt free to
  leave or otherwise terminate the encounter with the
  agents because his driver's license had not been
  returned to him. While we agree with the government
  that [Defendant] could have left the airport by plane,
  taxi, or simply walking down the street, as a practical

matter he was not free to go. [Defendant] was confronted by the agents as he was preparing to open the door to his car and drive away. He could not lawfully leave the parking lot in his car without his driver's license. The question of whether an individual has been detained turns on whether a person under the circumstances would reasonably feel at liberty to refuse the agents' questions or otherwise terminate the encounter." *U.S. v. Lambert*, 46 F.3d 1064, 1068 (10th Cir. 1995).

- "We consider a number of factors in determining whether a police-citizen encounter becomes a seizure: the location of the encounter, particularly whether the defendant is in an open public place where he [is] within the view of persons other than law enforcement officers, whether the officers touch or physically restrain the defendant whether the officers are uniformed or in plain clothes; whether their weapons are displayed; the number, demeanor and tone of voice of the officers; whether and for how long the officers retain the defendant's personal effects such as tickets or identification; and whether or not they have specifically advised defendant at any time that he had the right to terminate the encounter or refuse consent." *U.S. v. Zapata*, 997 F.2d 751, 756–57 (10th Cir. 1993).

§ 22:2   Grounds for stop: An airport stop must be based on reasonable suspicion; A drug courier profile alone may not supply reasonable suspicion

Supreme Court

- "A court sitting to determine the existence of reasonable suspicion must require the agent to articulate the factors leading to that conclusion, but the fact that these factors may be set forth in a profile does not somehow detract from their evidentiary significance as seen by a trained agent." *U.S. v. Sokolow*, 490 U.S. 1, 10, 109 S. Ct. 1581, 104 L. Ed. 2d 1 (1989).
- "Before the officers even spoke to the three confederates, one by one they had sighted the plain clothes officers and had spoken furtively to one another. One was twice overheard urging the others to get out of here. Respondent's strange movements in his attempt to

evade the officers aroused further justifiable suspicion, and so did the contradictory statements concerning the [suspects'] identities. [The Officer] had special training in narcotics surveillance and apprehension; like members of the Drug Enforcement Administration, the Narcotics Squad of the Miami Police Department is carrying out a highly specialized law enforcement operation designed to combat the serious societal threat posed by narcotics distribution. Respondent was approached in a major international airport where, due in part to extensive antihijacking surveillance and equipment, reasonable privacy exceptions are of significantly lesser magnitude. We hold, therefore, that the trial court was incorrect in its conclusion that there was no articulable basis for detaining respondent." *Florida v. Rodriguez*, 469 U.S. 1, 6, 105 S. Ct. 308, 83 L. Ed. 2d 165 (1984).

- "[N]ot all seizures of the person must be justified by probable cause to arrest for a crime. [C]ertain seizures are justifiable under the Fourth Amendment if there is articulable suspicion that a person has committed or is about to commit a crime." *Florida v. Royer*, 460 U.S. 491, 498, 103 S. Ct. 1319, 75 L. Ed. 2d 229 (1983).

- "Because of the inherently transient nature of drug courier activity at airports, allowing police to make brief investigative stops of persons at airports on reasonable suspicion of drug-trafficking substantially enhances the likelihood that police will be able to prevent the flow of narcotics into distribution channels." *U.S. v. Place*, 462 U.S. 696, 704, 103 S. Ct. 2637, 77 L. Ed. 2d 110 (1983).

- "We agree with the State that when the officers discovered that [Defendant] was travelling under an assumed name, this fact, and the facts already known to the officers—paying cash for a one-way ticket, the mode of checking the two bags, and [Defendant's] appearance and conduct in general—were adequate grounds for suspecting [Defendant] of carrying drugs and for temporarily detaining him and his luggage while they attempted to verify or dispel their suspicions in a manner that did not exceed the limits of an investigative detention." *Florida v. Royer*, 460 U.S. 491, 502, 103 S. Ct. 1319, 75 L. Ed. 2d 229 (1983).

- "[I]f the respondent was seized when the DEA agents approached her on the concourse and asked questions of her, the agents' conduct in doing so was constitutional only if they reasonably suspected the respondent of wrongdoing." *U.S. v. Mendenhall*, 446 U.S. 544, 551–52, 100 S. Ct. 1870, 64 L. Ed. 2d 497 (1980).

- "[T]he [lower] court thought it relevant that (1) the petitioner had arrived from Fort Lauderdale, which the agent testified is a principal place of origin of cocaine sold elsewhere in the country, (2) the petitioner arrived in the early morning, when law enforcement activity is diminished, (3) he and his companion appeared to the agent to be trying to conceal the fact that they were traveling together, and (4) they apparently had no luggage other than their shoulder bags. [T]he agent could not, as a matter of law, have reasonably suspected the petitioner of criminal activity on the basis of these observed circumstances. Of the evidence relied on, only the fact that the petitioner preceded another person and occasionally looked backward at him as they proceeded through the concourse relates to their particular conduct. The other circumstances described a very large category of presumably innocent travelers, who would be subject to virtually random seizures were the Court to conclude that as little foundation as there was in this case could justify a seizure. The agent's belief that the petitioner and his companion were attempting to conceal the fact that they were traveling together, a belief that was more an inchoate and unparticularized suspicion or hunch than a fair inference in the light of his experience, is simply too slender a reed to support the seizure in this case." *Reid v. Georgia*, 448 U.S. 438, 440–41, 100 S. Ct. 2752, 65 L. Ed. 2d 890 (1980).

Sixth Circuit

- "Defendant first aroused the curiosity of [officer] because of the way he was dressed. Upon reviewing the connecting flight information sheet, [the Officer] determined that defendant had booked a one-way ticket from New York to Cincinnati to Salt Lake City to Anchorage for cash forty-one minutes before the departure of the flight. This action is consistent with a drug courier profile—paying a large sum of cash for a ticket immediately before a flight. [The Officer] was aware of a large amount of cocaine being transported from New

York City to Anchorage. After defendant produced
identification the officers, determined that the identification was the type that was readily available from any
street vendor and was often carried by drug couriers to
provide an alias When questioned, defendant could not
remember his final destination until prompted by [the]
Officer. Although any one of these factors is not by itself
proof of illegal activity and is consistent with innocent
travelers, these same factors, when combined, amount
to reasonable suspicion to support a temporary
detention." *U.S. v. Bueno*, 21 F.3d 120, 125, 1994 FED
App. 0116P (6th Cir. 1994).

- "Airport stops and searches occur frequently and agents
often rely on the drug courier profile to justify stopping
and investigating people for possible drug activity.
While we recognize the governmental interest in stopping the drug traffic in our airports we also recognize
the need for careful protection of Fourth Amendment
freedoms from overly-intrusive law enforcement
activity." *U.S. v. Fifty-Three Thousand Eighty-Two
Dollars in U.S. Currency, $53,082.00*, 985 F.2d 245, 248
(6th Cir. 1993).

- "Prior to initially questioning [Defendant], the agents
only had two indicia of suspicion: (1) their own racially-
biased assumption that because [Defendant] was a man
of color wearing dreadlocks, he must have been an illegal alien from Jamaica; and (2) their long-discredited
drug source city rationale that because [Defendant] had
embarked from Los Angeles, he must have been a drug
courier. If the agents' approach in this case became
prevalent among law enforcement officers across the
nation, many black or Hispanic men boarding transcon-
tinental flights out of drug source cities, such as Los
Angeles, would be subject to virtually random seizures
regardless of innocence or guilt." *U.S. v. Grant*, 920
F.2d 376, 388 (6th Cir. 1990).

Eighth Circuit
- "In assessing whether the requisite degree of suspicion
exists, we must determine whether the facts collectively
establish reasonable suspicion. Once we discount the
facts with which we find weaknesses, we are left with
[Defendant's] arrival on a plane from a known source

1009

city, and her vagueness about the purpose of her trip. These facts are insufficient to demonstrate a reasonable articulable suspicion of criminal activity." *U.S. v. Green*, 52 F.3d 194, 199 (8th Cir. 1995).

Ninth Circuit

- "At the outset, we must determine whether Guam Customs officers have the statutory authority to stop an individual that they believe is violating Guam's drug laws . . . Guam Customs officers are statutorily authorized to arrest persons and seize methamphetamine "imported into Guam." The question then becomes whether methamphetamine arriving in Guam on a flight originating in Hawaii is "imported into Guam" within the meaning of the statutory scheme . . . (W)e think it is clear that Guam Customs officers have the statutory authority to stop and question an individual suspected of smuggling drugs into Guam, so long as the person is arriving from outside of Guam. It is immaterial whether the flight originated within the United States or in some other country: the statute prohibits "any bringing in" of drugs "into any area on Guam.""" *U.S. v. Rowland*, 464 F.3d 899 (9th Cir. 2006).

Tenth Circuit

- "The only information known to the agents prior to the their seizure was [Defendant]: (1) was flying alone; (2) had a one-way ticket he had purchased with cash shortly before departure from a drug-source city; (3) had checked one piece of luggage; and (4) appeared nervous and left the airport quickly after retrieving his suitcase. All of this is perfectly consistent with innocent behavior and thus, raises very little suspicion." *U.S. v. Lambert*, 46 F.3d 1064, 1070 (10th Cir. 1995).

- "Law enforcement officers may briefly detain a traveler and her luggage to pursue a limited course of investigation provided the officers have a reasonable, articulable suspicion justifying th e intrusion. Important government interests include effective crime detection and prevention, and minimizing the risk of harm to officers and the public. Nor is an impermissible detention caused simply because an officer approaches an individual and asks a few questions. During a *Terry* stop a police officer may ask [a] detainee a moderate number of questions to determine his identity and to try to obtain information confirming or dispelling the officer's suspicion." *U.S. v. Griffin*, 7 F.3d 1512, 1517 (10th Cir. 1993).

§ 22:3 Arrest: An arrest at an airport must be based on probable cause

Supreme Court

- "[P]robable cause to arrest [Defendant] did not exist at the time he consented to the search of his luggage. The facts are that a nervous young man with two American Tourister bags paid cash for an airline ticket to a target city. These facts led to inquiry, which in turn revealed that the ticket had been bought under an assumed name. The proffered explanation did not satisfy the officers. We cannot agree with the State, if this is its position, that every nervous young man paying cash for a ticket to New York City under an assumed name and carrying two heavy American Tourister bags may be arrested and held to answer for a serious felony charge." *Florida v. Royer*, 460 U.S. 491, 507, 103 S. Ct. 1319, 75 L. Ed. 2d 229 (1983).

Fourth Circuit

- "The fact that [Defendant] met a number of the drug courier profile characteristics—he traveled on a flight from Miami, a fertile source of narcotics, on a one-way ticket issued in a false name and paid for in cash and that there were no baggage claim checks—alone was not enough to constitute probable cause for arrest. [T]he policeman's observance of the bulge at the ankle in combination with the drug courier profile characteristics would constitute probable cause for arrest." *U.S. v. Aguiar*, 825 F.2d 39, 41 (4th Cir. 1987).

Fifth Circuit

- "[W]hen [the Officer] requested [Defendant] to come with him to the Delta office, the interrogation could no longer be characterized as 'brief' or 'on-the-spot.' Rather, the request signaled the beginning of a more extended interrogation which was to occur in a place other than

where it began. Second, . . . [Defendant] was never
informed that he was 'free to go,' and the circumstances
surrounding the request indicate that [he] would have
been physically restrained if he had refused to accompany [the Officer] or had tried to escape his custody.
Third, the circumstances indicate that the detention
involved here was for the purpose of interrogation. In
sum, the scope of the intrusion involved in [the Officer's]
request for [Defendant] to accompany him to the Delta
office was significantly greater than that involved in a
brief *Terry* stop, and therefore amounted to an arrest."
U.S. v. Hill, 626 F.2d 429, 435–36 (5th Cir. 1980).

Sixth Circuit

- "At the time [the Agent] seized [Defendant's] currency,
  he knew the following facts: [Defendant] was traveling
  to Miami; he arrived shortly before his flight and
  purchased a one-way ticket in his name with cash; although observed entering the terminal with a companion, [Defendant] attempted to present the appearance
  that he was traveling alone; [Defendant] constantly
  looked around as he walked through the airport; [the
  Agent's] search revealed that [Defendant] carried
  $14,190 in cash; and [Defendant] gave an unlikely
  explanation for the source of the money. While travel to
  an alleged drug source city, late arrival at the airport,
  and nervousness are inherently unsuspicious activities,
  this Court has held that these facts are probative in
  deciding whether the government has established probable cause. A defendant's attempt to conceal the fact
  that he is traveling with another also indicates possible
  criminal activity. Even when considered together,
  however, these factors alone did not provide [the Agent]
  with a reasonable ground for belief that the currency
  seized from [Defendant] was contraband or evidence of
  a crime." *U.S. v. Baro*, 15 F.3d 563, 567–68, 1994 FED
  App. 0029P (6th Cir. 1994).
- "The officers in the present case knew that at this point
  they did not have probable cause to arrest the defendant
  and therefore allowed him to leave after their brief
  detention. [W]e do not believe that the move from the
  concourse to the stairwell converted the brief detention
  based on reasonable suspicion into an arrest lacking

probable cause. Given that defendant consented to moving to the stairwell, there was no less intrusive means by which the police could have pursued their legitimate suspicions and the brief five-minute detention of defendant did not exceed the limited restraint permitted by the Fourth Amendment." *U.S. v. Bueno*, 21 F.3d 120, 126, 1994 FED App. 0116P (6th Cir. 1994).

- "At the point in time when the officers directed [Defendant] to accompany them to their airport office, they knew that [Defendant] had arrived in Memphis from a high-profile drug source city; had rapidly walked through the airport terminal; had glanced furtively in every direction as if conducting counter-surveillance; had no luggage beyond the new shoulder bag he carried, despite his asserted three-week sojourn in South Florida; had paid cash for his one-way air passage from Miami to Memphis; had acted nervously, sweated profusely, and had provided implausible answers to several of the officers' inquiries; and, notwithstanding his contention that his shoulder bag contained nothing but gifts for his children, was carrying two highly suspicious packages therein. [The Officer's] discovery of the taped balls, coupled with the full spectrum of facts known about [Defendant] when he was seized, not only gave rise to the reasonable suspicion necessary to subject [Defendant] to a limited investigative *Terry* stop, but, more importantly, also provided the officers with probable cause to arrest him." *U.S. v. Taylor*, 956 F.2d 572, 578 (6th Cir. 1992).

Ninth Circuit

- "Probable cause exists when the police have reasonably trustworthy information sufficient to lead a prudent person to believe that the accused has committed or is committing a crime. Police may use their experience, special training, and expertise to determine that probable cause existed. At the time of [Defendant's] arrest, the police knew that: 1) [Defendant] was wearing sunglasses at night; 2) he scanned the airport and acted nervous; 3) he paid cash for the airline tickets; 4) both [Defendant] and [Accomplice] said they would be gone for five days, but their bags contained no clothing; 5) [Defendant's] ticket had a false name on it; 6) [Defen-

dant] was accompanied by [Accomplice], who was found
to be carrying narcotics before [Defendant's] arrest; and
7) [Defendant] suggested his own complicity by assuming a handcuffed position after [Accomplice's] arrest.
The government established probable cause. Because
the totality of circumstances suggest that [Defendant]
was involved in a narcotics transaction, the subsequent
search of [Defendant] was incident to a lawful arrest."
U.S. v. Milner, 962 F.2d 908, 913 (9th Cir. 1992).

§ 22:4 Consent: Although most airport searches are conducted pursuant to consent, contraband found during a consent search may be suppressed if it is the 'fruit' of an unlawful stop or arrest

Supreme Court

- "[I]t is submitted that the entire encounter was consensual and hence [Defendant] was not being held against
  his will at all. We find this submission untenable. Asking for and examining [Defendant's] ticket and his driver's license were no doubt permissible in themselves,
  but when the officers identified themselves as narcotics
  agents, told [him] that he was suspected of transporting
  narcotics and asked him to accompany them to the police room, while retaining his ticket and driver's license
  and without indicating in any way that he was free to
  depart, [Defendant] was effectively seized for the
  purposes of the Fourth Amendment. These circumstances surely amount to a show of official authority
  such that a reasonable person would have believed he
  was not free to leave. [Defendant] was being illegally
  detained when he consented to the search of his luggage . . . . [W]e agree that the consent was tainted by
  the illegality and was ineffective to justify the search."
  Florida v. Royer, 460 U.S. 491, 501, 502, 103 S. Ct. 1319,
  75 L. Ed. 2d 229 (1983).
- "[T]he totality of the evidence in this case was plainly
  adequate to support the District Court's finding that
  the respondent voluntarily consented to accompany the
  officers to the DEA office. The respondent had twice
  unequivocally indicated her consent to the search, and
  when assured by the police officer that there would be

no problem if nothing were turned up by the search, she began to undress without further comment." *U.S. v. Mendenhall*, 446 U.S. 544, 558, 559, 100 S. Ct. 1870, 64 L. Ed. 2d 497 (1980).

Sixth Circuit

- "As the numerous airport search cases recently before this Court make clear, the Fourth Amendment is not violated when a police officer approaches a member of the traveling public, identifies himself as a law enforcement officer, and solicits information. Moreover, a request to search the passenger's luggage or person does not transform this initial questioning into a seizure. Against this backdrop, a court then confronts the question of whether the approached and questioned passenger actually consented to a search of his bag or person. Where, as here, the government alleges that consent was voluntarily given, the government bears the burden of proof on this issue and the consent must be unequivocal and intelligently given, untainted by duress or coercion." *U.S. v. Baro*, 15 F.3d 563, 566, 1994 FED App. 0029P (6th Cir. 1994).

- "[A]ccording to the officers' testimony, [his] initial approach to defendant at the airport was a permissible consensual encounter. [The Officer] approached defendant on the concourse, identified himself as a police officer, and then asked defendant a few short questions about his identity and travel itinerary, which defendant willingly answered. Defendant then consented while on the airport concourse to a search of his carry-on bag." *U.S. v. Bueno*, 21 F.3d 120, 124, 1994 FED App. 0116P (6th Cir. 1994).

Ninth Circuit

- "We have identified five factors to be considered in determining the voluntariness of consent to a search: (1) whether defendant was in custody; (2) whether the arresting officers have their guns drawn; (3) whether *Miranda* warnings have been given; (4) whether the defendant was told he has a right not to consent; and (5) whether defendant was told a search warrant could be obtained. The fact that some of these factors are not established does not automatically mean that consent was not voluntary." *U.S. v. Russell*, 664 F.3d 1279, 1281 (9th Cir. 2012) (citation omitted).

- "Any search, even a consensual one, is constrained by the bounds of reasonableness. The question here is whether a request to conduct a search of the person for narcotics reasonably includes the groin area. In other words, when [the defendant] consented to a search of his person, was it reasonable for [the officer] to assume the consent included the groin area? The scope of consent is benchmarked against an 'objective reasonableness' test. The factual context is key to our decision. [The officer] specifically advised [the defendant] that he was looking for narcotics. After consenting to the search, [the defendant] was more than cooperative. To facilitate the search, he lifted his arms to shoulder height and spread his legs. [The defendant] could have objected either of the two times he gave verbal consent before the search, or while [the officer] worked his way up from the ankles to the groin. Indeed, [the officer] purposely searched from the ankles up because 'it gives them an opportunity to say that they don't want the search . . . there is an opportunity to stop.' Instead [the defendant] said nothing and certainly did nothing to manifest any change of heart about his consent to search. He never objected, expressed any concern, nor did he revoke consent or call a halt to the search, nor did he complain to the officer after the fact. We hold that the search was reasonable. Narcotics are often hidden on the body in locations that make discovery more difficult, including the groin area. The search here did not extend inside the clothing. Finally, this case does not present a question of a body pat-down by an officer of the opposite gender. Not only would a reasonable person in [the officer's] situation understand that the general consent for a narcotics search of the person included a pat-down of all areas of the body, including the groin area, [the defendant's] unrestricted consent to the search and conduct during the search suggested nothing different." *U.S. v. Russell*, 664 F.3d 1279, 1282–83 (9th Cir. 2012) (citations omitted).

Tenth Circuit

- "Defendant's consent to search of his bag by airport security was voluntary; door of security office was open for most of the interview and search, and the officers never laid hands on defendant, or made any promises, and defendant continuously maintained possession of his bag until it was searched, and he was physically free to leave with his belongings at any time." *U.S. v. Davis*, 286 Fed. Appx. 574 (10th Cir. 2008).

- "A person who is being detained may still give a voluntary consent but if the detention is illegal, the government must prove that the primary taint has been purged and that the consent was in fact voluntary. The government's burden is therefore heavier if the detention is illegal." *U.S. v. McRae*, 81 F.3d 1528, 1537 (10th Cir. 1996).

- "We reject [Defendant's] argument that because [Defendant] was a woman traveling alone, she, as the defendant in *Ward*, would be more easily intimidated than some other person. And we reject any rule that would classify groups of travelers according to gender, race, religion, national origin, or other comparable status." *U.S. v. Little*, 18 F.3d 1499, 1505 (10th Cir. 1994).

Eleventh Circuit

- "Given the extremely intimidating nature of airport stops, this court has emphasized that verbal agreements acquiescing in officers' requests should be scrutinized exceptionally closely to ensure a complete absence of coercive influence." *U.S. v. Blake*, 888 F.2d 795, 799 (11th Cir. 1989).

D.C. Circuit

- "A consensual search cannot exceed the scope of the consent. The scope of the consent is measured by a test of objective reasonableness: it depends on how broadly a reasonable observer would have interpreted the consent under the circumstances. Here, [Defendant] clearly consented to a search of his body for drugs. We conclude that a reasonable person would have understood that consent to encompass the search undertaken here. Under *Jimeno*, the scope of a search is generally defined by its expressed object. In this case, [Defendant] authorized a search for drugs. Dealers frequently hide drugs near their genitals. [The Officer] testified that his colleagues make up to 75 percent of their drug recoveries from around the crotch area. For these reasons, we conclude that a request to conduct a body search for drugs reasonably includes a request to conduct some search of that area." *U.S. v. Rodney*, 956 F.2d 295, 297–98 (D.C. Cir. 1992).

§ 22:5 Boarding passengers and luggage: Warrantless searches of boarding passengers and their luggage are justified by the strong public interest in preventing air piracy

Supreme Court

- "We reiterate that where the risk to public safety is substantial and real, blanket suspicionless searches calibrated to the risk may rank as reasonable—for example, searches now routine at airports and at entrances to courts and other official buildings. But where, as in this case, public safety is not genuinely in jeopardy, the Fourth Amendment precludes the suspicionless search, no matter how conveniently arranged." *Chandler v. Miller*, 520 U.S. 305, 323, 117 S. Ct. 1295, 137 L. Ed. 2d 513, 12 I.E.R. Cas. (BNA) 1233, 145 A.L.R. Fed. 657 (1997).

First Circuit

- "Routine security searches at airport checkpoints pass constitutional muster because the compelling public interest in curbing air piracy generally outweighs their limited intrusiveness. Consequently, all carry-on luggage can be subjected to initial x-ray screening for weapons and explosives without offending the Fourth Amendment. In the event the initial x-ray screening is inconclusive as to the presence of weapons or explosives, the luggage may be hand-searched as reasonably required to rule out their presence." *U.S. v. Doe*, 61 F.3d 107, 109–10 (1st Cir. 1995).
- "Other contraband inadvertently discovered during a routine checkpoint search for weapons and explosives may be seized and introduced in evidence at trial even though unrelated to airline security. On the other hand, lawful airline security searches of carry-on luggage may not be enlarged or tailored systemically to detect

contraband (e.g., narcotics) unrelated to airline security." *U.S. v. Doe*, 61 F.3d 107, 110 (1st Cir. 1995).

Third Circuit

- "The Government concedes that an airport pre-boarding security screening is a search. But this concession obscures the difficult issue of whether [defendant, who had been subjected to both magnetometer search and frisk] experienced one prolonged search, or several individual searches. . . . [W]e find that [defendant] experienced a single, warrantless search, which was initiated without individualized suspicion. . . . [Defendant's] search at the airport checkpoint was justified by the administrative search doctrine. . . . Suspicionless checkpoint searches are permissible under the Fourth Amendment when a court finds a favorable balance between 'the gravity of the public concerns served by the seizure, the degree to which the seizure advances the public interest, and the severity of the interference with individual liberty.' . . . First, there can be no doubt that preventing terrorist attacks on airplanes is of paramount importance. Second, airport checkpoints also advance the public interest. . . . Third, the procedures involved in [defendant's] search were minimally intrusive. They were well-tailored to protect personal privacy, escalating in invasiveness only after a lower level of screening disclosed a reason to conduct a more probing search. . . . Lastly, the entire procedure is rendered less offensive—if not less intrusive—because air passengers are on notice that they will be searched." *U.S. v. Hartwell*, 436 F.3d 174 (3d Cir. 2006).

Fourth Circuit

- "[Defendant] had a choice of traveling by air or by some other means. The signs in the terminal gave him fair notice that if in the course of the total screening process a physical inspection of his hand luggage should be considered necessary to assure the safety of the traveling public, he could be required to submit it for that purpose. When he then voluntarily entered upon the screening process [Defendant] acquiesced in its full potential scope as represented to him, including physical inspection if, as developed, that should be requested.

Allowing him to withdraw his luggage when the x-ray raised the suspicions of the security officers would frustrate the regulation's purpose of deterring hijacking." *U.S. v. DeAngelo*, 584 F.2d 46, 47–48 (4th Cir. 1978).

Seventh Circuit

- "Clearly it is reasonable, regardless of the doctrinal rubric, for the government to require airline passengers to step through a metal detector even though there is no reasonable suspicion that a given passenger is carrying a weapon. In part because the search is not intrusive, and in part because of the danger that an armed passenger poses on an airplane in flight, this condition on the right to travel by air is reasonable." *Burgess v. Lowery*, 201 F.3d 942, 947, 85 A.L.R.5th 719 (7th Cir. 2000).

- "Given the unfortunate realities of today's world, where law enforcement authorities must combat a steady influx of illicit drugs, as well as guard against possible terrorist incidents accomplished with devices ranging from simple handguns to sophisticated bombs, it is not surprising that over the last few decades our society has accepted increased security measures (e.g., hand-held metal detectors used to scan one's torso) at many locations such as airports, courthouses, hospitals, and even schools. In light of these realities, we agree with other courts of appeal that have held that the reasonable expectation of privacy inherent in the contents of luggage is not compromised by a police officer's physical touching of the exterior of luggage left exposed in the overhead rack of a bus." *U.S. v. McDonald*, 100 F.3d 1320, 1325 (7th Cir. 1996).

Ninth Circuit

- "[A]n airport search remains a valid administrative search only so long as the scope of the administrative search exception is not exceeded; once a search is conducted for a criminal investigatory purpose, it can no longer be justified under an administrative search rationale. Thus, because TSA screeners are limited to the single administrative goal of searching for possible safety threats related to explosives, the constitutional

bounds of an airport administrative search require that
the individual screener's actions be no more intrusive
than necessary to determine the existence or absence of
explosives that could result in harm to the passengers
and aircraft. . . . [S]ome inquiry into the actual motivations behind an administrative search is permitted to
guard against wholly pretextual intrusions into the public's reasonable expectations of privacy. Nevertheless,
where—as here—the search is undertaken *pursuant to
a general scheme without individualized suspicion,*
consideration of the government actor's actual motivation has been limited to an inquiry into the *programmatic* purposes motivating the search. The Supreme
Court has cautioned that this inquiry is *not* an invitation to probe the minds of individual officers acting at
the scene. Accordingly, this court has held that where a
warrantless search is conducted pursuant to a lawful
administrative scheme with a constitutionally permissible motivation, the subjective motive of the individual
conducting the search will not invalidate the search.
. . . [I]t is undisputed that here there was no programmatic secondary purpose—[the screener] did not receive
any reward for finding contraband, and searching for
evidence of a crime was not part of her assigned duties.
The TSA search scheme under which she operated was
focused solely on the discovery of threats to air travel
safety. Thus, the inquiries into discretion and search
intent outlined in *Bulacan* and *$124,570 U.S. Currency*
are simply inapplicable here because the purpose inquiry in [the context of intrusions undertaken pursuant
to a general scheme without individualized suspicion] is
to be conducted only at the programmatic level and is
not an invitation to probe the minds of individual officers acting at the scene. Of course, to say that we
conduct the Fourth Amendment inquiry only at the
programmatic level is not to say that a lawful administrative search intent, engaged at the inception of the
search but later abandoned, provides carte blanche to
the searching officers to snoop to their hearts' content
without regard to the scope of their actions. The search
must still be in furtherance of the administrative goal,
no more extensive nor intensive than necessary, in the
light of current technology, to detect the presence of

weapons or explosives[,] . . . [and] confined in good
faith to that purpose. So, as long as (1) the search was
undertaken pursuant to a legitimate administrative
search scheme; (2) the searcher's actions are cabined to
the scope of the permissible administrative search; and
(3) there was no impermissible programmatic secondary
motive for the search, the development of a second,
subjective motive to verify the presence of contraband is
irrelevant to the Fourth Amendment analysis. Thus,
the presence here of a secondary desire to confirm that
the items searched might be contraband could not, in
and of itself, invalidate the initially constitutional
administrative search [the screener] conducted, at least
as long as she actually engaged in a search for explosives and her actions were no more intrusive than necessary to clear the bag of any safety concerns." *U.S. v.
McCarty*, 648 F.3d 820, 831–35 (9th Cir. 2011), as
amended, (Sept. 9, 2011) (inner quotations and citations omitted).

- "The crux of the issue [of defining the scope of the
search], then, involves two related questions: (1) when
did [the screener's] administrative search for explosives
truly end, and become a wholly independent search for
evidence of child pornography?; and (2) which of [the
screener's] actions exceeded the scope of the administrative search by becoming 'more extensive [or] intensive
than necessary, in the light of current technology, to
detect the presence of weapons or explosives'? [W]here
an action is taken that cannot serve the administrative
purpose—either because the threat necessitating the
administrative search has been dismissed, or because
the action is simply unrelated to the administrative
goal—the action clearly exceeds the scope of the permissible search. Here, the scope of the permissible search—
mandated by the TSA protocol—was defined by the
point at which the screener was convinced the bag posed
no threat to airline safety. . . . [The screener] did not
at any point state that she had abandoned her primary
search for aircraft safety hazards at the time she viewed
the *photographs* in the envelope. . . . Thus, the screener's review of the photographs in the packet occurred
within the scope of the ongoing lawful administrative
search. As a result, her discovery of their nature

coincided with her search for explosives, rather than followed the formation of an independent and exclusive intent to search for contraband. Accordingly, [the screener's] viewing of the photographs from the envelope was justified by and part of the lawful administrative search, and—as we clarified above—even the development of a secondary desire to confirm that the photographs evidenced contraband did not invalidate that search." U.S. v. McCarty, 648 F.3d 820, 835–38 (9th Cir. 2011), as amended, (Sept. 9, 2011) (citations omitted).

- "We must decide whether a prospective commercial airline passenger, who presented no identification at check-in, and who voluntarily walked through a metal detector without setting off an alarm, can then prevent a government-ordered secondary screening search by stating he has decided not to fly and wants to leave the terminal. We hold that such passenger cannot prevent the secondary search because such search comports with the Fourth Amendment's requirement that a search be reasonable where, as here, the initial screening was inconclusive. . . . ." U.S. v. Aukai, 440 F.3d 1168 (9th Cir. 2006), on reh'g en banc, 497 F.3d 955 (9th Cir. 2007).

- "Airport screenings of passengers and their baggage constitute administrative searches and are subject to the limitations of the Fourth Amendment. To judge reasonableness, it is necessary to balance the right to be free of intrusion with society's interest in safe air travel. . . . An airport screening search is reasonable if: (1) it is no more extensive or intensive than necessary, in light of current technology, to detect weapons or explosives; (2) it is confined in good faith to that purpose; and (3) passengers may avoid the search by electing not to fly." U.S. v. Marquez, 410 F.3d 612 (9th Cir. 2005), opinion amended, 2005 WL 1661572 (9th Cir. 2005).

- "Passengers rushing to board a plane can fairly be said to have consented to a search for weapons and explosives; any such devices found in their possession are fair game for seizure. But passengers would be surprised to learn that they are also submitted to a more generalized search for contraband or, broader yet, things that

are not in themselves illegal but merely look suspicious."
U.S. v. $124,570 U.S. Currency, 873 F.2d 1240, 1247,
108 A.L.R. Fed. 643 (9th Cir. 1989).

Eleventh Circuit

- "[T]he validity of a screening program does not 'turn[ ]
  on whether significant numbers of putative air pirates
  are actually discovered by the searches conducted under
  the program.' Instead, '[w]hen the Government's interest lies in deterring highly hazardous conduct, a low
  incidence of such conduct, far from impugning the validity of the scheme for implementing this interest, is
  more logically viewed as a hallmark of success.'" *Corbett
  v. Transportation Sec. Admin.*, 767 F.3d 1171, 1180–81
  (11th Cir. 2014), cert. denied, 135 S. Ct. 2867, 192 L.
  Ed. 2d 897 (2015) (citations omitted).

- "Contrary to Corbett's assertion, the scanners effectively
  reduce the risk of air terrorism. Although this proposition is self-evident, Corbett disputes it on the ground
  that he has circumvented the scanners and speculates
  that the rates of failure and false-positives are high.
  But the Fourth Amendment does not require that a
  suspicionless search be fool-proof or yield exacting
  results. The Supreme Court has explained that the
  evaluation of effectiveness is 'not meant to transfer from
  politically accountable officials to the courts the decision as to which among reasonable alternative law
  enforcement techniques should be employed to deal with
  a serious public danger.' Choosing which technique best
  serves the government interest at stake should be left
  to those with 'a unique understanding of, and a responsibility for, limited public resources, including a finite
  number of police officers.' '[W]e need only determine
  whether the [scanner] is a reasonably effective means
  of addressing the government interest in deterring and
  detecting a terrorist attack' at airports. Common sense
  tells us that it is." *Corbett v. Transportation Sec. Admin.*,
  767 F.3d 1171, 1181 (11th Cir. 2014), cert. denied, 135
  S. Ct. 2867, 192 L. Ed. 2d 897 (2015) (citations omitted).

- "The Fourth Amendment does not compel the Administration to employ the least invasive procedure or one
  fancied by Corbett. Airport screening is a permissible
  administrative search; security officers search all pas-

sengers, abuse is unlikely because of its public nature, and passengers elect to travel by air knowing that they must undergo a search. The 'jeopardy to hundreds of human lives and millions of dollars of property inherent in the pirating or blowing up of a large airplane' outweighs the slight intrusion of a generic body scan or, as a secondary measure, a pat-down." *Corbett v. Transportation Sec. Admin.*, 767 F.3d 1171, 1182 (11th Cir. 2014), cert. denied, 135 S. Ct. 2867, 192 L. Ed. 2d 897 (2015) (citations omitted).

- "Because of the danger of air piracy, . . . airport security checkpoints, like international borders, are critical zones in which special fourth amendment considerations apply. After an individual voluntarily presents himself at an airport security area, a resulting search does not require probable cause or even reasonable suspicion, but instead mere suspicion of possible illegal activity. The facts establishing the hijacker profile are sufficient to provide the requisite mere suspicion necessary to conduct the searches in this case." *U.S. v. Lopez-Pages*, 767 F.2d 776, 778 (11th Cir. 1985).

- "[A]irport security checkpoints and loading gates are sui generis under the fourth amendment. Due to the intense danger of air piracy, we have long held that these areas, like international borders, are critical zones in which special fourth amendment considerations apply." *U.S. v. Herzbrun*, 723 F.2d 773, 775 (11th Cir. 1984).

§ 22:6   Dogs: Using a dog to sniff a container at an airport to detect contraband does not normally constitute a search; thus, Fourth Amendment protections do not apply

Supreme Court

- "[W]e conclude that the particular course of investigation that the agents intended to pursue here—exposure of respondent's luggage, which was located in a public place, to a trained canine—did not constitute a search within the meaning of the Fourth Amendment." *U.S. v. Place*, 462 U.S. 696, 707, 103 S. Ct. 2637, 77 L. Ed. 2d 110 (1983).

- "We have affirmed that a person possesses a privacy

interest in the contents of personal luggage that is protected by the Fourth Amendment. A canine sniff by a well-trained narcotics detection dog, however, does not require opening the luggage. It does not expose noncontraband items that otherwise would remain hidden from public view, as does, for example, an officer's rummaging through the contents of the luggage. Thus, the manner in which information is obtained through this investigative technique is much less intrusive than a typical search. Moreover, the sniff discloses only the presence or absence of narcotics, a contraband item. Thus, despite the fact that the sniff tells the authorities something about the contents of the luggage, the information obtained is limited. This limited disclosure also ensures that the owner of the property is not subjected to the embarrassment and inconvenience entailed in less discriminate and more intrusive investigative methods." *U.S. v. Place*, 462 U.S. 696, 707, 103 S. Ct. 2637, 77 L. Ed. 2d 110 (1983).

Third Circuit

- "It is established that when a police officer or other law enforcement officer takes a piece of luggage from a person, a seizure within the meaning of the Fourth Amendment occurs. In *Place*, the Supreme Court analogized temporary seizures of persons, which were found to be constitutional in *Terry v. Ohio*, to temporary seizures of luggage, holding that the temporary seizure of luggage is constitutional so long as the seizure is not overly intrusive upon the person's privacy interest in the property, and so long as the property is not detained for a long period of time. The Court noted that because of the inherently transient nature of drug courier activity at airports, allowing police to make brief investigative stops of persons at airports on reasonable suspicion of drug-trafficking substantially enhances the likelihood that police will be able to prevent the flow of narcotics into distribution channels." *U.S. v. Frost*, 999 F.2d 737, 740–41 (3d Cir. 1993).

Fifth Circuit

- "We recognized that when airport security concerns are not implicated, every passenger who has luggage checked with an airline enjoys a reasonable expectation of privacy that the contents of that luggage will not be exposed in the absence of consent or a legally obtained warrant. That reasonable expectation of privacy, however, does not extend to the airspace surrounding the luggage. Therefore, we held that the use of a trained canine to sniff the exterior of luggage did not constitute a search. As a result, we concluded that reasonable and articulable suspicion is not required before a DEA agent may use a canine trained in drug detection to sniff luggage in the custody of a common carrier." *U.S. v. Lovell*, 849 F.2d 910, 913 (5th Cir. 1988).

Seventh Circuit

- "The officers' decision to detain [Defendant's] tote bag for a canine sniff was likewise justified. A narcotics detection dog would have quickly confirmed or dispelled the officers' suspicion that the bag contained narcotics without causing undue embarrassment or disturbing its other contents. Moreover, the proposed detention would have lasted no more than approximately fifteen minutes. Where the scope of the detention and the investigative technique employed is so carefully tailored to its underlying justification, there is no Fourth Amendment violation." *U.S. v. McCarthur*, 6 F.3d 1270, 1277–78, 39 Fed. R. Evid. Serv. 1126 (7th Cir. 1993).

Eighth Circuit

- "[A] dog sniff of luggage [does] not constitute a search implicating the Fourth Amendment. [A] dog sniff is less intrusive than a typical search. Furthermore, the information provided by a dog sniff is limited. It merely discloses the presence or absence of contraband." *U.S. v. Turpin*, 920 F.2d 1377, 1385 (8th Cir. 1990).

Ninth Circuit

- "As a general proposition, we agree with this statement—government agents who have no particular reason to believe that any particular drug suspect will be arriving on an incoming flight need not have a dog sitting continuously at the gate, the luggage area, or the nearby location where the search will be conducted. Where, though, government agents are at the airport

awaiting a particular individual who they know is coming on a particular flight and whom they suspect of drug
trafficking, they should arrange for a dog to be sent to
the appropriate location as soon as they decide to meet
the plane themselves. [C]learly the government must
have its dog either at the same airport or at a similarly
accessible location, so that the dog can sniff the
suspect's luggage with dispatch." *U.S. v. $191,910.00 in
U.S. Currency*, 16 F.3d 1051, 1061–62 (9th Cir. 1994).

§ 22:7 Seizure of luggage: A limited seizure of a traveler's luggage may be permissible when there is a reasonable suspicion that it contains seizable items

Supreme Court

- "In the ordinary case, the Court has viewed a seizure of
  personal property as *per se* unreasonable within the
  meaning of the Fourth Amendment unless it is accomplished pursuant to a judicial warrant issued upon
  probable cause and particularly describing the items to
  be seized. Where law enforcement authorities have
  probable cause to believe that a container holds contraband or evidence of a crime, but have not secured a
  warrant, the Court has interpreted the Amendment to
  permit seizure of the property, pending issuance of a
  warrant to examine its contents, if the exigencies of the
  circumstances demand it or some other recognized
  exception to the warrant requirement is present." *U.S.
  v. Place*, 462 U.S. 696, 701, 103 S. Ct. 2637, 77 L. Ed.
  2d 110 (1983).

- "[T]he Government asks us to recognize the reasonableness under the Fourth Amendment of warrantless
  seizures of personal luggage from the custody of the
  owner on the basis of less than probable cause, for the
  purpose of pursuing a limited course of investigation,
  short of opening the luggage, that would quickly confirm
  or dispel the authorities' suspicion. Specifically, we are
  asked to apply the principles of *Terry v. Ohio*, to permit
  such seizures on the basis of reasonable, articulable
  suspicion, premised on objective facts, that the luggage
  contains contraband or evidence of a crime. In our view,
  such application is appropriate." *U.S. v. Place*, 462 U.S.
  696, 702, 103 S. Ct. 2637, 77 L. Ed. 2d 110 (1983).

- "Given the fact that seizures of property can vary in intrusiveness, some brief detentions of personal effects may be so minimally intrusive of Fourth Amendment interests that strong countervailing governmental interests will justify a seizure based only on specific articulable facts that the property contains contraband or evidence of a crime." *U.S. v. Place*, 462 U.S. 696, 706, 103 S. Ct. 2637, 77 L. Ed. 2d 110 (1983).

- "[S]uch a seizure can effectively restrain the person since he is subjected to the possible disruption of his travel plans in order to remain with his luggage or to arrange for its return. Therefore, when the police seize luggage from the suspect's custody, we think the limitations applicable to investigative detentions of the person should define the permissible scope of an investigative detention of the person's luggage on less than probable cause. Under this standard, it is clear that the police conduct here exceeded the permissible limits of a *Terry*-type investigative stop. The length of the detention of respondent's luggage alone precludes the conclusion that the seizure was reasonable in the absence of probable cause. . . . [T]he New York agents knew the time of [Defendant's] scheduled arrival at LaGuardia, had ample time to arrange for their additional investigation at that location, and thereby could have minimized the intrusion on respondent's Fourth Amendment interests." *U.S. v. Place*, 462 U.S. 696, 708–09, 103 S. Ct. 2637, 77 L. Ed. 2d 110 (1983).

Second Circuit

- "It is clear that the agents seized the suitcase within the meaning of the fourth amendment when they informed [Defendant] that they intended to hold the suitcase for the purpose of obtaining a search warrant. Accordingly, the government must demonstrate that, at the point of the seizure, the agents had at least a reasonable suspicion based on specific and articulable facts that the suitcase contained contraband. To justify a *Terry* type detention, a law enforcement officer must have a reasonable suspicion supported by articulable facts that criminal activity may be afoot. The term reasonable suspicion is not capable of a precise definition. It is clear, however, than an inchoate and unparticular-

ized suspicion or hunch on the part of a law enforcement officer will not suffice to establish reasonable
suspicion. Rather, the officer must provide specific reasonable inferences which [the Officer] is entitled to draw
from the facts in light of his experience. In making this
determination, we consider the totality of the
circumstances. Acts that considered in isolation are consistent with innocent travel, nevertheless, when considered together, may establish cause for further
investigation." *U.S. v. Hooper*, 935 F.2d 484, 493 (2d
Cir. 1991).

Fifth Circuit

- "[A] Border Patrol agent's removal of a suspect's bag
  from an airport baggage area conveyor belt, his squeeze
  of the bag to procure a scent, and his subsequent sniff
  of that bag constituted neither a seizure nor a search."
  U.S. v. Garcia, 849 F.2d 917, 919 (5th Cir. 1988).

Seventh Circuit

- "Finally, we note that the brief detention of the
  defendant's bags (fifteen minutes) satisfies the dictates
  of *Place* that the limitations defining a *Terry* stop also
  define the limits of an investigative detention of luggage Here, the agents were diligent in the effectuation
  of their duties as less than a quarter of an hour passed
  before a drug-detection dog was brought to the scene."
  U.S. v. Edwards, 898 F.2d 1273, 1277–78 (7th Cir.
  1990).

Eighth Circuit

- "Police officers must have either the owner's consent or
  a reasonable suspicion supported by articulable objective facts that the luggage contains drugs in order to
  detain a person's luggage for a sniff search." *U.S. v.
  Tillman*, 81 F.3d 773, 775 (8th Cir. 1996).
- "Police officers are, of course, always free to approach
  citizens and question them if they are willing to stay
  and listen. Without at least reasonable suspicion,
  though, officers may not even temporarily seize a person
  or his luggage. For the reasonable suspicion standard to
  have meaning, officers must be required to have more
  than a hunch that a suspect is carrying drugs." *U.S. v.
  O'Neal*, 17 F.3d 239, 242 (8th Cir. 1994).

Tenth Circuit

- "The seven hour delay in the present case clearly goes beyond the brevity required for a *Place* seizure. Moreover, in examining whether the DEA agents could have minimized the intrusion on [Defendant's] Fourth Amendment interests, we note that unexplored alternatives to the course of action did exist. In addition, as in *Place*, the intrusion here was exacerbated by the failure of the agents to accurately inform [Defendant] of the place to which they were transporting the luggage, of the length of time he might be dispossessed, and of what arrangements would be made for return of the luggage if the investigation dispelled the suspicion." *U.S. v. Scales*, 903 F.2d 765, 769 (10th Cir. 1990).

Chapter 23

Mail Searches

Research References

West's Key Number Digest

Customs Duties ⊘126; Postal Service ⊘47; Searches and Seizures
⊘29

KeyCite®: Cases and other legal materials listed in KeyCite Scope can be
researched through the KeyCite service on Westlaw®. Use KeyCite to
check citations for form, parallel references, prior and later history, and
comprehensive citator information, including citations to other decisions
and secondary materials.

---

§ 23:1   First class mail: First class mail is accorded full Fourth Amendment protection and may only be opened pursuant to a search warrant

Supreme Court

- "The significant Fourth Amendment interest was in the
  privacy of this first-class mail; and that privacy [could]
  not [be] disturbed or invaded until the approval of the

magistrate was obtained." *U.S. v. Van Leeuwen*, 397 U.S. 249, 253, 90 S. Ct. 1029, 25 L. Ed. 2d 282 (1970).

- "[First class] letters and sealed packages of this kind in the mail are as fully guarded from examination and inspection, except as to their outward form and weight, as if they were retained by the parties forwarding them in their own domiciles. The constitutional guaranty of the right of the people to be secure in their papers against unreasonable searches and seizures extends to their papers, thus closed against inspection, wherever they may be. Whilst in the mail, they can only be opened and examined under like warrant, issued upon similar oath or affirmation, particularly describing the thing to be seized, as is required when papers are subjected to search in one's own household." *Ex parte Jackson*, 96 U.S. 727, 733, 24 L. Ed. 877, 1877 WL 18454 (1877).

Fifth Circuit

- "Individuals do not surrender their expectations of privacy in closed containers when they send them by mail or common carrier. The Supreme Court has long recognized that [l]etters and other sealed packages are in the general class of effects in which the public at large has a legitimate expectation of privacy. Both senders and addressees of packages or other closed containers can reasonably expect that the government will not open them." *U.S. v. Villarreal*, 963 F.2d 770, 773–74 (5th Cir. 1992).

- "[I]nvestigative detention of an overnight package, based only on reasonable suspicion, may violate the Fourth Amendment if the detention continues, without probable cause, for an unreasonable time after the package's delivery deadline." *U.S. v. Lewis*, 902 F.2d 1176, 1180, 30 Fed. R. Evid. Serv. 583 (5th Cir. 1990).

Sixth Circuit

- "The Community contends that the state is unable to seize tobacco products that are being shipped to it because it is immune from seizures as an independent sovereign . . . (C)ontrary to the Community's argument, the Supreme Court has clearly endorsed state seizures as a remedy where sovereign immunity prevents in-court remedies. This underscores the problem with the Community's argument here, as it appears that sovereign immunity only provides immunity from suit, not from seizures. Although the Community attempts to portray seizures with a search warrant as a type of judicial process, the Supreme Court has clearly taken the opposite view, and the Community's argument on this point is not availing." *Keweenaw Bay Indian Community v. Rising*, 477 F.3d 881, 2007 FED App. 0084P (6th Cir. 2007).

- "It is well established that letters are in the general class of effects protected by the Fourth Amendment. However, if a letter is sent to another, the sender's expectation of privacy ordinarily terminates upon delivery. This is true even though the sender may have instructed the recipient to keep the letters private." *U.S. v. King*, 55 F.3d 1193, 1195–96, 1995 FED App. 0170P (6th Cir. 1995).

Eighth Circuit

- "[A] seizure occurred when Drug Enforcement Administration agents took custody of a package and its contents from employees of a private carrier. '[T]he decision by governmental authorities to exert dominion and control over the package for their own purposes clearly constituted a seizure' . . . a package in the mail may be detained on the basis of reasonable suspicion to believe it contains contraband pending further investigation directed toward establishing probable cause which will support issuance of a search warrant." *Garmon v. Foust*, 741 F.2d 1069, 1072, 19 Ed. Law Rep. 872 (8th Cir. 1984).

Ninth Circuit

- "There is no expectation of privacy in the addresses on a package, regardless of its class. The Supreme Court has held that the inspection of the outside of first-class mail did not disturb any privacy interest. . . .[S]enders knowingly exposed the outsides of the mail to postal employees and others, and defendant could not keep those areas private." *U.S. v. Hinton*, 222 F.3d 664, 675 (9th Cir. 2000).

Tenth Circuit

- "A temporary detention of mail for investigative purposes is not an unreasonable seizure when authorities have a reasonable suspicion of criminal activity." *U.S. v. Lux*, 905 F.2d 1379, 1382, 115 A.L.R. Fed. 749 (10th Cir. 1990).

Eleventh Circuit

- "It is beyond dispute that mail is subject to Fourth Amendment protection." *U.S. v. Smith*, 39 F.3d 1143, 1144 (11th Cir. 1994).

§ 23:2   Other mail: Mail other than first class is not accorded the protection of the Fourth Amendment

Supreme Court

- "[F]irst-class mail such as letters and sealed packages subject to letter postage—as distinguished from newspapers, magazines, pamphlets, and other printed matter—is free from inspection by postal authorities, except in the manner provided by the Fourth Amendment." *U.S. v. Van Leeuwen*, 397 U.S. 249, 251, 90 S. Ct. 1029, 25 L. Ed. 2d 282 (1970).

First Circuit

- "[T]he package was not first-class but must have been accepted as either third- or fourth-class mail. The appellant might have protected the privacy of his package by marking it first class. [W]e see no constitutional question under the unreasonable search and seizure provision of the Fourth Amendment." *Santana v. U.S.*, 329 F.2d 854, 856 (1st Cir. 1964).

Fourth Circuit

- "[U]nlike first class mail, there is no expectation of privacy in the forwarding of fourth class mail. Such classification is not altered by the availability of preferential handling to the extent practicable in dispatch and delivery by payment of a special handling fee." *U.S. v. Riley*, 554 F.2d 1282, 1283 (4th Cir. 1977).

Sixth Circuit

- "[I]nspection by the Post Office Department of an un-

sealed package not having upon it stamps sufficient to
qualify it as first class mail was not an invasion of appellant's immunity from unreasonable search and
seizure." *Webster v. U.S.*, 92 F.2d 462 (C.C.A. 6th Cir.
1937).

§ 23:3   International mail: Mail arriving from foreign countries may be searched without a warrant under the rationale which justifies border searches

Supreme Court

- "[C]ustoms officials could search, without probable
  cause and without a warrant, envelopes carried by an
  entering traveler, whether in his luggage or on his
  person. Surely no different constitutional standard
  should apply simply because the envelopes were mailed,
  not carried. The critical fact is that envelopes cross the
  border and enter this country, not that they are brought
  in by one mode of transportation rather than another."
  U.S. v. Ramsey, 431 U.S. 606, 620, 97 S. Ct. 1972, 52 L.
  Ed. 2d 617 (1977).

Fifth Circuit

- "There appears to be no sound reason to distinguish between incoming mail and other property that crosses
  our border. Affixing a postage stamp to a parcel should
  not grant it immunity that would not be accorded a
  package carried by a traveller." *U.S. v. Richards*, 638
  F.2d 765, 772 (5th Cir. 1981).

- "Mail sorting rooms at a port of entry like New York
  are border areas. Thus, the instant search was reasonable simply because the package was searched at a border area after entering this country from Thailand."
  U.S. v. Pringle, 576 F.2d 1114, 1117 (5th Cir. 1978).

Seventh Circuit

- "The search at issue here, an airport search of a package sent from a foreign country into the United States,
  is the functional equivalent of an international border
  search. Federal agents are not restricted by Fourth
  Amendment standards when they conduct such routine
  searches. Indeed, [a]ny person or thing coming into the

United States is subject to search by that fact alone, whether or not there be any suspicion of illegality directed to the particular person or thing to be searched." *U.S. v. Smith*, 29 F.3d 270, 273–74, 24 Envtl. L. Rep. 21252 (7th Cir. 1994).

Ninth Circuit

- "Although it is undisputed that the officers did not follow the proper procedures for obtaining a mail cover, suppression is not the appropriate remedy for a failure to follow agency regulations. . . .In *Ani*, we held that the exclusionary rule was not triggered when a customs inspector searched a package sent via international mail without reasonable cause and contrary to postal regulations. Rather, we held that, because border searches of international mail do not require probable cause, the customs inspector's search did not violate a constitutional mandate." *U.S. v. Hinton*, 222 F.3d 664, 674 (9th Cir. 2000).

- "In applying the reasonable cause standard, the Supreme Court and this court have accorded considerable weight to the source country origin of an international package. Moreover, these cases and others make clear that once suspicion is triggered by source country origin, not much else is required to justify a search. The *Ramsey* Court's ruling that an agent had reasonable cause to suspect contraband in a letter was based on the letter's Thailand origin, its bulkiness, and the fact that it weighed considerably more than a normal airmail letter. In *Nates*, this court found reasonable cause to suspect, in a departing international flight case, where the bags were brand new, unusually heavy, without identification tags, and destined for Colombia, a known source-country for narcotics on a flight often used by currency smugglers. In *Most*, the customs agent based his decision to open the package on his knowledge that the package was coming from a source country for drugs, his observance that the label described an unusually cheap article; and the inference that the package contained something extra because it weighed more than expected for the labeled description." *U.S. v. Taghizadeh*, 87 F.3d 287, 289–90 (9th Cir. 1996), as amended, (Aug. 14, 1996).

- "Inspection of mail from abroad is a border search for which neither a search warrant nor probable cause is required. . . . Such searches are considered reasonable under the Fourth Amendment simply by virtue of the fact that they occur at the border." *U.S. v. Most*, 789 F.2d 1411, 1414 (9th Cir. 1986).

Tenth Circuit

- "[T]he interception and discovery of the hashish in New York was a legal border search. Furthermore, controlled or monitored deliveries of intercepted mail packages of foreign origin to the named addressee have been upheld." *U.S. v. Galvez*, 465 F.2d 681, 687 (10th Cir. 1972).

D.C. Circuit

- "Defendant concedes that no warrant was required for the initial opening of the box, as it arrived at the border via international mail." *U.S. v. Gbemisola*, 225 F.3d 753, 758 (D.C. Cir. 2000).

§23:4 Controlled mail deliveries: When law enforcement agents lawfully learn that there is contraband in a container, they may reseal the container and deliver it to the intended recipient

Supreme Court

- "The lawful discovery by common carriers or customs officers of contraband in transit presents law enforcement authorities with an opportunity to identify and prosecute the person or persons responsible for the movement of the contraband. To accomplish this, the police, rather than simply seizing the contraband and destroying it, make a so-called controlled delivery of the container to its consignee, allowing the container to continue its journey to the destination contemplated by the parties. The person dealing in the contraband can then be identified upon taking possession of and asserting dominion over the container." *Illinois v. Andreas*, 463 U.S. 765, 769, 103 S. Ct. 3319, 77 L. Ed. 2d 1003 (1983).

- "The threshold question, then, is whether an individual

has a legitimate expectation of privacy in the contents of a previously lawfully searched container. It is obvious that the privacy interest in the contents of a container diminishes with respect to a container that law enforcement authorities have already lawfully opened and found to contain illicit drugs. No protected privacy interest remains in contraband in a container once government officers lawfully have opened that container and identified its contents as illegal. The simple act of resealing the container to enable the police to make a controlled delivery does not operate to revive or restore the lawfully invaded privacy rights." *Illinois v. Andreas*, 463 U.S. 765, 771, 103 S. Ct. 3319, 77 L. Ed. 2d 1003 (1983).

- "The issue then becomes, at what point after an interruption of control or surveillance [should courts] recognize the individual's expectation of privacy in the container as a legitimate right protected by the Fourth Amendment proscription against unreasonable searches. In fashioning a standard, we must be mindful of three Fourth Amendment principles. First, the standard should be workable for application by rank and file, trained police officers. Second, it should be reasonable; for example, it would be absurd to recognize as legitimate an expectation of privacy where there is only a minimal probability that the contents of a particular container had been changed. Third, the standard should be objective, not dependent on the belief of individual police officers. A workable, objective standard that limits the risk of intrusion on legitimate privacy interests is whether there is a substantial likelihood that the contents of the container have been changed during the gap in surveillance. We hold that absent a substantial likelihood that the contents have been changed, there is no legitimate expectation of privacy in the contents of a container previously opened under lawful authority." *Illinois v. Andreas*, 463 U.S. 765, 772–73, 103 S. Ct. 3319, 77 L. Ed. 2d 1003 (1983).

Seventh Circuit

- "No protected privacy interest remains in contraband in a container once government officers lawfully have opened that container and identified its contents as illegal. The simple act of resealing the container to enable the police to make a controlled delivery does not operate to revive or restore the lawfully invaded privacy rights." *U.S. v. Koenig*, 856 F.2d 843, 853 (7th Cir. 1988).

Tenth Circuit

- "[T]he official seizure of the contraband occurred . . . when the government asserted dominion over it. Certainly, the seizure meets the Fourth Amendment requirement of probable cause, because the government agents involved knew that the substance was contraband before seizing it. But, the officers' failure to obtain a warrant to seize can be excused only if the circumstances at the time of the seizure were sufficiently exigent to make their course of action imperative. The officers had determined with certainty—and without violation of privacy—that the substance submitted for shipment was contraband. At that time, they could have ordered that the substance be detained until a magistrate could issue a warrant to seize it. The time delay required to obtain a warrant, however, might very well have warned the parties to the crime of the government's presence and prevented their apprehension. If the contraband had not been shipped immediately, the . . . addressee probably would have become suspicious and remained aloof, and the officers' investigation and arrest process would have proven unproductive." *U.S. v. Ford*, 525 F.2d 1308, 1313 (10th Cir. 1975).

§23:5 Detention of mail: Mail can be seized for a limited period of time based upon reasonable suspicion

First Circuit

- "[T]he inspector had reasonable suspicion to detain the package initially. When the inspector learned that the sender's address was fictitious, additional suspicion developed, justifying the further delay that it took to arrange for the dog sniff test. In addition to having reasonable suspicion, the officials did not unreasonably delay delivery of the package. To determine the reasonableness of the delay, we review the diligence of the investigators, the length of detention, and the information conveyed to the suspect." *U.S. v. Allen*, 990 F.2d 667, 671 (1st Cir. 1993).

Third Circuit

- "Postal authorities may seize and detain mailed items for a reasonable amount of time, if they have a reasonable suspicion of criminal activity. We look at the totality of the circumstances in determining whether the length of the detention was reasonable. Here, the length of the delay [four days] was reasonable because it was due to the investigation, scheduled leave, and the weekend, when postal operations, in ordinary course, cease or slow down considerably. Therefore, [Defendant's] argument is without merit and we will affirm the District Court's finding that the Parcel was not unreasonably seized." *U.S. v. Golson*, 743 F.3d 44 (3d Cir. 2014).

Fifth Circuit

- "[A] temporary seizure of a mailed package—removing it from the normal flow of mail—was not a Fourth Amendment violation because postal inspectors acted on legitimate suspicions." *U.S. v. Daniel*, 982 F.2d 146, 150 (5th Cir. 1993).

Sixth Circuit

- "Police detective, stationed in airport mail facility, had reasonable suspicion to justify detaining defendant's express mail package pending a dog sniff, which occurred approximately 20 minutes of the time detective first noticed the package; signature was waived with an X mark, package seemed dense, the label was handwritten, the package was coming from Las Vegas and going to Shaker Heights, and the return address was fictitious." *U.S. v. Alexander*, 540 F.3d 494 (6th Cir. 2008).

Seventh Circuit

- "[A]lthough a person generally maintains a reasonable expectation of privacy in mail sent or received using an alias and the use of an alias does not result in an outright loss of Fourth Amendment rights, a law enforcement officer or a court is certainly entitled to consider the use of an alias a relevant factor in deciding whether to detain mail for further investigation or issue a warrant authorizing search of a package." *U.S. v. Pitts*, 322 F.3d 449 (7th Cir. 2003).

- "The Supreme Court has recognized that individuals have a Fourth Amendment right to be free from unreasonable searches and seizures of items they place in the mail. . . . However, if law enforcement authorities possess reasonable suspicion to believe that a package contains contraband, they may detain that package for a reasonable length of time while investigating the package. . . . Thus, we may uphold the detention here if the postal inspector reasonably suspected that the package contained contraband and if the detention lasted for a reasonable duration." *U.S. v. Dennis*, 115 F.3d 524, 531–32 (7th Cir. 1997).

Eighth Circuit

- "[Defendant] contends the postal inspector lacked the requisite reasonable suspicion to detain and inspect the Express Mail package. ... It is clear under our precedent that when [postal inspector] moved the package to a separate room for a canine sniff, the package was seized for Fourth Amendment purposes. Having determined there was a seizure, we must decide whether there was a reasonable, articulable suspicion to support the seizure. ... Reasonable suspicion exists when 'an officer possesses a particularized and objective basis for suspecting that the package contains contraband', that is more than an 'inchoate and unparticularized suspicion or hunch.' The facts informing [the inspector's] decision to move the Express Mail package into a separate room are undisputed. The fighting issue is whether, taken together, these facts give rise to a reasonable suspicion. We believe they do. The Los Angeles postal inspector that forwarded the package to [the inspector] informed [him] that the package had identifying characteristics that indicated the presence of contraband. The package was typical of those used by drug dealers for shipping drugs. The address labels were handwritten rather than pre-printed as used by most Express Mail customers. The package came from a narcotics source city. Payment for delivery of the package was made with cash. The package was delivered to the airport by an individual driving a rental vehicle. The vehicle was rented by an individual that lived 60 miles from the airmail facility. Based on this information, his own inspection of the package, and his twenty-one years as a postal inspector, including nine years as a narcotics officer, [the inspector] requested and scheduled a canine sniff to determine if the package contained contraband. ... Each of the factors articulated by [the inspector], when considered alone, is consistent with innocent mail use. However, when those factors are viewed in the aggregate by a trained law enforcement officer, they give rise to the objectively reasonable suspicion needed to justify a canine sniff." *U.S. v. Walker*, 324 F.3d 1032 (8th Cir. 2003).

- "[L]aw enforcement authorities must possess a reasonable suspicion based on articulable facts that a package contains contraband before they may detain the package for investigation." *U.S. v. Vasquez*, 213 F.3d 425, 426, 55 Fed. R. Evid. Serv. 218 (8th Cir. 2000).

- "Individuals have a right to be free from unreasonable searches and seizures of items they place in the mail. . . . Law enforcement authorities must possess a reasonable suspicion based on articulable facts that a package contains contraband before they may detain the package for investigation. . . . Reasonable suspicion exists when, based on the totality of the circumstances, an officer possesses a particularized and objective basis for suspecting that the package contains contraband, that is, more than an inchoate and unparticularized suspicion or hunch." *U.S. v. Johnson*, 171 F.3d 601, 603 (8th Cir. 1999).

- "[I]ndividuals have a Fourth Amendment right to be free from unreasonable searches and seizures of items placed in the first-class mail, and law enforcement authorities must have a reasonable suspicion based on articulable, objective facts that a package contains contraband before detaining it from the mail without a warrant." *U.S. v. Sundby*, 186 F.3d 873, 875 (8th Cir. 1999).

- "[P]ostal authorities acting upon reasonable suspicion have been permitted to physically seize and remove items in the mail that are believed to contain narcotics and subject the items to canine drug sniffs." *U.S. v. Harvey*, 961 F.2d 1361, 1364 (8th Cir. 1992).

Ninth Circuit

- "The recipient of a mailed item… has a reasonable expectation that the mail will not be detained by postal employees beyond the normal delivery date and time. … [Defendant] argues that the detention of the package was unreasonable because [the postal inspector] waited twenty-two hours after receiving the parcel to call for a canine sniff. Even if the initial seizure of a mailed package is based on reasonable suspicion, a prolonged detention is unreasonable under the Fourth Amendment. … [Defendant] contends that the package was unreasonably detained for twenty-two hours, from the time [the inspector] received the package at 3 p.m. on March 29, until the time he requested a canine sniff at 1 p.m. on March 30. She asserts that the detention began at 3:00 p.m. when [the inspector] received the package after its arrival at the Honolulu Post Office. She fails to consider, however, that 3:00 p.m. was past the delivery time for express mail on that day. [Defendant's] package could not have been delivered until the following morning. Because [defendant's] possessory interest in the package was in the timely delivery of the parcel, [the inspector] did not interfere with that interest before the regular delivery time on March 30, 2000. The record does not indicate the precise time that [defendant's] packages would have been delivered but for the detention. Assuming, for the purposes of resolving this question, that the earliest time of delivery was 6:00 a.m. on March 30, 2000, the interference with [defendant's] possessory interest caused by the delay in calling for the canine sniff at 1:00 p.m. was only seven hours. A seven-hour interference with [defendant's] possessory interest, prior to obtaining probable cause to seize the package, was not unreasonable under the circumstances." *U.S. v. Hernandez*, 313 F.3d 1206 (9th Cir. 2002).

Tenth Circuit

- "In this Circuit, it is clear that a temporary detention of mail for investigative purposes is not an unreasonable seizure when authorities have a reasonable suspicion of criminal activity. Thus, the issue is whether the postal inspectors had a reasonable suspicion of criminal activity at the time they detained the package." *U.S. v. Glover*, 104 F.3d 1570, 1576 (10th Cir. 1997) (abrogated on other grounds by, Corley v. U.S., 556 U.S. 303, 129 S. Ct. 1558, 173 L. Ed. 2d 443 (2009)).

- "The temporary detention of mail for investigative purposes is not an unreasonable seizure when authorities have a reasonable suspicion of criminal activity. . . . In the present case, the package shared some of the characteristics of a profile developed to identify narcotics packages in that it contained a handwritten label; was going from an individual to an individual; was coming from a narcotics source state; bore no return zip code; had a misspelled return address street; contained a correction in the city portion of the return address; and was found to contain a nonexistent return address street number. . . . A combination of seemingly independent innocent factors may create a reasonable suspicion justifying detention for a dog sniff if the factors substantially reflect elements of a suspicious profile." *U.S. v. Scarborough*, 128 F.3d 1373, 1378, 47 Fed. R. Evid. Serv. 1395, 158 A.L.R. Fed. 725 (10th Cir. 1997).

Eleventh Circuit

- "The Supreme Court has held that no Fourth Amendment privacy interest in first-class mail is invaded by detaining such mail based on facts that create reasonable suspicion until a search warrant can be obtained. Reasonable suspicion results from specific and articulable facts and rational inferences therefrom that reasonably justify an intrusion." *U.S. v. Banks*, 3 F.3d 399, 401 (11th Cir. 1993).

Chapter 24

Canine Searches

Research References

West's Key Number Digest

Drugs and Narcotics ☞184 to 185; Schools ☞169.5; Searches and Seizures ☞13, 22, 192

KeyCite®: Cases and other legal materials listed in KeyCite Scope can be researched through the KeyCite service on Westlaw®. Use KeyCite to check citations for form, parallel references, prior and later history, and comprehensive citator information, including citations to other decisions and secondary materials.

---

§ 24:1 Private property: Private property located in public and semipublic places is subject to sniffing by a dog. Such an act is not a search

<u>Supreme Court</u>

- "An officer, in other words, may conduct certain unrelated checks during an otherwise lawful traffic stop. But contrary to Justice Alito's suggestion, he may not do so in a way that prolongs the stop, absent the reasonable suspicion ordinarily demanded to justify detaining an individual. . . . [A] dog sniff, unlike the routine measures just mentioned, is not an ordinary incident of a traffic stop. Lacking the same close connection to roadway safety as the ordinary inquiries, a dog sniff is not fairly characterized as part of the officer's traffic mission. . . . If an officer can complete traffic-based inquiries expeditiously, then that is the amount of 'time reasonably required to complete [the stop's] mission.' As we said in *Caballes* and reiterate today, a traffic stop 'prolonged beyond' that point is 'unlawful.' The critical question, then, is not whether the dog sniff occurs before or after the officer issues a ticket, as Justice ALITO supposes, but whether conducting the sniff 'prolongs'— *i.e.,* adds time to—'the stop.' " *Rodriguez v. U.S.*, 135 S. Ct. 1609, 1615–16, 191 L. Ed. 2d 492 (2015) (inner citations omitted).

- "Since the officers' investigation took place in a constitutionally protected area, we turn to the question of whether it was accomplished through an unlicensed physical intrusion. While law enforcement officers need not shield their eyes when passing by the home on public thoroughfares, an officer's leave to gather information is sharply circumscribed when he steps off those thoroughfares and enters the Fourth Amendment's protected areas. In permitting, for example, visual observation of the home from public navigable airspace, we were careful to note that it was done in a physically nonintrusive manner. *Entick v. Carrington,* a case undoubtedly familiar to every American statesman at the time of the Founding, *Boyd v. United States,* states the general rule clearly: [O]ur law holds the property of every man so sacred, that no man can set his foot upon his neighbour's close without his leave. As it is undisputed that the detectives had all four of their feet and all four of their companion's firmly planted on the constitutionally protected extension of Jardines' home, the only question is whether he had given his leave (even implicitly) for them to do so. He had not. A license may be implied from the habits of the country, notwithstanding the strict rule of the English common law as to entry upon a close. We have accordingly recognized that the knocker on the front door is treated as an invitation or license to attempt an entry, justifying ingress to the home by solicitors, hawkers and peddlers of all kinds. This implicit license typically permits the visitor to approach the home by the front path, knock promptly, wait briefly to be received, and then (absent invitation to linger longer) leave. Complying with the terms of that traditional invitation does not require fine-grained legal knowledge; it is generally managed without incident by the Nation's Girl Scouts and trick-or-treaters. Thus, a police officer not armed with a warrant may approach a home and knock, precisely because that is no more than any private citizen might do. But introducing a trained police dog to explore the area around the home in hopes of discovering incriminating evidence is something else. There is no customary invitation to do *that*. An invitation to engage in canine forensic investigation assuredly does not inhere in the very act of hanging a knocker. To find a visitor knocking on the door is routine (even if sometimes unwelcome); to spot that same visitor exploring the front path with a metal detector, or marching his bloodhound into the garden before saying hello and asking permission, would inspire most of us to—well, call the police. The scope of a license—express or implied—is limited not only to a particular area but also to a specific purpose. Consent at a traffic stop to an officer's checking out an anonymous tip that there is a body in the trunk does not permit the officer to rummage through the trunk for narcotics. Here, the background social norms that invite a visitor to the front door do not invite him there to conduct a search." *Florida v. Jardines*, 133 S. Ct. 1409, 1415–16, 185 L. Ed. 2d 495 (2013) (inner quotations and citations omitted).

- "Official conduct that does not compromise any legitimate interest in privacy is not a search subject to the Fourth Amendment. We have held that any interest in possessing contraband cannot be deemed legitimate, and thus, governmental conduct that only reveals the possession of contraband compromises no legitimate privacy interest. . . . Accordingly, the use of a well-trained narcotics-detection dog—one that does not expose noncontraband items that otherwise would remain hidden from public view—during a lawful traffic stop, generally does not implicate legitimate privacy interests." *Illinois v. Caballes*, 543 U.S. 405, 125 S. Ct. 834, 160 L. Ed. 2d 842 (2005).

- "It is well established that a vehicle stop at a highway checkpoint effectuates a seizure within the meaning of the Fourth Amendment. . . .The fact that officers walk a narcotics-detection dog around the exterior of each car at the Indianapolis checkpoints does not transform the seizure into a search. . . . Just as in *Place*, an exterior sniff of an automobile does not require entry into the car and is not designed to disclose any information other than the presence or absence of narcotics. . . . Like the dog sniff in *Place*, a sniff by a dog that simply walks around a car is much less intrusive than a typical search." *City of Indianapolis v. Edmond*, 531 U.S. 32, 40, 121 S. Ct. 447, 148 L. Ed. 2d 333 (2000).

- "The purpose for which respondent's luggage was seized, of course, was to arrange its exposure to a narcotics detection dog. Obviously, if this investigative procedure is itself a search requiring probable cause, the initial seizure of respondent's luggage for the purpose of subjecting it to the sniff test—no matter how brief—could not be justified on less than probable cause. The Fourth Amendment protects people from unreasonable government intrusions into their legitimate expectations of privacy. We have affirmed that a person possesses a privacy interest in the contents of personal luggage that is protected by the Fourth Amendment. A canine sniff by a well-trained narcotics detection dog, however, does not require opening the luggage. It does not expose noncontraband items that otherwise would remain hidden from public view, as does, for example, an officer's rummaging through the contents of the luggage. Thus, the manner in which information is obtained through this investigative technique is much less intrusive than a typical search. Moreover, the sniff discloses only the presence or absence of narcotics, a contraband item. Thus, despite the fact that the sniff tells the authorities something about the contents of the luggage, the information obtained is limited. This limited disclosure also ensures that the owner of the property is not subjected to the embarrassment and inconvenience entailed in less discriminate and more intrusive investigative methods. In these respects, the canine sniff is *sui generis*. We are aware of no other investigative procedure that is so limited both in the

manner in which the information is obtained and in the
content of the information revealed by the procedure.
Therefore, we conclude that the particular course of
investigation that the agents intended to pursue here—
exposure of respondent's luggage, which was located in
a public place, to a trained canine—did not constitute a
search within the meaning of the Fourth Amendment."
U.S. v. Place, 462 U.S. 696, 707, 103 S. Ct. 2637, 77 L.
Ed. 2d 110 (1983).

First Circuit

- "In *Place*, the Supreme Court held that a dog sniff of
  luggage in an airport was not a search. . . . [T]he
  important factor in applying *Place* is not whether the
  sniff occurs in a public place like an airport, but
  whether—as in an officer's plain view observation of
  contraband—the observing person or the sniffing canine
  are legally present at their vantage when their respective senses are aroused by obviously incriminating
  evidence." *U.S. v. Esquilin*, 208 F.3d 315, 318 (1st Cir.
  2000) (abrogated on other grounds by, Missouri v.
  Seibert, 542 U.S. 600, 124 S. Ct. 2601, 159 L. Ed. 2d
  643 (2004)).

Second Circuit

- "A police canine sniff of the front yard was not a search
  for Fourth Amendment purposes where the objects
  smelled by the dog were not located inside the dwelling
  or residence, the front yard of house was within plain
  view of the public road and adjoining properties, and
  there was no legitimate expectation of privacy in the
  front yard of the home insofar as the presence of the
  scent of the narcotics in the air was capable of being
  sniffed by the police canine." *U.S. v. Hayes*, 551 F.3d
  138 (2d Cir. 2008).

Fourth Circuit

- "The stop prior to the search, which lasted no more
  than fifteen minutes, was devoted to issuing an improper equipment notice and checking [Defendant's]
  license. It was while waiting for the report back on the
  license check that [the Defendant] and the officer
  engaged in the conversation which led to the dog's sniff

of the vehicle. Having the trained dog sniff the perimeter of [Defendant's] vehicle, which had been lawfully stopped in a public place, did not of itself constitute a search." *U.S. v. Jeffus*, 22 F.3d 554, 557 (4th Cir. 1994).

Sixth Circuit

- "The Supreme Court has held that a canine sniff does not unreasonably intrude upon a person's reasonable expectation of privacy. . . . This is so, because the manner in which information is obtained through this investigative technique is much less intrusive than a typical search. Moreover, the sniff discloses only the presence or absence of narcotics, a contraband item. . . . Therefore, the limited and discriminating nature of a sniff does not constitute a search within the meaning of the Fourth Amendment." *U.S. v. Reed*, 141 F.3d 644, 649, 1998 FED App. 0110P (6th Cir. 1998).

- "In *Place*, the Supreme Court held that exposure of an airline passenger's luggage to a drug-sniffing dog did not constitute a search within the meaning of the Fourth Amendment. . . . The Court based its ruling upon the fact that a canine sniff causes a very limited intrusion, in terms of both the manner in which the information is obtained, and the content of the information revealed. . . . The luggage need not be opened to conduct the canine sniff, and non-contraband items are not exposed to police or public view. Moreover, the only information obtained is whether or not the luggage contains drugs. No reasonable expectation of privacy is infringed, and therefore no search occurs. . . . This court has likewise held that a passenger on a common carrier has no reasonable expectation of privacy in the exterior of his luggage or the airspace surrounding it." *U.S. v. Gant*, 112 F.3d 239, 241, 1997 FED App. 0140P (6th Cir. 1997).

Seventh Circuit

- "A dog sniff in a public place is not a search because it is unique, in that it does not intrude on or disclose any information other than whether contraband is present, and a possessor of contraband cannot maintain a legitimate expectation that the contraband's presence will not be revealed." *U.S. v. Grogg*, 534 F.3d 807 (7th Cir. 2008).

- "Critical to our holding that the dog sniff in this case was not a Fourth Amendment search is the fact that police were lawfully present inside the common areas of the residence with the consent of [defendant's] roommate. While [defendant] contends that he had a legitimate expectation that the contents of his locked bedroom would remain private, he does not contest in any meaningful way [the roommate's] authority to allow police inside the common areas of their shared home. . . . Once [the roommate] authorized the police to explore the common areas of [the house], the entry of a narcotics-sniffing dog into that space did not infringe on any legitimate privacy interest. Everything behind [defendant's] locked bedroom door remained undetected except the narcotics, which [defendant] had no right to possess in the first place. The dog sniff from the common area of defendant's residence, where police were present by consent, did not violate defendant's Fourth Amendment rights, and the district court did not err in denying [defendant's] motion to suppress." *U.S. v. Brock*, 417 F.3d 692 (7th Cir. 2005).

- "As *Place* makes clear, a canine sniff does not expose non-contraband items within a bag to public view; consequently such an inspection does not constitute a search within the meaning of the Fourth Amendment when the bag is in a public place." *U.S. v. Ward*, 144 F.3d 1024, 1031 (7th Cir. 1998).

Eighth Circuit

- We decline to address whether *Jardines* casts doubt on those cases which hold a hotel parking lot is a place not regularly used for residential purposes. The Supreme Court issued its opinion in *Jardines* on March 26, 2013. The search of [Defendant's] truck occurred almost a full year earlier on May 8, 2012. Even assuming *Jardines* casts doubt on previous cases involving the search of a vehicle in a hotel parking lot—a question we need not address—suppression of the evidence discovered in [Defendant's] truck would not be appropriate; the police officers who searched [Defendant's] truck were entitled to an objective reasonable reliance on existing judicial precedent. We therefore conclude the district court did not err when it determined the search of [Defendant's] truck fell within the automobile exception to the search warrant requirement." *U.S. v. Holleman*, 743 F.3d 1152 (8th Cir. 2014).

- "[A] dog sniff of a car parked on a public street or alley does not amount to a search for Fourth Amendment purposes. . . . Similarly, other circuits have concluded that a dog sniff of the exterior of a car waiting at a roadblock established to check licenses and vehicle registrations is not a Fourth Amendment search." *U.S. v. $404,905.00 in U.S. Currency*, 182 F.3d 643, 647 (8th Cir. 1999).
- "The fact that the dog, as odor detector, is more skilled than a human does not render the dog's sniff illegal. . . . Just as evidence in the plain view of officers may be searched without a warrant . . . evidence in the plain smell may be detected without a warrant." *U.S. v. Roby*, 122 F.3d 1120, 1124–25 (8th Cir. 1997).
- "[T]he police officer must be able to point to specific and articulable facts which, taken together with rational inferences from those facts, reasonably warrant that intrusion. This same standard governs detention of luggage for purposes of a limited investigation such as a canine sniff." *U.S. v. Polk*, 97 F.3d 1096, 1099 (8th Cir. 1996).

Tenth Circuit

- "A canine sniff itself does not implicate Fourth Amendment rights because of the limited information it provides and its minimal intrusiveness. . . . Thus, we have held that a canine sniff of an already legitimately detained automobile is not a search within the meaning of the Fourth Amendment. . . . Likewise, detention of the driver at the scene to accomplish a canine sniff is generally reasonable where the driver is already under lawful arrest." *U.S. v. Hunnicutt*, 135 F.3d 1345, 1350 (10th Cir. 1998).
- "[T]he dog's sweep of the vehicle did not infringe on any constitutionally protected privacy interest. As this court recognized in *United States v. Morales-Zamora* when the odor of narcotics escapes from the interior of a vehicle, society does not recognize a reasonable privacy interest in the public airspace containing the incriminating odor. Where government officials have lawfully

detained a vehicle, a dog's sniff is not a search within the meaning of the fourth amendment." *Romo v. Champion*, 46 F.3d 1013, 1018 (10th Cir. 1995).

• "While Defendants were lawfully detained, the dog alerted on the trunk and the blue suitcase, thereby affording the agents probable cause to search. Because they were lawfully detained, Defendant's refusal of consent to the dog sniff was irrelevant. Consent is not required for a dog sniff of a lawfully detained vehicle. [Because,] dog sniff does not constitute a search." *U.S. v. Massie*, 65 F.3d 843, 849 (10th Cir. 1995).

Eleventh Circuit

• "In *United States v. Place* the Supreme Court determined that, because a canine sniff of a person's luggage indicated only the presence or absence of contraband, the canine sniff was only minimally intrusive and was no search within the meaning of the Fourth Amendment. Here, the dogs sniffed the exterior of plaintiffs' vehicles; they did not invade plaintiffs' homes or their bodily integrity. The sniffs occurred while plaintiffs were lawfully stopped in a public place; and because the sniffs occurred during the license check, plaintiffs were not delayed to conduct the sniffs. The sniffs also alerted the officers only to the potential presence of drugs; they did not expose the contents of plaintiffs' vehicles to public view. And, the privacy interest in possessing illegal drugs is not one that society recognizes as reasonable. As in *Place*, the external sniff of plaintiffs' vehicles was not a search within the meaning of the Fourth Amendment. So long as the use of the dogs did not make the delay caused by the roadblocks unreasonable—and we have no evidence to the contrary, the state's decision to use dogs at the roadblocks does not make the operation unconstitutional." *Merrett v. Moore*, 58 F.3d 1547, 1553 (11th Cir. 1995).

§ 24:2 Persons: The sniffing of persons by dogs may constitute a search protected by the Fourth Amendment

Fifth Circuit

• "Whether a non-contact dog sniff constitutes a search is

a question of first impression in this circuit. . . .
Construing the evidence in the light most favorable to
the government, as we are required to do, we accept the
testimony of Agent Morales that defendant and his
companion were approximately four to five feet away
from the dog when they exited the bus and the dog
alerted to an odor. Because the dog was not in close
proximity to the defendant at the time he alerted, the
dog's sniff was only minimally intrusive. Moreover,
there is no evidence that Agent Morales intended to
search the passengers exiting the bus or to have the
dog sniff them. He testified that he intended to wait for
everybody to get off and then put the dog inside the
bus. Considering that the sniff was unintentional and
that the dog was approximately four to five away from
the defendant at the time the sniff occurred, we
conclude that the sniff does not constitute a search with
the meaning of the Fourth Amendment." *U.S. v. Reyes*,
349 F.3d 219 (5th Cir. 2003).

- "The use of the dogs to sniff the students . . . presents
  an entirely different problem [from dogs' sniffing of lock-
  ers and automobiles]. After all, the fourth amendment
  protects people, not places." *Horton v. Goose Creek
  Independent School Dist.*, 690 F.2d 470, 477, 6 Ed. Law
  Rep. 950, 35 Fed. R. Serv. 2d 303 (5th Cir. 1982).

- "[S]ociety recognizes the interest in the integrity of one's
  person, and the fourth amendment applies with its full-
  est vigor against any intrusion on the human body. [W]e
  hold that sniffing by dogs of the students' persons . . .
  i.e., sniffing around each child, putting his nose *on* the
  child and scratching and manifesting other signs of
  excitement in the case of an alert . . . is a search within
  the purview of the fourth amendment." *Horton v. Goose
  Creek Independent School Dist.*, 690 F.2d 470, 478, 479,
  6 Ed. Law Rep. 950, 35 Fed. R. Serv. 2d 303 (5th Cir.
  1982).

Sixth Circuit

- "[W]e assume that the '*Terry* clock' was reset when the
  initial purpose of the stop was completed and, as a
  result, the further detention of Ms. Harris and Winters
  must have been supported by an independent reasonable and articulable suspicion that criminal activity

was afoot." *U.S. v. Winters*, 782 F.3d 289, 298 (6th Cir. 2015), cert. denied, 136 S. Ct. 170, 193 L. Ed. 2d 138 (2015).

- "The troopers' actions here are unconstitutional and unconscionable. If law enforcement officers are permitted to illegally seize persons in order to attempt to uncover evidence of criminal conduct, then the Fourth Amendment right of persons in this country to go about their business free from baseless interference from the police has been extinguished. Thus, we hold that a canine narcotics sniff made possible by an unconstitutional *Terry* seizure violates the Fourth Amendment." *U.S. v. Buchanon*, 72 F.3d 1217, 1228, 1995 FED App. 0362P (6th Cir. 1995).

Tenth Circuit

- "[W]hile the dog's sniff of plaintiffs' bodies was clearly more intrusive than its sniff of the vehicle, it nevertheless was reasonable in light of all the relevant circumstances. Again, plaintiffs' expectations in privacy were reduced because they were visiting a prison, and a dog's sniff of the area surrounding one's body is not terribly intrusive. To the extent that the dog's nose physically touched [the Passenger], that contact was purely incidental. Such a brief, unintentional touch cannot make an otherwise reasonable search unconstitutional." *Romo v. Champion*, 46 F.3d 1013, 1018 (10th Cir. 1995).

§24:3 Canine reactions as probable cause: In order for a dog's reaction to a person or container to provide probable cause to search or arrest, the reliability of the dog must be established

Supreme Court

- "Making matters worse, the decision below treats records of a dog's field performance as the gold standard in evidence, when in most cases they have relatively limited import. Errors may abound in such records. If a dog on patrol fails to alert to a car containing drugs, the mistake usually will go undetected because the officer will not initiate a search. Field data thus may not capture a dog's false negatives. Conversely (and more relevant here), if the dog alerts to a car in which the officer finds no narcotics, the dog may not have made a mistake at all. The dog may have detected substances that were too well hidden or present in quantities too small for the officer to locate. Or the dog may have smelled the residual odor of drugs previously in the vehicle or on the driver's person. Field data thus may markedly overstate a dog's real false positives. By contrast, those inaccuracies—in either direction—do not taint records of a dog's performance in standard training and certification settings. There, the designers of an assessment know where drugs are hidden and where they are not—and so where a dog should alert and where he should not. The better measure of a dog's reliability thus comes away from the field, in controlled testing environments. For that reason, evidence of a dog's satisfactory performance in a certification or training program can itself provide sufficient reason to trust his alert. If a bona fide organization has certified a dog after testing his reliability in a controlled setting, a court can presume (subject to any conflicting evidence offered) that the dog's alert provides probable cause to search. The same is true, even in the absence of formal certification, if the dog has recently and successfully completed a training program that evaluated his proficiency in locating drugs." *Florida v. Harris*, 568 U.S. 237, 133 S. Ct. 1050, 1056–57, 185 L. Ed. 2d 61 (2013) (citations omitted).

- "[E]vidence of a dog's satisfactory performance in a certification or training program can itself provide sufficient reason to trust his alert. If a bona fide organization has certified a dog after testing his reliability in a controlled setting, a court can presume (subject to any conflicting evidence offered) that the dog's alert provides probable cause to search. The same is true, even in the absence of formal certification, if the dog has recently and successfully completed a training program that evaluated his proficiency in locating drugs. . . . A defendant, however, must have an opportunity to challenge such evidence of a dog's reliability, whether by cross-examining the testifying officer or by introducing his own fact or expert witnesses. The defendant, for example, may contest the adequacy of a certification or training program, perhaps asserting that its standards are too lax or its methods faulty. So too, the defendant may examine how the dog (or handler) performed in the assessments made in those settings. . . . If the State has produced proof from controlled settings that a dog performs reliably in detecting drugs, and the defendant has not contested that showing, then the court should find probable cause. If, in contrast, the defendant has challenged the State's case (by disputing the reliability of the dog overall or of a particular alert), then the court should weigh the competing evidence. . . . The question—similar to every inquiry into probable cause—is whether all the facts surrounding a dog's alert, viewed through the lens of common sense, would make a reasonably prudent person think that a search would reveal contraband or evidence of a crime. A sniff is up to snuff when it meets that test." *Florida v. Harris*, 568 U.S. 237, 133 S. Ct. 1050, 185 L. Ed. 2d 61 (2013).

Fifth Circuit

- "We have repeatedly affirmed that an alert by a drug-detecting dog provides probable cause to search. Moreover, ... a showing of the dog's training and reliability is not required if probable cause is developed on site as a result of a dog sniff of a vehicle. Even if we were to address [defendant's] challenge of [the arresting officer and his dog's] qualifications, it would be of no avail. ... The district court determined that the evidence that the dog was certified was sufficient proof of his training to make an effective alert. Assuming that proof of the canine's reliability was required, there was sufficient evidence in the record to support the district court's finding that the dog's alert was reliable and established probable cause for a search of the vehicle." *U.S. v. Sanchez-Pena*, 336 F.3d 431 (5th Cir. 2003).
- "Evidence that is not obtained as a result of police illegality, but rather through a legal independent source, need not be suppressed. ... In this case, the officers did not obtain the evidence as a result of the alleged arrest; the evidence was the product of legal police activity... [T]he fact that [defendant] was handcuffed is irrelevant because handcuffing [defendant] did not cause the officers to find the evidence. The officers detained and questioned [defendant] while awaiting the results of the

check of his record. [Defendant's] detention was constitutionally permissible because an officer may detain an
individual until a check of his record is complete. ... The
officers had a drug-detecting dog sniff [defendant's] car,
which is also permissible because a dog sniff of a vehicle is not a Fourth Amendment 'search' requiring
individualized suspicion. The results of the dog sniff
gave the officers probable cause to search [defendant's]
car, so the search that uncovered the evidence was
justified. ... The evidence was obtained through an independent source and thus suppression of the evidence is
not appropriate in this case." *U.S. v. Moore*, 329 F.3d
399 (5th Cir. 2003).

- "We have held that a drug-dog's alert is sufficient to
  create probable cause for a search. . . . Our review of
  the case law, however, reveals that no federal court has
  ever confronted a situation where a dog's cast is used to
  justify a search, nor a situation where a weak alert on
  its own triggers a search." *U.S. v. Rivas*, 157 F.3d 364,
  368 (5th Cir. 1998).

- "The fact that the dog alerted provided probable cause
  to search. *Daniel* held that [the] theory that an affidavit
  must show how reliable a drug-detecting dog has been
  in the past is without jurisprudential support in this
  circuit. Because a showing of the dog's reliability is unnecessary with regard to obtaining a search warrant, a
  fortiori, a showing of the dog's reliability is not required
  if probable cause is developed on site as a result of a
  dog sniff of a vehicle." *U.S. v. Williams*, 69 F.3d 27, 28
  (5th Cir. 1995).

Sixth Circuit

- "In order for a dog's alert to support a determination of
  probable cause for a search, the training and credibility
  of the dog must be established, but the government need
  not produce actual certification records to establish the
  reliability of the dog; testimony about the dog's training
  and reliability suffices. Therefore, the government
  adequately demonstrated that the dog that alerted to
  the presence of drugs while walking around a van that
  had been stopped by a state trooper was reliable, and
  thus, the dog's alert provided probable cause to search
  the van; although the defense expert in animal behavior

testified that the Ohio certification process for drug sniffing dogs was inherently flawed, and that the dog's training failed to certify residual odors or small quantities, the dog's handler testified that the dog had been certified by three different agencies, including state accreditation programs in Ohio and Indiana, and that he had personally conducted more than 100 training sessions with the dog, which he documented." *U.S. v. Torres-Ramos*, 536 F.3d 542 (6th Cir. 2008).

- "A canine alert, however, does not constitute probable cause in a completely random setting, such as an airport, because of its questionable accuracy." *U.S. v. Galloway*, 316 F.3d 624, 2003 FED App. 0023P (6th Cir. 2003).

- "It is well-established in this Circuit that an alert by a properly-trained and reliable dog establishes probable cause sufficient to justify a warrantless search of a stopped vehicle." *U.S. v. Hill*, 195 F.3d 258, 273, 1999 FED App. 0351P (6th Cir. 1999).

- "We find these principles to be useful guides in evaluating the training and reliability of a drug detection dog for the purpose of determining if probable cause exists base d on the results of the dog's sniff. When the evidence presented, whether testimony from the dog's trainer or records of the dog's training, establishes that the dog is generally certified as a drug detection dog, any other evidence, including the testimony of other experts, that may detract from the reliability of the dog's performance properly goes to the credibility of the dog. Lack of additional evidence, such as documentation of the exact course of training, similarly would affect the dog's reliability." *U.S. v. Diaz*, 25 F.3d 392, 394, 1994 FED App. 0193P (6th Cir. 1994).

Eighth Circuit

- "In *Florida v. Harris*, ___ U.S. ___, 133 S.Ct. 1050, 185 L.Ed.2d 61 (2013), the Supreme Court discussed the framework courts should use to determine whether a drug dog sniff is reliable enough to give police officers probable cause to conduct a search. . . . Here, the record showed Henri and his handler were first certified through the Northern Michigan K—9 school as a narcotics detection team in October 2009. Henri and his

handler thereafter successfully completed annual re-
certifications between the time of their initial certification and the search of [Defendant's] vehicle. In addition, to the extent actual field performance is still
relevant, the record shows Henri's 'in-field' accuracy
record was 57%. . . . Considering 'all the facts surrounding [Henri's] alert[s], viewed through the lens of
common sense,' we conclude those facts 'would make a
reasonably prudent person think that a search would
reveal contraband or evidence of a crime.' *Florida v.
Harris*, 133 S.Ct. at 1058. We are thus satisfied Henri's
sniffs were 'up to snuff.' *Id*." *U.S. v. Holleman*, 743 F.3d
1152 (8th Cir. 2014).

- "To establish the dog's reliability, the affidavit need
  only state the dog has been trained and certified to
  detect drugs. . . . . An affidavit need not give a detailed
  account of the dog's track record or education." *U.S. v.
  Sundby*, 186 F.3d 873, 876 (8th Cir. 1999).

Ninth Circuit

- "In *United States v. Cedano-Arellano*, we held that when
  a defendant requests dog history discovery to pursue a
  motion to suppress, Federal Rule of Criminal Procedure
  16 compels the government to disclose the 'handler's
  log,' as well as 'training records and score sheets, certification records, and training standards and manuals'
  pertaining to the dog. These materials were held to be
  'crucial to [the defendant's] ability to assess the dog's
  reliability, a very important issue in his defense, and to
  conduct an effective cross-examination of the dog's
  handler' at the suppression hearing. These disclosures
  are 'mandatory' when the government seeks to rely on a
  dog alert as the evidentiary basis for its search." *U.S. v.
  Thomas*, 726 F.3d 1086 (9th Cir. 2013) (citations
  omitted).

- "[O]ur sister circuit declined to adopt a rule 'which
  would require the dog to give a final indication before
  probable cause is established.' Its rationale was on the
  mark: probable cause is measured in reasonable expectations, not certainties. Evidence from a trained and
  reliable handler about alert behavior he recognized in
  his dog can be the basis for probable cause. Whether a
  particular dog displays enough signaling behavior will

depend on the facts and circumstances of each case. The Supreme Court's *Harris* decision confirms the correctness of this view. In rejecting Florida's evidentiary checklist for a drug dog's reliability, the Court explained that '[a] gap as to any one matter . . . should not sink the State's case,' because that is 'the antithesis of a totality-of-the-circumstances analysis.' " *U.S. v. Thomas*, 726 F.3d 1086 (9th Cir. 2013) (citations omitted).

- "[T]his court has never held that the mere fact of a narcotics dog's positive alert to a large sum of money constitutes sufficient evidence to establish probable cause for forfeiture. Rather, probable cause is established only when an aggregate of facts—over and beyond the positive dog alert to a large sum of money— demonstrate the money's connection to drugs, with no single fact being dispositive." *U.S. v. U.S. Currency, $30,060.00*, 39 F.3d 1039, 1042 (9th Cir. 1994).

Tenth Circuit

- "Contrary to [Defendant]'s assertion, drug-detecting dogs have not supplanted the neutral and detached magistrate as the arbiter of probable cause." *U.S. v. Glover*, 104 F.3d 1570, 1577 (10th Cir. 1997) (abrogated on other grounds by, Corley v. U.S., 556 U.S. 303, 129 S. Ct. 1558, 173 L. Ed. 2d 443 (2009)).

- "The absence of a full alert by a narcotics dog does not negate probable cause of the presence of narcotics when other circumstances support such a finding." *U.S. v. Munoz-Nava*, 524 F.3d 1137 (10th Cir. 2008).

- "As a general rule, an alert from a canine with a sufficient accuracy record is sufficient to establish probable cause. . . . The problem in this case is that the canine had never been trained to alert on ephedrine. Rather the canine had been trained to alert on, among other drugs, methamphetamine, of which ephedrine is a component." *U.S. v. Patten*, 183 F.3d 1190, 1195 (10th Cir. 1999).

- "A canine alert provides the probable cause necessary for searches and seizures. . . . Here, the canine alerted twice to the inside of the defendant's car. Under *Ludwig*, that provided the probable cause necessary to arrest the defendant. Even if the subsequent fruitless search of the car diminished the probability of contraband being in the car, it increased the chances that whatever the dog had alerted to was on the defendants' bodies." *U.S. v. Anchondo*, 156 F.3d 1043, 1045 (10th Cir. 1998).

- "This court has consistently held that probable cause can be based on alerts by trained dogs. . . . Other courts have reached the same conclusion. . . . [W]ith a canine, the reliability should come from the fact that the dog is trained and annually certified to perform a physical skill. When the annual certification process involves actual field testing and grading of the canine's drug-detection skills . . . the canine's reliability is sufficient for a probable cause determination absent some circumstance that justifies a more complete examination of the canine's skill and performance. . . . We find that a 70–80% success rate meets the liberal standard for probable cause established in *Gates*." *U.S. v. Kennedy*, 131 F.3d 1371, 1378 (10th Cir. 1997).

- "An agent may not unlawfully enter an area in order to conduct a dog search. The warrantless entry of a car interior is unlawful unless there is probable cause to believe it contains contraband. The agent testified that the dog showed alert behavior immediately, that the dog was trained to sit when he got as close to the substance as he could, and that by sitting next to the rear driver's side door the dog was indicating that he was as close as he could get to the contraband in the car. Accordingly, the search of the car interior was supported by probable cause based on the dog's behavior outside the car." *U.S. v. Sukiz-Grado*, 22 F.3d 1006, 1009 (10th Cir. 1994).

§ 24:4   At the border: Canine inspection of vehicle permissible without suspicion or consent

Tenth Circuit

- "Agents are free to conduct canine inspections so long as the vehicles and their occupants are otherwise lawfully detained at the time of the inspection. At the border, canine inspections are permissible even in the absence of individualized suspicion and even without the consent of the vehicle's driver or occupants. A canine sniff on the exterior of a vehicle during a lawful traffic stop does not implicate legitimate privacy interests.

Moreover, a canine's alert to the presence of contraband during an exterior sniff of a vehicle gives rise to probable cause for agents to search that vehicle's interior. Notwithstanding these principles, other Fourth Amendment protections apply even at border checkpoints. Significantly, the Fourth Amendment unquestionably prohibits the search of a vehicle's interior unless law enforcement officials receive consent, have a warrant, or otherwise establish probable cause to support the search." *U.S. v. Forbes*, 528 F.3d 1273 (10th Cir. 2008).

Chapter 25

Electronic Surveillance

§ 25:1   Standard: The Fourth Amendment governs electronic surveillance that infringes on an individual's reasonable expectation of privacy

§ 25:2   Warrant requirements: A warrant authorizing electronic surveillance must be based on probable cause and meet particularity requirements

§ 25:3   Exceptions: There are some electronic surveillance devices and techniques which do not invade a reasonable expectation of privacy

§ 25:4   Electronic communications: User has reasonable expectation of privacy in text messages

§ 25:5   Accessing geolocation data from cell phones and satellite-based monitoring (SBM): reasonable grounds required

Research References

West's Key Number Digest

Constitutional Law ⬥319.5; Criminal Law ⬥394; Searches and Seizures ⬥13.1, 20 to 21, 25 to 26; Telecommunications ⬥491 to 541

KeyCite®: Cases and other legal materials listed in KeyCite Scope can be researched through the KeyCite service on Westlaw®. Use KeyCite to check citations for form, parallel references, prior and later history, and comprehensive citator information, including citations to other decisions and secondary materials.

---

§ 25:1   Standard: The Fourth Amendment governs electronic surveillance that infringes on an individual's reasonable expectation of privacy

<u>Supreme Court</u>

- "We have said that the Fourth Amendment draws a firm line at the entrance to the house. . .That line, we think, must be not only firm but also bright—which requires clear specification of those methods of surveillance that require a warrant. While it is certainly possible to conclude from the videotape of the thermal imaging that occurred in this case that no significant compromise of the homeowner's privacy has occurred, we must take the long view, from the original meaning of the Fourth Amendment forward. . . .Where, as here, the Government uses a device that is not in general public use, to explore details of the home that would previously have been unknowable without physical intrusion, the surveillance is a search and is presumptively unreasonable without a warrant." *Kyllo v. U.S.*, 533 U.S. 27, 121 S. Ct. 2038, 2046, 150 L. Ed. 2d 94 (2001).

- "This case thus presents the question whether the monitoring of a beeper in a private residence, a location not open to visual surveillance, violates the Fourth Amendment rights of those who have a justifiable interest in the privacy of the residence. Contrary to the submission of the United States, we think that it does." *U.S. v. Karo*, 468 U.S. 705, 714, 104 S. Ct. 3296, 82 L. Ed. 2d 530 (1984).

- "[T]he Fourth Amendment protects people, not places. What a person knowingly exposes to the public, even in his own home or office, is not a subject of Fourth Amendment protection. But what he seeks to preserve as private, even in an area accessible to the public, may be constitutionally protected. The Government's activities in electronically listening to and recording the petitioner's words violated the privacy upon which he justifiably relied while using the telephone booth and thus constituted a 'search and seizure' within the meaning of the Fourth Amendment. The fact that the electronic device employed to achieve that end did not happen to penetrate the wall of the booth can have no constitutional significance." *Katz v. U.S.*, 389 U.S. 347, 351, 353, 88 S. Ct. 507, 19 L. Ed. 2d 576 (1967).

- "[C]onversation [is] within the Fourth Amendment's protections, and. . .the use of electronic devices to capture it [is] a search within the meaning of the Amendment." *Berger v. State of N.Y.*, 388 U.S. 41, 51, 87 S. Ct. 1873, 18 L. Ed. 2d 1040 (1967).

Second Circuit

- "The interception of an oral conversation falls within the fourth amendment's protections, and capturing a conversation through the use of electronic devices is a search and seizure. [T]he underlying command of the Fourth Amendment is always that searches and seizures be reasonable. The determination of the standard of reasonableness governing any specific class of searches requires balancing the need to search against the invasion which the search entails." *U.S. v. Bianco*, 998 F.2d 1112, 1124 (2d Cir. 1993).

- "No provision specifically requiring notice of the execution of a search warrant is included in the Fourth Amendment. Accordingly, the Supreme Court [found] no basis for a constitutional rule proscribing all covert entries. [T]he Fourth Amendment does not prohibit *per se* a covert entry performed for the purpose of installing otherwise legal electronic bugging equipment." *U.S. v. Pangburn*, 983 F.2d 449, 453 (2d Cir. 1993).

Fourth Circuit

- "*White* underscored a second point pertinent to this appeal: that in the course of conversing with others, persons assume certain risks that may bear on the viability of any Fourth Amendment rights they subsequently assert. Inescapably, one contemplating illegal activities must realize and risk that his companions may be reporting to the police. If he sufficiently doubts their trustworthiness, the association will very probably end or never materialize. But if he has no doubts, or allays them, or risks what doubt he has, the risk is his. To be sure, there are differences between an informant and a cordless phone user at the other end of a communication. There exists, however, a crucial similarity between them for purposes of determining the existence of valid Fourth Amendment interests. The common characteristic of the government informant and the cordless phone user is that they are both unreliable recipients of the communicated information: one because he repeats the conversation to law enforcement officers and the other because he broadcasts the conversation over radio waves to all within range who wish to overhear. It is this general risk of unreliability of which *White* and *Hoffa* warn, not the specific risk that the listener is an informant per se." *In re Askin*, 47 F.3d 100, 105 (4th Cir. 1995).

Sixth Circuit

- "In Fourth Amendment cases the Supreme Court has long recognized a distinction between the content of a communication and the information necessary to convey it. Content, per this distinction, is protected under the Fourth Amendment, but routing information is not." *U.S. v. Carpenter*, 819 F.3d 880, 883-84 (6th Cir. 2016), cert. granted, 137 S. Ct. 2211, 198 L. Ed. 2d 657 (2017).

Seventh Circuit

- "As for statements that seizure within the meaning of the Fourth Amendment refers to an interference with possessory interests. . .that the Court means only that such an interference is actionable even if no invasion of privacy occurs, not that only possessory interests are protected. A person has no possessory interest in a telephone conversation. The interest that is invaded by wiretapping is an interest in privacy, not property, yet it is an interest that the Fourth Amendment has been interpreted to protect against seizure." *Platteville Area Apartment Ass'n v. City of Platteville*, 179 F.3d 574, 579 (7th Cir. 1999).

Eighth Circuit

- "As in *Scott*, the investigation in this case involved a widespread conspiracy requiring extensive surveillance to determine the precise scope of the enterprise. Also as in Scott, many of the calls not related to narcotics that appellants argue were improperly minimized were either short or ambiguous in nature. In a case such as this, it is not uncommon for a conversation to end before a monitor can determine if the call is narcotics related. In this case, the recorded calls were treated similarly to the contemporaneously minimized calls. Whether minimization was performed contemporaneously or after-the-fact, agents would stop listening once they determined the call was not narcotics related. Considering the facts and circumstances of the case, we conclude the district court did not err in finding that the agents did not act unreasonably in listening to entire recorded conversations of many non-narcotics related calls." *U.S. v. Padilla-Pena*, 129 F.3d 457, 464, 181 A.L.R. Fed. 829 (8th Cir. 1997).

- "Under either the fourth amendment or the Wiretap Act, the inquiry is 1) whether defendant manifested a subjective expectation of privacy, and 2) if so, whether society is prepared to recognize that expectation as reasonable. [W]hether a defendant's expectation of privacy is one that society is prepared to recognize as reasonable is a question of law subject to de novo review. Under the circumstances, we find that defendant's expectation of privacy while seated in the police car was not reasonable. A marked police car is owned and operated by the state for the express purpose of ferreting out crime. It is essentially the trooper's office, and is frequently used as a temporary jail for housing and transporting arrestees and suspects. The general public has no reason to frequent the back seat of a patrol car, or to believe that it is a sanctuary for private discussions. A police car is not the kind of public place, like a phone booth where a person should be able to reasonably expect that his conversation will not be monitored. In other words, allowing police to record statements made by individuals seated inside a patrol car does not intrude upon privacy and freedom to such an extent that it could be regarded as inconsistent with the aims of a free and open society." *U.S. v. Clark*, 22 F.3d 799, 801–02 (8th Cir. 1994).

Ninth Circuit

- "Congress passed the SCA in 1986 as part of the Electronic Communications Privacy Act. 'The SCA was enacted because the advent of the Internet presented a host of potential privacy breaches that the Fourth Amendment does not address.' To address these potential privacy breaches, the SCA 'creates a set of Fourth Amendment-like privacy protections by statute, regulating the relationship between government investigators and service providers in possession of users' private information.' Specifically, the statute protects the privacy of electronic communications by (1) placing limits on the government's ability to compel network service providers to disclose information they possess about their customers and subscribers, 18 U.S.C. § 2703, and (2) restricting the ability of network service providers to voluntarily disclose information about their customers and subscribers to the government, 18 U.S.C. § 2702. Violation of these provisions may result in criminal or civil liability, unless one or both of the SCA's statutory immunity provisions applies." *Sams v. Yahoo! Inc.*, 713 F.3d 1175, 1179 (9th Cir. 2013) (citations omitted).

- "Beepers could help police keep vehicles in view when following them, or find them when they lost sight of them, but they still required at least one officer-and usually many more-to follow the suspect. The modern devices used in Pineda-Moreno's case can record the car's movements without human intervention-quietly, invisibly, with uncanny precision. A small law enforcement team can deploy a dozen, a hundred, a thousand such devices and keep track of their various movements by computer, with far less effort than was previously needed to follow a single vehicle. The devices create a permanent electronic record that can be compared, contrasted and coordinated to deduce all manner of private information about individuals. By holding that this kind of surveillance doesn't impair an individual's reasonable expectation of privacy, the panel hands the government the power to track the movements of every one of us, every day of our lives." *U.S. v. Pineda-Moreno*, 617 F.3d 1120 (9th Cir. 2010). Kozinski, dissent.

- "The panel holds that the government can obtain this information without implicating the Fourth Amendment because an individual has no reasonable expectation of privacy in his movements through public spaces where he might be observed by an actual or hypothetical observer. But that's quite a leap from what the Supreme Court actually held in *Knotts,* which is that you have no expectation of privacy as against police who are conducting visual surveillance, albeit 'augmenting the sensory faculties bestowed upon them at birth with such enhancements as science and technology afford[s] them.' " *U.S. v. Pineda-Moreno*, 617 F.3d 1120 (9th Cir. 2010). Kozinski, dissent.

- "[V]ideo surveillance is subject to higher scrutiny under the Fourth Amendment. A person has a stronger claim to a reasonable expectation of privacy from video surveillance than against a manual search. Thus, we have held that the Fourth Amendment forbids warrantless videotaping of a private office and hotel rooms. However, video surveillance does not in itself violate a reasonable expectation of privacy. Indeed, videotaping of suspects in public places, such as banks, does not violate the [F]ourth [A]mendment; the police may record what they normally may view with the naked eye. We have not defined the precise contours of Fourth Amendment protection in the video context. However, in this case, given the public nature of the mailroom in a community hospital where individuals—even DEA agents—strolled nearby without impediment during the transaction, we conclude the defendant had no objectively reasonable expectation of privacy that would preclude video surveillance of activities already visible to the public." *U.S. v. Gonzalez*, 328 F.3d 543 (9th Cir. 2003).

- "Hidden video surveillance is one of the most intrusive investigative mechanisms available to law enforcement. The sweeping, indiscriminate manner in which video surveillance can intrude upon us, regardless of where we are, dictates that its use be approved only in limited circumstances. As we pointed out in *Taketa*, the defendant had a reasonable expectation to be free from hidden video surveillance because the video search was directed straight at him, rather than being a search of property he did not own or control. . . .and the silent, unblinking lens of the camera was intrusive in a way that no temporary search of the office could have been." *U.S. v. Nerber*, 222 F.3d 597, 603, 91 A.L.R.5th 763 (9th Cir. 2000).

- "Twenty-five years ago, the Supreme Court determined the Fourth Amendment governs wiretap surveillance. The Court made clear that if certain conditions were met, wiretapping authorized by warrant would pass constitutional muster. Congress codified the requirements of *Berger* and *Katz* in Title III of the Omnibus Crime Control and Safe Streets Act of 1968. Every circuit to address the issue, including our own, has upheld Title III against a challenge of facial unconstitutionality." *U.S. v. Petti*, 973 F.2d 1441, 1443 (9th Cir. 1992).

Tenth Circuit

- "The legislative history of Title III instructs that Congress intended this definition to parallel the reasonable expectation of privacy test articulated by the Supreme Court in *Katz v. United States.* . . . Accordingly, for Title III to apply, the court must conclude: (1) the defendant had an actual, subjective expectation of privacy—i.e., that his communications were not subject to interception; and (2) the defendant's expectation is one society would objectively consider reasonable." *U.S. v. Longoria*, 177 F.3d 1179, 1181–82 (10th Cir. 1999).

Eleventh Circuit

- "The legislative history of Title III directs that we consider oral communication in light of the constitutional standards expressed in *Katz v. United States.* The constitutional question is whether the person invoking its [Fourth Amendment] protection can claim a justifiable, a reasonable, or a legitimate expectation of privacy that has been invaded by government action." *U.S. v. McKinnon*, 985 F.2d 525, 527 (11th Cir. 1993).

§ 25:2 Warrant requirements: A warrant authorizing electronic surveillance must be based on probable cause and meet particularity requirements

Supreme Court

- "[W]e find nothing to persuade us that the Court of Appeals was wrong in its rejection of [the minimization] claim. Forty percent of the calls were clearly narcotics related. Many of the remaining calls were very short, such as wrong-number calls, [and] calls to persons who were not available to come to the phone. . . . In a case such as this, involving a wide-ranging conspiracy with a large number of participants, even a seasoned listener would have been hard pressed to determine with any precision the relevancy of many of the calls before they were completed. A large number were ambiguous in nature, making characterization virtually impossible until the completion of these calls. And some of the nonpertinent conversations were one-time conversations. Since these calls did not give the agents an opportunity to develop a category of innocent calls which should not have been intercepted, their interception cannot be viewed as a violation of the minimization requirement." *Scott v. U.S.*, 436 U.S. 128, 141–42, 98 S. Ct. 1717, 56 L. Ed. 2d 168 (1978).

- "The Fourth Amendment commands that a warrant issue not only upon probable cause supported by oath or affirmation, but also particularly describing the place to be searched, and the persons or things to be seized. The need for particularity and evidence of reliability in the showing required when judicial authorization of a search is sought is especially great in the case of eavesdropping. By its very nature eavesdropping involves an intrusion on privacy that is broad in scope." *Berger v. State of N.Y.*, 388 U.S. 41, 55, 87 S. Ct. 1873, 18 L. Ed. 2d 1040 (1967).

- "The government agents here ignored the procedure of antecedent justification. . .that is central to the Fourth Amendment, a procedure that we hold to be a constitutional precondition of the kind of electronic surveillance involved in this case. Because the surveillance here failed to meet that condition, and because it led to the petitioner's conviction, the judgment must be reversed." *Katz v. U.S.*, 389 U.S. 347, 359, 88 S. Ct. 507, 19 L. Ed. 2d 576 (1967).

- "Yet the inescapable fact is that this restraint was imposed by the agents themselves, not by a judicial officer. They were not required, before commencing the search, to present their estimate of probable cause for detached scrutiny by a neutral magistrate. They were not compelled, during the conduct of the search itself, to observe precise limits established in advance by a specific court order. Nor were they directed, after the search had been completed, to notify the authorizing magistrate in detail of all that had been seized. In the absence of such safeguards, this Court has never sustained a search upon the sole ground that officers reasonably expected to find evidence of a particular crime and voluntarily confined their activities to the least intrusive means consistent with that end." *Katz v. U.S.*, 389 U.S. 347, 356–57, 88 S. Ct. 507, 19 L. Ed. 2d 576 (1967).

- "[Statutes which give] broadside authorization rather

than being carefully circumscribed so as to prevent unauthorized invasions of privacy actually permit general
searches by electronic devices. [T]he statute here is
equally offensive. First, . . . eavesdropping is authorized without requiring belief that any particular offense has been or is being committed; nor that the property sought, the conversations, be particularly described.
. . . Secondly, authorization of eavesdropping for a two-
month period is the equivalent of a series of intrusions,
searches, and seizures pursuant to a single showing of
probable cause. Prompt execution is also avoided. Third,
the statute places no termination date on the eavesdrop
once the conversation sought is seized. Finally, the statute's procedure, necessarily because its success depends
on secrecy, has no requirement for notice as do conventional warrants, nor does it overcome this defect by
requiring some showing of special facts. Nor does the
statute provide for a return on the warrant thereby
leaving full discretion in the officer as to the use of
seized conversations of innocent as well as guilty
parties. In short, the statute's blanket grant of permission to eavesdrop is without adequate judicial supervision or protective procedures." *Berger v. State of N.Y.*,
388 U.S. 41, 58–60, 87 S. Ct. 1873, 18 L. Ed. 2d 1040
(1967).

- "[T]he statute's failure to describe with particularity
the conversation sought gives the officer a roving commission to seize any and all conversations. It is true
that the statute requires the naming of the person or
persons whose communications, conversations or discussions are to be overheard or recorded. But this does no
more than identify the person whose constitutionally
protected area is to be invaded rather than particularly
describing the communications, conversations, or
discussions to be seized. As with general warrants this
leaves too much to the discretion of the officer executing
the order." *Berger v. State of N.Y.*, 388 U.S. 41, 59, 87
S. Ct. 1873, 18 L. Ed. 2d 1040 (1967).

Fourth Circuit

- "The general presumption of constitutionality afforded
to duly enacted legislation has heightened significance
with regard to Title III. As the uses of technology

become more intrusive, claims of personal privacy will
grow in importance. As the methods of criminal enterprises become more sophisticated, the needs of law
enforcement in combatting them will also grow. Difficult judgments and trade-offs will be inevitable, just
as they were in the most recent piece of surveillance
legislation. In the fast-developing area of communications technology, courts should be cautious not to wield
the amorphous reasonable expectation of privacy standard, in a manner that nullifies the balance between
privacy rights and law enforcement needs struck by
Congress in Title III." *In re Askin*, 47 F.3d 100, 105–06
(4th Cir. 1995).

Seventh Circuit

- "Under 18 U.S.C. § 2518(1)(c), each application for wire
  surveillance must contain a full and complete statement as to whether or not other investigative procedures
  have been tried and failed or why they reasonably appear to be unlikely to succeed if tried or to be too
  dangerous. The government need demonstrate only one
  of the three alternatives. The burden of establishing necessity is not great, and we must review the government's compliance with the necessity requirement in a
  practical and common-sense fashion." *U.S. v. Gray*, 410
  F.3d 338 (7th Cir. 2005).

- "It is true that if government agents execute a valid
  wiretap order and in the course of executing it discover
  that it was procured by a mistake and at the same time
  overhear incriminating conversations, the record of the
  conversations is admissible in evidence. . . . It is just
  the plain view doctrine . . . translated from the visual
  to the oral dimension. It is as if government agents executing a conventional search warrant discover that they
  have the wrong address but before they can withdraw
  notice other illegal activity. . . . The discovery of the
  mistake does not make the search unlawful from its
  inception . . . because all that is required for a lawful
  search is probable cause to believe that the search will
  turn up evidence or fruits of crime, not certainty that it
  will. But in either case, the visual or the aural, once the
  mistake is discovered, the government cannot use the
  authority of the warrant, or of the order, to conduct a

search or interception that they know is unsupported by probable cause or is otherwise outside the scope of the statute or the Constitution. . . . No longer would they be merely discovering evidence of crime in the course of a lawful search." *U.S. v. Ramirez*, 112 F.3d 849, 851–52 (7th Cir. 1997).

Eighth Circuit

- "We first address whether a warrant was required for the use of a [Network Investigative Technique or NIT]. At least one district court in this circuit has determined that a warrant would likely be unnecessary for an NIT that exclusively searched for IP addresses, relying on a line of cases allowing third-party subpoenas of the same. A defendant's publicly available information may not be entitled to Fourth Amendment protection. But, '[t]he government is not permitted to conduct a warrantless search of a place in which a defendant has a reasonable expectation of privacy simply because it intends to seize property for which the defendant does not have a reasonable expectation of privacy.' This case differs from cases in which an IP address is voluntarily provided to third parties. In this case, the FBI sent computer code to the defendants' respective computers that searched those computers for specific information and sent that information back to law enforcement. Even if a defendant has no reasonable expectation of privacy in his IP address, he has a reasonable expectation of privacy in the contents of his personal computer. Moreover, the NIT retrieved content from the defendants' computers beyond their IP addresses. We conclude the execution of the NIT in this case required a warrant. 'Our answer to the question of what police must do before searching a [computerized device] . . . is accordingly simple—get a warrant.' " *United States v. Horton*, 863 F.3d 1041, 1046–47 (8th Cir. 2017) (citations omitted).
- "The probable cause required for allowing electronic interception of wire communications is the same as that required by the Fourth Amendment for a search warrant. . . . To that end we must determine that the affidavit included facts that would allow the issuing judge to believe (1) that an individual had committed or was about to commit a particular offense, (2) that com-

munication relating to that offense would be intercepted, and (3) that the residence was being used in connection with that offense or was commonly used by those whose communications were to be intercepted. . . . In determining probable cause we are bound to consider only the facts contained within the four corners of the affidavit." *U.S. v. Milton*, 153 F.3d 891, 894 (8th Cir. 1998).

Ninth Circuit

- "The fact that society is prepared to accept as reasonable defendants' expectation to be free from video surveillance while alone in the hotel room is confirmed by the way the law treats audio surveillance in identical circumstances. The government conceded that audio surveillance conducted after the informants departed was inadmissible, because the federal wiretap statute permits warrantless audio surveillance only if one of the participants in the monitored conversation consents. . . . The limitations in the wiretap statute reflect a societal determination that the threat to liberty inherent in audio surveillance requires that this intrusive investigative technique be permitted only in limited circumstances." *U.S. v. Nerber*, 222 F.3d 597, 604–05, 91 A.L.R.5th 763 (9th Cir. 2000).

- "In this case, the wiretap application contained sufficient information to establish probable cause to wiretap any cell phone associated with the phone number identified in the order, and the order had as its clear purpose the authorization to tap all such phones." *U.S. v. Duran*, 189 F.3d 1071, 1086 (9th Cir. 1999).

- "A district judge authorizing a wiretap must enter several statutorily-required findings of probable cause. The judge must find probable cause to believe (1) that an individual is committing, has committed, or is about to commit specified offenses, including product tampering and obstruction of justice, (2) that communications relevant to that offense will be intercepted through the wiretap, and (3) that the individual who is the focus of the wiretap investigation will use the tapped phone. Looking only to the four corners of the wiretap application, we will uphold the wiretap if there is a substantial basis for these findings of probable cause." *U.S. v. Meling*,

47 F.3d 1546, 1551–52, 41 Fed. R. Evid. Serv. 593 (9th
Cir. 1995).

Tenth Circuit

- "As an initial matter, we agree with the district court
  that nothing in the Fourth Amendment prevents us
  from considering whether certain facts in the affidavit
  support probable cause for the GPS data *in addition to*
  the wiretaps. Warrants frequently authorize a search of
  more than one place, and one set of facts may provide
  probable cause for both searches. Moreover, we are
  mindful that 'the Fourth Amendment's commands, like
  all constitutional requirements, are practical and not
  abstract.' '[C]ourts should not invalidate [a] warrant by
  interpreting the affidavit in a hypertechnical, rather
  than a commonsense, manner.' Thus, we reject Mr.
  Barajas's suggestion that our probable cause determination hinges on the government's failure to specifically
  request GPS data. However, it does not necessarily follow that the facts in the affidavit are sufficient for probable cause. We still must find the judge had a 'substantial basis,' to conclude that 'contraband or evidence of a
  crime will be found in a particular place.' The district
  court answered this question in the affirmative . . .
  We, however, are not so sure that Mr. Barajas's use of
  the phones for criminal activity is enough to authorize
  access to the GPS data. We require a 'nexus' between
  the criminal activity and the place to searched and
  demand that an affiant provide the judge with '[s]uf-
  ficient information.' Absent an explanation of how Mr.
  Barajas's location would reveal information about the
  workings of the conspiracy—or more accurately, Mr.
  Barajas himself—we cannot be certain that probable
  cause exists." *U.S. v. Barajas*, 710 F.3d 1102, 1109 (10th
  Cir. 2013) (citations omitted).
- [T]here are five requirements that must be satisfied
  before video surveillance will be permitted. An order
  permitting video surveillance shall not be issued unless:
  (1) there has been a showing that probable cause exists
  that a particular person is committing, has committed,
  or is about to commit a crime; (2) the order particularly
  describes the place to be searched and the things to be
  seized in accordance with the fourth amendment; (3)

the order is sufficiently precise so as to minimize the recording of activities not related to the crimes under investigation; (4) the judge issuing the order finds that normal investigative procedures have been tried and have failed or reasonably appear to be unlikely to succeed if tried or appear to be too dangerous; and (5) the order does not allow the period of interception to be longer than necessary to achieve the objective of the authorization, or in any event no longer than thirty days. *U.S. v. Apperson*, 441 F.3d 1162 (10th Cir. 2006).

- "Title III of the Omnibus Crime Control and Safe Streets Act of 1968, as amended, lays out a strict framework for authorizing electronic eavesdropping by law enforcement officials. . . .First, a law enforcement officer must obtain approval from the Attorney General of the United States or her designee to seek the appropriate order from a federal judge. . . .Second, the officer must submit to the judge a written application for the wiretap. . . .Third, the judge must issue an ex parte order granting the application and making specific supporting findings." *U.S. v. Garcia*, 232 F.3d 1309, 1312 (10th Cir. 2000).

- "The application and affidavit for wiretap authorization are subject to the requirements of *Franks v. Delaware*. . . . We have extended the holding of *Franks* to material omissions. . . . If a wiretap affidavit omits material information that would vitiate either the necessity or the probable cause requirements had it been included, the resultant evidence must be suppressed." *U.S. v. Green*, 175 F.3d 822, 828, 51 Fed. R. Evid. Serv. 1199 (10th Cir. 1999).

§ 25:3 Exceptions: There are some electronic surveillance devices and techniques which do not invade a reasonable expectation of privacy

Supreme Court

- "It is clear that the actual placement of the beeper into the can violated no one's Fourth Amendment rights. The can into which the beeper was placed belonged at the time to the DEA, and by no stretch of the imagination could it be said that respondents then had any legitimate expectation of privacy in it." *U.S. v. Karo*, 468 U.S. 705, 711, 104 S. Ct. 3296, 82 L. Ed. 2d 530 (1984).

- "The governmental surveillance conducted by means of the beeper in this case amounted principally to the following of an automobile on public streets and highways. Nothing in the Fourth Amendment prohibited the police from augmenting the sensory faculties bestowed upon them at birth with such enhancement as science and technology afforded them in this case. [T]here is no indication that the beeper was used in any way to reveal information as to the movement of the drum within the cabin, or in any way that would not have been visible to the naked eye from outside the cabin. [D]id monitoring the beeper signals complained of by respondent invade any legitimate expectation of privacy on his part? . . . [W]e hold they did not. Since they did not, there was neither a search nor a seizure within the contemplation of the Fourth Amendment." *U.S. v. Knotts*, 460 U.S. 276, 281, 282, 285, 103 S. Ct. 1081, 75 L. Ed. 2d 55 (1983).

- "[P]etitioner in all probability entertained no actual expectation of privacy in the phone numbers he dialed, and . . . even if he did, his expectation was not legitimate. The installation and use of a pen register, consequently, was not a search, and no warrant was required." *Smith v. Maryland*, 442 U.S. 735, 745–46, 99 S. Ct. 2577, 61 L. Ed. 2d 220 (1979).

- "Neither the Constitution nor any Act of Congress requires that official approval be secured before conversations are overheard or recorded by Government agents with the consent of one of the conversants." *U. S. v. Caceres*, 1979-1 C.B. 465, 440 U.S. 741, 744, 99 S. Ct. 1465, 59 L. Ed. 2d 733, 79-1 U.S. Tax Cas. (CCH) P 9294, 43 A.F.T.R.2d 79-872 (1979).

First Circuit

- "We are aware that there are cases holding that users of cellular phones are not protected by the Fourth Amendment. . . . The operative facts in these cases, however, took place before the provision in 18 U.S.C. Section 2510(1) expressly excluding the radio portion of a cordless telephone communication from the protection of the Act was deleted by amendment in 1994." *U.S. v. Pervaz*, 118 F.3d 1, 5 (1st Cir. 1997).

Second Circuit

- "[W]hat a person knowingly exposes to the public through an open door or window does not receive Fourth Amendment protection, yet what a person tries to keep private, even in a public place, may be entitled to constitutional protection. Accordingly, a defendant does not have a privacy interest in matters voluntarily revealed to a government agent, including a confidential informant. ... '[N]o interest legitimately protected by the Fourth Amendment is involved' where a defendant 'rel[ies] upon his misplaced confidence that [a government informant] would not reveal his wrongdoing.' A defendant likewise lacks a Fourth Amendment privacy interest in the recording of statements made to a government agent and, therefore, such consensual audio recordings do not require a warrant. ... [A]s with... audio recordings... , the videotape evidence, which merely showed scenes viewable by [a government informant], did not violate [defendant's] Fourth Amendment right to be free from unreasonable searches and seizures." *U.S. v. Davis*, 326 F.3d 361 (2d Cir. 2003).

Third Circuit

- "[Defendant] challenges the District Court's admission into evidence of tapes of meetings in his hotel suite. [Defendant] contends that the monitoring and recording of these meetings violated his Fourth Amendment rights because the government did not obtain a warrant. [Defendant's] argument, however, is inconsistent with well-established Fourth Amendment precedent concerning the electronic monitoring of conversations with the consent of a participant. . . . [I]f a person consents to the presence at a meeting of another person who is willing to reveal what occurred, the Fourth Amendment permits the government to obtain and use the best available proof of what the latter person could have testified about. . . . [T]here was no violation of [defendant's] Fourth Amendment rights. The monitoring devices were installed in the suite's living room at a time when [defendant] had no expectation of privacy in the premises. There is no evidence that conversations were monitored when [the informant] was absent from the room, and [the informant] was plainly there at the time of the incriminating meetings shown on the tapes that were introduced at [defendant's] trial. We are satisfied that the tapes do not depict anything material that [the informant] himself was not in a position to hear or see while in the room. Finally, we reject [defendant's] suggestion that the government was required, before resorting to video surveillance, to demonstrate that less intrusive investigative techniques were unlikely to succeed. Although this requirement applies to monitoring governed by the federal wiretapping statute, that statute does not apply to electronic surveillance conducted with the prior consent of a party to the communication. Similarly, judicial decisions considering a similar requirement in cases involving silent video surveillance conducted without a participant's consent are inapplicable in this context. We therefore reject [defendant's] argument that the tapes should have been suppressed." *U.S. v. Lee*, 359 F.3d 194, 63 Fed. R. Evid. Serv. 781, 93 A.F.T.R.2d 2004-993 (3d Cir. 2004).

- "We would not be so presumptuous as to limit *Smith*, a Supreme Court decision, in the manner suggested by [Defendant]. In any event, [Defendant] concedes that he has no evidence that the pen register was used to record any information other than telephone numbers. The mere suggestion that pen register equipment is now capable of misuse does not give us a basis to depart from the controlling precedent of the *Smith* case." *U.S. v. Veksler*, 62 F.3d 544, 549, 79 A.F.T.R.2d 97-886 (3d Cir. 1995).

Fifth Circuit

- "(Defendant) argues that video surveillance by or with the consent of a government informant constitutes a search within the gambit of the Fourth Amendment's protections, and a warrant is therefore necessary to legally conduct such video surveillance. We disagree . . . Once (defendant) invited the (informant) into his home, he "forfeited his privacy interest in those activities that were exposed to (the informant) The videotape evidence here only depicted what was viewable by the (informant), to whose presence (defendant) consented . . . Because (defendant) did not retain a privacy interest in the areas captured by the video surveillance conducted by an invited visitor, we hold that no Fourth Amendment violation occurred." *U.S. v. Brathwaite*, 458 F.3d 376 (5th Cir. 2006).

Sixth Circuit

- "[T]he government's collection of business records containing cell-site data was not a search under the Fourth Amendment." *U.S. v. Carpenter*, 819 F.3d 880, 890 (6th Cir. 2016), cert. granted, 137 S. Ct. 2211, 198 L. Ed. 2d 657 (2017).

Seventh Circuit

- "An officer's need to preserve evidence is an important law enforcement component of the rationale for permitting a search of a suspect incident to a valid arrest. Because of the finite nature of a pager's electronic memory, incoming pages may destroy currently stored telephone numbers in a pager's memory. The contents of some pagers also can be destroyed merely by turning off the power or touching a button. Thus, it is imperative that law enforcement officers have the authority to immediately search or retrieve, incident to a valid arrest, information from a pager in order to prevent its destruction as evidence. The motion to suppress was properly denied." *U.S. v. Ortiz*, 84 F.3d 977, 984 (7th Cir. 1996).

Eighth Circuit

- "Title I of the Electronic Communications Privacy Act of 1986... regulates the interception of wire, oral and electronic communications. Title I provides that it is not unlawful to intercept such a communication if a party to the communication has given prior consent to the interception. Nor does such an interception violate the Fourth Amendment. The government bears the burden of proving consent... Consent may be express or implied, but in either case, there must be actual consent. When someone voluntarily participates in a telephone conversation knowing that the call is being intercepted, this conduct supports a finding of implied consent to the interception... The Magistrate Judge inferred [informant's] consent to the telephone interception from her consent to cooperate in the controlled delivery and her participation in the elaborate preparations for that delivery, such as allowing herself to be wired for sound, giving the officers the keys to the Excursion, and consenting to the installation of videotaping equipment in the hotel room, all of which happened roughly contemporaneously with the telephone interception. This finding was bolstered by the trial testimony of the case agent, ... who testified about how [informant's] cell phone conversation was recorded: '[W]e had a little, mechanical attachment that attaches to the recorder, which an individual can place the other end into their-the ear and which will pick up the recording. ...' If [informant] was required to place a mechanical device into her ear in order to record the conversation, there can be little doubt that she was aware the conversation was being intercepted. [Informant] herself testified that the police were with her when she made the call. Furthermore, [officer] indicated that he and [informant] listened to the tape after the call was over... [The officer] would hardly have played the tape back for [informant] if he had taped it without her knowledge... We cannot say that the district court clearly erred in accepting the Magistrate Judge's recommendation of a finding of consent or in denying the motion to suppress the audiotape." *U.S. v. Corona-Chavez*, 328 F.3d 974 (8th Cir. 2003).

Ninth Circuit

● "Neither this nor any other circuit has spoken to the constitutionality of computer surveillance techniques that reveal the to/from addresses of e-mail messages, the IP addresses of websites visited and the total amount of data transmitted to or from an account. We conclude that the surveillance techniques the government employed here are constitutionally indistinguishable from the use of a pen register that the Court approved in Smith. First, e-mail and Internet users, like the telephone users in Smith, rely on third-party equipment in order to engage in communication. . . . Second, e-mail to/from addresses and IP addresses constitute addressing information and do not necessarily reveal any more about the underlying contents of communication than do phone numbers. . . . The government's surveillance of e-mail addresses also may be technologically sophisticated, but it is conceptually indistinguishable from government surveillance of physical mail. . . . . E-mail, like physical mail, has an outside address "visible" to the third-party carriers that transmit it to its intended location, and also a package of content that the sender presumes will be read only by the intended recipient. The privacy interests in these two forms of communication are identical. The contents may deserve Fourth Amendment protection, but the address and size of the package do not. . . . We therefore hold that the computer surveillance techniques that Alba challenges are not Fourth Amendment searches. However, our holding extends only to these particular techniques and does not imply that more intrusive techniques or techniques that reveal more content information are also constitutionally identical to the use of a pen register." *U.S. v. Forrester*, 512 F.3d 500 (9th Cir. 2008).

- "Like private telephone conversations, either party to a chat room exchange has the power to surrender each other's privacy interest to a third party. The nature of consent illustrates a reality of the Internet, namely, that a person initiating an Internet-based conversation does not control the recipient." *U.S. v. Meek*, 366 F.3d 705 (9th Cir. 2004).

- "We are also persuaded that the use of photographic equipment to gather evidence that could be lawfully observed by a law enforcement officer does not violate the Fourth Amendment. The use of a motion activated camera under these circumstances appears to us to be a prudent and efficient use of modern technology." *U.S. v. McIver*, 186 F.3d 1119, 1125 (9th Cir. 1999).

- "*Dow Chemical Co. v. United States*, establishes the relevant distinction as being between conventional equipment commonly availabl e to the public and without the ability to penetrate walls or windows, and highly sophisticated surveillance equipment not generally available to the public. A 35 mm camera with a 600 mm lens is a kind of vision enhancer commonly available to the public and used typically for telephoto landscape photography. Such helicopter surveillance as occurred here, not of an area immediately adjacent to a private home, does not amount to a search prohibited by the

Fourth Amendment." *U.S. v. Van Damme*, 48 F.3d 461, 463 (9th Cir. 1995).

Tenth Circuit

- "[W]e emphasize that like the phone numbers recorded by the pen register in *Smith*, [cell-service location information or CSLI] is not a record of conversations between individuals, but rather a record of the transmission of data that occurs to facilitate those conversations. As Judge Kethledge explained in *Carpenter*, 'federal courts have long recognized a core distinction' between the content of personal communications and the information necessary to convey that content. In other words, 'although the content of personal communications is private, the information necessary to get those communications from point A to point B is not.' Thus, like the numerical information in *Smith*, CSLI is not protected by the Fourth Amendment, because it functions merely 'as a means of establishing communication.'. . . In reaching our holding today, we recognize the difficulties inherent in applying longstanding precedent to new technology, which has progressed at an exponential pace in the four decades since *Miller* and *Smith* were decided. We are acutely aware of the privacy concerns accompanying technological advancement, particularly in our society, where using a cell phone has become a near necessity in the modern American economy. And we acknowledge that distinguishing between the content of communication and the means of transmission may be more difficult for other types of data, such as web-browsing history. But today we focus on the narrow question before us: whether Thompson has a reasonable expectation of privacy in his historical CSLI. And for the reasons above, we hold he does not." *United States v. Thompson*, 866 F.3d 1149 (10th Cir. 2017) (citations omitted).

- "It is well settled that a law enforcement agent can surreptitiously record conversations between the agent and another person without any violation of the Fourth Amendment." *U.S. v. Scott*, 37 F.3d 1564, 1582, 74 A.F.T.R.2d 94-6454 (10th Cir. 1994).

Eleventh Circuit

- "[A]t the time [Defendant]'s conversations were intercepted, federal statutory law recognized no reasonable expectation of privacy on a cordless telephone. [Defendant], in fact, has never argued that federal statutory or constitutional law at the time these recordings were made required officers to obtain prior judicial approval to intercept cordless telephone communications." *U.S. v. Mathis*, 96 F.3d 1577, 1583 (11th Cir. 1996).

- "In United States v. Ford we held that the ground surveillance of an unoccupied mobile home on leased land with a thermal infrared heat detector did not violate the Fourth Amendment. Three other circuits also have concluded that thermal infrared surveillance or FLIR is not an unconstitutional search." *U.S. v. Robinson*, 62 F.3d 1325, 1328 (11th Cir. 1995) (rejected on other grounds by, U.S. v. Kyllo, 140 F.3d 1249 (9th Cir. 1998)).

§ 25:4 Electronic communications: User has reasonable expectation of privacy in text messages

Sixth Circuit

- "This case involves an asserted privacy interest in information related to personal communications. As to that kind of information, the federal courts have long recognized a core distinction: although the content of personal communications is private, the information necessary to get those communications from point A to point B is not. . . . In the twentieth century, the telephone call joined the letter as a standard form of communication. The law eventually followed, recognizing that police cannot eavesdrop on a phone call—even a phone call placed from a public phone booth—without a warrant. But again the Supreme Court distinguished between a communication's content and the information necessary to send it. . . . Today, the same distinction applies to internet communications. The Fourth Amendment protects the content of the modern-day letter, the email. But courts have not (yet, at least) extended those protections to the internet analogue to envelope markings, namely the metadata used to route internet communications, like sender and recipient addresses on an email, or IP addresses. The business records here fall on the unprotected side of this line. Those records say nothing about the content of any calls. Instead the records include routing information, which the wireless providers gathered in the ordinary course of business. Carriers necessarily track their customers' phones across different cell-site sectors to connect and maintain their customers' calls. And carriers keep records of these data to find weak spots in their network and to determine whether roaming charges apply, among other purposes. Thus, the cell-site data—like mailing addresses, phone numbers, and IP addresses—are information that facilitate personal communications, rather than part of the content of those communications themselves. The government's collection of business records containing these data therefore is not a search. . . . The same things are true as to the locational information here. The defendants of course lack any property interest in cell-site records created and maintained by their wireless carriers. More to the point, when the government obtained those records, it did 'not acquire the *contents* of communications.' Instead, the defendants' cellphones signaled the nearest cell towers— thereby giving rise to the data obtained by the government here—solely 'as a means of establishing communication.' Moreover, any cellphone user who has seen her phone's signal strength fluctuate must know that, when she places or receives a call, her phone 'exposes' its location to the nearest cell tower and thus to the company that operates the tower. And any cellphone user who has paid 'roaming' (*i.e.,* out-of-network) charges—or even cellphone users who have not—should know that wireless carriers have 'facilities for recording' locational information and that 'the phone company does in fact record this information for a variety of legitimate business purposes.' Thus, for the same reasons that Smith had no expectation of privacy in the numerical information at issue there, the defendants have no such expectation in the locational information here. On this point, *Smith* is binding precedent. [T]he government action in this case is very different from the government action in *Jones*. That distinction matters: in applying *Katz,* 'it is important to begin by specifying *precisely the nature of the state activity that is challenged.'* Whether a defendant had a legitimate expectation of privacy in certain information depends in part on what the government did to get it. A phone conversation is private when overheard by means of a wiretap; but that same conversation is unprotected if an agent is forced to overhear it while seated on a Delta flight. Similarly, information that is not particularly sensitive—say, the color of a suspect's vehicle—might be protected if government agents broke into the suspect's garage to get it. Yet information that is highly sensitive—say, all of a suspect's credit-charges over a three-month period—is not protected if the government gets that information through business records obtained per a subpoena. . . . In sum, we hold that the government's collection of business records containing cell-site data was not a search under the Fourth Amendment." *U.S. v. Carpenter*, 819 F.3d 880, 886-90 (6th Cir. 2016), cert. granted, 137 S. Ct. 2211, 198 L. Ed. 2d 657 (2017) (citations omitted).

Ninth Circuit

- "The extent to which the Fourth Amendment provides protection for the contents of electronic communications in the Internet age is an open question. The recently minted standard of electronic communication via e-mails, text messages, and other means opens a new frontier in Fourth Amendment jurisprudence that has been little explored. Congress passed the Stored Communications Act in 1986 as part of the Electronic Communications Privacy Act. The SCA was enacted because the advent of the Internet presented a host of potential privacy breaches that the Fourth Amendment does not address. However, users of text messaging services have a reasonable expectation of privacy in their text messages stored on their service provider's network." *Quon v. Arch Wireless Operating Co., Inc.*, 529 F.3d 892, 27 I.E.R. Cas. (BNA) 1377, 91 Empl. Prac. Dec. (CCH) P 43233, 155 Lab. Cas. (CCH) P 60628 (9th Cir. 2008), rev'd and remanded on other grounds, 560 U.S. 746, 130 S. Ct. 2619, 177 L. Ed. 2d 216, 30 I.E.R. Cas. (BNA) 1345, 93 Empl. Prac. Dec. (CCH) P 43907, 159 Lab. Cas. (CCH) P 61011 (2010).

- "[E]-mail . . . users have no expectation of privacy in the to/from addresses of their messages . . . because they should know that this information is provided to and used by Internet service providers for the specific purpose of directing the routing of information. But users do have a reasonable expectation of privacy in the content of their text messages vis-a-vis the service provider." *U.S. v. Forrester*, 512 F.3d 500, 510 (9th Cir. 2008).

§ 25:5 Accessing geolocation data from cell phones and satellite-based monitoring (SBM): reasonable grounds required

Supreme Court

- "In *United States v. Jones,* we held that the Government's installation of a GPS device on a target's vehicle, and its use of that device to monitor the vehicle's movements, constitutes a search. We stressed the importance of the fact that the Government had physically occupied private property for the purpose of obtaining information. Under such circumstances, it was not necessary to inquire about the target's expectation of privacy in his vehicle's movements in order to determine if a Fourth Amendment search had occurred. Where, as here, the Government obtains information by physically intruding on a constitutionally protected area, such a search has undoubtedly occurred. We reaffirmed this principle in *Florida v. Jardines,* where we held that having a drug-sniffing dog nose around a suspect's front porch was a search, because police had gathered . . . information by physically entering and occupying the [curtilage of the house] to engage in conduct not explicitly or implicitly permitted by the homeowner. In light of these decisions, it follows that a State also conducts a search when it attaches a device to a person's body, without consent, for the purpose of tracking that individual's movements." *Grady v. North Carolina*, 135 S. Ct. 1368, 1370, 191 L. Ed. 2d 459 (2015) (inner quotations and citations omitted).

Second Circuit

- "This Memorandum and Order memorializes the rationale for authorizing access to prospective geolocation data for the defendant's cellular phone in these circumstances. This determination rests on two grounds. First, the Court is authorized to issue a search warrant where, as here, the Government demonstrates probable cause to believe that the information sought will aid in the apprehension of an individual subject to an arrest warrant. Second, given the ubiquity and celebrity of geolocation technologies, an individual has no legitimate expectation of privacy in the prospective location of a cellular telephone where that individual has failed to protect his privacy by taking the simple expedient of powering it off. Thus, in these circumstances, the Government may seek a search warrant for prospective geolocation data or, in the alternative, may obtain an authorization order under the Electronic Communications Privacy Act." *In re Smartphone Geolocation Data Application*, 977 F. Supp. 2d 129 (E.D. N.Y. 2013).

Fifth Circuit

- "[T]he Government, when determining whether an intrusion constitutes a search or seizure, draws a line based on whether it is the Government collecting the information or requiring a third party to collect and store it, or whether it is a third party, of its own accord and for its own purposes, recording the information. Where a third party collects information in the first instance for its own purposes, the Government claims that it can obtain this information later with a § 2703(d) order, just as it can subpoena other records of a private entity. We agree. This question of *who* is recording an individual's information initially is key because:

  [T]he individual must occasionally transact business with other people. When he does so, he leaves behind, as evidence of his activity, the records and recollections of others. He cannot expect that these activities are his private affair. To the extent an individual knowingly exposes his activities to third parties, he surrenders Fourth Amendment protections, and, if the Government is subsequently called upon to investigate his activities for possible violations of the law, it is free to seek out these third parties, to inspect their records, and to probe their recollections for evidence.
  . . . The third party can store data disclosed to it at its

discretion. . . . for any purpose[.] The Government does
concede that the subpoenaed third party must have possession of—the right to control—the records before officials can require it to turn them over. . . . Defining
business records as records of transactions to which the
record-keeper is a party also fits well with the historical
and statutory distinction between communications
content and addressing information. . . . Communications content, such as the contents of letters, phone
calls, and emails, which are not directed to a business,
but simply sent via that business, are generally
protected. However, addressing information, which the
business needs to route those communications appropriately and efficiently are not. Under this framework, cell site information is clearly a business record.
. . . A cell service subscriber, like a telephone user,
understands that his cell phone must send a signal to a
nearby cell tower in order to wirelessly connect his call.
. . . Finally, the ACLU argues that advances in technology have changed society's reasonable expectations of
privacy in information exposed to third parties. . . . At
the same time, '[l]aw enforcement tactics must be allowed to advance with technological changes, in order
to prevent criminals from circumventing the justice
system.' Therefore, '[i]n circumstances involving dra-
matic technological change, the best solution to privacy
concerns may be legislative. A legislative body is well
situated to gauge changing public attitudes, to draw
detailed lines, and to balance privacy and public safety
in a comprehensive way.' Congress has crafted such a
legislative solution in the SCA. The statute conforms to
existing Supreme Court Fourth Amendment precedent.
This precedent, as it now stands, does not recognize a
situation where a conventional order for a third party's
voluntarily created business records transforms into a
Fourth Amendment search or seizure when the records
cover more than some specified time period or shed light
on a target's activities in an area traditionally protected
from governmental intrusion. We decline to create a
new rule to hold that Congress's balancing of privacy
and safety is unconstitutional. We understand that cell
phone users may reasonably want their location information to remain private, just as they may want their

trash, placed curbside in opaque bags, or the view of their property from 400 feet above the ground, to remain so. But the recourse for these desires is in the market or the political process: in demanding that service providers do away with such records (or anonymize them) or in lobbying elected representatives to enact statutory protections. The Fourth Amendment, safeguarded by the courts, protects only reasonable *expectations* of privacy. Recognizing that technology is changing rapidly, we decide only the narrow issue before us. Section 2703(d) orders to obtain *historical* cell site information for specified cell phones at the points at which the user places and terminates a call are not categorically unconstitutional. We do not address orders requesting data from all phones that use a tower during a particular interval, orders requesting cell site information for the recipient of a call from the cell phone specified in the order, or orders requesting location information for the duration of the calls or when the phone is idle (assuming the data are available for these periods). Nor do we address situations where the Government surreptitiously installs spyware on a target's phone or otherwise hijacks the phone's GPS, with or without the service provider's help." *In re U.S. for Historical Cell Site Data*, 724 F.3d 600, 610–15 (5th Cir. 2013) (citations omitted).

• "Guerrero asserts that the district court should have suppressed the historical cell site location data that roughly indicated where he was, or at least where his cell phone was, on the afternoon that Mendez was killed. That data revealing 'the antenna tower and sector to which the cell phone sends its signal' was only available from third party communications providers. Congress has mandated a specific procedure that the government must follow to obtain that data. . . . Guerrero contends, and the government concedes, that this procedure was not followed; the government obtained the data from state officials who themselves had used a subpoena, not a Section 2703(d) order, to receive the information. The violation of the Act is clear. Guerrero's problem is that suppression is not a remedy for a violation of the Stored Communications Act. The Act has a narrow list of remedies, and—unlike the Wiretap Act, *see* 18 U.S.C. § 2515—suppression is not among them. There is no basis for judicial imposition of the exclusionary rule for a statutory violation when Congress has not provided that remedy. For Guerrero to suppress the cell site location data, he therefore must show that the cell site location data was obtained not just in violation of the Act, but also in violation of the Fourth Amendment." *U.S. v. Guerrero*, 768 F.3d 351, 357–58 (5th Cir. 2014), cert. denied, 135 S. Ct. 1548, 191 L. Ed. 2d 643 (2015) (citations omitted).

Sixth Circuit

- "The [Stored Communications]Act stakes out a middle ground between full Fourth Amendment protection and no protection at all, requiring that the government show 'reasonable grounds' but not 'probable cause' to obtain the cell-site data at issue here. The defendants and the ACLU effectively ask us to declare that balance unconstitutional. There is considerable irony in that request. The *Katz* standard asks whether the defendants' asserted expectation of privacy 'is "one that society is prepared to recognize as reasonable[.]"' Here, one might say that society itself—in the form of its elected representatives in Congress—has already struck a balance that it thinks reasonable. That is not to say that courts should defer to Congress's judgment on constitutional questions. But when the question itself turns on society's views, and society has in a meaningful way already expressed them, judges should bring a certain humility to the task of deciding whether those views are reasonable—lest judges 'confuse their own expectations of privacy,' with those that every reasonable person must hold." *U.S. v. Carpenter*, 819 F.3d 880, 889-90 (6th Cir. 2016), cert. granted, 137 S. Ct. 2211, 198 L. Ed. 2d 657 (2017) (citations omitted).
- "[S]uppression of evidence is not among the remedies available under the Stored Communications Act." *U.S. v. Carpenter*, 819 F.3d 880, 890 (6th Cir. 2016), cert. granted, 137 S. Ct. 2211, 198 L. Ed. 2d 657 (2017).

Eleventh Circuit

- "[W]e hold that the government's obtaining a § 2703(d) court order for production of MetroPCS's business records at issue did not constitute a search and did not violate the Fourth Amendment rights of Davis." *U.S. v. Davis*, 785 F.3d 498, 513 (11th Cir. 2015).

cords at issue did not constitute a search and did not
violate the Fourth Amendment rights of Davis. U.S. v.
Davis, 785 F.3d 498, 513 (11th Cir. 2015).

Chapter 26

Beeper Searches

§ 26:1   Definition: A beeper is a device that transmits radio signals. It can reveal locations but cannot record or transmit conversations

§ 26:2   Installation: Warrantless installations of beepers by methods that do not violate reasonable expectations of privacy are permissible

§ 26:3   Monitoring in a public place: The warrantless monitoring of a beeper's transmissions in a public place does not violate the Fourth Amendment

§ 26:4   Monitoring in a home: The warrantless monitoring of a beeper surreptitiously introduced into a home violates the Fourth Amendment

Research References

West's Key Number Digest

Searches and Seizures ☞21, 24, 61; Telecommunications ☞491 to 494, 511, 540

KeyCite®: Cases and other legal materials listed in KeyCite Scope can be researched through the KeyCite service on Westlaw®. Use KeyCite to check citations for form, parallel references, prior and later history, and comprehensive citator information, including citations to other decisions and secondary materials.

---

§ 26:1   Definition: A beeper is a device that transmits radio signals. It can reveal locations but cannot record or transmit conversations

Supreme Court

- "A beeper is a radio transmitter, usually battery operated, which emits periodic signals that can be picked up by a radio receiver." *U.S. v. Knotts*, 460 U.S. 276, 277, 103 S. Ct. 1081, 75 L. Ed. 2d 55 (1983).
- "Visual surveillance would have sufficed to reveal all of

these facts to the police. The fact that the officers in this case relied not only on visual surveillance, but also on the use of the beeper to signal the presence of Petschen's automobile to the police receiver, does not alter the situation. Nothing in the Fourth Amendment prohibited the police from augmenting the sensory faculties bestowed upon them at birth with such enhancement as science and technology afforded them in this case." *U.S. v. Knotts*, 460 U.S. 276, 282, 103 S. Ct. 1081, 75 L. Ed. 2d 55 (1983).

Fourth Circuit

- "In *United States v. Knotts*, an electronic tracking device was placed inside a five-gallon container of chloroform and sold by a Minneapolis chemical company to one of the defendants. A search warrant was obtained after three days of intermittent visual surveillance. Concluding that scientific enhancement raises no constitutional issues which visual surveillance would not also raise, the Supreme Court held that the monitoring was neither a search nor a seizure within the contemplation of the Fourth Amendment because the surveillance did not invade any legitimate expectation of privacy." *U.S. v. Jones*, 31 F.3d 1304, 1309 (4th Cir. 1994).

Eleventh Circuit

- "Moreover, actually calling a beeper does not violate the Fourth Amendment under any circumstances. There simply is no reasonable expectation of privacy in not having a beeper called. The only reason to obtain a beeper is to allow other people to call it. Beepers are obtained with the expectation, even the purpose, of letting other people call them. Therefore, there is no reasonable expectation of privacy in not having a beeper called, and calling a beeper does not implicate Fourth Amendment concerns." *U.S. v. Diaz-Lizaraza*, 981 F.2d 1216, 1223, 37 Fed. R. Evid. Serv. 1095 (11th Cir. 1993).

D.C. Circuit

- "[U]nder the Supreme Court's decisions in *United States v. Karo*. . .and *United States v. Knotts*. . .warrants are not always required for either the installation or use of

mobile tracking devices." *U.S. v. Gbemisola*, 225 F.3d
753, 758 (D.C. Cir. 2000).

§ 26:2 Installation: Warrantless installations of beepers by methods that do not violate reasonable expectations of privacy are permissible

<u>Supreme Court</u>

- "It is clear that the actual placement of the beeper into the can violated no one's Fourth Amendment rights. The can into which the beeper was placed belonged at the time to the DEA, and by no stretch of the imagination could it be said that respondents then had any legitimate expectation of privacy in it." *U.S. v. Karo*, 468 U.S. 705, 711, 104 S. Ct. 3296, 82 L. Ed. 2d 530 (1984).

- "Although the can may have contained an unknown and unwanted foreign object, it cannot be said that anyone's possessory interest was interfered with in a meaningful way. At most, there was a technical trespass on the space occupied by the beeper. The existence of a physical trespass is only marginally relevant to the question of whether the Fourth Amendment has been violated." *U.S. v. Karo*, 468 U.S. 705, 712–13, 104 S. Ct. 3296, 82 L. Ed. 2d 530 (1984).

- "The mere transfer to Karo of a can containing an unmonitored beeper infringed no privacy interest. It conveyed no information that Karo wished to keep private, for it conveyed no information at all. To be sure, it created a *potential* for an invasion of privacy, but we have never held that potential, as opposed to actual, invasions of privacy constitute searches for purposes of the Fourth Amendment." *U.S. v. Karo*, 468 U.S. 705, 712, 104 S. Ct. 3296, 82 L. Ed. 2d 530 (1984).

<u>Fourth Circuit</u>

- "[I]n *Karo*, the defendant was in legal possession of a non-contraband object in which the beeper had been placed. [T]here was an intrusion by the government into an area in which the defendant had a legitimate expectation of privacy, an intrusion which occurred originally when agents placed the beeper in the container of ether. and which continued as that container

was transported to his house and from there to other
places of concealment. [T]he Fourth Amendment does
not prohibit the placing of beepers in contraband and
stolen goods because the possessors of such articles have
no legitimate expectation of privacy in substances which
they have no right to possess at all." *U.S. v. Jones*, 31
F.3d 1304, 1311 (4th Cir. 1994).

- "[T]he inspectors never saw [the Defendant] place the
envelope containing the transmitter in his van. Their
sole grounds for suspicion consisted of (1) the fact that
[Defendant] had driven the mail on the other four
Saturdays when deposits had gone astray; and (2) the
fact that [Defendant] had taken longer than usual to
balance the load in the trailer at the Carrboro Post
Office. Absent the revelations of the tracking device,
they simply had no way of knowing that the transmitter, and the stolen mail pouch in which it was concealed,
might be inside [Defendant]'s van. Admissibility of the
evidence which was seized from [Defendant]'s van and
which convicted him of the crime charged, therefore,
turns squarely on the issue of the propriety of the postal
inspectors' use of the electronic tracking device. We
believe it would be a mistake, and a misreading of the
Supreme Court's guidance in *Knotts* and *Karo*, to
analyze this question solely in terms of [Defendant]'s
privacy expectation in the interior of his own van. While
we agree that [he] had a reasonable expectation of
privacy in the interior of his own van, we find no government intrusion there. The beeper was not planted in
the van; it was concealed in a mail pouch which
belonged to the government and in which [Defendant]
had no expectation of privacy whatsoever. The mail
pouch with the beeper found its way into [the] van only
because [Defendant] stole the pouch and hid it in the
van himself. We do not believe that *United States v.
Karo* compels the conclusion that there was a search of
[Defendant's] van." *U.S. v. Jones*, 31 F.3d 1304, 1310
(4th Cir. 1994).

Fifth Circuit

- "We find that the DEA agents' reasonable suspicion
that [Defendant] was engaged in criminal activity justified the placement and monitoring of the beeper. The

actual installation of the beeper was much less intrusive than the typical stop and frisk. [Defendant] was in the pizza restaurant when the installation took place. He was not detained or questioned; he suffered no indignity; nothing from the interior of the van was seized or searched; indeed, nothing even from the van's exterior was removed." *U.S. v. Michael*, 645 F.2d 252, 258 (5th Cir. 1981).

- "Applying this dual privacy and intrusiveness analysis to the facts of the instant case, we hold that the minimal intrusion involved in the attachment of a beeper to [Defendant]'s van, parked in a public place, was sufficiently justified so as to satisfy any of [Defendant]'s fourth amendment expectation of privacy concerns." *U.S. v. Michael*, 645 F.2d 252, 256 (5th Cir. 1981).

Ninth Circuit

- "We have previously held that the warrantless insertion of electronic devices pursuant to a lawful Customs search does not violate the Fourth Amendment." *U.S. v. Most*, 789 F.2d 1411, 1414 (9th Cir. 1986).

§ 26:3 Monitoring in a public place: The warrantless monitoring of a beeper's transmissions in a public place does not violate the Fourth Amendment

Supreme Court

- "[D]id monitoring the beeper signals complained of by respondent invade any legitimate expectation of privacy on his part? . . . [W]e hold it did not. Since it did not, there was neither a search nor a seizure within the contemplation of the Fourth Amendment." *U.S. v. Knotts*, 460 U.S. 276, 285, 103 S. Ct. 1081, 75 L. Ed. 2d 55 (1983).

Fifth Circuit

- "*Knotts* teaches us here that monitoring signals from an electronic tracking device that tells officers no more than that a specific aircraft is flying in the public airspace does not violate any reasonable expectation of privacy. Because this is so, no Fourth Amendment violation results from such public detection. The movement of an airplane in the sky, like that of an automobile on a highway, is not something in which a person can claim a reasonable expectation of privacy." *U.S. v. Butts*, 729 F.2d 1514, 1517 (5th Cir. 1984).

- "The subsequent monitoring also did not violate [Defendant's] reasonable expectation of privacy. The beeper only aided the agents in the performance of their lawful surveillance. The van traveled public roads and was exposed to public view. Monitoring the beeper while the agents had reasonable suspicion to believe [Defendant] was conspiring to manufacture MDA did not violate his fourth amendment rights." *U.S. v. Michael*, 645 F.2d 252, 258 (5th Cir. 1981).

D.C. Circuit

- "In *Karo*, the Supreme Court held that a warrant was required to monitor the location of a tracking device in a private home because of the legitimate expectation of privacy within a home. . . .However, the Court also held that no warrant was required for monitoring the device during the time it was en route to the house in a truck on a public road." *U.S. v. Gbemisola*, 225 F.3d 753, 758–59 (D.C. Cir. 2000).

§ 26:4 Monitoring in a home: The warrantless monitoring of a beeper surreptitiously introduced into a home violates the Fourth Amendment

Supreme Court

- "This case thus presents the question whether the monitoring of a beeper in a private residence, a location not open to visual surveillance, violates the Fourth Amendment rights of those who have a justifiable interest in the privacy of the residence. [W]e think that it does." *U.S. v. Karo*, 468 U.S. 705, 714, 104 S. Ct. 3296, 82 L. Ed. 2d 530 (1984).

- "Indiscriminate monitoring of property that h as been withdrawn from public view would present far too serious a threat to privacy interests in the home to escape entirely some sort of Fourth Amendment oversight." *U.S. v. Karo*, 468 U.S. 705, 716, 104 S. Ct. 3296, 82 L. Ed. 2d 530 (1984).

<u>Fourth Circuit</u>

- "The Supreme Court granted certiorari to answer a question it had left unresolved in *Knotts:* Whether monitoring of a beeper falls within the ambit of the Fourth Amendment when it reveals information that could not have been obtained through visual surveillance. Using the beeper monitor, law enforcement authorities determined that the can containing the monitoring device was inside the house, and obtained a warrant to search the house based in part on information derived through use of the beeper. The Supreme Court noted that it would be an unreasonable search to surreptitiously enter a residence without a warrant to verify that the container was there, and then continued: For purposes of the Fourth Amendment, the result is the same where, without a warrant, the Government surreptitiously employs an electronic device to obtain information that it could not have obtained by observation from outside the curtilage of the house. The beeper tells the agent that a particular article is actually located at a particular time in the private residence and is in the possession of the person or persons whose residence is being watched. Even if visual surveillance has revealed that the article to which the beeper is attached has entered the house, the later monitoring not only verifies the officers' observations but also establishes that the article remains on the premises. The Court thus answered affirmatively the question it had reserved in *Knotts,* holding that monitoring of a beeper falls within the ambit of the Fourth Amendment when it reveals a critical fact about the interior of premises that could not have been obtained through visual surveillance." *U.S. v. Jones,* 31 F.3d 1304, 1309–10 (4th Cir. 1994).

<u>Fifth Circuit</u>

- "The officers also missed no opportunity to obtain a valid warrant during a lengthy investigation—they did not know where the car was, nor that it contained the money, until they completed their tracking upon arrival at the house. The pursuit began shortly after the robbery, and continued until the signal was traced. When the officers arrived at [Defendant's] house, the trail was hot. Finally, the officers believed they needed to

deactivate the transmitter as soon as possible so it
would not hinder other potential investigations." *U.S. v.
Reed*, 26 F.3d 523, 529–30 (5th Cir. 1994).

D.C. Circuit

- "In *Karo*, the Supreme Court held that a warrant was
  required to monitor the location of a tracking device in
  a private home because of the legitimate expectation of
  privacy within a home." *U.S. v. Gbemisola*, 225 F.3d
  753, 758–59 (D.C. Cir. 2000).

Chapter 27

Body Searches

§ 27:1   Exterior intrusions: Intrusions on the body's
         surface (swabbing, hair samples, retrieval of
         evidence from the mouth, etc.) do not normally
         require a search warrant

§ 27:2   Interior intrusions: Intrusions into the body
         (blood tests, stomach pumping, surgery, etc.) are
         permitted by the Fourth Amendment only if they
         are conducted pursuant to a warrant, or if
         exigent circumstances exist and there is a clear
         indication that the desired evidence will be
         found

§ 27:3   Strip and body cavity searches: Strip searches
         and body cavity searches occur primarily in
         prisons or jails. They must be conducted in a
         reasonable manner and must be justified by the
         circumstances

§ 27:4   Strip searches at the border: Strip searches at the
         border may be conducted only pursuant to real
         or reasonable suspicion

§ 27:5   Body cavity searches at the border: Body cavity
         searches at the border must be based on a
         higher standard than strip searches

Research References

West's Key Number Digest

Arrest ⬤⇒71.1; Automobiles ⬤⇒414; Constitutional Law ⬤⇒262;
   Customs Duties ⬤⇒126; Prisons ⬤⇒4; Searches and Seizures
   ⬤⇒14, 23 to 24, 36, 39, 75, 78

KeyCite®: Cases and other legal materials listed in KeyCite Scope can be
researched through the KeyCite service on Westlaw®. Use KeyCite to
check citations for form, parallel references, prior and later history, and
comprehensive citator information, including citations to other decisions
and secondary materials.

---

§ 27:1 Exterior intrusions: Intrusions on the body's surface (swabbing, hair samples, retrieval of evidence from the mouth, etc.) do not normally require a search warrant

Supreme Court

- "It can be agreed that using a buccal swab on the inner tissues of a person's cheek in order to obtain DNA samples is a search. Virtually any intrusio[n] into the human body will work an invasion of cherished personal security that is subject to constitutional scrutiny. The Court has applied the Fourth Amendment to police efforts to draw blood, scraping an arrestee's fingernails to obtain trace evidence, and even to a breathalyzer test, which generally requires the production of alveolar or deep lung breath for chemical analysis. A buccal swab is a far more gentle process than a venipuncture to draw blood. It involves but a light touch on the inside of the cheek; and although it can be deemed a search within the body of the arrestee, it requires no surgical intrusions beneath the skin. The fact than an intrusion is negligible is of central relevance to determining reasonableness, although it is still a search as the law defines that term. . . . The legitimate government interest served by the Maryland DNA Collection Act is one that is well established: the need for law enforcement officers in a safe and accurate way to process and identify the persons and possessions they must take into custody. It is beyond dispute that probable cause provides legal justification for arresting a person suspected of crime, and for a brief period of detention to take the administrative steps incident to arrest. . . . [i]n every criminal case, it is known and must be known who has been arrested and who is being tried. An individual's identity is more than just his name or Social Security number, and the government's interest in identification goes beyond ensuring that the proper name is typed on the indictment. Identity has never been considered limited to the name on the arrestee's birth certificate. In fact, a name is of little value compared to the real interest in identification at stake when an individual is brought into custody. It is a well recognized aspect of criminal conduct that the perpetra-

tor will take unusual steps to conceal not only his
conduct, but also his identity. Disguises used while committing a crime may be supplemented or replaced by
changed names, and even changed physical features.
An arrestee may be carrying a false ID or lie about his
identity and criminal history records . . . can be inaccurate or incomplete. . . . Like a fingerprint, the 13
CODIS loci are not themselves evidence of any particular crime, in the way that a drug test can by itself be
evidence of illegal narcotics use. . . . Perhaps the most
direct historical analogue to the DNA technology used
to identify respondent is the familiar practice of
fingerprinting arrestees. From the advent of this
technique, courts had no trouble determining that
fingerprinting was a natural part of the administrative
steps incident to arrest. In the seminal case of *United
States v. Kelly,* Judge Augustus Hand wrote that routine fingerprinting did not violate the Fourth Amendment precisely because it fit within the accepted means
of processing an arrestee into custody. . . . We find no
ground in reason or authority for interfering with a
method of identifying persons charged with crime which
has now become widely known and frequently practiced.
By the middle of the 20th century, it was considered
elementary that a person in lawful custody may be
required to submit to photographing and fingerprinting
as part of routine identification processes. DNA identification is an advanced technique superior to fingerprinting in many ways, so much so that to insist on fingerprints as the norm would make little sense to either the
forensic expert or a layperson. The additional intrusion
upon the arrestee's privacy beyond that associated with
fingerprinting is not significant, and DNA is a markedly more accurate form of identifying arrestees."
Maryland v. King, 133 S. Ct. 1958, 1968–72, 1976, 186
L. Ed. 2d 1 (2013) (inner quotations and citations
omitted).
- "The respondent appealed his conviction, claiming that
the fingernail scrapings were the product of an unconstitutional search under the Fourth and Fourteenth
Amendments. On the facts of this case, considering the
existence of probable cause, the very limited intrusion
undertaken incident to the station house detention, and

the ready destructibility of the evidence, we cannot say that this search violated the Fourth and Fourteenth Amendments." *Cupp v. Murphy*, 412 U.S. 291, 292, 296, 93 S. Ct. 2000, 36 L. Ed. 2d 900 (1973).

- "The required disclosure of a person's voice is . . . immeasurably further removed from the Fourth Amendment's protection than was the intrusion into the body effected by the blood extraction in *Schmerber*." *U.S. v. Dionisio*, 410 U.S. 1, 14, 93 S. Ct. 764, 35 L. Ed. 2d 67 (1973).

First Circuit

- "The evolving case law governing unwanted bodily intrusions or manipulations has weighed several relevant considerations. Once it is established that, as here, the state is entitled to the information the bodily intrusions is designed to obtain, the means used will be measured by its reasonableness in light of the need to obtain the evidence in this way. To the degree the procedure would not be considered offensive even by the most delicate and is routine, it will be less likely to involve a constitutional violation. By contrast, nonroutine manipulative intrusions on bodily integrity will be subject to heightened scrutiny to determine, *inter alia,* whether there are less intrusive alternatives available. One does not have to cultivate particularly delicate sensibilities to believe degrading the process of having a strain gauge strapped to an individual's genitals while sexually explicit pictures are displayed in an effort to determine his sexual arousal patterns. The procedure involved bodily manipulation of the most intimate sort. There has been no showing regarding the procedure's reliability and, in light of other psychological evaluative tools available, there has been no demonstration that other less intrusive means of obtaining the relevant information are not sufficient." *Harrington v. Almy*, 977 F.2d 37, 45, 8 I.E.R. Cas. (BNA) 449, 8 I.E.R. Cas. (BNA) 457 (1st Cir. 1992).
- "There can be little doubt that an inspection of one's hands, under an ultraviolet lamp, is the kind of governmental intrusion into one's private domain that is protected by the Fourth Amendment. If the reach of the Fourth Amendment extends to fingerprinting, and a

search of one's clothing or personal effects, it should certainly encompass a detailed inspection, by special instrument, of one's skin. The protection afforded an individual by the Fourth Amendment would be eviscerated if, under authority of a warrant to search premises, government agents could scan an individual's body with sensitive instruments capable of picking up the most minute or intimate object lodged thereon." *U.S. v. Kenaan,* 496 F.2d 181, 182–83 (1st Cir. 1974).

Fourth Circuit

- "The crime of DWI presents a unique situation in that the most reliable evidence of whether a person is driving while legally drunk is contained in that person's body. The best means of obtaining evidence of the breath alcohol content, and the least intrusive way of testing, is the breathalyzer test. Given that the defendants were legally arrested at the time of the search, these limited intrusions to prevent the destruction of evidence were not unreasonable, as they were searches incident to lawful arrests." *U.S. v. Reid,* 929 F.2d 990, 994 (4th Cir. 1991).

Sixth Circuit

- "We too conclude that the DNA Act is not so punitive in effect as to override its regulatory purpose, and thus that applying it to [defendant] does not violate the *Ex Post Facto* Clause." *U.S. v. Coccia,* 598 F.3d 293 (6th Cir. 2010).

Seventh Circuit

- "It is apparent that had the agents not swabbed [Defendant]'s hands at the time, the opportunity may not have knocked again, especially if [Defendant] washed his hands. Accordingly, we find that the swabbing was no more offensive to Bridges' person than fingerprinting or photographing him. We hold that the swabbing was not an unreasonable search." *U.S. v. Bridges,* 499 F.2d 179, 184 (7th Cir. 1974).

Eighth Circuit

- "[T]he Fourth Amendment provides no protection for what a person knowingly exposes to the public, even in his own home or office. . . . Courts applying this principle have suggested that the protection of the fourth amendment may be wholly denied to voices, faces, and fingerprints." *Pace v. City of Des Moines*, 201 F.3d 1050, 1053 (8th Cir. 2000).

D.C. Circuit

- "[T]he [warrantless] search was reasonable since it was obviously necessary to conduct the test as promptly as possible because of the ease with which the evidence could be destroyed by a thorough washing. The simplicity of the [benzadine] test [conducted by swabbing the penis] makes it unnecessary to have it conducted by a physician. It is a chemical test not a medical test and was properly administered by a trained police technician. His qualifications were not questioned." *U.S. v. Smith*, 470 F.2d 377, 379 (D.C. Cir. 1972).

§ 27:2   **Interior intrusions: Intrusions into the body (blood tests, stomach pumping, surgery, etc.) are permitted by the Fourth Amendment only if they are conducted pursuant to a warrant, or if exigent circumstances exist and there is a clear indication that the desired evidence will be found**

Supreme Court

- "The question presented here is whether the natural metabolization of alcohol in the bloodstream presents a *per se* exigency that justifies an exception to the Fourth Amendment's warrant requirement for nonconsensual blood testing in all drunk-driving cases. We conclude that it does not, and we hold, consistent with general Fourth Amendment principles, that exigency in this context must be determined case by case based on the totality of the circumstances. . . . The State properly recognizes that the reasonableness of a warrantless search under the exigency exception to the warrant requirement must be evaluated based on the totality of the circumstances. But the State nevertheless seeks a *per se* rule for blood testing in drunk-driving cases. . . . It is true that as a result of the human body's natural metabolic processes, the alcohol level in a person's blood begins to dissipate once the alcohol is fully absorbed and continues to decline until the alcohol is eliminated. . . . This fact was essential to our holding in *Schmerber,* as we recognized that, under the circumstances, further delay in order to secure a warrant after the time spent investigating the scene of the accident and transporting the injured suspect to the hospital to receive treatment would have threatened the destruction of evidence. But it does not follow that we should depart from careful case-by-case assessment of exigency and adopt the categorical rule proposed by the State and its *amici.* In those drunk-driving investigations where police officers can reasonably obtain a warrant before a blood sample can be drawn without significantly undermining the efficacy of the search, the Fourth Amendment mandates that they do so. We do not doubt that some circumstances will make obtaining a warrant impractical such that the dissipation of alcohol from the bloodstream will support an exigency justifying a properly conducted warrantless blood test. That, however, is a reason to decide each case on its facts, as we did in *Schmerber,* not to accept the considerable overgeneralization that a *per se* rule would reflect. The context of blood testing is different in critical respects from other destruction-of-evidence cases in which the police are truly confronted with a now or never situation. . . . The State's proposed *per se* rule also fails to account for advances in the 47 years since *Schmerber* was decided that allow for the more expeditious processing of warrant applications, particularly in contexts like drunk-driving investigations where the evidence offered to establish probable cause is simple. The Federal Rules of Criminal Procedure were amended in 1977 to permit federal magistrate judges to issue a warrant based on sworn testimony communicated by telephone. As amended, the law now allows a federal magistrate judge to consider "information communicated by telephone or other reliable electronic means." States have also innovated. Well over a majority of States allow police officers or prosecutors to apply for search warrants remotely through various means, including telephonic or radio communication, electronic communication such as e-mail, and video conferencing. And in addition to technology-based developments, jurisdictions have found other ways to streamline the warrant process, such as by using standard-form warrant applications for drunk-driving investigations. We by no means claim that telecommunications innovations have, will, or should eliminate all delay from the warrant-application process. Warrants inevitably take some time for police officers or prosecutors to complete and for magistrate judges to review. Telephonic and electronic warrants may still require officers to follow time-consuming formalities designed to create an adequate record, such as preparing a duplicate warrant before calling the magistrate judge. And improvements in communications technology do not guarantee that a magistrate judge will be available when an officer needs a warrant after making a late-night arrest. But technological developments that enable police officers to secure warrants more quickly, and do so without undermining the neutral magistrate judge's essential role as a check on police discretion, are relevant to an assessment of exigency. That is particularly so in this context, where BAC evidence is lost gradually and relatively predictably. Of course, there are important countervailing concerns. While experts can work backwards from the BAC at the time the sample was taken to determine the BAC at the time of the alleged offense, longer intervals may raise questions about the accuracy of the calculation. For that reason, exigent circumstances justifying a warrantless blood sample may arise in the regular course of law enforcement due to delays from the warrant application process. But adopting the State's *per se* approach would improperly ignore the current and future technological developments in warrant procedures, and might well diminish the incentive for jurisdictions to pursue progressive approaches to warrant acquisition that preserve the protections afforded by the warrant while meeting the legitimate interests of law enforcement. In short, while the natural dissipation of alcohol in the blood may support a finding of exigency in a specific case, as it did in *Schmerber*, it does not do so categorically. Whether a warrantless blood test of a drunk-driving suspect is reasonable must be determined case by case based on the totality of the circumstances."

Missouri v. McNeely, 133 S. Ct. 1552, 1556, 1560–63, 185 L. Ed. 2d 696 (2013) (inner quotations and citations omitted).

- "In light of our society's concern for the security of one's person, it is obvious that this physical intrusion, penetrating beneath the skin, infringes an expectation of privacy that society is prepared to recognize as reasonable. The ensuing chemical analysis of the sample to obtain physiological data is a further invasion of the tested employee's privacy interests." *Skinner v. Railway Labor Executives' Ass'n*, 489 U.S. 602, 616, 109 S. Ct. 1402, 103 L. Ed. 2d 639, 4 I.E.R. Cas. (BNA) 224, 130 L.R.R.M. (BNA) 2857, 13 O.S.H. Cas. (BNA) 2065, 49 Empl. Prac. Dec. (CCH) P 38791, 111 Lab. Cas. (CCH) P 11001, 1989 O.S.H. Dec. (CCH) P 28476 (1989).

- "Subjecting a person to a breathalyzer test, which generally requires the production of alveolar or deep lung breath for chemical analysis, implicates similar concerns about bodily integrity and, like the blood-alcohol test we considered in *Schmerber*, should also be deemed a search." *Skinner v. Railway Labor Executives' Ass'n*, 489 U.S. 602, 616–17, 109 S. Ct. 1402, 103 L. Ed. 2d 639, 4 I.E.R. Cas. (BNA) 224, 130 L.R.R.M. (BNA) 2857, 13 O.S.H. Cas. (BNA) 2065, 49 Empl. Prac. Dec. (CCH) P 38791, 111 Lab. Cas. (CCH) P 11001, 1989 O.S.H. Dec. (CCH) P 28476 (1989).

- "A compelled surgical intrusion into an individual's body for evidence implicates expectations of privacy and security of such magnitude that the intrusion may be unreasonable even if likely to produce evidence of a crime." *Winston v. Lee*, 470 U.S. 753, 759, 105 S. Ct. 1611, 84 L. Ed. 2d 662 (1985).

- "Search warrants are ordinarily required for searches of dwellings, and, absent an emergency, no less could be required where intrusions into the human body are concerned. The importance of informed, detached and deliberate determinations of the issue whether or not to invade another's body in search of evidence of guilt is indisputable and great." *Schmerber v. California*, 384 U.S. 757, 770, 86 S. Ct. 1826, 16 L. Ed. 2d 908 (1966).

- "The interests in human dignity and privacy which the Fourth Amendment protects forbid any such intrusions [into the body] on the mere chance that desired evidence might be obtained. In the absence of a clear indication that in fact such evidence will be found, these fundamental human interests require law officers to suffer the risk that such evidence may disappear unless there is an immediate search." *Schmerber v. California*, 384 U.S. 757, 769–70, 86 S. Ct. 1826, 16 L. Ed. 2d 908 (1966).

- "[T]here is nothing brutal or offensive in the taking of a sample of blood when done, as in this case, under the protective eye of a physician. The blood test procedure has become routine in our everyday life. We therefore conclude that a blood test taken by a skilled technician is not such conduct that shocks the conscience, nor such a method of obtaining evidence that it offends a sense of justice." *Breithaupt v. Abram*, 352 U.S. 432, 435–37, 77 S. Ct. 408, 1 L. Ed. 2d 448 (1957).

- "It would be a stultification of the responsibility which the course of constitutional history has cast upon this Court to hold that in order to convict a man the police cannot extract by force what is in his mind but can extract what is in his stomach. . . . [T]he proceedings by which this conviction was obtained do more than offend some fastidious squeamishness or private sentimentalism about combatting crime too energetically. This is conduct that shocks the conscience. Illegally breaking into the privacy of the petitioner, the struggle to open his mouth and remove what was there, the forcible extraction of his stomach's contents—this course of proceeding by agents of government to obtain evidence is bound to offend even hardened sensibilities. They are methods too close to the rack and the screw to permit of constitutional differentiation." *Rochin v. California*, 342 U.S. 165, 172–73, 72 S. Ct. 205, 96 L. Ed. 183, 25 A.L.R.2d 1396 (1952).

First Circuit

- "When a medical procedure is performed at the instigation of law enforcement for the purpose of obtaining evidence, the fact that the search is executed by a medical professional does not insulate it from Fourth Amendment scrutiny." *Sanchez v. Pereira-Castillo*, 590 F.3d 31 (1st Cir. 2009).

Second Circuit

- "Plaintiffs allege that the Defendant Police Officers strip searched Green twice. Plaintiffs first allege that McKennie forced Green to strip off all of her clothing, and that Jane Doe and McKennie performed two vaginal searches of Plaintiff and later alleged that Jane Doe alone performed a vaginal search at the direction of Scott. A valid search warrant creates a presumption of reasonableness regarding an attendant search. However, the attendant search must still be reasonable. . . . Indeed, the Second Circuit has exhibited considerable regard for the right of any person—even a person who has been lawfully arrested and confined in a correctional facility pending trial—not to be subjected to a strip search unless there exists particularized suspicion that an individual is secreting contraband. Furthermore, no court has ever held that being arrested for a narcotics-related crime automatically gives rise to reasonable suspicion that drugs are being carried in an arrestee's body cavities, so as to justify a strip search or visual body cavity inspection. In fact, the Second Circuit has held that an arrest for a misdemeanor drug offense, alone, is insufficient to satisfy the reasonable suspicion requirement, and the same rule applies to felony narcotics arrestees. Here, Plaintiffs allege that the Defendant Police Officers did not levy any criminal charges as a result of the search, nor did they find any drugs or the two individuals referred to in the warrant. In such a case, where narcotics were not recovered during the initial sweep of the apartment, it is unreasonable to immediately suspect that the occupants of the apartment—none of whom were identified in the warrant—might be in possession of either narcotics or weapons. It is even plausibly more unreasonable to conduct a *second* strip search on Green, after the first one revealed nothing, when Green was allegedly handcuffed during the search of the apartment." *Green v. City of Mount Vernon*, 96 F. Supp. 3d 263, 291–93 (S.D. N.Y. 2015) (inner citations and quotations omitted).

- "Plaintiffs' Fourth Amendment challenge to New York's DNA-indexing statute is properly analyzed under the special-needs test. Although courts have unanimously upheld DNA-indexing statutes whether they have ap-

plied the special-needs test or the general Fourth
Amendment balancing test, the test applied continues
to matter, especially since the reasons for adopting a
particular test will inevitably have consequences in
other search contexts. We therefore continue to hold
suspicionless searches to the higher standard of review
embodied in the special-needs inquiry. . . . We therefore
ask whether a DNA-indexing statute that aims to create a DNA-identification index to assist in solving
crimes serves a special need, as that term has been
defined by the Court in its recent cases. There can be
little doubt that New York's statute serves a purpose
related to law enforcement, but we do not think that
fact automatically condemns the New York statute. . . .
[W]e find it crucial that the state, in collecting DNA
samples, is not trying to determine that a particular individual has engaged in some specific wrongdoing. . . .
Because the state's purpose in conducting DNA index-
ing is distinct from the ordinary crime detection activities associated with normal law-enforcement concerns,
it meets the special-needs threshold. . . . Having
concluded that New York's DNA statute serves a special
need, we now weigh that special need against the
privacy intrusion it effects to determine whether it is
reasonable within the meaning of the Fourth
Amendment. . . . There can be little doubt that New
York has a strong government interest in obtaining
identifying information from convicted offenders and
keeping a record of such information. Nor is there any
question that New York's statute is effective in advancing that state interest. Against these government
interests, the court must weigh the intrusion on
inmates, which is twofold. First, offenders are subject to
a physical intrusion when they are required to provide
the DNA sample, whether by blood sample or buccal
cheek swab. We conclude that this physical intrusion is
far outweighed by the government's strong interests in
obtaining from plaintiffs the uniquely effective identifying information that DNA provides. . . . The second
intrusion to which offenders are subject is the analysis
and maintenance of their DNA information in New
York's database. . . . [I]t is potentially a far greater
intrusion than the initial extraction of DNA, since the

state analyzes DNA for information and maintains DNA records indefinitely. It is this intrusion that has caused the greatest concern among those of our colleagues who would strike down DNA-indexing statutes as unconstitutional. Although we acknowledge these concerns, we ultimately conclude that the intrusion into plaintiffs' privacy resulting from state's practice of analyzing and maintaining DNA records does not outweigh the government's strong interests. . . . Relying on the special-needs test rather than the general balancing test employed by the district court, we hold that New York's DNA statute satisfies the Fourth Amendment." *Nicholas v. Goord*, 430 F.3d 652 (2d Cir. 2005).

- "Upon consideration of the minimal intrusion involved, the important state interest, and the lack of discretionary decisions, we conclude that the balance of interests in this case tips in defendants' favor and conclude that the DNA statute survives Fourth Amendment scrutiny." *Roe v. Marcotte*, 193 F.3d 72, 80 (2d Cir. 1999).

Third Circuit

- "There is no doubt that a compelled blood test like the one in this case is a body intrusion and a search within the meaning of the Fourth Amendment. . . . It must be reasonable in order to satisfy the Fourth Amendment and performed in a manner appropriate under the circumstances. . . . Consistent with the Fourth Amendment, the Act assures that government officials conduct tests only of individuals for which they have sufficient justification. . . . The Act requires that there be probable cause to believe that the subject of the search has sexually assaulted the victim in a manner which creates a risk of transmission of HIV. . . . The Act provides greater protection than the Fourth Amendment does." *U.S. v. Ward*, 131 F.3d 335, 340–41 (3d Cir. 1997).

Seventh Circuit

- "In determining whether a search that intrudes below the surface of the body is reasonable, courts must weigh a variety of factors to determine whether society's interest in conducting the search outweighs the individual's interest in privacy and security."... The... balancing test

1119

[set forth by the Supreme Court] requires the court to consider the following facts: (1) the extent to which the procedure may threaten the safety or health of the individual; (2) the extent of intrusion upon the individual's dignitary interests in personal privacy and bodily integrity; and (3) the community's interest in fairly and accurately determining guilt or innocence." *U.S. v. Husband*, 312 F.3d 247 (7th Cir. 2002).

- "In determining whether a search that intrudes below the surface of the body is reasonable, courts must weigh a variety of factors to determine whether society's interest in conducting the search outweighs the individual's interests in privacy and security." *U.S. v. Husband*, 226 F.3d 626, 630 (7th Cir. 2000).

Ninth Circuit

- "In the end, the LBPD conducted a warrantless forcible seizure of an unidentified item of unknown size from Fowlkes' rectum by non-medical personnel who (1) did nothing to assure that the removal was safe and performed under sanitary conditions; (2) were aided by the use of a taser but not by lubricant; (3) seized the object in the absence of exigent circumstances; and (4) acted in violation of LBPD policy. No single factor is dispositive, but under the totality of the circumstances presented here, we conclude that the manner of this seizure was unreasonable." *U.S. v. Fowlkes*, 804 F.3d 954, 967 (9th Cir. 2015).

- "Neither of the concerns that animated our reasoning in *Bull* or the Court's reasoning in *Florence* is present in this case. First, the government does not contend that it is necessary to physically penetrate the body cavities of every person booked into the Long Beach City Jail. Instead, it seeks to justify the warrantless intrusion into one inmate's body cavity. . . . The relatively small numbers of inmates concealing contraband in their body cavities shows there is not a 'special need' for officers to conduct warrantless searches into inmates' body cavities in general. These small numbers and the technological advancements that facilitate nearly immediate access to warrants, render the burden placed on the government to obtain a warrant negligible. Because officers likely will be able to establish probable cause based on their visual observations of the small number of individuals whom they suspect of secreting contraband, the time, feasibility, and practicability concerns underlying *Bull* and *Florence* do not apply here." *U.S. v. Fowlkes*, 770 F.3d 748, 757–58 (9th Cir. 2014), opinion withdrawn and superseded on reh'g on other grounds, 804 F.3d 954 (9th Cir. 2015) (citations omitted).

- "The 2004 Amendment does not provide the Government *carte blanche* to take buccal swabs from anyone and everyone. It applies only to persons arrested on suspicion of having committed a felony. *Before individuals can be required to give a buccal swab DNA sample under the 2004 Amendment, a law enforcement officer must determine that there is probable cause to suspect that person of having committed a felony.* Even critics of mandatory DNA sampling concede that a felony arrestee has a significantly diminished expectation of privacy. Upon arrest, individuals are often booked and placed in a jail cell pending arraignment or bail, and at that point they are typically subjected to numerous degrading physical and emotional intrusions. They may be subjected to visual body cavity searches; be monitored by guards of the opposite sex while they shower and use the toilet; be restrained and peppersprayed; have their telephone access restricted; occasionally be housed with violent detainees who leave them 'with facial injuries that require [ ] surgery,[']; and be 'in lockdown for as much as 23½ hours a day, always shackled in chains, even when taking a shower or making a phone call, and rarely being allowed to see daylight and breathe fresh air.' . . . We evaluate two distinct claims of privacy intrusion: the physical collection of the DNA, and the analysis of the information contained in that sample. . . . The buccal swab cannot seriously be viewed as an unacceptable violation of a person's bodily integrity. . . . In short, the physical extraction of DNA using a buccal swab collection technique is little more than a minor inconvenience to felony arrestees, who have diminished expectations of privacy. . . . Plaintiffs challenge not only the physical intrusion of the buccal swab, but the collection and use of the information contained in the DNA sample. Although Plaintiffs use the phrase 'DNA profile' to evoke images of an oppressive 'Big Brother' cataloguing our most intimate traits, the reality is far less troubling. A DNA profile contains only thirteen 'junk DNA' markers that are not linked to any genetic or physical trait. They are used only to identify the individual. Given the minimal amount of information contained in a DNA profile, we are persuaded that DNA, as collected and used under the 2004 Amendment, is substantially indistinguishable from traditional fingerprinting as a means of identifying arrestees and, incidentally, tying arrestees to criminal investigations. Although there are some distinctions between DNA and fingerprints, these distinctions do not implicate serious *privacy* concerns. These differences include, among others: DNA identification is more robust and reliable than fingerprint identification; DNA is more often left at crime scenes than fingerprints, thus enhancing DNA's investigative efficacy; and, as emphasized by Plaintiffs, DNA contains a much broader range of identifying information than fingerprints and is more susceptible to misuse. Nevertheless, the relative reliability and greater availability of DNA do not affect any cognizable privacy interests (as individuals do not have a 'privacy interest' *per se* in the efficiency of law enforcement operations), and the wider potential usage of DNA data (and accompanying potential for abuse) is carefully restricted by the strict limitations established in the DNA Act. Fingerprinting has been consistently upheld as constitutional. . . . Given the arrestee's diminished privacy interests; the *de minimis* nature of the physical intrusion entailed in the taking of a buccal swab; the carefully circumscribed scope of the DNA information being extracted; the stringent limits on the manner in which that information may be used; and the well-established law enforcement interest in obtaining arrestees' identifying information, and further, to deter future criminal acts and to exculpate innocent arrestees—the balance of interests tilts strongly in favor of upholding the constitutionality of the 2004 Amendment. We emphasize that our decision deals solely with DNA extraction, processing, and analysis as it presently exists, and is enforced. We acknowledge that future developments in the law could alter the constitutionality of the DNA Act, as amended. But we cannot test the amended DNA Act's *current* legality in light of uncertain *future* amendments to the law, which themselves would likely violate the DNA Act, as amended by the 2004 Amendment." *Haskell v. Harris*, 669 F.3d 1049 (9th Cir. 2012) (emphasis in original, citations omitted).

- "Intrusions into the human body, including the taking of blood, are searches subject to the restrictions of the Fourth Amendment." *U.S. v. Wright*, 215 F.3d 1020, 1025 (9th Cir. 2000).

- "When an arrestee has agreed to submit to a breath or urine test which is available and of similar evidentiary value, the government's need for a blood test disappears. Under such circumstances, it is unreasonable to require a blood test and the Fourth Amendment is violated. Further, when a DUI suspect agrees to take an available alternative test of equal evidentiary value, the risk that evidence will be lost disappears and the exigent circumstance that excused the police from obtaining a warrant likewise disappears, rendering a warrantless nonconsensual blood test in such circumstances unconstitutional." *Nelson v. City of Irvine*, 143 F.3d 1196, 1207 (9th Cir. 1998).

- "The Supreme Court has held that the taking of a blood sample while a person is unconscious by a qualified technician and in a controlled setting does not offend due process because there is nothing brutal or offensive in the taking of a sample of blood when done . . . under the protective eye of a physician. . . . The Court noted that, even if a person is unconscious when the blood is withdrawn, the absence of conscious consent, without more, does not necessarily render the taking a violation of a constitutional right." *Belgarde v. State of Mont.*, 123 F.3d 1210, 1214 (9th Cir. 1997).

Tenth Circuit

- "The [DNA Analysis Backlog Elimination Act of 2000, requiring the collection of a DNA sample as a condition of supervised release], while implicating the Fourth Amendment, is a reasonable search and seizure under the special needs exception to the Fourth Amendment's warrant requirement because the desire to build a DNA database goes beyond the ordinary law enforcement need." *U.S. v. Kimler*, 335 F.3d 1132, 61 Fed. R. Evid. Serv. 1024, 7 A.L.R. Fed. 2d 583 (10th Cir. 2003).

- "As in *Schmerber*, police had probable cause to suspect [plaintiff] of the crime of driving under the influence, and as in *Schmerber*, the delay necessary to obtain a warrant under the circumstances threatened destruction of the evidence. [Plaintiff's] brief can be liberally construed to argue that *Schmerber* is distinguishable in at least one important respect: state law does not authorize New Mexico police to compel a blood test in a misdemeanor case involving no physical injury, even with a warrant. . . . Under the facts of *Schmerber*—a serious accident with the potential of a felony prosecution—state law authorized police to procure a warrant for a blood test, and if time and circumstances had permitted, the police could have done so. It was only the delay necessary to obtain a warrant, which created the emergency, which justified the warrantless search. By contrast, in this case no warrant was available by law for a test of [defendant's] blood. . . . We can reasonably infer from the evidence, therefore, that Officer Porter would not have been able to obtain a search warrant under the circumstances of this case, even if he had time to do so. Because the exigent circumstances in Schmerber were based entirely on the 'emergency' circumstances created by the delay necessary to obtain a warrant, it follows that Schmerber is distinguishable. . . . If a state does not permit obtaining evidence from the bloodstream, even under the protection of a warrant based on probable cause, it perforce demonstrates minimal interest in the evidence to be obtained by the search. State actors then cannot turn around and seek shelter under the exigent circumstances exception to the Fourth Amendment's warrant requirement. This approach is assumed within *Schmerber* itself. After noting that warrants are generally required absent specific emergency circumstances, *Schmerber* held that 'The officer in the present case... might reasonably have believed that he was confronted with an emergency, in which the delay necessary to obtain a warrant, under the circumstances, threatened the destruction of the evidence.' Implicit in this holding is that exigent circumstances exist only when a warrant would be available but for the shortage of time. That is not true in this case." *Marshall v. Columbia Lea Regional Hosp.*, 345 F.3d 1157 (10th Cir. 2003).

- "[W]hile obtaining DNA samples implicates Fourth Amendment concerns, it is reasonable in light of an inmate's diminished privacy rights, the minimal intrusion involved, and the legitimate government interest in using DNA to investigate and prosecute crimes." *Shaffer v. Saffle*, 148 F.3d 1180, 1181 (10th Cir. 1998).

D.C. Circuit

- "Today we join this unanimous body of authority, and we conclude that the mandatory collection of [plaintiff's] DNA sample was 'reasonable' under the Fourth Amendment's balancing test. On one side of the balance, it is well settled that probationers have lesser privacy interests than do ordinary citizens. Moreover, the privacy invasion caused by a blood test is relatively small (even when conducted on a free citizen). . . . While we need not decide whether the Fourth Amendment permits the suspicionless collection of blood samples from every suspect arrested for a felony, it certainly permits the collection of a blood sample from a *convicted* felon, like [plaintiff], while he is still on probation. . . . Balancing [plaintiff's] reduced privacy interests against the government's interests in monitoring probationers, deterring recidivism, and protecting the public, we hold it was reasonable for the Appellees to collect [plaintiff's] DNA while on probation. [Plaintiff's] second argument is that the Fourth Amendment prohibits the government from storing his 'genetic fingerprint' in the CODIS database and 're-searching' it after he has left the probationary rolls (as he now has). . . . We conclude that accessing the records stored in the CODIS database is not a 'search' for Fourth Amendment purposes. . . . [A] felon's DNA fingerprint is more akin to a *snapshot*: It reveals identifying information based on a blood test conducted at a single point in time. Of course, even snapshots can raise Fourth Amendment concerns. However, if a snapshot is taken in conformance with the Fourth Amendment, the government's storage and use of it does not give rise to an independent Fourth Amendment claim. Accordingly, we conclude that ac-

cessing the DNA snapshots contained in the CODIS
database does not independently implicate the Fourth
Amendment." *Johnson v. Quander*, 440 F.3d 489 (D.C.
Cir. 2006).

§ 27:3 Strip and body cavity searches: Strip searches and body cavity searches occur primarily in prisons or jails. They must be conducted in a reasonable manner and must be justified by the circumstances

Supreme Court

- "[Plaintiff]'s subjective expectation of privacy against
  such a [strip] search is inherent in her account of it as
  embarrassing, frightening, and humiliating. The reasonableness of her expectation (required by the Fourth
  Amendment standard) is indicated by the consistent experiences of other young people similarly searched,
  whose adolescent vulnerability intensifies the patent
  intrusiveness of the exposure." *Safford Unified School
  Dist. No. 1 v. Redding*, 557 U.S. 364, 129 S. Ct. 2633,
  174 L. Ed. 2d 354, 245 Ed. Law Rep. 626 (2009).

- "In sum, what was missing from the suspected facts
  that pointed to [plaintiff] was any indication of danger
  to the students from the power of the drugs or their
  quantity, and any reason to suppose that [plaintiff] was
  carrying pills in her underwear. We think that the
  combination of these deficiencies was fatal to finding
  the search reasonable." *Safford Unified School Dist. No.
  1 v. Redding*, 557 U.S. 364, 129 S. Ct. 2633, 174 L. Ed.
  2d 354, 245 Ed. Law Rep. 626 (2009).

- "We do not underestimate the degree to which these
  searches may invade the personal privacy of inmates.
  The searches must be conducted in a reasonable
  manner. . . . But we deal here with the question
  whether visual body-cavity inspections as contemplated
  by the [prison] rules can ever be conducted on less than
  probable cause. Balancing the significant and legitimate security interests of the institution against the
  privacy interests of the inmates, we conclude that they
  can." *Bell v. Wolfish*, 441 U.S. 520, 560, 99 S. Ct. 1861,
  60 L. Ed. 2d 447 (1979).

First Circuit

- "[C]ourts have concluded that, to be reasonable under *Wolfish*, strip and visual body cavity searches must be justified by at least a reasonable suspicion that the arrestee is concealing contraband or weapons. . . . Accordingly, it is clear that at least the reasonable suspicion standard governs strip and visual body cavity searches in the arrestee context as well." *Swain v. Spinney*, 117 F.3d 1, 7 (1st Cir. 1997).

- "[A] strip search can hardly be characterized as a routine procedure or as a minimally intrusive means of maintaining prison security. Indeed, a strip search, by its very nature, constitutes an extreme intrusion upon personal privacy, as well as an offense to the dignity of the individual. Accordingly, a strip search cannot be justified absent some quantum of individualized suspicion. In determining the level of individualized suspicion against which to test the constitutionality of prison-visitor strip searches with a view to striking the proper balance between respecting the legitimate privacy expectations of prison visitors and the need to maintain prison security, courts have converged upon one common benchmark: the standard of reasonable suspicion." *Wood v. Clemons*, 89 F.3d 922, 928 (1st Cir. 1996).

Second Circuit

- "The Fourth Amendment requires an individualized reasonable suspicion that a misdemeanor arrestee is concealing weapons or other contraband based on the crime charged, the particular characteristics of the arrestee, and/or the circumstances of the arrest before she may be lawfully subjected to a strip search. To establish reasonable suspicion, officers must point to specific objective facts and rational inferences that they are entitled to draw from those facts in light of their experience; the standard requires individualized suspicion, specifically directed to the person who is targeted for the strip search." *Hartline v. Gallo*, 546 F.3d 95 (2d Cir. 2008).

- "The Fourth Amendment requires an individualized reasonable suspicion that a misdemeanor arrestee is concealing weapons or other contraband based on the crime charged, the particular characteristics of the ar-

1127

restee, and/or the circumstances of the arrest before the arrestee may be lawfully subjected to a strip search. To establish reasonable suspicion, officers must point to specific objective facts and rational inferences that they are entitled to draw from those facts in light of their experience; the standard requires individualized suspicion, specifically directed to the person who is targeted for the strip search. Whether a particular strip search is constitutional turns on an objective assessment of the facts and circumstances confronting the searching officer at the time, and not on the officer's actual state of mind at the time of the search." *Hartline v. Gallo*, 546 F.3d 95 (2d Cir. 2008).

- "[A]t the time of the strip search, under the law of the United States Supreme Court, the Court of Appeals for the Second Circuit, and the other circuit courts of appeals, a search of prison visitors without reasonable suspicion violated clearly established law. . . . [C]orrectional officers needed reasonable suspicion to strip search prison visitors without violating their constitutional rights. . . . The standard requires individualized suspicion, specifically directed to the person who is targeted for the strip search." *Varrone v. Bilotti*, 123 F.3d 75, 78–79 (2d Cir. 1997).

Third Circuit

- "Patdowns, frisks, luggage searches, and automobile searches, involving neither a high expectation of privacy nor a seriously invasive search, are routine searches that require no suspicion, whereas body cavity searches, strip searches, and x-ray examinations are considered nonroutine searches by virtue of their significant intrusion on an individual's privacy and require reasonable suspicion." *U.S. v. Whitted*, 50 V.I. 1081, 541 F.3d 480, 43 A.L.R.6th 771 (3d Cir. 2008).
- "Highly intrusive searches of the person that implicate the dignity and privacy interests of the person being searched require reasonable suspicion." *U.S. v. Whitted*, 50 V.I. 1081, 541 F.3d 480, 43 A.L.R.6th 771 (3d Cir. 2008).

Fourth Circuit

- "Because the invasiveness of [Defendant]'s search far

outweighed any potential justification for the scope, manner, and place under which it was conducted. . .we agree with the district court that the search was unreasonable and, therefore, unconstitutional. . . .[A] strip search or a body cavity search conducted in public violates an arrestee's Fourth Amendment right to a reasonable search. . . ." *Amaechi v. West*, 237 F.3d 356, 362 (4th Cir. 2001).

- "[W]e conclude that the search in question was not an unconstitutional strip search. The search did not occur on the street subject to public viewing but took place in the privacy of the police van. Since the police officers acted reasonably in attempting to locate the missing money, the contention that he was subjected to an unconstitutional strip search must fail." *U.S. v. Dorlouis*, 107 F.3d 248, 256 (4th Cir. 1997).
- "We conclude that the search conducted inside [the defendant's] underwear is properly characterized as a strip search, which includes 'the exposure of a person's naked body for the purpose of a visual or physical examination.' A movement of clothing to facilitate the visual inspection of a suspect's naked body, as occurred here, is a standard example of a strip search. A suspect need not have been fully undressed for the search to have characteristics of, or be treated as, a strip search. We also find instructive the Supreme Court's recent characterization of a strip search in *Safford Unified School District No. 1 v. Redding*. The Court held that a school official's order that a student 'remove her clothes down to her underwear, and then "pull out" her bra and the elastic band on her underpants . . . in the presence of the two officials who were able to see her necessarily exposed breasts and pelvic area to some degree,' constituted a search that could be fairly called a 'strip search.' " *U.S. v. Edwards*, 666 F.3d 877, 882 (4th Cir. 2011) (citations omitted).
- "In *Bell*, the Supreme Court developed 'a flexible test' to determine the reasonableness of a broad range of 'sexually invasive searches,' which included but was not limited to strip searches. . . . Under the *Bell* framework for determining the reasonableness of sexually invasive searches, the need for a particular search is balanced against the invasion of personal rights caused by the

search. Pursuant to *Bell,* we examine the search in its complete context and consider the following factors: 1) the place in which the search was conducted; 2) the scope of the particular intrusion; 3) the manner in which the search was conducted; and 4) the justification for initiating the search." *U.S. v. Edwards,* 666 F.3d 877, 883 (4th Cir. 2011) (citations omitted).

Fifth Circuit

- "[T]he classification of a crime as a misdemeanor has been treated by other circuits as a relevant or even determinative factor in ascertaining whether there is a reasonable suspicion requirement. In other settings, as well, misdemeanors have historically been considered minor offenses. In *Stewart,* we cited the applicability of the challenged policy to individuals arrested for misdemeanors in support of our conclusion that the challenged policy was unconstitutional because it applied to minor offenders when no reasonable suspicion existed that they might possess weapons or contraband. In *Stewart,* however, the detainees had been arrested pursuant to Class C misdemeanors, which, unlike the Class A misdemeanor in this case, were punishable only by fine. Nevertheless, in light of the persuasive authority, we hold that hindering apprehension—other than felony hindering apprehension under section 38.05(d), the status of which is not before us—is, given its misdemeanor status, a minor offense for these purposes and reasonable suspicion was therefore required for a strip search. Accordingly, any instruction to that effect did not amount to error." *Jimenez v. Wood County, Tex.,* 621 F.3d 372, 377–78 (5th Cir. 2010), on reh'g en banc, 660 F.3d 841, 80 Fed. R. Serv. 3d 1408 (5th Cir. 2011) (citations omitted).

- "A strip search is permissible only if the official has an individualized suspicion that the arrestee is hiding weapons or contraband. This suspicion must relate to the individual arrestee, not a category of offenders and does not arise merely because an arrestee fails to post bond immediately and police move him to general population. In short, pure speculation does not create a reasonable suspicion; nor does a generalized fear of a category of arrestees." *Kelly v. Foti,* 77 F.3d 819, 822 (5th Cir. 1996).

Sixth Circuit

- "[N]o clearly established principle of constitutional law . . . forbids a juvenile detention center from implementing a generally applicable, suspicionless strip-search policy upon intake into the facility. . . . . [T]he plaintiffs have failed to meet their burden of demonstrating that every reasonable official in June 2009 would have known that conducting a suspicionless strip search of a juvenile detainee during his or her intake into a detention facility violated the Fourth Amendment. Without this, their federal claims cannot survive the defendants' assertion of qualified immunity. We need not, and do not, opine on the constitutionality of the strip searches. The district court erred in denying summary judgment to the defendants on the plaintiffs' [42 USCA] § 1983 claims, and we therefore reverse." *T.S. v. Doe*, 742 F.3d 632 (6th Cir. 2014).

- "The natural extension of this principle is that prison authorities have much greater leeway in conducting searches of visitors. Visitors can be subjected to some searches, such as a pat-down or a metal detector sweep, merely as a condition of visitation, absent any suspicion. However, because a strip and body cavity search is the most intrusive search possible, courts have attempted to balance the need for institutional security against the remaining privacy interests of visitors. Those courts that have examined the issue have concluded that even for strip and body cavity searches prison authorities need not secure a warrant or have probable cause. However, the residual privacy interests of visitors in being free from such an invasive search requires that prison authorities have at least a reasonable suspicion that the visitor is bearing contraband before conducting such a search. [W]e do not think that a person consents to a strip and body cavity search by simply appearing at a visiting center. Instead, the same logic that dictates that such a search may be conducted only when there is reasonable suspicion also demands that the person to be subjected to such an invasive search be given the opportunity to depart." *Spear v. Sowders*, 71 F.3d 626, 630, 632, 1995 FED App. 0366P (6th Cir. 1995).

Eighth Circuit

- "Police chief's photographing of arrestee's tattoo did not amount to a strip search under Missouri strip search law, despite arrestee's contention that her underwear was revealed during the photographing, absent evidence that the search was for the purpose of inspecting her underwear, or even that her underwear was inspected." *Schmidt v. City of Bella Villa*, 557 F.3d 564 (8th Cir. 2009).

Ninth Circuit

- "The conduct of the search here was patently unreasonable. In determining whether an individual search is reasonable, we evaluate the 'totality of the circumstances,' including 'the scope of the particular intrusion, the manner of its conduct, and the justification for initiating it.' First, Sergeant Gibbs evinced an intent to conduct any body cavity search he thought necessary long before he saw the plastic bag protruding from Fowlkes's rectum or was privy to any other possible justification for such an intrusion. Gibbs, suspecting that Fowlkes had contraband in his person, made his way to the strip search room in the basement armed with his protective gloves, a stun gun taser, and additional officers—in short, everything he needed to conduct a cavity search, *except* a warrant. Second, the scope of the search intruded beyond the surface of Fowlkes's body, interfering with his bodily integrity. . . . Third, the manner in which this search was conducted was unreasonable. . . . In evaluating whether the manner in which a search is conducted is reasonable, we consider a variety of factors including hygiene, medical training, emotional and physical trauma, and the availability of alternative methods for conducting the search. As an initial matter, the officers violated the jail's own written policy for body cavity searches by failing to conduct the search 'under sanitary conditions' and by not using a 'Physician, Nurse Practitioner, Registered Nurse, Licensed Vocational Nurse, or Emergency Medical Technician.' There is no evidence that any of the officers had medical or any other relevant training on how to safely remove suspicious objects from an arrestee's rectum or how to evaluate whether such removal could cause serious physical harm or death. . . . As the Supreme Court accurately predicted forty-years ago, tolerating such searches does invite an unjustified element of personal risk-a risk that Fowlkes experienced first—hand and one that is constitutionally intolerable. . . . Here there was no effort to minimize the potential for internal physical trauma to Fowlkes or the emotional humiliation he suffered. *Schmerber* is again instructive. There the [Supreme] Court explicitly considered that the blood draw in question 'involves virtually no risk, trauma, or pain,' and that it 'was performed in a reasonable manner' because 'blood was taken by a physician in a hospital environment according to accepted medical practices.' Here by contrast, despite undisputed testimony by the officers themselves that Fowlkes posed no threat, much less an immediate threat to himself or the officers, and was not a flight risk (he was naked and bent over at the time), Sergeant Gibbs used a stun-gun taser to shock Fowlkes in an apparent effort to subdue him before conducting the physical search. Once Fowlkes was subdued, the officers proceeded with the degrading and dangerous removal of the as yet unidentified cocaine from Fowlkes's rectum. Such conduct is a far cry from *Cameron's* directive to 'allay the anxieties and concerns of the suspect,' or contemplate whether any 'less intrusive means of obtaining the evidence may properly have been considered.' " *U.S. v. Fowlkes*, 770 F.3d 748, 758–60 (9th Cir. 2014), opinion withdrawn and superseded on reh'g on other grounds, 804 F.3d 954 (9th Cir. 2015) (citations omitted).

• [W]e disagree with those other circuits that have held strip searches of arrestees entering the general jail population per se unreasonable unless the officials have individualized reasonable suspicion that the arrestees are smuggling contraband. These courts have purported to distinguish *Bell* on several grounds: that persons arrested on certain minor offenses do not represent a security concern, that persons who are arrested are less likely to smuggle contraband than detainees already in the general jail population who engage in contact visits, and that a blanket strip search policy for all arrestees entering the general jail population is unreasonable unless officials have demonstrated the existence of a significant smuggling problem and that a blanket policy has a significant deterrent effect. As explained above, this reasoning is inconsistent both with the general principles enunciated in *Bell* and *Turner,* and with the specific application of those principles to the strip search at issue in *Bell.* Moreover, these decisions are inconsistent with the Supreme Court's warning that federal courts must avoid substituting their judgment for the 'professional expertise of corrections officials' in 'determining whether restrictions or conditions are reasonably related to the Government's interest in maintaining security and order and operating the institution in a manageable fashion.' While federal courts may ' disagree[ ] with the judgment of [corrections] officials about the extent of the security interests affected and the means required to further those interests,' the Supreme Court's 'decisions have time and again emphasized that this sort of unguided substitution of judicial judgment for that of the expert prison administrators on matters such as this is inappropriate.' We agree with the reasoning of the Eleventh Circuit that the rights of arrestees placed in custodial housing with the general jail population 'are not violated by a policy or practice of strip searching each one of them as part of the booking process, provided that the searches are no more intrusive on privacy interests than those upheld in the *Bell* case,' and the searches are 'not conducted in an abusive manner.' We therefore overrule our own panel opinions in *Thompson* and *Giles.* We do not, however, disturb our prior opinions considering searches of arrestees who were not classified for housing in the general jail or prison population. The constitutionality of searches of arrestees at the place of arrest, searches at the stationhouse prior to booking, and searches pursuant to an evidentiary investigation must be analyzed under different principles than those at issue today." *Bull v. City and County of San Francisco,* 595 F.3d 964, 980–81 (9th Cir. 2010) (citations omitted).

- "[A]n arrestee could be strip searched without individualized suspicion if the arrestee would be introduced into the general jail population. (citation omitted) In those circumstances, the institutional need to prevent arrestees from bringing contraband into the jail justified the 'the invasion of personal rights that the search entails.' (citation omitted) *Bull,* however, left undisturbed our line of precedent requiring reasonable suspicion to strip search arrestees charged with minor offenses who are not classified for housing in the general jail population." *Edgerly v. City and County of San Francisco,* 599 F.3d 946 (9th Cir. 2010).

- "[Defendants] argue that the visual body cavity search violated no constitutional rights because Sheriff's Department officials are entitled to deference on jail security matters, and their interest in securing this jail during the booking process outweighs [plaintiff's] right to be free from a compulsory visual inspection of her genitalia and anus. . . . [Defendant] responds that drug charges alone are insufficient to justify such an extreme intrusion, where she was merely a misdemeanor arrestee charged with being under the influence of a controlled substance, who was detained for only a few hours and was never housed with the jail's general population. . . . The parties agree that the search took place in a private room, behind closed doors, with no one present but [plaintiff and defendant], and there is no issue about how it was conducted. . . . [Defendants] failed to show any link between their blanket strip search policy and legitimate security concerns for detainees such as [plaintiff]. They made only a conclusory submission that the purpose of the search protocol is 'to provide facility security and to ensure the inmate's health and safety,' and that inmates have 'sometimes' ingested drugs to evade detection. Nor did they adduce evidence of any deterrent effect on persons such as [plaintiff] who are spontaneously arrested and detained temporarily at the facility for being under the influence. In effect, they ask us to take security implications on faith. This we cannot do. [Defendants] maintain that all drug offenses inherently heighten security concerns because of the risk that persons arrested on drug charges will bring drugs with them. . . . We cannot see how the charge of being under the influence of a drug necessarily poses a threat of concealing (and thereby using or trafficking) additional drugs in jail during the limited time between booking and bail, or booking and placement in the general population. If not, it was unreasonable to assume that [plaintiff] harbored drugs in some cavity or other. . . . [Plaintiff] was under the control of the arresting officer from the time she was taken into custody at work until booking. The officer perceived no indication that she was carrying drugs or contraband. [Defendant] conducted a pat down search before obtaining permission for the visual cavity search, and it turned up nothing. [Plaintiff] was held with several other detainees, but was not in the facility for long and was never put into the general jail population. In these circumstances, we conclude that an arrest for being under the influence of a drug does not supply reasonable suspicion that drugs are concealed in a bodily cavity. . . . There was no individualized suspicion that [plaintiff] concealed drugs in a bodily cavity. Therefore, subjecting her to a strip search with visual cavity inspection offended her constitutional right to be free of an unreasonable search." *Way v. County of Ventura*, 445 F.3d 1157 (9th Cir. 2006).

- "Taken together one might read *Grummett*, *Michenfelder*, and *Sepulveda* to suggest that up close, frequent, and intentional viewings by guards of the opposite sex could violate a prisoner's privacy rights. In fact, the able magistrate judge in the instant case reached this very conclusion. In 1993, however, an en banc panel of our court took us in a different direction. In *Jordan v. Gardner* we stated: Whether such rights exist—whether the inmates possess privacy interests that could be infringed by the cross-gender aspect of otherwise constitutional searches—is a difficult and novel question, and one that cannot be dismissed lightly. But we cannot assume from the fact that the searches cause immense anguish that they therefore violate protected Fourth Amendment interests. Far from it, our prior case law suggests that prisoners' legitimate expectations of bodily privacy from persons of the opposite sex are extremely limited." *Somers v. Thurman*, 109 F.3d 614, 620 (9th Cir. 1997).

- "We have previously said that visual body cavity searches conducted after contact visits as a means of preventing prisoners' possession of weapons and contraband, even absent probable cause, have been found reasonable by the Supreme Court. [T]he prisoner bears the burden of showing that prison officials intentionally used exaggerated or excessive means to enforce security." *Thompson v. Souza*, 111 F.3d 694, 700 (9th Cir. 1997).

Tenth Circuit

- "The Fourth Amendment requires a balancing of the need for the particular search against the invasion of personal rights that the search entails. Courts must consider the scope of the particular intrusion, the manner in which it is conducted, the justification for initiating it, and the place in which it is conducted. With respect to the scope of the search, there can be no doubt that a strip search is an invasion of personal rights of the first magnitude. Courts have consistently recognized a distinction between detainees awaiting bail and those entering the jail population when evaluating the necessity of a strip search under constitutional standards." *Archuleta v. Wagner*, 523 F.3d 1278 (10th Cir. 2008).

- "We begin with the premise that inmates retain some right to privacy: 'Although the inmates' right to privacy must yield to the penal institution's need to maintain security, it does not vanish altogether.' A second well established premise is that 'a strip search is an invasion of personal rights of the first magnitude.' . . . [D]etermination of the constitutionality of a strip search 'requires a balancing of the need for the particular search against the invasion of personal rights that the search entails. Courts must consider the scope of the particular intrusion, the manner in which it is conducted, the justification for initiating it, and the place in which it is conducted.'. . . [W]e conclude that plaintiff has identified a well established right, the right not to be subjected to a humiliating strip search in full view of several (or perhaps many) others unless the procedure is reasonably related to a legitimate penological interest. We also conclude that the identified right of the plaintiff was clearly established at the time of the May 1993 search in question so that a reasonable officer would have known that a decision to subject inmates to demeaning searches in public requires justification. All of the principles were established in cases we have cited which were decided well before the

May 1993 conduct in question." *Farmer v. Perrill*, 288 F.3d 1254 (10th Cir. 2002).

- "We start from the irrefutable premise that a strip search is an invasion of personal rights of the first magnitude. . . . Undoubtedly, there are searches more intrusive than the exposure of one's breast in a public place, but we are hard-pressed to think of more than a few. . . . Nor do we believe the circumstances empowered the officers to conduct a road-side strip search. In fact, we cannot conceive of a set of circumstances allowing us to condone as reasonable an officer-imposed strip search in a public area such as a city street in the middle of the afternoon." *Nelson v. McMullen*, 207 F.3d 1202, 1206–07 (10th Cir. 2000).

- "It is not clearly unconstitutional to strip search persons arrested for possession of drugs but not placed in the general inmate population, at least if there is reasonable suspicion they have additional drugs or weapons on their persons. . . . However, it was clearly established in May 1994 that a strip search of a person arrested for driving while under the influence of drugs but not placed in the general jail population is not justified in the absence of reasonable suspicion that the arrestee has drugs or weapons hidden on his or her person." *Foote v. Spiegel*, 118 F.3d 1416, 1425 (10th Cir. 1997).

- "In this case, the dog alerted to plaintiff [Appellant] while sniffing her person. This court has held in several cases that a dog alert without more [creates] probable cause for searches and seizures. If a dog's alert gives authorities probable cause to conduct a search, it certainly satisfies the lesser standard of reasonable suspicion. [A]fter the dog alerted to [Appellant], prison officials possessed at least reasonable suspicion that she was concealing narcotics. Consequently, ordering her to submit to a strip search before entering the prison was clearly constitutional." *Romo v. Champion*, 46 F.3d 1013, 1020 (10th Cir. 1995).

Eleventh Circuit

- "[A]ssuming that arrestees being booked into a jail or detention facility retain some Fourth Amendment rights, those rights are not violated by a policy or practice of strip searching each one of them as part of the booking process, provided that the searches are no more intrusive on privacy interests than those upheld in the *Bell* case. We also assume, of course, that the searches are not conducted in an abusive manner." *Powell v. Barrett*, 541 F.3d 1298, 1314 (11th Cir. 2008) (citation omitted).

- "[W]e must conclude the search of Plaintiff cannot be justified under the Constitution on the single ground that Plaintiff was about to be placed in the Jail's general population. That conclusion, however, does not mean that Plaintiff's own constitutional rights were violated when she was searched: just because she was strip searched at a jail that had a search practice that would generally violate the Constitution does not mean every search that was conducted actually violated the Constitution. . . . Because we conclude that reasonable suspicion existed for this particular strip search, we also must conclude that no constitutional right was violated by the search. . . . Plaintiff was arrested and charged with family violence battery. . . . This crime is obviously one of violence. We accept that a person's being charged with a crime of violence is sufficient to evoke reasonable suspicion that the person may be concealing weapons or contraband. We know that both the arresting officer and the jail shift supervisor testified that they—based on their interactions with Plaintiff that evening—did not subjectively suspect Plaintiff of possessing weapons or drugs. But whether reasonable suspicion existed at the time is a question of law to be determined ultimately by judges, not policemen or jailers. And the question we are faced with here is not whether a specific arresting officer or jailer actually and subjectively had the pertinent reasonable suspicion, but whether, given the circumstances, reasonable suspicion objectively existed to justify such a search. . . . Plaintiff argues that the three cases cited by Defendants . . . are inapposite to whether [defendant officer] had reasonable suspicion to strip search Plaintiff based solely on an arrest charge. . . . We agree that those cases are not controlling, but for another reason: none of those cases involved an arrest for an obvious crime of violence. We conclude that the strip search performed on Plaintiff

violated no constitutional right." *Hicks v. Moore*, 422
F.3d 1246 (11th Cir. 2005).

- "Due to the extremely intrusive nature of a strip search,
  strip searches of arrestees based on less than probable
  cause have only been upheld where such searches were
  necessary to protect the overriding security needs of the
  institution—that is, where officials have a reasonable
  suspicion that a particular detainee harbors weapons or
  dangerous contraband. A detention center, police station, or jail holding cell is a place fraught with serious
  security dangers. These security dangers to the institution are the same whether the detainee is a juvenile or
  an adult. The considerations regarding contraband are
  the same whether the detainee is a juvenile or an adult.
  Likewise, we see no reason to differentiate between
  strip searches to discover contraband to protect the security of the institution and strip searches within the
  institution which may lead to contraband (drugs) to be
  used as evidence of a crime. The level of intrusion is the
  same. Consequently, we hold that law enforcement officers may conduct a strip search of a juvenile in
  custody, even for a minor offense, based upon reasonable suspicion to believe that the juvenile is concealing
  weapons or contraband." *Justice v. City of Peachtree
  City*, 961 F.2d 188, 193 (11th Cir. 1992).

§ 27:4   Strip searches at the border: Strip searches at the border may be conducted only pursuant to real or reasonable suspicion

Second Circuit

- "The light touching of appellant's back followed by a
  lifting of his shirt arguably straddles the line between
  the two categories of border searches—searching more
  than personal belongings or effects such as a purse,
  wallet, or even outer jacket was involved; but the search
  was not nearly as intrusive as a body cavity or full strip
  search. Since the potential indignity resulting from a
  pat on the back followed by a lifting of one's shirt simply
  fails to compare with the much greater level of intrusion associated with a body cavity or full strip search,
  we decline to hold that reasonable suspicion was here
  required." *U.S. v. Charleus*, 871 F.2d 265, 268 (2d Cir.
  1989).

- "[A]lthough anyone entering or leaving the country may expect to have his luggage and personal effects examined, he does not expect that his entry or departure, standing alone, will cause him to be subjected to a strip search. Before a border official may insist upon such an extensive invasion of privacy, he should have a suspicion of illegal concealment that is based upon something more than the border crossing, and the suspicion should be substantial enough to make the search a reasonable exercise of authority." *U.S. v. Asbury*, 586 F.2d 973, 975–76 (2d Cir. 1978).

Eighth Circuit

- "We join those circuits holding that a reasonable suspicion that a person is carrying drugs on the outside of the body may insulate a strip search from fourth amendment challenge. . . . Similarly, we concur with the conclusion reached by those circuits holding that a reasonable suspicion that a person is an alimentary canal smuggler may justify an involuntary x-ray examination." *U.S. v. Oyekan*, 786 F.2d 832, 837 (8th Cir. 1986).

Ninth Circuit

- "Strip searches and body-cavity searches are of course considered nonroutine, and, unlike luggage searches and patdowns, must be supported by reasonable suspicion. Once customs officials reasonably suspect that an international traveler is smuggling contraband, however, they may detain her and perform the searches necessary to either verify or dispel the suspicion that she will introduce a harmful agent into this country." *U.S. v. Gonzalez-Rincon*, 36 F.3d 859, 864 (9th Cir. 1994).

Eleventh Circuit

- "Border searches are not subject to the probable cause and warrant requirements of the Fourth Amendment; rather, they are simply subject to that amendment's more amorphous reasonableness standard. We have applied this reasonableness requirement by adopting a flexible test which adjusts the strength of suspicion required for a particular search to the intrusiveness of that search. In determining the level of intrusiveness of a search, extensiveness alone does not control. Rather, it is the personal indignity suffered by the individual searched that controls the level of suspicion required to make the search reasonable." *U.S. v. Villabona-Garnica*, 63 F.3d 1051, 1057 (11th Cir. 1995).

- "Reasonable suspicion to justify a strip search can only be met by a showing of articulable facts which are particularized as to the person and as to the place to be searched." *U.S. v. Vega-Barvo*, 729 F.2d 1341, 1349 (11th Cir. 1984).

- "At the border, a customs inspector must have a reasonable suspicion that a person is carrying contraband internally before a person's stomach may be searched either by x-ray or by detaining the person until he excretes his stomach's contents. The reasonable suspicion standard requires a showing of articulable facts which are particularized as to the person and as to the place that is to be searched." *U.S. v. Henao-Castano*, 729 F.2d 1364, 1366 (11th Cir. 1984).

§ 27:5 Body cavity searches at the border: Body cavity searches at the border must be based on a higher standard than strip searches

Supreme Court

- "We hold that the detention of a traveler at the border, beyond the scope of a routine customs search and inspection, is justified at its inception if customs agents, considering all the facts surrounding the traveler and her trip, reasonably suspect that the traveler is smuggling contraband in her alimentary canal. . . . It is also important to note what we do not hold. Because the issues are not presented today we suggest no view on what level of suspicion, if any, is required for nonroutine border searches such as strip, body cavity, or involuntary x-ray searches." *U.S. v. Montoya de Hernandez*, 473 U.S. 531, 541, 105 S. Ct. 3304, 87 L. Ed. 2d 381 (1985).

Second Circuit

- "We have recently seen a significant increase in alimentary-canal drug smugglers who, by swallowing drug-filled condoms, use their bodies to shield illegal drugs from the eyes of customs inspectors. Because of this unusual practice, our courts have been faced with novel legal issues in guiding law enforcement officials who seek to discover and apprehend the smugglers." *U.S. v. Onumonu*, 967 F.2d 782, 783, 36 Fed. R. Evid. Serv. 273 (2d Cir. 1992).

- "We hold that the detention of a traveler at the border, beyond the scope of a routine customs search and inspection, is justified at its inception if customs agents, considering all the facts surrounding the traveler and her trip, reasonably suspect that the traveler is smuggling contraband in her alimentary canal. The reasonable suspicion standard has been applied in a number of contexts and effects a needed balance between private and public interests when law enforcement officials must make a limited intrusion on less than probable cause. It thus fits well into the situations involving alimentary canal smuggling at the border: this type of smuggling gives no external signs and inspectors will rarely possess probable cause to arrest or search, yet governmental interests in stopping smuggling at the border are high indeed. Under this standard, officials at the border must have a particularized and objective basis for suspecting the particular person of alimentary canal smuggling." *U.S. v. Esieke*, 940 F.2d 29, 33 (2d Cir. 1991).

- "We disagree that the removal of an artificial leg for inspection is as intrusive as a body-cavity search. [T]he exposure of the stump to which the prosthetic device is attached, accompanied by a temporary lack of mobility, constitutes an embarrassment. But done in a medical setting, unaccompanied by exposure of intimate bodily parts, and without physical force is clearly less intrusive than a body-cavity search." *U.S. v. Sanders*, 663 F.2d 1, 3 (2d Cir. 1981).

Ninth Circuit

- "Routine searches at a United States international border require no objective justification, probable cause or warrant. Although routine border searches may proceed without probable cause or justification, reasonable suspicion is required for the detention of a traveler at the border beyond the scope of a routine customs search and inspection. [T]he degree of intrusiveness is a critical factor in distinguishing between routine and non-routine searches. Our past decisions highlight types of border searches that are so intrusive that they require at least reasonable suspicion. For example we held that a strip search at the border requires real suspicion, and that a body cavity search at the border requires a clear indication that the suspect is carrying contraband in a body cavity. And, in *United States v. Summerfield* we decided that an intrusion into an individual's body requires a clear indication that desired evidence will be found. These decisions are consistent with the Supreme Court's statement that strip searches, body cavity searches, and involuntary x-ray searches are examples of non-routine border searches. [A] border search goes beyond the routine only when it reaches the degree of intrusiveness present in a strip search or body cavity search. Border searches involving the removal of shoes do not entail the degree of intrusiveness present in strip and body cavity searches. The search of [Defendant's] shoes and baggage was a routine border search, and no reasonable suspicion was necessary." *U.S. v. Ramos-Saenz*, 36 F.3d 59, 61–62 (9th Cir. 1994), as amended, (Oct. 14, 1994).

- "Detention for a monitored bowel movement is justified if customs officers have a particularized and objective basis for suspecting the particular person of alimentary canal smuggling. The customs inspectors based their suspicion on several factors they learned through interviewing her that were not consistent with innocent travel. These factors include her nervous demeanor and her lies about the purpose of her trip and her occupation, which are not easily susceptible to rote profile recitations." *U.S. v. Gonzalez-Rincon*, 36 F.3d 859, 863 (9th Cir. 1994).

- "More, however, is required for a body cavity search at a border, a search which involves an intrusion beyond the body's surface. A clear indication or plain suggestion that the suspect is concealing contraband in his body cavity is required for such a search." *U.S. v. Aman*, 624 F.2d 911, 912 (9th Cir. 1980).

Tenth Circuit

- "It is necessary to show preliminarily that there is a clear indication of the presence of narcotics [in the body cavity]." *Yanez v. Romero*, 619 F.2d 851, 855 (10th Cir. 1980).

Eleventh Circuit
- "Once reasonable suspicion exists that a person entering the country is an internal drug smuggler, the government may detain the traveler until enough time has passed to allow the contents of the suspected smuggler's stomach to be excreted. The traveler-suspect often has some control over the length of his detention; for example, he could choose the usually speedier alternative of an x-ray examination. We accept that there may be limits on how long police can detain a suspected internal carrier (or how many bowel movements can be required); these limits, however, have not been approached in this case where the international traveler was held only ninety minutes and when only two bowel movements were involved." *U.S. v. Rodriguez*, 74 F.3d 1164, 1164–65 (11th Cir. 1996).
- "We recognize that the force of the seven cases decided today may well present the person entering the United States with somewhat of a *Hobson*'s choice. Once a particularized suspicion arises that you are an internal carrier, the agents can conduct a search sufficient to determine the accuracy of that suspicion, the type of search depending in part on what you consent to. In the absence of consent, the agents can detain you until nature reveals the truth or falsity of their suspicions. This is the reason, in our judgment, that the cases should not rest solely on whether there was consent or waiver in a particular case. Consent may heavily influence the determination as to the reasonableness of the manner of the search, but it does not completely foreclose the question of whether it was constitutional to search in some manner. A *Hobson's* choice may render a consent to an otherwise unconstitutional search ineffective. But it may render valid a search that could not otherwise be physically forced." *U.S. v. Pino*, 729 F.2d 1357, 1360 (11th Cir. 1984).

Chapter 28
Employee Drug Testing

§ 28:1   Fourth Amendment applies: The taking of a urine specimen constitutes a search within the meaning of the Fourth Amendment

§ 28:2   Balancing required: The constitutionality of urine testing is evaluated by balancing the need for the testing against the individual's expectation of privacy

§ 28:3   Individualized suspicion: Mandatory urinalysis may not require individualized suspicion

Research References

West's Key Number Digest

Searches and Seizures ⟜14, 23, 25.1, 78

KeyCite®: Cases and other legal materials listed in KeyCite Scope can be researched through the KeyCite service on Westlaw®. Use KeyCite to check citations for form, parallel references, prior and later history, and comprehensive citator information, including citations to other decisions and secondary materials.

---

§ 28:1   Fourth Amendment applies: The taking of a urine specimen constitutes a search within the meaning of the Fourth Amendment

Supreme Court

- "We begin our discussion of this case with an uncontested point: Georgia's drug-testing requirement, imposed by law and enforced by state officials, effects a search within the meaning of the Fourth and Fourteenth Amendments. As explained in *Skinner*, government-ordered collection and testing of urine intrudes upon expectations of privacy that society has long recognized as reasonable. Because these intrusions are searches under the Fourth Amendment, ibid., we focus on the question: Are the searches reasonable?" *Chandler v. Miller*, 520 U.S. 305, 313, 117 S. Ct. 1295, 137 L. Ed. 2d

513, 12 I.E.R. Cas. (BNA) 1233, 145 A.L.R. Fed. 657 (1997).

- "In contrast to the effective testing regimes upheld in *Skinner*, *Von Raab*, and *Vernonia*, Georgia's certification requirement is not well designed to identify candidates who violate antidrug laws. Nor is the scheme a credible means to deter illicit drug users from seeking election to state office. However well-meant, the candidate drug test Georgia has devised diminishes personal privacy for a symbol's sake. The Fourth Amendment shields society against that state action." *Chandler v. Miller*, 520 U.S. 305, 319, 322, 117 S. Ct. 1295, 137 L. Ed. 2d 513, 12 I.E.R. Cas. (BNA) 1233, 145 A.L.R. Fed. 657 (1997).

- "Taking into account all the factors we have considered above—the decreased expectation of privacy, the relative unobtrusiveness of the search, and the severity of the need met by the search—we conclude Vernonia's Policy is reasonable and hence constitutional. We caution against the assumption that suspicionless drug testing will readily pass constitutional muster in other contexts. The most significant element in this case is the first we discussed: that the Policy was undertaken in furtherance of the government's responsibilities, under a public school system, as guardian and tutor of children entrusted to its care. Just as when the government conducts a search in its capacity as employer the relevant question is whether that intrusion upon privacy is one that a reasonable employer might engage in, so also when the government acts as guardian and tutor the relevant question is whether the search is one that a reasonable guardian and tutor might undertake. Given the findings of need made by the District Court, we conclude that in the present case it is." *Vernonia School Dist. 47J v. Acton*, 515 U.S. 646, 664–65, 115 S. Ct. 2386, 132 L. Ed. 2d 564, 101 Ed. Law Rep. 37 (1995).

- "Because it is clear that the collection and testing of urine intrudes upon expectations of privacy that society has long recognized as reasonable, the Federal Courts of Appeals have concluded unanimously, and we agree, that these intrusions must be deemed searches under the Fourth Amendment." *Skinner v. Railway Labor Executives' Ass'n*, 489 U.S. 602, 617, 109 S. Ct. 1402,

103 L. Ed. 2d 639, 4 I.E.R. Cas. (BNA) 224, 130 L.R.R.M. (BNA) 2857, 13 O.S.H. Cas. (BNA) 2065, 49 Empl. Prac. Dec. (CCH) P 38791, 111 Lab. Cas. (CCH) P 11001, 1989 O.S.H. Dec. (CCH) P 28476 (1989).

- "Where the Government requires its employees to produce urine samples to be analyzed for evidence of illegal drug use, the collection and subsequent chemical analysis of such samples are searches that must meet the reasonableness requirement of the Fourth Amendment." *National Treasury Employees Union v. Von Raab*, 489 U.S. 656, 678–79, 109 S. Ct. 1384, 103 L. Ed. 2d 685, 4 I.E.R. Cas. (BNA) 246, 49 Empl. Prac. Dec. (CCH) P 38792, 1989 O.S.H. Dec. (CCH) P 28589 (1989).

Fourth Circuit

- "The first question is whether urinalysis is a search." *Carroll v. City of Westminster*, 233 F.3d 208, 211, 17 I.E.R. Cas. (BNA) 14, 142 Lab. Cas. (CCH) P 59124 (4th Cir. 2000).

Sixth Circuit

- "[I]n *Chandler* the Court clarified how suspicionless testing—presumably inherently suspect because by definition it is not accompanied by individualized suspicion—can comport with the Fourth Amendment . . . [W]here a Fourth Amendment intrusion serves special needs, it is necessary to balance the individual's privacy expectations against the Government's interests to determine whether it is impractical to require a warrant or some level of individualized suspicion in the particular context." *Knox County Educ. Ass'n v. Knox County Bd. of Educ.*, 158 F.3d 361, 373, 130 Ed. Law Rep. 62, 14 I.E.R. Cas. (BNA) 609 (6th Cir. 1998).

Seventh Circuit

- "The Fourth Amendment, as interpreted in the modern cases, protects privacy. Urination is generally a private activity in our culture, though, for most men, not highly private. Men urinate side by side in public restrooms without embarrassment even though there is usually very little, and often no, attempt to partition the urinals. In hospitals and physicians' offices, urine samples of both men and women are generally taken by female nurses or technicians under conditions of privacy similar to those prescribed by the racing board's rule (there are female as well as male jockeys). The affront to the cluster of emotions that define the sense of privacy that is caused by the giving of a urine sample is not the same for everybody and of particular relevance here it is slight for people who for whatever reason are subject to frequent medical examinations." *Dimeo v. Griffin*, 943 F.2d 679, 682, 6 I.E.R. Cas. (BNA) 1288, 6 I.E.R. Cas. (BNA) 1440, 120 Lab. Cas. (CCH) P 56789 (7th Cir. 1991).

Eighth Circuit

- "Defendant's consent for a urine sample was obtained lawfully where defendant, after first invoking his *Miranda* rights, independently reinstated communication with police officer, stated that he understood his rights, and stated that he wished to waive them." *U.S. v. Palega*, 556 F.3d 709 (8th Cir. 2009).
- "State-compelled collection and testing of urine constitutes a search subject to the demands of the Fourth Amendment." *Levine v. Roebuck*, 550 F.3d 684 (8th Cir. 2008).

Ninth Circuit

- "Urinalysis, when required by the government, is a search of the body that is constitutionally prohibited unless it is reasonable. What is reasonable depends upon the special needs of the government in terms of the government's requirements of those being tested and the reasonable expectations of privacy of those subjected to the test. A warrant is not necessarily a precondition. Particular suspicion of an individual is not necessarily a precondition. What the government must show is a reasonable accommodation of the tested employees' privacy expectations to the special needs the government serves by testing." *American Federation of Government Employees, AFL-CIO v. Roberts*, 9 F.3d 1464, 1466, 9 I.E.R. Cas. (BNA) 285 (9th Cir. 1993).
- "It is well established that a urinalysis drug test is a search within the meaning of the Fourth Amendment. To be deemed reasonable, a search generally must be

supported by a warrant issued upon probable cause. However, neither a warrant nor probable cause, nor, indeed, any measure of individualized suspicion, is an indispensable component of reasonableness in every circumstance. [W]here a Fourth Amendment intrusion serves special governmental needs, beyond the normal need for law enforcement, it is necessary to balance the individual's privacy expectations against the Government's interests to determine whether it is impractical to require a warrant or some level of individualized suspicion in the particular context." *Jackson v. Gates*, 975 F.2d 648, 652, 7 I.E.R. Cas. (BNA) 1249, 8 I.E.R. Cas. (BNA) 192 (9th Cir. 1992).

Tenth Circuit

- "Based on a detailed review of its decisions in *Skinner*, *Von Raab*, and *Acton*, the *Chandler* Court identified two general characteristics that we must now examine in the first instance, before any balancing occurs. First, the Court examined whether the proffered governmental concerns were real by asking whether the testing program was adopted in response to a documented drug abuse problem or whether drug abuse among the target group would pose a serious danger to the public. . . . Second, the Court examined whether the testing scheme met the related goals of detection and deterrence." *19 Solid Waste Dept. Mechanics v. City of Albuquerque*, 156 F.3d 1068, 1073, 14 I.E.R. Cas. (BNA) 629 (10th Cir. 1998).

- "It is well established that a urinalysis required by a government employer for the purpose of detecting illegal drug use is a search protected by the Fourth Amendment. In the two leading Supreme Court employee drug testing cases, *Skinner* and *Von Raab*, the justices concluded that the testing at issue was permissible without the usual protection of a warrant based on probable cause, and even without any measure of individualized suspicion In *Skinner*, the Court ruled that railroad employees' privacy expectations, which were limited because of the industry's pervasive regulation, were outweighed by the government's compelling interest in ensuring the safe operation of the rails. In *Von Raab*, the Court similarly found that the government's interests in safety and the integrity of its borders outweighed the individual privacy interests of customs officials who carry firearms or are involved in drug interdiction." *Rutherford v. City of Albuquerque*, 77 F.3d 1258, 1260, 11 I.E.R. Cas. (BNA) 737 (10th Cir. 1996).

D.C. Circuit

- "Government-compelled urinalysis is a search for purposes of the Fourth Amendment. . . . As such, it is impermissible if it is unreasonable. . . . In *Skinner* and *Von Raab*, however, the Court acknowledged that there are exceptions to the warrant requirement for cases where a search serves special governmental needs beyond the normal need for law enforcement. . . . In such cases the reasonableness of a search is determined by balancing the public interest in the . . . testing program against the privacy concerns implicated by the tests, without reference to the usual presumption in favor of the procedures specified in the Warrant Clause. . . . We have applied this same test to numerous other proposed drug testing programs in recent years." *Stigile v. Clinton*, 110 F.3d 801, 803, 12 I.E.R. Cas. (BNA) 1246, 133 Lab. Cas. (CCH) P 11790 (D.C. Cir. 1997).

- "[E]ven a current employee's expectation of privacy, while reasonable enough to make urine testing a Fourth Amendment search, can be so diminished that the search is not unreasonable. This simply recognizes that Fourth Amendment searches vary in their intrusiveness. Taking a person's fingerprints, for example, and ransacking a person's dwelling place, while both searches, may require different degrees of justification to make them reasonable." *Willner v. Thornburgh*, 928 F.2d 1185, 1188, 6 I.E.R. Cas. (BNA) 498, 118 Lab. Cas. (CCH) P 10635, 1991 O.S.H. Dec. (CCH) P 29280 (D.C. Cir. 1991).

§ 28:2 Balancing required: The constitutionality of urine testing is evaluated by balancing the need for the testing against the individual's expectation of privacy

Supreme Court

- "We reiterate that where the risk to public safety is

substantial and real, blanket suspicionless searches
calibrated to the risk may rank as reasonable—for
example, searches now routine at airports and at
entrances to courts and other official buildings. But
where, as in this case, public safety is not genuinely in
jeopardy, the Fourth Amendment precludes the suspicionless search, no matter how conveniently arranged."
Chandler v. Miller, 520 U.S. 305, 323, 117 S. Ct. 1295,
137 L. Ed. 2d 513, 12 I.E.R. Cas. (BNA) 1233, 145 A.L.R.
Fed. 657 (1997).

- "[W]here a Fourth Amendment intrusion serves special
governmental needs, beyond the normal need for law
enforcement, it is necessary to balance the individual's
privacy expectations against the Government's interests
to determine whether it is impractical to require a warrant or some level of individualized suspicion in the
particular context." *National Treasury Employees Union
v. Von Raab*, 489 U.S. 656, 665–66, 109 S. Ct. 1384, 103
L. Ed. 2d 685, 4 I.E.R. Cas. (BNA) 246, 49 Empl. Prac.
Dec. (CCH) P 38792, 1989 O.S.H. Dec. (CCH) P 28589
(1989).

- "In sum, we believe the Government has demonstrated
that its compelling interests in safeguarding our borders
and the public safety outweigh the privacy expectations
of employees who seek to be promoted to positions that
directly involve the interdiction of illegal drugs or that
require the incumbent to carry a firearm. We hold that
the testing of these employees is reasonable under the
Fourth Amendment." *National Treasury Employees
Union v. Von Raab*, 489 U.S. 656, 677, 109 S. Ct. 1384,
103 L. Ed. 2d 685, 4 I.E.R. Cas. (BNA) 246, 49 Empl.
Prac. Dec. (CCH) P 38792, 1989 O.S.H. Dec. (CCH) P
28589 (1989).

- "We think Customs employees who are directly involved
in the interdiction of illegal drugs or who are required
to carry firearms in the line of duty likewise have a
diminished expectation of privacy in respect to the
intrusion occasioned by a urine test. Unlike most
private citizens or government employees in general,
employees involved in drug interdiction reasonably
should expect effective inquiry into their fitness and
probity. Much the same is true of employees who are
required to carry firearms. Because successful perfor-

mance of their duties depends uniquely on their judgment and dexterity, these employees cannot reasonably
expect to keep from the Service personal information
that bears directly on their fitness. While reasonable
tests designed to elicit this information doubtless
infringe some privacy expectations, we do not believe
these expectations outweigh the government's compelling interests in safety and in the integrity of our
borders." *National Treasury Employees Union v. Von
Raab*, 489 U.S. 656, 672, 109 S. Ct. 1384, 103 L. Ed. 2d
685, 4 I.E.R. Cas. (BNA) 246, 49 Empl. Prac. Dec. (CCH)
P 38792, 1989 O.S.H. Dec. (CCH) P 28589 (1989).

Fourth Circuit

- "*Skinner* and *Von Raab* are clear in their holding that
  random, suspicionless workplace drug testing is allowed
  under certain circumstances. Just as the United States
  Customs officers in *Von Raab* and the railroad personnel *in Skinner*, police officers using illegal drugs have
  the potential to cause great harm to the public." *Carroll
  v. City of Westminster*, 233 F.3d 208, 213, 17 I.E.R. Cas.
  (BNA) 14, 142 Lab. Cas. (CCH) P 59124 (4th Cir. 2000).

Sixth Circuit

- "Having ruled that the public interest in suspicionless
  testing is very strong, an analysis of the employee's
  privacy rights is necessary to determine which of the
  competing values should prevail in this case. . . . .
  [B]ecause teachers' legitimate expectation of privacy is
  diminished by their participation in a heavily regulated
  industry and by the nature of their job, the public interest in suspicionless testing outweighs that private
  interest. . . . [W]e read the Supreme Court precedents
  assessing the privacy interests of employees as focusing
  on two central factors: (1) the intrusiveness of the drug
  testing scheme; and (2) the degree to which the industry
  in question is regulated." *Knox County Educ. Ass'n v.
  Knox County Bd. of Educ.*, 158 F.3d 361, 379, 130 Ed.
  Law Rep. 62, 14 I.E.R. Cas. (BNA) 609 (6th Cir. 1998).

Ninth Circuit

- "We consider whether police may conduct a search
  based on less than probable cause of an individual

released while awaiting trial . . . . Usually, Fourth Amendment reasonableness means that a search or seizure must be supported by probable cause, though pat-downs and similar minor intrusions need only be supported by reasonable suspicion . . . But we relax these requirements "when 'special needs, beyond the normal need for law enforcement,' " make an insistence on the otherwise applicable level of suspicion " 'impracticable.' " . . . . The government in this case has relied on nothing more than a generalized need to protect the community and a blanket assertion that drug-testing is needed to ensure (defendant's) appearance at trial. Both are insufficient . . . . We thus cannot validate (defendant's) search under the special needs doctrine . . . . Nevada's decision to test (defendant) for drugs without probable cause does not pass constitutional muster under any of the three approaches: consent, special needs or totality of the circumstances. Since the government concedes there was no probable cause to test (defendant) for drugs, (defendant's) drug test violated the Fourth Amendment. Probable cause to search (defendant's) house did not exist until the drug test came back positive. The validity of the house search, which led to both the shotgun and (defendant's) statement about the shotgun, is derivative of the initial drug test. That search is likewise invalid; its fruits must be suppressed." *U.S. v. Scott*, 450 F.3d 863 (9th Cir. 2006).

- "The United States argues here that searching pretrial releasees by testing them for drugs serves two special needs: (1) protecting the community from criminal defendants released pending trial and (2) ensuring that defendants show up at trial. But at . . . . The government's first identified purpose, protecting the community, presumably means protecting it from the criminal activities of pretrial releasees generally . . . . The dissent points out correctly that the ' "government's interest in preventing crime by arrestees is both legitimate and compelling," ' (citations omitted) But the government's interest in preventing crime by anyone is legitimate and compelling. (citations omitted) Crime prevention is a quintessential general law enforcement purpose and therefore is the exact opposite of a special need . . . . The second purpose, ensuring that pretrial releasees appear in court, fares somewhat better: While it has a law enforcement component a defendant's failure to appear in court when ordered to do so is a criminal offense, . . . it also implicates the efficient functioning and integrity of the judicial system, . . . a purpose separate from the general interest in crime control. . . . [T]he connection between the object of the test (drug use) and the harm to be avoided (non-appearance in court) is tenuous . . . . We are thus unable to conclude that the search regime to which [the defendant] was subjected was necessary to ensure his appearance at trial . . . . [P]retrial releasees are ordinary people who have been accused of a crime but are presumed innocent . . . . Because the government failed to demonstrate that Nevada had special needs for obtaining the drug-testing release condition, it cannot justify the search-testing [defendant] for drugs without probable cause-using this approach. .[W]e hold only that the government has not made the requisite special needs showing in this case: It has not, for example, demonstrated a pattern of "drug use leading to nonappearance" in court, . . . nor pointed to an individualized determination that [defendant's] drug use was likely to lead to his nonappearance. The government in this case has relied on nothing more than a generalized need to protect the community and a blanket assertion that drug-testing is needed to ensure [defendant's] appearance at trial. Both are insufficient. We thus cannot validate [defendant's] search under the special needs doctrine." *U.S. v. Scott*, 450 F.3d 863 (9th Cir. 2006).

- "We conclude that where prison officials select a large number of inmates for testing based upon legitimate criteria, the danger discussed in *Storms* and other cases—that correctional officials could harass particular inmates by subjecting them to repeated tests—is wholly illusory. We refuse to accept the proposition that a urine test of so many inmates (in this case, 124) conducted at the same time, under the same conditions, could constitute harassment of one of the inmates." *Thompson v. Souza*, 111 F.3d 694, 702 (9th Cir. 1997).

- "We recognize that significant privacy interests of DOL employees are infringed by urinalysis drug testing for off-duty drug use. Nevertheless, under the circumstances set forth above, we find these interests outweighed by the DOL's interest in preventing on- or off-duty drug use from impairing TDP employees in the performance of their duties. We also note that the threshold requirement of reasonable suspicion minimizes the intrusion on the employees' privacy interests. Reasonable suspicion drug testing of TDP employees is not random and unannounced. Rather, as the name suggests, such testing is based on objective evidence of on- or off-duty drug use. Furthermore, for purposes of testing for off-duty drug use under section 10-A(1), objective evidence must consist of credible eyewitness observations of illegal drug use or impairment. Finally, the Plan vests only minimal discretion in the officials charged with implementing reasonable suspicion testing. Supervisors are trained to recognize facts giving rise to reasonable suspicion. They also must document all such facts and circumstances including dates and times of off-duty drug use or impairment as reported by reliable and credible sources before recommending a drug test." *American Federation of Government Employees, AFL-CIO, Local 2391, (AFGE) v. Martin*, 969 F.2d 788, 793, 7 I.E.R. Cas. (BNA) 970, 122 Lab. Cas. (CCH) P 10257, 1992 O.S.H. Dec. (CCH) P 29748 (9th Cir. 1992).

Tenth Circuit

- "In the end, we must evaluate whether the safety and health concerns cited by the City would genuinely be advanced by the testing program. While we recognize that the City has important safety and health concerns in testing its mechanics for drug use, given that the scheme that the City devised would not effectively detect or deter drug use, we must conclude that the City has failed to show a special need for suspicionless drug testing. Because we find that the program is not based on a special governmental need, we do not need proceed to balance the parties' respective interests." *19 Solid Waste Dept. Mechanics v. City of Albuquerque*, 156 F.3d 1068, 1074–75, 14 I.E.R. Cas. (BNA) 629 (10th Cir. 1998).

- "Here, however, the officials who decided [Plaintiff]

should be tested did exercise significant discretion—indeed, departing from the literal language of the substance abuse policy. It also is of importance that [Plaintiff] was given no advance warning of the testing. Not only did the substance abuse policy on its face fail to alert him, but the city officials who called him in to work also did not tell him that the test would be administered the day he returned. This sort of unwarned testing is, we think, the most intrusive possible, contravening all of one's reasonable expectations of privacy. In *Skinner*, testing was triggered by accidents, other safety-related incidents, and rule violations. In *Von Raab*, testing was required only for employees who sought transfer or promotion to certain positions, and the employees were notified in advance of the scheduled sample collection. In both cases, the employees knew when testing would, or could, occur. Nor were other factors present to diminish [Plaintiff]'s expectation of privacy. The City's interest in ensuring safety, meanwhile, appears to have been at a fairly low ebb with respect to [Plaintiff]'s test. In sum, even conceding that the City has an important safety interest in ensuring that its heavy truck drivers are free from drugs, that interest in this case is considerably diluted by the factors we have just discussed. We conclude that, when balanced against the unusually intrusive nature of the testing as described above and the fact that a positive test leads inexorably to termination, this diluted interest must give way to [Plaintiff]'s expectation of privacy." *Rutherford v. City of Albuquerque*, 77 F.3d 1258, 1261–63, 11 I.E.R. Cas. (BNA) 737 (10th Cir. 1996).

• "A urinalysis constitutes a search for purposes of the Fourth Amendment and therefore must be conducted in a reasonable manner. In determining whether a search of a prisoner is reasonable, we must [balance] the significant and legitimate security interests of the institution against the privacy interests of the [prisoner], and give prison administrators wide-ranging deference in [their] adoption and execution of policies and practices that in their judgment are needed to preserve internal order and discipline and to maintain institutional security. The unauthorized use of narcotics in a detention center by inmates does pose a serious threat to prison officials' ability to maintain institutional security. Consequently, prison officials have a significant and legitimate interest in preventing unauthorized drug use among prison inmates. We therefore hold that the random urine collection and testing of prisoners is a reasonable means of combating the unauthorized use of narcotics and does not violate the Fourth Amendment." *Lucero v. Gunter*, 17 F.3d 1347, 1349–50 (10th Cir. 1994).

D.C. Circuit

- "Government-compelled urinalysis is a search for purposes of the Fourth Amendment. As such, it is impermissible if it is unreasonable. In *Skinner* and *Von Raab*, however, the Court acknowledged that there are exceptions to the warrant requirement for cases where a search serves special governmental needs beyond the normal need for law enforcement. In such cases the reasonableness of a search is determined by balancing the public interest in the testing program against the privacy concerns implicated by the tests, without reference to the usual presumption in favor of the procedures specified in the Warrant Clause. We have applied this same test to numerous other proposed drug testing programs in recent years." *Stigile v. Clinton*, 110 F.3d 801, 803, 12 I.E.R. Cas. (BNA) 1246, 133 Lab. Cas. (CCH) P 11790 (D.C. Cir. 1997).

- "Our conclusion is that for job applicants their privacy expectations in regard to the Justice Department's urine testing requirement are significantly diminished and are far less than those of incumbents. Unlike current employees, job applicants are routinely required to reveal considerable amounts of information about themselves, information the employer uses to make responsible hiring decisions. The urine testing procedure at the Justice Department minimizes the intrusion and the chemical analysis later performed on the urine sample reveals no information the applicant has a cognizable interest in keeping secret. An applicant may avoid even this minimal invasion of privacy by not seeking employment with the Justice Department. On the other hand, the Justice Department's interests, as an employer, in requiring applicants to undergo urinalysis are strong. Drug testing in the context of a job application is commonplace. Although an employer may monitor an incumbent's performance, and thus be required to have individualized suspicion before subjecting the employee to urinalysis, such a requirement for testing applicants would be impractical." *Willner v. Thornburgh*, 928 F.2d 1185, 1193–94, 6 I.E.R. Cas. (BNA) 498, 118 Lab. Cas. (CCH) P 10635, 1991 O.S.H. Dec. (CCH) P 29280 (D.C. Cir. 1991).

- "The government has ample latitude to intervene before its fears about off-duty drug use are realized in the form of poor work performance, as law enforcement officials may investigate the worker under appropriate constitutional and statutory restrictions. Similarly, the government may investigate and punish wrongdoing within the walls of its offices as an employer and as a law enforcer, again under applicable legal constraints. What the government may not do in the case of ordinary employees is justify drug testing procedures that intrude upon constitutionally protected privacy interests with speculation about possible future job impairment or rules violations. We hold, therefore, that the USDA Program is unconstitutional insofar as it authorizes mandatory drug testing of FNS workers who do not hold safety- or security-sensitive jobs, absent reasonable suspicion of on-duty drug use or drug-impaired work performance." *National Treasury Employees Union v. Yeutter*, 918 F.2d 968, 974, 5 I.E.R. Cas. (BNA) 1605, 1990 O.S.H. Dec. (CCH) P 29143 (D.C. Cir. 1990).

§ 28:3   Individualized suspicion: Mandatory urinalysis may not require individualized suspicion

Supreme Court

- "[A school district's policy of suspicionless drug testing for all students participating in extracurricular activities] is a reasonable means of furthering the School District's important interest in preventing and deterring drug use among its schoolchildren." *Board of Education of Independent School District No. 92 of Pottawatomie County v. Earls*, 536 U.S. 822, 122 S. Ct. 2559, 153 L. Ed. 2d 735, 166 Ed. Law Rep. 79 (2002).

- "Our precedents have settled that, in certain limited circumstances, the Government's need to discover such latent or hidden conditions, or to prevent their development, is sufficiently compelling to justify the intrusion on privacy entailed by conducting such searches without any measure of individualized suspicion." *National Treasury Employees Union v. Von Raab*, 489 U.S. 656, 668, 109 S. Ct. 1384, 103 L. Ed. 2d 685, 4 I.E.R. Cas. (BNA) 246, 49 Empl. Prac. Dec. (CCH) P 38792, 1989 O.S.H. Dec. (CCH) P 28589 (1989).

- "We conclude that the compelling government interests served by the FRA's regulations would be significantly hindered if railroads were required to point to specific facts giving rise to a reasonable suspicion of impairment before testing a given employee. In view of our conclusion that, on the present record, the toxicological testing contemplated by the regulations is not an undue infringement on the justifiable expectations of privacy of covered employees, the Government's compelling interests outweigh privacy concerns." *Skinner v. Railway Labor Executives' Ass'n*, 489 U.S. 602, 633, 109 S. Ct. 1402, 103 L. Ed. 2d 639, 4 I.E.R. Cas. (BNA) 224, 130 L.R.R.M. (BNA) 2857, 13 O.S.H. Cas. (BNA) 2065, 49 Empl. Prac. Dec. (CCH) P 38791, 111 Lab. Cas. (CCH) P 11001, 1989 O.S.H. Dec. (CCH) P 28476 (1989).

Third Circuit

- "[W]e conclude that a public employee union acting as exclusive bargaining agent may consent to drug testing on behalf of the employees it represents. Such consent may be manifested in several different contexts. The simplest example occurs when a union expressly agrees to drug testing during the negotiation of a collective bargaining agreement. As previously explained, individual employees are bound by such express consent." *Bolden v. Southeastern Pennsylvania Transp. Authority*, 953 F.2d 807, 828, 7 I.E.R. Cas. (BNA) 92, 139 L.R.R.M. (BNA) 2118, 120 Lab. Cas. (CCH) P 56772, 1993 O.S.H. Dec. (CCH) P 30008 (3d Cir. 1991).

- "It is clear that compulsory, suspicionless drug testing of a person holding [Plaintiff's] job falls outside the precedents discussed above. In all of those cases, the employees subjected to suspicionless testing were found to have diminished privacy expectations due to pervasive governmental regulation of the jobs they performed. Here, SEPTA has not shown that maintenance custodians are pervasively regulated or that they have diminished privacy expectations for any other reason. On the other side of the scale, SEPTA's brief asserts in passing that [Plaintiff's] duties posed a substantial risk of harm to others, but we find no factual support in the record for this contention. SEPTA did not include maintenance custodians among the employees in safety sensitive positions who are covered by its random-testing program. Moreover, the nature of a maintenance custodian's work does not appear to involve any great risk of causing harm to other persons." *Bolden v. Southeastern Pennsylvania Transp. Authority*, 953 F.2d 807, 823, 7 I.E.R. Cas. (BNA) 92, 139 L.R.R.M. (BNA) 2118, 120 Lab. Cas. (CCH) P 56772, 1993 O.S.H. Dec. (CCH) P 30008 (3d Cir. 1991).

Sixth Circuit

- "[W]e would be remiss if we did not point out that the safety sensitive nature of a teacher's or administrator's job is not limited to the necessity to act at the immediate time of a dangerous event. Rather, school personnel perform an essential monitoring role in preventing incidents from occurring in the first place. Teachers and administrators are in a unique position to observe children and learn if they are involved in activities which can lead to harm or injury to themselves or others. Clearly, if school personnel are themselves under the influence of, or involved in, drugs, their ability to perform this critical function is not only reduced, but they themselves are open to being compromised and undermined. Clearly, a school board has a very strong interest in preventing this as part of its responsibility to insure the safety and security of school children." *Knox County Educ. Ass'n v. Knox County Bd. of Educ.*, 158 F.3d 361, 379, 130 Ed. Law Rep. 62, 14 I.E.R. Cas. (BNA) 609 (6th Cir. 1998).

Eighth Circuit

- "While police officers enjoy a diminished expectation of privacy because of the importance of their position in society, it is clear that the action taken shows no respect for the safeguards present in *Von Raab*, *Rushton*, and other cases cited above: [Plaintiff] was not selected for urinalysis testing according to a random or routine program which guarded against discriminatory or arbitrary selection of employees to be tested. Consequently, as this Court held in *McDonell*, in the absence of uniform or systematic random selection of employees subject to drug testing, we will allow the Government to enforce drug testing where employees are chosen only on the basis of a reasonable suspicion." *Ford v. Dowd*, 931 F.2d 1286, 1291–92, 6 I.E.R. Cas. (BNA) 641, 6 I.E.R. Cas. (BNA) 960 (8th Cir. 1991).

Ninth Circuit

- "We do not deny that the government has a strong interest in random testing of nuclear industry employees who are in safety-sensitive positions. However, the government's blanket inclusion of all workers in protected areas may in some cases be overkill." *International Broth. of Elec. Workers, Local 1245 v. U.S. Nuclear Regulatory Com'n*, 966 F.2d 521, 526, 7 I.E.R. Cas. (BNA) 890 (9th Cir. 1992).

- "The Navy's random drug testing of civil employees holding TSA clearances directly furthers a compelling interest in protecting the security of our nation by ensuring that employees who come into close proximity to information the unauthorized disclosure of which reasonably could be expected to cause exceptionally grave damage to the national security do not use illegal drugs. Accordingly, we hold that the fourth amendment does not prohibit the Navy from randomly testing its civilian employees for drug use if the employees are also required by the Navy to hold security clearances giving them access to classified information." *AFGE Local 1533 v. Cheney*, 944 F.2d 503, 508–09, 6 I.E.R. Cas. (BNA) 1324 (9th Cir. 1991).

- "Based on our analysis of the statutory guidelines for issuance of rules respecting pipeline safety and the transportation of hazardous liquids, we conclude that the drug testing rules formulated by RSPA are not generally arbitrary and capricious. In our view, therefore, RSPA's decision to adopt random testing was not an arbitrary and capricious exercise of its rulemaking authority. We conclude by noting that seven circuit courts of appeal, including our own, have upheld random drug tests for employees with safety-sensitive, security-sensitive, or public-integrity-sensitive jobs. The government's interest in the safety of the pipeline industry is great. Random drug testing, as compared with other forms of testing, offers the best potential deterrent to drug use. This factor, coupled with the possibility of a catastrophic accident, is sufficient to show a strong governmental interest in random testing. Against this interest we must weigh the Fourth Amendment privacy concerns of the individuals to be tested. We conclude, however, that the level of intrusiveness does not justify striking down the random drug testing rule. Moreover, pre-employment and post-accident tests are less intrusive than random testing because they are triggered by the employee's own act or conduct, or by a definable event. Consequently, we find that such testing rules also withstand constitutional scrutiny." *International Broth. of Elec. Workers, Local 1245 v. Skinner*, 913 F.2d 1454, 1459–60, 5 I.E.R. Cas. (BNA) 1621, 14 O.S.H. Cas. (BNA) 1777, 14 O.S.H. Cas. (BNA) 1946, 119 Lab. Cas. (CCH) P 10783, 1990 O.S.H. Dec. (CCH) P 29079, 1991 O.S.H. Dec. (CCH) P 29391 (9th Cir. 1990).

Tenth Circuit

- "It is well established that a urinalysis drug test required by a government employer for the purpose of detecting illegal drug use is a search subject to the Fourth Amendment, and therefore must be reasonable. It is equally well settled that in the government employment context, as opposed to the criminal law context, a warrant will not be required where the intrusion is based on either reasonable suspicion or special needs. The Supreme Court has recognized that when special needs, beyond the normal need for law enforcement, make the warrant and probable cause requirement impracticable, it will be dispensed with. This special needs exception permits drug testing of employees in safety-sensitive positions, pursuant to a random or uniform selection process, and does not require probable cause or even reasonable suspicion that an employee might be impaired. In the absence of a special needs random or uniform selection process, drug testing o f a government employee does not require a warrant, but must be based on individualized suspicion, i.e., a reasonable suspicion that the employee was engaging in unlawful activity involving controlled substances." *Benavidez v. City of Albuquerque*, 101 F.3d 620, 623–24, 12 I.E.R. Cas. (BNA) 411 (10th Cir. 1996).

- "[A]lthough random urine testing of inmates does not violate the Fourth Amendment, the procedures for selecting inmates for testing must be truly random. Selection procedures are not truly random and thus violate the Fourth Amendment when the procedures leave the exercise of discretion as to selected targets in the hands of a field officer with no limiting guidelines." *Lucero v. Gunter*, 52 F.3d 874, 877, 32 Fed. R. Serv. 3d 297 (10th Cir. 1995).

Eleventh Circuit

- "Testing a urine sample, which can reveal a host of private medical facts about an employee, and which entails a process that itself implicates privacy interests, is a search. The basic question we are required to answer when confronted with a drug-testing policy is whether this search is reasonable. While [i]n the criminal context, reasonableness usually requires a showing of probable cause to obtain a search warrant, that standard is unsuited to determining the reasonableness of administrative searches where the Government seeks to *prevent* the development of hazardous conditions. The default rule in this context, therefore, is that [t]o be reasonable under the Fourth Amendment, a search ordinarily must be based on individualized suspicion of wrongdoing. While individualized suspicion is the normal requirement, particularized exceptions to the main rule are sometimes warranted based on special needs, beyond the normal need for law enforcement. When the government alleges that special needs justify this Fourth Amendment intrusion, courts must undertake a context-specific inquiry, examining closely the competing private and public interests advanced by the parties. In limited circumstances, where the privacy interests implicated by the search are minimal, and where an important governmental interest furthered by the intrusion would be placed in jeopardy by a requirement of individualized suspicion, a search may be reasonable despite the absence of such suspicion. Therefore, the test we apply is a job-category-by-category balancing of the individual's privacy expectations against the Government's interests with other relevant factors being the character of the intrusion—particularly whether the collection method affords a modicum of privacy—and the efficacy of the testing regime. At times, the Supreme Court has described the interests justifying suspicionless drug testing as compelling. [A] compelling interest is one *important enough* to justify the particular search at hand, in light of other factors that show the search to be relatively intrusive upon a genuine expectation of privacy. . . . The principle we draw from *Skinner* is that government employees . . . engaged in safety-sensitive tasks, particularly those involved with the operation of heavy machinery or means of mass transit, may be subject to suspicionless drug testing. In *Von Raab,* . . . the Supreme Court found that the Government ha[d] a compelling interest in ensuring that front-line interdiction personnel [we]re physically fit, and ha[d] unimpeachable integrity and judgment. The Supreme Court next approved of suspicionless drug testing in a far different context than government employment: schools. The Court upheld the constitutionality of two schools' policies of randomly drug testing student athletes and students participating in competitive extracurricular activities. The Supreme Court found that there was a special need in the public school context, where teachers were responsible for their young charges. . . . As for the students' privacy interests, the Court noted that the students by definition were (1) children, who (2) have been committed to the temporary custody of the State as schoolmaster. The State, acting *in loco parentis,* exercised a degree of supervision and control that could not be exercised over free adults. Those diminished privacy interests could not overcome the government's important interests in protecting children from drug use. . . . The crucial point is that, to affirm the district court's declaration and injunction in this case, we would have to find that none of the 85,000 current employees covered by the district court's relief belong to the special-needs categories identified by the Supreme Court." *American Federation of State, County and Mun. Employees Council 79 v. Scott*, 717 F.3d 851, 866–70, 35 I.E.R. Cas. (BNA) 1273 (11th Cir. 2013) (inner quotations and citations omitted).

D.C. Circuit

- "Because the government's interest in protecting the safety of the President and the Vice President within the White House security perimeter outweighs appellees' interest in not being subject to urinalysis, the suspicionless drug testing of OEOB passholders is not an unreasonable search. It does not, therefore, violate the Fourth Amendment." *Stigile v. Clinton*, 110 F.3d 801, 807, 12 I.E.R. Cas. (BNA) 1246, 133 Lab. Cas. (CCH) P 11790 (D.C. Cir. 1997).

Chapter 29

Non-Governmental Violations of Individual Rights

§ 29:1   No constitutional protection: Actions by private individuals are not within the purview of the Fourth Amendment

§ 29:2   No exclusionary remedy: The exclusionary rule does not apply to evidence seized by private individuals

§ 29:3   Government involvement: If a government official aids in a search or seizure by a private citizen, the Fourth Amendment applies

Research References

West's Key Number Digest

Criminal Law ☞394.2; Evidence ☞154; Searches and Seizures ☞7, 33

KeyCite®: Cases and other legal materials listed in KeyCite Scope can be researched through the KeyCite service on Westlaw®. Use KeyCite to check citations for form, parallel references, prior and later history, and comprehensive citator information, including citations to other decisions and secondary materials.

---

§ 29:1   No constitutional protection: Actions by private individuals are not within the purview of the Fourth Amendment

Supreme Court

- "The fact that positive test results were turned over to the police does not merely provide a basis for distinguishing prior special needs cases. It also provides an affirmative reason for enforcing the Fourth Amendment's strictures. While state hospital employees, like other citizens, may have a duty to provide the police with evidence of criminal conduct that they inadvertently acquire in the course of routine treatment, when

they undertake to obtain such evidence from their
patients for the specific purpose of incriminating those
patients, they have a special obligation to make sure
that the patients are fully informed about their constitutional rights, as standards of knowing waiver
require." *Ferguson v. City of Charleston*, 532 U.S. 67,
121 S. Ct. 1281, 1292, 149 L. Ed. 2d 205 (2001).

- "It is well established that the exclusionary rule, as a
  deterrent sanction, is not applicable where a private
  party or a foreign government commits the offending
  act." *U.S. v. Janis*, 1976-2 C.B. 615, 428 U.S. 433, 456
  n.31, 96 S. Ct. 3021, 49 L. Ed. 2d 1046, 76-2 U.S. Tax
  Cas. (CCH) P 16229, 38 A.F.T.R.2d 76-5378 (1976).

- "The exclusionary rules were fashioned to prevent, not
  to repair, and their target is official misconduct." *Coolidge
  v. New Hampshire*, 403 U.S. 443, 488, 91 S. Ct. 2022,
  29 L. Ed. 2d 564 (1971).

- "The Fourth Amendment gives protection against
  unlawful searches and seizures, and as shown in previous cases, its protection applies to governmental action.
  Its origin and history clearly show that it was intended
  as a restraint upon the activities of sovereign authority,
  and was not intended to be a limitation upon other than
  governmental agencies." *Burdeau v. McDowell*, 256 U.S.
  465, 475, 41 S. Ct. 574, 65 L. Ed. 1048, 13 A.L.R. 1159
  (1921).

First Circuit

- "The Fourth Amendment's protection against unreasonable searches and seizures applies only to government
  action and not to a search or seizure, even an unreasonable one, effected by a private individual not acting as
  an agent of the Government." *U.S. v. Silva*, 554 F.3d 13
  (1st Cir. 2009).

- "While the seizure of [Defendant] may have assisted
  the government, there is no suggestion that the government initiated or participated in the citizen action. In
  the absence of governmental action, the Fourth Amendment does not apply." *U.S. v. Mendez-de Jesus*, 85 F.3d
  1, 2–3 (1st Cir. 1996).

Fifth Circuit

- "The initial search, being private in nature, is not

subject to Fourth Amendment analysis, unless the private individual was acting as an agent of, or with the participation of, a government official." *U.S. v. Grimes*, 244 F.3d 375, 383, 56 Fed. R. Evid. Serv. 1048 (5th Cir. 2001).

Sixth Circuit

- "Factors in whether private party is acting as agent of government when conducting search are: (1) government's knowledge or acquiescence, and (2) intent of party performing search." *U.S. v. Hardin*, 539 F.3d 404 (6th Cir. 2008).

- "It is well established that evidence obtained by a private search is not subject to the Fourth Amendment exclusionary rule In *United States v. Jacobsen* the Supreme Court acknowledged that the Fourth Amendment protection against unreasonable searches and seizures is wholly inapplicable to a search or seizure, even an unreasonable one, effected by a private individual not acting as an agent of the Government or with the participation or knowledge of any governmental official." *U.S. v. Murdock*, 63 F.3d 1391, 1403, 1995 FED App. 0258P (6th Cir. 1995).

- "The Fourth Amendment does not apply to searches or seizures by private persons. Rather, it proscribes only governmental action and does not apply to a search or seizure, even an unreasonable one, conducted by a private individual not acting as an agent of the government or with the participation or knowledge of any governmental official." *U.S. v. King*, 55 F.3d 1193, 1196, 1995 FED App. 0170P (6th Cir. 1995).

- "When [the victim] searched the closet in order to find the location of the guns, the United States correctly asserts that her actions constituted a private search and no constitutional violation occurred as a result of her actions. However, the defendant argues that the officers' entry and seizure of the guns constituted an unconstitutional violation, not [the Victim]'s. Indeed, if [the Victim] had retrieved the weapons herself and then turned them over to the police, an entirely private search and seizure would have occurred and the defendant would have no cause to complain. However, the facts indicate that [the Victim] disclosed the location of the guns and then the officers seized the weapons and ammunition." *U.S. v. Johnson*, 22 F.3d 674, 679, 1994 FED App. 0134P (6th Cir. 1994).

Seventh Circuit

- "Although individuals have a right under the Fourth Amendment of the United States Constitution to be free from unreasonable searches and seizures by the Government, private searches are not subject to constitutional restrictions." *U.S. v. Hall*, 142 F.3d 988, 993 (7th Cir. 1998).

Eighth Circuit

- "When the government reexamines materials following a private search, the government may intrude on an individual's privacy expectations without violating the Fourth Amendment, provided the government intrusion goes no further than the private search." *U.S. v. Starr*, 533 F.3d 985 (8th Cir. 2008).
- "The Constitution does not apply to searches, reasonable or otherwise, by private individuals, so long as the private party is not acting as an agent of the Government or with the participation or knowledge of any governmental official. . . . Further, to be a Fourth Amendment search, a governmental intrusion must infringe on a legitimate expectation of privacy. . . . Because a private search frustrates such an expectation . . . an ensuing police intrusion that stays within the limits of the private search is not a search for Fourth Amendment purposes. . . . Thus, in a private search case, the legality of later governmental intrusions must be tested by the degree to which they exceeded the scope of the private search." *U.S. v. Miller*, 152 F.3d 813, 815 (8th Cir. 1998).
- "The Supreme Court has expressly held that the constraints of the Fourth and Fifth Amendments do not apply to purely private activity." *U.S. v. Garlock*, 19 F.3d 441, 442 (8th Cir. 1994).

Ninth Circuit

- "The technician's search of [defendant]'s hard drive was a private search that did not implicate the protections of the Fourth Amendment. (citation omitted) No governmental actors were present during the search. There were no agreements between the repair shop and the police department, and there is nothing to indicate that the technician initially searched [defendant]'s computer with the intent to aid law enforcement. The government's subsequent involvement did not change the private nature of the search, and [defendant] has not shown that the government's search expanded beyond the technician's search prior to the issuance of a warrant." *U.S. v. Carey*, 356 Fed. Appx. 988 (9th Cir. 2009).

Tenth Circuit

- "Bounty hunters do not qualify as state actors when they act without the assistance of law enforcement and for their own pecuniary interests." *U.S. v. Poe*, 556 F.3d 1113 (10th Cir. 2009).
- "It is clear that the Fourth Amendment does not apply to searches by private parties, absent governmental involvement." *U.S. v. Humphrey*, 208 F.3d 1190, 1203 (10th Cir. 2000).

Eleventh Circuit

- "A search by a private person does not implicate the Fourth Amendment unless he acts as an instrument or agent of the government. For a private person to be considered an agent of the government, we look to two critical factors: (1) whether the government knew of and acquiesced in the intrusive conduct, and (2) whether the private actor's purpose was to assist law enforcement efforts rather than to further his own ends. The district court's finding of probable cause for the search warrant was based on the information provided in the anonymous source's first and second e-mails, together with [the investigating officer's] affidavit describing how she personally corroborated that information. The information conveyed in those two e-mails was limited to that which the source had acquired before making any contact with [law enforcement officers]. Thus, even assuming *arguendo* that the [police] tacitly encouraged further nonconsensual searches, the information relied on in support of the warrant—graphic images showing [defendant] sexually abusing a young child and identifying information regarding [defendant] which [the investigating officer] thoroughly corroborated—more than sufficed to establish probable cause. We also reject [defendant's] argument for suppression based on [the investigating officer's] failure to advise the judge who issued the warrant how the source obtained the information he sent to the police. [Defendant] asserts that no judge would have found probable cause knowing that the source had hacked into his computer. But he supplies no authority for this assertion. To justify suppression of evidence seized under a warrant, the alleged deliberate or reckless failure to include material information in the affidavit must conceal information that would defeat probable cause. ... [The investigating officer] put the magistrate judge on notice regarding the manner in which she had received the information asserted in support of the warrant—i.e., that it came from an anonymous source who claimed to have found a child molester on the Internet. Because information obtained by a private person is not subject to the Fourth Amendment's exclusionary rule, a statement that the anonymous source had hacked into [defendant's] computer to obtain that information would not have affected the magistrate's finding of probable cause. *U.S. v. Steiger*, 318 F.3d 1039 (11th Cir. 2003).

§ 29:2 No exclusionary remedy: The exclusionary rule does not apply to evidence seized by private individuals

Supreme Court

- "[A] wrongful search or seizure conducted by a private party does not violate the Fourth Amendment and such private wrongdoing does not deprive the government of the right to use evidence that it has acquired lawfully." *Walter v. U.S.*, 447 U.S. 649, 656, 657, 100 S. Ct. 2395, 65 L. Ed. 2d 410 (1980).
- "The papers having come into the possession of the Government without a violation of petitioner's rights by governmental authority, we see no reason why the fact that individuals, unconnected with the Government, may have wrongfully taken them, should prevent them

from being held for use in prosecuting an offense where the documents are of an incriminatory character." *Burdeau v. McDowell*, 256 U.S. 465, 476, 41 S. Ct. 574, 65 L. Ed. 1048, 13 A.L.R. 1159 (1921).

Fourth Circuit

- "The Fourth Amendment is directed exclusively at state action and evidence secured by private searches, even if illegal, need not be excluded from a criminal trial." *U.S. v. Kinney*, 953 F.2d 863, 865 (4th Cir. 1992).

Sixth Circuit

- "Once a private search is conducted, the government's subsequent use of the information obtained in the private search does not implicate the Fourth Amendment as long as the government's use does not exceed the scope of the private search. This is true even if the private party betrayed a confidence in providing the information to the government." *U.S. v. King*, 55 F.3d 1193, 1196, 1995 FED App. 0170P (6th Cir. 1995).
- "The Fourth Amendment does not apply if the search is effected by a private individual not acting as an agent of the government. [W]here a private person delivers the fruits of his search to police, that evidence is not excludable at trial on the basis that it was procured without a search warrant." *U.S. v. Scarborough*, 43 F.3d 1021, 1025, 1995 FED App. 0007P (6th Cir. 1994).

Ninth Circuit

- "Since [the doctor] drew and analyzed [Defendant's] blood for purely medical reasons, he did not possess the requisite intent to engage in a search or seizure under the fourth amendment. In taking the blood, [the doctor] did not intend to elicit a benefit for the government in its investigative or administrative capacity. Rather, he acted for a reason entirely independent of the government's intent to collect evidence for use in [Defendant's] criminal prosecution. We therefore conclude that the district court properly refused to suppress the evidence of [Defendant's] blood alcohol level." *U.S. v. Attson*, 900 F.2d 1427, 1433 (9th Cir. 1990).

Tenth Circuit

- "It is well settled that independent searches by private citizens are unaffected by Fourth Amendment prohibitions against unreasonable searches and seizures, and that results thereof constitute admissible evidence." *U.S. v. Thomas*, 613 F.2d 787, 792 (10th Cir. 1980).

§ 29:3 Government involvement: If a government official aids in a search or seizure by a private citizen, the Fourth Amendment applies

Supreme Court

- "Although the Fourth Amendment does not apply to a search or seizure, even an arbitrary one, effected by a private party on his own initiative, the Amendment protects against such intrusions if the private party acted as an instrument or agent of the Government. Whether a private party should be deemed an agent or instrument of the Government for Fourth Amendment purposes necessarily turns on the degree of the Government's participation in the private party's activities a question that can only be resolved in light of all the circumstances." *Skinner v. Railway Labor Executives' Ass'n*, 489 U.S. 602, 614, 109 S. Ct. 1402, 103 L. Ed. 2d 639, 4 I.E.R. Cas. (BNA) 224, 130 L.R.R.M. (BNA) 2857, 13 O.S.H. Cas. (BNA) 2065, 49 Empl. Prac. Dec. (CCH) P 38791, 111 Lab. Cas. (CCH) P 11001, 1989 O.S.H. Dec. (CCH) P 28476 (1989).

- "The decisive factor is the actuality of a share by a federal official in the total enterprise of securing and selecting evidence by other than sanctioned means. It is immaterial whether a federal agent originated the idea or joined in it while the search was in progress. So long as he was in it before the object of the search was completely accomplished, he must be deemed to have participated in it. Evidence secured through such federal participation is inadmissable." *Lustig v. United States*, 338 U.S. 74, 79, 69 S. Ct. 1372, 93 L. Ed. 1819 (1949).

First Circuit

- "The key issue here is whether [private shipping company employee], acting pursuant to [company] policy and the FAA regulations, was effectively acting as an agent of the government when she opened [defendant's] package, thus triggering the provisions of the Fourth Amendment. . . . [We have] identified several factors that may be relevant, depending on the circumstances: the extent of the government's role in instigating or participating in the search, its intent and the degree of control it exercises over the search and the private party, and the extent to which the private party aims primarily to help the government or to serve its own interests. Applying these factors to the case at hand, we think it clear that [employee] was acting in a private, rather than governmental, capacity." *U.S. v. Momoh*, 427 F.3d 137 (1st Cir. 2005).

- "A person will not be acting as a police agent merely because there was some antecedent contact between that person and the police. . . . Rather, two facts must be shown. First, the police must have instigated, encouraged or participated in the search. . . . Second, the individual must have engaged in the search with the intent of assisting the police in their investigative efforts." *U.S. v. Pervaz*, 118 F.3d 1, 5 (1st Cir. 1997).

Fourth Circuit

- "The Fourth Amendment protects against unreasonable searches and seizures by Government officials and those private individuals acting as instruments or agents of the Government. It does not provide protection against searches by private individuals acting in a private capacity. Thus, evidence secured by private searches, even if illegal, need not be excluded from a criminal trial. Determining whether the requisite agency relationship exists necessarily turns on the degree of the Government's participation in the private party's activities, a question that can only be resolved in light of all the circumstances. This is a fact-intensive inquiry that is guided by common law agency principles. The defendant bears the burden of proving that an agency relationship exists. In order to run afoul of the Fourth Amendment, therefore, the Government must do more than passively accept or acquiesce in a private party's search efforts. Rather, there must be some degree of Government participation in the private search. . . . [T]hree major lessons emerge from the case law. First, courts should look to the facts and circumstances of each case in determining when a private search is in fact a Government search. Second, before a court will deem a private search a Government search, a defendant must demonstrate that the Government knew of and acquiesced in the private search and that the private individual intended to assist law enforcement authorities. Finally, simple acquiescence by the Government does not suffice to transform a private search into a Government search. Rather, there must be some evidence of Government participation in or affirmative encouragement of the private search before a court will hold it unconstitutional. Passive acceptance by the Government is not enough." *U.S. v. Jarrett*, 338 F.3d 339, 61 Fed. R. Evid. Serv. 1530 (4th Cir. 2003).

Fifth Circuit

- "[A] police view subsequent to a search conducted by private citizens does not constitute a 'search' within the meaning of the Fourth Amendment so long as the view is confined to the scope and product of the initial search. . . [T]he police exceed the scope of a prior private search when they examine a closed container that was not opened by the private searchers unless the police are already substantially certain of what is inside that container based on the statements of the private searchers, their replication of the private search, and their expertise. . . [T]he police's pre-warrant examination of the disks clearly exceeded the scope of the private search. The police could not have concluded with substantial certainty that all of the disks contained child pornography based on knowledge obtained from the private searchers, information in plain view, or their own expertise. . . [T]he police exceeded the scope of the private search in the instant case when they examined disks that the private searchers did not examine. [Defendant] further contends that the police exceeded the scope of the private search because they examined more files on each of the disks than did the private searchers. . . [T]he police do not exceed the scope of a prior private search when they examine the same materials that were examined by the private searchers, but they examine these materials more thoroughly than did the private parties. In the context of a closed container search, this means that the police do not exceed the private search when they examine more items within a closed container than did the private searchers. . . . Because we find that the police do not exceed the scope of a prior private search when they examine particular items within a container that were not examined by the private searchers, we accordingly determine that the police in the instant case did not exceed the scope of the private search if they examined more files on the privately-searched disks than [private citizens] had. Suppression of any such files is therefore unnecessary." *U.S. v. Runyan*, 275 F.3d 449 (5th Cir. 2001).

- "[W]e find that the proper Fourth Amendment inquiry, when confronted with a police search of a home that extends no further than a previously-conducted private party search, is to determine whether the homeowner or occupant continues to possess a reasonable expectation of privacy after the private search occurs. In making this determination, consideration must be given to whether the activities of the home's occupants or the circumstances within the home at the time of the private search created a risk of intrusion by the private party that was reasonably foreseeable. If indeed the private party's intrusion was reasonably foreseeable (based on such activities or circumstances), the occupant will no longer possess a reasonable expectation of privacy in the area or thing searched, and the subsequent police search will not trigger the Fourth Amendment. If, however, the private party's initial intrusion was not reasonably foreseeable, the occupant's reasonable expectation of privacy will survive, and the subsequent police search will indeed activate the Fourth Amendment." *U.S. v. Paige*, 136 F.3d 1012, 1020 (5th Cir. 1998).

Sixth Circuit

- "Factors in whether private party is acting as agent of government when conducting search are: (1) government's knowledge or acquiescence, and (2) intent of party performing search." *U.S. v. Hardin*, 539 F.3d 404 (6th Cir. 2008).

- "The Fourth Amendment, of course, proscribes only
  governmental action and does not apply to a search or
  seizure, even an unreasonable one, conducted by a
  private individual not acting as an agent of the
  government. A person will not be acting as a police
  agent merely because there was some antecedent
  contact between that person and the police. Rather, two
  elements must be shown in order to treat ostensibly
  private action as a state-sponsored search: (1) the police
  must have instigated, encouraged, or participated in
  the search; and (2) the private individual must have
  engaged in the search with the intent of assisting the
  police. Regarding this latter element of intent, we have
  explained that a private party is not an agent of the
  government where the intent of the private party
  conducting the search is entirely independent of the
  government's intent to collect evidence for use in a criminal prosecution." *U.S. v. Bruce*, 396 F.3d 697, 2005
  FED App. 0049P (6th Cir. 2005), vacated in part on
  other grounds on reh'g, 405 F.3d 1034 (6th Cir. 2005).

Seventh Circuit

- "A search or seizure by a private party does not
  implicate the Fourth Amendment unless the party is
  acting as an 'instrument or agent' of the government. In
  determining whether a private party acted as an 'instrument or agent' of the government, we consider several
  factors, including whether the government knew of and
  acquiesced in the intrusive conduct; whether the private
  party's purpose in conducting the search was to assist
  law enforcement; and whether the government requested the action or offered the private actor a
  reward. . . The first time [the delivery driver] opened
  the package, the police were not present, nor had the
  officers ever spoken with [the driver]. The police had
  merely notified area delivery services to watch for suspicious packages and contact authorities; they did not
  instruct anyone, including [the driver], to open any
  packages. The Fourth Amendment is not triggered when
  a private party initiates a search and contacts police after evidence is discovered. There is no evidence here
  that the police controlled, directed, condoned, or
  acquiesced in [the driver's] initial decision to open the

package. Accordingly, her actions cannot be imputed to the police." *U.S. v. Crowley*, 285 F.3d 553 (7th Cir. 2002).

- "When determining whether a private citizen has acted as a government agent, the question is whether in light of all the circumstances of the case [the person] must be regarded as having acted as an instrument or agent of the state. . . . The Court is called upon to determine whether: (1) the Government knew of and acquiesced in the intrusive conduct; and (2) the private party's purpose for conducting the search was to assist law enforcement efforts or further his own ends. . . . Another consideration is whether the Government offered the private party a reward." *U.S. v. Hall*, 142 F.3d 988, 993 (7th Cir. 1998).

- "A search or seizure by a private party does not implicate the Fourth Amendment. . . . However, the Fourth Amendment does apply to a search or seizure by a party (even if otherwise a private party) who is acting as an instrument or agent of the government. . . . This Court has explained that two critical factors in the instrument or agent analysis are whether the government knew of and acquiesced in the intrusive conduct and whether the private party's purpose in conducting the search was to assist law enforcement agents or to further its own ends. . . . Other useful criteria are whether the private actor acted at the request of the government and whether the government offered the private actor a reward." *U.S. v. Shahid*, 117 F.3d 322, 325 (7th Cir. 1997).

- "That a CI might also have intended to assist law enforcement does not transform him into a government agent so long as the private party has had a legitimate independent motivation for engaging in the challenged conduct. [A] party is subject to the fourth amendment only when he or she has formed the necessary intent to assist in the government's investigative or administrative functions; in other words, when he or she intends to engage in a search or seizure. However, under this test, the fourth amendment will not apply when the private party was acting for a reason that is independent of such a governmental purpose." *U.S. v. McAllister*, 18 F.3d 1412, 1417–18 (7th Cir. 1994).

<u>Eighth Circuit</u>

- "The difficulty with the government's position, we believe, is that it relies on a reading of Jacobsen that is much too broad. In that case, a private freight carrier opened a package, cut open a tube that was in it, and discovered a zip-lock plastic bag containing a white powder. When DEA agents arrived on the scene after employees of the carrier had called them in, they removed the zip-lock bag from the tube and inspected it. The Supreme Court held that the invasions of respondents' privacy by the Government agent must be tested by the degree to which they exceeded the scope of the private search. . . . The Court went on to observe that the Fourth Amendment is implicated only if the authorities use information with respect to which the expectation of privacy has not already been frustrated. . . . Because the actions of the federal officers' search in Jacobsen had not revealed to them anything that the freight carrier's employees had not already told them, the Court held that the Fourth Amendment had not been violated." *U.S. v. Rouse*, 148 F.3d 1040, 1041 (8th Cir. 1998) (rejected by, U.S. v. Runyan, 275 F.3d 449 (5th Cir. 2001)).

- "We recognize that the government can exercise such control over a private actor that a private action can fairly be attributed to the government for purposes of the Fourth and Fifth Amendment. [Defendant] must show that, in light of all the circumstances, [the Officer] or [Auditor] acted as an instrument or agent of the government. She may meet this test by showing that the government exercised such coercive power or such significant encouragement that it is responsible for their conduct, or that the exercised powers are the exclusive prerogative of the government." *U.S. v. Garlock*, 19 F.3d 441, 443 (8th Cir. 1994).

Ninth Circuit

- "The technician's search of [defendant]'s hard drive was a private search that did not implicate the protections of the Fourth Amendment. (citation omitted) No governmental actors were present during the search. There were no agreements between the repair shop and the police department, and there is nothing to indicate that the technician initially searched [defendant]'s computer with the intent to aid law enforcement. The government's subsequent involvement did not change the private nature of the search, and [defendant] has not shown that the government's search expanded beyond the technician's search prior to the issuance of a warrant." *U.S. v. Carey*, 356 Fed. Appx. 988 (9th Cir. 2009).

- "Whether a private party engaged in state action is a highly factual question. . . . Crucial is the nature and extent of the relationship between the [state actor] and the [media defendants who observed and reported on execution of search warrant at plaintiff's premises]. . . . [Plaintiff] asks us to consider three distinct tests. . . First, the 'joint action' test examines whether private actors are willful participants in joint action with the government or its agents. Second, and derivative of the joint action test, the 'symbiotic relationship' test asks whether the government has so far insinuated itself into a position of interdependence with a private entity that the private entity must be recognized as a joint participant in the challenged activity. Last, the 'public functions' test inquires whether the private actor performs functions traditionally and exclusively reserved to the States." *Brunette v. Humane Society of Ventura County*, 294 F.3d 1205, 30 Media L. Rep. (BNA) 2016 (9th Cir. 2002), as amended on denial of reh'g and reh'g en banc, (Aug. 23, 2002).

Tenth Circuit

- "When a private individual conducts a search not acting as, or in concert with, a government agent, the Fourth Amendment is not implicated, no matter how unreasonable the search. In some cases a search by a private citizen may be transformed into a governmental search implicating the Fourth Amendment if the government coerces, dominates or directs the actions of a private person conducting the search or seizure. The Court of Appeals uses a dual-pronged inquiry to decide if a search by a private individual constitutes state action; first, it determines whether the government knew of and acquiesced in the individual's intrusive conduct, and second, it considers whether the party performing the search intended to assist law enforcement efforts or to further his own ends." *U.S. v. Poe*, 556 F.3d 1113 (10th Cir. 2009).

- "To determine whether a private person's search becomes a Government search, the court examines (1) whether the Government knew of and acquiesced in the intrusive conduct, and (2) whether the person searching intended to assist law enforcement efforts or to further his or her own ends. [Defendant] does not contend that law enforcement officers coerced, dominated or directed [state university employee], or that she otherwise conducted her search pursuant to any law enforcement or other governmental objective. Rather, as he admits, [employee] simply became curious about the safe and its contents." *U.S. v. Soderstrand*, 412 F.3d 1146 (10th Cir. 2005).

- "In determining whether a search by a private person becomes a government search, the following two-part inquiry is utilized: 1) whether the government knew of and acquiesced in the intrusive conduct, and 2) whether the party performing the search intended to assist law enforcement efforts or to further his own ends. . . .Both prongs must be satisfied before the private search may be deemed a government search." *U.S. v. Souza*, 223 F.3d 1197, 1201 (10th Cir. 2000).

- "While private searches generally do not raise constitutional concerns, the Fourth Amendment would be seriously undermined if the search of the package in this case was described as anything other than orchestrated by the government." *U.S. v. Souza*, 223 F.3d 1197, 1202 (10th Cir. 2000).

- "[A] search by a private citizen may be transformed into a governmental search implicating the Fourth Amendment if the government coerces, dominates or directs the actions of a private person conducting the search or seizure. In such a case, the private citizen may be regarded as an agent or instrumentality of the police and the fruits of the search may be suppressed. [T]wo important inquiries to aid in the determination of whether a private person becomes an agent or instrumentality of the police are whether the government knew of and acquiesced in the intrusive conduct, and whether the party performing the search intended to assist law enforcement efforts or to further his own ends. It is clear that if a government agent is involved merely as a witness, the requisite government action implicating Fourth Amendment concerns is absent." *U.S. v. Smythe*, 84 F.3d 1240, 1242–43 (10th Cir. 1996).

- "We have stated the applicable test to determine when a search by a private person becomes government action as a two-part inquiry, 1) whether the government knew of and acquiesced in the intrusive conduct, and 2) whether the party performing the search intended to assist law enforcement efforts or to further his own ends. We hold this part of the test also requires that the court weigh the government's role in the search. A government agent must be involved either directly as a participant—not merely as a witness—or indirectly as an encourager of the private person's search before we will deem the person to be an instrument of the government." *U.S. v. Leffall*, 82 F.3d 343, 347 (10th Cir. 1996).

Chapter 30

Institutional Searches

Research References

West's Key Number Digest

Armed Services ⭠1, 11, 22, 28; Constitutional Law ⭠262, 278;
    Criminal Law ⭠308, 394; Military Justice ⭠1046, 1056; Prisons
    ⭠4, 13; Schools ⭠169.5; Searches and Seizures ⭠23, 24 to 25,
    55, 62, 78, 105; Sentencing and Punishment ⭠1961, 1992 to
    1993

KeyCite®: Cases and other legal materials listed in KeyCite Scope can be
    researched through the KeyCite service on Westlaw®. Use KeyCite to
    check citations for form, parallel references, prior and later history, and
    comprehensive citator information, including citations to other decisions
    and secondary materials.

---

§ 30:1   Military: The Fourth Amendment governs
        military searches, but does not limit the
        military's right to conduct inspections

Fourth Circuit

- "[T]he validity of closed base searches taken without particularized suspicion does not turn on the case-by-case application of a special needs or exigent circumstances balancing test. The case law makes clear that searches on closed military bases have long been exempt from the usual Fourth Amendment requirement of probable cause. The rationale is the same for why the base is closed in the first place: to protect a military installation that is vital to national security. The barbed-wire fence, the security guards at the gate, the sign warning of the possibility of search, and a civilian's common-sense awareness of the nature of a military base—all these circumstances combine to puncture any reasonable expectations of privacy for a civilian who enters a closed military base." *U.S. v. Jenkins*, 986 F.2d 76, 78–79 (4th Cir. 1993).

Seventh Circuit

- "It is too late in the day to suggest that the Fourth Amendment's basic protection against unreasonable searches and seizures does not apply to members of the armed forces. Nevertheless, the military implementation of that guarantee is different from that employed in civilian matters. In civilian cases, the warrant requirement has been abrogated by judicial decision only in certain carefully described situations. In the military situation, Congress has primary responsibility for the delicate task of balancing the rights of servicemen against the needs of the military. Congress has determined that an alternate procedure to a warrant issued by a magistrate is more compatible with the realities of military life." *U.S. v. Chapman*, 954 F.2d 1352, 1367 (7th Cir. 1992).
- "Members of the armed forces have considerably less of an expectation of privacy while living on a military installation, and a military commander has considerably more interest in being informed of all activities in the area under his command." *U.S. v. Chapman*, 954 F.2d 1352, 1369 (7th Cir. 1992).
- "Under Military Rule of Evidence 315, an investigatory search of a member's person or quarters may only be undertaken (absent exigent circumstances) when the investigator presents the military commander with in-

formation establishing that there is probable cause to believe that the area sought to be searched contains evidence of unlawful activity. The investigator may present that information orally or in writing. There is no explicit requirement that the person presenting the information be under oath, although it appears to be the preferred practice. [T]he military search authorization procedure is a finely tuned accommodation of the servicemember's privacy interests grounded in the Fourth Amendment and the specific needs, dictated by military necessity, for good order and discipline in the armed forces." *U.S. v. Chapman*, 954 F.2d 1352, 1368–69 (7th Cir. 1992).

Ninth Circuit

- "The disruptive effect of extending the exclusionary rule to military administrative discharge proceedings is a price which our society cannot afford to pay." *Garrett v. Lehman*, 751 F.2d 997, 1004 (9th Cir. 1985).

Tenth Circuit

- "Under Military Rule of Evidence 315, '[a]n 'authorization to search' is an express permission, written or oral, issued by a competent military authority to search a person or an area for specified property or evidence or for a specific person and to seize such property evidence or person.' An authority to search must be supported by probable cause, which can be determined on the basis of '[o]ral statements communicated to the authorizing official in person, via telephone, or by other appropriate means of communication.' M.R.E. Rule 315(f)(2)(B)." *U.S. v. Banks*, 451 F.3d 721 (10th Cir. 2006).

D.C. Circuit

- "GIs are entitled to the protection of the Fourth Amendment as are all other American citizens. To strike the proper balance between legitimate military needs and individual liberties we must inquire whether conditions peculiar to military life dictate affording different treatment to activity arising in a military context. [Here] warrantless inspections are reasonable and constitutionally permissible under the Fourth Amendment." *Committee for GI Rights v. Callaway*, 518 F.2d 466, 476, 477 (D.C. Cir. 1975).

Specialized Federal Courts

- "While the traditional military inspection which looks at the overall fitness of a unit to perform its military mission is a permissible deviation from what may be tolerated in civilian society generally—recognizing that such procedure is a reasonable intrusion which a serviceperson must expect in a military society—the shakedown inspection as earlier defined in search specifically of criminal goods or evidence is not such a permissible intrusion into a person's reasonable expectation of privacy, even in the military setting." *U. S. v. Roberts*, 2 M.J. 31, 36 (C.M.A. 1976).

- "[A]n inspection cannot be used as a pretext to cover up unlawful invasions of the personal rights of members of the armed services." *U.S. v. Lange*, 35 C.M.R. 458, 462, 1965 WL 4707 (C.M.A. 1965).

§ 30:2   **Parolees, probationers, and supervised releasees: Parolees, probationers, and convicted felons on conditional/supervised release have only limited Fourth Amendment protection**

Supreme Court

- "In *United States v. Jones,* we held that the Government's installation of a GPS device on a target's vehicle, and its use of that device to monitor the vehicle's movements, constitutes a search. We stressed the importance of the fact that the Government had physically occupied private property for the purpose of obtaining information. Under such circumstances, it was not necessary to inquire about the target's expectation of privacy in his vehicle's movements in order to determine if a Fourth Amendment search had occurred. Where, as here, the Government obtains information by physically intruding on a constitutionally protected area, such a search has undoubtedly occurred. We reaffirmed this principle in *Florida v. Jardines,* where we held that having a drug-sniffing dog nose around a suspect's front porch was a search, because police had gathered . . . information by physically entering and occupying the [curtilage of the house] to engage in conduct not explicitly or implicitly permitted by the homeowner. In light of these decisions, it follows that a State also conducts a search when it attaches a device to a person's body, without consent, for the purpose of tracking that individual's movements." *Grady v. North Carolina*, 135 S. Ct. 1368, 1370, 191 L. Ed. 2d 459 (2015) (inner quotations and citations omitted).

• "(P)arolees are on the "continuum" of state-imposed punishments..On this continuum, parolees have fewer expectations of privacy than probationers, because parole is more akin to imprisonment than probation is to imprisonment . . . Examining the totality of the circumstances pertaining to petitioner's status as a parolee, "an established variation on imprisonment," . . . including the plain terms of the parole search condition, we conclude that petitioner did not have an expectation of privacy that society would recognize as legitimate . . . California's ability to conduct suspicionless searches of parolees serves its interest in reducing recidivism, in a manner that aids, rather than hinders, the reintegration of parolees into productive society . . . Thus, we conclude that the Fourth Amendment does not prohibit a police officer from conducting a suspicionless search of a parolee." *Samson v. California*, 547 U.S. 843, 126 S. Ct. 2193, 165 L. Ed. 2d 250 (2006).

• "The State has a dual concern with a probationer. On the one hand is the hope that he will successfully complete probation and be integrated back into the community. On the other is the concern, quite justified, that he will be more likely to engage in criminal conduct than an ordinary member of the community. The view of the Court of Appeals in this case would require the State to shut its eyes to the latter concern and concentrate only on the former. But we hold that the Fourth Amendment does not put the State to such a choice. Its interest in apprehending violators of the criminal law, thereby protecting potential victims of criminal enterprise, may therefore justifiably focus on probationers in a way that it does not on the ordinary citizen. We hold that the balance of these considerations requires no more than reasonable suspicion to conduct a search of this probationer's house. The degree of individualized suspicion required of a search is a determination of when there is a sufficiently high probability that criminal conduct is occurring to make the intrusion on the individual's privacy interest reasonable. Although the Fourth Amendment ordinarily requires the degree of probability embodied in the term 'probable cause,' a lesser degree satisfies the Constitution when the balance of governmental and private interests makes such a standard reasonable. ... When an officer has reasonable suspicion that a probationer subject to a search condition is engaged in criminal activity, there is enough likelihood that criminal conduct is occurring that an intrusion on the probationer's significantly diminished privacy interests is reasonable. The same circumstances that lead us to conclude that reasonable suspicion is constitutionally sufficient also render a warrant requirement unnecessary." *U.S. v. Knights*, 534 U.S. 112, 122 S. Ct. 587, 151 L. Ed. 2d 497 (2001).

- "A State's operation of a probation system . . . presents special needs beyond normal law enforcement that may justify departures from the usual warrant and probable cause requirements. . . . To a greater or lesser degree, it is always true of probationers (as we have said it to be true of parolees) that they do not enjoy the absolute liberty to which every citizen is entitled, but only conditional liberty properly dependent on observance of special [probation] restrictions." *Griffin v. Wisconsin*, 483 U.S. 868, 873–74, 107 S. Ct. 3164, 97 L. Ed. 2d 709 (1987).

First Circuit

- "The standard dictionary definition of the term 'warrant' does not include a requirement that a warrant be supported by an oath or affirmation. Black's Law Dictionary defines 'warrant' as a 'writ directing or authorizing someone to do an act, esp. one directing a law enforcer to make an arrest, a search, or a seizure.' In addition, Black's Law Dictionary defines an 'arrest warrant' as a 'warrant, issued only on probable cause, directing a law-enforcement officer to arrest and bring a person to court. The Random House Dictionary defines 'warrant' as 'an instrument, issued by a magistrate, authorizing an officer to make an arrest, seize property, make a search, or execute a judgment.' The Oxford English Dictionary defines 'warrant' as a 'writing issued by the sovereign, an officer of state, or an administrative body, authorizing those to whom it is addressed to perform some act.' The Oxford English Dictionary's language was exactly the same in 1971 and thus likely served as the definitional backdrop to Congress's 1984 passage of the Sentencing Reform Act. [The defendant] argues that 'warrant' is a 'term of art,' which must be imbued with the interpretation given in the Constitution. In concluding that the term 'warrant' means 'a document that is based upon probable cause and supported by sworn facts,' the Ninth Circuit reasoned that '[i]t is a well-established canon of statutory construction that when Congress uses a term of art, such as "warrant," unless Congress affirmatively indicates otherwise, we presume Congress intended to incorporate the common definition of that term . . . .' The Ninth Circuit noted that section 3606's inclusion of probable cause '[b]y extension' required an oath or affirmation. The government responds that the term 'warrant' is not a term of art in the context of persons under the supervision of the court (i.e. on pretrial release, probation, or supervised release) where a warrant supported by oath or affirmation has not consistently been required for violations of terms of release. As the Fifth Circuit pointed out, explicit oath or affirmation requirements, such as those in the Fourth Amendment and the Federal Rules of Criminal Procedure, are 'not proof that there is an implicit sworn-facts requirement embedded in the very meaning of the word "warrant" as a legal term. If anything, such examples suggest the converse, i.e. that a valid warrant need not be supported by sworn facts unless a specific statutory provision requires such support.' . . . Significantly, prior to the advent of supervised release, administrative warrants to revoke a prisoner on parole did not require sworn facts. The governing statute under the parole regime provided that a 'warden, at any time within the term or terms of the prisoner's sentence, may issue his warrant to any officer hereinafter authorized to execute the same for the retaking of such prisoner.' . . . [C]ourts have continued to hold that the '[r]equirements contained in the Federal Rules of Crim-

inal Procedure that impose procedures for taking someone into custody do not necessarily apply to people who
. . . are under court supervision as part of a criminal
sentence.' They have explained that the reason these
rules for taking someone into custody do not necessarily
apply is that a convicted criminal on supervised release
(or parole) is already in 'constructive custody.' Because
Congress is presumed to have known that the parole
statute had no oath requirement, its failure to engraft
such a requirement onto section 3606 speaks volumes.
In light of this legislative history, the failure to include
an oath or affirmation requirement in section 3606 and
the inclusion of a probable cause requirement demonstrates congressional intent not to require sworn facts."
U.S. v. Collazo-Castro, 660 F.3d 516, 520–22 (1st Cir.
2011) (citations omitted).

- "We do not hold, as some courts have suggested, that
once a DNA sample is lawfully extracted from an individual and a DNA profile lawfully created, the individual necessarily loses a reasonable expectation of privacy
with respect to *any* subsequent use of that profile.
Instead, we narrowly hold that once a qualified federal
offender's profile has been lawfully created and entered
into CODIS under the DNA Act, the FBI's retention
and periodic matching of the profile against other
profiles in CODIS for the purpose of identification is not
an intrusion on the offender's legitimate expectation of
privacy and thus does not constitute a separate Fourth
Amendment search." *Boroian v. Mueller*, 616 F.3d 60,
68 (1st Cir. 2010) (citations omitted).

- "It is well established that identification records of
convicted felons, such as fingerprints or mugshots, are
routinely retained by the government after their sentences are complete and may be expunged only in narrowly defined circumstances . . . . Other precedents
hold that the government's matching of a lawfully
obtained identification record against other records in
its lawful possession does not infringe on an individual's legitimate expectation of privacy . . . . These longstanding practices and precedents on the retention and
matching of offenders' identification records inescapably
inform a convicted offender's reasonable expectation of
privacy with respect to his or her DNA profile. As with

the matching of records in a fingerprint database, the
government's use of CODIS to match Boroian's profile
against other profiles in the database is limited to a
comparison of the identification records already in its
lawful possession and does not reveal any new, private
or intimate information about Boroian. Moreover, the
government's comparison of Boroian's DNA profile with
other profiles in CODIS is precisely the use for which
the profile was initially lawfully created and entered
into CODIS under the DNA Act . . . . Boroian suggests
that the government does not need his DNA profile for
'identification' purposes because it already has other
means of identification, such as his fingerprints and
social security number. However, the fact that the
government may lawfully retain and access these more
traditional means of identifying Boroian only emphasizes that the government's retention and matching of
his DNA profile does not intrude on Boroian's legitimate expectation of privacy. At present, Boroian's DNA
profile simply functions as an additional, albeit more
technologically advanced, means of identification . . . .
Therefore, we join the other courts to have addressed
the issue in holding that the government's retention
and matching of Boroian's profile against other profiles
in CODIS does not violate an expectation of privacy
that society is prepared to recognize as reasonable, and
thus does not constitute a separate search under the
Fourth Amendment. Boroian has not cited, and our
research has not revealed, any decisions holding to the
contrary." *Boroian v. Mueller*, 616 F.3d 60, 67-68 (1st
Cir. 2010) (citations omitted).

• "In determining the reasonableness of a probation
search, the probationer's expectation of privacy may be
shaped by search conditions in the probation order
where the order clearly expresses the conditions and
the probationer is unambiguously informed of them."
U.S. v. Graham, 553 F.3d 6 (1st Cir. 2009).

• "This case presents a question of first impression in this
circuit: is it a violation of the Fourth Amendment's prohibition on unreasonable searches and seizures to
require an individual on supervised release to provide a
blood sample for purposes of creating a DNA profile and
entering it into a centralized database? Agreeing with

the eleven other circuits that have held similarly, we hold that it is not. In doing so, we interpret the Supreme Court's decision in *Samson v. California* [citation omitted] to require that we join the majority of the circuits in applying a 'totality of the circumstances' approach to the issues in this case, rather than the 'special needs' analysis used by the minority of circuits. . . . However, we also impose an important limitation on our holding. Because the appellant is currently on supervised release and will remain so until 2009, we do not resolve the question of whether it is also constitutional to retain the DNA profile in the database after he is no longer on supervised release. Mindful of the well-established principle that constitutional cases should be decided as narrowly as possible and the rapid pace of technological development in the area of DNA analysis, we reserve judgment on that issue for another day." *U.S. v. Weikert*, 504 F.3d 1, 2–3 (1st Cir. 2007).

- "(A) valid parole violation warrant, issued on the basis of reasonable grounds to believe that a parolee has violated the conditions of his parole, is adequate to support an entry into the parolee's domicile for the purpose of executing the warrant . . . On appeal the defendant has not attempted to argue that the warrant was issued on the basis of a constitutionally infirm predicate. We must, therefore, treat the parole violation warrant as valid and enforceable. Doing so, we conclude that the warrant provided the officers with lawful authority to enter the motel room for the purpose of arresting the defendant . . . That ends this aspect of the appeal. Because *Hudson* applies with equal force in the context of an arrest warrant, the district court did not err in refusing to order suppression based upon the officers' conceded violation of the knock and announce rule." *U.S. v. Pelletier*, 469 F.3d 194 (1st Cir. 2006).

Second Circuit

- "Parole search of defendant's bedroom, which was substantially connected to his arrest for dealing drugs, was reasonable under the Fourth Amendment." *U.S. v. Watts*, 301 Fed. Appx. 39 (2d Cir. 2008).
- "We revisit the issue here to consider whether the 2004 DNA Act violates the Fourth Amendment when applied

to individuals convicted of nonviolent crimes who were sentenced only to probation . . . (W)e analyze the constitutionality of the 2004 DNA Act as it applies to Appellants under the two-prong special-needs approach. First . . . we consider whether the search and seizure is justified by a special need beyond the ordinary needs of normal law enforcement. (Next), we examine . . . whether the search was reasonable in light of that special need . . . Taking and storing samples of DNA under the restrictions of the DNA Act fulfills many important governmental interests, only some of which are limited to the criminal history of the subjects of the DNA testing. The invasion of privacy, both immediate, and long term, from DNA testing of convicted felons-even those convicted of non-violent crimes and sentenced only to probation-is, given the safeguards of the 2004 DNA Act, relatively small. Accordingly we conclude that the 2004 DNA Act, as applied to appellants, does not constitute an unreasonable search or seizure and hence does not violate the Fourth Amendment . . ." *U.S. v. Amerson*, 483 F.3d 73 (2d Cir. 2007).

- "On appeal, [defendant] does not seriously challenge that parole officers were reasonably entitled under New York rules and regulations to conduct a warrantless search of his residence on January 9, 2001. Instead, he submits that the special needs of parole supervision do not extend to parole searches in which police officers participate. Alternatively, [defendant] asserts that his signed release certification consented to searches only by parole officers, not by the police. [Defendant's] first argument, a variation of what we have referred to as a 'stalking horse' theory, is largely foreclosed by our decision in *United States v. Reyes, 283 F.3d at 462-65*, which specifically rejected stalking horse challenges to warrantless searches by probation or parole officers accompanied by the police. [Defendant] attempts to distinguish *Reyes* on the ground that it did not involve a full search but only a less intrusive home visit. In fact, *Reyes's* rejection of challenges to coordinated efforts between probation/parole officers and other law enforcement officials turned not on the particular level of intrusion in that case, but on the legitimacy of the supervision objectives being pursued by the probation

officers. As *Reyes* recognized, the duties and objectives
of probation/parole officers and other law enforcement
officials, although distinct, may frequently be intertwined and responsibly require coordinated efforts. For
precisely that reason, *Reyes* noted that it is difficult to
imagine a situation in which a probation/parole officer
who entered a residence with other law enforcement officials based on information about a supervisee's illegal
activities would not be pursuing legitimate supervision
objectives. In [defendant's] case, the record amply
demonstrates that the initial decision to search his
mother's apartment was made by parole officers performing their statutory duty to investigate a report that
[defendant] was committing crimes in violation of his
parole. No evidence supports a conclusion that the challenged parole search was a ploy to help police evade the
Fourth Amendment warrant requirement." *U.S. v.
Newton*, 369 F.3d 659 (2d Cir. 2004).

- "The Supreme Court set out a particular exception when
  it held that a state's operation of a probation program
  presents 'special needs' beyond normal law enforcement
  that may justify departures from the usual warrant and
  probable-cause requirements. The Court based this view
  on its conclusion that probationers do not enjoy the
  absolute liberty to which the average citizen is entitled,
  but instead only enjoy a conditional liberty dependent
  upon their adherence to special probation restrictions.
  Accordingly, probationers can be subjected to burdens
  upon their privacy that would be unconstitutional were
  they applied to the general citizenry, as long as those
  burdens are imposed pursuant to a regulation that
  satisfies the Fourth Amendment's reasonableness
  requirement. The Supreme Court and this Circuit have
  extended this analysis to parolees as well as
  probationers. . . . [I]f plaintiff were a parolee and
  defendants' actions [of searching her house to arrest a
  parolee they had been informed was there] were
  rationally and reasonably connected to their duties as
  parole officers, there would be no violation of a clearly
  established constitutional right, and plaintiff's claim
  would fail. However. . . . [b]ecause plaintiff is not a
  parolee, she cannot be subjected to the same burdens
  upon her privacy, and the departures from the usual

warrant and probable-cause requirements allowed with respect to parolees are not justified for her." *Moore v. Vega*, 371 F.3d 110 (2d Cir. 2004).

Third Circuit

- "Under normal circumstances, the Fourth Amendment requires government officials to have both probable cause and a warrant to conduct a search. In the case of parolees, however, the requisite level of suspicion is reduced and a warrant is not required." *U.S. v. Baker*, 221 F.3d 438, 443 (3d Cir. 2000), as amended, (Sept. 21, 2000).

Fifth Circuit

- "(A) probation officer will necessarily have to perform some actions such as walking through a yard to conduct a home visit. Briefly walking through rooms in (defendant's) home is no different-(the probation officer) did not closely examine any room, did not rifle through (defendant's) belongings, and merely followed (defendant) as he was led around the home. His conduct was incidental to and a part of his interpersonal contact with (defendant). (Defendant), as a probationer with diminished expectations of privacy, cannot expect that a probation officer will not view the various rooms in his home while conducting a home visit to verify that his residence there is genuine and suitable . . . (The probation officer) thus did not cross the line from a home visit to a search, and on these facts was not required to show reasonable suspicion of criminal activity. We therefore affirm the district court's denial of the motion to suppress the firearm (found in plain view)." *U.S. v. LeBlanc*, 490 F.3d 361 (5th Cir. 2007).

- "The ultimate issue in this case is whether a home visit conducted by [defendant]'s probation officer violated the Fourth Amendment, which depends on: first, whether Louisiana's probation statutes and regulations are constitutional as reasonable guidelines for implementing the 'special needs' of the state's system for supervising probationers for purposes of their rehabilitation and the community's protection; and, second, whether the home visit and the plain view seizure at issue here complied with these state guidelines and with the

Fourth Amendment. . . . In 2003, [defendant] was
convicted in a Louisiana state court of contractor mis-
application of payments under Louisiana Revised
Statutes 14:202, a felony, and was placed on supervised
probation for five years. On July 29, 2004 a state probation officer, Todd Cruice, visited [defendant] at his small
semi-shotgun house in a rural area near Pointe A La
Hac in Plaquemines Parish, Louisiana. [Defendant]
does not challenge a Louisiana probation officer's
authority to conduct home visits at reasonable times
and intervals. Rather, he argues that Officer Cruice
exceeded the bounds of his authority by inspecting his
whole house without any reason to suspect him of a
crime or probation violation, instead of conversing with
him in his kitchen as another officer had done on a
previous occasion. . . . [During this] . . . home visit[,
after Cruice] . . . asked if he could 'look around,'
[defendant] did not object but showed him the entire
house while pointing out each respective room and
certain improvements he had made or undertaken. . . .
As he turned back to leave the bedroom, Cruice saw in
plain view what he immediately recognized as the bar-
rel of a .410 gauge shotgun sticking out from under
[defendant]'s bed. Cruice retrieved the gun, opened it,
and found it loaded with a shotgun shell. . . . Cruice
. . . seized the firearm as evidence of [defendant's violation of his probation. The home visit lasted for less than
ten minutes, while the 'walk-through' portion lasted
two to three minutes. The district court found that
Cruice 'did not physically move anything, open drawers,
or rifle through personal belongings; rather, he used
only his eyes.' [footnote omitted] . . . [Defendant]
moved to suppress the gun, arguing to the district court
that it was seized pursuant to an unlawful search. He
contended that the probation officer exceeded the scope
of the required home visit by asking to look around, and
that he did not have reasonable suspicion of a probation
violation to support a search of the premises. The
district court denied the motion to suppress, holding
that the actions of the probation officer did not constitute a search separate from the home visit and that
this visit was permissible under the Fourth Amendment given the reduced privacy expectations of

probationers. . . . [Defendant] argues that Cruice went
beyond the permitted 'home visit' authorized by Louisiana probation policies. He contends that a home visit is
limited to interpersonal contact, and that Cruice's actions violated his expectation of privacy under the
Fourth Amendment. . . . We think the District Court
correctly concluded that this home visit and seizure of a
dangerous weapon in plain view did not violate the
Fourth Amendment. As part of his sentence for the commission of a crime, [defendant] was subjected to supervision pursuant to the state laws, rules, regulations and
conditions governing Louisiana's probation system. The
visit and inspection of [defendant]'s home satisfied the
demands of the Fourth Amendment because it was carried out pursuant to laws and regulations that themselves satisfy the Fourth Amendment's reasonableness
requirement under well-established principles. [citation
and footnote omitted] . . . [In Samson v. California,
t]he Supreme Court . . . recognized a 'continuum' of
expectations of privacy under the Fourth Amendment
based on the degree of punishment a defendant is
subjected to. [citation omitted] 'Just as other punishments for criminal convictions curtail an offender's
freedoms, a court granting probation may impose reasonable conditions that deprive the offender of some
freedoms enjoyed by law-abiding citizens.' [citation
omitted] . . . Consequently, reasonable restrictions
upon liberty and privacy are allowed and are necessary
'to assure that the probation serves as a period of genuine rehabilitation and that the community is not
harmed by the probationer's being at large.' [citation
omitted] 'These same goals require and justify the
exercise of supervision to assure that the restrictions
are in fact observed . . . . Supervision, then, is a
'special need' of the State permitting a degree of im-
pingement upon privacy that would not be constitutional
if applied to the public at large.' [citation omitted]" *U.S.
v. LeBlanc*, 490 F.3d 361, 363–366 (5th Cir. 2007).

- "In reaching its conclusion that a sworn-facts requirement is implicit in the term 'warrant,' the Ninth Circuit
pointed to the Fourth Amendment's Oath or affirmation
requirement and multiple statutes that require arrest
warrants to be based upon sworn statements. Explicit

oath or affirmation requirements, however, are not proof
that there is an implicit sworn-facts requirement
embedded in the very meaning of the word 'warrant' as
a legal term. If anything, such examples suggest the
converse, i.e. that a valid warrant need not be supported
by sworn facts unless a specific statutory provision
requires such support. [The defendant] cites, and we
can find, no statute that does not contain a sworn-facts
requirement but that has been read to require support
by sworn facts anyway. By contrast, at least two
statutes have authorized the issuance of a warrant not
supported by sworn facts. Pursuant to 18 U.S.C.
§ 3148(b), a district court may issue a warrant for the
arrest of someone on pretrial release based solely on a
motion by the government. While this statute applies in
a context different from the one at issue in this case,
'its existence refutes [the] suggestion that issuing warrants based on unsworn allegation is statutorily
unprecedented.' The other statute, while not currently
in effect, is closer in legal context. 18 U.S.C. § 717, the
predecessor statute to today's 18 U.S.C. § 3606, authorized wardens to issue warrants for the arrest of
parolees and contained no express sworn-facts
requirements. Construing § 717, the Fourth Circuit
expressly held that a warrant issued for the arrest of a
parolee did not need to be supported by sworn facts. In
light of these statutes and the cases interpreting them,
[the defendant's] contention that any statute that
contains the word 'warrant' has always been and must
be read to include an implicit sworn-facts requirement
does not withstand scrutiny. [The defendant] next
contends that section 3583(i) should be read to incorporate the Fourth Amendment's Oath or affirmation
requirement to avoid an unconstitutional interpretation
of the statute. In other words, he argues that a warrant
for the arrest of a supervised releasee must comport
with the Oath or affirmation requirement. This proposition does not find support in the case law. The *Jarman*
court, for example, held that warrants for the retaking
of parolees are not true arrest warrants that must
comport with the Fourth Amendment. Other courts,
including this one, that have considered the constitutional status of parolees and supervised releasees have

also concluded that such persons do not enjoy the full spate of constitutional rights enjoyed by criminal defendants. Given the relaxed constitutional norms that apply in revocation hearings, a warrant for the arrest of a supervised releasee need not comply with the Oath or affirmation clause of the Fourth Amendment. Consequently, we reject [the defendant's] contention that, to avoid interpreting section 3583 in a way that would render it unconstitutional, we must read a sworn-facts requirement into the term 'warrant.' Neither the plain language of section 3583 nor the principle of constitutional avoidance suggests that the district court did not have jurisdiction over [the defendant] because the warrant was not supported by sworn facts." *U.S. v. Garcia-Avalino*, 444 F.3d 444, 445–47 (5th Cir. 2006) (citations omitted).

Sixth Circuit

- "[T]he policy provides that an officer may conduct a warrantless search if he has reasonable suspicion 'that the performance of the search may produce evidence to support [an alleged violation of Appellant's parole].' . . . [T]he reasonable-suspicion aspect of the policy remains reasonable under the Fourth Amendment. . . . Reasonable suspicion is based on the totality of the circumstances and has been defined as requiring articulable reasons and a particularized and objective basis for suspecting the particular person of criminal activity. The government argues that [officer] had reasonable suspicion that [defendant] did not live at his reported residence, in violation of a probation condition. . . . [T]he government relies on the following facts as evidence that [defendant] did not live at his reported address: (1) [defendant] was not present during the three times that [officer] visited [defendant's] reported address; (2) [defendant] was unemployed and received SSI payments; (3) in [officer's] experience, it is common for a probationer not to live at the address he reports to his probation officer; and (4) [defendant] appeared nervous when [officer] informed him that two probation officers would accompany him home to verify his residence. . . . [T]hese facts and the inferences that [officer] drew from them are inadequate to constitute reasonable suspicion

1203

that [defendant] no longer lived at his reported residence. . . .Because the government has pointed not to 'articulable reasons' and 'a particularized and objective basis' that [defendant] violated the residency condition of his probation but instead to a chain of tenuous inferences, we hold that the officers did not have the requisite reasonable suspicion to conduct the search." *U.S. v. Henry*, 429 F.3d 603, 2005 FED App. 0450P (6th Cir. 2005).

- "Although the parole officer is interested in the parolee's rehabilitation, the officer is also charged with monitoring compliance with various restrictions, including restrictions on the use of drugs. As in this case, parole officers often work closely with the police. Exempting evidence illegally obtained by a parole officer from the exclusionary rule would greatly increase the temptation to use the parole officer's broad authority to circumvent the Fourth Amendment. We therefore hold that evidence obtained by a parole officer in violation of the Fourth Amendment must be suppressed in a subsequent criminal proceeding." *U.S. v. Payne*, 181 F.3d 781, 788, 1999 FED App. 0229P (6th Cir. 1999).

- "A probation officer need not have a warrant to conduct a search of a probationer where the probation officer is properly carrying out her official responsibilities. Furthermore, police officers and probation officers can work together and share information to achieve their objectives. However, it is impermissible for a probation search to serve as subterfuge for a criminal investigation." *U.S. v. Martin*, 25 F.3d 293, 296, 1994 FED App. 0154P (6th Cir. 1994).

Seventh Circuit

- "The difference between those in custody and those under supervision is a distinction without a difference for the purposes of the DNA Act and the Fourth Amendment. Individuals under supervision are subject to control by the state, although to a lesser degree than those incarcerated . . . Those under supervised release 'do not enjoy 'the absolute liberty to which every citizen is entitled, but only . . . conditional liberty properly dependent on observance of special restrictions' . . . we conclude that because 'DNA testing of [supervised releasees] is ultimately for a law enforcement goal, it seems to fit within the special needs analysis the [Supreme] Court has developed for drug testing and searches of probationers' homes, since it is not undertaken for the investigation of a specific crime.'" *U.S. v. Hook*, 471 F.3d 766 (7th Cir. 2006), aff'd, 2006 WL 5152924 (N.D. Ill. 2006).

- "It is a long-recognized principle that the contours of the Fourth Amendment's protection against unreasonable searches are defined by society's conception of an individual's reasonable expectation of privacy. . . . In the case of parolees and probationers, that expectation is significantly limited by the supervisory relationship and restrictions imposed on the individual by the State." *U.S. v. Jones*, 152 F.3d 680, 686 (7th Cir. 1998).

Eighth Circuit

- "Because 'ordinary Fourth Amendment analysis' applies to a probationary search, the parole officers' subjective purpose for the search is irrelevant to our analysis, and we look only at whether the parole officers' conclusion that reasonable suspicion existed was objectively reasonable." *U.S. v. Hamilton*, 591 F.3d 1017 (8th Cir. 2010).

- "The Probation Office moved to modify the conditions of (defendant's) release to require (defendant's) cooperation in the DNA collection. (Defendant) resisted the motion, arguing collection of his DNA constitutes an unreasonable search and seizure in violation of the Fourth Amendment . . . . Given probationers' diminished privacy rights . . . the minimal intrusion involved in obtaining DNA samples, and the legitimate governmental interest in using DNA as a crime investigating tool, we . . . . hold, based on the totality of the circumstances, the collection of DNA under the DNA Act for inclusion in the CODIS database does not constitute an unreasonable search and seizure in violation of the Fourth Amendment." *U.S. v. Kraklio*, 451 F.3d 922 (8th Cir. 2006).

- "A probationer's home, like anyone else's, is protected by the Fourth Amendment's requirement that searches be reasonable. . . . Nevertheless, officers may search a person's home without a warrant based on probable

cause when special needs, beyond the normal need for
law enforcement, make the warrant and probable-cause
requirement impracticable. . . . A state's operation of a
probation system presents special needs. . . . Because
probationers enjoy only conditional liberty properly dependent on observance of special probation restrictions
. . . states may closely supervise probationers and
impinge on their privacy to a greater extent than the
general public to ensure the probationer observes the
restrictions. . . . The search of a probationer's home
without a warrant and with less than probable cause
does not violate the Fourth Amendment if the search is
conducted under state probation regulations that satisfy
the Fourth Amendment's reasonableness standard. . . .
In other words, regulations may establish reasonableness for probationary searches." *U.S. v. Vincent*, 167
F.3d 428, 430 (8th Cir. 1999).
- "We agree that a parole search is unlawful when it is
nothing more than a ruse for a police investigation.
. . . Parole and police officers may work together,
however, provided the parole officer is pursuing parole-
related objectives and is not merely a stalking horse for
the police." *U.S. v. McFarland*, 116 F.3d 316, 318 (8th
Cir. 1997).

Ninth Circuit

- "The requirement under DNA Analysis Backlog Elimination Act of 2000 that certain federal offenders who
were on parole, probation, or supervised release submit
to compulsory deoxyribonucleic acid (DNA) profiling, in
the absence of individualized suspicion that they had
committed additional crimes, is reasonable and does not
violate the Fourth Amendment. Reliance on a totality of
the circumstances analysis to uphold compulsory DNA
profiling of convicted offenders both comports with the
Supreme Court's recent precedents and is in concert
with the requirements of the Fourth Amendment."
Ellison v. Nevada, 299 Fed. Appx. 730 (9th Cir. 2008).
- "Defendant . . . appeals several conditions of supervised
release imposed as part of his sentence, following his
conviction by guilty plea for counterfeiting United
States federal reserve notes . . . We have made clear
that the government bears the burden of showing that

a discretionary condition of supervised release is appropriate in a given case . . . Even if a proposed condition meets this requirement, it still must "involve 'no greater deprivation of liberty than is reasonably necessary for the purposes' of supervised release"-that is, to achieve deterrence, public protection, or offender rehabilitation . . . Condition # 5 requires that (defendant) seek and obtain approval from his probation officer before using any particular computer or computer-related device, internet-service provider, or computer or internet account-such as a screen user name or email account . . . The breadth of condition # 5 is not reasonably related to the nature and circumstances of (defendant)'s counterfeiting offense or (defendant)'s history and characteristics . . . The government . . . asserts that condition # 6 is reasonably related to (defendant)'s offense. (A)s currently written the search and seizure provision purports to extend to "[a]ll computers, computer-related devices, and their peripheral equipment, used by the defendant" . . . Ostensibly, this includes machines used for work or personal purposes, whether owned by (defendant) or by others . . . Because (defendant) cannot be left to guess about the intended meaning of the terms of his supervised release, clarification is required . . . A computer monitoring condition in some form may be reasonable. However, to comply with the Fourth Amendment, it must be narrowly tailored-producing no greater deprivation of liberty than is reasonably necessary. At present, the text gives no indication as to what kinds or degrees of monitoring are authorized-and, as courts have noted, monitoring software and/or hardware takes many forms, with greatly varying degrees of intrusiveness . . . . The Supreme Court founded its holding in *Samson* on the conclusion that under a parole-search statute, such as California's, parolees do 'not have an expectation of privacy that society would recognize as legitimate' . . . If under the California parole-search statute, a parolee has no expectation of privacy in his person, we reason that a parolee has no legitimate expectation of privacy in his residence either, at least when the parolee is present. Any other rule would diminish the protection to society given by the search condition of parole, permitting search at any time." *U.S. v. Lopez*, 474 F.3d 1208 (9th Cir. 2007) (overruled on other grounds by, U.S. v. King, 687 F.3d 1189 (9th Cir. 2012)).

- "Every circuit to consider a Fourth Amendment challenge to the 2004 [amendment to the DNA] Act has reached the same conclusion: collecting DNA from nonviolent felons as authorized by the Act does not violate the Fourth Amendment . . . . The majority of circuits adopt a "totality of the circumstances" framework . . ., which examines the totality of the circumstances to determine whether a search is reasonable . . . Whether a search is reasonable is determined by assessing . . . the degree to which it intrudes upon an individual's privacy . . . and . . . the degree to which it is needed for the promotion of legitimate governmental interests . . . [A]s a convicted felon who currently continues to serve his term of supervised release, [the defendant] has a diminished privacy interest in the collection of his DNA for identification purposes . . . In sum, we . . . hold that in the case before us, requiring [the defendant] to comply with the 2004 amendment to the DNA Act is constitutional because the government's significant interests in identifying supervised releasees, preventing recidivism, and solving past crimes outweigh the diminished privacy interests that may be advanced by a convicted felon currently serving a term of supervised release." *U.S. v. Kriesel*, 508 F.3d 941 (9th Cir. 2007).

- "[I]n order to avoid any constitutional problems with § 3583(i), we construe it to mean that not all warrants or summonses will extend the district court's jurisdiction to revoke supervised release. Instead, the warrant issued must have been based upon sworn allegations that the person violated a condition of supervised release. The government argues that a parole violation warrant may issue without 'probable cause' supported by 'oath or affirmation' because parolees are subject to lesser or no Fourth Amendment protections. We disagree. Although, while on supervised release, [the defendant] was subject to lesser Fourth Amendment protection, he was nonetheless protected by the Fourth Amendment. The cases dealing with lesser Fourth Amendment protection are generally concerned with which searches and seizures are reasonable without a warrant. The cases do not address whether a warrant for violation of the terms of release must comply with the Warrant Clause. Here, by statute, a warrant was required to extend the court's jurisdiction. Unlike the Fourth Amendment's malleable restriction on unreasonable searches and seizures, the Warrant Clause is exceptionally clear and provides that 'no Warrants shall issue, but upon probable cause, supported by Oath or affirmation.' Thus while certain searches may be permissible when there is less than probable cause, under the Fourth Amendment, no warrant is valid unless there is probable cause supported by sworn facts." *U.S. v. Vargas-Amaya*, 389 F.3d 901, 906–07 (9th Cir. 2004) (citations omitted).

- "... [I]n order to determine if a parole search is objectively reasonable, we are required to balance the privacy interests of a parolee against the government's interest in the search. ... [Defendant's] expectation of privacy in his own home is not wholly defeated by virtue of his parole status. As the Supreme Court has recognized, 'A probationer's home, like anyone else's, is protected by the Fourth Amendment's requirement that searches be reasonable.'... It is thus too late in the day to assert that searches of parolees by their parole officers present no Fourth Amendment issues. Rather, such searches may be held illegal and the evidence obtained therefrom suppressed unless they pass muster under the Fourth Amendment test of reasonableness. ... It is true that [defendant's] parole status reduces the 'expectation of privacy... that society is prepared to recognize as reasonable.' However, a *reduced* expectation of privacy is substantially different from an *extinguished* expectation of privacy. ... We... reject the argument that a blanket 'Fourth Waiver' parole condition [agreeing to searches at any time as a condition of parole] eliminates a parolee's expectation of privacy so as to render any parole search reasonable. ... Under the circumstances of a parole search pursuant to a 'Fourth Waiver' condition, ... a search could be reasonable without strict adherence to the ordinary probable cause requirements. ... [R]easonable suspicion provide[s] a sufficiently high probability of criminal conduct to render the overall

balance reasonable and the search valid. ... [T]he fact
that a parole search invades the home must weigh heavily in the 'totality of the circumstances' that determines
whether such a search is reasonable. ... The Supreme
Court's 'special needs' jurisprudence... does not support
a different conclusion. ... Because permitting a suspicionless search of [defendant's] residence would offend
both the protected status of the home and the bar
against suspicionless searches for evidence of criminal
conduct, we conclude that some individualized suspicion
was required here. The appropriate standard in such
cases is reasonable suspicion. ... [A] search of a parolee's
home pursuant to a parole condition is reasonable only
if it is supported by reasonable suspicion. ... [A]
compulsory parole condition may not serve as a consent
to engage in otherwise unreasonable searches, and that
[defendant] therefore did not consent to the parole
search of his home. *U.S. v. Crawford*, 323 F.3d 700 (9th
Cir. 2003), on reh'g en banc, 372 F.3d 1048 (9th Cir.
2004).

- "A probation search is permissible if conducted pursuant to a state law that satisfies the Fourth Amendment's
reasonableness standard. . . . The Fourth Amendment's
reasonableness standard balances the special law
enforcement needs supporting the state law scheme
against the probationer's privacy interests. Wisconsin's
scheme met this test in *Griffin* because it required reasonable grounds to support a search." *U.S. v. Conway*,
122 F.3d 841, 842 (9th Cir. 1997).

- "With respect to probationers, we have long recognized
that the legality of a warrantless search depends upon
a showing that the search was a true probation search
and not an investigation search. . . . Unlike an investigation search, a probation search should advance the
goals of probation, the overriding aim of which is to
give the [probationer] a chance to further and to demonstrate his rehabilitation while serving a part of his
sentence outside the prison walls. . . . While the warrantless search of a probationer's home need not necessarily be initiated, conducted, or even supervised by a
probation officer to qualify as a probation search, it cannot be a mere subterfuge enabling the police to avoid
having to obtain a search warrant (oftentimes character-

ized as using probation officers as stalking horses for the police)." *U.S. v. Ooley*, 116 F.3d 370, 372 (9th Cir. 1997).

- "While parolees and probationers have greater privacy interests than prisoners, they do not enjoy the same degree of privacy expectations as the ordinary citizen. In some cases, probation officers may search probationers without obtaining a warrant and under circumstances when there is less than probable cause. However, the search must be reasonable and must be based upon the probation officer's reasonable belief that it is necessary to the performance of her duties." *Portillo v. U.S. Dist. Court for Dist. of Arizona*, 15 F.3d 819, 823 (9th Cir. 1994).

Tenth Circuit

- "A parolee's home, like anyone else's, is protected by the Fourth Amendment's requirement that searches be reasonable. But there are exceptions to the warrant and probable-cause requirements for searches of probationers and parolees and their homes. One such exception authorizes warrantless searches without probable cause (or even reasonable suspicion) when the totality of the circumstances renders the search reasonable. We have explained that this exception is predicated on (1) the reduced (or absent) expectation of privacy that the Court would recognize for probationers and parolees and (2) the needs of law enforcement. . . . Under Kansas law, a warrantless search of a parolee must be supported by reasonable suspicion. . . . Under the totality of the circumstances, we conclude that the search at issue here was reasonable, because (1) as a parolee, [the defendant] had a diminished expectation of privacy; (2) there was reliable information that [the defendant] had violated his parole and was involved with distributing drugs, which supports a reasonable suspicion to search the residence; and (3) the State had a strong interest in monitoring [the defendant's] behavior and preventing his recidivism, especially in light of his recent parole violations." *U.S. v. Mabry*, 728 F.3d 1163 (10th Cir. 2013) (internal citations omitted).
- "[The defendant] contends that the search was not lawful because it did not comply with Kansas Department

of Corrections Internal Management Policy and Procedure Section 14-164 III(a)(1), which requires an SEO
[Special Enforcement Officer] executing an arrest warrant to get prior approval from a supervisor to search
the residence. Under the totality of the circumstances,
the failure to comply with state policies governing
searches of parolees is a factor to consider. . . . In this
case, when considered in light of the totality of the circumstances, the alleged failure to get prior permission
from a supervisor had a minimal impact on [the
defendant's] expectation of privacy and the State's interest in supervising him. In light of the information
regarding [the defendant's] recent parole violations and
the conditions at the residence, the officers possessed a
reasonable suspicion that [the defendant] had violated
his parole, and his limited expectation of privacy was
outweighed by the State's strong interest in monitoring
his behavior and preventing his recidivism." *U.S. v.
Mabry*, 728 F.3d 1163 (10th Cir. 2013).

- "The Supreme Court has created two exceptions to the
Fourth Amendment's warrant requirement in the
context of parolee searches . . . Neither this Court nor
the Supreme Court has, however, blessed a search by
law enforcement acting independently of the parole officer under this rationale . . . Even evaluating these
factors based on the totality of the circumstances, as we
must . . . we cannot agree with the district court that
the officers had reasonable suspicion to search (defendant's) home without consent, without the presence of a
parole officer, and in violation of Kansas Department of
Corrections rules governing parolee searches." *U.S. v.
Freeman*, 479 F.3d 743 (10th Cir. 2007).

- "All of the Plaintiffs were convicted of non-violent
felonies . . . Given the Plaintiffs' diminished privacy
rights, the minimal intrusion involved in obtaining a
DNA sample, and the Act's restrictive provisions, and
given the legitimate governmental interests in accurately identifying offenders, solving past and future
crimes, and combating recidivism, we hold that collecting and profiling the Plaintiffs' DNA, as authorized and
regulated by the DNA Analysis Backlog Elimination
Act of 2000, as amended, does not violate the Fourth
Amendment. In doing so, we align ourselves with the

overwhelming weight of authority on this issue." *Banks v. U.S.*, 490 F.3d 1178 (10th Cir. 2007).

- "Generally, law enforcement officials should conduct searches pursuant to a warrant supported by probable cause. . . . The Supreme Court, however, has recognized exceptions to the warrant requirement for certain special needs of law enforcement, including a state's parole system. . . . Accordingly, a warrantless search of a parolee's residence will satisfy the Fourth Amendment's reasonableness requirement to the extent parole agents carry it out pursuant to state law which itself satisfies the Fourth Amendment's reasonableness requirement." *U.S. v. Cantley*, 130 F.3d 1371, 1375 (10th Cir. 1997).

- "Parolees do not enjoy the absolute liberty to which every citizen is entitled, but only conditional liberty properly dependent on observance of special parole restrictions. These restrictions are designed to ensure rehabilitation and protect the public. These twin aims justify the state limiting a parolee's Fourth Amendment rights and consequent expectations of privacy. To determine the lawfulness of a warrantless search, we balance the parolee's expectations of privacy against the state's interests to determine the level of individualized suspicion necessary to support a warrantless search. The search will satisfy the Fourth Amendment's reasonableness requirement to the extent parole agents carried it out pursuant to state law which itself satisfies the Fourth Amendment's reasonableness requirement." *U.S. v. Lewis*, 71 F.3d 358, 361 (10th Cir. 1995).

§ 30:3 Prisoners: Prisoners have very limited Fourth Amendment protection

Supreme Court

- "In addressing this type of constitutional claim courts must defer to the judgment of correctional officials unless the record contains substantial evidence showing their policies are an unnecessary or unjustified response to problems of jail security. . . . [A] regulation impinging on an inmate's constitutional rights must be upheld 'if it is reasonably related to legitimate penological interests.' . . . The Court [in *Wolfish*] explained that there is no mechanical way to determine whether intrusions on an inmate's privacy are reasonable. The need for a particular search must be balanced against the resulting invasion of personal rights. . . . The Court has also recognized that deterring the possession of contraband depends in part on the ability to conduct searches without predictable exceptions. . . . Officers who interact with those suspected of violating the law have an 'essential interest in readily administrable rules.' " *Florence v. Board of Chosen Freeholders of County of Burlington*, 566 U.S. 318, 132 S. Ct. 1510, 1513–16, 1522, 182 L. Ed. 2d 566 (2012) (citations omitted).

- "The Court has held that deference must be given to the officials in charge of the jail unless there is 'substantial evidence' demonstrating their response to the situation is exaggerated." *Florence v. Board of Chosen Freeholders of County of Burlington*, 566 U.S. 318, 132 S. Ct. 1510, 1518, 182 L. Ed. 2d 566 (2012).

- "[W]e hold that society is not prepared to recognize as legitimate any subjective expectation of privacy that a prisoner might have in his prison cell and that, accordingly, the Fourth Amendment proscription against unreasonable searches does not apply within the confines of the prison cell. The recognition of privacy rights for prisoners in their individual cells simply cannot be reconciled with the concept of incarceration and the needs and objectives of penal institutions." *Hudson v. Palmer*, 468 U.S. 517, 525–26, 104 S. Ct. 3194, 82 L. Ed. 2d 393 (1984).

- "[W]e have previously considered not only a Fourth Amendment challenge but a due process challenge to a room search procedure almost identical to that used at Central Jail, and we sustained the practice on both scores. We have no reason to reconsider that issue; the identical arguments made by respondents here were advanced by the respondents in *Bell*. The security concerns that we held justified the same restriction in *Wolfish* are no less compelling here." *Block v. Rutherford*, 468 U.S. 576, 591, 104 S. Ct. 3227, 82 L. Ed. 2d 438 (1984).

- "It may well be argued that a person confined in a detention facility has no reasonable expectation of privacy with respect to his room or cell and that therefore the Fourth Amendment provides no protection for such a person. In any case, given the realities of institutional confinement, any reasonable expectation of privacy that a detainee retained necessarily would be of a diminished scope. Assuming, *arguendo,* that a pretrial detainee retains such a diminished expectation of privacy after commitment to a custodial facility, we nonetheless find that the room-search rule does not violate the Fourth Amendment." *Bell v. Wolfish*, 441 U.S. 520, 556–57, 99 S. Ct. 1861, 60 L. Ed. 2d 447 (1979).

- "A detention facility is a unique place fraught with serious security dangers. Smuggling of money, drugs, weapons, and other contraband is all too common an occurrence. And inmate attempts to secrete these items into the facility by concealing them in body cavities are documented in this record. We do not underestimate the degree to which these searches may invade the personal privacy of inmates. Nor do we doubt, as the District Court noted, that on occasion a security guard may conduct the search in an abusive fashion. Such abuse cannot be condoned. The searches must be conducted in a reasonable manner. But we deal here with the question whether visual body-cavity inspections as contemplated by the [prison] rules can *ever* be conducted on less than probable cause. Balancing the significant and legitimate security interests of the institution against the privacy interests of the inmates, we conclude that they can." *Bell v. Wolfish*, 441 U.S. 520, 559–60, 99 S. Ct. 1861, 60 L. Ed. 2d 447 (1979).

Second Circuit

- "The special needs exception also applies to the prison setting. While convicted prisoners do not forfeit all constitutional protections by reason of their conviction and confinement, the rights they retain are subject to restrictions dictated by concerns for institutional security, order, and discipline." *Roe v. Marcotte*, 193 F.3d 72, 78 (2d Cir. 1999).

Third Circuit

- "Prisoners do not have a right to privacy and freedom from unreasonable searches during incarceration. . . .

Seizure of [petitioner's] legal property thus cannot constitute a Fourth Amendment violation." *Tindell v. Beard*, 351 Fed. Appx. 591 (3d Cir. 2009).

Fifth Circuit

- "The extraction of blood from a prisoner to collect a DNA sample implicates Fourth Amendment rights. Nonetheless, collection of DNA from prisoners under the DNA Act is reasonable under the Fourth Amendment." *Groceman v. U.S. Dept. of Justice*, 354 F.3d 411 (5th Cir. 2004).

- "A prisoner's rights are diminished by the needs and exigencies of the institution in which he is incarcerated. He thus loses those rights that are necessarily sacrificed to legitimate penological needs. . . . However, searches and seizures conducted of prisoners must be reasonable under all the facts and circumstances in which they are performed. . . . We must balance the need for the particular search against the invasion of the prisoner's personal rights caused by the search. . . . We must consider the scope of the particular intrusion, the manner in which it is conducted, the justification for initiating it, and the place in which it is conducted." *Moore v. Carwell*, 168 F.3d 234, 236–37 (5th Cir. 1999).

Sixth Circuit

- " '[A] strip search, by its very nature, constitutes an extreme intrusion upon personal privacy.' The act of a stranger examining the most private areas of one's body 'is "an offense to the dignity of the individual" that is "undoubtedly humiliating and deeply offensive to many[.]" ' Intrusive under ideal circumstances, strip searches are especially humiliating when they are conducted in front of other inmates: 'The wider an audience for a strip search, the more humiliating it becomes, especially when the stripped individual is exposed to bystanders who do not share the searching officers' institutional need to view her unclothed.' The same applies to strip searches conducted in a discourteous manner. . . .. These basic principles teach us that the Registry searches plaintiff endured constituted a significant intrusion into her bodily privacy. Graham's visual inspections of plaintiff's naked body, though only skin-deep, constituted a profound intrusion into her personal privacy, an intrusion only magnified by the fact that plaintiff was exposed to several other inmates during each search. Moreover, plaintiff testified that, while she did not believe Graham intended to humiliate or harass her, Graham made several rude comments about her body odor and hygiene, saying she '[s]mells like a funky monkey' and telling her she needed to clean herself better. These comments, while not dispositive of reasonableness, 'implicate the dignitary interest "inherent in the privacy component of the Fourth Amendment's proscription against unreasonable searches."' Taken together, the scope, manner, and location of the searches overwhelmingly support the conclusion that the searches plaintiff endured were especially intrusive. . .. Nevertheless, the nature of the intrusion is only part one of the inquiry. An intrusive search is not necessarily an unreasonable one, especially in the corrections setting, where an inmate's interest in being free from privacy invasions must yield to the realities of operating a safe and effective corrections system. In every case, corrections officials and reviewing courts must balance the intrusion against 'the need for the particular search at issue' to determine whether the search is constitutionally tolerable. We proceed, then, to the second step of the analysis to determine whether defendants have asserted a legitimate penological. justification for conducting the group searches." *Sumpter v. Wayne County*, 2017 WL 3568607, *5 (6th Cir. 2017) (citations omitted).

Seventh Circuit

- "Although the taking of a DNA sample is clearly a search, the Fourth Amendment does not proscribe all searches, only those that are unreasonable. In some instances where a search is not made pursuant to a warrant supported by probable cause, it may nonetheless be reasonable if it falls within an exception to the warrant requirement and is supported by some quantum of individualized suspicion. But even individualized suspicion is not always necessary to support a finding that a search is reasonable. Although the United States Supreme Court has yet to address the validity of DNA collection statutes under the Fourth Amendment, as we just noted, state and federal courts that have are almost unanimous in holding that these statutes do not violate the Fourth Amendment. Courts uphold these DNA collection statutes because the government interest in obtaining reliable DNA identification evidence for storage in a database and possible use in solving past and future crimes outweighs the limited privacy interests that prisoners retain. Also, courts generally conclude that the collection of biological samples is only a minimal intrusion on one's personal physical integrity. These courts find that the government has a special need in obtaining identity DNA samples. . . . Wisconsin's DNA collection statute is, we think, narrowly drawn, and it serves an important state interest. Those inmates subject to testing because they are in custody, are already 'seized,' and given that DNA is the most reliable evidence of identification—stronger even than fingerprints or photographs—we see no Fourth Amendment impediments to collecting DNA samples from them pursuant to the Wisconsin law. The Wisconsin law withstands constitutional attack under the firmly entrenched 'special needs' doctrine." *Green v. Berge*, 354 F.3d 675 (7th Cir. 2004).

- "So, does a prison inmate enjoy any protection at all under the Fourth Amendment against unreasonable searches and seizures? Although we acknowledge the tension between *Johnson* and *Canedy*, we think the answer is yes, but we hasten to add that given the considerable deference prison officials enjoy to run their institutions it is difficult to conjure up too many real-life scenarios where prison strip searches of inmates could be said to be unreasonable under the Fourth Amendment." *Peckham v. Wisconsin Dept. of Corrections*, 141 F.3d 694, 697 (7th Cir. 1998).

- "Lawful imprisonment necessarily makes unavailable many rights and privileges of the ordinary citizen, a retraction justified by the considerations underlying our penal system. But, though his rights may be diminished by the needs and exigencies of the institutional environment, a prisoner is not wholly stripped of constitutional protection when he is imprisoned for a crime. Thus, this court's precedents have long recognized that, while the

justifiable reasons for invading an inmate's privacy are
both obvious and easily established, the surrender of
privacy is not total and that some residuum meriting
constitutional protection survives the transfer into
custody. To this end, while the Supreme Court has
permitted prison officials to conduct body cavity
searches of prisoners after every visit with a person
from outside the prison, it has emphasized that the
searches must be conducted in a reasonable manner.
The judicial inquiry, then is to balanc[e] the significant
and legitimate security interests of the institution
against the privacy interests of the inmates." *Canedy v.
Boardman*, 16 F.3d 183, 185–87 (7th Cir. 1994).

<u>Ninth Circuit</u>

- "We have previously said that visual body cavity
  searches conducted after contact visits as a means of
  preventing prisoners' possession of weapons and contraband, even absent probable cause, have been found reasonable by the Supreme Court. [T]he prisoner bears the
  burden of showing that prison officials intentionally
  used exaggerated or excessive means to enforce
  security." *Thompson v. Souza*, 111 F.3d 694, 700 (9th
  Cir. 1997).

- "We conclude that where prison officials select a large
  number of inmates for testing based upon legitimate
  criteria, the danger discussed in *Storms* and other
  cases—that correctional officials could harass particular
  inmates by subjecting them to repeated tests—is wholly
  illusory. We refuse to accept the proposition that a urine
  test of so many inmates (in this case, 124) conducted at
  the same time, under the same conditions, could constitute harassment of one of the inmates." *Thompson v.
  Souza*, 111 F.3d 694, 702 (9th Cir. 1997).

- "[N]o prisoner should reasonably expect privacy in his
  outbound telephone calls. Although prisoners do not
  forfeit all their privacy rights at the jailhouse steps
  they do have those rights severely curtailed. In *United
  States v. Hearst* we rejected an inmate's Fourth Amendment challenge to the routine taping of telephone
  conversations on the grounds that such taping was reasonable we now hold that any expectation of privacy in
  outbound calls from prison is not objectively reasonable

and that the Fourth Amendment is therefore not triggered by the routine taping of such calls." *U.S. v. Van Poyck*, 77 F.3d 285, 290–91 (9th Cir. 1996).

Tenth Circuit

- "[W]hile obtaining DNA samples implicates Fourth Amendment concerns, it is reasonable in light of an inmate's diminished privacy rights, the minimal intrusion involved, and the legitimate government interest in using DNA to investigate and prosecute crimes." *Shaffer v. Saffle*, 148 F.3d 1180, 1181 (10th Cir. 1998).
- "Although we have stated that the frequency with which prison guards watch inmates of the opposite sex undressing, using toilet facilities, and showering is an important factor in assessing the constitutionality of prison practices we have also concluded that a prisoner's right to privacy may be violated by a single search." *Hayes v. Marriott*, 70 F.3d 1144, 1147 (10th Cir. 1995).

Eleventh Circuit

- "Because we believe that Georgia's legitimate interest in creating a permanent identification record of convicted felons for law enforcement purposes outweighs the minor intrusion involved in taking prisoners' saliva samples and storing their DNA profiles, given prisoners' reduced expectation of privacy in their identities, we. . . hold that the statute [requiring convicted, incarcerated felons to provide DNA samples for data bank] does not violate the Fourth Amendment." *Padgett v. Donald*, 401 F.3d 1273 (11th Cir. 2005).
- "Although prisoners have no Fourth Amendment right to be free from strip searches the Eighth Amendment prohibits the unnecessary and wanton infliction of pain. Thus, if strip searches are devoid of penological merit and imposed simply to inflict pain, the federal courts should intervene." *Harris v. Ostrout*, 65 F.3d 912, 915–16 (11th Cir. 1995).

§ 30:4   Prison visitors: Although prison visitors may have limited Fourth Amendment protection, strip searches of prison visitors must be based on particularized suspicion

First Circuit

- "Although a generous amount of deference is given to prison officials on matters of prison safety, security, and discipline it is clear that visitors do not relinquish their Fourth Amendment rights at the prison gates. Prison visitors retain the right to be free from unreasonable searches and seizures. The meaning of reasonableness for Fourth Amendment purposes is highly situational. A search that is reasonable in the prison environment may not be in other contexts less fraught with serious security dangers. The standard of reasonableness that governs searches in a given context depends, in general, upon a balancing of the need to search against the invasion which the search entails." *Wood v. Clemons*, 89 F.3d 922, 928 (1st Cir. 1996).

- "[A] strip search can hardly be characterized as a routine procedure or as a minimally intrusive means of maintaining prison security. Indeed, a strip search, by its very nature, constitutes an extreme intrusion upon personal privacy, as well as an offense to the dignity of the individual. Accordingly, a strip search cannot be justified absent some quantum of individualized suspicion. In determining the level of individualized suspicion against which to test the constitutionality of prison-visitor strip searches with a view to striking the proper balance between respecting the legitimate privacy expectations of prison visitors and the need to maintain prison security, courts have converged upon one common benchmark: the standard of reasonable suspicion." *Wood v. Clemons*, 89 F.3d 922, 928 (1st Cir. 1996).

- "[A] prison visitor confronted with the choice between submitting to a strip search or foregoing a visit cannot provide a legally cognizable consent. *Blackburn* rejected the argument that the visitor's right to leave rather than submit to search, or to decline to return after the first strip search, in any way affected the issue; for it is the very choice to which she was put that is constitutionally intolerable." *Cochrane v. Quattrocchi*, 949 F.2d 11, 14 (1st Cir. 1991).

Third Circuit

- "Because the government need not show probable cause or even reasonable suspicion to support a search under the special needs doctrine, the government must prove instead that its search meets a general test of 'reasonableness.' Under this standard, the constitutionality of a particular search is judged by balancing its intrusion on the individual's Fourth Amendment interests against its promotion of legitimate governmental interests beyond that of typical law enforcement. . . . [C]onsidering the relatively minor inconvenience of the searches, balanced against the [department of corrections] officials' special need to maintain the security and safety of the prison that rises beyond their general need to enforce the law, the prison officials' practice of engaging in suspicionless searches of prison visitors' vehicles is valid under the special needs doctrine. . . . The mere fact that a search may result in arrest and criminal prosecution, and thus have the ancillary effect of furthering ordinary law enforcement concerns, does not negate the applicability of the special needs doctrine. . . . We thus decline to hold unconstitutional the vehicle search program simply because [department] officials report any uncovered illegality to the police." *Neumeyer v. Beard*, 421 F.3d 210 (3d Cir. 2005).

Sixth Circuit

- "The natural extension of this principle is that prison authorities have much greater leeway in conducting searches of visitors. Visitors can be subjected to some searches, such as a pat-down or a metal detector sweep, merely as a condition of visitation, absent any suspicion. However, because a strip and body cavity search is the most intrusive search possible, courts have attempted to balance the need for institutional security against the remaining privacy interests of visitors. Those courts that have examined the issue have concluded that even for strip and body cavity searches prison authorities need not secure a warrant or have probable cause. However, the residual privacy interests of visitors in being free from such an invasive search requires that prison authorities have at least a reasonable suspicion that the visitor is bearing contraband before conducting such a search. [W]e do not think that a person consents to a strip and body cavity search by simply appearing at a visiting center. Instead, the same logic that dictates that such a search may be conducted only when there is reasonable suspicion also demands that the person to be subjected to such an invasive search be given the opportunity to depart." *Spear v. Sowders*, 71 F.3d 626, 630, 632, 1995 FED App. 0366P (6th Cir. 1995).

- "Absent independent evidence to support [the] alleged tip, status alone does not impart reasonable suspicion, nor does status combined with an anonymous tip and a tip from a non-existent person. This is especially true where neither the visitor nor the inmate had ever been suspected of previous smuggling activity and the corrections officer can not recall relaying the tip. The operative principle of Fourth Amendment is its prohibition against unreasonable searches and seizures. To allow the scant information presented in this case to justify an intrusive and humiliating strip search of a prison visitor renders the Fourth Amendment's protections meaningless." *Daugherty v. Campbell*, 33 F.3d 554, 557, 1994 FED App. 0285P (6th Cir. 1994).

- "The prison visitors' situation is analogous to that of air travellers going through airport security. Although they volunteer to board the airplane, they do not lose their right not to be subjected to something so invasive as a strip or body cavity search without so much as a hint of suspicion." *Long v. Norris*, 929 F.2d 1111, 1116 (6th Cir. 1991).

Seventh Circuit

- "In a long and unbroken series of decisions by our sister circuits stretching back to the early 1980s, it had become well established. . . .that strip searches of prison visitors were unconstitutional in the absence of reasonable suspicion that the visitor was carrying contraband." *Burgess v. Lowery*, 201 F.3d 942, 945, 85 A.L.R.5th 719 (7th Cir. 2000).

Eighth Circuit

- "Both *Hunter* and our subsequent case, *Smothers v. Gibson*, premise the State's ability to conduct warrantless strip searches of prison visitors on the State's interest in keeping contraband out of the prisons. The *Hunter* court expounded at length on the danger posed by visitors smuggling contraband into prisons, and this was its sole rationale for condoning warrantless strip searches. Nothing in the *Hunter* or *Smothers* cases suggests that prison visitors' fourth amendment rights not to be searched without a warrant are abridged after their visit and after the danger of smuggling has passed. The mere fact that this case and *Hunter* involved people who had gone to visit prisoners is a superficial similarity. That similarity does not justify an officer in relying on *Hunter* when the purpose for the *Hunter* rules does not exist." *Marriott By and Through Marriott v. Smith*, 931 F.2d 517, 520–21 (8th Cir. 1991).

Tenth Circuit

- "But every decision establishing a reasonable suspicion standard for searches of prison visitors has involved a strip search. A strip search is a far cry from the routine, rather nonintrusive search initially conducted by defendants at the roadblock. As this court has stated, the strip search of an individual by government officials, regardless how professionally and courteously conducted, is an embarrassing and humiliating experience. Requiring reasonable suspicion for strip searches of prison visitors is not inconsistent with our holding today that the routine preliminary search of plaintiffs and their vehicle, although executed without individualized suspicion, was reasonable." *Romo v. Champion*, 46 F.3d 1013, 1019 (10th Cir. 1995).

- "Prison visitors do not abandon their constitutional rights when they enter a penitentiary. To be sure, those visiting a prison cannot credibly claim to carry with them the full panoply of rights they normally enjoy. But neither may they constitutionally be made to suffer a wholesale loss of rights—nor even one commensurate with that suffered by inmates." *Boren v. Deland*, 958 F.2d 987, 988 (10th Cir. 1992).

Eleventh Circuit

- "Because of the character of prisoners and the nature of imprisonment, corrections facilities are volatile places, brimming with peril, places where security is not just an operational nicety but a matter of life or death importance. That is why the Supreme Court has decided that even when a prison restriction or practice infringes a specific constitutional guarantee, the practice must be evaluated in the light of the central objective of prison administration, safeguarding institutional security. Among the most critical security measures are those employed to keep contraband, like the loaded pistol and cocaine found in [defendant's] car, away from prison property and out of prison facilities. . . . There is a diminished expectation of privacy in an automobile to begin with. Subtract from that the reduction in privacy that one can reasonably expect when going onto prison grounds, and there is not much left. Whatever little expectation of privacy might otherwise remain is rendered negligible by the two signs warning visitors that cars entering the property are subject to search. [Defendant] drove past the two warning signs not once, which would have been enough, but eight times. She had no realistic expectation of privacy in the contents of her car. . . . [Defendant] contends that even if the search were reasonable had she insisted on completing her mission of picking up the inmate, it became unreasonable once she asked to leave without her car being searched. . . . Any policy that reduces the likelihood of a successful search will decrease the risk to the wrongdoer. A policy allowing the wrongdoer to back out on the brink of discovery reduces the risk to zero, leaving her free reign to probe the security measures until an opening is found." *U.S. v. Prevo*, 435 F.3d 1343 (11th Cir. 2006).

§ 30:5 Schools: Although the Fourth Amendment applies to searches conducted by school personnel, students have limited Fourth Amendment protection

Supreme Court

- "Perhaps the best that can be said generally about the required knowledge component of probable cause for a law enforcement officer's evidence search is that it raise a 'fair probability' or a 'substantial chance' of discovering evidence of criminal activity. (citations omitted) The lesser standard for school searches could as readily be described as a moderate chance of finding evidence of wrongdoing." *Safford Unified School Dist. No. 1 v.*

Redding, 557 U.S. 364, 129 S. Ct. 2633, 174 L. Ed. 2d
354, 245 Ed. Law Rep. 626 (2009).

- "The very fact of [plaintiff]'s pulling her underwear
away from her body in the presence of the two officials
who were able to see her necessarily exposed her breasts
and pelvic area to some degree, and both subjective and
reasonable societal expectations of personal privacy support the treatment of such a search as categorically
distinct, requiring distinct elements of justification on
the part of school authorities for going beyond a search
of outer clothing and belongings." *Safford Unified
School Dist. No. 1 v. Redding*, 557 U.S. 364, 129 S. Ct.
2633, 174 L. Ed. 2d 354, 245 Ed. Law Rep. 626 (2009).

- "We do mean, though, to make it clear that the *T.L.O.*
concern to limit a school search to reasonable scope
requires the support of reasonable suspicion of danger
or of resort to underwear for hiding evidence of wrongdoing before a search can reasonably make the quantum
leap from outer clothes and backpacks to exposure of
intimate parts. The meaning of such a search, and the
degradation its subject may reasonably feel, place a
search that intrusive in a category of its own demanding its own specific suspicions." *Safford Unified School
Dist. No. 1 v. Redding*, 557 U.S. 364, 129 S. Ct. 2633,
174 L. Ed. 2d 354, 245 Ed. Law Rep. 626 (2009).

- "Fourth Amendment rights, no less than First and
Fourteenth Amendment rights, are different in public
schools than elsewhere; the 'reasonableness' inquiry
cannot disregard the schools' custodial and tutelary
responsibility for children. For their own good and that
of their classmates, public school children are routinely
required to submit to various physical examinations,
and to be vaccinated against various diseases. Legitimate privacy expectations are even less with regard to
student athletes. Somewhat like adults who choose to
participate in a closely regulated industry, students
who voluntarily participate in school athletics have reason to expect intrusions upon normal rights and privileges, including privacy." *Vernonia School Dist. 47J v.
Acton*, 515 U.S. 646, 656–57, 115 S. Ct. 2386, 132 L. Ed.
2d 564, 101 Ed. Law Rep. 37 (1995).

- "Traditionally at common law, and still today, uneman-
cipated minors lack some of the most fundamental

rights of self-determination—including even the right of liberty in its narrow sense, i.e., the right to come and go at will. They are subject, even as to their physical freedom, to the control of their parents or guardians. When parents place minor children in private schools for their education, the teachers and administrators of those schools stand in loco parentis over the children entrusted to them. In T.L.O. we rejected the notion that public schools, like private schools, exercise only parental power over their students, which of course is not subject to constitutional constraints. While denying that the State's power over schoolchildren is formally no more than the delegated power of their parents, T.L.O. did not deny, but indeed emphasized, that the nature of that power is custodial and tutelary, permitting a degree of supervision and control that could not be exercised over free adults. Thus, while children assuredly do not shed their constitutional rights at the schoolhouse gate, the nature of those rights is what is appropriate for children in school." *Vernonia School Dist. 47J v. Acton*, 515 U.S. 646, 654–56, 115 S. Ct. 2386, 132 L. Ed. 2d 564, 101 Ed. Law Rep. 37 (1995).

- "In carrying out searches and other disciplinary functions pursuant to such policies, school officials act as representatives of the State, not merely as surrogates for the parents, and they cannot claim the parents' immunity from the strictures of the Fourth Amendment. [T]he Fourth Amendment applies to searches conducted by school authorities." *New Jersey v. T.L.O.*, 469 U.S. 325, 336–37, 105 S. Ct. 733, 83 L. Ed. 2d 720, 21 Ed. Law Rep. 1122 (1985).

- "A search of a child's person or of a closed purse or other bag carried on her person, no less than a similar search carried out on an adult, is undoubtedly a severe violation of subjective expectations of privacy. [S]choolchildren may find it necessary to carry with them a variety of legitimate, noncontraband items, and there is no reason to conclude that they have necessarily waived all rights to privacy in such items merely by bringing them onto school grounds. Against the child's interest in privacy must be set the substantial interest of teachers and administrators in maintaining discipline in the classroom and on school grounds. [T]he accommodation of the privacy interests of schoolchildren with the substantial need of teachers and administrators for freedom to maintain order in the schools does not require strict adherence to the requirement that searches be based on probable cause to believe that the subject of the search has violated or is violating the law. Rather, the legality of a search of a student should depend simply on the reasonableness, under all the circumstances, of the search." *New Jersey v. T.L.O.*, 469 U.S. 325, 337–39, 341, 105 S. Ct. 733, 83 L. Ed. 2d 720, 21 Ed. Law Rep. 1122 (1985).

- "Under ordinary circumstances, a search of a student by a teacher or other school official will be justified at its inception when there are reasonable grounds for suspecting that the search will turn up evidence that the student has violated or is violating either the law or the rules of the school. Such a search will be permissible in its scope when the measures adopted are reasonably related to the objectives of the search and not excessively intrusive in light of the age and sex of the student and the nature of the infraction." *New Jersey v. T.L.O.*, 469 U.S. 325, 341–42, 105 S. Ct. 733, 83 L. Ed. 2d 720, 21 Ed. Law Rep. 1122 (1985).

Second Circuit

- "We hold that where information possessed by a state officer would warrant a person of reasonable caution in the belief that a child is subject to the danger of abuse if not removed from school before court authorization can reasonably be obtained, the exigent circumstances doctrine too permits removal of the child without a warrant equivalent and without parental consent." *Tenenbaum v. Williams*, 193 F.3d 581, 605, 140 Ed. Law Rep. 24 (2d Cir. 1999).

Fourth Circuit

- "The Supreme Court has held that the existence of Fourth Amendment protections depends on whether the individual has a legitimate expectation of privacy in the thing or place to be searched. . . . . Like members of the public generally, schoolchildren enjoy a legitimate expectation of privacy in their persons and effects." *DesRoches by DesRoches v. Caprio*, 156 F.3d 571, 576, 129 Ed. Law Rep. 628 (4th Cir. 1998).

Fifth Circuit

- "[A]lthough the Fourth Amendment applies in schools, the nature of those rights is what is appropriate for children in school. . . .The reasonableness inquiry must take into account the schools' custodial and tutelary responsibility for children. . . .Furthermore, students in the school environment have a lesser expectation of privacy than members of the population generally." *Milligan v. City of Slidell*, 226 F.3d 652, 654–55, 147 Ed. Law Rep. 429 (5th Cir. 2000).

- "[The] fourth amendment right to be free from an unreasonable seizure. extend to seizures by or at the direction of school officials, but whether such a seizure is unreasonable depends on all relevant contextual circumstances. The Supreme Court has recognized the unique backdrop that schools present for the operation of the fourth amendment, specifically noting that the preservation of order and a proper educational environment requires close supervision of schoolchildren, as well as the enforcement of rules against conduct that would be perfectly permissible if undertaken by an adult. Thus, while school officials are subject to the limitations of the fourth amendment, the reasonableness of seizures must be determined in light of all of the circumstances, with particular attention being paid to whether the seizure was justified at its inception and reasonable in scope." *Hassan v. Lubbock Independent School Dist.*, 55 F.3d 1075, 1079, 100 Ed. Law Rep. 862 (5th Cir. 1995).

Sixth Circuit

- "A school official may detain a student if there is a reasonable basis for believing that the pupil has violated the law or a school rule; the detention must be reasonably related in scope to the circumstances which justified it in the first place." *S.E. v. Grant County Bd. of Educ.*, 544 F.3d 633, 238 Ed. Law Rep. 28 (6th Cir. 2008).

Seventh Circuit

- "Public high school students have a lesser expectation of privacy than the general public. However, students do not shed their constitutional rights at the schoolhouse door." *Joy v. Penn-Harris-Madison School Corp.*, 212 F.3d 1052, 1063, 144 Ed. Law Rep. 866 (7th Cir. 2000).

- "School officials do not need to establish probable cause to justify the search of a student; instead, such a search is permissible if it is both justified at its inception and reasonably related in scope to the circumstances which justified the interference in the first place. . . . To satisfy this requirement, a student's conduct must create a reasonable suspicion that a particular regulation or law has been violated, with the search serving to produce evidence of the violation." *Willis by Willis v. Anderson Community School Corp.*, 158 F.3d 415, 418, 130 Ed. Law Rep. 89 (7th Cir. 1998), as amended on denial of reh'g and reh'g en banc, (Oct. 28, 1998).

Eighth Circuit

- "Students presumptively have a legitimate, though limited, expectation of privacy in the personal belongings that they bring into public schools. Because subjecting students to full-scale, suspicionless searches eliminates virtually all of their privacy in their belongings, and there is no evidence in the record of special circumstances that would justify so considerable an intrusion, we hold that the search practice is unconstitutional." *Doe ex rel. Doe v. Little Rock School Dist.*, 380 F.3d 349, 191 Ed. Law Rep. 608 (8th Cir. 2004).

Ninth Circuit

- "In *New Jersey v. T.L.O.* . . . the Supreme Court held that school officials conducting student searches must act reasonably. The Court expressly left open whether individualized suspicion is an essential element of the reasonableness standard. . . . The Court has since approved a student search not based on individualized suspicion. . . ." *Smith v. McGlothlin*, 119 F.3d 786, 788, 120 Ed. Law Rep. 145 (9th Cir. 1997).

Tenth Circuit

- " 'Special needs' is the label attached to certain cases where special needs, beyond the normal need for law enforcement, make the warrant and probable-cause

requirement impracticable. In special needs cases, the
Court replaces the warrant and probable cause requirement with a balancing test that looks to the nature of
the privacy interest, the character of the intrusion, and
the nature and immediacy of the government's interest.
. . . At this stage in development of the doctrine, the
'special needs' category is defined more by a list of
examples than by a determinative set of criteria. Among
the cases said by the Court to involve 'special needs'
are: a principal's search of a student's purse for drugs
in school; a public employer's search of an employee's
desk; a probation officer's warrantless search of a
probationer's home; a Federal Railroad Administration
regulation requiring employees to submit to blood and
urine tests after major train accidents; drug testing of
United States Customs Service employees applying for
positions involving drug interdiction; schools' random
drug testing of athletes; and drug testing of public
school students participating in extracurricular
activities. The Supreme Court has not told us what,
precisely, this set of cases has in common, but the cases
seem to share at least these features: (1) an exercise of
governmental authority distinct from that of mere law
enforcement—such as the authority as employer, the in
loco parentis authority of school officials, or the post-
incarceration authority of probation officers; (2) lack of
individualized suspicion of wrongdoing, and concomitant
lack of individualized stigma based on such suspicion;
and (3) an interest in preventing future harm, generally
involving the health or safety of the person being
searched or of other persons directly touched by that
person's conduct, rather than of deterrence or punishment for past wrongdoing. It also appears significant
that each of these cases involved extraction of consent
through a threatened withholding of a benefit, rather
than lack of consent. It is not clear, therefore, that the
'special needs' doctrine has any place in this case
[involving nonconsensual physical examinations of children in the Head Start program]. To be sure, the Head
Start agency may have been exercising a form of in loco
parentis authority; there was no individualized suspicion of wrongdoing and hence no stigma from being
singled out for a search; and the stated purpose of the

examinations was to promote the health and educational readiness of the children. On the other hand, the claim in this case involves lack of consent rather than compelled consent. According to the plaintiffs, [defendant] simply used its power over the children to conduct the examinations. Had [defendant] instead required the parents to consent to an unscheduled examination, on condition of not permitting their children to enroll in the Head Start program, this case would more closely resemble a classic 'special needs' case. We need not resolve whether the 'special needs' doctrine applies, however, because it is plain that, if performed without the necessary consent, the searches were unconstitutional even if we employ the 'special needs' balancing test." *Dubbs v. Head Start, Inc.*, 336 F.3d 1194, 179 Ed. Law Rep. 92 (10th Cir. 2003).

Eleventh Circuit

- "The Supreme Court determined at the outset that the Fourth Amendment applied to searches conducted by school authorities. . . . The Court, however, rejected the proposition that searches within the school setting must be based on probable cause as that term is understood in the context of Fourth Amendment jurisprudence. . . . Specific application of the factors established to define the constitutionally permissible parameters of a school search—that is, that it be reasonably related to the objectives of the search and not excessively intrusive in light of the age and sex of the student and the nature of the infraction—is notably absent from the Court's discussion and conclusion with respect to T.L.O." *Jenkins by Hall v. Talladega City Bd. of Educ.*, 115 F.3d 821, 824–25, 118 Ed. Law Rep. 867 (11th Cir. 1997).

Chapter 31

Forfeiture

Research References

West's Key Number Digest

Constitutional Law ⚯278, 303, 311, 319.5; Double Jeopardy ⚯23 to 26; Drugs and Narcotics ⚯190 to 195; Evidence ⚯154; Fines ⚯1.3; Forfeitures ⚯1 to 5; Judgment ⚯549, 559, 648; Jury ⚯19

KeyCite®: Cases and other legal materials listed in KeyCite Scope can be researched through the KeyCite service on Westlaw®. Use KeyCite to check citations for form, parallel references, prior and later history, and comprehensive citator information, including citations to other decisions and secondary materials.

---

§ 31:1 Fourth Amendment: The prohibition against unreasonable searches and seizures and the exclusionary rule apply to forfeiture proceedings

Supreme Court

- "[T]he [quasi-criminal] nature of a forfeiture proceeding . . . and the reasons which led the Court to hold that the exclusionary rule is obligatory upon the States support the conclusion that the exclusionary rule is applicable to forfeiture proceedings such as the one involved here." *One 1958 Plymouth Sedan v. Com. of Pa.*, 380 U.S. 693, 702, 85 S. Ct. 1246, 14 L. Ed. 2d 170 (1965).

First Circuit

- "The courts have created various doctrines over the years intended to deal with the practical considerations of how best to effectuate the twin legislative objectives behind forfeiture: the deterrence of drug activities by forfeiture of property involved and the protection of the innocent from loss of their property interests by virtue of their association with drug criminals." *U.S. v. Real Property Located at 221 Dana Avenue, Hyde Park, MA*, 239 F.3d 78, 83 (1st Cir. 2001), on reh'g, 261 F.3d 65 (1st Cir. 2001).

Second Circuit

- "[W]hen a car is properly seized by the police pursuant to a forfeiture statute, the government has a greater possessory interest in the car than the owner, permitting law enforcement officers to search the seized vehicle without a warrant. . . . [L]aw enforcement officers may seize forfeitable vehicles from public places without a warrant if they have probable cause to believe that the vehicle is, in fact, subject to forfeiture. Thus. . . law enforcement officers who have probable cause to believe an automobile is subject to forfeiture may both seize the vehicle from a public place and search it without a warrant." *U.S. v. Gaskin*, 364 F.3d 438 (2d Cir. 2004).

- "[W]e hold that an illegal seizure of property does not immunize that property from forfeiture, that the property itself cannot be excluded from the forfeiture action, and that evidence obtained independent of the illegal seizure may be used in the forfeiture action." *U.S. v. $37,780 In U.S. Currency*, 920 F.2d 159, 163 (2d Cir. 1990).

Sixth Circuit

- "Absence of probable cause at the time of the seizure may result in the suppression of evidence in later proceedings, but the defendant property itself cannot be suppressed from the forfeiture action. In contrast, a failure to establish probable cause on the forfeiture issue will preclude forfeiture of the property altogether." *U.S. v. One 1974 Learjet 24D, Serial Number 24D-290, Mexican Registration XA-RMF*, 191 F.3d 668, 673, 1999 FED App. 0338P (6th Cir. 1999).

- "[W]here property declared by a federal statute to be forfeited because used in violation of federal law is seized by one having no authority to do so, the United States may adopt the seizure with the same effect as if it had originally been made by one duly authorized. [T]he forfeiture can proceed if the government can show probable cause with untainted evidence." *U.S. v. One (1) 1987 Mercury Marquis*, 909 F.2d 167, 168 (6th Cir. 1990).

Ninth Circuit

- "The exclusionary rule applies in civil forfeiture cases by barring the admission of evidence obtained pursuant to search and seizure in violation of the Fourth Amendment, as well as fruits of the poisonous tree." *U.S. v.*

$493,850.00 in U.S. Currency, 518 F.3d 1159 (9th Cir. 2008).

- "The burden of establishing probable cause is on the government. . . . To establish probable cause and pass the point of mere suspicion, the government must demonstrate by some credible evidence the probability that the seized asset was in fact connected to drugs. . . . The government cannot rely on suppressed evidence to establish probable cause." *U.S. v. Real Property Known As 22249 Dolorosa Street, Woodland Hills, Cal.*, 167 F.3d 509, 513 (9th Cir. 1999).

- "The Eighth Circuit has held that the appropriate remedy for the illegal seizure of forfeitable real property under *Good* is dismissal of the forfeiture action, with leave to file a new action if the statute of limitations has not run. The Second Circuit has followed the general rule that the illegal seizure of property, standing alone, will not immunize that property from forfeiture, and held that the only remedy for an illegal seizure of forfeitable property under the Fifth Amendment is suppression of any evidence impermissibly obtained as a result of the seizure." *U.S. v. Real Property Located at 20832 Big Rock Drive, Malibu, Cal. 902655*, 51 F.3d 1402, 1406 (9th Cir. 1995).

- "The mere fact that property was illegally seized does not immunize that property from forfeiture, we held that illegally seized property could not be introduced as evidence in a forfeiture proceeding: [A]ny evidence which is the product of an illegal search or seizure must be excluded in the forfeiture hearing. The Government must satisfy forfeiture requirements with untainted evidence. [T]he body or identity of a defendant or respondent in a criminal or civil proceeding is never itself suppressible as a fruit of an unlawful arrest, even if it is conceded that an unlawful arrest, search, or interrogation occurred. A similar rule applies in forfeiture proceedings directed against contraband or forfeitable property." *U.S. v. $191,910.00 in U.S. Currency*, 16 F.3d 1051, 1063 (9th Cir. 1994), *superseded by statute on another grounds*.

- "Seizures for the purpose of forfeiture are subject to the warrant requirement. Exigent circumstances, however, may excuse the failure to obtain a warrant." *U.S. v. Lingenfelter*, 997 F.2d 632, 640 (9th Cir. 1993).

Tenth Circuit

- "Although forfeiture proceedings are inherently civil in nature, they are not to be effectuated in derogation of one's constitutional rights. Thus, any defects in process used to secure the possession of defendant property may defeat the government's right to possession, inasmuch as the government will be barred from introducing evidence illegally seized in violation of the fourth amendment to prove a claim of forfeiture." *U.S. v. One Hundred Forty-Nine Thousand Four Hundred Forty-Two and 43/100 Dollars ($149,442.43) in U.S. Currency,* 965 F.2d 868, 872 (10th Cir. 1992).

§ 31:2   **Showing required: The government must show probable cause to believe the item subject to forfeiture was involved in criminal wrongdoing**

Supreme Court

- "[R]espondent contends that freezing the assets in question before he is convicted—and before they are finally adjudged to be forfeitable—raises distinct constitutional concerns. We conclude, however, that assets in a defendant's possession may be restrained in the way they were here based on a finding of probable cause to believe that the property will ultimately be proven forfeitable. Indeed, it would be odd to conclude that the Government may not restrain property, such as the home and apartment in respondent's possession, based on a finding of probable cause, when we have held that (under appropriate circumstances), the Government may restrain persons where there is a finding of probable cause to believe that the accused has committed a serious offense. Put another way: if the Government may, post-trial, forbid the use of forfeited assets to pay an attorney, then surely no constitutional violation occurs when, after probable cause is adequately established, the Government obtains an order barring a defendant from frustrating that end by dissipating his assets prior to trial." *U.S. v. Monsanto,* 491 U.S. 600, 616, 109 S. Ct. 2657, 105 L. Ed. 2d 512 (1989).

First Circuit

- "In practice, then, if the United States brings a forfeiture action against a parcel of real estate and a person claiming an interest in the real estate chooses to contest the forfeiture, the government bears the burden of demonstrating probable cause to support a belief that a nexus existed between the real estate and some specified illegal activity sufficient to justify forfeiture." *U.S. v. 15 Bosworth Street*, 236 F.3d 50, 54 (1st Cir. 2001).

Fourth Circuit

- "An unrebutted probable cause showing will suffice to justify the forfeiture." *U.S. v. Ahmad*, 213 F.3d 805, 809, 2001-2 U.S. Tax Cas. (CCH) P 50673, 89 A.F.T. R.2d 2002-2164 (4th Cir. 2000).

Sixth Circuit

- "To support a seizure, the government has the burden of showing probable cause that there was a connection between the defendant property and drug activity." *U.S. v. Real Property Known and Numbered as 415 East Mitchell Ave., Cincinnati, Ohio*, 149 F.3d 472, 476, 1998 FED App. 0217P (6th Cir. 1998).

Seventh Circuit

- "[A] court adjudicating a forfeiture claim employs a burden-shifting method of proof. . . .The government has the initial burden of establishing probable cause to believe that the property at issue has a connection with illegal drug activity and is therefore subject to forfeiture. . . .Probable cause exists if the government has established that the totality of the circumstances demonstrates a nexus between the property and illegal drug activity. . . .Once the government has met its burden, the ultimate burden shifts to the claimant to prove by a preponderance of the evidence that the property at issue has no connection with illegal drug activity and is therefore not subject to forfeiture." *U.S. v. Santiago*, 227 F.3d 902, 906 (7th Cir. 2000).
- "For the government to seize any property pursuant to § 981, it must first establish probable cause that the property was involved in an illegal transaction. . . . In order for the government to establish probable cause in a civil forfeiture case, it must demonstrate a reasonable

ground for the belief of guilt supported by less than prima facie proof but more than mere suspicion. . . . The government need not make an actual showing of illegality, but must only show a probability or substantial chance of criminal conduct. . . . The procedure for determining probable cause in civil forfeiture actions is similar to that for determining probable cause in a criminal setting; the court should look at the totality of the circumstances in making its decision." *U.S. v. U.S. Currency Deposited in Account No. 1115000763247 for Active Trade Co., Located at First Nat. Bank, Chicago, Ill.*, 176 F.3d 941, 944 (7th Cir. 1999).

- "Both the district court and the government base their belief that probable cause exists on seven undisputed factors: (1) an unusually large amount of cash was found at the pizzeria; (2) this large amount of cash was in small bill denominations; (3) this large amount of cash was unusually stored; (4) to date, no one has identified a legitimate source of the currency or explained the reason for the currency's unusual storage; (5) three unregistered handguns were found on the premises; (6) an informant identified a large amount of cocaine being delivered to the pizzeria (more on this later); and (7) a trained drug dog identified traces of narcotics on the defendant currency. In our opinion, none of these factors alone can constitute probable cause, and even taking them as true and considering them all together, they still do not constitute probable cause. . . . In sum, the government is unable to come up with the requisite narcotics-nexus to meet its initial burden of showing probable cause. . . . We reiterate that the government may not seize money, even half a million dollars, based on its bare assumption that most people do not have huge sums of money lying about, and if they do, they must be involved in narcotics trafficking or some other sinister activity." *U.S. v. $506,231 in U.S. Currency*, 125 F.3d 442, 452–54 (7th Cir. 1997).

Eighth Circuit

- "In a forfeiture action under section 881, the United States bears the initial burden of establishing probable cause to connect property to drug trafficking. . . . Establishing a connection to general criminality is not enough. . . . The government meets this burden by presenting evidence which creates more than a mere suspicion but less than prima facie proof that the seized property is related to drug trafficking." *U.S. v. $141,770.00 in U.S. Currency*, 157 F.3d 600, 603, 50 Fed. R. Evid. Serv. 148 (8th Cir. 1998).

Ninth Circuit

- "When a motion for return of property is made when the property in question is no longer needed for evidentiary purposes, either because trial is complete, the defendant has pleaded guilty, or the government has abandoned its investigation, the person from whom the property had been seized is presumed to have a right to its return and the government has the burden of demonstrating that it has a legitimate reason to retain the property by demonstrating that it is contraband or subject to forfeiture." *U.S. v. Harrell*, 530 F.3d 1051 (9th Cir. 2008).

- "Forfeiture actions . . . require the Government to provide the district court with a showing of probable cause for belief that a substantial connection exists between the property to be forfeited and the criminal activity. . . . This determination of probable cause is based on the aggregate of facts and may be established by circumstantial evidence. . . . The Government may establish probable cause by relying on otherwise inadmissible hearsay. . . . Probable cause to believe that the property is involved in some illegal activity is not enough-the government must have probable cause to believe that the property is involved in the activity subject to the specific forfeiture statute it invokes." *U.S. v. $405,089.23 U.S. Currency*, 122 F.3d 1285, 1289 (9th Cir. 1997).

- "Currency associated with drug trafficking is subject to forfeiture to the Government. . . . The Government must show probable cause that the currency seized . . . was specifically associated with drug trafficking, not just with illegal activity in general. . . . Determination of probable cause for forfeiture is based upon a totality of the circumstances or aggregate of facts test. . . . A finding of probable cause may be premised on the collective knowledge of all the officers working on the airport narcotics detail. . . . Moreover, because otherwise innocent-looking conduct may convey different messages to a trained observer, the experience and knowledge of the detail members can be taken into account when determining probable cause." *U.S. v. $129,727.00 U.S. Currency*, 129 F.3d 486, 489 (9th Cir. 1997).

Eleventh Circuit

- "We recently have reaffirmed that probable cause is the standard of proof the government must meet in forfeiture cases." *U.S. v. Land, Winston County*, 163 F.3d 1295, 1303 (11th Cir. 1998).

§ 31:3 Standing: A person claiming an interest in property which the government seeks to forfeit must demonstrate a possessory interest in the property

First Circuit

- "[C]ourts have held that an allegation of ownership and some evidence of ownership are together sufficient to establish standing to contest a civil forfeiture. . . . Courts generally do not deny standing to a claimant who is either the colorable owner of the res or who has any colorable possessory interest in it." *U.S. v. U.S. Currency, $81,000.00*, 189 F.3d 28, 35 (1st Cir. 1999).

Second Circuit

- "Although *Schwimmer* did not address whether a general creditor may achieve standing by virtue of being a bona fide purchaser for value we find it appropriate to extend *Schwimmer's* holding to answer this question of law in the negative. We therefore hold that, in order to have a Section 853(n)(6)(B) right, title or interest in the seized property, Appellants must demonstrate that they have a legal interest in the property as required by *Schwimmer*. [A]lthough general creditors can claim an interest in their debtors' estates, they cannot claim an interest in any particular asset that makes up that estate. In other words, the court intimated that an interest in property must be an interest in a particular, specific asset, as opposed to a general interest in an entire forfeited estate or account. Because petitioners lack an identifiable legal interest in the assets seized by the United States, they are general creditors who lack standing to contest the Order of Forfeiture." *U.S. v. Ribadeneira*, 105 F.3d 833, 836–37 (2d Cir. 1997).

- "A general creditor has no interest in a particular asset or particular funds that is either vested or superior to a defendant's. He may have a right to receive payment, but he does not have a property interest superior to defendant's in any particular asset or funds until he has obtained some judgment and secures that asset or those funds. At that point, he is no longer merely a general creditor. Thus, the property remains property of the defendant even as against the claim of a general creditor. The general creditor's interest therefore does not threaten to undermine the Court's jurisdiction over the property, and does not invalidate the order of forfeiture. Thus, a general creditor has no interest in particular assets or funds that warrants an amendment of an order of forfeiture under § 1963(1)(6)(A)." *U.S. v. Schwimmer*, 968 F.2d 1570, 1581, 23 Fed. R. Serv. 3d 224 (2d Cir. 1992).

Sixth Circuit

- "In order to contest a governmental forfeiture action. . . . [A] claimant must have a colorable ownership, possessory or security interest in at least a portion of the defendant property. . . . To contest a forfeiture action, an individual customarily bears the burden of demonstrating an interest in the seized item sufficient to satisfy the court of his standing. as a claimant." *U.S. v. $515,060.42 in U.S. Currency*, 152 F.3d 491, 497–98, 1998 FED App. 0161P (6th Cir. 1998).
- "With respect to Article III standing, a claimant must demonstrate a legally cognizable interest in the defendant property. A property interest less than ownership, such as a possessory interest, is sufficient to create standing." *U.S. v. Currency $267,961.07*, 916 F.2d 1104, 1107 (6th Cir. 1990).
- "[R]ecognition of state laws governing property rights does not contravene the federal forfeiture scheme, and that the application of state law is the most appropriate method of determining the interest of an innocent owner

under 21 U.S.C. § 881(a)(7)." *U.S. v. Certain Real Property Located at 2525 Leroy Lane, West Bloomfield, Mich.*, 910 F.2d 343, 347 (6th Cir. 1990).

Seventh Circuit

- "[S]tate law defines and classifies property interests for purposes of the forfeiture statutes." *U.S. v. One 1989 Stratford Fairmont*, 986 F.2d 177, 179 (7th Cir. 1993).

Eighth Circuit

- "Claimant to third-party rights to property that was subject to forfeiture, pursuant to defendant's plea asserting ownership of property and agreeing to forfeiture, lacked standing, under Article III case or controversy requirements, for Fourth Amendment challenge to seizure of property from claimant's residence, since claimant was not entitled to vicariously assert defendant's Fourth Amendment rights regarding search and seizure." *U.S. v. Porchay*, 533 F.3d 704 (8th Cir. 2008).
- "To manifest standing in the forfeiture context, a claimant must first show an ownership interest in the property. . . .An ownership interest is evidenced in a number of ways including showings of actual possession, control, title and financial stake." *U.S. v. 1998 BMW ""I" Convertible Vin No. WBABJ8324WEM 20855*, 235 F.3d 397, 399 (8th Cir. 2000).
- "Although an owner need not be a bona fide purchaser and ownership of personal property may be defined as having a possessory interest in the res, with its attendant characteristics of dominion and control these principles are inapplicable to this case. Possession of real property, even when coupled with an expectancy interest, does not equate with ownership in a forfeiture action. Ownership may be evidenced in a number of ways including showings of actual possession, title and financial stake." *U.S. v. One Parcel of Property Located at Tracts 10 and 11 of Lakeview Heights, Canyon Lake, Comal County, Tex.*, 51 F.3d 117, 120–21, 32 Fed. R. Serv. 3d 68 (8th Cir. 1995).
- "In order to have standing to contest a forfeiture, a claimant must prove that he or she has an ownership interest in the defendant property. An ownership interest, of course, may be evidenced in a number of ways

including showings of actual possession, control, title and financial stake. [B]are legal title by one who does not exercise dominion and control over the property is insufficient to establish ownership. A nominal owner who lacks possession of the defendant property and did not exercise dominion and control over it does not have an interest sufficient to have standing to challenge forfeiture." *U.S. v. One 1990 Chevrolet Corvette, VIN No. 1G1YY3384L5104361, with All Appurtenances and Attachments thereon,* 37 F.3d 421, 422 (8th Cir. 1994).

Ninth Circuit

• "To have standing to challenge a forfeiture, a claimant must allege that he has an ownership or other interest in the forfeited property." *U.S. v. Real Property Known As 22249 Dolorosa Street, Woodland Hills, Cal.,* 167 F.3d 509, 512 (9th Cir. 1999).

Eleventh Circuit

• "[T]he essential nature of forfeiture actions is such that the cause of action is not rendered moot by the Government settling with one potential claimant. A forfeiture proceeding is not an action against the claimant but rather is an *in rem* action against the seized property brought under the fiction that the property itself is guilty of facilitating the crime. By proceeding administratively with [another claimant], the Government merely settled with one party that had a claim to the money it was holding; it did not dispose of all possible claimants and did not judicially prosecute the underlying crime of which the property was accused. As long as the Government is still holding some of the property, it must give due process to parties claiming a right to have that property released. [Claimant], as a claimant to the property, had a right to insist that the Government file a judicial forfeiture complaint to contest the legality of the forfeiture. The Government still has possession of the property, thus [claimant's] injury is real and its claim is not moot." *Via Mat Intern. South America Ltd. v. U.S.,* 446 F.3d 1258 (11th Cir. 2006).

§ 31:4 Remission of forfeitures: Where the return of forfeited property is authorized, the claimant must show that he was not involved in criminal activity and that he exercised due care in controlling the property sought to be forfeited

Supreme Court

- "[A] long and unbroken line of cases holds that an owner's interest in property may be forfeited by reason of the use to which the property is put even though the owner did not know that it was to be put to such use. In *Calero-Toledo v. Pearson Yacht Leasing Co* the most recent decision on point, the Court concluded that the innocence of the owner of property subject to forfeiture has almost uniformly been rejected as a defense. Petitioner is in the same position as the various owners involved in the forfeiture cases beginning with *The Palmyra* in 1827. She did not know that her car would be used in an illegal activity that would subject it to forfeiture. But under these cases the Due Process Clause of the Fourteenth Amendment does not protect her interest against forfeiture by the government." *Bennis v. Michigan*, 516 U.S. 442, 446–49, 116 S. Ct. 994, 134 L. Ed. 2d 68 (1996).

- "[I]t would be difficult to reject the constitutional claim of an owner who proved not only that he was uninvolved in and unaware of the wrongful activity, but also that he had done all that reasonably could be expected to prevent the proscribed use of his property." *Calero-Toledo v. Pearson Yacht Leasing Co.*, 416 U.S. 663, 689, 94 S. Ct. 2080, 40 L. Ed. 2d 452, 1974 A.M.C. 1895 (1974).

- "When the forfeiture statutes are viewed in their entirety, it is manifest that they are intended to impose a penalty only upon those who are significantly involved in a criminal enterprise." *U.S. v. U.S. Coin and Currency*, 1971-1 C.B. 411, 401 U.S. 715, 721–22, 91 S. Ct. 1041, 28 L. Ed. 2d 434, 71-1 U.S. Tax Cas. (CCH) P 15979, 27 A.F.T.R.2d 71-1026 (1971).

First Circuit

- "Once the government carries its relatively modest

burden of showing probable cause, the devoir of persuasion shifts to the claimant, who must refute the government's prima facie case in one of two ways: either (1) by demonstrating that the property was not in fact used for the specified illegal activity, or (2) by proving that she (the claimant) neither knew about, nor consented to, the illicit activity." *U.S. v. 15 Bosworth Street*, 236 F.3d 50, 54 (1st Cir. 2001).

- "In a civil forfeiture case, lack of knowledge or consent is an affirmative defense. . . .Thus, the claimant bears the burden of proving the absence of knowledge or consent by a preponderance of the evidence." *U.S. v. 15 Bosworth Street*, 236 F.3d 50, 54 (1st Cir. 2001).

Second Circuit

- "Where it is undisputed that the claimant had knowledge of the drug-related activity, consent will be inferred unless the claimant can prove that he took all reasonable measures to rid the property of the illegal conduct. The sufficiency of a claimant's preventive actions involves a particularized case-by-case inquiry. Although claimants need not take heroic or vigilante measures to rid their property of narcotics activity they must take every action reasonable under the circumstances. Because the reasonableness test is used only to ascertain whether claimants have consented to the use of their property for illegal purposes, it is necessarily a subjective standard." *U.S. v. One Parcel of Property Located at 121 Allen Place, Hartford, Conn.*, 75 F.3d 118, 121 (2d Cir. 1996).

- "[T]hose who assert the innocent owner defense have unique access to evidence regarding such claims. They know precisely what information was brought to their attention and why facts of which owners are generally aware were unknown to them. If knowledge of drug transactions on the premises is conceded, they also know precisely what steps they took to prevent use of the premises for drug trafficking. Burden-shifting where one party has superior access to evidence on a particular issue is a common feature of our law." *U.S. v. One Parcel of Property Located at 194 Quaker Farms Road, Oxford, Conn.*, 85 F.3d 985, 990 (2d Cir. 1996).

- "Once the government has established probable cause

to believe the property has been used to facilitate such an offense, persons claiming to be innocent owners have the burden of proving, by a preponderance of the evidence, that the narcotics activity on the property occurred without their knowledge or, if they had knowledge of it, without their consent. Where an owner has engaged in willful blindness as to activities occurring on her property, her ignorance will not entitle her to avoid forfeiture." *U.S. v. Milbrand*, 58 F.3d 841, 844 (2d Cir. 1995).

Sixth Circuit

- "Upon a showing of probable cause, the burden of proof shifts to the claimant to demonstrate that the property is his and not the proceeds of drug transactions. The claimant may meet his burden by showing that the property was not the proceeds of illegal drug activities or that the claimant is an innocent owner and was unaware of the proceeds' criminal connection." *U.S. v. Dusenbery*, 201 F.3d 763, 766, 2000 FED App. 0017P (6th Cir. 2000).

Seventh Circuit

- "After the government makes an initial showing of probable cause, the burden shifts to the claimant to show, by a preponderance of the evidence, that the property is not subject to forfeiture, i.e. that it was not involved in an illegal transaction. . . . Without a sufficient rebuttal, the government's initial showing of probable cause will suffice to support the forfeiture." *U.S. v. U.S. Currency Deposited in Account No. 1115000763247 for Active Trade Co., Located at First Nat. Bank, Chicago, Ill.*, 176 F.3d 941, 945 (7th Cir. 1999).
- "Once the government meets its burden of establishing the existence of probable cause, the ultimate burden shifts to the claimant to prove by a preponderance of the evidence that the property is not subject to forfeiture by demonstrating that the property was not used in connection with drug activities. . . . If the claimant fails to rebut the government's proof, the probable cause showing, standing alone, will support a judgment of forfeiture. . . . The claimant, of course, need not do anything to rebut the government's proof if the govern-

ment's proof is insufficient to demonstrate the requisite nexus between the property and illegal narcotics activity." *U.S. v. $506,231 in U.S. Currency*, 125 F.3d 442, 451 (7th Cir. 1997).

Ninth Circuit

- "The government correctly points out that the burden lies entirely with the purchasers to establish that they are innocent owners. No threshold showing by the government is required." *U.S. v. Real Property at 2659 Roundhill Dr., Alamo, Cal.*, 194 F.3d 1020, 1027 (9th Cir. 1999).

Eleventh Circuit

- "Knowledge of an illegal activity may be attributed to a corporation only when the knowledge was obtained by an agent acting within the scope of his or her employment and for the benefit of the corporation. Acting within the scope of employment entails more than being on the corporate employer's premises, but rather also involves an intent to benefit the corporation. In sum, the case law suggests that the applicability of the innocent owner defense will often turn on the particular facts surrounding not the individual's ownership and authority over the corporate parcel, but rather whether the individual vested with such authority was acting within the scope of his corporate employment." *U.S. v. Route 2, Box 472, 136 Acres More or Less*, 60 F.3d 1523, 1527–28 (11th Cir. 1995).

§ 31:5 Due process constraints: Forfeiture proceedings are governed by the Due Process Clause but not the Double Jeopardy Clause of the Fifth Amendment

Supreme Court

- "*[I]n rem* civil forfeiture is a remedial civil sanction, distinct from potentially punitive *in personam* civil penalties such as fines, and does not constitute a punishment under the Double Jeopardy Clause." *U.S. v. Ursery*, 518 U.S. 267, 278, 116 S. Ct. 2135, 135 L. Ed. 2d 549 (1996).

- "In this case we consider whether a United States

District Court may strike the filings of a claimant in a forfeiture suit and grant summary judgment against him for failing to appear in a related criminal prosecution. The Court of Appeals for the Ninth Circuit held this to be a proper exercise of the District Court's inherent authority. We reverse. In an ordinary case a citizen has a right to a hearing to contest the forfeiture of his property, a right secured by the Due Process Clause. The question before us is whether the doctrine should be extended to allow a court in a civil forfeiture suit to enter judgment against a claimant because he is a fugitive from, or otherwise is resisting, a related criminal prosecution. The right of a citizen to defend his property against attack in a court is corollary to the plaintiff's right to sue there. For this reason we have held it unconstitutional to use disentitlement similar to this as punishment for rebellion against the United States We need not, and do not, intimate a view on whether enforcement of a disentitlement rule under proper authority would violate due process. It remains the case, however, that the sanction of disentitlement is most severe and so could disserve the dignitary purposes for which it is invoked. The dignity of a court derives from the respect accorded its judgments. That respect is eroded, not enhanced, by too free a recourse to rules foreclosing consideration of claims on the merits." *Degen v. U.S.*, 517 U.S. 820, 821–28, 116 S. Ct. 1777, 135 L. Ed. 2d 102 (1996).

- "The right to prior notice and a hearing is central to the Constitution's command of due process. We tolerate some exceptions to the general rule requiring predeprivation notice and hearing, but only in extraordinary situations where some valid governmental interest is at stake that justifies postponing the hearing until after the event. Whether the seizure of real property for purposes of civil forfeiture justifies such an exception requires an examination of the competing interests at stake, along with the promptness and adequacy of later proceedings." *U.S. v. James Daniel Good Real Property*, 510 U.S. 43, 53, 114 S. Ct. 492, 126 L. Ed. 2d 490 (1993).

First Circuit

- "[W]e are offered no reason to disagree with our sister

circuits that, to the extent a plaintiff may challenge on federal constitutional grounds the government's retention of personal property after a lawful initial seizure in circumstances such as these, that challenge sounds in the Fifth Amendment rather than in the Fourth Amendment. A different result may well obtain when the government seizes a person rather than property. But where property is concerned, it would seem that the Fifth Amendment's express protections for property provide the appropriate framework. In particular, the Takings Clause provides recourse where 'private property [is] taken for public use, without just compensation.'" *Denault v. Ahern*, 857 F.3d 76, 84 (1st Cir. 2017) (citations omitted).

- "Due process requires the government to afford an owner notice and an opportunity to be heard before civilly forfeiting his property. . . .but actual receipt of notice by the defendant is not automatically required. . . . .Rather, *Mullane* said that due process requires the provision of notice reasonably calculated, under all the circumstances, to apprise interested parties of the pendency of the action and afford them an opportunity to present their objections." *Whiting v. U.S.*, 231 F.3d 70, 76 (1st Cir. 2000).

Second Circuit

- "In addition to publishing notice of the seizure and its intent to forfeit, the government also must send written notice of seizure together with information on the applicable procedures . . . to each party who appears to have an interest in the seized article. . . . Because in a civil forfeiture case the interest of the property owner is potentially enormous . . . . the owner must be made aware of, and provided with a practical opportunity to challenge, the forfeiture." *Ikelionwu v. U.S.*, 150 F.3d 233, 237 (2d Cir. 1998).

Third Circuit

- "We hold that, while the government need not prove actual notice to the prisoner, if it chooses to rely on less than actual notice, it bears the burden of demonstrating the existence of procedures that are reasonably calculated to ensure that such notice will be given.

Thus, our rule requires the government to ensure that proper procedures are employed in the facilities where it chooses to house its prisoners." *U.S. v. One Toshiba Color Television*, 213 F.3d 147, 155, 46 Fed. R. Serv. 3d 1327 (3d Cir. 2000).

Sixth Circuit

- "Based upon the historic and continuing importance of the private interest at stake—the right to be free from governmental interference—and the absence of any convincing countervailing government needs, the Court held that, absent exigent circumstances, the Due Process clause requires the government to provide notice and a meaningful opportunity to be heard before seizing real property subject to civil forfeiture." *U.S. v. Real Property Located at 1184 Drycreek Road, Granville, Ohio 43023*, 174 F.3d 720, 727, 1999 FED App. 0153P (6th Cir. 1999).

Seventh Circuit

- "Notice of forfeiture by mail to the claimant's residence is inadequate if the government knew that the claimant would not receive it. . . .When the government mails a notice to an address at which it knows the claimant not to be, the notice typically violates due process because it is not reasonably calculated to apprise the claimant of the action. . . .Thus, the government violates due process when it purposely mails notice of forfeiture to the claimant's residence knowing that the claimant is incarcerated or in federal custody." *Krecioch v. U.S.*, 221 F.3d 976, 980–81 (7th Cir. 2000).

Eighth Circuit

- "[D]ue process requires that the government provide notice reasonably calculated, under all the circumstances to apprise interested parties of the pendency of a forfeiture action, and to afford the parties an opportunity to present their objections. . . . The means employed must be such as one desirous of actually informing the absentee might reasonably adopt to accomplish it. . . . Moreover, if the government is incarcerating the property owner when it initiates forfeiture proceedings, we have consistently held that fundamental fairness requires that the property owner or his or her counsel receive actual notice of the forfeiture in time to decide whether to compel the government to proceed by judicial condemnation." *U.S. v. Five Thousand Dollars in U.S. Currency*, 184 F.3d 958, 960, 44 Fed. R. Serv. 3d 1149 (8th Cir. 1999).

Eleventh Circuit

- "The Fifth Amendment. . .does not bar two prosecutions for the same conduct by separate sovereigns—in this case, the State of Florida and the United States. . . . Furthermore, despite holding that civil forfeitures can be punitive for Eighth Amendment purposes, the Supreme Court continues to hold to the view that civil in rem forfeiture actions are nonpunitive for Fifth Amendment purposes; therefore, a forfeiture action cannot serve as the basis for a claim under the Double Jeopardy Clause." *U.S. v. 817 N.E. 29th Drive, Wilton Manors, Fla.*, 175 F.3d 1304, 1311, 168 A.L.R. Fed. 739 (11th Cir. 1999).

D.C. Circuit

- "When the government knows (or can easily ascertain) where a person may be found, it must direct its notice there. . . . If . . . the government knows that a claimant is in prison, it . . . can easily . . . find out whether the prisoner has been moved or released (and if so, to what address), or whether some problem at the prison prevented delivery." *Lopez v. U.S.*, 201 F.3d 478, 481 (D.C. Cir. 2000).

- "Certainly, if . . . the government knows that a claimant is in prison, it cannot, with a straight face, claim it does not know where he is. The government can easily call the prison or the Bureau of Prisons, and find out whether the prisoner has been moved or released (and if so, to what address), or whether some problem at the prison prevented delivery. . . . That, or something like it, is what the United States should have done here; there is no indication that it would have been at all burdensome for the United States to take this route. Its failure to do so renders its efforts to give notice constitutionally inadequate, and invalidates the forfeiture." *Small v. U.S.*, 136 F.3d 1334, 1338 (D.C. Cir. 1998).

§ 31:6 Proportionality: In very limited circumstances, some courts have considered proportionality arguments in forfeiture cases

Supreme Court

- "The analysis applied by the *Halper* Court deviated from our traditional double jeopardy doctrine in two key respects. First, the *Halper* Court bypassed the threshold question: whether the successive punishment at issue is a criminal punishment. Instead, it focused on whether the sanction, regardless of whether it was civil or criminal, was so grossly disproportionate to the harm caused as to constitute punishment. In so doing, the Court elevated a single *Kennedy* factor—whether the sanction appeared excessive in relation to its nonpunitive purposes—to dispositive status. But as we emphasized in *Kennedy* itself, no one factor should be considered controlling as they may often point in differing directions. . . . The second significant departure in *Halper* was the Court's decision to assess the character of the actual sanctions imposed . . . rather than, as *Kennedy* demanded, evaluating the statute on its face to determine whether it provided for what amounted to a criminal sanction. . . . We believe that *Halper's* deviation from longstanding double jeopardy principles was ill considered. As subsequent cases have demonstrated, *Halper's* test for determining whether a particular sanction is punitive, and thus subject to the strictures of the Double Jeopardy Clause, has proved unworkable. . . . The . . . protection afforded by extending double jeopardy protections to proceedings heretofore thought to be civil is more than offset by the confusion created by attempting to distinguish between punitive and nonpunitive penalties." *Hudson v. U.S.*, 522 U.S. 93, 101–03, 118 S. Ct. 488, 139 L. Ed. 2d 450, 162 A.L.R. Fed. 737 (1997).
- "Congress plainly intended forfeiture of assets to operate as punishment for criminal conduct in violation of the federal drug and racketeering laws, not as a separate substantive offense. Our precedents have likewise characterized criminal forfeiture as an aspect of punishment imposed following conviction of a substantive criminal offense. In *Alexander v. United States* we

observed that the criminal forfeiture authorized by the RICO forfeiture statute is clearly a form of monetary punishment no different, for Eighth Amendment purposes, from a traditional fine. Similarly, in *United States v. $8,850* we recognized that a criminal proceeding may often include forfeiture as part of the sentence. And in *Austin v. United States* we concluded that even the *in rem* civil forfeiture authorized by §§ 881(a)(4) and (a)(7) [can be] punitive in nature, so that forfeiture imposed under those subsections is subject to the limitations of the Eighth Amendment's Excessive Fines Clause." *Libretti v. U.S.*, 516 U.S. 29, 39–40, 116 S. Ct. 356, 133 L. Ed. 2d 271 (1995).

- "Criminal fines, civil penalties, civil forfeitures, and taxes all share certain features: They generate government revenues, impose fiscal burdens on individuals, and deter certain behavior. All of these sanctions are subject to constitutional constraints. A government may not impose criminal fines without first establishing guilt by proof beyond a reasonable doubt. A defendant convicted and punished for an offense may not have a nonremedial civil penalty imposed against him for the same offense in a separate proceeding. A civil forfeiture may violate the Eighth Amendment's proscription against excessive fines. And a statute imposing a tax on unlawful conduct may be invalid because its reporting requirements compel taxpayers to incriminate themselves." *Department of Revenue of Montana v. Kurth Ranch*, 511 U.S. 767, 778, 114 S. Ct. 1937, 128 L. Ed. 2d 767, 73 A.F.T.R.2d 94-2140 (1994).

- "In light of the historical understanding of forfeiture as punishment, the clear focus of §§ 881(a)(4) and (a)(7) on the culpability of the owner, and the evidence that Congress understood those provisions as serving to deter and to punish, we cannot conclude that forfeiture under §§ 881(a)(4) and (a)(7) serves solely a remedial purpose. We therefore conclude that forfeiture under these provisions constitutes payment to a sovereign as punishment for some offense, and, as such, is subject to the limitations of the Eighth Amendment's Excessive Fines Clause." *Austin v. U.S.*, 509 U.S. 602, 621, 113 S. Ct. 2801, 125 L. Ed. 2d 488, 1994 A.M.C. 1206 (1993).

Second Circuit

- "[W]e join those courts that have concluded that appropriate excessiveness analysis entails a multi-factor test combining the principles of both instrumentality and proportionality. In our view, the factors to be considered by a court in determining whether a proposed in rem forfeiture violates the Excessive Fines Clause should include (1) the harshness of the forfeiture (e.g., the nature and value of the property and the effect of forfeiture on innocent third parties) in comparison to (a) the gravity of the offense, and (b) the sentence that could be imposed on the perpetrator of such an offense; (2) the relationship between the property and the offense, including whether use of the property in the offense was (a) important to the success of the illegal activity, (b) deliberate and planned or merely incidental and fortuitous, and (c) temporally or spatially extensive; and (3) the role and degree of culpability of the owner of the property." *U.S. v. Milbrand*, 58 F.3d 841, 847–48 (2d Cir. 1995).

Fourth Circuit

- "Just two terms ago, in *United States v. Bajakajian*. . .the Supreme Court again considered these questions, and, for the first time, articulated a test for determining whether a punitive forfeiture violates the Excessive Fines Clause. . . .the *Bajakajian* analysis and language significantly limit *Austin's* apparent conclusion that traditional civil in rem forfeitures generally are punitive to some degree. . . .[A] punitive forfeiture will be held to violate the Excessive Fines Clause only if it is grossly disproportional to the gravity of the offense. . . .Although the Supreme Court has not yet expressly so held, we believe that *Bajakajian's* grossly disproportional analysis applies when determining whether any punitive forfeiture—civil or criminal—is excessive." *U.S. v. Ahmad*, 213 F.3d 805, 812–13, 15, 2001-2 U.S. Tax Cas. (CCH) P 50673, 89 A.F.T.R.2d 2002-2164 (4th Cir. 2000).

Fifth Circuit

- "To determine whether a forfeiture proceeding is punitive for double jeopardy purposes, the court looks to whether Congress intended the forfeiture proceeding to be civil or criminal and to whether the forfeiture proceedings are in fact so punitive that they may not legitimately be viewed as civil in nature, despite Congress' intent." *U.S. v. Williams*, 132 F.3d 1055, 1061, 48 Fed. R. Evid. Serv. 777 (5th Cir. 1998).

Eighth Circuit

- "Criminal forfeitures are monetary punishments subject to the Eighth Amendment's Excessive Fines Clause. . . . Whether a forfeiture is grossly disproportionate and thus violates the Eighth Amendment is a fact-sensitive inquiry that depends on a number of factors. . . . These factors include, but are not limited to: the seriousness of the offense; an assessment of the personal benefit reaped by the particular defendant; the defendant's motive and culpability; and the extent that the defendant's interest and the enterprise itself are tainted by criminal conduct." *U.S. v. Van Brocklin*, 115 F.3d 587, 601–02 (8th Cir. 1997).
- "Civil forfeiture is subject to the limitations of the Excessive Fines Clause. The burden is on the Claimant to make a prima facie showing that the fine is grossly disproportionate to the illegal activity committed by the Claimant. A court must look at the specific facts of the case, including the extent of the criminal wrongdoing and the value of the property forfeited. Courts must also consider the amount of time the property owner engaged in illegal activity." *U.S. v. One 1970 36.9' Columbia Sailing Boat*, 91 F.3d 1053, 1057 (8th Cir. 1996).

Ninth Circuit

- "[A] forfeiture is unconstitutional unless it survives scrutiny under the Excessive Fines Clause of the Eighth Amendment. The Excessive Fines Clause limits the Government's power to extract payments, whether in cash or in kind, as punishment for some offense. Pursuant to this court's Excessive Fines Clause test, a forfeiture is constitutional if: (1) the property forfeited is an instrumentality of the crime committed; and (2) the value of the property is proportional to the culpability of the owner. Forfeiture of currency is unconstitutional when the crime to which the forfeiture is tied is a mere failure to report. In such situations, there simply is not an instrumentality relationship between the currency and the crime to satisfy the instrumentality prong of the Excessive Fines test." *U.S. v. Bajakajian*, 84 F.3d 334, 336–38 (9th Cir. 1996), judgment aff'd, 524 U.S. 321, 118 S. Ct. 2028, 141 L. Ed. 2d 314, 172 A.L.R. Fed. 705 (1998).

Tenth Circuit

- "As aptly noted by the Fifth Circuit, the forfeiture of proceeds of illegal drug sales serves the wholly remedial purposes of reimbursing the government for the costs of detection, investigation, and prosecution of drug traffickers and reimbursing society for the costs of combating the allure of illegal drugs, caring for the victims of the criminal trade when preventative efforts prove unsuccessful, lost productivity, etc. . . . Furthermore, on a macroeconomic level, the estimated proceeds of illegal drug sales are roughly equivalent to the yearly costs drugs inflict on society and government. . . . Finally, on a microeconomic level, the forfeiture of drug proceeds, contrasted with the types of properties considered by the Supreme Court in *Austin*, extracts from the particular drug trafficker with some precision an amount of money equivalent to the costs that the drug dealer has imposed on society." *U.S. v. One Parcel of Real Property Described as Lot 41, Berryhill Farm Estates*, 128 F.3d 1386, 1395 (10th Cir. 1997).

- "In *Calle de Madero*, we recognized that, in a forfeiture proceeding, the government bears the initial burden of proving the requisite connection between the forfeited property and the offense. If this instrumentality test is satisfied, the forfeiture will not be considered excessive unless the claimant or defendant then shows that the forfeiture is grossly disproportionate in light of the totality of the circumstances surrounding the forfeiture. In evaluating proportionality, courts must consider the severity of the offense with which the property was involved, the harshness of the sanction imposed, and the culpability of the claimant." *U.S. v. One Parcel Property Located at Lot 85, County Ridge*, 100 F.3d 740, 744 (10th Cir. 1996).

Eleventh Circuit

- "Because Congress is a representative body, its pronouncements regarding the appropriate range of fines for a crime represent the collective opinion of the American people as to what is and is not excessive. Given that excessiveness is a highly subjective judgment, the courts should be hesitant to substitute their opinion for that of the people. . . . Consequently, if the value of forfeited property is within the range of fines prescribed by Congress, a strong presumption arises that the forfeiture is constitutional." *U.S. v. 817 N.E. 29th Drive, Wilton Manors, Fla.*, 175 F.3d 1304, 1309, 168 A.L.R. Fed. 739 (11th Cir. 1999).

- "It has been established that the Excessive Fines Clause of the Eighth Amendment applies to in rem civil forfeiture proceedings under 21 U.S.C. § 881(a)(7). The tests laid out by lower courts since *Austin* generally fall into two categories. Some have followed Justice Scalia's suggestion and applied an instrumentality test, focusing on the use of the property in the commission of the illegal act, asserting that this test is the only way to preserve the guilty property fiction of traditional in rem forfeiture. A few have applied a proportionality test, the core of which is a comparison of the severity of the forfeiture with the seriousness of the crime. Many, including the district court in this case, have combined the two approaches in some fashion. These observations lead to the conclusion that application of the Excessive Fines Clause to civil forfeiture under 21 U.S.C. § 881(a)(7) requires a review of the proportionality of the fine imposed. That is, a court must ask: Given the offense for which the owner is being punished, is the fine (imposed by civil forfeiture) excessive? While the core of proportionality review is a comparison of the severity of the fine with the seriousness of the underlying offense, it would be futile to attempt a definitive checklist of relevant factors. The relevant factors will necessarily vary from case to case." *U.S. v. One Parcel Property Located at 427 and 429 Hall Street, Montgomery, Montgomery County, Ala.*, 74 F.3d 1165, 1170, 1172 (11th Cir. 1996).

§ 31:7   Civil forfeiture: Most forfeitures are civil in nature

Supreme Court

- "The question of whether a given sanction is civil or criminal is one of statutory construction. It appears that the § 1497 forfeiture is civil and remedial, and, as a result, its imposition is not barred by an acquittal of [criminal] charges of violating § 545." *One Lot Emerald Cut Stones and One Ring v. U.S.*, 409 U.S. 232, 237, 93 S. Ct. 489, 34 L. Ed. 2d 438 (1972).

- "Forfeiture of goods or their value and the payment of fixed or variable sums of money are other sanctions which have been recognized as enforcible by civil proceedings. In spite of their comparative severity, such sanctions have been upheld against the contention that they are essentially criminal and subject to the procedural rules governing criminal prosecutions." *Helvering v. Mitchell*, 1938-1 C.B. 317, 303 U.S. 391, 400, 58 S. Ct. 630, 82 L. Ed. 917, 38-1 U.S. Tax Cas. (CCH) P 9152, 20 A.F.T.R. (P-H) P 796 (1938).

- "This forfeiture proceeding is *in rem*. It is the property which is proceeded against, and, by resort to a legal fiction, held guilty and condemned as though it were conscious instead of inanimate and insentient." *Waterloo Distilling Corporation v. U.S.*, 282 U.S. 577, 581, 51 S. Ct. 282, 75 L. Ed. 558 (1931).

First Circuit

- "The six-year limitations period applying to civil forfeiture actions also applies to defendant's claims for return of seized property under criminal procedure rule. Where there has been a related criminal proceeding but no civil forfeiture proceeding, defendant's cause of action for return of seized property accrues at the end of the criminal proceeding." *Santiago-Lugo v. U.S.*, 538 F.3d 23 (1st Cir. 2008).

Second Circuit

- "[C]ivil forfeiture is a creature unto itself. It is an area of the law which is founded upon the many inherent fictions of our jurisprudence. Perhaps no area of the law embodies more legal fictions—and better illustrates their use and misuse—than does civil forfeiture. As perhaps the most obvious use of legal fiction, the civil forfeiture action is brought directly against the property as defendant. The conceptual basis of the forfeiture is, quite basically, that the property has perpetrated some wrong. Thus, as the action is against the property and not the owner, the action is *in rem* in nature. . . . The Government need not prove, within the criminal justice system, that the owner committed a crime." *U.S. (Drug Enforcement Agency) v. One 1987 Jeep Wrangler Auto. VIN No. 2BCCL8132HBS12835*, 972 F.2d 472, 476 (2d Cir. 1992).

- "A forfeiture proceeding may even be commenced where no criminal action is brought. Consequently, the determination of when the government is to proceed against a piece of property is seemingly discretionary and limited only by the relevant statute of limitations." *U.S. (Drug Enforcement Agency) v. One 1987 Jeep Wrangler Auto. VIN No. 2BCCL8132HBS12835*, 972 F.2d 472, 476–77 (2d Cir. 1992).

Fourth Circuit

- "[A] remand is required for proper application of the decisional standards ushered in by the Civil Asset Forfeiture Reform Act of 2000 (CAFRA). . . . Although CAFRA increased the government's burden of proof at trial from mere probable cause (the old standard) to the preponderance of the evidence, it made clear that the pleading requirements imposed by cases such as *One Lot of U.S. Currency ($36,634)* no longer apply. It did so by stating that no civil forfeiture complaint may be dismissed because the government lacked sufficient evidence of forfeitability at the time of filing, and that the government may use evidence gathered after filing to meet its burden of proof. As a consequence, the government no longer must plead facts sufficient to establish probable cause to forfeit; it need only satisfy Rule E(2)(a) of the Supplemental Rules for Certain Admiralty and Maritime Claims. In relevant part, the rule provides: 'In actions to which this rule is applicable the complaint shall state the circumstances from which the claim arises with such particularity that the . . . claimant will be able, without moving for a more definite statement, to commence an investigation of the facts and to frame a responsive pleading.' " *U.S. v. Lopez-Burgos*, 435 F.3d 1, 2–3 (1st Cir. 2006) (citations omitted).

- "Unlike criminal forfeiture cases, conviction for the underlying criminal activity is not a prerequisite for forfeiture of the property. In civil forfeiture cases, property is subject to forfeiture even if its owner is acquitted of—or never called to defend against—criminal charges." *U.S. v. One Parcel of Real Estate Located at 7715 Betsy Bruce Lane Summerfield, N.C.*, 906 F.2d 110, 111–12 (4th Cir. 1990).

Seventh Circuit

- "As the district court in this case noted, there is some debate as to whether the common-law exclusionary rule should apply in civil-forfeiture proceedings. However, Rule G(8)(a) of the Supplemental Rules for Admiralty or Maritime Claims and Asset Forfeiture Actions provides that '[i]f the defendant property was seized, a party with standing to contest the lawfulness of the seizure may move to suppress use of the property as evidence.' This rule, like others promulgated pursuant to the Rules Enabling Act, has the force of a statute. In re Dorner, 343 F.3d 910, 914 (7th Cir.2003) (citing 28 U.S.C. § 2072(b)). Thus, regardless of whether the common-law exclusionary rule applies, we must determine whether the district court should have granted the [truck owners'] motion to suppress under Rule G(8)(a)." *U.S. v. $304,980.00 in U.S. Currency*, 732 F.3d 812 (7th Cir. 2013) (citations omitted).

- "[I]t is somewhat misleading to consider whether *Moya-Gomez* applies to civil forfeiture: although civil and criminal forfeiture may have the same practical effects, they have distinct procedural guarantees and burdens of proof, stemming for the most part from adherence to the fiction that civil forfeiture is an in rem proceeding against guilty property rather than a penalty. For example, civil discovery is more extensive than criminal, and a civil case may provide more opportunities for a claimant to challenge the complaint. . . . . At the same time, civil forfeiture claimants usually have been unable to avail themselves of the constitutional guarantees afforded to criminal defendants." *U.S. v. Michelle's Lounge*, 39 F.3d 684, 696, 30 Fed. R. Serv. 3d 31 (7th Cir. 1994) (abrogated on other grounds by, Kaley v. U.S., 134 S. Ct. 1090, 188 L. Ed. 2d 46 (2014)).

Ninth Circuit

- "Whether claimants in civil forfeiture action had standing to challenge search warrant that resulted in seizure of property that was subject of forfeiture action presented mixed question of fact and law that Court of Appeals reviewed de novo, and findings of fact underlying that conclusion were reviewed for clear error." *U.S. v. $40,955.00 in U.S. Currency*, 554 F.3d 752 (9th Cir. 2009).

- "The exclusionary rule applies in civil forfeiture cases by barring the admission of evidence obtained pursuant to search and seizure in violation of the Fourth Amendment, as well as fruits of the poisonous tree. Consequently, illegally seized property may not be introduced as evidence in a forfeiture proceeding. However, the mere fact of the illegal seizure, standing alone, does not immunize the goods from forfeiture." *U.S. v. $493,850.00 in U.S. Currency*, 518 F.3d 1159 (9th Cir. 2008).

- "To determine whether a remedy denominated civil is actually a punitive criminal penalty subject to the prohibition of double jeopardy, the court should consider whether the sanction (1) involves an affirmative disability or restraint; (2) has historically been regarded as punishment; (3) requires a finding of scienter; (4) will promote retribution and deterrence; (5) applies to behavior that is already a crime; (6) can have an alternative purpose; and (7) appears excessive in relation to the alternative purpose. . . . These factors must be considered in relation to the statute on its face, and only the clearest proof will suffice to override legislative intent and transform what has been denominated a civil remedy into a criminal penalty." *Rivera v. Pugh*, 194 F.3d 1064, 1068 (9th Cir. 1999).

- "A civil forfeiture proceeding is an action *in rem,* and the court must have actual or constructive control of the res when a forfeiture proceeding is initiated." *U.S. v. $46,588.00 in U.S. Currency and $20.00 in Canadian Currency*, 103 F.3d 902, 904 (9th Cir. 1996).

- "A criminal forfeiture is an in personam judgment against a person convicted of a crime, while a civil forfeiture is an in rem proceeding in which liability attaches to particular property and not particular institutions or individuals. Thus, the defendant in a criminal forfeiture proceeding is the person, and the defendant in a civil forfeiture proceeding is the particular property." *U.S. v. $814,254.76, in U.S. Currency, Contents of Valley Nat. Bank Account No. 1500-8339,* 51 F.3d 207, 210–11 (9th Cir. 1995).

Eleventh Circuit

- "The classical distinction between civil and criminal forfeiture was founded upon whether the penalty assessed was against the person or against the thing. Forfeiture against the person operated in personam and required a conviction before the property could be wrested from the defendant. . . . Such forfeitures were regarded as criminal in nature because they were penal; they primarily sought to punish. Forfeiture against the thing was in rem and the forfeiture was based upon the unlawful use of the res, irrespective of its owner's culpability. These forfeitures were regarded as civil; their purpose was remedial." *U.S. v. Gilbert,* 244 F.3d 888, 919, R.I.C.O. Bus. Disp. Guide (CCH) P 10036 (11th Cir. 2001).

- "Generally speaking, civil forfeiture is the forfeiture of real or personal property to the state after that property is shown to be linked to a violation of the state's laws. Some trace the roots of civil forfeiture to the Old Testament. Blackstone, for example, noted the scriptural origin of one particular species of common law forfeiture—the deodand, according to which chattel was forfeit if it caused the death of a subject. At the time our Bill of Rights was ratified, the English common law recognized three kinds of forfeiture. Of these three, only statutory forfeiture became part of the American legal tradition. In the years since, Congress has authorized forfeiture to aid enforcement of many statutory schemes, including the navigation laws, food and drug laws, copyright laws, and antitrust laws." *U.S. v. One Parcel Property Located at 427 and 429 Hall Street, Montgomery, Montgomery County, Ala.,* 74 F.3d 1165, 1168 (11th Cir. 1996).

§ 31:8   Civil Asset Forfeiture Reform Act

Fifth Circuit

- "The courts may no longer rely on hearsay, absent an exception to the hearsay rule, when deciding the merits of a civil forfeiture proceeding brought under CAFRA; instead, any affidavits submitted by the parties must be based on personal knowledge." *U.S. v. $92,203.00 in U.S. Currency*, 537 F.3d 504 (5th Cir. 2008).

Ninth Circuit

- "CAFRA's enactment in 2000 did, of course, substantially revise the law governing civil asset forfeitures. Among the changes imposed by Congress was a requirement that, ordinarily, the United States institute a judicial forfeiture proceeding within 90 days of the submission of a claim for the return of seized property. A failure to institute a timely judicial forfeiture proceeding requires the return of the property and constitutes a waiver of the right to seek civil forfeiture in connection with the same underlying offense. In addition, Congress expressly provided for the recovery of attorney's fees, litigation costs, and *postjudgment interest* in certain circumstances of wrongfully seized property." *Carvajal v. U.S.*, 521 F.3d 1242 (9th Cir. 2008).
- "In a civil forfeiture proceeding, CAFRA requires the government to prove, by a preponderance of the evidence, that property is subject to forfeiture. The government may use evidence gathered after the filing of a complaint for forfeiture to establish, by a preponderance of the evidence, that property is subject to forfeiture. Once the government provides such proof, the burden shifts to the claimant to prove that he or she is an innocent owner of the property. While CAFRA sets forth a burden-shifting analysis for civil forfeiture actions, it does not eliminate the requirement that the government show probable cause to institute forfeiture actions by presenting evidence that, at the time the government filed the complaint, it had reasonable grounds to believe that the property was related to an illegal drug transaction." *U.S. v. $493,850.00 in U.S. Currency*, 518 F.3d 1159 (9th Cir. 2008).
- "To demonstrate Article III standing in a civil forfeiture

action, a claimant must have a sufficient interest in the property to create a case or controversy. This burden is not a heavy one, at least at the initial stages of a forfeiture suit. A claimant need demonstrate only a colorable interest in the property, for example, by showing actual possession, control, title, or financial stake. To do so at the motion to dismiss stage, a claimant must allege that he has an ownership or other interest in the forfeited property." *U.S. v. Real Property Located at 475 Martin Lane, Beverly Hills, CA*, 545 F.3d 1134 (9th Cir. 2008).

• "The interest payment provision of CAFRA, 28 U.S.C. § 2465(b)(1)(C), is triggered only when the government institutes civil forfeiture proceedings and a plaintiff substantially prevails." *Carvajal v. U.S.*, 521 F.3d 1242 (9th Cir. 2008).

D.C. Circuit

• "Statutory disentitlement under CAFRA requires a showing of five elements: (1) a warrant or similar process has issued in a criminal case for the claimant's apprehension; (2) the claimant had notice or knowledge of the warrant or process; (3) the criminal case is related to the forfeiture action; (4) the claimant is not confined or otherwise held in custody in another jurisdiction; and (5) claimant has deliberately avoided criminal prosecution by leaving the United States, declining to enter or reenter the country, or otherwise evading the criminal court's jurisdiction." *U.S. v. $6,976,934.65, Plus Interest Deposited into Royal Bank of Scotland Intern., Account No. 2029-56141070, Held in Name of Soulbury Ltd.*, 554 F.3d 123 (D.C. Cir. 2009).

§ 31:9 Jurisdiction: Since civil forfeiture is an *in rem* procedure, the court must have possession or control of the *res* when the action is commenced

Supreme Court

• "[I]t long has been understood that a valid seizure of the *res* is a prerequisite to the initiation of an *in rem* civil forfeiture proceeding." *Republic Nat. Bank of Miami v. U.S.*, 506 U.S. 80, 84, 113 S. Ct. 554, 121 L. Ed. 2d 474, 1993 A.M.C. 2010 (1992).

- "Fairly read, *The Brig Ann* simply restates the rule that the court must have actual or constructive control of the *res* when an *in rem* forfeiture suit is initiated. If the seizing party abandons the attachment prior to filing an action, it, in effect, has renounced its claim. The result is to purge away all the prior rights acquired by the seizure and unless a new seizure is made, the case may not commence. *The Brig Ann* stands for nothing more than this." *Republic Nat. Bank of Miami v. U.S.*, 506 U.S. 80, 87, 113 S. Ct. 554, 121 L. Ed. 2d 474, 1993 A.M.C. 2010 (1992).

- "In a civil forfeiture proceeding, . . . the right to appeal is a crucial safeguard against abuse. No settled rule requires continuous control of the *res* for appellate jurisdiction in an *in rem* forfeiture proceeding. Nor does the Appropriations Clause place the money out of reach. Accordingly, we hold that the Court of Appeals did not lose jurisdiction when the funds were transferred from the Southern District of Florida to the Assets Forfeiture Fund of the United States Treasury. The judgment of the Court of Appeals is reversed, and the case is remanded for further proceedings consistent with this opinion." *Republic Nat. Bank of Miami v. U.S.*, 506 U.S. 80, 92, 113 S. Ct. 554, 121 L. Ed. 2d 474, 1993 A.M.C. 2010 (1992).

Second Circuit

- "The conceptual underpinnings of civil forfeiture can be traced back to ancient Roman and medieval English law, both of which made objects used to violate the law subject to forfeiture to the sovereign. Our laws providing for official seizure of property used in criminal activity perpetuate the legal fiction that property used in violation of law was itself the wrongdoer that must be held to account for the harms it had caused. Because the property, or res, is considered the wrongdoer, it is regarded as the actual party to in rem forfeiture proceedings." *U.S. v. Daccarett*, 6 F.3d 37, 45, 72 A.F.T. R.2d 93-6248 (2d Cir. 1993).

Fifth Circuit

- "In *National Bank*, the government argued that the court lacked jurisdiction because the forfeited property

had been sold and the proceeds deposited in the
Treasury. Thus, the government argued, the venerable
admiralty rule that jurisdiction over an *in rem* forfeiture proceeding depends upon continued control of the
res deprived the court of jurisdiction. The Supreme
Court held to the contrary, ruling that no such rule
exists. Instead, the Court relied on its early case law to
reach the opposite conclusion—that continued possession was not necessary to maintain jurisdiction over an
in rem forfeiture action. According to the Court, the
well-settled rule is that jurisdiction, once vested, is not
divested, although a state of things should arrive in
which the original jurisdiction could not be exercised."
*U.S. v. 1988 Oldsmobile Cutlass Supreme 2 Door, VIN
1G3WR14W5JD323281*, 983 F.2d 670, 674 (5th Cir.
1993).

- "The basic requirement of jurisdiction *in rem* (and *quasi
  in rem*, for that matter) is that a court must have
  exclusive possession or control over the property in order to consider the suit and grant or deny the relief
  sought. The long-accepted purpose of this rule is to
  avoid conflicts in the administration of justice and the
  unseemliness of two courts vying simultaneously for
  control of the same property. The need for this rule is in
  no way diminished, nor the conflict any less unseemly,
  when, as here, a state court is the first to obtain the
  power to dispose of property seized pursuant to its warrant and subsequently a federal agency attempts to assert power over the same property in order to find it
  forfeit to the United States." *Scarabin v. Drug Enforcement Admin.*, 966 F.2d 989, 994 (5th Cir. 1992).

Sixth Circuit

- "The basis of claimant's argument that the District
  Court lacked jurisdiction is the well-settled principle
  that a court cannot exercise jurisdiction over a *res* that
  is already subject to the *in rem* jurisdiction of another
  court. According to this rule, the first court to exercise
  in rem jurisdiction over the *res* exercises jurisdiction to
  the exclusion of a second court that later attempts to
  proceed against the same *res*." *U.S. v. Certain Real
  Property 566 Hendrickson Blvd., Clawson, Oakland
  County, Mich.*, 986 F.2d 990, 993 (6th Cir. 1993).

Eleventh Circuit

- "The criminal forfeiture provisions of section 853 authorize the government to seek forfeiture of a defendant's
interest in subject property. . . . This is in contrast to
the civil forfeiture scheme embodied in 21 U.S.C. § 881,
involving an in rem proceeding, wherein the whole property (as opposed to a particular defendant's interest in
the property) is treated as being itself guilty of
wrongdoing." *U.S. v. Kennedy*, 201 F.3d 1324, 1329
(11th Cir. 2000).

§ 31:10 Criminal forfeiture: In criminal forfeitures, criminal constitutional rules apply

Supreme Court

- "[O]ur analysis of the nature of criminal forfeiture as
an aspect of sentencing compels the conclusion that the
right to a jury verdict on forfeitability does not fall
within the Sixth Amendment's constitutional protection.
Our cases have made abundantly clear that a defendant
does not enjoy a constitutional right to a jury determination as to the appropriate sentence to be imposed."
Libretti v. U.S., 516 U.S. 29, 49, 116 S. Ct. 356, 133 L.
Ed. 2d 271 (1995).

- "We are unpersuaded that the Rule 11(f) inquiry is necessary to guarantee that a forfeiture agreement is knowing and voluntary. Whether a stipulated asset forfeiture is factually based is a distinct inquiry from the
question whether the defendant entered an agreement
to forfeit assets knowingly and voluntarily. [A] plea of
guilty and a forfeiture provision contained in a plea
agreement are different matters altogether. Forfeiture,
as we have said, is a part of the sentence. If the
voluntariness of a defendant's concession to imposition
of a particular sentence is questionable, the relevant inquiry is whether the sentencing stipulation was informed and uncoerced on the part of the defendant, not
whether it is factually sound." *Libretti v. U.S.*, 516 U.S.
29, 42, 116 S. Ct. 356, 133 L. Ed. 2d 271 (1995).

First Circuit

- "We think that the genealogy of modern criminal forfeiture is important. The device is born out of the mating

of two historically distinct traditions. One parent is civil forfeiture, an in rem proceeding rooted in the notion that property used in, or intimately associated with, criminal activity acquires a taint, and that such property is therefore forfeitable even if not owned by the miscreant. The second parent is old-hat criminal forfeiture, which traditionally operated as an incident of a felony conviction in personam against a convicted defendant, requiring him to forfeit his property to the crown." *U.S. v. Saccoccia*, 58 F.3d 754, 783, 42 Fed. R. Evid. Serv. 355 (1st Cir. 1995).

Second Circuit

- "The Supreme Court. . .has determined that criminal forfeiture is part of the process of criminal sentencing. . . . Fact-finding at sentencing is made by a preponderance of the evidence. . . . It follows as a matter of logic that, absent any indication to the contrary in the statutory text, criminal forfeiture. . .depends on the preponderance of the evidence." *U.S. v. Bellomo*, 176 F.3d 580, 595, 138 Lab. Cas. (CCH) P 10433, 51 Fed. R. Evid. Serv. 1179, 83 A.F.T.R.2d 99-2328 (2d Cir. 1999).

Fourth Circuit

- "An in personam criminal forfeiture is an action against the person as distinguished from an in rem forfeiture which is an action against the property itself. In in personam criminal forfeitures, the person not the property is guilty of some offense. The Supreme Court has explained, in *Alexander v. United States*, that in personam criminal forfeitures are clearly a form of monetary punishment no different, for Eighth Amendment purposes, from a traditional fine. In other words, if an in personam criminal forfeiture is a fine, it follows that to determine whether the fine is excessive, the amount of the fine, i.e., the value of the property being forfeited, must by necessity be considered." *U.S. v. Wild*, 47 F.3d 669, 674 (4th Cir. 1995).

Sixth Circuit

- "We decide to follow existing federal circuit precedent on this close issue, and hold that the government must prove that property is subject to criminal forfeiture under section 853(a) by a preponderance of the evidence. We agree with *Sandini* that this holding best represents the nature of a criminal forfeiture proceeding as Congress intended it. However ambiguous section 853 may be, it expressly provides that a court shall order criminal forfeiture in addition to any other sentence at the time that it imposes the sentence. Although a criminal forfeiture proceeding bears some characteristics of a criminal matter, its purpose is to determine the proper punishment for the charged offense once the defendant's guilt on that charge has been proved beyond a reasonable doubt. By requiring proof by a preponderance of the evidence, we acknowledge the purpose of criminal forfeiture and ensure that it serves as the efficient alternative to civil forfeiture that Congress intended it to be." *U.S. v. Smith*, 966 F.2d 1045, 1052 (6th Cir. 1992).

Seventh Circuit

- "Procedurally, a forfeiture authorized by section 853 operates as a sanction against the defendant based upon his conviction. As such, forfeiture under section 853 is part of the sentencing and not an element of the crime. As a consequence, the government need not prove that property is subject to forfeiture beyond a reasonable doubt, the standard for elements of a crime, but only by a preponderance of the evidence, the standard for sentencing." *U.S. v. Ben-Hur*, 20 F.3d 313, 317 (7th Cir. 1994).

Eighth Circuit

- "[A]lthough charged as a count in the indictment, criminal forfeiture is neither an element of a criminal offense nor a criminal offense itself. Therefore, proof beyond a reasonable doubt is neither constitutionally nor statutorily mandated." *U.S. v. Bieri*, 21 F.3d 811, 822 (8th Cir. 1994).

Ninth Circuit

- "Under section 853(a)(1), the government need prove by only preponderance of the evidence, and not beyond a reasonable doubt, that property should be criminally forfeited. . . . This burden of proof is constitutional because the criminal forfeiture provision does not itself describe a separate offense, but is merely an additional penalty for an offense that must be proved beyond a reasonable doubt." *U.S. v. Garcia-Guizar*, 160 F.3d 511, 517–18 (9th Cir. 1998).

Tenth Circuit

• "We hold that impoundment of a vehicle located on private property that is neither obstructing traffic nor creating an imminent threat to public safety is constitutional only if justified by both a standardized policy and a reasonable, non-pretextual community-caretaking rationale. Our holding, like that of a majority of circuits, recognizes that *Bertine* makes the existence of standardized criteria the touchstone of the inquiry into whether an impoundment is lawful. However, *Bertine* did not purport to overrule *Opperman,* and *Opperman* envisioned a situation in which an impoundment is immediately necessary, regardless of any other circumstances, in order to facilitate the flow of traffic or protect the public from an immediate harm. But to hold, as have the First, Third, and Fifth Circuits, that standardized criteria are never relevant is to ignore the plain language of *Bertine,* which holds that police discretion to impound a vehicle is constitutional only 'so long as that discretion is exercised according to standard criteria.' Our holding follows our prior circuit precedent in *Taylor, Ibarra,* and *Maher* in recognizing the centrality of standardized criteria, yet allowing broader officer discretion to protect public safety. Our requirement that standardized criteria guide impoundments on private property ensures that police discretion to impound vehicles is cabined rather than uncontrolled. Imposing heightened requirements on police who seize vehicles from private property is consistent with our circuit precedent and caselaw from other circuits. Yet *Opperman* establishes that if a vehicle is obstructing or impeding traffic on public property, it can be impounded regardless of whether the impoundment is guided by standardized procedures. By recognizing that standardized procedures need not justify impoundments of such vehicles, our holding is also faithful to our circuit precedent holding that officers should be free to impound vehicles that threaten public safety. For example, our holding allows officers from a rural county lacking a specific policy to impound a vehicle obstructing a highway, if that impoundment is reasonable and not pretextual, without fear of liability. Moreover, because our holding requires all community-caretaking impoundments to be supported by a reasonable, non-pretextual justification, it guards against arbitrary impoundments. This rule ensures that even if the police were to adopt a standardized policy of impounding all vehicles whose owners receive traffic citations, such impoundments could be invalidated as unreasonable under our precedent. Protection against unreasonable impoundments, even those conducted pursuant to a standardized policy, is part and parcel of the Fourth Amendment's guarantee against unreasonable searches and seizures. Ascertaining whether an impoundment is justified by a reasonable and legitimate, non-pretextual community-caretaking rationale is not an easy task. We note that courts have considered the following non-exclusive list of factors: (1) whether the vehicle is on public or private property; (2) if on private property, whether the property owner has been consulted; (3) whether an alternative to impoundment exists (especially another person capable of driving the vehicle); (4) whether the vehicle is implicated in a crime; and (5) whether the vehicle's owner and/or driver have consented to the impoundment." *U.S. v. Sanders*, 796 F.3d 1241, 1248–50 (10th Cir. 2015) (citations omitted).

- "Under federal forfeiture laws, any person who is convicted of the offenses for which the defendant has been found guilty is required to forfeit to the United States the profits and instrumentalities of their illegal conduct. Specifically, the laws of the United States provide that any property, real or personal, involved in such offense or any property traceable to such property which belongs to the defendant is subject to forfeiture upon conviction of defendant for violation of title . . . 18 United States Code 1957." *U.S. v. Bornfield*, 145 F.3d 1123, 1133–34, 49 Fed. R. Evid. Serv. 601 (10th Cir. 1998).

Eleventh Circuit

- "[T]he preponderance standard defines the Government's burden of proof in section 853(a)(2) forfeitures. . . . The forfeiture is not intended to rectify the unjust enrichment of the individual, but to punish the defendant. . . . The preponderance standard ordinarily governs sentencing matters." *U.S. v. Dicter*, 198 F.3d 1284, 1289 (11th Cir. 1999).

D.C. Circuit

- "RICO criminal forfeiture differs from other types of forfeiture because it is targeted at the individual wrongdoer, rather than the property sought to be forfeited. . . . The forfeiture is not intended to rectify the unjust enrichment of the individual, but to punish the defendant upon conviction of violation of any provision of the section . . . by forfeiture of all interest in the enterprise." *U.S. v. DeFries*, 129 F.3d 1293, 1315, 156 L.R.R.M. (BNA) 2999 (D.C. Cir. 1997).

§ 31:11 Attorney's fees: Assets which may be necessary to pay attorney's fees are not exempt from forfeiture

Supreme Court

- "It is our view that there is a strong governmental interest in obtaining full recovery of all forfeitable assets, an interest that overrides any Sixth Amendment interest in permitting criminals to use assets adjudged forfeitable to pay for their defense. Otherwise, there would be an interference with a defendant's Sixth Amendment rights whenever the government freezes or takes some property in a defendant's possession before, during or after a criminal trial." *Caplin & Drysdale, Chartered v. U.S.*, 491 U.S. 617, 631, 109 S. Ct. 2667, 105 L. Ed. 2d 528 (1989).

- "We conclude that there is no exemption from Section 853's forfeiture or pretrial restraining order provisions for assets which a defendant wishes to use to retain an attorney. In enacting Section 853, Congress decided to give force to the old adage that crime does not pay. We find no evidence that Congress intended to modify that nostrum to read, crime does not pay, except for attorney's fees. If, as respondent and supporting *amici* so

vigorously assert, we are mistaken as to Congress'
intent, that body can amend this statute to otherwise
provide. But the statute, as presently written, cannot
be read any other way." *U.S. v. Monsanto*, 491 U.S.
600, 614, 109 S. Ct. 2657, 105 L. Ed. 2d 512 (1989).

- "Here, the language is clear and the statute
comprehensive: Section 853 does not exempt assets to
be used for attorney's fees from its forfeiture provisions.
In sum, whatever force there might be to respondent's
claim for an exemption from forfeiture under Section
853(a) of assets necessary to pay attorney's fees—based
on his theories about the statute's purpose, or the
implications of interpretative canons, or the understandings of individual members of Congress about the statute's scope—the short answer is that Congress did not
write the statute that way." *U.S. v. Monsanto*, 491 U.S.
600, 611, 109 S. Ct. 2657, 105 L. Ed. 2d 512 (1989).

- "If defendants have a right to spend forfeitable assets
on attorney's fees, why not on exercises of the right to
speak, practice one's religion, or travel? The full exercise
of these rights, too, depends in part on one's financial
wherewithal; and forfeiture, or even the threat of forfeiture, may similarly prevent a defendant from enjoying
these rights as fully as he might otherwise. Nonetheless, we are not about to recognize an antiforfeiture
exception for the exercise of each such right; nor does
one exist for the exercise of Sixth Amendment rights,
either." *Caplin & Drysdale, Chartered v. U.S.*, 491 U.S.
617, 628, 109 S. Ct. 2667, 105 L. Ed. 2d 528 (1989).

Second Circuit

- "The RICO criminal forfeiture statute has caused alarm
in a number of quarters, but two groups have felt
particularly vulnerable to this law: defense attorneys,
who risk non-payment if their clients' funds are found
subject to forfeiture, and third-party property holders,
who risk losing their property to the Government if
their property appears to be the defendant's and the
defendant is ordered to forfeit that property to the
Government. Although the Supreme Court held in
Monsanto and *Caplin & Drysdale* that the forfeiture of
funds for attorneys fees does not violate the Sixth
Amendment right to counsel, the Attorney General has

the authority under 18 U.S.C. § 1963(g)(2) to permit defendants to keep some assets otherwise forfeitable to the Government, in order to pay their attorneys. With respect to the rights of third-party property holders, § 1963(g) permits those parties to petition the Attorney General for remission of property, and § 1963(1) permits a narrow class of interest holders to petition a Court to amend an order of forfeiture so that their property may be returned directly to them." *U.S. v. Schwimmer*, 968 F.2d 1570, 1573, 23 Fed. R. Serv. 3d 224 (2d Cir. 1992).

Third Circuit

- "[F]ees may not be subject to forfeiture even if the attorney had known of the taint at the time the fee was received, as long as he or she did not know about the act creating the taint at the time it was committed. If an attorney would not lose the fee when he or she only discovers the taint after receiving the property, then the rule we fashion would create no disincentive for an attorney to investigate a client's case. It would merely create an incentive for an attorney to require payment of the fee (or retainer) up-front." *U.S. v. One 1973 Rolls Royce, V.I.N. SRH-16266 By and Through Goodman*, 43 F.3d 794, 811 (3d Cir. 1994).

Sixth Circuit

- "Here, as in *Caplin & Drysdale*, when the defendant claims that he has suffered some substantial impairment of his Sixth Amendment rights by virtue of the seizure or forfeiture of assets in his possession, such a complaint is no more than the reflection of the harsh reality that the quality of a criminal defendant's representation frequently may turn on his ability to retain the best counsel money can buy." *U.S. v. Sammons*, 918 F.2d 592, 598 (6th Cir. 1990).

Seventh Circuit

- "Of course, as *Moya-Gomez* made clear, a claimant need not have an absolute Sixth Amendment right to have a significant interest in the property. A civil forfeiture claimant might argue that even though the Sixth Amendment does not apply to civil cases, the Fifth Amendment's Due Process Clause requires appointment of counsel—or, as a corollary, an opportunity to retain counsel. But these cases only underscore that, for due process purposes, deprivations of liberty received different protections than deprivations of other rights. Accordingly, we find that a civil forfeiture claimant's interest is significantly diminished when he seeks assets to pay attorneys in the civil forfeiture action as opposed to a related criminal action." *U.S. v. Michelle's Lounge*, 39 F.3d 684, 698, 30 Fed. R. Serv. 3d 31 (7th Cir. 1994) (abrogated on other grounds by, Kaley v. U.S., 134 S. Ct. 1090, 188 L. Ed. 2d 46 (2014)).

- "The imposition of a pretrial restraining order freezing the assets of the defendant that the government believes are subject to forfeiture may well have the practical effect of rendering the defendant indigent. However, this possibility does not, when it occurs, constitute a denial of the defendant's absolute Sixth Amendment right to counsel. While a defendant whose entire assets are subject to a restraining order will not be able to retain counsel of choice, he has the right to have counsel appointed." *U.S. v. Moya-Gomez*, 860 F.2d 706, 725 (7th Cir. 1988).

Tenth Circuit

- "Our holding today is not at odds with the Supreme Court's decisions in *Caplin & Drysdale*. . . . Those companion cases only held that a criminal defendant has no Sixth Amendment right to use forfeitable assets to employ counsel. Neither case decided whether due process requires a hearing at which a defendant could challenge the forfeitability of assets. . . . For the reasons set forth above, we conclude that due process requires a district court to conduct a post-restraint, pretrial hearing before continuing to freeze assets if a defendant needs the assets for reasonable legal and living expenses and makes a prima facie showing that the grand jury erred in determining the assets are traceable to the underlying offense." *U.S. v. Jones*, 160 F.3d 641, 648–49 (10th Cir. 1998).

Eleventh Circuit

- "To preserve forfeitable assets for a possible conviction, the district court may restrain the defendant from using these assets before trial. The restraints may be imposed by way of a restraining order, an injunction, the execution of a performance bond, or a temporary seizure of certain assets which, because of their liquidity, can be readily transferred or hidden. As a consequence of the provisions of section 853, an attorney retained to defend one whose assets are subject to forfeiture and restraint may go uncompensated. If the defendant is convicted, the attorney will have no right to assets once in possession of his client because the government's title—vesting at the time of the offense— will usually predate the attorney's claim. This scenario may cause many lawyers to refuse representation of a defendant whose apparent assets are frozen before trial and which may be subject to forfeiture upon conviction. [W]e agree that 21 U.S.C. Section 853 reaches all illegal funds, including those earmarked for payment to attorneys." *U.S. v. Bissell*, 866 F.2d 1343, 1349, 1350 (11th Cir. 1989).

Chapter 32

Standing

§ 32:1   Requirement: The defendant must have been personally aggrieved by the search in order to object to the introduction of evidence obtained by unlawful search and seizure

§ 32:2   Standard: The person challenging the constitutionality of a search must show a legitimate expectation of privacy in the premises searched or the item seized

§ 32:3   Possession or ownership: Possession or ownership of a seized item will not automatically confer standing

§ 32:4   Standing to challenge stop: Passenger may challenge vehicle stop

Research References

West's Key Number Digest

Criminal Law ⬅️394.4 to 394.5; Searches and Seizures ⬅️25.1 to 26, 161 to 170

KeyCite®: Cases and other legal materials listed in KeyCite Scope can be researched through the KeyCite service on Westlaw®. Use KeyCite to check citations for form, parallel references, prior and later history, and comprehensive citator information, including citations to other decisions and secondary materials.

---

§ 32:1 Requirement: The defendant must have been personally aggrieved by the search in order to object to the introduction of evidence obtained by unlawful search and seizure

<u>Supreme Court</u>

• "The State concedes that the police had no adequate justification to pull the car over . . . . but argues that the passenger was not seized and thus cannot claim that the evidence was tainted by an unconstitutional stop. We resolve this question by asking whether a reasonable person in Brendlin's position when the car stopped would have believed himself free to "terminate the encounter" between the police and himself . . . We think that in these circumstances any reasonable passenger would have understood the police officers to be exercising control to the point that no one in the car was free to depart without police permission . . ." *Brendlin v. California*, 551 U.S. 249, 127 S. Ct. 2400, 168 L. Ed. 2d 132 (2007).

- "[I]n order to claim the protection of the Fourth Amendment, a defendant must demonstrate that he personally has an expectation of privacy in the place searched, and that his expectation is reasonable; i.e., one which has a source outside of the Fourth Amendment, either by reference to concepts of real or personal property law or to understandings that are recognized and permitted by society." *Minnesota v. Carter*, 525 U.S. 83, 88, 119 S. Ct. 469, 142 L. Ed. 2d 373 (1998).

- "Our Fourth Amendment decisions have established beyond any doubt that the interest in deterring illegal searches does not justify the exclusion of tainted evidence at the instance of a party who was not the victim of the challenged practices. [A] court may not exclude evidence under the Fourth Amendment unless it finds that an unlawful search or seizure violated the defendant's own constitutional rights." *U. S. v. Payner*, 1980-2 C.B. 749, 447 U.S. 727, 731, 735, 100 S. Ct. 2439, 65 L. Ed. 2d 468, 80-2 U.S. Tax Cas. (CCH) P 9511 (1980).

- "[T]he supervisory power does not authorize a federal court to suppress otherwise admissible evidence on the ground that it was seized unlawfully from a third party not before the court." *U. S. v. Payner*, 1980-2 C.B. 749, 447 U.S. 727, 735, 100 S. Ct. 2439, 65 L. Ed. 2d 468, 80-2 U.S. Tax Cas. (CCH) P 9511 (1980).

- "A person who is aggrieved by an illegal search and seizure only through the introduction of damaging evidence secured by a search of a third person's premises or property has not had any of his Fourth Amendment rights infringed. And it is proper to permit only defendants whose Fourth Amendment rights have been violated to benefit from the [exclusionary] rule's protections." *Rakas v. Illinois*, 439 U.S. 128, 134, 99 S. Ct. 421, 58 L. Ed. 2d 387 (1978).

- "Fourth Amendment rights are personal rights which, like some other constitutional rights, may not be vicariously asserted." *Alderman v. U.S.*, 394 U.S. 165, 174, 89 S. Ct. 961, 22 L. Ed. 2d 176 (1969).

First Circuit

- "Defendant did not have a reasonable expectation of privacy in storage locker after he failed to pay rent for several months, and thus defendant lacked standing to assert Fourth Amendment violation with respect to search of locker; storage facility operator had a lien on contents of locker, operator had scheduled a public auction, operator removed lock on space to permit government agents to search, and Massachusetts law allowed storage facility to exclude a lessee who failed to pay rent." *U.S. v. Lnu*, 544 F.3d 361 (1st Cir. 2008).
- "Consensual searches are a recognized exception to the Fourth Amendment's warrant requirement, but the government bears the burden to prove by a preponderance of the evidence that defendant or an authorized third party gave the consent voluntarily." *U.S. v. Vanvliet*, 542 F.3d 259 (1st Cir. 2008).
- "It is doctrinal bedrock that a police stop of a moving vehicle constitutes a seizure of the vehicle's occupants and therefore comes within the purview of the Fourth Amendment. . . . This principle applies equally to drivers and passengers. . . . Hence, each occupant of a car has a right to challenge the propriety of a traffic stop under the Fourth Amendment. Although courts occasionally use the term standing as a shorthand for this status, the real implication is that the individual's Fourth Amendment interests were affected by official actions." *U.S. v. Woodrum*, 202 F.3d 1, 5–6 (1st Cir. 2000).
- "[Defendant] was nothing more than a casual visitor in the apartment, and, as such, had no reasonable expectation of privacy there. . . . Since Fourth Amendment rights are personal to each defendant and may not be asserted vicariously. . . . [Defendant]'s failure to demonstrate his own legitimate expectation of privacy in the premises renders the exclusionary rule unavailable to him." *U.S. v. Torres*, 162 F.3d 6, 10 (1st Cir. 1998).

Second Circuit

- "Fourth Amendment rights are personal, and may be
  enforced only by persons whose own protection under
  the Amendment has been violated. . . . To contest the
  validity of a search, a defendant must demonstrate that
  he himself exhibited an actual subjective expectation of
  privacy in the area searched, and that this subjective
  expectation is one that society is willing to accept as
  reasonable. . . . A defendant lacks standing in the
  Fourth Amendment context when his contacts with the
  searched premises are so attenuated that no expectation of privacy he has in those premises could ever be
  considered reasonable." *U.S. v. Fields*, 113 F.3d 313,
  320 (2d Cir. 1997).

Third Circuit

- "Defendant had no legitimate expectation of privacy in
  vehicle, and thus lacked standing to challenge police
  search of vehicle, where vehicle, though parked in
  defendant's driveway, was not registered in his name,
  and, at the time of the search, defendant disavowed any
  ownership right in the vehicle and stated that he did
  not know to whom it belonged." *U.S. v. Patton*, 292 Fed.
  Appx. 159 (3d Cir. 2008).

Fourth Circuit

- "The voluntary return of property seized under a valid
  search warrant does not give rise to an adverse inference or tend to establish that the initial seizure violated
  Fourth Amendment." *U.S. v. Srivastava*, 540 F.3d 277,
  102 A.F.T.R.2d 2008-6088 (4th Cir. 2008).

Fifth Circuit

- "Because Fourth Amendment rights are personal, the
  Supreme Court has stated that there is no useful analytical purpose to be served by considering a matter of
  standing distinct from the merits of a defendant's
  Fourth Amendment claim. . . . ('Rigorous application of
  the principle that the rights secured by this Amendment are personal, in place of a notion of "standing,"
  will produce no additional situations in which evidence
  must be excluded.'). Despite this admonishment, for
  brevity's sake, courts often refer to the question of
  whether or not a defendant is asserting a violation of

his own Fourth Amendment rights as one of 'standing.' " *U.S. v. Pack*, 612 F.3d 341, 347 (5th Cir. 2010), opinion modified on denial of reh'g, U.S. v. Pack, 622 F.3d 383 (5th Cir. 2010).

Sixth Circuit

- "In order to qualify as a person aggrieved by an unlawful search and seizure, as required to establish standing to challenge the search and seizure, one must have been a victim of a search or seizure, one against whom the search was directed, as distinguished from one who claims prejudice only through the use of evidence gathered as a consequence of a search or seizure directed at someone else." *U.S. v. Pearce*, 531 F.3d 374 (6th Cir. 2008).

- "The plaintiffs allege that the NSA has, by conducting the warrantless wiretaps, violated the "plaintiffs' privacy rights guaranteed by the Fourth Amendment" . . . However, the Supreme Court has made clear that Fourth Amendment rights are "personal rights" which, unlike First Amendment rights, may not be asserted vicariously . . . . The plaintiffs do not, and cannot . . . assert that any of their own communications have ever been intercepted. Instead, they allege only a belief that their communications are being intercepted, based on their own assessment of their overseas contacts as people who are likely to fall within the NSA's broad, public description of its targets. As acknowledged by plaintiffs' counsel at oral argument, it would be unprecedented for this court to find standing for plaintiffs to litigate a Fourth Amendment cause of action without any evidence that the plaintiffs themselves have been subjected to an illegal search or seizure." *American Civil Liberties Union v. National Sec. Agency*, 493 F.3d 644 (6th Cir. 2007).

- "A person has standing to challenge the admissibility of contraband found in a suitcase or travel bag only if one has a legitimate expectation of privacy in the bag at the time of the search. . . . [O]ne who disclaims any interest in luggage thereby disclaims any concern about whether or not the contents of the luggage remain private." *U.S. v. Peters*, 194 F.3d 692, 695–96, 1999 FED App. 0357P (6th Cir. 1999).

Seventh Circuit

- "The search of the passengers was illegal, but normally
  A cannot challenge the legality of the search of B even
  when the search produces information used to convict
  A." *U.S. v. Johnson*, 380 F.3d 1013 (7th Cir. 2004).

Eighth Circuit

- "A person who is wrongfully on the premises may not
  object to the legality of a search. A person who the police find to be unlawfully occupying a building condemned for occupancy, and who refuses their command
  to vacate the premises, may not object to the legality of
  their entry and removal by arrest." *Cross v. Mokwa*,
  547 F.3d 890 (8th Cir. 2008).
- "Claimant to third-party rights to property that was
  subject to forfeiture, pursuant to defendant's plea asserting ownership of property and agreeing to forfeiture, lacked standing, under Article III case or controversy requirements, for Fourth Amendment challenge
  to seizure of property from claimant's residence, since
  claimant was not entitled to vicariously assert defendant's Fourth Amendment rights regarding search and
  seizure." *U.S. v. Porchay*, 533 F.3d 704 (8th Cir. 2008).
- "Fourth Amendment rights are personal and cannot be
  asserted vicariously. . . .A defendant who fails to prove
  a sufficiently close connection to the relevant places or
  objects searched. . .has no standing to claim that they
  were searched or seized illegally." *U.S. v. Pierson*, 219
  F.3d 803, 806 (8th Cir. 2000).
- "Even if the search of the bag were unconstitutional, we
  believe that [Defendant] has no standing to challenge
  the search. It is undisputed that to this day he disclaims
  any ownership interest in the bag. A person must have
  a reasonable expectation of privacy in a place searched
  before he or she may contest the validity of the search.
  . . . Fourth Amendment rights are personal
  and. . .may not be vicariously asserted." *U.S. v.
  Washington*, 197 F.3d 1214, 1216 (8th Cir. 1999).

Ninth Circuit

- "Parents/homeowners had legitimate expectation of
  privacy in house and therefore could challenge search
  warrant by authority of which police searched adult

son's bedroom within house, even though bedroom had separate entrance and son conducted drug trafficking business out of bedroom; parents did not have to have exclusive possessory interest in bedroom or exclusive right of access or exclusion to it, in order to claim expectation of privacy, and bedroom was not separated from rest of house via lock on door or son's payment of rent." *U.S. v. $40,955.00 in U.S. Currency*, 554 F.3d 752 (9th Cir. 2009).

- "Defendant lacked standing to challenge search of vehicle in which he was smuggling narcotics, where defendant fled vehicle that he neither owned nor leased, and that he had been in only once." *U.S. v. Ramos-Soto*, 304 Fed. Appx. 578 (9th Cir. 2008).

Tenth Circuit

- "We have recognized that an individual may have a reasonable expectation of privacy in a motel room. . . . In making this determination, we have traditionally considered whether the individual had lawful ownership or control of the premises searched. . . . Of importance is the status of the defendant as an overnight guest. . . . Thus, we have required a defendant to demonstrate that he was the registered occupant of the room or that he was sharing it with the person to whom the room was registered." *U.S. v. Gordon*, 168 F.3d 1222, 1226 (10th Cir. 1999).

- "Fourth Amendment rights are personal and may not be asserted vicariously. . . . Suppression of evidence is an appropriate remedy only when the search violates a person's constitutional rights. It is not enough that a person is aggrieved only by the introduction of damaging evidence derived from the search. . . . The proponent of a motion to suppress has the burden of adducing facts at the suppression hearing indicating that his own rights were violated by the challenged search." *U.S. v. Gama-Bastidas*, 142 F.3d 1233, 1238 (10th Cir. 1998).

Eleventh Circuit

- "[W]hen a police officer effectuates an arrest warrant in a third-party's abode, the officer may violate the Fourth Amendment rights of the third-party. But we agree with

our sister circuits that the subject of an arrest warrant
cannot challenge the execution of that warrant and the
later discovery of evidence in a third-party's home."
U.S. v. Hollis, 780 F.3d 1064, 1069–70 (11th Cir. 2015),
cert. denied, 136 S. Ct. 274, 193 L. Ed. 2d 200 (2015)
(citation omitted).

- "Fourth Amendment rights. . . .are personal, and only
  individuals who actually enjoy the reasonable expectation of privacy have standing to challenge the validity
  of a government search." *U.S. v. Cooper*, 203 F.3d 1279,
  1284 (11th Cir. 2000).

§ 32:2 Standard: The person challenging the constitutionality of a search must show a legitimate expectation of privacy in the premises searched or the item seized

Supreme Court

- "Our Fourth Amendment analysis embraces two
  questions. First, we ask whether the individual, by his
  conduct, has exhibited an actual expectation of privacy;
  that is, whether he has shown that he sought to
  preserve something as private. . . . Second, we inquire
  whether the individual's expectation of privacy is one
  that society is prepared to recognize as reasonable."
  Bond v. U.S., 529 U.S. 334, 338, 120 S. Ct. 1462, 146 L.
  Ed. 2d 365 (2000).

- "[N]either *Ross* itself nor the historical evidence it relied
  upon admits of a distinction among packages or containers based on ownership. When there is probable cause
  to search for contraband in a car, it is reasonable for
  police officers—like customs officials in the Founding
  era—to examine packages and containers without a
  showing of individualized probable cause for each one.
  A passenger's personal belongings, just like the driver's
  belongings or containers attached to the car like a glove
  compartment, are in the car, and the officer has probable cause to search for contraband in the car. . . . Passengers, no less than drivers, possess a reduced expectation of privacy with regard to the property that they
  transport in cars, which trave[l] public thoroughfares
  . . . seldom serve as . . . the repository of personal effects . . . . are subjected to police stop and examination

to enforce pervasive governmental controls as an every-day occurrence . . . . and, finally, are exposed to traffic accidents that may render all their contents open to public scrutiny." *Wyoming v. Houghton*, 526 U.S. 295, 302–03, 119 S. Ct. 1297, 143 L. Ed. 2d 408 (1999).

- "Property used for commercial purposes is treated differently for Fourth Amendment purposes than residential property. An expectation of privacy in commercial premises, however, is different from, and indeed less than, a similar expectation in an individual's home." *Minnesota v. Carter*, 525 U.S. 83, 90, 119 S. Ct. 469, 142 L. Ed. 2d 373 (1998).

- "[Defendant's] status as an overnight guest is alone enough to show that he had an expectation of privacy in the home that society is prepared to recognize as reasonable. To hold that an overnight guest has a legitimate expectation of privacy in his host's home merely recognizes the everyday expectations of privacy that we all share. Staying overnight in another's home is a longstanding social custom that serves functions recognized as valuable by society. [W]e think that society recognizes that a houseguest has a legitimate expectation of privacy in his host's home." *Minnesota v. Olson*, 495 U.S. 91, 96, 97, 98, 110 S. Ct. 1684, 109 L. Ed. 2d 85 (1990).

- "Petitioner, of course, bears the burden of proving not only that the search was illegal, but also that he had a legitimate expectation of privacy." *Rawlings v. Kentucky*, 448 U.S. 98, 104, 100 S. Ct. 2556, 65 L. Ed. 2d 633 (1980).

- "[T]his Court uniformly has held that the application of the Fourth Amendment depends on whether the person invoking its protection can claim a justifiable, a reasonable, or a legitimate expectation of privacy that has been invaded by government action. This inquiry normally embraces two discrete questions. The first is whether the individual, by his conduct, has exhibited an actual (subjective) expectation of privacy. The second question is whether the individual's subjective expectation of privacy is one that society is prepared to recognize as reasonable, whether the individual's expectation, viewed objectively, is justifiable under the circumstances." *Smith v. Maryland*, 442 U.S. 735, 740, 99 S. Ct. 2577, 61 L. Ed. 2d 220 (1979).

- "[T]he question is whether the challenged search and seizure violated the Fourth Amendment rights of a criminal defendant who seeks to exclude the evidence obtained during it. That inquiry in turn requires a determination of whether the disputed search and seizure has infringed an interest of the defendant which the Fourth Amendment was designed to protect." *Rakas v. Illinois*, 439 U.S. 128, 140, 99 S. Ct. 421, 58 L. Ed. 2d 387 (1978).

First Circuit

- "A taxi fare—who by definition has contracted to pay for both the right to exclude others from the cab and the right to control its destination in certain respects—has a reasonable expectation that he will not gratuitously be seized while en route. . . . Absent a warrant, the police can intrude on such an expectation only in a few carefully circumscribed kinds of situations." *U.S. v. Woodrum*, 202 F.3d 1, 6 (1st Cir. 2000).

Second Circuit

- "We do not need to reach the question of whether an unauthorized driver of a rental car ever has a reasonable expectation of privacy in the car, because Lyle was not just an unauthorized driver, but an unlicensed one. Accordingly, Lyle's use of the rental car was both unauthorized and unlawful. Lyle should not have been driving any car because his license was suspended, and a rental company with knowledge of the relevant facts certainly would not have given him permission to drive its car nor allowed a renter to do so. Under these circumstances, Lyle did not have a reasonable expectation of privacy in the rental car. Our decision in *United States v. Smith* is instructive. There, we held that Smith had no legitimate expectation of privacy in the trunk of a rental car, despite the fact that he was in the driver's seat of the car when he was stopped by law enforcement. Like Lyle, Smith 'had no driver's license and the car was registered in another's name.' Also like Lyle, Smith 'made no showing that he had any legitimate basis for being in the car at all.' Lyle's reliance on the Sixth Circuit's decision in *Smith* is misplaced. *Smith* presented unique facts. Specifically, Smith was not only the husband of the renter, but he also 'had a business relationship with the rental company' because he had 'called the rental company to reserve the rental vehicle,' 'was given a reservation number,' and 'provided the company with his credit card number, and that credit card was subsequently billed for the rental of the vehicle.' In light of these facts, the Sixth Circuit determined that 'Smith was the de facto renter of the vehicle' and that, therefore, he had a legitimate expectation of privacy in the rental car. Lyle was not the de facto renter of the car at issue here. Moreover, the Sixth Circuit also noted that Smith was a licensed driver. For these reasons, *Smith* is distinguishable. Accordingly, Lyle lacked a reasonable expectation of privacy in the rental car, and the district court did not err in denying his motion to suppress." *United States v. Lyle*, 856 F.3d 191, 201–02, 103 Fed. R. Evid. Serv. 450 (2d Cir. 2017) (citations omitted).

Third Circuit

- "[The defendant] did not have Fourth Amendment standing to challenge this search because he lacked an objectively reasonable expectation of privacy in the common areas of a multi-unit apartment building with a locked exterior door. In *Acosta,* we held that a resident of a multi-unit apartment complex lacks an objectively reasonable expectation of privacy in the common areas of the multi-unit apartment complex, at least where the exterior door is *unlocked*. We now extend *Acosta* and join a number of other Circuit Courts of Appeals in holding that a resident lacks an objectively reasonable expectation of privacy in the common areas of a multi-unit apartment building with a locked exterior door. Moreover, we think [the defendant] lacked a reasonable expectation of privacy in the building's common areas because he did not have control over these areas. After all, '[a]n expectation of privacy necessarily implies an expectation that one will be free of *any* intrusion, not merely unwarranted intrusions.' Here, any resident in the multi-unit apartment building could admit guests, delivery people, repair workers, postal carriers, custodians, and others into the common areas of the apartment building. Additionally, the purpose of the locked front door was to 'provide security to the occupants, not privacy in common hallways.' Finally, residents benefit from police protection in these common areas. Given the plethora of individuals who could access the common areas of the locked multi-unit apartment building and [the defendant's] inability to control these areas, [the defendant] 'could not have reasonably expected [his] privacy to extend beyond [his] apartment door.' Finally, we reiterate that Fourth Amendment standing turns on legitimate expectations of privacy and not—as [the defendant] argues—on concepts of property-law trespass. Indeed, many places designated as 'private' by the common law of property do not garner Fourth Amendment protection because they have been knowingly exposed to public view and lose a legitimate expectation of privacy. Here, the common areas of the apartment building are similarly 'public' spaces and not entitled to Fourth Amendment protection. [The defendant's] argument that the Task Force violated his Fourth Amendment rights by trespassing in the common areas of the locked, multi-unit apartment building misses the mark. The relevant question is whether [the defendant] had an objectively reasonable expectation of privacy in the common areas. For the reasons discussed, he did not. Therefore, no Fourth Amendment violation occurred, and we will affirm." *U.S. v. Correa*, 653 F.3d 187, 190–92 (3d Cir. 2011) (citations omitted).

- "The defendant had no legitimate expectation of privacy in vehicle, and thus lacked standing to challenge police search of vehicle, where the vehicle, though parked in defendant's driveway, was not registered in his name, and, at the time of the search, the defendant disavowed any ownership right in the vehicle and stated that he did not know to whom it belonged." *U.S. v. Patton*, 292 Fed. Appx. 159 (3d Cir. 2008).

Fourth Circuit

- "[Plaintiff] herself was never searched pursuant to [a public hospital's policy of testing new mothers for drug use]; rather, a search was conducted on the urine of her newborn child. Appellees assert that because [plaintiff] did not have a reasonable expectation of privacy in her child's urine, she lacks standing to claim a violation of the Fourth Amendment. We agree with Appellees that [plaintiff] suffered no violation of her Fourth Amendment rights. Fourth Amendment rights are personal rights which, like some other constitutional rights, may not be vicariously asserted. We are aware of no decision holding, or even suggesting, that a mother has a reasonable expectation of privacy in her newborn child's bodily fluids." *Ferguson v. City of Charleston, S.C.*, 308 F.3d 380 (4th Cir. 2002).

Fifth Circuit

- " '[A] person has no standing to challenge a search or seizure of property that was voluntarily abandoned.' In *Powell*, police searched defendants Booker Powell and April Akin's car for evidence of drug trafficking. The officers heard ringing during the search and discovered a phone near the driver's seat. 'Powell denied the phone was his,' and 'Akin said that it belonged to Powell.' We held that by 'disclaim[ing] personal connection to the phone,' Akin abandoned it, which deprived her of standing to challenge the admissibility of the phone and its records. Like the defendant in *Powell*, Escamilla expressly disclaimed ownership of the phone and left it in the possession of DEA agents. By doing so, Escamilla abandoned the phone and has no standing to challenge Agent Antonelli's Cellebrite search. Escamilla's reliance on a single out-of-circuit case, decided before *Powell*, is misplaced." *United States v. Escamilla*, 852 F.3d 474, 485–86 (5th Cir. 2017) (citations omitted).

- "The Government contends that [defendant] has no standing to challenge the search of the Chevy because [defendant] had no privacy interest in the car. However, we have previously held that while the search of an automobile does not implicate a passenger's Fourth Amendment rights, a stop results in the seizure of the passenger and driver alike. Therefore, while a passenger of a stopped automobile does not have standing to challenge the search of a car, he does have standing to challenge the seizure of his person as unconstitutional." *U.S. v. Grant*, 349 F.3d 192 (5th Cir. 2003).

Seventh Circuit

- "... [Defendant] was not simply an unauthorized driver, he was also an unlicensed one. [Defendant] should not have been driving any car, much less a rental car that Enterprise never would have given him permission to drive. As a result, [defendant's] expectation of privacy was not reasonable. ... Therefore, [defendant] lacked standing to challenge the search. *U.S. v. Haywood*, 324 F.3d 514 (7th Cir. 2003).

- "Today, we adopt the rule that a person listed on a rental agreement as an authorized driver has a protected Fourth Amendment interest in the vehicle and may challenge a search of the rental vehicle. We arrive at this conclusion by applying the two-pronged objective and subjective expectation-of-privacy test. A person listed as an approved driver on a rental agreement has an objective expectation of privacy in the vehicle due to his possessory and property interest in the vehicle." *U.S. v. Walker*, 237 F.3d 845, 849 (7th Cir. 2001).

Eighth Circuit

- "Russell asserts a possessory interest because the sedan was rented by his girlfriend and allegedly operated at his request. A 'defendant must present at least some evidence of consent or permission from the lawful owner/renter [of a vehicle] to give rise to an objectively reasonable expectation of privacy.' Russell provides no evidence that his girlfriend permitted him to drive the sedan or otherwise exercise any possessory control over it. Because he did not establish a reasonable expectation of privacy in the sedan, he has no standing to challenge the search." *United States v. Russell*, 847 F.3d 616, 618–19 (8th Cir. 2017) (citation omitted).

- "[Defendant] contends that the district court erred in denying his motion to suppress because the search warrant for his uncle's property lacked probable cause, but he has failed to demonstrate that he had a legitimate expectation of privacy there. (citation omitted) The evidence did not show that [defendant] either lived or stayed more than irregularly at his uncle's residence, that he stored personal effects there which he admitted to owning, or that he had exclusive access to or had taken precautions to maintain privacy in the gun cabinets or the room where the ammunition was found.

(citation omitted) He therefore lacks standing to challenge the search." *U.S. v. Davis*, 361 Fed. Appx. 704 (8th Cir. 2010).

- "Applying these principles to [defendant's] van, we conclude that the stop of the vehicle did not implicate his constitutional rights at all. A person who lends an automobile to another of course does not give up his or her fourth amendment interest altogether. The lender's right to possession when the bailment terminates, for instance, is a valuable property right. On the other hand, the lender's right to control the property during the bailment is greatly diminished, and he or she no longer has a reasonable expectation of a possessory interest in it for a time. When [defendant] lent the van to his stepson, he gave up any significant expectation related to controlling its movement. . . . Of course, he had a reasonable expectation that his stepson would maintain general control of the van, but this expectation is quite different from the stepson's own expectation in minute-to-minute control of the vehicle while driving. It is important to realize that a person's interest in his or her loaned effects is not identical to the possessory interest of the bailee who has direct control of the effects, and the lender cannot assert the bailee's independent fourth amendment right to have the bailee's interest protected from unreasonable government interference. A brief stop by the police of a loaned automobile being driven by a third party does not significantly impair the interests of the person who lent the automobile. . . . The burden that such stops impose on the bailor's interest, if burden at all, is too slight to amount to a fourth amendment seizure. So that there is no confusion about our holding, we point out that where a party is asserting his or her personal right to be free from government seizure, a different standard applies. For example, had [defendant] been driving the van when it was stopped, the case would be governed by *Terry*, and the police would need to demonstrate that they had a reasonable suspicion. In this case, however, the only rights of his that are implicated in the stop are his rights in the van itself." *U.S. v. Fuller*, 374 F.3d 617 (8th Cir. 2004).

- "A defendant moving to suppress evidence has the

burden of showing a legitimate expectation of privacy in the area searched. . . .Factors relevant to the determination of standing include: ownership, possession and/or control of the area searched or item seized; historical use of the property or item; ability to regulate access; the totality of the circumstances surrounding the search; the existence or nonexistence of a subjective anticipation of privacy; and the objective reasonableness of the expectation of privacy considering the specific facts of the case." *U.S. v. Pierson*, 219 F.3d 803, 806 (8th Cir. 2000).

- "Fourth Amendment rights may not be vicariously asserted. . . . In order to show a legitimate expectation of privacy in the searched premises, the person challenging the search has the burden of showing both a subjective expectation of privacy and that the expectation is objectively reasonable; that is, one that society is willing to accept. . . . Several factors are relevant to this showing: whether the party has a possessory interest in the things seized or the place searched; whether the party can exclude others from that place; whether the party took precautions to maintain the privacy; and whether the party had a key to the premises." *U.S. v. McCaster*, 193 F.3d 930, 933 (8th Cir. 1999).

Ninth Circuit

- "Fourth Amendment standing, unlike Article III standing, is a matter of substantive Fourth Amendment law; to say that a party lacks Fourth Amendment standing is to say that his reasonable expectation of privacy has not been infringed. It is crucial to Fourth Amendment standing relating property used for commercial purposes that the place searched be given over to the defendant's exclusive use. Except in the case of a small, family-run business over which an individual exercises daily management and control, an individual challenging a search of workplace areas beyond his own internal office must generally show some personal connection to the places searched and the materials seized; absent such a personal connection or exclusive use, a defendant cannot establish standing for Fourth Amendment purposes to challenge the search of a workplace beyond his internal office." *U.S. v. SDI Future Health, Inc.*, 568 F.3d 684, 103 A.F.T.R.2d 2009-2436 (9th Cir. 2009).

- "[I]t is crucial to Fourth Amendment standing that the place searched be 'given over to [the defendant's] exclusive use. . . . [M]ere access to, and even use of, the office of a co-worker 'does not lead us to find an objectively reasonable expectation of privacy.' . . . [A]n employee of a corporation, whether worker or manager, does not, simply by virtue of his status as such, acquire Fourth Amendment standing with respect to company premises. . . . [B]eing merely a shareholder of a corporation, without more, is also not enough. As always, a reasonable expectation of privacy does not arise ex officio, but must be established with respect to the person in question." *U.S. v. SDI Future Health, Inc.*, 568 F.3d 684, 103 A.F.T.R.2d 2009-2436 (9th Cir. 2009).

- " 'When a man chooses to avail himself of the privilege of doing business as a corporation, even though he is its sole shareholder, he may not vicariously take on the privilege of the corporation under the Fourth Amendment; documents which he could have protected from seizure, if they had been his own, may be used against him, no matter how they were obtained from the corporation. Its wrongs are not his wrongs; its immunity is not his immunity.' " *U.S. v. SDI Future Health, Inc.*, 568 F.3d 684, 696 n.5, 103 A.F.T.R.2d 2009-2436 (9th Cir. 2009).

- "Except in the case of a small business over which an individual exercises daily management and control, an individual challenging a search of workplace areas beyond his own internal office must generally show some personal connection to the places searched and the materials seized. The strength of such personal connection should be analyzed with reference to the following factors: (1) whether the item seized is personal property or otherwise kept in a private place separate from other work-related material; (2) whether the defendant had custody or immediate control of the item when officers seized it; and (3) whether the defendant took precautions on his own behalf to secure the place searched or things seized from any interference without his authorization. Absent such a personal connection or exclusive use, a defendant cannot establish standing for Fourth Amendment purposes to challenge the search of a workplace beyond his internal office." *U.S. v. SDI*

Future Health, Inc., 568 F.3d 684, 698, 103 A.F.T.R.2d 2009-2436 (9th Cir. 2009).

- "Defendant lacked standing to challenge search of vehicle in which he was smuggling narcotics, where defendant fled vehicle that he neither owned nor leased, and that he had been in only once." *U.S. v. Ramos-Soto*, 304 Fed. Appx. 578 (9th Cir. 2008).

- "In order to have standing to challenge the search of a hotel room under the Fourth Amendment, a defendant must establish a reasonable expectation of privacy in the room. . . .This court has held that a defendant has no reasonable expectation of privacy in a hotel room when the rental period has expired and the hotel has taken affirmative steps to repossess the room. . . .On the other hand, this court has concluded that the lessee of a rental car maintains a reasonable expectation of privacy in the car after the expiration of the lease, when the rental agency has taken no affirmative steps to repossess the car and when it has a policy of permitting lessees to keep cars and simply charging them for the extra time." *U.S. v. Dorais*, 241 F.3d 1124, 1128 (9th Cir. 2001).

Tenth Circuit

- "The Supreme Court has explained that overnight guests have a reasonable expectation of privacy in the home of their host. Further, we have held that even social guests who do not stay the night have a reasonable expectation of privacy in the host's home and may therefore challenge a search of the home on Fourth Amendment grounds. In contrast, a person who is present at another's home, with permission, simply for the purpose of consummating a business transaction does not have a reasonable expectation of privacy there." *U.S. v. Thomas*, 372 F.3d 1173 (10th Cir. 2004).

- "[Defendant's] relationship to [employer's] computer also does not suggest a reasonable expectation of privacy. [Employer] explicitly reserved ownership of not only its computer hardware, but also the data stored within. . . Because the computer was issued to [defendant] only for work related purposes, his relationship to [employer's] computer was incident to his employment. Reasonable people in [defendant's] employment context would expect [employer's] computer policies to constrain their expectations of privacy in the use of [employer]-owned computers. Additionally, the pornographic images seized by police were not within [defendant's] immediate control. . . [Defendant] did not have access to the seized data because he had previously attempted to delete the files from [employer's] computer's memory. Police only recovered the data through special technology unavailable to [defendant]. Finally, [defendant] did not take actions consistent with maintaining private access to the seized pornography. . . [Defendant] downloaded child pornography through a monitored . . . computer network. [Employer's] policy clearly warned computer users such data is 'fairly easy to access' by third parties. The policy explained network administrators actively audit network transmissions for such misuse. While [defendant] did attempt to erase the child pornography, [employer's] computer policy warned system administrators kept file logs recording when and by whom files were deleted. Moreover, given his transmission of the pornographic data through a monitored . . . network, deleting the files alone was not sufficient to establish a reasonable expectation of privacy." *U.S. v. Angevine*, 281 F.3d 1130 (10th Cir. 2002).

Eleventh Circuit

- "To determine whether an individual has a reasonable expectation of privacy in a hotel room, courts have looked to such indicia as whether the individual paid and/or registered for the room or whether the individual's personal belongings were found inside the room." *U.S. v. Cooper*, 203 F.3d 1279, 1284 (11th Cir. 2000).

- "To have standing to challenge a search, one must manifest a subjective expectation of privacy in the invaded area that society is prepared to recognize as reasonable. . . . The individual's expectation, viewed objectively, must be justifiable under the circumstances. . . . The individual challenging the search bears the burdens of proof and persuasion." *U.S. v. Cooper*, 133 F.3d 1394, 1398 (11th Cir. 1998).

§ 32:3   Possession or ownership: Possession or ownership of a seized item will not automatically confer standing

Supreme Court

- "The person in legal possession of a good seized during an illegal search has not necessarily been subject to a Fourth Amendment deprivation. [L]egal possession of a seized good is not a proxy for determining whether the owner had a Fourth Amendment interest for it does not invariably represent the protected Fourth Amendment interest. This Court has repeatedly repudiated the notion that arcane distinctions developed in property and tort law ought to control our Fourth Amendment inquiry." *U. S. v. Salvucci*, 448 U.S. 83, 91, 100 S. Ct. 2547, 65 L. Ed. 2d 619 (1980).
- "While property ownership is clearly a factor to be considered in determining whether an individual's Fourth Amendment rights have been violated, property rights are neither the beginning nor the end of this Court's inquiry." *U. S. v. Salvucci*, 448 U.S. 83, 91, 100 S. Ct. 2547, 65 L. Ed. 2d 619 (1980).
- "[In Jones v. U.S., 362 U.S. 257, 80 S. Ct. 725, 4 L. Ed. 2d 697, 78 A.L.R.2d 233 (1960) (overruled by, U. S. v. Salvucci, 448 U.S. 83, 100 S. Ct. 2547, 65 L. Ed. 2d 619 (1980))] the Court held that the defendant was not obliged to establish that his own Fourth Amendment rights had been violated, but only that the search and seizure of the evidence was unconstitutional. Upon such a showing, the exclusionary rule would be available to prevent the admission of the evidence against the defendant. We are convinced that the automatic standing rule of *Jones* has outlived its usefulness in this Court's Fourth Amendment jurisprudence. The doctrine now serves only to afford a windfall to defendants whose Fourth Amendment rights have *not* been violated. We are unwilling to tolerate the exclusion of probative evidence under such circumstances since we adhere to the view that the values of the Fourth Amendment are preserved by a rule which limits the availability of the exclusionary rule to defendants who have been subjected to a violation of their Fourth Amendment rights." *U. S. v. Salvucci*, 448 U.S. 83, 87, 95, 100 S. Ct. 2547, 65 L. Ed. 2d 619 (1980).

- "While petitioner's ownership of the drugs is undoubtedly one fact to be considered in this case, *Rakas* emphatically rejected the notion that arcane concepts of property law ought to control the ability to claim the protections of the Fourth Amendment." *Rawlings v. Kentucky*, 448 U.S. 98, 105, 100 S. Ct. 2556, 65 L. Ed. 2d 633 (1980).

- "[C]apacity to claim the protection of the Fourth Amendment depends not upon a property right in the invaded place but upon whether the person who claims the protection of the Amendment has a legitimate expectation of privacy in the invaded place." *Rakas v. Illinois*, 439 U.S. 128, 143, 99 S. Ct. 421, 58 L. Ed. 2d 387 (1978).

- "Capacity to claim the protection of the [Fourth] Amendment depends not upon a property right in the invaded place but upon whether the area was one in which there was a reasonable expectation of freedom from governmental intrusion." *Mancusi v. DeForte*, 392 U.S. 364, 368, 88 S. Ct. 2120, 20 L. Ed. 2d 1154, 68 L.R.R.M. (BNA) 2449, 58 Lab. Cas. (CCH) P 12756 (1968).

Second Circuit

- "Although the extent of a defendant's property or possessory interest in the place searched is a factor generally considered in determining the reasonableness of a defendant's expectation of privacy . . . a defendant's lack of such an interest does not rule out the possibility that he may still show a reasonable expectation of privacy. . . . Residence may give rise to an expectation of privacy . . . but an individual may also have a sufficient interest in a place other than his own home so that the Fourth Amendment protects him. . . . For instance, where a guest has permission to use an apartment, is given a key, and uses the apartment in the owner's absence, society may be prepared to recognize the guest's privacy, even though no property interest exists. . . . Indeed, society recognizes as legitimate the expectation of privacy possessed by an overnight guest—even though he has at best a fleeting connection to his host's home." *U.S. v. Fields*, 113 F.3d 313, 320 (2d Cir. 1997).

Fifth Circuit

- "We have recognized that 'passengers who assert[ ] neither a property nor a possessory interest in the automobile that was searched, nor any interest in the seized property, ha[ve] no legitimate expectation of privacy entitling them to the protection of the [F]ourth [A]mendment.' However, '[t]he owner of a suitcase located in another's car may have a legitimate expectation of privacy with respect to the contents of his suitcase.' A defendant who abandons or disclaims ownership of property *prior to the search* does not have standing to challenge a search subsequent to his abandonment or disclaimer of that property. Neither Gonzalez nor Meraz–Garcia denied ownership of the bag prior to its search, and therefore, neither has abandoned the luggage. We have recognized that passengers have standing to challenge searches to their luggage. Gonzalez and Meraz—Garcia have asserted a protectable privacy interest in their luggage based on *Jaras* and *Buchner.* Therefore, they have asserted a sufficient interest in the bag searched to support standing to allege a Fourth Amendment claim." *U.S. v. Iraheta,* 764 F.3d 455, 461–62 (5th Cir. 2014) (citations omitted).

- "This case presents an issue of first impression: whether a homeowner has a reasonable expectation of privacy in a vehicle owned and operated by a third party but parked on the homeowner's driveway. We conclude that [defendant] had that expectation, but only because the evidence seized not only was in a truck parked on his property, but also was known to him because it was the subject of the unlawful enterprise in which he took part. . . The difficult question is whether [defendant's] expectation of privacy in the truck is one which society would recognize as reasonable. . . [T]he fact that the truck was on [defendant's] property is undeniably relevant to the question whether he had a reasonable expectation of privacy. . . He had a strong possessory interest in the place searched, which was the real property on which his house was located. He plainly had the right to exclude others from the premises, which he owned, and thereby to exclude others—except possibly the renters of the truck—from the truck by excluding them from the real property. Although apparently it was not [defendant] who locked the truck, he had a subjective expectation of privacy in its contents; he obviously knew of the 170 pounds of marihuana stored there and was concerned that it not be discovered. The normal precautions to maintain his privacy included having the truck parked on his property to protect that privacy. Finally, it is undeniable that [defendant] was legitimately on the premises of his own house. . . Because of [defendant's] possessory interest in the land, and particularly because he and his associates had an overriding interest in privacy regarding the marihuana in the truck, we conclude, under the specific facts of this case, that he did indeed have a reasonable expectation of privacy sufficient to create standing for a Fourth Amendment challenge to the search of the truck." *U.S. v. Gomez*, 276 F.3d 694 (5th Cir. 2001).

Sixth Circuit

- "The government argues that [defendant], a mere guest at the home, had no expectation of privacy, and therefore lacks standing to challenge the officers' entry into the apartment. . . [W]e agree that [defendant] had no expectation of privacy in the home. . . It is well-established that a defendant claiming that a search violated his Fourth Amendment rights has the burden of demonstrating that he had a legitimate expectation of privacy in the place that was searched. And although an overnight guest may be able to establish a legitimate expectation of privacy in the home of his host, persons who are in another's home solely for business purposes—as opposed to being on the premises for a personal occasion-do not have such an expectation of privacy." *U.S. v. Talley*, 275 F.3d 560, 2001 FED App. 0438P (6th Cir. 2001).

- "The courts have considered a number of factors in identifying those expectations which qualify for Fourth Amendment protection. Although the most obvious among the factors is the person's proprietary or possessory interest in the place to be searched or item to be seized, a property right alone is not determinative of whether the individual reasonably expected freedom from governmental intrusion. . . .Other factors include whether the defendant has the right to exclude others from the place in question; whether he had taken

normal precautions to maintain his privacy; whether he
has exhibited a subjective expectation that the area
would remain free from governmental intrusion; and
whether he was legitimately on the premises." *U.S. v.
King*, 227 F.3d 732, 744, 2000 FED App. 0284P (6th
Cir. 2000).

Eighth Circuit

- "Russell asserts a possessory interest because the sedan
  was rented by his girlfriend and allegedly operated at
  his request. A 'defendant must present at least some
  evidence of consent or permission from the lawful
  owner/renter [of a vehicle] to give rise to an objectively
  reasonable expectation of privacy.' Russell provides no
  evidence that his girlfriend permitted him to drive the
  sedan or otherwise exercise any possessory control over
  it. Because he did not establish a reasonable expectation of privacy in the sedan, he has no standing to challenge the search." *United States v. Russell*, 847 F.3d
  616, 618–19 (8th Cir. 2017) (citation omitted).

- "[T]he district court did not err in holding that [defen-
  dant] lacked standing to challenge the search of the
  motel room and the subsequent seizure of the methamphetamine contained therein. The fact that [defendant's]
  lawful arrest prevented him from returning to the...
  [m]otel and either retrieving his goods before the rental
  agreement lapsed or extending his stay does not
  advance [defendant's] argument that his Fourth Amendment rights were violated. The court [in an earlier case]
  determined that the defendant had no standing to challenge the search of the room because his expectation of
  privacy was lost when the rental period expired. ... The
  court rejected the defendant's argument that he lost the
  opportunity to renew the rental agreement when he
  was arrested, noting that it 'was [the] defendant's own
  conduct that prevented his return to the motel.' " *U.S.
  v. Perez-Guerrero*, 334 F.3d 778 (8th Cir. 2003).

Ninth Circuit

- "[A] person does not have a privacy interest in information revealed to a third party and subsequently conveyed
  to governmental authorities, even if the information is
  revealed on the assumption that it will be used for a

limited purpose and that the third party will not betray
their confidence. . . . .The key factor, *Miller* held, is that
a person does not possess a reasonable expectation of
privacy in an item in which he has no possessory or
ownership interest." *U.S. v. Cormier*, 220 F.3d 1103,
1108 (9th Cir. 2000).

- "We do not hold that members of a conspiracy can never
  have standing to contest a search of items or places related to the conspiracy. However, conspirators must
  show that they personally have a property interest
  protected by the Fourth Amendment that was interfered
  with or a reasonable expectation of privacy that was
  invaded by the search." *U.S. v. Padilla*, 111 F.3d 685,
  688 (9th Cir. 1997).

- "Legal possession of a seized good is not a substitute for
  a factual finding that the owner of the good had a legitimate expectation of privacy in the area searched." *U.S.
  v. Zermeno*, 66 F.3d 1058, 1061 (9th Cir. 1995).

<u>Tenth Circuit</u>

- "To establish standing to challenge a car search, the
  defendant bears the burden of showing that he had a
  'legitimate possessory interest in or [a] lawful control
  over the car.' ... Because the focus of the inquiry is on
  reasonable expectations, however, a defendant need not
  submit legal documentation showing a chain of lawful
  custody from the registered owner to himself. In resolving standing issues of this type, we consider important,
  but not determinative, the following factors: '(1)
  whether the defendant asserted ownership over the
  items seized from the vehicle; (2) whether the defendant
  testified to his expectation of privacy at the suppression
  hearing; and (3) whether the defendant presented any
  testimony at the suppression hearing that he had a legitimate possessory interest in the vehicle.' ... Where
  the proponent of a motion to suppress is the car's driver
  but not the registered owner, mere possession of the car
  and its keys does not suffice to establish a legitimate
  possessory interest. Rather, at a minimum, the proponent bears the burden of establishing 'that he gained
  possession from the owner or someone with authority to
  grant possession.' [In this case, the defendant] was driving a vehicle borrowed from a relative of the registered

owner. ... [H]owever, [defendant] submits other evidence, in addition to the familial relationship between the lender and the registered owner, that would lead a reasonable person to conclude that the lender was in lawful possession. First, [defendant] stated that he presumed that [the lender] owned the car, and that if she didn't, it was only because she had not yet purchased the vehicle from her cousin. Second, [the lender] had used the car as her own during the full week of [defendant's visit, and kept it at her home address. Third, [defendant] knew the registered owner personally. These facts, assuming they were believed by the district court, ... lead to our conclusion that a reasonable person would assume that [the lender] was in lawful possession of the subject automobile. ... These facts also meet the requirements... that the defendant must establish that the lender was 'someone with the authority to grant possession.'... This, in conjunction with his statement that [the lender] openly used the car as her own during the entire week of [defendant's] visit, if believed, would lead a reasonable person to infer that [the lender] had authority to lend the car, and that [defendant] therefore had a reasonable expectation of privacy in the vehicle." *U.S. v. Valdez Hocker*, 333 F.3d 1206 (10th Cir. 2003).

- "A worker may have an objectively reasonable expectation of privacy in his workspace, or portions thereof, depending on the circumstances. In the circumstances here, however, we agree with the district court that [defendant's] work as part of a cleaning crew cannot serve as a basis for an objectively reasonable expectation of privacy in the whole of the premises. . . Moreover, [defendant] does not base his privacy claim on his employment but on his claimed intent to convert the premises into his residence. . . [Defendant] argues that he was a resident, albeit one who was not yet staying overnight because of the condition of the property. The matter of residency *at the time of the search*, however, is of considerable importance in this Fourth Amendment inquiry, and the attempt to minimize its significance is unavailing. Moreover, here the *reason* that [defendant] had not taken residence in the property—because it was uninhabitable—is also significant because it bears on whether [defendant's] expectation of privacy is one that society is willing to accept as reasonable. The undisputed fact is that the property was not being used as a residence by anyone and could not reasonably have been so used." *U.S. v. Higgins*, 282 F.3d 1261 (10th Cir. 2002).

- "A defendant has standing to challenge a search only if he or she has a reasonable expectation of privacy in the area being searched the Supreme Court held that a passenger who asserts neither a possessory nor a property interest in a vehicle would not have a legitimate expectation of privacy in the vehicle protected by the Fourth Amendment. Accordingly, we have held that a defendant in sole possession and control of a car rented by a third party has no standing to challenge a search or seizure of the car. Defendants here have not demonstrated that they had a legitimate possessory or ownership interest in the rented cars; accordingly, they lack standing to challenge the searches of the vehicles." *U.S. v. Shareef*, 100 F.3d 1491, 1499–1500 (10th Cir. 1996).

- "Clearly, a guest may possess an expectation of privacy in the premises of his host; and that expectation may meet the standard of societal reasonableness. The pivotal question in this case is whether [Defendant] presented sufficient evidence to show that he was an invited guest of the registered occupant of the motel room. In *Carr*, we held that where an occupant of a motel room registered to another person presented no evidence that he was in lawful possession of the room or that he was the invited guest of the person to whom the room was registered, he failed to establish a reasonable expectation of privacy in the room. Likewise, in this case the evidence failed to establish [Defendant]'s guest status and expectation of privacy in the motel room. Mere physical possession or control of property is not sufficient to establish standing to object to a search of that property. Although a defendant need not come forward with documentation establishing legal possession of the area searched he must at least demonstrate, in the case of a motel room, that he was the invited guest of the renter of the premises." *U.S. v. Conway*, 73 F.3d 975, 979, 43 Fed. R. Evid. Serv. 671 (10th Cir. 1995).

D.C. Circuit

- "[W]e conclude that appellant lacks standing to challenge the search of his knapsack. In the course of the investigatory stop, as duly explained above, the officers asked the driver of the car to open the trunk, which he did. [The] Officer removed the knapsack from the car. When [Defendant] was asked whether the bag was his, he denied ownership. On these facts, we need not reach the issue of whether the police officers had probable cause to search appellant's knapsack. Because [Defendant] disclaimed ownership of the bag, he abandoned his property and waived any legitimate privacy interest in it. Courts have long held that, when a person voluntarily denies ownership of property in response to a police officer's question, he forfeits any reasonable expectation of privacy in the property; consequently, police may search it without a warrant. Accordingly, [Defendant] has no standing to challenge the search of his bag on Fourth Amendment grounds." *U.S. v. Mangum,* 100 F.3d 164, 170 (D.C. Cir. 1996).

§ 32:4   Standing to challenge stop: Passenger may challenge vehicle stop

Supreme Court

- "[A] passenger is seized, just as the driver is, from the moment [a car stopped by the police comes] to a halt on the side of the road. . . . A passenger therefore has standing to challenge a stop's constitutionality." *Arizona v. Johnson,* 555 U.S. 323, 129 S. Ct. 781, 172 L. Ed. 2d 694 (2009).

Fifth Circuit

- "Because the defendant, who was in the vehicle, did not have a possessory or privacy interest in the vehicle, the district court correctly determined that she lacked standing to challenge the search of the vehicle. [citations omitted] Nevertheless, because the stop resulted in defendant's seizure, she did have standing to challenge the legality of the stop and the seizure of her person." *U.S. v. Lara,* 271 Fed. Appx. 404 (5th Cir. 2008).

Sixth Circuit

- "[I]f either the stopping of the car, the length of the passenger's detention thereafter, or the passenger's removal from it are unreasonable in a Fourth Amendment sense, then surely the passenger has standing to object to those constitutional violations and to have suppressed any evidence found in the car which is their fruit." *U.S. v. Campbell*, 549 F.3d 364 (6th Cir. 2008).

Eighth Circuit

- "Russell asserts a possessory interest because the sedan was rented by his girlfriend and allegedly operated at his request. A 'defendant must present at least some evidence of consent or permission from the lawful owner/renter [of a vehicle] to give rise to an objectively reasonable expectation of privacy.' Russell provides no evidence that his girlfriend permitted him to drive the sedan or otherwise exercise any possessory control over it. Because he did not establish a reasonable expectation of privacy in the sedan, he has no standing to challenge the search." *United States v. Russell*, 847 F.3d 616, 618–19 (8th Cir. 2017) (citation omitted).

Tenth Circuit

- "Fourth Amendment rights are personal, and, therefore, a defendant cannot claim a violation of his Fourth Amendment rights based only on the introduction of evidence procured through an illegal search and seizure of a third person's property or premise. As indicated, Mr. Romero was not the registered driver of the rental car stopped. He was not even a passenger in the car. Because he had no possessory or property interest in the van, it is clear that he lacked standing to challenge the Trooper stop of the car being driven by the Worthton, also not a authorized driver of the rental car." *U.S. v. Worthon*, 520 F.3d 1173 (10th Cir. 2008).

Chapter 33

Burdens of Proof

§ 33:1   Standing: A defendant seeking to suppress
        evidence bears the preliminary burden of
        proving that his or her own Fourth Amendment
        rights were violated by a preponderance of the
        evidence

§ 33:2   Search warrants: If a search or seizure is
        conducted pursuant to a warrant, the defendant
        bears the burden of demonstrating that the
        warrant is invalid once its existence has been
        proven

§ 33:3   Warrantless searches: If a search or seizure is not
        conducted pursuant to a warrant, the
        prosecution bears the burden of proving that the
        search or seizure falls within one of the
        exceptions to the Fourth Amendment warrant
        requirement

§ 33:4   Standards of appellate review: Clearly erroneous
        standard applies to findings of fact; de novo
        standard applies to legal findings; plain error
        standard applies to arguments not raised below

Research References

West's Key Number Digest

Criminal Law ⟜394.5 to 394.6, 1134.1–1134.4, 1134.27–1134.35,
   1139, 1141, 1144–1144.14, 1147, 1148, 1152, 1153, 1154, 1158,
   1158.1, 1158.2, 1158.12, 1158.20, 1158.21, 1158.25; Searches
   and Seizures ⟜23, 26, 78, 112, 192, 199; Sentencing and Punishment ⟜1961

KeyCite®: Cases and other legal materials listed in KeyCite Scope can be
researched through the KeyCite service on Westlaw®. Use KeyCite to
check citations for form, parallel references, prior and later history, and
comprehensive citator information, including citations to other decisions
and secondary materials.

---

§ 33:1 Standing: A defendant seeking to suppress evidence bears the preliminary burden of proving that his or her own Fourth Amendment rights were violated by a preponderance of the evidence

Supreme Court

- "[Defendant], of course, bears the burden of proving not only that the search of [codefendant's] purse was illegal, but also that he had a legitimate expectation of privacy in that purse." *Rawlings v. Kentucky*, 448 U.S. 98, 104, 100 S. Ct. 2556, 65 L. Ed. 2d 633 (1980).

- "The proponent of a motion to suppress has the burden of establishing that his own Fourth Amendment rights were violated by the challenged search or seizure." *Rakas v. Illinois*, 439 U.S. 128, 130 n.1, 99 S. Ct. 421, 58 L. Ed. 2d 387 (1978).

- "In the event that [defendant establishes] . . . the allegation of perjury or reckless disregard . . . by a preponderance of the evidence [at a suppression hearing], . . . the [court will set aside the] affidavit's false material set to one side[.] . . . [Where] the affidavit's remaining content is insufficient to establish probable cause, the search warrant must be voided and the fruits of the search excluded to the same extent as if probable cause w[ere] lacking on the face of the affidavit." *Franks v. Delaware*, 438 U.S. 154, 156, 98 S. Ct. 2674, 57 L. Ed. 2d 667 (1978).

- "[T]he controlling burden of proof at suppression hearings should impose no greater burden than proof by a preponderance of the evidence." *U.S. v. Matlock*, 415 U.S. 164, 177 n.14, 94 S. Ct. 988, 39 L. Ed. 2d 242 (1974).

First Circuit

- "[I]nformation supporting probable cause may be set out in an affidavit submitted with the application for a search warrant. Although '[t]here is . . . a presumption of validity with respect to the affidavit supporting the search warrant,' that presumption may be refuted during a so-called *Franks* hearing. However, to get a *Franks* hearing, a party must first make two 'substantial preliminary showings': (1) that a false statement or omis-

sion in the affidavit was made knowingly and intentionally or with reckless disregard for the truth; and (2) the
falsehood or omission was necessary to the finding of
probable cause. Failure to make a showing on either element dooms a party's hearing request. In the event
that a hearing is granted and 'at that hearing the allegation of perjury or reckless disregard is established by
the defendant by a preponderance of the evidence, and,
with the affidavit's false material set to one side [or the
omitted material included], the affidavit's . . . content
is insufficient to establish probable cause, the search
warrant must be voided and the fruits of the search
excluded to the same extent as if probable cause was
lacking on the face of the affidavit.' " *U.S. v. Rigaud*,
684 F.3d 169, 173 (1st Cir. 2012) (citations omitted).

- "It is well settled that a defendant who fails to demonstrate a legitimate expectation of privacy in the area
searched or the item seized will not have standing to
claim that an illegal search or seizure occurred. In order to make such a demonstration, the defendant must
show both a subjective expectation of privacy and that
society accepts that expectation as objectively
reasonable. The burden of proving a reasonable expectation of privacy lies with the defendant. The defendant
must demonstrate a privacy expectation in both the
item seized and the place searched." *U.S. v. Mancini*, 8
F.3d 104, 107 (1st Cir. 1993).

Third Circuit

- "Application of the exclusionary rule is instead limited
to those 'unusual cases' in which it may achieve its
objective: to appreciably deter governmental violations
of the Fourth Amendment. . . . However, while '[r]eal
deterrent value' is necessary for the exclusionary rule
to apply, there are other considerations and it alone is
not sufficient. Deterrence must also outweigh the
'substantial social costs' of exclusion. These costs often
include omitting 'reliable, trustworthy evidence' of a
defendant's guilt, thereby 'suppress[ing] the truth and
set[ting] [a] criminal loose in the community without
punishment.' As this result conflicts with the 'truth-
finding functions of judge and jury,' exclusion is a 'bitter pill,' swallowed only as a 'last resort.' Accordingly,

to warrant exclusion, the deterrent value of suppression must overcome the resulting social costs." *U.S. v. Katzin*, 769 F.3d 163, 170–71 (3d Cir. 2014), cert. denied, 135 S. Ct. 1448, 191 L. Ed. 2d 403 (2015) (citations omitted).

- "Simple, isolated negligence is insufficient to justify suppression." *U.S. v. Wright*, 777 F.3d 635, 638 (3d Cir. 2015).

Fifth Circuit

- "A defendant normally bears the burden of proving by a preponderance of the evidence that the challenged search or seizure was unconstitutional. In a case such as this one, however, in which the officer acted without a warrant, the government bears the ultimate burden of proving that the officer had probable cause." *U.S. v. Ho*, 94 F.3d 932, 936 (5th Cir. 1996).

Sixth Circuit

- "A defendant bears the burden of establishing that his own Fourth Amendment rights were violated. . . . The two-part test requires that a defendant show (1) he had a subjective expectation of privacy in the searched premises and (2) that society is prepared to recognize that expectation as legitimate." *U.S. v. McRae*, 156 F.3d 708, 711, 1998 FED App. 0303P (6th Cir. 1998).

Seventh Circuit

- "The party seeking suppression bears the burden of establishing that he had a reasonable expectation of privacy in the area and items searched. . . . In order to establish a reasonable expectation of privacy, the party must show that he had an actual, subjective expectation of privacy that society is prepared to recognize as reasonable." *U.S. v. Meyer*, 157 F.3d 1067, 1079, 49 Fed. R. Evid. Serv. 970 (7th Cir. 1998).

Eighth Circuit

- "A defendant moving to suppress evidence has the burden of showing a legitimate expectation of privacy in the area searched. . . .Factors relevant to the determination of standing include: ownership, possession and/or control of the area searched or item seized; historical use of the property or item; ability to regulate access; the totality of the circumstances surrounding the search; the existence or nonexistence of a subjective anticipation of privacy; and the objective reasonableness of the expectation of privacy considering the specific facts of the case." *U.S. v. Pierson*, 219 F.3d 803, 806 (8th Cir. 2000).

- "A defendant moving to suppress evidence on the basis of an unlawful search bears the burden of proving that he had a legitimate expectation of privacy that was violated by the challenged search. . . . To establish a legitimate expectation of privacy, the defendant must demonstrate: (1) a subjective expectation of privacy; and (2) that the subjective expectation is one that society is prepared to recognize as objectively reasonable." *U.S. v. Gwinn*, 191 F.3d 874, 878 (8th Cir. 1999).

- "The defendant moving to suppress bears the burden of proving he had a legitimate expectation of privacy that was violated by the challenged search. To establish a legitimate expectation of privacy, the defendant must demonstrate (1) a subjective expectation of privacy; and (2) that the subjective expectation is one that society is prepared to recognize as objectively reasonable." *U.S. v. Muhammad*, 58 F.3d 353, 355 (8th Cir. 1995).

Ninth Circuit

- "To establish standing to challenge the legality of a search or seizure, the defendants must demonstrate that they have a legitimate expectation of privacy in the items seized or the area searched. . . . To demonstrate this, the defendants must manifest a subjective expectation of privacy in the area searched, and their expectation must be one that society would recognize as objectively reasonable. . . . The defendants have the burden of establishing that, under the totality of the circumstances, the search or seizure violated their legitimate expectation of privacy. . . ." *U.S. v. Sarkisian*, 197 F.3d 966, 986 (9th Cir. 1999).

- "A defendant is not entitled to rely on the government's allegations in the pleadings, or positions the government has taken in the case, to establish standing. The government's assertions in its pleadings are not evidence. It was [Defendant]'s obligation to present evidence of his standing, or at least to point to specific evidence in the record which the government presented and which established his standing. He did not do so. Accordingly, he may not challenge the search as a violation of the Fourth Amendment." *U.S. v. Zermeno*, 66 F.3d 1058, 1062 (9th Cir. 1995).

Tenth Circuit

- "Fourth Amendment rights are personal and may not be asserted vicariously. . . . Suppression of evidence is an appropriate remedy only when the search violates a person's constitutional rights. It is not enough that a person is aggrieved only by the introduction of damaging evidence derived from the search. . . . The proponent of a motion to suppress has the burden of adducing facts at the suppression hearing indicating that his own rights were violated by the challenged search." *U.S. v. Gama-Bastidas*, 142 F.3d 1233, 1238 (10th Cir. 1998).

- "[I]f a party moves to suppress evidence obtained as a result of an allegedly unconstitutional search, he has the duty to demonstrate a subjective expectation of privacy that society is prepared to recognize as reasonable. This precept stems from the general rule that the proponent of a motion to suppress has the burden of establishing that his own Fourth Amendment rights were violated by the challenged search or seizure." *U.S. v. Conway*, 73 F.3d 975, 979, 43 Fed. R. Evid. Serv. 671 (10th Cir. 1995).

- "A proponent of a motion to suppress who relies upon the lawful possession factor bears the burden of presenting at least some evidence that his or her possession was lawful. While the proponent of a motion to suppress need not always come forward with legal documentation establishing that he lawfully possessed the area searched, the proponent must at least state that he gained possession from the owner or someone with the authority to grant permission." *U.S. v. Benitez-Arreguin*, 973 F.2d 823, 828 (10th Cir. 1992).

§ 33:2 Search warrants: If a search or seizure is conducted pursuant to a warrant, the defendant bears the burden of demonstrating that the warrant is invalid once its existence has been proven

Supreme Court

- "[W]here the defendant makes a substantial preliminary showing that a false statement knowingly and intentionally, or with reckless disregard for the truth, was included by the affiant in the [search] warrant affidavit, and if the allegedly false statement is necessary to the finding of probable cause, the Fourth Amendment requires that a hearing be held at the defendant's request." *Franks v. Delaware*, 438 U.S. 154, 155–56, 98 S. Ct. 2674, 57 L. Ed. 2d 667 (1978).

First Circuit

- "[I]nformation supporting probable cause may be set out in an affidavit submitted with the application for a search warrant. Although '[t]here is . . . a presumption of validity with respect to the affidavit supporting the search warrant,' that presumption may be refuted during a so-called *Franks* hearing. However, to get a *Franks* hearing, a party must first make two 'substantial preliminary showings': (1) that a false statement or omission in the affidavit was made knowingly and intentionally or with reckless disregard for the truth; and (2) the falsehood or omission was necessary to the finding of probable cause. Failure to make a showing on either element dooms a party's hearing request. In the event that a hearing is granted and 'at that hearing the allegation of perjury or reckless disregard is established by the defendant by a preponderance of the evidence, and, with the affidavit's false material set to one side [or the omitted material included], the affidavit's . . . content is insufficient to establish probable cause, the search warrant must be voided and the fruits of the search excluded to the same extent as if probable cause was lacking on the face of the affidavit.' " *U.S. v. Rigaud*, 684 F.3d 169, 173 (1st Cir. 2012) (citations omitted).

Second Circuit

- "In order to challenge successfully a search warrant based on an attack on the allegations in a supporting affidavit, a defendant must show by a preponderance of the evidence that the affidavit contained false statements that were material on the issue of probable cause. The defendant must further show that the alleged false statements were made intentionally, knowingly, or with reckless disregard for the truth." *U.S. v. Wapnick*, 60 F.3d 948, 955, 76 A.F.T.R.2d 95-5601 (2d Cir. 1995).

Fifth Circuit

- "The defendant challenging a search must show the warrant to be invalid by a preponderance of the evidence. Initially, the defendant must be a *prima facie* showing of illegality. The government must then present rebuttal evidence. However, the burden of persuasion remains at all times with the defendant." *U.S. v. Richardson*, 943 F.2d 547, 548–49 (5th Cir. 1991).

Sixth Circuit

- "In *Franks v. Delaware* the Supreme Court held that under certain limited circumstances, a defendant has a Fourth Amendment right to challenge the truthfulness of factual statements made in an affidavit supporting a warrant. A defendant who challenges the veracity of statements made in an affidavit that formed the basis for a warrant has a heavy burden. His allegations must be more than conclusory. He must point to specific false statements that he claims were made intentionally or with reckless disregard for the truth. He must accompany his allegations with an offer of proof. Moreover, he also should provide supporting affidavits or explain their absence. If he meets these requirements, then the question becomes whether, absent the challenged statements, there remains sufficient content in the affidavit to support a finding of probable cause." *U.S. v. Ursery*, 109 F.3d 1129, 1132–33, 1997 FED App. 0102P (6th Cir. 1997).

Eighth Circuit

- "A search warrant may be invalid if the issuing magistrate's probable cause determination was based on an affidavit that contained false statements made knowingly and intentionally or with reckless disregard for the truth. . . . In order to prevail on a *Franks* challenge a defendant must show: 1) that a false statement knowingly and intentionally, or with reckless disregard to the truth, was included in the affidavit, and 2) that the affidavit's remaining content is insufficient to provide probable cause. . . . A similar analysis applies to omissions of fact where a defendant must show: 1) that facts were omitted with the intent to make, or in reckless disregard of whether they thereby make, the affidavit misleading, and 2) that the affidavit, if supplemented by the omitted information, could not support a finding of probable cause." *U.S. v. Box*, 193 F.3d 1032, 1034–35 (8th Cir. 1999).

- "A defendant is entitled to a hearing to determine the veracity of a search warrant affidavit if he or she can make a substantial preliminary showing that a false statement was included in the affidavit (or that relevant information was omitted from it) intentionally or recklessly, and that the allegedly false statement was necessary to a finding of probable cause or that the alleged omission would have made it impossible to find probable cause." *U.S. v. Mathison*, 157 F.3d 541, 547–48 (8th Cir. 1998).

Ninth Circuit

- "The Fourth Amendment incorporates a strong preference for search warrants. Warrantless searches are *per se* unreasonable. While warrantless searches are not absolutely prohibited, the exceptions to the warrant requirement are jealously and carefully drawn. The burden is on the Government, moreover, to show the reasonableness of a warrantless search. This includes demonstrating that the search comes within one of the narrow exceptions to the warrant requirement." *U.S. v. Carbajal*, 956 F.2d 924, 930 (9th Cir. 1992).

Tenth Circuit

- "As a general matter, if the search or seizure was pursuant to a warrant, the defendant has the burden of proof; but if the police acted without a warrant the burden of proof is on the prosecution. Thus, the defendant has the burden of proving that a warrant was

invalidly issued in reliance on a deliberately or recklessly false affidavit. On the other hand, when the
defendant challenges a warrantless search or seizure
the government carries the burden of justifying the
agents' actions. In other words, the government has the
burden of proving that an exception to the warrant
requirement applies." *U.S. v. Maestas*, 2 F.3d 1485,
1490–91 (10th Cir. 1993).

Eleventh Circuit

- "To attack the veracity of a warrant affidavit, a defendant must make a preliminary showing that the affiant
  made intentional misstatements or omissions (or made
  misstatements with a reckless disregard for their
  truthfulness) that were essential to the finding of probable cause. . . . Once the defendant makes such a showing, he is entitled to an evidentiary hearing on the matter; if he prevails at the hearing, the search warrant is
  to be voided and the fruits of the search must be
  excluded." *U.S. v. Burston*, 159 F.3d 1328, 1333, 50 Fed.
  R. Evid. Serv. 700 (11th Cir. 1998).

**§ 33:3   Warrantless searches: If a search or seizure is
          not conducted pursuant to a warrant, the
          prosecution bears the burden of proving that
          the search or seizure falls within one of the
          exceptions to the Fourth Amendment warrant
          requirement**

Supreme Court

- "[O]nly in a few specifically established and well-
  delineated situations may a warrantless search of a
  dwelling withstand constitutional scrutiny, even though
  the authorities have probable cause to conduct it. The
  burden rests on the State to show the existence of such
  an exceptional situation." *Vale v. Louisiana*, 399 U.S.
  30, 34, 90 S. Ct. 1969, 26 L. Ed. 2d 409 (1970).

- "[T]he general requirement that a search warrant be
  obtained is not lightly to be dispensed with, and the
  burden is on those seeking [an] exemption [from the
  requirement] to show the need for it." *Chimel v. California*, 395 U.S. 752, 762, 89 S. Ct. 2034, 23 L. Ed. 2d 685
  (1969).

- "When a prosecutor seeks to rely upon consent to justify the lawfulness of a search, he has the burden of proving that the consent was, in fact, freely and voluntarily given." *Bumper v. North Carolina*, 391 U.S. 543, 548, 88 S. Ct. 1788, 20 L. Ed. 2d 797 (1968).

First Circuit

- "It is the prosecution's burden to establish, by a preponderance of the evidence, that consent was freely and voluntarily given; there must be more than mere acquiescence in the face of an unfounded claim of present lawful authority." *U.S. v. Perez-Montanez*, 202 F.3d 434, 438, 53 Fed. R. Evid. Serv. 400 (1st Cir. 2000).
- "[T]he government bears the burden of establishing that, at the time of the arrest, the facts and circumstances known to the arresting officers were sufficient to warrant a reasonable person in believing that the individual had committed or was committing a crime." *U.S. v. Reyes*, 225 F.3d 71, 75 (1st Cir. 2000).
- "A warrantless search of a private residence is presumptively unreasonable under the Fourth Amendment. The government therefore must prove that the initial search came within some recognized exception to the Fourth Amendment warrant requirement. Generally speaking, absent probable cause and exigent circumstances the Fourth Amendment bars warrantless, nonconsensual entries of private residences." *U.S. v. Tibolt*, 72 F.3d 965, 968–69 (1st Cir. 1995).

Second Circuit

- "If the place or object subjected to the warrantless search is one in which the defendant had a reasonable expectation of privacy, the burden of showing that the search fell within one of the exceptions to the warrant requirement is on the government." *U.S. v. Kiyuyung*, 171 F.3d 78, 83 (2d Cir. 1999).
- "[W]e are mindful that where, as here, the government asserts the good faith exception to the exclusionary rule, the burden is on the government to demonstrate the objective reasonableness of the officers' good faith reliance." *U.S. v. Santa*, 180 F.3d 20, 25, 52 Fed. R. Evid. Serv. 570 (2d Cir. 1999).

Third Circuit

- "However, certain circumstances can excuse the warrant requirement. Among these are an inventory search incident to a lawful arrest objects in plain view of the officers and exigent circumstances. To excuse the absence of a warrant, the burden rests on the State to show the existence of these exceptional situations." *Parkhurst v. Trapp*, 77 F.3d 707, 711 (3d Cir. 1996).

Fifth Circuit

- "As [Defendant] correctly points out, the district court erred in placing the burden of proof on him. [Defendant] had established, and it was always undisputed, that the stop and search were without a warrant. He had also adequately shown standing, and that, too, was never contested. In these circumstances, the burden shifts to the government to justify the warrantless search. The district court's findings hence may have been influenced by an erroneous view of the law." *U.S. v. Chavis*, 48 F.3d 871, 872 (5th Cir. 1995).

Seventh Circuit

- "Where the government obtains evidence in a search conducted pursuant to one of these exceptions, it bears the burden of establishing that the exception applies." *U.S. v. Basinski*, 226 F.3d 829, 833 (7th Cir. 2000).

Eighth Circuit

- "Because the search in this case was conducted without a warrant, the burden is on the government, as the district court recognized, to prove that the search comported with the requirements of the Fourth Amendment. That is to say, the warrantless search of luggage is presumptively unreasonable and thus presumptively unconstitutional." *U.S. v. Rouse*, 148 F.3d 1040, 1041 (8th Cir. 1998) (rejected on other grounds by, U.S. v. Runyan, 275 F.3d 449 (5th Cir. 2001)).

Ninth Circuit

- "Whether consent to a search was voluntary is a question of fact, subject to the clearly erroneous standard of review. While the Government bears the burden of showing at trial that consent was given freely and vol-

untarily, on defendant's appeal the evidence must be
viewed in the light most favorable to the Government."
U.S. v. Chischilly, 30 F.3d 1144, 1151, 40 Fed. R. Evid.
Serv. 289 (9th Cir. 1994) (overruled on other grounds
by, U.S. v. Preston, 751 F.3d 1008 (9th Cir. 2014)).

Tenth Circuit

- "When an allegedly consensual search is preceded by an
  unlawful arrest, the government must prove the consent
  was given voluntarily." *U.S. v. Reeves*, 524 F.3d 1161
  (10th Cir. 2008).

Eleventh Circuit

- "If accused successfully establishes expectation of
  privacy in area searched, burden shifts to government,
  as party defending propriety of warrantless search, to
  prove that search was reasonable based on recognized
  exception to warrant requirement." *U.S. v. Harris*, 526
  F.3d 1334 (11th Cir. 2008).

§ 33:4 Standards of appellate review: Clearly erroneous standard applies to findings of fact; de novo standard applies to legal findings; plain error standard applies to arguments not raised below

Supreme Court

- "We hold that as a general matter determinations of
  reasonable suspicion and probable cause should be
  reviewed de novo on appeal. Having said this, we hasten
  to point out that a reviewing court should take care
  both to review findings of historical fact only for clear
  error and to give due weight to inferences drawn from
  those facts by resident judges and local law enforcement officers. A trial judge views the facts of a particular case in light of the distinctive features and events of
  the community; likewise a police officer views the facts
  through the lens of his police experience and expertise."
  Ornelas v. U.S., 517 U.S. 690, 699, 116 S. Ct. 1657, 134
  L. Ed. 2d 911 (1996).

Fifth Circuit

- "[Defendant] challenges [the officer]'s initial stop of his

[Dodge] Durango. Because [defendant] did not raise this argument below, his argument is subject to the plain error standard of review. [citation omitted] 'This court finds plain error when: (1) there was an error; (2) the error was clear and obvious; and (3) the error affected the defendant's substantial rights.' [citation omitted] 'If all three conditions are met[, we]. . .may then exercise [our] discretion to notice a forfeited error but only if (4) the error seriously affects the fairness, integrity, or public reputation of judicial proceedings.' [citation omitted]" *U.S. v. Khanalizadeh*, 493 F.3d 479 (5th Cir. 2007).

Sixth Circuit

- " 'When reviewing a motion to suppress, [we] must consider evidence in the light most likely to support the district court's decision.' [citation omitted] '[A] district court's factual findings are accepted unless they are clearly erroneous; however, the district court's application of the law to the facts, such as a finding of probable cause, is reviewed de novo. [citation omitted]" *U.S. v. Garcia*, 496 F.3d 495, 502 (6th Cir. 2007).

Seventh Circuit

- "In *Ornelas*, the Supreme Court addressed the appropriate standard of appellate review for the reasonable suspicion and probable cause standards employed in determining the legality of searches and seizures under the Fourth Amendment. The Court began its analysis by noting that both of these standards are common-sense, nontechnical conceptions that deal with the factual and practical considerations of everyday life on which reasonable and prudent men, not legal technicians, act. . . . . In short, although holding that a deferential standard of review was appropriate with respect to the trial court's determination of the underlying historical facts, the Supreme Court held that the ultimate question of whether those facts satisfy the relevant standard was a mixed question of fact and law that ought to be subject to independent appellate review." *U.S. v. D.F.*, 115 F.3d 413, 415 (7th Cir. 1997).
- "We will reverse a refusal to suppress evidence seized pursuant to a search warrant only if, upon reviewing all of the evidence, we are left with the definite and

firm conviction that a mistake has been made." *U.S. v. Sleet*, 54 F.3d 303, 306 (7th Cir. 1995).

Ninth Circuit

- "A district court's denial of a motion to suppress is reviewed de novo. [citation omitted] The district court's factual findings underlying the decision are reviewed for clear error. [citation omitted] 'Where no findings of fact were made or requested, this court will uphold a trial court's denial of a motion to suppress if there was a reasonable view to support it.' [citation omitted]. . ." *U.S. v. Gooch*, 506 F.3d 1156, 1158 (9th Cir. 2007).

Tenth Circuit

- "In *Ornelas*, the Supreme Court held that Courts of Appeals must review de novo a district court's determinations of reasonable suspicion and probable cause. . . . As in custody determinations, the Court noted that determinations of reasonable suspicion and probable case entail two discrete inquiries: what events occurred leading up to the stop or search, and then the decision whether these historical facts, viewed from the standpoint of an objectively reasonable police officer, amount to reasonable suspicion or probable cause." *U.S. v. Erving L.*, 147 F.3d 1240, 1245–46 (10th Cir. 1998).
- "In reviewing a district court's denial of a motion to suppress, we should view the evidence adduced at the hearing on the motion in a light most favorable to the government and we should review a district court's findings of fact only for clear error. . . . However, questions concerning the reasonableness of a search under the Fourth Amendment, and the existence, or nonexistence, of probable cause, are subject to *de novo* review by us." *U.S. v. Hugoboom*, 112 F.3d 1081, 1085 (10th Cir. 1997).
- "A trial court is required to grant a suppression hearing only when a defendant presents facts justifying relief. A defendant who requests a hearing bears the burden of showing that there are disputed issues of material fact. To warrant an evidentiary hearing, the motion to suppress must raise factual allegations that are sufficiently definite, specific, detailed, and nonconjectural to enable the court to conclude that contested issues of fact going to the validity of the search are in issue. Similarly, a

hearing is not required when suppression is improper for a reason of law appearing on the face of the motion." *U.S. v. Chavez-Marquez*, 66 F.3d 259, 261 (10th Cir. 1995).

Eleventh Circuit

- "Rulings on motions to suppress evidence constitute mixed questions of law and fact." *U.S. v. Lightbourn*, 357 Fed. Appx. 259 (11th Cir. 2009).

Chapter 34

Derivative Evidence: The Fruit of the Poisonous Tree Doctrine

Research References

West's Key Number Digest

Arrest ⬤⇒63.4; Criminal Law ⬤⇒394, 412, 518, 1036; Federal Courts ⬤⇒444, 523; Searches and Seizures ⬤⇒202; Sentencing and Punishment ⬤⇒321, 960; Witnesses ⬤⇒277, 331.5, 398, 406

§ 34:1 Rule: Both direct and indirect evidence obtained by illegal police conduct is inadmissible

Supreme Court

- "[T]he exclusionary rule also prohibits the introduction of derivative evidence, both tangible and testimonial, that is the product of the primary evidence, or that is otherwise acquired as an indirect result of the unlawful search, up to the point at which the connection with the unlawful search becomes so attenuated as to dissipate the taint." *Murray v. U.S.*, 487 U.S. 533, 536–37, 108 S. Ct. 2529, 101 L. Ed. 2d 472 (1988).

- "In order to make effective the fundamental constitutional guarantees of sanctity of the home and inviolability of the person . . . this Court held nearly half a century ago that evidence seized during an unlawful search could not constitute proof against the victim of the search. The exclusionary prohibition extends as well to the indirect as the direct products of such invasions." *Wong Sun v. U.S.*, 371 U.S. 471, 484, 83 S. Ct. 407, 9 L. Ed. 2d 441 (1963).

First Circuit

- "In addition to the stop for questioning, *Terry* permits a pat-down search for weapons based on an objectively reasonable belief that the suspicious individual is armed and presently dangerous. . . .Such a protective search, designed to allow the officer to conduct his investigation without fear of violence, must be strictly limited to that which is necessary for the discovery of weapons. . . .Typically, this will be a limited patting of the outer clothing of the suspect for concealed objects which might be used as instruments of assault. . . .If the frisk goes beyond what is necessary to determine if the suspect is armed, its fruits will be suppressed." *U.S. v. Campa*, 234 F.3d 733, 737–38 (1st Cir. 2000).

Second Circuit

- "To 'safeguard Fourth Amendment rights generally,' the Supreme Court has crafted the exclusionary rule, requiring the exclusion of evidence '[w]hen the police exhibit deliberate, reckless, or grossly negligent disregard for Fourth Amendment rights.' '[A]n assessment of the flagrancy of the police misconduct constitutes an important step in the calculus of applying the exclusionary rule.' In this case, such an assessment reveals that law enforcement personnel made a deliberate decision to violate constitutional requirements. We assume that the officers had probable cause to arrest Stokes for participation in the murder of Porter. While such probable cause would have permitted them to arrest Stokes without a warrant had they encountered him in a public place, it has long been established that an entry into protected premises in order to search for or arrest a suspect requires an arrest or search warrant. There is little doubt that a warrant could have been obtained. Nevertheless, Assistant District Attorney Chase made a deliberate strategic choice to have the officers attempt to arrest Stokes without a warrant, in order to question Stokes outside of the presence of counsel. Detective Perrotta testified that he was familiar with this rule and knew that he needed a warrant or consent to enter Stokes's room. Despite this knowledge, however, rather than waiting for Stokes to leave the motel room, or seeking consent to enter, or attempting a ruse in an effort to lure Stokes out of the room, he deliberately entered the motel room without a warrant or consent. That deliberate, tactical choice to violate Stokes's constitutional rights was 'sufficiently deliberate that exclusion [could] meaningfully deter it.' We have no doubt that the exclusion of evidence is presumptively appropriate in such a clear case of illegal police action." *U.S. v. Stokes*, 733 F.3d 438 (2d Cir. 2013) (citations omitted).

- "The exclusionary rule generally prohibits admission at trial of evidence seized in searches deemed unreasonable under the Fourth Amendment, as well as of derivative evidence acquired as an indirect product or result of the unlawful search." *U.S. v. Santa*, 180 F.3d 20, 25, 52 Fed. R. Evid. Serv. 570 (2d Cir. 1999).

Third Circuit

- "The exclusionary rule mandates that evidence derived from constitutional violations may not be used at trial because illegally derived evidence is considered fruit of the poisonous tree." *U.S. v. Pelullo*, 173 F.3d 131, 136 (3d Cir. 1999).

Fifth Circuit

- "The exclusionary rule of the Fourth Amendment generally prohibits the introduction at trial of not only primary evidence obtained as a direct result of an illegal search or seizure, but also evidence discovered later that is derivative of an illegality, or constitutes fruit of a poisonous tree." *U.S. v. Grosenheider*, 200 F.3d 321, 327 (5th Cir. 2000).
- "If the arresting officers lacked probable cause and the arrest is invalid, evidence discovered as a result of the arrest is subject to suppression under the Fourth Amendment as the fruit of an illegal arrest." *U.S. v. Ho*, 94 F.3d 932, 935 (5th Cir. 1996).
- "Under the circumstances of the present case, [Defendant]'s consent to a search of the suitcases cannot be inferred from [Defendant]'s silence and failure to object because the police officer did not expressly or implicitly request [Defendant]'s consent prior to the search. As [the] Officer did not have consent to search the suitcases, the marijuana he seized was the fruit of an illegal search and should have been suppressed by the trial court." *U.S. v. Jaras*, 86 F.3d 383, 390–91 (5th Cir. 1996).

Sixth Circuit

- "An ordinary traffic stop by a police officer is a 'seizure' within the meaning of the Fourth Amendment. Accordingly, any evidence seized during an illegal traffic stop must be suppressed as fruits of the poisonous tree." *U.S. v. Jackson*, 682 F.3d 448, 453 (6th Cir. 2012) (citation omitted).
- "The general remedy for a Fourth Amendment violation is that evidence obtained due to the unconstitutional search or seizure is inadmissible. The scope of evidence to be excluded sweeps broadly, including both evidence obtained as a direct result of an unconstitutional search or seizure, as well as evidence that is considered the

fruit of a prior illegality that was come at by exploitation of the initial illegality." *U.S. v. Dice*, 200 F.3d 978,
983, 2000 FED App. 0005P (6th Cir. 2000).

Seventh Circuit

- "The Fourth Amendment . . . does not apply . . . to
searches or seizures performed by private individuals
. . . To determine whether an individual was acting as
a private party or as an "instrument or agent" of the
government, we examine 'whether the government
knew of and acquiesced in the intrusive conduct and
whether the private party's purpose in conducting the
search was to assist law enforcement agents or to further its own ends' . . . 'Other useful criteria are
whether the private actor acted at the request of the
government and whether the government offered the
private actor a reward.' . . . In this case . . . the brothers' (off-duty police officers) actions in entering the home
are consistent with concerned sons attempting to
prevent a misguided father from engaging in continued
destructive behavior. Particularly noteworthy, they did
not notify a police department before searching the
home, they did not act to obtain a reward, and they did
not collect evidence of the crimes while inside the home.
The brothers may ultimately have intended to turn
their father in to the authorities, but . . . their primary
objective was to protect the community from harm, not
to assist law enforcement." *U.S. v. Ginglen*, 467 F.3d
1071 (7th Cir. 2006).

- "If the arrest was legal, so was the search of the van,
not only because the van had been abandoned but also
because the police were entitled to impound it when
they found it (since the renter was in jail) and to
conduct an inventory search of it. But if the arrest was
illegal, evidence obtained by the discovery of the key
hidden by the arrested persons in the police car and the
ensuing discovery, impoundment, and search of the van
would be inadmissible, all that being a fruit of the
unlawful arrest." *U.S. v. Ienco*, 92 F.3d 564, 568, 45
Fed. R. Evid. Serv. 415 (7th Cir. 1996).

Eighth Circuit

- "The exclusionary rule reaches not only primary evidence obtained as a direct result of an illegal search or seizure but also evidence later discovered and found to be derivative of an illegality or fruit of the poisonous tree. Invalidating a search warrant because the magistrate was affected in some minor way by tainted information, when the warrant would have been granted even without the tainted information, would work against the principle that the fruit of the poisonous tree doctrine not be used to place the government in a worse position than it would have been in absent its illegal conduct." *U.S. v. Swope*, 542 F.3d 609 (8th Cir. 2008).

- " 'In our circuit, resistance to an illegal arrest can furnish grounds for a second, legitimate arrest' . . . . 'When a defendant commits a new and distinct crime during an unlawful detention, the Fourth Amendment's exclusionary rule does not bar evidence of the new crime' . . . 'A contrary rule would virtually immunize a defendant from prosecution for all crimes he might commit that have a sufficient causal connection to the police misconduct' . . . . In denying (defendant's) motion to suppress, the district court concluded (defendant) forfeited any Fourth Amendment protection by resisting and running away from the officers, thus creating probable cause to arrest (defendant) for obstructing a peace officer, in violation of Neb.Rev.Stat. § 28-906(1), and to search (defendant) incident to that arrest. We agree with this conclusion." *U.S. v. Sledge*, 460 F.3d 963 (8th Cir. 2006).

Ninth Circuit

- "Under the Fourth Amendment, an illegal stop taints all evidence obtained pursuant to the stop, unless the taint is purged by subsequent events. . . . Federal courts have invariably found that consents to search at the time of or shortly following an illegal stop of a vehicle are unlawful because the search is tainted by the primary illegality and the taint has not been purged." *U.S. v. Arvizu*, 232 F.3d 1241, 1251–1252 (9th Cir. 2000), judgment rev'd and remanded on other grounds, 534 U.S. 266, 122 S. Ct. 744, 151 L. Ed. 2d 740 (2002).
- "Consent by a defendant or a third party is tainted where the evidence indicates that it stemmed from the prior illegal Government action. . . . [W]here, as here,

the police confront a person with contraband that they have illegally found, the subsequent consent to search is fruit of the Government action." *U.S. v. Oaxaca*, 233 F.3d 1154, 1158 (9th Cir. 2000).

- "Because we conclude that the initial entry was impermissible and that the evidence seized pursuant to the warrant must be suppressed, all of the other evidence seized must also be suppressed. Consent to search that is given after an illegal entry is tainted and invalid under the Fourth Amendment. . . . Accordingly, all of the items seized pursuant to the consent form, including those forming the basis of the second count, must be suppressed. For the same reason, the government's argument that the seizure of the additional items was proper under the plain view doctrine, fails. The plain-view doctrine does not apply unless the initial entry is lawful, either pursuant to a valid warrant or under one of the recognized exceptions to the warrant requirement." *U.S. v. Hotal*, 143 F.3d 1223, 1228 (9th Cir. 1998).

Tenth Circuit

- "This appeal raises the question of whether evidence of a defendant's identity (including statements, fingerprints, and an A-file) may ever be suppressed as the "fruit" of an unlawful arrest . . . Our conclusion . . . is that the "identity" language in *Lopez-Mendoza* refers only to jurisdiction over a defendant and it does not apply to evidentiary issues pertaining to the admissibility of evidence obtained as a result of an illegal arrest and challenged in a criminal proceeding. Instead, we utilize the normal and generally applicable Fourth Amendment exclusionary rule to determine whether challenged identity-related evidence should be excluded under the circumstances present in the particular case . . . . The answer to whether Defendant's A-file "[was] come at by exploitation" of illegal conduct necessarily depends on whether Defendant's fingerprints were obtained for an investigatory purpose exploiting the unconstitutional arrest or whether they were obtained as part of a routine booking procedure not linked to the purpose of the illegal arrest. Because the officers used Defendant's fingerprints to obtain his A-file, if those

fingerprints are determined to be suppressible as fruits
of the poisonous tree, then it follows that the A-file
should also be suppressed." *U.S. v. Olivares-Rangel*,
458 F.3d 1104 (10th Cir. 2006).

- "Defendants do have standing to challenge their
detention. We distinguish passenger standing to directly
challenge a vehicle search from passenger standing to
seek suppression of evidence discovered in a vehicle as
the fruit of an unlawful stop, detention, or arrest. If the
physical evidence found in the vehicles was the fruit of
the defendants' unlawful detention, it must be
suppressed. This requires a two party inquiry: first,
whether the defendants were unlawfully detained, and
second, whether the discovered evidence was the fruit
of that unlawful detention. Only if both of those questions are answered in the affirmative will the physical
evidence found in the vehicles be suppressed." *U.S. v.
Shareef*, 100 F.3d 1491, 1500 (10th Cir. 1996).

§ 34:2   Policy: The courts suppress evidence obtained directly and indirectly by illegal police conduct in order to deter unlawful police activity and in order to maintain judicial integrity

Supreme Court

- "[U]nbending application of the exclusionary sanction
to enforce ideals of governmental rectitude would
impede unacceptably the truth-finding functions of
judge and jury. After all, it is the defendant, and not
the constable, who stands trial." *U. S. v. Payner*, 1980-2
C.B. 749, 447 U.S. 727, 734, 100 S. Ct. 2439, 65 L. Ed.
2d 468, 80-2 U.S. Tax Cas. (CCH) P 9511 (1980).

- "[The exclusionary] rule has primarily rested on the
judgment that the importance of deterring police
conduct that may invade the constitutional rights of
individuals throughout the community outweighs the
importance of securing the conviction of the specific
defendant on trial." *U. S. v. Caceres*, 1979-1 C.B. 465,
440 U.S. 741, 754, 99 S. Ct. 1465, 59 L. Ed. 2d 733, 79-1
U.S. Tax Cas. (CCH) P 9294, 43 A.F.T.R.2d 79-872
(1979).

- "[T]he exclusionary rule should be invoked with much

greater reluctance where the claim is based on a causal relationship between a constitutional violation and the discovery of a live witness than when a similar claim is advanced to support suppression of an inanimate object." *U. S. v. Ceccolini*, 435 U.S. 268, 280, 98 S. Ct. 1054, 55 L. Ed. 2d 268 (1978).

- "The deterrent purpose of the exclusionary rule necessarily assumes that the police have engaged in willful, or at the very least negligent, conduct which has deprived the defendant of some right. By refusing to admit evidence gained as a result of such conduct, the courts hope to instill in those particular investigating officers, or in their future counterparts, a greater degree of care toward the rights of an accused. Where the official action was pursued in complete good faith, however, the deterrence rationale loses much of its force." *Michigan v. Tucker*, 417 U.S. 433, 447, 94 S. Ct. 2357, 41 L. Ed. 2d 182 (1974).

- "[I]t is not deterrence alone that warrants the exclusion of evidence illegally obtained—it is the imperative of judicial integrity. The exclusion of illegally procured [evidence] obtained in its wake deprives the Government of nothing to which it has any lawful claim and creates no impediment to legitimate methods of investigating and prosecuting crime. On the contrary, the exclusion of evidence causally linked to the Government's illegal activity no more than restores the situation that would have prevailed if the Government had itself obeyed the law." *Harrison v. U.S.*, 392 U.S. 219, 224 n.10, 88 S. Ct. 2008, 20 L. Ed. 2d 1047 (1968).

- "[T]estimony as to matters observed during an unlawful invasion has been excluded in order to enforce the basic constitutional policies. [The aims are] deterring lawless conduct by federal officers, [and] closing the doors of the federal courts to any use of evidence unconstitutionally obtained." *Wong Sun v. U.S.*, 371 U.S. 471, 485–86, 83 S. Ct. 407, 9 L. Ed. 2d 441 (1963).

Second Circuit

- "The fruit of the poisonous tree doctrine is an evidentiary rule that operates in the context of criminal procedure. . . . The fruit of the poisonous tree doctrine is calculated to deter future unlawful police conduct and protect liberty by creating an incentive—avoidance of the suppression of illegally seized evidence—for state actors to respect the constitutional rights of suspects. . . . Like the exclusionary rule, the fruit of the poisonous tree doctrine is a judicially created remedy designed to safeguard Fourth Amendment rights generally through its deterrent effect, rather than a personal constitutional right of the party aggrieved." *Townes v. City of New York*, 176 F.3d 138, 145 (2d Cir. 1999).

Third Circuit

- "Application of the exclusionary rule is instead limited to those 'unusual cases' in which it may achieve its objective: to appreciably deter governmental violations of the Fourth Amendment. . . . However, while '[r]eal deterrent value' is necessary for the exclusionary rule to apply, there are other considerations and it alone is not sufficient. Deterrence must also outweigh the 'substantial social costs' of exclusion. These costs often include omitting 'reliable, trustworthy evidence' of a defendant's guilt, thereby 'suppress[ing] the truth and set[ting] [a] criminal loose in the community without punishment.' As this result conflicts with the 'truth-finding functions of judge and jury,' exclusion is a 'bitter pill,' swallowed only as a 'last resort.' Accordingly, to warrant exclusion, the deterrent value of suppression must overcome the resulting social costs." *U.S. v. Katzin*, 769 F.3d 163, 170–71 (3d Cir. 2014), cert. denied, 135 S. Ct. 1448, 191 L. Ed. 2d 403 (2015) (citations omitted).

- "The good faith exception to the exclusionary rule was developed to effectuate this balance and has been applied 'across a range of cases.' Where the particular facts of a case indicate that law enforcement officers 'act[ed] with an objectively "reasonable good-faith belief" that their conduct [was] lawful, or when their conduct involve[d] only simple, "isolated" negligence,' there is no illicit conduct to deter. In such circumstances, 'the deterrence rationale loses much of its force and exclusion cannot pay its way.' Alternatively, where law enforcement conduct is 'deliberate, reckless, or grossly negligent' or involves 'recurring or systemic negligence,' deterrence holds greater value and often outweighs the associated costs. Put differently, exclusion is appropriate only where law enforcement conduct is both 'sufficiently deliberate' that deterrence is effective and 'sufficiently culpable' that deterrence outweighs the costs of suppression. Thus, determining whether the good faith exception applies requires courts to answer the 'objectively ascertainable question whether a reasonably well trained officer would have known that the search was illegal in light of all of the circumstances.' " *U.S. v. Katzin*, 769 F.3d 163, 171 (3d Cir. 2014), cert. denied, 135 S. Ct. 1448, 191 L. Ed. 2d 403 (2015) (citations omitted).

- "Simple, isolated negligence is insufficient to justify suppression." *U.S. v. Wright*, 777 F.3d 635, 638 (3d Cir. 2015).
- "[W]e cannot say that Nardinger acted deliberately, recklessly, or with gross negligence in executing the warrant. Nardinger should have shown the attachment to [the defendant], but that misstep—stemming from his inexperience and misunderstanding of the magistrate judge's order—does not mean that he deliberately violated [the defendant]'s Fourth Amendment rights. In short, application of the exclusionary rule would provide little deterrent effect and would not justify the costs of suppression." *U.S. v. Franz*, 772 F.3d 134, 149 (3d Cir. 2014).
- "The exclusion of evidence illegally obtained is one of the cornerstones of federal criminal procedure. . . . Similarly, incriminating evidence derived from the illegally obtained evidence, colorfully termed the fruit of the poisonous tree, is also excluded." *U.S. v. Vasquez De Reyes*, 149 F.3d 192, 194 (3d Cir. 1998).

Fifth Circuit

- "Generally, the fruits of illegal searches and seizures are inadmissible under the exclusionary rule. . . . But the good-faith exception to the exclusionary rule allows the admission of the fruits of some illegal stops." *U.S. v. Lopez-Valdez*, 178 F.3d 282, 289 (5th Cir. 1999).
- "We have held that a defendant's INS file need not be suppressed because of an illegal arrest. . . . Other courts have indicated that an individual's identity is not suppressible. In *I.N.S. v. Lopez-Mendoza*. . .the respondent objected to being summoned to a civil deportation proceeding following his unlawful arrest. . . .

Rejecting the respondent's argument, the Supreme Court stated that the body or identity of a defendant or respondent in a criminal or civil proceeding is never itself suppressible as a fruit of an unlawful arrest." *U.S. v. Roque-Villanueva*, 175 F.3d 345, 346 (5th Cir. 1999).

Sixth Circuit

- "[S]uppression of evidence is not among the remedies available under the Stored Communications Act." *U.S. v. Carpenter*, 819 F.3d 880, 890 (6th Cir. 2016), cert. granted, 137 S. Ct. 2211, 198 L. Ed. 2d 657 (2017).

- "The 'exclusionary rule,' barring admission of any evidence obtained by an unlawful search and seizure, is supplemented by the fruit of the poisonous tree doctrine, which bars the admissibility of evidence that police derivatively obtain from an unconstitutional search or seizure. In order to exclude evidence obtained from an unlawful search or seizure under the exclusionary rule or the fruit of the poisonous tree doctrine, the defendant must show more than the mere fact that a constitutional violation was a but-for cause of the police's obtaining the evidence. In determining whether to exclude evidence, a court asks whether, granting establishment of the primary illegality, the evidence to which the objection is made has been come at by exploitation of that illegality or instead by means sufficiently distinguishable to be purged of the primary taint." *U.S. v. Pearce*, 531 F.3d 374 (6th Cir. 2008).

Seventh Circuit

- "Probable cause to issue a search warrant is established when the information in the supporting affidavit, taken as a whole, provides information that would lead a reasonable person to believe there is a fair probability that contraband or evidence of a crime will be found. Under the good-faith exception, it is inappropriate to suppress the fruits of a search conducted pursuant to a later-invalidated warrant provided the executing officers relied on the warrant in good faith. That the officers obtained a warrant is itself prima facie evidence of good faith. A defendant can rebut that presumption by demonstrating that the supporting affidavit was so lacking in indicia of probable cause as to render official belief in its existence entirely unreasonable." *U.S. v. Millbrook*, 553 F.3d 1057, 78 Fed. R. Evid. Serv. 551 (7th Cir. 2009) (overruled on other grounds by, U.S. v. Corner, 598 F.3d 411 (7th Cir. 2010)).

- "The goal of the poisonous tree doctrine is to ensure that the prosecution is not put in a better position by means of the illegality, but the countervailing consideration is that the prosecution must not be put in a worse position." *U.S. v. Swift*, 220 F.3d 502, 507 (7th Cir. 2000).

- "Under this exclusionary rule, a poisonous tree is a violation of one of a defendant's constitutional rights." *Winsett v. Washington*, 130 F.3d 269, 273 (7th Cir. 1997).

- "In striking a balance between society's interest in deterring police misconduct and its comparable concern that juries not be deprived of probative evidence, the Supreme Court has concluded that when the authorities have seized evidence in violation of statutory or constitutional protections, they should be placed in no better, but no worse, a position than they would have been had no impropriety occurred. The inevitable discovery doctrine exemplifies that balance. Whereas the exclusionary rule deprives the prosecution of evidence tainted by official wrongdoing and thereby discourages future improprieties, the inevitable discovery exception to the rule permits the introduction of evidence that eventually would have been located had there been no error, for in that instance there is no nexus sufficient to provide a taint." *U.S. v. Jones*, 72 F.3d 1324, 1330, 43 Fed. R. Evid. Serv. 708 (7th Cir. 1995).

Eighth Circuit
- "It is true . . . that if an illegal search taints a subsequent act of abandonment, evidence acquired after the abandonment ought to be suppressed as the fruit of the unlawful search." *U.S. v. Washington*, 146 F.3d 536, 537 (8th Cir. 1998).

Ninth Circuit
- "That same rationale applies when the police violate

Payton by ordering a suspect to exit his home at
gunpoint. The home receives special constitutional
protection in part because 'at the very core of the Fourth
Amendment stands the right of a man to retreat into
his own home and there be free from unreasonable
governmental intrusion.' When the police unreasonably
intrude upon that interest by ordering a suspect to exit
his home at gunpoint, the suspect's opportunity to collect himself before venturing out in public is certainly
diminished, if not eliminated altogether. In this context,
too, *Payton* 's protection of the privacy and sanctity of
the home would be incomplete if it didn't extend to the
person of a suspect forced to abandon the refuge of his
home involuntarily. For these reasons, evidence seized
during a pat-down search incident to an arrest made in
violation of *Payton* must be suppressed, whether the
search occurs inside the home, as in *Kirk* and *Blake,* or
outside the home, as in this case. In either scenario, evidence found on the suspect's person should be regarded
as 'the fruit of having been arrested in the home rather
than someplace else.' Accordingly, the cash and marijuana seized during the search incident to Nora's arrest
must be suppressed." *U.S. v. Nora*, 765 F.3d 1049,
1056–57 (9th Cir. 2014) (citations omitted).

- "Nora's incriminating statements followed immediately
  on the heels of the unlawful search of his person, which
  yielded marijuana and a large amount of cash. Whether
  the police questioned Nora about that evidence or not,
  his answers were likely influenced by his knowledge
  that the police had already discovered it. As in *Shetler,*
  the government produced no evidence to the contrary.
  Nor has the government shown that intervening circumstances rendered the connection between Nora's
  statements and the illegal search 'so attenuated as to
  dissipate the taint.' Nora's post-arrest statements must
  therefore be suppressed." *U.S. v. Nora*, 765 F.3d 1049,
  1057 (9th Cir. 2014) (citations omitted).

§ 34:3 Independent source exception: The 'fruit of the poisonous tree' doctrine will not be applied if the government learns of evidence from a source separate and distinct from the illegal source

Supreme Court

- "[Defendant's] statement taken at the police station was not the product of being in unlawful custody. Neither was it the fruit of having been arrested in the home rather than someplace else. The case is analogous to *United States v. Crews*. In that case, we refused to suppress a victim's in court identification despite the defendant's illegal arrest. The Court found that the evidence was not come at by exploitation of the defendant's Fourth Amendment rights, and that it was not necessary to inquire whether the taint of the Fourth Amendment violation was sufficiently attenuated to permit the introduction of the evidence. Here, likewise, the police had a justification to question [Defendant] prior to his arrest; therefore, his subsequent statement was not an exploitation of the illegal entry into [Defendant's] home." *New York v. Harris*, 495 U.S. 14, 19, 110 S. Ct. 1640, 109 L. Ed. 2d 13 (1990).

- "[S]eizure of tangible evidence already seized is no more impossible than rediscovery of intangible evidence already discovered. The independent source doctrine does not rest upon such metaphysical analysis, but upon the policy that, while the government should not profit from its illegal activity, neither should it be placed in a worse position than it would otherwise have occupied. So long as a later, lawful seizure is genuinely independent of an earlier, tainted one (which may well be difficult to establish where the seized goods are kept in the police's possession) there is no reason why the independent source doctrine should not apply." *Murray v. U.S.*, 487 U.S. 533, 537, 108 S. Ct. 2529, 101 L. Ed. 2d 472 (1988).

- "By contrast, the derivative evidence analysis ensures that the prosecution is not put in a worse position simply because of some earlier police error or misconduct. The independent source doctrine allows admission of evidence that has been discovered by means wholly independent of any constitutional violation." *Nix v. Williams*, 467 U.S. 431, 443, 104 S. Ct. 2501, 81 L. Ed. 2d 377 (1984).

- "[E]vidence discovered during the subsequent search of the apartment the following day pursuant to the valid search warrant issued wholly on information known to the officers before the entry into the apartment need not have been suppressed as fruit of the illegal entry because the warrant and the information on which it was based were unrelated to the entry and therefore constituted an independent source for the evidence." *Segura v. U.S.*, 468 U.S. 796, 799, 104 S. Ct. 3380, 82 L. Ed. 2d 599 (1984).

- "The exclusionary rule enjoins the Government from benefiting from evidence it has unlawfully obtained; it does not reach backward to taint information that was in official hands prior to any illegality. The pretrial identification obtained through use of the photograph taken during respondent's illegal detention cannot be introduced; but the in-court identification is admissible . . . because the police's knowledge of respondent's identity and the victim's independent recollections of him both antedated the unlawful arrest and were thus untainted by the constitutional violation." *U. S. v. Crews*, 445 U.S. 463, 476–77, 100 S. Ct. 1244, 63 L. Ed. 2d 537 (1980).

- "[T]he exclusionary rule has no application because the Government learned of the evidence from an independent source. . . . We need not hold that all evidence is fruit of the poisonous tree simply because it would not have come to light but for the illegal actions of the police. Rather the more apt question in such a case is whether, granting establishment of the primary illegality, the evidence to which instant objection is made has been come at by exploitation of that illegality or instead by means sufficiently distinguishable to be purged of the primary taint." *Wong Sun v. U.S.*, 371 U.S. 471, 487–88, 83 S. Ct. 407, 9 L. Ed. 2d 441 (1963).

- "Of course this does not mean that the facts thus obtained [from illegally procured evidence] become sacred and inaccessible. If knowledge of them is gained from an independent source they may be proved like any others, but the knowledge gained by the Government's own wrong cannot be used by it." *Silverthorne*

Lumber Co. v. U.S., 251 U.S. 385, 392, 40 S. Ct. 182, 64 L. Ed. 319, 3 A.F.T.R. (P-H) P 3016, 24 A.L.R. 1426 (1920).

First Circuit

- "The Fourth Amendment requires suppression not only of evidence seized during an unlawful search, but also of evidence 'that is the product of the primary evidence, or that is otherwise acquired as an indirect result of the unlawful search.' However, under the 'independent source' exception to the Fourth Amendment's exclusionary rule, 'evidence acquired by an untainted search which is identical to . . . evidence unlawfully acquired' is admissible. Accordingly, '[w]hether the initial entry [into a home] was illegal or not is irrelevant to the admissibility of the challenged evidence' where 'there was an independent source for the warrant under which that evidence was seized.'" *United States v. Dent*, 867 F.3d 37 (1st Cir. 2017) (citations omitted).

Third Circuit

- "The underlying rationale for the independent source rule is that the exclusionary rule ensures that the police should not be in a better position as a result of their illegal action, but neither should they lie in a worse position." *U.S. v. Vasquez De Reyes*, 149 F.3d 192, 194 (3d Cir. 1998).

Fifth Circuit

- "Records belonging to a bankruptcy debtor, which were obtained by a defrauded bank pursuant to its own subpoena, did not constitute inadmissible fruit of allegedly illegal search performed by the Internal Revenue Service." *In re McCann*, 268 Fed. Appx. 359, R.I.C.O. Bus. Disp. Guide (CCH) P 11455 (5th Cir. 2008).
- "[U]nder the 'independent source' exception to the exclusionary rule, the government must make two showings in order for a lawful search pursuant to a warrant to be deemed 'genuinely independent' of a prior illegal search: (1) that the police would still have sought a warrant in the absence of the illegal search; and (2) that the warrant would still have been issued (i.e., that there would still have been probable cause to support

the warrant) if the supporting affidavit had not contained information stemming from the illegal search. [citation omitted] In the instant case, the Government contends that the magistrate judge would have issued the two warrants permitting the police to search [defendant's computer and disks and [defendant's] home even if the police had never conducted a pre-warrant search of the storage media. According to the Government, the information that the police obtained from interviews . . . and from [defendant's] admissions in his statement to [a law enforcement officer] was sufficient to compel the police to seek a warrant and to establish probable cause for a warrant to issue. Thus, because the police obtained the same information acquired through their pre-warrant search of the disks from the subsequent, lawful searches pursuant to the warrant, these subsequent searches were an 'independent source' of the images on the disks and this evidence is admissible at trial." *U.S. v. Runyan*, 290 F.3d 223 (5th Cir. 2002).

- "[C]onsent to search may, but does not necessarily, dissipate the taint of a prior fourth amendment violation. . . . Where there has been a prior constitutional violation, the government's burden to prove that the defendant consented becomes all the more difficult. . . . [W]hen we evaluate consent given after a Fourth Amendment violation, the admissibility of the challenged evidence turns on a two-pronged inquiry: whether the consent was voluntarily given and whether it was an independent act of free will. Voluntariness focuses on coercion, and the second prong considers the causal connection between the consent and the prior constitutional violation." *U.S. v. Dortch*, 199 F.3d 193, 201 (5th Cir. 1999), opinion corrected on denial of reh'g, 203 F.3d 883 (5th Cir. 2000).

- "The Supreme Court has held that where evidence initially unlawfully seized is subsequently obtained pursuant to a search warrant based on independent information, the independent source doctrine applies not only to evidence seen for the first time during the warrant-authorized search, but also to evidence seen in plain view at the time of the illegal warrantless search." *U.S. v. Hassan*, 83 F.3d 693, 695 (5th Cir. 1996).

Sixth Circuit

- "[T]he Supreme Court has long provided that when knowledge or possession of evidence is gained from an independent and lawful source, that evidence is admissible. . . . To be admissible, the government must show that the evidence was discovered through sources wholly independent of any constitutional violation. . . . This doctrine is anchored in the notion that although the government should not profit from its illegal activity, neither should it be placed in a worse position than it would otherwise have occupied." *U.S. v. Dice*, 200 F.3d 978, 984, 2000 FED App. 0005P (6th Cir. 2000).

Seventh Circuit

- "Excluding evidence that the police ultimately obtained by independent legal means would not put the police in the same position they would have been in if they had not committed any illegal conduct; instead, it would put them in a worse position. . . .The independent source doctrine avoids this by allowing the introduction of evidence discovered initially during an unlawful search if the evidence is discovered later through a source that is untainted by the initial illegality." *U.S. v. May*, 214 F.3d 900, 906 (7th Cir. 2000).

Tenth Circuit

- "The fact that another investigation was already underway when a constitutional violation occurred is strong proof that it was independent of the illegal investigation, as *Nix* and *Griffin* illustrate. However, it is possible for an investigation that begins after the violation to be independent of the illegal investigation." *U.S. v. Larsen*, 127 F.3d 984, 987 (10th Cir. 1997).

§ 34:4 Attenuation exception: The courts will admit derivative evidence if there is no significant causal relationship between the unlawful police conduct and the discovery of the evidence

Supreme Court

- "The attenuation doctrine evaluates the causal link between the government's unlawful act and the discovery of evidence, which often has nothing to do with a defendant's actions. And the logic of our prior attenuation cases is not limited to independent acts by the defendant. It remains for us to address whether the discovery of a valid arrest warrant was a sufficient intervening event to break the causal chain between the unlawful stop and the discovery of drug-related evidence on Strieff's person. The three factors articulated in *Brown v. Illinois* guide our analysis. First, we look to the 'temporal proximity' between the unconstitutional conduct and the discovery of evidence to determine how closely the discovery of evidence followed the unconstitutional search. Second, we consider 'the presence of intervening circumstances.' Third, and 'particularly' significant, we examine 'the purpose and flagrancy of the official misconduct.' . . . . Applying these factors, we hold that the evidence discovered on Strieff's person was admissible because the unlawful stop was sufficiently attenuated by the pre-existing arrest warrant. Although the illegal stop was close in time to Strieff's arrest, that consideration is outweighed by two factors supporting the State. The outstanding arrest warrant for Strieff's arrest is a critical intervening circumstance that is wholly independent of the illegal stop. The discovery of that warrant broke the causal chain between the unconstitutional stop and the discovery of evidence by compelling Officer Fackrell to arrest Strieff. And, it is especially significant that there is no evidence that Officer Fackrell's illegal stop reflected flagrantly unlawful police misconduct." *Utah v. Strieff*, 136 S. Ct. 2056, 2061–62, 63, 195 L. Ed. 2d 400 (2016) (citations omitted).

- "Nothing in the reasoning of [*Payton*] suggests that an arrest in a home without a warrant but with probable cause somehow renders unlawful continued custody of the suspect once he is removed from the house. There could be no valid claim here that [Defendant] was immune from prosecution because his person was the fruit of an illegal arrest. Nor is there any claim that the warrantless arrest required the police to release [Defendant] or that [Defendant] could not be immediately rearrested if momentarily released. Because the officers had probable cause to arrest [Defendant] for a crime, [Defendant] was not unlawfully in custody when he was removed to the station house, given *Miranda* warnings and allowed to talk. For Fourth Amendment purposes, the legal issue is the same as it would be had the police arrested [Defendant] on his door step, illegally entered his home to search for evidence, and later interrogated [Defendant] at the station house. Similarly, if the police had made a warrantless entry into [Defendant's] home, not found him there, but arrested him on the street when he returned, a later statement made by him after proper warnings would no doubt be admissible." *New York v. Harris*, 495 U.S. 14, 18, 110 S. Ct. 1640, 109 L. Ed. 2d 13 (1990).

- "[A] confession obtained through custodial interrogation after an illegal arrest should be excluded unless intervening events break the causal connection between the illegal arrest and the confession so that the confession is sufficiently an act of free will to purge the primary taint. If *Miranda* warnings were viewed as a talisman that cured all Fourth Amendment violations, then the constitutional guarantee against unlawful searches and seizures would be reduced to a mere form of words." *Taylor v. Alabama*, 457 U.S. 687, 690, 102 S. Ct. 2664, 73 L. Ed. 2d 314 (1982).

- "In the typical fruit of the poisonous tree case, the challenged evidence was acquired by the police after some initial Fourth Amendment violation, and the question before the court is whether the chain of causation proceeding from the unlawful conduct has become so attenuated or has been interrupted by some intervening circumstance so as to remove the taint imposed upon that evidence by the original illegality." *U. S. v. Crews*, 445 U.S. 463, 471, 100 S. Ct. 1244, 63 L. Ed. 2d 537 (1980).

- "[S]ince the cost of excluding live-witness testimony often will be greater [than the cost of excluding inanimate evidence], a closer, more direct link between the illegality and that kind of testimony is required. [Here,] the degree of attenuation was sufficient to dissipate the connection between the illegality and the testimony. The evidence indicates overwhelmingly that the testimony given by the witness was an act of her own free will in no way coerced or even induced by official authority as a result of [the illegal police conduct]. Substantial periods of time elapsed between the time of the illegal search and the initial contact with the witness, on the one hand, and between the latter and the testimony at trial, on the other. While the particular knowledge to which [the witness] testified at trial can be logically traced back to [the illegal search], both the identity of [the witness] and her relationship with the [Defendant] were well known to those investigating the case." *U. S. v. Ceccolini*, 435 U.S. 268, 278, 279, 98 S. Ct. 1054, 55 L. Ed. 2d 268 (1978).

- "The *Miranda* warnings are an important factor in determining whether the confession is obtained by exploitation of an illegal arrest. But they are not the only factor to be considered. The temporal proximity of the arrest and the confession, the presence of intervening circumstances and, particularly, the purpose and flagrancy of the official misconduct are all relevant." *Brown v. Illinois*, 422 U.S. 590, 603–04, 95 S. Ct. 2254, 45 L. Ed. 2d 416 (1975).

- "Sophisticated argument may prove a causal connection between information obtained [unlawfully] and the Government's proof. As a matter of good sense, however, such connection may have become so attenuated as to dissipate the taint." *Nardone v. U.S.*, 308 U.S. 338, 341, 60 S. Ct. 266, 84 L. Ed. 307 (1939).

First Circuit

- "Under these facts, we need not address the legality of the frisk itself. We conclude that regardless of the legality of the frisk, the discovery of the gun was so tainted by the illegal stop that it should have been suppressed as 'fruit of the poisonous tree.' Evidence obtained during a search may be tainted by the illegality of an earlier Fourth Amendment violation, so as to render such evidence inadmissible as 'fruit of the poisonous tree.' This rule equally extends to both the direct and the indirect products of unlawful searches and seizures. '[T]he indirect fruits of an illegal search or arrest should be suppressed when they bear a sufficiently close relationship to the underlying illegality.' Suppression is not appropriate, however, if 'the connection between the illegal police conduct and the discovery and seizure of

the evidence is so attenuated as to dissipate the taint.'
Determining the consequences of unlawful police
conduct for seized evidence requires looking at both
causation and attenuation. The Supreme Court has
declined to adopt a simple 'but for' test that would
mandate suppression of any evidence that 'came to light
through a chain of causation that began with an illegal
arrest' or another Fourth Amendment violation. A strict
but-for rule would prove nearly limitless. 'Rather, the
more apt question in such a case is whether, granting
establishment of the primary illegality, the evidence to
which instant objection is made has been come at by
exploitation of that illegality or instead by means sufficiently distinguishable to be purged of the primary
taint.' When determining attenuation, 'temporal proximity [ ], the presence of intervening circumstances, and,
particularly the purpose and flagrancy of the official
misconduct are all relevant.' Here, [the officers] were
responding to 911 calls that described 'at most a misdemeanor assault and battery or disturbance of the peace'
that 'was not terribly serious.' The participants had already dispersed, so the police interest in investigating
suspected participants in the misdemeanor brawl was
minimal. Nonetheless, the officers pursued—without
reasonable suspicion—two men who were merely 'walking normally on a residential sidewalk.' Yet the officers
accosted the two men with a substantial show of authority, including: cutting off their path with an unmarked
police car, ordering [one defendant] to put his hands on
the hood, asking [the second defendant] 'accusatory'
questions, and ordering [the second defendant] to take
his hands out of his pockets. Up until at least that point,
the officers' conduct amounted to a flagrant violation of
the core of [the second defendant's] Fourth Amendment
right against unreasonable seizures. Without cause,
[one officer] reached out toward [the second defendant],
felt the gun, and yelled 'Gun!'. The only intervening action by [the second defendant] between the illegal stop
and the frisk was removing his hands from his pockets
at [the officer's] direction. After [the officer's] 'tap,' [the
second defendant] immediately responded by shoving
him. A brief struggle ensued, after which [the second
defendant] was arrested and the gun was seized. The

time elapsed between the illegal stop and the discovery
and seizure of the gun was minimal. The officers'
encounter with [the second defendant] and the discovery
of the gun 'were both results of the officers' unconstitutional conduct.' Discovery of the gun flowed directly
from the original unlawful seizure of [the second
defendant] and was not 'so attenuated as to dissipate
the taint' of the initial unlawful stop. Under these facts,
we conclude that the gun was fruit poisoned by the
unlawful seizure and, accordingly, should have been
suppressed." *U.S. v. Camacho*, 661 F.3d 718, 728–30
(1st Cir. 2011) (citations and inner quotations omitted).

Second Circuit

- "In *United States v. Ceccolini* . . . the Supreme Court
  held that the exclusionary rule does not invariably bar
  the testimony of a witness whose identity is revealed to
  the authorities as the result of an illegal search. The
  exclusion of such testimony depends on the degree of
  attenuation between the illegal search and the
  testimony. . . . In *United States v. Leonardi* . . . this
  Court interpreted *Ceccolini* to require consideration of
  the following factors: (a) the stated willingness of the
  witness to testify, (b) the role played by the illegally
  seized evidence in gaining his cooperation, (c) the
  proximity between the illegal behavior, the decision to
  cooperate and the actual testimony at trial, and (d) the
  motivation of the police in conducting the search." *U.S.
  v. Reyes*, 157 F.3d 949, 954, 50 Fed. R. Evid. Serv. 288
  (2d Cir. 1998).

Fourth Circuit

- "[W]e have little difficulty concluding that where, as
  here, the discovery of the challenged evidence follows
  an unlawful search, but precedes an independent criminal act on the part of the defendant, that criminal act is
  not an intervening event for the purpose of determining
  whether the 'taint' of the unlawful police action is
  purged." *U.S. v. Gaines*, 668 F.3d 170, 175 (4th Cir.
  2012).
- "As a general rule, evidence obtained as a result of a
  Fourth Amendment violation is inadmissible. . . . This
  broad exclusionary prohibition extends to verbal evi-

dence as well as physical evidence. . . . In *Wong Sun*, however, the Supreme Court noted that an intervening act of free will may purge the primary taint of the unlawful invasion. . . . Factors relevant to the inquiry include: (1) the amount of time between the illegal action and the acquisition of the evidence; (2) the presence of intervening circumstances; and (3) the purpose and flagrancy of the official misconduct. . . . Nevertheless, a finding with respect to attenuation . . . can only be made after consideration of all the circumstances of the case. . . . This requires a careful sifting of the unique facts and circumstances of each case. . . . Finally, the burden of showing admissibility rests . . . on the prosecution." *U.S. v. Seidman*, 156 F.3d 542, 548, 159 L.R.R.M. (BNA) 2211, 136 Lab. Cas. (CCH) P 10246 (4th Cir. 1998).

Fifth Circuit

- "In sum, even if [Defendant]'s consent was voluntarily given, and the district court's determination therefore was not clearly erroneous, the consent was not valid. Instead, because the causal chain between the illegal detention and [Defendant]'s consent to a third body search was not broken, the search was nonconsensual. And because there was no probable cause to search his person, the evidence obtained during that search should have been suppressed." *U.S. v. Dortch*, 199 F.3d 193, 202–03 (5th Cir. 1999), opinion corrected on denial of reh'g, 203 F.3d 883 (5th Cir. 2000).

Seventh Circuit

- "Even if police officer's seizure of defendant's computer became unreasonable due to the length of the delay in obtaining a search warrant for the computer, the defendant's telephone calls to the police station and statements made to the police were not derivative of the seizure of his computer, and thus the defendant's statements were not excludable as fruit of the poisonous tree. The defendant called the police station and volunteered that he had pretty graphic files on his computer, defendant agreed to come down for questioning, and defendant called the officer to clarify some of his previous statements." *U.S. v. Budd*, 549 F.3d 1140 (7th Cir. 2008).

- "Determining whether the causal chain has been sufficiently attenuated to dissipate the taint of the illegal act requires analysis of the temporal proximity of the illegal conduct to the evidence obtained, the presence of any intervening circumstances, and the purpose and flagrancy of the police misconduct. . . . [Defendant] argues that his statement after being shown the gun found inside his bedroom should be suppressed under the fourth amendment. This determination requires an analysis of whether the statement should have been excluded as the product of an illegal entry. . . . [T]he admissibility of the gun seized in the defendant's residence and the statement he made to police thereafter cannot be decided without an initial determination of the lawfulness of the entry into the residence." *U.S. v. Fields*, 371 F.3d 910 (7th Cir. 2004).

- "The test for determining the admissibility of evidence obtained through a chain of causation that began with an illegal arrest is whether, granting establishment of the primary illegality, the evidence to which instant objection is made has been come at by exploitation of that illegality or instead by means sufficiently distinguishable to be purged of the primary taint." *U.S. v. Ienco*, 182 F.3d 517, 526 (7th Cir. 1999).

- "[I]f the causal chain between the initial illegality and the evidence sought to be excluded is broken, the link to the evidence is sufficiently attenuated to dissipate the taint of illegal conduct. . . . It has been noted that the purpose of this attenuated connection test is to mark the point of diminishing returns of the deterrence principle inherent in the exclusionary rule. . . . Three factors for determining whether the causal chain is sufficiently attenuated to dissipate the taint of illegal conduct are: (1) the time elapsed between the illegality and the acquisition of the evidence; (2) the presence of intervening circumstances; and (3) the purpose and flagrancy of the official misconduct." *U.S. v. Ienco*, 182 F.3d 517, 526 (7th Cir. 1999).

- "Moreover, no intervening event of any significance occurred between the illegal seizure and the consent to break the causal chain. The testimony of the officers establishes that their conduct had a quality of purposefulness. In concluding that the illegal seizure in this case vitiated the appellants' subsequent consent, we follow the strong body of case law in our circuit, as well as in other circuits, that has held, typically after applying *Brown v. Illinois*, that the voluntary consents at issue were tainted by illegal stops, detentions or arrests." *U.S. v. Jerez*, 108 F.3d 684, 695 (7th Cir. 1997).

Ninth Circuit

- "The government has not shown that there was a break in the chain of events sufficient to refute the inference that the search and the resulting seizure of the cocaine were products of the stop. . . . The government has not shown that connection between the traffic stop and the search of the car was sufficiently attenuated to dissipate the taint caused by the illegality. . . . In this case, the interrogation and search were a direct result of the illegal stop. . . . This is a classic case of obtaining evidence through the exploitation of an illegal stop, as is the case when the officer's suspicions are aroused by what he observes following the stop, and on that basis obtains . . . consent." *U.S. v. Twilley*, 222 F.3d 1092, 1097 (9th Cir. 2000).

- "The attenuated basis exception is, at bottom, the manifestation of the courts' consistent rejection of a but for causation standard in fruit of the poisonous tree doctrine. . . . Rather, the taint inquiry is more akin to a proximate causation analysis. That is, at some point, even in the event of a direct and unbroken causal chain, the relationship between the unlawful search or seizure and the challenged evidence becomes sufficiently weak to dissipate any taint resulting from the original illegality. . . . In other words, at some point along the line, evidence might be fruit, yet nonetheless be admissible because it is no longer tainted or poisonous. Of course, the line between taint and attenuation is not an easy one to draw. As a leading treatise observes, there is not now and doubtless never will be any litmus-paper test for determining when there is only an attenuated connection between a Fourth Amendment violation and certain derivative evidence." *U.S. v. Smith*, 155 F.3d 1051, 1060, Fed. Sec. L. Rep. (CCH) P 90274 (9th Cir. 1998).

Eleventh Circuit

- "Three general exceptions to the fruit of the poisonous tree doctrine have been developed, under which the government may break that causal chain and defeat a motion to suppress. . . . Although the Government does not argue which of the three referenced exceptions breaks the causal chain in this instance, we find that 'circumstances independent of the primary illegality' have attenuated the causal connection and thus 'dissipate the taint' of the officer's unlawful search with regard to [the defendant's] statements during the 3:33 PM phone call." *U.S. v. Timmann*, 741 F.3d 1170 (11th Cir. 2013).

D.C. Circuit

- "An illegal search or seizure calls for suppression of evidence only if the seizure is a but-for cause of the discovery of the evidence (a necessary condition), and if the causal chain has not become 'too attenuated to justify exclusion,' or, to put the same point with another metaphor, if circumstances have not 'purged [the evidence] of the primary taint,' . . . In resolving whether the causal chain has become 'too attenuated,' the Court has identified three factors of special relevance: (1) the amount of time between the illegality and the discovery of the evidence, (2) the presence of intervening circumstances, and (3) the purpose and flagrancy of the illegal conduct. For this inquiry, the government bears the burden of demonstrating admissibility." *U.S. v. Brodie*, 742 F.3d 1058 (D.C. Cir. 2014) (citations omitted).

§ 34:5   Inevitable discovery exception: If the derivative evidence eventually would have been discovered through lawful means, it is admissible

Supreme Court

- "The inevitable discovery doctrine, with its distinct requirements, is in reality and extrapolation from the independent source doctrine: Since the tainted evidence would be admissible if in fact discovered through an independent source, it should be admissible if it inevitably would have been discovered." *Murray v. U.S.*, 487 U.S. 533, 539, 108 S. Ct. 2529, 101 L. Ed. 2d 472 (1988).

- "When the challenged evidence has an independent source, exclusion of such evidence would put the police in a worse position than they would have been in absent any error or violation. There is a functional similarity between these two doctrines in that exclusion of evidence that would inevitably have been discovered would also put the government in a worse position, because the police would have obtained that evidence if no misconduct had taken place. Thus, while the independent source exception would not justify admission of evidence in this case, its rationale is wholly consistent with and justifies our adoption of the ultimate or inevitable discovery exception to the Exclusionary Rule." *Nix v. Williams*, 467 U.S. 431, 443–44, 104 S. Ct. 2501, 81 L. Ed. 2d 377 (1984).

- "The ultimate or inevitable discovery exception to the Exclusionary Rule is closely related in purpose to the harmless-error rule. The harmless-constitutional-error rule serve[s] a very useful purpose insofar as [it] block[s] setting aside convictions for small errors or defects that have little, if any, likelihood of having changed the result of the trial. The purpose of the inevitable discovery rule is to block setting aside convictions that would have been obtained without police misconduct." *Nix v. Williams*, 467 U.S. 431, 443 n.4, 104 S. Ct. 2501, 81 L. Ed. 2d 377 (1984).

- "While neither [Defendant's] incriminating statements themselves nor any testimony describing his having led the police to the victim's body can constitutionally be admitted into evidence [because they w ere illegally obtained], evidence of where the body was found and its condition might well be admissible on the theory that the body would have been discovered in any event, even had incriminating statements not been [unlawfully] elicited from [Defendant]." *Brewer v. Williams*, 430 U.S. 387, 407 n.12, 97 S. Ct. 1232, 51 L. Ed. 2d 424 (1977).

First Circuit

- "The term inevitable, although part of the *Nix* doctrine's name, is something of an overstatement. The facts of *Nix* itself—a body hidden in an area of many square miles—show that what is required is a high probability that the evidence would have been discovered by lawful

means. The probability has not been quantified, but it
only confuses matters to pretend that the government
must prove to a certainty what would have happened
but for the illegally obtained admission." *U.S. v. Rogers*,
102 F.3d 641, 646 (1st Cir. 1996).

Second Circuit

- "The exclusionary rule is not without exceptions,
however. One such exception—the inevitable discovery
doctrine—provides that the fruits of an illegal search or
seizure are nevertheless admissible at trial if the
government can prove that the evidence would have
been obtained inevitably without the constitutional
violation. The government bears the burden of proving
inevitable discovery by a preponderance of the evidence.
We have made clear, however, that proof of inevitable
discovery involves no speculative elements but focuses
on *demonstrated historical facts capable of ready
verification or impeachment*. The focus on demonstrated
historical facts keeps speculation to a minimum, by
requiring the district court to determine, viewing affairs as they existed at the instant before the unlawful
search occurred, what *would have happened* had the
unlawful search never occurred. Evidence should not be
admitted, therefore, unless a court can find, with a high
level of confidence, that each of the contingencies necessary to the legal discovery of the contested evidence
would be resolved in the government's favor. . . . Here,
the district court, finding that there was only one real
contingency in this case, failed to account for all of the
demonstrated historical facts in the record, and in doing so, failed adequately to consider other plausible
contingencies that might not have resulted in the guns'
discovery. . . . A court may only speculate about the
likelihood that [another person] would have returned
and removed the guns, but that is precisely the problem:
a finding of inevitable discovery cannot rest on speculation about what [the other person] might or might not
have done. . . . [W]e note that unlike the more typical
application of the inevitable discovery rule, in which
the government seeks to invoke the doctrine on the
basis of standardized, established procedures such as
those requiring inventory searches or on the basis of an

investigation that was already underway, the district
court's inevitability analysis in this case is predicated
on an assessment of the actions that might have been
taken by third parties—Stokes, Fulmes, or motel staff—
not acting at the behest of the police. Such an analysis
is inherently speculative, and the district court's conclusions were not based on 'demonstrated historical facts
capable of ready verification.' . . . In short, on de novo
review, we conclude that the sheer number of contingencies that may not have been resolved in the government's favor undermines the conclusion that discovery
of the evidence pursuant to a lawful search was
inevitable. At bottom, the government's argument
amounts to little more than a contention that the officers were not leaving the motel without Stokes. That
the officers would not leave the motel without arresting
Stokes, however, does not compel the conclusion that
the officers would inevitably have discovered the guns."
U.S. v. Stokes, 733 F.3d 438 (2d Cir. 2013) (citations
and inner quotations omitted).

Fourth Circuit

- "Agent Willey provided sufficient testimony for the
district court to find that the DEA had a standard
inventory procedure pertaining to all impounded
vehicles and would have inevitably discovered the challenged evidence by conducting an inventory search according to routine and standard DEA procedures. Even
the most circumscribed inventory procedures call for an
inventory of unsecured items located in an unlocked vehicle's interior. Such basic procedures would have
uncovered the incriminating cellphone found on the passenger's seat and the documents strewn throughout the
unlocked Pontiac's interior. As for documents found in
the glove compartment, we note that both the Supreme
Court and lower federal courts have 'recognized that
standard inventories often include an examination of
the glove compartment, since it is a customary place for
documents of ownership and registration.' Here, although Agent Willey did not guide the district court
step-by-step through the DEA's impoundment-and-
inventory procedure, he did explain that identifying the
registered owner of the vehicle was part of standard

DEA practice. The district court did not clearly err in finding that the DEA would routinely search a glove compartment under these circumstances. . . .In short, we have never required the government to provide a written impoundment-and-inventory policy or elicit step-by-step testimony concerning such a policy to meet its burden under the inevitable-discovery doctrine. The government meets its burden and this court can affirm on inevitable-discovery grounds if the district court can assess the inevitability and reasonableness of a hypothetical inventory search from testimony provided by a law-enforcement official—such as DEA Agent Willey here. . . ." *United States v. Bullette*, 854 F.3d 261, 266–67 (4th Cir. 2017) (citations omitted).

- "[W]hen evidence could not have been discovered without a subsequent search, and no exception to the warrant requirement applies, and no warrant has been obtained, and nothing demonstrates that the police would have obtained a warrant absent the illegal search, the inevitable discovery doctrine has no place. In those circumstances absolutely nothing suggests, let alone proves by a preponderance of the evidence, that the illegally obtained evidence inevitably would have been discovered. The inevitable discovery doctrine cannot rescue evidence obtained via an unlawful search simply because probable cause existed to obtain a warrant when the government presents no evidence that the police would have obtained a warrant. Any other rule would emasculate the Fourth Amendment." *U.S. v. Allen*, 159 F.3d 832, 841–42 (4th Cir. 1998).

Sixth Circuit

- "[T]he exclusionary rule does not apply when the Government can demonstrate that evidence found because of a Fourth Amendment violation would inevitably have been discovered lawfully. . . .[A] successful inevitable discovery argument requires the government to proffer clear evidence of an independent, untainted investigation that inevitably would have uncovered the same evidence as that discovered through the illegal search." *U.S. v. Haddix*, 239 F.3d 766, 768–69, 2001 FED App. 0039P (6th Cir. 2001).

- "The inevitable discovery doctrine is conceptually more

problematic than the independent source doctrine because it involves a degree of deducing what would have happened rather than simply evaluating what actually happened. Under the inevitable discovery doctrine, evidence may be admitted if the government can show that the evidence inevitably would have been obtained from lawful sources in the absence of the illegal discovery. By its nature, the inevitable discovery doctrine requires some degree of speculation as to what the government would have discovered absent the illegal conduct. Speculation, however, must be kept to a minimum; courts must focus on demonstrated historical facts capable of ready verification or impeachment. The burden of proof is on the government to establish that the tainted evidence would have been discovered by lawful means." *U.S. v. Leake*, 95 F.3d 409, 412 (6th Cir. 1996).

Seventh Circuit

- "The challenged evidence was also admissible under the related doctrine of inevitable discovery, since the officer who did the on-site search credibly testified that he would have referred the case to the sex-crimes division regardless of what he had seen on the devices. In other words, even if the on-site search hadn't occurred, the federal warrant still would have issued based on C.T.'s statements during her interview, and the evidence from Fifer's electronic devices still would have been discovered as a result of that warrant." *United States v. Fifer*, 863 F.3d 759, 766–67 (7th Cir. 2017) (citations omitted).
- "The inevitable-discovery doctrine precluded exclusion of evidence illegally seized pursuant to a search warrant lacking a particular description of the things to be seized where the police conducted exactly the same search that they would have conducted had the warrant described with the requisite particularity the things for which they were searching; it was not remotely likely that the state judge would have refused to sign the warrant had it complied with the Fourth Amendment by listing those things." *U.S. v. Sims*, 553 F.3d 580 (7th Cir. 2009).
- "It is hard to understand how the discovery of evidence inside a house could be anything but inevitable once

the police arrive with a warrant; an occupant would hardly be allowed to contend that, had the officers announced their presence and waited longer to enter, he would have had time to destroy the evidence." *U.S. v. Jones*, 149 F.3d 715, 717 (7th Cir. 1998).

Eighth Circuit

• "The inevitable discovery doctrine is based on the concept that illegally obtained evidence that is sufficiently purged of its original taint is not subject to the exclusionary rule. . . . . The precarious balance struck by the Fourth Amendment's warrant requirement and the inevitable discovery doctrine recognizes that, while the exclusion of illegally obtained evidence both deters police officers from violating constitutional protections and prevents prosecutors from benefitting from the illegality, evidence that would have been inevitably discovered through independent, lawful means should be admitted so that the prosecutor is put in the same, not worse, position as though the original illegality had not occurred." *U.S. v. Madrid*, 152 F.3d 1034, 1037–38 (8th Cir. 1998).

• "To decide whether the cocaine inside the envelope would have been inevitably discovered, this Court must not only examine whether there was a reasonable probability that the evidence would have been discovered by lawful means if the police misconduct had not occurred, but it must also examine whether the government was pursuing a substantial, alternative line of investigation at the time of the police misconduct." *U.S. v. Hammons*, 152 F.3d 1025, 1029 (8th Cir. 1998).

Ninth Circuit

• "We hold that the search of Gorman's vehicle following the coordinated traffic stops violated the Constitution and affirm the district court's order granting Gorman's motion to suppress. Gorman's first roadside detention was unreasonably prolonged in violation of the Fourth Amendment. The dog sniff and the search of Gorman's vehicle, in turn, followed directly in an unbroken causal chain of events from that constitutional violation. As a result, the seized currency is the 'fruit of the poisonous tree' and was properly suppressed under the exclusionary rule. . ... The coordinated action at issue in Gorman's case offers a prime illustration of the value of the 'fruit of the poisonous tree' analysis. The analysis allows us to see the officers' conduct in Gorman's case as what it is: a single integrated effort by police to circumvent the Constitution by making two coordinated stops. When the result of one stop is communicated and, on that basis, another stop is planned and implemented, the coordinated stops become, in effect, one integrated stop that must as a whole satisfy the Constitution's requirements. An illegal police venture cannot be made legal simply by dividing it into two coordinated stops. The Constitution guards against this kind of gamesmanship because the Fourth Amendment's protections extend beyond the margins of one particular police stop and can extend to the integrated and purposeful conduct of the state. *United States v. Gorman*, 859 F.3d 706, 714, 719 (9th Cir. 2017) (citations omitted).

- "[W]hile the search cannot be upheld as incident to arrest in light of *Gant,* the deterrent rationale for the exclusionary rule is not applicable where the evidence would have ultimately been discovered during a police inventory of the contents of [defendant]'s car. . .. . We emphasize, however, that the inevitable discovery doctrine will not always save a search that has been invalidated under *Gant.* The government is still required to prove, by a preponderance of the evidence, that there was a lawful alternative justification for discovering the evidence. . . . Therefore . . . the district court must conduct a case-by-case inquiry to determine whether a lawful path to discovery—such as inevitability—exists in each case. To hold otherwise would create an impermissible loop-hole in the Court's bright-line *Gant* determination." *U.S. v. Ruckes*, 586 F.3d 713 (9th Cir. 2009).

- "As this court explained in *Mejia*, it has never applied the inevitable discovery exception so as to excuse the failure to obtain a search warrant where the police had probable cause but simply did not attempt to obtain a warrant. . . .Hence, the district court committed clear error in applying the inevitable discovery doctrine based on the agents' actual but unexercised opportunity to secure a search warrant." *U.S. v. Reilly*, 224 F.3d 986, 995 (9th Cir. 2000).

Tenth Circuit

- "As discussed above, a court may apply the inevitable discovery exception only when it has a high level of confidence that the warrant in fact would have been issued and that the specific evidence in question would have been obtained by lawful means. Inevitable discovery analysis thus requires the court to examine each of the contingencies involved that would have had to have been resolved favorably to the government in order for the evidence to have been discovered legally and to assess the probability of the contingencies having occurred. . . .The more contingencies there are, and the lower the probability that each would have been resolved in the government's favor, the lower the probability that the evidence would have been found by lawful means." *U.S. v. Souza*, 223 F.3d 1197, 1205 (10th Cir. 2000).

- "Like the independent source doctrine, the inevitable discovery doctrine is an exception to the general rule requiring exclusion of evidence that is the result of unlawful government conduct. Evidence found as a result of illegal police conduct that inevitably would have been lawfully discovered absent the illegal conduct need not be suppressed. . . . The inevitable discovery doctrine is based on the same rationale as the independent source doctrine—that the interest of society in deterring unlawful police conduct and the public interest in having juries receive all probative evidence of a crime are properly balanced by putting the police in the same, not a worse, position that they would have been if no police error or misconduct had occurred." *U.S. v. Larsen*, 127 F.3d 984, 986 (10th Cir. 1997).

Eleventh Circuit

- "Under the inevitable discovery exception, if the prosecution can establish by a preponderance of the evidence that the information would have ultimately been recovered by lawful means, the evidence will be admissible. [citations omitted] However, the mere assertion by law enforcement that the information would have been inevitably discovered is not enough. [citation and footnote omitted] This circuit also requires the prosecution to show that 'the lawful means which made discovery inevitable were being *actively pursued* prior to the occurrence of the illegal conduct.' [citation omitted; emphasis added in court's opinion] This second requirement is especially important. Any other rule would effectively eviscerate the exclusionary rule, because in most illegal search situations the government could have obtained a valid search warrant had they waited or obtained the evidence through some lawful means had they taken another course of action. [citation omitted] . . . . The Supreme Court first endorsed the inevitable discovery exception in Nix v. Williams, holding that evidence of the location and condition of a murder victim's body was admissible, even though it was learned through an illegal interrogation of the defendant, because search parties were already conducting systematic searches in the area near the body. [citation omitted] Finding this ruling consistent with [our] "active pursuit" requirement . . . ., we have continued to strictly apply this requirement. [citation omitted] . . . Here, the prosecution cannot evade the suppression of the evidence by utilizing the inevitable discovery exception to the exclusionary rule, because it cannot show that officers were actively pursuing any lawful means at the time of the illegal conduct. While a dog sniff can be used to give probable cause to search a vehicle [citation omitted], at the time Stinson decided to seize the car, he knew that the canine unit would be unavailable to meet him at the gas station for some time. The officers could not have indefinitely detained [defendant], who was then handcuffed in the back of a police car, at the gas station without arresting him. [citations omitted] However, the officers did not place [defendant] under arrest at the gas station, and there is no evidence that they planned to bring the canine unit to the scene in a reasonable time after learning of its unavailability. . . . The investigative team was engaged in no lawful investigatory actions which would have led to the search of [defendant]'s car. For the exception to apply, the prosecution needed to show that the police would have obtained the evidence 'by virtue of ordinary investigations of evidence or leads already in their possession.' [citation omitted] . . . In . . . the present case, there is no evidence that the team was pursuing [defendant] or his vehicle as part of their ongoing investigation. In fact Sgt. Stinson testified that [defendant] was completely unknown to the investigation prior to this stop. Furthermore, it is unlikely that any other future investigation would have discovered precisely this evidence given that vehicles are by nature mobile, and [defendant] was alerted to the police attention by the initial stop. [citation omitted] . . . When the officers learned that their lawful method of obtaining the evidence—bringing the canine unit to the scene in a reasonable time frame—would be unavailable, the officers decided to take an unlawful route to obtain the desired evidence because it was expedient, rather than determine an alternate lawful route. This is precisely the misconduct which the exclusionary rule is meant to deter. Therefore, the inevitable discovery exception does not apply under these circumstances. . . . Th[us], we find that the district court properly suppressed the evidence from the vehicle search. The search occurred only due to the vehicle's unconstitutional seizure. The police lacked the probable cause necessary to interfere with [defendant]'s possessory interest to such an extent. Furthermore, the evidence obtained cannot be saved from suppression by the inevitable discovery exception because the police were not engaged in any lawful investigatory activity which would have led to the search of the car." *U.S. v. Virden*, 488 F.3d 1317, 1322–1324 (11th Cir. 2007).

§ 34:6 Burden of proof: Once the defendant has made a prima facie showing of government illegality, the prosecution must prove an independent source by a preponderance of the evidence

Supreme Court

- "[T]he cases implementing the exclusionary rule begin with the premise that the challenged evidence is in some sense the product of illegal governmental activity. Of course, this does not end the inquiry. If the prosecution can establish by a preponderance of the evidence that the information ultimately or inevitably would have been discovered by lawful means then the deterrence rationale has so little basis that the evidence should be received." *Nix v. Williams*, 467 U.S. 431, 444, 104 S. Ct. 2501, 81 L. Ed. 2d 377 (1984).

- "The United States concedes that when an illegal search has come to light, it has the ultimate burden of persuasion to show that its evidence is untainted. But at the same time petitioners acknowledge that they must go forward with specific evidence demonstrating taint." *Alderman v. U.S.*, 394 U.S. 165, 183, 89 S. Ct. 961, 22 L. Ed. 2d 176 (1969).

- "The burden is on the accused in the first instance to prove to the trial court's satisfaction that wire-tapping was unlawfully employed. Once that is established the trial judge must give opportunity to the accused to prove that a substantial portion of the case against him was a fruit of the poisonous tree. This leaves ample opportunity to the Government to convince the trial court that its proof has an independent origin." *Nardone v. U.S.*, 308 U.S. 338, 341, 60 S. Ct. 266, 84 L. Ed. 307 (1939).

Third Circuit

- "It is the government's burden to show that the evidence at issue would have been acquired through lawful means, a burden that can be met if the government establishes that the police, following routine procedures, would inevitably have uncovered the evidence. . . . However, the Supreme Court made clear in *Nix* that the analysis should focus upon the historical facts capable of ready verification, and not speculation. . . . Inevitable discovery is not an exception to be invoked casually, and if it is to be prevented from swallowing the Fourth Amendment and the exclusionary rule, courts must take care to hold the government to its burden of proof." *U.S. v. Vasquez De Reyes*, 149 F.3d 192, 195–96 (3d Cir. 1998).

Fifth Circuit

- "To determine whether the causal chain was broken, we consider: (1) the temporal proximity of the illegal conduct and the consent; (2) the presence of intervening circumstances; and (3) the purpose and flagrancy of the initial misconduct. The burden of showing admissibility rests on the government." *U.S. v. Vega*, 221 F.3d 789, 801–02, 54 Fed. R. Evid. Serv. 1502 (5th Cir. 2000).

- "Consent to search may, but does not necessarily, dissipate the taint of a fourth amendment violation. The admissibility of the challenged evidence turns on a two-pronged inquiry: whether the consent was voluntarily given and whether it was an independent act of free will. The first prong focuses on coercion, the second on causal connection with the constitutional violation. Even though voluntarily given, consent does not remove the taint of an illegal detention if it is the product of that detention and not an independent act of free will. To determine whether the causal chain was broken, we consider: (1) the temporal proximity of the illegal conduct and the consent; (2) the presence of intervening circumstances; and (3) the purpose and flagrancy of the initial misconduct. The burden of showing admissibility rests on the government." *U.S. v. Chavez-Villarreal*, 3 F.3d 124, 127–28 (5th Cir. 1993).

Sixth Circuit

- "Here, the testimony about what the IRS would have done in investigating this case is inconsistent with what the IRS actually did. . . . As in *Leake*, the record does not substantiate the government's claim that it was hot on the trail of the disputed evidence. The government has not carried its burden of proving the inevitability of discovery." *U.S. v. Ford*, 184 F.3d 566, 578, 99-2 U.S. Tax Cas. (CCH) P 50724, 84 A.F.T.R.2d 99-5361, 1999 FED App. 0267P (6th Cir. 1999).

Seventh Circuit

- "As *Nix* itself makes clear, when the government relies on the inevitable discovery doctrine, it bears the burden of proving, by a preponderance of the evidence, that it would have found the challenged evidence through lawful means. [W]e wish to stress that the burden of proof *Nix* imposes on the government ordinarily will require the government to do more than it did in this case. *Nix*, we repeat, speaks in terms of proof by preponderance of the evidence that the government would have discovered the challenged evidence through lawful means; and typically that will entail testimony rather than mere argument. It is all too easy to imagine in retrospect lawful avenues through which the government might have obtained evidence that in reality it came upon in contravention of the Fourth Amendment. Speculation and assumption do not satisfy the dictates of *Nix*, however. Inevitable discovery is not an exception to be invoked casually, and if it is to be prevented from swallowing the Fourth Amendment and the exclusionary rule, courts must take care to hold the government to its burden of proof." *U.S. v. Jones*, 72 F.3d 1324, 1334, 43 Fed. R. Evid. Serv. 708 (7th Cir. 1995).

Eighth Circuit

- "[The defendant] bears the burden of establishing a nexus between the alleged constitutional violation and the discovery of the firearms. If [the defendant] sufficiently comes forward with specific evidence demonstrating taint, the ultimate burden of persuasion to show the evidence is untainted lies with the government. To meet this burden, the Government must show the evidence obtained after the illegal search was not come at by exploitation of that illegality [but] instead by means sufficiently distinguishable to be purged of the primary taint." *U.S. v. Hastings*, 685 F.3d 724, 728 (8th Cir. 2012) (quotations and citations omitted).

Ninth Circuit

- "The inevitable discovery exception to the exclusionary rule is available when the government demonstrates, by a preponderance of the evidence, that it would inevitably have discovered the incriminating evidence through lawful means. . . . The government can meet its burden by demonstrating that, by following routine procedures, the police would inevitably have uncovered the evidence." *U.S. v. Lopez-Soto*, 205 F.3d 1101, 1106–07 (9th Cir. 2000).

Tenth Circuit

- "To suppress evidence as the fruit of his unlawful detention, [defendant] must make two showings: (1) that the detention did violate his Fourth Amendment rights; and (2) that there is a factual nexus between the il-

legality and the challenged evidence. Only if the
defendant has made these two showings must the
government prove that the evidence sought to be suppressed is not 'fruit of the poisonous tree,' either by
demonstrating the evidence would have been inevitably
discovered, was discovered through independent means,
or was so attenuated from the illegality as to dissipate
the taint of the unlawful conduct." *U.S. v. DeLuca*, 269
F.3d 1128 (10th Cir. 2001).

- "To successfully suppress evidence as the fruit of an
  unlawful detention, a defendant must first establish
  that the detention did violate his Fourth Amendment
  rights. . . .The defendant then bears the burden of
  demonstrating a factual nexus between the illegality
  and the challenged evidence. . . . Only if the defendant
  has made these two showings must the government
  prove that the evidence sought to be suppressed is not
  fruit of the poisonous tree. . . ." *U.S. v. Nava-Ramirez*,
  210 F.3d 1128, 1131 (10th Cir. 2000).

- "Under the fruit of the poisonous tree doctrine, the
  exclusionary rule bars the admission of physical evidence and live witness testimony obtained directly or
  indirectly through the exploitation of police illegality.
  . . . The court may nevertheless admit evidence seized
  illegally, if the government shows that (1) the evidence
  was obtained from a source that was wholly independent of the illegal conduct . . . (2) that the evidence inevitably would have been discovered despite the illegal
  activity . . . or (3) that the link between the illegality
  and the evidence has become so attenuated as to dissipate the taint. . . . The government must make its
  showing by a preponderance of the evidence." *U.S. v.
  Lin Lyn Trading, Ltd.*, 149 F.3d 1112, 1116 (10th Cir.
  1998).

- "Even though voluntary consent may be given by a
  person who is detained if the consent is given after an
  illegal stop, the government carries a heavy burden of
  showing that the primary taint of the illegal stop was
  purged so that the subsequent consent was voluntary in
  fact. To satisfy this burden the government must prove,
  from the totality of the circumstances, a sufficient attenuation or break in the causal connection between
  the illegal detention and the consent. We find a lack of

attenuation sufficient to make defendant's subsequent consent voluntary. There were absolutely no intervening circumstances in the short period of time between the illegal detention and the defendant's subsequent consent." *U.S. v. Gregory*, 79 F.3d 973, 979–80 (10th Cir. 1996).

§ 34:7 Limited use of illegally seized evidence: Evidence obtained by illegal search or seizure may be used to impeach a defendant, presented to a grand jury, and offered in sentencing and post-sentencing proceedings

Supreme Court

- "[T]he use of evidence obtained in an illegal search and inadmissible in the Government's case in chief [may be] admitted to impeach the direct testimony of the defendant. [S]tatements taken in violation of *Miranda* and unusable by the prosecution as part of its own case [are] admissible to impeach statements made by the defendant in the course of his direct testimony. [P]ermitted impeachment by otherwise inadmissible evidence is not limited to collateral matters. [A] defendant's statements made in response to proper cross-examination reasonably suggested by the defendant's direct examination are subject to otherwise proper impeachment by the government, albeit by evidence that has been illegally obtained that is inadmissible on the government's direct case, or otherwise, as substantive evidence of guilt." *U.S. v. Havens*, 446 U.S. 620, 624–25, 100 S. Ct. 1912, 64 L. Ed. 2d 559, 6 Fed. R. Evid. Serv. 1 (1980).

- "[W]e [have] refused to require that illegally seized evidence be excluded from presentation to a grand jury. We have likewise declined to prohibit the use of such evidence for the purpose of impeaching a defendant who testifies in his own behalf." *U. S. v. Ceccolini*, 435 U.S. 268, 275, 98 S. Ct. 1054, 55 L. Ed. 2d 268 (1978).

First Circuit

- "It is well-settled that evidence obtained in violation of the Fourth Amendment can be admitted for the limited purpose of impeaching a testifying criminal defendant's credibility. The so-called impeachment exception to the exclusionary rule reflects a balance of values underlying that rule. Thus, while defendants are free to testify truthfully on their own behalf without opening the door to impeachment an affirmative resort to perjurious testimony may be exposed by impeachment with illegally obtained evidence. When a defendant opens the door to impeachment through his statements on direct, the government may try to establish that his testimony is not to be believed through cross-examination and the introduction of evidence, including tainted evidence, that contradicts the direct testimony. When the assertedly false testimony is first given on cross-examination, however, the trial judge must gauge how closely the cross-examination is connected with matters explored during direct before invoking the impeachment exception to the exclusionary rule." *U.S. v. Morla-Trinidad*, 100 F.3d 1, 4–5, 45 Fed. R. Evid. Serv. 1331 (1st Cir. 1996).

- "To date, five circuit courts of appeal have addressed the issue of whether the Fourth Amendment exclusionary rule prohibits a sentencing court from considering illegally seized evidence for purposes of determining or enhancing a defendant's Guidelines sentence. Each of these courts has held that the exclusionary rule does not generally apply in the sentencing context and that there is no blanket prohibition on the consideration of illegally seized evidence for purposes of making the findings required under the Guidelines." *U.S. v. Raposa*, 84 F.3d 502, 504 (1st Cir. 1996).

Second Circuit

- "If the unwarned statement could be considered by the police officers, then the arrest would be legal and the subsequently obtained statements and physical evidence would no longer be subject to taint analysis. As we examine the facts in this case to determine whether there was probable cause to arrest [Defendant], we can find no valid and useful purpose to be served by disregarding his pre-warning statement to the officers who were acting in good faith. Where, as here, there is no indication of trickery or coercion, there is no justification for requiring a police officer to ignore incriminating admissions in arriving at a conclusion that there is

probable cause for an arrest. Supression of the uncoun-
seled statements at the trial is sufficient to further the
purposes of *Miranda*." *U.S. v. Morales*, 788 F.2d 883,
885 (2d Cir. 1986).

Seventh Circuit

- "We held in United States v. Brimah, 214 F.3d 854 (7th
  Cir.2000), that the exclusionary rule does not apply at
  criminal sentencing. Every other court of appeals has
  come to the same conclusion. [Defendant] does not ask
  us to overrule *Brimah*. Instead he observes that a footnote, 214 F.3d at 858 n. 4, remarks that the appeal did
  not present the question whether an "egregious" violation of the fourth amendment might justify suppression
  at sentencing. [Defendant] wants us to call the search
  of his house "egregious" and hold that the evidence must
  be suppressed. He acknowledges, however, that this
  step would itself create a conflict among the circuits: No
  court of appeals has held that evidence is inadmissible
  at sentencing on account of an "egregious" violation
  (whatever that might mean in operation). See also 18
  U.S.C. § 3661, which provides that all evidence is
  admissible at sentencing. We could create an "egregious
  violation = suppression" rule only at the expense of holding § 3661 unconstitutional as applied, a step no court
  of appeals has taken. . . . In addition to footnote 4 in
  Brimah, this court has several times observed that it
  was unwilling to suppress evidence at sentencing when
  the defendant had not shown that the police knowingly
  violated the Constitution for the purpose of jacking up
  the sentence. But we have never held that such a
  purpose *does* justify suppression at sentencing. . . .
  [Defendant] wants us to create a novel distinction between "ordinary" and "egregious" violations that lacks
  any support in the holdings of the Court that created
  the exclusionary rule and defines its scope. . . . The
  search of [Defendant's] house was authorized by a
  warrant. That makes it difficult to see any space between ordinary and egregious violations of the fourth
  amendment for the purpose of sentencing. . . . [I]t is
  hard to understand how an "egregious" violation could
  be defined in a way that is both administrable and distinguishes severe from other violations. . . . [A]n

"egregious violation" exception is not necessary to deter officers from violating the fourth amendment—and deterrence is the goal of the exclusionary rule. When a violation of the fourth amendment really is beyond the pale, the offending officers will be liable in damages. Qualified immunity protects officers who commit "ordinary" violations of the fourth amendment, but not those who wilfully or blatantly violate the Constitution. . . . The exclusionary rule does not apply at sentencing. An "egregious violation" exception is not necessary to deter violations, as long as damages are available." *U.S. v. Sanders*, 743 F.3d 471 (7th Cir. 2014).

- "[A] violation of the knock and announce rule 'does not authorize exclusion of the evidence seized pursuant to the ensuing search.' " *U.S. v. Brown*, 333 F.3d 850 (7th Cir. 2003).

Ninth Circuit

- "*Harris* and *Hass* have been applied in a search and seizure case. Evidence obtained in violation of the 4th Amendment was used to impeach the defendant for statements he made on cross examination." *U.S. v. Tsinnijinnie*, 91 F.3d 1285, 1288, 45 Fed. R. Evid. Serv. 369 (9th Cir. 1996).

Tenth Circuit

- "[A]ll nine other circuits to have considered this issue have determined that, in most circumstances, the exclusionary rule does not bar the introduction of the fruits of illegal searches and seizures during sentencing proceedings." *U.S. v. Ryan*, 236 F.3d 1268, 1271 (10th Cir. 2001).

- "In the opinion of this court, extension of the exclusionary rule to sentencing or post-sentencing proceedings before federal agencies would, in the ordinary case, have a deterrent effect so minimal as to be insignificant. In the usual case, law enforcement officers conduct searches and seize evidence for the purpose of obtaining convictions, not for the purpose of increasing the sentence in a prosecution already pending or one not yet commenced. It is apparent that the significant deterrent to official lawlessness is the threat that an illegal search and seizure would render the prosecution ineffective. The additional threat that the sentence imposed in a future criminal prosecution might be less severe or that the defendant in a future case might be paroled earlier would appear to have little practical effect." *U.S. v. Graves*, 785 F.2d 870, 873 (10th Cir. 1986).

Table of Cases

Dunaway v. New York, 442 U.S. 200, 99 S. Ct. 2248, 60 L. Ed. 2d 824 (1979)—3:4, 4:1

Dunn, U.S. v., 480 U.S. 294, 107 S. Ct. 1134, 94 L. Ed. 2d 326 (1987)—16:1

Edwards, U.S. v., 415 U.S. 800, 94 S. Ct. 1234, 39 L. Ed. 2d 771 (1974)—7:4, 13:4

Ferguson v. City of Charleston, 532 U.S. 67, 121 S. Ct. 1281, 149 L. Ed. 2d 205 (2001)—29:1

Fernandez v. California, 134 S. Ct. 1126, 188 L. Ed. 2d 25 (2014)—17:4

Flippo v. West Virginia, 528 U.S. 11, 120 S. Ct. 7, 145 L. Ed. 2d 16 (1999)—6:1, 8:2

Florence v. Board of Chosen Freeholders of County of Burlington, 566 U.S. 318, 132 S. Ct. 1510, 182 L. Ed. 2d 566 (2012)—4:2, 30:3

Florida v. Bostick, 501 U.S. 429, 111 S. Ct. 2382, 115 L. Ed. 2d 389 (1991)—3:1, 3:2, 17:1, 17:2

Florida v. Harris, 568 U.S. 237, 133 S. Ct. 1050, 185 L. Ed. 2d 61 (2013)—24:3

Florida v. Jardines, 569 U.S. 1, 133 S. Ct. 1409, 185 L. Ed. 2d 495 (2013)—24:1

Florida v. Jimeno, 500 U.S. 248, 111 S. Ct. 1801, 114 L. Ed. 2d 297 (1991)—17:2, 17:5

Florida v. J.L., 529 U.S. 266, 120 S. Ct. 1375, 146 L. Ed. 2d 254 (2000)—5:7, 9:2, 9:4

Florida v. Riley, 488 U.S. 445, 109 S. Ct. 693, 102 L. Ed. 2d 835 (1989)—16:3

Florida v. Rodriguez, 469 U.S. 1, 105 S. Ct. 308, 83 L. Ed. 2d 165 (1984)—22:2

Florida v. Royer, 460 U.S. 491, 103 S. Ct. 1319, 75 L. Ed. 2d 229 (1983)—3:2, 3:4, 3:6, 3:12, 4:1, 4:2, 9:1, 9:2, 9:3, 17:1, 22:1, 22:2, 22:3, 22:4

Florida v. Wells, 495 U.S. 1, 110 S. Ct. 1632, 109 L. Ed. 2d 1 (1990)—13:3

Florida v. White, 526 U.S. 559, 119 S. Ct. 1555, 143 L. Ed. 2d 748 (1999)—1:1, 4:3, 11:2, 13:1

Franks v. Delaware, 438 U.S. 154, 98 S. Ct. 2674, 57 L. Ed. 2d 667 (1978)—5:16, 33:1, 33:2

Frisbie v. Collins, 342 U.S. 519, 72 S. Ct. 509, 96 L. Ed. 541 (1952)—4:10

Georgia v. Randolph, 547 U.S. 103, 126 S. Ct. 1515, 164 L. Ed. 2d 208 (2006)—17:4

Giordenello v. U.S., 357 U.S. 480, 78 S. Ct. 1245, 2 L. Ed. 2d 1503 (1958)—5:6

Grady v. North Carolina, 135 S. Ct. 1368, 191 L. Ed. 2d 459 (2015)—25:5, 30:2

Graham v. Connor, 490 U.S. 386, 109 S. Ct. 1865, 104 L. Ed. 2d 443 (1989)—1:6, 3:11, 4:9

Griffin v. Wisconsin, 483 U.S. 868, 107 S. Ct. 3164, 97 L. Ed. 2d 709 (1987)—30:2

Groh v. Ramirez, 540 U.S. 551, 124 S. Ct. 1284, 157 L. Ed. 2d 1068 (2004)—5:4

Grubbs, U.S. v., 547 U.S. 90, 126 S. Ct. 1494, 164 L. Ed. 2d 195, 31 A.L.R. Fed. 2d 635 (2006)—5:11

Harris v. U.S., 390 U.S. 234, 88 S. Ct. 992, 19 L. Ed. 2d 1067 (1968)—13:1

Harrison v. U.S., 392 U.S. 219,

Miller, U. S. v., 1976-1 C.B. 535,
425 U.S. 435, 96 S. Ct.
1619, 48 L. Ed. 2d 71, 76-1
U.S. Tax Cas. (CCH) P
9380, 37 A.F.T.R.2d 76-1261
(1976)—2:4

Mincey v. Arizona, 437 U.S. 385,
98 S. Ct. 2408, 57 L. Ed. 2d
290 (1978)—8:2

Minnesota v. Carter, 525 U.S.
83, 119 S. Ct. 469, 142 L.
Ed. 2d 373 (1998)—1:1, 1:2,
1:3, 32:1, 32:2

Minnesota v. Dickerson, 508
U.S. 366, 113 S. Ct. 2130,
124 L. Ed. 2d 334 (1993)—
6:1, 9:5, 9:6, 9:7, 14:1, 14:3

Minnesota v. Olson, 495 U.S. 91,
110 S. Ct. 1684, 109 L. Ed.
2d 85 (1990)—8:1, 32:2

Missouri v. McNeely, 569 U.S.
141, 133 S. Ct. 1552, 185 L.
Ed. 2d 696 (2013)—8:2, 27:2

Monsanto, U.S. v., 491 U.S. 600,
109 S. Ct. 2657, 105 L. Ed.
2d 512 (1989)—31:2, 31:11

Montoya de Hernandez, U.S. v.,
473 U.S. 531, 105 S. Ct.
3304, 87 L. Ed. 2d 381
(1985)—18:1, 18:12, 27:5

Muehler v. Mena, 544 U.S. 93,
125 S. Ct. 1465, 161 L. Ed.
2d 299 (2005)—3:14, 10:3

Mullenix v. Luna, 136 S. Ct.
305, 193 L. Ed. 2d 255
(2015)—1:2, 4:9

Murray v. U.S., 487 U.S. 533,
108 S. Ct. 2529, 101 L. Ed.
2d 472 (1988)—1:8, 34:1,
34:3, 34:5

Nardone v. U.S., 308 U.S. 338,
60 S. Ct. 266, 84 L. Ed. 307
(1939)—34:4, 34:6

Nathanson v. U.S., 290 U.S. 41,
54 S. Ct. 11, 78 L. Ed. 159
(1933)—5:2, 5:6

National Treasury Employees
Union v. Von Raab, 489 U.S.
656, 109 S. Ct. 1384, 103 L.
Ed. 2d 685, 4 I.E.R. Cas.
(BNA) 246, 49 Empl. Prac.
Dec. (CCH) ¶ 38792, 1989
O.S.H. Dec. (CCH) ¶ 28589
(1989)—28:1, 28:2, 28:3

New Jersey v. T.L.O., 469 U.S.
325, 105 S. Ct. 733, 83 L.
Ed. 2d 720, 21 Ed. Law Rep.
1122 (1985)—2:3, 30:5

New York v. Belton, 453 U.S.
454, 101 S. Ct. 2860, 69 L.
Ed. 2d 768 (1981)—6:1, 7:1,
7:3, 11:6, 11:7, 12:5

New York v. Burger, 482 U.S.
691, 107 S. Ct. 2636, 96 L.
Ed. 2d 601 (1987)—21:3

New York v. Class, 475 U.S. 106,
106 S. Ct. 960, 89 L. Ed. 2d
81 (1986)—10:7, 11:1

New York v. Harris, 495 U.S. 14,
110 S. Ct. 1640, 109 L. Ed.
2d 13 (1990)—34:3, 34:4

Nix v. Williams, 467 U.S. 431,
104 S. Ct. 2501, 81 L. Ed.
2d 377 (1984)—1:9, 34:3,
34:5, 34:6

North American Cold Storage
Co. v. City of Chicago, 211
U.S. 306, 29 S. Ct. 101, 53
L. Ed. 195 (1908)—21:4

O'Connor v. Ortega, 480 U.S.
709, 107 S. Ct. 1492, 94 L.
Ed. 2d 714, 1 I.E.R. Cas.
(BNA) 1617, 42 Empl. Prac.
Dec. (CCH) ¶ 36891
(1987)—21:1

Ohio v. Robinette, 519 U.S. 33,
117 S. Ct. 417, 136 L. Ed.
2d 347, 148 A.L.R. Fed. 739
(1996)—1:1, 3:2, 17:2, 17:3

Oliver v. U.S., 466 U.S. 170, 104
S. Ct. 1735, 80 L. Ed. 2d
214 (1984)—2:1, 16:1, 16:2,
16:3

2473, 189 L. Ed. 2d 430, 42 Media L. Rep. (BNA) 1925 (2014)—7:5

Robinson, U.S. v., 414 U.S. 218, 94 S. Ct. 467, 38 L. Ed. 2d 427 (1973)—7:1

Rochin v. California, 342 U.S. 165, 72 S. Ct. 205, 96 L. Ed. 183, 25 A.L.R.2d 1396 (1952)—27:2

Rodriguez v. U.S., 135 S. Ct. 1609, 191 L. Ed. 2d 492 (2015)—10:2, 10:3, 10:6, 24:1

Ross, U.S. v., 456 U.S. 798, 102 S. Ct. 2157, 72 L. Ed. 2d 572 (1982)—11:2, 11:3, 11:4, 11:5, 12:3, 12:4, 12:5

Ryder v. U.S., 515 U.S. 177, 115 S. Ct. 2031, 132 L. Ed. 2d 136 (1995)—1:9, 5:18

Sabbath v. U.S., 391 U.S. 585, 88 S. Ct. 1755, 20 L. Ed. 2d 828 (1968)—5:12

Safford Unified School Dist. No. 1 v. Redding, 557 U.S. 364, 129 S. Ct. 2633, 174 L. Ed. 2d 354, 245 Ed. Law Rep. 626 (2009)—1:7, 2:2, 27:3, 30:5

Salvucci, U. S. v., 448 U.S. 83, 100 S. Ct. 2547, 65 L. Ed. 2d 619 (1980)—2:1, 2:2, 32:3

Samson v. California, 547 U.S. 843, 126 S. Ct. 2193, 165 L. Ed. 2d 250 (2006)—30:2

San Francisco, Calif., City and County of v. Sheehan, 135 S. Ct. 1765, 191 L. Ed. 2d 856 (2015)—4:9, 8:4

Santana, U.S. v., 427 U.S. 38, 96 S. Ct. 2406, 49 L. Ed. 2d 300 (1976)—4:6, 8:2

Saucier v. Katz, 533 U.S. 194, 121 S. Ct. 2151, 150 L. Ed. 2d 272 (2001)—4:9

Schmerber v. California, 384

U.S. 757, 86 S. Ct. 1826, 16 L. Ed. 2d 908 (1966)—27:2

Schneckloth v. Bustamonte, 412 U.S. 218, 93 S. Ct. 2041, 36 L. Ed. 2d 854 (1973)—17:2

Scott v. Harris, 550 U.S. 372, 127 S. Ct. 1769, 167 L. Ed. 2d 686 (2007)—4:9

Scott v. U.S., 436 U.S. 128, 98 S. Ct. 1717, 56 L. Ed. 2d 168 (1978)—4:8, 25:2

See v. City of Seattle, 387 U.S. 541, 87 S. Ct. 1737, 18 L. Ed. 2d 943 (1967)—21:1, 21:2

Segura v. U.S., 468 U.S. 796, 104 S. Ct. 3380, 82 L. Ed. 2d 599 (1984)—1:6, 3:14, 34:3

Sgro v. U.S., 287 U.S. 206, 53 S. Ct. 138, 77 L. Ed. 260, 85 A.L.R. 108 (1932)—5:8

Sharpe, U.S. v., 470 U.S. 675, 105 S. Ct. 1568, 84 L. Ed. 2d 605 (1985)—9:3, 10:8

Shipley v. California, 395 U.S. 818, 89 S. Ct. 2053, 23 L. Ed. 2d 732 (1969)—7:2

Sibron v. New York, 392 U.S. 40, 88 S. Ct. 1889, 20 L. Ed. 2d 917 (1968)—7:2

Silverthorne Lumber Co. v. U.S., 251 U.S. 385, 40 S. Ct. 182, 64 L. Ed. 319, 3 A.F.T.R. (P-H) ¶ 3016, 24 A.L.R. 1426 (1920)—34:3

Skinner v. Railway Labor Executives' Ass'n, 489 U.S. 602, 109 S. Ct. 1402, 103 L. Ed. 2d 639, 4 I.E.R. Cas. (BNA) 224, 130 L.R.R.M. (BNA) 2857, 13 O.S.H. Cas. (BNA) 2065, 49 Empl. Prac. Dec. (CCH) ¶ 38791, 111 Lab. Cas. (CCH) ¶ 11001, 1989 O.S.H. Dec. (CCH) ¶

A.F.T.R.2d 5787 (1965)—5:6, 5:14

Verdugo-Urquidez, U.S. v., 494 U.S. 259, 110 S. Ct. 1056, 108 L. Ed. 2d 222 (1990)—1:1

Vernonia School Dist. 47J v. Acton, 515 U.S. 646, 115 S. Ct. 2386, 132 L. Ed. 2d 564, 101 Ed. Law Rep. 37 (1995)—28:1, 30:5

Villamonte-Marquez, U.S. v., 462 U.S. 579, 103 S. Ct. 2573, 77 L. Ed. 2d 22 (1983)—3:7, 18:7, 20:2

Virginia v. Harris, 558 U.S. 978, 130 S. Ct. 10, 175 L. Ed. 2d 322 (2009)—9:2

Virginia v. Moore, 553 U.S. 164, 128 S. Ct. 1598, 170 L. Ed. 2d 559 (2008)—1:1, 2:3, 4:3, 6:3

Walder v. U.S., 347 U.S. 62, 74 S. Ct. 354, 98 L. Ed. 503 (1954)—1:8

Walter v. U.S., 447 U.S. 649, 100 S. Ct. 2395, 65 L. Ed. 2d 410 (1980)—17:5, 29:2

Warden, Md. Penitentiary v. Hayden, 387 U.S. 294, 87 S. Ct. 1642, 18 L. Ed. 2d 782 (1967)—1:5, 8:1, 8:2

Washington v. Chrisman, 455 U.S. 1, 102 S. Ct. 812, 70 L. Ed. 2d 778, 1 Ed. Law Rep. 1087 (1982)—4:7, 7:1, 14:3

Waterloo Distilling Corporation v. U.S., 282 U.S. 577, 51 S. Ct. 282, 75 L. Ed. 558 (1931)—31:7

Watson, U.S. v., 423 U.S. 411, 96 S. Ct. 820, 46 L. Ed. 2d 598 (1976)—4:3, 17:3

Welsh v. Wisconsin, 466 U.S. 740, 104 S. Ct. 2091, 80 L. Ed. 2d 732 (1984)—1:3, 4:4, 4:6, 8:1

White v. Pauly, 137 S. Ct. 548, 196 L. Ed. 2d 463 (2017)—3:11

Whren v. U.S., 517 U.S. 806, 116 S. Ct. 1769, 135 L. Ed. 2d 89 (1996)—4:8, 10:1, 10:9, 13:3

Wilson v. Arkansas, 514 U.S. 927, 115 S. Ct. 1914, 131 L. Ed. 2d 976 (1995)—1:1, 5:12

Wilson v. Layne, 526 U.S. 603, 119 S. Ct. 1692, 143 L. Ed. 2d 818, 27 Media L. Rep. (BNA) 1705 (1999)—5:12

Winston v. Lee, 470 U.S. 753, 105 S. Ct. 1611, 84 L. Ed. 2d 662 (1985)—27:2

Wong Sun v. U.S., 371 U.S. 471, 83 S. Ct. 407, 9 L. Ed. 2d 441 (1963)—34:1, 34:2, 34:3

Wyoming v. Houghton, 526 U.S. 295, 119 S. Ct. 1297, 143 L. Ed. 2d 408 (1999)—2:3, 11:1, 11:3, 11:5, 12:4, 32:2

Ybarra v. Illinois, 444 U.S. 85, 100 S. Ct. 338, 62 L. Ed. 2d 238 (1979)—4:2, 5:4, 9:4, 9:5

Zurcher v. Stanford Daily, 436 U.S. 547, 98 S. Ct. 1970, 56 L. Ed. 2d 525, 3 Media L. Rep. (BNA) 2377 (1978)—1:5

First Circuit

Acosta-Colon, U.S. v., 157 F.3d 9 (1st Cir. 1998)—9:3

Allen, U.S. v., 469 F.3d 11 (1st Cir. 2006)—11:6

Allen, U.S. v., 990 F.2d 667 (1st Cir. 1993)—23:5

Almonte-Báez, United States v., 857 F.3d 27 (1st Cir. 2017)—8:2

Arthur, U.S. v., 764 F.3d 92 (1st Cir. 2014)—3:6

Barboza, U.S. v., 412 F.3d 15 (1st Cir. 2005)—9:5

Martin, U.S. v., 157 F.3d 46 (2d
Cir. 1998)—5:14

McCardle v. Haddad, 131 F.3d
43 (2d Cir. 1997)—6:2, 10:6

McCargo, U.S. v., 464 F.3d 192
(2d Cir. 2006)—9:4

Mendez, U.S. v., 315 F.3d 132
(2d Cir. 2002)—13:2

Milbrand, U.S. v., 58 F.3d 841
(2d Cir. 1995)—31:4, 31:6

Moetamedi, U.S. v., 46 F.3d 225
(2d Cir. 1995)—5:11

Moore v. Vega, 371 F.3d 110 (2d
Cir. 2004)—30:2

Morales, U.S. v., 788 F.2d 883
(2d Cir. 1986)—34:7

Navas, U.S. v., 597 F.3d 492 (2d
Cir. 2010)—1:4, 11:1, 11:2,
11:3, 21:3

Newton, U.S. v., 369 F.3d 659
(2d Cir. 2004)—30:2

Nicholas v. Goord, 430 F.3d 652
(2d Cir. 2005)—27:2

O'Brien, U.S. v., 303 Fed. Appx.
948 (2d Cir. 2008)—6:3

Oliveira v. Mayer, 23 F.3d 642
(2d Cir. 1994)—10:8

One Parcel of Property Located
at 194 Quaker Farms Road,
Oxford, Conn., U.S. v., 85
F.3d 985 (2d Cir. 1996)—
31:4

One Parcel of Property Located
at 121 Allen Place, Hart-
ford, Conn., U.S. v., 75 F.3d
118 (2d Cir. 1996)—31:4

Onumonu, U.S. v., 967 F.2d 782,
36 Fed. R. Evid. Serv. 273
(2d Cir. 1992)—18:13, 27:5

Padilla, U.S. v., 548 F.3d 179 (2d
Cir. 2008)—8:3

Pangburn, U.S. v., 983 F.2d 449
(2d Cir. 1993)—25:1

Perea, U.S. v., 986 F.2d 633 (2d
Cir. 1993)—13:4

Rahman, U.S. v., 189 F.3d 88,

52 Fed. R. Evid. Serv. 425
(2d Cir. 1999)—9:4

Raymonda, U.S. v., 780 F.3d 105
(2d Cir. 2015)—5:9

Reyes, U.S. v., 157 F.3d 949, 50
Fed. R. Evid. Serv. 288 (2d
Cir. 1998)—34:4

Reyes, U.S. v., 821 F.2d 168 (2d
Cir. 1987)—18:12

Ribadeneira, U.S. v., 105 F.3d
833 (2d Cir. 1997)—31:3

Rodriguez, U.S. v., 532 F.2d 834
(2d Cir. 1976)—19:2

Roe v. Marcotte, 193 F.3d 72 (2d
Cir. 1999)—21:5, 27:2, 30:3

Rogers, U.S. v., 129 F.3d 76 (2d
Cir. 1997)—10:7

Sanders, U.S. v., 663 F.2d 1 (2d
Cir. 1981)—27:5

Santa, U.S. v., 180 F.3d 20, 52
Fed. R. Evid. Serv. 570 (2d
Cir. 1999)—33:3, 34:1

Schwimmer, U.S. v., 968 F.2d
1570, 23 Fed. R. Serv. 3d
224 (2d Cir. 1992)—31:3,
31:11

Scopo, U.S. v., 19 F.3d 777 (2d
Cir. 1994)—14:2

Shi Yan Liu, U.S. v., 239 F.3d
138 (2d Cir. 2000)—5:17

Simels, U.S. v., 654 F.3d 161 (2d
Cir. 2011)—1:8, 1:9

Simko v. Town of Highlands,
276 Fed. Appx. 39 (2d Cir.
2008)—16:1

Simmons, U.S. v., 560 F.3d 98
(2d Cir. 2009)—3:6, 4:1, 9:4

Simms v. Village of Albion, N.Y.,
115 F.3d 1098 (2d Cir.
1997)—4:8

Simpson v. City of New York,
793 F.3d 259 (2d Cir.
2015)—4:2

Singh, U.S. v., 811 F.2d 758 (2d
Cir. 1987)—18:6

Smartphone Geolocation Data

Third Circuit

Wilson, U.S. v., 205 F.3d 720 (4th Cir. 2000)—10:1, 10:2

Wilson, U.S. v., 953 F.2d 116 (4th Cir. 1991)—22:1

Yanez-Marquez v. Lynch, 789 F.3d 434 (4th Cir. 2015)—1:2, 1:3, 1:8, 2:4, 5:4, 19:3

Yates v. Terry, 817 F.3d 877 (4th Cir. 2016)—4:9

Fifth Circuit

Adekunle, U.S. v., 2 F.3d 559 (5th Cir. 1993)—18:13

Afanador, U.S. v., 567 F.2d 1325 (5th Cir. 1978)—18:12

Alvarez, U.S. v., 127 F.3d 372 (5th Cir. 1997)—5:1

Andres, U.S. v., 703 F.3d 828 (5th Cir. 2013)—10:3, 11:8

Andrews, U.S. v., 22 F.3d 1328 (5th Cir. 1994)—12:6

Atwater v. City of Lago Vista, 195 F.3d 242 (5th Cir. 1999)—2:3

Baker, U.S. v., 47 F.3d 691 (5th Cir. 1995)—11:7

Blocker, U.S. v., 104 F.3d 720 (5th Cir. 1997)—21:2

Brathwaite, U.S. v., 458 F.3d 376 (5th Cir. 2006)—25:3

Broca-Martinez, United States v., 855 F.3d 675 (5th Cir. 2017)—10:2

Butts, U.S. v., 729 F.2d 1514 (5th Cir. 1984)—26:3

Campbell, U.S. v., 178 F.3d 345 (5th Cir. 1999)—9:6

Cardenas, U.S. v., 9 F.3d 1139 (5th Cir. 1993)—18:3, 18:4

Cardona, U.S. v., 955 F.2d 976 (5th Cir. 1992)—18:4

Castro, U.S. v., 166 F.3d 728 (5th Cir. 1999)—3:4

Cavazos, U.S. v., 288 F.3d 706 (5th Cir. 2002)—5:16

Cervantez-Valerio, U.S. v., 275 Fed. Appx. 417 (5th Cir. 2008)—18:1

Chapa-Garza, U.S. v., 62 F.3d 118 (5th Cir. 1995)—4:10

Chavez-Chavez, U.S. v., 205 F.3d 145 (5th Cir. 2000)—18:9

Chavez-Villarreal, U.S. v., 3 F.3d 124 (5th Cir. 1993)—34:6

Chavis, U.S. v., 48 F.3d 871 (5th Cir. 1995)—33:3

Conlan, U.S. v., 786 F.3d 380 (5th Cir. 2015)—14:3

Conroy, U.S. v., 589 F.2d 1258 (5th Cir. 1979)—20:1, 20:8

Cooper v. Brown, 844 F.3d 517 (5th Cir. 2016)—4:9

Daniel, U.S. v., 982 F.2d 146 (5th Cir. 1993)—23:5

D'Antignac, U. S. v., 628 F.2d 428, 6 Fed. R. Evid. Serv. 1012 (5th Cir. 1980)—20:3, 20:4

Darensbourg, U.S. v., 236 Fed. Appx. 991 (5th Cir. 2007)—9:6

Dortch, U.S. v., 199 F.3d 193 (5th Cir. 1999)—10:8, 34:3, 34:4

Dovali-Avila, U.S. v., 895 F.2d 206 (5th Cir. 1990)—18:7

Dukes, U.S. v., 139 F.3d 469 (5th Cir. 1998)—17:2

Ervin, U.S. v., 907 F.2d 1534 (5th Cir. 1990)—1:4

Escalante, U.S. v., 239 F.3d 678 (5th Cir. 2001)—10:9

Escamilla, United States v., 852 F.3d 474 (5th Cir. 2017)—17:3, 17:5, 18:1, 18:9, 32:2

Finley, U.S. v., 477 F.3d 250, 72 Fed. R. Evid. Serv. 377 (5th Cir. 2007)—7:1

Flores, U.S. v., 63 F.3d 1342, 42

Triplett, U.S. v., 684 F.3d 500 (5th Cir. 2012)—5:4, 5:5, 5:18

United States—(see opposing party)

U.S.—(see opposing party)

U.S. for Historical Cell Site Data, In re, 724 F.3d 600 (5th Cir. 2013)—25:5

Van Meter, U.S. v., 280 Fed. Appx. 394, 2008-1 U.S. Tax Cas. (CCH) ¶ 50373, 101 A.F.T.R.2d 2008-2482 (5th Cir. 2008)—5:4

Vega, U.S. v., 221 F.3d 789, 54 Fed. R. Evid. Serv. 1502 (5th Cir. 2000)—1:2, 8:1, 34:6

Villarreal, U.S. v., 963 F.2d 770 (5th Cir. 1992)—12:3, 12:5, 23:1

Virgil, U.S. v., 444 F.3d 447 (5th Cir. 2006)—8:3

Waldrop, U.S. v., 404 F.3d 365 (5th Cir. 2005)—14:3

Wallace, United States v., 857 F.3d 685 (5th Cir. 2017)—2:4

Wallace v. Wellborn, 204 F.3d 165 (5th Cir. 2000)—1:5

Webster, U.S. v., 162 F.3d 308 (5th Cir. 1998)—9:3

Wernecke v. Garcia, 591 F.3d 386 (5th Cir. 2009)—4:5

Williams, U.S. v., 365 F.3d 399 (5th Cir. 2004)—17:2

Williams, U.S. v., 132 F.3d 1055, 48 Fed. R. Evid. Serv. 777 (5th Cir. 1998)—31:6

Williams, U.S. v., 69 F.3d 27 (5th Cir. 1995)—24:3

Williams, U.S. v., 617 F.2d 1063, 1980 A.M.C. 2550 (5th Cir. 1980)—20:7, 20:9

Wilson, U.S. v., 306 F.3d 231 (5th Cir. 2002)—8:1

Wren v. Towe, 130 F.3d 1154 (5th Cir. 1997)—1:9

Zapata-Ibarra, U.S. v., 212 F.3d 877 (5th Cir. 2000)—18:9

Zimmerman, U.S. v., 303 Fed. Appx. 207 (5th Cir. 2008)—2:4

Zucco, U.S. v., 71 F.3d 188 (5th Cir. 1995)—11:5

Zuniga, United States v., 860 F.3d 276 (5th Cir. 2017)—3:5

Sixth Circuit

Abboud, U.S. v., 438 F.3d 554, 97 A.F.T.R.2d 2006-1142, 2006 FED App. 0066P (6th Cir. 2006)—5:4

Abdullah, U.S. v., 162 F.3d 897, 1998 FED App. 0348P (6th Cir. 1998)—17:1

Abernathy, United States v., 843 F.3d 243 (6th Cir. 2016)—5:2, 5:3

Akram, U.S. v., 165 F.3d 452, 1999 FED App. 0012P (6th Cir. 1999)—10:9

Alexander, U.S. v., 540 F.3d 494 (6th Cir. 2008)—23:5

Allen, U.S. v., 211 F.3d 970, 2000 FED App. 0157P (6th Cir. 2000)—5:6, 5:7

Allen, U.S. v., 106 F.3d 695, 1997 FED App. 0049P (6th Cir. 1997)—6:1

American Civil Liberties Union v. National Sec. Agency, 493 F.3d 644 (6th Cir. 2007)—32:1

Archibald, U.S. v., 589 F.3d 289 (6th Cir. 2009)—7:2, 8:3

Atkin, U.S. v., 107 F.3d 1213, 79 A.F.T.R.2d 97-1301, 1997 FED App. 0085P (6th Cir. 1997)—5:16

Avery, U.S. v., 137 F.3d 343,

1998 FED App. 0074P (6th Cir. 1998)—5:16

Cheatham, U.S. v., 577 Fed. Appx. 500 (6th Cir. 2014)— 1:8, 3:4, 4:2, 9:4, 10:3, 10:7, 10:8

Coccia, U.S. v., 598 F.3d 293 (6th Cir. 2010)—27:1

Coffee, U.S. v., 434 F.3d 887, 2006 FED App. 0030P (6th Cir. 2006)—5:7

Colbert, U.S. v., 76 F.3d 773, 1996 FED App. 0063P (6th Cir. 1996)—4:7

Courtright v. City of Battle Creek, 839 F.3d 513 (6th Cir. 2016)—3:6, 3:10, 4:2, 4:9

Crowder, U.S. v., 62 F.3d 782, 1995 FED App. 0241P (6th Cir. 1995)—17:3

Currency $267,961.07, U.S. v., 916 F.2d 1104 (6th Cir. 1990)—31:3

Daughenbaugh v. City of Tiffin, 150 F.3d 594, 1998 FED App. 0232P (6th Cir. 1998)—16:1, 16:3

Daugherty v. Campbell, 33 F.3d 554, 1994 FED App. 0285P (6th Cir. 1994)—30:4

Davis, U.S. v., 430 F.3d 345, 2005 FED App. 0449P (6th Cir. 2005)—10:3

Diaz, U.S. v., 25 F.3d 392, 1994 FED App. 0193P (6th Cir. 1994)—24:3

Dice, U.S. v., 200 F.3d 978, 2000 FED App. 0005P (6th Cir. 2000)—34:1, 34:3

Dillard, U.S. v., 438 F.3d 675, 2006 FED App. 0073P (6th Cir. 2006)—2:2

Dunning, United States v., 857 F.3d 342 (6th Cir. 2017)— 5:16

Durk, U.S. v., 149 F.3d 464,

1998 FED App. 0213P (6th Cir. 1998)—5:4

Dusenbery, U.S. v., 201 F.3d 763, 2000 FED App. 0017P (6th Cir. 2000)—31:4

Elbe, U.S. v., 774 F.3d 885 (6th Cir. 2014)—5:8, 5:9

Ellison, U.S. v., 462 F.3d 557, 2006 FED App. 0339P (6th Cir. 2006)—2:4

Erwin, U.S. v., 155 F.3d 818, 1998 FED App. 0291P (6th Cir. 1998)—3:7, 17:2

Ewolski v. City of Brunswick, 287 F.3d 492, 2002 FED App. 0133P (6th Cir. 2002)—8:2

Fifty-Three Thousand Eighty-Two Dollars in U.S. Currency, $53,082.00, U.S. v., 985 F.2d 245 (6th Cir. 1993)—12:2, 22:2

Figueredo-Diaz, U.S. v., 718 F.3d 568 (6th Cir. 2013)— 1:9

$515,060.42 in U.S. Currency, U.S. v., 152 F.3d 491, 1998 FED App. 0161P (6th Cir. 1998)—31:3

Ford, U.S. v., 184 F.3d 566, 99-2 U.S. Tax Cas. (CCH) ¶ 50724, 84 A.F.T.R.2d 99-5361, 1999 FED App. 0267P (6th Cir. 1999)—34:6

Foster, U.S. v., 376 F.3d 577, 65 Fed. R. Evid. Serv. 1, 2004 FED App. 0230P (6th Cir. 2004)—9:1

Fox v. Van Oosterum, 176 F.3d 342, 1999 FED App. 0164P (6th Cir. 1999)—3:13

Gaitan-Acevedo, U.S. v., 148 F.3d 577, 49 Fed. R. Evid. Serv. 590, 1998 FED App. 0143P (6th Cir. 1998)—8:2

Galloway, U.S. v., 316 F.3d 624,

$304,980.00 in U.S. Currency, U.S. v., 732 F.3d 812 (7th Cir. 2013)—31:7

Trevino, U.S. v., 60 F.3d 333 (7th Cir. 1995)—10:5

United States—(see opposing party)

Uribe, U.S. v., 709 F.3d 646 (7th Cir. 2013)—10:2

U.S.—(see opposing party)

U.S. Currency Deposited in Account No. 1115000763247 for Active Trade Co., Located at First Nat. Bank, Chicago, Ill., U.S. v., 176 F.3d 941 (7th Cir. 1999)—31:2, 31:4

Valance v. Wisel, 110 F.3d 1269, 46 Fed. R. Evid. Serv. 1127 (7th Cir. 1997)—9:1, 10:9

Van Dreel, U.S. v., 155 F.3d 902 (7th Cir. 1998)—5:18

Vega, U.S. v., 72 F.3d 507 (7th Cir. 1995)—10:8

Viilo v. Eyre, 547 F.3d 707 (7th Cir. 2008)—4:9

Walker, U.S. v., 237 F.3d 845 (7th Cir. 2001)—32:2

Walls, U.S. v., 225 F.3d 858 (7th Cir. 2000)—4:4

Ward, U.S. v., 144 F.3d 1024 (7th Cir. 1998)—3:13, 12:1, 12:2, 24:1

Wesela, U.S. v., 223 F.3d 656, 55 Fed. R. Evid. Serv. 552 (7th Cir. 2000)—17:5

West, U.S. v., 321 F.3d 649 (7th Cir. 2003)—17:2

Williams, U.S. v., 209 F.3d 940 (7th Cir. 2000)—7:1

Williams, U.S. v., 106 F.3d 1362, 46 Fed. R. Evid. Serv. 686 (7th Cir. 1997)—10:9

Willis, U.S. v., 61 F.3d 526 (7th Cir. 1995)—4:8

Willis by Willis v. Anderson

Community School Corp., 158 F.3d 415, 130 Ed. Law Rep. 89 (7th Cir. 1998)—2:3, 30:5

Wilson, U.S. v., 938 F.2d 785 (7th Cir. 1991)—12:6

Winsett v. Washington, 130 F.3d 269 (7th Cir. 1997)—34:2

Woods v. City of Chicago, 234 F.3d 979, 55 Fed. R. Evid. Serv. 912 (7th Cir. 2000)—1:7, 4:3

Yang, U.S. v., 286 F.3d 940 (7th Cir. 2002)—18:3, 18:4

Eighth Circuit

Abumayyaleh, U.S. v., 530 F.3d 641 (8th Cir. 2008)—14:4

Ahumada, United States v., 858 F.3d 1138 (8th Cir. 2017)—1:9

Alatorre, United States v., 863 F.3d 8110 (8th Cir. 2017)—8:3

Allegree, U.S. v., 175 F.3d 648 (8th Cir. 1999)—10:3

Allen, U.S. v., 713 F.3d 382 (8th Cir. 2013)—12:6

Allen, U.S. v., 705 F.3d 367 (8th Cir. 2013)—10:2

Almeida-Perez, U.S. v., 549 F.3d 1162 (8th Cir. 2008)—17:4

Alverez, U.S. v., 235 F.3d 1086 (8th Cir. 2000)—3:13, 12:5

Aquino, U.S. v., 674 F.3d 918 (8th Cir. 2012)—17:2

Armstrong, U.S. v., 554 F.3d 1159 (8th Cir. 2009)—6:3

Arrocha, U.S. v., 713 F.3d 1159 (8th Cir. 2013)—3:13

Baldenegro-Valdez, U.S. v., 703 F.3d 1117 (8th Cir. 2013)—13:2

Banks, U.S. v., 553 F.3d 1101, 78 Fed. R. Evid. Serv. 734 (8th Cir. 2009)—9:2

Terry, U.S. v., 400 F.3d 575 (8th Cir. 2005)—4:2

Tillman, U.S. v., 81 F.3d 773 (8th Cir. 1996)—12:2, 22:7

Tovar-Valdivia, U.S. v., 193 F.3d 1025 (8th Cir. 1999)—3:2

True v. Nebraska, 612 F.3d 676, 30 I.E.R. Cas. (BNA) 1537, 93 Empl. Prac. Dec. (CCH) ¶ 43931, 159 Lab. Cas. (CCH) ¶ 61021 (8th Cir. 2010)—21:5

Tugwell, U.S. v., 125 F.3d 600 (8th Cir. 1997)—15:2

Tuley, U.S. v., 161 F.3d 513 (8th Cir. 1998)—3:6, 10:1

Turpin, U.S. v., 920 F.2d 1377 (8th Cir. 1990)—22:6

United States—(see opposing party)

U.S.—(see opposing party)

Va Lerie, U.S. v., 424 F.3d 694 (8th Cir. 2005)—12:2

Van Brocklin, U.S. v., 115 F.3d 587 (8th Cir. 1997)—31:6

Vasquez, U.S. v., 213 F.3d 425, 55 Fed. R. Evid. Serv. 218 (8th Cir. 2000)—3:13, 12:1, 23:5

Vester v. Hallock, 864 F.3d 884 (8th Cir. 2017)—4:9

Vincent, U.S. v., 167 F.3d 428 (8th Cir. 1999)—30:2

Vore, U.S. v., 743 F.3d 1175 (8th Cir. 2014)—11:2

Walker, U.S. v., 555 F.3d 716 (8th Cir. 2009)—9:1

Walker, U.S. v., 324 F.3d 1032 (8th Cir. 2003)—5:11, 23:5

Warford, U.S. v., 439 F.3d 836 (8th Cir. 2006)—16:3

Washington, U.S. v., 197 F.3d 1214 (8th Cir. 1999)—32:1

Washington, U.S. v., 146 F.3d 536 (8th Cir. 1998)—15:2, 34:2

Weeks, U.S. v., 160 F.3d 1210 (8th Cir. 1998)—5:18

Weinbender, U.S. v., 109 F.3d 1327 (8th Cir. 1997)—5:10, 14:3

Wells, U.S. v., 347 F.3d 280 (8th Cir. 2003)—1:7

Whisenton, U.S. v., 765 F.3d 938 (8th Cir. 2014)—17:8

Whispering Oaks Residential Care Facility, LLC, U.S. v., 673 F.3d 813 (8th Cir. 2012)—21:2

White, U.S. v., 42 F.3d 457 (8th Cir. 1994)—10:3

Williams, U.S. v., 165 F.3d 1193 (8th Cir. 1999)—12:4

Williams, U.S. v., 139 F.3d 628 (8th Cir. 1998)—9:5, 9:6

Winarske, U.S. v., 715 F.3d 1063 (8th Cir. 2013)—1:7

Woolbright, U.S. v., 831 F.2d 1390, 23 Fed. R. Evid. Serv. 1277 (8th Cir. 1987)—13:4

Wright, United States v., 844 F.3d 759 (8th Cir. 2016)—11:3

Wright, U.S. v., 145 F.3d 972 (8th Cir. 1998)—5:14

Yousif, U.S. v., 308 F.3d 820 (8th Cir. 2002)—10:5

Zamoran-Coronel, U.S. v., 231 F.3d 466 (8th Cir. 2000)—17:2

Ninth Circuit

Abbouchi, U.S. v., 502 F.3d 850 (9th Cir. 2007)—18:3

Adjani, U.S. v., 452 F.3d 1140 (9th Cir. 2006)—5:10

AFGE Local 1533 v. Cheney, 944 F.2d 503, 6 I.E.R. Cas. (BNA) 1324 (9th Cir. 1991)—28:3

Albers, U.S. v., 136 F.3d 670, 1998 A.M.C. 1017 (9th Cir. 1998)—12:4

Choudhry, U.S. v., 461 F.3d 1097
(9th Cir. 2006)—10:2

Conway, U.S. v., 122 F.3d 841
(9th Cir. 1997)—30:2

Cormier, U.S. v., 220 F.3d 1103
(9th Cir. 2000)—17:3, 32:3

Cotterman, U.S. v., 637 F.3d
1068 (9th Cir. 2011)—18:1,
18:3, 18:11

Crawford, U.S. v., 323 F.3d 700
(9th Cir. 2003)—30:2

Cruz v. City of Anaheim, 765
F.3d 1076 (9th Cir. 2014)—
4:9

Cunag, U.S. v., 386 F.3d 888
(9th Cir. 2004)—2:2

Cunningham v. Gates, 229 F.3d
1271 (9th Cir. 2000)—4:9

Davis, U.S. v., 530 F.3d 1069
(9th Cir. 2008)—16:1

Davis, U.S. v., 332 F.3d 1163
(9th Cir. 2003)—12:3, 17:4

Davis, U.S. v., 905 F.2d 245,
1990 A.M.C. 2289 (9th Cir.
1990)—20:3, 20:7

Deeks, U.S. v., 303 Fed. Appx.
507 (9th Cir. 2008)—8:3

Delgado, U.S. v., 545 F.3d 1195
(9th Cir. 2008)—21:3

Deorle v. Rutherford, 272 F.3d
1272 (9th Cir. 2001)—4:9

Diaz-Castaneda, U.S. v., 494
F.3d 1146 (9th Cir. 2007)—
2:4

Dorais, U.S. v., 241 F.3d 1124
(9th Cir. 2001)—32:2

Dougherty v. City of Covina, 654
F.3d 892 (9th Cir. 2011)—
5:3, 5:7

Dubrofsky, U.S. v., 581 F.2d 208
(9th Cir. 1978)—18:5

Duran, U.S. v., 189 F.3d 1071
(9th Cir. 1999)—25:2

Eagon, U.S. v., 707 F.2d 362 (9th
Cir. 1982)—20:3

Edgerly v. City and County of

San Francisco, 599 F.3d 946
(9th Cir. 2010)—27:3

$814,254.76, in U.S. Currency,
Contents of Valley Nat.
Bank Account No. 1500-
8339, U.S. v., 51 F.3d 207
(9th Cir. 1995)—31:7

Elliott, U.S. v., 322 F.3d 710 (9th
Cir. 2003)—5:7

Ellison v. Nevada, 299 Fed.
Appx. 730 (9th Cir. 2008)—
2:1, 30:2

Espinosa v. City and County of
San Francisco, 598 F.3d 528
(9th Cir. 2010)—17:4, 17:6

Ewain, U.S. v., 88 F.3d 689 (9th
Cir. 1996)—5:10, 14:2

Ferguson, U.S. v., 33 Fed. Appx.
849 (9th Cir. 2002)—15:1

Fiorillo, U.S. v., 186 F.3d 1136,
48 Env't. Rep. Cas. (BNA)
1993, 29 Envtl. L. Rep.
21396 (9th Cir. 1999)—17:4

Fisher v. City of San Jose, 558
F.3d 1069 (9th Cir. 2009)—
8:2

Flores, U.S. v., 172 F.3d 695 (9th
Cir. 1999)—17:4

Forrester, U.S. v., 512 F.3d 500
(9th Cir. 2008)—25:3, 25:4

$46,588.00 in U.S. Currency
and $20.00 in Canadian
Currency, U.S. v., 103 F.3d
902 (9th Cir. 1996)—31:7

$40,955.00 in U.S. Currency,
U.S. v., 554 F.3d 752 (9th
Cir. 2009)—31:7, 32:1

4,432 Mastercases of Cigarettes,
More Or Less, U.S. v., 448
F.3d 1168, 28 Int'l Trade
Rep. (BNA) 1611 (9th Cir.
2006)—21:3

$405,089.23 U.S. Currency, U.S.
v., 122 F.3d 1285 (9th Cir.
1997)—31:2

$493,850.00 in U.S. Currency,

I.E.R. Cas. (BNA) 192 (9th Cir. 1992)—28:1

Jimenez-Medina, U.S. v., 173 F.3d 752 (9th Cir. 1999)—3:6

Johnson, U.S. v., 357 Fed. Appx. 29 (9th Cir. 2009)—7:1

Johnson, U.S. v., 990 F.2d 1129 (9th Cir. 1993)—12:1

Jones, U.S. v., 286 F.3d 1146 (9th Cir. 2002)—6:3

Juvenile (RRA-A), U.S. v., 229 F.3d 737 (9th Cir. 2000)—3:2, 18:4

Khan, U.S. v., 35 F.3d 426, 1996 A.M.C. 1213 (9th Cir. 1994)—20:7

Kindle, U.S. v., 293 Fed. Appx. 497 (9th Cir. 2008)—13:1, 13:3

Klarfeld v. U.S., 944 F.2d 583 (9th Cir. 1991)—21:5

Kow, U.S. v., 58 F.3d 423 (9th Cir. 1995)—5:17

Kriesel, U.S. v., 508 F.3d 941 (9th Cir. 2007)—30:2

Lacy, U.S. v., 119 F.3d 742 (9th Cir. 1997)—5:8

LaLonde v. County of Riverside, 204 F.3d 947 (9th Cir. 2000)—1:3, 8:1

Lingenfelter, U.S. v., 997 F.2d 632 (9th Cir. 1993)—31:1

Liston v. County of Riverside, 120 F.3d 965 (9th Cir. 1997)—3:8

Lopez-Rodriguez v. Mukasey, 536 F.3d 1012, 40 A.L.R. Fed. 2d 767 (9th Cir. 2008)—6:1

Lopez-Soto, U.S. v., 205 F.3d 1101 (9th Cir. 2000)—10:2, 34:6

Lopez, U.S. v., 474 F.3d 1208 (9th Cir. 2007)—30:2

Lowry v. City of San Diego, 858

F.3d 1248 (9th Cir. 2017)—4:9

Magallon-Lopez, U.S. v., 817 F.3d 671 (9th Cir. 2016)—4:8, 10:2

Mann, U.S. v., 389 F.3d 869 (9th Cir. 2004)—5:4

Marquez, U.S. v., 410 F.3d 612 (9th Cir. 2005)—22:5

Martinez-Garcia, U.S. v., 397 F.3d 1205 (9th Cir. 2005)—1:8, 5:12

Mattarolo, U.S. v., 209 F.3d 1153 (9th Cir. 2000)—9:6

Maybusher, U.S. v., 735 F.2d 366 (9th Cir. 1984)—20:3

Mayer, U.S. v., 490 F.3d 1129 (9th Cir. 2007)—2:4

McCartney, U.S. v., 357 Fed. Appx. 73 (9th Cir. 2009)—3:5

McCarty, U.S. v., 648 F.3d 820 (9th Cir. 2011)—22:5

McIver, U.S. v., 186 F.3d 1119 (9th Cir. 1999)—2:4, 16:3, 25:3

McLaughlin, U.S. v., 170 F.3d 889 (9th Cir. 1999)—7:2

McWeeney, U.S. v., 454 F.3d 1030 (9th Cir. 2006)—17:5

Meek, U.S. v., 366 F.3d 705 (9th Cir. 2004)—17:4, 25:3

Meling, U.S. v., 47 F.3d 1546, 41 Fed. R. Evid. Serv. 593 (9th Cir. 1995)—25:2

Mena v. City of Simi Valley, 226 F.3d 1031 (9th Cir. 2000)—3:8, 5:4

Mendez, U.S. v., 476 F.3d 1077 (9th Cir. 2007)—10:3

Meza-Corrales, U.S. v., 183 F.3d 1116 (9th Cir. 1999)—8:3

Milner, U.S. v., 962 F.2d 908 (9th Cir. 1992)—22:3

Miranda v. City of Cornelius, 429 F.3d 858 (9th Cir. 2005)—13:1

Ramos-Saenz, U.S. v., 36 F.3d 59 (9th Cir. 1994)—18:12, 27:5

Ramos-Soto, U.S. v., 304 Fed. Appx. 578 (9th Cir. 2008)—32:1, 32:2

Real Property at 2659 Roundhill Dr., Alamo, Cal., U.S. v., 194 F.3d 1020 (9th Cir. 1999)—31:4

Real Property Known As 22249 Dolorosa Street, Woodland Hills, Cal., U.S. v., 167 F.3d 509 (9th Cir. 1999)—31:1, 31:3

Real Property Located at 475 Martin Lane, Beverly Hills, CA, U.S. v., 545 F.3d 1134 (9th Cir. 2008)—31:8

Real Property Located at 20832 Big Rock Drive, Malibu, Cal. 902655, U.S. v., 51 F.3d 1402 (9th Cir. 1995)—31:1

Reeves, U.S. v., 210 F.3d 1041 (9th Cir. 2000)—5:16

Reid, U.S. v., 226 F.3d 1020 (9th Cir. 2000)—8:3, 17:1, 17:4

Reilly, U.S. v., 224 F.3d 986 (9th Cir. 2000)—34:5

Reyes-Bosque, U.S. v., 596 F.3d 1017 (9th Cir. 2010)—8:2

Reyes-Oropesa, U.S. v., 596 F.2d 399 (9th Cir. 1979)—19:1

Rivera v. Pugh, 194 F.3d 1064 (9th Cir. 1999)—31:7

Rodriguez-Preciado, U.S. v., 399 F.3d 1118 (9th Cir. 2005)—17:5

Rohde v. City of Roseburg, 137 F.3d 1142 (9th Cir. 1998)—10:7

Rojas-Millan, U.S. v., 234 F.3d 464 (9th Cir. 2000)—10:3

Romero-Bustamente, U.S. v., 337 F.3d 1104 (9th Cir. 2003)—16:1

Romm, U.S. v., 455 F.3d 990 (9th Cir. 2006)—18:1

Ross, U.S. v., 32 F.3d 1411 (9th Cir. 1994)—21:5

Rowland, U.S. v., 464 F.3d 899 (9th Cir. 2006)—22:2

Ruckes, U.S. v., 586 F.3d 713 (9th Cir. 2009)—34:5

Ruddell, U.S. v., 71 F.3d 331 (9th Cir. 1995)—5:11

Russell, U.S. v., 664 F.3d 1279 (9th Cir. 2012)—22:4

Ruvalcaba v. City of Los Angeles, 64 F.3d 1323 (9th Cir. 1995)—10:6

Salas De La Rosa, U.S. v., 366 Fed. Appx. 757 (9th Cir. 2010)—17:4

Sams v. Yahoo! Inc., 713 F.3d 1175 (9th Cir. 2013)—5:18, 25:1

Sanchez v. County of San Diego, 464 F.3d 916 (9th Cir. 2006)—2:1

San Jose Charter of Hells Angels Motorcycle Club v. City of San Jose, 402 F.3d 962 (9th Cir. 2005)—5:4

Santa Maria, U.S. v., 15 F.3d 879 (9th Cir. 1994)—18:8

Santopietro v. Howell, 857 F.3d 980 (9th Cir. 2017)—4:2

Sarkisian, U.S. v., 197 F.3d 966 (9th Cir. 1999)—33:1

Sayetsitty, U.S. v., 107 F.3d 1405, 46 Fed. R. Evid. Serv. 760 (9th Cir. 1997)—4:8

Schlotzhauer, U.S. v., 356 Fed. Appx. 56 (9th Cir. 2009)—1:3

Scott, U.S. v., 705 F.3d 410 (9th Cir. 2012)—11:2

Scott, U.S. v., 450 F.3d 863 (9th Cir. 2006)—28:2

SDI Future Health, Inc., U.S. v., 568 F.3d 684, 103

Index